the
Thirteen Colonies

TRAVEL ∗ HISTORIC ∗ AMERICA

Fodor's

First Edition

Fodor's Travel Publications
New York | Toronto | London | Sydney | Auckland
www.fodors.com

Fodor's Travel Historic America: The Thirteen Colonies

Editor: Robert I. C. Fisher

Writers: Thomas A. Chambers (introductory chapter and New York); Lynn Davis-Trier (Delaware); Joyce Eisenberg (Pennsylvania); Christopher T. George (Maryland and Washington, D.C.); Carolyn B. Heller (Massachusetts); Andrea Lehman (New Jersey); Diana Ross McCain (Connecticut); Tracey Minkin (Rhode Island); David and Steele Sartwell (Vermont); Laura V. Scheel (Maine); Kathy Smith (New Hampshire); Lea Lane Stern (South Carolina/Georgia); CiCi Williamson (Virginia); Cornelia B. Wright (North Carolina)

Production Editor: Linda K. Schmidt

Design: Tina Malaney

Cover Photo: U.S. National Archives and Records Administration (*top*), Kelly-Mooney Photography/ Corbis (*bottom*)

Maps: David Lindroth, cartographer; Rebecca Baer, Robert Blake, map editors

Production/Manufacturing: Angela McLean

Copyright

First Edition

ISBN 1–4000–1231–7
ISSN 1541–3217

Important Tip

Although all prices, opening times, and other details in this book are based on information supplied to us at press time, changes occur all the time in the travel world, and Fodor's cannot accept responsibility for facts that become outdated or for inadvertent errors or omissions. So always confirm information when it matters, especially if you're making a detour to visit a specific place.

Special Sales

Fodor's Travel Publications are available at special discounts for bulk purchases for sales promotions or premiums. Special editions, including personalized covers, excerpts of existing guides, and corporate imprints, can be created in large quantities for special needs. For more information, contact your local bookseller or write to Special Markets, Fodor's Travel Publications, 1745 Broadway, New York, NY 10019. Inquiries for Canada should be directed to your local Canadian bookseller or sent to Random House of Canada, Ltd., Marketing Department, 2775 Matheson Boulevard East, Mississauga, Ontario L4W 4P7. Inquiries from the United Kingdom should be sent to Fodor's Travel Publications, 20 Vauxhall Bridge Road, London SW1V 2SA, England.

PRINTED IN THE UNITED STATES OF AMERICA

10 9 8 7 6 5 4 3 2 1

Contents

About the Authors

✦ **Thomas A. Chambers** knows New York State from a trio of perspectives: native son, tour guide, and historian. Born in the old Dutch settlement of Schenectady, he grew up in Saratoga County and thrilled to the shrill of fifes, crack of muskets, and pungent stench of gunpowder during the United States' bicentennial celebrations. After emulating Benjamin Franklin's penchant for reading the dictionary, Chambers worked as a historic interpreter at Fort Ticonderoga, where he became adept at telling stories and firing off 18th-century artillery. Bitten by the history bug, Chambers took his doctorate in American history from the College of William and Mary. Noting similarities in social structure between Virginia's Tidewater gentry and the Dutch patron class of New York, he extended that comparison into the social mores of the early 19th century. *Drinking the Waters* (Smithsonian Institution Press), his 2002 book on class formation, sectionalism, and society at American mineral springs resorts, compares Southern and Northern elite tourists before, during, and after the Civil War. His writings on early America have appeared in *The Journal of the Early Republic* and *New York History*. As a professor, he is now a member of the history department of Niagara University, Lewiston, New York. An inveterate backroads driver, he has visited many of the hidden jewels of historic sites listed in his chapter on New York State. For this edition, he also wrote the "Forging a New Republic" essay and the multi-state driving tours for the introductory chapter.

✦ Like many a schoolteacher's child, **Lynn Davis-Trier** spent long summer vacations in the back seat of the family station wagon as the travel-bitten pedagogues up front debated the merits of Plimoth Plantation versus St. Augustine. Quizzes were mandatory. A seventh-generation Pennsylvanian, Lynn traces her roots to Palatine immigrants who fled to William Penn's Holy Experiment (a.k.a. the colonies of Pennsylvania and Delaware), following the repeal of the Edict of Nantes, and counts among her Colonial connections an ancestor scalped by the Minqua in 1758 and also the noted gunsmith John Bonewitz (whose long rifles were famed during the Revolution). Her fascination with the "Lower Counties on the Delaware," which she wrote about for this guidebook, began with yet another summer vacation—this time to Cape Henlopen, lured by its ghost ships and pirates and promise of buried treasure. Today Lynn is lucky enough to work at Winterthur. Lynn's musings on Delaware and beyond have appeared in *Art & Antiques*, *Antiques and the Arts Weekly*, the *Philadelphia Inquirer*, the *Boston Herald* and UNESCO's *Museum*.

✦ An editor, travel writer and tireless adventurer, **Joyce Eisenberg** has trekked through the poppy fields of northern Thailand (B.C., or Before Children) and the lava fields of Iceland (W.C., or With Children). In between she spent most of her career writing about her native Philadelphia: penning the first Fodor's guide to the city in 1985, serving as editor of the Delaware Valley edition of *Travelhost* magazine, and contributing to Philadelphia's tourism Web site. Author of the recently published *JPS Dictionary of Jewish Words*, she enjoyed chronicling the chutzpah of Pennsylvania's favorite sons for this book. Though her ancestors signed the register at Ellis Island, and not the Declaration of Independence, she still manages to interface with the Colonial era on a day-by-day basis: her office overlooks a park named for General "Mad Anthony" Wayne and her children attend one of the city's Friends' schools, which are based on William Penn's Quaker traditions.

✦ A Brit by birth, independent historian and freelance writer **Christopher T. George** first came to Baltimore, Maryland, in the mid-1950s with his parents and was promptly enrolled at a school named for Maryland Revolutionary War commander Gen. Mordecai Gist, where he gamely tolerated his classmates' ribbing about the 1814 bombardment of Fort McHenry by the British. He soon developed a passionate interest in the state's early history, and later pursued research on the Battle of Baltimore and the role played by Gen. Robert Ross, who famously set fire to Washington, D.C. in August 1814. In 2002, this focus resulted in *Terror on the Chesapeake: The War of 1812 on the Bay* (White Mane Publishers), a detailed account of the American campaign waged by the British Royal Navy under Admiral Cockburn. He continues to pursue his Maryland investigations in his role as an editorial associate with *Maryland Historical Magazine*. For the current edition, he researched and wrote the chapter on Maryland and Washington, D. C.

✦ "It's the quirky little details that make touring Massachusetts so much fun," says **Carolyn B. Heller,** author of the Massachusetts chapter and New England resident for more than 20 years. While visiting the State House in Boston she learned that Massachusetts has an official state insect (the ladybug), and Carolyn keeps tabs on all the amazing discoveries unearthed from the Colonial period at Boston's Big Dig. While she enjoyed blazing a Revolutionary trail across the state for this edition, she has long been a regular contributor to numerous Fodor's guides to Boston, Cape Cod, and New England. She also covers the area restaurant scene as the local editor for the Boston Zagat Survey, and her food and travel writing has appeared in the *Boston Globe, Los Angeles Times, Miami Herald, FamilyFun, Travelers' Tales Paris, Passport Newsletter,* and other publications.

✦ Writer, editor, history lover, and Trenton resident **Andrea Lehman** has called New Jersey home for 20 years. While writing for numerous Fodor's publications, she has explored the Garden State's farthest reaches, but didn't understand its richness until she tackled the New Jersey chapter of this guide. Today, she continues to focus on family travel as the author of *Fodor's Around Philadelphia with Kids*. Although she enjoys that Birthplace of the Revolution, this mother of two girls says she prefers the Greater Trenton area, or, as she puts it, with a historian's chuckle in her voice, "the Neonatal Intensive Care Unit of the Revolution."

✦ Author of the Connecticut chapter, **Diana Ross McCain** can't remember a time when she wasn't passionately interested in history. She might well have been the only fourth-grader in Ohio who was truly excited by coloring cloth replicas of the state flag, fashioning scarlet carnations (Ohio's state flower) out of tissue paper, and visiting President William McKinley's cavernous tomb in Canton. Her favorite historical era is the Revolutionary War (she is a self-described George Washington

"groupie"), which meant moving in 1977 to Connecticut was akin to opening a bottomless treasure chest. She earned graduate degrees in both library science and history, the latter from Wesleyan University, and was on the staff of The Connecticut Historical Society for twenty years, first as a librarian, then as an editor and publicist. Since 1997 she has worked full time as a freelance researcher and writer specializing in history.

✦ Local historians cued **Tracey Minkin,** author of this book's Rhode Island chapter, into the fact that her house sits at the easternmost corner of Roger Williams' original tract of land in Providence. Did this cosmic connection set her on the course to travel throughout her tiny state—crawling into the attics of stone enders, reading monument markers in pouring rain, pulling over on highways to mark driving tour mileages, and pestering everyone she knew for their favorite Colonial anecdotes—on behalf of Fodor's? More likely it was Roger Williams who turned Tracey into a borderline Colonial/ Revolutionary obsessive who never lets her school-age children complete a ride to school without hearing yet another historical anecdote. A graduate of the Columbia School of Journalism, Tracey has written for many publications, including *Travel & Leisure, Outside, Walking, Boston, Cooking Light, Yankee, American Way,* and *Rhode Island Monthly*.

✦ The Vermont chapter is truly DNA-authentic since authors **David Allen Sartwell** and **Steele Allen Sartwell** can trace their roots back to Vermont's founding years, being direct descendants of the famed "fair captive," Jemima Sartwell Howe, whose 18th-century saga of Indian capture, French release, and long trek home can be found in many state histories. Recently retired from Salem State College, Dr. David Sartwell still enjoys trekking the trails blazed by his earliest forefathers, including Ethan Allen, together with his son Steele, himself a budding historian and lawyer.

✦ Ever since she was a child, author **Laura V. Scheel**'s biggest regret in life was that she could never travel back in time. As crossing the Oregon Trail as a pioneer or settling a New England village were out of the question, travel activity and history have somewhat appeased this yearning. Her wide-reaching research during these pursuits produced this book's Maine chapter. Perhaps it is no surprise that her American ancestry can be traced all the way back to Mary Chilton, the 13-year-old girl believed to be the first woman to step on land from the Mayflower back in 1620. Also high in the branches of the family tree is unfortunate Susannah Martin, the sixth person to be convicted and hanged as a witch in Salem's infamous Witch Trials of 1692. Laura lives peacefully in Maine, restoring her antique home and barn, and writing for various publications.

✦ When freelance writer **Kathy Smith** settled for good in her native state in 1988, she spent the next 14 years jogging New Hampshire's undesignated trails and mining untold stories for veins of wisdom that would make up for the years she lost through her self-imposed exile. Having traveled from Sydney to San Philippe on missions as straightforward as German-language studies and as complicated as researching the Yellowstone buffalo wars for *The New Renaissance,* she has yet to find a somewhere that yields as much sense of place as her own New England turf. In writing the chapter on Revolutionary-era New Hampshire, Kathy, whose doctorate in literature is from the University of Massachusetts and who is currently at work on a book about the New England culture of hospitality, was guided by the satisfaction one takes in reliving history.

✦ Author of the South Carolina/Georgia chapter, **Lea Lane Stern** always appreciated the historic charm—though not the humidity—of the South. She has contributed to many Fodor's guidebooks (her curiosity and expressive observations have especially enlightened the *Naples, Capri, and the Amalfi Coast* and *Greece* editions), has appeared as a travel expert on radio, television, and fodors.com, was a travel columnist at Gannet Papers, and writes for the *Miami Herald* and other leading newspapers. Lea is an avid history buff, has lived in Georgia, and has traveled around the southeast dozens of times. In her explorations for her chapter, Lea learned that those pesky Revolutionary-era generals didn't have the proper respect for Colonial boundaries, crossing back and forth between South Carolina and Georgia at will. Following in their footsteps, sections of her chapter's driving tours help mesh the two states together.

✦ Never having liked history as taught in high schools, as an adult **CiCi Williamson** was bitten by Historicus virginica, the "Virginia history bug," while navigating through the state for numerous Fodor's guides and her most recent book, *The Best of Virginia Farms* (Menasha Ridge Press, 2003). To write the Virginia chapter for this guide, she explored the byways and highways of the state, at one point even stepping back to 1800 and "joining" Vice President Thomas Jefferson on his 125-mi journey from Washington, D.C. to Monticello, his home in the Piedmont. The trip today takes just over two hours by car, but in Jefferson's time it was a four-day ride in his phaeton carriage, leaving from the corner of C Street and New Jersey Avenue (where the widower lodged at Conrad and McMunn's boarding house), crossing the Potomac on the Georgetown ferry (no bridges back then), and heading southwest along the same path I–66 follows today. With stops at perhaps Manassas, Fairfax, Culpeper, or Montpelier—where he would overnight with his friends James and Dolley Madison—he forged on to the base of Monticello mountain. Needless to say, CiCi adores "TJ's neighborhood." She has written more than 1,500 newspaper and magazine features and six books.

✦ Author of the North Carolina chapter, **Cornelia B. Wright** always enjoyed history from the ground up, from an early start building sand castles on Rhode Island's rocky coast to many years spent as a medieval archaeologist in Germany. After living through one-too-many dusty excavations, she became a book editor. After being a peripatetic New Englander all her life, Cornelia moved to North Carolina in 1991 and discovered she was actually a Southerner manqué. As director of publications for Old Salem and the Museum of Early Southern Decorative Arts, she wrote and edited publications about the history of the South and its decorative arts. She is the co-author, with Penelope Niven, of the *Old Salem Official Guidebook.* Now a freelance writer, she contributes regularly to *Early American Life* magazine and other publications.

✦ The challenge of rallying a baker's dozen of historians brought *The Thirteen Colonies* editor **Robert I. C. Fisher** into near-telepathic communication with George Washington, admittedly commander of a much vaster, though no less dedicated, army. Still, the troops who gave their all to fashioning this readable account of the history of our nation's infancy never hesitated to embark on a dusty journey, track an elusive clue, wheedle an anecdote from a forgetful old-timer, or ponder the many forks that appeared in the road. To them, each of whom has added another star—13 in all—to Fodor's banner, he can only say "Hip, Hip, Huzzah!"—18th-century lingo for "Thank you for a great job." Stepping back into past centuries while living in present-day Manhattan allowed editor Fisher to experience a Rip van Winkle moment every day the book was in preparation. As a lifelong resident of New York City's "Village of Greenwich," he often found himself communing with van Winkle's creator, Washington Irving, whose town house still stands there on time-burnished Commerce Street.

Traveling Through History

From the beginning, America has been a land of travelers—settlers on the move in sailing ships, wagon trains, canal barges, railroad cars, and pack coaches—and there has never been a better time than now to partake of that tradition. There is a grand excitement in going to the very sites where the nation's character was formed and actually setting foot in momentous places you've until now only read about. When you're there you'll discover new things about the country's past, in the process deepening your understanding of America's historic events.

If you want to get to know what the United States is all about, nothing beats visiting the places where the nation's life story unfolded. When you stroll the streets of heritage-rich towns, gaze across battlefields where destiny was determined, and enter rooms where history was made, you travel back in time. Before your eyes, the past sheds its dusty mantle and becomes new again, a fresh and even thrilling experience for you to relive. You imagine you can see pioneers heading west, watch colonists going about their business, hear the militia practicing its maneuvers, and smell the powdery ink on the latest broadsheet. Whether you are a great-grandparent who's heard (and perhaps told) the story over and over, or a third-grader who's finding out about it for the very first time, a trip into the past can leave you with a whole new perspective on the people and events that made America what it is today.

And what about that third-grader (or sixth-grader or tenth-grader)? Even if your kids yawn their way through their history homework, a field trip to a place they've learned about in school is almost guaranteed not to bore them. Leave behind the textbook and head for the trail, and what they've read about immediately becomes real. Take the lesson out of the classroom and into the cabin, and suddenly even the most reluctant students can't resist the urge to join in. When you're face-to-face with the America of long ago, history bursts to life before your eyes, in illuminating and often unexpected ways. It makes for an unforgettable vacation.

LET US HEAR FROM YOU

Keeping a travel guide fresh and up-to-date is a big job, and we welcome any and all comments. We'd love to have your thoughts on places we've listed, and we're interested in hearing about your own special finds. Our guides are thoroughly updated for each new edition, and we're always adding new information, so your feedback is vital. Contact us via e-mail in care of editors@fodors.com (specifying the name of the book on the subject line) or via snail mail in care of *Travel Historic America: The Thirteen Colonies*, at Fodor's, 1745 Broadway, New York, NY 10019. We look forward to hearing from you. And in the meantime, have a wonderful trip.

HOW TO USE THIS GUIDE

▼▼

Travel Historic America: The Thirteen Colonies contains everything you need to know in order to plan and enjoy your trip into the American past. For a family on summer vacation, a retiree traveling the country by RV, a college student on break, or simply anyone who wants to be immersed in our country's history up close and in person, the book that you hold in your hands is a great tool. With it as your guide you can tour re-created Colonial villages, participate in Revolutionary battle reenactments, discover 18th-century inns and taverns, explore maritime museums and Shaker villages, and stroll elegant historic districts. Of course, the problem of containing a quart within a pint pot could hardly be better demonstrated than in the book's attempt to portray, in nearly 500 pages, all the beauty, breadth, and drama of the myriad Revolutionary and Colonial era sites in the founding states (indeed, there are *entire* books devoted to many single sites and museums included in this guide). As the joke goes, George Washington slept in so many places it is no wonder he is called "The Father of our Country." So it is not surprising that many taverns, cabins, and mansions couldn't be included, especially as our authors opted to drop lesser sites in favor of the real interest-grabbers. Already can be heard the advance-guard of protest among lovers of some omitted destinations, such as Virginia's Shenandoah Valley, the mountainous reaches of New Hampshire, and the far-western frontiers of Maryland and New York. In many ways, however, these regions were very much off the beaten path even in the 18th century, barely settled by pioneers during the central time-span of this guide. But as for the period's most enthralling sites and fascinating destinations, whatever your interests, this book will help you make the story of early America part of your personal history.

WHAT'S INSIDE

For each of the thirteen Colonies, you will find information on the cities, villages, and historic restorations where you can still glimpse Colonial America firsthand. *The Thirteen Colonies* includes as many authentically historic towns, attractions, events, restaurants, and lodgings as space allows, focusing on delivering to you the kind of in-depth, expert knowledge that you won't get anywhere else. The guide opens with an introduction to Early American history; this text is accompanied by a time line that highlights the pivotal moments of the story. A map of the region shows the original thirteen Colonies, along with the state lines of today. Also marked on the map are the routes of the regional driving tours described in the introduction; these itineraries take you deep into the past as you travel from state to state.

In alphabetical order by state name, the chapters of the guide contain everything you need to know to plan a fun and fulfilling Colonial American vacation. Whether you are trying to decide which part of the thirteen Colonies to explore or have already chosen a destination, the opening sections of the state chapters can answer your questions. A historical overview of the state, accompanied by a time line of events, opens each chapter, followed by a Regional Gazetteer that gives you an overview of the differing regions within each state. On a state map are marked the towns listed within the chapter, plus major roads and landmarks and the routes of the state driving tours.

The driving tours mapped out for each state are an excellent trip-planning tool. To help you customize your trip according to your interests, the driving tours trace themes such as Revolutionary battlefields, the homeland of such figures as George Washington, and coastal Colonial ports. Each is an efficient yet adventurous itinerary for a road trip, complete with recommendations on which routes to take for a great drive, interesting places to stop along the way, and towns that are best for overnight stays. The towns visited on the driving tours, along with the many other communities of historical interest included in the guide, are listed in alphabetical order within the chapters. As you peruse the town listings you will also come across boxes filled with fascinating anecdotes and legends that will enrich your "Colonial" experience.

The final chapter of the guide, "Resources," directs you to a wealth of sources for further information on the history of the Colonies and contacts who can help you plan your trip. There are both general sources, which can inform you about Colonial America as a whole, and state-specific sources, which can tell you what you need to know about the state you plan to visit. Organizations listed under "Historical and Tourism Organizations" specialize in supplying information, while those under "History Tours and Packages" can set you up on a preplanned trip or can customize a guided itinerary for you. Under "Further Reading" are the kind of solidly researched yet enjoyably readable books that can put you in the mood for your Revolutionary-era adventure months ahead of time—or prolong the excitement for months afterward.

Where to Find It Town by Town

It's easy to find the city you are looking for in *The Thirteen Colonies,* because the towns within each state are listed in alphabetical order. You can quickly cross-reference to nearby towns: just look below the town name to find the list of nearby towns that are also listed in the chapter.

TOWN LISTINGS, A TO Z
A brief description of each town summarizes its place in history and its character today. Some of the towns included in the guide played an important role in history, whereas others represent towns typical of the period. You can get more information before you visit by contacting the organizations—chambers of commerce, visitor bureaus, historical associations, and the like—listed below the town introduction.

ATTRACTIONS AND EVENTS
These headings point you to the historically oriented things you can see and do in and around each town. From farmsteads and historic homes to heritage festivals and battle reenactments, it's all here, and it's all true to history. You won't find hokey theme parks or bogus roadside attractions in these pages: every destination listed is of genuine historical significance. You'll learn about museums, walking tours, hands-on activities, state and national parks, theatrical performances, and annual events. Note that attractions in smaller nearby towns are sometimes listed under larger towns, and that when a nearby town is of interest in its entirety but is too small to have its own heading, it may appear as an attraction under a larger town.

HISTORIC DINING AND LODGING
In this section you will find reviews of dining and lodging options of historical interest in and near the town. Not every town has such accommodations, but those that do are worth considering as a stopover for lunch, dinner, or a night's sleep. These distinctive restaurants, hotels, inns, B&Bs, and watering holes have been selected for their combination of authenticity and quality. Some of these properties have served the public continuously; others have been restored after years of disuse, or converted from other uses, with meticulous respect for history. Furnishings may be antiques or reproductions and food may be old-fashioned or updated, but your overall experience will be transporting, allowing you to remain immersed in the past even when your day of touring is done.

By Robert I. C. Fisher

Liberty's Road

ot's in it fer me?" "Och, lad, a Paradise! A veritable Eden where Game and Fish and all manner of Harvest appear as if by Magick! No tax-gathereres, no Sherriffs; only Gold and Good Weather."

Thus were they convinced; those poor farmers, those indifferent apprentices, those younger-son gentlemen, and those sailors who went anywhere a ship took them. The several convicts in the group had not been convinced; they had been shipped. There were 144 men aboard the *Susan Constant,* the *Godspeed,* and the *Discovery* as the outgoing morning tide of December 20, 1606, carried them away from the farewells of their sponsors on the London dock to head for the New World across the great ocean.

Captain Christopher Newport, commander of the little fleet, had chosen to sail south-west from England, between the Azores and the Canaries, then due west across the Atlantic, following the route that Columbus had taken more than a hundred years before. But winter squalls and Spanish dominion over the waters of the West Indies made them turn northward; by mid-April they entered Chesapeake Bay. The three ships, trip-weary and provision-scarce, crawled into the bay, tiptoeing, as it were, past the resident "Indians." Eventually they sighted a river—a broad, deep, fresh river, pouring itself into the bay around a wooded peninsula. Captain Newport ordered the three ships to be moored six fathoms off the coast. A first foray on shore revealed a dense forest with more than enough trees to help them build their new settlement, which they were to call Jamestown. That night they returned to the boats and, in their excitement, sleep was light for all of them. In the fading twilight, one man thought he had seen an Indian crossing the beach. Then, as darkness gathered at the river's edge, the noises of the night began. Insects hummed, owls screeched, a fox yelped, and other things proclaimed their presence with weird noises. Eden had some unknowns, too.

Fast-forward five centuries. On your family's vacation, you have chosen to see the sights connected with America's founding years in the "colonie" of Virginia. Here at Jamestown, you discover the *Susan Constant,* the *Godspeed,* and the *Discovery* moored to a pier in a tiny cove. These are not models; they are exact reproductions of the ships that sailed from England to Virginia. They are seaworthy, but they are *so* small. You lean back against a bulkhead and try to imagine five months in passage, 144 men, cold and wet days and nights, moldy food, brackish water, and sickness and death.

In elegant Williamsburg, you marveled at one of its many gorgeously restored "buildings of publick necessity," Christiana Campbell's Tavern, where George Washington really did eat—10 times in two months, according to his own diary. You visited the battlefield at Yorktown, where General Cornwallis surrendered the entire British Army to the Continental troops. Given the size of those British redoubts—oversize foxholes, really—it is hard to picture several hundred attackers and defenders occupying each one, although you find it very easy to imagine being one of the troops (if one might be forgiven the pun, bloody easy). And a meadow away, the Moore House witnessed the climax of the Revolutionary War— here, in this altogether plain-looking little farmhouse, a great power gave up its claim to dictate ever again the fortunes of its American Colonies.

As you have discovered journeying through Virginia, time travel *is* feasible—and in your own car at that. A simple trip from the first fort at Jamestown to Williamsburg's English fineries to the Yorktown battlefield traces another incredible journey—our nation's—made by six generations and marked by rugged hardship and Revolutionary battles. Over the decades, millions of dollars and the efforts of thousands of planners, builders, artisans, and craftspeople have restored and re-created countless Colonial and Revolutionary War sights. So your trip makes history truly come alive—for your children and for yourself.

This book is written to help "put you in the picture"—to give you an overview of where you are, where you're going, and where you may want to travel from there to the important, the intriguing, and the beautiful places where the United States was born and struggled through its youth. In it, we trace the trajectory of European settlement that spanned two centuries from the first Colonies at Jamestown and Plymouth. The guide's main focus is the European colonization of the continent—a land, it must be underscored, that had already witnessed the magnificent birth (and sometimes also the decline) of many native cultures. Approximately 1820 is the cutoff period, a date that allows us to study the great homes and decorative arts of the Federal era as well as to get a sense of the stormy early years of the new republic. As we must remember, the Revolutionary War was simply a prelude to another ferocious battle— the one between Republican forces, which wanted states to have more power, and the Federalists who wanted a heavily centralized goverment.

As you visit Independence Hall, Salem's Rebecca Nurse House, Mount Vernon, Fort Ticonderoga, Plimoth Plantation, and hundreds of other sites, you can begin to understand the fever pitch of patriotism that compelled men to offer "their Lives, their Fortunes, and their sacred Honor" to the cause of liberty—eventually, that is. Revisionist historians have now discerned that the first men who left England for "Paradise" did so for riches, not freedom. The families who then followed often did so for survival and benefit, not for a chance to be self-governing. When Virginia's first House of Burgesses met in the 1620s, the members knew that they were to imitate all things English and didn't mind. They knew they had to answer to London for any fault and thought it proper. They knew they were to meet just once a year to ensure that things were going smoothly and they were content to do so. They were an extension of England—everybody knew that. The small difference, which would soon become an enormous one, was that these representatives were elected by all males over 16, not just by landowners. Nobody seemed to notice the divergence from Mother England; they had simply gotten used to the idea that anyone who pulled his weight could have his say.

So, now it is time to draw up a cup of tea (or rather—if you want to pay respects to the tenets of the Boston Tea Party—a cup of coffee) and get acquainted with a saga undertaken not only by brave generals but also by blacksmiths, farmers, merchants, and frontier women; one lived not just by the English but also by a multicultural array of French, Swedes, Hessians, Native "Indian" tribes, and peoples from Africa. The best way to start out on your own journey back in time is to refresh your memory of Colonial America's history. Thomas

I'm a Yankee Doodle Dandy

Get out your tricornes, load up your muskets, and get those red-dye capsules ready (for your "wounds"). The reenactment boom has swept the land. Whether riveted by history, channeling an ancestor who fought in the Battle of Monmouth, or simply enjoying an escape from 21st-century life, thousands of teachers, doctors, lawyers, and salespeople have "joined the Revolution" by becoming reenactors. In full regalia—redcoat, rifle, and cellphone—they thrill in re-creating everything from the Battle of Bunker Hill to Washington's Crossing of the Delaware. How can *you* become a Private Yankee Doodle? First, find a Unit. Go to the main Web sites—such as www.revwar.com/reenact or www.reenactor.net—to uncover hundreds of area regiments and militias. Some of the leading networks are: the Continental Line (www.continentalline.org), the Brigade of the American Revolution (www.brigade.org), and the British Brigade (www.britishbrigade.org). Track down the one in your neighborhood, attend their next reenactment, and start asking questions. Only when you're really ready to "enlist" should you invest in gear. Invest is the word: a uniform coat, cocked hat, and musket can add up to $1,000, and that's just for starters (tip: get a loaned uniform for your trial period). If you're serious, search out the vendors (called Sutlers) who sell "period" clothing at reenactments. Then come the days of mustering and drill work, the breaks for "liberty tea" (made with herbs), and the adrenalin-filled charges of battle. Not everyone gets to "be" Gen. Nathanael Greene—first-timers are usually foot soldiers, and women and children charmingly dress up as "followers of the army." Musicians can join a company of fifers and drummers. Be it drum or rifle, don't leave those earplugs at home.

Chambers's essay in the introductory chapter, "Forging a New Republic," sketches out our country's first growth, trials, and accomplishments in broad strokes. The pages that follow tell you about the many hundreds of structures scattered across the former and first thirteen Colonies, the best of many thousands of these relics, that reveal what happened, when it happened, and where it happened during "the times that try men's souls" (in the famed words of Thomas Paine, the Revolutionary-era pamphleteer). We have omitted most of the "why" since ours is a story and travel book, not a history lesson. But, most important, although a list of "Who" it happened to would probably fill an entire book itself, we hope that this guide will, vicariously, make *you* one of them.

By Thomas A. Chambers

Forging a New Republic

The American Revolution did not begin with one cataclysmic event. Rather, it started with a series of tiny measures, like individual stones pulled from a levee that weakened the British hold over the land until the trickle of water spilling over the dam became a torrent that no one could stop. It's easy to forget that even after British and American soldiers—men from a common culture and ethnic group—spilled each other's blood at Bunker Hill, Ticonderoga, Québec, Norfolk, Charleston, and elsewhere in 1775 and 1776, many in America continued to seek a compromise. As fate would have it, the Colonies' Continental Congress was willing to concede too little, and King George III was so outraged that his subjects resisted his rule that he refused to read even so much as their Olive Branch Petition. The political wind was blowing toward independence when, early in 1776, a Philadelphia activist named Thomas Paine issued a decisive pamphlet entitled *Common Sense*. In plain and forceful language Paine decried the inequities of British rule and forcefully argued for the necessity of independence. In Paine's writing, an island should not rule a continent, the revered King was a "royal brute" and, as he cogently put it, "T'is Time to Part!" The pamphlet became a bestseller, read aloud in taverns and public squares, and soon, the people clamored for independence. The Second Continental Congress drafted a Declaration of Independence, which was passed on July 2, then issued on July 4, 1776. But with a British army menacing American soil, the Declaration was worth only as much as the paper it was printed on.

The rest is history. Already in the 18th century, discussion had been much bruted about this fledging country. "What then, is the American, this new man?" asked J. Hector St. John de Crevecoeur, a French immigrant to America during the Revolutionary War period. A farmer in what is now upper New York State, he chose a sylvan life after unsuccessfully seeking his fortune as a surveyor and soldier in New France. But it was his background as a French aristocrat that led him to ask his question, one that many people in Europe and the new Colonies pondered: how did this new nation compare to Europe, from where most of the new arrivals (with the notable exception of African slaves) came? According to Crevecoeur,

Roll Call: The Thirteen Colonies (plus Two)

Why do we call them the *thirteen* Colonies? Answer: that was the number of Colonies that rebelled against the Crown at the time of the American Revolution. The thirteen, however, started out as only two—in the very beginning, the Colonies of Massachusetts and Virginia comprised the *entire* eastern seaboard of the United States. With time, more settlements led to smaller Colonies *and* major boundary disputes, most notably with the territories that came to be known as Vermont (originally claimed by New York, Massachusetts, and Maine) and Maine (originally claimed by Massachusetts). Below is the roll call of these states and their entrances upon the national stage, listed in order of precedence of settlement. **Virginia:** The first settlement by England in the New World was established by the London Company of Virginia in 1607, becoming a Crown Colony in 1629. **Massachusetts:** After the Plymouth Colony was founded in 1620 by the Pilgrims and the Massachusetts Bay Colony was established by the Puritans in 1630, both united in 1691. They proceeded to annex Maine, which had been colonized by the New England Council in the 1620s. **New York:** Founded in 1624 as Nieuw Netherland by the Dutch West India Company, this territory was then seized by the English. It was merged with New Jersey for a time as the Dominion of New England to strengthen control against French forces. **New Jersey:** Initially settled by the Dutch in 1624, it was then taken over by the English in 1664. **New Hampshire:** First settled in 1631 as part of the territories now known as Maine, New Hampshire was annexed by the Massachusetts Bay Colony in 1642, becoming its own Colony in 1679. **Pennsylvania:** Initially settled by Dutch and Swedes in 1631, the territory came under English rule in 1644 and was granted to William Penn by Charles II in 1681. **Maryland:** In 1632 King Charles II granted the Maryland Charter to the Lords Baltimore. For a time before 1732, Proprietory Maryland included all of Delaware. **Connecticut:** Initial settlers arrived here from Massachusetts in 1635. In 1638 the New Haven Colony was founded, then annexed in 1662 to the larger territory when it was chartered by the Crown. **Rhode Island:** In 1636 two settlement groups branched off from Massachusetts to settle this territory, uniting in 1644 and then receiving a charter from Charles II in 1663. **Delaware:** First settled by the Swedes in 1638, the territory was seized by the Dutch in 1655 and by the English in 1664, then granted to William Penn in 1682. Fearing Quaker control, the Colony set up its own government. **North Carolina:** While a claimant for the very first English settlement in the New World, the Roanoke Island colonies (1584–90) were abandoned or destroyed. In 1663 Charles II granted the Carolina Colony to eight Lords Proprietor. In 1712 South Carolina was partitioned off and North Carolina became a royal Colony in 1729. **South Carolina:** Founded in 1670 as part of Carolina Colony, it became its own territory in 1711 and a royal province in 1729. **Georgia:** King George II granted this territory to a private company of eight Lords Proprietor in 1732. In 1752 it was transformed into a Crown Colony. **Vermont:** During the 17th and 18th centuries this territory was basically claimed as part of New Hampshire or New York. After initial settlements dating back to the 1640s, two adjacent Colonies—New York and New Hampshire—began to stake out land grants in this territory during the 1740s. **Maine:** After some initial English settlements, the Massachusetts Bay Colony claimed this territory as its own in 1652, then granted the Province of Maine its own government in 1680 but maintained control. In 1741 its border was set, freeing New Hampshire to become its own province.

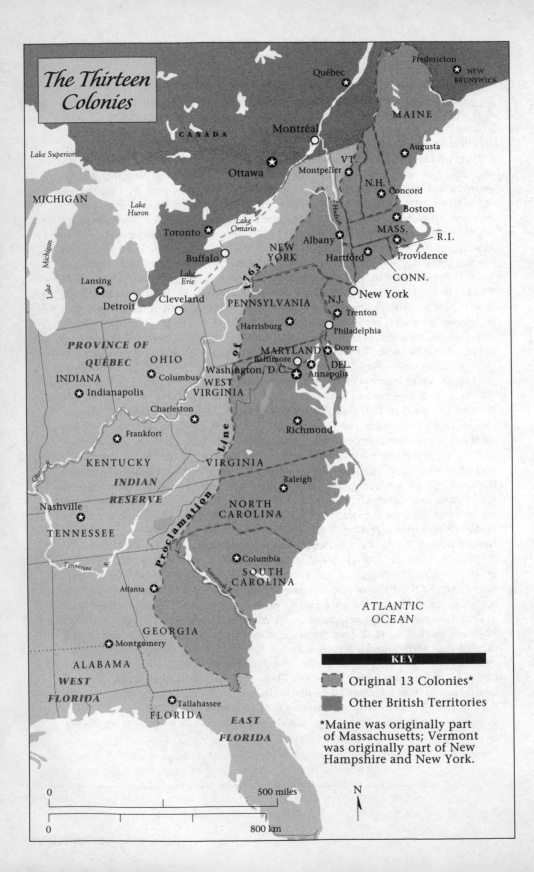

The Thirteen Colonies

CANADA

Québec

Montréal

Ottawa

Lake Superior

MICHIGAN

Lake Huron

Lake Ontario

Toronto

Buffalo

Lake Erie

Lansing

Detroit

Cleveland

MAINE

Augusta

VT.

Montpelier

N.H.

Concord

Boston

MASS.

R.I.

Albany

Hartford

Providence

NEW YORK

CONN.

New York

N.J.

Trenton

PENNSYLVANIA

Harrisburg

Philadelphia

PROVINCE OF QUÉBEC

OHIO

Columbus

INDIANA

Indianapolis

MARYLAND

Dover

Baltimore

DEL.

Washington, D.C.

Annapolis

WEST VIRGINIA

Charleston

Frankfort

KENTUCKY

VIRGINIA

Richmond

INDIAN RESERVE

Raleigh

Nashville

NORTH CAROLINA

TENNESSEE

Tennessee R.

Ohio R.

Proclamation Line of 1763

Hudson

Columbia

SOUTH CAROLINA

Atlanta

Savannah R.

GEORGIA

Montgomery

ALABAMA

WEST FLORIDA

Tallahassee

FLORIDA

EAST FLORIDA

Fredericton

NEW BRUNSWICK

ATLANTIC OCEAN

KEY

Original 13 Colonies*

Other British Territories

*Maine was originally part of Massachusetts; Vermont was originally part of New Hampshire and New York.

| 0 | 500 miles |
| 0 | 800 km |

N

America was an egalitarian nation that ignored a citizen's religion, his national origin, and even his wealth. "He is an American," wrote Crevecoeur, "who, leaving behind him all his ancient prejudices and manners, receives new ones. Here individuals of all nations are melted into a new race of men." The new country was proving to be a land of labor, opportunity, and social mobility. Yet reaching that reward involved countless struggles, disasters, setbacks, lost and ruined lives, conquered peoples, brutalities, and sacrifices. It also entailed incredible triumphs of spirit and arms, small victories achieved through stubbornness and sheer force of will, and miraculous successes—against all odds.

✦ IT ALL BEGAN WITH A COLLISION

The contact between Europeans and Indians was a collision of two peoples migrating in opposite directions—the Indians eastward across North America and the Europeans westward across the Atlantic Ocean. Unfortunately for the Indians, and fortuitously for the Europeans, the peoples that the Europeans met on North America's eastern margins had comparatively much less advanced social organizations, tools, and political systems. The conquest of North America was never an equal fight.

The reasons that Europeans invaded North America are many and complex, but they mostly relate to European society in the 15th, 16th, and 17th centuries. Having just emerged from a period of disease, isolation, feudal power, and decentralization, Europe was poised to expand. With the demographic and political brakes released, Europeans quickly rolled across the continent uniting nations and expanding trade. Italian cities like Venice, Florence, and Genoa amassed great fortunes by trading for silks and spices with Arabs and Turks across the Mediterranean. They now had excess capital they wished to invest to further trade, and other cities and nations sought to emulate their wealth. For instance, the tiny kingdom of Portugal, dangling on Europe's western edge, sent ships down the African coast, discovering lucrative trade in gold and slaves. Portuguese ships realized their dream of finding a shortcut to Asia that bypassed hostile Muslim lands when they rounded Africa's southern tip in 1487, but did not reach the valuable Spice Islands until ten years later. By that time, someone else had discovered an equally valuable trade route.

A Genoese captain sailing under the Spanish flag, Cristoforo Columbo (Christopher Columbus in Latin), sailed west—the opposite direction of the Portuguese—and in 1492 landed on what would become the West Indies. Incorrectly assuming that he had reached Asia, he called the Arawaks he met "Indians," and the name stuck. His return to Spain created a sensation—no one had ever seen human beings like those Columbus brought back with him, and his promises of endless wealth launched one of the most costly invasions the world has ever seen. Spain grew rich from gold and plunder taken from New World tribes and great civilizations such as the Aztec and Incas. It wasn't long before other European nations begin to swarm across the Atlantic Ocean. England was among them.

✦ FOOTHOLDS IN THE NEW WORLD

After a long period of unification and religious quarrels, England established the first *permanent* Colony in the original thirteen Colonies on the swampy banks of the James River at Jamestown, Virginia, in 1607. It barely survived—two-thirds of the initial settlers died from disease or starvation in the first few years. Sited 40 mi inland as protection against Spanish raids, the Jamestown fort lacked a supply of fresh water, adequate sanitation, and enough men willing to raise crops (or able to do so, for that matter—they had virtually no experience with farming or fishing). The men of Jamestown preferred instead to raid Indians and hunt for gold. Only the arrival in 1609 of a relief convoy with 600 new settlers—which met the colony's survivors as they sailed down the James River headed back to England—saved Jamestown. The colony, established by the Virginia Company in London with the expressed purpose of making its investors rich, had to sacrifice profit for survival in the early years, until 1612, when it started to grow tobacco under the tutelage of John Rolfe's wife, the Powhatan Pocahontas (sorry, fans of legend—and the Disney movie—she was *not* in love with John Smith). Exporting that crop Virginia prospered, and thousands of settlers arrived over the next several decades. Some were drawn by promises of self-government and free land for each man who paid his own passage, some by the prospect of freedom and land-holding after seven years or more of indentured servitude (an exchange of labor for the ship's fare); after 1619, some were hauled across the Atlantic Ocean in ships' hulls, barbarically chained together and treated as property—America's first African slaves.

England soon established another Colony along the northern coast of New England at Massachusetts Bay. The Pilgrims who landed there in 1620, headed for Virginia, had been blown off course. After landing on the tip of Cape Cod—named "Providence" for what they saw as their miraculous arrival—the 100 colonists found recently ploughed fields near what is now Plymouth. In truth, disease carried earlier by European traders had decimated the local Patuxet Indians before they could plant their crop. The Pilgrims believed that God had ordained that they settle the spot and signed a "compact" before leaving their boat, the *Mayflower,* outlining a godly commonwealth that adhered to the strictest tenets of Protestantism. The two-thirds of the passengers added at the last minute by the ship's London investors had no special desire for religious freedom; they were there to make money and provided some of the first tensions between the secular and spiritual in American history.

✦ THE "NEW" ENGLAND

Money was perhaps the one common thread that united the first European Colonies in North America. Joint stock companies—a financial innovation of the 16th and 17th centuries—backed Virginia, Massachusetts Bay, Nieuw Netherland (New York), and New Sweden (modern Delaware), all established before 1638. Commercial and imperial rivalries between European powers motivated nations to plant Colonies—but North America never returned the fantastic profits that Caribbean sugar islands did, much less the treasure fleets of Spain's possessions. Instead, eastern North America remained a moderately prosperous land of farmers and merchants, primarily subsisting on trade within the Colonies or by sending ships' masts and pine tar to England, furs and tobacco to the international market, or foodstuffs to the more thriving Caribbean plantations (who made so much money growing sugar that they could not afford to devote land to wheat or corn). The original Colonies belonged to a larger transatlantic world of trade but remained on its margins as a sparsely settled and economically modest area.

That all changed by the late 17th and early 18th centuries. Two things happened. First, the Colonies gained political stability. Second, they became part of a unified economic system. By the late 1600s European Colonies had enough people and security to vanquish the Indians who had once roamed the lands England had claimed. Metacom's War in Massachusetts, the final Powhatan uprising in Virginia, the Dutch alliance with the Iroquois against Hudson River valley Algonquians, the Yamasee War in South Carolina, and William Penn's friendly relations with the Delaware all set a pattern on the new land: Europeans would rule there, and Indians could either acquiesce or be vanquished. Squabbles among settlers were also resolved, with Bacon's Rebellion guaranteeing gentry domination of Virginia and the Chesapeake, and the Halfway Covenant ensuring that a godly commonwealth would continue to prevail in Massachusetts and New England.

Perhaps more important was the establishment of English rule over the thirteen Colonies and the imposition of a uniform trading system. By the end of the 17th century England had emerged from the cauldron of civil war to achieve a limited monarchy with Parliamentary rule. After nearly a century of internal strife, having resolved domestic problems, England directed its gaze on its vast North American Colonies. It conquered Nieuw Netherland, thus expelling the only non-English entity among the Colonies (the Dutch controlled all of what is now New Jersey and parts of Pennsylvania and Delaware in the mid-17th century). Now the Crown wanted a greater role in overseeing its possessions and ruled through royal charters and a series of laws known as the Navigation Acts. The mother country limited trade with other European powers, created its own monopoly in valuable crops like tobacco and sugar, and insisted that the Colonies import finished goods only from England. This system not only granted a significant advantage to English merchants and shippers but also gave Americans a protected market and stimulated an economic boom that brought prosperity on both sides of the Atlantic. So long as England regulated trade and left the Colonies to rule themselves, the relationship worked perfectly.

Much of this changed when religious conflict—that old nemesis of peace and prosperity—once again injected intolerance and self-righteousness into politics. In England, Protestants suspected King James II of hatching a "popish plot" to establish a Catholic dynasty and invited William of Orange and his wife Mary, a Protestant claimant to the English throne, across the English Channel in 1688. The following year William and Mary deposed James II and established religious toleration—but only for Protestants—in England. Across the Atlantic, without political stability in the mother country, chaos ensued. Rebellions in New England and New York upset the peace, and Protestants overthrew Catholic government in Maryland, ending religious toleration there. Religious strife simultaneously divided Europe into enemy camps as England and the Netherlands joined in war against Catholic France, ushering in nearly a century of bloodshed on both sides of the Atlantic.

✦ WARS FOR EMPIRE

War was the norm in the Colonies between 1689 and 1763; they were at peace for only 36 of those 74 years. Named after kings and queens that modern American students struggle to remember, the wars of this era erupted for control of land and royal dynasties in Europe. Americans fought in these wars because land to the north and south of their borders were controlled by Britain's rivals—Catholic France and Spain. Acting as an auxiliary of the British army, American troops invaded Florida and Acadia (modern Nova Scotia) in the early 1700s, attacked Spanish possessions in the Caribbean, South America, and Florida (again) in the 1740s, and captured the French citadel at Louisbourg on Cape Breton Island in 1745. Americans sustained significant losses during these conflicts, but more costly was the war at home. During constant raids on frontier settlements, the French and their Indian allies burned towns, took hundreds of colonists captive, and ended countless lives. From Maine to Georgia, the frontier lived in fear of surprise attack from the Abenaki, Iroquois, or Cherokee. Out of these decades of war Americans learned two lessons: that they could defend themselves with little help from the British, and that the French and Indians were mortal enemies who must be defeated.

The chaos of war came to mock English attempts to exert royal authority in North America. Britain ruled its American possessions through federalism and salutary neglect—a compromise that in essence allowed the Colonies to govern their own affairs while recognizing British sovereignty and control of trade and diplomacy. Attempts to regulate trade generally fared miserably, and the Colonies quickly engaged in commerce with whomever they pleased. In this way both Britain and its colonies prospered as Spain's colonial possessions never imagined; Britain's financial revolution was built on trade, debt, banks, a stock market, and taxes, all the while extending wealth beyond the ruling class into the minor gentry and even the middle class.

Then the bubble of inflation and debt burst. Once again, war was the culprit. The Colonies' fantastic growth over the course of the 18th century—from 250,000 people in 1700 to 2.5 million in 1775—pushed borders ever westward to the spine of the Appalachian Mountains. Just over their crest and along the shores of Lakes Ontario and Erie were ancient enemies—the French and their Indian allies—who were simultaneously moving eastward. Europe's two greatest empires clashed yet again, but this time the war began in North America when a young Virginia officer, George Washington, fired on French troops. He was near the forks of the Ohio River at present-day Pittsburgh, Pennsylvania, an area the French insisted was their own. They had built a string of forts on their borders to resist American incursions into contested territory in northern New York, Nova Scotia, and the Ohio country. With both nations expanding at the same time and desiring the same land, war seemed inevitable.

The fighting began in earnest with seasoned regiments of crack British troops. But at Fort

Duquesne, at Lake George, and along countless wilderness trails, the vaunted Redcoats bled and suffered like any other soldier. Marching and fighting alongside the British, American soldiers—"provincials" in the derisive 18th-century parlance—no longer viewed the imperial troops as infallible. In addition, disputes over whether American officers should hold equal rank with their British counterparts, harsh military discipline, and what pious New Englanders considered the raunchy conduct, foul language, and moral turpitude of British soldiers highlighted the differences between British and American values. To win the war, the British depended on American troops, money, and supplies. The Americans assisted only grudgingly while insisting on their political independence, something few Britons recognized. More than one British general flew into a rage when Colonial assemblies demanded that the Crown had to pay them for supplies or when a provincial officer refused to follow an order because it was not part of the contract he made in joining the campaign.

Victory came at last after epic campaigns up the Lake George–Lake Champlain corridor, brutal fighting on the southern frontier, and the decisive Battle of Québec, where both the French and British commanders fell. With the 1763 Treaty of Paris, England controlled almost all of North America east of the Mississippi River. But this moment of imperial triumph quickly turned to Colonial disintegration when colonists surged westward, no longer fearing French and Indian raids. The British quickly reacted with a proclamation that restricted American expansion to the east of the Appalachians, a concession to England's Indian allies. Americans felt betrayed, for they had little love for the peoples they had fought against for generations. The more serious break between England and its Colonies came when the bill for winning the war arrived.

✦ UPRIVER IN A TEAKETTLE

Like an ungrateful, penny-pinching friend at a fine restaurant, Americans dickered over their share of the check. Servicing the staggering debt amassed in defeating France and its European allies required more than half of England's annual revenues. Someone had to contribute to the costs of war, and the already highly taxed British Isles could not bear any further burden. So Parliament turned to the part of its empire that had benefited most from the war and asked America to pay its share. But Colonial Americans opposed any tax (even if it brought them handsome dividends). In the 1760s and 1770s taxes imposed on items as obscure as painters' pigments and as rudimentary as paper outraged the colonists.

It was not so much the items taxed or the amounts but the *type* of levies that proved so objectionable. Since the days of the Navigation Acts, Americans had assumed that Parliament had the right to regulate external trade—that between the Colonies and Britain or any other nation. But within the Colonies, Americans insisted that only they themselves could raise revenue. In a technical distinction that only an IRS official might understand, Americans accepted external taxes but denied Parliament's right to levy internal ones. The British insisted that they had the ultimate authority to tax the Colonies "in all cases whatsoever." Britain's Stamp Act and Townshend Acts were opposed with boycotts, non-importation, political maneuverings, and, most effectively, mob violence. In Boston the Sons of Liberty intimidated customs officials, tarred and feathered opponents, burned government buildings, and destroyed private property. Britain repealed some of the laws but refused to concede its right to tax. When resistance in Boston became too much—and especially after protestors destroyed the powerful East India Company's tea, dumping it overboard during the famous Tea Party— Parliament sent troops to quell the disturbances. The Boston Massacre and subsequent firing at Lexington and Concord were part of the same attempt to impose imperial authority by force on an increasingly belligerent populace.

The events that led to the American Revolution were more than disputes over taxes, however. They constituted fundamental disagreements and misunderstandings about the nature of government and representation. Americans were heir to an ancient strand of republican thought hostile to governmental power and constantly vigilant against conspiracies. Where the British saw a simple attempt to raise revenue, Americans imagined a plot to destroy their liberties. Citing precedents dating back to Engalnd's Magna Carta, Americans also insisted that representation must be actual, that each citizen must have a legislator that he elected. But the British Parliamentary system assumed differently. The empire was too vast and too populous, government ministers declared, for every single citizen to elect his representative. Instead, legislators worked for the common good of all of the empire's citizens, a kind of "virtual" representation. This approach made sense to the colonists when generic trade policies or imperial diplomacy were at stake, but not when the issue became taxes that colonists would pay. Just as they had failed to comprehend their differences over imperial federalism, military matters, and taxation, Britons and Americans misunderstood each other on representation. The result was rebellion.

After evacuating Boston and being repulsed at Charleston in 1775 and 1776, the British won almost every battle. Their superior numbers, training, and supplies drove George Washington's army from New York and nearly ended the Colonies' bid for independence. But Washington's daring raid on Trenton, New Jersey, on Christmas Eve 1776, and the decisive American defeat of the British invasion of New York State in 1777 turned the tides of war. Great Britain learned that it had a worthy foe in the American army, which had learned to fight in strict ranks like Europeans—especially after France recognized the United States. French arms, money, and ships proved decisive. Great Britain managed some victories in Pennsylvania and New Jersey, but spent the remainder of the war hunkered down in New York City, hoping to defeat the Americans by strangling trade—and it almost worked. In Connecticut, Rhode Island, and Virginia, British raids destroyed property and crops. The British blockade and rampant inflation caused household income to drop 40% over the course of the war. Indian raids reduced harvests and once again struck fear into the hearts of frontiersmen. During the winter of 1779–1780 Washington's army was down to 3,600 men, he did not have enough horses to pull his artillery, and several regiments nearly deserted. But somehow, desperately, the Americans hung on and did the only thing that kept the Revolution alive—they maintained an army that the British could not decisively defeat. Deadlocked in the North, the British hoped to win over at least part of the Colonies to the south.

✦ THE SOUTHERN CRUCIBLE

One of Great Britain's greatest wartime successes had been capturing Savannah, Georgia, in 1778 and reestablishing royal government in that Colony. British generals and policymakers believed that Georgia was the model for conquering the South. There were enough loyal men there, the theory went, to defeat the rebellion and welcome the return of British rule. After capturing the south's richest and most populous city, Charleston, in January 1780, British General Clinton returned to New York City and left Lord Cornwallis in charge of 8,300 troops, a formidable army. While their regular troops chased the American army, first Clinton and then Cornwallis relied on Loyalists to police the countryside and reestablish British authority. But these men had lost homes, farms, property, and sometimes parts of their family, and wanted vengeance. At Waxhaws on the North Carolina border, Loyalist troops cut down 350 Patriots who had already surrendered; "Tarleton's quarter," named after the British Loyalist commander, became the rallying cry for the Patriots. Americans on both sides embarked on orgies of violence, mutilating corpses, burning farms, and terrorizing the civilian population of the Carolinas. Meanwhile, as Cornwallis' troops swept the ragtag American army from the South, civil war in the backcountry claimed many men on both sides. Frontiersmen angered by Britain's limits on settlement and alliance with Indians defeated the Loyalist forces in the west. Retreating to the coast with his flank exposed, Cornwallis lost a series of small battles and watched the might of his army dissipate. By summer 1781 the British held only Savannah and Charleston in the South, and Cornwallis was racing toward Virginia.

There he fortified Yorktown, a small tobacco-trading village on the Chesapeake Bay. Washington snuck his army south from near New York City and bottled Cornwallis up on the Yorktown peninsula. The French navy defeated a British relief force, and French troops directed a classic European siege of the surrounded British army. On October 19, 1781, Cornwallis surrendered his entire army, and the last major battle of the Revolution was over. The British prime minister resigned, and King George III contemplated abdication. Peace negotiations in Paris yielded the Americans almost everything they desired. Most significantly, the United States gained possession of British lands east of the Mississippi. In 1783 the new nation controlled half of a continent.

✦ POISED FOR GREATNESS

First America had to establish a government and to heal. The Revolution had fundamentally altered society. Women, African-Americans, and the poor demanded and won many new liberties. Rich planters and powerful merchants no longer exercised absolute control. Democracy prevailed to such an extent that when Pennsylvania lacked an executive, the state was ruled by a committee. At the national level, the Articles of Confederation Congress voted by state, with tiny Delaware holding the same power as expansive New York. The government could not even pass a 5% tax on imports; real power remained with the states. This system proved so untenable that nationalists like Alexander Hamilton called for a convention to draft a stronger governing structure.

The result was the Constitution of 1787, a document of startling reach and political sophistication that blended demands for a strong national government with concerns over protecting rights and limiting power. Even the creation of the document had been radical, as the constitutional convention had been charged only with amending the previous Articles of Confederation, not overturning them. In addition, the convention changed the rules in the middle of the game: three-quarters of the states could ratify the new Constitution, not the unanimous consent required for amending the Articles. It almost didn't work, as the vote to approve the Constitution was close in every state and two, North Carolina and Rhode Island, defeated it outright. The key states were Virginia and New York, whose population and wealth were crucial for the nation's survival. Monumental debates in each state called forth eloquent political rhetoric from such luminaries as James Madison, Patrick Henry, Alexander Hamilton, and John Jay. The New York newspapers carried the debates and promulgated the pro-Constitution essays known as the *Federalist Papers,* a classic of American political thought. But New Hampshire beat them to the punch when it became the ninth state to ratify the Constitution, thus meeting the three-fourths requirement. Virginia and New York quickly followed, with North Carolina and Rhode Island joining in 1789 and 1790, after the Bill of Rights was introduced to protect individual liberties. The Constitution was a wholly illegal act that bloodlessly overthrew one government and replaced it with another. It was also radical in that it sought to put power in the hands of the people.

In the years that followed, the radical spirit mellowed. Building a nation, expanding its boundaries, fostering commerce and trade, and solidifying political coalitions were far less momentous tasks than defeating the world's greatest power and launching an experiment in democracy. Yet in the decades after the Revolution Americans took the question of values very seriously and quarreled over the Revolution's legacy and meaning. Everyone could agree that George Washington represented the Revolution's ideals of service and selfless leadership, but few concurred on what shape his government should take. Congress debated for nearly a month before deciding what to call Washington. Such trivial matters gave way to graver concerns as two political parties emerged based on whether followers supported strong or weak central government—the Federalists and Republicans, respectively. Their disputes over a national bank, debt, the French Revolution, and civil rights resulted in one of the most bitter and partisan presidential elections of all time in 1800. Thomas Jefferson defeated John Adams but tied his running mate, Aaron Burr, in the Electoral College. After 35 ballots and endless backroom politicking, Jefferson won. He called his takeover of power the "Revolution of 1800," because an administration hostile to its predecessor had assumed governmental control without violence or a coup d'état. This kind of transition became the foundation of American democracy.

Jefferson oversaw the expansion of American territory that his predecessor, John Adams, had begun. Treaties with Great Britain and Spain solidified boundaries to the north and south and ratified America's claim to the Great Lakes region. But Jefferson's purchase of Louisiana from France doubled the size of the United States. Vast new territories west of the Mississippi River were now open to American settlement. It was to be an "empire of liberty" that stretched across the continent, promising land and opportunity for future generations. By the second decade of the 19th century, America was no longer "the Thirteen Colonies"—there were 24 states in 1821—and much of nation's population and agricultural production came from west of the Appalachian Mountains. Getting from the Revolution to that point was no easy task: first the United States had to fight European nations on the high seas, defeat the British during the War of 1812, crush Indian revolts, establish judicial and financial systems, and, most important, unite the people behind a single government.

But by 1817, when newly elected President James Monroe toured New England and journalists proclaimed an "Era of Good Feelings," the nation was in an optimistic mood. Monroe presided over a time of fewer partisan divides and a sense of promise and opportunity. One of Monroe's first acts as President was to paint over the smoke stains on the Executive Mansion left when British troops attempted to burn it a few years earlier. Its brilliant color earned the building the name "White House," and the structure seemed to symbolize the republic's bright future. Inside, Monroe brightened the mansion with formal dinners, balls, and opulent decorations. The country had come a long way from the early, desperate days of Jamestown, when settlers fought over weevil-infested flour and died from starvation and infectious disease. We need only ponder that contrast to understand the scope of the achievement represented by the birth of our nation.

Colonial America's Superhighway

A DRIVING TOUR ON THE "POST ROAD" FROM BOSTON TO VALLEY FORGE

▼▼▼

Distance: 245 mi (one way)   **Time:** 14 days (13 nights)
Breaks: Overnight stays are best planned for Boston, Providence, Ledyard, Stamford, New York City, Princeton, Philadelphia, and Valley Forge

In the age of e-mail, instant messaging, cell phones, regular phones, pagers, and whatever electronic gadget that emerges next week, we forget how vital and difficult communication once was. Before the dot-com Information Revolution there was another transformation in communication that relied on far simpler technology, the printing press. Although they were scarce in Colonial America until the mid- to late-18th century, printing presses helped serve to disseminate mainly business and political news. Therefore, Colonists still relied on the written word to conquer physical distance between people who wanted to transmit a message. The technology of moving a letter from one place to another was simple: a man placed the letter in a bag, mounted a horse, and carried the letter to its recipient. But creating a system to regularly carry letters and mail proved far more complicated. Beginning in 1673 royal officials hacked marks into trees between major cities, creating a route for the mail carriers to follow. The Crown set standard rates in 1711, and Benjamin Franklin regularized the chaotic American postal system after his appointment as the Colonies' postmaster general in 1753. One of Franklin's greatest accomplishments was to establish a Post Road between major cities. It ran from Portland in Maine to Annapolis in Maryland, the approximate route of U.S. 1 today. Along this horse path the ideas of revolution and missives of commerce once passed. In its modern incarnation the Post Road is jammed with cars, businesses, and signs more complex than ax cuts on a tree—but along its route are some of the earliest and most important cultural sites of Colonial America. Follow U.S. 1 and you follow American history.

Begin your tour in Colonial America's cultural capital, **Boston.** Its Puritan founders decreed it "a city on a hill," setting an example of pious accomplishment for others to imitate. Boston's astounding number of colleges and universities, as well as computer companies, help it maintain its claim as one of America's most intellectual cities, a veritable "Athens of America." There is so much Colonial and Revolutionary-era history here that you'll have to skip a large chunk of it in order to do the whole town in a reasonable number of days—but since Boston was once a spit of land connected by a narrow isthmus to the mainland, most of the important sites are within a relatively small area. Around downtown—the area just east of Boston Common—are the places where radical patriots pushed America toward rebellion. The Old South Meeting House, the Old State House, and Fanueil Hall all held fiery meetings during the 1760s–70s where leaders like Samuel Adams and James Otis railed against the evils of British taxation. All are within easy walking distance of each other and open to the public. If you feel like walking more, follow the Freedom Trail into the North End, where the Paul Revere House and Old North Church tell the tale of his famous midnight ride in 1775. If you can remember Longfellow's poem, now is the time to impress (or embarrass) your companions and recite it. Across the Charlestown bridge is another Revolutionary War icon, the Bunker Hill Monument. Perhaps no other defeat in American history gets this much attention. Also here is the U.S.S. *Constitution,* a stalwart of the American navy, first launched in 1797. Two days should suffice to get a feel for Boston's role in the nation's creation, although side trips to Lexington and Concord or Plymouth are certainly worthwhile. A visit to the grounds of Harvard University is also time well spent, as the United States' oldest college was and still is the training ground of many Massachusetts' leaders, as well as many of the nation's.

If you can deal with the twisting streets and erratic drivers of downtown Boston, leave the city south via U.S. 1/I–93. Take Exit 9, Adams Street, to **Quincy** and the birthplace of a key revolutionary, cousin of the more fiery Samuel Adams, and second President of the United States, the John Adams National Historic Site. His home is open for tours, and you can imagine the man who fancied himself a gentleman farmer—if never, thanks to David McCullough, the subject of one of the bestselling biographies ever written—walking his daily 10-mi constitutional around the grounds. Return to U.S. 1/I–93 until its intersection with I–95, then follow that highway south toward Providence. U.S. 1 is a much more scenic drive through quaint New England towns, but your goal is the same Roger Williams as was over three centuries earlier—get away from Massachusetts as fast as you can!

Williams fled Massachusetts in 1636 after his arguments for religious toleration and stricter version of Calvinism earned him banishment. His followers founded aptly named **Providence,** a sprawling metropolis off I–95. The Memorial Boulevard exit crosses the Providence River and heads you toward the historic district. Turn left onto Canal Street to the Roger Williams National Memorial, with cogent displays on Rhode Island's history and a lovely park that is a good base for a walking tour of surrounding sites. Benefit Street, one block east and then south, is one long row of brightly colored 18th-century clapboard houses. Impressive Colonial and Revolutionary-era houses include the famed John Brown House, and Joseph Nightingale House. The city's rich cultural heritage is on display at the Providence Athenaeum, with its impressive collection of early books, and it seems to ooze from the stones on the Brown University campus. Providence has many other historic sites, but a Colonial post rider had no time to dawdle.

After an overnight, continue south on U.S. 1 to **North Kingston** and Smith's Castle, just past the junction with Route 403. Burned during Metacom's War in 1676, it is now a restored period house with frequent tours. Farther south on the Post Road is the Gilbert Stuart Birthplace, where Revolutionary America's greatest portraitist grew up. The grounds and herb gardens are exquisite, as is the house itself. Return to U.S. 1 and then turn right about 3 mi south onto Route 138. This road meanders through Kingston, the home of the University of Rhode Island, and swampland. Past West Kingston turn left onto Great Neck Road and drive a few miles south to South Kingston, continuing west on Route 138 to return you to I–95 after a 10-mi ride. Take Exit 90, Route 27, and follow this road north toward Mashantucket and the eye-popping Foxwoods Casino and Hotel. If you dare bring down the hellfire and damnation that Puritan preachers predicted for those who gambled, you can see what your losses can build the following day. Casino profits have allowed the Pequot to build one of the finest and most high-tech museums of Native American history in the country, the Mashantucket Pequot Museum and Research Center, located in the township of **Ledyard.** Entertaining and instructional, the facility gives incredible insights into the people who once dominated this coast. Return to I–95 and cross the Thames River into **New London,** settled by the English in the late 1600s. Three Colonial mansions, the Joshua Hempsted House, the Nathaniel Hempsted House, built by Joshua's grandson, and the Shaw-Perkins Mansion relate both the difficulty and comfort of Colonial life. Choose to stay either in New London or follow U.S 1 through charming New England towns; there are several inns along the way that offer a decidedly non-commercial feel.

The next morning your mail bag feels heavier and you must mount up for another spring on I–95 at a pace much faster than a horse's walk. Jump off the interstate at Exit 58 and take Route 77 south to **Guilford** and the Henry Whitfield House. English Puritans moved to this area in the 1630s fleeing religious persecution and built this stone house to guard against Indian attack. It contains a wealth of historic artifacts from the Colonial period. Press on to **New Haven,** where signs from Route 34 direct you to the Yale University campus. Find a parking spot and walk around the impressive grounds, even if most surfaces are covered with cement. The collections of both the Yale University Art Gallery and the Paul Mellon Center for British Art are replete with 18th-century American and English treasures. Also walk on The Green in the city center and imagine Connecticut's leaders rubbing shoulders with the ordinary farmers who once grazed their cows here. After finding sustenance in one of New Haven's many restaurants, get back on I–95 and drive 45 minutes to the Stamford/Greenwich area. There are many modern hostelries in the area so you can opt to overnight hereabouts. Or, instead, forge on directly to New York.

The drive south on U.S. 1 from Stamford toward the New York City area goes quickly but is crowded. Entering New York State you hit Interstate 95 and posh suburban Westchester County. Plan to stop at St. Paul's Church National Historic Site on Route 22 (I–95 Exit 13) in Mount Vernon, across the county from **Yonkers,** where key debates about the freedom of the press took place and injured British troops received treatment during a 1776 battle. From here, stick to I–95 to Manhattan. If you don't want to drive in the city, park in Westchester County and take a commuter train in; stations and schedules for the Metro-North commuter rail line are available on-line (www.mta.nyc.ny.us/mnr/). Make a reservation at a Manhattan hotel and get ready to tour the key historic sites at Manhattan island's tip of **New York City.**

Rise early the next morning and navigate the urban jungle where post riders once had only cows and birds for company. Of the dozens of sights you could see, make sure to visit the Federal Hall National Memorial, Fraunces Tavern Museum, and St. Paul's Chapel at Fulton Street; also nearby are Castle Clinton, the South Street Seaport Museum, and the beautifully restored City Hall. You can quickly walk to all three before catching a cab or subway back to your hotel. It seems a shame to limit yourself to one day in one of the world's greatest cities, so take in a few other cultural treasures if time permits. Just be sure to resume your journey on U.S. 1 (take the Holland Tunnel to reach New Jersey from Lower Manhattan, the Lincoln Tunnel from Midtown), lest the mail be late.

U.S. 1 wends its way through urban and suburban New Jersey towns like Newark, Elizabeth, and New Brunswick where Dutch and English farmers once eked a living from the land; consumerism and light industry now hold sway. One of America's oldest colleges lies about 20 mi away on U.S. 1 in the posh and tidy town of **Princeton.** Most of the key historic sites and Princeton University buildings are near Nassau Street. Just outside of town on the Princeton Pike is the Princeton Battlefield State Park, where Washington's troops defeated the British after his Christmas raid on Trenton. This is a good place to spend the night before the final push into Philadelphia. Trenton is the state capital, the site of George Washington's only tactical victory. From Princeton, follow Route 206 to I–95 south. Exit at the last point in New Jersey, Route 29. Follow that road north to **Washington Crossing** and its state park, where the American commander led his ragged and demoralized Continental Army on a midnight raid. After traversing the ice-choked Delaware River the army marched nearly a dozen miles south to Trenton, where they surprised the still-sleeping Hessian troops. You can visit the Old Barracks, where the German soldiers slept off their Christmas revelry before being surprised.

But you have no time to nap. You are bound for Colonial America's largest city and commercial center, **Philadelphia,** another wonderful 18th-century city where the key sites are in easy walking distance of each other. Book a room in the City of Brotherly Love (a rough translation of its Latin root words) and plan to spend two nights. William Penn converted his father's old political debt into a Colonial charter and planned a city on the western shore of the Delaware River in 1681. Penn's descendents exerted a strong influence on the Colony and earned the enmity of many less well-connected citizens, especially those in the hinterlands. It was those people, many of them religious dissenters attracted to the Quaker Penn's religiously tolerant settlement, whose agricultural products enriched Philadelphia. Trade with the West Indies and Europe made this city America's greatest, and the place where colonists gathered beginning in 1774 to debate independence. This improbable course of events is accurately and dramatically presented at the Independence National Historical Park, which includes such icons of American history as the Liberty Bell and Independence Hall. Be sure to venture to the Betsy Ross House on Arch Street as well as the Todd House near Independence Hall. Stand outside this building where the Declaration of Independence was written and imagine how long it took for word to reach Boston via the Post Road, where you began this tour. The differences in travel and communication between the 18th-century and today are profound enough to make you wonder how Colonial Americans ever got anything done.

If you feel like seeing more, visit **Valley Forge National Historical Park,** about 20 mi northwest of Philadelphia, where Washington's troops spent the crucial winter of 1777–78, or the Pennsylvania Dutch Country, an hour's drive west, where a variety of German and Swiss immigrants established their unique brands of 18th-century Protestantism, which still include prohibitions on certain technologies.

Mel Gibson Slept Here

A DRIVING TOUR OF SOUTHERN REVOLUTIONARY WAR SIGHTS FROM CHARLESTON TO YORKTOWN

▼▼▼

Distance: 830 or 1,000 mi (one way)   **Time:** 13–14 days (12–13 nights)
Breaks: Overnight stays are best planned for Charleston, Camden, Spartanburg, Charlotte, Greensboro, Wilmington, and Williamsburg

The release of Mel Gibson's blockbuster 2000 film, *The Patriot,* rekindled Americans' interest in the Revolutionary War, especially in the fighting in the South. Beautifully shot, with a dramatic story line that included patriotism, romance, and good versus evil, the movie combined Hollywood drama with historic realism. When historians declared open season on the film for its egregious errors in interpretation and fact, most Americans did not care— they loved a good story well told. But the one thing that movie fans and historians agreed on was that Mel Gibson's character, Benjamin Martin—a conglomeration of several historical figures spiced with a dash of Hollywood myth—brought to life the nature of the Revolutionary South. Martin's fight was bloody, ruthless, and partisan, dividing the South even before the Civil War. However, unlike the fictional Martin's men, who traversed the humid Carolinas on horseback and foot, you can visit key Revolutionary War sites in the comfort of your car. Once you've recruited the troops and laid in sufficient provisions for your journey, set forth to retrace steps of the Revolution's most important campaigns—the guerrilla war to wrest control from the British.

Begin your campaign in the city that was the South's largest and wealthiest during the Revolution, **Charleston.** Plantation owners made fortunes from rice, cotton, and indigo grown by their slaves and traded across the Atlantic. Their mansions line the Battery, the tip of Charleston's peninsula, which is still a pleasant stroll. The British realized the city's importance and sought to capture it as the base of their invasion of the South. After taking Savannah in 1778 and reestablishing royal rule there, British officials felt they could convince other Southerners to resume their allegiance to King George. The British Navy blockaded the city while 10,000 Redcoats sealed off landward escape routes, forcing the 5,000-soldier strong American army to surrender. Generals Clinton and Cornwallis made cosmopolitan Charleston their headquarters and delegated much of the fighting to Loyalist troops. Plan to spend two or three days in the Charleston area. Be sure to see the Powder Magazine, where munitions were stored for much of the Colonial period and into the Revolution, and The Old Exchange and Provost Dungeon. This site saw the election of delegates to the First Continental Congress and the result of that heady moment, and Americans held as prisoners by the British in its dungeon. The extensive exhibits are a nice introduction to the history of the Revolution.

A half-day side trip outside of town complements Charleston's Revolutionary history. North of the city across the Cooper River on U.S. 17 is Mount Pleasant, once a rural outpost but now a thriving suburb. Turn right onto Route 703 to the resort village of **Sullivan's Island.** Turn right on Middle Street to Fort Moultrie National Historic Site, where patriots scored one of the first victories in the Revolution. Although better known for its role in the Civil War, Fort Moultrie interprets the Revolutionary-era history and the evolution of seacoast defenses and boasts excellent seashore views. Once you've tired of Charleston's fine food and polite manners (if such a thing is possible), head upcountry to the land where the Revolution was fought and won. Take U.S. 1 south to **Camden,** where American troops suffered a humiliating defeat in August 1780, and Cornwallis made his headquarters in the Kershaw Cornwallis House. This building is part of the Historic Camden organization, which maintains several sites pertaining to the British occupation. After Cornwallis marched his army north early in 1781, a small British force remained here fighting a series of battles.

Plan to spend two overnights, sandwiching a day of touring, in Camden, with Mel Gibson lurking on the outskirts ready to pounce. Then hit the highway on I–20 toward Columbia. Continue past I–26 to Exit 58, where U.S. 1 takes you through Lexington. Continue on Route 378 when it splits from U.S. 1 and follow it to Saluda, where Route 178 heads northwest toward Greenwood. About 20 mi past Saluda is Route 248; turn right toward **Edgefield** and the Ninety Six National Historic Site. In 1775 the first battle south of New England took place at this settlement named after its distance from a Cherokee town to the west. Remains of Colonial villages and Revolutionary earthworks make this strategically important post a compelling stop. When Cornwallis headed north, remote British outposts like this one were ripe for picking. In fact, American troops under Nathanael Greene let Cornwallis go and focused on retaking the countryside in South Carolina. Once strategic Ninety Six fell, the British remained in control of only Charleston and Savannah. Greenwood, a dozen miles west on Route 178, is your best bet for its modern lodgings.

The key to victory was not so much battles between American and British troops as it was guerrilla warfare among Americans. Vicious battles at Waxhaws and Hanging Rock on the North Carolina–South Carolina border north of Camden were just as brutal as anything Mel Gibson conjured up in *The Patriot*, although neither side burned civilians inside a church as in one of the film's most horrific scenes. But unlike that movie, almost all of the combatants in South Carolina were Americans. Patrick Ferguson and Thomas Sumter led Loyalist and Patriot troops, respectively, who showed little mercy to their enemies, whether military or civilian. Countless little skirmishes across the Carolinas are the real story of the Revolution in the South, and actually delayed Cornwallis' northward march. He never found the level of Loyalist sentiment he had expected.

To get to the legendary Cowpens National Battlefield, near **Spartanburg,** the next major Revolutionary War site, go east on Route 34 (North Main Street) in Ninety Six, toward Route 248 (Cambridge Street). Turn left onto Route 246 (Cambridge Street North). Continue, and turn right onto U.S. 221 north (Laurens Highway Route 72 east) and merge onto I–26 west. Then merge onto I–85 north via Exit 188, toward Charlotte. Take U.S. 221 Exit 78 toward Chesnee and follow signs to park. In January 1781 the Americans won their only set-piece battle against British troops in the South here. Equally matched armies met in a clearing where a Loyalist farmer had kept his cattle and engaged in back-and-forth charges before the Loyalist and British soldiers ventured too far and were overwhelmed by an American counterattack. Although the hated Banastre Tarleton (this villain's nickname was even more perfect—"Bloody") escaped, the British had suffered a costly blow and Cornwallis continued northward, convinced that he could not hold South Carolina. Just three months earlier another Loyalist force had been defeated. An earlier victory near **York** at Kings Mountain National Military Battlefield can be reached by returning to I–85 and driving west into North Carolina. Take Exit 2 to Route 216 and follow the signs, but don't be confused by the nearby state park unless you plan to camp there. In 1780 Patriot troops from the backcountry and mountain regions, angered by Loyalist raids and the British alliance with the Cherokee, decimated Loyalist troops here, killing some after they had surrendered and hanging others. This was the first civil war in the South, and halted the British advance.

By this point in time one battlefield may be blending into another, and a bit of cultural enrichment of the urban variety might be in order. Forty miles from Kings Mountain on I–85 is **Charlotte,** a vibrant New South city bustling with shops, restaurants, entertainment, some of the region's most powerful banks, and several fascinating historic sights, including the Reed Gold Mine. Even super-patriot Mel Gibson needed an occasional respite, so take two overnights in one of the city's modern hotels to reinvigorate the troops for the drive north on I–85 to **Greensboro** and the Guilford Courthouse National Military Park. In Greensboro turn onto I–40 west and take Exit 213 to Guilford College Road. Go right onto New Garden Road and follow signs to the battlefield. The British under Cornwallis chased the Americans across North Carolina and even into Virginia before American General Greene attacked here in March 1781. Cornwallis won a technical victory but suffered so many casualties that he had no choice but to retreat to the coast where British ships might resupply and reinforce him. He had lost the strategic initiative. Pause at one of Greensboro's modern hostelries for the night.

At this point you must make much the same choice that Cornwallis did—head to the coast or press on to your final destination. If time permits, follow the British retreat to **Wilmington.** A twenty minute drive east on I–40 will lead you to Moore's Creek National Battlefield. A patriot victory here in February 1776, discouraged a planned British invasion and helped convince North Carolina to vote for independence later that year. Although not part of Cornwallis' campaign, Moore's Creek was one of the Revolution's first patriot victories. Reach it via Exit 408 to Route 210 west. The park is just past the hamlet of Currie. A short drive away is the small city of Wilmington and the spectacular beaches nearby. Return to the main tour via I–40 to I–95 north toward Richmond, then follow the directions below. This detour involves several hundred miles of driving, so don't take it without planning ahead.

If you'd rather march double-time, like those movie viewers who fast-forward through the cheesy romantic sections of *The Patriot,* follow I–40 east from Greensboro, which is also I–85. Continue on I–85 when it splits before Durham and continue into Virginia. In Petersburg follow signs to I–95, then I–295. British raids led by Loyalist troops and the infamous traitor Benedict Arnold reached as far west as Charlottesville in 1781, but no sites commemorate those events (after all, the Americans lost!). Head east on I–64 toward **Williamsburg,** where you can experience both the beginning and end of the Revolution. The area offers a plethora of lodging ranging from dirt-cheap to luxurious, making it a good base for the next two days of touring. Exit 238 takes you into the heart of Colonial Williamsburg, Virginia's re-created capital of the early 1770s. Of special interest are the Governor's Palace and Capital, which interpret British Colonial rule and the coming of the Revolution. The Powder Magazine offers military drills and demonstrations on occasion. Stop at the visitor center to get your bearings and tickets. Interpreters avoid the topic, but Lord Dunmore, the British governor in 1775, issued a proclamation promising freedom to slaves who aided the British cause, a major factor in Virginia's joining the Revolution. Plan to spend the day here.

Start the next day with a bucolic drive along the Colonial National Parkway to **Yorktown,** a dozen miles to the east, where Lord Cornwallis ended his campaign. A combined American and French army cornered the British here and forced Cornwallis to surrender after a long siege. There are two different entities here—the Yorktown Victory Center, run by a private foundation, and Yorktown Battlefield, operated by the National Park Service. Each is worth a visit and offers excellent interpretations and tours. Your best bet is to get a map from the National Park Visitor Center and drive the battlefield tour road. Yorktown itself contains several Revolutionary-era buildings and quaint shops. If you have a DVD player in your vehicle, pop in *The Patriot* and see how unlike the movie Yorktown looks. Then pat yourself on the back with the knowledge that you conquered the South—unlike Cornwallis.

Thirteen Colonies Timeline

1492 Christopher Columbus crosses the Atlantic Ocean from Spain. Before his trip, he had visited England and probably heard tales of the fishing banks "to the west."

1507 The New World is named after explorer Amerigo Vespucci.

ca. 1550 The Iroquois Confederacy is formed in New York State.

1585 An English Colony at Roanoke Island is established, and abandoned in 1586. Colonists reestablish Roanoke in 1587 but later disappear.

1607 First permanent English Colony at Jamestown.

1608 French Colony founded at Québec. Alliance with local Algonquians earns the French the lasting enmity of the Iroquois.

1609 Henry Hudson sails up the North River, which later bore his name, at the same time that Samuel de Champlain moves down his eponymous lake, just a few dozen miles away. Virginia Colony experiences the "starveing tyme."

1619 The House of Burgesses, the New World's first representative assembly, elected at Jamestown. The first African slaves were brought to America by Dutch traders at Jamestown.

1620 Missing landfall in Virginia, religious separatists head north and arrive on the *Mayflower* to found Plymouth on December 21; half the colonists die over the following winter.

1624 The Dutch ship, *New Netherland,* left eight crewmen on Manhattan Island (New York Harbor) and sail upriver as far as the future city of Albany.

1626 Pieter Minuit purchases the Isle of Manhatta from local tribes for $24 worth of "trinkets" and wampum.

1634 Maryland colonists aboard the *Arc* and the *Dove* land at the mouth of the Potomac to found a Catholic Colony based on religious tolerance.

1636 Connecticut and Rhode Island founded, the latter as a "democratic Colony" with greater religious tolerance than Massachusetts.

1660 Charles II restores monarchy to England.

1662 Halfway Covenant adopted in Massachusetts. Allows descendants of church members to be baptized without attaining full church membership (and sustains Puritan influence in the New England Colonies).

1663 Carolina proprietors receive royal charter.

1664 Pieter Stuyvesant surrenders harbor Colony of New Amsterdam to British troops, and it is renamed New York. New York and New Jersey are created from Nieuw Netherland and placed under English rule.

1675–76 Metacom (King Philip to the English) leads an Indian uprising that burns New England towns within 20 mi of Boston before being defeated. In Virginia, Nathaniel Bacon's Rebellion fizzles out against British rulers.

1679 New Hampshire separates as a "special province" from Massachusetts.

1681 William Penn receives charter for a Colony along the Delaware River.

1688–89 Glorious Revolution in England overthrows Catholic rule and places William and Mary on throne. Chaos in North America as rebellions in New York, Massachusetts, and Maryland threaten royal government.

1689–97 King William's War brings raids between Carolina and Spanish Florida as well as border raids in New England.

1691–92 Massachusetts absorbs Plymouth Colony. Salem witchcraft trials take 19 lives.

1701 French forces defeat the Iroquois, who pledge neutrality in coming wars and allow French influence in the Great Lakes region and Illinois territory.

1703 Delaware separates from Pennsylvania and becomes a Colony.

1732 Georgia is founded as a debtor's Colony with no slavery. Carefully planned Savannah is laid out the following year.

1732 Benjamin Franklin's *Poor Richard's Almanack* issued. George Washington born in Virginia.

1744–48 King George's War highlighted by the capture of Louisbourg, France's massive fortress on the Atlantic, but the peace treaty returned it to France. Embittered New Englanders face forced enlistment in the British navy. French and Indian troops burn Saratoga, New York.

1752 Benjamin Franklin flies his kite and discovers the electric conductor.

1754–63 Seven Years' War, also known as the French and Indian War in British North America, rages. Fighting starts when George Washington fires on French troops along the Monongahela River.

1758 Massive British failures at Fort Duquesne, Lake George, Crown Point, Fort William Henry, and Ticonderoga are reversed after this year.

1759 British invade Canada and capture the capital city, Québec, ending French rule in North America.

1764 Sugar and Currency Acts tax American Colonies to raise revenue for Colonial administration and to repay war debt; these taxes hurt an economy already in recession.

1765 Stamp Act taxes Colonies further, and resistance mounts. The Stamp Act Congress unites many colonists to protest "taxation without representation."

1766 Parliament repeals Stamp Act but passed the Declaratory Act, retaining its right to tax the Colonies. Royal surveyors Mason and Dixon establish the boundary between Maryland and Pennsylvania, as well as Delaware's northern border.

1766–71 North and South Carolina Regulator movements seek to establish order in backcountry districts through vigilante justice.

1767 Townshend Acts levies duties on finished goods imported from Great Britain.

1770 Surrounded by a mob hurling insults and snowballs, British troops fire on Bostonians, killing five men. Crispus Attucks, a multiracial sailor, is first American to die in the Revolution.

1773 Protestors opposed to the tax on tea burn a tea-laden ship in Annapolis, Maryland. Later in Boston, thinly disguised "Indians"—actually leading citizens and anti-tax patriots—dump a cargo of tea into the harbor.

1774 Coercive Acts close port of Boston and suspend self-rule in Massachusetts. The First Continental Congress meets to discuss resisting British taxes and to promote "civil disobedience." Rhode Island abolishes slavery.

1775 The Revolutionary War begins when British troops fire on the Lexington militia outside Boston. Paul Revere's Ride to Concord on April 18th. The Battle of Bunker Hill is waged in Boston in early June. Americans capture the British fortress at Ticonderoga and invade Canada.

1775 The Second Continental Congress meets to organize a government and army, with Seven Years' War veteran George Washington at its head.

1776 Thomas Paine publishes his crucial pamphlet, *Common Sense,* that helps propel movement for independence. British troops evacuate Boston but capture New York City. The war looks dim for Americans until

Washington crosses the Delaware Christmas night to win a victory at Trenton.

1776 At the Continental Congress in Philadelphia, Richard Henry Lee of Virginia moves "that these united Colonies are and of right ought to be free and independent states," a resolution adopted on July 2, with the Declaration of Independence approved two days later.

1777 British troops occupy Philadelphia as Washington harasses them in New Jersey. At Saratoga British General Burgoyne surrenders his entire army to American forces. The Marquis de Lafayette arrives with first French troops, as his nation recognizes the United States.

1778 France and the Netherlands sign treaties of alliance trade with the United States. Western New York State experiences civil war. British invade Georgia after withdrawing from Philadelphia.

1780–81 British strategy shifts south. Charleston falls in 1780 and Lord Cornwallis begins his march across the Carolinas. Partisan guerrilla warfare between Loyalists and Patriots lead to brutal atrocities on both sides.

1781 Cornwallis surrenders to an American and French army at Yorktown, Virginia, after a series of costly victories and scant American victories.

1783 Treaty of Paris ends the war and recognizes American independence.

1787 Drafted in Philadelphia, the Constitution goes to states for ratification.

1787–88 Debates over the Constitution result in *The Federalist Papers* and passage by 11 states. North Carolina and Rhode Island join later.

1789–90 The United States begins organizing a government. George Washington wins unanimous election as the nation's first President, and Congress meets for the first time. Swampland on the Potomac River is selected as the nation's permanent capital.

1791 Bill of Rights is ratified to satisfy Anti-Federalist concerns about the Constitution's lack of protection for individual rights.

1793 The United States attempted to stay out of the war between Great Britain and its enemies, France and Spain. Eli Whitney invents the cotton gin, revolutionizing southern agriculture.

1798–1800 Quasi-War with France is fought on the high seas. Republicans claim that Federalists, proponents of strong centralized government led by President John Adams, oppose the Revolution's principles.

1800 Washington, the District of Columbia, becomes the nation's capital. Thomas Jefferson is elected President in an intensely partisan campaign.

1803 Jefferson purchases Louisiana from France for $15 million, doubling the size of the United States. He doubts he had the authority to do so, but Congress approves the purchase anyway.

1804–06 Meriwether Lewis and William Clark lead the Corps of Discovery up the Missouri River and across the Rocky Mountains to the Pacific Ocean, seeking to chart the Louisiana Purchase and study its vast expanse.

1806–09 American attempts to remain neutral during the Napoleonic Wars in Europe rely on old strategies of nonimportation and embargo. Jefferson's policies fail to halt British and French attacks on American shipping, and cripple seaport economies.

1812–14 The United States declares war on Great Britain.

1816 President Monroe oversees prosperity and peace, the "Era of Good Feelings."

1818 The Erie Canal begins and the National Road is completed, ushering in a transportation revolution that spurs trade and westward migration.

By Diana Ross McCain

Connecticut

~

The Constitution State

"Anything you can do, I can do better" has been the mind-set of Connecticut since its founding in the 1630s. Residents rarely encountered a concept, a process, or a product they didn't try to improve or even replace with something entirely new. Noah Webster of West Hartford compiled the first dictionary of American English in 1806; David Bushnell of Saybrook invented the first submarine in 1776; Tapping Reeve established the first American law school in Litchfield in 1784; Eli Terry of Terryville developed, during the early 1800s, the mass-production and marketing techniques that put a clock in just about every American home; the Episcopal Church was founded in Woodbury in 1783; and in 1809 Mary Ann Kies of Killingly became the first woman to receive a U.S. patent (for an improved method of weaving straw with silk or thread). The roll call of Connecticut ingenuity goes on and on. But it was Connecticut's earliest innovation—refined, redefined, and zealously defended generation after generation—that proved the most profound of all: independence.

Connecticut, in fact, was still in its infancy when it first savored, then boldly refashioned, liberty's sweetness. That early taste went on to become a craving for charting its own destiny, first as a British colony, later as a player in the experiment in self-government that was the United States of America. In the 1630s, the fledgling towns of Windsor, Hartford, and Wethersfield heroically banded together to adopt the Fundamental Orders of Connecticut and organize themselves as the independent commonwealth known as the Connecticut Colony. These orders many now regard as the world's first constitution.

Today visitors who explore the third-smallest state's 5,000 square mi—a surprising two-thirds of them forested—will discover historic vistas of gentle grandeur, and an abundance of centuries-old, beautifully preserved homes, churches, schools, public buildings, town greens, burying grounds, museums, and monuments. Many of these sights eloquently evoke the often contradictory qualities—heroism and treachery, faith and intolerance, grand vision and short-sighted provincialism, ingenuity and stubbornness, to mention but a few—of a

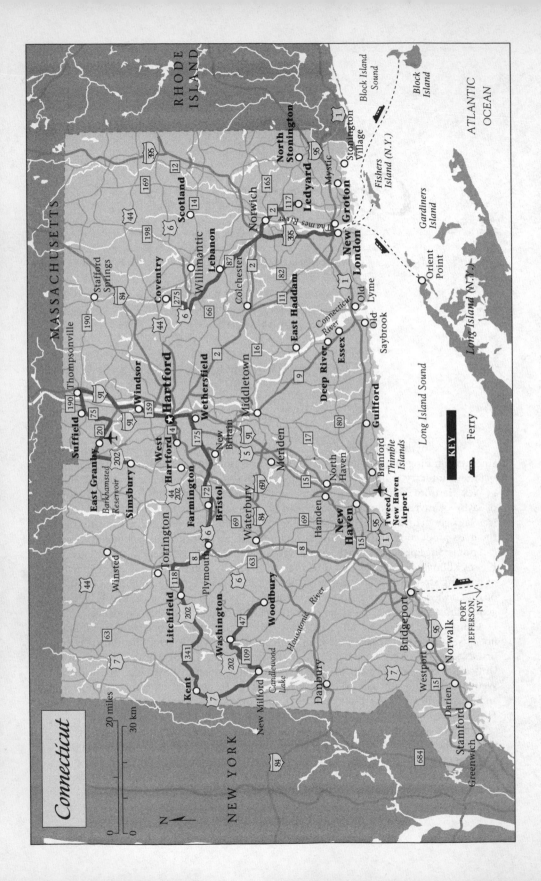

dozen generations who crafted Connecticut's unique identity. While the slot machines in casinos in the southeastern woods of Connecticut are giving Mystic Seaport's 19th-century sailing ships a run for their money, the Foxwoods Casino near Ledyard has funded an eye-knocking history museum devoted to the tribe that runs the outfit, the Mashantucket Pequots. As might be expected, the Indian saga of the Colonial era was not a pretty one. While Native Americans lived in Connecticut for more than 10,000 years before English settlers arrived, by 1700 two brutal conflicts, the Pequot War of 1637 and King Philip's War of 1675–76, along with the ravages of disease and the decimation wrought by slavery, had severely reduced many tribes.

✦ UNDER THE SHADE OF THE CHARTER OAK

Nevertheless, the name of the state itself comes from the Indian *Quinnetucket,* a reference to the "long, tidal river" that runs 45 mi through the center of the state. Native Americans lived off the bounty of Connecticut's land long before the year 1633 saw the arrival of the first permanent Europeans. A party of Dutch from New Netherlands successfully navigated that long tidal river and established a trading post near what would eventually become Connecticut's capital, Hartford. Then, English Connecticut was brought into being in the 1630s by bands of Puritans who, discontent with the religious and political leadership of Massachusetts Bay, splintered off. In 1636 the Rev. Thomas Hooker moved his congregation 100 mi from Cambridge, Massachusetts, to Hartford and with that, colonization began in earnest. In 1638 a fourth group established the New Haven Colony, an entity independent of Connecticut.

Connecticut Colony citizens promptly erected a milestone on humankind's road to democracy by adopting in 1639 the Fundamental Orders. The Fundamental Orders embodied the then-radical principle, proclaimed by Hartford founding father Reverend Thomas Hooker, that "the free consent of the people" was the source of governmental authority. By 1660 the Connecticut Colony had expanded along the Connecticut River from the Sound to Massachusetts, while the New Haven Colony had spread along 50 mi of the coast. The enduring influence of these immigrants' medieval English roots and the spareness of their lifestyle on what remained a frontier through the 1600s are reflected in the clapboards weathered dark with age and the small diamond-paned casement windows of the 1678 Joshua Hempsted House in New London and the circa 1710 Buttolph-Williams House in Wethersfield.

In 1660 the Puritan Commonwealth in England collapsed, and King Charles II ascended the throne—creating a crisis for Connecticut and New Haven, neither of which had formal permission from the English crown to exist. Connecticut Governor John Winthrop, Jr., secured from King Charles II the Royal Charter of 1662, which not only legitimized his colony's existence, but granted it a degree of self-government that made it all but independent of England. Connecticut was not so much striving for independence as it was protecting what it had enjoyed for two generations. When the Declaration of Independence severed political bonds with Great Britain, Connecticut kept the Royal Charter of 1662, minus references to the king, as the foundation of its government. Today an original copy of the Royal Charter is displayed at the Connecticut State Library in Hartford. A generation later Connecticut had to defend its independence yet again, when in 1687 King Charles II's successor, James II, sought to revoke the Charter. When Connecticut's leaders refused to return the document, royal representative Sir Edmund Andros came to Hartford to seize it. But Andros left Hartford empty-handed. Why he did is the keystone of Connecticut's heritage.

Legend says that Connecticut's leaders stubbornly debated with Andros until nightfall. Finally the Charter was laid upon a table. Suddenly candles were extinguished; when they were relit, the Charter had vanished. During the moments of darkness someone handed it out a window to a waiting conspirator, who hid it in the hollow of a gigantic, ancient tree that came to be known as the Charter Oak. This, in turn, became the definitive icon of Connecticut independence, reflected by its selection to grace the Connecticut state quarter minted in 1999.

✦ FAMILY, FARM, AND FAITH

During the Revolutionary War, the fever for freedom burned hottest in eastern Connecticut. And it is at three sites here that the veil between the present and the Revolutionary past seems very thin. In Lebanon, on the town green, stands the home of Jonathan Trumbull, Sr., the only Colonial governor to side with the patriots. A few steps away is the War Office, a small, simple building that was the nerve center of Connecticut's considerable contribution to the struggle for American independence. Here Governor Trumbull met more than 1,000 times with the Connecticut Council of Safety to coordinate recruitment of troops and production of food, clothing, cannon, and equipment for the patriot forces. It kept Washington's troops fortified during the winter of 1777–78 at Valley Forge and through the winter of 1779–80 in Morristown, New Jersey. Family, farm, and faith were the center tenets that embodied the life from which many Revolutionary soldiers came, and they are brought vividly to life in the Georgian house at the Nathan Hale Homestead in Coventry. The site's pastoral charm makes even more poignant the fate of Nathan Hale, who grew to manhood here. After enlisting in the Continental Army, Hale volunteered in 1776 to spy behind British lines. Captured and facing the hangman's noose, Hale, only 21, uttered those words of courageous patriotism that resonated down the ages, elevating him to the status of one of the Revolution's best-known heroes: "I only regret that I have but one life to lose for my country."

When the need for a stronger national government became desperately evident following America's victory in the Revolution, Connecticut provided a key player to the team that crafted the solution. In 1787 the Constitutional Convention was deadlocked over how representation in Congress should be determined. Roger Sherman of New Haven saved the day with the Connecticut Compromise, providing for representation based on population in the House of Representatives and equal representation for each state in the Senate. Connecticut ratified the U.S. Constitution in 1788, becoming the fifth state.

A REGIONAL GAZETEER
▼▼

✦ HARTFORD AND THE CONNECTICUT RIVER VALLEY

Dutch explorer Adriaen Block first explored the Connecticut River area in 1614, and in 1633 a trading post was set up in what is now Hartford. Within five years throngs of restive Massachusetts Bay colonists had settled in this fertile valley. Less touristy than the coast and northwest hills, the Connecticut River valley is a swath of small villages and uncrowded state parks punctuated by a few small cities and a large one: the capital city of Hartford. To the south of Hartford, with the exception of industrial Middletown, distinctive hamlets vie for a share of Connecticut's tourist crop with antiques shops, scenic drives, and trendy restaurants and elegant Colonial-era homesteads built by rich merchants and sea captains. The essence of the era when maritime trade dominated Connecticut Valley life is best sensed in **Wethersfield,** which boasts dozens of handsome structures built before 1820. The highlight is the Webb-Deane-Stevens Museum, comprising three important 18th-century houses. Farther down the Valley, sites in several towns also reflect that close connection with the river. The Connecticut River Museum in **Essex** chronicles four centuries of that mighty waterway's heritage—displays include a full-scale model of the *American Turtle,* the one-man wooden submarine invented on the banks of the Connecticut River during the American Revolution by David Bushnell.

Connecticut's significant contribution to the founding of the American Republic is reflected at the 1740 **Windsor** home of Oliver Ellsworth, one of the authors of the U.S. Constitution and third chief justice of the U.S. Supreme Court. The Noah Webster House in **West Hartford** is the restored birthplace of the "schoolmaster to America," whose "blue-backed speller" and pioneering dictionary of American English helped unite citizens of the new nation

Connecticut Timeline

1634–1636 Puritans from Massachusetts Bay Colony settle towns of Windsor, Wethersfield, and Hartford.

1637 Pequot Indians are nearly exterminated in Pequot War with English colonists.

1639 Hartford, Windsor, and Wethersfield adopt Fundamental Orders as framework for joint civil government.

1662 Royal Charter granted to Connecticut Colony by King Charles II.

1665 New Haven Colony absorbed by Connecticut Colony according to provisions of Royal Charter of 1662.

1687 King James II sends Sir Edmund Andros to Hartford to seize the Connecticut Royal Charter of 1662. Connecticut officials refuse to hand over the document. Legend says the Charter was hidden from Andros in hollow of ancient tree that became famous as Charter Oak.

1701 Yale College founded in Saybrook; moved to New Haven in 1717.

1764 Publication begins in Hartford of the *Connecticut Courant* newspaper, today the *Hartford Courant.*

1776 June: Connecticut General Assembly votes to authorize delegates to Continental Congress to propose that the Congress "declare the United American Colonies Free and Independent States."

1776 July: Connecticut delegates to Continental Congress vote in favor of independence.

1781 1,800 British troops commanded by Benedict Arnold burn much of New London and massacre 150 surrendering militiamen at Fort Griswold in Groton.

1783 Noah Webster publishes in Hartford his "blue-backed speller," a reading text designed for American students that will sell tens of millions of copies.

1787 At the Constitutional Convention in Philadelphia, Roger Sherman of New Haven resolves deadlock over representation in Congress with Connecticut Compromise.

1788 Connecticut ratifies the U.S. Constitution, becoming fifth state.

in the decades following the American Revolution via a shared version of English distinct from that of Great Britain. While Ellsworth was adjudicating and Webster educating, one-time peddler Oliver Phelps was speculating so successfully in western wilderness lands that he could afford to enlarge and renovate his **Suffield** house in cutting-edge style—the Phelps-Hatheway House is considered one of the most important pre-1820 homes in the Connecticut Valley.

In **Hartford** the Old State House, a dignified brick-and-brownstone Neoclassical structure designed by Charles Bulfinch, was built in 1796. The 1782 Butler-McCook House, Hartford's oldest surviving structure, is furnished with possessions of the four generations of the same family who lived here. Prior to 1807, just about every Hartfordite was interred in the Ancient Burying Ground. Its more than 400 surviving gravestones constitute an open-air museum of early Connecticut history and folk art. Splendid examples of paintings, furniture, silver, glass, and ceramics from the 1600s and 1700s are on view at the Wadsworth Atheneum Museum of Art. *Towns listed: Deep River, Essex, East Granby, East Haddam, Farmington Hartford, Simsbury, Suffield, West Hartford, Wethersfield, Windsor.*

✦ SEA-SHAPED: CONNECTICUT'S COAST

In an era when travel by water was faster, cheaper, and more convenient than overland transportation, the Long Island Sound coastline was a logical first stop for English settlers. The first English newcomers set down at the mouth of the Connecticut River in 1635, and within 15 years almost the entire coast, from Rhode Island to New York, had been settled. The Henry Whitfield House in **Guilford,** built of stone in 1639, and the 1678 Joshua Hempsted House in **New London** provide visitors with rare glimpses of daily existence in early Colonial Connecticut. Towns like New London and New Haven became important ports for international trade. On the rare occasions when war came to Connecticut during the Revolution and the War of 1812, coastal towns like Fairfield, New London, Groton, and New Haven bore the brunt of British amphibious assaults.

The Fort Griswold Battlefield State Park across the Thames River in **Groton** bears witness to Connecticut's steadfast support of the fight for American independence, and the cruel price sometimes exacted for that support. The Shaw-Perkins Mansion was Connecticut's naval headquarters during the Revolution. In 1781 New London was targeted for a British invasion in part because of the damage privateers docked there were wreaking on British vessels. When the 1,600 British soldiers retreated, much of New London had been destroyed by fire, and 160 defenders of Fort Griswold across the Thames River in Groton had been slaughtered while trying to surrender. Two years earlier the British had torched **Fairfield,** reducing almost the entire town to ruins—the Ogden House is one of the few survivors of that conflagration. Yale University, America's third institution of higher education, was founded in Saybrook in 1701, moving to **New Haven** in 1716. Connecticut Hall, built in 1752, is the oldest surviving structure on campus—it was home to Nathan Hale, Noah Webster, and Eli Whitney during their student days. *Towns listed: Groton, Guilford, Mystic, New Haven, New London, North Stonington.*

✦ HOTBED OF REVOLUTION: EASTERN CONNECTICUT

Most of Connecticut east of the Connecticut River was not settled by English pioneers until the late 1600s and early 1700s. The region lacked easy access to transportation by water and its land was not the best. The history of the Native American peoples who had occupied Connecticut for more than 10,000 years prior to the arrival of the first Europeans is explored in sites both extravagant and humble in this area. The Mashantucket Pequot Museum and Research Center in **Ledyard** is a state-of-the-art facility, pulling out all the stops in recounting the heritage of Eastern Woodland Indian tribes in general, and the Pequots in particular.

New settlers' willingness to defy authority was demonstrated when in 1765 the British Parliament imposed, without the Colonists' consent, a stamp tax on documents used in the Colonies. Eastern Connecticut spawned the band of Sons of Liberty who, 500 strong, "persuaded" Connecticut's stamp-tax collector to resign. When war finally broke out, firebrands from eastern Connecticut were in the forefront of the state's role in realizing American independence. From his home and the War Office on the **Lebanon** Green, Connecticut Governor Jonathan Trumbull, Sr., the only Colonial governor to side with the Patriot cause, and the Connecticut Council of Safety directed Connecticut's considerable contribution of men and supplies to the fight for liberty. A rebel of a different stripe was Governor Trumbull's son John, born in the Lebanon house in 1756, who went on to become one of the new nation's greatest painters. Lebanon was also the birthplace of one of Connecticut's four signers of the Declaration of Independence, William Williams. One of the most enduringly famous heroes to emerge from the Revolution was Nathan Hale—the patriot spent most of his tragically short life at the Nathan Hale Homestead in **Coventry.** *Towns listed: Coventry, Lebanon, Ledyard, Scotland.*

✦ FINAL FRONTIER: WESTERN CONNECTICUT

Western Connecticut's rugged, hilly terrain, poorly suited for agriculture, meant that this region was the last part of the Colony to be settled. English pioneers didn't begin arriving in large numbers until the early 1700s. The Institute for American Indian Studies in **Washington** highlights the culture of the Native Americans who occupied southern New England for thousands of years before that European influx. Undaunted by the land's inferior fertility, enterprising settlers during the 18th century found ways to profit from the area's natural resources, establishing fledgling manufacturing enterprises that were harbingers of Connecticut's future as an industrial giant. The Sloane-Stanley Museum and Kent Iron Furnace in **Kent** tells the story of the region's iron industry as it continued into the 19th century. Another natural resource, copper, was mined in **East Granby** beginning in 1707. During the Revolution, Connecticut's leaders converted this facility into Old New-Gate Prison, a chilly hellhole where prisoners of war and suspected Tories were incarcerated 60 ft underground. In the 1810s clockmaker Eli Terry developed a process for making clocks cheaper, faster, and in a smaller, portable size—using the water power of a stream in the town of **Plymouth** to run the machinery, Terry was soon turning out affordable clocks by the thousands, thus earning Connecticut worldwide fame as the "clock state." The American Clock and Watch Museum in **Bristol** explains this important chapter in local history. Over in **Litchfield,** attorney Tapping Reeve established America's first law school in 1784. Another intellectual first for the nation is remembered at the Glebe House in **Woodbury**—here in 1783 10 clergymen of the Church of England met secretly to elect the first bishop of a new religious denomination, the Protestant Episcopal Church. *Towns listed: Bristol, Kent, Litchfield, Washington, Woodbury.*

The Litchfield Hills
to the Connecticut Valley
A DRIVING TOUR FROM WOODBURY TO HARTFORD

▼▼▼

Distance: approx. 130 mi (one-way)   **Time:** 3 days (2 nights)
Breaks: Waterbury (6 mi south of the outlined route between Litchfield and Bristol) is a convenient location to spend the night, and there are many hotels in Hartford and Wethersfield.

"I have spent this Morning in Riding thro Paradise," future president John Adams rhapsodized about his journey along the Connecticut River between Windsor and Wethersfield in June 1771. "Nothing can exceed the Beauty and Fertility of the Country. The Lands upon the River, the flat low Lands, are loaded with rich, noble Crops of Grass, and Grain and Corn." Today's travelers often feel similarly when they venture through some of Connecticut's most time-stained counties and towns to discover Revolutionary byways and highways, from the Litchfield Hills to the famed Connecticut Valley. Two highways, I–84 and Route 8, form the southern and eastern boundaries of the Litchfield Hills region. Here in the foothills of the Berkshires is some of the most spectacular and unspoiled scenery in Connecticut. Grand old inns are plentiful, as are sophisticated eateries. Sweeping town greens and stately homes anchor Litchfield and New Milford. Kent, New Preston, and Woodbury draw avid antiquers, and Washington, Salisbury, and Norfolk provide a glimpse into New England village life as it might have been two centuries ago.

Begin in **Woodbury,** appropriately time-burnished with probably more antiques shops than in all the towns in the rest of the Litchfield Hills combined. Five magnificent churches line U.S. 6; they represent some of the best-preserved examples of Colonial religious architecture in New England. Check out the Glebe House, a large gambrel-roof Colonial in which Dr. Samuel Seabury was elected America's first Episcopal bishop in 1783; on view is a fine collection of antiques and renowned British horticulturist Gertrude Jekyll designed the historic garden. Follow Route 47 northwest for 8 mi to **Washington**—one of the best-preserved Colonial towns in Connecticut and the first town in the United States to be named for the first president (in 1779). If you're looking for a luxe blow-out, enjoy a meal or stay at the famed Mayflower Inn, south of the Gunnery on Route 47. Head south along Route 109, then 202 for 6 mi to **New Milford.** Here, in 1743, a cobbler named Roger Sherman opened his shop where Main and Church streets meet—as a Declaration of Independence signer, Sherman also helped draft the Constitution. You'll find old shops, galleries, and eateries all within a short stroll of New Milford's green—one of the longest in New England.

Follow Route 7 northwest for 11 mi to **Kent,** home to art galleries, antiques shops, and the Sloane-Stanley Museum. Artist and author Eric Sloane was fascinated by early American woodworking tools, and his collection ranges from the 17th to the 19th century. Head 20 mi northwest, along Route 341 and U.S. 202 to arrive at the next stop, **Litchfield,** hub of the Litchfield Hills—everything here seems to be on a larger scale than in neighboring burgs, especially the impressive Litchfield Green and the white Colonial and Colonial Revival homes that line the broad elm-shaded streets. The top draw here for history seekers is the Tapping Reeve House and Law School, where, in 1784 Judge Tapping Reeve established the first law school in the country. The well-organized galleries at the Litchfield History Museum display decorative arts, paintings, and antique furnishings.

Seventeen miles southeast of Litchfield, following Routes 118, 8, and 6, is **Bristol.** You can set your watch at the famed American Clock & Watch Museum where more than 3,000 timepieces are on display in an 1801 house. Now head eastward 13 mi along Routes 72, 9, and 175 to **Wethersfield,** a vast Hartford suburb. Dating from 1634, it has the state's largest—and, some say, most picturesque—historic district, with more than 100 buildings from before 1840. Wethersfield allows you to take a plunge into Connecticut's Colonial and Revolutionary past. Headliners here include the Buttolph-Williams House—although it was built around 1710, everything about the house inside and out bespeaks the early Puritan settlers' roots in medieval England.

Three miles to the north along I–91 is **Hartford**'s Main Street neighborhood, which offers a wealth of sites, most within walking distance. The new Main Street History Center is attached to the 1782 Butler-McCook House, the oldest surviving documented structure in the city. The celebrated Wadsworth Atheneum Museum of Art features magnificent displays of furniture, painting, and silver from the Colonial and Revolutionary eras. The handsome, dignified Old State House, built in 1796 and designed by Boston architect Charles Bulfinch, bespeaks the conservative Federalism that prevailed in Connecticut in the decades following adoption of the federal Constitution. Cater-corner from the Old State House is the First Church of Christ and the Ancient Burying Ground, and the Raymond Baldwin Museum of Connecticut History houses the "holy grail" of Connecticut history: an original copy of the Royal Charter of 1662 framed in wood from the Charter Oak.

Five miles to the west along I–84, you reach **West Hartford** and the Noah Webster House. The house reflects life during the pre-Revolutionary era, when Noah—creator of the first American dictionary—was growing up here. Northeast 10 mi along I–84 and I–91 is **Windsor,** with the first stop the Windsor Historical Society, whose offerings include the 1758 Strong House and the 1769 Dr. Hezekiah Chaffee House. The 1781 Oliver Ellsworth Homestead, also in Windsor, is the restored home of one of the framers of the U.S. Constitution and a chief justice of the U.S. Supreme Court. The Phelps-Hatheway House in **Suffield** 9 mi north of Windsor along Routes I–91, 20, and 75 remains one of the finest pieces of architecture in the Connecticut River valley. For the most dangerous Tories, and men who committed such serious crimes as rape and robbery, punishment was often confinement in Old New-Gate Prison in **East Granby,** 4 mi west along Routes 168 and 187. End your tour by heading southwest 8 mi along Routes 20 and 10 to gracious **Simsbury** to visit the Simsbury Historical Society's Phelps Tavern Museum & Homestead, the period-furnished 1771 Colonial home of Elijah Phelps and his family. After this dip into the Colonial era, it's now time to head back east 11 mi along Routes 10 and 44 to Hartford—and modern-day reality.

Nathan Hale, Benedict Arnold, and Company

A DRIVING TOUR FROM LEDYARD TO GROTON

▼▼▼

Distance: approx. 50 mi (one-way)   **Time:** 2 days (1 night)
Breaks: Norwich is a convenient location for a night's stay, as are New London and Groton.

A driving tour of Colonial and Revolutionary sites in southeastern Connecticut should begin, most appropriately, with the beginning: the Mashantucket Pequot Museum and Research Center in **Ledyard,** which chronicles the history and culture of the Mashantucket Pequot Tribal Nation and other Native American tribes. Visitors can take an escalator through the heart of a "glacier" of the type that covered most of Connecticut 11,000 years ago and walk through a life-size recreation of a Pequot village from the 1500s. Eight miles northwest along Route 2 you come to **Norwich,** site of the ancient Native American Burial Grounds and the Christopher Leffingwell House, a gathering place for revolutionaries. Follow Route 87 7 mi northwest to **Lebanon,** the nerve center of Connecticut's contribution to the Revolutionary war effort. Lebanon looks remarkably like it did more than 200 years ago. The Town Green, a mile long, has not been tidied up into a park as have so many others, but continues to be used as a hayfield. The Jonathan Trumbull, Sr., House on the Lebanon green, built in 1710, was the home of the only Colonial governor to side with the Patriots during the Revolution.

Continue on Routes 87, 6, and 275 another 9 mi to **Coventry,** home to a soldier who never returned from the war but left a legacy of last words that would inspire generations to come. Nathan Hale was born in 1755 and grew to manhood at the site today known as the Nathan Hale Homestead. In 1776, Hale, a captain in the Continental Army, was captured behind enemy lines by the British who, after learning his true identity and mission, hanged the 21-year-old spy on September 22, 1776, in New York City. Set on 12 acres of fields and woods adjacent to a state forest, the Hale Homestead seems to have been frozen in time. Head back 16 mi along Route 87 to Norwich, then follow Route 2A south and Route 82 west a total of 17 mi along Route 82, then southeast along Route 85, brings the visitor to **New London,** where the stark, unpainted clapboards, high gables, and tiny diamond-paned casement windows of the 1678 Joshua Hempsted House reflect the English roots of Connecticut's 17th-century residents. A short distance from the Hempsted House stands the granite Shaw-Perkins Mansion—George Washington did indeed sleep here during a visit to New London in 1776.

Like Nathan Hale, most of the sons Connecticut sacrificed to the struggle for liberty died far from home, for the state was largely spared the ravages of combat inflicted upon Pennsylvania, New Jersey, New York, or Virginia. What fighting occurred on Connecticut soil consisted of sporadic British raids on coastal towns. One of these assaults, the 1781 attack on Fort Griswold in **Groton,** just a mile east on Route I-95 across the Thames River, was one of the darkest days in Connecticut history, as Benedict Arnold led a raiding party of 1,600 British and Hessian troops who proceeded to kill Fort Griswold's garrison even though they attempted to surrender. Fort Griswold Battlefield State Park encompasses that hallowed ground where so many Connecticut men died defending their homeland. Heading eastward on Route 1 about 8 mi you will reach Mystic, famed for its enormous restoration of seafaring America, complete with tall ships, acres of sail, and a bevy of restored historic structures that might have even enchanted Herman Melville, but nearly all of it falling beyond our time frame of Colonial and Federalist America.

BRISTOL

▼▼▼

"In every dell in Arkansas and in every cabin where there is not a chair to sit in, there is sure to be a Connecticut clock," a foreign visitor to America observed in the 1840s. That phenomenon had its origins in Plymouth, Connecticut, next to Bristol, where in the early 1800s entrepreneur Eli Terry—for whom nearby Terryville is named—developed a process for manufacturing clocks that were cheap enough for ordinary people to afford and small enough for Connecticut peddlers to include in the wares they hawked across the country. The region for many decades was supplier to the world of affordable clocks. In time, there were some 275 clockmakers in and around Bristol during the late 1800s—it is said that by the end of the 19th century just about every household in America told time to a Connecticut clock. Seth Thomas, for whom nearby Thomaston is named, learned under Terry and carried on the tradition. *Contact Litchfield Hills Visitors Council / Box 968, Litchfield 06759 / 860/567–4506 / fax 860/567–5214 / www.litchfieldhills.com.*

American Clock and Watch Museum. This is the only museum of its kind in the country— and an astounding place to be when the big hand hits the 12. This museum boasts the world's best collection of American-made clocks, many of them examples made in and around Bristol. Indeed, during the 1800s, Connecticut was known as "the clock state" since so many manufacturers of clocks and watches were manufactured in this area, first with wooden gears, then with brass. The collection has more than 3,000 timepieces—more than 1,400 on display— and also includes antique watches and clocks from other countries. Bristol was famous for its "Dollar" watches—a fancy term to indicate they were unjeweled. | 100 Maple St. | 860/583–6070 | www.clockmuseum.org | $5 | Apr.–Nov., daily 10–5.

COVENTRY

▼▼▼

The farming community of Coventry, settled around 1700, produced an extraordinary crop of secular and spiritual leaders. At a time when most boys' formal education consisted of a few years attendance at a one-room schoolhouse, more than half a dozen sons of Coventry graduated from colleges that included Yale and Princeton. Several went on to become influential ministers and lawyers. Coventry gave its all to the struggle for American independence; Deacon Richard Hale, for example, sent all six of his sons into military service—most notably, the hallowed Nathan. *Contact Northeast Connecticut Visitors District / 13 Canterbury Rd., Suite 3, Box 145, Brooklyn 06234 / 860/779–6383 / www.ctquietcorner.org.*

Nathan Hale Homestead. Nathan Hale was born and grew up on this farmstead, until fate took him first to Yale, then into the Continental Army, and finally to his historic rendezvous with death in New York in 1776 at the age of only 21. Hale had volunteered for an espionage mission behind enemy lines. But he was captured, and when the British learned his true identity and purpose, they hanged him as a spy (without trial). Hale's last words have echoed down the centuries as one of the noblest expressions of courage and patriotism: "I only regret that I have but one life to lose for my country." As it turns out, Hale never saw the spacious Georgian house that stands at the Homestead today—it was under construction while he was on his mission. However, Hale's father, the Deacon Richard Hale (1717–1802, who had come to Coventry around 1740 from Newburyport, Massachusetts), several of his siblings, and their offspring occupied it for decades—indeed, the deacon had 12 children by his first wife, then welcomed his second wife's seven children, so little wonder a larger house was required.

Nathan became the schoolmaster of the Latin School in New London, much respected by his male students for his atheleticism, much adored by his female students for his handsome visage. With war approaching, he signed up with the troops, and was ultimately stationed to New York where he witnessed the defeat of Washington's forces on August 27 and probably played a role in ferrying the Americans back across the East River to New York Island (today's Manhattan). Soon after, as a Knowlton Ranger, he was sent to spy behind British lines on Long Island. Betrayed (some historians conjecture) by his Loyalist cousin, Samuel, and arrested—he carried his diploma at the time and refused to lie about his identity to his captors (an ethical education at work?)—he was hung on September 22, 1776, at a gallows in "Artillery Park" (present-day 3rd Avenue at 66th Street), where his body hung for two days as a warning to rebels. Those famous last words were not entirely his. Many souls were given to quoting Joseph Addison's play *Cato*, a drama set in ancient Rome with many speeches given to sacrificing one's life for liberty. *"How beautiful is death when earned by virtue? Who would not be that youth? What woe is it that we can die but once to serve our country."* Hale's famous last words were, in truth, a spin on Addison's ringing words. Today, his family's Homestead is furnished to reflect life in the period following the American Revolution, with antiques that include Nathan Hale's Bible and fowling piece. The house's site on 12 acres, next to a 400-acre state forest, evokes the landscape of widely spaced farms that was Connecticut in the 18th century. | 2299 South St. | 860/742–6917 | www.hartford.org/als/nathanhale/homestead | $5 | May–Oct., Wed.–Sun. 1–4.

✦ ON THE CALENDAR: July **Encampment and Muster.** This weekend historical encampment takes place on the grounds of the Nathan Hale Homestead. On Saturday there is a reenactment of a Revolutionary War battle (with the outcome always uncertain). On Sunday afternoon the Nathan Hale Ancient Fife and Drum Corps hosts a muster (individual corps play and then all join in for a stirring grand finale). Colonial crafts are demonstrated, and reenactors share the realities of life in the 18th century. | 2299 South St. | 860/742–6917.

DEEP RIVER
▼▼

Deep River takes its dramatic-sounding name not, as might be expected, from the majestic Connecticut River, which it borders, but from a tributary that has been known as Deep River since 1721. Another unexpected twist is that this community, characterized by quiet, small-town charm, annually hosts what is probably the noisiest event in the state—"The Deep River Ancient Muster." *Contact Connecticut River Valley Shoreline Visitors Council | 393 Main St., Middletown 06457 | 800/486–3346 | fax 860/704–2340 | www.cttourism.org.*

✦ ON THE CALENDAR: July **Deep River Ancient Muster.** The world's largest and oldest fife and drum parade, featuring 70 corps representing various eras of history, takes place on the third Saturday of July. More than 2,000 fifers and drummers participate in what has been called a "Colonial Woodstock," held annually since 1953. A "tattoo"—a concert by various corps—takes place the night before. | 860/526–0058 | Free | Parade, Sat. noon; tattoo, Fri. 7 | www.moxie comp.com/dram.

EAST GRANBY
▼▼

The local names of "Turkey Hills" and "Salmon Brook" testify to the abundance of wildlife in East Granby during the 1700s, but it was copper below the ground that was the town's greatest draw. For more than a century that metal was mined on and off, but never with great success. In 1737 and 1739 a local blacksmith by the name of Higley fashioned his own coins from East Granby copper, which, although of no legal value, were some of the first coins made in America. Today the few surviving "Higley coppers" are numismatic treasures. *Contact Connecticut's North Central Tourism Bureau | 111 Hazard Ave., Enfield 06082 | 800/248–8283 | www.ctheritagevalley.com.*

Old New-Gate Prison and Copper Mine. As if the Colonies' rapidly unraveling relationship with Great Britain weren't headache enough, in 1773 Connecticut faced a domestic dilemma: there were more convicted criminals than the state's jails could hold. The quintessentially Yankee solution, both practical and economical, was to purchase abandoned copper mines in East Granby (then part of Simsbury) for the "purpose of confining, securing, and profitably employing such criminals and delinquents." Following the outbreak of the American Revolution two years later, Connecticut began incarcerating a new category of offenders in the copper mines: British prisoners of war and Tories, including several of the latter sent by George Washington, who called them "flagrant and atrocious villains." The prisoners spent their nights in the dark, dank caverns—where the temperature is always a chilly 52°F—carved out 60 ft below the surface by the original miners. During the day they there were brought up to the surface, chained to blocks, and put to work making wagons, nails, and shoes. Old New-Gate was used for nearly half a century, during which a total of more than 800 criminals did hard time—really hard time. Today visitors can descend into the shafts in which the prisoners slept and explore the ruins of the stone buildings in which they labored during the day. | 115 Newgate Rd. | 860/653–3563 | www.chc. state.ct/usold_new.htm | $4 | Mid-May–mid-Oct., Wed.–Sun. 10–4:30.

EAST HADDAM

▼▼

While East Haddam's defining attraction is the Goodspeed Opera House, a white-wedding-cake Victorian known to be the birthplace of the American musical, there are other sites, such as the Nathan Hale Schoolhouse, that reveal the town's Colonial history. *Contact Connecticut River Valley and Shoreline Visitors Council | 393 Main St., Middletown 06457 | 800/ 486–3346 | fax 860/704–2340 | www.cttourism.org.*

St. Stephen's Church and Nathan Hale Schoolhouse. This church, built in 1794 and moved to its present site in 1890, is listed in the *Guinness Book of World Records* as having the oldest bell in the United States. It was supposedly crafted in Spain in 815, but most historians think it was really made in the 1400s. Behind the church is the one-room schoolhouse where Nathan Hale is said to have taught from 1773 to 1774, after his graduation from Yale (*see* the Nathan Hale Homestead in Coventry, *above*)—so bored was he by his existence out here in the wilderness, he took off for the bustling streets of New London and, thence, to his appointment with destiny by signing up with the Continental Army. | Main St. | 860/873–9547 | Free | Call for hrs.

Sundial Herb Gardens. The three formal gardens here—a knot garden of interlocking hedges, a typical 18th-century geometric garden with a central sundial, and a topiary garden—surround an 18th-century farmhouse. A Colonial barn serves as a formal tea room and a shop where you'll find herbs, books, and rare and fine teas. Sunday afternoon teas and special programs take place throughout the year. | 59 Hidden Lake Rd., Higganum | 860/345–4290 | www. sundialgardens.com | $1 | Jan.–mid-Oct. and early Nov.–late Nov., weekends 10–5; late Nov.– Dec. 24, daily 10–5.

ESSEX

▼▼▼

The picture-perfect river village of Essex owes many of the handsome houses that contribute to its charm to the shipbuilding that flourished during the late 1700s and early 1800s—but that same industry was the catalyst for the darkest day in the town's early history. Starting in 1775 with Connecticut's first warship of the Revolution, the *Oliver Cromwell* (fitted with 24 cannon), Essex shipyards turned out scores more ships over the next decades. Their production took on special importance when the War of 1812 broke out between the United States and Great Britain, so in spring 1814 the British decided to eliminate the threat. Before dawn on April 8, more than 130 British marines and sailors landed at the bottom of Main Street and seized control of a completely surprised and unprepared Essex. The British agreed not to torch the town if locals would not interfere with their mission. By noon the enemy was gone, having burned 28 ships that were either anchored in the river or under construction, and taken two others with them. Essex bounced back and continued to be an important shipbuilding center for many years. Gone are the days of steady trade with the West Indies, when the aroma of imported rum, molasses, and spices hung in the air. Whitewashed houses—many the former roosts of sea captains—line Main Street, whose shops sell clothing, antiques, paintings and prints, and sweets. *Contact Connecticut River Valley and Shoreline Visitors Council | 393 Main St., Middletown 06457 | 800/486–3346 | fax 860/704–2340 | www.cttourism.org.*

Connecticut River Museum. This small gem of a museum is housed in a converted former warehouse on the dock right next to the majestic waterway whose history it chronicles. A permanent exhibition explores the rich and varied activity that occurred over the past four centuries along the length of the waterway early Colonists referred to simply as the "Great River." That story, which includes the lucrative and risky trade with the West Indies and Atlantic coast ports during the 1700s, and the building of ships for private trade in peacetime and for national defense during the Revolution and the War of 1812, garnered the Connecticut recognition by the federal government as one of only 10 "American Heritage Rivers" in the country. Most visitors will be astonished by the full-size reproduction of the *Turtle*, a one-man, egg-shape wooden submersible vessel invented by David Bushnell of nearby Westbrook in 1776. It was in the waters of the Connecticut River that Bushnell conducted his experiments that resulted in the world's first successful submarine. The *Turtle* was designed as a stealth weapon that could attach timed explosive charges to the hulls of enemy British vessels anchored in American harbors. Despite several attempts, it never fulfilled that mission, through no fault of its inventor. | 67 Main St. | 860/767–8269 | www.ctrivermuseum.org | $4 | Tues.–Sun. 10–5.

Museum of Fife and Drum. This self-described "visual and musical history of America on parade" features displays of fifes and drums that have set American hearts pounding for more than 250 years, along with music, uniforms, swords, and much more. It is sponsored by the Company of Fifers & Drummers, an international service organization that coordinates more than 150 traditional fife and drum corps throughout the United States, Canada, and even Europe. | 62 N. Main St. | 860/767–2237 | http://companyoffifeanddrum.org/museum.html | $3 | June 30–Labor Day, weekends 1–5; 3rd weekend of July and 4th weekend of Aug., reserved for private activities.

HISTORIC DINING AND LODGING

Bee and Thistle Inn. Set 5 mi to the southeast of Essex in Old Lyme, this 1756 Colonial inn comes with candlelight, firelight, floral prints, and landscaped lawns that lead to the Lieutenant River. Some of the antiques-filled guest rooms have four-poster beds or canopy beds, while all have wingback chairs, hardwood floors, Oriental rugs, and views of plants and flowers from the sunken garden. The bay-windowed dining room (closed Tues.) is considered one of the state's most romantic dining spots. Restaurant. No smoking. | 100 Lyme St. | 860/434–1667 | www.beeandthistleinn.com | 11 rooms | $79–$159 | AE, DC, MC, V.

Griswold Inn. Established in 1776 and billed as America's oldest continuously operating inn, this famous and lovely white clapboard building a short walk from the Connecticut River mixes Colonial, Federal, and Victorian decor. Some guest rooms have fireplaces and most are furnished with antiques. Downstairs are some five historic dining salons; the incomparable Covered Bridge was constructed from, yes, an abandoned New Hampshire covered bridge and is now virtually wallpapered with dazzling Currier & Ives prints, Endicott & Co. steamboat prints, temperance banners, and maritime memorabilia. Restaurant, complimentary breakfast. | 36 Main St. | 860/767-1776 | fax 860/767-0481 | www.griswoldinn.com | 16 rooms, 15 suites | $95–$125; $150–$200 suites | AE, MC, V.

FARMINGTON
▼▼▼

"There are about one hundred handsome dwelling houses within the limits of something more than a mile, some of which are elegant edifices," historian John Warner Barber wrote of Farmington in 1836. His praise could still apply to Farmington. Although the town is now a large, upscale suburb, many of the homes that impressed Barber more than 165 years ago still stand along Main Street and its side streets, some dating back to the 1600s. The stately clapboard Congregational meetinghouse, built in 1771, is one of the oldest surviving houses of worship in the state. Also of reknown is Miss Porter's School, the late Jacqueline Kennedy Onassis's alma mater, and the spectacular Hill-Stead Museum, a Colonial Revival mansion built by Theodate Pope Riddle, and now hung with a stunning collection of Impressionist paintings, with notable works by Degas and Monet. *Contact Greater Hartford Tourism District | 31 Pratt St., Hartford 06103 | 800/793–4480 | fax 860/244–8180 | www.enjoyhartford.com.*

Stanley-Whitman House. One of the most stunning relics of Connecticut, this house is a veritable icon of Early Colonial architecture, complete with lean-to roof and brown clapboard. English immigrants to Connecticut in the 1600s brought with them ideas about architecture that were rooted deep in their native land's past. Thus, this house, with medieval features that include a massive stone center chimney and a second floor extending out over the first to create an overhang from which are suspended four carved wooden pendant drops, was for decades believed to have been built around 1660, just 20 years after Farmington was settled. But by the 1980s increased knowledge of historical architecture made it clear that the house in fact dated from around 1720. Undaunted, the house's stewards commissioned what may be the most meticulous and accurate restoration of a Colonial dwelling in New England. Today, the Stanley-Whitman House showcases Farmington of the 1700s on guided tours; collections on hand number more than 3,000 items, but only a selection are on display—rooms are sparingly furnished. Special events are held through the year, including delightful Living History tours ("January 10: The Lines are Drawn! Townspeople form a Committee of Inspection to enforce patriot activities—but not everyone agrees. Meet William Judd, Chairman of this powerful committee, and Mathias Leaming, who must vote his conscience—even if it means losing everything."). There is also a full-scale research library. | 37 High St. | 860/677-9222 | www.stanleywhitman.org | $5 | May–Oct., Wed.–Sun. noon–4; Nov.–Apr., weekends noon–4.

GROTON
▼▼▼

Groton's location on the east side of the mouth of the Thames River determined its destiny, for good and ill. In the 1700s it became a center of maritime trade and fishing. It was also home to a number of "wreckers"—vessels that cruised as far as the West Indies seeking damaged or "wrecked" ships and cargo that they could salvage for profit. During time of war its strategic position made Groton an important defensive post. *Contact Southeastern Connecticut Tourism District | 470 Bank St., Box 89, New London 06320 | 860/444–2206 | fax 860/442–4257 | www.mysticmore.com.*

Fort Griswold Battlefield State Park. This is Connecticut's most hallowed ground of the American Revolution. Here on September 6, 1781, approximately 160 hastily assembled local men and boys fought to defend Fort Griswold against an invading British force that outnumbered them five to one—with tragic results. Fort Griswold's defenders held their position with a stubborn defiance that infuriated the enemy. When at last it became clear that hoped-for reinforcements would not arrive in time, and that the fort would fall, the patriots attempted to surrender. But most were brutally shot or bayonetted by the enraged enemy, who then looted and in some cases mutilated the corpses, and at last set fire to the fort. The patriot fatalities included Fort Griswold's commander, Colonel William Ledyard, who according to legend was run through by the British officer to whom he had just handed his sword in submission. The tragedy was rendered even more bitter—if such a thing were possible—by the fact that the attackers were part of a British raiding party commanded by traitor Benedict Arnold, a native of nearby Norwich. The state park encompasses the remnants of Fort Griswold, and a museum now chronicles the battle. From atop a 135-ft-tall stone monument, erected in 1830, visitors can look out over Long Island Sound, from which the British came on that grim day. | Monument St. and Park Ave. | 860/445–1729 | www.revwar.com/ftgriswold/ | Free | Memorial Day–Labor Day, daily 10–5; Labor Day–Columbus Day, weekends 10–5.

GUILFORD
▼▼

The search for the classic New England villagescape often ends in Guilford, one of Connecticut's oldest towns. The 12-acre Town Green, one of the largest in New England, is at the heart of blocks of dozens of structures dating back as far as the 17th century, more than 50 built before 1820—three are open to the public. The buildings surrounding the Green itself include several houses from the 1700s and early 1800s, most now converted into shops or offices. The architectural gem of the green that is the key to its quintessential look is the pristine white First Congregational Church, with its soaring steeple and pillared portico, built in 1829. Down Whitfield Street from the Green is the town marina on Long Island Sound, from which can be seen the lighthouse built in 1802 on Faulkner's Island 2 mi off shore. *Contact Guilford Visitors Information Center | 32 Church St., Guilford 06437 | 203/458–0408.*

George Hyland House. A gorgeous, red-clapboard, and lead-pane-windowed saltbox, this was built during the late 1600s or early 1700s. Between 1916 and 1918 it was restored by pioneering architectural historian and preservationist Norman Isham. Today it is a museum of Colonial life and architecture, replete with furnishings dating from the 1600s and 1700s, its original five fireplaces, and hand-hewn floors and walls. | 84 Boston St. | 203/453–9477 | www.hylandhouse.com | $2 | June–Aug., Tues.–Sun. 10–4:30; Sept.–mid-Oct., weekends 10–4:30.

Henry Whitfield State Museum. Built in 1639 for Guilford founding father, the Rev. Henry Whitfield, this massive stone house's medieval, fortresslike appearance is a reminder of the fact that when it was built the Atlantic coast was still a wilderness up for grabs among competing powers that included the English, Dutch, Spanish, French, and Native Americans. A small diamond-paned casement window in the corner of a second-floor room served as an observation post on Long Island Sound a short distance away, the direction from which enemies were likely to approach. The oldest stone house in New England, the Henry Whitfield

Museum underwent two Colonial Revival restorations during the 20th century, which have made it impossible to know for certain its original exact appearance. It is furnished, in typical spare Colonial fashion, with objects dating from the 1600s and 1700s, and it mounts changing exhibitions on Guilford and Connecticut history. | 248 Whitfield St. | 203/453–2457 | www.hbgraphics.com/whitfieldmuseum | $3.50 | Feb.–mid-Dec., Wed.–Sun. 10–4:30.

Thomas Griswold House Museum. This classic New England saltbox was built in 1774 by Thomas Griswold III for two of his sons. Thomas's descendants lived in the house until 1958. Today it is a museum reflecting life in the early 1800s, when Thomas Griswold's grandson George occupied the house. Furnishings include several of the actual objects listed in the inventory taken of George Griswold's possessions when he died, among them a parlor mirror and a dressing table. The gardens are planted with plants used prior to 1820. | 171 Boston St. | 203/453–3176 | www.thomasgriswoldhouse.com | $2.50 | June–Sept., Tues.–Sun. 11–4; Oct., weekends 11–4.

HARTFORD
▼▼

Hartford was a center of political, economic, social, cultural, and religious activity almost from the moment the Rev. Thomas Hooker arrived in 1636 with his congregation of about 100 Puritans from Cambridge, Massachusetts. Hartford shares with the two other original towns of Windsor to the north and Wethersfield to the south a friendly rivalry over which can rightfully claim the honor of being the "first" or "oldest" town in Connecticut—if only by a few months.

Thomas Hooker started making history in Hartford in 1638 when he preached a sermon declaring that government derived its authority from the consent of the people. That radical concept was incorporated the next year into a framework of common government adopted by the three river towns, known as the Fundamental Orders, which some consider the first written constitution in history. Hartford was the capital of the Connecticut Colony, which reaped a windfall of unimaginable import in 1662, when King Charles II granted it a phenomenally liberal Royal Charter. The document made Connecticut all but independent of the British Crown, and if that weren't enough, it threw in the New Haven Colony as a bonus.

By the 18th century Hartford was a thriving riverport, trading with the West Indies and towns along the Atlantic coast. That fact, combined with Hartford's position as Colonial capital, made Hartford a remarkably cosmopolitan place, home to some important benchmarks. The town's *Connecticut Courant* newspaper was for a time during the war the country's most influential journalistic voice for the Patriot cause (today it is the *Hartford Courant,* the oldest continuously published newspaper in America); in 1783 in West Hartford Noah Webster published his famous "blue-backed speller"; in 1796 the first cookbook written by an American was published here; in 1788 local merchant Jeremiah Wadsworth founded his Hartford Woolen Manufactory to help relieve American reliance upon imported textiles (George Washington gave the endeavor his personal endorsement by prominently wearing a suit of brown cloth from this company for his first inauguration); and in 1810 the American insurance industry was born in Hartford, primarily to provide a degree of security for those involved in the high-risk maritime trade. *Contact Greater Hartford Tourism District | 31 Pratt St., Hartford 06103 | 800/793–4480 | fax 860/244–8180 | www.enjoyhartford.com.*

Ancient Burying Ground. "Remember me as you pass by/ As you are now so once was I/ As I am now so you must be/ Prepare for death and follow me." Those who accept—figuratively, of course—that "invitation" found on many an early Connecticut gravestone and visit this Ancient Burying Ground will discover a splendid open-air museum of early Connecticut history

"Remember Me as You Pass By"

Graveyards may seem the unlikeliest places to learn about life in Connecticut two or three centuries ago, but in fact they are among the very best. These collections of stones into which trained and talented cutters chiseled images and epitaphs are fascinating open-air museums of history and folk art. Best of all, every town has at least one, most are open 24 hours year-round, you can touch the objects, and admission is free. Tiptoeing among tombstones may at first seem a tad ghoulish, but these markers were intended as missives to the living.

Just the bare facts of an epitaph can speak volumes. The gravestone in Hartford's Ancient Burying Ground for Mary Skinner, who died in 1772 at the age of 41, reports that she was buried "with 10 of her Children by her Side who all Died Soon After they were Born." That stark description of a tragedy experienced by most parents two centuries ago—although rarely on such a horrific level—testifies to the tenuousness of life during that era and suggests the physical, emotional, and spiritual strength required to survive in a world in which death came frequently, often swiftly and without warning, to young and old alike. Some gravestones speak of long lives lived well. When the "aged and venerable" David Robinson died in 1780 at the age of 79, the epitaph on his tombstone in the Old Durham Cemetery proclaimed proudly that, "The whole Number of his Children, Grand and Great-Grand children was One hundred and Seventy, of which one Hundred forty and eight Survived him."

The nature and evolution of gravestone imagery illustrates how completely Puritanism, later known as Congregationalism, dominated every aspect of life in early Connecticut. By far the most common decorative motif on tombstones prior to 1800 was a stylized human head flanked by wings. On gravestones dating from the late 1600s and early 1700s, the head is often a grimacing skull with batlike wings, reflecting, some students of gravestones believe, early Puritans' obsession with the grim inevitability of death and the decay of mortal flesh. Later in the 18th century, particularly following the intensely emotional revival of the 1730s and 1740s known as the Great Awakening, the faces on the stones became less fearsome, more human, with feathery wings and often a crown, perhaps of righteousness. These more appealing images, possibly symbolizing an angel, or the soul's flight to heaven, are thought by some scholars to express an optimistic hope for eternal bliss beyond the grave. Around 1800 the angels abruptly vanished from Connecticut gravestones, replaced by classical urns and weeping willows. The change reflected both an increasing secularization of Connecticut society.

Practical Puritans spurned art for art's sake, but gravestones served a purpose, and thus provided an creative outlet for trained and talented stonecutters, who often developed personal styles so distinctive that their work is immediately identifiable. For those seeking an evocative encounter with Connecticut's past, few experiences can rival a simple stroll through an old burying yard in any season. Self-guided walking tour brochures are available for a number of Connecticut's historic graveyards, and some offer tours led by real-live guides, especially around Halloween. But remember—do not make rubbings of gravestones, as rubbings damage the stones. For more information: **Association for Gravestone Studies** | 413/772–0836 | www.gravestonestudies.org. The **Connecticut Gravestone Network** | 860/643–5652 | www.ctgravestones.com.

and folk art. The epitaphs on the more than 400 gravestones in the Burying Ground, which is Hartford's oldest surviving historic site, speak not just of death, but of life in the 1600s, 1700s, and early 1800s. Many stones, decorated with evocative symbols carved by talented stonecutters, are rare examples of early folk sculpture—gravestones were a luxury during this time (although an estimated 6,000 individuals were interred in the graveyard, a tombstone marked the final resting place of perhaps only one in ten). A free illustrated self-guided walking tour brochure guides you to a baker's dozen of the most interesting stones and tells the stories behind several, including the accidental explosion that destroyed a local schoolhouse and left half a dozen young men dead and a 300-year-old scandal marked by adultery, insanity, death threats, and divorce involving members of Colonial Connecticut's elite. A touching tribute to some of those early Hartford residents who lie in unmarked graves is a black slate memorial stone erected in 1998 through the efforts of Hartford schoolchildren to commemorate the more than 300 African-Americans interred here. | Main and Gold Sts. | 860/561–2585 | www.ancientburyingground.org | Free | May–Oct., Mon.–Sat. 10–4, Sun. 9–1.

Butler-McCook House and Garden/Main Street History Center. The place to start experiencing Hartford's earliest centuries is this complex, which includes the city's oldest surviving structure and an adjacent brand-new museum. The Butler-McCook House, built in 1782, was home to four generations of the same family and is now furnished with artifacts original to the site, including furniture and paintings from the 1700s and early 1800s. The Main Street History Center, opened in 2002, features the keystone exhibition, "Witnesses on Main Street." It chronicles downtown Hartford's development from a wilderness settlement in the 1630s to a major urban center in the early 20th century. | 396 Main St. | 860/522–1806 | www.hartnet.org/als | $5 | Wed.–Sat. 10–4, Sun. 1–4.

Connecticut Historical Society. For one of the most delightful peeks into 18th-century Connecticut, take in this museum's extraordinary collection of hand-painted tavern signs: gilded and painted depictions of rearing lions, patriotic eagles, and majestic oak trees that were handy landmarks in an age before street signs and were among the earliest American advertisements. Tavern and inn signs helped transform everyday streetscapes into "democratic, open-air galleries, with a common set of images accessible to the gaze of all citizens," as the museum puts it. Coded messages—a yellow sun over a pine tree, a common 18th-century symbol of Liberty—were sometimes involved. Other exhibitions explore more than 360 years of Connecticut history. The interactive exhibition "Tours and Detours Through Connecticut History" uses artifacts, a sound-and-light show, and hands-on activities to introduce everyday life during the Colonial era. Selections from the Society's renowned, handsome collection of furniture are regularly displayed, with a show of furniture by Connecticut Valley cabinetmakers of the 1600s and 1700s planned for 2004. | 1 Elizabeth St. | 860/236–5621 | www.chs.org | $6 | Tues.–Sun. noon–5.

Museum of Connecticut History. The "holy grail" of Connecticut history—an original copy of the Royal Charter of 1662 granted by King Charles II, which made the Colony almost completely independent of crown control—is on display in Memorial Hall along with other of the state's most precious historic treasures. The exhibition "Liberties and Legends" recounts how in 1687 Connecticut leaders defied an attempt by King Charles' successor, King James II, to revoke the Charter. After repeated messages ordering Connecticut to hand over the Charter were evaded or ignored, 70 armed soldiers arrived in Hartford to seize the document in late October. That they left empty-handed the next day is known for a fact, but how the Charter was kept from their clutches is Connecticut's most cherished legend. Tradition says Connecticut's leaders stubbornly debated the issue with the royal representative until darkness fell, and the room was lit only by candles. When they could stall no longer, the Charter was brought out and placed on a table. Then suddenly, the candles were snuffed out—one version says a man feigned faintness and fell forward, knocking the candles off the table—and when relit, the Charter was gone. Legend says it had been handed out the window to a waiting man who hid the document in the hollow of an enormous, ancient oak tree about a mile away.

The Charter Oak became famous far beyond Connecticut. When a windstorm toppled it in 1857—a monument marks the spot—it was mourned by many, and its wood was crafted into all manner of souvenirs, from goblets to a special chair for the lieutenant governor in the State Capitol across the street. The Charter Oak remains a symbol of resistance to tyranny and Connecticut's premier icon, as demonstrated by the decision to use its image on the Connecticut state quarter produced by the U.S. Mint in 1999. The State Museum's "Connecticut Collections" display from its major areas of collecting, which include Connecticut governmental, military, and industrial history. Objects on view range from the state's original manuscript copy of the Declaration of Independence to Connecticut-made firearms and pottery to weapons and memorabilia from the American Revolution and the War of 1812. | 231 Capitol Ave. | 860/757–6535 | www.cslib.org | Free | Weekends 9–4, Sat. 10–4, Sun. noon–4.

Old State House. Restored for its 200th birthday in 1996, the brick-and-brownstone Old State House serves as a museum of Connecticut history, much of it momentous, some of it mirthful. Much of what it commemorates actually occurred in this building or on this site, including construction of the first meetinghouse in 1636. Costumed guides in character as figures from Connecticut's past conduct tours that highlight important events that occurred in the Old State House, designed by renowned Boston architect Charles Bulfinch. Here delegates from New England states, unhappy with the depressing course of the War of 1812, met in 1814 to propose major changes to the federal government—only to look foolish when news arrived shortly after their adjournment of Andrew Jackson's crushing defeat of the British in the Battle of New Orleans. An unexpected, wonderfully engaging feature of the Old State House is the re-created Hartford Museum. The second museum in all of America, it opened in 1797 on the top floor of the Old (then brand-new) State House. Much of the museum's collections consisted of oddities donated by travelers who brought them back from faraway lands. Curiosities ranged from an armadillo to a "unicorn's horn" to a two-headed calf. And there is a want list of objects originally in the Museum that are being sought—does anyone have the shoes of the god Bacchus? | 800 Main St. | 860/522–6766 | www.ctosh.org | Free Weekends 10–4, Sat. 11–4.

Wadsworth Atheneum Museum of Art. The country's oldest public art museum, founded in 1842, features marvelous displays of early American fine and decorative arts. Paintings include magnificent 18th-century portraits by John Singleton Copley, John Trumbull, and Ralph Earl. A particular highlight is the celebrated Wallace Nutting Collection, the country's largest assemblage of American furniture and domestic arts dating from the decades between 1690 and 1730. Nutting (1861–1941) was a Harvard-educated Congregational minister who wound up being an influential tastemaker in the early 20th century, thanks to its hand-tinted photos of New England landscapes and Colonial interiors, "States Beautiful" books, and a reproduction line of furniture that distilled "Pilgrim-Century" America for consumers for the first time. His vast collection was donated to the museum by J. P. Morgan, Jr., in 1925. Atheneum visitors can also step into one of the 18th-century Connecticut Valley's most lavishly crafted rooms, a parlor removed in its entirety from the Judge Seth Wetmore house in Middletown. Note that the Atheneum will close for expansion early in 2004. | 600 Main St. | 860/278–2670 | www.wadsworthatheneum.org | $7 | Tues.–Sun. 11–5.

KENT

▼▼

"Kent is characteristically mountainous." Historian John Warner Barber's 1836 description, while arguably an exaggeration—-the tallest peak in Connecticut is less than 3,000 ft above sea level—-helps explain why Kent was way down on the list of farmers looking for land to cultivate, and as a result wasn't settled until 1738. Kent was for a number of years the site of several iron furnaces, but they ceased operation early on. Kent remains a relatively rural portion of the Litchfield Hills, home to the beautiful Kent Falls. Kent is the ancestral home of the Schaghticoke tribe of Indians—during the Revolutionary War, 100 Schaghticokes helped defend the Colonies by transmitting messages of army intelligence from the Litchfield Hills to Long Island Sound, along the hilltops, by way of shouts and drum beats. *Contact Litchfield Hills Visitors Council | Box 968, Litchfield 06759 | 860/567–4506 | fax 860/567–5214 | www.litchfieldhills.com.*

Sloane-Stanley Museum. Eric Sloane, a renowned 20th-century artist and author, had a deep appreciation for the tools early settlers used for working wood. Often the craftsman himself fashioned or even designed the tool, which could be as fine a piece of workmanship as anything it was used to make. Sloane's extensive collection of woodworking tools dating from the 1600s through the 1800s is on display. | U.S 7 | 860/927–3489 | www.chc.state.ct.us/sloanestnleymuseum.htm | $4 | Mid-May–Oct., Wed.–Sun. 10–4.

LEBANON
▼▼

Don't be fooled by modern Lebanon's placid, bucolic landscape. This town was a cauldron of radical political activism that swept Connecticut into the American Revolution, then served as the command center for the state's considerable contribution toward victory in that war. The center of historic Lebanon is the Town Green, which is little changed from its original appearance of three centuries ago— hay is still grown and mown on it. Around the Green stand an array of historic structures that bear witness to the town's key role in charting the destiny of Connecticut, and of the United States, during the turbulent 1700s. *Contact Northeast Connecticut Visitors District | 13 Canterbury Rd., Suite 3, Brooklyn 06234 | 888/628–1228 | www.ctquietcorner.org.*

Jonathan Trumbull, Jr., House Museum. Jonathan Trumbull, Jr., namesake son of Connecticut's Revolutionary War governor, built this handsome residence in 1769 on the opposite side of the Town Green from his father's home. During the Revolution Jonathan Trumbull, Jr., served in the Continental Army, including a stint as an aide to George Washington. After the war he involved himself in state politics, and in 1797 was himself elected governor, a post he held until his death in 1809. The house has been restored to its appearance during Trumbull's lifetime, and features hands-on tours and exhibits that relate how a house and the people who occupy it interact. | 780 Trumbull Hwy. | 860/642–6100 | http://jtrumbulljr.org | $2 | May–Oct., weekends 1–5.

Jonathan Trumbull, Sr., House Museum. Jonathan Trumbull, Sr., was the only Colonial governor to side with the Patriots during the American Revolution. Trumbull became governor in 1769 and was an ardent advocate of Colonial rights. Several of Trumbull's six children played their own important roles in American history. His son Joseph died early in the Revolution, worn out by his work as commissary responsible for securing supplies for the Continental Army. Jonathan Trumbull, Jr., served in the Revolution and later became governor of Connecticut himself. The youngest child, John, born in this house, defied his father's practical advice, became an artist, and went on to glory, dedicating much of his career to documenting for posterity the major events of the War for Independence in meticulously researched paintings, of which the most famous is *The Signing of the Declaration of Independence.* His first major painting, *The Death of General Warren at the Battle of Bunker's Hill* (1786), now in the Yale University Art Gallery, is just one of many gracing great museums. His friendship with Jefferson and John Adams gave him unique insights to the events of his day. | 169 W. Town St. | 860/642–7558 | www.lebanonct.org/historic_sites.html | $2 | May 15–Oct. 15, Tues.–Sat. 1–5.

Revolutionary War Office. Within the walls of this small, plain gambrel-roofed structure, Connecticut's considerable might was marshalled and applied toward the Patriot cause. Constructed around 1730 to serve as a store for Jonathan Trumbull, Sr., then a merchant, it was converted in 1775 by now-Governor Trumbull into the command post for the state's participation in the Revolution. Here the Council of Safety, which in cooperation with Governor Trumbull oversaw the war effort, met more than 500 times. Under their supervision, Connecticut provided men, materiel, and other supplies to the Continental Army; authorized more than 200 privateers who seized close to 500 British vessels; and answered a desperate George Washington's appeals for food for his starving soldiers at Valley Forge and Morristown by arranging for herds of cattle to be driven to the camps in the dead of winter. | 149 W. Town St. | 860/878–3399 | Donation suggested | Hrs limited; phone ahead.

LEDYARD
▼▼

The town separated from Groton in 1836 and took the name of Ledyard, in honor of Colonel William Ledyard, commander of Fort Griswold in Groton on the day in 1781 when invading British troops slaughtered most of the Patriot troops, including more than two dozen men from what would become Ledyard. *Contact Southeastern Connecticut Tourism District | 470 Bank St., Box 89, New London 06320 | 860/444–2206 | fax 860/442–4257 | www.mysticmore.com.*

Mashantucket Pequot Museum and Research Center. This enormous, state-of-the-art museum, opened in 1998, explores the history and culture of Northeastern Woodland tribes in general and the Pequots in particular. Highlights include a re-created caribou hunt from 11,000 years ago, a 17th-century Native American fort, and a full-size, walk-through recreation of a Pequot village from the 1500s, populated by dozens of lifelike figures and enhanced with authentic smells and sounds. Interactive computer stations and films throughout the museum supply additional information. | 110 Pequot Trail | 800/411–9671 | www.mashantucket.org | $12 | Memorial Day–Labor Day, daily 10–6; Labor Day–Memorial Day, Wed.–Mon. 10–5.

LITCHFIELD
▼▼

Litchfield was settled in 1720, relatively late compared to many other Connecticut towns, but it more than made up for lost time, attracting ambitious and talented individuals who made it a renowned center of religion, education, and patriotism. Litchfield was the birthplace of Ethan Allen, commander of New England's Green Mountain boys when they captured Fort Ticonderoga for the Patriot cause in 1775. Here also resided Oliver Wolcott, Sr., one of Connecticut's signers of the Declaration of Independence. Wolcott was responsible for one of Litchfield's most unusual activities. On July 9, 1776, a New York crowd—riled up by just having heard the Declaration of Independence for the first time—pulled down a giant lead equestrian statue of King George III, and Wolcott arranged for most of the statue to be sent to Litchfield, where it was melted down and molded into more than 40,000 musket balls—known as "melted majesty"—to be fired at the enemy British. *Contact Litchfield Hills Visitors Council | Box 968, Litchfield 06759 | 860/567–4506 | fax 860/567–5214 | www. litchfieldhills.com.*

Litchfield History Museum. Historic artifacts including clothing, furniture, paintings, and household objects are among the items displayed in seven galleries that explore domestic life and "making a living" in Litchfield during the decades following the American Revolution. | 7 South St. | 860/567–4501 | www.litchfieldhistoricalsociety.org | $5 | Mid-Apr.–Nov., Tues.–Sat. 11–5, Sun. 1–5.

Tapping Reeve House and Law School. Among Connecticut's many gifts to the nation is that venerable institution, the law school. In 1784, in a small building next to his home, Judge Tapping Reeve opened the first such educational institution in the United States. Prior to that landmark event, all attorneys trained by apprenticing themselves to a practicing lawyer. The Litchfield Law School, in existence until 1833, counted an astonishing number of movers and shakers among its 1,000 students, including Noah Webster, Horace Mann, John C. Calhoun, and a slew of congressmen, governors, and jurists. Today a new exhibition employing role-playing and hands-on activities enables visitors to follow the experience of a real student at the law school in the 1800s. Both the house and law school building are open to the public. | 82 South St. | 860/567–4501 | www.litchfieldhistoricalsociety.org | $5 | Mid-Apr.–Nov., Tues.–Sat. 11–5, Sun. 1–5.

MYSTIC

The village of Mystic has tried with dedication to recapture the seafaring spirit of the 18th and 19th centuries—and succeeded. Some of the nation's fastest clipper ships were built here in the mid-19th century and today the town is home to **Mystic Seaport** (860/572–0711; www.mysticseaport.org), the collection of antique buildings that comprises the country's largest maritime history museum, along with the showy, modern, and utterly fascinating Mystic Aquarium and Institute for Exploration. However, although the Boardman School dates from 1768 and the ropewalk from 1824, nearly all the buildings and exhibits in the Mystic Seaport complex date from the mid-19th-century, so it falls outside the scope of this book. Still, to gain a picture of post-Revolution America in the early years of its commercial development, which was so inextricably linked to the sea, a visit to Mystic Seaport is a must.

NEW HAVEN

New Haven was a community of innovators and risk-takers from its founding by Puritans in 1638. The town was not settled haphazardly as were most, but was laid out in a grid of nine squares in 1640. The center square was reserved to serve as a public "common," and it survives to this day as the New Haven Green, which has been the site of many events, celebrations, and protests over the past 360 years. On Temple Street, which bisects the Green, stand three splendid examples of early 19th-century architecture: the First Congregational Church, built between 1812 and 1814 according to a design by renowned architect Ithiel Town, modeled on the church of St. Martin's in-the-Fields on Trafalgar Square in London; Trinity Church, built in 1815 and also designed by Ithiel Town; and United Church, erected in 1815.

Interestingly, beneath the First Church is a crypt containing a small, humble gravestone that bears witness to New Haven's willingness to defy a king's fury. When the Puritan Commonwealth that had ruled England for more than a decade collapsed in 1660, King Charles II ascended the throne that had been left empty by the beheading of his father, King Charles I, in 1649. One of his priorities was to track down and punish the Puritan judges who had signed his father's death warrant. Three of them—Edmund Whalley, William Goffe, and John Dixwell—fled to New England, where their fellow Puritans hid them. Dixwell settled in New Haven in 1673 and was known as James Davids, and his gravestone in the crypt bears only the initials "J. D."—even in death it was not safe to reveal his true identity.

The 18th century saw New Haven flourish in many ways. In 1701 it was elevated to the status of co-capital of Connecticut with Hartford, in 1716 Yale College (founded in 1701) moved here as only the third college established in all of British North America, while the first newspaper published in the Colony, the *Connecticut Gazette,* came off the press in 1755. By the eve of the American Revolution, New Haven had become an important hub of maritime trade, particularly with the West Indies, thanks to its fine harbor. New Haven plunged right into the fight between Great Britain and the Colonies. When word arrived that British regulars and Minutemen had clashed at Lexington and Concord, a local merchant named Benedict Arnold (the same man who five years later would turn traitor) forced the local leaders to give him the keys to the gunpowder magazine and then armed his company of militia to march to support the Patriots in Massachusetts. New Haven's reputation as a stronghold of Patriot support earned it an unwelcome visit from the British on the morning of July 5, 1779. Forty-eight enemy vessels landed several thousand troops, who marched right into the heart of New Haven and spent the day engaged in "Ravage & Plunder"—but some sources say that New Haven was largely spared in response to the pleas of local Tories. On July 6 the British sailed away from New Haven, headed for Fairfield, where they would wreak the almost complete destruction that New Haven had escaped. *Contact New Haven Convention and Visitors Bureau | 59 Elm St., New Haven 06510 | 203/777–8550 | fax 203/782–7755 | www.newhavencvb.org.*

New Haven Colony Historical Society. Exhibits explore the history of the towns strung along the Long Island coast that were included in the New Haven Colony during its brief life between 1639 and 1665, with an emphasis on the city of New Haven. Intriguing artifacts include the cotton gin invented by Yale graduate Eli Whitney during a stay in Georgia in 1793. | 114 Whitney Ave. | 203/562–4183 | $2 | Sept.–June, Tues.–Fri. 10–5, weekends 2–5; July and Aug., Tues.–Fri. 10–5, Sat. 2–5.

Yale University Art Gallery. Yale is home to one of the world's best assemblages of American paintings and decorative arts. The gallery got its start in 1832 when artist John Trumbull, a Connecticut native (and a Harvard graduate), gave Yale many of the paintings and portraits he had created during nearly half a century spent documenting American history and personalities on canvas. Trumbull's works at Yale include his famous *The Signing of the Declaration of Independence.* In addition to paintings, Yale houses an internationally renowned collection of Early American silver and furniture. For the flip side of the coin, check out the famed Paul Mellon Center for the Study of British Art, also on the Yale campus; this museum has a noted collection of 18th-century paintings by great British masters and often mounts important exhibitions on British art. | 1111 Chapel St. | 203/432–0600 | www.yale.edu/artgallery | Free | Sept.–May, Tues., Wed., Fri., and Sat. 10–5; Thurs. 10–8; Sun. 1–6. June, Tues.–Sat. 10–5, Sun. 1–6. July and Aug., Tues.–Sat. 10–5.

Yale University, Connecticut Hall. For 250 years Yalies have been learning and sometimes living in Connecticut Hall. The three-story brick building was considered the most splendid structure in all of Connecticut when it was completed in 1752. Students who lodged here included Revolutionary War patriot Nathan Hale (whose statue is out front), lexicographer Noah Webster, and inventor Eli Whitney. Connecticut Hall is included on guided tours of the campus offered by the University. | 149 Elm St. | 203/432–2000 | www.yale.edu | Free | Tours weekdays at 10:30 and 2, weekends at 1:30.

NEW LONDON
▼▼

From its settlement in the mid-1640s, New London made the most of its splendid harbor, developing into a center of shipbuilding, maritime trade, whaling, and sealing. With the outbreak of the American Revolution, that seafaring heritage made it a critical point in the patriots' offensive and defensive efforts—for which the town would pay dearly. Captain Nathaniel Shaw of New London was placed in charge of Connecticut's fledgling naval operations, the strongest arm of which were the "privateers"— private vessels officially commissioned by Connecticut to seize both private and military shipping belonging to the enemy British. New London was the home port of dozens of privateers that captured hundreds of British ships, inflicting considerable damage on the enemy's war effort. In the summer of 1781, the British decided to clean them out and they had just the right man for the job: Benedict Arnold, the hero-turned-traitor who was now a general in the British army. Arnold was a native of nearby Norwich and on September 6, 1781, Arnold led an invasion force of approximately 1,600 British troops. Their goal was to burn the privateers anchored in New London Harbor and warehouses filled with supplies, but the flames quickly spread out of control, and almost all of New London burned to the ground—one more cruel betrayal to be laid at Benedict Arnold's doorstep. *Contact Southeastern Connecticut Tourism District | 470 Bank St., Box 89, New London 06320 | 860/444–2206 | fax 860/442–4257 | www.mysticmore.com.*

Hempsted Houses. Joshua Hempsted was born in the house that bears his name in 1678, the year that it was built, and died in it in 1758. Hempsted was a colonial jack-of-all-trades—farmer, judge, gravestone carver, and shipwright. Life in this house three centuries ago doesn't have to be imagined or re-created, for it was documented in a diary maintained by Joshua Hempsted for nearly 50 years—a rare source of information about life within the walls of one of New England's oldest dwellings and throughout southeastern Connecticut during the first half of the 18th century. Hempsted recorded the mundane and momentous, including the births of several of his nine children and the death of his wife in 1716. He remained a widower for the rest of his long life, raising his large family alone. Next door is the rare stone house built in 1758 by Joshua Hempsted's grandson Nathaniel Hempsted. Both houses's furnishings include original Hempsted family objects. | 11 Hempstead St. | 860/443–7949 | www.hartnet.org/als | $5 | May–Oct., Thurs.–Sun. noon–4.

Shaw-Perkins Mansion. This stone mansion was home to Captain Nathaniel Shaw and headquarters of Connecticut's considerable naval force, both warships and privateers, during the American Revolution. Furnishings include 18th-century furniture and portraits. Guided tours explore New London's history, particularly the town's lucrative trade with the West Indies. | 11 Blinman St. | 860/443–1209 | $5 | Wed.–Fri. 1–4, Sat. 10–4.

NORTH STONINGTON

▼▼

North Stonington was one of many Connecticut communities rocked by the religious revival of the 1740s known as the Great Awakening, which was a highly emotional reaction to the stale, uninspiring practices into which the established churches, presided over by college-educated clergy, had fallen. In 1742 many members of the North Stonington Congregational Church broke away to form their own church, declaring that "God had redeemed their souls, and that they were not bound to rites and forms." In the Great Awakening's defiance of the powerful religious establishment were the seeds of defiance of British power that would sprout a generation later. *Contact Southeastern Connecticut Tourism District | 470 Bank St., Box 89, New London 06320 | 860/444–2206 | fax 860/442–4257 | www.mysticmore.*

HISTORIC DINING AND LODGING
Randall's Ordinary. At Randall's Ordinary they cook the real old-fashioned way—and we mean some three-centuries old-fashioned. Open-hearth cooking guarantees authentic results. Why not opt for a delicious hot buttered rum as you enjoy such welcoming nibbles as Vermont

cheese and crackers and hearth-roasted popcorn? Sit back by the fireplace, be lulled by a harpist playing 18th-century tunes, then feast on such specialties as butternut squash soup with spider cornbread, Nantucket scallops, roasted capon with wild-rice stuffing, and Thomas Jefferson bread pudding—served by a waitstaff garbed in period clothing. After you savor your last glass of port, Madeira wine, or hot cider, you can—having booked in advance— head to one of the 15 elegant guest rooms with stenciled walls and wide wooden plank floors. Some are in the 1685 farmhouse, where antique canopy beds, hand-woven bedspreads, rocking chairs, and a fireplace in every room would even make Washington purr; the others are in the 1819 barn and silo and all are set on 250 bucolic acres. Restaurant. No smoking. | Rte. 2 | 860/599–4540 | fax 860/599–3308 | www.randallsordinary.com | 12 rooms, 3 suites | $125–$350 | AE, MC, V.

SCOTLAND

▼▼▼

Early settler Isaac Magoon named Scotland in 1706 in honor of his native country. Although it never grew larger than a rural village, it managed to produce not only one of the nation's founding fathers but a successful artist, Samuel Lovett Waldo, who studied in Europe with Benjamin West and John Singleton Copley and whose paintings are part of the collections of major museums. *Contact Northeast Connecticut Visitors District | 13 Canterbury Rd., Suite 3, Box 145, Brooklyn 06234 | 860/779–6383 | www.ctquietcorner.org.*

Huntington Homestead. The birthplace of Samuel Huntington, a signer of the Declaration of Independence, this severe, strikingly white clapboard house has undergone astonishingly little change since its construction around 1700. Situated on farmland that includes old-growth trees and stone walls, it evokes Connecticut of the 18th century. The house remained in private hands until the mid-1990s, when local residents formed a nonprofit trust that purchased it to serve as a museum of early Connecticut life. This is a research project in process, with ongoing structural study and archaeological excavations that reveal much about the site, which was once occupied by Native Americans, and of the evolution of the building itself. | 36 Huntington Rd. | 860/456–8381 | www.huntingtonhomestead.org | $4 | May–Oct., 1st and 3rd Sat. of each month 11–4.

SIMSBURY

▼▼▼

Simsbury's early years were perilous. Settled in the 1660s, it was still an exposed frontier outpost when the conflict with Native Americans known as King Philip's War broke out in 1675. Twice the pioneering residents fled; following the second evacuation, in 1676, the Indians torched the town, destroying more than 40 buildings. Before the year was out the English settlers had triumphed over the Native Americans, and Simsbury's citizens returned for good. *Contact Greater Hartford Tourism District | 234 Murphy Rd., Hartford 06114 | 860/244–8181 | fax 860/244–8180 | www.enjoyhartford.com.*

Phelps Tavern Museum and Homestead. Life in a roadside tavern two centuries ago is depicted in the installation of "The Entertainment of Strangers, 1786–1849." Taverns were the nerve centers of early New England towns. Here residents gathered to pick up the latest news and gossip, discuss issues of politic concern, conduct business, take part in court proceedings, mingle with travelers who had stopped for the night—and, of course, eat and drink. The main dining room here is fetchingly decorated with regional antiques of the 18th century. Several other historic structures reflect varying aspects of early life, including the meetinghouse, a one-room schoolhouse, and the Hendrick Cottage with its period herb garden. | 800 Hopmeadow St. | 860/658–2500 | www.phelpstavernmuseum.com | $6 | May 15–Columbus Day, Tues.–Sat. 10–4; guided tours 1–4.

SUFFIELD
▼▼▼

A mistake made by two (lazy?) surveyors hired to lay out the boundary between Massachusetts and Connecticut in the 1600s resulted in Suffield, Enfield, Woodstock, and Somers being erroneously (in Connecticut's opinion at least) included in Massachusetts. In 1749, in a movement spearheaded by Phineas Lyman of Suffield, the four towns "seceded" from Massachusetts and joined Connecticut. Massachusetts protested the switch for more than 50 years, but in vain. Other early Suffield men of ambition and distinction included Gideon Granger, appointed United States postmaster in 1801, and Oliver Phelps, who with a partner purchased more than 2 million acres of wilderness lands in western New York. *Contact North Central Connecticut Chamber of Commerce | Box 294, Enfield 06083 | 860/741–3838 | fax 860/741–3512 | www.ncccc.org.*

Alexander King House. Dr. Alexander King, prominent local physician and longtime public servant, erected his 11-room house in 1764. Furnished with 18th- and early 19th-century artifacts, the home is notable for its separate doctor's office, hand-carved corner cupboard, and overmantel painting in the dining room. | 232 S. Main St. | 860/668–5286 | www.suffield-library.org/localhistory/king.htm | $1 | May–Sept., Wed. and Sat. 1–4.

Phelps-Hatheway House and Garden. The dramatic swings of fortune that could be experienced during the Revolution and the decades following it are reflected in this structure. It was built in 1764 by a prosperous, Yale-educated lawyer, who had to sell it in 1788 after his Tory sympathies cut into his livelihood. The buyer was a self-made man: former peddler Oliver Phelps, who was growing rich investing in wilderness lands to the west that had opened up following the Revolution. Phelps added a wing in 1794—complete with wallpaper imported from Paris—to make the house one of the finest in the Connecticut River valley. Phelps's investments in western lands failed, and by 1802 he had left his splendid Suffield home. Today the house is furnished with outstanding examples of 18th-century Connecticut furniture and has formal flower gardens. | 55 S. Main St. | 860/685–0055 | www.hartnet.org/als | $4 | May–Oct., Wed., Fri., and weekends 1–4. Last tour starts at 4.

WASHINGTON
▼▼▼

In 1779, this town, settled in 1734, became one of the first in America named in honor of George Washington. To do so required no small amount of confidence and courage, for at that time George Washington was no more than the military leader of a rebellion whose success was far from certain. Industrialization passed Washington by, leaving it exceptionally charming and full of handsome homes dating from before 1820. The Mayflower Inn, a fine hotel, draws the wealthy. *Contact Litchfield Hills Visitors Council | Box 968, Litchfield 06759 | 860/567–4506 | fax 860/567–5214 | www.litchfieldhills.com.*

Institute for American Indian Studies. An authentically reconstructed outdoor Algonkian village, with three wigwams, a longhouse, and a garden planted with corn, beans, and squash, is a highlight of this gem of a small museum's exploration of the history of the Eastern Woodland Indians. Also offered are exhibitions on the art and culture of Native Americans. | 38 Curtis Rd. | 203/868–0518 | $4 | Mon.–Sat. 10–5, Sun. 12–5.

WEST HARTFORD

▼▼▼

Hartford settlers began expanding into the western portion of the town from their original location on the Connecticut River in the 1680s. But West Hartford did not become a separate town until 1854. Its most famous son is Noah Webster. *Contact Greater Hartford Tourism District | 31 Pratt St., Hartford 06103 | 800/793–4480 | fax 860/244–8180 | www. enjoyhartford.com.*

Noah Webster House/Museum of West Hartford History. Within the walls of this house, colonial farm boy Noah Webster dreamed of one day being able to attend Yale. Webster achieved that goal, then went on to compile two seminal works of American culture: the "blue-backed speller," first published in 1783, and the first dictionary of American English. Webster was one of those bright young individuals of the Revolutionary era who understood that political independence from Great Britain meant little if the nation continued to be dependent upon Britain economically and culturally. Webster's "blue-backed speller" taught American spelling and pronunciation rather than English and helped standardize the language in the new nation and bring people closer. Costumed guides lead visitors through the house, which is furnished and interpreted to illustrate life in the years immediately preceding the American Revolution. Several of Webster's possessions are on display. | 227 S. Main St. | 860/521–5362 | http://noahwebsterhouse.org | $5 | Sept.–May, Mon., Thurs.–Sun. 1–4; June–Aug., Mon., Thurs.–Fri. 11–4, weekends, 1–4. Last tour at 3.

WETHERSFIELD

▼▼▼

With its hundreds of well-preserved structures dating from the 1600s, 1700s, and 1800s, Wethersfield is a must for visitors seeking a close encounter with Connecticut's Colonial and Revolutionary past. One of the three original Connecticut River towns settled in the 1630s, Wethersfield was carrying on a lively maritime trade with the West Indies and ports along the Atlantic coast by the 1700s and early 1800s; the proceeds from the commerce paid for many of the handsome sea captains' and merchants' houses that still line the streets. Wethersfield for many years was renowned for one particular export: red onions, grown in such numbers that a visitor reported their aroma was "wafted far and wide upon every passing breeze." Many of these vegetables were cultivated by young, single women, known as "onion maidens," who used the profits to purchase necessities and some of the small luxuries of life. Wethersfield's handsome brick meetinghouse, built in 1764, was known popularly as the "church that onions built," because some members of the congregation made their contribution toward its construction with ropes of the valuable red onions. *Contact Greater Hartford Tourism District | 31 Pratt St., Hartford 06103 | 800/793–4480 | fax 860/244–8180 | www.enjoyhartford.com.*

Buttolph-Williams House. With its weathered clapboards, overhanging second floor, and small diamond-paned casement windows, the Buttolph-Williams House, built around 1720, reflects the enduring influence of the medieval roots of the first generations of English settlers. Many visitors will recognize this evocative building as the setting and inspiration for Elizabeth George Speare's classic children's novel, *The Witch of Blackbird Pond.* | 249 Broad St. | 860/529–0460 | www.hartnet.org/als | $5 | Mid-May–mid-Oct., Wed.–Mon. 10–4.

Webb-Deane-Stevens Museum. These three splendid 18th-century structures offer just about everything a visitor could ask for in a historic site. Each house reflects a different architectural style of the 1700s, has been carefully furnished with appropriate artifacts, and two of the three are closely connected to individuals and events that helped determine the outcome of the American Revolution. The Joseph Webb House, a massive gambrel-roofed structure, was built in 1752 by a successful merchant in the West Indies trade. It earned its place in history in May of 1781, when General George Washington spent five days here, conferring with the Comte de Rochambeau, commander of forces sent by France to assist the patriots in their war with Britain. The two military leaders (allegedly) planned the campaign that led to the surrender six months later of the British army at Yorktown, Virginia, a coup that guaranteed American victory in the War for Independence. Imported red wallpaper put up in anticipation of Washington's visit can still be seen on the wall of the chamber in which he slept. The Silas Deane House was built next door to the Webb House in 1764 by the lawyer who was selected as one of Connecticut's representatives to the Continental Congress. Congress dispatched Silas Deane to Paris on a secret mission to secure French support for the colonists' rebellion—it was Deane who signed up the young Marquis de Lafayette for the fight for American independence. The Stevens House, built around 1788 on the opposite site of the Webb House, reflects the lifestyle of a tradesman in the decades following the American Revolution. | 211 Main St. | 860/529–0612 | www.webb-deane-stevens.org | $8 | May–Oct., Wed.–Mon. 10–4; Nov.–Apr., weekends 10–4. Last tour at 3.

Wethersfield Historical Society Museum. A visit to Wethersfield should start with a tour of this museum's exhibition "Legendary People, Ordinary Lives." Original artifacts and modern objects explore major themes from the town's past, such as "Serving the Nation" and "Pursuing Prosperity." Each section concludes with a "Signpost to History" that directs visitors to sites around town, some open to the public, others private, related to that particular theme. | 200 Main St. | 860/529–7656 | $3 | Tues.–Sat. 10–4, Sun., 1–4.

WINDSOR

▼▼

Two 18th-century restored homesteads here are both impressive in their own right. The town was established in 1633 at the confluence of the Farmington and Connecticut rivers by settlers who had come from Plymouth, in Massachusetts; the land that originally formed it has been subdivided many times—Litchfield is one of its offshoots. *Contact North Central Connecticut Chamber of Commerce | Box 294, Enfield 06083 | 860/741–3838 | fax 860/741–3512 | www.ncccc.org.*

Oliver Ellsworth Homestead. American history was made not only by victorious generals and gifted orators, but by men who performed the less glamorous but no less crucial task of developing rules by which the new nation would govern itself. One such low-profile patriot was Oliver Ellsworth. He was one of the framers of the U.S. Constitution in 1787, contributed to the composing of the Bill of Rights, wrote the Judiciary Act that was the foundation of the modern federal judicial system, and was chief justice of the U.S. Supreme Court. This house, which Ellsworth built in 1781 and lived in until his death in 1807, is furnished with many family heirlooms, including some of Ellsworth's personal items. | 778 Palisado Ave. | 860/688–8717 | $2 | May 15–Oct. 15, Tues., Wed., Sat. noon–4:30.

Windsor Historical Society. The Society's Strong House dates from around 1758, and its historic furnishings include the board of wooden pigeonholes that served as Windsor's first post office. A few steps brings the visitor to the brick Dr. Hezekiah Chaffee House, built in 1765 and furnished with antiques, many from the shops of local craftsmen. Adjacent to the Strong House is the Society's modern museum building, which houses three galleries that show permanent and changing exhibitions on Windsor's past. | 96 Palisado Ave. | 860/688–3813 | $3 | Tues.–Sat. 10–4.

WOODBURY

▼▼▼

Woodbury started out in 1672 as an exposed frontier settlement, from which the first inhabitants fled in 1675 for fear of attack by Indians during King Philip's War. The town has come a long way since then and now proclaims itself "the antiques capital of Connecticut." Today, this posh town has some of Connecticut's most celebrated and distinguished dealers of 18th- and 19th-century American decorative arts, including the shops of Wayne Pratt and David Schorsch. *Contact Litchfield Hills Visitors Council / Box 968, Litchfield 06759 / 860/567–4506 / fax 860/567–5214 / www.litchfieldhills.com.*

Glebe House. "Glebe" means the farm land given to a minister as part of his compensation. His home, if located on that land, was, consequently, the glebe house. This house, built around 1750, acquired that designation in 1771, when the Rev. John Marshall and his wife took up residence. Reverend Marshall was a priest in the Anglican Church, of which the British monarch is the temporal head, a fact that in many minds automatically raised suspicions about the minister's loyalty to the cause of colonial rights. The event that made this house a landmark in American religious history occurred in 1783, when 10 Anglican ministers from around Connecticut met to form a new denomination, the Episcopal Church, which did not acknowledge the king's authority. They elected the Reverend Samuel Seabury as the first bishop of the Episcopal Church. Today the Glebe House is furnished as it would have been during the turbulent Revolutionary War years, when Reverend Marshall and his wife were in residence. | Hollow Rd. | 203/263–2855 | www.woodburyct.org | $4 | Apr.–Oct., Wed.–Sun. 1–4, Nov., weekends 1–4.

By Lynn Davis-Trier

Delaware

The First State

The tiny state sandwiched between Pennsylvania and Maryland is more than just a rest stop on history's highway. Ah, the ships that have heeded the beckoning finger of Cape Henlopen and the shore winds that seemed to whisper, "Come closer, boys, and check this out." Check out the tales of our life under the flags of three different nations—first the Dutch, then the Swedes, then the English (actually, this game of Sovereignty Tag went more like Dutch-Swedish-Dutch-Swedish-English). And check out the great minds—and great men—who went forth from Delaware to frame a nation, defending and defining its values and ensuring that no foreign flag would ever again fly over its marshy hummocks, its village greens, and its market towns. From the ruins of a 17th-century Dutch fort on Lewes's sandy shore to the mansions of the intoxicatingly named Brandywine Valley on the state's northern-most edge, Delaware is filled with small sites that made a big difference in America's political, cultural, religious, economic, and industrial landscape. Many of these sites—places like Lewes and Dover and New Castle—are today often overshadowed by big-ticket, capital "C" for Colonial attractions full of Pilgrims and plantations, but nevertheless retain an undeniable, if quiet, authenticity.

While Delaware played a leading role in the drama of patriotism and independence, only one Revolutionary skirmish—the Battle of Cooch's Bridge—was played out on her stage. The cast of characters essential to any telling of the Delaware story, however, is studded with Colonial stars: Pieter Minuit, the Walloon who bought the island of Manhattan for $24 worth of Dutch guilders as a prelude to founding New Sweden on the site of present-day Wilmington, his last blaze of glory before perishing during a Caribbean hurricane; Swedish Governor Johan Printz, a 400-pound cavalry officer (think of his poor horse), who arrived in 1643 and led the Colony through an era of growth and stability; Pieter Stuyvesant, the hot-tempered, one-legged governor of New Amsterdam who attacked New Sweden, bringing it back under Dutch rule; Quaker governor William Penn, in his long coat and broad-brimmed hat, the man Thomas Jefferson called "the greatest law-giver the world has produced"; George Washington, of course, who planned his strategy for the Battle of the Brandywine from a house near present-day Newark and who marched his troops across the fertile fields of northern New Castle County on his way to fight at Chadd's Ford; the Marquis de Lafayette, not only during the war, but also during his triumphant return in 1824; another Frenchman, by the name of du Pont, whose attempts to improve the American gunpowder industry fueled America's defense in the War of 1812 (as well as subsequent wars) and whose explosive wealth created a lasting dynasty on the banks of the Brandywine; other patriots (John Dickinson, Caesar Rodney, Thomas McKean, George Read); as well as pirates (Captain Kidd, Blackbeard).

Historically speaking, Delaware begins in the bay of the same name. Enter one Henry Hudson, explorer extraordinaire, sailing under the flag of Holland in 1609 and seeking a shortcut to the "Western Sea" (a.k.a. the Pacific Ocean). Over the next few years, Dutch and English explorers continued to trade with the tribes on Delaware's peninsula, but not until 1631—11 years after the landing of the Pilgrims at Plymouth—did the Dutch establish the settlement of Zwaanendael (near present-day Lewes). Meanwhile, back in the Old World, King Gustavus Adolphus of Sweden set his country's sights on becoming an important trading nation like Holland and England. The New Sweden Company then established a foothold in the New World near Wilmington and called it Fort Christina. The Dutch, more than a little miffed, built a stronghold a few miles south, Fort Casimir. Over the next decade, the Dutch and the Swedes challenged each other for control of the Delaware River and Bay. Then in 1664, the English captured New Amstel. During this time, the Calverts of Maryland tried to seize the Colony, claiming that it was part of their charter. Back in England, however, King Charles II had just created a new Colony and granted its charter to the Quaker William Penn. Called Pennsylvania, the new Colony also included the three counties on the Delaware peninsula. Penn arrived on Delaware's shores in 1682 and created a general assembly to govern his Colony. In theory, it sounded like a good idea—two colonies, one government. But in practice, it didn't work. The residents of the lower counties lived in fear of the privateers and pirates who raided their shores. They petitioned Penn's government to organize a militia and set up cannons to protect themselves. But the Quakers—100 mi upstream from the scenes of the crimes—refused. Reluctantly, Penn agreed to let the Lower Counties separate from Pennsylvania.

As the move toward independence gained momentum, the Lower Counties became increasingly alarmed at England's arrogance and demands. John Dickinson, who owned farms in Kent County, emerged as one of the movement's most eloquent writers. Following the Stamp Act Congress, he drafted the 14-point Declaration of Rights and Grievances, and his subsequent series of letters in the Pennsylvania Chronicle catapulted the cause of American liberty onto the global stage. On June 15, 1776, the Delaware assembly suspended all royal authority in the three counties. A month later, Caesar Rodney's decisive vote kickstarted the War for American Independence. During the Revolution, Delaware saw just one battle on its soil—the Battle of Cooch's Bridge in 1777, where the Stars and Stripes supposedly made its debut—but the Delaware regiment fought in many campaigns. The Colony had its share of Loyalists—enough to keep the militia busy and to warrant Congress dispatching Continental troops to Delaware twice.

✦ BETWEEN NORTH AND SOUTH

Generally considered a border state between north and south, Delaware is more accurately categorized as being both northern *and* southern. Wilmington and its surrounding area have close ties—physical, topographical, economic, and social—with Pennsylvania, just across the uniquely curving border. This region was industrialized early, and still exhibits some Quaker traits, despite the blessed excesses of the du Pont family's "chateau country" on its northern edge. Somewhere roughly south of the Chesapeake and Delaware Canal, however, Delaware becomes a southern state. A salty tang fills the air. People talk differently. The land is flat, the streams flow slowly. You have entered, as the locals of these lower parts punningly call it, "Slower Delaware." Instead of walking through its towns, such as Laurel and Milford and even Odessa, you start to *meander*. Like the Tidewater states that share this peninsula,

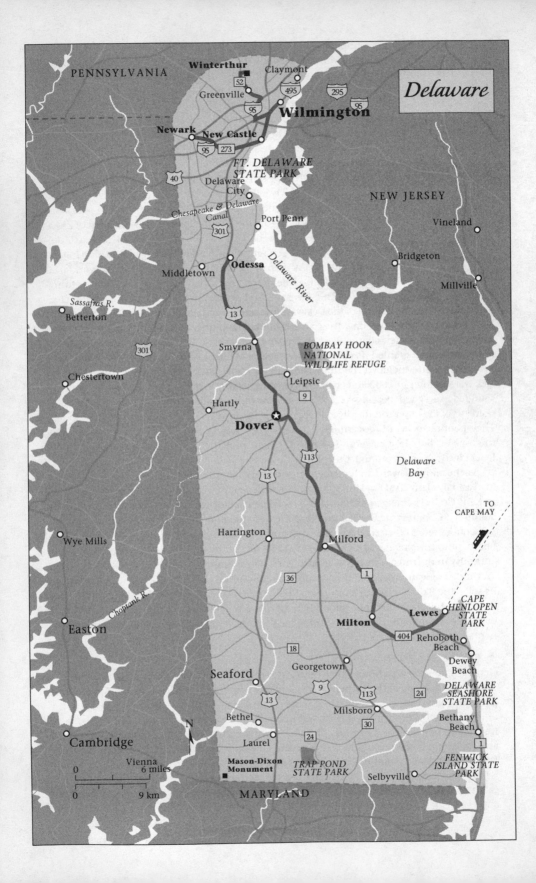

Delaware Timeline

1609 Henry Hudson, an Englishman employed by the Dutch East India Company, sails into what is now Delaware Bay and River on the *Half Moon.*

1631 The Dutch establish the Colony and fort of Zwaanendael, just inside Cape Henlopen, as a whaling venture, complete with fort.

1632 Native Americans attack and burn Fort Zwaanendael. All colonists are killed.

1638 Pieter Minuet leads two ships of Swedish and Finnish settlers up the Delaware River, where they establish Fort Christina (now Wilmington), the first permanent settlement on the Delaware.

1651 Pieter Stuyvesant, Dutch governor of New Netherland, sends 11 ships and a small army to challenge the Swedes. Fort Casimir is built by the Dutch on site of present-day New Castle, a few miles south of Fort Christina.

1654 The Dutch surrender Fort Casimir to the Swedes.

1655 The Dutch defeat the Swedes by reclaiming Fort Casimir and capturing Fort Christina, marking the demise of the New Sweden Colony as Delaware becomes part of New Netherland.

1664 The English capture New Amstel, renaming it New Castle, and claiming the land for James, Duke of York.

1682 The Duke of York creates the new Colony of Pennsylvania—which includes present-day Delaware—and gives it to the English Quaker William Penn, who sets foot on the new continent at New Castle.

1701 The Colony—officially known as the Three Lower Counties Upon Delaware—petitions William Penn for its own assembly.

1764 Two English surveyors, Charles Mason and Jeremiah Dixon, draw the boundary lines between Delaware, Pennsylvania, and Maryland.

1767 John Dickinson, Delaware farmer and lawyer, writes *Letters from a Farmer in Pennsylvania,* a powerful protest against George III's policies toward the Colonies.

1776 On June 15, Delaware declares its separation from England and Pennsylvania. Caesar Rodney makes his heroic July 1–2 overnight ride from Dover to Philadelphia, where he cast Delaware's deciding vote for independence. Delaware adopts its first state constitution.

1777 September 3: General William Maxwell and his Continental troops are defeated by British at the Battle of Cooch's Bridge. English march toward Pennsylvania, where General Washington's army awaits them at Chadd's Ford for the Battle of Brandywine. After winning the Battle of Brandywine on September 11, English troops occupy Wilmington until mid-October.

1787 Delaware is the first state to ratify the new United States Constitution.

lower Delaware has traditionally been more agricultural than industrial and more Presbyterian than Quaker and has had higher rates of slave ownership and a greater number of loyalists. Only one act in history galvanized Delawareans of every background and political stripe—the fateful ratification that took place in a tavern one day in 1787.

The ink had scarcely dried on the Constitution when 30 Delaware gentlemen convened for a meeting in the Golden Fleece in Dover. Landowners and lawyers, farmers and physicians, merchants and mill owners united in a common mission: to vote on whether or not to approve the law that would govern their young country. While Mrs. Battell, the owner of the tavern, poured the claret, the men debated. The minutes of the meeting have not survived, but surely someone must have mentioned taxes. And someone else—probably a farmer—must have brought up foreclosures. And several people probably chimed in with the 18th-century equivalent of "things can't go on like this," possibly followed by a spirited "Hear! Hear!" One thing is certain—the Delaware delegates, Federalist or otherwise, wanted the chaos of the post-Revolution years to cease. And so Delaware—quickly, unanimously—voted to ratify the Constitution. Pennsylvania and New Jersey followed their neighbor's lead, but the small state's decisive moment on December 7, 1787, earned it the right to call itself "The First State."

A REGIONAL GAZETEER

▼▼

✦ WILMINGTON, NEW CASTLE, AND THE NORTH

The hills roll down from Pennsylvania, bringing with them a fast-moving stream that soon becomes a river. Called Brandywine by the Dutch, the river gave rise to flour mills, paper mills, cotton mills, and a gunpowder mill. The mills, in turn, gave rise to incredible wealth, especially in the case of the du Pont family, whose black-powder mill at Hagley fueled the War of 1812 and provided the blasting power essential for westward expansion. The mansions and gardens of the du Ponts dot the hillsides today, and some of them—including **Winterthur,** with its magnificent collection of early American decorative arts, and Nemours, a Louis XVI-style chateau that houses some portraits by Charles Willson Peale and ephemera documenting Pierre Samuel du Pont's relationships with Thomas Jefferson and the Marquis de Lafayette—are open to the public.

Even the highways have history here. In the 1750s, the Kennett Pike (Route 52) was little more than a dirt path used by farmers to transport their goods from southeastern Pennsylvania to the port and markets of Wilmington. Washington's troops are said to have passed along here on their way to the Battle of the Brandywine. Given the road's position near the Delaware/Pennsylvania border, it's quite likely that they did. In 1811 it became a privately operated turnpike. Today the Kennett Pike—designated as Delaware's first historic highway—still offers charm and scenic beauty.

The Brandywine River empties into the Delaware at **Wilmington,** where it is joined by the Christina, the river that the Swedes sailed into in 1638. From Wilmington south to Odessa on Appoquinimink Creek, this section of New Castle County thrived because of its easy access to water and its close relationship—physically, economically, and philosophically—with Philadelphia. The state's earliest history lies along the river between New Sweden's Fort Christina, or today's Wilmington, and New Amsterdam's Fort Casimir, or today's **New Castle.** A few miles south, the town of Delaware City owes much of its development to the creation of the Chesapeake and Delaware Canal. South of the canal, but still in New Castle County, the picture-perfect town of Odessa served as a grain-shipping port on the Appoquinimink. An early but strong wave of anti-slavery sentiment swept **Odessa,** home of the 1783 Appoquinimink Friends Meeting House, several of whose members were stationmasters for the Underground Railroad. As a result, the "slave's path to liberty" often ran through Odessa, from which boats would carry the slaves northward to Wilmington, Philadelphia, and freedom. *Towns listed: New Castle, Newark, Odessa, Wilmington, Winterthur.*

✦ CENTRAL KENT: CAPITAL PLEASURES

Many of Kent County's early settlers were actually from Maryland. Perhaps this accounts for the Tidewater feel and seemingly slower pace of life. You are miles away from the industrialized north, however, traveling through towns where people still earn their livelihoods as their ancestors did—off the bounty of the land and the water. Fields of soybeans and corn cover the fertile soil of the coastal plain. Weathered watermen pull crab traps from the shallow inlets. Don't be surprised if you stop in a restaurant and see muskrat on the menu—these are still trapping towns, especially around Smyrna, Leipsic, and Little Creek. In the Amish communities west of **Dover** the sight of a horse and buggy may transport you to an earlier day, while the sounds of Thunderbirds and other military planes heading for Dover Air Force Base will keep you grounded in the present. The capital city of Dover seems to straddle past and present—even government business is conducted in handsome Georgian Revival buildings on grassy quads, giving the legislative heart of the state an almost collegiate feel. *Town listed: Dover.*

✦ SUSSEX COUNTY: DELAWARE'S DIXIE

From the hopping resort towns on the Atlantic Ocean and Delaware Bay to the quiet small towns of its interior, Sussex County has been both sculpted and sustained by water. The Mispillion River—a legendary stopping point of Henry Hudson—separates Sussex from Kent to the north, while 30,000 acres of swampland make the border with Maryland feel more like Louisiana. More than any other part of Delaware, Sussex reflects the manner and mindset of its neighbors on the peninsula, Maryland and Virginia. Once you move away from the coast, you'll find more people with English roots—as opposed to Swedish or Dutch. Wherever you are in southern Delaware, the water is never far away. With the arrival of Europeans, Sussex's waterways supported sawmills, gristmills, shipyards, and fisheries. The past decade has seen towns look to their rivers for recreation and revitalization. Backwater villages that were little more than a boat ramp and a bait shop now boast a bed-and-breakfast and an antiques emporium or two, as more and more visitors—mostly from Wilmington and Washington, D.C.—escape to the slower pace of lower Delaware. *Towns listed: Lewes, Milton.*

The Tides of Time: Coastal Delaware

A DRIVING TOUR FROM LEWES TO ODESSA

▼▼▼

Distance: 200 mi (one-way)   **Time:** 5 days (4 nights)
Breaks: Overnight stops in Milton, Milford, and Dover

Delaware has more than 260 mi of shoreline (ocean, bay, and river)—an amazing fact considering that the state is just 100 mi long by 30 mi wide. Proximity to the water made Delaware a strategic settlement, shaped its economy, and at the same time left it vulnerable to invasion. This tour begins at Lewes, near where the Atlantic Ocean enters the Delaware Bay and follows the waters inland to port and mill towns shaped by their relationships with rivers, creeks, and swamps. You'll cross the Delmarva Peninsula's last "wild" river on a 200-year-old ferry, learn how the water made trade possible between the capital city of Dover and the nation's capital at Philadelphia, and wind up your tour in the prosperous shipping port of Odessa.

Start your tour at the spot where the first European set foot in Delaware—at the picture-perfect resort town of **Lewes** (to add an authentic touch, you can even approach the town by water if you take the ferry across the bay from Cape May, New Jersey). A visit to the Zwaanendael Museum will lay out the story of Delaware and give you a good sense of context for the sites that follow. After lunch at one of the pleasant restaurants on 2nd Street, take a walking tour of the town that includes the Lewes Historical Society complex at 3rd and Shipcarpenter streets or—if the weather's nice—head out of town on U.S. 9 toward Cape Henlopen and visit the beach where Captain Kidd supposedly buried his treasure. Check to see if the tall ship *Kalmar Nyckel* is docked in Lewes; if so, you can experience a taste of the sea journey made by the Swedes and Finns who settled Wilmington in 1638.

Leave the 17th century behind and follow U.S. 9 south out of town, picking up Route 5 north toward **Milton** and the 198 buildings of its historic district, which include several bed-and-breakfasts for an overnight stay. In the morning savor the small-town atmosphere so that you can compare it with that of yet another inland mill town, **Milford,** less than 10 mi to the north via Route 5 and Route 1. Explore the Mispillion River, a source of food for the area's native tribes and a source of power and transportation for European colonists, before visiting the Parson Thorne Mansion and the Milford Museum to learn about the town's early days and maritime history. Spend the night in town at either the Greek Revival Causey Mansion B&B or the flamboyant Towers B&B.

In the morning head toward the much-contested Maryland border by taking Route 14 west until you reach U.S. 13 south in the direction of Seaford. The road is lined with antiques shops offering remnants of Delaware's agrarian and maritime past and farm markets that tempt summer tourists with tasty seasonal produce, such as juicy Delaware peaches. Pick up provisions for a lunch by the side of the Nanticoke River before crossing on the **Woodland Ferry,** a free, 200-year-old cable-drawn boat that carries two or three cars at a time across one of the least spoiled feeder waters into the Chesapeake Bay. The Woodland Ferry may well be the oldest still in use in the country—when this area was still part of Maryland (back in 1658), a law was passed requiring that all counties must maintain free passage ferries for making "rivers, creeks, branches, and swamps passable for horse and foote." To get to Wood-land Ferry from Seaford, turn onto Route 20 west (McDonald's at the intersection) and travel for about 6 mi through the town. At Gethsemane United Methodist Church, you'll see a sign for the ferry. Turn left here and proceed a little more than 3 mi to Woodland.

From the ferry crossing, take Route 78 to U.S. 9 north toward Laurel. Pick up Route 24, which skirts the edges of the mysterious, primeval Great Cypress Swamp, and head toward Millsboro, where the Nanticoke Indian Museum displays vestiges of life before European settle-ment. Leave Millsboro via U.S. 113 and continue north to Dover, where you'll spend the night. A day in **Dover,** Delaware's compact capital, should center on The Green and the sites that surround it—the spot where the Golden Fleece Tavern (where the Delaware delegation ratified the constitution) once stood; the State House; then (just steps away) the Biggs Museum with its outstanding examples of Colonial portraiture and Delaware furniture and decorative arts. Lunch at The Blue Coat Tavern in an atmosphere of Colonial kitsch. Spend the afternoon at either the Delaware Agricultural Museum or Woodburn, the governor's mansion. Return to your hotel for the night.

For the next day's excursion along the coast, you'll need to doubleback on U.S. 113 south. Shortly after you pass the Dover Air Force Base, you'll see a sign for Kitts Hummock Road, where you'll begin the day by touring the home of patriotic pensman John Dickinson. After-ward, head north along coastal Route 9 through Bombay Hook National Wildlife Refuge. If the privately owned Allee House, located in the refuge just past Dutch Neck Crossroads, is open, stop for a tour of one of the best-preserved farmhouses in the state. Continue on Route 9 until you hit Route 6, which will take you into the inland port town of Smyrna. Drive down Mount Vernon Street, a short wide boulevard flanked by homes built between the mid-1700s and the late 1900s. From Smyrna, you can doubleback to Route 9 or proceed to U.S. 13 north, both of which lead to the well-preserved town of **Odessa,** an early grain shipping port with close religious, social, and economic ties to Philadelphia.

Three Centuries in the First State: Dutch Settlement to Du Pont Splendor

A DRIVING TOUR FROM WILMINGTON TO NEW CASTLE TO CHATEAU COUNTRY

▼▼▼

Distance: 50 mi (one-way)   **Time:** 3 days (2 nights)
Breaks: Base yourself in Wilmington for both nights

The Swedish, Dutch, English, and French roots of the Delaware Colony converge in the north-ernmost corner of the state. Time-travel through some of the highlights of Delaware's history, beginning with the site of the earliest settlement in New Sweden, then travel to the New Castle region, where the Swedish, Dutch, and English roots of the Colony converge. Walk along cobblestone streets once walked by William Penn, George Washington, and the Marquis de Lafayette. See the courtroom where representatives of the dueling Calverts of Maryland and Penns of Pennsylvania fought for custody of the Delaware counties, and travel the roads on which American General William Maxwell planted his troops for an ambush on General Cornwallis's column leading into the Battle of Cooch's Bridge. Using Wilmington as a hub city, venture out in a different direction each day to experience three centuries of life in the first state.

From the heart of Wilmington, look for signs for the Christina River Trail, which will take you to the site where Pieter Minuit and his boatload of Swedes and Finns established **Fort Christina** in 1638. Fort Christina State Park, here on the landing site known as "The Rocks," commemorates the Colony of New Sweden. A monument by sculptor Carl Milles that was presented by the people of Sweden perpetuates the memory of these first settlers, and an early log cabin stands as testament to the Swedes' saga of survival. To reach this rather rough-and-tumble part of town, take Martin Luther King Parkway past the Wilmington Train Station, through an industrial area, until you arrive at Church Street. You'll see signs for the park, which is at the foot of 7th Street, as well as for Old Swede's Church (Holy Trinity), built in 1698 and still in use for regular worship.

Now that you've seen the site where the Swedes defended their Colony, it's only fair that you should check out the stronghold of their rivals, the Dutch who built Fort Casimir in the town formerly known as New Amstel, but now known as **New Castle.** Take I–95 south toward New Castle and continue past the U.S. 13 and the U.S. 40 overpass. At the intersection of Routes 9 and 273, turn left onto Route 9 north. Go ½ mi to the next light and bear right onto Delaware Street. Look for a parking space in the center of town so that you can cross the Village Green and stop by The Arsenal on the Green for a Von Steuben Reuben if it's lunchtime, or—if it's Sunday—brunch on Eggs Benedict Arnold before exploring this pretty town on foot. Plan on a very full afternoon in Old New Castle, with tours of the George Read II House, Amstel House, Dutch House, and the 1732 Court House. Be sure to allow time to wander among the graves in the church yard at Immanuel Church, looking for names of such Delaware statesmen as George Read and Caesar Rodney. Walk along the atmospheric length of The Strand and down to The Battery, a riverfront park where the fine folk of New Castle congregate for jogging, rollerblading, and dogwalking. Before returning to Wilmington, make a detour toward **Newark** and the site of the only Revolutionary battle fought on Delaware soil.

To see the Cooch's Bridge Battle Monument, take I–95 south to the exit for Route 896 north. Turn right on Delaware Route 4, and start to imagine the British troops heading into battle along this road. You may have to view the monument from the comfort and safety of your own car, because there is no parking area and the shoulder of the road is narrow, with cars zooming near at a very fast clip. Return to Route 896 to I–95 north, which will lead you to the heart of **Wilmington.** Dine at the Hotel du Pont, either on regional American cuisine in The Brandywine Room or with a formal French meal in the more luxurious Green Room. Spend the night in grand style at this historic hotel, built with the wealth the du Pont family amassed from providing the gunpowder essential to fighting the War of 1812.

You'll explore the history of that wealth and learn more about the black powder industry in the morning, when you visit Hagley Museum and Library, where the du Pont story begins. From downtown Wilmington, follow 12th Street, which turns into Route 52 North. Take the exit for Route 141 north. After crossing Route 100, watch for Hagley's main entrance on the left. Afterward, it's just a two-minute drive north on Route 100 for lunch at Krazy Kat's in Montchanin, a restored village that was once home to some of the families who worked on du Pont estates. One of the grandest of these estates is just around the corner at Winterthur. From Montchanin, take Kirk Road and turn right onto Route 52, recently designated Delaware's first historic and scenic highway, which will lead you to the front gate of

Winterthur. Spend the afternoon touring Henry Francis du Pont's fabled estate and its incomparable collections of American decorative arts before returning to Wilmington via Route 52. On your final day, head back out Route 52, turning north on Route 141 to visit **Nemours,** the extravagant masterpiece of yet another member of the du Pont family. On your way back into the city, stop for lunch at the circa 1790 Columbus Inn. If time allows, head back into the heart of town and conclude your Delaware experience at the Delaware History Museum on Market Street.

DOVER
▼▼

There's a reason why Dover's historic heart—with its rectilinear streets, redbrick buildings, and patches of green—echoes that of Philadelphia, its distant neighbor 80 mi to the north. Both were laid out by William Penn within 35 years of each other (Philadelphia in 1682, Dover in 1717). After living through London's bubonic plague of 1665 and Great Fire of 1666, Penn envisioned New World cities as "greene townes" that "will never be burnt and always be wholesome."

Dover offers all the assets of Penn's ideal city, but on an intimate scale (you can even stand at the foot of Legislative Mall on Federal Street and gaze at a near-clone of Independence Hall—the Colonial Revival Legislative Hall—complete with a reproduction Liberty Bell that is a dead ringer, minus the crack, for the Philadelphia bell). Dover became the second capital of the first state in 1777, when the threat of sea invasions at New Castle forced a move inland. From Monday through Friday the city bustles with official government business, its streets and restaurants packed with state-employed workers. On weekends, however, the town—for in the absence of working-day activity Dover is more town than city—seems sparsely populated and sleepy. The shopping district is away from the Green, on Loockerman Street, but a few specialty shops, such as Delaware Made at 214 State Street, offer icons of the state's proud heritage, including blue hens made of salt-glazed stoneware.

Perhaps because of this quiet pace (along with proximity to fertile farmland) Dover has seen an influx of Amish families—descendants of an Anabaptist sect that came to the New World in the early 18th century seeking religious freedom as part of Penn's Holy Experiment. In fact, there are today more Amish in the countryside west of Dover than there are in Lancaster, Pennsylvania. *Contact Delaware State Visitor Center | 406 Federal St., Dover 19901 | 302/739–4266 | www.destatemuseums.org. Delaware Tourism Office | 99 Kings Hwy., Dover 19901 | 302/739–4271 or 800/441–8846 | www.visitdelaware.com. Kent County Tourism Convention and Visitors Bureau | 9 E. Loockerman St., Dover 19901 | 302/734–1736 or 800/233–5368 | www.visitdover.com.*

Allee House. Located in the 16,000-acre Bombay Hook National Wildlife Refuge, this well-preserved Georgian farmhouse has overlooked the fields and marshes of coastal Kent county since 1753. | Whitehall Neck Rd., Smyrna | 302/653–6872 | Free | Spring and fall, weekends 2–5.

Barratt's Chapel. Methodists consider this 1780 church their "Independence Hall," for it was at Barratt's Chapel that a near-legendary meeting between lay minister Francis Asbury and Thomas Coke, personal emissary of the founder of Methodism, John Wesley, took place. The meeting resulted in the creation of the Methodist Episcopal Church in America. The museum features a collection of Methodist memorabilia. | 6362 Bay Rd., Frederica | 302/335–5544 | Free | Weekends 2–4.

Biggs Museum of American Art. Tucked away on the second and third floors of the modern brick building that houses the Delaware State Visitor Center, the Biggs is the state's only art museum south of the Chesapeake and Delaware Canal. Visitors are seen to idly wander upstairs, perhaps intent on a casual glance, to emerge an hour or two later, surprised at having stumbled upon a collection that spans two centuries of American art and includes works by Benjamin West, Gilbert Stuart, and Charles Willson Peale. Other members of the famed Peale family of painters are represented by still lifes. The 14 galleries are arranged in chronological order and include decorative arts as well as paintings and sculpture. | 406 Federal St. | 302/674–2111 | www.biggsmuseum.org | Free | Wed.–Sat. 10–4, Sun. 1:30–4:30.

Christ Episcopal Church. Many a Delaware patriot prayed in this 1734 church's pine pews, including Nicholas Ridgely, one of the ratifiers of the Constitution. There's a monument to Caesar Rodney, whose remains are buried in the graveyard here. The church itself, altered numerous times over three centuries, is an interesting conglomerate of architectural fashion. | South and Water Sts. | 302/734–5731 | Free | Weekdays 9–3.

Delaware Agricultural Museum and Village. During the 1600s, peaches were so plentiful in these parts that colonists used them as feed for hogs. The story of the peach and how it caused central Delaware's economy to both blossom and wither is just one of the many tales told at this intriguing site dedicated to the state's agricultural heritage. Exhibitions include Loockerman Landing—a re-created Delmarva town of the past—and a one-room log dwelling moved here from its original site in New Castle County. | 866 N. DuPont Hwy. | 302/734–1618 | www.agriculturalmuseum.org | $3 | Tues.–Sat. 10–4, Sun. 1–4.

Delaware State House. Along with its impressive legislative legacy, this 1792 Georgian building—which underwent major restoration in the 1970s—is so beautiful that its aesthetic appeal alone accounts for a steady stream of visitors. The freehanging double staircase is a breathtaking marvel of lightness and stability, of engineering and grace. A gilt sunflower medallion adorns the ceiling. Portraits by Thomas Sully honor Delaware's heroes of the War of 1812. But there are lessons to be learned here as well—guided tours (which depart from the visitor center) help visitors understand how legislative and judicial actions impacted the lives of men, women, children, slaves, and free blacks 200 years ago. | The Green | 302/739–4266 | www.destatemuseums.org | Free | Tues.–Sat. 10–4:30, Sun. 1:30–4:30.

The Green and the Golden Fleece Tavern. A silent, sylvan witness to galvanizing moments in the history of Delaware and the nation, the grovelike square known as The Green offers a peaceful respite from touring. Relax on one of its wooden benches and try to imagine what it was like to be a member of Delaware's Colonial regiment, which assembled here in 1775 before marching off to join General George Washington. Or think of the liberating feeling Dover residents must have felt when they gathered here on July 29, 1776, to hear the Declaration of Independence read to them for the first time (not to mention the sense of exhilaration they must have felt when they tore down the sign from King George's Tavern—now the Kent County Court House—burning the King's portrait on The Green and replacing it with one of George Washington). The surroundings evoke a poignant sense of respect for the officers and soldiers of the Delaware line who were reviewed on The Green here in 1780, just prior to their march to the immortal Southern Campaign. Few of them returned.

A sign on the far corner of The Green marks the site of the Golden Fleece Tavern, where 30 legislators met on December 7, 1787, to ratify the United States Constitution and gain Delaware lasting acclaim as the first state to do so. Anchored by the State House at one end, The Green is surrounded by private residences and offices that range from Georgian to Federal to Italianate, from brick to clapboard, making for an especially pleasing architectural countenance. Outdoor concerts are held here in the summer. | South State St. | Free.

John Dickinson Plantation. "Here then, my dear country men *rouse* yourselves, and behold the ruin hanging over your heads." So wrote John Dickinson in a series of newspaper essays titled *Letters from a Farmer in Pennsylvania to the Inhabitants of the British Colonies*. Not only did Dickinson succeed in motivating his fellow colonists, but his passionate and powerfully reasoned message attracted international attention and support. He was the talk of Paris salons.

Voltaire compared him to Cicero. Paul Revere made an engraving of his likeness. He was America's first native hero, at a time when the war was still being fought with words.

When he heard the first rumblings of war, Dickinson—who was of a cautious, conservative nature, cool-headed even in the heat of rebellious fervor—abandoned his law practice and devoted himself to furthering the interests of the Colonies. He belonged to a core group of thinkers, speakers, and writers that included Patrick Henry and Sam Adams, whose eloquence inspired Americans to take action to defend their rights and liberties.

Dickinson divided most of his time between Philadelphia and Wilmington, but he grew up here on the banks of the St. Jones River. When the 1740 brick homestead on the property burned down in 1804, Dickinson rebuilt it, specifying that it should be furnished "in the finest manner, as the best houses in Wilmington." The mansion, which is once again undergoing restoration, is furnished with period antiques, although the fine pair of camelback Chippendale sofas once belonging to Dickinson were purchased by Henry Francis du Pont for his home at Winterthur, where they are now on display. Dickinson inherited the estate and at least 59 slaves after his father's death in 1760. Influenced by Quaker teachings, he executed a manumission—or conditional freeing—of his slaves in 1777. In 1785, he unconditionally freed all of his slaves. Guides in historic clothing discuss the role of slaves and tenant farmers, as well as the daily life of the Dickinson family. Warning: if you arrive late in the day, the rather surly attendant may threaten to lock you in for the night! | 340 Kitts Hummock Rd. | 302/739–3277 | www.destatemuseums.org | Free | Tues.–Sat. 10–3:30, Sun. 1:30–4:30.

Woodburn. The Underground Railroad, an impudent ram, and a wine-guzzling ghost all figure in the story of this 1790 Georgian mansion, which today serves as the Governor's executive residence. In the past, Woodburn was home to a long line of important Delawareans, including gentleman farmers, an abolitionist, and a dentist. One of the finest Middle Period Georgian homes in Delaware, Woodburn is a massive but well-proportioned structure of Flemish-bond brickwork. The interiors are suitably ample and spacious, with fine paneling and molding. So where does the ram come into the picture? Jacob Stout, governor of Delaware from 1820 to 1821, operated a tannery on the property. One day while he was looking into one of the tanning vats, his pet ram butted him into the vat. He reportedly stated, "Look at the impudence of that damned ram to butt the Governor of Delaware into a tan vat!" The abolitionist was Daniel Cowgill, a Quaker who purchased the home in 1825, freeing all of his slaves and allowing them to meet in the great hall at Woodburn. Records from the Harriet Tubman Society later showed Woodburn as a station on the Underground Railroad. Allegedly, a tunnel ran from a secret room in the basement out onto the St. Jones River, where slaves were covertly hidden in waiting boats and transported north to freedom in Pennsylvania and New Jersey.

The first documented ghost appeared around 1815, when the house was owned by Dr. and Mrs. Martin Bates. They had as a guest an itinerant Methodist preacher, who described meeting a gentleman in knee breeches and a powdered wig on the staircase—an exact sketch of Mrs. Bates's late father, Charles Hillyard, the builder of Woodburn. According to Woodburn legend, if a glass of wine left downstairs at night is found empty in the morning, Mr. Hillyard—a heavy tippler—is on the prowl again. | 151 Kings Hwy. | 302/739–5656 | www.state.de.us/woodburn | Free | By appointment only, weekdays 8:30–4.

✦ ON THE CALENDAR: May **Old Dover Days.** A fife and drum corps leads the morning parade, and even the Governor gets into the spirit and dons Colonial garb, as generations of local families light upon The Green for traditional crafts, costumed reenactments, and maypole dancing. | 800/233–5368.

HISTORIC DINING AND LODGING

Blue Coat Inn. In a low-ceilinged setting decorated with a nautical theme, the Blue Coat Inn specializes in seafood, both traditional (oysters Rockefeller, crab cakes, mushrooms stuffed with crab Imperial) and enlightened (many dishes are available broiled instead of fried). Service is pleasant, if a bit pokey. | 800 N. State St. | 302/674–1776 | $8–$15 | AE, DC, MC, V.

Village Inn Restaurant. Windsor chairs and exposed ceiling beams lend Colonial credibility to this restaurant just 2 mi east of Dover on Route 8. Specialties include crabmeat strudel and fish chowder, along with a full line of pastas. | Little Creek | 302/734–3238 | $18–$25 | MC, V | Closed Mon. No lunch.

Cowgill Corner B&B. The original part of the house on this working farm was built in 1760. Guests looking for a country setting and willing to share it with a flock of sheep and llamas, beef cattle, and Border Collies can reserve one of the two guest rooms, which are decorated in a contemporary interpretation of country style. There are also two campers on site for those who wish to be closer to nature. Homey but pristine, and with a sparkling swimming pool, Cowgill Corner can accommodate dogs and horses, along with their owners. Pool. | 7299 Bayside Dr. | 302/734–5743 | www.cowgillsb-b.com | 2 rooms | $55–$85 | No credit cards.

Little Creek Inn. Furnished with antiques and reproductions that run the stylistic gamut from Queen Anne to Empire, this inn also has a swimming pool on the premises. | 2623 N. Little Creek Rd. | 302/730–1300 | www.littlecreekinn.com | 4 rooms | $200–$250 | MC, V.

LEWES

▼▼

Awash in history—and with a pirate past to boot—the coastal town of Lewes (loo-is) is justified in calling itself "The First Town in the First State." Located just inside Cape Henlopen, Lewes was the site of one of the earliest, if shortest-lived, Dutch settlements in the New World. In 1631, after years of small-scale, friendly trading with the native Lenni Lenape, the Dutch established a whaling Colony on the site and named it Zwaanendael, or Valley of the Swans, after the beautiful waterfowl they saw there. But when Captain David Pietersen DeVries arrived one year later to lead the Colony, he found it destroyed, and the remains of men and animals scattered about.

Because of its strategic location, Lewes has always been vulnerable to invasion. During the 1690s, privateers and pirates began terrorizing the people who lived near the Bay. Captain Kidd supposedly hid a treasure chest of gold in the dunes of nearby Cape Henlopen, but since the ecologically vulnerable dunes are protected and metal detectors prohibited, the pirate's booty will most likely remain buried treasure. While the region remained relatively calm during the Revolution—despite the infestation of enemy ships in the Bay—it was the War of 1812 that put the town in peril again. In April 1813, a British squadron began a 22-hour bombardment of Lewes, but did surprisingly little damage to the town. Today the quaint town is more likely to be bombarded by tourists than cannonballs. Although Lewes is still tranquil compared to the neighboring resort of Rehoboth Beach, more and more visitors are discovering its quaint streets and bayside charm. Second Street between Market Street and Savannah Road is especially lively, with plenty of restaurants to choose from as well as shops selling books, antiques, vintage jewelry, ice cream, and coffee. A walking tour brochure—available free from the Chamber of Commerce—offers a glimpse of the town's four centuries of history and architecture. *Contact Lewes Chamber of Commerce and Visitors Bureau | Box 1, Lewes 19958 | 302/645–8073 | www.leweschamber.org.*

1812 Memorial Park. The site of a defense battery during the War of 1812, this waterfront green commemorates the defense of Lewes and offers a terrific view of the harbor, where the tall ships *Jolly Rover* and *Kalmar Nyckel* are often docked. | Front St., across from the Post Office | Free.

Fisher-Martin House. This charming frame house with the gambrel roof (circa 1730) is the official visitor center for Lewes and the perfect place to pick up a visitor guide and begin your walking tour of the town. | 120 Kings Hwy. | 302/645–8073 | www.leweschamber.org | May–Oct., weekdays 10–4, Sat. 9–3, Sun. 10–2; Nov.–Apr., weekdays 10–4.

Lewes Historical Society Complex. Ranging from an early log cabin to an 18th-century farm-house, the historical society's tidy buildings exhibit a variety of architectural styles and furnishings. A few blocks away from the main complex is the Cannonball House (118 Front Street), which takes its name from the calling card left by one of the British fleet's 241 cannons during the bombardment. | Shipcarpenter and 3rd Sts. | 302/645–7670 | www.historiclewes.org | $6 | Mid-June–Labor Day, Tues.–Fri. 10–4, Sat. 10–12:30.

Preservation Forge. A tiny working blacksmith shop where you can watch smithy John Austin Ellis create pokers, door latches, and weathervanes, Preservation Forge also features a mini-museum of early blacksmith-made ironwares. | 114 West 3rd St. | 302/645–7987 | Hrs vary.

Zwaanendael Museum. The museum's stepped gable and highly ornamented facade—a replica of the town hall in the Netherlands town of Hoorn—adds an unexpected Dutch air to streets more accustomed to traditional resort architecture. Inside you'll find exhibits on the history of Lewes, including the 1813 bombardment, along with fascinating artifacts from the British brig *HMS DeBraak,* which hit a violent squall and sank off the coast in 1798. | Shipcarpenter and 3rd Sts. | 302/645–1148 | Free | Tues.–Sat. 10–4:30, Sun. 1:30–4:30.

✦ ON THE CALENDAR: Sept. **Cape Henlopen Howard Pyle Festival.** Named in honor of the Delaware artist and illustrator whose paintings helped shape the romantic image of pirates, this event features an encampment and reenactment, cannon and musket demonstrations, and music. | 302/645–6852.

MILTON
▼▼

Settled in 1672 by English colonists, this village packs a lot of historic architecture into one square mile—198 homes are on the National Historic Register. *Contact Milton Chamber of Commerce | 424 Mulberry St., Milton 19968 | 302/684–1101 | www.historicmilton.com.*

✦ ON THE CALENDAR: Dec. **Holly Festival.** Milton was once the leader in the commercial holly business—turning the Delaware state tree into glossy holiday wreaths and decorations. The town celebrates the tree's commercial success with a festival featuring handmade Christmas decorations, a house tour, and caroling. | 302/684–1101.

NEW CASTLE
▼▼

With its shaded village green, cobblestone streets, and charming alleys, old New Castle greets the visitor gently. Don't be dismayed by the strip malls and subdivision sprawl that mar the approach to this riverside gem. Once you leave the highway behind, you'll enter a uniquely authentic village, one that shuns the blatant come-ons of many an ersatz "historical" site in favor of a subdued, yet well-appointed atmosphere that allows 21st-century residents to dwell quite comfortably in a town that has existed for more than 300 years (and where no skateboarding is allowed, in deference to the redbrick sidewalks).

New Castle's pristine appearance can be attributed to what were considered two strokes of misfortune in the 19th century—the railroad bypassed the town and the county seat was moved to Wilmington. The resulting economic loss meant that residents didn't have the means to make serious alterations to their homes. New Castle remained virtually untouched until it was rediscovered in the 1920s, when the town narrowly escaped being transformed into a large-scale living museum by the Rockefeller family, which—when rebuffed by the locals—turned its gaze southward to Williamsburg, Virginia.

The rest, as they say, is history. New Castle remains a modest town with an enviable pedigree. Many of its historic structures—including the Rising Sun Tavern on Harmony Street—are, in fact, private residences. Just a handful of stores dot the historic district, including Common Goodes & Embellishments (204 Delaware Street), which boasts of offering "Needful items for the commonfolk and gentry alike" and sells such period artifacts as perukes, fichus (ladies' shoulder wraps), and pigtails of tobacco. *Contact Historic New Castle Visitor's Bureau | Box 465, New Castle 19720 | 800/758–1550 | www.visitnewcastle.com.*

Amstel House. Don't let the name mislead you—the Amstel House is not a rowdy tavern serving Dutch beer, but rather an early example of the elegant architectural style known as American Georgian. During an era when colonists looked to London for design cues, the stately symmetry of double-hung windows flanking a pedimented center entry bespoke the prosperity and taste of Dr. John Finney, for whom the house was built in 1738. Tours and exhibitions focus on 18th- and 19th-century life in New Castle and incorporate artifacts associated with the town's early history. According to local legend, the mansion is haunted by an unknown spirit who also frequents a house down the street that was owned by Finney's son. George Washington attended a wedding at Amstel House in 1784—no word on whether or not he spied the anonymous incubus. | 2 E. 4th St. | 302/322–2794 | $4 | Mid-Mar.–Dec., Tues.–Sat. 11–4, Sun. 1–4.

Battery Park. Even before the Dutch established Fort Casimir, they bestowed the name "Sandhuken" or Sand Hook on this long, unbroken stretch of sandy shoreline. The park—a 2-mi strip of green that hugs the coastal salt marshes—is a popular place for jogging, in-line skating, and walking. During the War of 1812, when every American town situated on water was subject to attack by the British fleet, a force of artillery was camped nearby; hence, the name "The Battery." | Delaware St. at Delaware River | Free.

Dutch House Museum. Facing the village green laid out by Pieter Stuyvesant, the tiny 17th-century Dutch house—a steep-roofed structure that remains relatively intact after more than three centuries—offers a glimpse of what life was like when the town was the Dutch haven of New Amstel. Dutch Colonial and European antiques, including delftware and pewter, offer clues to everyday life; the open hearth kitchen is as much a focal point for visitors today as it was for residents in 1700. | 32 E. 3rd St. | 302/322–9168 | $4 | Mid-Mar.–Dec., Tues.–Sat. 11–4, Sun. 1–4.

George Read II House and Garden. A trophy house for the Federal era, this Neoclassical mansion—with its marble fireplace, mahogany doors, and silver-plated doorknobs—would cost approximately $2.5 million to build today. More than 75 craftsmen and suppliers built the 22-room house for George Read II, son of the patriot who signed the Declaration of Independence. Some historians suggest that the younger Read commissioned the magnificent house to compensate for his failure to achieve his father's fame. Make of it what you will, but when his father's house was destroyed by fire in 1824, George Read II added his father's land to his own newly created domain. Today the Read House garden blooms where George Read's childhood home once stood. The oldest surviving garden in the region, it encompasses 1½ acres and is divided into three sections: a formal parterre, a specimen garden filled with exotic and native plants, and a large fruit orchard and kitchen garden, set off by allées of pear trees, trellised grapes, and boxwood hedges.

In 1920, Phillip and Lydia Laird, relatives of the du Pont family, purchased the property and renovated the house to accommodate their lifestyle, which included frequent entertaining. During Prohibition, the Lairds flew seaplanes to Cuba to stock their own private speakeasy in the basement. Of the 12 rooms open to the public, three have been preserved as redecorated by the Lairds in the 1920s. | 42 The Strand | 302/322–8411 | www.hsd.org | $5 | Mar.–Dec., Tues.–Sat. 10–4, Sun. noon–4; Jan.–Feb., weekends noon–4.

The Green, or Commons. After New Castle's conquest by the British, the Dutch-designed village green took on an English air, with market days and fairs, as well as public whippings and hangings. In 1731 a woman named Catharine Bevan was sentenced to be hanged over a fire for conspiring with her lover (who was also her servant) to poison her elderly husband. Instead, the fire burned her noose and she fell into the flames, where it was reported that "she was seen to struggle." Bevan is thought to be the only white woman in the country to have been executed in this way. Although the last public whipping in Delaware took place in 1952, the whipping law remained on the books until 1973. | Market and Delaware Sts.

Old New Castle Court House. Defiant proclamations and heated political debate once echoed through the chambers of this 1732 structure, which served as the meeting place for Delaware's Colonial Assembly until 1777. Within these walls, representatives of Lord Baltimore and William Penn argued over Maryland and Pennsylvania's conflicting claims to the Delaware counties; the Colonial Assembly swore its commitment to a new nation by authorizing Caesar Rodney, Thomas McKean, and George Read to vote for independence at the Second Continental Congress. The courthouse's cupola was designated as the center of a 12-mi arc defining Delaware's northern border with Pennsylvania. Tours and exhibitions focus on Colonial history, early systems of law and government, and important jury trials and verdicts. | 211 Delaware St. | 302/322–4453 | Free | Tues.–Sat. 10–3:30, Sun. 1:30–4:30.

Packet Alley. A tiny lane that runs from The Strand to the banks of the Delaware River, Packet Alley has captured the imagination of Delaware schoolchildren since the 1950s, when a book called *Packet Alley: A Magic Story of Now and Long Ago* portrayed the Alley as a kind of time tunnel. With the help of a little Dutchman and a pair of magic eyeglasses, two youngsters peer into Packet Alley's past, witnessing visits by Lafayette, Andrew Jackson, Louis Napoléon, Henry Clay, and the Native American leaders Osceola and Black Hawk en route to visit the "Great Father" in Washington, D.C. In reality, Packet Alley did observe this parade of history, for it was at the alley's wharf that packet boats from Philadelphia arrived to meet stagecoaches bound for Frenchtown, Maryland—the chief corridor for communication and travel between the northern and southern Colonies. | Between The Strand and the Delaware River | Free.

✦ ON THE CALENDAR: May **A Day in Old New Castle.** The oldest house tour in America, with many private homes and gardens open for public viewing. | 877/496–9498.

HISTORIC DINING AND LODGING

Arsenal on the Green. The Arsenal has had a long and varied life. Built between 1809 and 1811 as—of all things—an arsenal, the building has also served as soldiers' quarters, a hospital, and a high school. As a restaurant, the Arsenal is fully armed with a historically themed menu that ranges from casual fare in The Eagle & Cannon Tavern (Caesar Rodney Salad, Von Steuben Reuben) to elegant entrées (Duck Pear William Penn, Fort Delaware Filet) in the 1812 Dining Room. | 30 Market St. | 302/328–1290 | $18–$25 | AE, MC, V.

Jessop's Tavern. The "tag, you're it" aspect of New Castle's ethnic history converges on the menu of this renovated 1724 tavern and restaurant. Swedish sauces, Dutch cheeses, and traditional English entrées such as fish-and-chips and shepherd's pie give diners the chance to sample three centuries' worth of three cultures. | 114 Delaware St. | 302/322–6111 | $16–$22 | MC, V | Closed Sun.

Terry House. This four-story Federal town house is noted for its porches that run the length of one side and offer unobstructed views of Battery Park and the Delaware River. Air-conditioned rooms are furnished with antiques and reproductions and include such modern amenities as computer data ports, telephones, and cable TV. Breakfast is served in a long dining room furnished in a melange of Chippendale and Federal styles. | 130 Delaware St. | 302/322–2505 | www.terryhouse.com | 4 rooms | $90–$110 | AE, D, MC, V.

William Penn Guest House. William Penn slept here—in one of the four rooms available for guests today. This guest house—just steps from the Green where Penn took part in the ceremony that added the Delaware counties to his holdings—is one of the rare inns housed in a building that dates from the 1600s. | 206 Delaware St. | 302/328–7736 | 4 rooms | $60–$85 | MC, V.

NEWARK

▼▼

The present-day home of the University of Delaware has been a seat of higher learning since the establishment of its forerunner, Newark Academy, in the 18th century. Early advertisements for the school assured parents that Newark (say it "New Ark") offered no "remarkable instances of profligacy and vice to draw the attention of youth, divert them from their studies, or turn them aside from the paths of virtue." The original building still stands at the corner of Main and Academy. Just a block away you'll find the Deer Park Inn, built on the site of an 18th-century inn that hosted such travelers as Charles Mason and Jeremiah Dixon. Although its Main Street feels more collegiate than Colonial, Newark's claim to revolutionary fame is both valid and unique: the Battle of Cooch's Bridge took place on the outskirts of town in September of 1777. Nearby Iron Hill provided the lookout point where Washington and his most trusted general—the Marquis de Lafayette—risked capture to personally reconnoiter the enemy. *Contact Greater Wilmington Convention and Visitors Bureau | 100 West 10th St., Suite 20, Wilmington 19801 | 800/422–1181 | www.wilmcvb.org.*

Cooch's Bridge Battle Monument. There are still Cooches living in the homestead at Cooch's Bridge—the site of the only Revolutionary battle fought on Delaware soil. The private residence (which served as temporary headquarters for the Hessian General Knyphausen) is off-limits to tourists, and the battlefield is accessible only during periodic reenactments. The site of the battle is marked by a monument flanked by cannons. | Cooch's Bridge Rd., off Old Baltimore Pike (south of Newark, between Rtes. 896 and 72.

Hale-Byrnes House. George Washington was here. Really. When the Continental general learned that British ships had landed near Elkton, Maryland, to begin their march toward Philadelphia, Washington positioned his troops between the British line and the capital city. This brick building along the White Clay Creek is the documented meeting place of Washington and Lafayette's war council. | 606 Stanton Christiana Rd. | 302/998–3792 | Free | By reservation only.

ODESSA

▼▼

One of the best-preserved towns in Delaware, the pristine village of Odessa has worn many names over the centuries. The Lenni Lenape called it "Apequnimy," which meant "the place where we carried our canoes." For here at the narrowest point of the peninsula (just 7 mi from a Delaware River feeder stream to the headwaters of the Chesapeake), they would disembark and carry their canoes, a shortcut that eliminated 400 mi of strenuous water travel around the entire peninsula. The first European settlers were Dutch, lured here in 1662 by the possibilities of a trade route that would give them easy access to Maryland and its lucrative tobacco trade. The marshy creeks teemed with muskrat and beaver, prized for both their meat and their pelts, which brought high prices on the European market. Despite building a fort to keep out the English and the pirates (Blackbeard supposedly sailed the back streams, looking for places to stash his loot), the Dutch lost their Colony to the English in 1664. With the growth of the English presence in "Appoquinimee"—the town's Anglo name—a man named Sir Richard Cantwell built a toll bridge and the settlement became known as Cantwell's Bridge.

During the early part of the 18th century, many people regarded lower New Castle County as a last outpost of civilization, malaria-infested in the summer and isolated in the winter. Cantwell's Bridge, however, became a prosperous town, due in large part to a flourishing wheat trade and its location at the junction of two trade routes—the Appoquinimink Creek and the King's Highway. By the time of the Revolution, it was a large settlement for its day, populated by 125 inhabitants whose habitations ranged from Georgian mansions to log cabins. The town saw no direct action during the Revolutionary War and emerged unscathed. It continued to grow and prosper well into the 19th century, when the advent of train travel shifted the critical trade route inland to Middletown. To win back prosperity and prominence, the town's citizens voted to change its name to Odessa, in honor of the famous grain port on the Black Sea.

By the 20th century, Odessa had started to decay. Foresighted preservationists—most notably H. Rodney Sharp, who made his fortune with the DuPont Company—recognized the merit of the surviving structures and began acquiring and restoring them. Ultimately, he gave the properties to Winterthur, which bestowed his name upon two of them and continues to operate a core group of buildings known as Historic Houses of Odessa. Most of the Winterthur properties are open to the public; other historic houses in the town— such as The Pump House—are maintained as private residences, but can be seen on a self-guided walking tour (available in a booklet sold in the gift shop in the Brick Hotel). *Contact Greater Wilmington Convention and Visitors Bureau | 100 West 10th St., Suite 20, Wilmington 19801 | 800/422–1181 | www.wilmcvb.org.*

Brick Hotel. As Cantwell's Bridge grew in the years of the early Republic, a man named William Polk built himself a "commodious brick house" for use as both a residence and a hotel. This straightforward building of the Federal period features classic lines, a central doorway, and an elliptical fanlight. No longer a hotel, it now has exhibition space and a collection of quintessential Victorian furniture. The ticketing office and gift shop for Historic Houses of Odessa are here. | Main St. | 302/378–4069 | www.winterthur.org | $8 (includes 3 other Historic Houses of Odessa properties) | Mar.–Dec., Tues.–Sat. 10–4, Sun. 1–4. Last tour departs at 3.

Collins-Sharp House. No one knows the exact date of this low, plank-covered house with the gambrel roof, but the asymmetrical weatherboards and large cooking hearth reflect construction techniques and domestic interiors of the 1730s. Despite its small size and humble appearance to today's eyes, the house falls within the category of plantation house and would have belonged to a gentleman, as it features fine paneling and moldings and quaint window cupboards. The Collins-Sharp house is not original to Odessa; it was moved here in 1962 to save it from demolition. | 2nd St. | 302/378–4069 | www.winterthur.org | $8 (includes 3 other Historic Houses of Odessa properties) | Mar.–Dec., Tues.–Sat. 10–4, Sun. 1–4. Last tour departs at 3.

Corbit-Sharp House. Although he lived here on the banks of the Appoquinimink, William Corbit could have been called a "Philadelawarean," a term used to describe those with close business and social ties to the City of Brotherly Love. This division of life and affinities is evident in the house that Corbit, a Quaker whose business was tanning, built in 1774. Regarded as Colonial Delaware's finest Georgian mansion, the Corbit-Sharp House would be right at home in Philadelphia or Wilmington, so it's a little surprising to find a house of this size and elegance in a relatively isolated marsh town. Much of the furniture in the mansion has Corbit family associations. There are also numerous examples of the work of local and regional craftsmen, including Odessa's premier cabinetmaking family, the Janviers, and clockmaker Duncan Beard. Once outside, be sure to take in the graceful Chinese lattice balustrade on the roof and note the fine brickwork (90,000 bricks were used). | Main St. | 302/378–4069 | www.winterthur.org | $8 (includes 3 other Historic Houses of Odessa properties) | Mar.–Dec., Tues.–Sat. 10–4, Sun. 1–4. Last tour departs at 3.

Wilson-Warner House. The Wilsons were a merchant family. As the owner of a dry-goods store specializing in imported goods, David Wilson built a home in 1769, one that—while simpler than the Corbit house next door—reflected his position and prosperity. By the time the house passed into his son's hands, however, the family's finances had taken a downturn. David Wilson, Jr. went bankrupt in 1828, an occurrence that, while unfortunate for him, was fortunate for posterity because the legal process produced hundreds of documents that provide an extremely detailed account of the contents of each room in the house. Through these records, we know that David Wilson's wall-to-wall Brussels carpet—assessed at a lavish $82— was by far the most expensive item in his house, and, quite possibly, the entire town. | Main St. | 302/378–4069 | www.winterthur.org | $8 (includes 3 other Historic Houses of Odessa properties) | Mar.–Dec., Tues.–Sat. 10–4, Sun. 1–4. Last tour departs at 3.

WILMINGTON
▼▼

Delaware's largest city wears its considerable history like a slightly tattered undergarment beneath spanking-new threads, revealing it only to those who can appreciate the substantial foundation that the older garment provides for the new. To follow the city's evolution, start at "The Rocks," where the first European settlers landed in 1638, and end in Rodney Square, where you can admire a statue of the Delaware patriot amidst a canyon of mid-rise towers that house the banks and corporations that power the city today.

From Rodney Square, it's just a short way to Willingtown Square, which honors Thomas Willing, who founded the town in 1731. A few blocks away, the area near 2nd and Shipley streets, known today as the Quaker Hill Historic District, was settled in 1738. Soon afterward, the settlement received a charter from William Penn, who changed its name to Wilmington to honor a friend. So many Quakers were attracted to the new town that a new meetinghouse had to be built in 1748. Wilmington, with its thriving port, grew to become a handsome brick city on a hill, overlooking the Christina and Delaware rivers. French officers in Rochambeau's army passed through on their way to Yorktown and commented on its appeal. Following their victory at the Battle of the Brandywine, the British occupied Wilmington, but were disappointed at the lack of provisions to be had (a result of General Washington's request that all mills hide their flour and millstones).

Most of the mills have closed, their buildings converted into loft apartments or art galleries. Today Wilmington's prosperity is tied to banks and credit-card companies drawn here by the favorable business climate and liberal laws of incorporation. The DuPont Company, founded in 1802, still has a significant presence, although it has greatly diversified from its gunpowder roots, giving the world such products as nylon, Teflon, Lycra, Kevlar, and Tyvek. North of the city, a concentration of du Pont family mansions-turned-museums, many surrounded by stunning gardens, has earned the area the sobriquet "chateau country." *Contact Greater Wilmington Convention and Visitors Bureau | 100 W. 10th St., Suite 20, Wilmington 19801 | 302/652–4088 or 800/422–1181 | www.wilmcvb.org. Historical Society of Delaware | 505 Market St., Wilmington 19801 | 302/655–7161 | www.hsd.org.*

Delaware History Museum. More "five-and-dime" than "shilling-and-farthing"—due to its home in a renovated Art Deco–era Woolworth's store—the Delaware History Museum exhibits artifacts that range from stone tools used by the Lenni Lenape to a Revolutionary War flag captured by a British officer. A hands-on section called "Grandma's Attic" aims to show children that history is both fascinating and fun. | 504 Market St. | 302/656–0637 | www.hsd.org | $4 | Weekdays noon–4, Sat. 10–4.

Fort Christina Monument. The log cabin may be an icon of the American frontier, but the durable dwelling—introduced by the Finns—played a key role in the success of the Colony of New Sweden. The log cabins built by the Swedes and Finns when they landed at this rocky riverbank sheltered them from extremes of temperature. In commemoration of the contributions of the earliest Finnish and Swedish settlers, a log cabin and a black granite monument form the core of this urban park. | East 7th St. at Christina River | 302/652–5629.

Hagley Museum and Library. The du Pont story starts here, on the banks of the Brandywine River, where Eleuthère Irénée du Pont recognized in 1802 that the narrow span combined with the rapid descent of the river would make it an excellent source of waterpower. Because the history of the Brandywine Valley is so intertwined with the history of the du Pont family, it's a good idea to tour Hagley before visiting any of the other du Pont mansions, just to get a sense of context and to unravel the genealogical strands of this influential clan. The du Pont mills produced their first gunpowder in 1804, earning a reputation for consistently reliable gun and blasting powder. Thomas Jefferson was among the fans of E. I. du Pont's powder; he used it to clear the land at Monticello. By 1811, DuPont was the largest gunpowder manufacturer in the fledgling republic and sold powder to the army and the navy for the War of 1812. The powder used by the Delaware Militia in 1813, when it fired on English ships at Lewes, came from the DuPont mills. As the young nation expanded, increasing quantities of DuPont powder were needed to blast canals, tunnels, mines, and railways.

A tour of the site's remaining powder mills reveals fascinating facts about the intricacies of making gunpowder (one ounce of black powder had to be capable of sending a 24-pound cannonball a distance of 250 yards). Massive stone mills, storehouses, and a waterwheel also illustrate the formidable power of water. Machinists demonstrate a water turbine, steam engine, powder tester, and a working machine shop. Exhibits trace the economic and technological history of the region. Outbuildings still standing on the estate include the Gibbons House on Blacksmith Hill, which served as home to powder-yard foremen and their families, and the 1817 Brandywine Manufacturer's Sunday School, where millworkers' children were given lessons.

Eleutherian Mills, the first du Pont family home in the New World, is also on the Hagley property and is open for tours. The Georgian-style residence is furnished with antiques and memorabilia from five generations of du Ponts. Despite his success as an industrialist, E. I. du Pont's true passion was botany. In fact, on his passport he listed his profession as *"botaniste."* Soon after he moved his family into the new home, Eleuthere Irenée begged his father to send him some seeds. The gardens at Eleutherian Mills were *très* French, with boxwood parterres, manicured allées, and espaliered fruit trees. The house and gardens were renovated by Louise du Pont Crowninshield in the 1900s. Today, the Crowninshield garden at Hagley blends the formal with a naturalistic style inspired by the terrain of the Brandywine Valley. | Rte. 141 north of Wilmington | 302/658–2400 | www.hagley.lib.de.us | $6.50–$12 | Mar. 15– Dec. 30, daily 9:30–4:30; Jan.–Mar. 14, weekends 9:30–4:30, weekdays guided tour at 1:30.

Kalmar Nyckel. Sweden's answer to the *Mayflower*, the *Kalmar Nyckel* was the only Colonial ship to complete more than two crossings to the New World. And it's a good thing she proved seaworthy—no women or children sailed on the ship's first passage, so subsequent trips were essential to the propagation of New Sweden. Re-created by a master shipbuilder in the 1980s, the vessel on view is authentic in every detail from stem to stern. Because the *Kalmar Nyckel* is a fully functioning sailing vessel, it's best to call ahead to see when she'll be in port. | 1124 E. 7th St. | 302/429–7447 | www.kalnyc.org.

Nemours Mansion and Garden. Inspired more by Versailles than by Monticello, Nemours is yet another du Pont family mansion, one that—in contrast to Eleutherian Mills and Winterthur—is most decidedly and emphatically French. Built by Alfred I. du Pont, a great-grandson of Eleuthere, the 102-room chateau is exquisitely rendered in ivory-pink Indiana limestone and surrounded by fountains, sculpture, and formal gardens. Alfred I. du Pont's eclectic collections include a James Peale portrait of George Washington, a pair of Gilbert Stuart sketches of Pierre Samuel du Pont and Thomas Jefferson, and a large, 18th-century French crystal chandelier said to have belonged to the Marquis de Lafayette, who, like Jefferson, was a friend of Pierre Samuel du Pont. In a small display room in the basement—near the bowling alley and just down the hall from the ice-making room—is an array of ephemera relating to Pierre Samuel, Jefferson, and Lafayette, including a plaque that Jefferson presented to du Pont for helping the United States acquire the Louisiana Territory. Tours of Nemours take a minimum of two hours, and visitors must be at least 16 years old. Reservations are recommended. | 1600 Rockland Rd. | 302/651–6912 | www.nemours.org | $10 | Tour May–Oct., Tues.–Sat. at 9, 11, 1, and 3 and Sun. at 11, 1, and 3.

Old Swedes (Holy Trinity) Church. Despite the legendary Swedish hardiness, worshipers at Old Swedes often brought heated rocks or pans of hot coals into their pews to keep themselves warm during services. Built in 1698 on the site of an old burial ground (the altar rail rests on the graves of five children), the church has exterior walls made of locally mined Delaware blue granite, supplemented with bricks made in Sweden and brought over on ships as ballast. Look closely at the walls and you can see oyster shells in the mortar. During the occupation of Wilmington that followed the Battle of the Brandywine in 1777, British Redcoats were quartered in the church; small cannonballs in the churchyard testify to their presence. Recent efforts to restore the church's doors revealed carved graffiti from as early as 1798, when the congregation was too small to properly protect the property from vandals. The 1690 Hendrickson House next to the church was moved here from Chester, Pennsylvania, and is open for tours. | 606 Church St. | 302/652–5629 | www.oldswedes.org | $2 | Mon.–Sat. 10–4.

Willingtown Square. Bond. Flemish bond. That's the style of brickwork that can be seen in the four buildings of Willingtown Square. The structures, which date from 1748 to 1801, were moved here from various sites throughout Wilmington to escape demolition. In Flemish bond brickwork, each row consists of headers (the short end of the brick) and stretchers (the long side) laid alternately. The headers were often glazed, giving the building a checkerboard appearance. At Willingtown Square, this type of brickwork provides unity for an otherwise disparate group of houses. Although the houses aren't open to the public, a walk through the adjoining square offers a taste of 18th-century atmosphere. Although the buildings are not open to the public, entrance to the square is free | 500 Block on Market St. | 302/655–7161 | www.hsd.org | Mon.–Sat. 10–4.

✦ ON THE CALENDAR: Aug. **August Quarterly.** This celebration of African-American heritage and pride dates back to 1814, when Peter Spencer, father of the Independent Black Church Movement and a former slave, started holding a combined reunion–religious revival for both slaves and free blacks. August Quarterly was often the one day that slave owners would allow their slaves to take off; some slaves used it as a starting point from which to escape to freedom. | 302/658–3838.

Nov. **Delaware Antiques Show.** Featuring more than 50 dealers in Early American antiques. | 800/448–3883.

Dec. **Sankta Lucia Celebration at Old Swedes Church.** The Swedish celebration of Saint Lucia's Day honors Sankta Lucia, whose name is derived from the Latin word for light. Offerings are made of lusse-bread, coffee, and ginger cookies. The Lucia celebration at Old Swedes also includes tours of the Hendrickson House, which is decorated for a Swedish Christmas. | 302/652–5629.

HISTORIC DINING AND LODGING
Columbus Inn. This former tollgate stop on the Kennett Pike dates from the 1790s, when it was a bakery (the original ovens are still in the basement). Chef Dave Peterson's cuisine reflects an eclectic mix of influences—swordfish is served with warm salad Niçoise, pork tenderloin

comes with wasabi mashed potatoes. | 2216 Pennsylvania Ave. | 302/571–1492 | $20–$30 | AE, MC, V | Closed Sun., May 26–Sept. 8.

Darley Manor Inn. Once known as "The Chimneys," this inn was built between 1775 and the 1790s and sits on property deeded by William Penn, Jr. in 1713. The surrounding North Wilmington neighborhood, called Claymont, features several unsung Revolutionary-era sites, including Robinson House (currently closed to the public), where Washington, Lafayette, "Light Horse" Harry Lee, and "Mad" Anthony Wayne were guests. A homey mishmash of Colonial Revival and Victorian styles, the inn offers one suite (the Wren's Nest) with a private stair and working fireplace. The exuberant owners will serve tea and sherry in the afternoon and tell you all about F. O. C. Darley, the popular illustrator who lived here in the 19th century and after whom the inn is named. | 3701 Philadelphia Pike | 302/792–2127 | www.dca.net/darley | $95–$119 | D, MC, V.

Hotel du Pont. Expect to be pampered at Wilmington's version of the Grand Hotel. Oversized guest rooms feature reproduction four-poster beds and separate sitting areas. The hotel is also worth a visit for its art collection—on hand are more than 700 original paintings representing 250 artists, including three generations of Wyeths. | 11th and Market Sts. | 800/441–9019 | www.dupont.com/hotel | $179–$599 | AE, MC, V.

WINTERTHUR
▼▼

An oasis of green in one of the nation's most heavily developed corridors, Winterthur is the country estate of the famed collector, horticulturist, and gentleman farmer Henry Francis du Pont. Those who know the name Winterthur as it applies to the museum and its collection of early American decorative arts might be surprised to learn that Winterthur was historically a self-sustaining county estate community, with its own post office and railroad station. The post office still serves the greater Winterthur community, but while the picturesque train depot still stands, only freight trains pass by.

Archaeological evidence indicates that the Winterthur land, with low-lying streams to attract animals and rolling high ground for espying them, was a Lenni Lenape hunting ground. The woodland at Winterthur is a second-growth forest that has been thinned and cut for at least two centuries, perhaps even longer. The land came into the du Pont family in the early 1800s. DuPont Company founder Eleuthere Irenée passed it on to his daughter Evelina and her husband, James Antoine Bidermann. They named the estate Winterthur, after Bidermann's ancestral home in Switzerland. *Contact Greater Wilmington Convention and Visitors Bureau | 100 W. 10th St., Suite 20, Wilmington 19801 | 302/652–4088 or 800/422–1181 | www.wilmcvb.org.*

Winterthur Museum. A walk through Henry Francis du Pont's fabled home is a virtual walk through two centuries and 13 Colonies. Du Pont's collection of some 89,000 American antiques spans the years 1640 to 1860. In addition to collecting objects, du Pont also collected entire rooms of period architecture, which he then installed in a long empty wing of his house-turned-museum. From low-ceilinged 17th-century New England rooms through to the airy opulence of a 19th-century dining room from Georgia, the museum includes architecture from all the original Colonies. Furniture styles run from the massive Jacobean cupboards seen in the earliest days of settlement through to the highly carved Rococo style of the mid-18th century and on to the Neoclassical styles of the Early Republic. Du Pont also collected accessories—porcelain, ceramics, and glass; textiles and needlework; paintings; and silver and other metals—that complemented his furntiure.

Du Pont began collecting in the 1920s, at a time when most of his contemporaries considered American antiques unfashionable. He was proven to be in the vanguard, however; soon every Rockefeller, Vanderbilt, and Hearst sought to collect examples of American

In Vogue: A Hit Parade of American Style at Winterthur

The war is over, independence has been declared, and suddenly, all your furniture—the ornate mahogany pieces carved by Philadelphia's best craftsmen—looks wrong. It now looks too heavy, too ornate, too . . . *English*. What's a fashionable and patriotic matron to do?

The post-Revolutionary era ushered in a new style that looked to ancient Greece and Rome—prototypes for the government and values of the new democracy—for inspiration. Inlaid woods; geometrical patterning; and classical motifs such as eagles, urns, swags, and allegorical figures replaced the Rococo richness of the Chippendale style. Throughout our history, the objects that Americans acquired or discarded tell us nearly as much about them as the words they have spoken, or written. The museum at Winterthur, home to Henry Francis du Pont's extensive collection of American antiques, traces the evolution of American style from the days of the early European settlements to just before the Civil War.

Consider the court cupboard, an item of furniture found in the most affluent 17th-century homes. These massive wooden cupboards were used for the display of silver, delftware, and other treasured possessions, making a public statement about the prosperity and status of the owner of the house. Traveling chronologically, we arrive at the William and Mary style, named after the Dutch stadtholder William III of Orange and his wife, Mary II of England, who became joint monarchs of England in 1689. The decorative arts of this period are influenced by exotica and wares from the Far East, as well as by the French court of Louis XIV at Versailles. Chairs featured high relief carvings, elaborate turnings, cane backs, and severe curves. The American Colonies, although they lagged behind European countries, also began adopting such new forms as the wing chair, high chest, and day bed. And what better way to boast of your literacy and importance than by acquiring that new form of furniture, the desk?

The next style of furniture to emerge on the American scene was also named after a monarch, in this case Queen Anne, who ruled England from 1702 to 1714. Although Queen Anne was reputed to be pious and dull, the style that shares her name produced some of the most curvaceous and sensuous furniture—characterized by shapely cabriole legs and an "S"-shape profile. Japanned (pseudo-lacquered) high chests, bat-shape back splats, and pie-crust tea tables reflected the West's continued fascination with the East. Furniture and accessories designed especially for the tea ritual announced that a household placed a high value on this social ceremony and evidence of wealth. The most fashionable style of the pre-Revolutionary years took its name from the influential patterns of a cabinetmaker named Thomas Chippendale, whose catalogue, *The Gentleman and Cabinetmakers Directory*, was a compendium of the new French- and Chinese-influenced Rococo style, most often rendered in mahogany, a dense wood that could withstand intense carving. In truth, the Federal style that followed the Revolution and appealed so strongly to the new nation's republican sensibilities did not entirely eschew English fashion. Following the War of 1812, however, Americans once again rejected English style and turned in the direction of France, enthusiastically adopting the darker, heavier Empire style, the style famously promulgated by Napoléon.

design and craftsmanship. In fact, in 1930 du Pont battled William Randolph Hearst at auction, finally outbidding him on the stunning Van Pelt high chest, an outstanding example of pre-Revolutionary Philadelphia craftsmanship, and setting a staggering record price—$44,000—that went unsurpassed for years. Du Pont also collected items for their historical association, including a rare set of six tankards made by Paul Revere; a matching pair of Chippendale sofas made for John Dickinson; a bedspread believed to have been owned by John Hancock;

Benjamin West's unfinished portrait of the American commissioners (John Jay, Benjamin Franklin, and John Quincy Adams, among others) at the signing of the Treaty of Paris—unfinished because the signers representing England refused to sit for the portrait; a set of Chinese porcelain that belonged to George Washington; John Trumbull's 1782 painting *Washington at Verplanck's Point,* showing the general reviewing the French troops after the victory at Yorktown; and an English earthenware statue of Ben Franklin, amusingly mislabeled "Washington." Be forewarned that Winterthur offers an array of guided tours—you won't see all of these objects on every tour. There's so much to see here that it would be impossible to cover it in a single day. Fortunately, the basic ticket package is good for two days.

In addition to the collection displayed in the period rooms of the mansion, Winterthur also has a gallery wing, offering both chronological and regional explorations of furniture styles, and special exhibitions on a wide range of themes. Just across the way from the museum, in the house that du Pont moved into when he opened the mansion to the public, is the Museum Store, where you can purchase—among other things—an exact reproduction of the high chest that du Pont outbid Hearst for in 1930. The repro sells for about $41,000—$3,000 less than the record-breaking price du Pont paid for the original, but this being Delaware, at least you won't have to pay sales tax. | Kennett Pike, Rte. 52 | 302/888–4600 or 800/448–3883 | www.winterthur.org | $10 | Mon.–Sun. 10–5. Last tour ticket sold at 3:45.

✦ ON THE CALENDAR: May **Point-to-Point Races.** Taking a cue from our forebears, who kept their horses in shape by racing from church steeple to church steeple, this day of steeplechase racing features some of the best amateur riders in the country and a parade of antique carriages—four-in-hands, phaetons, surreys. | 302/658–3838.

Sept. **Craft Festival.** From theorem painting to pottery, floorcloths to furniture, this high-end crafts festival features more than 100 invited artisans offering fine traditional work. | 800/448–3883.

Nov.–Dec. **Yuletide at Winterthur.** A holiday tour featuring decorations and traditions from America's past. | 800/448–3883.

HISTORIC DINING AND LODGING

Buckley's Tavern. The simple white-clapboard building on Kennett Pike just north of Winterthur fits right in with Centreville's Colonial past as a resting station for those traveling between Wilmington and the Pennsylvania communities across the border. The friendly tavern offers tasty pub fare, ranging from juicy burgers to individual pizzas. The pasta and seafood dishes served in the dining room—a little bit country, a little bit elegant—use fresh, often local, ingredients. | 5812 Kennett Pike, Rte. 52, Centreville | 302/656–9776 | AE, MC, V.

Inn at Montchanin Village. Once part of Winterthur, this early 19th-century hamlet of worker's housing has remained in du Pont family hands. The current proprietors, Dan and Missy Lickle, have preserved and enhanced the property, turning it into a fine country inn that is listed on the National Register of Historic Places. Rooms and suites are luxuriously furnished with antique four-posters and canopy beds made up with Frette linens. Some rooms have Jacuzzis or wet bars. Krazy Kat is an innovative and quirky restaurant, highly recommended. | Rte. 100 and Kirk Rd., Montchanin | 302/888–2133 | www.montchanin.com | 27 rooms | $135–$375 | AE, MC, V.

By Laura V. Scheel

Maine

❧⟶⟵❧

The Down East Dominion

aine's climate is invigorating and healthful." So states the pleasant observation of a Depression-era author, writing for the Federal Writer's Project on the topic of Maine,
New England's largest state. Indeed, it was this healthful climate that produced the vast display
of natural resources that attracted explorers to the region as early as the year 1003. From its
original inhabitants to the trade-hungry Europeans, Maine's wealth of fur, fish, and timber
was the reason behind both settlement and conflict. In many ways, well up into the mid-
1600s, Maine was the new frontier—a wild region viewed as a place to pluck the fruits of
commerce rather than maintain them. Much of the history of the central and northern coast
of Maine can be likened to the altering tides that mark its thousands of miles of shoreline:
in a restless and violent cycle that endured for nearly 200 years, settlements and fortunes were
made, only to be abandoned by the warlike forces of both humans and nature.

Well before the arrival of settlers, traders, and warfare, the area was home to various Indian
tribes that wandered at the whim of the seasons. The earliest known natives, the Red Paint
People, were named for their practice of coloring the bodies of their dead with red ochre at
burial. Later Indians, the Wabenaki "People of the Dawn" were the first to encounter the white
visitors and settlers and eagerly aided travelers by sharing food and trading goods. The good-
will would be short-lived; already by the early 1600s, when Captain George Waymouth
kidnapped five Indians from Monhegan to bring home to England as living showpieces, relations between whites and Indians were deteriorating quickly. Embroiled in continual battle
with the French against the English and with the settlers for more than a century, the Indians
were devastatingly subdued by 1724, after two fierce colonial victories left them powerless.

✦ RICHES IN THE WILDERNESS

The first English settlers at Popham in 1607 lasted only until the rigors of winter drove them
back across the ocean. A bit hardier, the French founded a colony at St. Croix Island,
concerned primarily with establishing a base for the lucrative fur trade. Scattered English

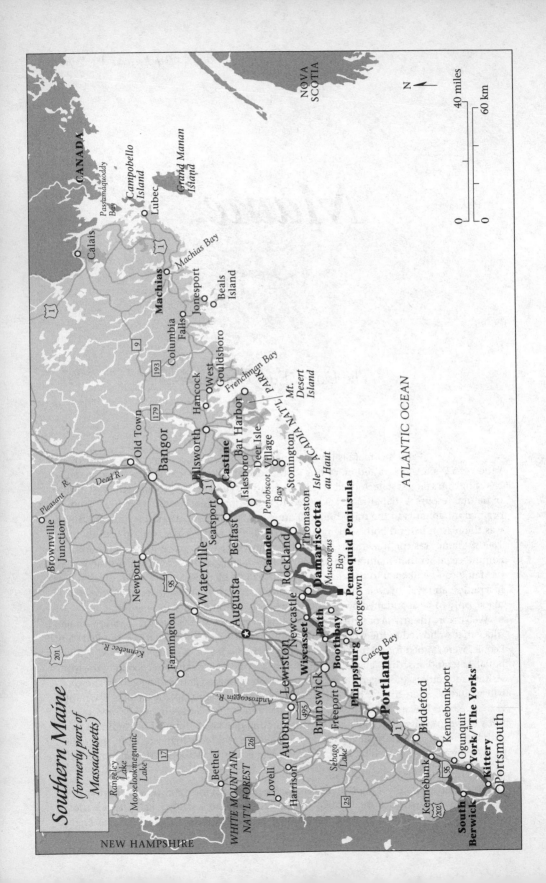

Southern Maine
(formerly part of Massachusetts)

NEW HAMPSHIRE

CANADA

NOVA SCOTIA

ATLANTIC OCEAN

N

40 miles
60 km

Calais

Passamaquoddy Bay
Campobello Island
Lubec
Grand Manan Island

Machias Bay
Machias
Jonesport
Beals Island
Columbia Falls
West Gouldsboro
Hancock
Frenchman Bay
Bar Harbor
Mt. Desert Island
PARK Bay
Deer Isle
ACADIA NAT'L
Stonington
Isle au Haut
Penobscot Village
Castine
Islesboro
Ellsworth
Old Town
Bangor
Brownville Junction

Pleasant R.
Dead R.

Newport
Waterville
Searsport
Belfast
Camden
Rockland
Thomaston
Damariscotta
Muscongus Bay
Pemaquid Peninsula
Newcastle
Wiscasset
Bath
Boothbay
Georgetown
Phippsburg
Casco Bay

Augusta
Farmington
Kennebec R.

Lewiston
Auburn
Brunswick
Freeport
Androscoggin R.

WHITE MOUNTAIN NAT'L FOREST
Bethel
Lovell
Harrison
Sebago Lake

Rangeley Lake
Mooselookmeguntic Lake

Portland
Biddeford
Kennebunkport
Kennebunk
Ogunquit
York/"The Yorks"
Kittery
Portsmouth
South Berwick

and French settlements were temporary and seasonal, exploiting the abundant fishing stocks while fattening livestock in the pastoral lands along the coast. Extensive fur trading with the Indians at the mouths of the Kennebec and Piscataqua rivers further encouraged exploration for more and more natural resources. With more than 5,000 rivers and streams, thousands of miles of coastline and hundreds of protected coastal harbors, Maine was an ideal place to make a fortune. Its secret would not last for long. More permanent settlement began with the strengthening of the Massachusetts Bay Colony, which granted Maine lands to Pilgrims eager to move elsewhere. The English crown also gave away millions of acres to noblemen, notably Sir Ferdinando Gorges, who envisioned the creation of a massive feudal estate that never happened. The first permanent settlements cropped up along the southern coast, in Saco, York, Kittery, and the nearby island called Appledore. (The Massachusetts Bay Colony officially took Maine under its ownership in 1652, buying out Gorges's heirs and further inflaming strained relations with the British.)

Remoteness from the ruling Massachusetts government, both geographically and in sentiment, flavored the settlements with a distinctive character of raucous independence. Though the church was the mainstay of social life, Mainers were generally more tolerant, and did not adhere to rigid Puritan ways as did their neighbors in Massachusetts. Despite Maine's growing resentment of the ruling Massachusetts Bay, the settlers were always willing and ready to fight on behalf of the Colonial governments. Indeed, there was so much fighting in Maine between the French, the Indians, and the British that it wasn't until the later half of the 1700s that the province actually experienced significant growth and development.

✦ WAR AND SEPARATION

While the Revolutionary War was fought mostly elsewhere, Maine settlers were well represented on the battlefields. One incident did take place in Maine, and is heralded as the first naval battle of the Revolution. Faced with the arrogance of British rule, the residents of Machias erected a liberty pole. Ordered to remove it, they refused and planned an attack. Armed with guns, axes, pitchforks, and other implements, the men sailed out to the *Margaretta*. No match for their scrappy, hand-to-hand fighting ways, the British surrendered after little resistance. The wounded and the dying British captain were taken ashore to the local tavern, while the *Margaretta* was captured and renamed the *Machias Liberty*. The fervor for separation from Massachusetts increased during the War of 1812. Led by Maine's governor William King, an attempt to break off failed. It wasn't until 1820 that Maine was admitted to the Union as a free state. Along that long road to legitimacy and self-rule, Mainers fought battles, built thriving industries in shipbuilding, fishing, and timber and created their own brand of Yankee ingenuity.

A REGIONAL GAZETEER
▼▼

✦ STEADY AND STALWART AGAINST THE CHANGING TIDES:
THE YORK COUNTY COAST

Despite its numerous 17th-century settlements and fruitful economy fed by fishing, timber, and shipbuilding, the south coast of Maine was still generally regarded as part of the vast frontier. It was, at times, a perilous place to be, although today's visitors would be hard pressed to picture generations of raiding Indians, French, or British soldiers where they now find tidy white-clapboard houses, calm harbors sheltering fishing boats and sailing sloops, well-kept churches, and myriad antiques shops and restaurants catering to travelers. For nearly two centuries wars with royal names like Queen Anne's (1703–13), King George's (1744–48), King Philip's (1675), and the French and Indian War (1754–60) raged wildly and vengefully upon settlements, destroying many several times over. Thus, while little 17th-century architecture remains owing to the constant warfare, there are many opportunities to explore glimpses

1497-1524 Various exploratory voyages from England and France stake royal claims on the region, laying the foundation for what would amount to immense future conflict.

1607 The English create a short-lived settlement at Popham; the unprepared abandon the site once the rigors of a Maine winter become apparent, but not without building the first ship ever constructed in the New World.

1652 The powerful Massachusetts Bay government boldly takes ownership of Maine, irritating both the independent settlers and the English crown.

1675 King Philip's War begins far south of the Maine Province, but strained relations between local Indians, British soldiers, and settlers incite an extension of the war. Within a decade, few of the region's settlements are spared destruction.

1675-1730s Continual warfare between Colonials, the French, and the Indians keep the Maine region from much growth; eventually both the Indians and French are brutally subdued.

1680 The Massachusetts Bay Colony grants the Province of Maine its own acting government and appoints those in charge.

1741 Maine's border is established, freeing New Hampshire to become its own province.

1775 Angry residents of Machias capture a British ship in rebellion; the act is held to be the first naval battle of the American Revolution. Later that year, Falmouth (now Portland) was nearly completely destroyed by the British.

1775 The long, hard, and ultimately fruitless journey of Benedict Arnold and troops to capture Québec winds through Maine.

1779 The hugely disastrous Penobscot Expedition, led by Commodore Saltonstall to recapture Castine from the British, leads to the loss of hundreds of soldiers and nearly 50 ships.

1783 Maine's northern boundaries are defined by the Treaty of Versailles.

1812 The northern coast of Maine is temporarily occupied by the British during the War of 1812.

1820 After many decades of separatist sentiment, Maine finally secedes from Massachusetts and is admitted to the Union as a free state. Portland is the original capital of the new state but later (1832) unwillingly relinquishes the position to Augusta.

of Maine's Colonial development. In **Kittery,** the Kittery Historical and Naval Museum brings back to life the ingenuity of the early shipbuilders. Military garrisons are plentiful in Maine, and here Fort McClary stands boldly atop the rise of Kittery Point, its sturdy and imposing hexagonal granite frame was enough to keep the British at bay during the Revolution. Also in Kittery is Maine's oldest church, the First Congregational Church and Old Parsonage House, dating from 1730. The William Pepperell House reflects the great wealth with which it was built in 1720; its owner made his fortune in lumber; on his death, his widow moved out and built her own white mansion, the now famed Lady Pepperell House, overlooking Portsmouth Harbor.

Just to the north are **the Yorks.** Here, in York Village is a restoration of seven wonderful 18th-century buildings, including the fabled Old York Gaol, one of the oldest public buildings in the nation, the John Hancock House, home of the prominent signer of the Declaration of the Independence, and the Emerson-Wilcox House, dating from 1742. Continuing up the coast, **South Berwick** survived numerous attacks but several fine examples of 18th-century building remain. Despite a climate of ongoing strife, higher education was not forgotten; Berwick Academy, a secondary school, was established in 1791. Not far away is the Sarah Orne Jewett House, the home of the beloved Maine writer known for her tales of life in a small Maine harbor town. *Towns listed: Kittery, South Berwick, the Yorks.*

✦ FROM ASHES TO GRANDEUR: GREATER PORTLAND

Balancing vulnerability with advantage, the greater Portland area experienced both growth and destruction throughout the Colonial years. Blessed with deep harbors and the sheltering shores of the Casco Bay Islands, the region at once benefited and suffered from its position, witnessing significant advancement, only to have it leveled by aggressive Indian raiders in 1676 and again by British troops in 1775. Fires swept throughout the town, wiping out homes and businesses, but hardy settlers refused to give up the promise and potential of prosperity. And prosper they did: enough for the brand new state of Maine to designate the city as its capital in 1820. **Portland** itself was originally settled in the late 1600s, though it took time for faith and fortitude to gather enough momentum to make it a significant township. Those who found wealth built grand homes here, including the Wadsworth House (home of General Peleg Wadsworth, the grandfather of renowned poet Henry Wadsworth Longfellow) and the McLellan-Sweat House. *Town listed: Portland.*

✦ KILLING FIELDS AND CALM HARBORS:
THE MAINE COAST (INCLUDING DOWNEAST)

In more than any other region in Maine, this coastal area was the target of a near constant tug of war between the English, the French, and the Indians. The French were the first to explore and settle, establishing a fur trading colony in 1604 at the mouth of the St. Croix River. In 1605 the English explorer George Weymouth stopped at Monhegan Island, and was so impressed with the area's potential for colonization that he kidnapped five Indians to bring back to England as living examples of the good health and fortune to be found there. The British settled in in 1607 in Popham, at the mouth of the Kennebec River. The settlers, paroled prisoners from England, fled after experiencing the brutality of a Maine winter.

These small tastes were enough to whet the appetites of others. The British, the French, and newly arriving colonists all wanted to sit at the head of the table and perpetual rivalry left the Maine coast in a tenuous position. However, the economy proved promising, thanks to fishing, lumber, and shipbuilding, the latter centered since the 18th century in Bath. That original batch of prisoners didn't leave Popham Colony until they had built the first ship in the Colonies, the *Virginia*. The Popham site is also where Benedict Arnold began his near 200-mi trek to invade Québec in 1775. Here, outside **Phippsburg,** the Fort Popham State Historic Site contains much information on this ill-fated journey.

Ship captains, builders, and tradesman profited handsomely, and their homes are a testament to their good fortune. Many towns along the coast take pride in venerable mansions: **Wiscasset** has the Nickels-Sortwell House and a well-kept historic district, while **Damariscotta** has the Chapman-Hall House. Farther north, in **Castine,** the British built Fort George in 1779 after seizing control of the town during the Revolution. This is also the site of one of the worst American naval battles in history.

Early Maine history is in evidence in the towns of Bristol and along the **Pemaquid Peninsula.** The Nahanda Village Site is believed to be the remains of a Native American site from nearly 2,000 years ago. Nearby, at Colonial Pemaquid, is another area rich in history; it was here that an early 17th-century English settlement was founded. Downeast in the coastal town of **Machias** is the Burnham Tavern, where rambunctious settlers brought the wounded and also the dying British captain of the ship *Margaretta*. Settlers attacked the British ship and were victorious, and the event is heralded as the first naval battle of the Revolution. *Towns listed: Camden, Castine, Damariscotta, Castine, Machias, Pemaquid Peninsula, Wiscasset.*

Built on a Ship's Fortune:
Midcoast to Downeast Maine

A DRIVING TOUR FROM BATH TO CASTINE

▼▼

Distance: approx. 80 mi (one-way)   **Time:** 4 days (3 nights)
Breaks: Overnight stays in Damariscotta, Camden, and Castine

Head out from Bath, Maine's shipbuilding capital. The industry began heartily in 1762 when the first commercial shipyard opened, although the trade was active long before. Ship enthusiasts will love the Maine Maritime Museum here, with nearly four centuries of shipbuilding history is on display, while many of the grand sea captain and merchant mid-1800s homes of the town are now lodging establishments. Head south on Route 209 from Bath along marshland to **Phippsburg** and down to Popham Beach. This is the site of the ill-fated 1607 colony that, though they didn't make it through a year, the settlers managed to build the *Virginia*, the first ship built in America. The granite Fort Popham structure, built during the Civil War, sits on the site of a long-gone fortification originally constructed during the Revolution.

Backtrack to Route 1 north on your way to **Wiscasset,** a village first settled in the early 1700s, evacuated during the times of fierce Indian battles, resettled, that now proclaims to be Maine's "prettiest village." It may well be. Prosperity came to the town in the late 18th century, resulting in the building of grand homes throughout the village historic district and near the waterfront. An excellent example is the Federal styled Nickels-Sortwell House (Maine and Federal streets), built by sea captain William Nickels in 1807. Just off Route 1 across the Davey Bridge (over the Sheepscot River) is Fort Edgecomb State Memorial, constructed in 1809—a great place for a picnic lunch. For more sybaritic delights, head south on Route 27 to the resort of Boothbay, about a dozen miles, but if you just want to continue your Colonial trek, continue north on Route 1 from Wiscasset to the neighboring town of **Damariscotta.** Yet another town that found shipbuilding to be the path to fortune, Damariscotta experienced a big boom in the early 19th century; misfortune came in the guise of a great fire that destroyed many of its early buildings. Some early structures did survive, though much of the town was rebuilt soon after the fire. The Chapman-Hall House, from 1754 did make it through the fire and is worth touring. St. Patrick's (Academy Road), constructed in 1808, still makes home to a bell cast by no other than beloved patriot and silversmith Paul Revere.

Leaving Damariscotta, take Route 130 south toward the **Pemaquid Peninsula.** Dating back to the 17th century, the Colonial Pemaquid site on Pemaquid Point is an active archaeological dig area. The remains of the 1692 Fort William Henry rest here; on-site is a modern reproduction of the old fortification. Continuing as far south on Route 130 as one can go, Pemaquid Point Lighthouse stands watch over the water from its 1827 beginnings. Adjacent to the light is the Fishermen's Museum, which has a fascinating display illustrating Maine's 400-year old fishing industry.

Head back up toward Bristol and take Route 32 north to the town of Waldoboro, then Route 1 north to around Rockland, where, just to the south, is Thomaston, the town where America's first Secretary of War and Bunker Hill veteran Major General Henry Knox made his home back in 1795. To get to his estate of Montpelier, take Route 131 south just out of town. Walk through the town's historic district, which has a good display of 19th-century architectural styles encouraged by seafaring wealth. For a break, a night's stay or to tour some of its excellent (though more modern) art museums, backtrack to Rockland on Route 1 north (the Farnsworth Art Museum's Wyeth Center is world-famous). Farther up Route 1 north is the tidy and much touristed town of **Camden.** While little evidence of Colonial history can be found here, it is perhaps the quintessential Maine coastal town.

To delve deeper into Maine's Downeast coast, continue north on Route 1 past the town of Belfast (notable for its Church Street historic district), through Searsport, and—it's a bit of a detour, but worth it for the sake of history—continue on Route 1 to the town of Orland, to join Route 175 south (this turns into Route 166) to reach **Castine.** During the Revolutionary War, the British occupied the area and built Fort George in an attempt to maintain control. The American mission to unhinge the British proved to be about the worst defeat in our nation's naval history. The remains of the fort can be toured. In town, the John Perkins House managed to survive the many battles, dating from 1763.

The Spirited Southern Coast

A DRIVING TOUR FROM KITTERY TO PORTLAND

▼▼▼

Distance: 70 mi (one-way)   **Time:** 3 days (2 nights)
Breaks: Overnight stays in the Yorks and Portland

The southern coast of Maine was the area in which colonists settled first, suffered greatly yet survived with enough spirit to not only hold on to their settlements, but actually prosper. Its reliance on the surrounding calm harbors that led to the open sea provided their livelihoods—but also their repeated vulnerability. Because of repeated attacks, the modest amount of remaining 18th-century architecture belies the region's history of inhabitance, which goes back to the early 1600s. Yet fear not, for there is plenty to see and study throughout the region.

Heading north on I–95 through Portsmouth, New Hampshire, follow the exit for Route 1B just before crossing the Piscataqua River bridge into Maine. If you have been driving along coastal Route 1A through New Hampshire, continue until it reconnects to U.S. 1, heading toward **Kittery,** the first stop in Maine. Officially Maine's oldest town (1647), much of Kittery is now dominated by the long stretch of outlet shopping centers up U.S. 1, but there are great pockets of history tucked in along the water. Take winding Route 103 east and head toward Kittery Point, a major shipbuilding port since the U.S. Navy opened the Portsmouth Naval Shipyard in 1800. Look for the white, 1730 First Congregational Church and Old Parsonage, Maine's oldest, which overlooks Portsmouth Harbor. Nearby, the privately owned, gambrel-roofed William Pepperrell House was built in 1729 with the immense wealth made from Maine's lumber trade, as was the nearby Lady Pepperrell House.

Also at the height of Kittery Point is Fort McClary, easy to spot for its unusual hexagonal shape. The fort witnessed multiple garrisons; the first as protection during the constant French and Indian raids around 1715. Head back west on Route 103 to rejoin U.S. 1 north. At the rotary where Route 236 meets U.S. 1, look for signs for the Kittery Historical and Naval Museum on Rodgers Road. Ship enthusiasts will marvel at the displays, old photographs, and the history of both Maine's and the nation's early shipbuilding industries.

For relief from outlet heaven, take Route 101 north from U.S. 1 and relax amid farmland on your way to the town of **South Berwick.** Take a right onto Route 236 (approximately 8 mi on Route 101) and continue until the road meets Route 91. Look for signs for Vaughan Woods State Park and the Hamilton House. Surrounded by woods but with impeccable formal gardens, this 1785 Georgian-style home was once in terrible disrepair. Local author and neighbor Sarah Orne Jewett convinced some wealthy friends to gather the funds for the efforts to restore this beauty in 1896, and this was done in earnest. The author's home is also run by the Society; follow Route 236 until you reach the center of South Berwick; at the division of Routes 236 and 4, look for signs for the Sarah Orne Jewett House, right in the center of town. Another sturdy Georgian home, this one reflects the shipbuilding wealth of its time, 1774.

Retrace your steps on Route 236 out of town and take Route 91 south toward **the Yorks.** Rejoin U.S. 1 north briefly; follow signs for Route 1A to York Village. Within easy reach and all owned by the Old York Historical Society are seven of the aged gems of history that dot the village, including the Jefferds Tavern (1750) and Emerson-Wilcox House (1742). The village itself is full of old and well-kept homes, many of them private but several now functioning as inns and restaurants. Follow Route 1A from the village toward York Harbor, turn right onto Route 103, a left onto Barrell Lane and discover the 1718 Georgian elegance of the Sayward-Wheeler House. Hop back onto U.S. 1 from York and head north through Wells and passing endless antiques shops and roadside flea markets, or opt for Route 9 for a more scenic jaunt on your way to Kennebunkport. Made famous by former President George Bush's estate just out of town, the port itself had quite a successful history as a major shipbuilding site. Little of this architectural history is publicly accessible, but the impeccable Colonial, Victorian, Georgian and Federal style homes on the town's side streets attest to its former heyday that continued well into the late 1800s.

The traveler has a choice here: either continue east out of Kennebunk on Route 9A directly back to Interstate 95 to get to Portland, or backtrack to Kennebunkport to Route 9. The latter is a bit longer, though more scenic. In Saco, head onto Route 195, which will take you to **Portland,** Maine's largest city with a still thriving seaport. On Congress Street, an excellent place to begin is Henry Wadsworth Longfellow House, childhood home of the beloved poet who moved there as a baby in 1807. Not far, on Spring Street, is the 1800 McClellan-Sweat House, another house that proved how civilized life could be up in the wildernesses of Maine.

CAMDEN
▼▼▼

Yet another photo-perfect town on the Maine coast, Camden offers little for the Colonial history enthusiast but plenty for those in search of leisure. Boats, boats, and more boats are what you (and the others who throng here each summer) will find in Camden's famed harbor. But popular tourist spots don't happen by accident. The deep, secluded harbor surrounded by rolling hills has made Camden a popular destination since the days steamships brought wealthy urbanites to vacation here. Once a shipbuilding hub, Camden's shady streets are lined with graceful, well-maintained homes from that era, many of which have been turned into B&Bs. *Contact Camden-Rockport-Lincolnville Chamber of Commerce | Commercial St., Public Landing, Camden 04843 | 207/236–4404 or 800/223–5459 | fax 207/236–4315 | www.visitcamden.com.*

Old Historical Conway House Complex. This is an 18th-century restored farmhouse and barn, furnished with authentic period materials. It has a working blacksmith shop, an 1820 maple sugar house, a Victorian privy, and the Camden Rockport Historical Society collection. | U.S. 1 near Rockport border | 207/236–2257 | $3 | July–Aug., Tues.–Fri. 10–4.

HISTORIC LODGING
Camden Maine Stay. This 1802 Greek Revival clapboard inn is listed on the National Register of Historic Places. It has manicured gardens, hiking trails at the edge of the property, comfortable common areas and guest rooms, and trademark hospitality that makes you feel relaxed and at home. Complimentary breakfast. No kids under 10. | 22 High St. | 207/236–9636 | fax 207/236–0621 | www.mainestay.com | 8 rooms | $100–$150 | AE, MC, V.

CASTINE
▼▼▼

Castine's tranquil pace belies its historical torment. For nearly 200 years, Castine was the center of conflicts among the French, Dutch, British, and Colonists for control of the Acadian peninsula. Numerous forts were built and leveled and both grand and ignominious battles were fought here. In what is still considered to be the worst naval defeat in American history, the attempt to overthrow the British takeover of the area in 1759 resulted in complete disaster. In command of the naval force, Commodore Saltonstall was later court-martialed for his part. Paul Revere was also part of the desperately failed mission but was exonerated. Castine fell back into the hands of the British in 1814 when American troops there could not defend the area. Within a year, the British gave up the town. Things are much quieter today. The town is peppered with helpful historical markers to keep all well informed. *Contact Castine Town Office | Court St., Castine 04421 | 207/326–4502.*

Castine Historical Society. Once the town's high school, the building is now home to this museum and town welcome center (a good place to get maps of the area). | Abbott School Building, Town Common | 207/326–4118 | Free | July–Labor Day, Tues.–Sat. 10–4, Sun. 1–4.

Fort George. Now an exquisite, waterfront spot for a picnic, this was the site of one of several of the town's former forts. The earthworks foundations are still in view; detailed signs give a history of the fort's former happenings. Visitors can also watch marching Maine Maritime Academy cadets and tour the U.S. Navy *State of Maine,* a training vessel, weekdays in July and August. | Waterfront | Free | Memorial Day–Labor Day; daily dawn–dusk.

Wilson Museum. This small museum has some interesting finds, ranging from an 1805 kitchen display to a selection of locally gathered Native American artifacts. Nearby, the museum maintains the historic Hearse House and the Blacksmith Shop; both are open Wednesday and Sunday only in July and August. | Perkins St. | 207/326–9247 | www.wilsonmuseum.org | Free | Late May–late Sept., Tues.–Sun. 2–5.

The **John Perkins House,** also part of the museum complex, is the only surviving pre-Revo lutionary home in the area. Inside are period furniture and craft displays. | Perkins St. | 207/ 326–9247 | www.wilsonmuseum.org | $4 | July–Aug., Wed. and Sun. 2–5.

HISTORIC LODGING
Castine Inn. This stately, three-story, 1898 Georgian-Federal–style inn with views of Penob-scot Bay is surrounded by elaborate, manicured gardens. Rooms are furnished in the New England summer-resort style; some on the third floor have harbor views. Restaurant, compli-mentary breakfast. No kids under 8. | Main St. | 207/326–4365 | fax 207/326–4570 | www. castineinn.com | 16 rooms | $85–$210 | MC, V | Closed Oct.–Apr.

DAMARISCOTTA
▼▼▼

This pretty village just off U.S. 1 is the gateway to the Pemaquid Peninsula and is on the banks of the Damariscotta River. The town's name, meaning "meeting place of the alewives," came from the rich harvests of herring found at the river. With the right timing, you can still see the magnificent spring runs of these fish. Although tourist trade is brisk, Damariscotta preserves small-town life with its tidy white-clapboard houses and snug downtown. *Contact Damariscotta Region Chamber of Commerce | Main St., Damariscotta 04543 | 207/563–8340 | www.drcc.org.*

Chapman-Hall House. The oldest-surviving homestead in the region, this house was completed in 1754. Period furnishings, the original kitchen, and exhibits about shipbuilding will all entice. Outside is a lush herb garden along with an 18th-century planting of heirloom roses. | Main St. at Church St. | 207/442–7863 | $1 | July–early Sept., Mon.–Sat. noon–4.

Oyster Shell Heaps. Long, long before the "white man" came, the areas around present-day Damariscotta and neighboring Newcastle were first inhabited by Native Americans. Fossilized shell heaps—evidence of their fondness for oysters—can be found embedded in the banks of the Damariscotta River. The shells date back 2,400 years. The best place to view these is from the Salt Bay Preserve Heritage Trail, a 3-mi path maintained by the Damariscotta River Association. | Heritage Center Farm, Belvedere Rd. | 207/563–1393.

HISTORIC LODGING

Mill Pond Inn. This 1780s Colonial, 2½ mi north of Damariscotta, has antiques-filled rooms and lakeside views. Loons, otters, and bald eagles reside on the lake, and you can arrange a trip with the owner, a Registered Maine Guide, on the inn's 17-ft antique lapstrake boat. The rooms are warm and inviting and there's a pub for guests, though you may find it hard to tear yourself away from the hammocks-for-two overlooking the pond. Complimentary breakfast. No kids under 10. | 50 Main St., Nobleboro | 207/563–8014 | www.millpondinn. com | 5 rooms | $110 | No credit cards.

KITTERY

▼▼

One of the earliest settlements in the region, Kittery suffered its share of British, French and Indian attacks, yet rose to prominence as a vital shipbuilding center. The town has much to share of this history, and enthusiasts will be rewarded with its offerings. In recent years, Kittery—the gateway to Maine—has come to be known as one thing: Outlet Heaven (or Hell, depending on your orientation). Flanked on either side of U.S. 1 are over 120 stores, which attract hordes of shoppers year-round. Prior to Liz Claiborne and Dansk, however, Kittery had long been known as the home of the Portsmouth Naval Shipyard. Yet Kittery (Maine's oldest town) and Kittery Point have some noted historic sights and buildings. *Contact State of Maine Visitor Information Center | I–95 and U.S. 1, Box 396, Kittery 03904 | 207/439–1319. Greater York Region Chamber of Commerce | Box 526, Kittery 03904 | 207/439–7545 | www. gatewaytomaine.org.*

Fort McClary. Built in 1690 to protect the mouth of the Piscataqua River, the fort's prominent historical feature is its famous 1812 hexagonal blockhouse. Once commanded by William Pepperell, a Loyalist who was the dominant figure in Maine's early history, the complex was first named Fort William in his honor, then renamed in Revolutionary days for a victim who fell at the Battle of Bunker Hill. Extensive renovations were carried out through the 1840s but the blockhouse here remains satisfyingly Colonial in aura. The fort, which successfully countered pirates, Indians, French, and British, sits on a scenic harbor and has ocean views. | Rte. 103, Kittery Point | 207/439–2845 | www.state.me.us/doc/parks | $1 | Memorial Day–end Sept., daily 9–8.

Kittery Historical and Naval Museum. Kittery's rich naval history is represented with this interesting collection of all things nautical. | U.S. 1 at Rogers Rd. | 207/439–3080 | $3 | June–Oct., Tues.–Sat. 10–4.

Lady Pepperell's Mansion. One of the most elegant houses in America, this essay in "Clapboard Palladian" was built in 1760, as it so proudly proclaims above the doorway, itself framed by two glorious two-story fluted pilasters. Set just past Fort McClary, this was meant to be the grandest mansion in the Piscataqua Valley, as befits a "lady." The immensely rich widow of Sir William Pepperrell—one of the J. Paul Gettys of his day—she retained the honorary title bestowed on her husband's family due to his great exploits leading "Pepperell's Yokells" in the French and Indian Wars even after the British were sent packing in the 1780s. While private and not open for tours, the house may be visited a few times during the year—make inquires in the town. Opposite the estate is a noted 1730 Meeting House. | Rte. 103, Kittery Point.

HISTORIC DINING AND LODGING

Cap'n Simeon's Galley. The dining room has a nautical theme with a heavy-beamed ceiling and a panorama embracing the pier, lighthouses, islands, and historic forts. | 90 Pepperell Rd., (Rte. 103), Kittery Point | 207/439–3655 | $10–$25 | AE, D, MC, V | Closed Tues. Columbus Day–Memorial Day.

Inn at Portsmouth Harbor. This brick Victorian home, with many antiques, is fully modernized. The inn offers a view of the Piscataqua River and Portsmouth Harbor, and is an ideal getaway for couples. Complimentary breakfast. No kids under 16. | 6 Water St. | 207/439–4040 | fax 207/438–9286 | www.innatportsmouth.com | 5 rooms | $135–$175 | MC, V.

MACHIAS

▼▼

The Machias River flows through historic Machias, the seat of Washington County. Machias is Micmac Indian for "bad little falls," and those very falls boil in the town's center. The first Revolutionary War naval battle took place here in 1775, when feisty local patriots took the British man-of-war *Margaretta*. The town grew prosperous with the lumbering and shipbuilding boom, but the blueberry is now top dog. (There's a large-scale blueberry festival held here each summer.) The downtown is a hilly ramble of stores, and the town claims a branch of the University of Maine. Machias also serves as a good base for exploring the area's scenic coastline. *Contact Machias Bay Area Chamber of Commerce | 112 Dublin St., Machias 04654 | 207/255–4402 | www.nemaine.com/mbacc.*

Bad Little Falls Park. These falls, for which Machias is named, are a must-see. Right in the center of town, there is also a small park with picnic benches, and a bridge spanning the gorge of this lovely stretch of the river. Nearby is the town cemetery, with some noted headstones from the 18th century. | U.S. 1 | Free | Daily dawn–dusk.

Burnham Tavern Museum. The oldest building in eastern Maine and the only one with a Revolutionary War history, this tavern served as a meeting place for planning the first naval battle of the Revolution. The gambrel-roof tavern was built in 1770 by Mary and Joe Burnham. It contains authentic furnishings from the period, many of them donated by Burnham descendants. | Main St. | 207/255–4432 | $2.50 | June–Sept., weekdays 9–5.

Gates House. Built by Nathan Gates in 1810, this abode houses the Machiasport Historical Society, replete with an extensive collection of photographs, tools, period furniture, housewares, memorabilia, and a genealogical library. | Rte. 92, Machiasport | 207/255–8461 | $1 donation | Mid-June–early Sept., Tues.–Sat. 12:30–4:30.

Fort O'Brien. Built in 1775 and destroyed by the British that same year, the four-gun Fort O'Brien was rebuilt, then destroyed by the British again in 1814. The first naval battle of the Revolutionary War was fought off this site, 5 mi east of town, five days before Bunker Hill. | Rte. 92 | 207/941–4014 | www.state.me.us/doc/parks | Free | Daily.

HISTORIC DINING AND LODGING
Riverside Inn. This 1805 inn is right on the East Machias tidal river, allowing you frequent sightings of eagles, seals, and other wildlife. The grounds have splendid vegetable and flower gardens, as well as a pond and waterfall. The inn also runs a fine restaurant—the small and large dining rooms have Victorian furnishings and river views. Restaurant, complimentary breakfast. No kids under 12. | U.S. 1 | 207/255–4134 | fax 207/255–3580 | www.riversideinn-maine.com | 4 rooms | $85–$95 | AE, MC, V.

PEMAQUID PENINSULA

▼▼

Long before the white settlers arrived, the Pemaquid Peninsula was a very active and well-populated Wabanaki Indian settlement. As explorers discovered the area's vital fish stocks and potential for profit, many established seasonal settlements. The first permanent year-round settlement cropped up around 1625, though the constant battling that would blacken the next century wreaked havoc on these homesteads. The region has had a lively Colonial history, including the legend that pirate Dixy Bull raided the settlement in 1632 with the far-fletched hopes of starting a pirate colony. Much of that history is still in evidence, particularly at the ongoing restoration project at the peninsula's point. A quiet calm prevails in its small fishing villages, wooded winding roads, and its majestic point that boldly juts out into the Atlantic and is home to the famed 1827 Pemaquid Lighthouse. *Contact Friends of Colonial Pemaquid | Box 304, New Harbor 04554-0304 | 207/677–2423 (Apr.–Oct.) or 207/624–6075 (Nov.–Mar.) | www.friendsofcolonialpemaquid.org.*

Colonial Pemaquid Restoration. Set on a small peninsula jutting into the Pemaquid River, the restoration preserves relics from the days when English mariners established a fishing and trading settlement here in the early 17th century. The excavations at Fort William Henry, begun in the mid-1960s, have turned up thousands of artifacts from the Colonial settlement, including the remains of an old customs house, a tavern, a jail, a forge, and homes. Some items are from even earlier Native American settlements. The state operates a museum displaying many of the artifacts. | Off Rte. 130, New Harbor | 207/677–2423 | www.state.me.us/doc/parks | $2 | Memorial Day–Labor Day, daily 9:30–5.

Pemaquid Historical Society and Museum. The 1772 Harrington Meetinghouse, the first of what would be three such establishments to provide a place of worship and council for area settlers, now houses this museum. The building was moved from its original site in the 1840s, though the structure is the same. Local exhibits depicting early life in the region are maintained by the Society. | Old Harrington Rd., Pemaquid | 207/677–2193 | July–Aug., Mon., Wed., Fri.–Sat. 2–4:30.

Pemaquid Point Light. Route 130 now terminates at this lighthouse, which looks as though it sprouted from the ragged, tilted chunk of granite that it commands. The former lighthouse-keeper's cottage is now the Fishermen's Museum, with photographs, models, and artifacts that explore commercial fishing in Maine. Here, too, is the Pemaquid Art Gallery, which mounts exhibitions from July to Labor Day. Museum: | Rte. 130 | 207/677–2494 | $1 | Memorial Day–Columbus Day, Mon.–Sat. 10–5, Sun. 11–5.

✦ ON THE CALENDAR: Sept. **Maine Heritage Days.** An annual historical gala that commemorates the Colonial wars between the French and the English in 1747. Living history portrayals include reenactments, displays, and lectures as well as demonstrations of the Colonial crafts of field surgery, arts, and blacksmithing. | Colonial Pemaquid, Pemaquid | 207/677–2423 (Apr.–Oct.) or 207/624–6075 (Nov.–Mar.) | www.friendsofcolonialpemaquid.org.

PHIPPSBURG
▼▼

The expansive white sands of Popham Beach might be what first attracted the initial European settlers to Phippsburg in 1607. Had the winter not been so severe as to drive the settlers home (those it didn't kill), this settlement could have given Jamestown a run for its money as the first permanent English settlement in America. Winters aside, visitors have continued to return ever since—including film crews for two major motion pictures (*Message in a Bottle* and *Head Above Water*). This 18-mi, history-rich peninsula has sand beaches, authentic fishing villages, nature trails, a major resort, and craggy cliffs for exploring. *Contact Chamber of Commerce of Bath-Brunswick Region | 59 Pleasant St., Brunswick 04011 | 207/725–8797 or 207/443–9751 | www.midcoastmaine.com.*

Fort Popham. One of three forts built since 1607 at the mouth of the Kennebec River, 16 mi south of Bath, the current Fort Popham dates from the Civil War. It was from this locale that

Benedict Arnold set out with troops to make an unimaginable trek through snow and ice over 350 mi to try to effect a surprise attack on Québec. Exhibits at the fort deal with this saga. | 10 Perkins Farm La. | 207/389–1335 | $1 | Apr.–Sept., daily 9–dusk.

HISTORIC LODGING

Popham Beach Bed and Breakfast. The weathered exterior of this restored 1883 Coast Guard station gives little indication of its stylish interior. The Library, one of five guest rooms, is particularly spacious, with a bay window looking out on Popham Beach. So quiet is this little spot, you'll hear the waves breaking on the shore and a bell buoy clanging at sea. Two-night minimum required July–August. Complimentary breakfast. | 4 Riverview Ave., Popham Beach | 207/389–2409 | www.pophambeachbandb.com | 3 rooms | $80–$145 | MC, V | Closed Nov.–Apr.

PORTLAND

▼▼▼

A city of many names throughout its history—Casco, Falmouth, and Portland—this area has had just as many transformations. Sheltered by the nearby Casco Bay Islands and blessed with a deep port, Portland was a very significant settlement from its early 17th-century beginnings. Settlers thrived on fishing and lumbering, repeatedly establishing the area while the British, French, and Indians continually sacked the lively settlements. Portland has seen disaster many times from its beginnings in the 1600s. In October of 1775, the British attack on the town, then called Falmouth, was pure devastation. George Washington called it "An outrage exceeding in barbarity and cruelty every hostile act among nations." During the attack, 130 homes were destroyed, churches, meetinghouses, and businesses were burned, nearly a dozen ships in the harbor were sunk and the citizens had no homes, food, or supplies to get them through the coming winter. As a result, the city did not see real prosperity again until around the 1820s. But the city has always had spirit, and each time its residents rebuilt from the ashes. Once peace was finally established, unfortunately, more disasters lay ahead. The city suffered through three major fires, the last in 1866. As a result, little remains from the Colonial period—but there are actually a few gems to be discovered, including the Wadsworth-Longfellow House. Today, Portland is Maine's largest city. Once Maine achieved statehood in 1820, it served as its capital, though in later years the seat was moved north to Augusta. *Contact Convention and Visitors Bureau of Greater Portland | 305 Commercial St., Portland 04102 | 207/772–5800 | www.visitportland.com.*

Portland Head Light. Built in 1791 and commissioned by George Washington, Portland Head is Maine's oldest lighthouse. It has great views of crashing surf, particularly after a storm. | 1000 Shore Rd., in Fort Williams Park | 207/799–2661 | Free | Daily dawn–dusk.

Tate House. This magnificent house fully conjures up the style—yes, even high style—of Colonial Maine. Built astride rose granite steps and a period herb garden overlooking the Stroudwater River on the outskirts of Portland, the 1755 house was built by Captain Captain George Tate, who had been commissioned by the English Crown to organize "the King's Broad Arrow"—the marking and cutting-down of gigantic forest trees, then transported over land to water and sent to England to be fashioned as masts for English fighting frigates (of course, with the English decimating the American forests for such purposes, it wasn't long before the natives put a stop to this practice during the Revolutionary War). The house has several period rooms, including a sitting room with some fine English Restoration chairs. With its clapboard still gloriously unpainted, its impressive Palladian doorway, dogleg stairway, unusual clerestory, and gambrel roof, this house will delight all lovers of Early American decorative arts. | 1270 Westbrook St. | 207/774–9781 | www.tatehouse.org | $5 | Mid-June–Sept., Tues.–Sat. 10–4, Sun. 1–4. Open weekends in Oct.

Wadsworth-Longfellow House. The Wadsworths and the Longfellows were two of the founding Pilgrim families and came together, with worldwide impact, in the works of the famed poet, Henry Wadsworth Longfellow, laureate of *Hiawatha* and countless other tales beloved by 19th-century Americans newly fascinated with their nation's early history. Built in 1785 by the poet's grandfather, Gen. Peleg Wadsworth, this 1785 structure was the first brick house in Portland and today contains many original furnishings, although most of them date from the 1850s. Still and all, the rooms here are alluring, and adorned with family portraits, heirloom instruments, and period wallpapers. Around the time the poet moved in with his parents, the Georgian ground floor had been topped off with Federal-style stories. After spending his childhood here, the poet took off for Bowdoin College and immortality. There's also a peaceful garden courtyard. Tours lasting 45 minutes are offered through the house. | 489 Congress St. | 207/772–1807 | www.mainehistory.org | $6 | June–Oct., daily 10–4.

HISTORIC LODGING

The Danforth. This beautiful, 1821 brick home has white columns, a cupola, and a prominent place in the Spring Street Historic District. Rooms have fireplaces and are plush with simple Colonial furnishings and couches. Complimentary breakfast. | 163 Danforth St. | 207/879–8755 | fax 207/879–8754 | www.danforthmaine.com | 10 rooms | $139–$329 | AE, MC, V.

SOUTH BERWICK
▼▼▼

Birthplace of famed 19th-century author Sarah Orne Jewett, this town has some claim to fame as inspiration for her beloved novels, such as *The Country of the Pointed Firs* (1896). But more important for readers of this book, it was the place where she conjured up her once-upon-a-timefied vision of 18th-century America, soon to take hold of the 19th-century American imagination and then inspiring, in its wake, the "Colonial Revival" that was to bear fruit in Colonial Williamsburg and other historic restorations across the country. Jewett's magisterial and moving prose captured Protestant New England in its earlier glow—her short stories of village spinsters, genteel widows, and aged sea captains inspired many with their poetry and burnished nostalgia. Some of that remains here in the noted houses of her home region. *Contact Greater York Region Chamber of Commerce | Box 526, Kittery 03904 | 207/439–7545 | www.gatewaytomaine.org.*

Hamilton House. Little wonder Sarah Orne Jewett (1849–1909) set part of her Revolutionary War novel, *The Tory Lover,* here—sitting on a bluff overlooking the Salmon Falls River, this shimmeringly white, Georgian Colonial "mini-palace" enjoys one of the most picture-perfect settings in New England. Bookended with four giant chimneys, fronted with three dormer windows, and topped with a suave mansard roof, this mansion was built in 1785 by shipbuilder Jonathan Hamilton to receive noted guests (including John Paul Jones) in regal splendor. Then in 1898, Mrs. Emily Tyson and her stepdaughter, Elise, purchased the house and, inspired by their famous author friend, Miss Jewett, resurrected and decorated it to conjure up Ye Olde Colonial Days, but with a Victorian spin—the true beginning of Colonial Revival Americana. Noted pieces of Piscataqua-area furniture, bird-and-vine wallpaper, and more "modern" touches as Currier and Ives prints, make Hamilton House's rooms eminently elegant. Within the formal gardens, "Sundays in the Garden" offers a summer concert series ranging from classical to folk. | Vaughan's La., South Berwick | 207/384–2454 | www.spnea.org | $4 | June–mid-Oct., Wed.–Sun. 11–5.

Sarah Orne Jewett House. Home to Sarah Orne Jewett, this fairly modest Georgian residence dates from 1774, and the Jewett family lived here when author Sarah born in 1849. She stayed on for much of her life—the view from her desk in the top floor hall looks down on the town's major intersection, which indeed gave her material for her novels, including *The Coun-*

try of the Pointed Firs. Jewett was at the forefront of the movement toward Colonial Revival. Cultural historians now have determined that "proper" New Englanders back then had been casting aspersions on newly arrived immigrants who, they claimed, were ruining landmark towns—thus the rush to find secluded hamlets like South Berwick and preserve them in their relatively pristine glory. Now a museum, the house contains period furnishings. Jewett's bedroom remains as she left it, but the author would probably be aghast to learn that a pizza parlor has set up shop a few feet away from her front door. | 5 Portland St., South Berwick | 207/384-2454 | www.spnea.org | $4 | June–mid-Oct., Wed.–Sun. 11–5.

WISCASSET

Built astride the Sheepscot River, Wiscasset ("meeting of the three tides or rivers") was first settled in the mid-17th century. Known as Pownalborough until 1802, the town was a major port during the mid-19th century. It still has many fine examples of ship captains' homes, churches, and public buildings from this era. There are also a number of interesting shops and museums to mosey through in the compact downtown. Self-proclaimed as the "prettiest village in Maine," Wiscasset could very well be termed Maine's "prettiest bottleneck." U.S. 1 traffic creeps at a crawl through town in the high summer months. *Contact Visitors Center | U.S. 1 N, West Bath 04530 | 207/725–8797 or 207/443–9751 | www.midcoastmaine.com.*

Castle Tucker. Built in 1807, this Georgian-style mansion includes Federal and Victorian furnishings and household items, as well as a freestanding elliptical staircase. | 2 Lee St. | 207/882–7364 | www.spnea.org | $4 | June–mid-Oct., Wed.–Sun. 11–4.

Fort Edgecomb. On Davis Island on the Sheepscot River, this fort was built in 1808 to protect Wiscasset, at the time the most important shipping port north of Boston. | 66 Fort Rd. | 207/882–7777 | www.state.me.us/doc.parks | $1 | Memorial Day–Labor Day, daily 9–5.

Nickels-Sortwell House. An outstanding example of Federal architecture, this house, built in 1807, was once the residence of Maine shipmaster William Nickels, whose fortune was made in the pine lumber trade. Today it contains Sortwell family furnishings, and an outstanding pinewood staircase. | Main and Federal Sts., (U.S. 1) | 207/882–6218 or 617/227–3956 | www.spnea.org | $4 | June–Oct., Wed.–Sun. 11–4.

HISTORIC DINING AND LODGING
Squire Tarbox Inn. This restored 18th-century farmhouse is set on a working dairy goat farm that's 8½ mi south of Wiscasset. You can view dairy operations and sample the goats' distinctive cheese. The Federal-style dining room serves a prix fixe menu that changes nightly but always includes a vegetarian entrée and a sampling of the inn's own goat cheese. Complimentary breakfast. | 1181 Main Rd., Westport | 800/818–0626 | fax 207/882–7107 | www.squiretarboxinn.com | 11 rooms | $115–$185 | AE, D, MC, V | Closed Nov.–Apr.

THE YORKS

The Yorks, first settled in 1624 as Agamenticus, have a long history in Maine. One of the first permanently settled areas, it was also witness to great destruction and fierce fighting. Colonial York citizens enjoyed a prosperity from fishing and lumber as well as a penchant for politics. The first cries for independent statehood from ruling Massachusetts were heard here, in the late 1700s, though these would not be answered until the next century. Angered by the British imposed taxes, York held its own and little-known tea party in 1775 in protest.

Today's York is made up of three small burgs, each with a distinct feel. York Beach, the most garrulous of the three, is a classic, old-time beach town, with a long stretch of sand beach, a zoo, and a carnivalesque downtown. York Harbor, dotted with imposing Victorian "cottages," is more reserved—more an exclusive enclave than a tourist spot. Best of all, York Village is a splendidly preserved Colonial village, which includes a seven-building historic museum. *Contact Yorks Chamber of Commerce | 571 U.S. 1, Yorks 03909 | 207/363–4422 or 800/639–2442 | fax 207/363–7320 | www.yorkme.org.*

Old York Historical Society. York Village was the nation's first city to be chartered (1641) and the site of the nation's first sawmill (1623). Sawmills are vitally important to Maine's history; a house can be made with round logs, but not a ship, and shipbuilding has always been a Maine mainstay from the beginning. Today, the wealth engendered by this industry is preserved in three centuries of maritime heritage and cultural history on view in seven historic museum buildings, most set picturesquely along both sides of the York River. There are a bevy of historic houses here to discover and treasure. Jefferds Tavern (Lindsay Road) is a Colonial-era hostelry that features cooking demonstrations and an introductory video tour of Old York—it also serves as a visitors center and is the place you purchase your tickets to the seven museum buildings. A 1730 farmhouse, the Elizabeth Perkins House (Sewall's Bridge), has antiques from an impressive collection formed in Colonial Revival 19th-century days. First constructed in the mid-1700s, the putty-hued Emerson-Wilcox House (U.S. 1A) has been added to over the years, resulting in an interesting mishmash of architectural styles—all, however, which will make readers of *This Old House* magazine drool. With its checkered history—the house was once a post office, tavern, and tailor's shop—there are more than 10 period rooms to savor, some adorned with samples of a celebrated crewelwork collection. Costumed guides provide tours. Originally a general store on the Hancock Wharf, the George Marshall Store (140 Lindsay Road) now serves as a gallery for revolving historical exhibits. Named for the famous Boston businessman who owned it, the John Hancock Warehouse (Lindsay Road) captures the early seafaring days of this coastal community and is part of a museum complex. Famously one of the oldest public buildings (1719) in North America, the Old Gaol (U.S. 1A) is equipped with old dungeons and cells. Costumed guides chill the young and not so young. Live demonstrations, decorative arts, period schoolhouse, museum shop, the Old Burying Ground, nature preserve, and tours round out the experience. | Lindsay Rd. (U.S. 1A), York Village | 207/363–4974 | www.oldyork.org | $7 for all 7 sites, $2 for individual sites | June–mid-Oct., Tues.–Sat. 10–5, Sun. 1–5.

Sayward-Wheeler House. Built in 1718, this house mirrors the fortunes of a coastal village in the transition from trade to tourism. Jonathan Sayward prospered in the West Indies trade in the 18th century; by 1860 his descendants had opened the house to the public to share the story of their Colonial ancestors. The house, accessible only by guided tour, reflects both these eras. | 79 Barrell La. Extension, York Harbor | www.spnea.org | 603/436–3205 | $4 | June–mid-Oct., weekends 11–4.

✦ ON THE CALENDAR: July–Aug. **York Days Celebration.** This annual summer event features concerts, tournaments, historical reenactments, crafts fair, parade, and fireworks. | 207/363–1040.

HISTORIC DINING AND LODGING

York Harbor Inn. Set across from the ocean, this inn is centered around a 1637 house and now includes mid-17th-century fishing cabin, complete with antiques, dark timbers, and a fieldstone fireplace. In the Harbor Hill building, all the rooms have fireplaces, whirlpool tubs, and ocean views. The dining room (no lunch off-season) has great views and top Maine crab cakes. Restaurant, complimentary breakfast. | U.S. 1A, York Harbor | 800/343–3869 | fax 207/363–7151 | www.yorkharborinn.com | 33 rooms | $99–$239 | AE, DC, MC, V.

By Christopher T. George

Maryland and Washington, D.C.

"Our Flag Was Still There!"

The coastline of Maryland is tortuous yet soft. Molded from clay, mud, marsh, and sand, it begins at Fenwick on the Atlantic shore and, with a break at the Virginia line, runs uninterrupted up the eastern and down the western shores of Chesapeake Bay, then up along the Potomac where it ends. Into the Chesapeake Bay, America's largest estuary, flows the broad Patapsco River, site of the famous port of Baltimore. Here in Maryland's largest city, landmarking its Mount Vernon district, you'll find the nation's first significant monument to George Washington. Set atop a graceful classical column, the stone figure of the first president was completed in 1829 at public expense to adorn Mount Vernon Place. Looking out over the calm vista of Chesapeake Bay, George is no doubt proud of the contributions made by Maryland to the nation he led. In fact, Maryland's nickname of the "Old Line State" had been conferred on it by the grateful general to honor the Maryland Line, those troops of regulars who fought for the patriotic cause in the American Revolution.

These men who fought to secure the independence of the United States in both northern and southern theaters achieved cinematic immortality in the climactic scene of the movie *The Patriot*. Noted actor Mel Gibson portrayed a gritty American leader much like the Maryland Line's commander, Lt. Col. John Eager Howard, who played a pivotal role in the outcome of the Battle of Cowpens, fought in South Carolina on January 17, 1781. As it turns out, war hero Howard's dramatic equestrian statue can also be seen in the Mount Vernon district, and rightly so, for at one point he owned much of it. Today this district—graced as it is with dozens of Georgian town houses—still conjures up the Colonial past at its Hollywoodian best. The good news for the Colonial buff is that Baltimore's Mount Vernon Square is just one of hundreds of sights that bring the early days of America alive for today's heritage traveler in Maryland.

✦ ALSO STARRING WASHINGTON, D.C.

As it happens, Maryland was regarded as the "keystone" of the new country due to its central coastal location among the thirteen original Colonies. Because of this, its city of Annapolis

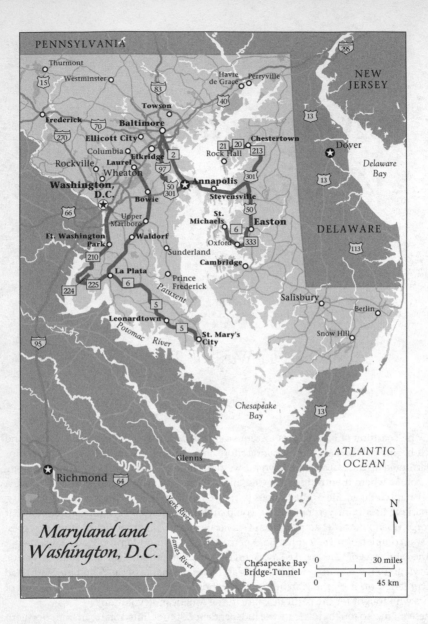

PENNSYLVANIA

NEW JERSEY

Thurmont
Westminster
Havre de Grace   Perryville
Towson
Frederick   Baltimore
Ellicott City   Chestertown   Dover
Columbia   Rock Hall   Delaware Bay
Rockville   Elkridge
Laurel
Wheaton   Annapolis
Washington, D.C.   Stevensville
Bowie
Upper Marlboro   St. Michaels   Easton   DELAWARE
Ft. Washington Park   Waldorf   Oxford
Sunderland   Cambridge
La Plata   Prince Frederick   Salisbury   Berlin
Leonardtown   Snow Hill
St. Mary's City

Chesapeake Bay

Glenns

Richmond   ATLANTIC OCEAN

Potomac River
Patuxent
York River
James River

N

Maryland and Washington, D.C.

Chesapeake Bay Bridge-Tunnel

0   30 miles

0   45 km

vied with others to become the permanent capital of the United States. But political considerations in the early 1790s led instead to the selection of a site on the banks of the Potomac, and it was Maryland that ceded territory for the new capital—a town designed by French engineer Pierre L'Enfant that was baptized Washington, D.C.

Maryland had been named in honor of Queen Henrietta Maria, consort of King Charles I of England, in 1632. Today, the influence of Maryland's English settlers is still evident—streets in Annapolis (Duke of Gloucester, for instance) and many towns and counties across the state still bear royal names; Prince Frederick, Prince George's, Queen Anne. English settlers arrived in 1631, establishing the first permanent trading post and farming community on what is now Kent Island, the largest island in the Chesapeake Bay. A year later King Charles I granted the Maryland Charter to Cecil Calvert, the second Lord Baltimore. In 1634, passengers on the ships *Ark* and *Dove,* landed on St. Clements Island in the Potomac River. They

Maryland and Washington, D.C., Timeline

1632 King Charles I grants Maryland Charter to Cecil Calvert, second Lord Baltimore.

1634 March 25. The first colonists land at St. Clement's Island in the Potomac River. They shortly build St. Mary's City, which becomes the capital.

1694 Governor Francis Nicholson moves the capital to Annapolis.

1729 Baltimore Town is chartered.

1755 General Edward Braddock marches through Maryland to attack the French at Fort Duquesne, but is defeated by the French and Indians at the Battle of Mononogahela. The French and Indian War begins.

1766 The Sons of Liberty organize in Baltimore County and Annapolis.

1774 October 14: The brig *Peggy Stewart*, containing a cargo of tea, is burned by its owner in Annapolis to prevent the patriotic mob from getting hold of his vessel.

1776 June 23: Governor Sir Robert Eden is forced to leave for England.

1776 July 4: Marylanders Charles Carroll of Carrollton, Samuel Chase, Thomas Stone, and William Paca sign the Declaration of Independence in Philadelphia.

1791 Maryland cedes land for the creation of the District of Columbia.

1797 City of Baltimore incorporated. USS *Constellation* is launched at Harris Creek, Canton, Baltimore City, first ship of the new U.S. Navy.

1814 August 24: British defeat Brig. Gen. William H. Winder's force of mainly militia at Bladensburg, Maryland. In Washington, they burn the Capitol and President's Mansion and other public buildings.

1814 September 12–14: Battle of Baltimore, including the bombardment of Fort McHenry. Francis Scott Key writes "The Star-Spangled Banner." British defeat at Baltimore helps end War of 1812.

eventually settled on the mainland, building a fort at St. Mary's City, the fourth permanent British settlement in the New World; it soon became Maryland's first capital. But in 1694 the General Assembly designated Anne Arundel Town—later renamed Annapolis—as the new state capital. Today, Annapolis still largely retains the flavor of a Colonial brick-built town—indeed, it has has extant more Georgian-era houses than the city of London. By the late 18th century, as the Tidewater tobacco culture gave way to a grain economy from inland farms, Baltimore overtook Annapolis as the state's major port and would soon rank as the third-largest city in the nation.

Today's traveler, like the settlers of yore, can escape the bustle of these economic hubs and head to still rural regions, where the Colonial past doesn't seem too far distant. You can drive in rural southern Maryland, with its tobacco farms, to the banks of the lower Potomac River, where the Calvert family first established the Colony. At re-created St. Mary's City you can watch craftspeople demonstrate the skills that made the colonists strong in a hostile new world. Or you can discover the Tidewater of the Eastern Shore of Maryland, an area that once saw tobacco boats plying their way to riverside plantations and British landing parties burning and pillaging nearby towns in the War of 1812.

✦ "BY THE DAWN'S EARLY LIGHT"

The War of 1812 brought perilous times to the region. It suffered more from British depredations in that conflict than during the Revolution. On August 24, 1814, at Bladensburg,

Prince George's County, a British army of 4,000 under Major General Robert Ross routed an American force of 6,000, comprised largely of hastily assembled militia. The British marched into and occupied Washington, burning the Capitol and the President's Mansion and other public buildings.

However, in three weeks lament for that national tragedy was turned to rejoicing when Baltimore repelled a British attack on September 12–14. The failed British bombardment of Baltimore's Fort McHenry was immortalized in a poem by Frederick County–born lawyer Francis Scott Key. Key had gone out to the British fleet to secure the release of an Upper Marlboro doctor who had been arrested by the enemy, and saw, though bombs were "bursting in air," that the flag was still flying after a day-long attack. His poem, set to the tune of a British drinking song and renamed "The Star-Spangled Banner," was later sung in a Baltimore theater. The anthem stands as testimony to the patriotism and endurance of the city's citizens during the "Second War of Independence." Today's visitor to the ramparts of Fort McHenry will see the flag still there, as Key wrote. A tour of this and other local sites hallowed by the spirits of noted Maryland patriots—Robert Morris (1734–1806), "financier" of the American Revolution; Lt. Col. Tench Tilghman (1744–81), aide to George Washington; Charles Carroll of Carrollton, Samuel Chase, Thomas Stone, and William Paca, all signers of the Declaration of Independence—provides abundant evidence that Maryland's history is still "gallantly streaming."

A REGIONAL GAZETEER
▼▼

✦ BALTIMORE
What began as a 17th-century settlement of a few houses clustered near Jones Falls, a branch of the Patapsco River, is today a lively city centered around the bustling and exciting Harborplace complex, complete with shopping pavilions, restaurants, and other attractions. Here, you'll find the sloop of war USS *Constellation,* an 1854 rebuild of the frigate launched at Baltimore in 1797. Along with the *Pride of Baltimore II,* a replica War of 1812 schooner, it provides a reminder of the days when the city's harbor was filled with a forest of sails. The seaport area of Fells Point features Colonial and Federal-era buildings and is important for having built the privateer schooners that were a scourge to the British in the Revolution and War of 1812. Other top historic sites include two historic homes belonging to the family of the last surviving signer of the Declaration of Independence, Charles Carroll of Carrollton: Mount Clare and Homewood. Of course, Baltimore is famed as the birthplace of Francis Scott Key's *"Star-Spangled Banner,"* which became the U.S. national anthem. Walking the ramparts at Fort McHenry under the huge 30-ft-by-42-ft flag—a replica of the flag (possibly) seen by Francis Scott Key that inspired his poem—still brings thrills to Americans and foreign visitors alike. Along with the fort, a must-see is the Star-Spangled Banner Flag House, the 1793 home of flagmaker Mary Pickersgill, where the famed flag was made. Fort commander Major George Armistead told Mary in 1813 he wanted a flag big enough for the British to see out in the Bay (as it turns out, they probably were flying a much smaller flag during the battle).
Towns listed: Baltimore, Elkridge, Towson.

✦ EASTERN SHORE: A WORLD APART
Maryland's Eastern Shore with its low-lying tidewater land stands as a world apart from the Western Shore. During both the Revolution and the War of 1812 the region was at times cut off from the rest of Maryland and vulnerable to British attack, particularly during the later conflict, when the British raided and pillaged small communities and plantations, destroying anything of military value, burning private homes and carrying off tobacco and slaves. Until the building of the Chesapeake Bay bridge in the 1950s, the area was even more isolated than today.

This part of the Colony grew as Lord Baltimore made land grants to settlers. In turn, English names such as Oxford, Cambridge, and Salisbury came to mingle exotically with Native American names given to rivers, such as Choptank, Pocomoke, and Nanticoke. When you walk the brick sidewalks of quiet **Chestertown** or **Oxford** you can almost sense the ghosts of local heroes Tench Tilghman and Robert Morris. The "Shore" was also the birthplace of War of 1812 naval hero Commodore Stephen Decatur and the great African-American leaders Frederick Douglass and Harriett Tubman. **St. Michaels** is studded with Federal-period houses, specialty shops, and restaurants, while over at Navy Point a steamboat wharf and canning plant have been turned into the impressive Chesapeake Bay Maritime Museum. *Towns listed: Cambridge, Chestertown, Easton, St. Michaels.*

✦ SOUTHERN MARYLAND: MARYLAND'S COLONIAL BEGINNINGS
Southern Maryland is where the Colony of Maryland first took root and is consequently an area rich in history leading up to and including the Revolutionary War. On **St. Clement's Island,** a huge memorial cross still celebrates the arrival of the first colonists. Here Jesuit father Andrew White officiated at the Feast of the Assumption on March 25, 1634, giving thanks for the settlers' safe arrival. The state's first capital was then established at **St. Mary's City,** near the mainland's southernmost point. In the town's museums you can see recent archaeological finds—a Jesuit crucifix, armor, muskets, and cannonballs, all bearing mute testimony to the religious and military upheavals suffered by this region. Here you'll also find homes of Declaration of Independence signer Thomas Stone and General William Smallwood. And while you are exploring down this way, why not visit nearby Chaptico, site of a British raid in 1814—the British are said to have ghoulishly broken into graves in its churchyard and torn the winding cloth off the body of an aunt of Francis Scott Key. As you travel the back roads, note the tobacco fields—the economy for most of the Colonial period relied solely on this crop (it was even used as a form of currency).

The headliner hereabouts, of course, is Maryland's present capital, **Annapolis.** Laid out in 1695 and later called "the Athens of America" and the "Venice of the New World," Annapolis's Georgian-style town houses lend the city great dignity. Maryland is the only state in which the homes of all its signers of the Declaration of Independence still stand—you can tour three of the four—the homes of Charles Carroll, Samuel Chase, and William Paca. In addition, there are other historical delights, such as the Hammond-Harwood House and the London Town House and Gardens. This is a town where George Washington once gambled before the Revolution and, today, of course, remains the home of the famed U.S. Naval Academy. Alma mater to Francis Scott Key, St. John's College also has some 18th-century structures. *Towns listed: Annapolis, La Plata, Leonardtown, St. Mary's City, Waldorf.*

✦ WASHINGTON, D.C.: FEDERAL HEART OF THE NATION
The site of the nation's capital, **Washington, D.C.,** was ceded by the state of Maryland to the Federal government in 1791 and surveyed by Maryland Quaker Andrew Ellicott and his African-American assistant Benjamin Banneker. Some of the nation's most impressive Federal-era homes still stand in the capital, including the White House, the Decatur House, and the Octagon House, home to Dolley and James Madison after the British burned the White House. Maryland's suburban counties around Washington, D.C., are also included in this region—Frederick, Prince George's, and Montgomery. All three have historic sites dating back to Colonial times. In **Frederick,** the Hessian Barracks were built by British and Hessian prisoners in 1777 and British prisoners in the War of 1812. The city's Roger Brooke Taney Home and Francis Scott Key Museum houses artifacts associated with Supreme Court justice Taney and his brother-in-law Francis Scott Key, born at Terra Rubra (private), a house 16 mi northeast. *Towns listed: Bowie, Frederick, Laurel, Washington, D.C.*

Star-Spangled Maryland

A DRIVING TOUR FROM BALTIMORE TO THE EASTERN SHORE

▼▼

Distance: 73 mi (one-way)　　**Time:** 3 days (2 nights)
Breaks: Overnight stays in Baltimore and Annapolis

This tour highlights Baltimore and historic Annapolis, with a quick trip over the Chesapeake Bay to the Eastern Shore and the history-rich towns of Queen Anne's County. Begin the tour in **Baltimore**'s Inner Harbor (access from I–95, Exits 52–55; I–83 ends at Inner Harbor). The city's bustling waterfront features museums, water taxis and boat cruises, famous restaurants, and shops, all within walking distance of one another. For a shopper's paradise be sure to visit Harborplace and its sister complex across the street, the multilevel Gallery. Just to the west is the 1854 sloop of war USS *Constellation,* a rebuild of the original frigate launched in Baltimore in 1797. The Star-Spangled Banner Flag House, the 1793 home of Mary Pickersgill, who made the giant flag that flew over Fort McHenry, is a must-see at Pratt and Albemarle streets. It is near Little Italy (a great place for restaurants), two blocks west of the Inner Harbor. Follow this with a ride on a water taxi to the old waterfront area of Fells Point, where patriots plotted against the British at the London Tavern and ships' carpenters built the fast privateer schooners that bedevilled British merchant ships. Here, too, is Fort McHenry National Monument and Historic Shrine, scene of the bombardment of 1814, whose flag Georgetown lawyer Francis Scott Key celebrated in his poem "The Star-Spangled Banner." If you wish, you can drive to the fort instead—take St. Paul south until it turns into Light Street, then left onto Key Highway, right on Lawrence Street one block to Fort Avenue, which takes you 2 mi to the fort.

When you're ready to leave the Inner Harbor area, head up to the Homewood House Museum (go one block north to Lombard then west to Charles; proceed north on Charles Street past Art Museum Drive to just north of 33rd Street to the campus of the Johns Hopkins University) to see a fine Federal-era house, the 1801 home of Charles Carroll, son of the noted barrister and signer of the Declaration of Independence. Farther north in Towson is Hampton Mansion (take Charles Street north to I–83 to Baltimore Beltway I–695 east, exit onto Dulaney Valley Road, take a right, and approach the mansion by way of Hampton Lane, 10 mi), the spectacular Colonial-era home of the Ridgely family, ironmasters, who made cannon to help the American war effort in both the Revolution and the War of 1812. On your way south out of the city, stop at the Mount Clare Museum House, southwest of the Inner Harbor, another Carroll family home, completed in 1760 (take Lombard Street west to Greene Street, then left on Greene, bearing right by the Orioles' ballpark Camden Yards to follow signs to Washington Boulevard; then take Washington Boulevard to Carroll Park, which is on your right just north of Monroe Street, 2 mi).

Leave Baltimore on I–97 south and proceed for 29 mi to U.S. 50/301 to reach **Annapolis,** a great destination for historic homes and mansions, Colonial streets, and the U.S. Naval Academy. Start at the Visitors Bureau and join a guided walking tour of the city. Visit the historic Maryland State House and the Hammond-Harwood House, the only verified full-scale example of the work of William Buckland, one of Colonial America's most prominent architects. The Chesapeake Bay Bridge (9 mi east of Annapolis on U.S. 50/301) connects Maryland's mainland with the Eastern Shore. **Chestertown** (24 mi northeast of Bay Bridge on U.S. 301 to 203) is a quiet town with Colonial and Federal-era buildings, home to Washington College, off Route 203, founded in 1782 in honor of George Washington. Emmanuel Episcopal Church, at High and Cross streets, was erected in 1768. Caulk's Field Battlefield lies 6 mi west on Route 20 to Route 21 and Caulk's Field Road—here in the early morning hours of August 31, 1814, 200 militiamen under Colonel Philip Reed defeated a naval raiding party under Captain Peter Parker of the Royal Navy. **Easton** (24 mi east and south from

Bay Bridge on U.S. 50) is another important Eastern Shore town with interesting buildings from the Colonial and Federal eras.

Oxford (6 mi southwest of Easton on Route 333), a charming tree-lined town, is proud of its connection to native son Robert Morris (1734–1806), the "financier" of the American Revolution. The town's main street is named for the financier's father, Robert Morris, Sr. The remains of the Morris home (1774) were incorporated into the Robert Morris Inn, a recommended local hostelry. At the water's edge on Tilghman Street is Byberry, a house said to have been built in 1695.

St. Michaels, on the Miles River (8 mi northwest of Oxford by toll ferry across the Tred Avon River), prides itself as the "Town that Fooled the British" by placing lights in the trees during a British naval raid of August 10, 1813. The British aim cannot have been so poor, because Cannonball House (privately owned), a circa 1800 Flemish-bond structure on Mulberry Street, got its name from the cannonball that crashed through the roof and bounced down the stairs. The Chesapeake Bay Maritime Museum traces the history of the bay and its traditions of boatbuilding, commercial fishing, and waterfowling. To return to Baltimore, backtrack west on U.S. 50/301 to Route 2, and head north into the city limits.

Life Styles of the Rich and Revolutionary

A DRIVING TOUR FROM WASHINGTON, D.C., TO ST. MARY'S COUNTY

▼▼

Distance: Approx. 75 mi (one-way)   **Time:** 3 days (2 nights)
Breaks: Overnight stays in Washington, D.C., and St. Mary's City

This tour focuses on the nation's capital, Maryland's Colonial origins and Revolutionary War contributions, and War of 1812 history. It starts out in Washington, D.C, follows the creeks and rivers of the area inhabited by Maryland's original residents—the Indians who sold land to Lord Baltimore's settlers to found Colonial Maryland in 1634. It goes on to contemplate the state's rebuilt Colonial capital of St. Mary's City on the Potomac River (with its replica of the 1676 redbrick state house) and archaeological finds in the visitor's center. Visits are made to the southern Maryland homes of Thomas Stone, signer of the Declaration of Independence, and General William Smallwood, of the Maryland Line, who supported George Washington at the Battle of Long Island in 1776.

In **Washington, D.C.,** various tour companies offer motorized tours around the city. After viewing the exterior of that grand Federal-era manse, the White House, begun in 1792 by Irish architect James Hoban and originally known as the President's Mansion, head over to Decatur House, at 748 Jackson Place NW, to see some grand Federal-style interiors. This was the home of War of 1812 naval hero Stephen Decatur. More splendor awaits at Octagon House at 1799 New York Avenue NW, built circa 1800 by architect William Thornton—James and Dolley Madison famously lived here while the British-burned White House was being rebuilt. To the west of downtown Washington is elegant Georgetown. Visit Dumbarton House, 2715 Q Street NW, built circa 1798, one of the oldest large houses in Georgetown, now home to the National Society of Colonial Dames of America, and Tudor Place, 1644 31st Street NW, the 1816 home of the Peter family, built by William Thornton. The Old Stone House at 3051 M Street NW, is Georgetown's oldest building (1766).

Near **Waldorf,** Fort Washington National Park (south approximately 12 mi on Route 210 out of central Washington) contains Fort Washington, built to protect the Potomac River approach to Washington, D.C. The fort was blown up in late August 1814 by Captain Samuel Dyson, U.S. Army, on the approach of a British squadron (Dyson paid the price by being court-martialed). Rebuilt after the war, the fort has Civil War–era cannons and improvements.

Port Tobacco in **La Plata** (south approximately 2 mi on Rose Hill Road) is one of Maryland's earliest Colonial towns. Built on the site of an Indian settlement, it was the scene of a 1681 rebellion. Also near La Plata is **Smallwood's Retreat** (south approximately 14 mi on Routes 210 and 224), a lovely little house that honors Revolutionary War commander General William Smallwood (1732–92), who lived here. It was lovingly restored in 1956. Nearby is the **Thomas Stone National Historic Site** (east approximately 8 mi on Routes 224 and 225), which includes Haberdeventure, the plantation home of Thomas Stone (1743–87), the youngest of Maryland's four signers of the Declaration of Independence. Then check out redbrick Christ Church, in Chaptico (southeast approximately 24 mi on Route 6, U.S. 301, and Route 231). The church dates from 1735 and was damaged by British troops in the War of 1812. St. Clements Island (south approximately 10 mi on Route 242 to Coltons Point), scene of the first landing by Lord Baltimore's colonists, is commemorated by a large memorial cross visible from the visitor center on the mainland. **Leonardtown** (northeast approximately 12 mi on Routes 242 and 234), dating to the mid-18th century, is one of those rare Maryland towns to still have an intact town square of that era. Old Sotterley Plantation (northeast approximately 11 mi on Route 245), the only working 18th-century plantation in the state, features a charming manor house modeled on (or the inspiration for) George Washington's Mount Vernon.

At **St. Mary's City** (approximately 48 mi southeast on Routes 245, 235, and 5) we turn the interior decoration clock back another century to capture the flavor of Maryland's Colonial beginnings. The first state capital was built on land purchased from the local Yaocomaco Indians. Get oriented at the St. Mary's City Visitors Center and Archeological Exhibit Hall—then explore the rebuilt State House of 1676, the re-created Van Sweringen's Tavern, and the Godiah Spray Tobacco Plantation. Bel Air Mansion and Stable Museum in **Bowie** (northwest approximately 100 mi on Routes 5, 235, and U.S. 301 to Belair Drive) provides the chance to examine the imposing mansion of Samuel Ogle (1694–1752), three-term Colonial governor of Maryland, as well as racing stables with exhibits that tell the history of 250 years of American thoroughbred racing history. Then head to **Laurel** to visit Montpelier Mansion (northwest approximately 12 mi on Route 197 to Montpelier Drive), a grand Georgian house built between 1781 and 1785. It provides a look at the life of a family who entertained distinguished visitors such as George Washington and Abigail Adams. To return to Washington, D.C., drive south on Interstate 495.

ANNAPOLIS
▼▼

Few cities have such a high concentration of 18th-century architecture, more than 50 pre-Revolutionary War structures (many of them still in use), including the famous homes of some of Maryland's prominent patriots, such as William Paca and Samuel Chase, both signers of the Declaration of Independence. Annapolis traces its founding to the late 17th century. Puritan settlers relocating from Virginia in 1649 established the town of Providence at the mouth of the Severn River, a tributary of the Chesapeake Bay. Anne Arundel Town was established in 1684 on the south side of the Severn, across from Providence. Ten years later, the town became Annapolis, the Colonial capital. For a brief time (1783 to 1784), Annapolis served as the nation's capital—the young country's first peacetime capital. The city's seafaring history dates back two centuries, to when Annapolis was a port of call for merchant ships from around the world. In Colonial times, the harbor saw slaves being traded. Today to be seen by the City Dock the Kunta Kinte–Alex Haley Monument honors the African slave Kunte Kinte, and his descendant, Alex Haley (1921–92), author of *Roots*. The author's 1976 book told the story of his ancestor's capture in Africa and sale at Annapolis. The 16-year-old African had been one of 98 Gambians who arrived in the city in September 29, 1767 aboard the ship *Lord Ligonier*.

For the walker, Annapolis's most historic streets, laid out in 1695, fan out from Church and State circles. Following Rowe Boulevard (off U.S. 50/301) will lead you to the historic center of Annapolis, on the south side of the Severn River. *Contact Annapolis and Anne Arundel County Conference and Visitors Bureau | 26 West St., Annapolis 21401 | 410/280–0445 | www. visit-annapolis.org.*

Charles Carroll House. This birthplace and city home of the only Catholic to sign the Declaration of Independence has 18th-century terraced gardens that overlook Spa Creek. The Marylander was one of the wealthiest men in Colonial America. The restored 1720 house contains a wine cellar that was added in the 19th century. | 107 Duke of Gloucester St. | 410/269–1737 | $4 | Fri. and Sun. noon–4, Sat. 10–2.

Chase-Lloyd House. William Buckland, a prominent Colonial architect, built the Chase-Lloyd House, with its gracefully massive facade—sheer except for a center third beneath a pediment. Work on the house was begun in 1769 for Samuel Chase, a signer of the Declaration of Independence and future Supreme Court justice. Five years later, tobacco planter and revolutionary Edward Lloyd IV had the building completed. The first floor is open to the public and contains more of Buckland's handiwork, including a parlor mantelpiece with tobacco leaves carved into the marble—a common motif in early Maryland homes. Buckland was famous for his interior woodwork; you can see more of it in the Hammond-Harwood House across the street and in George Mason's Gunston Hall in Virginia. The house is furnished in a mixture of 18th-, 19th-, and 20th-century pieces, and its staircase parts dramatically around an arched triple window. For more than 100 years the house has served as a home for elderly women who live upstairs. | 22 Maryland Ave. | 410/263–2723 | $2 | Mar.–Dec., Mon.–Sat. 2–4.

Hammond-Harwood House. Built in 1774 for Mathias Hammond, a noted Patriot, this magnificent Georgian mansion offers a full-blown glimpse of the elegance of pre-Revolutionary War Annapolis. The only verified full-scale example of the work of William Buckland—Colonial America's most prominent architect at the time of his 1774 death—the mansion features a fine collection of fashionable 18th- and early 19th-century furniture, but it is the rooms themselves—lavishly decorated throughout with ornate mouldings—that make this Buckland's masterpiece. As you walk through the salons, you sense how rich life was in Colonial-period Annapolis, where the gentry enjoyed wine, punch, and sweetmeats while playing cards, dice and backgammon (George Washington was known as a gambler, and he would often wail his losses when attending the city's theater and dance balls). All these luxuries were meant to be a manorial wedding present from Matthias Hammond, a planter and revolutionary, to his fiancée, who jilted him before the house was finished. Hammond never lived in the home and died a bachelor in 1784. The Loockermans moved into the house in 1811; their daughter would marry William Harwood, coincidentally William Buckland's great-grandson, and the couple made their home here. | 19 Maryland Ave. | 410/263–4683 | www.annapolis.net/hammondharwood | $5 | Mon.–Sat. 10–4, Sun. noon–4.

Historic London Town and Gardens. Maryland's largest archaeological site, this National Historic Landmark is on the South River, 8 mi from Annapolis. The three-story brick house at London Town, built by William Brown in 1760, shares a dramatic waterfront setting with 8 acres of landscaped and woodland gardens. Archaeological work here continues in search of the lost town of London—40 dwellings, shops, and taverns that made up a 17th-century tobacco port that slowly began to decline and disappear (the buildings were abandoned and left to decay) in the 18th century. Docents conduct house tours (which last 45 minutes to one hour); allow a half-hour to wander the grounds. | 839 Londontown Rd., Edgewater | 410/222–1919 | www.historiclondontown.com | $5 | Apr.–Dec., weekdays 9–4, Sat. 10–4, Sun. noon–4.

Maryland State House. Maryland's capitol, completed in 1780, holds a whole lot of history and boasts a few claims to fame as well: It's topped by the nation's largest wooden dome and is the oldest state capitol in continuous legislative use; it's also the only one in which the U.S. Congress has sat (1783–84). It was here that General George Washington resigned as commander in chief of the Continental Army and that the Treaty of Paris was ratified, ending the Revolutionary War. Both events took place in the Old Senate Chamber, which is filled with intricate woodwork (featuring the ubiquitous tobacco motif) attributed to Colonial architect William Buckland. Also decorating this room is Charles Willson Peale's painting *Washington at the Battle of Yorktown,* considered the masterpiece of the Revolutionary War period's finest portrait artist. The Maryland Senate and House now hold their sessions in two other chambers in the building. Look at the gold-leafed acorn atop the cupola and the 17th-century "saker" cannon near the south entrance, one of several early cannons recovered from St. Mary's County and believed to have come to the Colony with the first Maryland settlers. The State House Visitors Center has travel information for all of Maryland. Also on the grounds is the oldest public building in Maryland, the tiny redbrick Treasury, built in 1735. Note that special security precautions are in place at the State House and other state buildings in the Annapolis complex. | State Circle | 410/974–3400 | www.mdarchives.state.md.us | Free | Weekdays 9–5, weekends 10–4.

Shiplap House Museum. Built in 1715, this museum is in one of the city's oldest buildings. Originally a sailor's tavern, it is now devoted to maritime art and artifacts as well as local history. | 18 Pinkney St. | 410/267–7619 | Free | Weekdays 10–5.

United States Naval Academy. Founded in 1845, the academy was built on Windmill Point, the site of Fort Severn, which protected the city during the War of 1812. You can view a 12-minute film and join a one-hour guided tour or explore independently. The U.S. Navy Chapel, with its conspicuous dome, contains the remains of Revolutionary War hero John Paul Jones in the downstairs crypt. The Navy Museum in Preble Hall to the north of the chapel contains relics of early naval heroes and battles. | 121 Blake Rd. | 410/263–6933 | www.navyonline.com/tours.htm | Free | Jan.–Feb., daily 9–4; Mar.–Dec., daily 9–5.

William Paca House and Gardens. It is always a special thrill to step into this house of a signer of the Declaration of Independence and see just what William Paca (1740–90) could have lost if the Patriots had lost the fight for independence. Paca's elegant 37-room redbrick mansion is certainly the most impressive of the restored 18th-century mansions in Annapolis. Constructed 1763–65, the five-part Georgian residence was built as a town home for the wealthy young planter. Characterized by a modern historian as "a large heavyset fellow of strong ambition," Paca led protests against the Stamp Act in 1765 and was one of Maryland's delegates to the Continental Congress in September 1774. Today you can see his restored 2-acre pleasure garden featuring five terraces, fish-shaped pond, and the "wilderness." The mansion contains authentic period furnishings, including many imported from England, plus silverware and decorative arts. | 186 Prince George St. | 410/267–7619 | www.annapolis.org | $8 | Jan.–mid-Mar., Sat. 10–4, Sun. noon–4; mid-Mar.–Dec., Mon.–Sat. 10–5, Sun. noon–5.

✦ ON THE CALENDAR: July **Fourth of July Block Party.** Celebrate the great day at the Historic William Paca House (186 Prince George Street). Fife and drum performances, reenactments, roving entertainment, music, games, and other family fun are offered at this home of a signer of the Declaration of Independence. | 410/267–7619.

Aug. **Kunte Kinte Heritage Festival.** Since 1989 people have traveled to Annapolis, Maryland to enjoy a weekend of fun and festivities in celebration of the life of Kunte Kinte, hero of Alex Haley's *Roots,* who arrived as a slave on the dock in Annapolis in 1767. Come share in the celebration and preservation of rich African traditions. | www.kuntakinte.org/ | 410/349–0338.

HISTORIC LODGING

Georgian House. Built in 1747, this two-story stone house with black shutters and white trim is one of the older houses in town, offering quiet repose on its garden patio (especially after a day of sightseeing). The rooms—with sleigh beds, private decks, claw-foot tubs, and gas fireplaces—are similarly soothing. Complimentary breakfast. No kids. | 170 Duke of Gloucester St. | 410/263–5618 or 800/557–2068 | fax 410/263–5618 | 4 rooms | $95–$165 | AE, MC, V.

Maryland Inn. This vintage building was built in 1776 and has porches and a marble-tiled lobby. Some rooms are reminiscent of the Revolutionary era; all have antique furniture or reproductions and are hued in Williamsburg colors and wallpapers. Restaurant. | Church Cir. and Main St. | 410/263–2641 | fax 410/268–3613 | www.annapolisinns.com/marylandinn. html | 44 rooms | $169–$189 | AE, D, MC, V.

BALTIMORE

▼▼

To visit the Star-Spangled Banner City is a heart-stirring experience—after all, this is the city that proved that "our flag was still there." But it gives pause to realize that the city that gave the United States its national anthem hardly existed 65 years before Francis Scott Key wrote the words that would become its lyrics. In the mid-18th century, Baltimore comprised a handful of about 25 houses—this, when Boston, Philadelphia, and New York were already major cities. In fact, this was early on but one of several places around Chesapeake Bay named for Lord Baltimore—although the only one to survive and thrive. By the time of the Revolution, Baltimore Town became a place of significance, largely because the grain trade replaced tobacco as the major commodity in the region, and the economic balance shifted from Annapolis to Baltimore. Irish and German immigrants and free blacks swelled the town. Before long, Patriots were demonstrating against the Crown, with some opponents soundly tarred and feathered. Printer Mary Katherine Goddard published the first printed version of the Declaration of Independence. When Congress met in Baltimore in 1777, a disgruntled John Adams bewailed the muddy streets of the town. The British meanwhile declared Baltimore a "nest of pirates" because of the privateers operating out of the port. Baltimore suddenly had reached world significance, an importance resoundingly emphasized in the War of 1812 with the valiant defense of 1814, which gave the country "The Star-Spangled Banner." *Contact Baltimore Area Convention and Visitors Association | 100 Light St., Baltimore 21202 | 410/ 659–7300 | fax 410/727–2308 | www.baltimore.org.*

Fells Point. With its narrow lanes, redbrick buildings, and the air of an 18th-century seafaring village, Fells Point allows you to step back in time. Running from Gough Street to the waterfront, between Caroline and Chester sts, this district dates back to 1726 when William Fell, a Quaker from England, bought land here that he named "Fell's Prospect." Colonial homes grace the streets—many of these brick abodes were the lodging houses of ships' captains and sailors who sailed from the wharves here to ports around the world. Patriots plotted against the British authorities at the London Coffee House (at the corner of Bond and Thames streets; now under renovation). A Fells Point shipyard in 1775 built the first frigate of the Continental Navy, the *Virginia,* and this and other yards the fast schooners that harassed British shipping in the Revolution and the War of 1812. Ships such as Captain Joshua Barney's *Rossie* took a grievous toll on British merchant ships in the opening months of the War of 1812. When the British attacked Baltimore in 1814 one of their intentions was to burn the shipyards of Fells Point. Today, the district offers antiques shops, boutiques, restaurants, and inns, and is a popular nightlife destination. Begin by visiting the Robert Long House, which dates to 1765 and is styled in Flemish bond. Now the visitors center for the area, the house is Baltimore's oldest surviving urban residence and features an 18th-century garden. | Robert Long House: 808 S. Ann St. | 410/675–6750 | www.baltimorefellspoint.org. | Daily 12:30–3:30.

Fort McHenry National Monument and Historic Shrine. Here, if you're lucky, you can help the National Park Service rangers haul up the huge 42-by-30-ft garrison flag, a replica of the very "Star-Spangled Banner" now in the Smithsonian Institution's Museum of American History on the Mall in the nation's capital. The star-shaped, brick-and-earth structure, built in 1803, is most famous for its role in the War of 1812 as celebrated in the writing of the words for

With Bombs Bursting in Air:
Creating "The Star-Spangled Banner"

Today Fort McHenry's flag flies 24 hours a day in homage to that "star-spangled" banner that Francis Scott Key sighted fluttered above the fort from a distant ship even after 25 hours of cannonading by British ships. The fact that "our flag was still there" meant that the American forces held, the fort was kept, and the nation survived another ordeal. The events leading up to Key's poetic creation, however, are not as well known.

It all began with kindly Dr. Beanes. Making himself accommodating to the British invaders when they occupied Upper Marlboro on August 22, 1814, he allowed General Robert Ross to use his house as headquarters. Lieutenant George Gleig recalled going to the doctor's back door and being given tea, sugar, and a bottle of milk—kindness, indeed. After the Redcoats had burned the Capitol, the White House, and other buildings in Washington D.C., it was thus a shock to the 18-year-old lieutenant to see the old man being ridden into his camp on the back of a horse and treated with indignity. Beanes, it seemed, had detained some British stragglers, angering General Ross. The British commander now believed him to be a Yankee of "low cunning" and put him in the hold of the British flagship.

President James Madison personally asked Key to help negotiate the doctor's release. Key and U.S. Agent for Prisoner Exchange Colonel John S. Skinner sailed south from Baltimore aboard a truce ship to find the enemy fleet. They encountered the British fleet near Tangier Island in the lower Chesapeake Bay on September 7. Key and Skinner brought with them letters from British officers who had been wounded at the Battle of Bladensburg—letters testifying to how well the doctor had treated the wounded officers. General Ross released him, but the three Americans were kept with the fleet as it sailed north up the Bay to attack Baltimore. The British landed their troops at North Point, and their bombardment squadron worked its way past the shoals to attack Fort McHenry. Key and his companions were kept on board ship. This was probably in Old Roads Bay near North Point, not by today's Francis Scott Key Bridge, where a marker buoy painted with the Stars and Stripes symbolically marks his alleged position.

The bombardment began at 7:00 AM on September 13 and lasted 25 hours, during which time it was stormy and rainy. For that reason it is questionable whether Key actually saw the flag flying over the fort during the bombardment. The fact that the words of "The Star-Spangled Banner" say "the bombs gave proof that our flag was still there" suggests Key knew the flag must still be flying because the onslaught was continuing. But during a torrential rain a smaller storm flag would have been flying, not the grand 30-ft-by-42-ft "garrison flag" in the Smithsonian's National Museum of American History that fort commander Major George Armistead had commissioned from flagmaker Mary Pickersgill. Key only saw "a" tattered flag as he and his companions sailed into the harbor after the British had failed in their attempt to "reduce" the fort and sack Baltimore. Key's poem celebrating that "our flag was still there" was published in city newspapers soon afterward. It was sung on October 19 to the tune of a British drinking song in the Holliday Street Theater. Key recalled later, "The song came from my heart and made its way to the hearts of men."

the national anthem, "The Star-Spangled Banner" by Georgetown lawyer Francis Scott Key. Inside the visitors center and in the fort, exhibits bring to life the ferocious British bombardment of September 1814. The present fort stands on the site of a Revolutionary War earthen fort known as Fort Whetstone and was named for Irish-born Baltimorean James McHenry, President Washington's Secretary of War. It was erected under a congressional act of 1794 calling for a series of seacoast fortifications. After the 25-hour bombardment, which caused minimal casualties, the fort never again came under attack. However, it remained an active military post off and on for the next 100 years. The fort came under the administration of the National Park Service in 1933, two years after "The Star-Spangled Banner" became this country's national anthem. The visit includes a 15-minute history film. | F. Fort Ave. | 410/962–4290 | www.nps.gov/fomc | $5 | Daily 8–8.

Homewood House Museum. This small but exquisite Federal-era mansion, now located on the Johns Hopkins campus, was originally part of a 130-acre farm located 2 mi from the center of Baltimore. A classically inspired house, it was built in 1801 as the home of Charles Carroll, Jr. (1775–1825), only son of Declaration of Independence signer Charles Carroll of Carrollton. It was a wedding present in 1800 from the signer to his son and bride, Harriet Chew Carroll. Designed as a country house or villa, Homewood reflects the lifestyle of a cosmopolitan young couple of early 19th-century Baltimore. The symmetrical five-part plan expresses the ideals of Federal architecture in its balance and equipoise, with the house's main block flanked by two arcades and wings. The Reception Hall, Dining Room, and Drawing Room easily outshine the other salons. | 3400 N. Charles St. | 410/516–5589 | www.jhu.edu | $6 | Tues.–Sat. 11–4, Sun. noon–4.

Maryland Historical Society. This society's collection tells the fascinating story of the origins of Maryland from the Indian past through the Colony begun at St. Mary's City in 1634 to the present day through displays of its more than 200,000 cultural artifacts and everyday objects, including paintings, furniture, costumes, toys, sports memorabilia, period furniture, and the Radcliffe Maritime Collection. The Colonial Room displays paintings of Maryland's leading gentry, including signers of the Declaration of Independence William Paca and Samuel Chase, both in portraits by famed painter Charles Willson Peale. In addition, several rare paintings by African-American painter Josiah Johnson capture the images of Baltimore's leading families. The War of 1812 Room contains the original manuscript of "The Star-Spangled Banner" as well as paintings of the Battle of Baltimore, cannonballs, officers' epaulets, and other military memorabilia. | 201 W. Monument St. | 410/685–3750 | www.mdhs.org | $3 | Wed.–Fri. 10–5, 1st Thurs. of month 10–8, Sat. 9–5, Sun. 11–5.

Mount Clare Museum House. Experience the only pre-American Revolution mansion still standing in Baltimore City, built in 1760 by Charles Carroll, a barrister (lawyer) and distant relative of Charles Carroll of Carrollton, a signer of the Declaration of Independence. The original 800-acre plantation included wheat fields, a grist mill, racing stables, brick kilns, and a shipyard (his ships carried iron ore Carroll mined on this property). Mount Clare's north or front facade is quite the showpiece, complete with projecting portico, Neoclassical entablature, Palladian window, and pedimented gable roof. The National Society of Colonial Dames in Maryland have operated the house since 1917; the City of Baltimore reconstructed the wings. Despite the fact that the property left family hands, the mansion has been restored with much original Carroll furnishings and artifacts, including the family's silver teapot and china, chocolate warmer, and gambling tables. | 1500 Washington Blvd. | 410/837–3262 | www.users.erols.com/mountclaremuseumhouse | $6 | Tues.–Fri. 11–3, weekends 1–3.

Star-Spangled Banner Flag House and 1812 Museum. In the summer of 1813, an early woman entrepreneur, the widow Mrs. Pickersgill, had a flag-making business supplying ships' colors when she was asked by Fort McHenry commander Major George Armistead to make a garrison flag so big "that the British will have no difficulty seeing it from a distance." This is the house where she fashioned this amazing flag, which came to inspire the words for a national anthem. Built in 1793, this Federal home (now on the edge of Little Italy) was where Mary Young Pickersgill (1776–1857) hand-sewed the giant 42-by-30-ft "garrison flag" that flew over Fort McHenry during the British bombardment of September 1814. Note the fact that the 15-star, 15-stripe flag is unique in having a red stripe under the blue canton with the stars. Mary's mother, Rebecca Flower Young, had been a flagmaker in Philadelphia and had passed the trade to her daughter, and it is believed mother and daughter both created the flag along with Mary's daughter Caroline and niece Eliza. Because of the size of the flag, it had to be laid out on the floor of the malt house of a nearby brewery—the site of Claggett's brewery can be seen northwest of the Flag House property. The Flag House collection includes a full-length portrait by Charles Willson Peale of Mary Pickersgill's uncle, Colonel Benjamin Flower, Commissary General of Military Stores under George Washington. Other treasures of the house are a silk shawl printed with the Declaration of Independence, made to honor Lafayette on his return to the city in 1824, a walking stick once owned by George Washington, and Francis Scott Key's christening dress made by the poet's mother Anne Key for his christening in 1779. | 844 E. Pratt St. | 410/837–1793 | www.flaghouse.org | $4 | Tues.–Sat. 10–4.

Washington Monument. Erected in 1829, this marble Doric column is arguably the oldest formal monument to the nation's first president. The 178-ft obelisk was designed by Robert Mills, who later designed the famous Washington Monument in the nation's capital. You may climb 228 steps to its top for a bird's-eye view of the city. On a hill 100 ft above sea level, it was once a landmark for ships sailing into harbor. The four lovely gardens surrounding the monument form a Greek cross. In Colonial times, this area, known as Howard's Park, is believed to have been used as a dueling ground. Revolutionary War hero Colonel John Eager Howard (1752–1827) donated the land for the monument in 1815 after the original plan to build the monument at Fayette and Calvert streets (where the Battle Monument now resides) was protested by local citizens who feared the monument might fall on their houses. A plaque on the Mount Vernon Place United Methodist church northeast of the Washington Monument marks the site of the mansion where Francis Scott Key died. The author of "The Star-Spangled Banner" died while visiting his daughter, wife of Charles Howard, son of the Revolutionary War hero. | N. Charles St. | 410/396–0929 | www.wam.umd | $1 | Wed.–Sun. 10–4.

✦ ON THE CALENDAR: Sept. **Star-Spangled Banner Weekend.** Large War of 1812 reenactment and living history encampment at Fort McHenry National Monument on a mid-September weekend. Musket firing, artillery demonstrations, lectures, plus children's programs. On Saturday evening there are military pageantry and fireworks. | 410/962–4290 | www.nps.gov/fomc.

HISTORIC DINING AND LODGING

Henninger's Tavern. An antique china closet and an eclectic display of photos fill this circa 1800 building in picturesque Fells Point. White tablecloths mute the effect of the bright green and pink sponge-painted walls. The menu changes biweekly, with crab cakes always on tab. | 1812 Bank St. | 410/342–2172 | $14–$20 | AE, DC, MC, V | Closed Sun.–Mon.

Admiral Fell Inn. Near the busy nightlife spots of Fells Point, this hotel consists of eight buildings dating back to the 1700s and 1800s. All rooms are furnished with 19th-century Federal pieces as well as antique reproductions. 3 restaurants, complimentary breakfast. | 888 S. Broadway | 410/522–7377 | fax 410/522–0707 | www.admiralfell.com | 80 rooms | $139–$199 | AE, DC, MC, V.

BOWIE
▼▼▼

Bowie, originally known as Huntington, is the largest municipality in Prince George's County, a suburban enclave of Washington, D.C. The area around the city has been associated with Thoroughbred horses since Colonial times. The powerful Ogle family were largely responsible for important blood lines that have made Maryland racing famous nationwide. *Contact Prince George's County Conference and Visitors Bureau | 9200 Basil Ct., Suite 101, Largo 20774 | 301/925–8300 | www.cityofbowie.org.*

Belair Mansion. A majestic avenue of venerable tulip poplars leads you to a 1746 plantation mansion, once home-base for great men of power in Colonial Maryland. Belair was originally the estate of Samuel Ogle (1694–1752), three-term governor of Maryland between 1731 and 1752. The handsome Georgian house was built by Ogle's father-in-law, wealthy local landowner Colonel Benjamin Tasker (1720–60) for 47-year-old Ogle and his 18-year-old bride, Anne Tasker Ogle. Highlighting the collection (replete with important family objects) are allegorical paintings of the Four Seasons, hanging in the hall as they hung there in the mid-18th century, and painted by Philippe Mercier, principal painter to Britain's Prince of Wales. | 12207 Tulip Grove Dr. | 301/262–6200 | www.cityofbowie.org | Free | Thurs.–Sun. 1–4.

Belair Stable Museum. Maryland is celebrated for setting down the roots of American Thoroughbred horse racing and this museum, housed in a historic stable, allows a close and fascinating look at this fabled sport. Governor Samuel Ogle bred horses on this estate, having imported two famous Thoroughbreds from England in 1747, Spark and Queen Mab, the latter a brood mare. From these two horses are descended much of the stock that has made Maryland famous on American tracks. | 2835 Belair Dr. | 301/262–6200 | www.cityofbowie.org | Free | May–June and Sept.–Oct., weekends 1–4.

Marietta Manor. Built by U.S. Supreme Court Justice Gabriel Duvall in 1812, the Federal brick mansion houses Duvall family heirlooms, antiques from the late-18th and 19th centuries, and reproductions. | 5626 Bell Station Rd. (off Rte. 193), Glenn Dale | 301/464–5291 | www.pgheritage.org | $3 | Mar.–Dec., Fri.–Sun. noon–4.

CAMBRIDGE
▼▼▼

On the southern shore of the Choptank River, Cambridge has a rich history as Maryland's second-largest port. Besides being a shipbuilding and canning center, Cambridge was a mill town and a stop on the Underground Railroad. Its historic district reflects its prosperous past with Georgian and Federal buildings clustered on High Street. Mansions, many in the Queen Anne and Colonial Revival styles, line Oakley and Locust streets. Though its good fortune has waned, Cambridge remains an important port with vessels still seen on scenic Cambridge Creek. *Contact Wicomico Convention and Visitor Bureau | 8480 Ocean Hwy., Delmar 21875 | 410/548–4914 | www.wicomicotourism.org.*

Meredith House. This three-story, 18th-century Georgian is headquarters of the Dorchester County Historical Society and a mini-museum. Chippendale, Hepplewhite, and Sheraton period antiques fill the first floor. The Children's Room holds an impressive doll collection, cradles, miniature china, and baby carriages. Portraits and effects of six former Maryland governors from Dorchester County adorn the Governor's Room. There's also a restored smokehouse, blacksmith's shop, and medicinal herb garden. | 902 La Grange Ave. | 410/228–7953 | Free | By appointment.

Old Trinity Church, Dorchester Parish. Built in 1675 but altered in the 19th century, this Episcopal church, one of the denomination's oldest in continuous operation, has been restored to its original appearance. | Rte. 16 near Cherry Creek | 410/228–2940 | Free | Mon., Wed., Fri., and Sat. 10–4; Sun. 1–4.

Spocott Windmill. This post windmill for grinding grain is the only one in Maryland today, though they were common in the 1700s. This mill is a replica of one destroyed in the blizzard of 1888. | 1610 Hudson Rd. (Rte. 343) | 410/228–7090 | Free | Mon.–Sat. 10–5.

HISTORIC LODGING
Glasgow Inn. You'll feel like the Lord of the Domain staying in this Colonial plantation house set picturesquely on the Choptank River. Surrounded by 7 acres of grounds, the Glasgow had its origins before the Revolution with Scottish immigrant William Murray Ward—in 1760,

he purchased the tract of land known as "Ayreshire" and renamed it "Glasgow" after his native city. It was built that year with thick walls of English brick, painted white (a later wing was built in 1881 of white clapboard). Wingback chairs and fireplaces give the house a formal yet comfy air. Complimentary breakfast. | 1500 Hambrooks Blvd. | 410/228–0575 | fax 410/221–0297 | 7 rooms (4 with shared bath) | $100–$150 | No credit cards.

CHESTERTOWN

Quintessentially Maryland, charmingly Colonial, Chestertown—seat of Kent County since 1706—is one of the loveliest spots on the Eastern Shore. Its historic district is easily traveled on foot, affording glimpses of well-maintained Federal town houses, Georgian mansions, and a stone house reportedly built from a ship's ballast. This river town grew elegant, prosperous, and daring by the time of the American Revolution. On May 13, 1774, angered by British duties on tea, residents staged their own version of the Boston Tea Party in broad daylight, tossing tea brought into port by the brigantine *Geddes* into the Chester River. The event is commemorated each May at the Chestertown Tea Party. Today, tourists, sailors, and boat enthusiasts still flock to Chestertown. The town is also home to Washington College, chartered in 1782 and named for the nation's first president. *Contact Kent County Tourism | 100 N. Cross St., Suite 3, Chestertown 21620 | 410/778–0416 | www.kentcounty.com.*

Caulk's Field Battlefield. An experience to savor is a visit to site of a small War of 1812 battlefield to the west of Chestertown, marked by a stone monument. Situated on a quiet country lane, the area could not have changed much from the time of the battle on the night of August 30, 1814, which helped restore bruised American pride after the burning of Washington, D.C., by the British a week earlier. Captain Sir Peter Parker, of HMS *Menelaus* leading about 200 Royal Navy veteran seamen and Royal Marines advanced up the road from the Bay intent on attacking a militia camp. However, around 400 militiamen under Lt. Col. Philip Reed, a Revolutionary War veteran, lay in wait. Parker was killed along with 14 of his men against minimal American casualties. Parker's cousin, Lord Byron, later wrote an elegy memorializing his dead kinsman. A monument from 1902 commemorates the British dead in the battle. The Caulk House, a 1743 farmhouse (private), stands north of the battlefield. | Old Caulks Field Rd., west of Rte. 21 | Free | Daily 24 hours.

✦ ON THE CALENDAR: May **Chestertown Tea Party.** Reenactment of the town's 1774 Tea Party (originally May 13th), with Colonial parade, distance run, art show, and entertainment. | 410/778–0416.

HISTORIC LODGING
Inn at Mitchell House. This 18th-century manor house on 10 acres overlooking a pond has wide, highly polished floorboards and fireplaces in some of the rooms. Complimentary breakfast. | 8796 Maryland Pkwy. | 410/778–6500 | fax 410/778–2861 | www.chestertown.com/mitchell | 6 rooms | $90–$110 | MC, V.

EASTON

Easton has historical roots going back to the late 17th and 18th century. Quakers established the Third Haven Meeting House here in 1682–83. The town of Easton really began to grow after 1711, when the first courthouse for Talbot County was established here. Many of its buildings, dating from the late 19th and early 20th centuries, are cradled by large shade trees.

The downtown boasts small specialty shops and elegant Victorian homes—for the Revolutionary era buff, there are some notable sights. *Contact Talbot County Conference and Visitors Bureau | 210 Marlboro Ave., Suite 3, Easton 21606-1366 | 410/822–4606 | www.eastonmd.org.*

Historical Society of Talbot County. The society's museum features a three-gallery exhibit of Talbot County history. In addition, guided tours of three restored houses are offered: the James Neall House, built in 1810, the Joseph Neall House, built in 1795, and a 17th century reconstruction named Ending of Controversie. The Society's Federal- style gardens have won state and national acclaim, and a restored 18th century house serves as a consignment antique shop, with proceeds to benefit the Society. Self-guided walking tour maps of historic downtown Easton are available. | 25 S. Washington St. | 410/822–0773 | www.hstc.org | $3 | Tues.–Fri. 11–3, Sat. 10–4.

Talbot County Courthouse. Rebellious citizens gathered here to protest the Stamp Act in 1765 and to adopt the Talbot Resolves, a forerunner of the Declaration of Independence. Today, the courthouse, built in 1712 and expanded in 1794, along with two wings added in the late 1950s, is still in use. This was the center of the legislature for "the Colonial Capital of the Eastern Shore" during the Federal period, and now houses the seat of government for Talbot County. | 11 N. Washington St. | 410/770–8001 | www.eastonmd.org | During courthouse hrs, weekdays 9–5 | Free.

HISTORIC DINING AND LODGING
Restaurant Columbia. Located in a Federal brick townhouse dating from 1795, this restaurant serves roast rack of lamb as one of its specialties. | 28 S. Washington St. | 410/770–5172 | $22–$28 | AE, MC, V.

Inn at Easton. This upscale inn is a 1790 Federal-style mansion in the historic district. Each room has original artwork, featherbeds, and down comforters; suites have private sitting rooms and claw-foot bathtubs. Complimentary breakfast. No kids under 9. | 28 S. Harrison St. | 410/822–4910 | fax 410/822–4910 | www.theinnateaston.com | 7 rooms | $100–$300 | AE, MC, V.

ELKRIDGE
▼▼▼

This corner of Howard County encapsulates the story of early industrial Maryland. The area's first settler, a Puritan named Adam Shippley settled near here on land granted by Lord Baltimore in 1687. Iron works sprang up and the river provided a great means of transporting goods inland. The Great Falls of the Patapsco River, on the northwest edge of what is today Elkridge, terminated the navigable route up the river—Elk Ridge Landing soon became the largest Colonial seaport north of Annapolis. Around 1750, Caleb Dorsey constructed an iron smelting furnace and in 1810 the Ellicott family added an elegant Federal-style brick mansion, which they attached to an existing tavern. Nearby Ellicott City is a well-preserved 19th-century mill town on the Patapsco River popular with tourists who patronize its antiques stores, boutiques, and restaurants. The town's sloping streets makes it resemble an English industrial village, complete with sturdy granite buildings. *Contact Howard County Tourism Council | 2367 Main St., Ellicott City 21401 | 800/288–8747 | www.visithowardcounty.com.*

HISTORIC DINING AND LODGING
Elkridge Furnace Inn. Now one of the very best French restaurants in Maryland, the menu here is as nearly delicious as the historic ambience. This inn was first established as a tavern by Caleb Dorsey in 1744, then expanded into an iron-smelting furaceworks around 1750. The inn's dramatic height offers vistas of the Patapsco River from the second and third floors. The entrance to the red-sided Main House features fine transitional Federal–Greek Revival

detailing and consists of double leaf doors with five panes each flanked by narrow sidelights within a broad architrave. The menu is classic French, done with great style and elan. | 5745 Furnace Ave. | 410/379–9336 | $24–$28 | AE, MC, V.

FREEDERICK

Frederick beckons to you to come enjoy its links to the hardy German and English settlers who settled this area in the first half of the 18th century. Daniel Dulany began to lay out Frederick Town, named for Frederick, sixth Lord Baltimore in 1745. The town was active in the patriotic movement prior to the American Revolution, and in November 1765 the Frederick County Court declared the Stamp Act illegal. Frederick contributed to the Revolutionary War effort, most notably with its local men, painted like "red Indians," making an epic march to Boston where they fought alongside Massachusetts Minutemen and astonished New Englanders by shooting down the British "even at more than double the distance of common musket shot." *Contact Tourism Council of Frederick County, Inc. | 19 E. Church St., Frederick 21701 | 301/663–8687 or 800/999–3613 | www.visitfrederick.org.*

Beatty Cramer Architectural Museum. The only extant historic house that was standing in Frederick County when it was founded in 1748, this abode is unusual because of its timber framing, brick nogging, and European-styled carpentry. | 9010 Liberty Rd. | 301/668–2086 | $2 | Apr.–Nov., 1st Sat. of the month 10–4.

Frederick National Historic District Tour. Take a 90-minute, guided walking tour of the 50 blocks of restored and protected Victorian and Federal architecture. | 19 E. Church St. | 800/999–3613 | www.visitfrederick.org | $4.75 | Weekends 1:30.

Hessian Barracks. Located on the grounds of the Maryland School for the Deaf, these barracks were built in 1777 at the time of the Revolution. The barracks served as a Revolutionary War and War of 1812 prison to contain British prisoners. In 1803, they were a staging point for the Lewis and Clark expedition. | 101 Clarke Pl. | 301/228–2888 | www.visitfrederick.org | Free | By group appointment only.

Mt. Olivet Cemetery. Many American history buffs will want to pay homage at the final resting place of Francis Scott Key (1779–1843), author of "The Star-Spangled Banner," who is buried below a dramatic statue by the gates of this graveyard. Key was originally buried in the Howard family vault in Old St. Paul's Cemetery, Baltimore, but the people of Frederick petitioned to bring home the native son who was born east of Frederick at the Terra Rubra estate (private) and who had a law office in the city. | 515 S. Market St.

HISTORIC LODGING
Catoctin Inn. Built in 1780, this inn's antiques give it both an 18th- and 19th-century flavor. With meeting space and a computer available, the inn attracts business travelers as well as vacationers. Restaurant, complimentary breakfast. | 3613 Buckeystown Pike (Rte. 85), Buckeystown | 301/874–5555 | fax 301/874–2026 | www.catoctininn.com | 19 rooms | $109–$159 | AE, D, MC, V.

LA PLATA

This growing southern Maryland community, known as La Plata as early as 1866, has some Colonial and Revolutionary War era sites. *Contact Charles County Tourism | Box 2150, La Plata 20646 | 800/766–3386 | www.charlescounty.org/tourism.*

Port Tobacco. Shown as the site of an Indian town in Captain John Smith's 1608 map of the Chesapeake Bay, Port Tobacco became an English settlement soon after the arrival of Lord Baltimore's colonists in 1634. By the end of the 17th century it was a major seaport and had been the site of a 1681 uprising by supporters of former governor Josias Fendall against the government of Charles, third Lord Baltimore. The Proprietor's soldiers quelled the rebellion and Fendall was found guilty by a provincial court of plotting to kidnap Lord Baltimore. The plotters were dismissed as "rank Baconists"—a reference to the 1676 rebellion of Nathaniel Bacon in Virginia against Royal governor Sir William Berkeley. Historic sites in the hamlet of Port Tobacco include a 19th-century courthouse with displays of artifacts, a restored one-room schoolhouse and Catslide House, a restored 18th-century home. | Rte. 6, 3 mi west of La Plata | 301/934–4313 | $2 | Apr.–mid-Oct., Wed.–Sun. 11–4.

Smallwood's Retreat. Smallwood State Park is home to the gorgeous (but small) redbrick-and-clapboard restored plantation home of Revolutionary War general and Maryland governor William Smallwood (1732–1792). As commander of the Maryland Line, Smallwood supported George Washington at the Battle of Long Island in 1776 and in the Carolinas in the 1780s. Unfortunately, he died in debt and his home was sold at auction, a sad tale that many other patriots (including Thomas Jefferson) suffered since they had put their own money into the cause for independence. | Chicamuxen Rd. (4 mi east of Rte. 225), Marbury | 301/888–1410 | www.dnr.state.md.us/publiclands/southern/smallwood.html | $2 weekends, May–Sept., free weekdays | Daily dawn to dusk.

Thomas Stone National Historic Site. Haberdeventure, the plantation home of Thomas Stone (1743–87)—the youngest of Maryland's four signers—offers a chance to learn about one of the less well known signers of the Declaration of Independence. | Rose Hill Rd., between Rtes. 6 and 225 | 301/392–1776 | www.nps.gov/thst | Free | Mid-June–Sept., Wed.–Sun. 9–5.

LAUREL

▼▼

Laurel grew up round a stone grist mill on the Patuxent River that operated in the early 1800s, and was originally known as Laurel Factory, named after the area's mills and abundant mountain laurel. *Contact Prince George's County, Maryland Conference and Visitors Bureau | 9200 Basil Ct., Largo 20774 | 301/428–9702 | fax 301/925–2053 | www.visitprincegeorges.com.*

Montpelier Mansion. A grand Georgian mansion built between 1781 and 1785 provides a look at the life of a family who entertained distinguished visitors such as George Washington and Abigail Adams. The house was constructed for Major Thomas Snowden and his wife Anne. Located in 70 acres of parkland near the city of Laurel, the gardens of the house have been carefully re-created, complete with a boxwood-lined pathway. Select rooms are furnished as they would have appeared from the late 18th century through 1830. | 9401 Montpelier Dr. | 301/953–1376 | www.pgparks.com/places/historic/montpelier.html | $3 | Tues.–Sat. 10–6, Sun. noon–4.

LEONARDTOWN

▼▼

One of the oldest county seats in the United States, Leonardtown can trace its history back to the mid-18th century and is one of the few Maryland towns to have an intact town square. The town was among a number of communities in southern Maryland to be ransacked by marauding British during the War of 1812. *Contact St. Mary's County Division of Travel and Tourism | Box 653, Governmental Center, Washington St., 2nd floor, Leonardtown 20650 | 301/475–4411 or 800/327–9023 | www.co.saint-marys.md.us.*

Christ Episcopal Church, Chaptico. This brick church, dating from 1735, is situated in the oldest village in Maryland outside of St. Mary's City. The land for the church was donated by Philip Key, High Sheriff of the Colony of Maryland and grandfather of Francis Scott Key. Although damaged by British troops during the War of 1812, the church survived and prospered. Chaptico was once a port with warehouses, but the bay on which the town was situated has silted up and become marshland. In 1689, Chaptico was a rallying point where soldiers were mustered as part of the Protestant Rebellion in Maryland. | Rte. 234, Chaptico | 301/884–3451 | www.christepiscopalchaptico.org.

Old Sotterley Plantation. The only working 18th-century plantation in Maryland, the mansion is famously reminiscent of—or perhaps served as a model for!—Mount Vernon. The Chinese Chippendale staircase and the shell alcoves in the drawing room, both carved by Richard Boulton, then an indentured servant, are considered among the finest examples of 18th-century American woodwork. In 1717, James Bowles began building this house using post-in-ground construction, a method of house construction once common in the Tidewater regions. Two years after the death of Squire Bowles in 1727, his young widow, Rebecca, married George Plater II. Over the years, the Plater family converted the simple residence into a charming 18th-century manor house, which they named after their ancestral home, Sotterley Hall, in Suffolk, England. It was under George Plater III, sixth governor of Maryland, that the house reached its distinctive form that was so much admired by George Washington. The Plantation had one of the largest communities of enslaved African-Americans in the Southern Maryland region. While the Slave Cabin dates from the 1840s its conventional single-room plan is typical of the type seen in the region from the early 18th century. | 44300 Sotterley Main Rd., (Rte. 245), Hollywood | 301/373–2280 | www.sotterley.com | $7 | May–Oct., Tues.–Sun. 10–4.

Tudor Hall. This 1756 Georgian mansion overlooking Breton Bay boasts a beautiful "hanging" staircase in the main hall and a valuable research library. Of the many influential people who have called Tudor Hall home, the most well known is none other than Francis Scott Key, author of the "Star-Spangled Banner." | Camalier Dr. and Tudor Hall Pl. | 301/475–2467 | Free | Thurs.–Fri. noon–4, Sat. 10–4.

ST. MARY'S CITY
▼▼

Following their sighting of what is today Point Lookout, an intrepid group of 140 English settlers sailed the *Ark* and the *Dove* up the Potomac where they landed on an island that became St. Clement's. Their exploration, however, soon found them on a course into a tributary of the Potomac, the St. Mary's River. About halfway up, on an east bank, they founded St. Mary's City, the fourth permanent settlement in British North America and eventually the first capital of Maryland, albeit short-lived. Long before a Constitution or a Bill of Rights, the first law of religious tolerance in the New World was enacted in St. Mary's City, guaranteeing the freedom to practice whatever religion one chose. Here, too, almost three centuries before American women achieved suffrage, Mistress Margaret Brent challenged the status quo and requested the right to vote (she didn't get it). The settlement served as Maryland's capital city until 1695, when the legislature moved to Annapolis and the county seat moved to Leonardtown. St. Mary's City virtually vanished, its existence acknowledged only in historical novels and textbooks.

In 1934, in commemoration of the 300th anniversary of Maryland, the Colony's imposing State House, originally built in 1676, was reconstructed, the first step in the rebirth of St. Mary's City. In the early 1970s, a vast archaeological-reconstruction program began in earnest, a project that has revealed nearly 200 individual sites. You're encouraged to explore other "exhibits-in-progress" such as the town center, the location of the first Catholic Church in the English Colonies, a "victualing" and lodging house (a Colonial-era B&B), and the woodland Native American hamlet. *Contact St. Mary's County Division of Travel and Tourism | Box 653, Governmental Center, Washington St., 2nd floor, Leonardtown 20650 | 800/ 327–9023 | www.co.saint-marys.md.us.*

Historic St. Mary's City. Eight hundred–plus acres have become a living-history museum and archaeological park. The historic complex includes several notable reconstructions and reproductions of buildings. The State House of 1676, like its larger and grander counterpart in Williamsburg, has an upper and a lower chamber for the corresponding houses of parliament. This 1934 reproduction is based on court documents from the period; the original was dismantled in 1829 (many of the bricks were used for Trinity Church nearby).The small square-rigged ship, *Maryland Dove,* docked behind the State House is an accurate replica of the original *Dove,* one of two vessels (the other being the *Ark*) that conveyed the original settlers from England. The nearby Farthing's Ordinary is a reconstructed inn. Godiah Spray Tobacco Plantation depicts life on a 17th-century tobacco farm in the Maryland wilderness. Interpreters portray the Spray family—based on a family that lived about 20 mi away—and its indentured servants, enlisting passive onlookers in such household chores as cooking and gardening or in working the tobacco field. The buildings, including the main dwelling house and outbuildings, were built with period tools and techniques. Call for special events, which are scheduled for March through December—work alongside professional archaeologists, churn butter, watch a militia drill, or shoot a bow and arrow. Historic St. Mary's remains one of America's best-preserved Colonial archaeology sites—on display are the recently discovered lead coffins of the Calvert family members and early cannonballs, relics of Ingle's Rebellion of 1645. | Rte. 5 | 800/762–1634 | www.stmaryscity.org | $7.50 | Late Mar.–late Nov., Wed.–Sun. 10–5.

Leonard Calvert Monument. This obelisk in Trinity Episcopal Church cemetery celebrates the vision of religious tolerance advocated by Maryland's first governor, Leonard Calvert. | Off Rte. 5 | 301/862–4597 | Free.

HISTORIC DINING AND LODGING

Brome-Howard Inn. Set on 30 acres of farmland, this 19th-century farmhouse provides a trip through time to life on a tobacco plantation. Rooms are decorated with original family furnishings. Relax on one of the big outdoor porches or patios and watch the lazy St. Mary's River 200 ft away. In the evening, there are two candlelit dining rooms—the foyer or the formal parlor. Hiking trails lead to St. Mary's City, and the inn has bikes for guests to use. The dining rooms, open to guests and nonguests, specialize in seafood and occasionally serve such exotic items as bison, ostrich, or shark. Restaurant. | 18281 Rosecroft Rd. | 301/866–0656 | fax 301/ 866–9660 | www.bromehowardinn.com | 3 rooms | $95–$160 | AE, MC, V.

ST. MICHAELS
▼▼

St. Michaels will provide you with a unique Eastern Shore experience, surrounded as it is by tributaries of the Chesapeake Bay. One of the Eastern Shore's most popular sailing destinations, St. Michaels began to make its name as a shipbuilding center during the American Revolution. The town came under attack twice during the War of 1812, and in a battle on the morning of August 10, 1813 local legend is that residents diverted British fire by adroitly placing lanterns in the trees so the British would fire high—as it turns out, the aptly named Cannonball House was struck during the shelling. Built in 1805, the house is private, but you can see it from the outside, as you can other historic Federal-period houses dating to the early 1800s. Specialty shops, restaurants, and the impressive Chesapeake Bay Maritime Museum all entice. *Contact Talbot County Conference and Visitors Bureau | 210 Marlboro Ave., Suite 3, Easton 21606-1366 | 410/822–4606 | www.tourtalbot.org.*

Chesapeake Bay Maritime Museum. A complex of 10 buildings on 17 acres contains the history of the bay and its boatbuilding traditions. Exhibits document Chesapeake Bay vessels from Colonial times onward. Included is in the museum's Bay History Building is a reconstruction of the deck of the Baltimore-built schooner *Lynx,* showing a typical carronade. This lethal naval weapon, developed shortly after the American Revolution, could be loaded and fired rapidly and was particularly effective at close range. | Navy Point, Mill St. | 410/745–2916 | www.cbmm.org | $7.50 | Apr.–May and Sept.–Oct., daily 9–5; June–Aug., daily 9–6; Nov.–Feb., daily 9–4.

HISTORIC LODGING

Inn at Perry Cabin. Built right after the War of 1812, this white Colonial-style mansion is perched on the banks of the Miles River. Each room is distinct. Some have Laura Ashley fabrics and wallpaper, while others are furnished with English and Early American antiques. The hotel gets its name from Commodore Oliver Hazard Perry, the War of 1812 veteran. Restaurant, complimentary breakfast. No children under 10. | 308 Watkins La. | 410/745–2200 | fax 410/745–3348 | www.perrycabin.com | 35 rooms, 6 suites | $295 | AE, DC, MC, V.

TOWSON
▼▼▼

William and Thomas Towson founded this community in 1750 when they began farming the area. In 1768, Thomas' son, Ezekiel, built a large tavern at the crossroads of York and Joppa roads, which is still a major intersection, and the small village of "Towsontown" began to grow around it. *Contact Baltimore County Conference and Visitors Bureau | 435 York Rd., Towson 21204 | 800/570–2836 | www.visitbacomd.com.*

Hampton National Historic Site. At this significant site, 1 mi north of Towson, you can immerse yourself in one of the best-preserved and striking Federal-era mansions in the nation, the home of a family that made a significant contribution to the founding of our nation. The Ridgely family were ironmasters who cast cannons for the nation in the American Revolution and the War of 1812 and made other important contributions to the war effort. When completed in 1790, their elegantly furnished Late Georgian mansion, set amid formal gardens and shade trees, was the largest house in the United States, and it remains today the largest Georgian-style residence in the country. The sumptuous rooms in the mansion, with their brightly colored hues, are testament to the entertaining done by the Ridgelys. The Great Hall measures 51 ft by 21 ft and could seat more than 50 dinner guests. English visitor Richard Parkinson noted in 1805 that Ridgely was said to "keep the best table in America." An ongoing project is documenting the lives of the African-American slaves and white indentured servants who worked for the family on the plantation and at the ironworks. After you tour the spectacular mansion, the slave quarters, family cemetery, carriages, and state champion trees await your discovery. | 535 Hampton La. | 410/823–1309 | www.nps.gov/hamp | $5 | Daily 9–4.

WALDORF
▼▼▼

Once a farming community, Waldorf is now a fast-growing suburb of Washington, D.C. This area of southern Maryland, however, contains several sites of Colonial and Revolutionary War interest. *Contact Charles County Tourism | Box B, La Plata 20646 | 301/645–0558 or 800/ 766–3386 | www.charlescounty.org/tourism.*

Fort Washington National Park. A military installation from 1808 to 1946, Fort Washington is built on a bluff overlooking the Potomac River, a site chosen in 1790 to protect the new nation's capital by George Washington himself. The fort was threatened by a British Royal Navy squadron sailing up the Potomac River on August 27, 1814, soon after the British burned Washington, D.C. The commander of the fort, Captain Samuel Dyson, fearing that the British Army would attack him in the rear, chose to abandon the fort and blow it up—afterward, he was court-martialed. The defenses were later rebuilt beginning in 1815 by Major Pierre L'Enfant, who laid out Washington, D.C. Guided tours only. | Fort Washington Rd. in Fort Washington | 301/763–4600 | www.nps.gov/fowa | $4 per vehicle | Daily dawn–dusk.

Friendship House. Now part of the Charles County Community College campus, this small Tidewater-style house with brick interior was built around 1680, making it one of the oldest structures in the county. In 1968, it was dismantled, moved from its original site, and reassembled eight years later on this campus. | Charles County Community College | 301/870–3008 | Free | Weekends noon–4.

National Colonial Farm. This full-scale working farm, founded in 1958, is a replica of a typical 18th-century middle-class farm and gives you the opportunity to understand what life in the region was like 200 years ago for the great majority of people. Part of the National Park Service's Piscataway Park, the farm is managed by the Maryland-based Accokeek Foundation and has livestock and a tobacco barn as well as special events. | Bryan Point Rd., Accokeek | 301/283–2113 | www.accokeek.org | $2 | Tues.–Sun. 10–5.

WASHINGTON, D.C.

▼▼▼

Amid the majesty and bustle of our nation's capital today it's hard to imagine that barely over two centuries ago Washington, D.C. was brand new—indeed, to put it less elegantly, it was out and out a crude and unfinished place disliked by many in the Federal government. In 1800, First Lady Abigail Adams lost her way in the Maryland woods on her way to the new capital and then wrote despairingly to her daughter, Abby Smith, "Woods are all you see from Baltimore until you reach *the city,* which is so in name only." Woods and marshland still covered much of the Maryland land set aside for the capital even then, 10 years after the area formally became the nation's capital in 1790, a compromise location favored by President Washington because of its central location on a north–south axis between the states that grew from the 13 breakaway British Colonies.

Snaking through part of the area in what is now the Mall was the Tiber Creek, a waterway now entombed by the city and a name made an object of fun to the invading British in 1814 who thought the name showed the pretensions of Americans in naming a creek for the great river in Rome. In fact, the name "Tiber" was a marker of the area's Colonial past, deriving from an early landowner Francis Pope, who named the 400-acre land grant he had received from Lord Baltimore, "Rome." If the new capital laid out by French engineer Pierre L'Enfant was unfinished—a mere "sheep's meadow" in the words of one government official—this was partly because the Frenchman's design was so grandiose, "splendidly expansive" with landmark buildings and monuments set widely apart on grand avenues. What would become Capitol Hill, an oak-covered hill some 80 ft above the swampland, was the Frenchman declared, "a pedestal waiting for a monument." This was the origins of the Federal capital, important vestiges of which remain today in significant Federal-era buildings such as the White House, Decatur House, and Octagon House—the few original buildings of the new American capital still extant. Of course, there are also the Colonial and Federal buildings of Georgetown, which, together with Alexandria, Virginia, made up only one of two important towns in the area that predated Washington, D.C.'s founding in 1790. Although Georgetown is now a section of the nation's capital, it retains its old-world charm, making it a joy to walk around and enjoy, with its brick sidewalks, neat and elegant row houses, many of them exclusive addresses for congressmen and U.S. government officials. *Contact Washington, D.C., Convention and Tourism Corp. | 1212 New York Ave. NW, Suite 600, Washington, DC 20005 | 202/789–7000 | fax 202/789–7037 | www.washington.org.*

Decatur House Museum. The Decatur House offers you the chance to taste the elegance and political power of Federal-era Washington, D.C., and to touch a heroic and tragic story. The former home of naval hero Commodore Stephen Decatur and his wife, Susan, completed in 1818, is one of the oldest surviving homes in Washington, D.C. Tragically, the Decaturs only occupied the house for 14 months because the hero was mortally wounded in a duel with Commodore James Barron at the dueling grounds at Bladensburg on March 22, 1820. The elite address on Lafayette Square across from the White House is one of only three remaining residential buildings in the country designed by Benjamin Henry Latrobe, the father of American architecture. The nearly square, three-story Neoclassical town house is constructed in redbrick in the austere Federal fashion of the day. Inside, the elegant salons hold the Decatur House collections, ranging from paintings to noted pieces of furniture, including 18th-century Chippendale chairs and Stephen Decatur Jr.'s Louis XVI *secretaire à guillotine*. Entry to the house is gained through at 1600 H Street NW. Guided tours are available every 30 minutes. | 748 Jackson Pl. NW | 202/965–0920 | www.decaturhouse.org | Free | Tues.–Fri. 10–3, weekends 12–4.

Dumbarton House. Set on the heights of Georgetown, the vast estate offers you the opportunity to enjoy a fine Federal-period house that showcases furniture and decorative arts of the late-18th and early 19th centuries. The name of the house derives from the Colonial designation for the property, "Rock of Dumbarton," a name from Ninian Beall, a Scottish immigrant, who was granted by the Maryland Assembly a 795-acre tract for services "upon all incursions and disturbances of neighboring Indians." Beall apparently named the property after a distinctive geologic feature near Glasgow in his native Scotland. The house itself was built in 1800 above Rock Creek by Joseph Nourse, first Register of the U.S. Treasury, who lived here 1804–13, when it was purchased by Charles Carroll, a cousin of Charles Carroll of Carrollton, signer of the Declaration of Independence. Carroll renamed the house "Belle Vue." The mansion famously provided sanctuary for First Lady Dolley Madison on the terrifying night of August 24, 1814, during the British invasion of Washington, D.C., in the War of 1812. Charles Carroll escorted Dolley Madison from the President's mansion to Belle Vue, ahead of the British torching of the executive's mansion. When you visit Dumbarton House you will see a wealth of furniture, paintings, textiles, silver, and ceramics that were made and used in the republic's formative years. Guided tours only at 10:15, 11:15, and 12:15. | 2715 Q St. NW | 202/337–2288 | www.dumbartonhouse.org | Free | Labor Day–July, Tues.–Sat. 10–1.

Octagon House. Dolley Madison was fabled for her polished sense of style, and this house allows us a rare peek at Washington's first "Hostess with the Mostest." Fourth president James Madison and his wife Dolley lived here after the British burned the President's mansion in 1814 during the War of 1812. Col. John Tayloe III's home had been designed by Dr. William Thornton, first architect of the U.S. Capitol, in an American adaptation of the elegant Adam style of Neoclassicism. Colonel Tayloe and his wife, Ann Ogle Tayloe, began to entertain in the Octagon during the 1801 Washington "social season," making the residence one of the most important homes in Washington, D.C. President Madison and First Lady Dolley took up residence in the Octagon after the British sacked the President's house on the night of August 24, 1814. In the upstairs parlor President Madison signed the Treaty of Ghent on February 17, 1815, ending the War of 1812. Following the Madisons' six-month residency, the Tayloe family lived in the Octagon until 1855. Sold to the American Architectural Foundation in 1968, it opened as a museum of architecture and design in 1970. | 1799 New York Ave. NW | 202/638–3105 | www.archfoundation.org | $5 | Tues.–Sun. 10–4.

Old Stone House. Here's a taste of Colonial life in Georgetown before the Revolution—a house built in 1765 and believed to be the oldest structure in the District of Columbia. You'll find the Old Stone House in the midst of the shops and restaurants on Georgetown's busiest street. Step inside for the period-furnished rooms upstairs, then enjoy a brief interlude in the lovely English-type garden with its seasonal plantings. Administered by the National Park Service, the Old Stone House offers crafts demonstrations and programs relating to Colonial life. | 3051 M St. NW | 202/426–6851 | www.nps.gov/rocr/oldstonehouse | $5 | Wed.–Sun. noon–4.

Tudor Place Historic House and Garden. Georgetown elegance is epitomized in this magnificent 1816 mansion, considered one of the foremost Federal-era mansions in United States, built by Martha Washington's granddaughter, Martha Custis Peter. The house, designed by William Thornton, was the home to six generations of the Peter family. Friends of the Peter family included such distinguished figures as George Washington, the Marquis de Lafayette, and Robert E. Lee. These associations, as well as the family life of the Peters through the generations, are depicted in the paintings and furniture as well as documents and other artifacts found in the house. Washingtoniana includes pieces from the Washington's Sèvres porcelain dinner service and Martha Washington's Chinese Chippendale tea table. A round, temple-style portico with a domed roof and Tuscan columns dominates the exceptional south facade, designed by the first architect of the U.S. Capitol, Dr. William Thornton. On the sloping South Lawn, the stunning gardens of Tudor Place reflect the continuity of the Peter family. The basic design of the Federal period remains and includes some of the trees and boxwoods planted by Martha Custis Peter herself. Tours are given hourly of the house. | 1644 31st St. NW | 202/965–0400 | www.tudorplace.org | $6 | Mon.–Sat. 10–4, Sun. noon–4.

United States Capitol. Major Pierre L'Enfant, the city's planner, had declared Jenkin's Hill, later known as Capitol Hill, to be "a pedestal waiting for a monument." After George Washington laid the foundation stone in 1793, the first Capitol was for some years a single free-stone building. When the British attacked the city in August 1814, it was two separate buildings, the Senate and the House of Representatives, linked by a 100-ft wooden bridge. The British burned the Capitol along with other public buildings in the city, an act that scandalized opinion both in the United States and in Europe. The Senate and House of Representatives were carefully restored by architect Benjamin Henry Latrobe (1756–1820) and may be visited today as part of the tour of the Capitol. Both now serve as halls of statuary linking the new Senate and House chambers with the Capitol's great Rotunda, under the big dome. Be sure to get the guide to tell you about a neat architectural feature in the former House legislative chamber: a slight whisper uttered on one side of the hall can be heard across the polished marble on the other side of the hall due to the shape of the elliptical ceiling. As might be expected, this design oddity that was both exploited by and irritated early legislators. | 1st St. SW and Independence Ave. | 202/225–6827 | www.aoc.gov | Free | Mon.–Sat. 9–4:30 (guided tours only).

White House. No home in the United States and not many in the world can offer the thrill of being so close to history as does the President's Mansion, today known as "The White House." Originally constructed 1792–1800, to a design of Irish architect James Hoban, the mansion has been the home of every president of the United States since John Adams. It was reconstructed in 1815 after being burned by British soldiers during the War of 1812 in the wake of the fleeing President Madison and his First Lady, Dolley. British Rear Admiral George Cockburn is said to have taken a cushion from the house, and referring to Mrs. Madison, to have remarked that the cushion "will remind me of her seat." The mansion is significant for its Federal architecture, as a symbol of the presidency, and for the important decisions made within its walls over the years. | 1400 Pennsylvania Ave. NW | 202/208–1631 | www.nps.gov/whho | Due to security restrictions, the White House tours have been suspended until further notice.

HISTORIC DINING AND LODGING

Hotel Tabard Inn. Three Victorian town houses make up this quaint, popular hotel in Dupont Circle, with old Victorian and American Empire furniture, fireplaces, and outdoor patio. Rooms vary in size, and some share bathrooms. Restaurant. | 1739 N St. NW | 202/785–1277 | fax 202/785–6173 | www.tabardinn.com/home.htm | 40 rooms, 25 with bath | $140–$175 | AE, D, MC, V.

Jefferson Hotel. This downtown hotel has elegant 18th-century European furnishings. Some rooms have fireplaces and partial views of monuments and The White House. The superb restaurant is adorned with Jeffersonian-era documents. Restaurant. | 1200 16th St. NW | 800/368–5966 | fax 202/331–7982 | www.camberleyhotels.com | 132 rooms | $279–$589 | AE, D, MC, V.

By Carolyn B. Heller

Massachusetts

❦

From Pilgrims to Presidents

*M*assachusetts: *Because of You, Our Land Is Free"*—that's the official patriotic state song of the sixth Colony to join the Union. And while other states certainly played a part in the birth of the nation, the Bay State, named for the Massachusett tribe of Native Americans (who lived south of what is now Boston), can claim a starring role in the United States's early history. The state capital is Boston, 370 years old and far older than the republic it helped to create. The city's most famous buildings are not merely civic landmarks but national icons; its great citizens are the Adamses, Reveres, and Hancocks who continue to live at the crossroads of history and myth. But Massachusetts's story starts far away from Boston's historic Faneuil Hall, Quincy Market, and Old State House.

The saga begins with refugees from England who left 17th-century religious and economic constraints on a wing and a prayer (a prayer, certainly). In the 1600s, a series of English colonists passed through Massachusetts waters, encouraged in their profit-seeking adventures by a king and parliament anxious to trump the New World empires then being established by Spain and France. For the English, success finally came with one of the least prepared groups to make the attempt: a small boatload of religious dissidents, entrepreneurs, and indentured servants now collectively known to history as the Pilgrims. After making landfall at the tip of Cape Cod in November 1620, the *Mayflower* passengers finally disembarked at Plymouth Rock. As it turns out, neither of these spots were their goal. The coast around Virginia, hundreds of miles south, was their target, but a storm drove them northward to around Provincetown (where they stayed nearly a month), only to find the tip of the cape inhospitable. Then, by a series of misadventures, they ended up in Plymouth, once again blown in by inclement weather. They did not flock ashore blessing the land at every step but instead sent a few men to build shelters on the site of an abandoned Patuxet village, its fields already cleared for cultivation. Everyone else remained aboard the ship in incredibly crowded and unsanitary conditions—not unexpectedly, nearly half the colony perished in the unforgiving

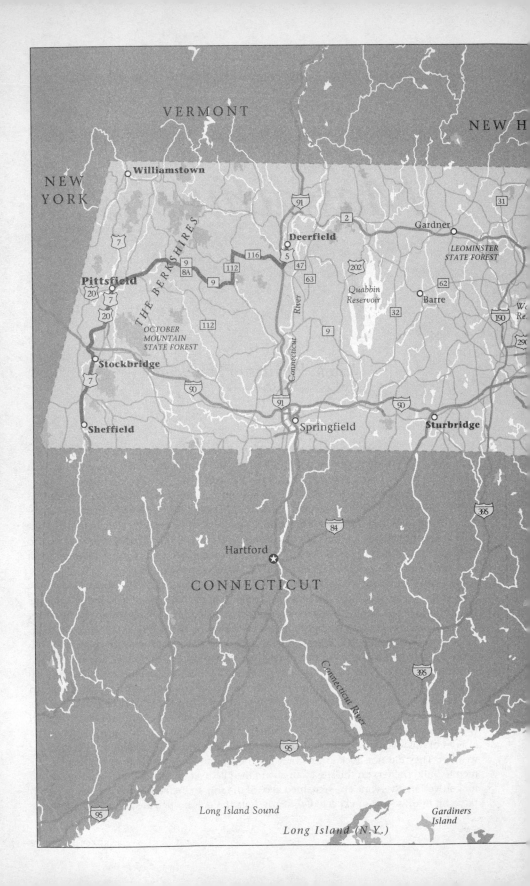

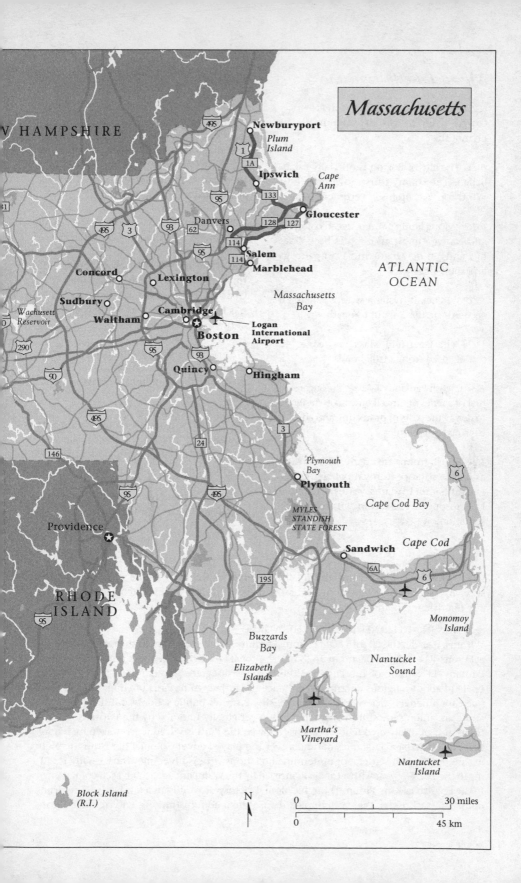

Massachusetts

NEW HAMPSHIRE

495

Newburyport

1

Plum Island

1A

Ipswich

Cape Ann

133

Danvers

95

93

62

128

127

Gloucester

495

3

114

95

114

Salem

Marblehead

ATLANTIC OCEAN

Concord

Lexington

Massachusetts Bay

Sudbury

Waltham

Cambridge

41

Wachusett Reservoir

290

95

93

Boston

Logan International Airport

90

Quincy

Hingham

495

146

24

3

Plymouth Bay

95

495

Plymouth

6

Cape Cod Bay

Providence

MYLES STANDISH STATE FOREST

Sandwich

Cape Cod

RHODE ISLAND

195

6A

6

95

Monomoy Island

Buzzards Bay

Nantucket Sound

Elizabeth Islands

Martha's Vineyard

Nantucket Island

Block Island (R.I.)

N

0   30 miles

0   45 km

Massachusetts Timeline

1620 Mayflower Pilgrims arrive in Province-town, then establish settlement at Plymouth.

1630 The city of Boston is officially established. The colony's first governor, John Winthrop, sets up his government here.

1675–76 King Philip's War between colonists and Native Americans cripples both sides but ends in defeat for the Wampanoags and their allies.

1692 Witchcraft hysteria sweeps Salem; 20 accused witches are put to death.

1704 The Deerfield Massacre leaves 48 settlers dead from a tribal raid.

1764 English Parliament passes the Sugar Act, first of a series of unwelcome taxes designed to defray the costs of protecting and administering the Colonies.

1768 British troops are quartered in Boston as local resistance to royal policies grows. Patriot Samuel Adams writes a Circular Letter opposing taxation without representation.

1770 The Boston Massacre heightens tensions between Colony and Crown.

1773 Angry about new duties on imported tea, Bostonians empty a cargo of it into their harbor during what becomes known as the Boston Tea Party.

1774 England closes Boston Harbor to all shipping to punish the colonists.

1775 "The shot heard 'round the world" touches off the American Revolution at Concord. Two months later, American militias inflict severe casualties on the British at the Battle of Bunker Hill.

1776 After an eight-month siege, British troops evacuate Boston without a shot. No further battles are fought on Massachusetts soil.

1780 Commonwealth of Massachusetts constitution is ratified, and John Hancock is elected the first governor under this new constitution.

1788 Massachusetts ratifies the federal constitution and enters the union as the sixth state.

winter that followed, almost ending the Colonial experiment before it began. But the survivors persevered, overcoming natural obstacles and their own shortcomings to eventually flourish and multiply.

✦ THE "SHOT HEARD 'ROUND THE WORLD"

Within a decade, the Pilgrim "Old Colony" acquired a new neighbor to the north: the Massachusetts Bay Colony, begun in 1628 under a royal charter granted to a group of so-called Puritans. Like some of the Pilgrims, the Puritans disagreed enough with the Church of England about religious doctrine to embrace the unknown hazards of emigration in their quest for a perfect society. Harvard University, Boston's public schools and the state legislature are among the still-thriving institutions originally founded by the Puritans. Tens of thousands of disaffected fellow citizens followed the Puritans' lead, encouraged by reports that played up New England's natural assets and played down Colonial hardships. Rapidly expanding English settlement undermined relations with Native Americans, finally resulting in the 1675–76 war with a tribal alliance led by the Wampanoag sachem Metacom, known to the English as King Philip. Though Colonial victory drove all but a few Native Americans out of Massachusetts, the cost crippled the Colonial administrations, ending their autonomy from England. In the war's aftermath the English crown revoked both the Pilgrim and Puritan charters, and by the end of the 17th century took direct control over its most populous holdings in North America by combining them into the royally governed Province of Massachusetts.

Mother England proceeded to spend the 1700s draining its treasury with expensive wars against other European powers. Massachusetts merchants, particularly those in the provincial capital of Boston and Salem, grew prosperous on foreign trade, much of it illegal competition against domestic British firms. The cash-strapped king and his ministers, resenting the flagrant smuggling and perceiving a huge cost to the crown in defending the American frontier from French and Indian aggression, attempted to grab a slice of the traders' profits through a series of taxes, such as the 1764 Sugar Act, the 1765 Stamp Act, and the 1768 Townshend Acts. Chafing at having their liberties pruned back after decades of lax oversight, pugnacious Massachusetts led the Colonial resistance to the unpopular new levies, arguing that "taxation without representation is tyranny." The right to raise revenue, insisted the Colonies, belonged to their own elected assemblies rather than to England's Parliament. In reply, Parliament dissolved the Massachusetts assembly, among others, and in 1768 sent soldiers to Boston to enforce the royal policies.

Hair-trigger passions on both sides of this constitutional debate were inflamed by such watershed events as the 1770 Boston Massacre, in which fearful British troops slew five members of a garbage-throwing mob, and the 1773 Boston Tea Party, in which colonists scuttled crates of tea in the harbor to protest a new set of import duties. Parliament retaliated with the 1774 Coercive Acts, which included closing Boston's port to all trade, but the move backfired. Instead of yoking his subjects to his will, King George III only ignited more Colonial anger with his inflexibility. And so on the afternoon of April 19, 1775, by a bridge on the Concord River, west of Boston, local militia shot back at startled English Redcoats—"the shot heard 'round the world" that plunged Massachusetts, and very soon all 12 of its Colonial counterparts, into a long and costly war of independence.

✦ ADAMS, REVERE, AND COMPANY

Massachusetts was at the vanguard of the Revolution, but after the morale-boosting Battle of Bunker Hill, in June 1775, and the British evacuation from Boston eight months later, the battlefields shifted permanently out of state. Massachusetts contributed as significantly to the new American republic's political framework after the war as it had to starting the conflict, which is why so many of the state's most popular historic sites—such as the homes of John Adams and Paul Revere, or landmarks along Boston's Freedom Trail—are national monuments. Modern preservation of luxurious Federal-style mansions and museums filled with collections begun by local merchant princes lent additional perspective on the spoils of war, as Massachusetts shipowners and traders, unfettered by royal restraints, amassed huge fortunes in overseas freight after the Revolution ended. But Thomas Jefferson's 1807 Embargo Act, halting all foreign trade, and "Mr. Madison's War" of 1812, which disrupted access to European markets, altogether torpedoed the state's reliance on maritime commerce and industry. Fortunately for the state economy, in 1814 an inventive engineer named Francis Cabot Lowell replicated an English-style power loom on the banks of the Charles River in Waltham, just upstream from Boston. It was the final machine Lowell and his partners required to create the nation's first fully automated textile factory. With it, Lowell singlehandedly jump-started America's fledgling Industrial Revolution to wind up supplying scores of mass-produced products for a growing nation. In the end, you'll find few other states offer such a rich and stirring panoply of Colonial and Revolutionary sites, as nearly every square mile of Massachusetts—studded with historic manors, taverns, meetinghouses, and museums—will prove.

A REGIONAL GAZETEER

▼▼▼

✦ THE HUB OF THE UNIVERSE: BOSTON AND CAMBRIDGE

In 1858 Dr. Oliver Wendell Holmes, author of *The Autocrat of the Breakfast-Table,* called **Boston** "the hub of the solar system"; social inflation, however, soon raised the ante to "hub of the universe." And for history buffs, Boston is certainly the hub of any Massachusetts explorations. If you have even a passing acquaintance with American history, you'll find plenty of familiar sights in Boston, one of the early settlements in the Massachusetts Bay Colony and a key player in the events leading up to the American Revolution. You can stand at the spot where colonials and British soldiers faced off in what became known as the Boston Massacre. You can sit in the Old State House where patriot leaders resisted the tax on tea and then head for the harbor where crates of the British leaf were dumped overboard. You can visit the 17th-century home of silversmith Paul Revere and the nearby Old North Church—of "one if by land, two if by sea" fame—where Revere began his ride to warn the minutemen that the British redcoats were marching on Lexington and Concord. Or you can climb to the top of the Bunker Hill Monument, site of an early Revolutionary battle, or head for Dorchester Heights where the colonists finally drove the British from Boston. Although it is mostly a 19th-century city, Boston is studded with Revolutionary-era historic houses, burying grounds, churches, and Colonial-era art, and many of its attractions are linked by the 2½ mi Freedom Trail. Boston's compact downtown, narrow and irregular 17th-century streets, and old-world architecture make it a genuine pleasure to traipse around on foot. Attractions not within easy walking distance are readily accessible by public transit, including ferries that shuttle around the city's busy inner harbor. Across the Charles River, and connected to downtown Boston by subway, is **Cambridge.** Like neighboring Boston, Cambridge was an important community in the years leading up to the American Revolution. A number of Tory sympathizers built elegant mansions here along Brattle Street, a tony road that was known as "Tory Row." Cambridge is home to the nation's first college—Harvard—and the city has literary roots as well. Henry Wadsworth Longfellow, famous in these parts for his poem about Paul Revere's Midnight Ride, lived here for many years; his Cambridge home is now a National Historic Site. Nine miles north of Boston is **Saugus,** site of a famed 18th-century ironworks. *Towns listed: Boston, Cambridge, Saugus.*

✦ "LET IT BEGIN HERE": LEXINGTON AND CONCORD

The now-suburban communities of Lexington and Concord, northwest of Boston, are forever etched into America's memory as the places where Colonial minutemen faced off against British soldiers in the first battles of the American Revolution. In **Lexington,** you can walk across the Battle Green and visit taverns and Colonial-era homes where John Adams and Paul Revere may really have slept. In nearby **Concord,** the Old North Bridge claims "the shot heard 'round the world." Many of the spots where these battles were fought and where other events of the era took place are now part of the Minute Man National Historic Park, with two visitor centers and a variety of special programs to help interpret these early revolutionary times. To the west lies **Sudbury,** home to that beloved Colonial icon Longfellow's Wayside Inn. *Towns listed: Concord, Lexington, Sudbury.*

✦ PURITANS, WITCHES, AND MILLIONAIRES: SALEM AND THE NORTH SHORE

The coastal inlets and protected harbors along the Atlantic shores north of Boston became some of the first town sites of the 17th-century Puritans, in the years before they founded Boston. The region's unparalleled number of surviving First Period dwellings—perhaps due to the Yankee "waste not, want not" credo—has earned it recognition as a National Heritage Area. The North Shore, as this area is known, became a center for maritime trade in the 1700s, a legacy that remains in the sea captains' homes and maritime museums that dot the shore. Here you'll discover such historic treasures as **Salem**—the "Witch City"; **Marblehead,** still reminiscent of Cornish fishing villages; **Gloucester,** the oldest seaport in America; **Newbury-**

port, with its redbrick center and rows of clapboard Federal mansions; and **Ipswich,** site of Castle Hill Mansion and a notable district of 17th-century houses. *Towns listed: Gloucester, Ipswich, Marblehead, Newburyport, Salem.*

✦ JOHN ADAMS COUNTRY: PLYMOUTH, QUINCY,
AND THE SOUTH SHORE

In December 1620 the *Mayflower* anchored at **Plymouth** Harbor, and its voyagers came ashore to found the first permanent European settlement north of Virginia. Although half of these original settlers, now known as the Pilgrims, died during their first winter in the New World, the Colony eventually stabilized and grew. Today, the town's star attraction, a living history museum known as Plimoth Plantation, vividly re-creates the life of these 17th-century Pilgrims. You can also visit a replica of the *Mayflower* as well as historic homes and small museums that illustrate what this remote outpost would have been like in the 1600s. Fifteen miles south, **Cape Cod** is the king of New England summer resorts. But the town of **Sandwich,** close to the mainland, is like a snapshot in time. This 1637 settlement is the Cape's oldest town, and even today this pretty village recalls the Colonial era. Closer to Boston, **Quincy** bills itself at the "City of Presidents" because it was the home of two: John Adams, the second president, and his son, John Quincy Adams, who was the sixth. Their birthplaces, their family home, and their tombs are all open to visitors as part of the Adams National Historical Park. Nearby **Hingham** is a must-do, thanks to three gorgeous buildings dating back to the 17th and 18th centuries: the Old Ship Meetinghouse, the Old Ordinary, and the Old Derby Academy. *Towns listed: Hingham, Plymouth, Quincy, Sandwich.*

✦ THE MASSACHUSETTS FRONTIER: FROM THE BERKSHIRES
TO THE PIONEER VALLEY

West of the almost sea-level basin occupied by Greater Boston is the undulating upland plateau of central Massachusetts. Most of this region was cleared for agricultural use by the early 19th century, and in **Sturbridge** an interpretive historic village takes you back to a central Massachusetts settlement of the early 1800s. Farther west, the Pioneer Valley is the state's farm country. Lured by this fertile land, pioneers headed west from the coastal towns in the 1700s and established settlements throughout the region. One such community is now an elaborately restored living history museum, known as Historic **Deerfield.** In Colonial times, the western end of the Massachusetts Bay Colony, extending into the rolling hills of the Berkshires, was its rough-and-ready frontier, a place defined by relations between the settlers and the Native American population. While many of the region's notable attractions today—a summer cornucopia of live music, dance, and theater, as well as Victorian mansions converted to inns and museums—date to more recent eras, Colonial history is still alive in such towns as **Sheffield** (the oldest in the Berkshires) and Norman Rockwellian **Stockbridge.** Also in the Berkshires, near **Pittsfield,** is Hancock Shaker Village, a former religious community where its occupants' devotion to creating "worldly perfection" led to a variety of modern innovations, now on view in this preserved settlement. *Towns listed: Deerfield, Pittsfield, Sheffield, Stockbridge, Sturbridge.*

Merchant Ships, Fishing Skiffs, and the Country's First Millionaires

A DRIVING TOUR FROM SALEM TO NEWBURYPORT

▾▾▾

Distance: 60 mi (one-way)   **Time:** 3 days (2 nights)
Breaks: Overnight stops in Marblehead or Newburyport

The area referred to as the North Shore stretches along the coast from Boston to the New Hampshire border. It is here in the towns of Salem, Marblehead, Gloucester, and Newburyport that the country's fishing and overseas trading industries developed in the 17th and early 18th centuries. Any of these towns can be easily visited as a day trip from Boston, but this tour allows exploration in all four towns over several days. While some North Shore attractions are open year-round, many close between mid-October and May, and the winter months can be quite chilly and raw. Summer and early fall are prime time in these seaside towns.

Start in **Salem** (from Boston, take I–93 north to I–95 north to Route 128 north; exit at Route 114 and continue to Salem—the latter stretch of this route is rather confusing, so watch carefully for the signs to the Salem Historic District). Your first stop is the National Park Service Regional Visitor Center on New Liberty Street, where you can watch a short film about the area and get information from the rangers on duty. A short walk from the Visitor Center is the Peabody Essex Museum, filled with exhibits on maritime art and history, with a special emphasis on the Asian export trade. The museum also offers tours of several historic houses. Next, head for the waterfront—it's a pleasant walk or a short drive—and visit the Salem Maritime National Historic Site, near Derby Wharf, to learn more about Salem's role as a major Colonial-era seaport; you can also tour Derby House, home of the country's first millionaire. Farther down Derby Street is the must-see House of the Seven Gables, immortalized in Nathaniel Hawthorne's classic novel of the same name. Make a detour to the nearby village of Danvers—where the witch craze really began—to visit the Rebecca Nurse Homestead, home of one of the unfairly accused (and executed) "witches." Here, too, is the famously gorgeous Derby Summer House, a masterpiece of the Federal style.

From Salem, it's only 4 mi east along Route 114 to **Marblehead,** a lovely seaside village with plenty of options for dining and lodging, including the 1729 Harbor Light Inn. While in Marblehead, take a peek into Abbot Hall to see the noteworthy painting, *The Spirit of '76,* and nearby is the Jeremiah Lee Mansion, the high-style home of a shipowner who was one of the richest people in the Colonies. To continue north to **Gloucester,** return to Salem, follow Route 114 back to Route 128, and take 128 north; it's about 20 mi from Salem to Gloucester. Or for a more scenic drive, head north from Salem on Route 1A. When you cross the bridge into Beverly, bear right onto Cabot Street and right again onto Route 127, which meanders north along the coast through Beverly, Manchester, and finally into Gloucester. In Gloucester, the Cape Ann Historical Museum is worth a stop for its collections of regional art and maritime artifacts, as is the nearby Sargent House Museum, which was home to one of America's first feminist writers. Spend the night nearby in Rockport.

The next day, take another scenic drive. From Gloucester follow Route 133 west to **Ipswich,** where several houses, including the abode of John Whipple, are magnificently frozen in amber from the 17th century. Then continue on Route 1A north, which becomes High Street in **Newburyport.** You can stop en route to tour the 1690 Spencer-Peirce-Little Farm or the 1654 Coffin House. After a lunch break in downtown Newburyport—its attractively restored commercial district is a pleasant place for a stroll—visit the maritime history exhibits at the Custom House Maritime Museum or follow Merrimac Street northwest into Amesbury to tour Lowell's Boat Shop, the nation's oldest continuous boat-building. Or you could simply stroll along Newburyport's waterfront and contemplate the current maritime scene.

The Massachusetts Frontier

A DRIVING TOUR FROM SHEFFIELD TO DEERFIELD

▼▼▼

Distance: 100 mi (one-way)   **Time:** 3–4 days (2–3 nights)
Breaks: Overnight stops in Stockbridge and Deerfield

You may not think of the "Wild West" when you think of Massachusetts, but in the 1700s, Massachusetts' western regions were pioneer country, where life was hard and encounters— friendly or not—between the settlers and the Native Americans were frequent. This tour begins in the state's southwest corner and travels through the Berkshires and the Pioneer Valley. Summer or fall are the best times to visit here, when the weather is warm and everything is open; spring is pleasant but can sometimes be cool and rainy. **Sheffield,** on U.S. 7 just north of the Connecticut line, is the Berkshires' oldest town. A good place to start a tour is at the Dan Raymond House/Sheffield Historical Society, a 1775 house whose furnishings illustrate 17th-century life in the Berkshires. Five miles south of Sheffield in the village of Ashley Falls is the Colonel Ashley House, one of the area's oldest homes, which played a role in several late 18th-century events: the Sheffield Declaration, a precursor to the Declaration of Independence, was drafted here, and an Ashley family slave became the first to sue for her freedom under the Massachusetts Constitution of 1780.

Follow U.S. 7 north to the charming village of **Stockbridge,** where two more historic homes reflect Colonial-era events. The Mission House belonged to Rev. John Sergeant, an early settler who aimed to convert the local Native Americans to Christianity; behind the house is a small museum about Native American life in the region. Almost across the street is Merwin House, an 1820s Federal-style brick home that was among the first in town to be turned into a summer vacation house, after the area became popular with tranquillity-seeking New Yorkers. If you're in search of your own tranquillity, stay the night at one of the historic inns nearby.

Get an early start, so you have most of the day to tour the Hancock Shaker Village, near **Pittsfield,** a living-history museum on the site of a Shaker religious community that was active from 1803 until the mid-1900s. To reach the village from Stockbridge, the more scenic route is to take Route 102 west to Route 41 north; you can also take U.S. 7 north to Pittsfield and then go west on U.S. 20. The village is west of Pittsfield (about 15 mi north of Stockbridge), near the intersection of U.S. 20 and Route 41. Then go east to **Deerfield** to spend the night at the historic Deerfield Inn. From Pittsfield, take Route 9 east, then turn north in Goshen on Route 112 and around Ashfield head east again on Route 116; when you hit U.S. 5, take it north to Deerfield. As you approach the Deerfield area, U.S. 5/Route 10 leads south to the Deerfield Inn. Try to do the Route 2 drive while it's still daylight, since this winding road through the mountains is one of the state's prettiest. A tour of Historic Deerfield, where 14 restored buildings have been converted into a walk-through interpretive museum of Colonial and post-Colonial life, can occupy several hours, though tickets to the village are good for two consecutive days. Save time for a peek into the Memorial Hall Museum, or if you're traveling with kids, visit the Children's Museum at the Indian House Memorial, which offers children's programs about Native American and Colonial life.

BOSTON

▼▼

With its narrow streets landmarked by important Colonial-era homes and monuments recalling the fledgling American republic's struggle for independence, Boston is a history buff's dream, offering peeks into the past around every corner. Its English Puritan founders, who established the city back in 1630, were attracted to the land because it was originally surrounded on nearly all sides by water, making it easy to defend. A deepwater harbor at its front door and a river at its back also made the town a natural choice for the Colonial capital, since 17th-century transportation and communication were largely dependent on boats. For its first 150 years, Boston was the leading Colonial port in North America, its wharves crowded with sailing vessels bound to and from every continent on the globe.

The political and economic heart of the Massachusetts Bay Colony, Boston was a lead actor in the events leading up to the American Revolution. It was the place where Colonial blood was spilled in an early skirmish between colonists and British soldiers, in what became known as the Boston Massacre. Where tea, too, was spilled—into the harbor—to protest British taxation. Where Paul Revere's ride began, alerting the colonists that British troops were marching on Lexington and Concord. And where many other names from the history books—

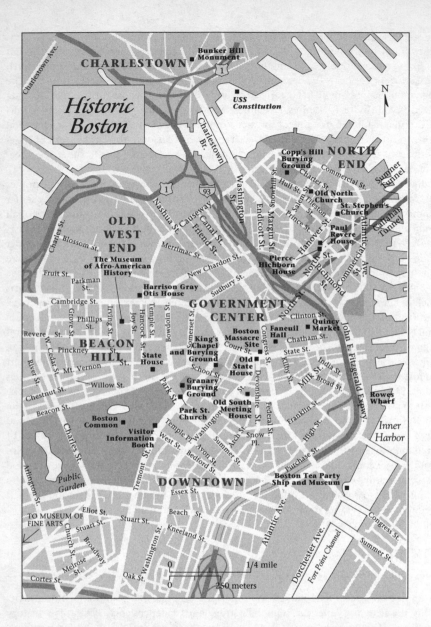

Historic Boston

from politicians John Adams, John Hancock, Samuel Adams, and Benjamin Franklin; to early iconoclasts Anne Hutchinson and Mary Dyer; to artists and architects Charles Bulfinch, Gilbert Stuart, and John Singleton Copley—all lived and walked the same serpentine streets that visitors and residents walk today.

Boston is a city of firsts. In 1634, the country's first public park—the still-green Boston Common—was established. The first public school in America opened in Boston in 1635. In 1652, the first American coin was produced here. The country's first newspaper, the *Boston News-Letter,* began publishing in 1704. Early vaccines against the deadly smallpox disease were developed here in 1721. The nation's first commercial bank, the Massachusetts Bank, began supplying capital to local merchants here in 1784, just after the Revolution. And that's just before the 18th century. This history—of politics and the arts, of education and innovation, indeed of the very foundations of the American Republic—is very much a part of present-day Boston. And as you walk these narrow streets and seek out these all-American landmarks, you'll discover history, legends, and more around every corner. *Contact Greater Boston Convention and Visitors Bureau | 2 Copley Pl., Suite 105, Boston 02116 | 617/536–4100 or 888/733–2678 | www.bostonusa.com. Boston Common Visitor Information Center | 147 Tremont St. | 800/888–5515. Boston National Historical Park Visitor Center | 15 State St., Boston 02109 | 617/242–5642 | www.nps.gov/bost.*

✦ NEIGHBORHOODS

Boston is a fairly compact city, and within the city center, it's much easier to navigate the narrow, congested streets on foot—as the Colonials might have—than to burden yourself with the modern automobile. The majority of Boston's 18th- and 19th-century attractions are concentrated in the following neighborhoods, most within or quite close to the city center.

Beacon Hill: A delightful maze of cobblestoned streets with gas lanterns, redbrick sidewalks, and time-burnished town houses, the area came to be known as Beacon Hill after citizens erected a mast holding a bucket of tar, which could be set afire to warn of enemy approach. The south slope overlooking Boston Common was settled by Boston's elite, including John Hancock and Mayor Harrison Gray Otis. The north slope was home to Boston's free African-American community and is part of the Black Heritage Trail. **Charlestown:** Charlestown was settled in 1629, making it a year older than Boston. Charlestown was once home to an active Navy Yard, which is now a National Historical Park, and to the oldest commissioned warship in the U.S. Navy, "Old Ironsides." Also in Charlestown is the Bunker Hill Monument, which commemorates one of the first major battles of the American Revolution. **Fenway:** A late 19th-century neighborhood, this is home to Boston's Museum of Fine Arts, where one of its many outstanding collections is devoted to Early American paintings and decorative arts. **Downtown and the Financial District:** Since the 18th century, Boston's financial district has been a birthplace of invention, innovation, and financial services. The Boston Stock Exchange, the third oldest in the country, was founded here in 1834. **Government Center:** Although this area is dominated by bleakly modern office buildings, including Boston City Hall, it's also home to two of Boston's most popular historic sights: Faneuil Hall and the three former warehouses turned food courts, Quincy Market (aka Faneuil Hall Marketplace). **North End:** The North End is Boston's oldest residential neighborhood and is remembered for its most famous residential house—that of Paul Revere—and the role the Old North Church played in the American Revolution.

Boston African American National Historic Site/Black Heritage Trail. Beginning in the early 1800s and continuing through the end of the 19th century, the north side of Beacon Hill was home to a vibrant community of free blacks—more than 8,000 at its peak—who built houses, schools, and churches that stand to this day. Fourteen of these sites are linked as the Black Heritage Trail, a 1½-mi self-guiding walking tour; brochures are available at the Museum of Afro-American History or the Boston National Historical Park Visitor Center. National Park Service rangers also give tours of the Trail daily from Memorial Day through Labor Day (and by appointment the rest of the year) at 10 AM, noon, and 2 PM, starting from the corner of Beacon and Park streets in the Boston Common. All but two buildings on the Trail are private residences, but the walk gives you a flavor of the era. | Beacon Hill | 617/725–0022 | www.nps.gov/boaf.

Boston Common. Nothing is more central to Boston than the Common, the oldest public park in the United States and undoubtedly the oldest of the town commons around which New England settlements were traditionally arranged. Dating from 1634, it's nearly as old as the city around it. Its roughly 50 acres were originally communal grazing land, used for military exercises and public executions (cows were banned in 1830). | Bounded by Tremont, Boylston, Charles, Beacon, and Park Sts. | www.cityofboston.gov/parks.

Central Burying Ground. This cemetery was established in 1756 to reduce crowding in the Copp's Hill, Granary, and King's Chapel burying grounds. However, it was considered less desirable than these cemeteries, because it was farther from the town center. It's the final resting place of Tories and Patriots alike, as well as many British casualties of the Battle of Bunker Hill. Gilbert Stuart, the portraitist best known for his likenesses of George and Martha Washington, is buried here; he died in 1828. | Boylston St. near Tremont St.

Boston Massacre Site. Tensions between colonists and British soldiers escalated throughout the 1760s, and in 1768, regiments of soldiers were sent to Boston to enforce the unpopular customs laws. These tensions erupted into violence on the evening of March 5, 1770, when nine British soldiers fired in panic on a taunting mob of more than 75 Bostonians. During this incident, which became known as the Boston Massacre, five townsmen died, including African-American sailor and runaway slave Crispus Attucks. In the legal action that followed, the defense of the accused soldiers was undertaken by John Adams and Josiah Quincy, both of whom vehemently opposed British oppression but were devoted to the principle of fair trial. All but two of the nine regulars charged were acquitted; the others were branded on the hand for the crime of manslaughter. A circle of cobblestones—on a traffic island in front of the Old State House—marks the Massacre site. | State and Devonshire Sts., on the traffic island.

Boston National Historical Park Visitor Center. A number of Boston historic sites are managed under the auspices of the National Park Service. Park Service rangers offer many interpretive programs throughout the year, particularly abbreviated guided walking tours of the Freedom Trail, the famous 2½-mi route weaving together 16 historic sites around Boston. These walking tours are generally offered from mid-April through November; call for seasonal schedules. The visitor center has brochures, maps, and other information, as well as rest rooms. | 15 State St. | 617/242–5642 | www.nps.gov/bost | Free | Daily 9–5.

Boston Tea Party Ship and Museum. Ever wonder why Americans drink coffee and not tea every morning? It all goes back to the Tea Act and the fact that tea became virtually unpatriotic to drink during the War of Independence. In May 1773, the British Parliament passed the Tea Act, which enabled the British East India Company to sell its tea in the American Colonies directly, bypassing American merchants. Although the act potentially meant lower tea prices, colonists feared that this preferential treatment to a British company would lead to monopolies not only on tea but on other goods, ultimately putting the colonists further under the dominion of the British crown. On November 27, 1773, three ships from the East India Co.—the *Dartmouth, Eleanor* and the *Beaver*—docked in Boston Harbor, inciting crowds to urge the ship captains to return to England, a protest strategy that had worked in New York and other ports. This time, however, Massachusetts Governor Thomas Hutchinson refused to allow the ships to leave the harbor without unloading their cargo. Bostonians then assembled at Old South Meeting House for several mass meetings to debate the crisis, but at the December 16 assembly, Samuel Adams declared, "This meeting can do nothing more to save the country." A band of more than 100 colonists and Sons of Liberty headed for the waterfront, disguised as Mohawk Indians, and bearing axes and tommyhawks. From the South Meeting House, they headed towards Griffin's Wharf, boarded the tea ships, cracked open the crates, and proceeded to make Boston Harbor into a large teapot. By nine PM, the Sons of Liberty had emptied 342 crates of tea overboard. Today, the Tea Party museum, on the waterfront at Fort Point Channel, is located on the *Beaver II*, a reconstruction of one of the three vessels. Unfortunately, the ship and museum are closed for renovations until spring 2004. At that time, once again, all guests may be pressed into donning feathers and war paint to reenact the tea drop every half hour. | Congress St. Bridge (closed for repairs until spring 2004; call before visiting) | 617/269–7150 | www.bostonteapartyship.com.

Bunker Hill Monument. Three classic errors surround this famous monument. First, the Battle of Bunker Hill was actually fought on Breed's Hill, which is where the monument sits today. (The real Bunker Hill is about ½ mi to the north of the monument; it's slightly taller than Breed's Hill). Bunker was the original planned locale for the battle and for that reason its name stuck—back then, the troops themselves originally called it the Battle of Charlestown). Second, although the battle is generally considered a Colonial success, the Americans lost. It was a Pyrrhic victory for the British redcoats, who sacrificed nearly half of their 2,200 men; American casualties numbered 400–600. And third: the famous war cry, "Don't fire until you see the whites of their eyes," may never have been uttered by American Colonel William Prescott or General Israel Putnam, but if either one did shout it, he was quoting an old Prussian command made necessary by the notorious inaccuracy of the musket. No matter. The Americans did employ a deadly delayed-action strategy on June 17, 1775, and conclusively proved themselves worthy fighters, capable of defeating the forces of the British Empire. Among the dead were the brilliant young American doctor and political activist Joseph Warren, recently commissioned as a major general but fighting as a private, and the British Major John Pitcairn, who two months before had led the Redcoats into Lexington. Pitcairn is believed to be buried in the crypt of the Old North Church. The beloved Warren, one of the Colony's foremost patriots, sent his friend Paul Revere off on his midnight ride. After his death his body lay in a shallow grave on Breed's Hill until the British evacuated Boston in 1776, when his remains were disinterred and buried ceremoniously in the Granary. His grave was moved by his descendants several more times, before he reached his final resting place, Forest Hills Cemetery, in the Jamaica Plain section of Boston. And how was his body originally identified? Warren's "dentist," Revere, recognized his own handiwork: the silver springs in Warren's false teeth.

In 1823, the committee formed to construct a monument on the Breed's Hill site of the battle chose the form of an Egyptian obelisk. Architect Solomon Willard designed a 221-ft-tall obelisk; due to a nagging lack of funds, it wasn't dedicated until 1843. The monument's zenith is reached by a flight of 294 steps. There is no elevator, but the views from the observatory are worth the effort of the arduous climb. A statue of Colonel Prescott stands guard at the base. In the lodge at the base, dioramas tell the story of the battle, and ranger programs are conducted regularly. | Monument Sq., Charlestown | 617/242–5641 | www.nps. gov/bost/bunker_hill.htm | Free | Lodge daily 9–5; monument daily 9–4:30.

Chestnut Street. Boston architect Charles Bulfinch (1763–1844) designed several of the delicate, graceful homes on this Beacon Hill street, including Nos. 13, 15, and 17, which Hepzibah Swam commissioned in the early 1800s as dowry gifts for her three daughters. Complete with Adam-style entrances, marble columns, and recessed arches, they are Chestnut Street at its most beautiful. | Beacon Hill.

Copp's Hill Burying Ground. An ancient and melancholy air hovers like a fine mist over this Colonial-era burial ground. The North End graveyard incorporates four cemeteries established between 1660 and 1819. Near the Charter Street gate is the tomb of the Mather family, the dynasty of church divines (Cotton and Increase were the most famous sons) who held sway in Boston during the heyday of the old theocracy. Also buried here is Robert Newman, who crept into the steeple of the Old North Church to hang the lanterns warning of the British attack the night of Paul Revere's ride. Look for the tombstone of Captain Daniel Malcolm; it is pockmarked with musket-ball fire from British soldiers, who used the stones for target practice. | Between Hull and Snowhill Sts. | www.cityofboston.gov/parks | Free | Apr.–Nov., daily 9–5; Dec.–Mar., daily 9–dusk.

Dorchester Heights Monument. In 1776, Dorchester Heights commanded a clear view of central Boston, where the British had been under siege since the preceding year. Here George Washington set up the cannons that Henry Knox, a Boston bookseller turned soldier, and later secretary of war, had hauled through the wilderness after their capture at Fort Ticonderoga. The artillery did its job of intimidation, and the British troops left Boston, never to return. The views from the top of the monument, a Georgian Revival white marble tower, stretch from the Blue Hills to the Harbor Islands. | Thomas Park near G St. | 617/242–5642 | Free | Grounds with interpretive plaques, daily. Monument, May–Labor Day, Wed. 4–8, weekends 10–4.

Faneuil Hall. In some ways Faneuil Hall is a local Ark of the Covenant; a considerable part of Boston's spirit resides here. Learning to pronounce its name is the first task of any newcomer—say "Fan'l" or "*Fan*-yuhl." Like other Boston landmarks, Faneuil Hall has evolved over many years. It was erected in 1742, the gift of wealthy merchant Peter Faneuil, who wanted the hall to serve as both a place for town meetings and a public market. It burned in 1761 and was immediately reconstructed according to the original plan of its designer, the Scottish portrait painter John Smibert. In 1763 the political leader James Otis helped inaugurate the era that culminated in American independence when he dedicated the rebuilt hall to the cause of liberty. In 1772 Samuel Adams stood here and first suggested that Massachusetts and the other Colonies organize a Committee of Correspondence to maintain semiclandestine lines of communication in the face of hardening British repression.

Faneuil Hall was substantially enlarged and remodeled in 1805 according to a Greek Revival design of the noted architect Charles Bulfinch; this is the building you see today. Its purposes remain the same: the balconied Great Hall is available to citizens' groups on presentation of a request signed by a required number of responsible parties; it also plays host to regular concerts. Inside Faneuil Hall are the mural *Webster's Reply to Hayne,* Gilbert Stuart's portrait of Washington at Dorchester Heights, and dozens of other paintings of famous Americans. Faneuil Hall has always sat in the middle of Boston's main marketplace: when such men as Andrew Jackson and Daniel Webster debated the future of the Republic here, the fragrances of bacon and snuff—sold by merchants in Quincy Market across the road—greeted their noses. Brochures about Faneuil Hall's history, distributed by the National Park Service, make light-hearted references to the ongoing commercialism nearby by reprinting a 1958 ditty by Francis Hatch: "Here orators in ages past / Have mounted their attack / Undaunted by the proximity / Of sausage on the rack." Note the gold-plated weather vane atop the cupola is in the shape of a grasshopper. One apocryphal story has it that Sir Thomas Gresham—founder of London's Royal Exchange—had been discovered in 1519 as a foundling babe by children chasing grasshoppers in a field. He later placed a gilded metal version of the insect over the exchange to commemorate his salvation. Years later Peter Faneuil saw the critter, liked it (it's the traditional symbol of good luck), and had a model of the Royal Exchange's grasshopper mounted over Faneuil Hall. | Corner of Congress and North Sts. | 617/635–3105 | www.nps.gov/bost | Free | Daily 9–5.

Ancient and Honorable Artillery Company of Massachusetts. On Faneuil Hall's top floors are the headquarters and museum of the oldest militia in the Western Hemisphere (it was founded in 1638). Arms, uniforms, and other artifacts are on display. | 617/227–1638 | Free | Weekdays 9–3:30.

Freedom Trail. The Freedom Trail is much more than a 2½-mi route of historic sites. As an eager army of the curious discovers every year, it's a walk into history, to the events that exploded on the world during the Revolution. Its 16 way stations allow you to reach out and touch the very wellsprings of U.S. civilization. If you want an in-depth treatment, pick up a copy of the 80-page *Complete Guide to Boston's Freedom Trail,* by Charles Bahne. It intersperses Trail directions with copious quotes from original sources, charming line drawings, and helpful maps. It's available at the Greater Boston Convention and Visitors Bureau on Tremont Street, which is where the Freedom Trail begins; at nearly all Freedom Trail sites with a gift shop; and at the National Park Service Visitor Center at 15 State Street. It really takes a full day to complete the entire route comfortably, and many visitors, particularly those with kids, may prefer to pick and choose among the attractions or break up the walk over two or three days. Perhaps some of its sights are more interesting than others, and perhaps it lacks the multimedia bells and whistles now becoming the norm at historic attractions. But that's what makes the Freedom Trail unique: it allows history to speak for itself.

Despite the labyrinthine quality to Boston's downtown streets, this walk is made easy: all you have to do is follow the red line, that is, the red bricks embedded in the pavement, which mark the route of the full Freedom Trail through the city. Begin at the corner of Beacon and Park streets, in front of the gold-domed **State House.** Follow the red line down the hill along Park Street to the 1809 **Park Street Church,** at the corner of Tremont Street, a center for the 19th-century abolition movement. Designed by Peter Banner, the church is distinguished by a 217-ft-tall steeple, an imitation of the needle-spired London works by Banner's fellow English church architect Christopher Wren. On Tremont Street next to the church is the **Granary Burying Ground,** one of Boston's 16 historic cemeteries and the final resting place for such notable figures as Samuel Adams, John Hancock, James Otis, and Paul Revere.

Continue to Tremont Street and **King's Chapel.** Its architect, Peter Harrison, was a prolific Colonial designer of royal governors' mansions and houses of worship, including Newport's historic Truro Synagogue. The red line takes a brief side trip to the chapel's burying ground, and then continues down School Street. Behind King's Chapel, in the first of School Street's two short blocks, is the ornate mansard-roof Old City Hall, in front of which stands a **statue of Benjamin Franklin.** Old Ben is commemorated here because he was born about a block away. On the sidewalk in front of him is a plaque honoring the **site of the first U.S. public school.** Although it has since moved elsewhere in the city, the 1635 Boston Latin School is still in operation as one of the most prestigious components of the Boston public school system. Resume walking down School Street to its intersection with Washington Street. There to the right is the attractive redbrick **Old South Meeting House,** built in 1729 and for many decades the largest building in Boston—it is famous as the site of the heated assembly that precipitated the Boston Tea Party in 1773. Follow the red line down Washington Street to the 1713 **Old State House,** on State Street next to the National Park Service Visitor Center. As Boston's oldest public building, it has an excellent and often overlooked museum inside. Opposite the front of the building, on its east side, notice the slightly raised cobblestone ring on the small traffic island. This marks the **site of the Boston Massacre,** one of the most incendiary events leading up to the American Revolution.

Turn back to the Old State House and note the balcony on the second floor, from which the Declaration of Independence was given its first public reading to cheering Bostonians, an event repeated every July 4. Continue on the red line across the busy intersection and down New Congress Street to the "Cradle of Liberty," **Faneuil Hall,** behind the statue of Sam Adams. The present 1763 building has hosted many famous orators from early patriots to John F. Kennedy. Leaving behind the colorful hubbub of Quincy Market's food courts and shops, behind Faneuil Hall, follow the red line until finally emerging in the historic North End. After a short stroll along restaurant-lined Hanover Street, turn right on Richmond Street and then left on North Street. On the left midway up the block facing cobbled North Square—actually a triangle—is the **Paul Revere House,** built around 1680. If the structure seems small now, consider how much smaller it would have been with a family of six children. Follow the red line back to Hanover Street, up three blocks, and left through the Paul Revere Mall, an irregular walled plaza better known to the neighborhood's Italian residents as the Prado. Towering over the back of the plaza is the famous **Old North Church,** whose role on the night before the outbreak of the American Revolution is immortalized in Longfellow's poem "Paul Revere's Ride." From the front of the church, head up Hull Street to **Copp's Hill Burying Ground,** the final resting place of many Colonial North End and Beacon Hill residents. Back on Hull Street, follow the red line downhill to Commercial Street and the Charlestown Bridge over the mouth of the Charles River. On the opposite side the line soon splits; turn left through City Square and the narrow Colonial streets of this historic neighborhood, zigzagging up the hill to the **Bunker Hill Monument.** Continue back down to the waterfront, staying to the left when the red line splits at the former militia training field, now a small park. After crossing Chelsea Street, enter the **Charlestown Navy Yard,** home to the world's oldest commissioned warship, the **U.S.S. *Constitution.*** The 1797 frigate salutes the "striking of the colors" with a shot from her cannon in the late afternoon. You can return to downtown by way of a short $1 harbor cruise aboard an MBTA commuter ferry from the Navy Yard's Pier 4. Return to the center of Boston using the ferry to Long Wharf and the

New England Aquarium. For Freedom Trail information, contact the **Boston National Histor-ical Park Visitor Center** | 15 State St. | 617/242–5642.

Granary Burying Ground. If you had found a resting place in this 1660 cemetery next to the Park Street Church, your neighbors would have been an impressive lot: among them patri-ots and politicians Samuel Adams, John Hancock, James Otis, and Paul Revere, along with Benjamin Franklin's parents, as well as the victims of the Boston Massacre. | Entrance on Tremont St. near Park St. | www.cityofboston.gov/parks | Dec.–Apr., daily 9–dusk; May–Nov., daily 9–5.

Harrison Gray Otis House. Built in 1796, this Federal-style house just beyond the north slope of Beacon Hill was designed by noted early American architect Charles Bulfinch for his friend Harrison Gray Otis, a wealthy local lawyer and real-estate speculator who served in Congress and eventually became mayor of Boston. Guided tours show off the opulent style that prevailed among Boston's affluent at the turn of the 19th century. The furnishings, textiles, wall coverings, and even the interior paint, specially mixed to match old samples, are faith-ful to the Federal period, circa 1790–1810. The dining room is set up as though Harry were about to come in and pour a glass of Madeira. But Otis lived here only four years before moving to more sumptuous digs, also designed by Bulfinch, higher up on Beacon Hill. | 141 Cambridge St. | 617/227–3956 | www.spnea.org | Guided tours $5 | Wed.–Sun., tours on the hr 11–4.

King's Chapel. Both somber and dramatic, King's Chapel looms over the corner of Tremont and School streets. The first chapel on this site was erected in 1688, when Sir Edmund Andros, the royal governor whose authority temporarily replaced the original Colonial charter, appropriated the land to establish an Anglican place of worship. This rankled the Puritans, who had left England to escape Anglicanism and had until then succeeded in keeping it out of the Colony. In the 1750s, construction began on the current Quincy-granite building, a fine example of Georgian architecture, which took five years to complete. Its distinctive shape, with a boxy protuberance above the front columns, wasn't achieved by design; for lack of funds, it was never topped with the steeple that architect Peter Harrison had planned. The pulpit, built in 1717 by Peter Vintoneau, is the oldest pulpit in continuous use on the same site in the United States. To the right of the main entrance is a special pew once reserved for condemned prisoners, who were trotted in to hear a sermon before being hanged on the Common. The chapel's bell is Paul Revere's largest and, in his judgment, his sweetest sound-ing. | 58 Tremont St., at School St. | 617/227–2155 | www.kings-chapel.org | Mid-Apr.–Nov., Mon. and Fri.–Sat. 10–4; Dec.–mid-Apr., Sat. 10–4.

King's Chapel Burying Ground. Legends linger in this oldest of the city's cemeteries, estab-lished in 1630, the same year that Boston itself was found. Glance at the handy map of famous grave sites (posted at the entrance) and take the path to the right from the entrance and then left by the chapel to the gravestone (1704) of Elizabeth Pain, the model for Hester Prynne in Nathaniel Hawthorne's *The Scarlet Letter*. Note the winged death's head on her stone. Also buried here is William Dawes, Jr., who, with Dr. Samuel Prescott, rode out to warn of the British invasion the night of Paul Revere's famous ride (due to Longfellow's stirring poem, Revere's the one who gets all the glory today). This is also the final resting place of John Winthrop, the first governor of Massachusetts Bay Colony and Mary Chilton Winslow, the first woman to step off the *Mayflower*. | 58 Tremont St., at School St. | 617/227–2155 | www. cityofboston.gov/parks | Mid-Apr.–mid-Sept., daily 9–5; mid-Sept.–mid-Apr., daily 9–dusk.

Museum of Afro-American History. Focusing on African-American contributions to New England, particularly during the period from the Colonial era through the 1800s, this museum includes two adjacent buildings on Beacon Hill—the Abiel Smith School and the African Meet-ing House. The museum in conjunction with the National Park Service offers tours of the Black Heritage Trail. | 46 Joy St., at Smith Ct. | 617/725–0022 | www.afroammuseum.org | $5 suggested donation | Late May–early Sept., daily 10–4; early Sept.–late May, Mon.-Sat. 10–4.

African Meeting House. Built in 1806 and centerpiece of Beacon Hill's African-American community, this is the oldest black church building still standing in the United States. It was constructed almost entirely with African-American labor, using funds raised in both the white and the black communities. The facade is an adaptation of a design for a town house published by the Boston architect Asher Benjamin. In 1832 the New England Anti-Slavery Society was formed here under the leadership of William Lloyd Garrison. For the fervent antislavery activism that started within its walls, it came to be known as the "Black Faneuil Hall." | 8 Smith Ct., off Joy St. | 617/725–0022 | www.afroammuseum.org | Free | Memorial Day–mid-Sept., daily 10–4; mid-Sept.–Memorial Day weekdays 10–4.

Museum of Fine Arts (MFA). This is one of the world's greatest repositories of American painting, sculpture, and decorative arts. Its acres of other world treasures make this a great palace of art, but American historians will particularly enjoy the 60 works by John Singleton Copley (1738–1815), Boston's—and Colonial America's—foremost portrait artist, including his *Paul Revere*. New England decorative arts are amply represented as well; rooms of period furniture show the progression of taste from the earliest Pilgrim pieces through the 18th-century triumphs of the Queen Anne, Hepplewhite, Sheraton, and Empire styles. To top it all off, the museum also houses silver teapots, sauceboats, and other tableware crafted by native son Paul Revere. | 465 Huntington Ave. | 617/267–9300 | www.mfa.org | $15; Wed. 4–9:45, free (donations accepted) | Entire museum Mon.–Tues., weekends 10–5:45, Wed.–Fri. 10–9:45. West Wing only Thurs.–Fri. 5–10. 1-hr tours available weekdays.

Old North Church. Standing at one end of the Paul Revere Mall is a church famous not only for being the oldest one in Boston (built in 1723) but for housing the two lanterns that glimmered from its steeple on the night of April 18, 1775. This is Christ Church, or the Old North, where Paul Revere and the young sexton Robert Newman managed that night to signal the departure by water of the British regulars to Lexington and Concord. Longfellow's poem aside, the lanterns were not a signal *to* Revere but *from* him to Charlestown across the harbor. Newman, carrying the lanterns, ascended the steeple (the original tower blew down in 1804 and was replaced; the present one was put up in 1954 after the replacement was destroyed in a hurricane), while Revere began his clandestine trip by boat across the Charles. Although William Price designed the structure after studying Christopher Wren's London churches, the Old North—which still has an active Episcopal congregation (including descendants of the Reveres)—is an impressive building in its own right. Inside, note the gallery and the graceful arrangement of pews (reserved in Colonial times for the families that rented them); the bust of George Washington, pronounced by the Marquis de Lafayette to be the truest likeness of the general he ever saw; the brass chandeliers, made in Amsterdam in 1700 and installed here in 1724; and the clock, the oldest still running in an American public building. The pews—No. 54 was the Revere family pew—are the highest in the United States due to the little charcoal-burning foot warmers (used to accommodate parishioners back when). Try to visit when changes are rung on the bells, after the 11 AM Sunday service; they bear the inscription, "We are the first ring of bells cast for the British Empire in North America." Every April 18, the raising of the lanterns in the church belfry is reenacted.

One of the most peculiar mementos in the annals of U.S. history is displayed in the small gift shop and museum next to the church. A glass container holds a vial of tea purportedly decanted from the boots of a participant in the notorious Boston tea-party fracas. Delightful souvenirs are for sale here, including parchment copies of Longfellow's 1863 poem, "Paul Revere's Ride." Behind the church is the Washington Memorial Garden, where volunteers cultivate a plot devoted to plants and flowers favored in the 18th century. | 193 Salem St. | 617/523–6676 | www.oldnorth.com | June–Oct., daily 9–6; Nov.–May, daily 9–5.

Old South Meeting House. Some of the fieriest town meetings that led to the Revolution were held in this 1729 brick building, culminating in the gathering of December 16, 1773, which was called by Samuel Adams to confront the crisis of three ships, laden with dutiable tea, anchored at Griffin's Wharf. The activists wanted the tea returned to England, and the governor would not permit it. To cries of "Boston Harbor a tea-pot tonight!" and John Hancock's "Let every man do what is right in his own eyes," the protesters poured out of the Old South, headed to the wharf with their waiting comrades, and dumped £18,000 worth of tea into the water. The exhibition "Voices of Protest" highlights Old South as a forum for free speech from Revolutionary days to the present, and the 20-minute audio program "If These Walls Could Speak" offers a reenactment of the major events that occurred here. Also on exhibit is a model of the city of Boston as it looked during the pre-Revolutionary days. The church suffered no small amount of indignity in the Revolution: its pews were ripped out by occupying British troops, and the interior was turned into a riding school. Aside from the windows and doors, the only original interior features surviving today are the tiered galleries above the main floor. | 310 Washington St. | 617/482–6439 | www.oldsouthmeetinghouse. org | $5 | Apr.–Oct., daily 9:30–5; Nov.–Mar., daily 10–4.

Old State House. This Colonial-era landmark has one of the most distinctive facades in Boston, with its State Street gable adorned by a brightly gilded lion and unicorn, symbols of British imperial power. The original figures were pulled down in 1776. For proof that bygones are bygones, consider not only the restoration of the sculptures in 1880 but also that Queen Elizabeth II was greeted by cheering crowds on July 4, 1976, when she stood on the Old State House balcony (from which the Declaration of Independence was first read in public in Boston and that overlooks the site of the Boston Massacre).

This was the seat of the Colonial government from 1713 until the Revolution, and after the evacuation of the British from Boston in 1776 it served the independent Commonwealth until its replacement on Beacon Hill was completed in 1798. John Hancock was inaugurated here as the first governor under the new state constitution. In the 1830s the Old State House served as Boston's City Hall. When demolition was threatened in 1880 because the real estate was so valuable, the Bostonian Society organized a restoration, after which the Old State House reopened with a permanent collection that traces Boston's Revolutionary War history and, on the second floor, changing exhibits. A comprehensive self-guiding audio tour gives a detailed round-up of the Massachusetts events that led up to the Revolution. | 206 Washington St. at the corner of State | 617/720–3290 | www.bostonhistory.org | $5 | Daily 9–5.

Park Street Church. This 1809 Congregational church, designed by English architect Peter Banner, stored gunpowder in its basement during the War of 1812, giving rise to the site's nickname, "Brimstone Corner." The country's oldest musical organization, the Handel & Haydn Society, was founded here in 1815, and Samuel Smith's hymn "America" was first sung here on July 4, 1831. | 1 Park St. | 617/523–3383 | www.parkstreet.org | Tours mid-June–Aug., Tues.–Sat. 9:30–3:30.

Paul Revere House. Stepping into Paul Revere's house takes you back 200 years—here are the hero's own saddlebags, toddy-warmer, and a pine cradle made from a molasses cask (Paul was papa to 16 children). Although he became forever immortalized for his famous horseback ride from Boston to Lexington in April 1775, warning the Colonial militiamen that the British soldiers were marching toward Concord, Paul Revere (1734–1818) was not a statesman or a military man. He earned his living as a silversmith and an engraver. He had a large family to support: eight children with his first wife, Sarah Orne, who died in childbirth, and eight more with his second wife, Rachel Walker (eleven of Revere's children survived infancy). Originally on the house's site was the parsonage of the Second Church of Boston, home to the Rev. Increase Mather, the Second Church's minister. Mather's house burned in the great fire of 1676, and the house that Revere was to occupy was built on its location about four years later, nearly 100 years before Revere's midnight ride through Middlesex County. Revere owned it from 1770 until 1800, although he lived there for only the first 10 years, renting it out the rest. The clapboard sheathing is a replacement, but 90% of the framework is original; note the Elizabethan-style overhang and leaded windowpanes. A few Revere furnish-

"Listen, My Children, and You Shall Hear"

This is a test: Paul Revere was (1) a patriot whose midnight ride helped ignite the American Revolution; (2) a part-time dentist; (3) a silversmith who crafted tea services; (4) a printer who engraved the first Massachusetts state currency; or (5) a talented metallurgist who cast cannons and bells. The only correct response is "all of the above." But there's more, much more, to this outsize Revolutionary hero—bell ringer for Old North Church, founder of the copper mills that still bear his name, and father of 16 children.

Although his life spanned eight decades (1734–1818), Revere is most famous for that one night, April 18, 1775, when he became America's most celebrated Pony Express rider. *"Listen, my children, and you shall hear / Of the midnight ride of Paul Revere"* are the opening lines of Henry Wadsworth Longfellow's poem, which placed the event at the center of American folklore. Longfellow may have been an effective evangelist for Revere, but he was an indifferent historian.

Revere wasn't the only midnight rider. As part of the system set in motion by Revere and William Dawes Jr., also dispatched from Boston, there were an unknown number of riders—at least several dozen—so that the capture of any one of them wouldn't keep the alarm from being sounded. It's also known that Revere never looked for the lantern signal from Charlestown. He told Robert Newman to hang two lanterns from Old North's belfry since the redcoats were on the move by water, but by that time, Revere was already being rowed across the Charles River to begin his famous ride.

Revere and Dawes had set out on separate routes but the same mission: to warn patriot leaders Samuel Adams and John Hancock that British regular troops were marching to arrest them, and alarm the countryside along the way. The riders didn't risk capture by shouting the news through the streets—and they never uttered the famous cry "The British are coming!," since Bostonians still considered themselves British—but instead went door to door, stopping at houses where other riders then carried the news to outlying villages and farms. When Revere arrived in Lexington a few minutes past midnight and approached the house where Adams and Hancock were lodged, a sentry challenged him, requesting that he not make so much noise. "Noise!" Revere replied. "You'll have noise enough before long. The regulars are coming out!"

Despite Longfellow's assertion, Revere never raised the alarm in Concord, for he was captured en route, along with Dawes and a third rider, both of whom escaped. Revere was held and questioned by the British patrol, and eventually released, without his horse, to walk back to Lexington in time to witness part of the battle on Lexington Green.

Poetic license aside, this tale has become part of the collective American spirit. Americans dote on hearing that Revere forgot his spurs, only to retrieve them by tying a note to his dog's collar, then awaiting its return with the spurs attached. The resourcefulness he showed in using a lady's petticoat to muffle the sounds of his oars while crossing the Charles is greatly appreciated. Little wonder that these tales—which may be less than historically accurate—resonate in the hearts and imagination of America's citizenry, as well as in Boston's streets on the third Monday of every April, Patriots' Day, when Revere's ride is reenacted—in daylight—to the cheers of thousands of onlookers.

ings are on display here, and just gazing at his silverwork—much more of which is displayed at the Museum of Fine Arts—brings the man alive. Special events are scheduled throughout the year, many designed with children in mind. During the first weekend in December, the staff dresses in period costume and serves up apple-cider cake and other Colonial-style goodies. From May through October, there's something going on every Saturday afternoon:

a silversmith or broommaker may be on hand, a hammer-dulcimer player could entertain, or the reenactment group the 10th Regiment of Foot—in full antique British regalia—might muster on the premises. And if you go to the house on Patriots' Day, chances are you'll bump into the Middlesex Fife and Drum Corps. The immediate neighborhood has Revere associations. The little park in North Square is named after Rachel Revere, his second wife, and the adjacent brick Pierce-Hichborn House once belonged to relatives of Revere. The garden connecting the Revere house and the Pierce-Hichborn House is planted with flowers and medicinal herbs favored in Revere's day. | 19 North Sq. | 617/523–2338 | www.paulreverehouse.org | $3; $4.50 with Pierce-Hichborn House | Jan.–Mar., Tues.–Sun. 9:30–4:15; Nov.–Dec. and first 2 wks of Apr., daily 9:30–4:15; mid-Apr.–Oct., daily 9:30–5:15.

Pierce-Hichborn House. One of the city's oldest brick buildings, this structure, adjacent to the Paul Revere House, was once owned by Nathaniel Hichborn, a boatbuilder and Revere's cousin. Built about 1711 for a glazier named Moses Pierce, the Pierce-Hichborn House is an example of early Georgian architecture. The home's symmetrical style was a radical change from the wood-frame Tudor buildings, like the Revere house, then common. Its four rooms are furnished with modest 18th-century furniture, providing a peek into typical middle-class life. | 29 North Sq. | 617/523–2338 | $3; $4.50 with Paul Revere House | Daily guided tours; call for schedule.

Quincy Market. Also known as Faneuil Hall Marketplace, this historic complex of market buildings consists of three block-long annexes: Quincy Market, North Market, and South Market, each 535 ft long and across a plaza from Faneuil Hall. The structures were designed in 1826 by Alexander Parris as part of a public-works project instituted by Boston's second mayor, Josiah Quincy, to alleviate the cramped public market on the first floor of Faneuil Hall. In the 1970s, the market buildings were restored and turned into one of Boston's most popular tourist attractions. Restaurants and shops now purvey all manner of goods, while quintessential Boston remains here only in Durgin-Park restaurant, opened in 1826 and known for its plain interior, surly waitresses, and large portions of traditional New England fare. | Bordered by Clinton, Commercial, and Chatham Sts. | 617/338–2323 | www.faneuilhallmarketplace.com | Mon.–Sat. 10–9, Sun. noon–6 (restaurants varying hrs).

St. Stephen's. This is the only Charles Bulfinch church still standing in Boston, and a stunning example of the Federal period. Built in 1804, it was first used as a Unitarian Church; since 1862 it has served a Roman Catholic parish. When the belfry was stripped during a major 1960s renovation, the original dome was found beneath a false cap; it was covered with sheet copper and held together with hand-wrought nails and later authenticated as being the work of Paul Revere. | 401 Hanover St. | 617/523–1230 | Daily 7:30–5.

State House. On July 4, 1795, the surviving fathers of the Revolution were on hand to enshrine the ideals of their new Commonwealth in a graceful seat of government designed by Charles Bulfinch. Governor Samuel Adams and Paul Revere laid the cornerstone; Revere would later roll the copper sheathing for the dome. Bulfinch's State House, which was completed in 1798, is one of the greatest works of Neoclassical architecture in America, so striking that it hardly suffers from having had appendages added in three directions by bureaucrats and lesser architects. The design is poised between Georgian and Federal; its finest features are the delicate Corinthian columns of the portico, the graceful pediment and window arches, and the vast yet visually weightless golden dome. Inside the State House are Doric Hall, with its statuary and portraits; the Hall of Flags, where an exhibit shows the battle flags from all the wars in which Massachusetts regiments have participated; the Great Hall, an open space used for state functions that houses 351 flags from the cities and towns of Massachusetts; the governor's office; and the chambers of the House and Senate. Despite its civic function, the building also holds its share of art. Perhaps the best known is the carved wooden *Sacred Cod*, mounted in the Old State House in 1784 as a symbol of the commonwealth's maritime wealth. It was moved, with much fanfare, to Bulfinch's structure in 1798. Tours of the State House, which last about 40–45 minutes, are free, but call in advance; school and civic groups sometimes occupy the available tour times. Note the two statues of American women that stand on the front lawn. One is of Anne Hutchinson, who challenged the religious hierarchy of the Massachusetts Bay Colony. She was excommunicated in 1638 and sentenced to banishment; after leaving the Colony she became one of the founders of Rhode Island. Her supporter, Mary Dyer, was also excommunicated; she later converted to the Quaker faith and was finally hanged for defending her beliefs. Her statue on the State House grounds overlooks the spot on the Boston Common where she mounted the gallows. | Beacon St. between Hancock and Bowdoin Sts. | 617/727–3676 | www.state.ma.us/sec/trs | Free | Tours weekdays 10–3:30. Call in advance.

U.S.S. Constitution. Better known as "Old Ironsides," the U.S.S. *Constitution* rides proudly at anchor in her berth at the Charlestown Navy Yard. The oldest commissioned ship in the U.S. fleet is a battlewagon of the old school, of the days of "wooden ships and iron men"— when she and her crew of 200 succeeded at the perilous task of asserting the sovereignty of an improbable new nation. Every July 4 and on certain other occasions she's towed out for a turnabout in Boston Harbor, the very place her keel was laid in 1797. The venerable craft was launched on October 21, 1797, as part of the nation's fledgling navy. Her hull was made of live oak, the toughest wood grown in North America; her bottom was sheathed in copper, provided by Paul Revere at a nominal cost. Her principal service was during Thomas Jefferson's campaign against the Barbary pirates, off the coast of North Africa, and in the War of 1812. In 42 engagements, her record was 42–0. The nickname "Old Ironsides" was acquired during the War of 1812, when shots from the British warship *Guerrière* appeared to bounce off her tough oaken hull. Today she continues, the oldest commissioned warship afloat in the world, to be a part of the U.S. Navy. The men and women who look after the *Constitution,* regular navy personnel, maintain a 24-hour watch. Sailors show visitors around the ship, guiding them to two of her three belowdecks, including the turrets where the desperate, difficult work of naval war was waged. Don't forget to visit the adjacent museum: one section takes you step by step through the *Constitution*'s most important battles, while old meets new in a video-game battle "fought" at the helm of a ship. You can talk a bus and subway out here, or opt for the Boston Harbor Cruise water shuttle from Long Wharf to Pier 4. | Charlestown Navy Yard, 55 Constitution Rd., Charlestown | 617/242–5670 | www. ussconstitution.navy.mil | Free | Apr.–Oct., daily 10–4; Nov.–Mar., Thu.–Sun., 10–4; tours on the half-hr 10:30–3:30.

Charlestown Navy Yard Visitors Information Center. At the entrance to the Charlestown Navy Yard, this National Park Service visitor center shows "Whites of Their Eyes," a multimedia presentation about the Battle of Bunker Hill, every half hour 9:30–4:30. | Charlestown Navy Yard, 55 Constitution Rd., Charlestown | 617/242–5601 | www.nps.gov/bost | Free | July–Aug., daily 9–6; rest of year, daily 9–5.

✦ ON THE CALENDAR: Mar. **Boston Massacre Ceremony.** On March 5, 1770, British soldiers killed five Bostonians in what became known as the Boston Massacre. This event is reenacted annually outside the Old State House. | 617/720–3290 | www.bostonhistory.org.

Apr. **Lantern Celebration.** A ceremony in the North End's Old North Church commemorates the hanging of the two lanterns on April 18, 1775, that alerted Paul Revere that British troops were crossing the Charles River en route to Lexington. The ceremony includes the reading of "Paul Revere's Ride" and the carrying of the lanterns to the steeple. | 193 Salem St. | 617/ 523–6676 | www.oldnorth.com | 3rd Sun. in Apr. at 8.

June **Bunker Hill Weekend.** On June 17, 1775, British regulars faced Colonial militiamen at the Battle of Bunker Hill. The British victory was hard-won: the Colonial militia proved worthy adversaries. This battle is commemorated with 18th-century manual of arms and musket firing demonstrations, and with a parade that ends at the Bunker Hill Monument. | Charlestown Navy Yard, Charlestown | 617/242–5601 | www.nps.gov/bost.

July **Harborfest.** Boston celebrates Independence Day with an entire week of special events, from historic reenactments, to a public reading of the Declaration of Independence, to an annual Fourth of July concert with the Boston Symphony Orchestra that culminates in a dramatic fireworks display. | 617/227–1528 | www.bostonharborfest.com.

July–Oct. **Paul Revere Tonight.** David Conner plays Paul Revere at the Old North Church in the North End. At this event, Revere tells the stories of his life in Boston before and during the revolution and talks about the Old North Church and his famous midnight ride. | Old North Church, 193 Salem St. | 617/523–6676 | www.oldnorth.com | $12 | Thurs. and Fri. at 8 PM.

HISTORIC DINING AND LODGING

Durgin-Park. "Established before you were born"—that's the motto of this local institution that's been dishing up square meals of New England classics since 1826, in a come-as-you-are atmosphere of long, communal tables and famously no-nonsense waitstaff. Try the Yankee pot roast. | 340 Faneuil Hall Marketplace. North Market Bldg. | 617/227–2038 | $7–$25 | AE, D, DC, MC, V.

Ye Olde Union Oyster House. Billing itself as America's oldest continuously operating restaurant, this 1826 seafood house near Faneuil Hall is full of tourists and true-blue Boston accents. The raw bar is a pleasant spot to stop for a drink and, of course, some oysters. The rest of the menu runs to basic New England fried, baked, or broiled fish. | 41 Union St. | 617/227–2750 | $17–$30 | AE, D, DC, MC, V.

Warren Tavern. Legend has it that Paul Revere really did drink at this 1780 tavern, not far from the Bunker Hill Monument. It looks old and Colonial, with a menu of basic American fare. | 2 Pleasant St., Charlestown | 617/241–8142 | www.warrentavern.com | $7–$15 | AE, D, MC, V.

Harborside Inn. Created in a 19th-century former mercantile warehouse, this small, stylish inn in the Financial District near Faneuil Hall has exposed brick walls, hardwood floors, Oriental rugs, original story-high windows, and an eight-floor skylit atrium. Restaurant, complimentary breakfast. | 185 State St. | 617/723–7500 | fax 617/670–2010 | www.hagopianhotels.com | 54 rooms | $165–$210 | AE, D, DC, MC, V.

John Jeffries House. Dr. John Jeffries cofounded the Massachusetts Eye and Ear Infirmary in 1824, and this Beacon Hill inn that bears his name was constructed in the early 1900s as a residence for nurses at that institution. Many of the rooms, furnished with Colonial- and Victorian-style pieces, are tiny, but the suites are a good value. The parlor has a spectacular view of the Charles River. Complimentary breakfast. | 14 David G. Mugar Way | 617/367–1866 | fax 617/742–0313 | www.johnjeffrieshouse.com | 46 rooms | $95–$175 | AE, D, DC, MC, V.

CAMBRIDGE

▼▼▼

Cambridge was settled in 1630, when the Puritan leader John Winthrop chose this meadowland as the site of a carefully planned, stockaded village he named Newtowne. Eight years later the town was renamed in honor of the university in England at which most Puritan leaders had been educated. In 1636, the Massachusetts Bay Colony established the country's first college here, which was later named after one of its first benefactors, John Harvard. That original college, now Harvard University, has grown into one of the most recognized names in higher education. In the 1770s, Cambridge's mansion-lined Brattle Street was dubbed Tory Row, because several of its elegant homes were owned by staunch supporters of King George III. Poet Henry Wadsworth Longfellow (1807–82), known for such works as "Paul Revere's Ride," later lived on Brattle Street for more than 40 years. His home is open to the public as the Longfellow National Historic Site, and he is buried nearby in Mt. Auburn Cemetery. Cambridge's part in the Revolutionary War began in 1775, following the April battles at Lexington and Concord. Militias began to assemble on Cambridge Common (on the edge of Harvard Square, it has been a park since the 1630s), and in July, General George Washington arrived here to assume command of the Continental Army. *Contact Cambridge Office for Tourism | 4 Brattle St., Cambridge 02138-3728 | 617/441–2884 or 800/862–5678 | fax 617/ 441–7736 | www.cambridge-usa.org. Visitor Information Booth | 0 Harvard Sq., Cambridge | 617/ 497–1630.*

Christ Church. The oldest church in Cambridge was built in 1761 by Anglicans loyal to the English crown. It was designed by Peter Harrison, architect of Boston's Anglican Church, King's Chapel. After the Tory congregation was chased out of town in the months leading up to the Revolution, Christ Church was used to house patriot soldiers and then reopened for holiday services in 1775, with George and Martha Washington in attendance. | 0 Garden St. | 617/876–0200 | www.cccambridge.org | Free | Sun.–Fri. 7:30–6, Sat. 7:30–3.

Dawes Island. This Harvard Square traffic island is named for Paul Revere's fellow rider, William Dawes, the tanner who galloped through Cambridge in April 1775 spreading the alarm that the British were en route to Concord. | Garden St. at Massachusetts Ave.

Dexter Pratt House. Also known as Blacksmith House, this clapboard building was the home of Dexter Pratt, the village blacksmith immortalized in Henry Wadsworth Longfellow's poetic lines: "Under a spreading chestnut tree, the village smithy stands." The building now houses the Cambridge Center for Adult Education and a bakery. | 56 Brattle St. | 617/547–6789 | Free | Mon.–Sat. 9–6.

Harvard University. Chartered in 1636 to "advance Learning and perpetuate it to Posterity," and named two years later in honor of a local Puritan minister who bequeathed his library to the young school, Harvard is the oldest—and one of the most respected—institutions of higher education in the country. At the university's heart is Harvard Yard, with its tree-filled quadrangles of dorms, classrooms, and administrative offices; the oldest buildings in the Yard date to the early 18th century. | Harvard Sq. | 617/495–1573 | www.harvard.edu.

Harvard Information Center. This office stocks publications related to the university, including descriptive self-guided tour brochures for Harvard Yard, campus maps, and illustrated guides to the university museums. During the academic year free public tours are given weekdays at 10 and 2 and Saturdays at 2; from mid-June through August, tours are held Monday through Saturday at 10, 11:15, 2, and 3:15. | Holyoke Center Arcade, 1350 Massachusetts Ave. | 617/495–1000 | www.harvard.edu | Sept.–mid-June, Mon.–Sat. 9–5; mid-June–Aug., Mon.–Sat. 9–7, Sun. noon–5.

Massachusetts Hall. This brick building is Harvard's oldest, built in 1720. It has always housed students, and during the Revolutionary War it served as a barracks for Continental Army soldiers. It is not open to the public. | Harvard Yard.

Wadsworth House. On the perimeter of Harvard Yard, this yellow clapboard structure was built in 1726 as a home for Harvard presidents. It served as the first headquarters for George Washington, who took command of the Continental Army in Cambridge in July, 1775. Closed to the public, it houses administrative offices. | 1341 Massachusetts Ave.

University Hall. Completed in 1815, this is one of two buildings in Harvard Yard designed by Charles Bulfinch, America's first professional architect and a Harvard graduate. A prime example of the Federal style begun by Bulfinch, the granite University Hall is currently an administration building. | Harvard Yard.

Hooper-Lee-Nichols House. Built between 1685 and 1690, and now headquarters of the Cambridge Historical Society, this is one of two "Tory Row" stronghold homes on Brattle Street open to the public. (Longfellow's home is the other.) Its interior salons are appointed with period books, portraits, and wallpaper. | 159 Brattle St. | 617/547–4252 | Guided tours $5 | Tues. and Thurs. 2–5.

Longfellow National Historic Site. This mid-Georgian house, constructed in 1759, is one of the seven original "Tory Row" homes on Brattle Street. George Washington lived here during the siege of Boston from July 1775 to April 1776. But its current legacy belongs to a later tenant, poet Henry Wadsworth Longfellow, whose verses about the Village Blacksmith, Evangeline, Hiawatha, and Paul Revere's midnight ride thrilled 19th-century America. The mansion was Longfellow's home between 1837 and 1882. | 105 Brattle St. | 617/876–4491 | www.nps.gov/long | Guided tours $3 | May–Oct., Wed.–Sun., 10–4:30.

HISTORIC LODGING

Mary Prentiss Inn. This Greek Revival–style mansion was built in 1843 as a country estate. Today, it houses a small upscale inn on a shady residential street north of Harvard Square. The rooms are furnished with a mix of antiques and period reproductions, and several have working fireplaces. The spacious back deck may not be historic, but it's a beautiful spot to enjoy a sunny day. Complimentary breakfast. | 6 Prentiss St. | 617/661–2929 | fax 617/661–5989 | www.maryprentissinn.com | 20 rooms | $169–$249 | AE, D, MC, V.

CONCORD

▼▼▼

This suburban community, incorporated in 1635 and 21 mi northwest of Boston, is deeply engraved in the national memory due to its almost accidental role at the outset of the American Revolution. Because of the shots that were fired there on the morning of April 19, 1775, the small wooden bridge over the placid Concord River on the north side of town is one of the cornerstones of American history. Colonial buildings that witnessed the events of that day still stand around the town green, and the town includes both a national park—the Minute Man National Historical Park—and a number of historic houses that memorialize the Revolutionary era.

Concord is actually "Act 2" in the fabled and bloody day that opened the Revolutionary War. The Redcoats had already marched on nearby Lexington from Boston—"to teach rebels a lesson"—arriving at dawn, where the very first skirmish resulted in the death of eight minutemen. Finding few arms and munitions hidden in Lexington—in truth, Colonists had already removed many of them to Concord by oxen—the Redcoats made haste to Concord. And it was here that the tables were turned on them, not only in the encounter by the Old North Bridge. By the end of that day, the Redcoats were on retreat back to Boston, Minutemen kept up a sniper attack on them, peppering the retreating "lobster backs" with musket fire from behind low stone walls and tall pine trees. In the second half of the 19th century, Concord earned a permanent place in American letters as the home of numerous literary luminaries, including Louisa May Alcott (*Little Women*), essayist Ralph Waldo Emerson, Nathaniel Hawthorne (*The Scarlet Letter, House of the Seven Gables*), and Henry David Thoreau (*Walden*)—today, the houses of these great writers are open as museums. *Contact Concord Chamber of Commerce | 58 Main St., Concord 01742 | 978/369–3120 | fax 978/369–1515 | www.concordmachamber.org.*

Concord Museum. Just east of the town center, this museum—set in a 1930 Colonial Revival building—provides a good overview of the town's history from its original Native American settlement to the present. Start with the permanent "Why Concord?" exhibit, which considers why so many important historical events happened in this area, or with the 15-minute "Exploring Concord" film, which features places that played prominent roles in the town's history. Other highlights include Native American artifacts, several period rooms illustrating life in the 18th and 19th centuries, and—best of all—one of the two lanterns hung at Boston's Old North Church to signal that the British were coming by sea. | 200 Lexington

Rd. (entrance on Cambridge Tpke.) | 978/369–9763 | www.concordmuseum.org | $7 | Apr.–Dec., Mon.–Sat. 9–5, Sun. noon–5; Jan.–Mar., Mon.–Sat. 11–4, Sun. 1–4.

Minute Man National Historical Park. On April 19, 1775, British troops marched from Boston to Concord to seize a suspected cache of rebel arms. Although the initial Revolutionary War sorties were in Lexington, word of the American losses spread rapidly to surrounding towns, and when the British finally marched into Concord, more than 400 rebels—minutemen—were waiting for them on Punkatasset Hill, the high ground overlooking the Concord River and the Old North Bridge. This vast, two-parcel park, spanning more than 800 acres in Concord, Lincoln, and Lexington, contains many of the sites important to Concord's role in the Revolution, including the North Bridge, as well as two visitor centers, one each in Concord and—5 mi to the east—Lexington (many of the special daily programs and events are held at the Lexington visitor center and at the Hartwell Tavern on Route 2A. For information about the sites in Lexington, see that town listing below.

North Bridge Visitor Center. A two-minute stroll from the Old North Bridge, this small visitor center has exhibits and information about Concord's role in the Revolution. | 174 Liberty St. | 978/369–6993 | www.nps.gov/mima | Free | May–Oct., daily 9–5; Nov.–Apr., daily 9–4.

Old North Bridge. At this hallowed spot, ½ mi from Concord center, the Concord minutemen fired "the shot hear round the world," officially beginning the American Revolution on the morning of April 19, 1775. The Americans didn't fire first, but when two of their own fell dead from a Redcoat volley, Major John Buttrick of Concord roared, "Fire, fellow soldiers, for God's sake, fire." The minutemen released volley after volley, and the Redcoats fled. Daniel Chester French's famous statue *The Minuteman* (1875) honors the country's first freedom fighters. The lovely wooded surroundings give a sense of what the landscape was like in more rural times. Of the confrontation, Ralph Waldo Emerson wrote in 1837: "By the rude bridge that arched the flood / Their flag to April's breeze unfurled / Here once the embattled farmers stood / And fired the shot heard round the world." (The lines are inscribed at the foot of *The Minuteman* statue.) Concord claims the right to the "shot," believing that native son Emerson was, of course, referring to the North Bridge standoff. Park Service officials skirt the issue, saying the shot could refer to the battle on Lexington Green, when the very first shot rang out from an unknown source, or to Concord when minutemen held back the Redcoats in the Revolution's first major battle, or even to the Boston Massacre. What's important is Emerson's belief that here began the modern world's first experiment in democracy. | Off Monument St.

Old Manse. Rev. William Emerson, who built this house in 1770, watched the opening battle of the American Revolution spill over onto his fields from the North Bridge. Decades later, his grandson, author Ralph Waldo Emerson (1803–82), moved in for a year before buying a house on the other side of town. The Old Manse was occupied constantly by the Emerson family, except for the 3½-year period during which another notable occupant resided here—Nathaniel Hawthorne, who rented the house with his wife and wrote the stories that gave the property its name. Furnishings date from the late 18th century. Tours last about 45 minutes. | 269 Monument St. | 978/369–3909 | www.thetrustees.org | Guided tours $7 | Mid-Apr.–Oct., Mon.–Sat. 10–5, Sun. noon–5. Last tour departs 4:30.

Wright Tavern. Built in 1747, this served as headquarters first for the minutemen, then the British, both on April 19. It is closed to the public. | 2 Lexington Rd.

✦ ON THE CALENDAR: Apr. **Battle Road Reenactment and Commemorations.** On the Saturday before Patriots' Day, militia and British redcoats reenact the skirmish that sent the British retreating to their Boston garrison, marking the beginning of the Revolutionary War. The Patriots' Day Parade takes place on Monday, Patriots' Day. Contact the Minute Man National Historical Park for details and locations. | 978/369–6993.

HISTORIC DINING AND LODGING

Colonial Inn. Rooms in the 1716 main inn have exposed-beam ceilings, decorative fireplaces, and four-poster beds; in the 1960s Prescott Wing, the feel is more modern country inn. Traditional stick-to-your-ribs Yankee fare, including prime rib and seafood, is served in the neo-Colonial dining rooms. Restaurant. | 48 Monument Sq. | 800/370–9200 | fax 978/371–1533 | www.concordscolonialinn.com | 47 rooms | $159–$225 | AE, D, DC, MC, V.

DEERFIELD
▼▼

As a result of Historic Deerfield's pioneering restoration efforts, Deerfield's main thoroughfare, simply known as "The Street," is one of the finest Colonial townscapes in America. Such beauty hides one of New England's bloodiest pasts. For when English families came in the 1670s to homestead the fertile lands between the Deerfield and Connecticut rivers, this was the very edge of the dangerous Massachusetts frontier. Native Americans had been farming the region for thousands of years, although by the 1640s, diseases that early English explorers had brought largely eliminated the local Pocumtucks, who lived in what is now the Deerfield area. However, other tribes repeatedly attacked the early Deerfield settlements, as the settlers became unwitting pawns in the deadly wars between England and France. Local Native American tribes, on their own anti-Colonial initiative and later as proxies for the French, repeatedly destroyed the town during its infancy. In 1675, during King Philip's War, more than 60 English settlers, including 14 from Deerfield—more than a third of the village's men—were killed at Bloody Brook (now known as South Deerfield). Then, on February 28, 1704, the streets ran red during the so-called Deerfield Massacre, when local tribes descended on the town (48 settlers were murdered, more than 100 others were captured and taken to Canada, and the village was abandoned). Three years later, Rev. John Williams, the town's first minister, who was one of those captured, managed to return with a party of settlers, and Deerfield was repopulated. Even when resettled, more strife arrived in the form of Whig vs. Tory sympathies among the town populace—Tories hosted tea parties in support of King George III while patriot supporters built Liberty poles (a replica of one still stands on The Street). By and large, the town ultimately rallied to the Patriot cause and sent men to fight at the Battle of Bunker Hill.

Today much of the village is known as Historic Deerfield, a walk-through interpretive museum of Colonial and post-Colonial life that was established in 1952 through the initiative of Henry and Helen Flynt. Interestingly, these historic buildings stand side-by-side with private homes and several schools (most notably, Deerfield Academy, a well-regarded college preparatory school founded in 1798). Deerfield's time-burnished streets and houses continue to cast their spell over visitors and moviegoers—its streets are often used as film sets (most notably for the 1994 version of *Little Women*). *Contact Franklin County Chamber of Commerce | 395 Main St., Greenfield 01302 | 413/773–5463 | fax 413/773–7008 | www.co.franklin.ma.us.*

Historic Deerfield. With more than fifty structures on 93 acres and 25,000 antiques to its name, Historic Deerfield is rightfully regarded as one of the nation's premier repositories of Colonial Americana. The Street—the town's famous tree-lined avenue of 18th- and 19th-century houses—is protected and maintained as a museum site, with 14 of the preserved buildings open to the public year-round (in winter, homes are shown according to interest). Highlights include the Allen House (1725); the Frary House (circa 1750); the Dwight House (1725); the Sheldon-Hawks House (1743); and the Ashley House (1730), home of the Tory minister Jonathan Ashley (locked out of his church by townsmen, legend has it he axed his way in). To see more than 100 years of settlement in a single building, tour the Wells-Thorn House; each of its rooms has been furnished to reflect life in a different generation between 1725 and

1850. No house is extant, however, from 1704 when the town was visited by "Ye Barbarous Enemy" and the streets ran red with blood from the native tribal Deerfield Massacre. Purchase of an all-house admission ticket includes access to the Flynt Center of Early New England Life (at 37-D Old Main St.), a large collections center and exhibit area, which displays some of the many treasures not on view in its houses (take a peek into the "museum's attic," with its huge assortment of chairs, dressers, china, toys, and other accoutrements of Colonial life). The best place to get an overview of Historic Deerfield is in the (circa-1760) Hall Tavern Visitor Center, which shows a 12-minute film about the town's history and homes. Because many of the homes and furnishings are of the "don't touch" variety, the village is best suited for adults and older children. However, throughout the year, there are "Hands-On History" programs with special activities for kids, and at press time, a new children's discovery center was in the works, slated to open in 2004. | The Street | 413/774–5581 | www.historic-deerfield.org | Individual houses or the Flynt Center $6. Combined admission to all of Historic Deerfield and Memorial Hall Museum $12 (ticket good for 2 consecutive days) | Daily 9:30–4:30.

Memorial Hall Museum. Founded in 1880, in a 1798 building that was the first home of Deerfield Academy, this museum preserves the area's history through extensive collections of furnishings, tools, costumes, quilts, kitchen wares, toys, and assorted other artifacts of daily life in early rural America. There is also an excellent Indian Room, whose exhibits not only describe regional Native American history but explain the errors in how the museum's Indian artifacts were interpreted in the past. That noted, the most unforgettable artifact here is the massive oak door to John Sheldon's residence, still imbedded with tomahawk scars from the night of February 28, 1704 | 8 Memorial St. | 413/774–3768 | www.deerfield-ma.org | $6, combined admission with Historic Deerfield $12 | May–Oct., daily 9:30–4:30.

Children's Museum at the Indian House Memorial. If you've brought the kids, stop by this small museum in a reproduction 1690s house that operates under the auspices of the Memorial Hall Museum. Various children's programs focus on Native American and Colonial life; you might make an 18th-century toy, grind corn, try quill pen calligraphy, or learn about herbal home remedies; tours of the Indian House are also offered throughout the day. | The Street | 413/774–3768 | www.deerfield-ma.org | $3, combined admission with Memorial Hall Museum $6 or with Historic Deerfield $12 | July–Labor Day, daily 11–4:30; Labor Day–Oct., weekends 11–4:30.

HISTORIC DINING AND LODGING

Deerfield Inn. Set right in the middle of Historic Deerfield, this dignified 1884 building with tall white pillars and a large porch was originally a stagecoach stop. Guest rooms are done in an upscale Colonial style, with patchwork quilts, floral wallpapers, and plenty of antiques. Afternoon tea is served daily, and the stately dining room offers regional American cuisine with French influences. Lunch is available in the casual, self-service Terrace Café, while the main restaurant serves up some very stylish vittles, including pan-seared pheasant with crushed peppercorns and wild mushrooms in a cognac cream sauce. Restaurant, bar, complimentary breakfast. No smoking. | 81 Old Main St. (The Street) | 413/774–5587 | fax 413/775–7221 | www.deerfieldinn.com | 23 rooms | $235–$255 | AE, DC, MC, V.

Whately Inn. Antiques and four-poster beds slope gently on old-wood floors of the guest rooms at this informal Colonial inn. The dining room (no lunch) has a fireplace and exposed beams, tables on a raised stage at one end, and some booths; it's dimly lighted, with candles on the tables. The full menu is also served in the more casual lounge. Restaurant. | Chestnut Plain Rd., Whately Center | 413/665–3044 or 800/942–8359 | www.whatelyinn.com | 4 rooms | $85–$95 | AE, D, MC, V.

GLOUCESTER

▼▼▼

On Gloucester's seaside promenade is *The Fisherman,* an iconic statue of a man steering a ship's wheel, his eyes searching the horizon. Commissioned by the town in celebration of Gloucester's 300th anniversary, this 1923 statue honors those "who go down to the sea in ships." Gloucester was the second permanent settlement of early Pilgrims in America (after Plymouth), and it's the oldest seaport in the nation. Located 37 mi northeast of Boston, it's still a major fishing port; Sebastian Junger's 1997 book, *The Perfect Storm,* recounted the fate of the *Andrea Gail,* a Gloucester fishing boat caught in "the storm of the century" in October 1991. The city's working waterfront, wooded surroundings, scenic harbor, and picturesque lighthouses have also inspired numerous painters, from Fitz Hugh Lane and Winslow Homer, to contemporary residents of Rocky Neck, the nation's oldest artist colony. Among other Gloucester notables is Judith Sargent Murray, who was a writer and one of the country's earliest feminists. Her husband, Rev. John Murray, started the Universalist faith in Gloucester and built its first church in 1807. Although Gloucester doesn't offer much in the way of Colonial-era accommodations, nearby Rockport, a well-touristed seaside village just a few miles to the northeast, has several appealing, moderately priced inns that date to the early 1800s. *Contact Cape Ann Chamber of Commerce | 33 Commercial St., Gloucester 01930 | 978/283–1601 or 800/321–0133 | www.capeannvacations.com.*

Cape Ann Historical Museum. Maritime artifacts, Colonial silverware, Chinese porcelain, and antique furnishings—particularly from the Federal period—are the highlights of this community museum. The museum also has a noteworthy art collection: paintings, drawings, and sculpture by local artists such as Winslow Homer and Milton Avery, with pride of place going to seascape painter, Fitz Hugh Lane (1804–65); the museum owns the largest number of his paintings. | 27 Pleasant St., off Main St. | 978/283–0455 | www.cape-ann.com/historical-museum | $5 | Mar.–Jan., Tues.–Sat. 10–5.

Sargent House Museum. This 18th-century Georgian house was home to Judith Sargent Murray (1751–1820), one of America's first feminist writers, whose many works—such as her 1790 essay "On the Equality of the Sexes"—argued for equal rights and education for women. She penned a widely read column called "The Gleaner" in *Massachusetts Magazine,* a monthly literary publication. She was also a tireless letter writer, who kept copies of the more than 2,000 letters she wrote between the 1770s and the early 1800s. The house museum is furnished with 1790s textiles, personal objects, and china; there are also works by Judith's great-great nephew, the painter John Singer Sargent. | 49 Middle St. | 978/281–2432 | www.sargenthouse.org | $5 | Memorial Day–Columbus Day, Fri.–Mon. noon–4.

Stage Fort Park. This pretty park with a small beach, children's playground, and the Gloucester Visitor Welcome Center was the site of the original settlement of the Dorchester Company, which sailed to Gloucester in 1623. | Hough Ave. off Western Ave. | 978/281–8865 | Visitor center May–Oct., daily 9–6.

HISTORIC LODGING

Inn on Cove Hill (Caleb Norwood Jr. House). Set on a hillside near the Rockport town center, a few miles from Gloucester, this Federal building dates from 1771. Its construction was reportedly paid for with gold from a pirate's booty. Some of the guest rooms are small, but all are cheerful, with bright floral-print wallpaper, Oriental rugs, patchwork quilts, and old-fashioned beds—some brass, others canopy four-posters. Complimentary breakfast. | 37 Mt. Pleasant St., Rockport | 978/546–2701 or 888/546–2701 | fax 978/546–1095 | www.innoncovehill.com | 8 rooms | $75–$140 | MC, V.

HINGHAM

▼▼

Few towns have as venerable a Colonial history as Hingham or such spectacular remnants of that fabled past. Settled in 1635 by families from Charlestown—many of their names, such as Hobart, Lincoln, Beal, Loring, Otis, and Cushing, still grace mailboxes here—the community found early success as a center of coopering and cordage, leading to its sobriquet, Bucket Town. Before riches, however, heaven needed to be attended to, and the Reverend Peter Hobart arrived to mastermind the construction of a magnficent meetinghouse, still extant. Also built in later years was the Old Ordinary, a tavern famous even in Federal days and now a museum; the Old Derby Academy; and the stylish historic houses that line the town's main road, once called "the most beautiful main street in America" by Eleanor Roosevelt. *Contact Hingham Historical Society | 34 Main St., Hingham 02043 | 781/749-7721 | www.hinghamhistorical.org.*

Old Derby Academy. First envisioned by Madame Sarah Derby in 1784, this academy was meant to be a school for boys and girls and was perhaps the first coeducational institution in America. Torn down in 1818, her structure was replaced by this eminently elegant Federal building, complete with Palladian window. Today it is the headquarters of the Hingham Historical Society and its extensive archives. | 34 Main St. | 617/749–7721 | By appointment.

Old Ordinary. Originally one of Colonial America's most exquisite period taverns, this 14-room Federal-period mansion was the favored grog stop for many notables, including Daniel Webster. With its weathered clapboards, charming period Colonial-style gardens (designed by Frederick Law Olmsted, Jr., no less), and beautiful period rooms, this ordinary (18th-century parlance for "tavern") now contains the Hingham Historical Society's decorative-arts collection. Replete with Sheraton sideboards, historic wallpapers, 18th-century portraits, and chipped Chippendale chairs, the period chambers include the Tap Room, the Kitchen, the Parlor, and the Bedchamber. | 21 Lincoln St. | 617/749–0013 | $3 | Mid-June–Labor Day, Tues.–Sat. 1:30–4:30; by appointment Labor Day–mid-Oct.

Old Ship Meetinghouse. A glorious monument of the 17th-century Elizabethan Gothic style, Old Ship still looms over Hingham's Lower Main Street. Puritans recognized no division between church and state, and town meetinghouses often served as temples of worship. No more striking example from that stormy era survives than this meetinghouse. It has echoed with congregants' prayers since ships' carpenters raised the main hall's massive timbers in 1681; side galleries were built in 1730 and 1755. The name is derived from the shape of the wood ceiling, which resembles a ship's hull. Today you can visualize the watchful tithingman prowling the aisles, ready to poke snoozing worshippers in pews with his long pole (one end was covered in fur to awaken females). Puritans disavowed altars, so pews—once lined with foot warmers—focus on the (very) grand pulpit. Outside are the parish house, a timeworn graveyard, and the Memorial Bell Tower. | Lower Main St. | 617/749–1679 | July–Aug., Tues.–Fri. 1–4; other times by appointment.

✦ ON THE CALENDAR: May **Historic Hingham Homes Tour.** Sponsored by the Hingham Historical Society, this mid-May tour features a sampler of the town's most elegant private homes, ranging from Colonial to Second Empire in style. | 781/749–1851

IPSWICH

▼▼

Founded in 1633, this coastal community 28 mi north of Boston is one of the oldest towns in America, home to the aptly named Castle Hill mansion and an elegant district of 17th-century houses. America's first poetess, Ann Bradstreet, lived here in the 1630s. She was the wife of Simon Bradstreet, noted governor of the Massachusetts Bay Colony. Many of Ipswich's most historic houses line South Main, High, and East streets near Choate Bridge, which spans South Main and dates from 1764. *Contact Ipswich Business Association | Box 94, Ipswich 01938 | 978/356–4400 | www.ipswichma.com*

Castle Hill. Commonly known as the Great House, this may be New England's most magnificent mansion. A 59-room Stuart-style palace, it was built in 1927 by Chicago industrialist Richard T. Crane, Jr., but remains a veritable homage to 17th- and 18th-century England. The views of Ipswich Bay from the eye-popping Grand Allee and the estate's landscaping are nearly as impressive as the house itself. Inside, the grand salons remain sumptuous tributes to the English decorative styles of William and Mary and Queen Anne, although filtered through a 20th-century eye. | Argilla Rd. | 978/356–4351 | $8 | Grounds daily 8–dusk, house tours Memorial Day–early Sept., Wed.–Thurs. 10–4.

Ipswich Historical Society Museums. Ipswich has the greatest number of First Period houses in the country, most identified by markers. You can visit two houses maintained by the town's historical society (report to the society first). The organization's staff can also help suggest walking tours through the town's four historical districts. | 54 S. Main St., 01938 | 978/356–2811 | $7 for one or both houses | May–Columbus Day, tours on the hour Wed.–Sat. 10–4, Sun. 1–4.

John Heard House. This stately Federal home was built in the 1790s for a ship's captain whose West Indies trade established a mercantile dynasty. Five generations of Heards occupied the house, furnishing it with decorative art and work by local artist Arthur Wesley Dow. Also of interest are the collections of nautical instruments, children's toys, and carriages. | 40 S. Main St., 01938 | 978/356–2641 | $7 | May–Columbus Day, tours on the hour Wed.–Sat. 10–4, Sun. 1–4.

John Whipple House. The very quintessence of Puritan style (if that is not an oxymoron), this dark and weathered clapboard home was built around 1655. A First Period residence, it reflects the personal tastes of six generations of Whipples. The collection of early handmade bobbin lace is a highlight. The grounds include a Colonial "housewife's garden" and antique shrub roses. Architecturally speaking, this abode has a "cousin" in the beautiful Parson Capen House in nearby Topsfield. | 53 S. Main St., 01938 | 978/356–2811 | $7 | May–Columbus Day, tours on the hour Wed.–Sat. 10–4, Sun. 1–4.

HISTORIC LODGING
1640 Hart House. One of the oldest buildings in the country (it was built in 1640), the Hart House retains its Early American touches such as original hand-carved beams and floorboards and five working fireplaces. | 51 Linebrook Rd. | 978/356–9411 | $13–$19 | AE, D, MC, V.

LEXINGTON
▼▼

The first English settlers came to Lexington in 1642, and the town, which was incorporated in 1713, became a farming community. However, it wasn't until 1775, when discontent in the British-ruled American Colonies burst into action, that Lexington earned its place in the history books. In response to the increasingly repressive actions of the British government in the 1770s, Colonial towns began to form or reactivate their local militias, comprised of all adult males between the ages of 16 and 60. One-third of each town's militiamen were designated "minutemen," so-called because they would be able to prepare for battle at a moment's notice. The British commander-in-chief in North America, Thomas Gage, who was also to be the last royal-appointed governor in Massachusetts, decided to quash this brewing unrest with a surprise attack on the town of Concord (with its well-known stockpile of armaments). The patriots were able to learn the destination of the planned attack, but they did not know whether the British would approach the town by land or would cross the Charles River by boat into Cambridge, and then march on through Lexington to Concord.

On April 18, 1775, when the Colonists discovered that the British troops were preparing to travel by boat, two lanterns were hung in the Old North Church to signal the soldiers' route. Patriot leader Paul Revere then set out for Lexington on horseback around midnight to alert the town that British soldiers were approaching (*see* "Listen, My Children, and You Shall Hear" box). The next morning, as the British advance troops, led by Major John Pitcairn, arrived in Lexington on their march toward Concord, a small group of minutemen were waiting to confront the Redcoats in what became the first skirmish of the Revolutionary War.

Modern Lexington, 16 mi northwest of Boston, has preserved many of the historical buildings that played bit parts in the events of that fateful spring morning in 1775. During the town's annual Patriot's Day celebration—the third Monday in April—costume-clad groups re-create the minutemen's battle maneuvers, "Paul Revere" rides again, and the streets are alive with the cries of "The Regulars are coming! The Regulars are coming!" *Contact Lexington Chamber of Commerce | 1875 Massachusetts Ave., Lexington 02421 | 781/862–1450 | www. lexingtonchamber.org.*

Battle Green. Once a simple town common, this patch of land was forever transformed at sunrise on the morning of April 19, 1775. After Paul Revere rode from Boston during the night to rouse local militiamen, minuteman captain John Parker assembled a company of about 77 men to meet the British soldiers, who were en route to Concord to seize a suspected rebel cache of arms. Captain Parker reportedly told his men, "Stand your ground, don't fire unless fired upon; but if they mean to have war, let it begin here." The British major John Pitcairn, commanding several hundred soldiers, ordered his troops to surround the minutemen and disarm them but not to fire. A shot did ring out—though no one knows who fired first. When the smoke cleared, eight minutemen were dead and 10 others wounded. The British, with only one solider injured, regrouped and continued their march to Concord.

At one corner of the Battle Green stands Henry Hudson Kitson's idealized 1900 statue of Parker—*The Minuteman* (set in a traffic island and therefore a difficult photo op). Captain Parker's famous command to his troops is emblazoned on The Line of Battle boulder, which marks where the men stood (just to the right of the statue). But after that first shot did ring out, history's questions are left unanswered. Who fired first? Why did Parker, a 45-year-old veteran of the French and Indian Wars (and noted for his guerilla tactics) place his men behind the barnlike, two-story meetinghouse, which sat where the Minuteman statue sits today? (A large memorial marks the meetinghouse site, behind the statue; Parker's grave is in the Old Burying Ground, behind the First Parish Church, at the fork of Harrington Road and Massachusetts Avenue). The minutemen couldn't see the advancing British columns, much less make a forcible show of resistance. Indeed, why didn't Captain Parker tell his men to take to the hills overlooking the British route? Seventy-seven men against 700 Redcoats? It was an absurd situation—and one of history's most-recorded mishaps. The Revolutionary Monument, near the statue, marks the burial site of minutemen killed in battle. | Massachusetts Ave. | Free | Daily.

Buckman Tavern. This circa 1710 tavern has been restored to look much the way it did on the night of April 18, 1775, when local militiamen gathered inside to discuss facing British troops on the march from Boston. Later that night, in the predawn hours, Paul Revere and fellow alarm rider William Dawes refreshed themselves here after confirming the approach of the British. A half-hour tour takes in the tavern's seven rooms; among the objects on display is an old front door with a hole made by a British musket ball. | 1 Bedford St. | 781/862–5598 | www.lexingtonhistory.org | $5; $12 combination ticket includes Hancock-Clarke House and Munroe Tavern | Mid-Mar.–Nov., Mon.–Sat. 10–5, Sun. 1–5.

Hancock-Clarke House. Two revolutionary leaders, Samuel Adams and John Hancock, were staying at this 17th-century parsonage as guests of Rev. Jonas Clarke, in April 1775 while they were attending the Provincial Congress in nearby Concord. On the night of April 18, Paul Revere rode here to warn them that the British were marching out of Boston. John Hancock's grandfather, Rev. John Hancock, had built the original section of the house around 1698 when he came to Lexington as a minister. The house contains artifacts from the Revolution, including pistols that belonged to British major John Pitcairn, as well as period furnishings and household items from the clerical families who lived here over the years. Tours run about 30 minutes. | 36 Hancock St. | 781/861–0928 | www.lexingtonhistory.org | $5; $12 combination ticket includes Buckman Tavern and Munroe Tavern | Mid-Apr.–Oct., Mon.–Sat. 10–5, Sun. 1–5.

Jason Russell House. As the Redcoats retreated from Lexington and Concord on April 19, 1775, they traveled through the town of Arlington (now a suburb between Cambridge and Lexington), where minutemen peppered them with musket fire. Patriot troops used aggressive (most commentators of the day would have called them "unhonorable") guerilla tactics—jumping ahead to turns in the road, hiding behind stone walls and pine trees—and managed to pick off more than 200 retreating Redcoats as they marched back along what is now Massachusetts Avenue. This stretch became known as "the bloodiest half mile of that Battle Road." The bullet-ridden Jason Russell House marks the spot where 10 minutemen and more than 20 British soldiers were killed during the Battle of the Foot of the Rocks (which involved about 1,700 minutemen and militia and a similar number of British soldiers). Russell himself was bayoneted to death by British soldiers outside his front door. Today the interior displays period kitchenware, spinning wheels, and even a cannonball that once hit the house. | 7 Jason St., at Massachusetts Ave., Arlington | 781/648–4300 | www.arlingtonhistorical. org | $3, includes the George Abbott Smith History Museum | Mid-Apr.–Oct., Fri.–Sun. 1–5.

   George Abbott Smith History Museum. Adjoining the Jason Russell House and open the same hours, this small museum has changing exhibits on Massachusetts and Arlington history. Displays include a Revolutionary-era musket, a statement of town expenses from 1811, and photos of historic area homes.

Lexington Visitors Center. After picking up maps or other information about the area, check out the diorama showing the 1775 confrontation between British regulars and the minutemen on Lexington Green. | 1875 Massachusetts Ave. | 781/862–1450 | www.lexingtonchamber. org | Free | Mid-Apr.–Nov., daily 9–5; Dec.–mid-Apr., daily 10–4.

Minute Man National Historical Park. This informative and entertaining 800-acre park, which commemorates the beginning of the American Revolution, begins just outside Route 128, west of the Lexington town center, and extends into nearby Lincoln and Concord. The park has two visitor centers, one in Lexington and one in Concord.

   Minute Man National Historical Park Visitor Center. Begin your park visit at this information center in Lexington to see the free multimedia presentation, "The Road to Revolution," a captivating introduction to the events of April 1775; it's shown daily every half hour starting at 9 AM. The rangers can also provide suggestions for touring the park and information about special events. | Rte. 2A, ½ mi west of Rte. 128 | 978/369–6993 or 781/862–7753 | www. nps.gov/mima | Free | May–Oct., daily 9–5; Nov.–Apr., daily 9–4.

   Battle Road Trail. This 5-mi walking and biking trail enables visitors to tour sections of the Minute Man National Historic Park without a car. The trail starts at Fiske Hill—on Route 2A just west of Route 128 (and east of the park visitor center in Lexington)—and continues to Meriam's Corner in Concord, which was the site of an April 19, 1775 clash between Colonists and the British. The trail runs roughly parallel to Route 2A, and although it isn't paved, the surface is fairly smooth. Pick up a trail map at the visitor center. Periodic guided walks are also offered; call the visitor center for schedules. | Rte. 2A | Daily, sunrise–sunset.

Hartwell Tavern. This restored 1732 tavern, which belonged to Ephraim and Elizabeth Hartwell, is staffed by National Park employees in period costume. They frequently demonstrate musket firing, open-hearth cooking, or other elements of early 18th-century life. Kids can play with reproduction Colonial toys. | Rte. 2A, just west of Bedford Rd. | May–Oct., daily 10–5.

Paul Revere Capture Site. Paul Revere's midnight ride on April 18, 1775 ended when he was captured by the British. The site of his capture, a short distance west of the Minute Man National Park Visitor Center on Route 2A (and along the Battle Road Trail), is marked with a boulder and plaque. Revere was set free when British officers realized that he had already completed his main mission—alerting the local militia of the British march on Concord. | Rte. 2A, just west of Mill St.

Munroe Tavern. As April 19, 1775, dragged on, British forces met fierce resistance in Concord. Dazed and demoralized after the battle at Concord's Old North Bridge, the British backtracked and regrouped at this 1695 tavern, while the Munroe family hid in nearby woods. The troops then retreated through what is now the town of Arlington. After a bloody battle there, they returned to Boston. The tavern is 1 mi east of Lexington Common; tours last about 30 minutes. | 1332 Massachusetts Ave. | 781/674–9238 | www.lexingtonhistory.org | $5; $12 combination ticket includes Hancock-Clarke House and Buckman Tavern | Call for hrs.

National Heritage Museum. This small institution devoted to the nation's cultural heritage displays artifacts from all facets of American life. An ongoing exhibit, "Lexington Alarm'd," outlines events leading up to April 1775 and illustrates Revolutionary-era life through everyday objects such as blacksmithing and farming tools, scalpels and bloodletting paraphernalia, and dental instruments, including a "tooth key" used to extract teeth. | 33 Marrett Rd. (Rte. 2A at Massachusetts Ave.) | 781/861–9638 | www.monh.org | Free; donation suggested | Mon.–Sat. 10–5, Sun. noon–5.

✦ ON THE CALENDAR: Apr. **Lexington Green Battle Reenactment.** Thousands of people gather each year in downtown Lexington's chilly darkness to witness the reenactment of the 1775 confrontation between British soldiers and defiant Lexington militiamen, a spectacle complete with cannons, horses, and full regalia. You should arrive at Battle Green by 4:30 AM to claim a viewing spot for the battle at 5:30 AM on Patriot's Day. | Massachusetts Ave. | 781/862–1703.

MARBLEHEAD
▼▼▼

Long before its volunteers rowed George Washington across the Delaware, Marblehead had an uncommon devotion to boats and sailing, a passion that continues to this day. Although it has fewer than 20,000 residents, the town has six yacht clubs, whose members, friends, and fellow enthusiasts fill the harbor with thousands of sails each summer. Back when, a 1660 report to the King of England described Marblehead as "the greatest Towne for fishing in New England." With its narrow and winding streets, old clapboard houses, and sea captains' mansions, this affluent seaside community 17 mi north of Boston retains much of the character of the village founded in 1629 by fishermen from Cornwall and the Channel Islands. During the Colonial period, Marblehead became a base for merchant trade along the American coast, to the Caribbean, and across the Atlantic, selling Massachusetts' fish and timber for rum, salt, and English manufactured goods. The proud spirit of these ambitious merchant sailors who made Marblehead prosper in the 18th century remains in the many impressive Georgian mansions that line the downtown streets. In addition to the sights below, of note architecturally is the Georgian-style King Hooper Mansion (housing an art gallery) on Hooper Street and the Old Town House on Market Square, a circa-1727 building that is the second-oldest municipal structure in America. The Chamber of Commerce has a visitor guide with a suggested walking tour of the city. Marblehead may be a little diffi-cult to reach—it's not on any major highway routes and, once there, the circuitous local streets can be confusing—but a stop here can easily be combined with a visit to Salem, just 4 mi to the west. *Contact Marblehead Chamber of Commerce | 62 Pleasant St., Marblehead 01945 | 781/631–2868 | www.marbleheadchamber.org.*

Abbot Hall. What makes this brick Victorian town hall notable is its exhibit room filled with art and historical documents, including the original deed to Marblehead from the Native American Nanapashemets. The must-see here, of course, is Archibald Willard's celebrated painting of three Revolutionary veterans with fife, drum, and flag, *The Spirit of '76,* commis-sioned for the nation's centennial in 1876. | 188 Washington St. | 781/631–0528 | Free | May–Oct., Mon.–Tues. and Thurs. 8–5, Wed. 7:30–7:30, Fri. 8–6, Sat. 9–6, Sun. 11–6; Nov.–Apr., Mon.–Tues. and Thurs. 8–5, Wed. 7:30–7:30, Fri. 8–1.

Jeremiah Lee Mansion. Built in 1768 by a wealthy shipowner and patriot, this mansion exem-plifies Marblehead's 18th-century high society. Colonel Jeremiah Lee became one of the rich-est people in the Colonies, thanks to his involvement in trade with England, the West Indies, and the other American Colonies in the years before the Revolutionary War. Although few furnishings original to the house remain, the mahogany paneling, rare hand-painted English wallpaper, and other appointments, as well as a fine collection of traditional North Shore furniture, provide clues into the life of an American gentleman. | 161 Washington St. | 781/631–1069 | Guided tours $5 | June–mid-Oct., Tues.–Sat. 10–4, Sun. 1–4.

HISTORIC LODGING

Harbor Light Inn. This classic New England inn, which dates to 1729, is filled with stately 18th-century antiques, four-poster and canopy beds, carved arched doorways, and wide-board floors. Most rooms have fireplaces, and four have private sundecks. Iced tea or lemonade—or hot cider in winter—is served in the afternoons, along with fresh-baked cookies. Compli-mentary breakfast. Pool. No kids under 8. No smoking. | 58 Washington St. | 781/631–2186 | fax 781/631–2216 | www.harborlightinn.com | 21 rooms | $135–$275 | AE, MC, V.

NEWBURYPORT

▼▼▼

Founded in 1635 by the mouth of the Merrimack River, Newburyport grew to prominence in the 18th century through shipbuilding and the industrious trade of its merchant ships. The fortunes amassed by local traders built the many grand homes that give the city its distinc-tive character. High Street, in particular, a short walk from the town's restored brick-front center, is lined with some of the finest examples of Federal-period mansions in New England. A characteristic of these three-story homes is that they appear square, with five windows—or on the first floor, a door—evenly spaced on the front side. Newburyport, 38 mi north of Boston, is a good walking city, and there's free all-day parking in a large lot on the water-front. *Contact Greater Newburyport Chamber of Commerce and Industry | 29 State St., Newbury-port | 978/462–6680 | www.newburyportchamber.org.*

Coffin House. Tristram Coffin, one of Newburyport's first settlers, built this house as a simple two-room dwelling in 1654. In 1700, the Coffin family, which by then included a married son and his offspring, expanded the house to more than double its size. Over the years, the house grew again as several generations opted to live under one roof. A good example of First Period architecture, the house illustrates how domestic needs and tastes changed from the 17th to 19th centuries. | 14 High Rd. | 978/462–2634 | www.spnea.org | Guided tours $5 | July–Labor Day, weekends 11–4 (tours hourly).

Custom House Maritime Museum. This 1835 building could perhaps be considered the Internal Revenue Service of the 17th century—in it, the federal government collected taxes on imported goods that Newburyport ship captains brought home from ports abroad. Robert Mills (1781–1855), who designed the Washington Monument, was also the architect of this building. Today, its maritime-history exhibits include ship models, nautical instruments, maritime-themed art, and ship captains' memorabilia. | 25 Water St. | 978/462–8681 | $5 | Apr.–Dec., Mon.–Sat. 10–4, Sun. 1–4.

Lowell's Boat Shop. In 1793 on the Merrimack River banks, Simeon Lowell and his sons, Stephen and Benjamin, set up this wooden boat-building shop, now the oldest continuous boat-building operation in the nation. It is the birthplace of the fisherman's dory—a sturdy, seaworthy boat that was used by the United States Life Saving Service—and one of the first mass production builders. It is now a working museum where you can observe wooden boat construction. To reach the boat shop from downtown Newburyport, follow Merrimac Street northwest and cross the river into Amesbury. | 459 Main St., Amesbury | 978/388–0162 | www.lowellboatshop.org | Wed.–Sat. 8–4.

Spencer-Peirce-Little Farm. Most other houses in this area were made of wood when this august stone-and-brick manor house was built in 1690 on this (now) 230-acre farm estate. Its construction costs became the stuff of local legend. From the late 17th century through the 19th century, it was home to several wealthy merchant families, and the furnishings reflect the lives of those families throughout those eras. It's located off Route 1A, south of Newburyport's town center. | 5 Little's La. | 978/462–2634 | www.spnea.org | Guided tours $5 | June–mid-Oct., Wed.–Sun. 11–4 (tours hourly).

HISTORIC LODGING

Clark Currier Inn. This meticulously restored 1803 Federal mansion is one of the nicest inns on the North Shore. It has an elegant "good morning" staircase, so-called because two small staircases join at the head of a large one, permitting people to greet one another on their way down to breakfast. Most of the guest rooms are spacious and furnished with antiques, including one with a glorious, late 19th-century sleigh bed. Out back is a pretty Federal-style garden with English roses and formal boxwood hedging. Complimentary breakfast. No kids under 10. | 45 Green St., | 978/465–8363 | www.clarkcurrierinn.com | 8 rooms | $95–$165 | AE, D, MC, V.

PITTSFIELD

▼▼

Pittsfield, named after English parliamentarian and patriot sympathizer William Pitt, is the Berkshires' largest and most commercial community. It became a significant manufacturing center during the 19th and early 20th centuries, especially after inventor William Stanley moved his electric-generator factory to Pittsfield in the late 1800s (it eventually became General Electric). But back in the late 18th century, when the Pittsfield area was frontier territory on the far western edge of the Massachusetts Bay Colony, a small religious community took up residence here. Established in 1747 in Manchester, England, by a group of Quakers, a religious society that took on the heady name of the United Society of Believers in Christ's Second Appearing welcomed into its fold Ann Lee, the daughter of a blacksmith. Lee became the leader of this religious community, which was known (disparagingly) as the Shaking Quakers, and later as simply the Shakers. Lee, who church members dubbed Mother Ann, immigrated to the New World in 1774 and settled near Albany, New York. During the 1780s, Mother Ann traveled through Massachusetts and Connecticut preaching her gospel, and in 1783 stayed for a month near the town of Pittsfield. Although Ann Lee died the following year, a Shaker community began to grow in Hancock, outside of Pittsfield, influenced by her visit. Hancock became the third of 19 Shaker settlements established in the United States, including three others in Massachusetts—in the towns of Harvard, Tyringham, and Shirley. The Hancock Shaker Village opened as a living history museum in 1961. *Contact Berkshire Visitors Bureau | Berkshire Common, plaza level, Pittsfield 01201 | 413/443–9186 or 800/ 237–5747 | www.berkshires.org.*

Hancock Shaker Village. Five miles west of downtown Pittsfield, this was the third of 19 U.S. communities founded by the United Society of Believers in Christ's Second Appearing, more commonly known as the Shakers. In the 1960s, the whole village was converted into a family-friendly living history museum dedicated to interpreting this religious order's agrarian lifestyle, domestic industry, and enduring design skills. The Shakers were a communal society, believing in common ownership of property and in celibacy; they adopted children or took in converts to maintain their numbers. They also believed in "worldly perfection"— making their communities as "close to heaven" as possible—a doctrine some scholars believe led to their ongoing quest for efficiency. On view at the village are the fruits of this quest, including double rolling pins (to roll out two pie crusts at once), a water wheel and turbine system that brought power to the village machine shop, and the 1826 Round Stone Barn (the only one of its kind), which was built to improve the process of feeding and milking the community's large herd of dairy cows. Professional artisans demonstrate spinning, weaving, basket-making, and other Shaker crafts (and the results are sold in the village museum shop). Admission for children under 18 is free year-round. | U.S. 20 | 413/443–0188 | www. hancockshakervillage.org | Memorial Day–late Oct., $15; late-Oct.–Memorial Day, $12 | Self-guided tours, Memorial Day–late Oct., daily 9:30–5; guided tours, late Oct.–Memorial Day, daily 10–3.

✦ ON THE CALENDAR: Sept.–Dec. **Shaker Suppers.** On several fall evenings, Hancock Shaker Village hosts Shaker Suppers, candlelight dinners with dishes made from original Shaker recipes, followed by performances of traditional Shaker music. Call for schedule and reservations, which are required. | 413/443–0188 or 800/817–1137.

PLYMOUTH
▼▼▼

On December 26, 1620, 102 weary men, women, and children disembarked from the *Mayflower* to found the first permanent European settlement north of Virginia. (In fact, Virginia was their intended destination, but storms pushed the ship off course.) Of the settlers, now known as the Pilgrims, a third were members of a Puritan sect of religious reformers known as the Separatists, because they wanted to establish their own church distinct from the national Church of England. This treasonous separation led the group to first flee to the city of Leiden in the Netherlands. After more than 10 years there, the group joined with other emigrants to start a new life in the New World.

Before coming ashore, the expedition's leaders drew up the Mayflower Compact, a historic agreement binding the group to the law of the majority. This compact became the basis for the Colony's government. After a terrible start (half of the original settlers died during the first winter), the Colony stabilized and grew under the leadership of Gov. William Bradford. Two other founding fathers—military leader Myles Standish and John Alden—acquired mythical status thanks to the poem by Henry Wadsworth Longfellow, "The Courtship of Miles Standish," which recounts the fable of Alden's winning the heart of Priscilla while proposing to her on behalf of his tongue-tied friend, Standish. The town's star attraction, Plimoth Plantation, is alone worth a detour from almost anywhere in the state, particularly if you have kids in tow. A re-creation of a 17th-century Puritan village, Plimoth Plantation vividly dramatizes the everyday lives of the first English settlers: you can watch them make cheese, forge nails, and explain where and when they bathed (hint: it wasn't often). And while the town of Plymouth, beyond the Plantation, is not without its touristy elements, there are many other attractions as well, from historic homes to small museums. Forty miles south of Boston (an hour by road or commuter rail), Plymouth is also less than 15 mi from Cape Cod. *Contact Destination Plymouth | 170 Water St., Suite 10C, Plymouth 02360 | 800/872–1620 | www.visit-plymouth.com. Plymouth Waterfront Visitor Information Center | 130 Water St., at U.S. 44, Plymouth 02360 | 508/747–7525.*

John Alden House Museum. The only standing structure in which original Pilgrims are known to have lived is about 10 mi north of Plymouth in the town of Duxbury, settled in 1628 by Pilgrim colonists Myles Standish and John Alden, among others. Alden, who served as assistant governor of Plymouth Colony, his wife Priscilla, and eight or nine of their children occupied this house, which was built in 1653 and is furnished with pieces that were authentic to the era. One bedroom has a "seven-day dresser," with a drawer to hold clothes for each day of the week; the Sunday drawer, which held formal church wear, is the largest. | 105 Alden St., Duxbury | 781/934–9092 | www.alden.org | Guided tours $4 | Mid-May–mid-Oct., Mon.–Sat. noon–5.

Mayflower II. The crew and passengers—that is, staff in period dress—who greet visitors to this replica of the most renowned ship in American history are "stuck" in the year 1621. They describe their voyage across the Atlantic and the events that precipitated that trip. They'll tell you about their own particular circumstances, too, or gossip about fellow passengers, if prompted. The *Mayflower II* was built in England, then sailed across the Atlantic in 1957. | State Pier, Water St. | 508/746–1622 | www.plimoth.org | $8 | Apr.–Nov., daily 9–5.

Pilgrim Hall Museum. The largest collection of Pilgrim-related artifacts in existence is this museum's principal claim to fame. It occupies two floors of an imposing Greek Revival building in the heart of Plymouth. The only portrait of a *Mayflower* passenger is among its prized 17th-century possessions, but the museum, which was established in 1824 and remains one of the country's oldest public museums, also makes an effort to shed light on the lives of the Native Americans who were here when the Pilgrim migration began and are still here today. | 75 Court St. | 508/746–1620 | www.pilgrimhall.org | $5 | Feb.–Dec., daily 9:30–4:30.

Plimoth Plantation. Over the entrance of this intriguing (and justifiably popular) living history museum is the caution: "You are now entering 1627." Believe it. Against the backdrop of the Atlantic Ocean, a Pilgrim village has been carefully re-created, from the thatch roofs, cramped quarters, and open fireplaces to the long-horned livestock. A large cast of costumed interpreters enact the daily lives of some 30 of the original Plymouth settlers, who converse with visitors in 17th-century dialect while they go about their chores—plucking ducks, cooking rabbit stew, making cheese, or tending their gardens. The "residents," who never break out of character, reveal a storehouse of information about their Colonial characters, from politics and religious beliefs to their arrival in their new homeland. Feel free to engage them in conversation about their lives, but expect only curious looks if you ask about anything that happened after 1627. Elsewhere in the Plantation complex are exhibition galleries, a replica of a Native American homesite, and regular demonstrations of early 17th-century English crafts. Special programs are offered, among them a Colonial Thanksgiving dinner. Dress for the weather, since many exhibits are outdoors. | Warren Ave. (Rte. 3A) | 508/746–1622 | www.plimoth.org | $20 | Apr.–Nov., daily 9–5.

   Carriage House Craft Center. This 19th-century carriage house, part of the Plimoth Plantation, is staffed by shoemakers, basketmakers, potters, and joiners. The artisans do not wear period costumes, but do use period tools.

   Hobbamock's Homesite. Hobbamock, a Wampanoag Indian, lived with his extended family near the original Plymouth settlement and served as an interpreter and guide for the colonists. The homesite provides an example of the typical 17th-century dwellings used by the local Wampanoags. Costumed interpreters, many of whom are of Native American descent, are on hand to explain and answer questions about Wampanoag culture, theology, and interactions with the English settlers. While the interpreters are not "in character" as the Pilgrim interpreters are—they'll speak to you in modern English—they frequently demonstrate Wampanoag crafts and food preparation.

Nye Barn. Most of the animals housed in this barn on the grounds of the Plimoth Plantation were bred from 17th-century gene pools, making it likely that these sheep, goats, cows, pigs, and chickens are similar to those raised in the original plantation.

Plymouth Rock. This surprisingly diminutive stone may seem overwhelmed by the classical open-sided temple that has been built around it, but the touchstone of English settlement in the New World need not pretend to be humble. The rock was identified 125 years after the fact by Elder Faunce, who told the story as it was passed down to him by his forefathers. | Water St. | Free | Daily.

Richard Sparrow House. Dating back to 1640, this is the oldest-surviving house in Plymouth. The lean-to at the rear was added later; originally the structure was a two-room design two stories tall, with an attic space. It is furnished in the spartan style of the Pilgrims' era. Perhaps somewhat incongruously, there's also a contemporary crafts gallery on the premises. | 42 Summer St. | 508/747–1240 | $2; gallery free | Apr.–late Nov., Thurs.–Tues. 10–5.

1749 Spooner House. After its construction in the late 1740s, this cozy structure became home to five generations of the Spooner family. Nothing, it seems, was ever thrown out in those 200 years. Furnishings and decorations acquired over the generations, sometimes side-by-side with whatever they were meant to replace, are mixed and matched for aesthetic rather than historical interest. | 27 North St. | 508/746–0012 | $4 | June–early Oct., Thurs.–Sat. 10–4.

Site of First Houses. The Pilgrims' first houses were built on short, steep Leyden Street, running up Cole's Hill from the harbor near Plymouth Rock. The private homes that stand here today each have plaques affixed to them identifying those original predecessors, now long vanished. The Pilgrims buried their dead on Cole's Hill—at night, so the Native Americans could not count the dwindling numbers of survivors. | Leyden St.

✦ ON THE CALENDAR: Aug. and Nov. **Pilgrims' Progress.** The 51 costumed marchers in this procession represent the survivors of the Pilgrim's first winter in Plymouth. The procession begins at 6 PM every Friday in August (and some dates in November) at the Mayflower Society House on North St. | 800/872–1620.

Oct.–Nov. **Autumnal Feasting.** Plimoth Plantation offers several fall dining events. Visitors can attend a dinner set in Plymouth, England in 1620, just before the *Mayflower* sail, where "passengers" discuss their hopes for the New World. There's also a Victorian Thanksgiving dinner, complete with period entertainment, and a New England Thanksgiving buffet with everything from soup to nuts. Reservations are required. | 508/746–1622 | www.plimoth.org.

HISTORIC DINING AND LODGING

Barker Tavern. If you're looking for sustenance en route between Plymouth and Boston, detour to this classic tavern-style restaurant, overlooking the harbor in the town of Scituate. The original section of the building dates to 1634, and the rather formal setting is Colonial-style, with beamed ceilings and large fireplaces. The menu runs to New England classics. Scituate is about 20 mi north of Plymouth and about 20 mi south of Quincy. | 21 Barker Rd., Scituate | 781/545–6533 | $20–$34 | AE, D, DC, MC, V | Closed Mon. No lunch.

John Carver Inn. This three-story, Colonial-style redbrick building is just a short walk from Plymouth's main attractions. This family-friendly inn has, of all things, a Pilgrim-theme pool with a water-slide replica of the *Mayflower*. At its Hearth 'n Kettle Restaurant, staff in Colonial attire serve a huge selection of American favorites, including seafood and hearty sandwiches. Restaurant. | 25 Summer St. | 508/746–7100 | fax 508/746–8299 | www.johncarverinn. com | 85 rooms | $139–$189 | AE, D, MC, V.

QUINCY
▼▼▼

Settled by English traders in 1625, the town that encompasses modern-day Quincy—a sprawling urban suburb about 8 mi south of downtown Boston—was originally known as Braintree. In 1792, Braintree was split into several smaller towns, one of which was named Quincy in honor of Col. John Quincy, a Revolutionary War leader who served as a Speaker of the Massachusetts House of Representatives (John Quincy's granddaughter, Abigail Smith, would go on to marry another Quincy notable, John Adams). Legend has it that Colonel Quincy pronounced his name "Quin-zee"—and that's how locals pronounce the town's name today.

Quincy calls itself the "City of Presidents," because it was the home of two: the second president, John Adams, and his son, John Quincy Adams, who was the sixth. Their birthplaces, their long-standing family home, and their tombs are all open to visitors as part of the Adams National Historical Park, run by the National Park Service. Another Quincy native son is John Hancock, who was born here in 1737. Hancock served in the Continental Congress (from 1775 to 1780), and he's perhaps best known for being the first signer of the Declaration of Independence. He died in Quincy, a very wealthy man, in 1793 while serving his ninth term as Massachusetts governor. In addition to sending its native sons to serve the nation, the city provided high-quality paving and building stone from its granite quarries for more than 200 years. Quincy granite was used to build King's Chapel in Boston and the Bunker Hill Monument in Charlestown. *Contact South Shore Chamber of Commerce | Box 690625, Quincy 02269 | 617/479–1111 | www.southshorechamber.org.*

Abigail Adams House. "Remember the ladies" was Abigail Adams's famous rejoinder to her husband as he laid the foundations for his fledging country's indepedence. Few, thankfully, have forgotten Abigail Smith (1744–1818), daughter of a Weymouth clergyman who went on to attain a lasting place in history as the wife of America's second president, John Adams, and mother of the sixth, John Quincy Adams. Biographers have long shown that she deserves attention on her own merits as political advisor, diarist, and correspondent—her letters are much prized by historians (as you can see if you read David McCullough's best-selling 2001 biography, *John Adams* and Lynn Withey's 2002 *Dearest Friend: A Life of Abigail Adams*). The small 1685 farmhouse—hip-roofed and fetchingly painted in robin's-egg blue and red trim—in which she was born, and located in the nearby township of Weymouth, has been restored to its mid-1700s appearance, thanks to wood paneling salvaged from nearby historic period taverns and Colonial-era furnishings. Built in 1685 for a Reverend Torrey, the house was bought in 1737 by the township's new Rev. William Smith, who had married Elizabeth Quincy of Braintree in 1740 and then sizeably enlarged it to educate his four children and other family members. Abigail married John Adams, then a lawyer, in 1764 and moved to Braintree (now Quincy) Massachusetts. The house is set 4 mi south of Quincy. | 180 Norton St., Weymouth | 781/335–4205 | www.abigailadams.org | $1 | July–Labor Day, Tues.–Sun. 1–4.

Adams National Historical Park. Administered by the National Park Service, these sites encompass five generations (1720–1927) of the illustrious Adams family, including two presidents and first ladies, three ministers, historians, and writers. A trolley connects the visitor center with the other sites in the park, including the birthplaces of John Adams and of his son John Quincy Adams; Peace Field, the home of several generations of Adamses, and the United First Parish Church, where the tombs of John and John Quincy Adams and their wives are located. | 1250 Hancock St. | 617/770–1175 | www.nps.gov/adam | $3 | Mid-Apr.–mid-Nov., daily 9–5. Last tour departs visitor center at 3:15.

John Adams and John Quincy Adams Birthplaces. These two saltbox houses date from the 17th century. The elder Adams was born (in 1735) and raised at 133 Franklin Street. After John and Abigail Adams married in 1764, they moved to the second house nearby at 141 Franklin Street, where their son was born (in 1767). Both houses are rather sparsely furnished, with period reproductions, although the tour guides provide historical background about the Adams family.

Peace Field (the Old House). When John and Abigail Adams moved here in 1788, they became the first of several generations of Adamses to live in this stately 1731 wood-frame house set amidst orchards and gardens; John Quincy Adams and his wife later used it as their summer home, and it remained an Adams residence until 1927. Though it had only four rooms when John and Abigail moved in, they and other family members continued to enlarge it—it now has 22 rooms. Everything in the house, from Abigail's china, to John's writing desk, to John and Abigail's canopy bed, belonged to the Adams family. The Stone Library, a separate building that John's grandson Charles Francis Adams had constructed directly behind the Old House, contains more than 14,000 volumes in a magnificent chamber, many of which belonged to John Quincy Adams (and include his notations in the margins). John Adams died in his second-floor study in the Old House on July 4, 1826, exactly 50 years to the day after he voted for the Declaration of Independence. Unbeknownst to Adams, his successor as President, Thomas Jefferson, had died just hours earlier at his home in Virginia. Both men had long cherished the dream of living to see the Declaration's 50th anniversary and both did so—barely.

United First Parish Church and the Adams Crypt. Designed by Alexander Parris, the Boston architect who also designed Quincy Market, and built in 1828 from granite quarried in Quincy, this is the only church in the United States in which two former presidents (and their wives) are buried. The simple tombs of John Adams, Abigail Adams, John Quincy Adams, and Louisa Catherine Adams rest in the church basement. The Adamses were all originally buried across the street in Hancock Cemetery; the remains of John and Abigail were moved to the church tomb in 1828, after the church's construction was completed, and those of John Q. and Louisa Catherine were transferred to the church in 1858. Tours of the church, which houses a Unitarian congregation, are offered separately from the National Park tour. | 1306 Hancock St. | 617/773–1290 | www.ufpc.org | $3 | Tours mid-Apr.–mid-Nov., Mon.–Sat. 9–5, Sun. 1–5.

Hancock Cemetery. Named for John Hancock's father, the Rev. John Hancock, who served as First Parish Church minister from 1726 until his death in 1744, this cemetery dates to the 1630s. Reverend Hancock is buried here, as are several generations of Adamses and Quincys, including Col. John Quincy, who gave the town its name; patriot and merchant Josiah Quincy; Henry Adams, John Adams' great-great-grandfather, whose 1646 grave is the earliest identifiable one in the burying ground; and John Adams and Susannah Boylston Adams, John Adams' father and mother. You can pick up a cemetery map at the nearby Adams National Historical Park Visitor Center. | Hancock St., opposite the United First Parish Church | Free | Daily, dawn–dusk.

Josiah Quincy House. This fine Georgian house was the home of the Quincy family. It is furnished with period wall paneling, fireplaces surrounded by English tile, and family heirlooms. | 20 Muirhead St. | 617/227–3956 | $2 | June–mid-Oct., tours on the hr weekends 11–4.

Quincy Historical Society. Occupying a former boys' school donated to the town by John Adams, this historical museum is located on the site where John Hancock, Revolutionary War–era president of the Continental Congress, was born. Exhibits detail Quincy's evolution from country retreat to industrial city, illustrated by artifacts, photos, and ephemera from the society's collections. There is also a research library. | Adams Academy Building, 8 Adams St. | 617/773–1144 | Free | Weekdays 9–4, 1st Sat. of each month 1–4.

Quincy Homestead. Four generations of Quincys lived here, including Dorothy Quincy, who became the wife of John Hancock. Two of the rooms were built in 1686, the others in the 18th century. Admire period furnishings and the herb garden. | 1010 Hancock St. | 617/472–5117 | $3 | May–Oct., Wed.–Sun. noon–5.

✦ ON THE CALENDAR: Oct. **Birthday of John Adams.** Lectures, dramatic performances, and a ceremony at United First Parish Church honor the life and public service of the second U.S. president, John Adams. | 617/770–1175.

Oct. **Spirits of Quincy's Past.** Behind the iron gates of the Hancock Cemetery, park rangers and volunteers take visitors on a candlelight tour of one of New England's oldest burying grounds. Historic figures "come back to life" to talk about what they did to help their community and their nation prosper. | 617/770–1175.

SALEM
▼▼▼

First settled in 1626, Salem was likely the richest city per capita in America by the late 1700s. It built its wealth as a trading port, where merchant ships departed for "the farthest port of the rich East," as the city's motto proclaimed. Frigates out of Salem opened the Far East trade routes and generated the wealth that created America's first millionaires. Its citizens prominent in the maritime world included wealthy merchant Elias Hasket Derby (1739–99), who was perhaps the Bill Gates of his day, and navigator Nathaniel Bowditch (1773–1838), who published *The New American Practical Navigator* in 1802, correcting more than 8,000 errors in British navigational materials.

Despite its history as a maritime power, Salem today is best-known for an event that occurred on land—the infamous Salem witch trials of 1692. The incident began in January 1692, when the 9-year-old daughter, Elizabeth, and 12-year-old niece, Abigail Williams, of Salem's Reverend (no less) Samuel Parris's began to fall into fits, visited by "spectral evidence" and haunted by accounts given to them by their governess, the West Indian slave Tituba. Village doctor William Griggs pointed to witchcraft as the cause and, under questioning, the girls and their friends came to accuse villagers Sarah Osburn, Sarah Good, and Tituba as "witches." On March 1, 1692, court officials John Hathorne and Jonathan Corwin convened investigations at the Salem Meetinghouse. While the accused protested their innocence, Tituba's graphic descriptions of "meetings with the devil"—highly seasoned with her Voodoo heritage—had the three women soon jailed.

By May, Governor William Phips convened a court to try accused witches who had not confessed—some 150 people were brought before the court, which condemned 19 people to death by September (18 were hanged and one, Giles Cory, pressed to death); five others died in jail. By early 1693, the horror of the made-up charges had pervaded the community; when trials were reconvened, they were quickly disbanded and several years later, the township offered an official apology. Today, historians continue to obsess over the trials. In 2002, Mary Beth Norton's *In the Devil's Snare: The Salem Witchcraft Crisis of 1692* posited that "the craze" was in part due to the the fallout of massacres and mischief witnessed by family retainers, children, and town officials who had all relocated to Salem from the outer reaches of Maine, where Indian raids had terrorized settlers during the conflict known as King Philip's War. But the ultimate words on Salem are to be found in two ground-breaking books, *Salem Possessed* (1974), by Paul Boyer and Stephen Nissenbaum, and *Salem Story* (1993), by Bernard Rosenthal. These authors discovered that the motivating forces behind many of the "witchcraft" charges were political, economic, and legal, *not* religious. The Parris and Putnam families shamefully used the trumped-up charges in their ongoing litigation against the accused, several members of whom wanted the church of Salem Village to merge with that of Salem

Town (thereby omitting the job of Reverend Parris). The Putnam family had much to gain economically by destroying many people they were suing. The truth gets even uglier: It is now known that the presiding magistrates could appropriate the property of the accused, thereby growing richer with every hanging. Such evil effectively blew the all-mighty force of Puritanism out of the water in 17th-century New England and it all but died out shortly after the Salem trials.

Although much of the witch hysteria actually occurred outside modern-day Salem in what is now neighboring Danvers, this inconvenient little fact hasn't prevented a large number of Salem's shops from masquerading as witch-themed "museums," displaying small doses of historical facts or artifacts and selling every imaginable kind of Halloweenlike merchandise. The city does have a somber, reflective monument, the Salem Witch Trials Memorial, as well as several sites where—if you can ignore the hokey hype—you can learn something about the society that fell under the spell of witch paranoia. Author Nathaniel Hawthorne was also born in this small city 16 mi north of Boston, and you can visit the relentlessly picturesque 17th-century House of the Seven Gables, which inspired his novel of the same name. Another Salem notable is architect Samuel McIntire (1757–1811), who built many of the city's stately Federal mansions. Either the National Park Service Regional Visitor Center or Destination Salem (the city's visitor bureau) can provide copies of the "McIntire Historic District Walking Trail" brochure, which outlines a self-guided walk past a number of McIntire's buildings.

Now most noted for its outlet marts, nearby Danvers—home to two must-dos, the Rebecca Nurse Homestead and the Derby Summer House at Glen Magna Farms—is about 5 mi from Salem and can be reached by heading northeast up Route 35. *Contact Destination Salem | 63 Wharf St., Salem 01970 | 978/741–3252 or 877/725–3662 | www.salem.org.*

Derby Summer House at Glen Magna. Considered by many connoisseurs to be the most beautiful Federal-style building in America, the diminutive Derby Summer House today crowns the gardens of the vast Glen Magna Farms estate (it was moved from its original location 4 mi away in 1901). Owned by the Danvers Historical Society and once an expansive working farm, albeit a "gentleman's seat," Glen Magna provided wealthy Salem merchant Joseph Peabody and his family with sanctuary from the War of 1812. The much-restored mansion is only "Colonial Revival," but head to the garden to see the Derby Summer House, the masterwork of designer Samuel McIntire, Salem's most prominent architect and furniture builder. Built in 1793 by maritime tycoon Elias Hasket Derby (the country's first millionaire, his ships were the first to ferry back treasures from Canton, China), it was conceived as a summer teahouse. A masterpiece of the Adamesque style, the small two-story pavilion is spectacularly ornamented, with figures of *The Milkmaid* and *The Reaper* upon its roofline. Delicate columns and second-story window festoons enchant the eye below. Truly the Federal style as seen through a jeweler's loupe, this structure is a must-see for all lovers of 18th-century America. Back in Salem, Derby's own mansion still stands on Derby Street. | Ingersoll St. (Endicott Park entrance), Danvers | 978/777–1666 | www.glenmagnafarms.org | House and garden tour $6, grounds $2 | June–Sept., Tues. and Thurs. 10–4; house tour Wed. at 10 and 2; garden tour Wed. at 11.

House of the Seven Gables. Immortalized in Nathaniel Hawthorne's classic 1851 novel of the same name, this celebrated 1668 wooden mansion is one of the oldest in New England and now comprises the centerpiece of a complex of Colonial-era houses and gardens that is nonpareil for evoking the mysteries of Salem's still spirit-warm past. "The aspect of the venerable mansion has always affected me like a human countenance, bearing the traces not merely of outward storm and sunshine, but expressive also, of the long lapse of mortal life, and accompanying vicissitudes that have passed within," wrote Hawthorne, and today it is easy to see why this forbidding brown-clapboard house—stunningly surrounded by 18th-century Jacobean-style gardens most famed for their lilac bushes—so haunted the writer, who set his saga of the Pyncheon family here. Hawthorne, in fact, grew up just down the block in a house that has now been moved adjacent to The Gables. The author's birthplace—with its highly contrasting, bright-red clapboard—dates from the late 18th century, and it was here that Nathaniel was born July 4, 1804. The Gables house—or the Turner-Ingersoll Mansion (to give its official name)—at that point belonged to a cousin of the novelist, whose ancestor, John Hathorne, was a judge at Salem's witchcraft trials. The Gables is today furnished in period style, but its pièce de résistance is the authentic secret staircase, something out of a horror flick starring Vincent Price (who, in fact, filmed a version of the Hawthorne novel). Costumed interpreters are on site to explain the house's 2,000 artifacts and objects, as well as point you to the seaside gardens, the Hawthorne homestead, and the Retire Becket House (now the site tea room), which also stood during the hysteria. | 54 Turner St. (off Derby St.) | 978/744–0991 | www.7gables.org | Guided tours $10; $16 combination ticket includes Salem 1630 Pioneer Village | Late Jan.–Mar., Mon.–Sat. 10–5, Sun. noon–5; Apr.–June, Nov., and Dec, daily 10–5; July–Oct., daily 10–7.

National Park Service Regional Visitor Center. In recognition of its many historic sites, the whole of Essex County, of which Salem is a part, has been designated a National Heritage Area. In this visitors' center, which serves as the gateway to the region, you'll find an introductory film, brochures that map out the area's sights, helpful rangers to answer questions, and a well-stocked gift shop and bookstore. | 2 New Liberty St. | 978/740–1650 | www.nps.gov/sama | Free | Daily 9–5.

Peabody Essex Museum. Salem's seafaring past is on display at this 200-year-old museum. Its galleries are filled with maritime art and history and spoils of the Asian export trade, ranging from 16th-century Chinese blue porcelain to an entire Japanese carrying litter to Indian colonial silver. The museum also offers tours of several nearby historical houses. At press time, the museum was completing a major renovation and expansion, designed by architect Moshe Safdie, expected to be completed in summer 2003. | East India Sq. | 978/745–9500 or 800/745–4054 | www.pem.org | $10 | Apr.–Oct., Mon.–Sat. 10–5, Sun. noon–5; Nov.–Mar., Tues.–Sat. 10–5, Sun. noon–5.

  Crowninshield-Bentley House. In one half of this 1720s Georgian home, Hannah Crowninshield ran a basic boardinghouse. In the more opulent other half lived her wealthy merchant son, Benjamin. The restoration of the building emphasizes this dichotomy. Noted diarist and thinker Rev. William Bentley lodged with Mrs. Crowninshield. | 132 Essex St. | 978/745–9500 | www.pem.org | $12 | Apr.–Oct., Mon.–Sat. 10–5, Sun. noon–5; Nov.–Mar., Tues.–Sat. 10–5, Sun. noon–5.

  Gardner-Pingree House. Built in 1804 by famous architect and woodcarver Samuel McIntire, this three-story Georgian Federal house is a fine example of that era's style. It's been restored to circa 1815, when it was inhabited by local merchant John Gardner. | 128 Essex St. | 978/745–9500 | www.pem.org | $12 | Apr.–Oct., Mon.–Sat. 10–5, Sun. noon–5; Nov.–Mar., Tues.–Sat. 10–5, Sun. noon–5.

  John Ward House. Farmer and tanner John Ward had front row seats for the horrifying events of 1692—he lived with his family opposite the gaol used in the witch trials. The house was built around 1684. | Brown St. | 978/745–9500 | $12 | Apr.–Oct., Mon.–Sat. 10–5, Sun. noon–5; Nov.–Mar., Tues.–Sat. 10–5, Sun. noon–5.

Rebecca Nurse Homestead. Perhaps the most historically pure and spiritually evocative house extant of the Early Colonial era, this First Period saltbox house would be a must-visit even if it weren't for the fact it remains a unique relic of the Salem witchcraft craze. Several miles northwest of present-day Salem, the homestead is set in the town of Danvers, established in 1630 and one of Massachusetts's earliest Puritan settlements (which found glory in the next century, when many volunteers from the village's Alarm Company headed to Lexington to fight at the first battle of the Revolutionary War). In those days it was known as Salem Village, part of what was a very large Salem township. Rebecca Nurse was a respected elder in the village, until, that is, March 19, 1692, when hysteric girls pointed to this 71-year-old matriarch as one of their tormentors. Rebecca responded, ". . . as to this thing, I am as innocent as the child unborn, but surely what sin hath God found out in me unrepented of that He should lay such an affliction upon me in my old age?" Her First Period saltbox house is one of a complex of buildings, which also includes the Meetinghouse—actually a recent edifice constructed for the 1985 Vanessa Redgrave film, *Three Sovereigns for Sarah,* which memorably depicted the trials that were held in the town meetinghouse (long since destroyed)—and the Endicott Barn, where a short film outlining the witchcraft hysteria is shown. In the end, goodly and godly Rebecca Nurse was hanged in 1692—her family secretly buried her body somewhere on the homestead's grounds. Also to be seen on the 32-acre estate are a small graveyard and 17th-century vegetable and herb gardens. This famed homestead is now run by the Danvers List Alarm Company, an 18th-century reenactment group. | 149 Pine St., Danvers | 978/774–8799 | www.rebeccanurse.org | $4 | Mid-June–early Sept., Tues.–Sun. 1–4:30; early Sept.–Oct., weekends 1–4:30; Nov.–mid-June, by appointment.

Salem 1630 Pioneer Village. In this small living history museum, costumed interpreters re-create the Salem of the early 17th century, when it was a fishing village and the Commonwealth's first capital. Replicas of thatch-roof cottages, period gardens, and wigwams have been constructed at the site. If you've been to Plimoth Plantation, you might find this exhibit rather modest, but it's refreshingly low-key compared with Salem's more commercial attractions. | Forest River Park, (follow Rte. 114 east, then turn left onto West Ave.) | 978/744–0991 | www.7gables.org/pv.htm | $7.50; $16 combination ticket includes House of the Seven Gables | July–Labor Day, Mon.–Sat. 10–5, Sun. noon–5.

Salem Maritime National Historic Site. Located near Derby Wharf, this National Historic Site—the first in the National Park System—illustrates Salem's heritage as a major seaport with a thriving overseas trade. Starting at the orientation center (with an 18-minute film), exhibits there and in several nearby restored houses document the development of shipping in the New England Colonies from the settlement era through the Revolutionary War and beyond. Also on site is a replica of *The Friendship,* a 171-ft, three-masted 1797 merchant vessel. | 174 Derby St. | 978/740–1660 | www.nps.gov/sama | Free. Tour of the buildings: $5 | Daily 9–5.

Custom House. Nathaniel Hawthorne worked in the (now restored) offices of this 1819 Custom House from 1846–49, a location made famous in *The Scarlet Letter.* | Derby St.

Derby House. Built in 1762, this house belonged to maritime merchant Elias Hasket Derby, reputed to be the country's first millionaire. | Derby St.

Narbonne House. Built in 1672, this is the oldest frame house of its type in Massachusetts. Over the years, it was home to craftsmen, seamen, and longshoremen. Its last inhabitants, seamstress sisters Sarah and Marie Narbonne, left behind many artifacts (currently on display) relating to their work and lives. | 170 Essex St.

Salem Witch Museum. This museum presents an informative, if somewhat hokey, introduction to the 1692 witchcraft hysteria. A half-hour multimedia exhibit re-creates key scenes, using 13 sets, life-size models, and an ominous taped narration. A short walk-through exhibit describes witch history and witch hunts through the years. | Washington Sq. N | 978/744–1692 | www.salemwitchmuseum.com | $6.50 | Sept.–June, daily 10–5; July–Aug., daily 10–7.

Salem Witch Trials Memorial. This melancholy space, dedicated in 1992 on the 300th anniversary of the witchcraft trials, honors those who died not because they were witches but because they refused to confess. A stone wall is studded with 20 stone benches, each inscribed with a victim's name. Look for the flagstones at one end of the plot that are engraved with protestations of innocence, sometimes cut off in mid-sentence. | Off Liberty St. near corner of Charter St. | www.salemweb.com/memorial.

Witch Dungeon Museum. Observe a live reenactment of a witch trial, taken from the transcripts of 1692. Then tour a re-created dungeon where accused witches were kept. | 16 Lynde St. | 978/741–3570 | www.witchdungeon.com | Guided tours $6 | Apr.–Nov., daily 10–5; evening hrs around Halloween; tours every half-hr.

Witch House. The name of this house is tragically inappropriate. No witch ever lived at this 1670s home; it belonged to Jonathan Corwin, the judge who presided over the Salem witch trials. The interior is strikingly authentic to the period. Tours, led by guides in period dress, run 35–40 minutes. | 310½ Essex St. | 978/744–0180 | Guided tours $5 | Mid-Mar.–June and Sept.–Nov., daily 10–4:30; July–Aug., daily 10–6.

✦ ON THE CALENDAR: July **Maritime Festival.** Learn how to cane a chair, watch shipwrights create masts and rigging to re-create a 1797 tall ship, and participate in other interactive demonstrations of historical trades at this event. | 978/740–1660.

HISTORIC LODGING
Hawthorne Hotel. Although it wasn't built until the 1920s, this imposing Federal-style brick building next to Salem Common is furnished with stately 18th-century reproductions. The formal, chandelier-bedecked restaurant, Nathaniel's, has an ambitious contemporary menu while the more casual tavern serves lighter bites. Restaurant. | 18 Washington Sq. W | 800/729–7829 | fax 978/745–9842 | www.hawthornehotel.com | 89 rooms | $125–$199 | AE, D, MC, V.

SANDWICH (CAPE COD)
▼▼▼

Established in 1637 by some of the Plymouth Pilgrims and incorporated in 1639, Sandwich is the oldest town on Cape Cod. Located about 60 mi south of Boston, just over the Sagamore Bridge, which crosses the Cape Cod Canal, the town is exceptionally blessed with period architecture, from Early Colonial to Victorian. Stroll up and down Main and Water streets in the center of the village for a mini-architectural tour. *Contact Cape Cod Canal Regional Chamber of Commerce | 70 Main St., Buzzards Bay 02532 | 508/759–6000 | www.capecodcanalchamber. org.*

Aptucxet Trading Post Museum. In 1627, Plimoth Plantation leaders established a way station in what is now Bourne, about 5 mi south of Sandwich, that became a center of trade between the Native American encampment at Great Herring Pond, 3 mi to the northeast; Dutch colonists in New Amsterdam (New York), to the south; and English colonists on Cape Cod Bay. The Native Americans traded furs; the Dutch traded linen cloth, metal tools, glass beads, sugar, and other staples; and the Pilgrims traded wool cloth, clay beads, sassafras, and tobacco (which they imported from Virginia). Wampum, made from polished fragments of hard-shell clams, was the medium of exchange. The museum that stands on the site today is a replica of the original trading post. Inside, 17th-century cooking utensils hang from the original brick hearth; beaver and otter skins, furniture, and other artifacts such as arrowheads, tools, and tomahawks are displayed. | 24 Aptucxet Rd., Bourne | 508/759–9487 | www.bournehistoricalsoc. org | $4 | May–June and Sept.–Columbus Day, Tues.–Sat. 10–5, Sun. 2–5; July–Aug., Mon.–Sat. 10–5, Sun. 2–5.

Dexter Gristmill. Where Shawme Pond drains over its dam, a little wooden bridge leads to this waterwheel-powered mill built in 1654. In season the miller demonstrates and talks about the mill's operation and also sells its ground corn. | Water and Grove Sts. | 508/888–4910 | $2; combination ticket with Hoxie House, $3 | Late May, Labor Day–late Sept., Sat. 10–4:45; June–Labor Day, Mon.–Sat. 10–4:45.

Heritage Plantation. A stop here at this complex of museum buildings on 76 beautifully land-scaped acres satisfies varied interests. Americana buffs, particularly those with a military bent, should check out the American History museum, which houses antique firearms, a collection of 2,000 hand-painted miniature soldiers, and military uniforms, as well as Native American arts. The art museum has an extensive Currier & Ives collection, with works dating to the mid-1800s, as well as a folk art gallery that includes Early American weathervanes, portraits (many of children), and 1800s scrimshaw (works made of whalebone or whale teeth). Families visiting with youngsters should ask at the ticket office for the Family Funpacks with children's activities, or the Clue tours, scavenger-hunt games for exploring the grounds. | 67 Grove St. | 508/888–3300 | www.heritageplantation.org | $12 | May–Oct., Sat.–Wed. 9–6, Thurs.–Fri. 9–8; Nov.–Apr., Tues.–Sun. 10–4.

Hoxie House. This old saltbox, one of the oldest houses on Cape Cod, was virtually unal-tered since it was built in 1675. Today it's a small museum, furnished to reflect daily life in the 17th century. | 18 Water St., [Rte. 130] | 508/888–1173 | $2, combination ticket with Dexter Gristmill $3 | Memorial Day–mid-June, Sat. 10–5, Sun. 1–5; mid-June–mid-Oct., Mon.–Sat. 10–5, Sun. 1–5.

Sandwich Glass Museum. The main industry in 19th-century Sandwich was producing vividly colored glass. This museum contains relics of the town's early history, as well as thousands of examples of blown and pressed glass. Glassmaking demonstrations are held in summer. | 129 Main St. | 508/888–0251 | $3.50 | Apr.–Dec., daily 9:30–5; Feb.–Mar., Wed.–Sun. 9:30–4.

SHEFFIELD
▼▼

Settlers reportedly purchased Sheffield and the surrounding land from the Mohicans (to be historically accurate, the name was actually Mahican) for three barrels of cider, 30 quarts of rum, and 460£. Perched near the Connecticut state line in the southwestern corner of Massachusetts, the town, which was established in 1733, is the oldest in Berkshire County. This small community, which also includes the adjacent village of Ashley Falls, was largely an agricultural area. More recently, it has attracted a large number of antiques shops. However, during Colonial times, Sheffield earned its place in history with three events: the drafting of the Sheffield Declaration, a precursor to the Declaration of Independence; a court case that led to the outlawing of slavery in Massachusetts; and the final battle of Shays' Rebellion.

In 1773, Colonel John Ashley, Theodore Sedgwick, and nine other Sheffield citizens met in Ashley's home to draft the Sheffield Declaration, a document describing the rights of man and detailing grievances against English rule. With such assertions as "Mankind in a State of Nature are equal, free, and independent of each other," it is considered to be a model for the Declaration of Independence. It also influenced the language of the Massachusetts Constitution, adopted in 1780, which declared that "all men are born free and equal." The Ashleys' house was also the setting for another quest for freedom. A slave woman called Bett worked for the Ashley family for many years and was present in the house during many of the discussions about freedom that led to the Sheffield Declaration. After an incident in 1781 in which John Ashley's wife Hannah struck Bett, the slave escaped and fled to Theodore Sedg-wick's home, where she asked Sedgwick to represent her in a suit for her freedom, spurred in part by the discussions about liberty that she had overheard. While historians are uncer-tain why Sedgwick agreed to take on Bett's case, in opposition to his friend Ashley, Sedg-wick convinced the jury that the 1780 state constitution forbid the keeping of slaves. The panel ruled in Bett's favor, effectively outlawing slavery in Massachusetts. Then, in 1787, Sheffield was the site of the last battle in Shays' Rebellion, the post-Revolutionary uprising by farmers looking for debt relief. Though you can visit Colonel Ashley's home and several other historic buildings, all that remains of the Shays' battle is a marker by the side of the road. *Contact Southern Berkshires Chamber of Commerce | 362 Main St., Great Barrington 01230-1804 | 413/528–1510 | www.greatbarrington.org.*

Colonel Ashley House. John Ashley (1709–1802) was a lawyer and land surveyor when he had this house built in 1735 in anticipation of his wedding to Hannah Hogeboom. Ashley became a wealthy man—he built an iron works nearby, as well as a gristmill and a sawmill; he was a prominent landowner; and he was a leader in the local militia—and the furnishings and personal effects that remain in the home reflect the affluent styles of the era, including a large collection of redware that dates to the late 1700s. One of the area's oldest homes, about 5 mi south of Sheffield proper, the house itself is a fine example of 18th-century craftsmanship. It also played a role in several events of the late 18th century. In 1773, the Sheffield Declaration, considered a precursor to the Declaration of Independence, was drafted here in the second floor study that still retains its beautiful wood paneling. In 1781, Colonel Ashley's slave Bett was the first to sue for her freedom under the Massachusetts Constitution of 1780. | Cooper Hill Rd., Ashley Falls | 413/298–8146 | www.thetrustees.org | Guided tours $5 | Late May–early Oct., weekends and Mon. holidays 10–5.

Dan Raymond House/Sheffield Historical Society. This circa 1775 house, which is now the headquarters of the local historical society, belonged to Dan Raymond, a businessman and real estate dealer, who built the home from bricks he made himself. The Raymonds were among Sheffield's wealthier families in the late 1700s, and while Raymond was thought to be a Tory sympathizer, he eventually joined a Revolutionary regiment. The house is full of quirky articles that illustrate 17th-century life in the Berkshires, including wooden dishes, two-pronged forks (the three-prong variety didn't come into use till the 1800s), spinning wheels, rope beds, and a courting mirror, angled so that dating couples could sneak peaks at each other. Visitors can also tour several other 19th-century structures on the property. | 159 Main St. | 413/229–2694 | www.sheffieldhistory.org | Guided tours $5 | Late May–Oct., Thurs.–Sun. 11–4.

Shays' Rebellion Monument. Located along the side of the road between South Egremont and Sheffield, this modest memorial marks the site of the final battle of Shays' Rebellion, which took place on February 26, 1787. | Sheffield-Egremont Rd.

HISTORIC LODGING
Egremont Inn. Built as a tavern in 1780, this rambling Colonial building still includes a friendly tavern room (serving light meals), but it's also a comfortable inn. Though some of the guest rooms are quite small, they're cheerfully furnished with simple period pieces and reproductions. There's plenty of common space, too, including several sitting areas (with fireplaces), a wraparound front porch, and a restaurant serving gourmet country cuisine. About 3 mi southwest of Great Barrington and 3 mi northwest of Sheffield. Restaurant. Complimentary breakfast. | 10 Old Sheffield Rd., South Egremont | 413/528–2111 | fax 413/528–3284 | www.egremontinn.com | 19 rooms | $140–$180 | AE, D, MC, V.

STOCKBRIDGE
▼▼▼

In the heart of the southern Berkshires region, Stockbridge may be better known for its post-Colonial attractions—painter Norman Rockwell lived here from the 1950s until his death in 1978, and majestic summer "cottages", dating to the Gilded Age, line many of the leafy back roads. But back in the 1700s, Stockbridge was an outpost on the Massachusetts frontier that had long been home to the Native Mohican people. In 1739, the same year that the town of Stockbridge was incorporated, Rev. John Sergeant built a home here and began working as a missionary to the Mohicans. He learned to speak the Mohican language and during his time in Stockbridge, relations between the Mohicans and the English settlers were peaceful. After Sergeant's death in 1749, however, this peaceful coexistence began to erode, and by the 1780s, the Mohicans had begun a westward migration into New York State and eventually to Wisconsin where their descendents live today as the Stockbridge-Munsee Band of the Mohican Nation. *Contact Stockbridge Chamber of Commerce | 6 Elm St., Stockbridge 01262 | 413/298–5200 | www.stockbridgechamber.org. Stockbridge Visitors Center | 41 Main St. | 413/298–4662.*

Merwin House. This 1820s Federal-style brick home, nicknamed "Tranquility," was among the earliest in the area to be turned into a summer vacation house, after the newly built railroads of the late 19th century opened up the bucolic Berkshires to tranquillity-seeking New Yorkers. The furnishings reflect the eclectic tastes of the well-traveled owners, and hint at the leisure they enjoyed during the growth of the local resort community. | 14 Main St. | 413/298–4703 | www.spnea.org | Guided tours $4 | June–mid-Oct.; weekend tours on the hr, 11–4.

Mission House. The Rev. John Sergeant, an early settler who aimed to convert the Mohicans, the local Native Americans, to Christianity, built this house in 1739. The meticulously restored home includes ornate wooden paneling in the parlor, furnishings that date to the 1700s (a number of which belonged to Sergeant), and the elaborately scrolled Connecticut Valley doorway out front. Behind the house is a small but detailed museum area that contains exhibits on Mohican life and history, with clothing, jewelry, tools, and other artifacts. | 19 Main St., at Sergeant St. | 413/298–3239 | www.thetrustees.org | Guided tours $5 | Memorial Day–Columbus Day, daily 10–5.

HISTORIC DINING AND LODGING
Historic Merrell Inn. This former stagecoach stop, built in the 1790s, is now a stately brick-front inn filled with antiques and period reproductions. Walk down the broad lawn to the screened gazebo for a view of the Housatonic River. The inn is a mile from Stockbridge. Complimentary breakfast. | 1565 Pleasant St. (Rte. 102), South Lee | 413/243–1794 | fax 413/243–2669 | www.merrell-inn.com | 10 rooms | $95–$180 | MC, V.

Red Lion Inn. Established in 1773 as a stagecoach stop on the Boston–Albany route, this vast and rambling clapboard inn has an impressive collection of antiques and china, although the rooms themselves—which vary from spacious to extremely compact—are furnished with "Colonial" reproductions. The sweeping front porch, right across the street from the Episcopal church, is ideal for people-watching. The adorably old-fashioned, antiques- and pewter-filled dining room conjures up America in much more innocent days (is it a time-warp from 1936?) and serves solid New England cuisine—order up a yummy hot buttered rum for a libation and finish off your feast with Indian pudding. You can also dine in the more informal tavern room or in the Lion's Den pub. Restaurant. | 30 Main St. | 413/298–5545 | fax 413/298–5130 | www.redlioninn.com | 103 rooms | $95–$215 | AE, D, DC, MC, V.

STURBRIDGE
▼▼▼

Founded in 1738, Sturbridge followed the trajectory of many central Massachusetts towns, evolving from a purely agrarian community to one that depended to a large extent on the earnings of water-powered mills built along the Quinebaug River. After the various local industries followed suppliers, buyers, or profits out of the region, the town shrank, losing more than a third of its population between the 1860s and the 1920s. Today, the town is best known as the home of Old Sturbridge Village, a simulated 1830s rural American town composed of authentic structures gathered from around New England and peopled with costumed interpreters who re-create life in the early 19th century. Sturbridge is about 60 mi southwest of Boston. *Contact Tri-Community Chamber of Commerce | 380 Main St., Sturbridge 01566-1057 | 508/347–2761 or 888/788–7274 | www.sturbridge.org.*

Old Sturbridge Village. As one of America's most famous living museums, a visit here is a veritable rite of passage for any child from a self-respecting, Early American history–interested family. Grouped around The Green, and presided over by a magisterial white-clapboard, steeple-topped Meetinghouse, about 40 historic structures from around New England have been collected here on 200 acres to create a small but complete 1830s-era village. Costumed interpreters describe and demonstrate different occupations that were typically found in a rural New England community in the 18th and early 19th centuries. You can see farmers, blacksmiths, shoemakers, shopkeepers, printers, and lawyers all going about their daily lives, and if you enter one of the homes, you may find the lady of the house cooking supper. A gristmill, a sawmill, and a pottery shop are all in operation as well. The village also has a sizable museum of artifacts from the early 19th century, including an outstanding collection of antique clocks. Special evening events are held in the Tavern at Old Sturbridge Village, including hearth cooking demonstrations, a visit with literary figures (perhaps Nathaniel Hawthorne or Emily Dickinson), and a 19th-century music and games night; call for evening event schedules and fees. | 1 Old Sturbridge Village Rd. | 508/347–3362 or 800/733–1830 | www.osv.org | $20 (valid for 2 consecutive days) | Apr.–Oct., daily 9 5; Nov.–Dec. and mid–Feb.–Mar., Tue.–Sun. 9:30–4; Jan.–mid-Feb., weekends 9:30–4.

✦ ON THE CALENDAR: July **Independence Day Celebration.** Celebrate the Fourth of July 19th-century-style, with a dramatic reading of the Declaration of Independence, a fife and drum band, and a parade. | Old Sturbridge Village | 508/347–3362.

HISTORIC DINING AND LODGING
Publick House Historic Inn. This 1771 inn on Sturbridge Common retains its Colonial charms with period furnishings and gardens. In the main dining room, lobster pie, prime rib, or the "Every Day is Thanksgiving" turkey dinner are good choices. Ebenezer's Tavern also serves a lighter pub menu. Under the same management is the nearby Colonel Ebenezer Crafts Inn (Fiske Hill Road), a Colonial farmhouse built around 1786, that now houses eight guest rooms. Restaurant. No smoking. | Rte. 131 | 508/347–3313 or 800/782–5425 | fax 508/347–5073 | www.publickhouse.com | 15 rooms, 2 suites | $125–$165 | AE, DC, MC, V.

SUDBURY
▼▼▼

A growing suburb of Greater Boston, Sudbury is fast filling up its open space with contemporary homes and shopping plazas with names intended to evoke the landscape they are replacing. Yet there will always be one corner of town that will forever evoke the past, thanks to the foresight of Henry Ford. Ford's interest in preserving Americana led him to the threshold of Sudbury's Wayside Inn, a 1716 stagecoach inn immortalized by poet Henry Wadsworth Longfellow. *Contact MetroWest Chamber of Commerce | 1671 Worcester Rd., Framingham, 01701 | 508/879–5600 | www.metrowest.org*

Hosmer House. Once a post office, this 18th-century house in the town center retains a few of the features from its postal service days, such as sorting boxes, but it has been restored to its earlier domestic specifications. | Concorde Rd. and Old Sudbury Rd., 01776 | 978/443–8891 | Free | Weekends 10–dusk.

Longfellow's Wayside Inn. This late-17th–early-18th-century historical and literary shrine is America's oldest operating inn. It's decorated with period furnishings and now operates as a restaurant and hotel. | 76 Wayside Inn Rd., off U.S. 20 | 978/443–1776 | Daily.

Gristmilll. The waterwheel here continues to turn the stones that grind wheat and corn for the inn's bakery. | Apr.–Nov., Wed.–Sun. 9–5; Mon.–Tues. by appointment.

Redstone School. A 1798 schoolhouse that is the very little red schoolhouse immortalized in "Mary Had a Little Lamb." | May–Oct., Wed.–Sun. by appointment.

✦ ON THE CALENDAR: Apr. **Reenactment of March of Sudbury Minutemen to Concord on April 19, 1775.** When the sleeping townfolk of Sudbury were roused on April 19, 1775, many proceeded to North Bridge in Concord to fight the Redcoats. Today this event is commemorated by a historical group, the Sudbury Companies of Militia and Minute, who assemble at 3:45 AM at the First Parish Church in Wayland to read the original roll call by the light of an 18th-century lantern. They march to the music of the Sudbury Fife and Drum Corps, arriving in Concord by mid-morning. | 978/369–6993.

July **Fourth of July Parade.** This annual Independence Day event departs from Boston Post Road and follows a 2-mi route that winds up at town center. Approximately 40 floats and as many as 10 bands and fife and drum corps march. | 978/579–0000.

Sept. **Annual Muster of Fife and Drum.** Step back into the 18th century on the last Saturday of September for this muster featuring 18th-century military encampments as well as children's games, crafts, and contra dancing of the period. The most popular event is the parade of fife and drum companies from all over New England. | 978/443–1776.

HISTORIC DINING AND LODGING

Longfellow's Wayside Inn. In operation since 1716, this legendary inn was a stop on the Underground Railroad and was once owned by Henry Ford. Its fame was first spread by the poet Henry Wadsworth Longfellow, who visited it in 1861 and found it so spooky he called it Hobgoblin Hall. The central hearth of the inn was the "setting" for the poet's famous *Tales of a Wayside Inn*—the most famous of its poems was his retelling of Paul Revere's ride ("Listen, my children, and you shall hear."). The inn is furnished with antiques and period pieces. Be sure to visit the Ford Room, where the illustrious magnate entertained guests such as Calvin Coolidge and Thomas Edison. Although added to the historic 18th-century stagecoach inn in 1929 (and restored in the 1950s after a disastrous fire), the main dining room upholds the classic New England style of this literary landmark. The fare—from seafood to prime rib—is prepared with time-honored simplicity. The guest rooms upstairs are on the snug side but just down the hallway from a spacious ballroom built by Colonel Ezekiel Howe in 1800. Outside on the grounds are the Wayside Gristmill, the Martha Mary Chapel, and the Redstone School (Mary of "Mary Had a Little Lamb" fame attended this school), which Ford had moved here from Sterling, Massachusetts. Restaurant, bar, complimentary breakfast. | 76 Wayside Inn Rd. | 978/443–1776 | fax 978/443–8041 | www.wayside.org | 10 rooms | $120–$146 | AE, D, DC, MC, V.

By Kathy Smith

New Hampshire

"Live Free or Die"

Not a single battle was joined on New Hampshire soil during the American War for Independence. Yet, at the Battle of Bennington in 1777, Commander of New Hampshire forces General John Stark sounded the clarion call "Live Free or Die" that still echoes down the corridors of revolutionary history. He could not have known that his fighting words would be adopted as the state motto, still inscribed on license plates today. Or that the phrase would become something of a nettlesome icon, tempting image-makers to parody the high-minded idealism with their own catchy slogans. ("Live Freeze or Die" has become popular among North Country residents, and for good reason—meteorologists in the observatory atop Mount Washington, the highest peak in New England, record the coldest temperatures and highest winds in the world). But despite or maybe because of its ring of artless patriotism, the phrase has become somewhat axiomatic in New Hampshire. It has helped shape the state's native character and remind its citizens of the pioneer struggles for statehood.

New Hampshire loves a paradox. Perhaps no New England state has been more often caricatured as stubbornly Yankee in its conservatism, socially renegade in its policies of taxation, education, and welfare, and monolithically "white" in its ethnic make-up. New Hampshire has always been home to free-thinkers. It was the first revolutionary state to form a new government after the war, and the ninth and deciding state to ratify the U.S. Constitution. In the tiny hamlet of Dixville Notch in the still wild Great North Woods, the 16 or so townspeople are the very "first in the nation" to go to the polls to elect the President.

In the early years of town founding, adventurers and profiteers migrated to New Hampshire to tap its substantial resources and to escape the tyranny of social and religious orthodoxy in Massachusetts. In the 18th century, a highly inventive and charismatic religious order, the Shakers, established utopian communities in Canterbury and Enfield, upon magnificent hills and sweeping lakeside meadows. Their knowledge of herbal medicine, their industry and invention, their form of ecstatic singing and worship, and their furniture admired worldwide still fascinate. Now as then, New Hampshire is rich in beauty. The gran-

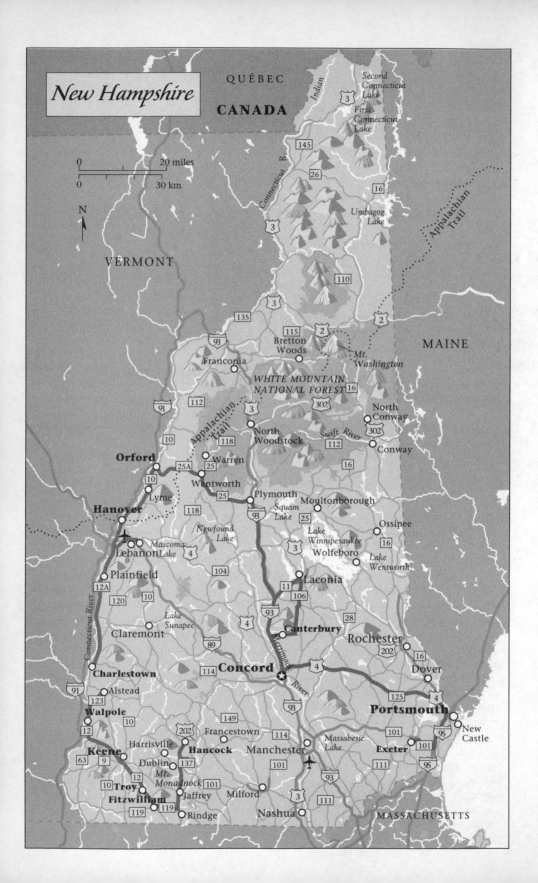

New Hampshire

QUÉBEC
CANADA

VERMONT

MAINE

Connecticut R.

Second Connecticut Lake
First Connecticut Lake
Indian

145
26
16
3

Umbagog Lake

Appalachian Trail

110

3

2
2

135
93

115
Bretton Woods

Mt. Washington

WHITE MOUNTAIN NATIONAL FOREST

Franconia

112
91
3

Appalachian Trail

16

302
North Conway

North Woodstock
Swift River
112
302
Conway

118
25
Warren

Orford
25A
25
10
Wentworth
Lyme
118
25
Plymouth
Moultonborough
93
Squam Lake
25

Hanover
Newfound Lake
Mascoma Lake
Lebanon
4

16

Lake Winnipesaukee
3
Wolfeboro
Ossipee
16
Lake Wentworth

Plainfield
104
12A
120
10
Lake Sunapee
Claremont
89
4

11
106
Laconia

93
4
28
Canterbury

Charlestown
91
114
Concord
Rochester
202
16
Dover

Alstead
123
Walpole
10
12

149
Francestown
114

Merrimack River

125
4
Portsmouth

202
Harrisville
Hancock
Manchester
101
Massabesic Lake
101
101
New Castle

Keene
63
9
Dublin
137
Mt. Monadnock
101
Jaffrey
Milford
93
111
Exeter
111
95

Troy
10
12
Fitzwilliam
119
119
Rindge
Nashua
3
111

MASSACHUSETTS

0   20 miles
0   30 km

N

ite in her earth is the very stuff from which the state takes its name. Even the constructed landscape rises organically from the natural one and rivals it charm for charm. The stone walls immortalized by poet Robert Frost were loosed rock by rock with backbreaking labor by early settlers. They remind us of the original clearing of the land for farms and the boundary making that has been a vexing theme throughout New Hampshire's history, surrounded as she is by Vermont, Maine, Massachusetts, and Canada. Off country lanes and beyond many of these stone walls, early farmhouses of the country vernacular style command a view of working fields. They combine houses, barns, and sheds in a functional but picturesque building style that grew out of the traditions of the Colonial period.

In the original towns of the Piscataqua region along the coast—Newcastle, Rye, Exeter, Hampton, and Portsmouth—17th-century dwellings, churches, and mills of wood-frame construction still stand. On the village greens of any country town you are sure to find the signature white-clapboard and steepled bell towers of the Congregational meeting house that was once required for a town charter. While no "first period" examples survive, "second period" buildings, or Federal style structures from the early 18th century, superseded these and can be seen in rural Rockingham County towns. Old parsonages, town halls, taverns, and one-room schoolhouses also date from this period. Citizens of "old" New Hampshire pride themselves on their droll wit, their storytelling ability, their financial cunning and thrift, their work ethic, and their individuality. While "good fences make good neighbors," there is never a shortage of helping hands in a jam. The diction of Robert Frost poetry is alive and well in the North Country, and Emerson's "poets of the tavern hearth" will still bend your ear given half a chance.

✦ FROM PISCATAQUA TO REVOLUTION

In the White Mountains, legends are associated with the great Indian sachems Passaconaway, Chocorua, and Wannalancet. New Hampshire's first Europeans settled at Odiorne Point on the Piscataqua in 1623. The Piscataqua region, rich in natural resources and trade opportunities, attracted residents from Massachusetts Bay and England, and by 1679, when New Hampshire became a royal Colony separate from Massachusetts, European settlers had founded four towns: Hampton, Portsmouth, Dover, and Exeter. It was natural that the first settlements should be established near the Piscataqua River, on the "Great Island" of Newcastle, and in Strawbery Banke (the historic district in Portsmouth now nationally known for its house museum). Its protected harbors would prove pivotal to New Hampshire's shipping trade, and the rich fishing grounds at the Isles of Shoals would translate into gold. Today the Pisquataqua region, particularly Newcastle, Exeter, and Portsmouth, survives as a living-history museum, a reminder of the Colonial period's struggles for social order, religious stability, and popular local governance.

The Wentworths governed New Hampshire from 1717 to the mid-1770s, establishing an oligarchy that strains the stereotypical perception of the Colonies as seedbeds of American democracy. Indeed, the Wentworth-Coolidge House, Colonial residence of Benning Wentworth and home to the council chambers of the provincial government, sits still on one of the most pristine harborside properties in Portsmouth. Despite continued warfare with the French and Indians that ended momentously in 1763 with the Treaty of Paris and the annexation of Canada by the British, New Hampshire prospered and population in its northern territory grew. The Wentworth power base, however, collapsed in the fervid patriotism that led up to the Revolution.

In the Granite State the Revolution was prelude to a constitutional government, and New Hampshire was the first of the Colonies to form a new government with the purpose of preserving local autonomy and traditional liberties. When the Revolution began, New Hampshire consisted of four regions: the Old Colony in and around Portsmouth, the central watershed of the Merrimack River, the Connecticut River Valley along the Vermont border, and the Frontier to the north. They were loosely held together by the provincial government, but often in conflict over borders and representation. The Boston Tea Party

New Hampshire Timeline

1614 Captain John Smith visits the Isles of Shoals (for years known as Smith's Isles) and Piscataqua, promoting the idea of settlement.

1629 Captain John Mason is formally granted land between Merrimack and Piscataqua after splitting his Maine patent jointly owned with Sir Ferdinando Gorges. He names the territory New Hampshire.

1629–34 Residents from Massachusetts Bay move north to settlements at Strawbery Banke and the "Great Island" (Newcastle) in increasing numbers to exploit economic resources and to escape dictates of the Bay Colony.

1689 Indians attack the settlement in Dover, the opening skirmish in frontier warfare that continues into second decade of the 18th century.

1690 New Hampshire reannexed to Massachusetts, but in 1691 she becomes a royal Colony once more under the governorship of Samuel Allen.

1699–1715 Governors Lord Bellomont and Joseph Dudley govern Massachusetts and New Hampshire jointly, cooperating closely with local leaders.

1717–75 Wentworth oligarchy begins when John Wentworth assumes lieutenant gover-

norship of the province until his death in 1730. His son Benning becomes independent governor from 1741 to 1766. Nephew John assumes governorship until his ouster at the start of the Revolution.

1765 Portsmouth "Sons of Liberty" resist the stamp tax and Townshed duties, and passed in 1767 to replace revenue from the repealed Stamp Act.

1773–74 New Hampshire responds to the Tea Act, boycotts merchants, and denounces taxes as unjust. Paul Revere arrives in Portsmouth with news that British troops plan to take possession of Fort William and Mary, the fort at Newcastle protecting Portsmouth harbor.

1775 New Hampshire militiamen flood south to help Massachusetts. John Sullivan and John Langdon are appointed to Continental Congress. Nathaniel Folsom is named commander in chief of New Hampshire troops.

1776 New Hampshire is the first state to frame a constitution.

1776–1805 Federalists maintain ascendancy despite passionate political conflicts with Republican coalition, led by John Langdon. Freehold farmers support President Adams and governor John Taylor Gilman.

and the "Intolerable Acts" it provoked, however, created a new patriotic zeal and unity. When Paul Revere arrived in Portsmouth on December 13, 1773, to warn of a British attack on Fort William and Mary, 400 men led by John Langdon assembled, overpowered the fort commander, and removed the gunpowder from the fort. When news of hostilities at Concord and Lexington reached New Hampshire, men by the hundreds, alone and as militia units, joined the fighting. In the meantime, Josiah Bartlett and John Langdon had gone to Philadelphia to join the Second Continental Congress. Revolutionary war hero John Stark led the New Hampshire militia in the Battle of Bunker Hill. Three of New Hampshire's 10 counties are named for Revolutionary War figures: Belknap, for Dr. Jeremy Belknap, who served as a chaplain for the army; Carroll, for a Maryland signer of the Declaration of Independence; and Sullivan, for Major General John Sullivan. Towns are also named after Bartlett and Thornton, both signers of the Declaration.

Back in New Hampshire, Langdon received contracts to build the first three ships for the Continental Navy: the *Raleigh,* the *Ranger* (readied by John Paul Jones), and the *America,* given to America's former enemy and now ally, France. John Paul Jones sailed for France on November 1, 1777, bearing news of Burgoyne's surrender at Saratoga, which led to the Franco-American alliance of February 1778. The Portsmouth Naval Shipyard has continued to be one of the nation's primary shipbuilding and ship repair sites. Although New Hampshire was staunchly republican in its independence, in 1788 it became the ninth and deciding state to ratify the U.S. Constitution.

When the War of 1812 broke out, William Plumer was governor. Two fronts were vulnerable to attack: Portsmouth harbor, with its two run-down forts, Constitution and McClary, and the northern frontier border with Canada. Luckily, there was no invasion of New Hampshire. But the outbreak of hostilities did occasion the rise of New Hampshire's famous Federalist, Dartmouth graduate Daniel Webster, who spoke out against the war. Webster went on to serve in the U.S. Senate and was Secretary of State under presidents Harrison and Fillmore. "America's greatest orator" and probably a legendary president if destiny had led him that way, Webster was famous for his ringing words, which not only defeated the devil (as Stephen Vincent Benét's famous short story would have it) but set the tone for American government well into the 19th century.

A REGIONAL GAZETEER

▼▼

✦ THE OLD COLONY: 18 MILES OF REVOLUTIONARY HISTORY

They came to fish but they stayed to conquer. **Portsmouth** (originally Strawbery Banke), seat of Colonial power and home to merchants and shipbuilders who made fortunes in the lusty, fractious, and profitable maritime economy, is the breathtaking harbor town still very much animated by the sights, sounds, and tidal activities reminiscent of Revolutionary New Hampshire. The 300-year history of Portsmouth and environs, complete with a Paul Revere ride all its own, and a famous shipyard where John Paul Jones oversaw the construction of of two major warships, is easily read in its architecture, its busy ship traffic, its walking tours and house museum. "Puddle Dock," once a seedy, sailor haunt and notorious red-light district, was saved from urban redevelopment in the 1950s to become Strawbery Banke, a 10-acre house museum that encloses 42 of the most important buildings of the Colonial and Federal periods. The Piscataqua River separates Portsmouth and New Castle from Kittery, Maine, by one of the strongest tidal currents in the world. Ten miles out are the **Isles of Shoals,** site of the first fishery, one of the earliest pioneer settlements (and setting for the still unsolved Smuttynose murder case). Along the narrow, winding streets of Portsmouth, New Castle, and **Exeter,** passersby can see themselves reflected in the windows of Colonial, Georgian, and Federal dwellings, meetinghouses, churches, and commercial structures. Spy closets, 300-year old apple orchards, and widow's walks offer beachniks and tourists smitten by Portsmouth's shops and nightlife a behind-the-looking-glass adventure in another century. *Towns listed: Exeter, Portsmouth.*

✦ SECESSION WITHIN: THE DEVIL AND DANIEL WEBSTER

The Connecticut River separates New Hampshire from Vermont, but the boundary wasn't always so clearly or politely drawn. In **Hanover,** the philosophical seat of its fertile Upper Valley, lies the ninth oldest college and the last institution of higher learning to be established under Colonial rule. Dartmouth College, founded in 1769 by the Reverend Eleazar Wheelock, gave what was then the frontier a powerful political stronghold. Isolated from the Old Colony and the Merrimack Valley regions, inhabitants had incorporated some 50 towns by 1780 and made up 27 percent of the population—but they did not consider themselves a part of New Hampshire. In 1781, in serious defiance of the new state constitution,

35 towns seceded from the state at the instigation of Dartmouth professors to join the self-styled State of Vermont. Civil war was averted only by congressional intervention. Today New Hampshire citizens can shout across the river to their Vermont neighbors or paddle up the Connecticut and be in two states at once.

Two dozen towns of the Upper Valley stretch along the Connecticut River, the area's only highway in the 18th century. In 1793, 17 years before Fulton, Samuel Morey invented the internal combustion engine and built the first steamship, launched at Orford. The river, by mandate of King George III, still belongs to New Hampshire, which maintains 10 bridges that link Vermont and New Hampshire, one of which is the longest covered bridge in the United States. In **Charlestown,** five dozen structures comprise a national historic district that includes the vintage-1800 Stephen Hassam House, built by the great-grandfather of impressionist painter Childe Hassam. The French and Indian War stockaded outpost at **Fort at Number 4** replicates the settlement of 1740. North through sleepy green dales and farm fields to **Lyme, Orford,** and **Haverhill,** country gives way to small towns with their handsome Federal-style Congregational churches, and village greens. The streets are quiet, and the river follows you wherever you want to go. *Towns listed: Charlestown, Enfield, Hanover.*

✦ ENCOUNTERS ALONG THE CROOKED RIVER

New Hampshire's central valley follows the crooked Merrimack River, the grand highway for early settlers who established a trading outpost in **Concord,** now the state's capital, in the mid-1600s. Today I–93 follows the river north, past the same cities and towns established 300 years ago and destined to become one of the most important industrial mill regions in the country. Dominating the built landscape, Concord's statehouse, built in 1819 of local granite, brings together the third-largest legislative body in the English-speaking world. At the time the valley was being settled, predominately by English and Scotch-Irish, an unorthodox religious community sprang up in **Canterbury,** 15 mi north of Concord. The Shakers, so called for their ecstatic form of worship, quickly became known for their inventiveness, ingenuity, and superior skills in husbandry, furniture-making, and herbal healing, and here created a utopian community that prospered well into the 19th century—25 original buildings still make up this National Historic Landmark high atop green hills fringed by fields and woods. *Towns listed: Canterbury, Concord.*

✦ IN THE SHADOW OF MONADNOCK

By all accounts, the region that now occupies much of Cheshire County in the southwestern part of the state was at such a distance from the Colonial seat of power that settlement was too dangerous until well into the 18th century. **Keene,** the economic center of the region, was settled by Nathan Blake and 40 other families in the 1730s, but the population was dispersed by marauding Indians. In the 1750s, the white man returned, and in 1762 Isaac Wyman established a tavern that served as a launching place for the Keene minutemen on their march into Massachusetts. Mount Monadnock (believe it or not, the second most-climbed peak in the world after Mount Fuji) lords it over the surrounding hill towns. Below the mountain, rural villages make suitable covers for *Yankee Magazine* (in fact, the original offices of both that journal and the *Old Farmer's Almanac* are located in the middle of Dublin village). Towns like **Fitzwilliam, Walpole,** and **Hancock** artlessly offer up their secret gardens, handsome Colonial and Federal houses, their roadside streams and ravines, and public clusters of bandstands and greens like kind grocers handing penny candy to a child. *Towns listed: Fitzwilliam, Hancock, Keene.*

Colonial Nooks and Crannies:
The Grand Monadnock Steeplechase

A DRIVING TOUR FROM WALPOLE TO HANCOCK

▼▼

Distance: 40 mi (one-way)   **Time:** 2 days (1 night)
Breaks: Regal overnights can be yours in Walpole, Keene, and Hancock.

Nowhere else in New England are you likely to feel so bewitched by villages. Spirited by the feeling of early settlement, out of the way of striving and undue haste, and well clad with acres of clean country beauty, the southwest stretch of Cheshire County is an explorer's dream. Come around the storied mountain, over granite uplands, and circle the domed hills. Climb down the low, wide-cornered roads notched into the valleys where the hiss of highway traffic is well out of earshot. We'll take a look at some well-preserved churches, meetinghouses, and original buildings of the 18th and 19th centuries, traveling at drift speed through some of the most artlessly pretty villages in the region. Start not far from the Vermont border in **Walpole** (home of filmmaker Ken Burns). A long view of the broad Connecticut River Valley, tree-shaded streets, and handsome white-clapboard houses, some dating from the 1700s, have charmed such Walpole visitors as Louisa May Olcott. Continue south on Routes 12/123 past Westmoreland Depot to Route 63 in Westmoreland, where the Park Hill Meeting House is considered one of the most beautiful churches in New England. Route 63 takes you south past Spofford Lake where it meets Route 9. Go east, passing Chesterfield Gorge, to the city of **Keene.** The Wyman Tavern was a central meeting place for patriots who marched from here in 1775 to join the battle at Lexington. See two other Colonial-era taverns in Keene—the Goodnow Tavern (1777) on the Old Walpole Road (Route 12A) and Sawyer Tavern (1803) at 63 Arch Street and Bradford Road. Then head southeast on Route 12 through **Troy** where the Troy Meeting House was raised in 1814 on the Common. From Troy continue south, past Rhododendron State Park, to **Fitzwilliam,** a village surrounded by lovely hills and graced by a green common that shows its pillared and Federal-style homes to great advantage. Take 119 east to the junction of Route 202. Follow it north to 137 north and **Hancock,** the next-to-last stop on the tour. Hancock is named after the President of the Continental Congress and first signer of the Declaration of Independence. In the village center is one of the country's oldest continuously operating inns, and along Route 123 the collection of late 18th century and early 19th century architecture is the best in southern New Hampshire. Not to be missed are the the Charles Symonds House (1809), a two-story brick Federal-style house that houses the historical society; the Meetinghouse (1820), a wood-frame structure built by renowned churchbuilder Elias Carter; the stately brick-ended Federal double house built by Jacob Ames in 1812 (east of the Hancock Inn); the John Hancock Grange; and the Sheldon House (1781).

River to Summit, Valley to Sea:
Romancing the Colonial Stone

A DRIVING TOUR FROM CHARLESTOWN TO EXETER

▼▼

Distance: 210 mi (one-way)   **Time:** 7 days (6 nights)
Breaks: Overnight stays in Hanover, Canterbury, Enfield, Portsmouth, and Exeter

For the sheer promise of it, travel this route as you'd read a well-crafted mystery, and you'll come to feel in your bones why New Hampshire is the fastest-growing state in New England. The road takes you along riverbanks, through mountain passes, around one of the largest lakes in the East, through the central valley, and out again to islands in the sea. Start on the

New Hampshire/Vermont border in **Charlestown.** The old elms are gone, but remnants of this once-strategic outpost of the French and Indian Wars have been carefully preserved. Colonial troops under General Stark mustered at Fort Number 4 to launch the campaign in Crown Point, New York, and the battle of Bennington. On Main Street (200 ft wide and a mile long) you'll find the national historic district, including the former Charlestown Inn (1817) and the 18th-century mansion now home to the Foundation for Biblical Research. Drive north along scenic Route 12A, passing Saint Gaudens National Historic Site, which nourished a colony of artists with its unimpeded view of Vermont's Mt. Ascutney. Continue through Plainfield (up River Road to hug the Connecticut River) to the junction of U.S. 4 and swing east to **Enfield,** taking U.S. 4A to the "Chosen Vail" of the Shakers, where 13 buildings, including the austere "Great Stone House," survive the celibate religious community established on Lake Mascoma in 1793. Retrace your steps along U.S. 4 back to Lebanon, then take Route 120 north to nearby **Hanover** and Dartmouth, the ninth-oldest college in the country. Four green-roofed, black-shuttered white-clapboard buildings (Dartmouth Row) located on the town common are the oldest academic structures on campus.

Take Route 10 north through Lyme. The River Road is a scenic alternative to Route 10. After about 25 mi, stop in Orford to view the seven Ridge Houses, built between 1773 and 1839. It was here that the first steam-powered paddle boat was developed by resident Samuel Morey, whose pattern was later imitated by (and credited to) Robert Fulton. Take rollercoaster Route 25A east about 20 mi to Wentworth, which skirts the edge of the White Mountain National Forest. From here you could detour eastward up into the mountains to tour the famously scenic Kancamagus Highway. But to continue on the tour, head south. Continue on Route 25 from Wentworth southeast about 15 mi to Plymouth, meet up with Interstate 93, then take it south 25 mi to meet up with Route 11. Take that east 10 mi to Laconia, then head 15 mi south on Route 106 toward **Canterbury.** Take Exit 18 and follow the signs to rural Canterbury Shaker Village. Its 24 buildings and 694 acres now comprise a sublime museum—back in the late 18th and early 19th centuries the complex housed a utopian community of celibate, devout believers.

From the village, follow signs west to I–93, and head south to **Concord,** the state capital since 1808, situated on the west bank of the Merimack River. Note the Federal-style state building with its gilded eagle, erected on Main Street between 1816 and 1819. The Concord Coach, manufactured by the Abbot and Downing Company, was the chief method of transportation on the western overland trails from 1813 until after the Civil War. An hour's drive east on U.S. 4 brings you to the original settlements of the Seacoast area. In **Portsmouth,** park your car and walk around town to get a feel for the narrow streets and to take in the sights, sounds, and smells of the old harbor town and busy seaport. Three- hundred-year-old homes, six-story warehouses, and the din of history are all around you. From Portsmouth you can ferry out to the eight islands known as the Isles of Shoals, 10 mi off the coast—Capt. John Smith was one of the first voyagers here in 1614.

Travel east on Route 1A to the island village of New Castle—on the way take Little Harbor Road to the Wentworth-Coolidge Mansion, built in 1650, and once the seat of royal government. In New Castle, the narrow streets flanked by 18th-century houses only periodically hide the view of the ocean. New Castle's Fort Stark has protected the harbor since 1746. Back on Route 1A, take the beach road, stopping at Odiorne State Park, site of a 1623 settlement. Continue south, and at Hampton Beach take Route 101 west to the junction of Route 108. Head south to **Exeter,** the last stop on the tour. Exeter, a center of nonconformism and fomenter of American liberty, was settled in 1638 and shaped by its founder, John Wheelwright. Because Exeter's Revolutionary fervor figured so largely in the struggle for independence, the capital was moved here from Portsmouth in 1775. The brick and clapboard historic homes on Front Street and the Phillips Exeter Academy buildings reflect three centuries of architectural diversity.

CANTERBURY

▼▼

Canterbury's chief contribution to the early historic record was a commune. On a high ridge overlooking hills and dales a cluster of 24 white, wood-frame buildings comprising "Shaker village" was established in 1792. "Don't lag and suspend, and postpone; be ambitious to appear well in every sense of the word." So wrote Marcia E. Hastings, a Canterbury Shaker, who, like her brethren, lived a life of celibacy, pacifism, equality, hard work, and ritual worship, a utopian experiment that flourished here into the late 19th century.

Canterbury Shaker Village. This outdoor museum and National Historic Landmark showcases the original meeting house, living quarters, infirmary, schoolhouse, laundry, creamery, and other facilities of the Shaker religious community that existed here for two centuries. Shakers invented household items such as the clothespin and the flat broom and were famous for their furniture. With "hands to work and hearts to God" they labored long but lived simply, pragmatically, and with the integrity born of their spiritual beliefs. Members of the sect lived here until 1992 when the 694-acre property was left in trust as a museum. Tours last 90 minutes, and you'll find a shop selling Shaker reproductions. | 288 Shaker Rd. | 603/783–9511 | www.shakers.org | $12 | May–Oct., daily 10–5; Apr., Nov.–Dec., weekends 10–5.

✦ ON THE CALENDAR: Aug. **Mother Ann Day.** An annual celebration features traditional music in the chapel during the Shaker holiday that commemorates the arrival of Ann Lee, who came to these shores to found the Shaker sect. | Canterbury Shaker Village | 603/783–9511.

HISTORIC DINING AND LODGING

Creamery Restaurant. A Shaker motto goes, "No cook is really good without a lively imagination and the will to use it." There's abundant imagination on display at this restaurant in Canterbury's Shaker Village, where menu options include vegetarian potpie with turnips, carrots, potatoes, and shiitake mushrooms or Granny Smith apple–and–rhubarb crisp with spearmint whipped cream. Herbs and vegetables are locally grown, and meals are served family style at long wooden tables. Reservations are required for Friday and Saturday night dinner service. | 288 Shaker Rd. | 603/783–9511 or 866/783–9511 | AE, MC, V | Closed Jan.–Mar.; closed weekdays in Apr., Nov., and Dec.; no dinner Sun.–Thurs.

Wyman Farm. A hop, skip, and a jump from Canterbury Shaker Village, this hilltop Cape abode is a comfortable, unpretentious 200-year-old beauty that will satisfy your shutterbug impulses. (Even the owner's golden retriever, Dunklee, posed for a Nordstrom catalog.) Features such as small-paned windows and antique furnishings whisk you back to a simpler age. | Wyman Road Loudon (4 mi south of Canterbury) | phone/fax 603/783–4467 | 3 rooms | No credit cards.

CHARLESTOWN

▼▼

A stockaded outpost during the French and Indian Wars, Charlestown was a mustering point for troops under General Stark. On April 7, 1747, a party of French and Indians besieged the fort for three days. Despite fires and relentless attacks, the militia held the fort. This was later the site from which General Stark launched the Revolutionary War campaigns in Crown Point, New York, and the Battle of Bennington. On Main Street, 63 Federal, Greek Revival, and Gothic Revival homes span a mile-long national historic district, the state's largest. *Contact Charlestown Economic Development Association | Box D, Claremont 03603 | 603/826–5237.*

Fort at No. 4. This fort was a lonely outpost, northernmost of any British settlement—villagers were safe only within its massive walls. Today, costumed interpreters demonstrate hearth cooking, weaving, herb gardening, and candlemaking. Each year, volunteers reenact militia musters and battles. It's a wonderful learning experience for families and kids. | 267 Springfield Rd. (Rte. 11) | 888/367–8284 | www.fortat4.org | $10 | Mid-May–Oct., daily 10–4:30.

✦ ON THE CALENDAR: July **Sutler's Market.** Coopers, blacksmiths, harness makers, basket weavers, spinners, and hearth bakers demonstrate 18th-century talents and trades at this reenactment of a Colonial market at the Fort at No. 4. The handcrafts—everything from soap to pistols—are all for sale. | 267 Springfield Rd. (Rte. 11) | 888/367–8284.

HISTORIC LODGING

Home Hill Country Inn. "Small cheer and great welcome makes a merry feast." So wrote Shakespeare, in a line that has become the motto of this French-inspired inn, a stunning Federal-style brick mansion that has been touted as one of the 10 best inns in New England by any number of critics. The mood is romantic and gracious, the rooms lavishly appointed at this new member of the Relais & Chateaux chain. Lest we forget the role of the French in the settling of New England, each guest room is named after a village in France, and the dining in the superb restaurant is French cuisine and so fine you'll want to spring for the prix-fixe. | 703 River Rd., Plainfield (20 mi from Charlestown, 5 mi north of Cornish) | 603/675–6165 | www.homehillinn.com/inn.html | $150–$315 | 8 rooms | AE, D, MC, V.

CONCORD

▼▼

The gold-domed State House, built in 1819 on busy Main Street, is the single most imposing structure in Concord's skyline. On its plaza, entered through a granite memorial arch, are statues of New Hampshire native sons Franklin Pierce, Daniel Webster, General John Stark, and Sen. John P. Hale. The city's defining natural feature is the mighty Merrimack River, along whose banks the Pennacook Indians fished and hunted (because of the bend in the river, they called it "the crooked place") and the first pioneers settled in 1725. Naturally, politics and business are primary concerns in the city that has been the state capital since 1808. New Hampshire's legislature numbers more than 400 members, reputedly making it the third-largest deliberative body in the world. But Concord was not an influential city in the early days of the state's history, when most of the wealth and political power was concentrated along the seacoast. Concord was relatively unscathed by the French and Indian Wars, the most marked incident being the slaying of five men in the Bradley Massacre of 1746. Until the 1800s, the most widely told Concord tale was of Hannah Dustin, who was kidnapped from Haverhill, Massachusetts, by Indians but managed to escape from—and scalp—her captors on the banks of the Merrimack in the dead of night. Concord came to prominence due to water power and transportation lines. In 1815, the Middlesex Canal connected it with Boston, and in 1842, a steam railroad was completed. Today it has 40,000 residents and lies at the intersection of I–89 and I–93, linking New Hampshire to Vermont and Boston to Montreal. *Contact The Greater Concord Chamber of Commerce | 40 Commercial St. (just off Exit 15, I–93), Concord 03301 | 603/224–2508 | fax 603/224–8128 | www.concordnhchamber.com.*

Museum of New Hampshire History. Exhibits in this 19th-century stone warehouse take you on a chronological tour of the state's history, with artifacts dating from before European settlement (hunting implements and dugout canoes) through to contemporary life. Learn about Abenaki life or how the infant "Ocean Born Mary" captivated pirates. See White Mountain art, war muskets, and an original Concord Coach. New Hampshire residents such as poet Robert Frost and Christian Science founder Mary Baker Eddy tell their own stories. | 6 Eagle Sq. | 603/226–3189 | www.nhhistory.org | $5 | Tues.–Sat. 9:35–5, Sun. noon–5.

New Hampshire State House and Plaza. Completed in 1819, this structure, noted for its eagle-topped gold dome, is the oldest state capitol in which the legislature still meets in its original chambers. There are tours daily. | 107 N. Main St. | 603/271–1110 | Free | Weekdays 8–4:30.

HISTORIC DINING AND LODGING

Crystal Quail. Dinner at this 18th-century post house is strictly four-star and by reservation only. The five-course prix-fixe meals offer three entrée choices, which often feature game dishes, such as pheasant. Vegetables are homegrown and organic, and the delectable desserts are made from scratch. Ask for directions when making your reservation; the location is hidden on back roads—but it's worth the detective work required to get there. Bring your own wine. | Pitman Rd., Center Barnstead, between Pittsfield and Alton (25 mi from Concord) | 603/269–4151 | $55 | No credit cards | Closed Mon., Tues. No lunch.

Temperence Tavern. Long on history and even longer on comfort, this inn in the center of Gilmanton's white-sided historic district served for 100 years as the overnight stagecoach stop on the Canada-to-Dover Road. Rooms used in the early 1820s as Masonic meeting rooms have been converted to guest accommodations. In the tap room notice the period wall stencils. The Indian shutters, wide floorboards, brass beds, vaulted ceilings, and six working open-hearth fireplaces are authentic 18th-century Americana. | Gilmanton Four Corners, Box 369, at junction of Rtes. 140 and 107, Gilmanton (25 mi from Concord) | 603/267–7349 | 5 rooms | $100–$135 | AE, MC, V.

ENFIELD
▼▼

Guided by their spiritual philosophy of simple gifts, the Enfield Shakers put their hands to work. They built more than 200 structures (including the six-story Great Stone Dwelling, the largest Shaker dwelling ever built), farmed more than 3,000 acres, educated, healed, created domestic work tools and furniture, and ecstatically worshiped God. Founded in 1793, this village was the ninth of 18 Shaker communities to be established in the United States. *Contact Selectman's Office | 23 Main St., Box 373, Enfield 03748 | 603/632–4201 | fax 603/632–5182 | www.enfield.nh.us.*

Dana Robes—Wood Craftsmen, Inc. Handcrafted and signed traditional Shaker furniture and decorative pieces made on site range from beds to armoires, from decorative boxes to coat racks. | Lower Shaker Village, U.S. 4A | 603/632–5385 | Showroom open weekdays 9–5, Sun. 10–5.

Enfield Shaker Museum. In 1923, after 130 years of communal living, declining membership forced the Shakers to put their Enfield property up for sale. They sold the site to the LaSalettes, an order of Catholic priests, thus preserving the tradition of spiritual, communal life there. A self-guided walking tour encompasses 13 of the remaining buildings. The museum preserves and explains Shaker culture, and artisans demonstrate Shaker crafts. | 24 Caleb Dyer La. | 603/632–4346 | www.shakermuseum.org | $7 | Memorial Day–Oct., Mon.–Sat. 10–5, Sun. noon–5; Nov.–Memorial Day, Sat. 10–4, Sun. noon–4.

HISTORIC DINING AND LODGING

Shaker Inn. So gorgeous its rooms were featured in *House Beautiful,* this six-story stone inn overlooks Lake Mascoma on the grounds of the Enfield Shaker Museum. Reproduction Shaker furnishings and some original features, such as built-in drawers, bifold shutters and peg rolls, characterize the guest rooms. Incorporated into the museum setting, the restaurant serves creative, Shaker-influenced dishes appropriate to the season, such as country-fried veal with sweet pepper–apple sauce and roasted corn polenta. Restaurant. | 447 U.S. 4A | 603/632–7810 | www.theshakerinn.com | 24 rooms | $125–$155 | AE, D, MC, V.

EXETER

▼▼

It is hard to understate the importance of the independent spirit shown by Exeter citizens during the Revolutionary period. Following the lead of the town's founder, the Rev. John Wheelwright, Exeter's defiance of royal government never wavered. As early as 1682, an attempt to collect taxes sent the marshall home with insults and an empty purse. In 1734, Exeter Colonials dressed as Indians dragged 10 of the British Crown's men from Samuel Gilman's tavern, threatening any who would cut the best trees for the king's navy. British ministers were burnt in effigy as the village committed itself to the struggle for liberty. The first Provincial Congress met in Exeter, and on January 6, 1776, the representatives wrote a constitution, thus becoming the first independent colony in the new world. Seven months later, John Taylor Gilman (who would become governor for 14 years), read the Declaration of Independence to the people. From 1775 to 1808, Exeter was the capital of New Hampshire. Today, it's largely residential and perhaps best known as home to the prepatory school Phillips Exeter Academy. *Contact Chamber of Commerce | 120 Water St., Exeter 03833 | 603/772–2411 | fax 603/772–9965.*

American Independence Museum. This is a fascinating group of buildings that is being renovated to be the premier center in New Hampshire for the study of the American Revolution. It will focus on the role that one family played in the founding of the new republic, and so it is fitting that such a repository should be housed here at the pretty yellow and white-clapboard Ladd-Gilman House (1721). The Ladds and Gilmans are both old families. The Ladds were somewhat eccentric. Nathaniel Ladd sounded the trumpet in Gove's Rebellion against Royal Governor Cranfield and was killed in a battle with Indians. Simeon, three generations later, claimed fame as president of a society of spirits called the "Nip Club," and his father kept a ready coffin in his house for emergencies. Like Icarus, he made a pair of wings, which failed to keep him aloft when he jumped from an upper window. The Gilmans produced two governors and a senator. Nicholas Gilman, treasurer of the Colony, issued all the state's currency during the Revolution from a room in this house, and Nicholas Jr. was a signer of the Constitution. Collection highlights include the Dunlap Broadside of the Declaration of Independence, two drafts of the U.S. Constitution; portraits of George Washington, and Nicholas Gilman, Jr; letters and documents by Washington, and Knox; and furnishings, tableware, silver and decorative arts from the period, along with textiles, military uniforms and weaponry of the Revolution. Renovations of the adjacent Folsom Tavern (1775) is ongoing—the finish woodwork that remains from the 18th century shows fine detail by craftsmen of the region, complete with double-faced doors, full classical cornices, and Greek Revival touches. George Washington famously had breakfast here on November 4, 1789. When the Georgian-style dining room gets up and running, you will be able to enjoy mutton stew, roast pork, local hard cider, wine and beer during one of the 18th-century dinner events being planned. | 1 Governors La. | 603/772–2622 | www.independencemuseum.org | $5 | Guided tours only, May–Oct., Wed.–Sun. noon–5.

Gardner House, Perry-Dudley House, and Sleeper House. Three houses along Front Street illustrate "the persistence of the Federal style," as historian Bryant Tolles writes. One of the earliest owners of the Perry House was Dr. William Perry, whose daughter, author Sarah Orne Jewett, grew up here. Also located in this historic district are the First Parish Meeting House, the Granite Bank, the Otis-Gorham House, and the Amos Tuck House. | 47 Front St. | 603/778–2335 (Exeter Historical Society) | Tues., Thurs., and Sat 2–4:30, or by appointment.

Gilman-Garrison House. The main part of this sprawling "wooden castle," built of massive timbers, may date to as early as 1658. It functioned originally as a fortified house, with windows that were hardly more than loopholes. About 1772, Brig. Gen. Peter Gillman added the long wing toward Water Street, used for entertainment and business of state. It is worth seeing the paneling and elaborate moldings. Daniel Webster boarded here as a student in 1796. He was apparently taught table etiquette here and his crude manners corrected by Ebenezer Clifford, the famous woodworker who then owned the home. Contact the owner, the Society for the Preservation of New England Antiquities (617/227–3956) in Boston for an appointment to view this "study house." | 12 Water St. | 603/436–3205 | www.spnea.org.

✦ ON THE CALENDAR: July **Revolutionary War Festival.** Celebrate independence from British rule with battle reenactments, music, and other festivities. | Downtown Exeter | 603/772–2411.

HISTORIC LODGING
Governor Jeremiah Smith House Inn. This bright, two-story 1730s Colonial inn, listed in the National Historic Register, was the home of New Hampshire governor Jeremiah Smith, who delivered the eulogy at George Washington's funeral. Period fire chambers, custom lace window treatments, and woven George Washington bedspreads complement many modern amenities. | 41 Front St. | 603/778–7770 | fax 603/778–7771 | www.portsmouthnh.com/jeremiahsmithinn | 8 rooms | $199–$129 | MC, V.

FITZWILLIAM
▼▼▼

Around the quintessentially New England green here, early Federal-style buildings and an elegantly spired church preserve the feeling of Colonial times. The first settlers were a couple who came in an ox-cart in 1762 with no shelter except the cart itself; under the cart their daughter was born. Next to settle was James Reed, later a brigadier general in the Continental Army. Yarn production was important to the town in its first 50 years, succeeded by the palm-leaf hat industry, and, with the coming of the railroad, granite. The town is small, with fewer than 3,000 souls, and wears its country demeanor with ease. *Contact Greater Peterborough Chamber of Commerce | Box 401, 10-B Wilton Rd., Peterborough 03458 | 603/924–7234 | fax 603/924–7235 | www.peterboroughchamber.com.*

Fitzwilliam Historical Society–Amos J. Parker House. At this small museum set in the mid-1800s home of renowned New Hampshire legislator, lawyer, and Fitzwilliam resident Amos J. Blake, each room is dedicated to a different aspect of life in Fitzwilliam: you'll find a doctor's office, a schoolroom, a nursery, two kitchens, and a business office, all furnished with period furniture and memorabilia. | On the Common, Rte. 119 | 603/585–7742 | Memorial Day–Columbus Day, Sat. 10–4.

HISTORIC DINING AND LODGING
Fitzwilliam Inn. The Fitzwilliam Inn has meant warmth and sustenance to weary travelers for more than 200 years. It was known as the Goldsmith Tavern in the late 18th century when it was a stop for stagecoach passengers traveling from Boston. Its English-style pub and adjoining dining room still provide tasty succor, and guest rooms are smartly appointed with antiques and period furnishings. Restaurant. | On the Common, Rte. 119 | 603/585–9000 | fax 603/585–3495 | www.fitzwilliaminn.com | 23 rooms | D, MC, V.

HANCOCK
▼▼▼

The town took the name of the president of the Continental Congress and the first man to sign the Declaration of Independence, John Hancock. Manufacturing was important here. Hancock produced nearly half of all cotton used in the state and much of its rifles and fowling pieces. Along Route 123, the old stagecoach road, you'll find some of the area's most carefully preserved architecture of the 18th and early 19th centuries. Every building on Main Street is listed on the National Register of Historic Places and this summer resort has been long acclaimed as one of the state's prettiest towns. Peterborough—the model for "Our Town" in Thorton Wilder's play—is just over the road past Mount Monadnock. *Contact Hancock Historical Society | Box 138, 7 Main St., Hancock 03449 | 603/525–9379.*

Charles Symonds House. At the east end of Hancock's main thoroughfare, where U.S. 202 enters the village, sits a two-story brick Federal building (1809) housing the Hancock Historical Society. Nearby the Hancock Inn, the Sheldon House, the John Hancock Grange (a frame house once used by the Hancock Artillery Company), and the congregational church demonstrate the changes in domestic architecture from the 1780s to the 1820s. | 7 Main St. | 603/525–9379.

HISTORIC DINING AND LODGING

Hancock Inn. The state's oldest inn—and possibly its most beautiful—was built the first year of George Washington's presidency. Over the years it has hosted elegant balls, served as a wayside stop for Concord Coaches, and been a hostelry for the first riders of the railroad. In the present day you can luxuriate in beds with handmade quilts, while braided rugs, rockers, and 1830s stencil patterns create a homey ambience. The guest rooms are stunners. The Norway Plain room takes the cake, complete with a wraparound 17th-century scenic mural on the walls; a pastoral view of the white spires of the church steeple where Paul Revere's bell No. 236 still rings the hour; and a cherry, cannonball four-poster bed. Downstairs enjoy Shaker cranberry pot roast by candlelight in the dining room, a setting shimmering in Colonial wood trim and blazing red walls. Nearby, the tavern serves libations and casual bites. Is this not Ye Olde Bliss? Restaurant. No children under 12. | 33 Main St. | 800/525–1789 | www.hancockinn.com | 13 rooms | $215–$250 | AE, MC, V.

HANOVER

▼▼▼

When Eleazar Wheelock founded Hanover's Dartmouth College in 1769, only 20 families lived here, making Dartmouth's motto, *Vox Clamantis in Deserto* (a voice crying in the wilderness), especially apt. In 1771 the first class of four men graduated, occasioning Gov. John Wentworth to build a road through the wilderness from Wolfeboro, 75 mi east, when he found the dusty trails rough going. In 1815, the New Hampshire legislature established a separate governing body for the college and changed its name to Dartmouth University. The trustees challenged the action and the case was argued in the United States Supreme Court by Daniel Webster, a graduate in the Class of 1801. The landmark decision handed down by Chief Justice John Marshall in 1819 is considered one of the most formative documents in United States constitutional history, strengthening the contract clause of the Constitution and paving the way for private institutions to conduct their affairs without interference from the state. Daniel Webster subsequently became so well known as a persuasive orator that Stephen Vincent Benét was to cast him in his 1937 short story as the hero of the common man who could out-wit the very devil.

The Hanover Gazette was one of the first newspapers to appear in the 18th century; by the turn of the century the village supported two general stores, an inn, and other trade establishments. The queen of the Connecticut River, Hanover has prospered in concert with the college and is the undisputed cultural center of Upper Valley life. The center of Hanover is characterized by a graceful Green with crisscrossing walks, symmetrical white Colonials and Georgian buildings. *Contact Chamber of Commerce | 216 Nugget Bldg., Box 5105, Hanover 03755 | 603/643–3115 | fax 603/643–5606 | www.hanoverchamber.org.*

Dartmouth College. The energetic collegiate atmosphere of this northernmost Ivy League school dominates the town. The four classroom buildings on Dartmouth Row (east side of Green), one of which dates from 1784, are among the oldest structures on campus. The first building that the Reverend Eleazar Wheelock commissioned for the transplanting of his charity school for Indian youth was a simple log hut. The endowment that enabled the founding of Dartmouth was raised by Samson Occom, a former Indian student who preached and charmed his way around England to the tune of 11,000 pounds sterling. Among the buildings clustered around the Green is the Baker Memorial Library (1 Elm Street), which houses historical pamphlets, broadsides, and literary gems such as 17th-century editions of Shakespeare's works. Murals painted by José Clemente Orozco depict the story of civilization on the American continents. The college's famed Hood Museum of Art has some pieces by silversmith Paul Revere. | Main and Wheelock Sts. | 603/646–1110 | www.dartmouth.edu.

Webster Cottage. This farm house was built for Reverend Ripley and his wife Abigail, daughter of Eleazar Wheelock. It has passed through many hands and appears to have been rented from 1802 until 1816, during the time Daniel Webster reportedly occupied an upstairs bedroom. The Hanover Historical Society maintains a collection of period antiques and memorabilia related to Webster. | 32 N. Main St. | 603/646–3371 | Free | June–mid-Oct., Wed., weekends 2:30–4:30.

HISTORIC LODGING

Hanover Inn. This four-story neo-Georgian tries hard for an eiderdown and brass-candlestick feel, but you can only take this so far when you offer 124 rooms. Zins Wine Bistro and the more formal Daniel Webster Room serve three meals a day. While some might carp at how modernized the hotel is, generation after generation of Dartmouth parents return happily. Restaurant. | Main and Wheelock Sts. | 603/643–4300 | fax 603/646–3744 | www.dartmouth.edu/inn | 124 rooms | $250–$310 | AE, D, DC, MC, V.

KEENE

▼▼▼

When Keene was first settled in 1736, the 40 original families deliberately built their homes to the rear of their lots thus leaving a large Main Street, the largest, in fact, in New England. Ten years later, Indians attacked the town, killing two and capturing Nathan Blake, the town's first settler. The village (then called Upper Ashuelot) was abandoned, the Indians burned it to the ground, and a permanent settlement was not reestablished until mid-century. Glassmaking was an important industry in the early 19th century, and earlier Keene was known for its pottery production. Notable Keene citizens include Cynthia Dunbar, the mother of Henry David Thoreau; John Dickson, who delivered the first antislavery speech in Congress; and artist Barry Faulkner, known for his murals. Today, Keene is a small city and college town of just more than 22,000. It is the cultural and economic hub of the region whose wide, tree-lined Main Street is adorned with immaculately kept historic buildings. *Contact Chamber of Commerce | 48 Central Sq., Keene 03431 | 603/352–1303 | www.keenechamber.com.*

Colonial Theatre. This theater rose out of the remains of what was once the Colonial Inn, built by local lawyer Peleg Sprague in 1793. During the heady days of Roaring Twenties optimism, Charles C. Baldwin razed the old Colonial Inn building in order to build a majestic movie theater. Today it's home to dance, music, and theater productions. | 95 Main St. | 603/352–2033 | www.colonial.org.

Horatio Colony House Museum. The house was built by Abel Blake, one of the first permanent settlers, then passed into the hands of Horatio Colony, grandson and namesake of Keene's first mayor. Visitors will find an eclectic mix of heirlooms and souvenirs from Colony's extensive travels. | 199 Main St. | 603/352–0460 | Free | June–mid-Oct., Tues.–Sat. 11–3; mid-Oct.–May, Sat. 11–3.

Wyman Tavern. The tavern was built by a veteran of the French and Indian Wars, Capt. Isaac Wyman. For 40 years it served as a tavern, famous as a meeting place for historical events such as the first meeting of the trustees of Dartmouth College under President Wheelock (1770) and the march of Captain Wyman and his minutemen who left from the tavern to fight in the battles at Lexington and Concord in April of 1775. Guided are tours available. | 339 Main St. | 603/357–3855 | June–Aug., Thurs.–Sat. 11–4.

◆ ON THE CALENDAR: July **Revolutionary War Living History.** Experience the American Revolution through the eyes of Joseph Chapman, a New Hampshire militiaman from Campbell's Gore in the Province of New Hampshire. The living history program uses reproduction artifacts from the 18th century and includes demonstrations of period cooking. | Rte. 32, Swanzey Center (6 mi south of Keene) | 603/352–0697.

HISTORIC DINING AND LODGING

Chesterfield Inn. Just reading the menu at this former farmhouse dating from the 18th century makes your mouth water—hazelnut-roasted chicken, wild game sausages, cider-braised scallops. Herbs are from the garden and the seafood is fresh from Boston. Located 10 mi west of Keene, it's worth a drive for fine dining. You can spend the night and awake to a view of a dozen perennial gardens and stunning views into Vermont. The house itself is "olde" with many modernized additions. Inside, touches of traditional and repro decor grace the guest rooms. Restaurant. | Rte. 9, Chesterfield | 800/365–5515 | fax 603/256–6131 | www.chesterfieldinn.com | 15 rooms | $150–$250 | AE, DC, MC, V.

Goose Pond Guest House. A pretty rural road leads north from the center of town to a meticulously maintained and classically furnished 1790 Colonial. It sits atop a knoll on a 13-acre property near Goose Pond, perfect for swimming or skating. | East Surry Rd., Keene | 603/357–4787 | www.goosepondguesthouse.com | 3 rooms | $190–$140 | V.

PORTSMOUTH
▼▼▼

Among the first white men to explore New Hampshire was Martin Pring, whose trip up the Piscataqua River in 1603 in search of sassafras led to the eventual opening of the territory by Capt. John Mason and the first settlement at Odiorne's Point in 1623. Called Piscataqua, then Strawbery Banke, and finally Portsmouth, the town was the powerful seat of the provincial government and home to the Wentworth family, whose three royal governors controlled the political and economic life of New Hampshire for several generations prior to the Revolutionary War. With the help of Daniel Fowle's *Portsmouth Gazette,* arguably the oldest continuously printed newspaper in the country, the spirited voice of Revolution was heard very loud here, and from here sprang some of the period's most notable early patriots, including John and Samuel Langdon, Samuel Livermore, John Paul Jones, and Tobias Lear. It was the seat of government until 1808, but it also harbored all the strong odors and bawdy color of a seaport, with a brisk slave trade, bars and brothels for sailors, the fishing industry, shipbuilding, and a dizzying mercantile trade in lumber, livestock, farm products, and oil. Later, private shipping declined; the development of the U.S. Navy Shipyard compensated in part for the loss, along with the rise of other trades and industries such as beer brewing. Today, Portsmouth is a virtual museum of Colonial days and the nerve center of the Seacoast's cultural life. Because of its seaside beauty, its diverse possibilities for recreation and entertainment, and its historic character, it has become a popular destination for summer wayfarers. *Contact Chamber of Commerce | 500 Market St., Portsmouth 03802 | 603/436–1118 | www.portsmouthchamber.org.*

Black Heritage Trail. Some of Portsmouth's most affluent citizens owned slaves, and Africans were sold, along with other merchandise, on a regular basis in Portsmouth's market. The town's slave population grew from a reported 52 in 1727 to about 4% of the total population in 1767. Now, the Black Heritage Trail gives you their stories. It's a self-guided walking tour that takes you to a variety of sites where black residents lived, worked, prayed, and played. Log onto the Web site or stop at the tourist office to get a run-down of its 20 sites. | Box 7158, Portsmouth 03802 | 603/427–2020 | www.seacoastnh.com.

Emery Farm. This is one of the country's oldest farms, established in 1655, and located on 12 acres between Durham and Portsmouth. It's open to the public and known locally as a good place to pick your own berries. Kids will like the farm's planned activities and petting zoo. | U.S. 4, Durham | 603/742–8495 | Apr.–Jan., daily 9–6.

Fort Constitution. Long known as Fort William and Mary, this National Historic Site on the island of New Castle was a principal British fort that patriots raided in 1774 in one of the first overt acts of aggression against the crown, months before the incidents at Concord and Lexington. The rebels later used the captured munitions against the British at the Battle of Bunker Hill. The base of the walls still remains from this fort (originally called William and Mary) built in 1600s and it was a major fortification during the French and Indian Wars. It was on December 13, 1774 that Paul Revere himself rode from Boston to say that the fort at Rhode Island had been dismantled and troops were coming to take over Fort William and Mary. The following day the Sons of Liberty and 400 men from Portsmouth, Rye and New Castle raided the fort and removed 5 tons of gun powder, cannon, and military stores. Governor John Wentworth immediately sent to Boston for the sloop Canceaux and 100 British marines, taking refuge in the fort with his family until he departed on the eve of the Revolution. | Rte. 1B at the Coast Guard Station, New Castle (4 mi east of Portsmouth) | 603/436–1552 | Free | Daily 10–5.

Ft. Stark State Historic Site. This 10-acre site 5 mi east of Portsmouth overlooks Little Harbor and was first used for defensive purposes in 1746. It was an active fortification in every war from the Revolutionary War through World War II. | Wild Rose La., New Castle | 603/436–1552 | $2.50 | Daily 10–4.

Harbor Cruises. One of the best views of Portsmouth is from the water. You can take an amusing and informative narrated tour of the harbor and estuary system to learn more about everything from birdlife to local folklore. Bring a lunch or get a snack on board. Reservations are recommended. | Ceres St. Dock | 800/776–0915.

There's nothing like a salty wind in summer on the open ocean, especially if your destination is the ancient Isles of Shoals. On a cruise with **Isles of Shoals Steamship Co.,** it's possible to make a stopover on Star Island, one of the nine land masses 10 mi out of Portsmouth. You also can go whale-watching. If you don't like crowds, visit Little Bay Buffalo Farm on a Great Bay foliage excursion in the fall. | Barker Wharf, 315 Market St. | 603/431–5500 or 800/441–4620 | www.islesofshoals.com | Mid–June–Labor Day, daily. Call for off-season schedules and reservations.

Historic District. Portsmouth's historic district is large and impossible to appreciate in one day. Every corner of the city has its charms, from the old harbor area of Bow and Ceres streets, against the backdrop of old warehouses, quaint shops, and working tugboats, to the narrow streets that pass by the white picket fences bordering one of the country's largest and most visited historic house museums, to Market Square and the old North Church, which played a major role in the abolition of slavery in New Hampshire. | Take Exit 7 from I–95 and follow signs for historic district.

Isles of Shoals. Nine islands (eight at high tide) ride the surf 10 mi off the coast of Portsmouth. Some, like Hog Island, Smuttynose, and Star Island, retain the earthy names given by the transient fishermen who visited them in the early 17th century. A colorful history of piracy, murder, and ghosts surrounds the archipelago, long populated by an independent lot. Celia Thaxter, a native islander, romanticized these islands with her poetry in *Among the Isles of Shoals* (1873). In the late 19th century, Appledore Island became an offshore retreat for her coterie of writers, musicians, and artists. Star Island has a nondenominational conference center and is open to guided tours. For information about visiting the Isles of Shoals, use the Isles of Shoals Steamship Co. to make a stopover on Star Island, one of the nine land masses 10 mi out of Portsmouth. | Isles of Shoals Steamship Co., Barker Wharf, 315 Market St. | 800/441–4620 | www.islesofshoals. com | Mid–June–Labor Day, daily. Call for off-season schedules and reservations.

Portsmouth Historic Homes. Given its early settlement and its dramatic role in the struggle for independence, Portsmouth is one of the best places to see old homes and learn about their architecture and the people who lived here and changed history. The Society for the Preservation of New England Antiquity conducts tours at a number of Portsmouth's magnificently restored homes.

John Langdon was a three-time governor of the state, a signer of the Constitution, and the first president of the Senate. His 1784 Georgian mansion, the **Governor John Langdon House,** was described by George Washington in 1789 as "the finest house in Portsmouth." It contains ornate woodwork and period furniture. | 143 Pleasant St. | 603/436–3205 | www.spnea.org | $5 | June–mid-Oct., Wed.–Sun. 11–5; visits by hourly tour only.

The oldest surviving structure in the state is the **Jackson House,** located on Portsmouth's historic Christian Shore. This home was built in 1664 by Richard Jackson, a cooper and shipwright. His heirs lived here for more than 250 years. | 50 Mechanic St. | 603/436–3205 | www. spnea.org | $5 | June–mid-Oct., weekends 11–5; tours on the hr, last tour at 4.

Costumed guides conduct tours of the 1758 **John Paul Jones House,** a boardinghouse that Jones called home while supervising the outfitting of two ships for the Continental Navy. The yellow, hip-roof house is the headquarters of the Portsmouth Historical Society. Exhibits include costumes, glass, guns, portraits, and late-18th-century documents. | 43 Middle St. | 603/436–8420 | www.seacoastnh.com/jpj | $5 | Mid-May–mid-Oct., Sat. 10–4, Sun. noon–4.

Built in 1763 by wealthy sea merchant Capt. John Moffatt as a wedding gift for his son, the Georgian **Moffatt-Ladd House** is one of the finest such specimens in the country. It was also the home of William Whipple, one of the signers of the Declaration of Independence. The Moffatt-Ladd House tells the story of Portsmouth's merchant class through portraits, letters, and furnishings. | 154 Market St. | 603/436–8221 | $5 | June–mid-Oct., Mon.–Sat. 10–4, Sun. 1–4.

The three-story **Rundlet May House,** a Federal mansion, is a testimony to the mercantile success of James Rundlet, who spared no expense in furnishing and adorning his home. The formal gardens, orchard, and outbuildings have remained unchanged. | 364 Middle St. | 603/436–3205 | www.spnea.org | $5 | June–mid-Oct., weekends 1–5; visits by hourly tour only.

The murals lining the hall staircase of the imposing 1716 **Warner House** might be the oldest-known murals still in their original place in the United States. The house itself is a noted example of Georgian architecture, with 18-inch-thick brick walls. The west wall lightning rod is believed to have been installed in 1762 under the supervision of Benjamin Franklin. | Daniel St. at Chapel St. | 603/436–5909 | www.warnerhouse.org | $5 | June–Oct., Tues.–Sat. 10–4, Sun. 1–4; visits by tour only.

The **Wentworth Coolidge Mansion,** a National Historic Landmark, was originally the home of Benning Wentworth, New Hampshire's first royal governor (1753–70). Notable among the period furnishings is the carved pine mantelpiece in the council chamber. Wentworth's imported lilac trees, believed to be the oldest in North America, bloom each May. There are contemporary arts exhibits here and gift shop in the visitor's center. | 375 Little Harbor Rd. | 603/436–6607 | $2.50 | June–Oct., Tues., Thurs., Fri., Sat. 10–3, Sun. 1–5.

Wentworth Gardner House. This lovely blocked-front 1760 house is said to rank among the finest Georgian-style buildings in the country. Its wood carvings are one of its best features. | 50 Mechanic St. | 603/436–4406 | $4 | Mid-June–mid-Oct., Tues.–Sun. 1–4.

Portsmouth Livery Co. Take a horse-drawn carriage through Colonial Portsmouth and Strawbery Banke to hear local legends and see some of the best-preserved sights from Colonial times. Look for carriages at stand in Market Square. | 603/427–0044 | Memorial Day–Labor Day, daily; Labor Day–mid-Oct., weekends.

Strawbery Banke Museum. New Hampshire's most famous historic restoration village was baptized by its first English settlers, who came to the area around what's now Portsmouth for the abundant wild strawberries they found along the Piscataqua River. This glorious 10-acre museum with period gardens, exhibits, and craftspeople includes 46 buildings that date from 1695 to 1820; 10 furnished homes represent 300 years of history in one continuously occupied neighborhood. Here are some of the highlights of the complex, which rose in the district picturesquely known as Puddle Duck. The 1762 Chase House is a Georgian-style showpiece, with a doorway capped by a curved pediment, framed by fluted pilasters and supported by paneled pedestals in the early Georgian manner; inside, note the carved frieze over the fireplace in the parlor, as well as full-length sliding shutters, wainscoting, denticulated mantelpiece and cornice, and the arches on either side of the fireplace. Spanning the Georgian and Federal periods is the elegant red-clapboard Joshua Jones House, which used to anchor the Puddle Duck area. The Pitt Tavern, dating from 1766, was a stop for the Portsmouth Flying Stage Coach and consequently had rooms upstairs for boarders, now exquisitely renovated. The earliest abode, with a melancholy post-medieval English feel, is the dramatically weathered, clapboard 17th-century Sherburne House. The light and spiffy 1800 Captain Walsh House shows the captain to have earned a tidy sum at sea. Perhaps the most opulent home is the Goodwin Mansion, former home of Governor Ichabod Goodwin, decorated in period Victorian style though built during the War of 1812. Surrounding many of these houses are lovely Colonial-style gardens. All in all, this is must-do for heritage travelers. | Marcy St. across from Prescott Park | 603/433–1100 | www.strawberybanke.org | $12 pass good for 2 consecutive days | Mid-Apr.–Oct., daily 10–5; 1st 2 weekends in Dec., 4–9 for candlelight strolls.

✦ ON THE CALENDAR: July–Aug. **Chautauqua.** A tableau of living history organized by the New Hampshire Humanities Council takes place under the big tents in a revival of old time entertainment. Shake hands with Sojourner Truth or Thomas Jefferson and hear the story of nationhood. | Strawbery Banke Museum | 603/224–4071.

HISTORIC LODGING

Inn at Strawbery Banke. Superbly located, this light-filled, comfortable inn was built in 1800 and has been updated for visitor's comfort. The guest rooms are rather plainly decorated but four-posters and quilts help the allure. | 314 Court St. | 603/436–7242 or 800/428–3933 | 7 rooms | AE, MC, V.

Martin Hill Inn. Friendly hospitality, inviting gardens, and homey antique comfort are to be found at these two adjacent Greek Revival homes, complete with white picket fence and brick garden path within walking distance of the historic district. The rooms are decorator-magazine in prettiness, with period antiques, canopy beds, opulent wallpapers, and an enchanting garden. | 404 Islington St. | 603/436–2287 | www.portsmouthnh.com/martinhllinn | 10 rooms | $120–$135 | MC, V.

WALPOLE
▼▼

Home to fillmmaker Ken Burns, and once a popular resort where Louisa May Alcott summered and the reclusive poet Emily Dickinson visited, Walpole holds its Colonial history dear and dates some of its village houses back to the 1790s. The town's history is closely associated with the Bellows family. Col. Benjamin Bellows founded the town, and one of his sons, Col.

John Bellows, was a prominent name in Revolutionary War activities and in the events leading up to the Declaration of Independence. The town's location in the Connecticut River valley affords pretty country vistas of southern Vermont. *Contact Walpole Historical Society | 33 West St., Walpole 02081 | 603/756–3308.*

Deacon Willard Lewis House. Built in 1826, this is Walpole's only home on the National Register and site of the Walpole Historical Society. You'll find here paintings, furniture, and memorabilia of local historical interest. | 33 West St. | 603/756–3308 | May–Oct., Wed. and Sat. 2–4.

HISTORIC DINING AND LODGING

Walpole Inn. You dine stylishly at this old, white clapboard, country inn and former home to Col. Benjamin Bellows, where the atmosphere is enhanced by exposed brick and white linen. The menu, which changes weekly, spotlights traditional New England fare and nouvelle novelties. The somewhat standard guest rooms are decorated with antique reproductions. Restaurant. | 297 Main St. | 603/756–3320 | fax 603/756–0987 | www.walpoleinn. com | 8 rooms | $145–$165 | AE, MC, V.

By Andrea Lehman

New Jersey

❦

Crossroads of the Revolution

*T*he year was 225 B.E. (Before E-Z Pass), and the state that today is thought of as a corridor between New York City and Philadelphia was already a busy thoroughfare. In late 1776 George Washington led a disheartened Continental Army across New Jersey for the first time, retreating southwest from New York to Pennsylvania. The army marched north in quasi-victory in early 1777 and east to attack in 1778, and for several years traveled the Colony's "highways" and byways, pausing for rest stops at key moments. As a result of this revolutionary traffic, there are plans afoot to designate parts of New Jersey as the Crossroads of the American Revolution National Heritage Area. Even the New Jersey state quarter proclaims the Colony's position as a revolutionary crossroads. A surprisingly modern-sounding sobriquet found in older texts declares New Jersey the "Cockpit of the Revolution," but "Crossroads" is a much better fit. Then, as now, one of the state's defining themes was its betweenness.

Betweenness, of course, can give a state an inferiority complex. Virginia has Yorktown and the early presidents. Pennsylvania has Independence Hall and the Liberty Bell. Massachusetts has too much to mention. And poor New Jersey has . . . Washington crossing the Delaware (though let's face it, how many people know that he was coming not to Delaware but to New Jersey—and on purpose?). The state's history lacks a defining event. Think of an army hunkered down for a cold winter, and chances are you'll think of Valley Forge, not Morristown. In fact, picture the American Revolution in general, and chances are you'll think of many, many places before you'll think of New Jersey. More's the pity. New Jersey saw more military engagements (296, according to a National Park Service report) than any other colony, and the Continental Army under Washington spent more time on Garden State soil—nearly half the war—than anywhere else.

✦ TEN CRUCIAL DAYS . . . AND COUNTING

Frankly, the importance of New Jersey's role in the revolution is underappreciated. Early on, the tide was turned in the Ten Crucial Days between the battles of Trenton and Princeton.

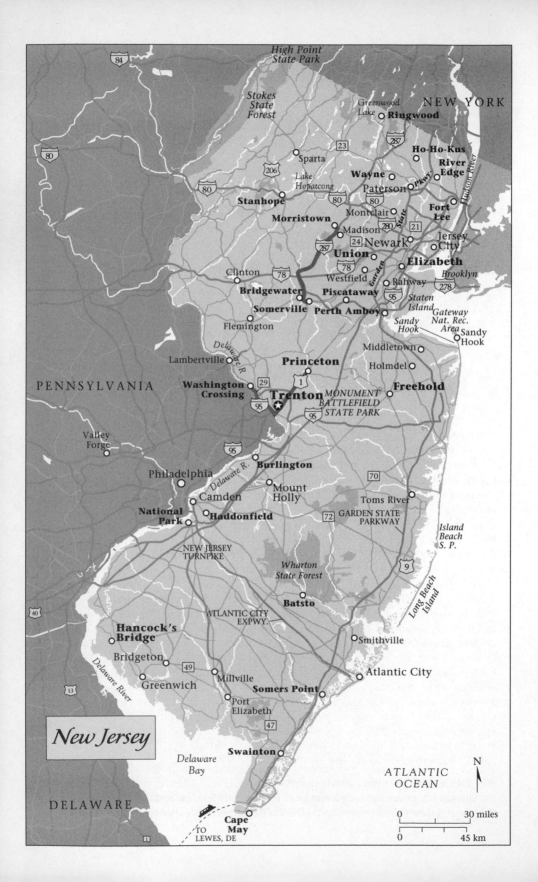

Though, truthfully, it would have to be turned several more times before final victory; were it not for those battles, the war would have been lost soon after it began. For three long winters the Continental Army was encamped in New Jersey (in Morristown and Middlebrook), and depending on what source you agree with, the Battle of Monmouth (1778) or the Battle of Springfield (1780) was the last major battle the army fought in the North. But the tale of New Jersey's Revolutionary role goes far beyond the exploits of Washington and Co. and their British and Hessian counterparts. Militias and other loose bands of Tories and Patriots wreaked their havoc, too, leaving bodies and plundered countryside behind centuries before the Sopranos.

In many ways, the lack of a defining event, individual, or group makes New Jersey a good lens through which to view the Revolution—and the emerging country. Settled not by one ethnicity but by a mix of nationalities and religious groups (albeit mostly Protestants), New Jersey was a melting pot long before the term was coined.

The first inhabitants were the Lenni Lenape (translation: "original people"). Dutch settlements started dotting the area nearest New Amsterdam (New York City) in the early 17th century, when both sides of the Hudson were part of New Netherland. Swedish settlers found their way to the banks of the Delaware (New Sweden), as did Quakers. As New Netherland gave way to New Jersey, first under the government of New York and then independent from it, immigrants continued to appear from such places as Scotland and Ireland, England and New England, and later, Germany. Together they represented the Dutch Reformed, Presbyterian, Anglican, Lutheran, Baptist, Congregational Puritan, and, of course, Quaker religions. It's fitting that in 1665, and again in 1677, early attempts at a provincial constitution, called the Concessions and Agreement, intended to grant residents extraordinary rights for the time—among them freedom of religion. But the Concessions were never fully implemented. Instead, they fell victim to a confusing power struggle between the Colonial governor and the Colonial "proprietors," both of whom felt the Crown had granted them control of the province.

Ultimately, the proprietary era would end, but it left behind a legacy that continues to this day. Back then, a province line stretching from Little Egg Harbor to the northwestern corner of the Colony divided it into the proprietorships of East and West Jersey. Today these regions are roughly what we tend to think of as North and South Jersey or the spheres of influence of New York City and Philadelphia.

✦ A HOUSE DIVIDED

As war came, New Jersey politics remained complicated, and the Colony remained a house divided. Though its five-man delegation to the Continental Congress in Philadelphia all signed the Declaration of Independence, it's estimated that there were nearly equal numbers of Patriots and Loyalists at home, including those, especially the Quakers, who simply had no appetite for war. (Among the Tories, the most ironic bit of casting was the role of royal governor, played by William Franklin, Ben's illegitimate son.) The Revolutionary War in New Jersey became as much a civil war as a war for independence. Militias and impromptu groups clashed in skirmishes that sometimes pitted neighbor against neighbor. Under-supplied armies on both sides conducted foraging expeditions (foraging sounds so much nicer than pillaging), taking from both those opposed to and sympathetic to their cause. And in the end, the victors confiscated the property of the losers, many of whom fled to England or Canada. Out of the conflict grew a new country and a new New Jersey.

In the ensuing debate about what form the new national government should take, New Jersey, being a small state, favored equal representation for each state (referred to as the New Jersey Plan), rather than representation by population. Eager to relieve itself of financial obligations to support the new government but without a port in which to levy tariffs, New Jersey pushed for a strong federal government that could raise its own funds. Once a compromise was reached, New Jersey was third to ratify the constitution and first to ratify the Bill of Rights.

The most unfortunate thing about New Jersey history is not that important things didn't happen here (they did), or even that people today don't know about them, but rather that

New Jersey Timeline

1638 Swedish settlers establish forts along the lower Delaware River, founding New Sweden.

1655 Under Pieter Stuyvesant, the Dutch force Swedes to give up forts in South Jersey. New Netherland is established.

1664 Dutch surrender New Netherland to England; proprietorship is granted to Lord Berkeley and Sir George Carteret (Hudson River to Delaware River).

1738 New Jersey becomes a royal Colony separate from New York and receives its own governor, Lewis Morris.

1776 July 2: Abraham Clark, John Hart, Francis Hopkinson, Richard Stockton, and John Witherspoon add their names to the Declaration of Independence.

1776 December 25–26: Washington and his troops cross the half-frozen Delaware River on Christmas night and surprise the Hessians in the Battle of Trenton.

1777 January 3: Battle of Princeton provides another victory, though Gen. Hugh Mercer is mortally wounded.

1777 January 6: Continental Army begins first winter encampment at Morristown.

1777 October 22: Battle of Red Bank is a victory for the Americans, but they're forced to abandon Fort Mercer within the month.

1778 June 28: Battle of Monmouth is fought to a costly draw in blazing heat; Molly Pitcher may or may not have taken part (or even existed).

1779-80 Continental Army encamps for second time at Morristown; it's the coldest winter of the century.

1783 June–November: The Continental Congress, fleeing Philadelphia because of disgruntled soldiers demanding to be paid, meets in Princeton's Nassau Hall.

1784 fall: The Continental Congress meets, albeit briefly (less than two months), in a Trenton tavern, making Trenton New Jersey's second "national capital." Plans to locate the permanent national capital in the area are considered but eventually lose out to Washington, D.C.

1787 December: New Jersey is the third state to ratify the constitution.

1789 New Jersey is the first state to ratify the Bill of Rights.

1790 Trenton selected as state capital.

1804 July 11: To defend his honor, Aaron Burr duels with Alexander Hamilton at Weehawken in what was euphemistically called an "interview." Burr shoots Hamilton above the hip (literally) and himself in the foot (figuratively). Neither Hamilton's body nor Burr's reputation recovers.

there is so much modern development encroaching on or obliterating historic sites. This chapter strives to help the avid historical traveler uncover remaining treasures and avoid sites whose value lies more in memory than in reality. (For example, we omit the site of a defunct fort nestled between two Gloucester County oil refineries, but it can be found, along with a more comprehensive list of sites, in *A Guide to New Jersey's Revolutionary War Trail*.) Luckily, there are enough preserved or re-created battlefields, barracks, houses, villages, and other historical wonders to keep you busy for quite a few weekends. And thanks to New Jersey's betweenness, these sites are not only easily accessible to residents of the Eastern Seaboard, but can serve as a microcosm of a young country's struggle. Why not rediscover American history by discovering New Jersey's?

A REGIONAL GAZETEER
▼▼

✦ EAST (NORTH) JERSEY: IN THE SHADOW OF NEW YORK
Nowhere is the assertion that New Jersey was a Colonial breadbasket more surprising than in today's Big Apple 'burbs. The area that is now a web of bedroom communities and industrial cities, shopping malls and shipping terminals, was once a rich agricultural region dotted with small towns. Tank farms were just plain farms in 1772, when William Livingston brought his family across the Hudson to Liberty Hall, his newly constructed Georgian manor house in Elizabethtown (now **Union**). The area was so rural compared to New York that his daughter complained that she would be forced to live a cloistered existence in what amounted to the boonies. Most of the land has been gobbled up and covered up (a classic example being the high-rises that stand where **Fort Lee** once stood . . . and fell). You'll find more elbow room and a different Colonial resource—iron—in the more mountainous areas farther north and west of "the city" across the Hudson. North Jersey's iron age is reflected in places like the Long Pond Ironworks in **Ringwood** and Waterloo Village in **Stanhope.**

Among the diverse groups that settled the area, the Dutch stand out. They came when this part of New Jersey was part of New Netherland, and they left their wooden shoeprints all over the region, particularly in Bergen and Somerset counties. They farmed (many owned slaves), attended Dutch Reformed churches, and built the Flemish-influenced homes generally called Dutch Colonials—often of stone with gambrel roofs, overhanging eaves, stoops, and sometimes Dutch doors. Examples in **River Edge**'s Historic New Bridge Landing Park include the Steuben House, which also happens to be an example of a home confiscated from a Tory and given to a Patriot.

In general, generalizations about New Jersey history are to be avoided. Not all people of Dutch heritage built Dutch Colonials, for example, as is demonstrated by the Georgian Dey Mansion, in **Wayne.** Though we could go on at length about group tendencies to embrace the Whig or Tory cause, the truth is that loyalties were divided within the same ethnic, religious, and socioeconomic groups, the same towns, and even the same families. The most notorious family schism divided Ben Franklin and son William, who lived two of his years as royal governor in the Proprietary House in **Perth Amboy.** The Hermitage in **Ho-Ho-Kus** stands as another example of a house divided, this time by its savvy owner. In the hodgepodge of regional Loyalist-ness and Patriot-ism, Morris County was a significant pocket of the latter, one of several factors that made it a good spot for the Continental Army's winter encampments. Today the famed National Historical Park in **Morristown** makes it North Jersey's best spot for a revolutionary experience. *Towns listed: Bridgewater, Elizabeth, Fort Lee, Ho-Ho-Kus, Morristown, Perth Amboy, Piscataway, Ringwood, River Edge, Stanhope, Union, Wayne.*

✦ CENTRAL JERSEY: DOWN TO THE CROSSROADS
Cinched tight in her corset, New Jersey boasts an hourglass figure whose constricted, conflicted wasp waist is an ambiguous area known as Central Jersey. If in-betweenness is New Jersey's identity, then Central Jersey is in-betweenness squared, a gray area with a redundancy of TV stations, where the *New York Times* gradually yields to the *Philadelphia Inquirer* and allegiances stretch to both north and south.

It wasn't much different in Colonial times. The old line dividing East and West Jersey bisected the region northwest to southeast. Geographically, the line dividing piedmont from coastal plain runs northeast–southwest, essentially following U.S. 1, Central Jersey's main artery. The quickest route across the state from Philadelphia to New York and shore to shore is across this midriff, a fact not lost on either the British or Americans. It's precisely the route the British were taking in June 1778, when the Americans, coming from Lambertville, intercepted them at Monmouth, instigating the biggest battle fought when the adversaries crossed paths. With apologies to the relative skirmishes fought in north and south, all major New Jersey battles took place in Central Jersey, making must-see war-related sights (in chronological order) of the Washington Crossing State Park in **Washington Crossing,** the Old Barracks in **Trenton,** the Princeton Battlefield State Park in **Princeton,** and the Monmouth Battlefield State Park in **Freehold.** *Towns listed: Freehold, Princeton, Trenton, Washington Crossing.*

✦ WEST (SOUTH) JERSEY: SHORE, BAY, AND PINELANDS

When the boundary between the proprietorships of East and West Jersey was established in 1676, East Jersey extended west to the Delaware in the north, while West Jersey included the Atlantic shore in the south. So much for appropriate names. After the Mason-Dixon Line was drawn in the 1760s, New Jersey's lower tier became, by inference, part of the South. Strangely enough, it's not as inappropriate as it sounds.

Except for Philadelphia suburbs and Turnpike traffic, South Jersey moves at a slower speed than the rest of the state. Visitors relax along the southern shore, within reach of such living-history sites as **Batsto** and **Historic Cold Spring Village,** which re-create an even slower-paced era. In the Pinelands and along Delaware Bay, the mood is decidedly rural and isolated. Marshes extend to the horizon along the bay. By contrast, dense scrubby woods and the twisty Mullica keep sightlines short despite the flat terrain of the Pine Barrens, which aren't barren at all. Agriculture maintains its toehold in the sandy soil of blueberry farms and the watery world of cranberry bogs. Do not assume, however, that South Jersey's Southernness extends to a pervasive acceptance of slavery. Though New Jersey as a whole had a lot of slaves for a northern state, its southern reaches, especially its southwest, were populated by many Quakers, known for their opposition to both war and slavery. That opposition was far from universal, however. See a homestead of Quaker lifestyles, beliefs, and architecture at Hancock House (in **Hancock's Bridge** near the mouth of Delaware Bay). And lest you think the revolution didn't set foot on southern shores, pay a visit to **National Park**'s Red Bank Battlefield. *Towns listed: Batsto, Burlington, Cape May, Haddonfield, Hancock's Bridge, National Park, Swainton.*

Ten Crucial Days:
Trying Men's Souls in Trenton and Princeton

A DRIVING TOUR FROM WASHINGTON CROSSING TO PRINCETON

▼▼▼

Distance: 26 mi (one-way)   **Time:** 2 days (1 night)
Breaks: Trenton's new Marriott Lafayette Yard Hotel, Princeton's classic hotel, and numerous chains along Route 1 are all good choices for a night's stay.

When the illustrious part that your Excellency has borne in this long and arduous contest becomes a matter of history, fame will gather your brightest laurels rather from the banks of the Delaware than from those of the Chesapeake. –Cornwallis to Washington, upon defeat at Yorktown

It took Washington and his army 10 days to save the Revolution. Assuming you have a car and your feet are clad in more than rags, you can do it in a weekend. First, let's get in our time machines and head back to the 18th century. In late 1776, the Patriot prognosis did not look good. Defeats in New York coupled with inadequate supplies and the gathering winter had led to a demoralized Continental Army. What's more, many soldiers' enlistments were due to expire at year's end. After retreating across New Jersey and crossing the Delaware into Pennsylvania (taking all the nearby boats), Washington conceived a bold stroke. To paraphrase a famous New Jerseyan, genius can be the result of 1% inspiration and 99% desperation.

After crossing the ice-choked Delaware throughout Christmas night, Washington's troops marched south to Trenton, where they surprised the sleeping and hung-over Hessians

(German mercenaries) barracked there. Securing a quick victory, the army lacked the manpower to hold the town and returned to Pennsylvania.

By January 2, the Continental Army was again in Trenton, but Cornwallis's larger British army was making its way there, too. Washington dispatched forces to delay the Redcoats, so that by the time the Brits arrived at Trenton, it was near dusk. A brief fight (the Second Battle of Trenton) transpired at a bridge over the Assunpink Creek, but nightfall cut it short. With his back to the river, Washington knew he would be in trouble come morning, so while a detachment stayed behind burning fires to throw off Cornwallis, the bulk of the army snuck out of town along a little-known, circuitous route to Princeton.

As Colonial forces approached Princeton from the south the next day, they encountered British troops under Lt. Col. Mahwood. The Battle of Princeton was the result, and though considered yet another American victory, it claimed the life of Brig. Gen. Hugh Mercer, after whom Mercer County would later be named. The Continental Army continued into Princeton proper (and proper it is), where they again beat up on British troops, looted and pillaged a bit, and then moved north before the snookered Cornwallis could catch up. They encamped at Morristown for the rest of the winter, their chain of victories providing the boost the Colonial cause so desperately needed.

Today, you can start where Washington started, at what is now referred to as **Washington Crossing** and was then called Johnson Ferry, one of many ferry crossings along the river. The answer to the first question your children will ask is obvious: "To get to the other side." The answer to the next question, "Why didn't he just take that cute little bridge?" is also easy: it hadn't been built yet. Their third question (assuming they have seen a picture of Emanuel Leutze's famous painting), "Why did Washington stand up during the crossing?" is better left unanswered.

If you choose, you can start at the **Washington Crossing Historic Park** on the Pennsylvania side (warning: SUVs should pull in their mirrors while crossing the bridge), but the Jersey side has its own lovely state park and visitor center. Here you can walk the walk the soldiers took in the wee hours of the night, and picnic in lovely surroundings. The easiest route to Trenton is via Route 29 south. For those desiring strict historical accuracy (except, of course, for the car thing), check out the actual routes the Continental Army took on the Ten Crucial Days Web site. You'll know you're on the right road if you see signs displaying a tricorne-hatted patriot and the phrase "Washington Victory Trail." It's unlikely you'll be able to surprise anyone in **Trenton** nowadays, but you can see where some of the Hessians were quartered at the Old Barracks and ascend the Battle Monument for a view of the surrounding countryside (now cityscape). While in town, check out Trent House, the restored Colonial home of Trenton's eponym. If it's summer, you might feel like returning to Washington Crossing's evening show in the open-air theater. Otherwise, spend the night in Trenton or en route to Princeton.

Again, there are more direct routes to Princeton than the one the Continental Army followed (that was the whole point, after all). U.S. 1 to Province Line Road (yes, that province line) to Quaker Road to Princeton Pike puts you at the Quaker Meetinghouse, where Declaration-signer Richard Stockton is buried in an unmarked grave. If you want to follow Washington's actual route, get those directions beforehand, too. In addition to "Washington Victory Trail" signs, this part of the route is marked by 12 stone obelisks, but they're not easy to spot. According to one local historian, you can see one in a field along Quaker Road as long as the corn's not too high. Just up Princeton Pike are the quiet of Princeton Battlefield State Park and the interpretive Thomas Clarke House. From there, continue up Princeton Pike into the heart of **Princeton** (and its parking nightmare). Here you can easily walk to see the Princeton Battle Monument, Morven, Bainbridge House, and Nassau Hall, all essentially along Nassau Street, as well as the Princeton Cemetery. Finish your day wandering the campus, shopping in Princeton's myriad upscale stores, or dining in one of its myriad restaurants, and congratulate yourself on your well-fought victories.

Washington Slept Here . . . and Slept Here and Slept Here: Winter Encampments in North Jersey

A DRIVING TOUR FROM MORRISTOWN TO SOMERVILLE

▼▼

Distance: 25 mi (one-way) **Time:** 2 days (1 night)
Breaks: Spend the night where the troops spent so many, in Morristown.

Battles schmattles. Yes, we know we've been bragging about all those important New Jersey battles, but despite their significance it wasn't battles that won the Revolution. It's now generally accepted that even key Patriot victories only served to prolong the war until the British finally got tired enough and quit. In essence, the American Revolution was a war of attrition. Nowhere is that more evident than at the two New Jersey locales where Washington and the Continentals encamped for three long winters. (It was customary in the 18th century not to fight through the winter.) And long they were. The army generally "rested" from December or January through May or June, and with the exception of Valley Forge in 1777–78, Washington's guys spent every winter in New Jersey from early 1777 to mid-1780, much of the time struggling to survive.

Despite close proximity to British-occupied New York (though perhaps seeming less close before the advent of New Jersey Transit), Morris County was firmly Patriot territory. That coupled with an advantageous, defensible position in the Watchung Mountains made Morristown an ideal spot to hunker down. It was so ideal, in fact, that Washington not only came here after the Battle of Princeton in January 1777 but returned again for the brutal winter of 1779–80. And a few brigades even returned in 1780–81. But we digress . . .

In May 1777 the army moved from Morristown to Middlebrook (around today's Bound Brook) and remained there until July. This also must have been a good spot to encamp, because Washington's army returned to the area for what turned out to be the mild winter of 1778–79. But that relatively pleasant memory would soon be erased by the reality of 1779–80 in Morristown, probably the coldest winter in the 18th century. Men huddled in huts and foraged in the countryside to ward off starvation, despite official sanctions against it. But the army survived. It even survived two mutiny attempts the following year, by brigades stationed at Morristown for part of the winter. With the army preserved, Washington eventually headed south to victory.

You can create your own encampment exploration experience in a weekend. Start in **Morristown.** The town centerpiece is The Green, where Washington's 1777 headquarters once stood, but the centerpiece of any historical visit is Morristown National Historical Park, the country's first such park. If you have extra time, you can see 18th- and 19th-century decorative arts in Macculloch Hall or head to nearby Madison for the Museum of Early Trades and Crafts. It will be hard to find a dinner like the ones the soldiers ate—when they ate—in 1779–80. So you may have to console yourself with Morris County's fine dining options.

On your second day, after finishing your explorations of Morristown, follow the soldiers' May 1777 itinerary by heading to **Bridgewater** and what's left of the second Middlebrook encampment: the grassy park that's called Washington Campground. Though light on interpretation, the park offers room to spread a blanket for a picnic. To get your daily Washington's headquarters fix, go to Somerville, home to the Wallace House and the adjacent Old Dutch Parsonage. You may not have covered much ground physically, but you will have covered three winters (and about 19 months) in two relatively unhurried days.

BATSTO

▼▼▼

Batsto is in the heart of the Pine Barrens region, within Wharton State Forest. The town is on the map as a former center of iron mining, and the historic village that grew up around the mining operation is a reminder of a once-very-different time. History, not iron, is the draw today, with visitors coming to view the ironmaster's mansion as well as demonstrations of crafts that were once performed here as part of daily life. *Contact Wharton State Forest /4110 Nesco Rd., Hammonton 08037 /609/561–0024 /www.state.nj.us/dep/forestry/parks/wharton.*

Batsto Village. Think that iron mining is only done in dark, deep shafts? Think again. Instead, picture the Pine Barrens—yes, the sandy, flat Pine Barrens. This reconstructed village, part of Wharton State Forest, was once home to an ironworks fueled by bog ore deposits in local streambeds. Charles Read built a furnace here in 1766, turning ore into iron—first for kettles, stoves, and other household goods and later for munitions for the Revolution and the War of 1812. Start in the visitor center, where you can pick up a map for a self-guided village tour and check out Batsto history and artifacts (even a cannonball) in the museum gallery. (Warning: the museum is slated for an overhaul, so it may not be open when you visit. The same is true of the ironmaster's mansion, whose earliest section dates to the 1780s, but is mostly a late-19th-century Italianate building; after its restoration—possibly in 2004— it will once again be open for guided tours.) Next, head out to explore the village and its 33 historic structures. Try to imagine the hundreds of people who once lived and worked here, even during wartime, since contributing to the war effort excused men from military service. Though much of what you see dates from the 19th century, still, an ore pile is an ore pile. There was an early sawmill here, too, even if it wasn't the one you see today. Workers' cottages date to the early 19th century. On weekends from Memorial Day through October, you might happen upon a weaver, potter, and spinner plying their trades. | Rte. 542 | 609/ 561–3262 | www.batstovillage.org/village.htm | Free | Grounds daily sunrise–sunset, historic buildings daily 9–4.

BRIDGEWATER

▼▼▼

At the southern end of the Watchung Mountain range, the area around Bridgewater, Somerville, and Bound Brook hosted two separate visits by the Continental Army, referred to as the Middlebrook encampments: the six-week encampment (May–July) of 1777 and the six-month encampment (December–June) of 1778–79. The only Middlebrook you'll find on a map today, however, is the Middle Brook (a stream). Instead, the encampment location is generally translated as modern-day Bound Brook, which had already been the site of a small battle in April 1777, before the army had come down from Morristown. In reality, though, the brigades were spread around the area, and Washington made his headquarters in Somerville in 1778–79. Today the area is quintessential New Jersey, filled with bedroom communities within commuting distance of many different work hubs: New York City, New Brunswick, Princeton, and the vast spread of corporate offices around this part of the state. *Contact Somerset County Historical Society / Van Veghten House, 9 Van Veghten St., Bridgewater 08807 /908/218–1281 / home.att.net/~somersetcountyhistoricalsociety.*

Old Millstone Forge Museum. Clang goes the hammer, while rapt kids (and kids at heart) watch volunteer blacksmiths mold hot metal into hooks or horseshoes. That's the big attraction at this museum on the blacksmithing trade, located in Millstone. The two-story brick and shingle museum was actually America's longest-operating blacksmith's shop, probably running from sometime in the mid- to late 1700s up until 1959. It still doesn't have electricity. What it does have are tools—on shelves, on the floor, some even dating to the 1600s—but the main draw is definitely the demonstrations of the disappearing art of the anvil. | N. River St., Millstone (6 mi south of Bridgewater) | 732/873–2803 | Donations suggested | Apr.–June and late Sept.–Nov., Sun. 1–4.

Van Horne House. If you're dying to learn what brick nogging is, this is the place to find out. Exhibits at this Heritage Trail Association headquarters include "Our Sacred Ground," about Revolutionary War sites in Somerset County; "The Forage War," about the Battle of Bound Brook; and "What a Story These Walls Tell," about the house itself. Though the earliest parts date to approximately 1750, the house is fundamentally a Colonial Revival (early 20th-century) structure. However, the association has added "windows on the past," actual windows that peek into the home's walls and reveal such early features as horsehair plaster, posts that still have their bark, hand-wrought nails, and, yes, brick nogging. The association occasionally offers bus and walking tours with a revolutionary theme. | 941 E. Main St. | 732/356–8856 | Donations suggested | www.heritagetrail.org | Sat. 10–noon, Sun. noon–2.

Wallace House and the Old Dutch Parsonage. These two 18th-century houses, set in Somerville, make up one state historic site, and though they don't share a historically significant moment, they do make for a nice tour. Tours start when people show up to take them, and on Sundays (and other days now and then) guides dress up in their Sunday best costumes. The Georgian mansion that is the Wallace House, the biggest house built in New Jersey during the revolution, is first. Washington used it as his headquarters during the second Middlebrook encampment, giving the Wallace family $1,000 in exchange. Much of the focus here isn't on Washington, though, but on life for the Wallaces in the wake of having the commander-in-chief and his entourage take over their house for half a year. The furniture here is genuine don't-touch period antiques. The Old Dutch Parsonage is a work in progress. Home to Jacob Hardenbergh, founder and first president of Queen's College (now known by the name of patriot and donor Col. Henry Rutgers), it is furnished as a clergyman's residence. In contrast to its neighbor, there are no barriers at the doors, and furnishings are good-quality reproductions that you can actually touch and sit on. It's a hands-on experience, 18th-century style. | 71 Somerset St., Somerville (2 mi south of Bridgewater) | 908/725–1015 | Donations suggested | Wed.–Sat. 10–noon and 1–4, Sun. 1–4.

Washington Campground. The brigades of the Continental Army were all over the place, literally, during the Middlebrook encampments. Unfortunately, this 3-acre hillside park in a residential area is all that remains. There are no buildings, no picnic pavilions, and no bathrooms. (Just think of it as historically accurate.) What there is is signage describing both encampments and an 80-ft flagpole flying a 13-star flag 24/7. The significance of the flag is that it commemorates the first official 13-star flag, flown over the first Middlebrook encampment in 1777. The irony of the flag is that this particular site was used in the second Middlebrook encampment in 1778–79. Still, it's a nice bit of symbolism in a nice spot for a brief symbolic encampment. | Middlebrook Rd. between Bosseler Ave. and Rte. 527 | Free | Daily sunrise–sunset.

✦ ON THE CALENDAR: Mar.–May and Sept.–Dec. **Candlelit Concerts at the Old Dutch Parsonage.** Period music is illuminated by candlelight and the glow of the fireplace. Concerts are given one Sunday evening (usually the first Sunday) each month. | 908/725–1015.

HISTORIC DINING

Ryland Inn. The cost of your meal might well be greater than the annual salary of the workers who built this circa-1800 country farmhouse and stagecoach stop. Chef Craig Shelton's top-rated modern regional French cuisine is special-occasion fare. The decor leans more to hunt club than period authenticity, but the 50-acre setting features vintage outbuildings (barn, stone and milk houses) and a Revolutionary War burial ground across the road. The inn is about 8 mi west of Somerville. | U.S. 22 W, Whitehouse | 908/534–4011.

BURLINGTON

▼▼▼

Almost like a miniature Philadelphia, this Quaker, industrial, port city actually predates its neighbor across the river. First settled in 1624, and permanently settled by the Quakers in 1677, Burlington retains its 17th- and 18th-century layout (High Street is the main drag) and the charm of an old town. You won't be able to find your way to its key sights just by looking for old brick buildings. The city is full of them—many dating from the 19th century but several from before that.

Start at the historical society's complex to get a grasp of city and county history and the names embedded in it—William Penn, William Franklin (royal governor and son of Ben), the Lawrence family, James Fenimore Cooper, Joseph Bonaparte, Francis Hopkinson, Thomas Paine, and John Woolman. You can learn about Burlington's tenure as the capital of West Jersey (the Provincial Congress alternated between Burlington and Perth Amboy through much of the 18th century and enacted the first state constitution here on July 2, 1776, before relocating to Trenton six days later) as well as its role in the war. Next, take a walk down High Street to the riverfront promenade, where you can see old waterfront homes and across to Bristol, Pennsylvania, and Burlington Island, supposedly the site of an early murder (a Native American killed a Dutchman). Along High Street and the parallel Wood Street, you'll spy some notable buildings. The Burlington Quaker Meeting House (340 High Street) is a refurbished mid-1780s structure built on the site of an earlier 1683 hexagonal building. Old St. Mary's Church (W. Broad and Wood streets) became the new kid on the block—and the first Episcopal Church in New Jersey—when it arrived in 1703. (It's called Old St. Mary's because there's a newer St. Mary's, circa 1846–54, across the courtyard.) Quite a fuss was made when many young Quakers were lured away to the new old Anglican church. Then there's the Thomas Revel House (217 Wood Street), considered the oldest existing house in the county, dating to 1685, though not at its original location. It's worth walking these few blocks along roads that were here (though not in their present form) long before the country was. *Contact Burlington County Historical Society. See below.*

Burlington County Historical Society. Begin your visit at the library and museum center, where you can explore an exhibit on the American Revolution as a global conflict on your own. Or go directly to the tour of the three houses operated by the historical society: the free-standing Bard-How House and the birthplaces of the two James, James Lawrence and James Fenimore Cooper. (Though attached to one another, these last two houses were built about 40 years apart.) Eventually, each house will interpret a different century in Burlington history—roughly the 1750s, 1850s, and 1950s—but for the near future, these 18th-century structures still tell tales of earlier times. | 451 High St. | 609/386–4773 | www.geocities. com\burlcohs | $5 | Tues.–Sat. 1–5.

Bard-How House. We hope you're not tired of mid-18th-century, South Jersey Quaker vernacular architecture, because here's another example. The oldest section of this three-story brick and frame home with a Flemish bond facade and pent roof dates to 1743. The interior represents the household of a mid-18th-century Quaker merchant. Notable among the period antiques is a signed Isaac Pearson tall clock (c. 1740) in a walnut case.

James Fenimore Cooper House. Though he's associated with upstate New York, writer James Fenimore Cooper was born in this house in 1789 and lived here for 13 months. We doubt he remembered much about it. Attached to the James Lawrence birthplace but built decades later, it contains period furnishings on the first floor and an exhibit on Joseph Bonaparte—Napoléon's brother and onetime king of Spain—on the second. After the Battle of Waterloo in 1815, Joseph fled to Bordentown, New Jersey, of all places, where he built himself a mansion, destroyed long ago.

James Lawrence House. Like Cooper, Capt. James Lawrence is famous not for what he did while living in this house (he moved when he was 13) but for his later career. A naval hero in the War of 1812, Lawrence uttered the famous line "Don't give up the ship" before giving up the ghost himself. The home where he and his family lived, built starting in 1742, was the site of a 1776 meeting between Lawrence's father, John, and the Hessian commander von Donop. Today the house, stucco-faced brick with lines struck to look like stone, is furnished in keeping with late-18th-century styles. It's noticeably different from Bard-How, especially in its Neoclassical Revival–influenced architecture and furnishings.

CAPE MAY

▼▼▼

Believed to be the oldest ocean resort in New Jersey, Cape May was first sighted in 1620 by the Dutch explorer Captain Cornelius Mey, who modestly named the entire peninsula after himself. Following the example of the Lenape people, who summered in the area for the good fishing, vacationers have been coming here for centuries. As early as the 1760s, guest houses began to appear, but it was in the 19th century that large numbers of southern gentry and northeastern industrialists made Cape May the "Queen of the Seaside Resorts." As a result, most local historical pride is reserved for Victoriana, but the summer-only Colonial House Museum, home to the Greater Cape May Historical Society, and a re-created living-history village north of the Cape May Canal are two exceptions. *Contact Greater Cape May Historical Society | 653½ Washington St., Cape May 08024 | 609/884–9100 | www.capemayhistory.org.*

Historic Cold Spring Village. She sat regally atop her high perch, her tall pointed hat the envy of all around her. Just then, she giggled. Was it a mistake? Would the schoolteacher make her take off the dunce cap and stand with her nose in the nose notch, a picture of abject humility in front of everyone in the one-room, shell-plastered Marshallville School? She truly hoped so. Discipline had never been so fun.

This outdoor living-history museum strives to re-create a small 19th-century South Jersey farm village. Over 20 antique structures, built between 1702 and 1897, were brought in from sites throughout Cape May and Cumberland counties, but their function today does not necessarily mirror yesterday's. Though most buildings here were once typical 18th- and 19th-century homes, nowadays many of them house workshops for old-time trades. There are shops for the bookbinder, blacksmith, printer, potter, and weaver as well as the schoolhouse (and its community-fostering, five-seater outhouse), barn, and country store, where a 1797 penny was found during renovation. Roam around at your own pace. You'll encounter village craftspeople in period costume demonstrating their trades with traditional tools, methods, and materials. Though the intended period of the recreation is approximately the 1820s to 1840s (post-Colonial but preindustrial except for a small railroad), many of the structures as well as the ageless crafts also represent an earlier time in South Jersey life. This restoration village is far enough outside Cape May's Victorian District that you will probably need to drive there. | 720 Rte. 9 (north of the Cape May canal) | 609/898–2300 | www.hcsv.org | $7 | Late May–late June and early–mid-Sept., weekends 10–4:30; late June–early Sept., Tues.–Sun. 10–4:30.

✦ ON THE CALENDAR: Sept. **Revolutionary War Encampment.** Reenactors re-create camp life, conduct weapons demonstrations (cleaning a gun, firing a cannon), and engage in a small skirmish. | 609/898–2300.

HISTORIC DINING AND LODGING

Daniel's on Broadway. The Hearth Room here, with all of five tables, dates from about 1765–1790 (the rest is a century later). Reserve ahead if you hope to eat with a view of the low ceiling, exposed beams, random-width pine floors, old windows with wavy glass, and the huge brick and stone fireplace complete with a swinging crane for holding kettles. | 416 S. Broadway, West Cape May | 609/898–8770 | $18–$27 | MC, V.

Wooden Rabbit. This pretty inn distinguishes itself from the crowd by virtue of the fact that it is *not* Victorian. A Federal house built in 1838, the inn is named for the many rabbits—from illustrations to stuffed toys—that grace its rooms. Fireplaces warm up the common rooms (decor is mainly Victorian), and afternoon tea is served on the glassed-in sunporch. Complimentary breakfast. | 609 Hughes St. | 609/884–7293 | fax 609/898–0842 | 2 rooms, 2 suites | $170–$200 | D, MC, V.

ELIZABETH

▼▼

If one were conducting a smell tour of New Jersey, Elizabeth would surely be on it. Close to the New Jersey Turnpike, Elizabeth is the quintessential industrial New Jersey town, the kind that the unenlightened may think is representative of the state. In truth, it does make a rather large impact, especially since it's one of the first things many visitors see if they come into Newark Airport and head south. But the city has a long and colorful history. Settled in 1664, Elizabethtown, as it was then known, was the first provincial capital and the first home of Princeton University. Like much of New Jersey, it was largely agricultural, though its port was and still is an important commercial center. *Contact Union County Division of Cultural and Heritage Affairs | 633 Pearl St., Elizabeth 07202 | 908/558–2550 | www.unioncountynj. org/econdev/cultural.htm.*

Boxwood Hall. Their signatures may be scrawled all over the documents that founded this country, but their footprints are all over Boxwood Hall. Built around 1750, this was the home of Elias Boudinot, president of the Continental Congress in 1781 (he signed the peace treaty with England) and brother-in-law of Richard Stockton, one of the Declaration signers. Alexander Hamilton boarded with the Boudinots his first year in America, and George Washington visited on his way to his inauguration in 1789. In the early 19th century, the house was sold to Jonathan Dayton, the youngest signer of the Constitution and longtime friend of Aaron Burr (who grew up in Elizabeth). Dayton welcomed General Lafayette to Boxwood Hall in 1824. The list is impressive, and so is what's left of the house—the eight-room center portion of what was an 18-room Georgian mansion (the wings were torn down in the 1870s). Guided tours cover a lot of ground: the home's inhabitants and visitors; the "forgotten" (pre-Constitution) presidents, such as Boudinot; the period (1760–1840) furnishings and decorative arts on display, including a New Jersey–made Brokaw clock; such original architectural details as 10-ft ceilings (very high for the time), hand-carved woodwork, and marble fireplaces; and the story of the hall's early 20th-century restoration. Kids especially seem to like playing detective and learning how researchers discovered the original red color of the wood shingles or the original roof line underneath a later mansard structure. | 1073 E. Jersey St. | 908/282–7617 | Free | May–Oct., Mon.– Sat. 9–noon and 1–5; Nov.–Apr., weekdays 9–noon and 1–5.

✦ ON THE CALENDAR: Oct. **Four Centuries in a Weekend.** Union County's 22 historical houses/museums open their doors on the same weekend. Included are attractions that are normally open by appointment only, including Elizabeth's Belcher-Ogden Mansion, one of two royal governor's residences in New Jersey. (Proprietary House, in Perth Amboy, is the other.) | 908/558–2550.

FORT LEE

▼▼

Perhaps it was a bad omen that George Washington named the fort that once stood here after Charles Lee, the ill-fated general who was later court-martialed for his failure at the

Battle of Monmouth. In fall 1776, before there were victories at Trenton and Princeton, there was the loss of Fort Lee. Perched high atop the Palisades, Fort Lee the fort, for which Fort Lee the town was named, was built in summer 1776 as a mate to Fort Washington, across the Hudson in New York City. Together they were meant to keep control of the river from the British, and the formidably sheer Palisades should have provided a good defensive position. Unfortunately, it wasn't good enough. A local Tory knew of a route up the cliffs, and superior British numbers managed to wrest both forts from American hands in quick succession. Washington's men were forced to abandon Fort Lee—and substantial provisions and munitions—and begin their first trip, in retreat, across New Jersey. Today, Fort Lee is a classic commuter town, while looming above it all is the great gray bridge named for the illustrious general and president whose record was hardly illustrious at the time he was here. *Contact Greater Fort Lee Chamber of Commerce | 210 Whiteman St., Fort Lee 07024 | 201/944-7575 | www.fortlee.com.*

Fort Lee Historic Park. Where the fort once stood, high-rises stand today, but the mighty Hudson remains as it was. As a result, most people who come to this park do so not to see authentic revolutionariana but to drink in the beautiful views across to Manhattan. A visitor center contains exhibits and a short film on the happenings of fall 1776. To the south are reconstructed gun batteries and an 18th-century soldiers' hut with a well, woodshed, and baking oven. This is the site of occasional interpretive programs and demonstrations of 18th-century ways. (The Kearney House, another Palisades park attraction north of Fort Lee in Alpine, was thought to have been Cornwallis's headquarters during the November 1776 landing. However, recent research has concluded that the landing spot was farther south and that the earliest section of the house may not have even been built by then.) | Hudson Terr. | 201/461–1776 | www.njpalisades.org | Free | Grounds daily 8–sunset; visitor center Mar.–Dec., Wed.–Sun. 10–5.

FREEHOLD
▼▼

Founded in 1715, Freehold is not quite on the Jersey shore, but it does provide a glimpse of Monmouth County's pastoral scenery of horse farms and county parks. To the west, straddling Freehold and Manalapan townships, is Monmouth Battlefield State Park, where the fighting was once hot and heavy. Molly Pitcher (*see* Misses and Legends box *below*) rose to fame here. *Contact Monmouth County Historical Association.* See below.

Covenhoven House. It should come as no great surprise that General Clinton would take Freehold's fanciest house for his headquarters before the Battle of Monmouth. Check out the exterior siding, almost like cake frosting, and the beautiful blue-and-white painted interior walls upstairs. in addition to the appropriate period furnishings. | 150 W. Main St. | 732/462–1466 | $2 | May–Sept., Tues., Thurs., Sun. 1–4, Sat. 10–4.

Monmouth Battle Monument. This Patriot-topped memorial across from the historical association museum is decorated with bronze bas-reliefs of various battle-related scenes, including Molly manning (or should we say womanning?) her cannon. Like most depictions, it's highly mythologized. | Court St.

Monmouth Battlefield State Park. There's a good reason why New Jersey residents head "down the shore" on hot summer days; they want to avoid what happened here 225 years ago. On June 28, 1778, what turned out to be the longest, hottest, and biggest (nearing 20,000 British and over 13,000 Continental troops) battle of the Revolution was fought amid the hilly farmland and hedgerows of what is now a 2,000-acre park. The British under General Henry Clinton had evacuated Philadelphia and were heading to New York, traipsing yet again through the core of New Jersey. Washington, having spent the winter at Valley Forge, decided to inflict a little damage before the Brits got away. They collided near Monmouth Court House. Actually, the first American commander to engage the British was Charles Lee, but when he ordered a retreat and defied Washington's order to attack (he was later court-martialed), Washington took over. The battle lasted much of the day, and soldiers died from heat stroke as well as wounds. In the end, the battle was nearly a draw, but the next day the British continued on to New York, lending a veneer of victory to the American cause. You can get oriented at the hilltop visitor center, which has maps, charts, and artifacts, such as musket balls excavated from the park. A landscape restoration project is re-creating fences, lanes, and woodlots as they would have been during the Revolutionary War period. Picnic areas, a nature center, hiking and bridle trails, and a restored Revolutionary War farmhouse round out the facilities. The adjacent Old Tennent Church, which was hit during the battle and served as a field hospital, has some soldiers' graves. | 347 Freehold-Englishtown Rd., Manalapan | 732/462–9616 | www.state.nj.us/dep/forestry/parks/monbat.htm | Free | Daily sunrise–sunset; visitor center daily 9–4.

Craig House. About 2½ mi from the visitor center, this Colonial farmhouse, occupied by the Craig family at the time of the battle, is furnished with antiques of the time. A note to architecture buffs: the 1746 kitchen has Dutch framing, while the two-story addition is English-framed. A note to architecture boneheads: ask the staff here to show you what this really means. | Sun. 12–4, other days depending on funding.

Monmouth County Historical Association Main Museum and Library. If you liked Emanuel Leutze's painting of *Washington Crossing the Delaware,* you'll probably like his depiction of the valiant general at the Battle of Monmouth. A second original is on display here. (In contrast to the first original, at the Cal-Berkeley museum, this canvas is a little smaller, and Washington's expression is more placid.) A permanent exhibit treats the battle, but rotating exhibits could cover any aspect of county history. In addition, the association maintains four historic houses around the county that are open to the public: the Covenhoven House, Holmes-Hendrickson House, Allen House, and Marlpit Hall. | 70 Court St. | 732/462–1466 | www.monmouth.com/~mcha | $2 | Tues.–Sat. 10–4, Sun. 1–4.

✦ ON THE CALENDAR: June **Battle of Monmouth Reenactment.** Men, women, and children in 18th-century attire camp at Monmouth Battlefield State Park and reenact the long, hot battle the last weekend of the month. | 732/462–9616.

HISTORIC DINING

Moore's Tavern and Restaurant. What better to do after a hot afternoon re-creating the Battle of Monmouth (in body or spirit) than to knock down a cool frosty one in a late 18th-century tavern? Though the restaurant here is a modern creation, everything in the 1787 tavern except the floor and bar are original. Lighting illuminates the peg joinery in the ceiling's open beams. And don't worry, you can get everything off the restaurant's menu in the tavern, in addition to that cool frosty one. | 402 W. Main St. | 732/863–0555.

HADDONFIELD

▼▼

Now one of the area's most affluent communities, Haddonfield started out as a stopover along the main road between Burlington and Salem. (A 1773 stone marker still stands by the town's main intersection.) A historic district containing more than 400 structures includes much of the central business district, but, as usual, virtually all the buildings are Victorian or later, since most earlier structures were torn or burned down. *Contact Visitor Center | 114 Kings Hwy. E, Haddonfield 08033 | 856/216–7253 | www.haddonfieldnj.org.*

Indian King Tavern. It's strange to think of sober history being made in a tavern, but in the 18th century, taverns were *the* center of community communication. News was disseminated and ideas exchanged in them. However, this particular 1750 tavern, named for the local Lenni Lenape people, was not just your typical community meeting place. In 1777 it was also the meeting place for a not-so-typical group—the New Jersey legislature—and it was here that the state seal was adopted and that the term "state" officially replaced that of "colony" in state documents. Guided tours, generally lasting 45 minutes to an hour, cover two floors of the tavern, furnished in a mix of antiques and reproductions. The private dining room contains gateleg tables set for a better class of patrons, while middling sorts ate in the public dining room—not to be confused with the public room (a bar, in modern parlance). Also here are the innkeeper's bedroom, the keeping room (not quite a kitchen, as cooking was done elsewhere), and the assembly/ball/meeting/banquet room (as its name suggests, a multipurpose profit center). | 233 Kings Hwy. E | 856/429–6792 | www.levins.com/tavern.html | Free | Wed.–Sat. 10–noon and 1–4, Sun. 1–4.

✦ ON THE CALENDAR: May, July, Sept., Dec. **Open Houses at Indian King Tavern.** During festivities for Great Seal Day in May, the Fourth of July, Colony to State Day in September, and the Music of Christmas in December, costumed docents stationed in the tavern's rooms tell stories. At the December open house a dulcimer group and fiddlers play 18th-century music. | 856/429–6792.

HANCOCK'S BRIDGE
▼▼▼

Area history goes back to 1675, when Quaker John Fenwick established the first English settlement around Salem. (Legend has it that Fenwick met with the local Lenape people beneath the now-400-plus-year-old Salem Oak, a local landmark.) The name Salem, by the way, comes from ancient Hebrew for "peace." The origin of the name Hancock's Bridge is easier to guess: shoemaker William Hancock bought property from Fenwick, and his son John built a bridge across the Alloways Creek. Though the land changed hands, the Quaker influence remained. *Contact Salem County Historical Society | 79–83 Market St., Salem 08079 | 856/935–5004 | www. salemcounty.com/schs.*

Hancock House. Hawks and doves will both find something to their liking at this early 18th-century, two-story brick home. War buffs will appreciate the story of the massacre that transpired here on March 21, 1778, when, in retribution for local resistance to British foraging activities, Maj. John Simcoe and about 300 British troops attacked. (The house had been used as militia headquarters since its Tory owner, Judge William Hancock, great-great-nephew of the original William Hancock, had been forced to leave.) The British bayoneted everyone they found (accounts differ as to number, but somewhere between 10 and 30), including Hancock, who had returned to his home. Guided tours tell about the massacre but don't ascend to the attic, where legend has it the floor is stained with blood. However, even if the attic were open, the floorboards have been turned over, so there's no way to verify the unlikely existence of 225-year-old bloodstains.

Peace-lovers, on the other had, might like the exterior's patterned brickwork, an excellent example of the common (and uncommon) bonds used in local Quaker vernacular architecture. Built in 1734 by yet another William Hancock and his wife, Sarah, it features a front facade with two different brick patterns and two different types of brick: common red bricks and vitrified blue bricks. Most of the facade is done in Flemish bond, a pattern of alternating stretchers (bricks laid with their long edge facing out) and headers (bricks with their short ends facing out) within each course. The bottom features English bond: alternating courses of stretchers and headers. On the end walls, the brickwork has a herringbone pattern, and a gable bears the monogram H above WS (for William and Sarah Hancock) and 1734. Furnishings are mostly intended to capture the period of the massacre, though one room reflects the home's tavern period. Also on the property are a 17th-century Swedish cabin and a Colonial herb and vegetable garden. | Locust Island Rd. | 856/935–4373 | www.geocities.com/hancockhousenj | Free | Wed.–Sat. 10–noon and 1–4, Sun. 1–4.

✦ ON THE CALENDAR: Mar. **Commemoration of the Massacre.** The massacre is reenacted, and Hancock House hosts tours and Colonial music played by a Colonial ensemble. | 856/935–4373.

HO-HO-KUS
▼▼

What's with the name? Ho-ho-kus is generally considered a contraction of the Delaware Indian word Mehokhokus—translation: "red cedar." (As elsewhere in New Jersey, the Lenni Lenape people were the area's first inhabitants.) Ho-Ho-Kus the town was founded in 1790, but a small piece of history walked through its central jewel, the Hermitage, a dozen years before. Today Ho-Ho-Kus is a quiet, upscale community that likes its tranquillity. *Contact Ho-Ho-Kus Chamber of Commerce | Box 115, Ho-Ho-Kus 07423 | 201/444–6664 | www.hohokuschamber.com.*

The Hermitage. One look at the gingerbread trim hanging from the eaves, and you might think you're in the wrong place. Both the home's Gothic Revival architecture and Victorian furnishings, reflecting the era when the Rosencrantz family lived here, are far from the mid-18th-century vintage of the house's core. If you're willing to tolerate Victoriana, take a tour anyway, to learn about the interesting history of an earlier homeowner, Theodosia Prevost. In July 1778, Theodosia's husband, James, was a British army officer, but this strong woman could see which way the wind was blowing. After the Battle of Monmouth, Prevost invited Washington and his men to stay at her house, which they did (not all his men, of course) for about four days in mid-July. She established a friendship with Washington, Hamilton, and other notables, who helped her keep her home from being confiscated at war's end. Ironically, she ended up wedding Aaron Burr in the house after her husband died. Ask your docent to show you as much of the pre-Victorian as possible. There's 18th-century stonework on the exterior, a desk of Aaron Burr's, remnants of an open-hearth fireplace in the kitchen, and a section of dining room wall that opens to reveal the posts and beams of the original ceiling. If you look past the 19th-century embellishments, you can see all the way to 1778. | 335 N. Franklin Tpk. | 201/445–8311 | www.thehermitage.org | $4 | Wed.–Sun. 1–4.

✦ ON THE CALENDAR: July **Revolutionary War Living History Day.** To commemorate the time of Washington's stay here, the Hermitage briefly focuses on its revolutionary history. Reenactors interact with the modern populace (perhaps conducting a musket firing or two). Children's events include period games and crafts. And tours truly focus on the home's 18th-century heritage. | 201/445–8311.

HISTORIC DINING
Ho-Ho-Kus Inn. There are contradictory stories about the origin of this Dutch Colonial sandstone landmark, but it seems to have been built in the late 1790s as a private home for the Zabriskie family and was later turned into an inn. Today's restaurant has five dining rooms (three upstairs, two down) with an original staircase and fireplaces. Much of the interior has been renovated, however. Cuisine is Continental/Italian. | 1 E. Franklin Tpk. | 201/445–4115 | $19–$26 | AE, DC, MC, V | Closed Sun. No lunch Sat.

MORRISTOWN

▼▼

You'd have to be on a fast or seriously underdressed to experience any privations in this affluent area today. The seat of Morris County is loaded with restaurants, shops, clubs, theaters,
and antiques, but most importantly, the town is loaded with history—mind- and body-numb-
ing, hut-huddling cold-war history, laid bare at the nation's first national historical park.
Not all of Morristown's historical significance lies within the confines of either 1777–80 or
the national park, however. The village green was the heart of town long before it played
host to Washington's first local headquarters (Arnold's Tavern—no longer standing). During
the Gilded Age, Morristown is said to have housed more millionaires than any other city in
the United States. Alfred Vail and Samuel Morse first demonstrated the telegraph at Historic
Speedwell in 1838, and Thomas Nast created his 19th-century political cartoons (many on
display at Macculloch Hall) and famous Santa Claus in town. If you have extra time, you
may want to check out this other local history. *Contact Morris County Historical Society / Acorn
Hall, 68 Morris Ave., Morristown 07960 / 973/267–3465 / www.acornhall.org.*

Macculloch Hall Historical Museum. This columned mansion, built between 1810 and 1819
on a 1765 foundation, is part historic home and part museum. Yes, there's the requisite family
history (of the Macculluchs and Millers), but you'll also find changing exhibits and period
rooms showcasing 18th- and 19th-century American and English fine and decorative arts.
A Charles Willson Peale portrait of George Washington from the 1790s hangs in the drawing room. The museum is perhaps best known, however, for the Thomas Nast collection of
some 2,000 19th-century political cartoons. The garden, the oldest in the county, is another
popular spot. | 45 Macculloch Ave. | 973/538–2404 | www.machall.org | $4 | Wed., Thurs.,
Sun. 1–4.

Morristown National Historical Park. This 1,000-acre homage to endurance has four discrete
sections: the Washington's Headquarters area, Fort Nonsense, Jockey Hollow, and the New
Jersey Brigade area. Together they tell of Morristown's considerable role in keeping the army
intact through the war, with an emphasis on the bitter winter of 1779–80. (During their 1777
sojourn, troops were put up in homes all over the area, and by 1780–81, only the Pennsylvania line, followed by the New Jersey Brigade, were stationed here.) You can start at either
the Washington's Headquarters Museum or the Jockey Hollow Visitor Center, depending on
whether you want to begin by looking at life for Washington and his officers or for the common
footsoldier (by 1779, uncommonly tough). Either way, take time for a brief orientation, get
information from rangers, check a calendar for demonstrations and other programs (usually
on weekends), pick up a brochure/map, and be off. Some of the sites below are adjacent to
each other, such as the Ford Mansion and Washington's Headquarters or Jockey Hollow and
Wick House. | 30 Washington Pl. | 973/539–2016 recording, Ext. 210 voice | www.nps.
gov/morr | $4 | Grounds daily 8–sunset.

    Ford Mansion. Though the circa-1772 Georgian home of Jacob Ford Jr.'s widow and four
children did house troops in 1777, it's more famous as Washington's headquarters in 1779–
80. Today the house is furnished to look as it might have during Washington's stay. Some
rooms were used by George and Martha, some by staff officers, and some by the Ford family.
Furnishings are primarily representative period antiques, but a dressing table, secretary desk,
and mirror actually belonged to the Fords. Just imagine who might have gazed into that
mirror. To see inside the mansion, pick up a tour (30–45 minutes) at the adjacent museum.
| Tours daily 10–11 and 1–4, on the hr.

    Fort Nonsense. The first reference to the name Fort Nonsense didn't appear until the 1820s,
along with the story that the compound of trenches and embankments Washington had
soldiers build in spring 1777 was just busy work. The more likely story, according to ranger
and historian Eric Olsen, is that he had them build the earthwork fortification as a strate-

Misses and Legends

For proof that Molly Pitcher really existed, look no further than the New Jersey Turnpike. After all, to get your name on a service area, you must be a flesh-and-blood famous New Jerseyan, right? Well, maybe.

Legend gives us multiple Mollys. There's Tailgunner Molly, who took over her husband's cannon when he was felled in the Battle of Monmouth, eventually earning commendation from Washington himself. There's Aquarian Molly, bringing water to soldiers on the battlefield. (There are fully seven park locations where Molly supposedly got her water.) Then there's Symbolic Molly, the name Molly standing for women in general and Pitcher representing a water-carrier. What appears to be true, according to park historian Garry Stone and first-hand accounts, is that a woman named Mary (nickname: Molly) Hays did help her husband, William, at the Battle of Monmouth (probably as an assistant bombardier and courier). The rest is likely embellishment. The real Hayses lived well past the battle.

Morristown's Tempe (Temperance) Wick doesn't need a rest stop named for her to keep her tale alive and mutating. The daughter of Henry Wick, she lived near the encamped Americans at Jockey Hollow. That much is true. The rest of the tale—which didn't appear until the 1870s, long after Tempe had died—has it that Tempe was accosted by soldiers who wanted her horse. She refused and rode off, hiding the steed in her house so the soldiers wouldn't find it. Depending on who's weaving the yarn, the soldiers were either American, British, Hessian, or even Polish. She hid the horse for a day, three days, a week, three weeks, a month (do I hear a year?). And the horse stayed in a downstairs room, in the cellar, in the attic (imagine getting a horse up and down those stairs!), in her bedroom, under her bed, or in bed dressed as a girl (the Little Red Riding Wick version). To judge the story's likelihood, ranger Eric Olsen suggests you imagine the 45 pounds of manure the horse would have produced daily. Still the Tempe Wick legend, like that of Molly Pitcher, will not die—a testament to the endurance of a good Revolutionary War heroine and our desire to contribute to the cause, even if a few centuries late.

gic overlook and place of refuge for those troops who would be left behind when the main army moved out. Though the fort has been eroded by time, a Belgian block outline reveals its size and shape, and interpretive signs provide details. | Behind county courthouse.

Jockey Hollow. Try to picture upward of 10,000 Continental Army soldiers encamped here, first building their own log huts in the freezing winter of 1779–80 and then clustered around the fire when they weren't drilling, training, or conducting other soldierly chores. What's amazing is that despite the horrible weather (much colder than at Valley Forge two years before) and lack of food (sometimes they'd go days without eating), only about 100 men died, as opposed to 1,000–3,000 in 1777–78. The encampment-hardened troops built better huts, used better sanitation, had better immunities against smallpox, and were just plain better at doing without. The visitor center here contains a furnished model of a hut, a mural showing what camp looked like, and a small theater that screens a short movie with a lot of moaning. Five empty replica huts are located outside at the Pennsylvania line. Other facilities at Jockey Hollow include wooded hiking trails and the Wick House. | Off Tempe Wick Rd., Harding Twp. | 973/543–4030 | Visitor center daily 9–5.

New Jersey Brigade. A few miles southwest of Jockey Hollow, 900 troops of the New Jersey Brigade encamped here in 1779–80. Though this area is not staffed, there is interpretive signage. There are also wooded trails for walking and remembering. | Off Old Jockey Hollow Rd., Bernardsville.

Washington's Headquarters Museum. Here you can pick up the requisite printed matter; take in the museum's exhibits, including a cannon captured at Princeton and two of Washington's swords; watch a 20-minute movie; and keep an ear cocked for the start of the Ford Mansion tours. | Daily 9–5.

Wick House. When the Continental Army plunked itself down on Henry Wick's farm (along with those of his neighbors), the Wick family's home became headquarters for General Arthur St. Clair. The prosperous Wicks had built the roomy, well-constructed house, reminiscent of their New England origins, around 1750. Today it displays two rooms set up for the general and his staff, two for the Wick family, and a shared kitchen. The most famous Wick might well be Henry's daughter, Tempe (*see* the "Misses and Legends" box). | Daily 9:30–noon and 1:30–4:30.

Schuyler-Hamilton House. Strangely, this white-clapboard 1760 home is known not by the name of its 18th-century owner, Revolutionary War doctor Jabez Campfield, nor of Washington's personal physician, Dr. John Cochran, who stayed here during 1779–80. It's named for Betsy Schuyler, Cochran's niece, and Col. Alexander Hamilton, who courted her here during that long winter. Period furnishings from 1720 to 1835 include four major tiger-maple pieces. | 5 Olyphant Pl. | 973/267–4039 | www.morrisig.com/vgreen/schuyler.htm | $4 | Sun. 2–4.

✦ ON THE CALENDAR: Dec. **Holly Walk.** One ticket gets you in to eight or so area historical museums and the national park over three days. The museums are decorated (if holiday decorations were appropriate to their period), and some special activities (perhaps weaving demonstrations or choral performances) are on tap. | 973/539–2016.

HISTORIC DINING AND LODGING

Grain House. History has it that grain for Washington's troops at Jockey Hollow was stored in what is now this restaurant's Grain Room; that the upstairs dining rooms comprised the haymows; and that the Coppertop Pub was a stable. The only horses here today, however, are on the walls. A Colonial ambience comes courtesy of a mix of the original and the reproduction: wide-plank floors, beamed ceilings, Currier & Ives prints, and smoke-blackened fireplaces now running on gas. American fare includes such "country food for the weary traveler" as Patriot's Stew. For the crowning (or should we say democratic?) glory, come for a Revolutionary Affair, held once or twice a year. A historic personage (maybe Abigail Adams or Martha Washington) is in attendance, and the food is genuine, perhaps from Abigail or Martha's own cookbooks. Adjacent to the restaurant on the 10-acre estate is the Olde Mill Inn (225 Route 202 and N. Maple Avenue, 866/836–9330), a newly built essay in traditional comfort and a greatly favored hostelry for this posh area. | 225 Rte. 202, Basking Ridge | 908/221–1150 | $17–$22 | AE, MC, V.

Parrot Mill Inn. This B&B's namesake was not a bird but George Parrot, the original owner of the 1780s section of this white clapboard, gambrel-roofed building. (A 1959 addition was tastefully blended in.) Thick walls, slanted floors, and antiques, including a 250-year-old settle, maintain the centuries-old feel. | 47 Main St., Chatham | 973/635–7722 | 5 rooms | $80–$110 | MC, V.

NATIONAL PARK
▼▼▼

Yes, it's confusing. Red Bank Battlefield Park, which contains the remnants of Fort Mercer and is located in National Park, is nowhere near Red Bank (on the Navesink River not far from Sandy Hook), is not in Mercer County (it's in Gloucester), and isn't a national park (it's operated by the county). But that shouldn't keep you from visiting this 44-acre passive-recreation park, which had its 40 minutes of fame 225 years ago. *Contact Gloucester County Parks and Recreation | 6 Blackwood-Barnsboro Rd., Sewell 08062 | 856/853–5120 | www.co.gloucester.nj.us.*

Red Bank Battlefield Park. In fall 1777, New Jersey's Fort Mercer and its partner across the river, Fort Mifflin, were key Patriot defenses, necessary to keep supplies from reaching the British in Philadelphia. For a while, it worked. When 1,200 Hessians under Col. Kurt von Donop attacked Fort Mercer on October 22, they were met by a smaller force under Col. Christopher Greene and, more importantly, by the well-fortified earthwork fort. Hundreds of Hessians, including von Donop, died after 40 minutes of fighting, but though American casualties were few, the fort could not be held forever. By November 20, both forts were abandoned, with the Americans attempting to burn everything at Fort Mercer as they fled. That's the bad news. The good news is that the Red Bank victory gave the Patriot cause some prestige, and the delay put a crimp in British plans. The other good news is that the sites of both forts are today open to the public. Though Fort Mifflin was subsequently rebuilt, Fort Mercer was not. Instead what you see today are trenches constituting the fort's remains. Memorials include a Patriot-topped monument dedicated to Colonel Greene and a memorial wall in honor of Gen. Hugh Mercer, for whom the fort was named. There's also a building with pieces of cheveaux-de-frise, used in the Delaware defense. Picnic areas, playgrounds, a riverfront path, a pier with a nice view across the river, and the absence of the airplane noise you'd find at Fort Mifflin complete a peaceful scene at a spot that was once anything but peaceful. | 100 Hessian Ave. | 856/853–5120 | www.co.gloucester.nj.us | Free | Daily sunrise–sunset.

Whitall House. It's said that Quaker Ann Whitall kept spinning yarn while the Battle of Red Bank raged outside her home. She just moved downstairs. After the battle, the circa-1748 Georgian was used as a field hospital where Ann nursed the wounded. Today you can take a tour of the home with a costumed interpreter and see a re-created military hospital along with the great room (set up as it would have been in the 18th century), a huge kitchen with working fireplace, and an herb garden. | Apr.–Oct., Wed.–Fri. 9–noon and 1-4, weekends 1–4; Nov.–Mar., Wed.–Fri. 9–noon and 1–4.

✦ ON THE CALENDAR: Oct. **18th-Century Field Day.** Though the day's highlight is a battle reenactment, there are also site-specific crafts, children's activities, and a 10k run that commemorates Jonas Cattell's run from Haddonfield to warn the fort that the British—okay, the Hessians—were coming. | 856/853–5120.

PERTH AMBOY
▼▼▼

When water was the highway of choice, Perth Amboy was a prominent port. Well-situated just across the Arthur Kill from Staten Island and where the Raritan River empties into Raritan Bay, it served as a capital for the province, colony, and state from the town's founding in 1683 until 1790, when the capital moved west to Trenton and New Jersey's other shore. Today Perth Amboy's waterfront location is largely industrial and serves to anchor one end of the Outerbridge Crossing. *Contact Perth Amboy Chamber of Commerce | 214 Smith St., Perth Amboy 08861 | 732/442–7400.*

Proprietary House. If it's war and peace you're after, go to Princeton or Trenton. For fathers and sons, come to Perth Amboy, where the story of William Franklin, Ben's son and the last royal governor of New Jersey, is told. Built by the East Jersey Proprietors, Proprietary House is the only remaining authentic official Colonial governor's residence. (Translation: some residences, like Elizabeth's Belcher-Ogden Mansion, were unofficial; Williamsburg's is a re-creation.) Construction began the same year Franklin became royal governor—1762—but he lived here only from 1774 to 1776. By most accounts, he was a well-respected royal governor for many years. He simply backed the wrong side, remaining loyal to the crown even as his father became an outspoken advocate of independence. In 1776 Franklin was arrested and eventually fled to England, never to return to New Jersey or repair the rift with his father. It's said Franklin's ghost is one of several that inhabit Proprietary House, possibly because it's where he spent his best years. Those memories must be bittersweet nevertheless, as he's been seen pacing the floor in an agitated state. You'll probably have to content yourself with seeing what's in the present-day English Palladian mansion and hearing about its 1762–1846 history. Tours take in the Franklin drawing room, dining and breakfast rooms, housekeeper's room, Colonial kitchen, servants' hall, and wine cellar, where afternoon tea is served. Keep your eye peeled for documents signed by Franklin; paintings of Franklin, including one in which he presents the king's charter for Queen's College; and, just maybe, Franklin himself. | 149 Kearny Ave. | 732/826–5527 | www.proprietaryhouse.org | Donations accepted | Wed. 10–4, Sun. 1–3.

✦ ON THE CALENDAR: June **Arrest of William Franklin.** Each year the drama plays out again as the arrest of William Franklin is re-enacted. House tours and people in period costume are constants. Other programs, such as demonstrations of Colonial firearms, vary from year to year. | 732/826–5527.

PISCATAWAY
▼▼

Like many 18th-century river towns, Piscataway was a center of trade. Then called Raritan Landing, for the river that provided its livelihood, it was a thriving merchant community settled mostly by people of Dutch descent. Today it's a typical Middlesex County suburb with its share of sprawl. *Contact Middlesex County Cultural and Heritage Commission | 703 Jersey Ave., New Brunswick 08901 | 732/745–4489 | www.cultureheritage.org.*

Cornelius Low House/Middlesex County Museum. Walk up the winding interpretive path intended to mirror the curvy Raritan River. Read the bronze plaques, and examine the models and silhouettes. It's a good first taste of the different layers of history on the menu here. You can learn about the families who once called this 1741 Georgian manor house home, including Isaac and Nicholas Low, sons of the home's builder (well-to-do merchant Cornelius Low, Jr.) who ended up on opposite sides during the revolution. If you're more interested in architecture, you can appreciate the 350 tons of stone used to build the 2½-story house, with square-cut stones on the front (river-facing) facade and more random shapes on the other sides. Inside are the original paneled stairs and wainscoting; Georgian and Greek Revival fireplaces, some with Delft tile surrounds; and rooms returned to their original paint colors. Or you can come to see the annually changing exhibit on some aspect of state history, from Cornelius Low's time to the present. | 1225 River Rd. | 732/745–4177 | Free | Tues.–Fri. and Sun. 1–4.

East Jersey Olde Towne Village. If you rebuild it, they will come to learn about the "history, traditions, folk arts, and artisanship of the people who lived and worked throughout the [Central Jersey] region." That's the goal of this 12-acre village and its 11 restored, relocated, and replicated structures. Representing a cross-section of 18th- and 19th-century vernacular architecture (stone and clapboard construction with Dutch and English influences), buildings here include a one-room schoolhouse, church, reconstructed mid-18th-century barracks (à la Trenton's Old Barracks), and the homes of merchants and farmers. The buildings are only open on the guided tour, given daily at 1:30 (except on those Sundays when there are special programs). If you come at other times, you'll have to be content with picking up brochures about each structure from the visitor center (currently in the barracks) and wandering around the village grounds. | 1050 River Rd. | 732/745–3030 | Free | Tues.–Fri. 8:30–4:15, Sun. 1–4.

HISTORIC DINING

O'Connor's Beef 'n Chowder House. Steak, ribs, and meat loaf are examples of the good ol' American cooking you can get in this good ol' American farmhouse—good new American when it was built in 1793. Look at the section cut out of the wall in the Fireplace Room to see the mud and hay used as insulation. Also reportedly hidden in the house are two ghosts: a revolutionary war soldier and a woman affectionately known as Grace. | 1719 Amwell Rd., Somerset | 732/873–3990 | $10–$22 | AE, MC, V.

PRINCETON

▼▼▼

This sophisticated and chichi university town was settled in the late 17th century as "Prince Town," in honor of Prince William of Orange and Nassau. You'll see a lot of both—orange and Nassau, that is. Nassau Street is the main drag, Nassau Hall an important university building, the Nassau Inn the local hotel, and orange and black the ubiquitous school colors.

Enough history happened here and enough famous historical figures lived here to make most large cities jealous. (The shortest of short lists includes two signers of the Declaration of Independence, John Witherspoon and Richard Stockton; three presidents, including James Madison; and Albert Einstein.) Still, Princeton University is such a dominant force that the Revolutionary history that happened here seems almost an afterthought. You'll have to pick between the nouvelle Colonial facades and upscale shops and restaurants to uncover the bastions of true Colonialism.

Start at Bainbridge House, across Nassau Street from the university. Then take a stroll around campus, especially Nassau Hall, before reemerging on Nassau Street farther south. Morven and the Princeton Battle Monument anchor the southern end of Nassau Street, but should you get peckish en route, just take a detour around Palmer Square or Witherspoon Street. Here you'll find great dueling ice cream and coffee shops (this is a college town, after all). And speaking of duels, a walk up Witherspoon brings you within range of the Princeton Cemetery, final resting place of poor Aaron Burr—poor because in Princeton, being just a vice president relegates you to near anonymity. *Contact Chamber of Commerce of the Princeton Area | Princeton Forrestal Village, 216 Rockingham Row, Princeton 08540 | 609/520–1776 | www. princetonchamber.org. Historical Society of Princeton.* See *Bainbridge House,* below.

Bainbridge House. Here's a rare Colonial-era home that isn't just a Colonial-era room with 19th- and 20th-century additions obscuring its original form. This largely preserved, generous mid-Georgian house was built in 1766. Nearly 70% of the interior woodwork is original, the trim paint has been returned to its original color, and even the restoration of the facade used 18th-century bricks. The house is the headquarters of the Historical Society of Princeton and mounts an annually changing exhibit on some aspect of Princeton history from its collections of furniture, paintings, clothing, household objects, and other objects. In addition, the house contains a library, photo archives, and the Princeton Gallery, covering the Lenape to the present. Battle of Princeton fans should look for the James Peale painting of same. The society conducts a two-hour walking tour of town on Sundays at 2, and a self-guided tour is available on its Web site. | 158 Nassau St. | 609/921–6748 | www. princetonhistory.org | Free | Mar.–Dec., Tues.–Sun. noon–4; Jan., Feb., weekends noon–4.

Morven. Unlike Bainbridge House, Morven has changed significantly with the times. The oldest part of the house was built in 1758 by Richard Stockton, a Declaration signer in July 1776 and very nearly New Jersey's first governor in August. But by year's end he had been captured by the British and signed (quite likely under duress) a sort of oath of re-allegiance to the Crown. He died in 1781. Generations of Stocktons lived at Morven and continued to alter it, encasing older portions in a newer shell to the point where which sections date from which period is debatable. More recently, from 1945 to 1981, the mansion served as the governor's residence. Today Morven is undergoing a major restoration, and what you see will depend on when you visit. The grounds have already been restored, with gardens representing three periods in Morven history: 18th century, 19th century, and Colonial Revival. Restoration of the interior—with high ceilings, plaster cornices, carved mantels, and fanlights—should be complete in 2003 or even 2004. | 55 Stockton St. | 609/683–4495 | www.historicmorven.org | Donations suggested; fees for special exhibits | Apr.–Oct., Wed.–Fri. 11–2, Sun. 1–4; Nov.–Mar., by appointment.

Nassau Hall, Princeton University. According to local lore, the dents on the south side of this brown stone university building were made by American cannonballs directed at the Redcoats holed up here after the Battle of Princeton. A further piece of the story—which actually appears to be true—has it that a cannonball came through a window and "beheaded" a portrait of King George II. Ironically, the frame that held that picture now surrounds a Charles Willson Peale portrait of Washington that hangs in the Faculty Room, along with the portraits of Princeton presidents and such prominent alumni as James Madison. The problem for curious history buffs is that the Faculty Room is kept locked. Even the historical society's tours cannot venture inside, though the university's Orange Key tours can. (The problem with this solution is that Orange Key tours are designed primarily for prospective students.) | 609/258–3603 or 609/258–1776 Orange Key Tours | www.princeton.edu | Free | Campus daily.

Princeton Battle Monument. Oh, the gory glory of it all! Hugh Mercer mortally wounded. Lady Liberty (or Victory) leading a mounted George Washington, who in turn is leading his men into battle. That's the main romanticized tableau depicted on this limestone monument, designed by the prominent Beaux Arts sculptor Frederick MacMonnies and dedicated in 1922. | Stockton and Bayard Sts. | 609/683–4495 | Free | Daily.

Princeton Battlefield State Park. Looking out across this peaceful field, it's a little hard to imagine the mayhem that went on here on January 3, 1776. Fierce fighting ended with an American victory but a Pyrrhic one. Gen. Hugh Mercer fell (and later died) not far from the Mercer oak, which itself finally fell only in the last decade. (You can see its stump and one of its offspring growing in a fenced area.) Interpretive signs and a ceramic map tell the story of the battle. Across the road, tall white columns, called the Colonnade, today serve both as a wedding photo backdrop and as a quasi-marker for the nearby unmarked grave of 21 British and 15 American soldiers killed in the battle. | 500 Mercer Rd. | 609/921–0074 | www.state.nj.us/dep/forestry/parks/prince.htm | Free | Daily sunrise–sunset.

Thomas Clarke House. British troops already occupied this Quaker farmer's home when Hugh Mercer, George Washington, and a cast of thousands arrived to make a bloody mess in Thomas and his brother William's fields and orchard. The wounded Hugh Mercer was brought to the house, where he died nine days later. Today the home's oldest section is furnished much as an 18th-century Quaker farmhouse would have been. Two rooms contain the "Arms of the Revolution" exhibit. | Wed.–Sat. 10–noon and 1–4, Sun. 1–4.

Princeton Cemetery. Aaron Burr, vice president under Thomas Jefferson and famous duelist, can rest easy, since Hamilton Avenue changes its name to Wiggins Street before it passes by the cemetery where he is buried. The graves of John Witherspoon (Declaration signer and College of New Jersey president) and other Princeton notables are here, too. Pick up a map on your way in. | 29 Greenview Ave. | 609/924–1369 | Free | Daily.

Rockingham. Like one of the general's soldiers, this circa-1710 home and 1783 Washington headquarters has done its share of moving around the outskirts of Princeton. Recently settled on its fourth site, after a nearby quarry's expansion forced its third relocation, a restored Rockingham is scheduled to open in late 2003. Washington's sojourn is a significant part of the interpretation of the huge home (upward of 20 rooms). It was here that he waited for the signing of the Treaty of Paris while the Continental Congress was meeting in Princeton. (Rooms are set up as an office, bedroom, and space to entertain—the Washingtons even hosted a party for 200 people.) It was here that he wrote his farewell orders to his troops. (Two copies are here.) Other items of interest include a Bible Washington used and a washbowl he carried through the war. But the house and the guided tour tell other tales, too. The 18th-century decorative arts collection reflects local history, and the story of how Rockingham was saved speaks volumes about the role of women in historic preservation. | 84 Laurel Ave., Kingston | 609/921–8835 | www.rockingham.net | Free | Wed.–Sat. 10–noon and 1–4, Sun. 1–4.

✦ ON THE CALENDAR: July 4 **Independence Day Celebration.** Princeton Battlefield is the site of musket and artillery demonstrations, domestic arts in the Clarke House, children's games, a talk on the battle, and the reading of the Declaration of Independence. | 609/921–0074.

HISTORIC DINING AND LODGING

Cranbury Inn. Plate rails displaying the inn's 364-plate collection thread through the various dining rooms, which date from the mid-1700s to the early 1900s. Antique guns go back to the Revolution, murals depict life in Colonial times, and a section of exposed wall reveals the timber-frame structure. All this vintage decor is a backdrop to the American cuisine: steaks, seafood, venison, and the not-so-vintage ostrich. | 21 S. Main St., Cranbury (10 mi from Princeton) | 609/655–5595.

Nassau Inn. There was a Nassau Inn as far back as 1756. This isn't it. For the sake of creature comforts, travelers will be happy about that. The original inn, up on Nassau Street, made way for Palmer Square, but this 20th-century incarnation still tries to recall its predecessor. Down a Sam Adams in the wood-paneled Yankee Doodle Tap Room, which has a Norman Rockwell painting of the Yankee Doodle soldier and a fireplace big enough to roast a large pig or small Jersey cow. Rooms, half of which are in what they term the "Colonial Wing," are a luxe combo of antique repros and modern traditional. | 10 Palmer Sq. | 609/921–7500 or 800/862–7728 | fax 609/921–9385 | www.nassauinn.com | 180 rooms, 30 suites | $99–$345 | AE, MC, V.

RINGWOOD
▼▼▼

"Ringwood is to industry what Williamsburg is to politics," asserts the Ringwood Manor Web site, a decidedly overzealous statement that yet rightfully champions the importance of iron-making to Early America. Even before the revolution, this area tucked against the Ramapo Mountains was an iron ore–mining center. When war broke out, ironmaster Robert Erskine sided with the Colonial cause, and his three local ironworks supplied the Continental Army with iron products, including chain intended for the Hudson at West Point, cheveaux-de-frise, and camp ovens. Erskine himself served as Washington's surveyor-general (i.e., mapmaker). The iron industry continued here into the 1950s, a fact that still shapes the landscape. Because ironmaking required huge amounts of land, large tracts, since turned over to the state for parkland, remained undeveloped. Today Ringwood is both a pastoral Passaic County oasis and a hub of activity whose open space and lower taxes (not to mention a few bears) attract many Bergen County residents. (New York is only 30 mi away.) You'll find good restaurants, strip malls, big houses, lots of parkland, and a few sights that recall the halcyon days when iron was golden. *Contact Ringwood State Park | 1304 Sloatsburg Rd., Ringwood 07456 | 973/962–7031 | www.state.nj.us/dep/forestry/parks/ringwood.htm.*

Long Pond Ironworks Historic District. Four miles from Ringwood Manor lie the remains of one of the area's three ironmaking plantations. This was a true company town. Because of ironmaking's labor intensiveness, the workers lived near the ironmaking facilities. Today 12 buildings still stand, though only one, the visitor center/museum is open to the public. Start here to learn about the ironworks and the ironmaking process as well as the lives of the iron-masters and iron workers from Long Pond's beginnings in Colonial times through the Civil War and Industrial Revolution. Pick up a brochure for a self-guided tour (about a mile) that takes you through the workers' village to the ruins of the industrial site, including a revolutionary-era furnace. The quiet wooded setting belies the industrial empire that once flourished here. | 1334 Greenwood Lake Tpk., West Milford | 973/657–1688 | www.longpondironworks.org | Donations suggested | Grounds daily sunrise–sunset; visitor center Mar.–Nov., weekends 1–4.

Ringwood Manor. Hiking trails, streams, and a botanical garden would be reason enough to come to 5,237-acre Ringwood State Park, but history hounds and metal mavens will find an added treasure: Ringwood Manor. This former ironmasters' home was begun in 1810 as a Federal-style house and enlarged to a 51-room Victorian mansion by mid-19th-century ironmaster Abram S. Hewitt (of Cooper-Hewitt Museum fame). A tour of the house covers the Federal architecture and furnishings along with the Victorian, and an exhibit of Washingtonia collected by the Hewitts includes prints, maps, and paintings. When you're done at the house, don't miss the lovely walk out to the cemetery, where Revolutionary War soldiers are buried. | 1304 Sloatsburg Rd. | 973/962–2240 | www.ringwoodmanor.com | Donations suggested | Grounds daily sunrise–sunset; house Wed.–Sun. 10–4.

✦ ON THE CALENDAR: July **July 4 at Ringwood Manor.** Robert Erskine's militia drills. A rider on horseback delivers the Declaration of Independence, which is read amid boos and huzzahs from the crowd. A cannon is fired, a flag raised, and a bell rung—all to celebrate American independence. | 973/962–2240.

Sept. **Revolutionary War Living History Weekend.** Civilians and soldiers bring Long Pond's village back to life the second weekend of the month. British forces conduct a raid at about 2 (but are repelled by the valiant townspeople, naturally). An evening candle lantern tour leads through the village, where you encounter dramatic vignettes. Perhaps you'll watch as British forces arrest a man while his family screams, or you might meet the ghost of an iron worker. Storytellers and balladeers provide additional entertainment. | 973/657–1688.

RIVER EDGE
▼▼▼

If you were abandoning Fort Lee today with a destination of New Brunswick, Princeton, and Trenton, you'd take I–80 to the Turnpike and settle in for a drive through the Meadowlands and past Newark Airport. In 1776 Washington didn't have that option, yet he still had to get his troops across the Hackensack River. The crossing he chose was northwest of Fort Lee, at a place once known as Aschatking ("where the river narrows"), which had a bridge: New Bridge. Because of the strategic crossing, both British and American forces came through this Bergen Dutch mill community several times during the war. Today a park lies here, partly in the bedroom community of River Edge, whose fine restaurants and active cultural scene are still only a handful of miles from the Hudson and Big Apple. *Contact Bergen County Historical Society | Box 55, River Edge 07661 | 201/343–9492 | www.carroll.com/bchs.*

Historic New Bridge Landing Park. Straddling the Hackensack River, 22 acres, and three municipalities, this park contains not only the usual parkland ripe for recreation but also five historical structures, including three classic but different gambrel-roofed, Bergen Dutch sandstone (a.k.a. Dutch Colonial) residences, operated by different organizations. At present, only the Steuben House is open with regularity. Future plans for the park include increased acreage and a new visitor center and museum. | Main St. | 201/816–0585 | www. carroll.com/bchs | Free | Daily.

Steuben House. This 1752 Bergen Dutch sandstone home could have been called the Zabriskie House, after its once and future owners. However, if you picked the wrong side in the revolution—and Jan Zabriskie did—you were generally out of luck and out of property. To the victor go not only the spoils but the naming rights, especially when the victor is the famous General Baron von Steuben. But in the case of this spoil, fate took an interesting turn. The abridged version of the house's story begins with the Zabriskies, Loyalists of Dutch heritage, who abandoned their farm during the war. The house was used by both the Americans and British, and Washington came through not only in November 1776 but again in September 1780. At war's end, the home was confiscated and given to von Steuben in thanks for war services rendered, but he lived here only from 1783 to 1788. When he grew short on funds, he sold it, ironically, to the Zabriskies' son. The 12-room (née five-room) house is now owned by the state. You can take a guided tour of its dwelling room and parlor or wander them on your own. Though the home showcases collections representing the 1680s to the 1860s, the focus is squarely on the Colonial Bergen lifestyle. The parlor's ornate kass (linen closet) and a spoonboard, on which couples hung their children's christening spoons, are typical Bergen Dutch treats. | 1209 Main St. | 201/487–1739 | http://apollo.carroll. com/bchs/Pages/steubenhsehistory.html | Free | Wed.–Sat. 10–noon and 1–5, Sun. 2–5.

◆ ON THE CALENDAR: Feb. **Washington's Birthday.** A small tea party with music and dancing honors General George, who made the Steuben House his headquarters. The usually shuttered Campbell-Christie and Demarest houses are also open. | 201/487–1739.

May **Pinkster.** A Dutch version of May Day comes complete with a May pole, dancing, and the three houses open for visitors. | 201/487–1739.

STANHOPE
▼▼

The completion of the Morris Canal in 1831 transformed Stanhope into a major outlet for goods shipped into upper Sussex County. Remains of the canal can be seen today, and the canal itself is on the National Register of Historic Places, yet the big lure here for the heritage traveler is the nearby Waterloo Village. *Contact Sussex County Historical Society | 82 Main St., Newton 07860 | 973/383–6010 | www.sussexcountyhistory.org.*

Waterloo Village. The heart of a visit to this living-history village is just that—a village. Buildings speak to life in a hamlet that essentially "began" in the 1760s, when later-to-be-Loyalists William Allen and Joseph Turner started the Andover Iron Works here (it was confiscated for the American cause in 1778) and evolved with the arrival of the Morris Canal in 1831. Some structures are re-creations, some were relocated, some aren't open at all, but most are staffed by guides who together interpret over 300 years of village history. Early structures include the Homestead, a converted horse barn; the blacksmith shop; 1760 Stagecoach Inn, which originally housed ironworkers; and the Rutan farmsite, reflecting a premechanized subsistence farm in the early 19th century. This is the place for a usual caveat about the Waterloo clock ticking well past the early days of nationhood into the latter 19th century. But what's refreshing about Waterloo is that the clock doesn't start with the arrival of Europeans. Waterloo acknowledges the people who were here first through a re-created Lenape (Minisink) village circa 1625. It's a short walk away from the main village on an island in Waterloo Lake. Here you'll find reproduced longhouses, dugout canoes, and demonstrations of crafts and gardening. | 525 Waterloo Rd. | 973/347–0900 | www.waterloovillage.org | $9 | Late May–early Sept., Wed. noon–4, Thurs.–Fri. 11–4, weekends 11–5.

HISTORIC DINING AND LODGING

Inn at Millrace Pond. In the old Moravian village of Hope, a millrace flows from a small millpond through a chasm of slate to a 1769 stone gristmill, which once supplied flour to the troops at Jockey Hollow and is now a country inn. From the foyer, you can look down a story and a half at the skeleton of the old wheel. This 18th-century hostelry includes the gristmill, which contains a fine restaurant plus a stunning Colonial tavern (lower-price menu) complete with huge roaring fireplace and flour chute, and several guest rooms with exposed beams. Additional rooms are in the Millrace House and Stone Cottage. Complimentary breakfast. | 313 Johnsonburg Rd., (Rte. 519 N), Hope | 800/746–6467 | www.innatmillracepond.com. | 6 rooms, 2 cottages | $120–$170 | AE, D, MC, V.

SWAINTON

▼▼

Head here for a true Colonial forgetaway—Leaming's Run Gardens. *Contact Cape May County Department of Tourism | 4 Moore Rd., Cape May Court House 08210 | 800/227–2297 | www. thejerseycape.net.*

Leaming's Run Gardens and Colonial Farm. Do you know what a Black Cochin is? Or a Silver-Spangled Hamburg? How about a White-Crested Polish? (Hint: it looks like a cross between Tina Turner and Rod Stewart.) Give up? They're all historic chickens. And just what makes a chicken historic? Its breed was brought to the New World by explorers or settlers and managed to avoid being cross-bred into the more common American breeds of today. You'll find these fabulous fowl along with goats, sheep, and the other usual barnyard suspects in the replica Colonial farm that's part of this larger botanic garden. The Colonial Farm buildings—a cabin, barn, outhouse, smokehouse, and two buildings that house the animals—are all recent reproductions, but they convincingly re-create a circa-1700 homestead. There's a vegetable and herb garden that grows what early settlers grew (no tomatoes here), and tobacco, corn, and peanuts mirror typical turn-of-the-18th-century crops. Bona fide vintage buildings at the gardens include an early 1700s barn, the Cooperage, which houses the gift shop, and a 1706 whaler's home that's not open to the public. Leave time, too, to stroll through the relaxed, casual flower gardens, which make up the largest annual garden in the United States. | 1845 Rte. 9 N | 609/465–5871 | www.njsouth.com/leamingsrun.htm | $7 | Mid-May–mid-Oct., daily 9:30–5.

TRENTON

▼▼

There are 19 other Trentons around the country, all named for this capital city and what went on here in the winter of 1776–77. But the town itself began nearly a century earlier, in 1679, when it was called Ye Ffalles of Ye De La Warr because of its location at a tiny waterfall marking the head of navigation of the Delaware River. (Early Trent's town history is found at Trent House.) Then came those two important Revolutionary War battles (or, more accurately, about a battle-and-a-half). To learn more about them, you can visit the Old Barracks Museum and Trenton Battle Monument on your own or take either of two two-hour walking tours. One, given the first Saturday of each month, visits the sights involved in those battles. The other, on Sunday afternoons April–October, covers Trenton history 1679–present, with an emphasis on those crucial 10 days. Contact the Convention and Visitors Bureau for both or for *any* local lore (including the fact that the city is considered the world's largest per capita consumer of pencil points).

But there's more to Trenton than December 26, 1776, and January 2, 1777. The city's heyday would come later, during a revolution when industry was king. Names like Roebling and Lenox made the city a manufacturing center, though now the biggest industry is government: Trenton is both the state capital and county seat. (You might be tempted to tour the New Jersey State House, the second-oldest capital building still in use, but be warned that you'd probably have to be buddies with Jim McGreevey to see any of the original 1792 structure.) By day, the city hums with state workers; by night, the city struggles to forge a renaissance. Still, where else can you get a terrific tomato pie? (For that matter, where else can you get a tomato pie, period?) *Contact Trenton Convention and Visitors Bureau. | Lafayette and Barrack sts., Trenton 08608 | 609/777–1771 recording; 609/777–1770 voice | fax 609/292–3771 | www.trentonnj.com.*

Old Barracks Museum. Even before 1776, Colonials were tired of the British—more specifically, tired of quartering British troops. So a series of barracks was built to house soldiers during the French and Indian Wars, of which the Old Barracks (built in 1758 but since modified and reconstructed) is the only one remaining. The barracks are perhaps best known for housing Hessians—in actuality, mainly their wives and children—at the time of the Battle of Trenton. By 1777, with Trenton back in Patriot hands, it was used as a military hospital where new recruits were inoculated against smallpox. Notice we didn't say "vaccinated." They got the real thing: a minor case of the disease—hopefully. Different periods in barracks history are explored on tours led by guides in period clothing: the building's construction, its time as an induction center for new soldiers, its role in the Battle of Trenton, and its life as a military hospital. Typically furnished quarters let you compare the life of a soldier (bunk beds with 15 to a room) to that of an officer (that canopy bed sure looks comfy). Judge for yourself if you'd have wanted to be treated in the surgeon's office. For kids (9–12) in need of mustering and drilling, there's a popular summer day camp. | Barrack St. | 609/396–1776 | www.barracks.org | $6 | Daily 10–5; last tour at 4.

Trenton Battle Monument. Washington stretches out his hand atop this 148-ft-tall, early Beaux Arts–style column, as if to say, "The Hessians are over there; point the cannons that way." Erected in 1893 on the site where Colonial artillery first fired on the Hessians, it contains an elevator to an observation platform. To get the most from a visit here, go to the Old Barracks first, and learn the details of the Trenton battles. Then from high above this transitional neighborhood, you can see the same roads (okay, so they're paved now) where all the action took place. A brochure is available, and interpretive signage is planned. Two bronze plaques are copies of the Thomas Eakins originals, which now reside at the state museum. | Broad and Pennington Rds. | 609/737–0623 (Washington Crossing State Park) | Free | Fri.–Sat. 10–12 and 1–4, Sun. 1–4.

William Trent House. Trenton wasn't settled by William Trent; it was just named by and for the rich merchant and New Jersey chief justice. In 1719 he built this grand (by early 18th-century standards) brick Georgian as a summer estate and began laying out what were to become the downtown streets. Within two years, however, he moved here full-time and lived in luxury (he even had a "bathing tubb") for only three more years. Currently undergoing restoration, the home is being returned more closely to its Colonial roots and will be decorated with period antiques and reproductions in keeping with what was here at the time of Trent's death. And speaking of his death (on Christmas Day 1724), it was originally thought that he died of a heart attack or stroke. But 14 years later, a group of slaves asserted that they'd heard that Trent's own slaves had poisoned him. Nothing like a little colonial dirt. | 15 Market St. | 609/989–3027 | $2.50 | Daily 12:30–4.

✦ ON THE CALENDAR: Feb. **Washington's Birthday.** The highlight of this day of special programs at the Old Barracks is when Washington cuts his birthday cake with his saber. | 609/396–1776.

Dec. **Ten Crucial Days.** The weekend after Christmas, a scaled-down and telescoped reenactment of the Ten Crucial Days is held. On Saturday, a daybreak crossing is followed by the

9-mi march to Trenton and the two Trenton battles. On Sunday, the shelling of Nassau Hall, in Princeton, is commemorated. | 609/777–1770.

UNION
▼▼

Of all the cities named Union, this town claims the honor of being the first. Union was known as Connecticut Farms until it separated from Elizabeth in 1808. At that time the area's nutrient-rich soil produced bountiful crops of all kinds. Today, the area sustains pharmaceutical companies and a hospital. A large retirement community resides here as well, and there's a small but active nightlife scene downtown with a few sports bars and theaters. Union is also home to Kean University (a familiar name in this town). *Contact Union Township Chamber of Commerce | 355 Chestnut St., Union 07083 | 908/688–2777 | www.unionchamber.com.*

Liberty Hall. The names Livingston and Kean could fill a who's who of New Jersey politics. The family produced governors and senators, they married into the families of Lewis Morris (New Jersey's first royal governor) and John Jay, and for over 200 years they lived in this 14-room Georgian manor house that grew up to become a 50-room Italianate mansion. It was William Livingston, member of the Constitutional Convention and New Jersey's first elected governor, who first built Liberty Hall in 1772 as a country estate. Today it's a house museum on 23 acres containing, among other things, a horse chestnut tree as old as the home. What's so unusual about Liberty Hall is that since it stayed in the same family for all those years, it's full of their stuff—items that chronicle the everyday right alongside the historically significant. You can trace the evolution of ironing by looking at irons and boards or imagine the Hessians who once raided the house in a bounty hunt for Livingston by looking at the saber cuts they left in the banister. After a brief video in the Blue House, you take the hourlong standard guided tour, covering 14 rooms. Alternatively, you can opt for the Wednesday tea and tour (reservations required), consisting of a little touring, some scones and tea with clotted cream on the porch, and a little more touring—much as Mrs. Kean would have entertained 60 or 70 years ago. | 1003 Morris Ave. | 908/527–0400 | www.libertyhallnj.org | $10 | Apr.–Dec., Wed.–Sat. 10–4, Sun. noon–4.

✦ ON THE CALENDAR: May **The Life and Times of William Livingston.** Liberty Hall's earliest days are recalled during this weekend of special activities. Reenactors might set up a Revolutionary War camp, Washington might come for a visit, and a storyteller might weave tales of the Three Graces (Livingston's three daughters) or of the Liberty Hall ghost (check out her likeness in one of the closets). This event is not held every year. | 908/527–0400.

WASHINGTON CROSSING
▼▼

Frankly, aside from the 19th-century D&R canal, which draws walkers, joggers, and cyclists to its towpath, the main reason to visit the hamlet of Titusville is the wonderful state park, named for and largely devoted to a certain dark and stormy night. Just about everyone refers to the area as Washington Crossing, and then they pause and specify New Jersey or Pennsylvania.

Washington Crossing State Park. Rising on a hill above the Delaware, this 991-acre park provides a deceptively bucolic setting for the interpretation of the Continental Army's middle-of-the-night crossing (during a sleet storm, no less) and its aftermath. We suggest you come in nicer weather and bring a picnic. Walk the trails, enjoying the woods or retracing the soldiers' steps up from the river and along Continental Lane. Okay, so you can't exactly retrace their steps. You'll have to cross on the footbridge over Route 29, which separates the lower river-front strip from the forest and fields of the main park. The park's key historical sights are the visitor center and Johnson Ferry House, but there is also an interpretive nature center and charming open-air theater that stages mostly musicals on summer evenings—*1776*, anyone? Also see the listing for Washington Crossing Historic Park in New Hope in the Pennsylvania chapter. | 355 Washington Crossing-Pennington Rd., Titusville | 609/737–0623 | www.state.nj.us/dep/forestry/parks/washcros.htm | Memorial Day–Labor Day, weekends and holidays, $3 per car; otherwise free | Memorial Day–Labor Day, daily 8–8; early Sept.–late May, daily 8–various times.

Johnson Ferry House. Believed to be where Washington and his officers discussed military strategy during the crossing, the Johnson Ferry House interprets the 18th-century life of the ferry keeper and his family and the impact of the crossing on them. Rooms are furnished with local period pieces. Demonstrations of domestic life are given on weekends. | 609/737–2515 | Wed.–Sat. 10–noon and 1–4, Sun. 1–4.

Visitor Center. If you need to brush up on your Ten Crucial Days trivia, this is a good spot. In the north gallery a timeline runs from the months leading up to the crossing through the months that followed, and artifacts from the 500+-item Swan Historical Foundation Collection help illustrate daily life and important events. As for the former, you'll see powder horns, quill pens, and money. Highlighting the latter is the order, signed by GW on December 1, 1776, directing that all the boats for 70 mi along the Delaware be gathered and brought to Trenton for the retreat into Pennsylvania. American, British, French, and Hessian weaponry on display includes a rare Ferguson rifle; the British breach-loading firearm was accurate but expensive, so only about 200 were made during the war and only six can be seen today in the United States. | 609/737–9304 | Wed.–Sun. 9–4:30.

✦ ON THE CALENDAR: Dec. **George Washington's Crossing of the Delaware.** A reenactment of this famed 1776 event is held on Christmas Day at 1 (PM, that is—authenticity goes only so far) as well as at daybreak the Saturday after Christmas. The latter is followed by a march to Trenton and the battles there. | 609/737–0623.

WAYNE

▼▼

The first European got a glimpse of Wayne, or Pompton Valley, around 1694. Before that the land had been inhabited by the Lenni Lenape tribe. Their legacy can be read in the names of the natural sites and the streets of the area. In 1695 Wayne was purchased from the East Jersey Company by the English in New York, and it remained a simple farming community throughout the 18th and 19th centuries. Once the railroad was built in the early 20th century, vacationers from New York City began to explore this natural haven. Now many of Wayne's 50,000 citizens commute to Manhattan. Though the town's main period attraction is the Dey Mansion (mansion staffers use the Dutch pronunciation "Die" rather than "Day," but you won't be tied to a windmill if you use the latter), there are a couple of other local 17th- and 18th-century homes open by appointment. *Contact Township of Wayne Department of Parks and Recreation | 475 Valley Rd., Wayne 07470 | 973/694–1800 Ext. 3258*

Dey Mansion. There are scads of New Jersey sights with 1776 in their phone numbers. This one, however, is a misnomer. Washington and several of his prominent officers (Lord Stirling, Lafayette, Anthony Wayne, Benedict Arnold) actually passed through in July, October, and November of *1780*. Still, this Georgian mansion and Washington headquarters certainly has the spirit of '76, and Washington et al. take center stage on the 30- to 45-minute guided tour. The other star is the house itself. Built between 1740 and 1750 by Dutch-born planter

Dirck Dey, the mansion had the comfort level that Washington preferred. Notice the "dressier" front facade (an inspiration for contemporary tract mansion design?), made mostly of brick with brownstone around the windows, and the "more casual" sides and rear, where the local stone plays a more prominent role. Inside the eight-room home are fine Chippendale- and Queen Anne–style furnishings, some on loan from the Metropolitan Museum of Art. An over-300-year-old mahogany kass (of Dutch origin, used for storing linens) is in the spinning room along with an assortment of salesman's furniture samples, smaller versions of fine furniture a craftsman would take orders for and deliver in four or five years. The three canopy beds are smaller than modern beds not because their inhabitants were shorter but because they slept in a semi-reclining position to aid their breathing. | 199 Totowa Rd. | 973/696–1776 | $1 | Wed.–Fri. 1–4, weekends 10–noon and 1–4.

✦ ON THE CALENDAR: Feb. **Washington's Birthday.** Open house at the Dey Mansion includes crafts demonstrations and a visit from reenactors to celebrate the general's big day. | 973/696–1776.

Oct. **Revolutionary War Encampment.** The local militia re-creates area skirmishes and shows off its firearms, while demonstrations of cooking and trades (gunsmithing, blacksmithing) add to the Dey Mansion's period feel. | 973/696–1776.

By *Thomas A. Chambers*

New York

Building an Empire

*S*ay "New York" and most people imagine skyscrapers, Times Square, the Statue of Liberty, or the Yankees. If you think that all these "icons" came long after New York City's—much less New York State's—Colonial and Revolutionary history, you're only partially correct. In point of fact, the Yankees have a connection to Dutch Nieuw Netherland and English New York, but theirs is not exactly a polite one. Pieter Stuyvesant, the mid-17th-century Dutch governor known for his irritability and wooden leg, used "Yankees"—a Dutch term that roughly translates as "land pirates"—to derisively refer to the English Puritan settlers who were beginning to occupy Dutch territory. This kind of contest for control lies at the center of Colonial and Revolutionary New York's history. Four powers—the Iroquois Indians, Dutch, French, and English—battled to rule New York and establish their own "Empire State." That name itself comes not from New York City's once-again tallest structure, the Empire State Building, but from George Washington's 1784 reference to New York State's vast geographic expanse and economic power.

If New York State's history is one of empire *building*, it is not of a specific place but of an idea. Every major group in New York State's history tried to create its own empire, each succeeding and failing in turn. The ruins of those attempts provide some of the most fascinating landmarks and relics of the days when America was young. In New York City, you can trace the life of the earliest Dutch settlers, see the spot where George Washington was sworn in as first U.S. president, and stroll around the restored site of America's greatest 19th-century seaport. Wending your way up the Hudson Valley, you'll encounter the prosperous homesteads of early Dutch farmers. Venture upstate to discover many splendors, including the Leatherstocking Country landscapes immortalized by James Fenimore Cooper and innumerable Federal-era mansions. And in the Upper Hudson Valley and Champlain Valley, American independence was won along the shores of waterways and forested knolls, which once echoed with the beat of drums, the tweet of fifes, the shrill of bagpipes, the slap of oar against water, and thud of bullet against flesh. Major battles, such as those waged at Fort Ticonderoga and

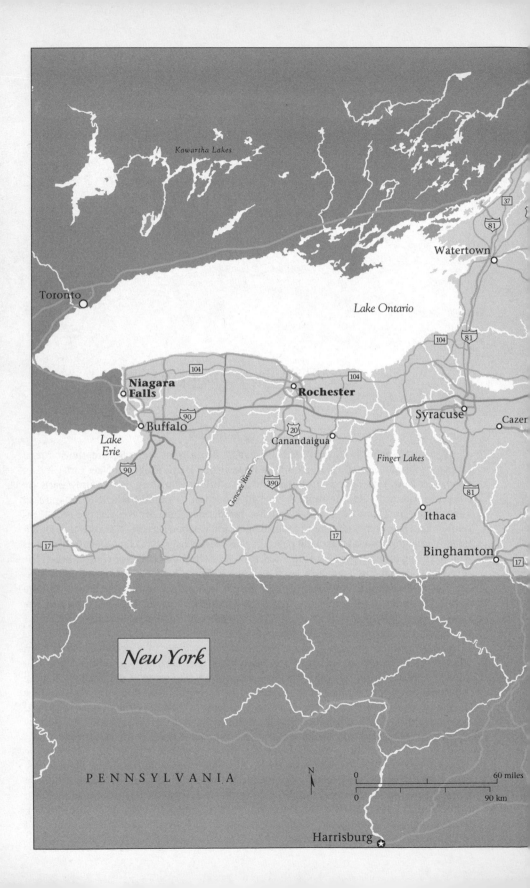

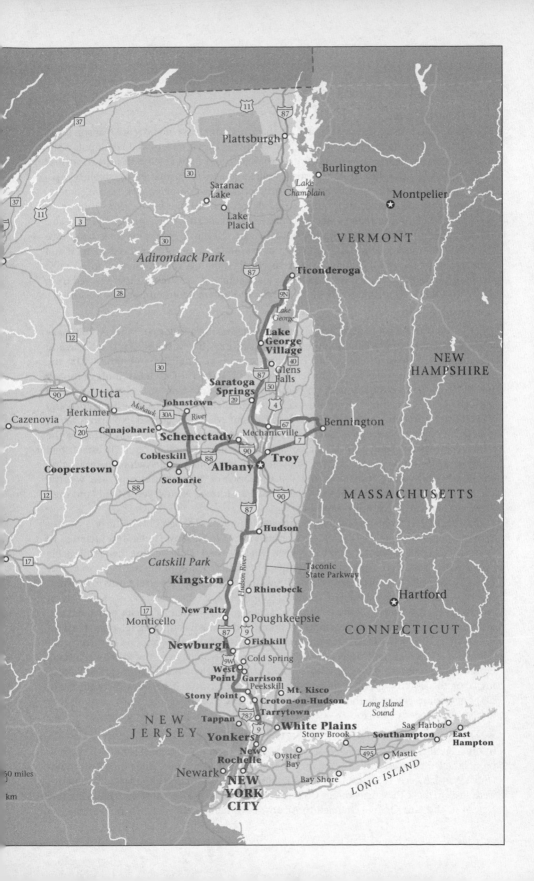

Saratoga, during the Seven Years' War and the American Revolution were fought here, making this region one of the great military history sections of the country. Taking the time to explore these sites—and the countrysides that lie in between—is a great way to understand New York's and America's history.

✦ WHOSE EMPIRE?

The story of New York's "olden days" actually begins many years before Henry Hudson's *Half Moon* ventured up his namesake "great streame." Before Dutch traders could depopulate the forests of beaver, before French and British soldiers could fight epic battles for control of North America, before the victorious British could founder in their attempts to establish imperial control and lose the most important battle of the Revolutionary War, before some of the nation's greatest political rhetoric could debate the passage of the Constitution, or before American homesteaders and canal builders could construct a commercial juggernaut, Native Americans had already knit together a vast, powerful empire of their own. Five nations—the Mohawk, Oneida, Onondaga, Cayuga, and Seneca—united into the largest and most militarily fearsome nation in eastern North America, the Iroquois Confederacy. Benjamin Franklin later used the Iroquois as an example of the strength that derived from unity, and Dutch, French, and British diplomats and generals courted Iroquois alliances.

✦ THE DUTCH ON THE HUDSON

Our story properly begins with Henry Hudson. After taking a "shortcut" that would make any modern American father captaining his minivan across the vast interstate high seas and treacherous backroad shoals proud, Hudson—in fact, an Englishman chartered by the Dutch—arrived in Lower New York Bay on September 2, 1609. The Dutch East India Company had directed Hudson to find a short route to Asia via Scandinavia, a sort of North*east* Passage. But when contrary winds slowed his progress, Hudson took a massive U-turn and headed west. Unwilling to admit he was lost, Hudson eventually arrived in North America and sailed up the "North" river to just above present-day Albany. Hudson's return to the Dutch commercial capital, Amsterdam, created a sensation. Merchants quickly established temporary fur-trading posts along the Hudson and Connecticut Rivers before incorporating the Dutch West India Company in 1621. At the center of the new company's seal was the image of a beaver, the buck-toothed rodent that transformed Nieuw Netherland (and then New York) into an economic powerhouse.

But Nieuw Netherland's population increased more slowly than did the furry source of its wealth because Dutch settlers never swarmed the Colony. Most Hollanders preferred to stay put (having their portraits painted by great Dutch Masters while wearing their fashionable beaver hats). In the New World, Dutch settlement clustered around the trading post at Fort Orange (modern-day Albany), the docks of Nieuw Amsterdam, and a few river towns in between. Incentives that would make a 21st-century "country home" shopper drool—such as 18 mi of land along the Hudson River or 9 mi on facing shores—failed to attract many settlers. With the Netherlands' home economy booming and residents enjoying religious freedom at this time, the Dutch lacked reasons to leave Europe. But war, economic hardship, and religious persecution drew others: French Huguenots, Germans from the Rhine Palatinate, Protestant Walloons from the Catholic-controlled southern Netherlands, and Scots. Still needing labor, the Dutch imported enslaved Africans, who constituted 10% to 15% of the Colonial population. Nieuw Netherland was truly a diverse place that might not seem all that foreign to a modern New Yorker—Colonial residents spoke at least 18 languages.

✦ FROM NIEUW NETHERLAND TO NEW YORK

In time, English merchants peered across the English Channel and grew jealous of the tidy profits the Dutch West India Company was reaping and, as a result, three different Anglo-Dutch Wars between 1652 and 1674 led to English control of Nieuw Netherland. The English were quick to make their mark on the Colony's two leading towns—Nieuw Amsterdam became New York and Fort Orange changed to Albany, both named after English noblemen. The

New York Timeline

1609 Englishman Henry Hudson sails up the river that will bear his name and claims the area for the Dutch East India Company.

1626 Governor Pieter Minuit buys Manhattan Island from Native Americans for 60 guilders (about $24).

1664 English forces conquer New Netherland; the Colony named New York after the Duke of York, King Charles II's brother, who holds a charter to colonize land between the Connecticut and Delaware Rivers plus nearby islands.

1758 15,000 British troops attack 3,500 French defenders at Carillon (Ticonderoga) and suffer nearly 3,000 casualties.

1765 Representatives from nine Colonies send delegates to the Stamp Act Congress in New York City, which challenges Parliament's right to tax the Colonies and defends Colonial assemblies.

1776 A British army of 32,000 men lands on Staten Island. Americans are soon defeated on Long Island, in Manhattan, and at White Plains. British occupation of New York City begins as the American army flees to New Jersey, and a remnant fortifies the Hudson River Highlands.

1776 Lacking instructions from home, the New York delegation is the only one not to approve (by abstention) the July 2 Declaration of Independence.

1777 After recapturing Ticonderoga and moving toward Albany, "Gentleman Johnny" Burgoyne surrenders his British and Hessian army to "Granny" Gates's American troops after two battles near Saratoga.

1787-88 New York City papers are full of the debate about ratifying the Constitution. Supporters Alexander Hamilton, John Jay, and James Madison write essays now known as *The Federalist Papers*.

1788 New York becomes the nation's 11th state by narrowly ratified the Constitution after bitter debate. Vote is 30–27 in special convention, split largely along rural (con) and urban (pro) lines.

1789 President-elect George Washington crosses the Hudson to Manhattan in a festooned barge and is greeted by thousands of cheering supporters. New York remains the nation's capital until 1790.

1804-05 New Yorker George Clinton is elected Vice President; outgoing Vice President Aaron Burr is defeated for Governor of New York. Burr kills key opponent and long-time nemesis Alexander Hamilton in a duel (held in New Jersey to skirt New York's anti-dueling laws).

1825 Erie Canal completed.

North River gained the name of its discoverer, the Englishman Hudson. New Jersey and Delaware were created as separate Colonies. Then, as the Glorious Revolution of 1689 ended in England, the Mother Country began cracking down in New York. English law, culture, and language became paramount—after all, New York was now a royal Colony, and no longer a private company's domain.

New York City became a major cosmopolitan center and home to such eccentrics as famed pirate William Kidd and Edward Hyde, Lord Cornbury, the governor fond of parading the city's streets in drag. Land incentives and a booming economy helped New York's population to grow to 97,000 by 1756. Ironically, the Dutch, who had founded New York on commercial principles, remained the most agrarian residents. They turned into a subject for parody by 19th-century author Washington Irving, who characterized New York's Dutch residents as short, balding, fat, superstitious, nearly illiterate farmers with poor grooming habits, archaic speech, and omnipresent pipes. Rip Van Winkle, the prototypical lazy, fun-loving Dutchman, became a curiosity in his hometown. Whatever the truth of Irving's stereotype, New York expanded in the 18th century, as did the French in Canada. Caught in the middle were the Iroquois as all three sides sought to control the remnant of western fur trade. The quarter-century between 1739 and 1765 brought war to North America for all but six years, turning Manhattan and Albany into imperial centers pulsing with scarlet-clad British troops on their way to battle. In epic battles at Lake George and Ticonderoga, many "Yorkers" died. By the end of 1759 New York considered itself secure from French attack and the powerful Iroquois were now an ally.

✦ TURNING POINTS

Yet just as British North America seemed on the verge of extended peace and prosperity, the empire fell apart. New taxes designed to pay for England "Great War"—the French and Indian Wars—crippled port cities and merchants. As every schoolchild knows, boycotts and petitions failed to solve the problem, and the British opened fire in Boston. Few remember that the first offensive action of the Revolution took place in New York, at the old Ticonderoga fortress, on May 10, 1775. A year later news of the Declaration of Independence prompted a New York City mob to topple the statue of King George III they had recently erected on Bowling Green. The next eight years brought hardship and suffering to New York, where one-third of the Revolutionary War's battles took place. A massive British army descended on New York City in 1776. Though George Washington lost New York City, the British failed to land a knock-out blow and destroy the American army.

The war's most important battle took place upstate along the banks of the Hudson River near Saratoga. In 1777 American forces halted a British invasion from Canada. Never before had a British army surrendered in the field, and the failed campaign to divide the Colonies in half ended British attempts to conquer New York. Soon France recognized the new nation and sent money, guns, ships, and troops to aid the rebellion, greatly aiding the cause of American independence. But fighting became bitter as it pitted neighbor against neighbor. Thousands of New Yorkers remained loyal to Great Britain, and and many fought for King George III. In the Lower Hudson valley tenants turned in landlord Frederick Philipse for treason; Irregular militias operated as quasi-bandits in the no-man's-land between American and British forces on the Hudson.; and many Iroquois towns were destroyed because of their loyalty to Great Britain (this, in turn, freed western lands for future white settlement). The Revolutionary War in New York ended in a whimper. Washington's desperately bored, cold, ill-fed, and rarely paid troops and officers nearly launched a coup d'etat in 1783 before Washington quashed it with an appeal to their patriotism. After the peace treaty, British forces evacuated New York City, and Washington, whose gray hair and deteriorating eyesight showed the war's personal cost, rode his horse home to Virginia.

Peace brought calm to New York, but not prosperity. A weak national government, confiscated farms and homes, worthless paper currency, and a debt crisis meant that few New Yorkers felt confident. Adopted New Yorker Alexander Hamilton proposed a new, stronger government. New York City's newspapers carried the classic political dialogue of the Federalist Papers as the debate over whether or not to ratify the Constitution raged. New York State barely ratified the Constitution and became the 11th state in July, 1788, and Manhattan the nation's first capital. The economic salvation for the state lay not in New York City but in Governor George Clinton's proposal to build a canal linking Albany with the state's western regions. Mocked as "Clinton's Ditch," the Erie Canal opened up western New York to settlement and, more importantly, provided a link to the expanding Midwest. Albany, New York City, and countless settlements along the canal boomed. The sudden availability of raw oysters—a treat usually limited to the seashore—in Buffalo announced a new age of prosperity. New York's empire now extended not just to its borders, but across much of the northern United States. By 1825 New York had become the United States' most populous, economically powerful, and politically influential state.

A REGIONAL GAZETEER

▼▼▼

✦ THE CAPITAL REGION: ALBANY TO SARATOGA

The Hudson and Mohawk rivers meet just north of this region's major city, Albany, forming a natural hub for commerce and empire-building: the Dutch established their first settlement on the west shore of the Hudson River to trade for furs with the Mohawk; during the 18th century Great Britain's imperial armies viewed Albany as the starting point for invading New France, and later the base for defeating the American rebellion. Geographically, the region sits astride the Hudson River corridor, which runs almost due north–south between New York City and Glens Falls, where Lakes George and Champlain complete a virtually uninterrupted waterway—Colonial America's interstate highway system—to Montréal. The Mohawk River leads west across the only significant break in the Appalachian Mountains between Maine and Georgia. The river system that trappers and armies once traversed gave way to the Erie Canal in the early 19th century, and ensured that the Capital Region would remain an economic force in New York's history. The Dutch set up a trading post at **Albany** in 1614, then called Fort Orange, and by the mid-17th century it was the leading fur-trading settlement in the Colonies, which were by now under British control. The city's Crailo State Historic Site interprets much of this history in a restored 18th-century mansion, as do several excellent house museums: Bronck Museum, Historic Cherry Hill, Schuyler Mansion State Historic Site, Ten Broeck Mansion. **Schenectady**'s historic core, the Stockade District, includes many older homes and churches.

French attacks and British armies heading north to Canada reminded 18th-century residents that they were on the frontier between two empires. The Battle of Saratoga in 1777 provided the turning point during the Revolution, preventing the British from controlling the key Hudson River valley and dividing the Colonies, and helping to convince France to support the American rebellion against its frequent foe, Britain. Undeveloped fields and stunning battlefield vistas at the Saratoga National Historic Park outside **Saratoga Springs** and the Bennington Battlefield near **Troy** help recapture the fighting. Nearby Saratoga Springs became one of the nation's premier resorts during the 19th century, and remains a cultural and recreational draw with horse racing and summer music festivals. *Towns listed: Albany, Saratoga Springs, Schenectady, Troy.*

✦ LIQUID HISTORY: THE HUDSON RIVER VALLEY

Navigator Henry Hudson hoped he'd found a route through North America to Asia when he sailed up what would become his namesake waterway in 1609. By the time his ship "Half Moon" ran aground just north of Albany, Hudson noticed what the Algonquians had long known: the Hudson River is really an estuary, with tides felt as far north as the dam in Troy (the incoming tide helped to free his boat—you can see a re-creation of Hudson's ship at the Hudson River Maritime Museum in Kingston). Much early settlement actually bypassed this region and sparse settlement preserved the river's beauty and provided inspiration for many of America's early landscape painters, collectively known as the Hudson River School. Wealthy merchants also admired the scenery and built mansions overlooking the Hudson, many of which are open to the public, including such Colonial-to-Federal period delights as Boscobel Restoration outside **Garrison,** Clermont State Historic Site near **Hudson,** and Montgomery Place not far from **Rhinebeck.** Colonial and Revolutionary-era life comes alive if you venture to explore the Huguenot Street Old Stone Houses in **New Paltz,** Mount Gulian Historic Site near **Fishkill,** and the remarkable cluster of buildings around the national historic district in **Kingston.** The Revolutionary War spared this region much warfare, but three significant sites related to the war's end are scattered around **Newburgh,** where Washington's Headquarters guarded against a British advance. "Mad Anthony" Wayne's daring midnight assault on the bluff at **Stony Point** and the grounds of the United States Military Academy at **West Point** are sites of military importance. *Towns listed: Fishkill, Garrison, Hudson, Kingston, Newburgh, New Paltz, Rhinebeck, Stony Point, Tappan, West Point.*

✦ LEATHERSTOCKING COUNTRY: ALONG THE MOHAWK VALLEY

The curious name of this region is a reminder of the area's pioneer past; it comes from the leather leggings the frontiersmen wore to protect their ankles and shins from brambles, as well as the name of 19th-century novelist James Fenimore Cooper's series on westward expansion, *The Leatherstocking Tales.* But before Europeans arrived, this area constituted the heart of Iroquoia, home to thousands of Mohawk and Oneida residents. Several important Iroquois cultural sites are clustered around **Cobleskill.** Fur trapping provided sustenance for the Indians and profits for Dutch traders in Albany and investors in Holland. The strength of the Iroquois Confederacy—they held the balance of power between Britain and France from initial contact through the 18th century—allowed them to retain their land and extract recognition from Europeans. The British appointed William Johnson, a wealthy landowner in the valley and recent war hero, as Indian superintendent. Johnson sought to mediate disputes with the Iroquois rather than fight, in part because his vast fortune depended on Indian trade. His opulent manor, Johnson Hall, in **Johnstown,** is a stunning reminder of how pluck and connections can make a man rich. By the early 19th century Iroquois villages (called "castles") had nearly vanished and the few natives who remained became the subject of romantic tales; Cooper's Uncas is thought to be modeled on an Indian living near the author's home on Lake Otsego, near **Cooperstown.** In Rome the Erie Canal Village offers a taste of the 19th-century glory days of the canal. *Towns listed: Canajoharie, Cobleskill, Cooperstown, Johnstown.*

✦ LONG ISLAND: COLONIAL FOOTHOLD

When most people envision Long Island they think of the swank beachfront mansions of the Hamptons. Few remember its role in New York's early settlement, the conflict between Dutch and English settlers, and the area's Loyalist government during the Revolution. The island—some 120 mi long—juts like a scabbard to the east of New York City along the southern coast of Connecticut before splitting into two forks at its far eastern end. The island's beaches provided the currency of most of North America before and well after European arrival, the colored seashells that Indians called wampum. Long Island's oldest history is actually the farthest away from New York City on the island's eastern tip. In the mid-1600s English settlers from Connecticut established farms and fishing villages near the coast and beyond the reach of Dutch authority, considering themselves part of Connecticut. Old farmhouses in and around **East Hampton** and **Southampton** evoke much of the eastern island's early history. The New Netherlands attempted to exert control but was never successful, and in 1665 English conquest of New York meant greater political freedom. *Towns listed: East Hampton, Southampton.*

✦ NEW YORK CITY AND THE LOWER HUDSON VALLEY: FREEDOM'S CAPITAL

During the Colonial era, **New York City** consisted of bustling Lower Manhattan, a fledgling village in Brooklyn, and a few scattered farms on Staten Island. Lower Manhattan's layout reflects this history and its spiderweb of streets contain several notable historic sites, including Fraunces Tavern Museum, St. Paul's Chapel—the latter two great relics from the days of George Washington—and the Federal-style palace of City Hall. By Central Park is the fascinating New-York Historical Society, while near the upper regions of the island are two houses whose owners infamously engaged in a duel to the death: Alexander Hamilton's Hamilton Grange and, 20 blocks away, the Morris-Jumel Mansion, a lavish house once the residence of Hamilton's arch enemy, Aaron Burr, and one that captures the lifestyles of the rich and Revolutionary better than any other still extant in the city. A short ferry ride to **Staten**

Island brings tourists to Historic Richmond Town, a collection of more than 25 historic structures. A key Revolutionary War battle took place in **Brooklyn** at Brooklyn Heights on Long Island's western edge, fueled by spy rings on both the British and American sides.

While Lower Manhattan prospered as a vibrant and diverse trading center throughout the Colonial period, much history took place just to the north as well, in the formerly rural stretches of the Lower Hudson valley. Fortunes made in Indian trade, international commerce, and land speculation are on display at several opulent mansions, notably the Van Cortlandt House in the Bronx, the Van Cortlandt Manor in **Croton-on-Hudson,** and Philipse Manor in **Yonkers,** while in **Tarrytown** the golden age of the Dutch Manorial Period is paid homage at the Old Dutch Church and Washington Irving's snuggery, Sunnyside. The British capture of New York City in 1776 occurred on land that is now almost completely developed, and only Washington's Headquarters and Museum in **White Plains** remains as a historic site. *Towns listed: Croton-on-Hudson, Mt. Kisco, New York City, Tarrytown, White Plains, Yonkers.*

✦ UPPER HUDSON RIVER AND CHAMPLAIN VALLEY: INTO THE ADIRONDACKS
Sitting on the shoulder of the Adirondack Mountains and offering a lush, flat valley and expansive lake that seems to blend into the Green Mountains of Vermont, this area first saw the conflicts between Algonquian tribes, allied with Samuel de Champlain who canoed down Lake Champlain in 1609, and their Iroquian enemies. His arquebus—a fluted musket that ignited with a fuse—fired the first of many shots the region would see. French settlers inhabited Crown Point into the 1750s, but the British finally conquered the region after epic battles at the fort at **Ticonderoga** and **Lake George.** *Towns listed: Lake George Village, Ticonderoga.*

✦ "LOW BRIDGE, EVERYBODY DOWN!": THE WESTERN ERIE CANAL
When early 19th-century Erie Canal boats neared a town, the boat's guide—usually a young boy leading a mule on the towpath—shouted "Low Bridge, Everybody Down!" lest the passengers abovedecks be struck by low-hanging bridge structures. This canal region stretches across the fertile farmland of western New York State near the Lake Ontario shore. While among the largest regions in New York State, its Colonial and Revolutionary-era history is brief, as almost no Europeans (beyond a few French soldiers at the impressive stone fortress of **Niagara Falls'** Old Fort Niagara State Historic Site) lived here until the 1780s. The Erie Canal brought a much larger explosion of settlement and economic activity, which can be seen in **Rochester,** outside of which you can find perhaps the most spectacular historic restoration in New York State, the Genesee Country Village and Museum. *Towns listed: Niagara Falls, Rochester.*

Empire and Independence: Warfare in the Mohawk and Hudson River Valleys

A DRIVING TOUR FROM JOHNSTOWN TO FORT TICONDEROGA

▼▼▼

Distance: approx. 250 mi (one-way)   **Time:** 4 days (3 nights)
Breaks: Overnight stays are best in Schenectady, Saratoga Springs, Ticonderoga

During the quarter century between the outbreak of the Seven Years War and the end of the Revolution's Northern Campaign, the Upper Hudson and Mohawk River valleys drew the attention of military planners in Paris, London, and up and down the Thirteen Colonies. No other region saw as much fighting, and no other was as important to securing Britain's possession of North America or securing the United States' independence. Today many of the places where empire and nation were contested are preserved as historic sites, whether grassy fields or stone bastions. This driving tour takes you past these sights and into the heat of battle. So rent classic movies like *Drums Along the Mohawk* or *Last of the Mohicans,* don your tricorn cap, shoulder your musket, and march in step; the pathways of 18th-century warfare await!

Your tour begins at the seat of British power in the Mohawk River valley and the edge of European settlement. The city of **Johnstown** lies just north of New York State Thruway Exit 28 and 40 mi northwest of Albany. Its namesake, William Johnson, led British troops during the Seven Years War. Johnson Hall served as the headquarters for British relations with western Indians. That Johnson both held that office and controlled the settlement of the region only made affairs neater and more efficient. Imagine the impression the stately manor house made on Iroquois delegations who came to parley with Johnson, or the hundreds of Mohawk, Oneida, or others nations crowding the front lawn as alliances and battle plans were discussed. Plan to spend the morning here and in transit to the next site.

Head south on Route 30A for 20 mi out of the **Mohawk Valley,** taking in some breath-taking bucolic views; near Central Bridge, just south of where Route 30A crosses I–88, turn onto Route 30 south. Near **Cobleskill,** before you enter the village of Schoharie, the Old Stone Fort museum complex is off a side road to your right. The farmers who lived in the Schoharie Valley pushed the edge of European settlement westward and angered the Iroquois who considered this area their own. Back across I–88 and south on Route 7 toward Cobleskill is the excellent Iroquois Indian Museum, which tells the story of Indian displacement. But while the Seven Years War pitted Indians and French against the British, the Revolutionary War matched British settlers against Indians *and* their British neighbors who sided with the Crown. Those men, led by William Johnson's descendents, laid siege to the Old Stone Fort in 1780. Take I–88 northeast to the Thruway east to I–890 into **Schenectady,** where the Historic Stockade District awaits, along with an array of hotels and restaurants.

Wake the troops up early this morning because the general has a long march planned. Return to the Thruway and take it east to Exit 24, where I–90 carries you around the city of **Albany,** New York's capital and the target of French and British invasions in two different wars. Head north on I–787 to the Route 7 east exit (which leads to Troy). Route 7 crosses the Hudson; tides brought Henry Hudson and his ship this far north, as well as legions of British troops in the 1750s. Continue through **Troy** on Route 7 toward Bennington, climbing out of the Hudson River valley. This stretch of road is highly commercial in the beginning but quickly transforms into rural farmland. After 20–30 minutes of pleasant scenery, and a host of ice cream stands, turn left onto Route 22 north toward Hoosick Falls. Just north of town turn right onto Route 67 east; a few miles later on your left is the entrance to the Bennington Battlefield State Historic Site. Here German troops fighting for British King George III, himself ethnically German, fell before a detachment of militia from Vermont and New Hampshire led by John Stark in 1777. Fierce fighting killed almost every member of the British army's detachment and helped seal General Burgoyne's defeat at Saratoga. Looking across the fields, you can almost imagine the desperate Hessian troops wondering, in their last moments, what had brought them to die in this remote corner of America.

Returning on Route 67, head west down the Hoosick valley past farm villages and mill towns that were the subject of folk artist Grandma Moses's paintings. Cross the Hudson River into Mechanicville and turn north on U.S. 4 until you arrive at **Saratoga Springs** and the Saratoga National Historic Park. On this spot the Colonies took an important step toward winning their independence. The visitor center and tour recount the two battles that helped defeat General Burgoyne's army, a surrender which led to French recognition of the United States. Follow U.S. 4 to Route 29 west, which after a dozen or so miles brings you to Saratoga Springs, a 19th-century resort that is a bustling college and tourist town today.

The following day, prepare to step backward in time as your car heads northward up I–87 (the Northway to locals)—follow it north to Exit 21, **Lake George Village.** In the heart of town overlooking the lake is Fort William Henry. This log fort and the nearby Lake George Battlefield Picnic Area were the sites of key Seven Years War battles and offer an intensely developed and unspoiled look at 18th-century forts, respectively. Resist the pressure to spend too much time here, however, as your marching orders have you 35 mi north at Lake George's tip by nightfall, in **Ticonderoga.** Fortunately, you don't have to paddle up the lake as soldiers once did, and you can choose between the scenic but slow Route 9N up the west shore or a quick jaunt up the Northway to Exit 28 and Route 74 into Ticonderoga.

Begin the final day of your campaign with a strategic overview—literally. Mount Defiance offers a commanding view of the Champlain Valley and Fort Ticonderoga below. Looking down, you can see why American troops evacuated the fort when British cannons glinted on this summit. If you peek through the trees behind you, Lake George may be visible, demonstrating the strategic importance of this waterway. A winding drive through town on Route 74—follow the signs—brings "the column" to Fort Ticonderoga, one of the most impressive military sites in North America. Its importance covers both wars and such significant events as the 1758 British defeat and Ethan Allen's 1775 sneak attack. Be sure to catch a fife-and-drum performance and the cannon demonstration, as well as the many outstanding exhibits on martial life inside the museum. By the middle of the afternoon the troops will be ready to assemble for one last campaign—the trip back home.

Old Nieuw York: The Dutch in the Hudson River Valley

A DRIVING TOUR FROM ALBANY TO NEW YORK'S STATEN ISLAND

▼▼

Distance: approx. 225 mi (one-way)   **Time:** 3 days (2 nights)
Breaks: Overnight stays in Hudson or Kingston, Tarrytown, and New York City

The Hudson River valley has been Dutch since Henry Hudson, albeit an Englishman working for a Dutch company, sailed up the river in 1609. Even after the English conquered Nieuw Netherland in 1664, the Dutch influence persisted in architecture and culture. Today a remarkable collection of Dutch buildings—some original and some replicas—depict the valley's Colonial history and bear witness to the grandeur of the Dutch Manorial Period. Consider starting your tour in early May, when Albany celebrates all things Dutch with Tulipfest. Local women even perform a ceremonial scrubbing of the streets in wooden shoes and traditional Dutch clothing.

Normally, you might think that colonial settlement began at the coast, but the Dutch chose to establish their first fur-trading post 150 mi from the Atlantic Ocean, where tides still raised and lowered the Hudson River (and still do today). Fort Orange—today's **Albany**— became the seasonal rendezvous for Dutch traders and Iroquois trappers as early as 1614. The best place to start your visit is the Crailo State Historic Site, housed in an old Dutch house that helps re-create the flavor and history of the early settlers. In downtown Albany the Albany Visitors Center and Henry Hudson Planetarium provides an excellent overview of the city's history and information on other nearby historic sites. Twenty minutes west of Albany on the New York State Thruway is the city of **Schenectady,** a much smaller Dutch settlement best known for surviving a French and Indian attack. The Historic Stockade District abuts the Mohawk River and includes several early homes.

Heading south down the Thruway alongside the Hudson River, swing off Exit 21B to the Bronck Museum, a 1663 farmhouse near Coxsackie (30 minutes south of Albany), off U.S. 9W South. Continue south on 9W to Catskill and cross the Hudson River via Route 23. To the north on U.S. 9 is the city of **Hudson,** where the Columbia County Historical Society maintains the Luykas Van Alen House, an excellent example of vernacular Dutch architecture (and a featured locale in the film of *The Age of Innocence*). Hudson has more than 50 antiques shops, so many people will want to make an overnight stay, especially if they want to make a side trip to Kinderhook and its many notable historic buildings (the figure that inspired Ichabod Crane of the *Legend of Sleepy Hollow* was schoolmaster here). But if you want to get to a more commercial city at your next stop, press on to **Kingston.** The easiest way to get there is to return to the Thruway and head south to Exit 19, although the scenic route down the east shore of the Hudson on Route 9G (crossing back over the Route 199 bridge) is pleasant. Plan to spend a full day in Kingston, because the sites are outstanding. Chronologically, the Stockade Historic District is the place to start. Originally built on a rise of land as protection from local Indians, this area contains 21 historic homes, although not all of them are from the Dutch period. The smallness of the houses and streets may surprise you. Moving forward in time, the Senate House State Historic Site interprets the 1777 meeting of the state senate in this house built by Dutch settler Abraham Van Gaasbeek. Save the rest of Kingston's Dutch sites for another day and wander around the Rondout area's shops and restaurants.

West of Kingston on U.S. 209 is the Hurley Patentee Manor, an extension of Kingston's settlement—the 1696 stone cottage you can tour is remarkable. Return to the Thruway and drive south to Exit 19, **New Paltz.** Unlike the Dutch at Albany or Kingston, the French Huguenots who settled here were not interested in connecting to the outside world—as refugees from war and religious persecution, they were content to establish farming communities here. The Huguenot Street Old Stone Houses date to the 1660s and are one of the region's best examples of the way ordinary people lived at that time. Return to the Thruway and continue south to Exit 17, then U.S. 6 east. Once over the Hudson River follow U.S. 9 south to **Croton-on-Hudson,** where Van Cortlandt Manor depicts tenant farming on the Hudson River valley's most productive estate during the 18th century. A similar site is 20 minutes south at Philipsburg Manor in **Tarrytown.** This farm was the northern portion of the wealthy Philipse family's holdings, and their palatial Philipse Manor Hall State Historic Site in Yonkers shows how the rich lived. Just a mile or so to the south you'll find the Hudson Valley's most relentlessly picturesque abode, Sunnyside, built by Washington Irving (creator of Ichabod Crane and Rip van Winkle) to conjure up a Dutch snuggery of old.

Probably all but the most ardent Holland-philes will have tired of historic houses and farms by this time, but there are several more excellent sites that might make keeping your wooden shoes on worthwhile. New York City contains a number of excellent examples of Dutch architecture and historic farms, almost all in outlying sections of the city, which makes driving to them possible. For specific directions, go to the Historic House Trust of New York City Web page: www.preserve.org/hht/map.htm. Your first stops after leaving Philipse Manor are in New York City's borough of the **Bronx,** about 15 minutes drive to the south. The Van Cortlandt House combines Dutch and English styles at the seat of one of New York's most powerful families. Nearby, the Valentine-Varian House is a far simpler home of a local blacksmith and farmer—its exhibits are top-notch. On **Manhattan**'s upper tip, the Dyckman Farmhouse Museum is the only surviving Dutch farmhouse on Manhattan. Not too many blocks away, on a bluff of Washington Heights, is the famous Morris-Jumel Mansion, a veritable Mount Vernon of New York, replete with palatial Federal-era salons and the requisite spirits of Washington, Gouverneur Morris, Aaron Burr, and other famous folk who once visited and lived here. Skirting the congestion of downtown, loop around Manhattan to **Brooklyn,** where the Lefferts Homestead combines Dutch farmhouse architecture with American influences. Nearby, the Claesen Wyckoff House Museum is the oldest home in New York City, dating to 1652. Both sites interpret Dutch farm life and local history. Complete your circle of Manhattan island by crossing the Verazzano Narrows Bridge to **Staten Island,** where Historic Richmondtown has more than two dozen buildings representing Colonial life and 19th-century periods. It is a fitting end to this tour because the living history museum links Dutch settlement to later developments in New York State history. Imagine, as you gaze out across the Verazzano Narrows, Henry Hudson's ship *Halfmoon* sailing by or a Dutch trading ship hauling beaver pelts past you to Amsterdam. A largely vanished European civilization once passed by here, leaving only a few of their houses behind.

ALBANY

▼▼

Albany's first European settlers looked up from the bank of the Hudson River and saw wilderness. While a small, seasonal trading post had operated on this spot for 10 years, nothing but woods lay beyond the immediate shoreline, which served as pier for 270 settlers' ships and a few Indian canoes. Modern visitors see none of this, and re-creating colonial Fort Orange, as the Dutch called the settlement, requires a huge leap of imagination. Interstate 787 runs along much of Fort Orange's original site and sadly obscures the few older pieces of architecture with its elevated spans. Beyond Albany's modern skyline, however, is a rich history. After all, this is the second-oldest permanent European settlement within the original 13 Colonies. One of the city's jewels is its collection of 18th-century mansions, some of which are open to the public and re-create the manners and life of some of Revolutionary America's wealthiest and most powerful families.

Throughout the 17th century, Fort Orange (Albany's name until the 1664 English takeover) was a key fur-trading post dominated by its owner, the Dutch West India Company. Soldiers, fur trappers, merchants, African slaves, and a variety of Indians went back and forth between the city's stockaded walls, the surrounding farm fields, and the tidal shoreline. Then Albany's strategic location at the head of navigation on the river made the city a focal point for French and British armies during the 18th century. The place to start your visit to Albany's sites is the Albany Country Convention and Visitors Bureau (which is adjacent to the Henry Hudson Planetarium), set in the heart of downtown's restaurants and shops. *Contact Albany County Convention and Visitors Bureau | 25 Quackenbush Sq., Albany 12207 | www.albany. org | 518/434–1217.*

Albany Institute of History and Art. This collection ranges from an Egyptian mummy to contemporary painting, but history buffs will be drawn by the American decorative arts and paintings collections. Here they will find a superlative repository of Albany-made silver, including Dutch tankards, mugs, salts, brandy bowls and funeral spoons. Chinese Export porcelain, Albany-made stoneware and redware, and over 40 examples of 18th-century Hudson Valley portraiture will entice. These collections help give an excellent interpretation of regional history, including such gems as the Albany area's domination of iron-stove manufacturing. | 125 Washington Ave. | 518/463–4478 | fax 518/462–1522 | www.albanyinstitute.org | $5 | Wed.–Sat. 10–5, Sun. noon–5.

Bronck Museum. Located in Coxsackie—about 30 minutes south of Albany off the New York State Thruway's Exit 21B—this museum offers a collection of structures related to the Hudson River valley's history, including the region's oldest surviving home, built in 1663 by Pieter Bronck. The Katskill Indians allowed him to build a tiny, single-room structure, which today has miraculously retained its original wood beams, wide floor boards, cellar hatchway, storage garret, and early Dutch door. Eight generations of the Bronck family came to settle on the property, enlarging the house in 1738 into a full-scale brick manor, complete with "hyphen hallway" and kitchen dependency; the interior is furnished with Federal, Empire, and Victorian-era family heirlooms (note the selection of Colonial textiles and spinning utensils). Also on the property are a 13-sided barn from the early 19th century and a Dutch-style barn from the colonial period, complete with 50-ft-long beams. Today, the museum houses collections of the Greene County Historical Society, including paintings by such artists as John Frederick Kensett and Ammi Philips. | Pieter Bronck Rd., off U.S. 9W, Coxsackie | 518/731–6490 | www.gchistory.org/ | $4 | Memorial Day–Oct. 15, Tues.–Sat. 10–4, Sun. 1–5; open Labor Day and Columbus Day.

Crailo State Historic Site. Follow the spiderweb of highway ramps across the Hudson River to the city of Rensselaer, named after the owner of Crailo, Hendrick Van Rensselaer. Hendrick was the grandson of the initial settler, Kiliaen, who arrived to make this area one of the only successful Dutch "patroonships" in New York State. Today Crailo—the name roughly translates to "crow's wood" and was the name of the Van Rensselaer homestead in the Netherlands—is a museum dedicated to the Dutch history of the greater Albany area, with displays of archaeological finds from the latest area digs. Costumed house tours on special days, educational programs, and guided tours are offered. An 18th-century, Federal-style wing addition shows the growing English cultural influence. | 9½ Riverside Ave., Rensselaer | 518/463–8738 | nysparks.state.ny.us | $3 | Early Apr.–Oct., Wed.–Sat. 10–5, Sun. 1–5.

Historic Cherry Hill. Driving south out of Albany on I–787 you might notice an immaculate yellow mansion perched on a hill overlooking an otherwise mundane neighborhood. This was the home of Philip Van Rensselaer, scion of one of the region's original Dutch settler families. It was built in 1787 and occupied by the family until the mid-20th century. Its strength is the remarkable continuity of one family in one house—changing fashion, style, and social mores are on full display here, along with some touching stories of the residents' struggles and triumphs. | 523½ S. Pearl St. | 518/434–4791 | www.historiccherryhill.org | $4 | Apr.–June and Oct.–Dec., hourly tours Tues.–Fri. 12–3, Sat. 10–3, Sun. at 1, 2, 3; July–Sept., Tues.–Sat., hourly tours 10–3, Sun. at 1, 2, 3.

Schuyler Mansion State Historic Site. This is the Georgian mansion of Philip Schuyler, a Revolutionary War general and member of one of New York's oldest and most powerful families. After its completion in 1763 many dignitaries visited here, including son-in-law Alexander Hamilton. In a display of the politeness of 18th-century warfare, Schuyler entertained captured British General John Burgoyne after the Battle of Saratoga, and Burgoyne had nothing but praise for his host. Restoration to the 1790s decor is in progress. Tours on the hour. | 32 Catherine St. | 518/434–0834 | www.nysparks.com | $3 | Mid-Apr.–Oct., Wed.–Sat. 10–5, Sun. 1–5.

Ten Broeck Mansion. This 200-plus-year-old house is in one of Albany's oldest and once most exclusive neighborhoods. It offers local history exhibits, house tours, and gardens. Individual rooms are decorated to evoke periods of the city's past. The Greek Revival building is also home to the Albany County Historical Society. That group hopes to make the mansion part of a historic and neighborhood revival, so stop by to support its efforts. | 9 Ten Broeck Pl. | 518/436–1489 | www.tenbroeck.org | $3 | May–Dec., Thurs.–Sun. 1–4.

✦ ON THE CALENDAR: May **Tulip Festival.** Thousands of tulips are at their peak during this three-day festival celebrating Albany's Dutch heritage in Washington Park on Madison Avenue. Traditions include scrubbing the streets and crowning a Tulip Queen. | 518/434–2032.

HISTORIC DINING AND LODGING

Nicole's Bistro at the Quackenbush House. Once the home of Pieter Quackenbush, one of Albany's original Dutch settlers, the 17th-century building that houses this French-American bistro has been standing longer than any building in Albany. Try the rack of lamb with rosemary Dijon crust, or the roast lamb or pheasant served with garlic mashed potatoes. The grounds include the recreation of a colonial herb garden. Right next door is the Albany Visitor's Cultural Center. | 25 Quackenbush Sq. | 518/465–1111 | $25–$30 | AE, D, DC, MC, V | Closed Sun. No lunch Sat.

Mansion Hill Inn and Restaurant. This inn in the heart of downtown Albany was built in 1861 and has a central courtyard. Guest rooms are large and uncluttered, with reproduction antique pieces and tasteful watercolor prints. Restaurant, complimentary breakfast. | 115 Philip St. | 518/465–2038 | fax 518/434–2313 | www.mansionhill.com | 8 rooms | $155–$175 | AE, D, MC, V.

CANAJOHARIE

▼▼▼

Roll down the windows and smell the chewing gum as you pull into town. The Beech-Nut food-processing plant is Canajoharie's main employer, and you can't miss the plant nestled against the New York State Thruway. That highway cuts through town and separates the town's buildings from Canajoharie's former thoroughfares and economic engines, the Mohawk River and Erie Canal. Its 1730 founders were most concerned with trading furs and getting along with the Mohawk tribe. The town's past wealth is evident in the Canajoharie Library and Art Gallery, which has a collection of fine art (mostly devoted to the late 19th century). This surrounding area was the frontier in mid-18th-century America, with European settlers just beginning to establish a foothold. *Contact Montgomery County Chamber of Commerce | Box 144, St. Johnsville 13452 | 518/842–8200 or 800/743-7337 | www.montgomerycountyny.com.*

Fort Klock. Thirty acres of farm buildings, a trading post, and the centerpiece 1750 limestone house and fort make Fort Klock an essential site for understanding the Mohawk Valley's settlement. Johannes Klock built this outpost—located west of Canajoharie on Route 5 about 2 mi east of St. Johnsville—to trade with the Mohawks; it later protected settlers from the Iroquois during the French and Indian War. The 2-ft-thick stone walls, built atop solid rock, did the trick. Extensive interpretive programs, displays of early American tools and farming techniques, a gathering room, and living history tours. | Rte. 5, St. Johnsville | 518/568–7779 | $1 | Late May–early Oct., Tues.–Sun. 9–5.

Fort Plain Museum. You can see Revolutionary War artifacts and Indian collections at this museum housed in a Greek Revival home on the west side of Fort Plain. David Lupe built the 1½-story stone building in 1848 on what had been the site of a Revolutionary War fortification. Collections span the early history of the Mohawk valley. | 389 Canal St., Ft. Plain (5 mi northwest of Canajoharie) | 518/993–2527 | Free | May–Sept., Wed.–Sun. noon–5.

COBLESKILL

▼▼▼

Cobleskill was a farming town from its start and still is today. Indians grew hemp along the creek that runs through town and European settlers established a farming community here in the late 1700s. The Revolutionary War brought raids from Loyalists and Indians, but their defeat led to a settlement boom. Dairy farming and SUNY-Cobleskill, a two-year college focusing on agriculture, make this town a center of Schoharie County. Nearby sites depict the early settlement and Native American history of the area. *Contact Schoharie County Chamber of Commerce | 243 Main St., Schoharie 12157-0400 | 518/295–7033 | www.schohariechamber.com.*

Iroquois Indian Museum. Located near the famous (and pleasantly cool) Howe Caverns, this museum takes an anthropological approach to Iroquois history. Exhibits range from archaeological relics to ancient and modern art. The museum is housed in a building that evokes an Iroquois longhouse, with skylights representing ceiling smoke holes. A truly innovative and intelligent museum, it hosts a number of cultural exhibits and events, including Iroquois dances. | Caverns Rd., Howe Caverns (6 mi northeast of Cobleskill off Rte. 7) | 518/296–8949 | www.iroquoismuseum.org | $7 | July–Aug., Mon.–Sat. 10–6, Sun. noon–5; Apr.–June and Sept.–Dec., Tues.–Sat. 10–5, Sun. noon–5.

Old Stone Fort Museum Complex. This collection of buildings in the town of Schoharie covers three centuries of rural life. Its centerpiece is the 1772 stone church that later served as a fort. When a stockade was built in 1777 to protect against British attack, the names of Loyalist builders were removed from the foundation where the masons had chiseled their handiwork. A 1780 attack by Loyalist forces left a cannonball dent that is still visible. A carriage house, law office, Greek Revival home, schoolhouse, and Dutch barn are also part of the complex. This is one of the best and most comprehensive sites for understanding early New York's rural history. Reenactments and festivals in the late summer and fall. | Rte. 30A, Schoharie (10 mi northeast of Cobleskill) | 518/295–7192 | fax 518/295–7187 | www.schohariehistory. net | $5 | May–June, Sept.–Oct., Tues.–Sat. 10–5, Sun. noon–5; July –Aug., Mon.–Sat. 10–5, Sun. noon–5.

HISTORIC DINING

Bull's Head Inn. This white, woodframe 1802 building is the oldest extant structure in Cobleskill, as the original posts and beams attest. It stands at the town's historic center along an old turnpike and on the site of log cabins that were destroyed during the Seven Years War. The restaurant, as well as a more casual pub, serve hearty fare, so don't be dissuaded by the "Sturdy Drink" sign above the entrance. | 2 Park Pl. | 518/234–3591 | $10–$25 | AE, MC, V | Closed Mon. No lunch Sat.

COOPERSTOWN
▼▼▼

William Cooper moved to the shores of Otsego Lake in the 1790s hoping to make a fortune. Land speculation, lawyering, and several business ventures succeeded, although Cooper never became the country squire he aspired to be (perhaps because he was known to wrestle with adversaries in the town's muddy streets?). His mansion, Fenimore House, still stands, and several other lovely homes and grand hotels speak to the town's popularity as a summer destination, but most of the sites in this town are from the mid- to late 19th century. But the New York Historical Association has its headquarters here, which includes its research library, and the Fenimore Art Museum and the Farmers Museum will please history buffs. Because of the town's National Baseball Hall of Fame and Museum, be sure to stay away on Hall of Fame weekend (late July) unless you love crowds (or baseball). Cooperstown is about a 30-minute drive from I–88—via Exit 17 and Route 28 or Exit 24 to Route 20 west and Route 80 south—or 45 minutes from the Thruway via Exit 30 and Route 28 south. *Contact Cooperstown Chamber of Commerce | 31 Chestnut St., Cooperstown 13326 | 607/547–9983 | www. cooperstownchamber.org.*

Farmers Museum. Walk through the gates of this working museum and you're instantly transported back to the mid-19th century, "young" for this guide book but redolent of vanished times. The re-created village and farm depict life in 1845 with an array of crafts, trades, and every barnyard animal imaginable. Covering 10 acres and 26 buildings, it is an engrossing place. The museum also has one of the oddities of the 19th century: the 10-ft-tall, 3,000-pound stone "Cardiff Giant," said to be a petrified, prehistoric man or an ancient statue. It was actually a hoax fabricated by a Binghamton cigar maker, but people came from miles around to see it. Today the giant is displayed much as he was "discovered" by workmen in 1869. | Lake Rd. (1 mi north of downtown off Rte. 80) | 607/547–1450 | www.farmersmuseum. org | $9 | May–Oct., daily 10–5; Apr. and Nov., Tues.–Sun. 10–4.

Fenimore Art Museum. In addition to a collection of artifacts and memorabilia of James Fenimore Cooper—the famous early 19th-century American author of such classics as *Last of the Mohicans* and *The Leatherstocking Tales* and son of Cooperstown's founder—this museum has strong collections of American folk art, fine art, and Indian art, with a strong emphasis on the early 19th century. The downstairs gallery on native peoples is especially excellent. The death-mask collection, including those of several founding fathers, is fascinating. Follow the lawn to the lakeshore during the summer months to see a re-created Iroquois longhouse. |

Lake Rd. (just north of town, off Rte. 80) | 607/547–1400 | www.nysha.org | $9 | June–Sept., daily 10–5; Apr.–May and Oct.–Dec., Tues.–Sun. 10–4.

HISTORIC LODGING

Mohican Motel. Two blocks from Main Street, this motel overlooks old village homes dating back to the founding of the town. It is made up of three buildings, including a Federal-style building that has been transformed into accommodations. | 90 Chestnut St. | 607/547–5101 | 11 rooms | $74–$135 | D, MC, V | Closed Thanksgiving–Easter.

CROTON-ON-HUDSON
▼▼▼

A town of contrasts, Croton-on-Hudson is a small town village with beautiful country homes and nostalgic shops as well as easy access to the world's greatest city through one of the busiest railroad stations north of New York City. At only 5 mi square, it might not seem like much, but Croton-on-Hudson has been home to many famous artists, including world-renowned sculptor Alexander Calder and poet Edna St. Vincent Millay. Located in the heart of Sleepy Hollow Country, the town has one Colonial-era crown jewel—the Van Cortland Manor. *Contact Croton Chamber of Commerce | Box 111, Croton-on-Hudson 10520 | 914/271–2196.*

Van Cortlandt Manor. A trip here has been a rite of passage for countless New York City school-children eager to see what Ye Olde Colonial Days were like (after reading all those dryasdust history textbooks). Set with a two-story porch and built in 1749 by Pierre Van Cortlandt—the fourth generation in a dynasty of super-successful Manhattan merchants, which had ingratiated itself with the English Crown (even after the British had booted the Dutch out from ruling over New York City)—this pretty and quaint (though far from opulent) 18th-century manor house does whisk you back to the 18th century. Here, Pierre, wife Joanna, and their eight children settled into a stone manor house, the anchor of a vast working estate on the banks of the Croton River farmed by tenants who rented the land, as well as African slaves. Excellent period furnishings of the Colonial and Federal periods include many artifacts original to the house. The high point for many is the remarkable kitchen complete with beehive oven and smokehouse. On the grounds is an 18th-century tavern, situated along a stretch of the historic Albany Post Road, at the site of a ferry crossing by the Croton River. Adjacent to the tavern is the adorably snug Tenant House, where cooking, spinning and weaving demonstrations are held. Blacksmiths and brickmakers also "ply their trade" during the summer months, which is also when the heirloom vegetable gardens are at their best. Guides dressed in Federal-period garb escort tours through the house, and really get into the act during the special events held throughout the year. Log onto the Web site for a fascinating and detailed history of the fabulous Van Cortlandts, who in many ways were the first (and richest) founding family of New York State. Even though it was right in the middle of Neutral Ground—the "demilitarized zone between British-held Manhattan and the largely Patriotic upper Hudson Valley"—the Cortlandt family fled this manor during the Revolution; after the war, they returned to find the house largely intact. | S. River Side Ave., off Croton Point Ave. | 914/271–8981 | www.hudsonvalley.org | $8 | Apr.–Oct., Wed.–Mon. 10–5 (last tour at 4); Nov.–Dec., weekends 10–4 (last tour 3).

✦ ON THE CALENDAR: July **Independence Day Celebration.** Relive a Revolutionary-era (1799) Fourth of July celebration at Van Cortlandt Manor. Cannon fire begins the festivities and everyone can join in the parade along with the costumed residents of the manor. Patriotic songs and speeches, country cooking and picnics, and demonstrations of military drills and musketry round out the day. | 914/271–8981.

EAST HAMPTON

▼▼

"Perhaps you think that East Hampton was put on the map by potato field-chateaux-building-yuppies from New York." Well, as East Hampton's nifty *Town Crier* Web site goes on to point out, the actual saga of East Hampton is history-soaked and extends back to the mid-16th century. The village was first settled by the English, and this region was never under Dutch influence or more than nominal control (architecture is a ready clue: New England saltboxes dominate rather than stepped-gable houses). That noted, East Hampton came to be populated by windmills (several still charmingly extant), along with a Common Whipper ("three shillings a whipping"), a Lord of the Manor, and (perhaps) Captain Kidd's treasure. While East Hampton is a single township, it comprises several villages, most famously, Amagansett to the east and Bridgehampton to the west, all situated on Long Island's South Fork.

Founded in 1648 by a group of English Puritans who had first settled in Massachusetts and Hartford (Connecticut) Colonies in the early 17th century and then purchased this land—then called "Maidstone" after their home base in England—from the Montauket tribe, the "plantation" initially attempted to merge with Connecticut (way across the sound on the mainland) but decided to merge with the English Colony of New York. Today, wealthy New Yorkers come here for summer weekends, yet the area has managed to retain some of its simplicity and historic charm. The beauty of the Hamptons is celebrated—more than one writer has compared its look to that of New England, replete with centuries-old elms and grey-shingled, 18th-century houses. *Contact East Hampton Chamber of Commerce | 79A Main St., East Hampton 11937 | 631/324–0362 | www.easthampton.com. East Hampton Historical Society | 101 Main St., East Hampton 11937 | 631/324–6850 | www.hamptonsweb.com/ehhs.*

Clinton Academy. One of the three oldest schools in New York State, this elegant Academy opened its doors for classes on January 1, 1785, schooling men for college or such trades as seafaring and surveying, while also teaching young women "the finer points of being a lady." Students boarded with families up and down Main Street in East Hampton Village. The academy closed in 1881 and was altered to become a town hall known as Clinton Hall, incorporating a theater wing, designed by James Renwick, Jr. With early 20th-century restorations, the building returned to its 18th-century appearance and this Late Georgian structure is once again reminiscent of Yale and Harvard's edifices. Constructed of brick and wood, topped with a gambrel roof, and welcoming all with its symmetrical front facade, the building has such gracenotes as a paneled front door centered by windows (note the early graffiti etched in some of the panes). At the top, a cupola holds a bell given to the school by New York's first governor, George Clinton. Be sure to explore the wildflower garden installed by the Garden Club of East Hampton. | 149 Main St. | 631/324–1850 | $4 | July 6–Columbus Day, weekends 1–5.

"Home Sweet Home" House. Picturesquely adorned with a windmill (one of three extant in East Hampton), this is a spectacular 1720s saltbox house that found lasting fame as the home to the 19th-century poet, playwright, and actor John Howard Payne, who wrote the words to "Home Sweet Home." Its construction is lean-to style—one side of the roof reaches almost to the ground while the other stops at the second story. Oak was used for framing, pine for paneling—the main salon was done up in the mid-1700s—and cedar was used for shingling (they remained unpainted because that's how the genteel did things on 18th-century Long Island). Inside, rooms are graced with period and regional antiques, including a mulliner chest, a water clock, lustreware, American chairs, and textiles. Guided tours inform about the history of the house and of Payne, who was born in New York City in 1791 and first came to East Hampton to be educated at the Clinton Academy, the third oldest school in the state. Payne later went to England as an actor, warbled "Home Sweet Home" at Convent Garden Opera House in 1822, then died in Tunis as an American consul. This lovely house and museum sits on East Hampton village green, within walking distance of other historic sites. | 14 James La. | 631/324–0713 | $4 | May–Sept., Mon.–Sat. 10–4, Sun. 2–4; Apr., Oct.–Nov., Fri.–Sat. 10–4, Sun. 2–4.

Miss Amelia's Cottage Museum. Right on Amagansett's Main Street is this petite, white salt-box house, built in 1725. Its sits on property once owned by Amagansett's founders and is full of period furniture. The antique clock is a fine Dominy piece, a relic from the famed Dominy dynasty of East Hampton clockmakers, furniture makers and millwrights, whose head factory, now long gone, was based in East Hampton. The Dominy family's windmills are among the finest in the area. Behind the house is the Roy K. Lester Carriage Museum—both sites illustrate early Amagansett life. | 129 Main St. | 631/267–3020 | $2 | Fri.–Sun. 10–4.

Osborn-Jackson House. Named for the first and last owners, originally built in 1723 as the abode of "Deacon" Daniel Osborn, this house was enlarged in 1760, while later improvements included "winder" stairs set into the back of the chimney, the left and right parlors, and an early open-hearth fireplace. It now serves as the headquarters for the East Hampton Historical Society and as a period house-museum for lovers of American decorative arts. Inquire here about information and directions to the other wonderful holdings of the society, including Mulford Farm and Amagansett's Marine Museum. | 101 Main St. | 631/324–6850 | $4 | Weekdays 9–5.

Water Mill Museum. Originally built in 1644, the oldest operating water mill on Long Island is still fully operational today, although its three stories of unfinished wood don't appear rather timeworn. Southampton was founded by migrants from Lynn, Massashusetts, who knew milling from their old residences, so it's no surprise that Edward Howell chose this pond to start grinding corn and wheat. You can work the lathe and learn the arts of quilting and weaving here. | 41 Old Mill Rd., Water Mill (3 mi south of East Hampton, 500 ft off Rte. 27) | 631/726–4625 | $3 | June–Sept., Thurs.–Mon. 11–5, Sun. 1–5.

HISTORIC LODGING

Hunting Inn. Old elms and maples surround this charming white-clapboard inn in the center of town, originally built in 1699. Set amid charming gardens and spacious grounds, each room is individually furnished with reproduction antiques. The Palm restaurant is well noted. Restaurant, complimentary breakfast. | 94 Main St. | 631/324–0410 | fax 631/324–8751 | 19 rooms | $275–$350 | AE, D, DC, MC, V.

1770 House. Rooms at this inn built in the 1700s have canopy beds and an eclectic personal collection of early American and English antiques. Outside is a patio and yard. The restaurant preserves its historic charm with wooden tables and oriental rugs. Restaurant, complimentary breakfast. No kids under 12. | 143 Main St. | 631/324–1770 | fax 631/324–3504 | 8 rooms | $165–$350 | AE, MC, V.

FISHKILL

▼▼▼

In the late 1990s the animal-rights group People for the Ethical Treatment of Animals launched a campaign to change this nearly 330-year-old town's name, insisting that the word "Fishkill" implied cruelty toward animals. Historians and townspeople quickly pointed out that the town's name derives from two Dutch words, "vis-kill," translated as "fish creek," and the name remains (of course, no one asked for the fishes' opinion). Dutch merchants purchased the land from Wappinger Indians in 1683 for trade goods but did not settle the area until 1709. Farming and trade maintained the town throughout the 18th century until it became a garrison town for the Continental Army during the Revolutionary War. New

York State made its capital here in 1788, and the first copies of the new state constitution rolled off the presses of local printer Samuel Loudon in 1777. Nearby sites include buildings used during the Revolutionary War and one of the town's original houses. Its former occupant, Madam Brett, cultivated a cordial relationship with local Indians and may have been one of America's first businesswomen. *Contact Chamber of Commerce | 300 Westage, Business Center 100, Fishkill 12524 | 845/897–2067.*

First Reformed Protestant Church. "Reformed" churches derived from the original Dutch congregations in Nieuw Netherland, but they have changed much in theology and membership since. This congregation began around 1731, when the church building was constructed. Sunday worship takes place at 10 AM, but tours can be arranged by appointment. The New York Provincial Congress met here and the structure served as a prison during the Revolutionary War. | 1153 Main St. | 845/896–9836 | Free.

Madam Brett Homestead. Set in Beacon (5 mi southwest of Fishkill) and one of the oldest houses in Dutchess County, this manse was home to seven generations of the Brett family from 1709 to 1954. The original portion was built by Catheryna and Roger Brett, who had settled on a plot from their father, Francis Rombout, one of the three patentees of southern Dutchess County. The widow Brett went on to "civilize the wilderness," raising three sons, operating a mill, and forming a trade cooperative. During the Revolutionary War, the homestead was used to store military supplies, and Washington and Lafayette attended a Christmas party here. In 1954, the Daughters of the American Revolution took possession of the house. Graced with handmade scalloped shingles, sloped dormers, hand-hewn beams and an early kitchen fireplace, the house is also fetchingly adorned with a large China-Trade Porcelain collection and 18th- and 19th-century furniture; outside there are formal gardens and herb gardens. | 50 Van Nydeck Ave., Beacon | 845/831–6533 | $4 | Sept.–Dec., 1st Sun. of each month 1–4.

Mount Gulian Historic Site. One of the Hudson Valley homesteads of the fabled Verplanck family—among the very richest and oldest of New York City (many members were immortalized in portraits painted by John Singleton Copley)—this house looks Dutch from the moment you approach it: the sloped gabled roof, four chimneys, and stone walls evoke an architectural style far different than English saltboxes. Located in Beacon and built in the 1730s by Gulian Verplanck, it served as headquarters for General George Washington's officer Baron von Steuben, who helped train the Continental Army to "fight like Europeans," from 1776 to 1783. He and his officers formed the Society of Cincinnati, the famous fraternal organization that held great sway in early national America. The 14-acre site includes a Colonial Dutch barn, restored gardens, exhibit space, and a dining room with period furnishings. Costumed interpreters re-create the life of Revolutionary War–era Dutch settlers, African-Americans, and Native Americans. Located 5 mi southwest of Fishkill, the site hosts a crafts fair and Revolutionary War weekend. Take I–84 to Exit 11 (Wappingers Falls/Beacon), then Route 9D North for a third of a mile, turn left into Hudson View Park Apartments, then left onto Lamplight Street, leading into Sterling Street to find Mount Gulian. | 145 Sterling St., Beacon | 845/831–8172 | $3 | Mid-Apr.–Dec., Wed. and Sun. 1–5.

Van Wyck Homestead Museum. The original three–room house was built in 1732, with the west wing added before 1757. This unassuming wood structure served as headquarters for General George Washington's officers from 1776 to 1783 and hosted a string of luminaries including Lafayette and Alexander Hamilton. Soldiers received their uniforms here, and Tory spy Enoch Crosby was tried here. His tale is said to have inspired James Fenimore Cooper's novel, *The Spy.* The house includes a research library, gift shop, and displays of period artifacts and paintings. | Junction of U.S. 9 and I–84 | 845/896–9560 | $2 | Memorial Day–Labor Day, weekends 1–5.

GARRISON

▼▼

Garrison sits on the east shore of the Hudson River almost directly across from the United States Military Academy at West Point. Famously, American troops stretched a massive chain across the river from West Point to keep the British south of the Hudson Highlands. The town is surrounded by restored, historic homes, including nearby Boscobel from the Federal era. The riverfront rail station and town park—set with picturesque 19th-century buildings and once used as a stand-in for Yonkers in the Barbra Streisand film of *Hello, Dolly!*—offers views of majestic cliffs in either direction. Garrison is located a few miles north of the Bear Mountain Bridge, among some of the most beautiful mountain scenery in the Hudson River valley. *Contact Southern Dutchess Chamber of Commerce | 300 Westage, Business Center 100, Fishkill 12524 | 845/897–2067.*

Boscobel Restoration. The quintessential Federal-era mansion of America, this famously gorgeous and meticulously restored house commands sweeping views of the Hudson River and the Constitution Marsh Sanctuary (itself one of the most unique landscapes along the river). The estate was designed as a political statement perhaps as much as a showpiece of beauty by States Morris Dyckman. Dyckman was both a Loyalist and a Quartermaster in the British Army during the Revolution, only returning to New York after the 1789 amnesty for Tories. He started buying up land In Montrose, overlooking Haverstraw Bay—15 mi south of the present site (the house was moved in the early 1960s)—in an attempt to re-create an English (i.e., un-American) country estate. English annuities and legacies then allowed him to furnish his mansion in the most luxurious style possible, and Dyckman promptly ordered boatloads of glorious furnishings from London. Construction began in 1804, with his widow Elizabeth Corne Dyckman (1776–1823) supervising most of the interior decoration—she moved in 1808. Unbelievably, the house was sold to a demolition expert for $35 in the 1950s, only to be saved by Lila Acheson Wallace and others. Inside a grand entry hall with an imposing staircase makes a suitable first impression, with numerous salons positively aglitter with masterpieces crafted by Duncan Phyfe and other recognized New York cabinetmakers of the day. The Dyckman English china, silver, glass and library are also on view. Outside, there are magnificent gardens, threaded by brick walkways, apple orchards, rose plantings (more than 140 varieties), and a belvedere over the river. A few minutes' stroll away is the town of Cold Spring, with its flea-market shops, restaurants, and, across the train tracks right by the river, a charming promontory set under the Hudson River's most awe-inspiring bluffs. Here, in the summer, not far to the right of the Hudson House hotel, be sure to head to the open-air terrace set with tables for dining to enjoy the Hudson River shore at its most beautiful. | Rte. 9D, Garrison-on-Hudson | 845/265–3638 | www.boscobel.org | $8 | Grounds: Apr.–Dec., Wed.–Mon. 9:30–dusk; house (by tour only): Apr.–Nov., Wed.–Mon. 1st tour 10 AM, last tour 4:15 (Dec., last tour 3:15).

HISTORIC DINING AND LODGING

Bird and Bottle Inn. Warren's Tavern first opened on the old Albany–New York Post Road in 1761. The two-story wooden structure has 18th-century wood floors and antique furniture. Canopied four-poster beds and working fireplaces adorn each of four rooms. Downstairs, wainscoting and candlelight lend an 18th-century ambience. Excellent game birds, open-air dining, and Sunday brunch are all on tap. Restaurant, complimentary breakfast. No kids under 12. | Old Albany Post Rd. (U.S. 9) | 845/424–3000 | fax 845/424–3283 | www.birdbottle. com | 4 rooms | $200 | AE, DC, MC, V.

Hudson House. Set in the charmingly idyllic promontory section of Cold Spring—a few miles to the south of Garrison—this three-story clapboard inn with wraparound porch is right on the river and near a host of antiques shops. It catered to steamboat passengers beginning in

1832 and has been an inn ever since. Comfortable rooms are furnished with antiques as well as modern conveniences. The restaurant here competes with the cheaper river café at the end of Main Street and Garrison's super-luxe Plumbush restaurant, set opposite the gates to Boscobel. Note that Metro-North trains rumble by a few blocks away from this hotel. Restaurant. | 2 Main St., Cold Spring | 845/265–9355 | fax 845/265–4532 | www.hudsonhouseinn. com | 13 rooms | $140–$225 | AE, DC, MC, V.

HUDSON

▼▼▼

Look up at the street signs, fashioned from little silhouettes of whales, and you'll see the reason for Hudson's founding, thanks to the whalers from Nantucket and New Bedford, Massachusetts, who moved here in 1783. By 1790, 25 schooners sailed from this port—more than 100 mi from the ocean yet still tidal and deep enough for big ships—for the whaling fields and the West Indian trade. Manufacturing machinery, matches, clothing, and cement took over in the 19th century, and the beautiful Federal-style homes along some streets reflect the town's wealthy past. Prostitution and drugs made Hudson's red-light district infamous during the first half of the 20th century. Today, weekenders have restored and transformed the old brothels into proper houses and the town is a mecca for antique shoppers—you can nearly go blind perusing the goods here, as there are more than 50 shops. The Parade Hill promenade at the western end of Warren Street—the main drag, which even Henry James once rhapsodized about—has river views. Many people take the train to Hudson just in order to catch a taxi from the station to Frederic Edwin Church's Olana, the famed Moorish mansion of the noted 19th-century American painter, but the town itself is a winner. In addition, surrounded as it is by historic villages and houses, Hudson is the best gateway to Columbia County's attractions found in nearby Kinderhook and Germantown. The Columbia County Historical Society is in stewardship of many historic sites here and has a small museum at 5 Albany Avenue in Kinderhook (518/758–9265, www.berk.com/cchs). *Contact Columbia County Chamber of Commerce | 507 Warren St., Hudson 12534 | 518/828–4417 | www.columbiachamber-ny.com.*

Clermont State Historic Site. One of the great Hudson River valley estates, this was the country address of the Livingston family, whose pedigree is among the bluest in America. Robert R. Livingston, who helped draft the Declaration of Independence, administered the oath of office to George Washington, negotiated the Louisiana Purchase, and helped Robert Fulton develop the steamship, was just one of New York's powerful Livingstons who made their home here. Other members of the family served in the Continental Congress and were delegates to the Constitutional Convention; all held important positions in New York's social and political circles. The house—located in Germantown, some 5 mi south of Hudson—reflects the changes made by several generations: it was burned by the British during the Revolutionary War and rebuilt on the original foundations. Further changes came in the 19th century. The rooms are furnished with family heirlooms; there are beautiful examples of decorative objects and of cabinet making. Outside, carriage ride trails and picnic dells beckon but all are drawn to the stunning views of the Catskill Mountains across the river—the Livingston family once owned nearly all the Catskill Mountain land visible to the west of the Hudson and this view, in fact, inspired Clermont's name, which means "Clear Mountain" in French. Special events are held on July 4 and at Christmas. | U.S. 6, west from Rte. 9G, Germantown (7 mi south of Hudson) | 518/537–4240 | $3 | April–Oct., Tues.–Sun. 8:30–5; Nov.–Dec. 15, 11–4 (tours start at 11); visitor center only Jan.–Mar., 11–4 on weekends.

James Vanderpoel House. This two-story brick house in downtown Kinderhook, 9 mi north of Hudson, is an example of the Federal style at its most fashionable. Green shutters and an imposing picture window set off the exterior, while inside, historic exhibits on life in Columbia County and furnishings represent the life of a prosperous attorney in an 1820s village. The rooms have plasterwork ceilings and graceful mantelpieces, and the second-floor window mirrors the doorway directly below. Tours highlight the ongoing restoration project. | 5 Albany Ave., Kinderhook (10 mi north of Hudson) | 518/758–9265 | $3 | Memorial Day–Labor Day, Thurs.–Sat. 11–5, Sun. 1–5.

Luykas Van Alen House. A set-designer's dream, this 1737 house found Hollywood fame when it was featured as the lovers' retreat in Martin Scorsese's *Age of Innocence* film. From outside its glorious redbrick walls, visitors can't see the entire second story of the house, hidden by a steeply pitched, parapet-gabled roof. The land-rich Luykas Van Alen (his family owned more than 15,000 acres) had the fortune to create a sumptuous abode in the Olde Niederland style—indeed, this house is the very spit of many houses still standing in Holland. Historic touches abound: fireplaces in each room, surprisingly high ceilings, magnificently sashed windows, bright red cupboards, a "senility cradle" (used for aged elders and now stored in the house's garret), Dutch half-doors, and an array of Delftware dishes, pewter chargers, brass candlesticks, and earthenware pots—all shown imposingly on a Hudson Valley *pottebank*—or pottery shelf. All in all, this house is more than camera-ready (as anyone can see from the wonderful photographs captured by Geoffrey Gross in Rod Blackburn's *Dutch Colonial Houses in America*, Rizzoli, 2002). To bring alive the sense of rural Dutch life in the 18th century, cooking and spinning demonstrations are held in season by the Columbia County Historical Society, who run the estate. (Sorry, even though there are all those fireplaces, the house is not heated per se, and so is closed during cold-weather months.) For lovers of Ye Olde New York, this is a must-stop.

Also on site, and moved here from a nearby location, is the **Ichabod Crane Schoolhouse.** Dating from the early 19th century, it served as a classroom into the 1940s. It is named after the famous itinerant schoolmaster and nemesis of Brom Bones of Washington Irving's "Legend of Sleepy Hollow" (published in the author's famous *Sketch Book* in 1819). Irving's Crane was modeled, many historians believe, after Jesse Metwin, the schoolmaster who was based in this school district at the time of the author's journeys to this area. Irving's story was, in truth, a parable against Puritan severity; few remember that his hero survived his encounter with the headless Hessian Horseman and went on to live a long and peaceful life in New York City. Tours of the schoolhouse are included with the Van Alen house museum—indeed, a delightful touch is lent by the fact that groups are welcome to enjoy it for a "one-room schoolhouse" experience. | Rte. 9H, Kinderhook (10 mi north of Hudson, off Rte. 9H) | 518/758–9265 | $3 | Memorial Day–Labor Day, Thurs.–Sat. 11–5, Sun. 1–5.

Robert Jenkins House and Museum. This 1811 Federal-style home contains a museum containing local historic memorabilia, including whaling and military artifacts. | 113 Warren St. | 518/828–9764 | July–Aug., Sun.–Mon. 1–3.

JOHNSTOWN
▼▼

Johnstown was founded in 1760 by Sir William Johnson, an Irish-born landowner and British superintendent of all Indians north of the Ohio River. His massive mansion stands as a testament the power and wealth he accumulated as lord of the Mohawk River. He had lived in the area since the 1730s as a trader with the Mohawks and manager of his uncle's lands. He established a strong friendship with the Mohawk through trade and familial connections, even becoming an honorary member of that nation. The stone mansion he built served as both a manor house for his vast landholdings and the diplomatic center for various negotiations with the Iroquois. In 1781, Johnstown was the site of a Revolutionary War battle that took place a few days after General George Cornwallis's 1781 surrender at the Battle of Yorktown. *Contact Fulton County Regional Chamber of Commerce and Industry | 2 N. Main St., Gloversville 12078 | 800/676–3858 | www.johnstown.com/city.*

Johnson Hall State Historic Site. This 1763 building looks like stone, but is actually made of wood. The valley's largest landowner and hero of the Seven Years' War erected it to encourage settlement and to represent Sir William Johnson's power in the region. Johnson sought to mediate disputes with the Iroquois rather than fight, in part because his vast fortune depended on Indian trade. Several important conferences with the Iroquois took place on the grounds, including one in 1774 whose negotiations proved so tough that Sir William died. When his family remained loyal to Great Britain during the Revolution, New York State confiscated and auctioned the property. House tours and a collection of buildings on the grounds interpret the 18th-century world of a man who fancied himself a feudal lord. | Hall Ave. | 518/762–8712 | $3 | May–Oct., Wed.–Sat. 10–5, Sun. 1–5.

HISTORIC DINING

Union Hall Inn. A French military officer, Capt. Vaumane Jean Baptist de FonClaire, erected a tavern here in 1798. Legend has it that Joseph Bonaparte dined here. Right off Main Street, the two-story red wood building has one of the curiosities of 18th-century architecture—a basically flat roof that extends well past the building. Antiques fill the three formal dining rooms. The food is excellent and innovative. | 2 Union Place | 518/762–3210 | $12–$25 | AE, MC, V.

KINGSTON

▼▼

Dutch settlers moved down from Albany during the 1650s and built a stockaded town on the rise above the Esopus Creek's floodplain. With the English takeover of the Colony in 1664, the town's name changed from Wiltwyck ("wild woods") to the more mundane Kingston, to emphasize that the Crown was in charge. Grain from surrounding farms made its way to sugar plantations in the Caribbean, and Kingston prospered. Nearby fields also fed Washington's army, and the city served as New York's first capital, both reasons for the British to burn the town in 1777. Quickly rebuilt—after all, most of the houses were stone and only burned partially—Kingston became a thriving commercial port with the 1828 completion of the D& H Canal. The Rondout/West Strand area on the river's edge includes many extant buildings from the canal era and has a lively arts and dining scene, stately historic homes, and river cruises from the pier at the foot of Broadway. There are several historic districts here that make Kingston worthy of at least a day's visit. Weekend festivals from May to October celebrate everything from the shad running to the British burning of Kingston. *Contact Chamber of Commerce of Ulster County | 7 Albany Ave., Suite G3, Kingston 12401 | 845/338–5100.*

Hudson River Maritime Museum. The Hudson has been a working river since the earliest Algonquians arrived here, and this fascinating museum does an excellent job of interpreting that history. A re-creation of Henry Hudson's ship, the *Halve Maen* (Half Moon), sometimes docks here—it seems like an awfully tiny craft for 20 men to cross the Atlantic Ocean in. Other exhibits discuss the steamboat era and the modern river, while there are changing (and fascinating) displays of boats of every description. You can also take a river cruise to the 19th-century Rondout Lighthouse. | 1 Rondout Landing | 845/338–0071 | $3 | May–Oct., daily 11–5.

Hurley Patentee Manor. If Kingston's Stockade District hasn't given you your fill of stone houses, head just outside of the city to the village of Hurley. Originally called Nieu Dorpf, Hurley was one of the earliest Dutch settlements in the Hudson River valley, and some of its original buildings survive. Patentee Manor combines a 1696 stone cottage with a 1745 Georgian attachment to offer a glimpse of 18th-century life and furnishings. Nearby houses reflect the time period but are not open to the public. | 464 Old Rte. 209 (Rte. 29) | 845/331–5414 | $2 | Mid-July–Labor Day, Wed.–Sat. 11–4, Sun. 1–5.

Senate House State Historic Site. This low-slung limestone building seems an unlikely place to form a new state government—but with New York City occupied by the British and General Burgoyne threatening Albany, New Yorkers held the first State Senate meeting in Abraham Van Gaasbeek's 17th-century Dutch house during September and October of 1777. The State Assembly was not so lucky and gathered in a nearby tavern. New York State has preserved the Senate House to its 1777 appearance, and the modern two-story visitor center and gallery next door interpret the site's Revolutionary-era history and feature artwork by John Vanderlyn and others. | 296 Fair St. | 845/338–2786 | $3 | Mid-Apr.–Oct., Wed.–Sat. 10–5, Sun. 1–5.

Stockade Historic District. Because of land disputes between Dutch settlers and the Esopus Indians in 1658, Peter Stuyvesant ordered settlers to move up to this bluff, where they built a 1,200-ft-by-1,300-ft wall on three sides of their enclave. Twenty-one historic structures still stand within the stockade area, including the Fred Jay Johnston House, Hoffman House, Matthew Jansen House, Franz P. Roggen House, Kingston Academy, Matthew Person House, Ulster County Courthouse, Henry Sleight House, and Old Dutch Church. This impressive collection of structures spans Kingston's history from its Dutch settlement to the early 19th century and is easily visited on a walking tour, which leave from the Urban Cultural Park Visitor Center, 308 Clinton Avenue. Some houses charge admission to enter, and the exhibits of period furniture and 18th-century life are certainly worth the price. | Bounded by Wall, John, and N. Front Sts. | 845/338–5100 | Free | Daily.

HISTORIC DINING

Hoffman House Tavern. Take a break from walking around the Stockade for lunch or dinner at this restored 1711 home and restaurant. Although built long after English conquest, it still reflects the Dutch architectural style that makes New York unusual. Fireside dining is offered in winter, while patio tables beckon in summer. | 94 N. Front St. | 845/338–2626 | $15–$19 | AE, D, DC, MC.

LAKE GEORGE VILLAGE
▼▼

Don't let the T-shirt shops, wax museum, popcorn and cotton-candy vendors, arcades, pleasure boats, or motorcyclists fool you; Lake George Village is full of history. The southern end of Lake George has been a resort since the early 1800s, and its history dates back even further. Because of its position on Lake George, the village area was inhabited before European settlers came, and once they arrived, it immediately became a strategic location. Water transit—the 18th-century interstate—between French Canada and English New York passed by this spot; boatmen carried their cargo the dozen or so miles between the Hudson River and this lake. To defend the carrying place and protect against French invasion, the British erected a fort at the lake's southern tip in 1755. An initial French defeat was followed two years later by the famous "massacre" at Fort William Henry. *Contact Lake George Chamber of Commerce | Box 272, Lake George 12845 | 518/668–5755 or 800/705–0059 | www.lgchamber.org.*

Fort William Henry Museum. This is a restoration of the original French and Indian War fort that James Fenimore Cooper wrote about in *The Last of the Mohicans*. The massacre was never as bloody as Cooper depicted it, but the French victory struck fear into the hearts of Colonists all the way to Albany. The site includes barracks, stockades, dungeons, and fort artifacts. You can take a guided tour or watch the demonstrations. Some of the presentations are geared more toward beach-goers than historians, but recent archaeological digs have provided for an improved museum. | Canada St. | 518/668–5471 | $9.30 | May–June and Labor Day–Oct., daily 10–5; July–Labor Day, daily 9–10.

Lake George Battlefield Picnic Area. Where else can you barbecue in the shadow—literally—of a 1759 fort? The remains of the original Fort George are here, along with a monument to Jesuit missionary Father Jogues and another to Mohawk Chief Hendrick and Sir William Johnson. Remarkably, you can still walk on the fort's ramparts. You can also get great views of Lake George from the Hendrick/Johnson Monument. But get here early if you want a prime picnic spot. | Beach Rd. off U.S. 9 | 518/623–3671 | Free; parking $5 | Late June–Labor Day, daily 9–8; early May–late June, weekends 9–5.

MT. KISCO
▼▼

Originally settled in 1719 as a farming area, it is now the commercial center of northern Westchester County and is dotted with the mansions of wealthy landowners. One of the earliest hereabouts, John Jay, put down roots in 1801 in a gorgeous homestead in the neighboring village of Katonah. *Contact Mt. Kisco Chamber of Commerce | 3 N. Moger Ave., Mt. Kisco 10549 | 914/666–7525 | www.mountkisco.org.*

John Jay Homestead State Historic Site. Located in adjacent Katonah—and set on one of the most spectacular greenwards in America—the house of John Jay, the first Chief Justice of the United States Supreme Court among many other important offices, features period furnishings and traces Jay's life and career. Perhaps best known as the author of several of the *Federalist Papers,* Jay retired here in 1801 and lived the life of a widowed gentleman farmer until his death in 1829. The furnishings are opulent, but we'll take the porch seats—their view extends over a manicured lawn that even Louis XIV would have envied. There are also Colonial-style garden plots to explore. | 400 Jay St. (Rte. 22), Katonah | 914/232–5651 | $3 | Apr.–Oct., Wed.–Sat. 10–4, Sun noon–4; grounds open year-round.

NEWBURGH
▼▼

Newburgh occupies a strategic bluff on the Hudson River's west shore. Just 60 mi north of New York City, it became the headquarters for George Washington's attempts to keep the British bottled up in Manhattan. It was here in 1783 that he averted a coup d'etat by his officers and later disbanded the Continental Army. An early 19th-century turnpike and early 20th-century manufacturing made the town prosper. This historic Hudson River town has lost much of its old architecture to urban renewal, but preservation efforts are saving houses and buildings. Several important Revolutionary War sites are located nearby. *Contact Chamber of Commerce | 47 Grand St., Newburgh 12550 | 845/562–5100.*

Knox's Headquarter's State Historic Site. The portly General Henry Knox commanded Washington's artillery throughout the Revolution and made his headquarters at this 1754 mansion—built by grain merchant John Ellison—several times. The longest was 1782–83, while American troops eyed the British in New York City. Major Gen. Horatio Gates made this his home when he was oversaw the many thousands of troops stationed at nearby New Windsor Cantonment. This estate also presents the house's later history as a flour mill and has a plant sanctuary. Log on to the Web site for directions. | Vail's Gate (12 mi south of Newbergh) | 845/561–6577 | www.bigchalk.com | $3 | Memorial Day–Labor Day, Wed.–Sat. 10–5, Sun. 1–5.

New Windsor Cantonment State Historic Site. While Generals Washington and Knox and other officers slept in elegant mansions nearby, nearly 7,000 American soldiers erected 600 log huts for their quarters at this "cantonment," or military enclave. It was here on April 19, 1783, that Washington issued cease-fire orders that ended the eight-year War of Independence. Conditions here were better than at Valley Forge or any other military encampment, but life was still rough. The presence of nearly 500 women and children, in some cases the soldiers' families and in others washerwomen and prostitutes, certainly helped and may have calmed the troops when they were all dispersed from here—without pay. A visitor center and staff in period dress present camp life and military demonstrations; you can tour the cantonment's chapel, the reconstructed Temple Building. Log on to the Web site for directions. | 374 Temple Hill Rd., north of junction of Rtes. 94 and 32, Vail's Gate (12 mi south of Newbergh) | 845/561–6577 | www.bigchalk.com | $3 | Mid–Apr.–Oct., Wed.–Sat. 10–5, Sun. 1–5.

Washington's Headquarters State Historic Site. After the British surrender at Yorktown, George Washington and his wife Martha remained at this site for 1½ years, until the last of the British left New York City. The home and grounds were designated a National Historic Site in 1848. Guided tours point out where Washington, his troops, and his slaves lived and worked. There are displays of clothing and equipment, as well as audio-visual presentations on the site's history. | 84 Liberty St. | 845/562–1195 | $3 | Apr.–Oct., Wed.–Sun. 10–5.

✦ ON THE CALENDAR: June **The General's Lady.** This festival at Washington's Headquarters celebrates the birthday of Martha Washington with music, food, and crafts demonstrations. | 845/562–1195.

NEW PALTZ
▼▼

Home to the State University of New York at New Paltz, this is an energetic college town with eclectic shopping and dining downtown. The town was founded in 1677 by French Protestant refugees—Huguenots—who purchased land in the Walkill valley from the Esopus Indians. Presenting their acquisition to the English governor as a fait accompli, they were awarded the right to establish a settlement. New Paltz is farther away from the Hudson River than most Colonial settlements because the 11 Huguenot families who founded it wanted to live separately; preserving their culture, language, and religion was no easy task. Huguenot Street preserves many of the original buildings, a blend of Dutch and French architectural styles. *Contact New Paltz Chamber of Commerce | 257½ Main St., New Paltz 12561 | 845/255–0243.*

Huguenot Street Old Stone Houses. This collection of stone houses is one of the oldest continuously inhabited group of homes in the United States. Structures date to 1692 and represent Dutch vernacular architecture of the Colonial period. Some houses have been adapted for modern use, but the stone foundations and walls evoke a more rustic time. New Paltz's remote location spared this unparalleled collection of buildings when others in the region were razed by development or destroyed by war. Many feature original furnishings. Access to the houses is by guided tour only, although you can freely walk up and down Huguenot Street and admire them. Start at the visitor center at the DuBois Fort, which has ample parking. | 64 Huguenot St., DuBois Fort | 845/255–1889 | $3–$10 | May–Oct., Tues.–Sun. 9–4.

Locust Lawn. The Huguenot Historical Society maintains three homes connected with Huguenot settlement and the Hasbrouck family in the New Paltz area; Josiah Hasbrouck's 1814 Federal-style mansion, Locust Lawn, is the best. Its striking three-story central hall leads to a collection of 18th- and 19th-century furniture. Note the marbleized plaster walls. Next door is the 1738 Terwilliger House and farm museum, which contains an ox cart that was used to carry supplies to the Continental Army at Valley Forge. | 400 Rte. 32, Gardiner | 845/255–1660 | $7 | Call for hrs.

NEW YORK CITY

▼▼

If Pieter Minuit could only see what he bought for $24 dollars worth of trade goods. His 1626 purchase of Manhattan Island from local Indians is now perhaps the modern age's greatest city. New York City has *always* been a city of immigrants—indeed, by the year 1650, barely 25 years after it was settled and when the population was only 4,500, there were already 18 languages spoken in Manhattan. Today's amazing polyglot of people might not surprise a Nieuw Amsterdam (as the stockade at the bottom of Manhattan was called) resident transported from the 17th century.

Visits by Giovanni da Verrazano in 1524, and, a year later, Esteban Gomez, a Portuguese Moor sailing for Spain, marked initial European discovery of New York, but it wasn't until Henry Hudson arrived in 1609 that the area was settled. The Dutch West India Company set up the first trading post here in 1615, and in 1626 Pieter Minuit finagled his land-for-beads-and-trinkets deal. Conflicts with indigenous peoples and a succession of incompetent or corrupt Dutch governors followed. Pieter Stuyvesant, the last Dutch governor of Nieuw Amsterdam, inherited a miserable, struggling town in 1647 yet made considerable headway in improving living conditions and fostering trade with the Caribbean. His attempts to improve the city's defenses failed, however, and merchants handed over a now thriving city to the English in 1664. They preferred negotiating a surrender to taking up arms. The island was promptly renamed in honor of the Duke of York.

During the Revolution, British forces occupied the city but for the first year. Manhattan was a haven for British sympathizers, mostly wealthy merchants and shippers who prospered as suppliers to the British army. "Insurrectionists" who were unable or unwilling to flee suffered the indignities of occupation, including the forced quartering of British troops in their homes. Despite local support, the British occupiers torched Manhattan in 1776, burning a quarter of it. By the time the Loyalists and British surrendered New York to the Americans on November 25, 1783—eight months after the end of the war—the city was ravaged, its population decimated (at half its prewar level of 25,000), and its economy in ruins.

Two years after the surrender, New York City had recovered enough of its grandeur to become the capital of the United States, which it would be for the next five years, from 1785 to 1790. Federal Hall still stands as a monument to that early role. From 1789 to roughly 1800, the city's population doubled to almost 70,000 people. By the middle of the 19th century, many of the developments that were to make New York a world-class city were already in place. In 1801, Alexander Hamilton founded the *New York Post*—not the city's first newspaper, but the oldest one still publishing. The New York Stock Exchange began in 1792 with traders gathering under a buttonwood tree near its present-day site of business. In the first decade of the next century, Robert Fulton successfully harnessed steam power, and, with the opening of the Erie Canal in 1825, New York became the nation's busiest seaport, eventually surpassing Philadelphia as a center of business. Since then, America's largest city has rarely looked back, one reason why Colonial and Revolutionary-era landmarks remain relatively scarce on the ground.

The Colonial-era heart of New York continues to be dominated by Wall Street, which is both an actual street and a shorthand moniker for the huge and powerful financial community that is clustered around the New York and American stock exchanges. In fact, its name dates back to the wooden wall built across the lower island in 1653 to defend the Dutch Colony against hostile Algonquins tribes. The Battery covers the southernmost tip of Manhattan, where Nieuw Amsterdam once stood. Streets ranging from here northward to 14th Street (beyond which the 1811 grid pattern takes hold) may be aligned with the shoreline or twist along the route of an ancient cow path—consider this a bemusing remnant of Colonial America. *Contact New York Convention and Visitors Bureau | 810 7th Ave., at W. 53rd St., New York 10019 | 212/484–1222 | www.nycvisit.com.*

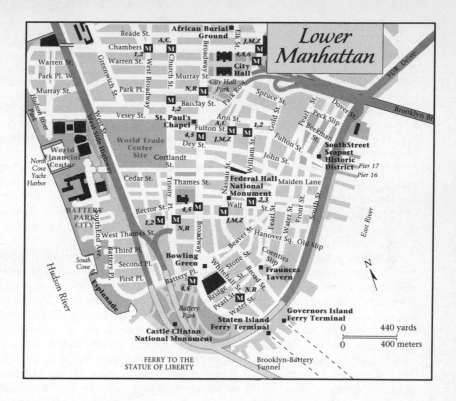

African Burial Ground. This grassy corner is part of the original area used to inter the city's earliest African-Americans—an estimated 20,000 were buried here until the cemetery was closed in 1794. The site was discovered during a 1991 construction project, and by an act of Congress it was made into a National Historic Landmark, dedicated to the people who were enslaved in the city between 1626 and Emancipation Day in New York, July 4, 1827. | Duane and Elk Sts.

Bowling Green. This oval greensward at the foot of Broadway became New York's first public park in 1733. On July 9, 1776, a few hours after citizens learned about the signing of the Declaration of Independence, rioters toppled a statue of British King George III that had occupied the spot for 11 years; much of the statue's lead was melted down into bullets. In 1783, when the occupying British forces fled the city, they defiantly hoisted a Union Jack on a greased, uncleated flagpole so it couldn't be lowered; patriot John Van Arsdale drove his own cleats into the pole to replace the flag with the Stars and Stripes. | Broadway, between Battery Place and Beaver St.

Castle Clinton National Monument. Jutting out as if it were Manhattan's green toe, Battery Park (so named because a battery of 28 cannons was placed along its shore in Colonial days to fend off invaders) is built on landfill and has gradually grown over the centuries to its present 22 acres. The park's main structure is Castle Clinton National Monument, the take-off point for ferries to the Statue of Liberty and Ellis Island. The "castle" is a circular, red-stone fortress on an island 200 ft from the shore, built originally to defend New York Harbor during the War of 1812 and named after DeWitt Clinton, then mayor of the city. But the British never attacked New York and the structure was transformed into Castle Garden, an entertainment center and opera house (Jenny Lind became world-famous here). In 1855 it became in immigrant landing station and welcomed more than 8 million—yes, that's million—people before it closed in 1890. Now, it has a small museum—programs offered

Who Swindled Whom? The Manhattan Land Deal

It was a swap that would make headline-making New York dealmaker Donald Trump green with envy. The tale is familiar: Pieter Minuit, director-general of the Dutch West India Company's outpost in what would become New York State, purchased Manhattan island for $24 in beads and trade goods. At roughly 1¢ for every 10 acres, it was one heck of a deal. The problem is, it may never have happened and, even if it did, the Indians thought *they* were ripping off the Dutch.

First of all, Minuit's role in this transaction is suspect. The directors of the Dutch West India Company had instructed his predecessor, Willem Verhulst, to buy the island in 1625. The historic record is unclear on who actually made the purchase, and whether Verhulst or Minuit was in charge of the Colony at the time. And unlike the roughly simultaneous purchase of Staten Island, no written deed records the sale. So the first part of the legend, Minuit's involvement in the deal, lacks certitude.

Second, while the Dutch thought they had driven a great bargain, the Indians believed they had hoodwinked the Dutch. The goods traded held far different values for each culture. To the Dutch, $24 of kettles, axes, hoes, wampum, drilling awls, Jew's harps, and other items was a small price to pay for valuable real estate. But these items (similar goods historians know were traded for Staten Island) held immense values for the Indians. Kettles and axes were metal goods that Indians could not make for themselves. Like the drilling awls, these items outperformed any the gourds, sharpened stones, and shells normally used for basic tasks like cooking, cutting, or piercing holes. Scarcity and utility made these items, that seemed mundane to Europeans, highly desirable. Likewise, Jew's harps were musical instruments that Indians could not produce themselves; their aural culture prized such novelties. Finally, the reputed glass beads may not have been the cheap items imagined by later historians, but wampum, the basic currency of native North America. These small shell beads were produced in small quantities on eastern Long Island and Narragansett Bay—scarcity makes any monetary system valuable. After first boring a hole in their middle (thus the importance of drilling awls in the Staten Island deal), Indians wove the shells together to tell stories and represent alliances.

If the Indians placed a higher value than the Dutch did on the goods exchanged, they also held a different conception of land ownership. The Dutch believed that they had purchased complete rights to Manhattan island. Most Indian cultures believed that no individual could own land; he could only allow people to use it. A better way to term the deal might be to say that the Indians "leased" Manhattan to the Dutch. Without European conceptions of real estate, the Indians figured they had just received a highly valuable collection of goods. How stupid of the Dutch to give them so much in exchange for the right to use land, something that most Indians granted freely! It was as if the two sides left the bargaining table thinking they had swindled the other, only to discover later that the entire deal was a grave misunderstanding. In any event, the Dutch didn't have much time to enjoy their "triumph"—only 38 years later, Governor Pieter Stuyvesant surrendered New Amsterdam to British troops, and it was renamed New York.

include ranger-led tours of the fort.Outside, at one end of the park mall stands the Netherlands Memorial Flagpole, which depicts Dutch traders offering beads to Native Americans in 1626 for the land on which to establish Fort Amsterdam. As it turns out, historians have now discerned that this event actually happened more than 20 mi away, at the far northern tip of Manhattan in the forest that is today known as Inwood Hill Park. There—under a giant tulip tree, legend has it—Pieter Minuit brokered the deal. Revisionist historians now believe that while it seems the Manhatta tribe got a bum rush, they actually did very well considering that Native Americans then (and now) often believe they never can "own" any part of nature and, therefore, the isle was never theirs to "sell" in the first place. For more information, *see* the "Who Swindled Whom?" box. In any event, inscriptions on the flagpole describe the event in English and Dutch. | State St. and Battery Pl. in Battery Park | 212/344–7220 | Castle Clinton free; ferry $7 round-trip | Daily 8:30–5.

City Hall. Reflecting not big-city brawn but the Neoclassical refinement and civility of Enlightenment Europe, New York's surprisingly decorous City Hall is a diminutive palace with a facade punctuated by arches and columns and a cupola crowned by a statue of Lady Justice. Built between 1803 and 1812, it was originally clad in white marble only on its front and sides, while the back was faced in more modest brownstone because city fathers assumed the city would never grow farther north than this. A magnificent, sweeping, marble double staircase leads from the domed rotunda to the second-floor public rooms. The small, clubby City Council Chamber in the east wing has mahogany detailing and ornate gilding and is headlined by the towering, early 19th-century portrait painted by Samuel F. P. Morse of the Marquis de Lafayette; the Board of Estimate Chamber, to the west, has Colonial-era paintings and church-pew–style seating; and the Governor's Room at the head of the stairs, used for ceremonial events, is a stunning showpiece of the Federalist style, filled with historic portraits and furniture, including a writing table that George Washington used in 1789 when New York was the U.S. capital. The Mayor's Wing remains private. The year 2003 is the 200th anniversary of the laying of City Hall's cornerstone so the building has now been sumptuously restored, with historic portraits by John Trumbull and other assorted treasures—such as the flag used for Washington's 1789 inauguration at nearby Federal Hall—newly on view. Best of all, guided tours (twice a month; reserve well in advance) are once again offered by arrangement with the City Hall sergeant. Outside, City Hall Park was originally used as a sheep meadow, known in the 18th century as the Fields or the Common. It went on to become a graveyard for the impoverished, the site of an almshouse, and then the home of the notorious Bridewell jail. Even as a park the locale was far from peaceful: it hosted hangings, riots, and political demonstrations. A bronze statue of patriot Nathan Hale, who was hanged in 1776 as a spy by the British troops occupying New York City, stands facing City Hall, so please pay your respects. | City Hall Park, Lower Manhattan | 212/788–6865 | Free | Tours at 2 on 2nd and 4th Fri. of each month.

Dyckman Farm House Park and Museum. Manhattan's last surviving Dutch farmhouse, this picturesque stone-and-fieldwood abode is now hemmed in by the dreary apartment houses of Inwood. The British burned the Dyckman family's first farmhouse, one reason why they built this one in 1784 well out of harm's way—in fact, all the way near the northern end of Manhattan. With its sloping gambrel roof, the house was once the center of Manhattan's largest farm. Today, its six rooms contain a museum of Dutch New York, featuring Dutch and English antiques as well as Revolutionary War artifacts. | 4881 Broadway, at 204th St. | www.preserve.org/hht/dyckman/farmhouse.htm | 212/304–9422 | $1 | Tues., Wed., Sun. 10–5, Thurs. 10–8.

Federal Hall National Memorial. Originally the City Hall of New York, this became the hallowed place where George Washington's first presidential oath was administered, where John Peter Zenger was tried and acquitted of libel in 1735 for exposing government corruption in his newspaper—the first triumph of the "freedom of the press" in America—and where the Stamp Act Congress came together in October 1765 to protest "taxation without representation." Grandly designed by architect Pierre L'Enfant (initial designer of Washington, D.C.), Federal Hall was a fitting showcase—it had to be, since New York had become the national capital when the Constitution was ratified in 1788. But after the First Congress gathered to write the Bill of Rights and Washington was inaugurated on April 30, 1789, the capital was moved to Philadelphia in 1790 and the building soon demolished. The current structure—a favorite symbol of Wall Street and used in countless TV commercials—was created as a customs house and depository for American gold (sorry, there's none left here). It now houses a memorial and museum devoted to its glory-stained history. Out front, the statue of Washington stands on the spot where he took the oath of office. | 26 Wall St., at Nassau St. | www.nps.gov/feha | Free | Weekdays 9–5.

Fraunces Tavern Museum. Incongruent among the surrounding skyscrapers at the southern tip of Manhattan, this tavern-cum-museum is indeed a relic of the glory days of the Revolution. Preserved not far away from the site of the World Trade Center, it was here that Washington bid a tearful farewell to his officers in 1783. Look for the pale yellow door on the 1719 three-story brick building—Washington might, in fact, recognize its pretty exterior, picked out with white columns and sash trim. Inside the entrance is a portrait of original patron Samuel Fraunces—little did he know that before long his watering hole would become a leading gathering place for "Insurrectionists." Indeed, taverns often played the role of mini-"City Halls" back then, and here, in 1768, the first New York Chamber of Commerce was born and the Sons of Liberty often galvanized popular support for the fledging revolution. During such events, Fraunces developed a deep friendship with Washington, so deep that he was soon appointed Chief Steward of the President's Household (Washington's house was just a short stroll away). Fittingly, it was in the tavern's Long Room in 1783 that General George made his emotional farewell address to his officers. In truth, the name of the tavern back then was the "Queen's Head," referring to a portrait of England's Queen Charlotte that long hung outside (up to 1783!).

Besides the restaurant—still going strong—the museum here includes a study center, archive, and full library. The collections include more than 200 replicas of Revolutionary War flags, 50 paintings of the era, a goodly array of weapons of the period, and personal effects of George Washington and his compatriots. Best of all are several period rooms that have been magnificently restored. The Long Room itself has been re-created as a loving reproduction of an 18th-century Publick Dining Room, complete with communal table and Windsor chairs. The Clinton Room is named after George Clinton, the first American governor of New York, who hosted a dinner party for Washington at the tavern in November 1783 to celebrate the British evacuation from New York, and this salon glows with spectacular period-scenic wallpaper and 19th-century Empire-style furniture. Unfortunately, you can't enjoy a meal at the Clinton Room's dinner table, so repair to one of three dining rooms. For dessert, don't miss the exhibition on view at the museum entitled, "George Washington: Down the Stream of Life." New York's most prominent monument to The George lies north: Washington Square Park, at the foot of 5th Avenue in the heart of Greenwich Village and presided over by Stanford White's magnificent marble arch in honor of the first president. | 54 Pearl St., at Broad St. | www.frauncestavernmuseum.org | 212/425–1778 | $2.50 | Weekdays 10–4:45.

Hamilton Grange National Memorial. Born on the Caribbean island of Nevis, Alexander Hamilton came to New York City at age 17 to study at King's College (now Columbia University). Named "The Grange" after his family's ancestral home in Scotland, this pretty Federal-style frame house was designed by architect John McComb, Jr., as the centerpiece of Hamilton's 32-acre estate; today, the house is hemmed in by mean city streets. The Grange served as Hamilton's residence for only two years after its 1802 completion—tragically, Hamilton's life was cut short by bitter political rival Aaron Burr (whose "country" residence in Manhattan, the gilded Morris-Jumel Mansion, was not far away), who killed him in a famous duel in Weekhawen, New Jersey on July 11, 1804. Guided tours of the house focus on Hamilton's time there. | 287 Convent Ave., at W. 141st St. | www.nps.gov/hagr | Free | 212/283–5154 | Fri.–Sun. 9–5.

Metropolitan Museum of Art. One of the greatest museums in the world, the Met is the largest museum in the Western Hemisphere. It seems unfair to recommend only one section, but the American Wing has a gigantic wing devoted to American painting, sculpture, and the decorative arts. Famous paintings of the Colonial period, and later—including that 1851 showstopper, Emanuel Leutze's mammoth *Washington Crossing the Delaware*—are on view. And don't miss the magnificent portraits of early New York society, including that masterpiece, John Singleton Copley's *Daniel Crommelin Verplanck,* which captures the spoiled young son of New York's richest 18th-century family playing with his pet squirrel on a gold chain in front of the family estate, Mount Gulian, in Fishkill-on-Hudson. The crowning jewels of the American Wing, however, are the 15 period rooms, which spectacularly capture the finest decors and antiques of early America, from the Pilgrim era to the luxe of the Federal period. All in all, a must-do for lovers of American beauty. | 5th Ave. at 82nd St. | 212/535–7710 | www.metmuseum.org | $10 suggested donation | Sun. and Tues.–Thurs. 9:30–5:30, Fri.–Sat. 9:30–9.

Morris-Jumel Mansion. One of New York City's greatest "time-machines" and the oldest surviving private dwelling in Manhattan, this mansion with a two-story colossal portico was built in 1765 as a summer villa for British officer Roger Morris and wife, a member of the powerful Philipse family. As a showpiece, its greatest architectural flourish was an elongated octagonal drawing room—the first of its kind in America, and a lovely touch of the Palladian style, soon to be the most fashionable of the Pre-Revolutionary period. The Morrises entertained in high style but abandoned the house at the outbreak of the Revolutionary War, when it was taken over by George Washington as headquarters during his upper Manhattan skirmishes, then later defaulted to British and Hessian soldiers. In 1810, a rich French merchant, Stephen Jumel, and his wife Eliza, bought the estate, and bestowed many elegant American-French Empire furnishings on the house. Eliza went on to marry the notorious Aaron Burr, who despatched Alexander Hamilton in a New Jersey duel (Hamilton's residence still stands 20 blocks to the south). The house remained in the family until 1865.

The house has 12 period rooms but their restoration has been done with a heavy hand. Blatantly bold wall colors (yes, we know they are "authentic" to the period, but still), "faux" (i.e., modern) fabrics, and overly waxed furniture do not an alluring impression make. Gouveneur Morris, a member of the family and the leading tastemaker of his day, might be aghast. Still and all, this house is positively unique as a domestic residence-museum for New York City, and all aficionados of American decorative arts should make the trek up to the far northern reaches of Manhattan to see it. As an added plus, the house in set in a lovely garden, replete with iron fence and gates. When leaving, ask the museum staff for directions to the adjacent Jumel Terrace Historic District, which includes Jumel Terrace, a block lined with early 19th-century wooden row-houses (near Edgecombe Avenue, between West 160th and 162nd streets)—an exceptional sight and now some very coveted real estate. South of this area lies the district of Harlem. | 65 Jumel Terrace, Roger Morris Park, at W. 161st St. | www.preserve.org/hht/jumel.htm | 212/923–8008 | $3 | Wed.–Sun. 10–4.

Mount Vernon Hotel Museum and Garden. Back in the late 18th century, this spot—just a few blocks from Bloomingdale's store—was considered "rural" and an escape from the bustle of the big city miles to the south. This 1799 carriage house sitting on land owned by Col. Smith and his wife Abigail Adams Smith (daughter of President John Adams) was thus converted in 1826 into a hotel for weary citydwellers. Today, surrounded by its stone walls and offering a beautifully restored stone-and-clapboard house with nine period rooms of Federal-style decor, it still remains a lovely retreat. Surrounded by the glitz of New York's Upper East Side, it is an amazing relic from days gone by. | 421 East 61st St. | 212/838–6878 | $5 | Tues.–Sun. 11–4; June, July, Tues., 11–9.

Museum of the City of New York. The unique history of New York City, from its Native American roots to the complex present-day metropolis, is carefully chronicled in this enormous Georgian mansion, thanks to collections rich in costume, furniture, paintings, decorative arts, oral histories, and toys. There are hundreds of documented pieces from New York cabinet shops and warerooms, ranging in date from a dressing bureau made by Samuel Prince of New York, 1770 and including pieces from cabinetmakers of Federal New York, including Michael Allison, John T. Dolan, Charles-Honoré Lannuier, and Duncan Phyfe. The collection of historic silver is one of the top 10 in the country. As for paintings, highlights include the van Mierevelt portrait of Katrina van Cortlandt, circa 1630; several fine specimens of early 18th-century Hudson Valley Patroon painting; and a tasty Whitman's Sampler of Colonial portraitists, such as Wollaston, Copley, and Trumbull, including two of George Washington by Gilbert Stuart. Today, many curatorial concerns at the museum focus on exhibits dealing with "modern" New York, but the Colonial buff will find treasures enough. | 1220 5th Ave., between E. 103rd and 104th Sts. | 212/534–1672 | www.mcny.org | $7 | Wed.–Sat. 10–5, Sun. noon–5.

National Museum of the American Indian. Seven stories high and covering three city blocks, this imposing structure was once home to the U.S. Customs House. High-tech exhibits and a treasure trove of artifacts present the history and current cultures of native peoples from throughout the Americas. This museum is a branch of the Smithsonian Institute in Washington D.C., where a second, larger museum will open in 2004. | Alexander Hamilton U.S. Custom House, 1 Bowling Green | 212/668–6624 | www.si.edu/nmai | Free | Mon.–Sun. 10–5, Thurs. 10–8.

New York Historical Society. Where else could you see Benjamin Franklin's glasses, Napoléon Bonaparte's signature, 250 Tiffany lamps (the largest collection in the world), and the Louisiana Purchase contract? And let's not forget George Washington's camp bed at Valley Forge. No, this is not some sort of glorified attic (although the museum's new Henry Luce III Center for the Study of American Culture certainly has the stuffings for one), but a very august and scholarly institution, with myriad top-notch temporary exhibitions ("Independence and Its Enemies in New York: The 225th Anniversary of the Declaration of Independence" was one show), an important library, and full calendar of concerts and walking tours. | 2 W. 77th St., at Central Park West | 212/873–3400 | www.nyhistory.org. | $5 | Tues.–Sun. 11–5

St. Paul's Chapel at Fulton Street. In 1766 this church stood at the city's northern edge, yet its columned stone facade seems ancient amid the skyscrapers that dwarf its steeple. The *New York Times* noted in July 2002 that this chapel is New York City's "most exquisite keystone of national history." Built in 1766, it certainly remains Manhattan's oldest public building in continuous use. Standing on the corner of Broadway and Fulton streets, it is a glorious exercise in the Georgian architectural style (closely resembling the famous St. Martin-in-the-Fields, which presides over Trafalgar Square in London). Inside, the church is fully Federal in style, glowing in bright pink and blue hues, authentic in restoration if not calming in spirit. St. Paul's most hallowed for its Revolutionary claims-to-fame, most momentously when George Washington strolled here for a service after his inauguration at nearby Federal Hall 1789 (you can see the pew he sat in). On the other side of the coin, British generals worshiped here during their occupation of the city. The gilded crown adorned with plumes above the pulpit is thought to be the city's only vestige of British rule. St. Paul's became one of the main centers of recovery efforts for the World Trade Center, which stood just two blocks away. You can continue to deliberate on weighty matters by walking through the church's vast graveyard, which has headstones dating back to the 17th century and now overlooks Ground Zero. | Fulton St. and Broadway | 212/602–0874 | Weekdays 9–3, Sun. 7–3.

South Street Seaport Museum. This "museum without walls" fills 11 square blocks on the East River with its cobblestone streets, magnificent historic sailing ships, 18th- and 19th-century architecture, a boatbuilding center, a children's crafts center, and much more. What South Street lacks in authenticity it makes up in bustle—on weekends, crowds arrive to enjoy the clothing stores and food courts here. Along with a nifty bookstore, the South Street Seaport Museum offers small exhibitions on nautical themes. But the largest objects in its collection are the great ships parked at the adjacent pier by water's edge—the "Street of Ships" is now home to the nation's largest fleet of privately maintained historic vessels. Pride of place is given to the gigantic, four-masted barque *Peking,* which while only built in 1911 distills all the magic and glory of centuries of merchant vessels powered only by wind. Visitors can go below deck to the restored living quarters; a film on view includes footage of one of Peking's voyages around storm-tossed Cape Horn. Competing for glamor is the *Wavertree*, built in 1885 as one of the last large sailing ships built of wrought iron (today, she is the largest afloat). Just to the left of Fulton Street, at 211 Water Street, is Bowne & Co. Stationers, a reconstructed working 19th-century print shop. Continue down Fulton around to Front Street, which has wonderfully preserved old brick buildings— some dating from the 1700s. On the south side of Fulton Street is the seaport's architectural centerpiece, Schermerhorn Row, a redbrick terrace of Georgian- and Federal-style warehouses and countinghouses built in 1811–12. | Visitors center: 12 Fulton St., at South St. | 212/748–8600 | www.southstseaport.com | $6 | Apr.–Oct., Fri.–Wed. 10–6, Thurs. 10–8; Nov.–Mar., Wed.–Mon. 10–5.

HISTORIC DINING AND LODGING

Fraunces Tavern. George Washington proved a chowhound here on many an occasion, so today a sign with his profile hangs over the entrance to this historic tavern. Samuel Fraunces built this gathering place in 1763, and its current decor evokes that earlier era. There are three dining salons to choose from: the informal Tavern, set with Revolutionary muskets, historic flags, a truly thrilling mural depicting the Battle of Brooklyn, and, yes, a plasma-screen TV; the Tallmadge Room, replete with glowing fireplace and paneled walls; and the Bissell Room, centered around a grand early 19th-century mural showing New York Harbor in 1727. We are not sure what The George would have made of such nouvelle entrées as ahi tuna and chili-rubbed porterhouse, but he would undoubtedly cottoned to the roast turkey breast with creamed fingerlings, smoked bacon, and Madeira gravy. And where else in New York City can you dine with muskets on the wall? | 54 Pearl St. | 212/968–1776 | $35–$41 | AE, DC, MC, V | Closed weekends.

Ye Waverly Inn. Ye olde quaintest tavern in the city, this 150-year-old Greenwich village town house has been a restaurant since 1920, always retaining its Colonial-tavern feel. Only a Pilgrim would feel comfortable in the high-back booths of the first dining room, while the adjoining mini-salons are very 1820 in feel—wallpapered, cozy, and lighted by fireplaces. Look for passable potpies, Southern fried chicken, and other traditional American dishes. Afterward, take a stroll up and down the block on Bank Street—lined with gorgeous 19th-century town houses, it has always been a favored address for the rich and famous. | 16 Bank St. (at Waverly Pl.) | 212/269–0144 | $12–$19 | AE, DC, MC, V.

Inn at Irving Place. Despite its plethora of hotels and thriving tourist trade, Manhattan lacks any historic lodgings from the Colonial or Revolutionary eras (consult the New York Convention and Visitors Bureau for the vast array of modern hotels)—but the nearest in date is this 1830s charmer, a luxurious town house set on Manhattan's Irving Place opposite a former residence of Washington Irving. Each elegantly appointed room in this landmark has a view of either the inn's gardens or Gramercy Park. The salons are adorned with antiques, all guest rooms are embued with historic chic, while the hotel's Lady Mendl's Tea Salon is a connoisseur's delight. Restaurant, bar, complimentary breakfast. No kids under 12. | 56 Irving Pl., between 17th and 18th Sts. | 800/685–1447 | fax 212/533–4611 | www.innatirving.com | 12 rooms (2 with shower only) | $300–$500 | AE, DC, MC, V.

OUTER BOROUGHS

Because they blossomed into full-fledged communities much later than Manhattan, New York City's outer boroughs contain historic sites that focus on rural life. As paradoxical as they may seem in a thriving, hyper-modern, and densely packed city, the houses and restorations listed below are well worth visiting.

✦ BRONX

Often depicted as the roughest of New York City's boroughs in popular culture, the industrial, gritty, and irrepressible Bronx has a history almost as old as the entire Dutch Colony.

Sea captain Jonas Bronck was the first European to settle here, in 1639. His name still describes the area, although Dutch settlers failed to predominate. Perhaps that is why calling the Bronx's baseball team the Yankees (from the Dutch "Jankes," a colloquial term for robbers and thieves) is so appropriate—after the 1650s English settlers from New England established farms here. Wealthy landowners like the Van Cortlandt and Philipse families managed to establish large manors in the Bronx, and the area remained largely agricultural into the 19th century.

Valentine-Varian House. Imagine the Bronx as a more rural, tranquil place as you wander through this 1758 fieldstone farmhouse. Its 2 ½ stories were typical of the architecture of the everyday houses of middle-class people in its era. Isaac Valentine, a blacksmith and farmer, abandoned the house as battles raged around it. Exhibits trace the history of the borough through the Revolution. | Varian House Park, 3266 Bainbridge Ave. | 718/881–8900 | $2 | Sat. 10–4, Sun. 1–5.

Van Cortlandt House. Frederick Van Cortlandt erected this brick mansion in 1748 and it stands as the oldest residence in the Bronx. Today, it has been stunningly restored and is the suavest monument to 18th-century domestic taste in New York City, magnificently adorned with Queen Anne tea tables, William and Mary chests, Chippendale chairs, and even a bedroom chicly covered in printed papers "en suite" for walls and chairs. Designed in homage to then-British rulers, this house was conceived in Georgian taste, but it is also studded with Dutch objects and ornaments in homage to the family's Old World roots—the family was one of the grandest in New York and intermarried with other patrician families, such as the Schuyler, Philipse, Jay, DePeyster, and White dynasties. Guests were often famous—George Washington initiated his triumphal return to Manhattan from this estate in 1783. The East Parlor is graced by an elaborately carved Rococo mantelpiece, a portrait of Augustus Van Cortlandt (1728–1823), a 1770 mahogany low-boy that bears the label of William Savery (noted Philadelphia cabinetmaker), and a great Chippendale-style five-legged card table— all perfectly aligned in Colonial simplicity and splendor. The Colonial kitchen is a wonder. Upstairs are bedrooms and a Dutch Chamber, an all-purpose room, with a fireplace tiled in Delftware and with a traditional Dutch cabinet bed (parents slept in the top compartment while children were warmed below by trapping their body heat inside). Don't miss the Georgian-style painted pine dollhouse in the nursery—one of the earliest known American examples and dating from 1740. | Broadway at West 246th St. | 718/543–3344 | $2 | Fri., 10–3, weekends 11–4.

✦ BROOKLYN

Nieuw Netherland's third suburban settlement, Breuckelen, received its government charter in 1646. Primarily a small farming settlement across the East River from the tip of Manhattan, it grew and expanded haphazardly. Dutch farmers composed most of Brooklyn's early settlement in scattered hamlets and crossroads that have now congealed into a continuous urban area. Overlooking New York harbor today is the Fort Greene Park Prison Ship Martyrs Monument, a soaring Doric column designed in 1908 by Stanford White to honor the 11,500 American soldiers and sailors who died lingering deaths on British prison ships anchored in Wallabout Bay of New York harbor between 1775 and 1782. Housing their recovered bones, which had first been buried on the shore below, the monument stands near the site of Fort Putnam, erected by Gen. Nathaniel Greene in 1776, used in the Battle of Brooklyn, and later renamed for the Revolutionary War hero.

Lefferts Homestead. The bell-shaped gambrel roof and porches prove what your eyes hinted— this is a Dutch house. Built in 1783 by Flatbush landowner Peter Lefferts, it combines Dutch and American influences and is a fine example of rural farmhouses–yes, this urban hustle of a neighborhood was once the boonies. The house was moved from its original site several blocks away in 1918. Furnishings reflect the early national period, one important room now resides in full state at the Brooklyn Museum of Art, and demonstrations re-create farm life. | Prospect Park, Flatbush Ave. at Empire Blvd. | 718/789–28229 | Free | Apr.–Nov., Thurs.–Fri. 1–4, weekends 1–5.

Old Stone House/Battle of Brooklyn Site The Battle of Brooklyn, one of the Revolution's earliest battles, took place near this site in August 1776. Roughly 32,000 British troops crossed from Staten Island to meet the approximately 20,000 American troops encamped here. George Washington stationed his troops in the woods and passes among the Brooklyn hills, but the British routed them. Maryland troops counterattacked British positions here, with much loss of life. The two-story structure that stands today is a replica of the 1699 farmhouse with 2-ft-thick walls. A first-floor interpretive center chronicles the Battle of Brookyn. | J.J. Byrne Park, 4th Ave. and 3rd St. | 718/768–3195 | Free. | Sat. noon–3.

Wyckoff House. Twelve years after arriving in America from the Netherlands at age 17, Pieter Claessen Wyckoff built this house in 1649. He and his wife raised 11 children in this low-slung building as Wyckoff rose from indentured servant to successful farmer and local official, finally becoming the wealthiest citizen of New Amersfoort, later the town of Flatlands. Subsequent additions expanded the size, but the wide floorboards and overhanging eaves are typical of the Wyckoff's time. Saved by city efforts in 1951, the house has been restored and quaintly furnished in 17th-century style. | 5816 Clarendon Rd. | 718/629–5400 | $2 | Tues.–Sun. 10–4.

✦ STATEN ISLAND

Settled by Dutch farmers in 1661, Staten Island today still feels provincial and even old-fashioned compared with the rest of the city; indeed, time stands still in the re-created village of Richmondtown. Although it is less convenient to get here than to the other boroughs, the 20-minute ferry ride across New York Harbor affords phenomenal views of lower Manhattan and the Statue of Liberty. Staten Island was named to honor of the governing body of the Netherlands, the States General. Indian opposition and the Anglo-Dutch prevented any permanent Colony from taking root until the 1660s, and it remained a farming area for many years. The Dutch roots of the island were spread far and wide through the local family of the Van der Bilts, who, through succeeding generations, grew into the mighty Vanderbilt dynasty of the 19th century.

Historic Richmond Town. One of New York City's finest and most extensive trips back in time, this is an historic restoration, which incorporates some 25 time-burnished buildings with the avowed purpose "not to freeze a single moment in time, but to create a journey through time." The story starts back in 1685, when Dutch, French, and English settlers founded Richmond Town, later to become the seat of county government. A crossroads settlement among the scattered farms of Staten Island, its central location was chosen by the Dutch Reformed congregation for a meeting house. With the explosion of trade and wealth in Manhattan in 1800, this area became populated and the town a center for commerce. Two dozen historic buildings—some from the hamlet, many others moved from around the island—and dating from 1690 to 1890 re-create past eras. The oldest-known elementary school building in the country, Voorlezer's House, is a prime attraction, allowing you to return to the 1690s. Fast forward to the 1820s to visit the farmhouse of Elizabeth Lake Tysen. Other historical treats are the Van Pelt Cemetery, a Queen Anne gatehouse, a Gothic Revival Parsonage (now the museum's restaurant), a fieldstone farmhouse from Revolutionary days, a basketmaker's house, a Dutch cottage, and Tinsmith shop. There is a delightful calendar of events, including summer crafts demonstrations and winter (January–April) concerts in a period tavern lit only by candles and heated solely by a wood-burning stove. | 441 Clarke Ave., Richmond and Arthur Kill Rds. | 718/351–1611 | $4 | Apr.–June and Sept.–Dec., Wed.–Fri. and Sun. 1–5; July–Aug., Wed.–Fri. 10–5 and weekends 1–5; Jan.–Mar., call for hrs.

NIAGARA FALLS

▼▼▼

Niagara Falls bridges the border between the United States and Canada. Historically, there is not much to see around the falls itself but head north to find one of the few Colonial-era outposts of the region, Old Fort Niagara. *Contact Niagara Falls Area Chamber of Commerce | 345 3rd St., 14303 | 716/285–9141 | www.nfachamber.org.*

ATTRACTRIONS

Old Fort Niagara State Historic Site. This strategic spot controlled access to the Great Lakes. The French built the first fort in 1679 and the main "castle" structure in 1726. Captured by the British in 1759 and 1812, the fort housed U.S. troops until 1963. The site provides an introduction to the fort's 300-year history with cannon and musket firings, historical reen-actments, 18th-century military demonstrations, and archaeological programs. The fort's build-ings date from 1726, and include a multi-story French fort that resembles a European castle. There are a museum shop, snack bar, and picnicking in the state park that surrounds the fort. The site is in Youngstown, 10 mi north of Niagara Falls; follow signs from Robert Moses Parkway. | Ft. Niagara State Park, Youngstown | 716/745–7611 | $6.75. | Nov.–Mar., daily 9–4:30; Apr., daily 9–5:30; May, weekdays 9–5:30, weekends 9–6:30; June, weekdays 9–6:30, weekends 9–7:30; July–Aug., daily 9–7:30; Sept., weekdays 9–5:30, weekends 9–6:30; Oct., daily 9–5:30.

HISTORIC DINING AND LODGING

Olde Fort Inn. Youngstown was one of the original settlements around Fort Niagara in the 1700s, and some of the historical flavor remains. This Colonial inn features a pressed-tin ceiling pocked by a few bullet holes and is close to Old Fort Niagara. | 110 Main St., Youngstown | 716/745–7141 | Closed Mon. No lunch | $10–$25 | AE, MC, V.

Red Coach Inn. An Old English Tudor house in kitschy Niagara Falls? Banish your thoughts of anachronism and stop here for some historic charm. During his early 19th-century tour of America the French aristocrat and Revolutionary War hero Lafayette stopped at a tavern across from this spot, riding in a red coach. Since 1923 this replica of the Old Bell Inn in Finedon, England, has offered guest rooms—with names like the London Room, Bristol Suite, and Windmere Suite—that are faux history, but a step back in time nonetheless. A mural in the main dining room commemorates Lafayette's visit. Old-world service includes cham-pagne and a cheese tray presented when you arrive. Even if you don't stay here, be sure to try the cozy tavern-restaurant—the main attraction is the amazing view of the falls' rapids from your table. Restaurant, bar, complimentary breakfast. | 2 Buffalo Ave. | 716/282–1459 | fax 716/282–2650 | www.redcoach.com | 2 rooms, 12 suites | $79–$220 | AE, D, DC, MC, V.

RHINEBECK

▼▼▼

Just off U.S. 9 and across the river from Kingston is Rhinebeck, an affluent village full of picture-perfect Georgian and Victorian houses. Dutch colonists carved the settlement out of the forest in the 1680s. The Beekman family received significant land patents in the area and recruited refugees from Europe's Palatine region as settlers. Important paths, turnpikes, and roads have brought travelers through ever since. Once known as "Violet Town" because hothouse violets were grown here, the village today has restaurants, crafts and jewelry shops, and the oldest inn in the area, the Beekman Arms. Modern travelers will find this former stage-coach stop a convenient resting place as they make their way up the east side of the Hudson River. *Contact Rhinebeck Chamber of Commerce | 19 Mill St., Box 42, Rhinebeck 12572 | 845/876–4778 | rhinebeckchamber.com.*

Montgomery Place. General Richard Montgomery is one of the great heroes of the Revolutionary War. He led American armies in their 1775 invasion of Canada and died trying to capture Québec City that winter. His widow, Janet Livingston Montgomery, purchased this 434-acre tract on the banks of the Hudson River in 1805. The stunning 23-room mansion, with its sweeping half-circle portico, was once the estate of the Livingston family, one of early New York State's most wealthy and powerful families. The original building was Federal, but in the mid-19th century, it was remodeled into a Greek Revival mansion and its main salons are treasure houses overflowing with gilded and glittering antiques. The grounds include a visitor center, gardens, hiking trails, orchards, a farm stand, and impressive views of the Hudson River and Catskill Mountains. The rose garden is notable. | River Rd., Annandale | 845/758–5461 | $6 | Apr.–Oct., Wed.–Mon. 10–5; Nov.–Dec., weekends 10–4; Dec.–mid-Dec., weekends 10–5.

HISTORIC DINING AND LODGING

Beekman Arms. Famously known as the oldest operating inn in the United States, the "Beek"—as locals call it—is one of the noted landmarks of the Hudson River valley. Opened in 1766 by William Traphagen to board and feed travelers—Rhinebeck had become the main stopping point between Albany and New York City—the inn welcomed George Washington (who stayed in Room No. 21), Philip Schuyler, Benedict Arnold, Alexander Hamilton, the Marquis de Lafayette, and even the 4th Regiment of the Continental Army, who drilled on its front lawn. A sturdy stone building originally built to withstand possible Indian attacks, the inn has grown gracefully over the years—upstairs guest rooms are luxurious, furnished with antiques, and some have working fireplaces. The inn's Long Room was a prominent meeting place for teas, public auctions, and Sunday services conducted by traveling preachers. In 1918 the inn received a full-scale renovation under the ownership of Tracy Dowes (his son, Olin Dowes, painted murals re-creating the town's beginnings on the walls of the Rhinebeck post office). The restaurant today is still called the Traphagen Tavern. In spite of all the changes, the lobby's wide-plank floorboards, exposed beams, and a stone fireplace still proclaim the inn's venerable age. Restaurant, bar. | 63–87 Mill St. | phone/fax 845/876–7077 | www.beekmanarms.com | 63 rooms | $85–$145 | AE, D, MC, V.

Beekman 1766 Tavern. Inside this popular restaurant, you'll be surrounded by 18th-century fixtures and portraits. It's been a watering hole since 1766, when Arent Traphagen moved his father's tavern to this crossroads set alongside the Hudson River. The building has served as Rhinebeck's town center through the years, including stints as a post office, theater, church, newspaper office, and political gathering place. | 4 Mill St. | 845/871–1766 | $18–$25 | AE, DC, MC, V.

Old Drovers Inn. Cattle herders (a.k.a. drovers, who brought their stock to New York in the 18th century along this route), Elizabeth Taylor back in the 1960s, and many monied weekenders have helped make this a noted landmark for more than two centuries. *Historic Preservation* meets *Architectural Digest* at this Relais et Châteaux outpost a good 20 mi southeast of Rhinebeck in a quiet patch of New York State favored by off-duty celebrities. Witty antiques, "Colonial" scenic wall murals, lush cashmere throws, and hurricane lanterns make the main salons here picture-perfect, and two of the four guest chambers—the Sleigh Room and the Cherry Room—are seductive exercises in 19th-century chic. Downstairs is the restaurant, where in winter much of the light comes from the large fireplace. The adjacent Tavern Room has tall straight-back banquettes, pewter mugs, and tilted pine floors, but the period ambience doesn't pervade the inn's menu, seasoned as it is with Thai spices and French sauces. Still, even those 18th-century cattle herders would have recognized the inn's Old Drovers' Turkey Hash. Lunch is a bargain compared to the pricey dinner. Restaurant, complimentary breakfast. | Old Rte. 22, Dover Plains (15 mi south of Millbank), 12522 | 845/832–9311 | fax 845/832–6356 | www.olddroversinn.com | $190–$475 | DC, MC, V.

Olde Rhinebeck Inn. Centuries-old buttermilk finishes, wide plank floors, beamed guest rooms, cossetting armchairs, and the most glorious Colonial fireplace parlor imaginable—you can imagine why this place has many fans. Built by German Palatine settlers more than three decades before the Revolutionary War, the building retains many of its original architectural details (although its exterior has been restored to within a inch of its life) and is on the National Register of Historic Places. Outside, a stocked-with-bass pond and Mudpie, the goat, beg you to relax. Breakfast, sometimes including baked French custardy pear pancake, sweet potato Frittata, and smoked bacon from Pennsylvania, all served up on a trestle-table made from James Cagney's former barn, would please that stylehound Thomas Jefferson himself. Complimentary breakfast. | 340 Wurtemburg Rd., Germantown (about 3 mi from Rhinebeck) | 845/871–1745 | fax 845/876–8809 | http://rhinebeckinn.com | 3 rooms | $195–$225 | AE, D, MC, V.

ROCHESTER
▼▼

The third-largest city in the state, Rochester has carved out a niche as a high-tech and industrial center with cultural offerings and a fine university. The city itself is modern, so historic America buffs head hereabouts only to visit one attraction—the fabulous Genesee Country Village and Museum. *Contact Visitors Information Center | 45 East Ave., Suite 400, Rochester 14604-1102 | 716/546–3070 or 800/677–7282 | www.visitrochester.com.*

Genesee Country Village and Museum. Although largely post-Colonial, this spectacularly lovely museum-village is dotted with Federal houses and shops whose restored historic beauty will make you gasp—readers of *This Old House* or any Revolutionary War history will have to make a beeline here. Set 25 mi southwest of Rochester and founded in 1976 as New York State's largest living history museum, this site glowingly re-creates the bygone era of Genesee country life of the 1820s and 1820. Rivaling the stature of Massachusetts's famed Old Sturbridge Village, this hamlet first began as a simple cluster of log cabins. The surrounding area soon became dotted with villages that provided many commercial and communal services to settlers—rich in taverns, stores, mills, tanneries, and smiths, as well as churches, libraries, and academies, the region's extant relics have in many cases been moved and set up here. Striking homes include the 1836 Foster-Tufts House, the shimmering white Federal 1825 Mackay Homestead, the "framed" 1797 Amherst-Humphrey House, several very early log cabins (paging Henry Fonda in *Drums Along the Mohawk*), the Greek-templed George Eastman Birthplace (he was founder of Kodak), plus a slew of shops (bookseller, dressmaker, cooper, physician), often ensconced in adorable little structures. Towering over all are houses of worship, including the 1823 Wheatland Friends Meeting House, the Romolus Female Seminary, and the 1844 Brooks Grove Methodist Church. The cynosure of all remains the cupola-topped Town Hall from 1822—the very quintessence of early 19th-century American elegance. Adorning the entire place are nine period-perfect gardens. The site features interpreters in period dress and crafts demonstrations, as well as a 175-acre nature center with walking trails. Go! From Rochester, head southwest to Scottsville, hooking up with Route 383 toward Mumford, or, alternatively from Rochester, take Expressway 390 south to Avon, then Route 5 West 12 mi to Caledonia and past the Civil War monument to Mumford, where a left turn at George Street will bring you to Genesee in about a mile. | Flint Hill Rd., Mumford | 585/538–6822 | www.gcv.org | $12.50 | May–June and Labor Day–Oct., Tues.–Fri. 10–4, weekends and holidays 10-5; July–Labor Day, Tues.–Sun. and holidays 10–5.

HISTORIC DINING AND LODGING

Spring House. Once a stop on the Underground Railroad, this four-story structure has served meals since Erie Canal days. Slate floors, brick walls, historic oil paintings, and columned porch—the entry is on the second floor up a curved staircase—ooze historic ambience. Remodeling and a hipper menu combine history with haute cuisine. | 3001 Monroe Ave. | 716/586–2300 | $18–$28 | AE, DC, MC, V.

Oliver Loud's Inn. When this property, 6 mi southeast of Rochester on the Erie Canal, was restored, every effort was made to copy the original wallpaper, borders, and moldings from 1812. Rooms have reproduction furniture and paintings. The common room has a fireplace, and there are rocking chairs on the porch that overlooks the canal. Richardson's Canal House is the noted hotel restaurant. Restaurant, complimentary breakfast. No kids under 12. | 1474 Marsh Rd., Pittsford | 716/248–5200 | fax 716/248–9970 | 8 rooms | $135–$155 | AE, DC, MC, V.

SARATOGA SPRINGS

▼▼▼

Sir William Johnson became the first European to sample Saratoga's famed mineral waters when his Mohawk allies carried him here after the Battle of Lake George in 1755. Miraculously, his debilitating leg wound healed and he walked more than 20 mi to his home. Since that date longshots of every description have found a home in Saratoga Springs, including race horses—the August meet of the Saratoga racetrack is known as "the graveyard of champions." Studded with Gilded Age mansions, Saratoga remains the summer home to the Philadelphia Orchestra and New York City Opera and Ballet. Locals use "Saratoga" to refer to the city of Saratoga Springs, not the location of the famous 1777 battle. Colonial-era (17th- and 18th-century) "Saratoga" was about 15 mi away on the banks of the Hudson River, where Schuylerville now stands. To make things even more confusing, both lay within Saratoga County. *Contact Saratoga County Chamber of Commerce | 28 Clinton St., Saratoga Springs 12866 | 518/584–3255 | www.saratoga.org. Urban Heritage Area Visitor's Center | 297 Broadway, Saratoga Springs 12866 | 518/580–0980 | www.saratoga.org/visitorcenter | Free | Mon.–Sat. 9–4.*

Saratoga National Historical Park (Battlefield). The 1777 Battles of Saratoga—there were two, one on September 19 and another on October 7—were fought on the bluffs above the Hudson River and were the scene of General Benedict Arnold's triumphant victory over the British (he later attempted to turn the tables by becoming traitor). The stirring saga began when Burgoyne's 7,000 British forces decided to do battle with American troops on the Freeman Farm clearing on September 19th; only German reinforcements permitted the Brits to finally overpower the Americans in three hours of lethal combat. Today, near Neilson Farm, you can find a line of red-topped poles to mark the British position and a line of blue-topped poles to mark the American. But by October 7, with promised reinforcements nowhere in sight, Burgoyne knew he had to either retreat or advance, and battle was ensued again on Barber Farm. Benedict Arnold proved the hero here when he led a daring charge—even though he had been relieved of command by General Gates—on Balcarres Redoubt and then on Breymann Redoubt, where he suffered his grievous leg injury (the only monument to Arnold is a statue of a boot representing the leg he lost here—to add further insult, it is hard to find). With Arnold's troops rallying for a final assault, Burgoyne had no choice upon nightfall but to retreat behind the Great Redoubt. His troops had suffered 1,000 casualties (the Americans, 500) after very valiant fighting so he headed to nearby Schuylerville to regroup, but there he found American forces had grown to nearly 20,000 troops. He had no choice but to surrender and order his forces to lay down their arms, the "turning point" of the American Revolution because the British surrender convinced France to openly support the rebellion with money and materiel. The site—set 14 mi west of modern Saratoga Springs—includes a 9½-mi road tour marked with all the farms and redoubts, along with impressive views of the Hudson and an excellent visitor center. Interpreters dress in period clothing, and the John Neilson House depicts life in the American Army during the battles. | 648 Rte. 32, Stillwater (14 mi west of Saratoga Springs) | 518/664–9821 | www.nps.gov/sara | $4 per vehicle | Grounds daily; visitor center daily 9–5; tour road open to cars Apr.–mid-Nov., daily.

Saratoga Monument. The three statues in the niches of this monument, built in 1877 to commemorate the centennial of the Battle of Saratoga, are of American Generals Schuyler, Gates, and Morgan. The fourth niche, designated for a statue of Benedict Arnold would have gone, remains empty to signify his later treason at West Point. The monument was not completed and dedicated until 1912, and the rickety iron stairs inside had been closed for years until the completion of a recent renovation. | 53 Burgoyne St. | 518/664–9821 | www.nps.gov/sara | Free | Fri.–Sun. 9–4:30.

General Philip Schuyler House. The country estate of one of New York's great Dutch families was destroyed by the British in 1777, but General Schuyler and his soldiers rebuilt the structure in 29 days. Furnishings and guided tours interpret the life of this wealthy family and their servants up to 1837. The wooden house is 7 mi north of the battlefield (just before the village of Schuylerville). Tours are limited to 10–12 people, so either get there early or be prepared to wait. | 1072 U.S. 4, Schuylerville | 518/664–9821 | Free | June–Sept., Wed.–Sun. 10–4:30; tours every half hr.

HISTORIC DINING AND LODGING

Olde Bryan Inn. This 1825 tavern-restaurant has big fireplaces, exposed beams, and rustic furnishings. Located in one of the city's oldest buildings, it sits near the site of Saratoga Springs' first mineral fountain just north of the present downtown. | 123 Maple Ave. | 518/587–2990 | www.oldebryaninn.com | $14–$22 | AE, D, MC, V.

Inn at Saratoga. This 1848 inn has an old-fashioned hand-operated elevator and 38 rooms done in Victorian style. Fireside dining and a sinful Jazz Brunch recall an earlier era of ease, as does the Grand Ballroom with room for 150. Located south of downtown yet close enough to walk. Restaurant, complimentary breakfast. | 231 Broadway | 800/274–3573 | fax 518/583–2543 | www.theinnatsaratoga.com | 38 rooms | $110–$150 | AE, D, MC, V.

SCHENECTADY

▼▼

Famed for its historic Stockade District, Schenectady was founded in 1661 by the Dutch just west of Albany on the Mohawk River. French and Indian raids and frequent floods failed to stop this town from growing into a trade center and one of Colonial New York's most important settlements. Farmers in the surrounding Mohawk Valley marketed their crops here, and boatmen unloaded their cargo into wagons bound for Albany; Schenectady was the last stop before a dozen miles of windy river and a major waterfall. Many of its original 18th- and 19th-century buildings are still standing in the Stockade district. Tireless efforts to achieve urban renewal have failed, but the industrial city of 65,000 retains pride in its heritage and great old-fashioned ethnic restaurants and markets. *Contact Schenectady Chamber of Commerce | 306 State St., Schenectady 12305 | www.schenectadychamber.org | 800/962–8007 | fax 518/370–3217.*

Historic Stockade District. Some of the houses in this district, among the oldest continuously occupied neighborhoods in the nation, date back to the 1690s, when the French and Indians burned the town. More than 20 of the 80 buildings date to before the Revolution, including some excellent examples of Dutch architecture. The winding, narrow streets converge on a central rotary and statue of Lawrence, the Mohawk who helped the townspeople after the attack 1690 Massacre mounted by the Alqonquin tribes. Walking tour information is available through the historical society and chamber of commerce; both are located in the neighborhood. Getting lost is not a problem—you'll eventually end up by the Mohawk River, and quickly realize that this low-lying settlement is still prone to spring flooding. | Off State St. | 518/374–0263 | www.historicstockade.com | Schenectady Museum and visitor center Tues.–Fri. 10–4:30, weekends noon–5; chamber of commerce weekdays 8–5; Schenectady County Historical Society weekdays 1–5, Sat. 9–1.

SOUTHAMPTON
▼▼▼

The town of Southampton was established in 1640 by British colonists who had originally sailed from the English port of the same name. The farming community grew along with nearby Sag Harbor, as whaling captains built their homes here. The Chamber of Commerce offers maps that detail a walking tour of Southampton's many historic homes. The Job Lane's shopping district mixes hip shops with tree-lined streets, blending the modern with the historic. American troops maintained a headquarters here during the Revolution. *Contact Southampton Chamber of Commerce | 72 Main St., Southampton 11968 | 631/283–0402 | fax 631/283–8707 | www.southamptonchamber.com.*

Old Halsey House. The Old Halsey Homestead was built in 1648 by town founder Thomas Halsey. It may be New York State's oldest English-style house, and it is filled with furniture, ceramics, and textiles from the 17th and 18th centuries. An interpretive gallery presents the site's story. Be sure to tour the beautiful gardens and orchard. | 189 S. Main St. | 631/283–2494 | $2 | Mid-June–early Sept., Tues.–Sun. 11–5.

Southampton Historical Museum. The museum boasts seven historic sites, including a whaling captain's home built in 1843. There is also a country store, an old-fashioned drugstore, a pre–Revolutionary War barn, and a blacksmith shop. Most of the exhibits focus on late-19th-century Southampton, but this is a good place to get a feel for the area's history, mostly because the museum's scope is so broad. | 17 Meeting House La. | 631/283–2494 | $3 | Mid-June–Sept., Tues.–Sat. 11–5, Sun. 1–5.

HISTORIC LODGING
1708 House. Above ground, this bed-and-breakfast was built in 1708 (and remodeled beginning in 1993); below is a cellar dating to 1648, now the dining room of this hostelry. Antiques from the owner's nearby shop fill the house and its nine guest rooms. Exposed beams, stone walls, and historic charm abound without sacrificing comfort. Dining room, complimentary breakfast. No kids. No smoking. | 126 Main St. | 631/287–1708 | fax 631/287–3593 | www.1708house.com | 9 rooms | $175–$395 | AE, MC, V.

STONY POINT
▼▼▼

Set above the Hudson River, this picturesque Rockland County town of 13,000 has a hilly landscape dotted with boutiques and eateries. Local attractions include the Hudson's oldest lighthouse and Stony Point Battlefield, where General "Mad Anthony" Wayne defeated British troops. *Contact Rockland County Office of Tourism | 3 Main St., Nyack 10960 | 845/353–5533 | www.rockland.org.*

Stony Point Battlefield State Historic Site. Sir Henry Clinton's British garrisons—1,000 strong—had captured the peninsula of Stony Point in May 1779 in order to protect the adjacent King's

Ferry service across the Hudson. American General "Mad" Anthony Wayne then led his Corps of Light infantry on an assault on the British fortifications under cover of night on July 15, 1779, ordering his men not to load their muskets lest a misfire awaken the British troops. Fixed-bayonets were their only weapons, along with the element of surprise. An African-American by the name of Pompey—who had obtained the British password under the guise of trips to sell farm produce—distracted the sentinels and thus allowed the Continental Army to storm the Point. Historians have now determined that Wayne actually thought this attack was suicidal—he left instructions for the care of his family after his death. But in a battle lasting less than an hour, Wayne captured the fort—but soon abandoned it when Washington determined it could not be held against the combined might of the British navy and army. This was essentially the last major battle in the North, and it kept the British from launching another campaign up the Hudson River. A museum features audiovisual exhibits, guided tours, and musket demonstrations, while the site is helpfully studded with numbered markers detailing the story of the battle. Don't forget to visit the restored 1826 lighthouse, the oldest on the Hudson, for spectacular views of the river. | Rte. 9W, ½-mi north of town | 845/786–2521 | www.lhric.org/spbattle/spbattle.htm | Free | Apr.–Oct., Wed.–Sat. 10–5, Sun. 1–5.

TAPPAN

One of the prettiest and most historic of Rockland County towns, Tappan has several historic structures of note, including one of Washington's most exquisitely restored headquarters and two sites that witnessed the trial of the notorious spymaster Major John André, the co-conspirator of Benedict Arnold and his aborted coup at West Point: the Dutch Reformed Church of Tappan, first erected in 1694 (the current redbrick, Georgian-style church dates from 1835) and site of the trial in 1780, and the Old '76 House, a former tavern where André was sequestered before his trial and execution. *Contact Rockland County Office of Tourism | 18 New Hempstead Rd., New City 10956 | 845/708–7300 | www.rockland.org.*

De Wint House. The oldest surviving structure in Rockland County and a picture-perfect specimen of Colonial Dutch architecture, this small but gorgeous house, officially known as the George Washington Masonic Historic Site, served as Washington's headquarters four times between 1780 and 1783. Most famously he was in residence here from September 28 to October 7, 1780, during the trial of Major John André, the spy who had attempted to deliver the fortifications of West Point into the hands of the British with the aid of American General Benedict Arnold. Three years later, May 4 through 8, 1783, Washington headquartered here to negotiate the final withdrawal of British troops from New York City with British General, Sir Guy Carleton (Samuel Fraunces, owner of New York City's Fraunces Tavern, came to prepare their dinner). Finally, the general was caught here on November 11 to 14, 1783, by a severe snowstorm on his way to West Point (on his route to New York City to tender his resignation). Adjacent to the De Wint House, a carriage house contains exhibits about Washington, while a copy of the personal flag used by the general during his tenure as Commander-in-Chief flies over the site's elegant garden. | 20 Livingston Ave. | 845/359–1359 | Free | Daily 10–4.

TARRYTOWN

Tarrytown's fame spread far and wide thanks to local resident and muse, the great storyteller and author, Washington Irving, who built his gorgeous Dutch snuggery, Sunnyside, on the town's outskirts (today, a separate village called Irvington). Set on the east bank of the Hudson

River a half-hour north of New York City, Tarrytown was first settled as a farming village by the Dutch in the mid-1600s and remains the heart of "Sleepy Hollow" country, since Irving both lived and died here (he is buried in the town's historic churchyard). But don't go looking for his Ichabod Crane or Rip van Winkle hereabouts—those two great fictional characters were set higher north along the Hudson around Kinderhook (although the Van Tassel family was one of the finest of 18th-century Tarrytown). Tarrytown made real history when three American militiamen captured John André, the British handler of Gen. Benedict Arnold's attempt to surrender West Point. André was hanged while Arnold joined the British side, then earning both infamy and a handsome reward. Today, festooned with boutiques and antiques shops (and Jay Gould's robber-baron castle-estate, Lyndhurst), Tarrytown has views of the Hudson River, here called the Tappan Zee (Dutch for "sea"), at its widest point. *Contact Tarrytown/North Tarrytown Chamber of Commerce, Sleepy Hollow Chamber of Commerce, Tarrytown and Sleepy Hollow | 80 S. Broadway, Tarrytown 10591 | 914/631–1705 | fax 914/631–1512 | www.sleepyhollowchamber.com.*

Old Dutch Church of Sleepy Hollow. Built in 1685, this whitewashed church on a lofty green knoll across the street from Philipsburg Manor is the oldest church in New York State. Yet it is far better known as the church that Ichabod Crane galloped toward while being chased by the headless Hessian Horseman in Washington Irving's *The Legend of Sleepy Hollow*. In 1697 a congregation was first organized to worship here in the Colonial Dutch–style building built by Frederick Philipse on his Manor of Philipsburgh (later known as North Tarrytown and recently baptized, to encourage higher real-estate sales, as "Sleepy Hollow"—a name that had only been a figment of Irving's imagination). Adjacent to this beautiful and evocative church is the famous Sleepy Hollow Cemetery, which serves as the final resting place for Irving and, indeed, some of the characters from his immortal tale. Weekend tours available. | 430 N. Broadway, Sleepy Hollow | 914/631–1123 | www.rctodc.org | Free | Grounds daily; church by appointment.

Philipsburg Manor Upper Mills. Originally named Flypse or Flypsen, Frederick Philipse arrived in New Amsterdam in the 1650s as Governor Pieter Stuyvesant's carpenter. Before long, he had become head of one of New York's wealthiest families, having amassed a 52,000-acre grant from England, which he worked with both European tenant farmers and one of the largest concentrations of African slaves in Colonial New York. His agricultural operation, entered over a long wooden bridge across the millpond, was centered around this still-standing stone manor house. Its gristmill, slave garden, and barn offer excellent windows into farming in the Hudson River valley. Farmers brought their corn and wheat here to be ground and shipped to New York City. The house's rooms are alluringly decorated with 18th-century pieces, including Dutch Delft ceramics, imported brassware, four-postered beds, and quaint kitchen. Interpreters in period clothing offer house tours and demonstrations of farm chores. Seasonal festivals include Pinksterfest in May, Sleepy Hollow Legend Weekend in October, and St. Nicholas Day in December. The palatial residence of the Philipse family still stands in nearby Yonkers (*see below*). | 381 N. Broadway (on Rte. 9), Sleepy Hollow (1 mi north of Tarrytown) | 914/631–8200 | www.hudsonvalley.org | $8 | Apr.–Oct., Wed.–Mon. 10–5; Nov.–Dec., Wed.–Mon. 10–4; Mar., weekends 10–4.

Sunnyside. "A little old-fashioned stone mansion, all made up of gable ends and as full of angles and corners as an old cocked hat" is how Washington Irving described the simple stone Dutch farmhouse he purchased in 1832 and, with the help of landscape painter George Harvey, then transformed into one of the most adorably picturesque houses of the 19th century. America's first successful, internationally known author, Irving found lasting fame with his *Sketchbook* tales, which include "The Legend of Sleepy Hollow"—the beloved story about Ichabod Crane, Katrina van Tassel, Brom Bones, and the Headless Horseman— and "Rip van Winkle," but he also wrote a bulging bookshelf of tomes devoted to history, notably a biography of George Washington and *Astoria,* a multivolume saga of the settling of the Northwest. Originally a tenant farmer's house on the Philipsburg Manor, the house was expanded by Jacob van Tassel and became known as "Wolfert's Roost," a famous gathering place for Patriots. After the Revolutionary War, it was then sold to Irving, who heavily remodeled it with Dutch-stepped gables in homage to the Van Tassel homeland. Tours are given through the house's snug and suavely restored 17 rooms, including Irving's library. Outside, picnicking is encouraged along the stream that flows through the landscape from a pond Irving called his "Little Mediterranean." Special events include a delightful candlelit Christmas display, but the best time to come here may be the spring, when the house's stepped-gable entrance is covered in wisteria planted by the bard himself, who lived here until his death in 1859. | West Sunnyside Lane, off Rte. 9, Irvington (1 mi south of Tarrytown) | 914/631–8200 | www.hudsonvalley.org | $9 (grounds only pass $4) | Apr.–Oct., Wed.–Mon. 10–5 (last tour at 4); Nov.–Dec., Wed.–Mon., 10–4 (last tour at 3); Mar., weekends only 10–4 (last tour at 3).

TICONDEROGA
▼▼▼

Ticonderoga is a Native American term, meaning "land of many waters." The town of Ticonderoga sits in between Lake George and Lake Champlain, with the LaChute River cascading through the town as Lake George empties into Lake Champlain. A key attraction for visitors is Fort Ticonderoga, where reenactments and an extensive, professional museum make history come alive. The village's proximity to graphite mines and abundant lumber made its name—of course—synonymous with pencils for much of the 20th century. Tourism and a paper mill provide most jobs; a giant discount store has created more at the expense of the once quaint downtown. Ticonderoga loves history, and local teenagers take great pride in marching in the Fort's fife and drum corps. *Contact Ticonderoga Area Chamber of Commerce | 108 Lake George Ave., Ticonderoga 12883 | 518/585–6619.*

Fort Ticonderoga. Drive through the fort's stone gates and imagine yourself storming the earthworks that appear quickly on your right. The road carries you through the forest and down a ravine and into the parking lot, where you catch a glimpse of fluttering flags and the fort's roof. Originally named Fort Carillon when it was built by Michael Chartier de Lotbinère for the French in 1755, this fort was captured by the British in 1759 and renamed Fort Ticonderoga. In between, a savage battle cost the British several thousand casualties in a futile frontal assault on the French lines; the Battlefield of Carillon, where the British suffered their defeat at the hands of the Marquis de Montcalm on July 8, 1758, is located not far from the fortifications. During the Revolution American troops captured the fort and in the winter of 1775–76, Col. Henry Knox organized the legendary "Noble Train of Artillery" to haul some 59 cannon by oxen from Ticonderoga to far-off Boston. The fort later fell to the British on July 5, 1777, when American garrisons spotted cannon that had been daringly set up by General Burgoyne's troops upon Sugar Loaf Hill—a vantage point that overlooked the fort (now named Mount Defiance—*see below*). Today the site on Lake Champlain presents living-history demonstrations, which include cannon-fire drills, fife-and-drum exhibitions, encampments, and wildly popular reenactments, notably the "Grand Encampment of the French and Indian War" held in late June and a "Revolutionary War Encampment" in early September. In addition, 18th-century native tribal lifeways are the subject of the annual Harvest Moon Festival in early October, while the season opening is always marked by an Annual War College of the Seven Years' War, an intensive seminar devoted to 18th-century military history. The beautifully restored King's Garden is just below the fort's walls on the grounds of the former Pell family estate, who restored the fort almost 100 years ago. On the ground is an archival study center with scholarly library and the world's largest collection of Colonial-era military artifacts and guns. Consult the Fort's Web page for frequent special events. | 518/585–2821 | www.fort-ticonderoga.org | $12 | Early May–mid-Oct., daily 9–5. Gardens open June–mid-Sept.

Fort Ticonderoga Ferry. Cross Lake Champlain to Shoreham, Vermont, in 6 minutes. This open-deck ferry service has been in operation since the mid-1700s. Pedestrians pay more than livestock. | Shorewell Ferries, Inc., Rte. 74 | 802/897–7999 | May–Oct., daily 7 AM–8 PM.

Hancock House. Local paper magnate and philanthropist Horace Moses donated this reproduction of John Hancock's Boston home to the local community in 1926. Today it houses the Ticonderoga Historical Society and important exhibits on local history, including a 19th-century post office. | 3 Wicker St. | 518/585–7868 | Free | Wed.–Sat. 10–4.

Heritage Museum. Learn about the industrial history of Ticonderoga and its pencils through exhibits, demonstrations, and a self-guided tour, all located in an old mill building near the falls. The adjacent park offers pleasant walking paths and a covered bridge. | Montcalm St. at Bicentennial Park | 518/585–6366 | Free | July–Aug., daily 10–4; mid-May–June, Sept.–mid-Oct., weekends 10–4.

Mount Defiance. View Fort Ticonderoga, the Green Mountains, and much of the Champlain Valley, from up above. During the Revolutionary War, British troops scaled this mountain with a cannon and forced the Americans to evacuate the fort, a major embarrassment that some feared would crush the rebellion. The British motto was: "Where a goat can go, a man can go. Where a man can go, a cannon can go." Somehow, the Americans never figured this out. Obtain a driving map at Fort Ticonderoga. | Mt. Defiance St. | 518/585–6619 | Free | Early May–mid-Oct., daily 9–5.

✦ ON THE CALENDAR: June **Grand Encampment of the French and Indian War.** Battle reenactments and living-history demonstrations by hundreds of British, French, American, and Indian reenactors. Because of the Fort's location on a peninsula and preserved wilderness, there are spots and moments when you see and hear nothing but "the 18th century." | 518/585–6619.

July **Best Fourth in the North.** Ticonderoga celebrates July 4 weekend with parades, carnivals, chicken BBQs, strawberry socials, live local bands, an Elvis impersonator, and fireworks. The parade is a spectacle of small-town America, with more firetrucks than you imagine existed and marching bands from as far away as Québec. | 518/585–6619.

HISTORIC LODGING
Latchstring Motel. This quaint motel sits at the west end of Ticonderoga village and is within walking distance of several restaurants—but be prepared to negotiate hills. Really a 1950s-era drive-up motel (sorry), it features cut-outs of uniformed Colonial soldiers by every room. | 420 Montcalm St. | 518/585–2875 | 9 rooms | $50–$80 | AE, MC, V.

TROY
▼▼

Troy is a few miles north of Albany on the east bank of the Hudson River, and is noted for its historic architecture, restaurants, and Rensselaer Polytechnic Institute, the nation's oldest engineering college. The Wharton block downtown has been used to film numerous films, including Scorcese's *The Age of Innocence*—but Revolutionary War buffs head here to visit the Bennington Battlefield. *Contact Troy's RiverSpark Visitor Center | 251 River St., Troy 12180 | 518/270–8667 | www.troyvisitorcenter.org | fax 518/270–1119 | Free | May–Sept., Tues.–Fri. 10–6, weekends 10–5; Oct.–Apr., Tues.–Sat. 11–5.*

Bennington Battlefield State Historic Site. A detachment of Hessian and British troops set off from Saratoga to capture American supplies in Bennington, Vermont. Greatly underestimating the rebels' strength and marching in cumbersome high leather cavalry boots, the Hessians lost most of their men in a brutal battle with Vermont and New Hampshire forces. This National Historic Landmark proved a key development in the 1777 defeat of Burgoyne's invasion from Canada. Offers interpretive markers, picnicking, and views of Vermont's Green Mountains. Thirty minutes from downtown Troy: Route 7 east, Route 22 north, Route 67 east. | Rte. 67, RD2, Hoosick Falls | 518/686–7109 (summer); 518/279–1155 | Free | May 1–Labor Day, daily 10–7; Labor Day–Columbus Day, weekends only 10–7.

WEST POINT
▼▼

America's oldest and most distinguished military academy, West Point, is on the bluffs overlooking the Hudson River and during the Revolutionary War this position became paramount in importance. Today, just walking onto the grounds of this highly regimented institution makes you stand up straighter. The academy has been the training ground for U.S. Army officers since 1802, but prior to its establishment, this site was protected by Fort Clinton, down by the river plain, and Fort Putnam, high on a ridge 500 ft over the river. It was these fortifications that American Gen. (and hero of the Battle of Saratoga) Benedict Arnold traitorously sought to deliver into the hands of the British (some revisionist historians now conjecture that Arnold was driven to this deed by the fact that America had "betrayed" Arnold's patriotic love and interests first). On the grounds you'll find memorials and cannons, while the restored lookout of Fort Putnam can be visited in the summer. Admission to West Point is free, although there is a fee for tours (a photo I.D. is required for all adults wishing to take a tour). *Contact West Point Visitor Center | Building 2107, West Point 10996 | 845/938–2638 | www.usma.edu.*

Fort Putnam. Initially, the noted bend in the Hudson called West Point was protected by a series of fortifications and earthen redoubts built some 500 ft over the river plain, the most notable element of which was Fort Putnam, erected by Colonel Rufus Putnan in 1778. If there is little left of the fort—the government stepped in and restored its few remaining walls and arched casemates during the 1976 Bicentennial—its view remains to enthrall. To quote famed British actress Fanny Kemble, who hiked up to the fort in 1832, "The beauty and sublimity of what I beheld seemed almost to crush my faculties—I felt dizzy as though my senses were drowning." Signs at West Point will direct you to the parking lot for Fort Putnam, which can only be accessed by a steep and long path. | 845/938–2203 | www.usma.edu | Free | Mid-May–Mid-Oct., Thurs.–Mon. 11–3.

Trophy Point. Offering nearly Cinerama vistas (ranging from Newburgh Bay to the north to Bannerman's Island to the south), Trophy Point looks down upon the Hudson River from the Plain (or parade grounds) at West Point. From here on April 30, 1778, famously, "The Great Chain"—a gigantic 500-yard-long, 65-ton chain link forged at Sterling Ironworks in Warwick, N.Y.—was strung across the river to the banks of Constitution Island (floated on rafts of giant logs). It was hoped that the chain would blockade British ships, bringing them to full stop and allowing engagement by troops hidden along river banks. American Gen. Benedict Arnold, then in charge of the West Point fortifications, notably pooh-poohed how effective a barrier the chain was, claiming that a fully loaded ship would have no problem breaking the chain. In the end, the British chose not to dare it. A circular memorial of chain links stands at the rise of Trophy Point, overlooking the earthen "amphitheater," which slopes down the hill— site for band concerts in the summer (and the finale scene in the 1969 Barbra Streisand film of *Hello, Dolly!*) and not far from the few ruins of Fort Clinton. | Free.

West Point Museum. Founded upon captured British militaria brought to West Point after the British defeat at Saratoga in 1777, this museum collection includes many Revolution-

Traitor and Patriot: Benedict Arnold

Every American knows that Benedict Arnold ranks as the nation's most notorious traitor. Indeed, his actions were reprehensible: while in command of the vital West Point fortifications—a vital key post on the Hudson River that kept the British bottled up in New York City—he attempted to surrender them into British hands in 1780. Handsomely rewarded by the Crown, he received a commission in the British army and led devastating raids into Connecticut and Virginia before the war's end. Yet other events that took place in New York State and elsewhere establish Arnold as one of the Revolutionary War's great heroes, and may even explain his eventual treason.

Born in Norwich, Connecticut in 1741 to an ancient and prosperous New England family, Arnold saw his father suffer financial collapse and was forced to apprentice to the local apothecary. The 1757 French invasion of New York State gave him a chance to join the army and extend his business into the Caribbean trade. With Britain taxes imposed to pay for the Seven Years' War mounting, Arnold became a leader of the Sons of Liberty, rushing to arms after the British opened fire at Lexington and Concord.

His first commission was to capture Fort Ticonderoga, the British fortress on faraway Lake Champlain. His Canadian victories in Crown Point and St. Johns earned Arnold fame and George Washington's confidence. Arnold's men soon undertook one of the most harrowing marches in American military history, rowing leaky boats against the current of icy Maine rivers, across swamps and mountains before descending upon Québec in December 1775. Though wounded in a New Year's Eve assault, he besieged the city, then headed into New York State, eventually building what may have been the first United States Navy at Whitehall, New York.

Expecting to be rewarded for his bravery and efforts, however, Arnold became enraged when Congress refused to promote him to Major General, favoring men with better political connections. Denied command in favor of Horatio Gates, Arnold swallowed his pride and lifted the siege at Fort Stanwix and personally led charges at Saratoga—despite Gates' orders confining Arnold to his tent—that won the battle for the Americans. His leg was later amputated because of a musket ball that had shattered Arnold's left femur, as well as his military career.

Assigned to command the American garrison at Philadelphia, he came to enjoy the city's sophisticated social swirl and, in June 1778, married Peggy Shippen, the daughter of one of Philadelphia's wealthiest families that many suspected of Loyalism. Shippen had befriended John André, a young British officer who persuaded Arnold to betray his country. Arnold's motives for becoming a turncoat were complex. He resented Congress's ill treatment of him, and he smarted from the amputation that confined him to what was in essence a civilian command. His own business having foundered, he needed cash to maintain his, and his wife's, position in high society. Political infighting in Pennsylvania and disgust with the alliance with Catholic France—Arnold was a stern Protestant— all persuaded him to begin slipping information to the British in 1779. His reassignment to West Point provided the perfect opportunity to settle old scores—but Arnold's plan was discovered and he escaped aboard a British ship while his handler, Major Andre, swung from a tree in Westchester County. The fact remains that without Arnold's military exploits the United States might not have come into being. Without question Benedict Arnold is one of America's great traitors, but he is also one of its great patriots.

ary War trophies once used for cadet instruction. Today, the museum spans the entire history of American warfare but the "American Wars" gallery includes the British drum surrendered at Saratoga and George Washington's pistols. | Olmsted Hall at Pershing Center | 845/938–2203 | Free | Daily 10:30–4.

WHITE PLAINS
▼▼

White Plains is caught between the city and the suburbs, and doesn't quite seem sure which it is. Even back when, founded in 1735, White Plains was a major crossroads between New York and New England. It was also the site of an important Revolutionary War battle. *Contact Westchester County Chamber of Commerce | 235 Mamaroneck Ave., White Plains 10605 | 914/948–2110 | www.westchester.org.*

Washington's Headquarters and Museum. This simple wooden house of the Elijah Miller family served as George Washington's headquarters during the November 1776, Battle of White Plains. Built in the Rhode Island–style of low, overhanging roofs, it was erected in 1738 and expanded in 1770. Already sent reeling from Long Island and Manhattan, Washington retreated here to his last chance to hold the lower Hudson River valley—and blew it. Westchester became a no-man's land between the two armies for the rest of the war. Middle-class furnishings include Washington's table and chairs. If you make an appointment, you can tour the house and visit Miller Hill Restoration, the excavated and restored earthworks built by George Washington's troops during the battle. | 140 Virginia Rd. | 914/949–1236 or 914/242–6324 | www.co.westchester.ny.us | $3 | By appointment only.

YONKERS
▼▼

This city of 180,000 people derives its name from Adrian Van der Donck, who received the surrounding area as a patroonship from the Dutch West Indian Company in 1646. Known as "jonkheer ("young gentleman") because of his status in Holland, this appellation gradually became associated with the settlement on the east bank of the Hudson River before evolving into "Yonkers." The town's location at the confluence of the Nepperhan and Hudson rivers made it a key transportation center, and settlement thrived by the early 1700s. Stately Philipse Manor harkens back to Colonial glory, but Yonkers is very much a modern city of industry and commerce. *Contact Yonkers Chamber of Commerce | 20 S. Broadway, Yonkers 10701 | 914/963–0332 | www.yonkerschamber.com.*

Philipse Manor Hall State Historic Site. Three generations of men named Frederick Philipse helped make this imposing three-story brick palace. The first came to Nieuw Netherland in the 1650s as a carpenter and made a fortune through trade, land speculation, and marriage. He purchased a sawmill near this site in 1672 and began amassing what later became a semi-feudal manor granted by England. Philipse's main residence was in Manhattan, and the family maintained the 1680s manor house as their summer home. By the time the third Frederick inherited the land it was turning a tidy profit, but he cared little for commerce or agriculture. Under Frederick Philipse III this home became a showplace of English gentility and Americans' aspirations to aristocracy. Unfortunately, the Philipse family's taste for high living depended on the rent of tenants, which peaked just at the historical moment when the American Revolution overthrew such hierarchical relationships. Sick of high rents and Frederick Philipse III's lordly manner, the tenants turned him in as a traitor in 1776. He and his family later fled to England and the manor was confiscated and sold at auction. Today

New York State operates the manor house and its impressive collection of portraiture and period furnishings. The papier-mache ceiling designs are particularly fascinating. | 29 Warburton Ave., at Dock St. | 914/965–4027 | Free | Apr.–Oct., Wed.–Sat. noon–5, Sun. 1–4.

St. Paul's Church National Historic Site. Set in nearby Mount Vernon, this is one of New York State's oldest churches and was established in 1665 (services were held until 1980). The current stone and brick structure was built in 1763 and served as a military hospital for British and Hessian soldiers after the 1776 battle at Pell's Point. Debates regarding freedom of the press took place nearby in the 1740s, and the visitor center houses the Bill of Rights Museum. Be sure to take the guided tour up the bell tower and stroll through 300 years worth of graves in the cemetery. | 897 S. Columbus Ave., Mount Vernon (2 mi east of Yonkers) | 914/667–4116 | Free | Weekdays 9–5.

Sherwood House. Thomas Sherwood leased the farmland surrounding this house from the Philipse family. Sherwood built the house himself, and served as constable and tax collector for the Town of Yonkers. Built in 1740, the structure contains period furnishings and offers tours by guides in period clothing. Even though Sherwood was fairly well off for the 18th century, his home seems spartan in comparison to Philipse Manor. | 340 Tuckahoe Rd. | 914/961–8940 | www.yonkershistory.org | Free | Early June–early Oct., Sun. 1–4.

By Cornelia B. Wright

North Carolina

"The Goodliest Soil Under the Cope of Heaven"

*N*orth Carolina has been called "the valley of humility between two towering mountains of conceit," Virginia and South Carolina. This compliment, if that's what you want to call it, is thanks to the independence and downright feistiness of many of its denizens, from wealthy planters to small farmers and tradesmen. Humility for many North Carolinians went hand-in-hand with authenticity—whether to their roots, their religion, or the way a representative government, both as a colony and as a republic, should be run. And the fascinating, gorgeous places you can visit here still share that authenticity—from the harborfront at Beaufort to the neat shop-lined streets of Old Salem.

Explorers and settlers coming to North Carolina experienced it as a series of frontiers, taming first the coastal plain, then the rolling hills of the Piedmont, and finally the mountains. Well, *taming* is maybe not the right word. There is still plenty of the wilderness present in every part of the state that we can sense the excitement and awe of the first people to set foot here. The state's farmsteads and towns, harbors and mountain forests, even some city streets, echo with the voices of those who breached both the physical wilderness and the frontier of liberty for a new land.

✦ MYSTERIES AND HOSTILITIES

In the 1500s North Carolina was eyed as a glittering prize by European explorers vying for a toehold—and control of the rich resources—in the New World. After the initial forays of Verrazano and DeSoto, the English established the first permanent claim in the Carolinas— but that's not to say things went swimmingly. The first settlement at Fort Raleigh, on Roanoke Island on the Outer Banks (1585–86), lasted only for a winter before the adventurers packed up and sailed back to England.

When you visit Fort Raleigh, is it fog you see, or a ghostly pale—or, more likely, a misty reflection—of the biggest mystery of early America, the Lost Colony of Roanoke? In 1587, 117 men, women, and boys sailed up to Fort Raleigh, ready to establish a permanent commu-

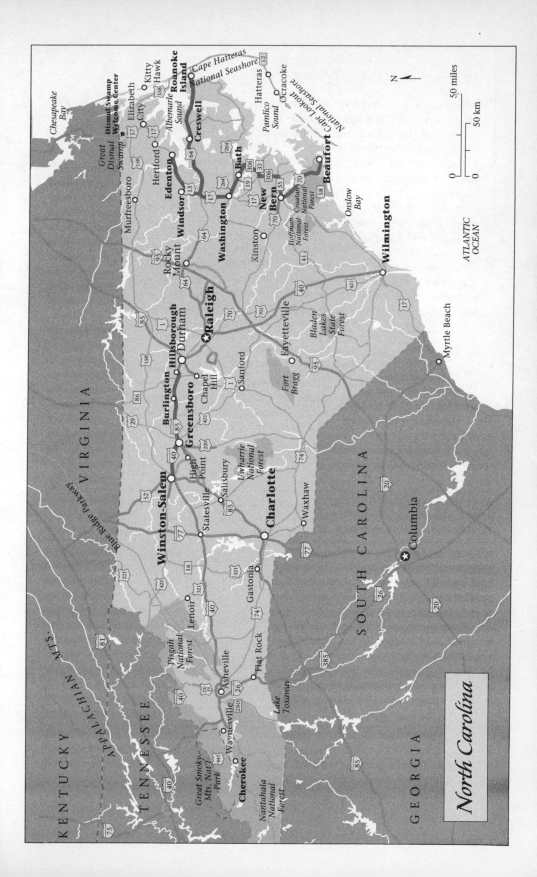

North Carolina

What's in a (Royal) Name?

What exactly do we mean by "Carolina"? Therein lies a story, for what we now call North Carolina was part of a vast southern colony that changed names and boundaries with the turn of the political tides. England's Elizabeth I—the fabled Virgin Queen—had named Virginia for herself in 1584 after Sir Walter Raleigh masterminded an expedition to the New World. After Charles I came to the throne, however, what is now the Carolinas and Georgia was divided from Virginia in 1629 and renamed Carolana in honor of the king.

In 1663 Charles II named this land Carolina and granted it to eight members of the nobility who had helped him regain the throne—the Lords Proprietor, they collected all the duties and taxes from their colony. In 1712, to make the large, unruly province more manageable, the colony was split in two, North and South Carolina, each with its own royal governor. Cities boasted noble names, too. When Charlotte was established in 1768, it was named in honor of George III's consort. It is still called the Queen City to this day. It may be only fitting that after the American Revolution, when the legislators of the new state chose a capital, they named it after the man who started it all, Sir Walter Raleigh.

---

nity. They hunkered in for the winter while the governor of the colony, John White, sailed back to England to procure supplies. Piracy, bad weather, and the defeat of the Spanish Armada delayed White's return until August 1590. He arrived at Roanoke to find the settlement abandoned. Myths abound about the settlers' fate, and while some historians venture imaginative guesses, most concede that we will never really know.

From the first shot fired by explorer Ralph Lane in 1586, relations between the native Algonquin peoples and the English swung between hospitality and hatred. Ultimately some tribes, especially the Tuscarora, were fed up with English encroachment on their lands and attacks on their people. They launched a full-scale attack on settlers in 1711–12, which in turn provoked retaliation, decimating the Tuscarora. What bullets failed do in wiping out the native peoples of the coast, disease did. Place names remain as an evocative reminder of the people who met the settlers: Roanoke, Hatteras, Pamlico, Manteo, Pasquotank, and Chowan, to name only a few.

A serious threat to the North Carolina coast was piracy—although if truth be told early colonists were not above a little smuggling to avoid import duties on whiskey or a cracking good blunderbuss. But they were no match for Blackbeard, Stede Bonnet, and the other pirates who haunted the sounds and inlets of the coast, "liberating" fat privateers and merchant ships of their cargoes. A fine figure of a man, Blackbeard enhanced his imposing stature by twisting hemp rope in his long black hair and luxuriant beard, which, on important attacks, he was reputed to light up in a halo of flame. His amorous exploits rivaled his piracy: rumor has it he was "married" 13 or 14 times. In 1717, to take advantage of a royal pardon for pirates, Blackbeard scuttled his ship, the *Queen Anne's Revenge,* on a sandbar (the remains of which, according to archaeologists, now grace the Maritime Museum in Beaufort), and promised to forsake his evil ways. Guess what? He didn't—in 1718 two Royal Navy ships ambushed him outside Ocracoke and beheaded him. His head sailed into Bath harbor on the bowsprit of a Navy battleship, hair and beard flying.

Once he was out of the picture it was clear sailing, and the ships arriving in port would most likely be heavily laden with wines and fine porcelain from Europe and China destined for Colonial households. As the 18th century progressed, life for planters and ship captains got downright comfortable. Yes, life in the thriving harbor towns of Bath, Beaufort, New Bern, and Halifax lacked the grandeur of London, but their denizens did their best to enjoy its importable cosmopolitan luxuries. They had indentured servants and slaves to do their bidding, imported china and furniture to fill their well-built Georgian houses, and balls and hunting parties to amuse their friends. Plantations produced two crops a year. Slaves became part of the essential fabric of life in towns and on plantations, interweaving their ancestral African identity with their workaday roles as artisans, caregivers, and farmers.

✦ SETTLEMENT AND SEDITION IN THE PIEDMONT

By the mid-18th century, the land along the coast had been bought up, so johnny-come-lately settlers turned their eyes to the Piedmont, also called the Backcountry. These folk established homesteads and farms, trading their goods at the new towns of Charlotte and Salisbury, New Garden (now Greensboro), Hillsborough, and Salem.

But life in the Piedmont could be dangerous. During the French and Indian War (1754–59) the pacifist Moravians built a fortified palisade at Bethabara to protect themselves from raids by northern Indians spurred on by the French to attack. What drove settlers to face the challenges of the frontier? Economic opportunity and religious freedom were only part of it. Many pioneers were sick of the hoity-toity attitudes and outright corruption of the colonial government and the coastal planters—the "plantocracy" who enjoyed inherited wealth and a lifestyle that depended on the labor of others, especially slaves. Call it grit, call it integrity, Backcountry folk were proud of the fact that they had created a life with the sweat of their brow.

In 1767, Governor William Tryon began to build a permanent seat of government in New Bern. This magnificent edifice, which he dubbed the "Governor's Palace," was declared one of the finest public buildings in America at the time. But when Governor Tryon levied a hefty tax to pay for his fine palace, the Regulators and other Backcountry folk flat-out refused. Most of them lived in cabins with dirt floors and slept on straw rather than in featherbeds and as for stays and powdered wigs, homespun linen and coonskin caps were more likely. When they were living like that, why should they pay for a magnificent palace they would never see? After a series of confrontations with government officials in and around Hillsborough, in 1771 the Regulators faced the Colonial militia at Alamance Battleground. Today you can pace the battlefield and imagine the gunshots and clash of weapons as the Regulators were defeated by the well-trained militia, and their leaders imprisoned or hanged.

By the early 1770s other problems were brewing for England. As events leading to the American Revolution stirred patriots' hearts, many North Carolinians, from the coast to the mountains, displayed imagination and verve in the fight for liberty.

✦ TEA, ANYONE?

By April 1774, events in Boston sent a ripple of protest up and down the Atlantic coast. Penelope Barker, a wealthy woman of Edenton, wasn't going to sit and drink tea while the men had all the fun arguing about the Boston Tea Party. In October 1774 she gathered 51 women in her elegant house overlooking Edenton Bay for a tea party of their own. They drafted and signed an agreement to support the cause of the colonies in whatever way they could. London newspapers had a heyday satirizing these colonial dames (of course, their families were secretly very proud of them). As the Revolution picked up steam, the first battle on North Carolina soil was a decisive one. If you visit Moore's Creek National Battlefield north of Wilmington at dawn, you can envision the rout of the Loyalists that was hailed as the "Lexington and Concord of the South." The Tories stormed the bridge over the creek before daybreak on February 27, 1776. They discovered too late that the Patriots had removed the bridge's planks and greased the log supports—and the Redcoats rolled into the creek in humiliating defeat. This single victory gave heart to patriots up and down the Eastern Seaboard.

Four long years later Cornwallis chose Charlotte in 1780 as the base of operations from which he would add North Carolina to his string of southern trophies. After his forces' embarrassing defeat at Kings Mountain at the hands of the colony's Overmountain men, Cornwallis gradually moved north to Guilford Courthouse, on the edge of present-day Greensboro. There Nathanael Greene, General Washington's most trusted general, had mustered the North

North Carolina Timeline

1584 English explorers led by Captains Arthur Barlowe and Philip Amadas are sent to North Carolina by Sir Walter Raleigh.

1585 The first attempt to establish an English colony is made on Roanoke Island. It fails, but an earthfort built by soldiers of fortune and named Fort Raleigh survives.

1587 A second English colony is established, with John White as leader.

1590 John White returns to Roanoke from a supply trip to England, but all the colonists have disappeared without a trace.

1663 King Charles II grants the Carolina colony to eight noblemen, known as Lords Proprietor, who had helped him regain the throne of England.

1706 Bath, the colony's first town, is founded.

1712 North Carolina and South Carolina become separate colonies.

1713 The Tuscarora War ends as Native Americans are defeated.

1729 Seven of the Lords Proprietor (with the exception of Lord Granville) sell their interests in North Carolina, and it becomes a royal colony.

1753 Moravians from Pennsylvania purchase nearly 100,000 acres from Lord Granville, which they name "Wachovia."

1754–63 The French and Indian War rages throughout the colonies.

1771 The Regulators fight the colonial militia over fair taxation and representation. It is the first act of protest against the state's colonial government.

1774 North Carolina sends delegates to the First Continental Congress.

1776 North Carolina is the first colony to vote for independence. The Battle of Miller's Creek Bridge is called the "Lexington and Concord of the South."

1781 British troops declare victory at Guilford Battleground (March 15), but suffer heavy losses. Cornwallis surrenders to General Washington at Yorktown, Virginia (October 19).

1789 North Carolina becomes the 12th state.

1792 Raleigh, the state's capital, is founded.

1808 Andrew Johnson, 17th president of the United States, is born in Raleigh.

Carolina troops. When the two forces engaged in fierce battle, the Patriots inflicted heavy casualties on the British forces. Unwilling to sacrifice more of his men, General Greene pulled back, leaving Cornwallis in possession of the field. Cornwallis had won the day, but it was a hollow victory. He headed north to Virginia, ultimately to surrender to General Washington at Yorktown.

✦ THE CHALLENGES AHEAD

Post-revolutionary days in the new state were not happy-ever-after. Lands were confiscated, former Loyalists rampaged, and state leaders struggled to establish order and establish fair representation for all North Carolinians. A big issue was the location of the state capital. In Colonial days, the capital had moved wherever the royal governor lived—from Bath to Edenton, back to Bath, to Wilmington, and finally to Tryon's Palace in New Bern. Ultimately the logic that underlies so many political decisions ruled the day. In 1792, legislators decided that the capital should be within a 10-mi radius of Isaac Hunter's tavern, which served a particularly delectable punch, and they named the new town Raleigh. In another noteworthy decision, the legislature chartered the University of North Carolina, which was built at Chapel Hill. When it opened its doors in 1795, it was the first state university in the country.

North Carolina stubbornness and independence had raised its head in the state's debate over ratifying the Constitution at Hillsborough in 1788. It finally did so in November 1789—the next-to-last state before Rhode Island.

A REGIONAL GAZETEER

▼▼

✦ THE COASTAL PLAIN

To put it mildly, Carolina had potential. The rich soil and wide grassy plains led an early settler to eloquently declare Carolina "the goodliest soil under the cope of heaven," and settlers were starry-eyed over the thought of two harvests a year in the mild climate. The tall pine forests in particular caught the eye of explorers in search of economic potential as the source of tar, pitch, and turpentine, critical naval stores for building and repairing a fleet of wooden ships. But the reality of settling the new land was more difficult. The carefully reconstructed Fort Raleigh on **Roanoke Island,** originally built in 1585 on the leeward side of Roanoke Island, is a mute witness to hardship and to the unsolved mystery of the "Lost Colony."

The Albemarle Sound, cutting into the northern Coastal Plain, is dotted with beautiful harbor towns that grew up around the rich plantation economy in the first half of the 18th century. **Bath** (the first town in North Carolina, incorporated in 1706), boasts the oldest church in the state, as well as many other early 18th-century buildings; **Edenton,** a seat of the colonial government from time to time before it found its permanent home at New Bern, boasts the 1758 Cupola House, the finest example of Jacobean architecture in the South, and many other gems along its shaded waterfront. Near Edenton is Merchants Millpond State Park, which offers a unique perspective on the Great Dismal Swamp, a place even George Washington found fascinating.

New Bern, at the mouth of the Neuse River, gained prominence in the years before the Revolution as the site chosen for the colonial capital—royal governor William Tryon's Governor's Palace was and is acclaimed as one of the finest Colonial buildings in America. Outside towns like New Bern, farms and plantations were bustling mini-towns in their own right. Along the coast, elegant **Beaufort** became famed for its high 18th-century style. South of "the graveyard of the Atlantic"—Cape Hatteras—the Cape Fear River offered deep-port moorings and shelter from storms. The ruins of Brunswick Town, which was settled in 1724 and destroyed by Cornwallis's troops during the Revolution, are dominated by the roofless walls of St. Phillip's Church. Nearby, **Wilmington,** whose Chandler's Wharf district beckons with the bustle and industry of early seafaring days, was established in 1732 and quickly became the favored port for big ships. *Towns listed: Bath, Beaufort, Creswell, Edenton, New Bern, Roanoke Island (Manteo), Washington, Wilmington, Windsor.*

✦ THE PIEDMONT

By the mid-18th century, all land on the coast had been snapped up by planters. Settlers looking for a stake of their own looked inland. They streamed into the Piedmont by two major routes: up the Cape Fear and the Pee Dee/Yadkin rivers, and from Pennsylvania down the Shenandoah Valley along the Great Wagon Road. Who came? Scotch-Irish, Quakers, German Lutherans, and others. Market towns quickly developed at Salisbury and Salem and were connected by road to **Charlotte,** settled in 1767, which linked the Backcountry to the cosmopolitan port of Charleston, South Carolina. **Hillsborough,** now a peaceful, tree-lined town, proved a hotbed of political activity in the pre-Revolutionary period. Here the Regulators confronted the colonial government with words, later facing them, unsuccessfully, with weapons in 1771 at Alamance Battleground, south of Burlington. After the Revolution the capital was built in the new town of **Raleigh.**

Many settlers valued the religious freedom the backcountry offered. The Moravians who settled first at Bethabara in 1753 and in Salem in 1771—now **Winston-Salem**'s Old Salem, the great historic restoration—came to build church-centered towns and establish industrious trading centers. Quakers settled the community of New Garden—now in **Greensboro**— in the vicinity of the modern-day Quaker-affiliated Guilford College. During the Revolution this peaceable community witnessed the turning point of the Southern Campaign at Guilford Battleground. *Towns listed: Burlington, Charlotte, Greensboro, Hillsborough, Raleigh, Winston-Salem.*

From Sound to the Sea:
Colonial Sites of the Coastal Plain
A DRIVING TOUR FROM ROANOKE ISLAND TO BEAUFORT

▼▼

Distance: approx. 160 mi (one-way)   **Time:** 5 days (4 nights)
Breaks: Spend one night on Roanoke Island (Manteo), two nights in Edenton, and one night in New Bern.

This five-day tour takes you from the earliest English settlement on Roanoke Island to the peak of colonial grandeur at Tryon Palace in New Bern. Feel free to pick and choose from the bounty of colonial sites and atmosphere as you immerse yourself in the measured charm of these beautifully preserved towns. And to put it all in context of Mother Nature, take time here and there to smell the roses breaking over a New Bern garden fence, trail an oar in the Great Dismal Swamp, or stand on the windswept shore of Albemarle Sound or the docks of Beaufort Harbor, smelling the breeze off the water and imagining the ships sailing into port, their sails full and flags fluttering in the breeze.

Reach **Roanoke Island** from Raleigh or I–95 by U.S. 64. You will find it a sleepy, well-kept place that hasn't succumbed to full-scale commercialism—much of the 12-mi-long island remains wild, with the village of **Manteo** used as the transportation hub. Fort Raleigh National Historic Site, at the north end of the island, is a re-creation of the original 1585 earthwork fortification built by the first soldiers who attempted to put down roots here. It is also the site where the Lost Colony was last seen by its governor John White in 1587. Roanoke Island Festival Park includes the *Elizabeth I* State Historic Site, a replica of the 16th-century vessel that crossed the Atlantic to the New World; a re-created Settlement Site, where interpreters describe the colonists' early life; and the Roanoke Adventure Museum, an interactive, hands-on center. Nearby, visit the lush Elizabethan Gardens, a 16th-century-style English garden, and, also in season, the spectacular outdoor drama *The Lost Colony*.

Leaving Roanoke, take U.S. 64 west to **Creswell** and follow signs to Somerset Place, an 18th-century plantation that gives credit to the slaves who made it what it was. Then drive to **Edenton** by Route 64 west, turning onto Route 32 north. Enjoy the view as you drive over the Albemarle Sound, into Edenton. This charming town will be your base of operations for two nights. Get information on walking tours and sights in Edenton at the Historic Edenton Visitor Center. While the streets of Edenton and the shore of Edenton Bay are rife with beautiful colonial and Federal houses, must-sees include the 1758 Cupola House, the 1767 Chowan Country Courthouse, the 1734 St. Paul's Church, and the 1800 James Iredell House State Historic Site. If you're ready to get away from it all, head west on Route 158 (from Edenton, take Route 32 north to U.S. 158) to **Merchants Millpond State Park,** which shares characteristics with the famous Great Dismal Swamp Park; you can canoe and wander nature trails, musing on how early mill owners and merchants shaped this thousand acres of paradise. Next morning, head west on U.S. 17 from Edenton to **Windsor** and visit Hope Plantation, whose two Colonial-era houses are both carefully furnished with the finest eastern North Carolina-made furniture and decorative arts.

From Windsor, take U.S. 17 south to **Washington,** which boasts many 18th- and early 19th-century houses in its historic district, and then head east on Route 92 to **Bath.** Stop at the

Historic Bath Visitor Center for information about walking tours within the bounds of the original 1706 town. After you pull yourself away from Bath's quiet charms, head east on Routes 92 and 306, and take the free ferry over the Pamlico River. Follow Route 306 to Route 55 west into **New Bern,** enjoying the view of the city from the bridge over the Neuse River. Signs will direct you to the historic district and the visitor center on the corner of George and Pollock Streets. Tryon Palace is the main attraction here, with the 1770 palace, its decorous gardens, and several other 18th- and early 19th-century buildings where history comes alive. If you are ready for a breath of fresh sea air, head for **Beaufort** from New Bern on U.S. 70. At the Beaufort Historical Association at 138 Turner Street, pick up a walking tour guide to the Old Town Beaufort Historic Site, with eight historic buildings from 1732 to 1859. The North Carolina Maritime Museum describes every aspect of life at sea, from whelks to whales to wooden ships. It also chronicles the fascinating 1997 discovery of what archaeologists strongly believe is Blackbeard's ship, the *Queen Anne's Revenge*. Keep an eye out—his ghost may be lurking.

In Search of Liberty
A DRIVING TOUR FROM HILLSBOROUGH TO OLD SALEM

▼▼▼

Distance: approx. 80 mi (one-way) **Time:** 3–4 days (2–3 nights)
Breaks: Spend the first night in Hillsborough and the second (and third, if you have time) in Winston-Salem.

This three- to four-day tour carries you from the first stirrings of dissent at Hillsborough to the battlefields where blood was shed and patriots' mettle was tested, to a town—Salem—whose colonial roots thrived after the Revolution. (And since history never comes in neat packages, expect forays into other times and places along the way!) To begin with, **Hillsborough,** which you can reach from I-40 at Exit 261 or I-85 at Exit 164, saw Regulators clashing with colonial tax collectors, British troops bivouacking during the Revolution, and state legislators debating the pros and cons of the Constitution. Now one of the most charming towns in North Carolina, its sleepy streets belie its passionate history. You can stroll the town on your own or in the company of a guide in colonial garb. You can also visit the reconstructed Occaneechi Village, with palisade, dwellings, and sweat lodge, on the site of an original settlement on the Eno River.

The next day, take I-85/I-40 west to **Burlington** and head south on Route 62 to Alamance Battleground. Here the Regulators squared off against royal governor William Tryon and his troops. Walk the lay of the battle lines and learn the outcome of the fight through field markers and a multimedia presentation in the visitor center. From this field of battle, head to another: Guilford Courthouse National Battleground in **Greensboro.** (Return to I-40 and head west, taking Exit 213 to Guilford College Road; continue past Guilford College, and bear right at the fork onto New Garden Road; cross Battleground Avenue.) Here British general Cornwallis held the field against General Nathanael Greene's troops, but at great cost. Don't miss Mendenhall Plantation in nearby Jamestown, a Quaker farm from 1811, which may have been a stop on the Underground Railroad. The plantation boasts a false-bottomed wagon that was used to spirit slaves North to freedom. (Take Guilford College Road south past I-40 and follow it to where it ends, and turn right on Main Street; Mendenhall Plantation is on the left.)

I-40 is also your magic carpet to **Winston-Salem** and its historic center of Salem, a pacifist Moravian town that avoided combat during the Revolution and flourished after the threat of war was over. At the living-history museum of **Old Salem,** you can visit a restored Moravian town of artisans and tradesmen. In beautiful houses of brick or wood, along streets lined with brick walkways and gaslight, authentically costumed interpreters demonstrate gunsmithing and weaving, soapmaking and gardening. But to get an idea of what Moravian life was like before there was a Salem, visit Historic Bethabara, about 8 mi north of Old Salem (follow

Cherry Street north to University Parkway and turn at the sign for Historic Bethabara). The first settlement in Wachovia, the 100,000-acre tract the Moravians purchased in 1752, Bethabara boasts foundations of the village's tavern, apothecary, and many other buildings. You can also visit a beautiful Moravian church (the Gemeinhaus) built in 1788, a potter's house from 1782, and a palisade (reconstructed) from the era of the French and Indian War. Bethabara also boasts the oldest documented colonial gardens in America.

BATH
▼▼

Surveyed and incorporated in 1705, Bath is the oldest town in North Carolina. Whenever the royal governors were in residence, early representatives of the fledgling colony convened here. The town thrived as a port until deeper harbors such as Wilmington drew away trade; its economic decline has ensured its tranquil and historic appearance. Today much of the tiny town, with its green open spaces and tall Colonial houses, occupies its original boundaries. Bath's calm demeanor belies its role at the center of some of the early 18th century's most vehement conflicts—Carey's Rebellion, fought over the governance of the Colony, and the Tuscarora Wars, in which the Tuscarora Indians rose up in brutal retaliation for years of bad treatment at the hands of the English. The town also witnessed Blackbeard's short-lived attempt at life as a law-abiding citizen in 1717, before he was bested by the Royal Navy off Ocracoke. *Contact Historic Bath Visitor Center | 207 Carteret St., Bath 27808 | 252/923–3971 | www.ah.dcr.state.nc.us.*

Bath State Historic Site. Bath's original village limits are now the boundaries of a National Register historic district. The early buildings still extant represent the wealth of the merchants and shipowners who made their fortunes from the sea: the 1751 Palmer-Marsh House, the 1830 Bonner House, and the Van Der Veer House. Bath is also home to the oldest church in North Carolina: St. Thomas Church, a modest brick structure built in 1734. Arrange a self-guided or guided tour through the visitor center. | Historic Bath Visitor Center, 207 Carteret St. | 252/923–3971 | www.ah.dcr.state.nc.us | House tours (2 homes) $2 | Visitor center Apr.–Oct., Mon.–Sat. 9–5, Sun. 1–5; Nov.–Mar., Tues.–Sat. 10–4, Sun. 1–4.

HISTORIC LODGING
Pirate's Den B & B. This house isn't old, but its location on the waterfront, mingling with its architectural elders, gives it charm beyond its years. After borrowing one of the inn's bicycles to explore Bath, you can relax in a rocking chair on the front porch. Complimentary breakfast. | 116 S. Main St. | 252/923–9571 | www.bbonline.com/nc/piratesden | 4 rooms | $75–$85 | AE, D, MC, V.

BEAUFORT
▼▼

The third oldest town in the state (1714), beautiful Beaufort is a small seaport with an impressive historic district. There are striking examples of double-porched Georgian houses and cottages that date back to the British occupation. The Caribbean influence on its houses, with their graceful proportions, is readily apparent, as is the English influence on the names of its streets and buildings. Beaufort retains much of the zest of a traditional seaport, with crafts bringing their catch to the docks on Front Street and shipbuilders plying their trade (they love an audience). One of the most notorious ships to meet its end in Beaufort's waters was Blackbeard's flagship, which he scuttled as part of his attempt to give up piracy. Archaeologists are 99.4% sure they have discovered the ship, and you can follow the story of their search—and see relics from the ship—at the North Carolina Maritime Museum. *Contact Beaufort Historic Site Visitor Center | 138 Turner St., Beaufort 28516 | 800/575–7483 | www. historicbeaufort.com.*

Beaufort Historic Site. Vintage double-decker English buses shuttle you between the historic spots of this 2-acre complex. Sights include the apothecary shop and doctor's office (circa 1859), the jail (circa 1829), and the county's oldest remaining public building (circa 1796). You can also opt to tour on foot. Of note here and throughout adjacent streets are jewels of early North Carolinian history, including the Circuit Courthouse (1796); some impressive double-porched houses, such as the Nelson House (1790) and the Rumley House (1770); the Easton House (1771), with its unique foundation of ship ballast stone; and venerable St. Paul's Church, whose construction reveals the influence of native shipbuilding trades. | 130 Turner St. | 252/728–5225 or 800/575–7483 | Bus tour $6, house tour $6, bus-walking tour $10 | Bus tours Mon., Wed., and Fri. at 11 and 1:30; house tours Mon.–Sat. at 10, 11:30, 1, and 3; visitor center Mon.–Sat. 9:30–5.

North Carolina Maritime Museum. Crammed with information about everything from shipwrecks—most notably, Blackbeard's flagship, the *Queen Anne's Revenge*—and hurricanes to saltwater estuaries and the creatures who inhabit them, this collections is replete with harpoons, duck decoys, outboard motors, pirate-related artifacts, and a vast trove of seashells. You can also see how wooden boats are built and restored in the watercraft center. Educational exhibits, programs, and field trips further enhance your visit. | 315 Front St. | 252/728–7317 | Free | Weekdays 9–5, Sat. 10–5, Sun. 1–5.

Old Burying Ground. One of the state's oldest cemeteries, the Old Burying Ground has legible dates on grave stones going back as far as 1756. The town's historical association has pamphlets to guide visitors to the more interesting graves, including that of a little girl buried in a rum keg and that of Otway Burns, the famous privateer. | Ann and Taylor Sts.

✦ ON THE CALENDAR: June **Old Homes Tour.** On the last weekend of the month some of the town's most historic (and private) homes and buildings are open for narrated tours, and there are crafts, music, demonstrations, and reenactments. Tours begin at the Beaufort Historic Site. | 800/575–7483.

HISTORIC DINING AND LODGING

Clawson's 1905 Restaurant and Pub. Antiques decorate this restaurant that was a general store in the early 1900s. Ribs and local seafood keep this restaurant crowded in summer. | 425 Front St. | 252/728–2133 | $12–$25 | D, MC, V | No lunch Sun.

Cedars Inn by-the-Sea. Two side-by-side homes (circa 1768 and 1851) make up this B&B. In the historic district, this inn is close to shops and restaurants. Rooms have private baths, many have antiques, and no two are quite alike. Complimentary breakfast. | 305 Front St. | 252/728–7036 | fax 252/728–1685 | www.cedarsinn.com | 7 rooms, 4 suites | $115–$155 | AE, D, MC, V.

BURLINGTON

▼▼▼

Burlington is the heart of the North Carolina textile belt that boomed in the 19th century. The modern town is nondescript, but its Colonial claim to fame lies south of the city at the Alamance Battleground State Historic Site. Here the Regulator Movement—the first cry for "no taxation without representation" in the American colonies—met a tragic end at the hands of the reigning militia. *Contact Burlington-Alamance County Convention and Visitors Bureau | Drawer 519, Burlington 27216 | 800/637–3804 | www.burlington-area-nc.org.*

Alamance Battleground State Historic Site. In the 1750s the settlers of the North Carolina Piedmont (considered the "backcountry" then) began to chafe at the way the county government ignored their interests while helping itself to their taxes. By the mid-1760s, a group banded together to protest these abuses and called itself the Regulators. Leading citizens all but regarded them as a "mob" and historians now believe they practiced "terrorist" activities, threatening all who obeyed British rule with violent and threatening confrontation. Leading targets of their anger were the brutal and corrupt tax collectors and bailiffs appointed by the royal governor—notoriously, the most insulting of these was the special tax levied to help pay for the Governor's Palace being built in New Bern in the most regal English style. After riots in Hillsborough and confrontations at the General Assembly in New Bern, the Regulators—some 2,000 strong—faced the state militia at Alamance Battleground but met with crushing defeat at the hands of Governor William Tryon (who promptly repaired back to his palace and began having his courts hang captured prisoners). At the same site today, you can walk the battlefield, visit the Allen House log cabin, and see a video describing the struggle that anticipated the conflict that led to American independence. | Rte. 62, 6 mi south of Burlington | 336/227–4785 | www.ah.dcr.state.nc.us/sections/hs/alamanc.htm | Free | Weekdays 9–5.

✦ ON THE CALENDAR: May **Anniversary of the Battle of Alamance.** Every year the battle is commemorated with ceremonies and reenactments of colonial domestic and military life. Call for details. | 336/227–4785.

June–Aug. **Sword of Peace.** Quakers during the American Revolution are the subject of this outdoor drama. | Historic Snow Camp Outdoor Theatre, 1 Drama Rd. (Rte. 49), Exit 145 | 336/376–6948.

CHARLOTTE

▼▼

Settled in 1765 at the convergence of two Indian trading paths, Charlotte was named for the German-born consort of George III, its county named after her place of birth, Mecklenburg. The region, however, did not remain loyal to England's king for long. In 1775, North Carolinians composed the Mecklenburg Resolves, a list of resolutions opposing the king's and Parliament's authority. While the Resolves document has been lost, scholars feel it may have strongly influenced the wording of the Declaration of Independence. During the Revolution, British general Cornwallis used Charlotte as his base of operations in 1780. After his successes in South Carolina and Georgia, he was unpleasantly surprised at the resistance he met in North Carolina, calling Charlotte "an agreeable village but damned rebellious country" and a "hornet's nest." The gold rush that began at Reed Gold Mine in 1799 brought an unprecedented period of growth and prosperity. In and around Charlotte, you can visit sites that illustrate the lively, varied society of the southern Piedmont. *Contact Visitor Center | 330 S. Tryon St., Charlotte | 704/331–2753 or 800/231–4636 | www.charlottecvb.org.*

Charlotte Museum of History and Hezekiah Alexander Homesite. This 8-acre homesite features the 1774 house of Hezekiah Alexander, a signer of the Mecklenburg Resolves and a blacksmith-turned-farmer. The imposing 2½-story house has been restored and furnished as it would have appeared in the late 18th century. A spring house and a hand-hewn log kitchen with a rock fireplace give an authentic sense of life in the Carolina backcountry. Costumed docents are happy to fill in the details. | 3500 Shamrock Dr. | 704/568–1774 | $6 | Tues.–Sun. 10–5; tours Tues.–Sun. at 1:15 and 3:15.

Historic Latta Plantation. The 1800 river plantation home of James Latta, a prosperous merchant, is set outside Charlotte in a plantation complex of detached kitchen, smokehouse, slave house, and other outbuildings. The Federal house boasts fine architectural details and carefully selected period furnishings. The house is only open by guided tour. Fields, farm animals, gardens, and interpreters in period clothing complete the experience. | 5225 Sample Rd., Huntersville | 704/875–2312 | www.lattaplantation.org | $4 | Tues.–Fri. 8–4, Sat. 12:30–4, Sun. 1:30–5.

Reed Gold Mine State Historic Site. In 1799 a lad named Conrad Reed brought home a pretty rock he found while fishing in his family's creek. A jeweler appraised it as gold and purchased it from his father for the sum of $3.50 (far below its actual worth—his father later sued and was awarded $1,000). Today at the site you can visit exhibits describing the gold rush that followed this discovery (until the 1849 California gold rush, North Carolina was the biggest gold-producing state in the country), and try your luck panning for gold. | 9621 Reed Mine Rd., Stanfield | 704/721–4653 | Free; gold panning $2 per pan | Apr.–Oct., Mon.–Sat. 9–5, Sun. 1–5; Nov.–Mar., Tues.–Sat. 10–4, Sun. 1–4.

CRESWELL

▼▼▼

A few miles outside Creswell, off U.S. 64, Somerset Place offers a unique perspective on southern plantation life, with a focus on the life and toil that were the fate of enslaved Africans. Their skill and hard work greatly contributed to the success of most plantations in the south.

Somerset Place State Historic Site. Blacksmith, gardener, canal engineer, seamstress, carpenter—these are only a few of the job descriptions of the slaves who made Somerset Place what it is today. The site describes the roles slaves played here, tracing their history from 80 Africans brought from West Africa in 1785. The 20-ft-wide canal leading to the 1830s mansion of the plantation's owners, the Collins family, was built by estate retainers in the 1780s. The mansion and outbuildings are open for guided tours. | 2572 Lake Shore Rd., Creswell | 252/797–4560 | fax 252/797–4171 | www.ah.dcr.state.nc.us | Free | Apr.–Oct., Mon.–Sat. 9–5, Sun. 1–5; Nov.–Mar., Tues.–Sat. 10–4, Sun. 1–4

EDENTON

▼▼▼

Incorporated in 1722, Edenton was the seat of North Carolina's Colonial government from 1722 to 1757 and, then again, in 1740–41 and 1743. It was an important port for the plantations of the Albemarle region, shipping out goods to Virginia, New England, and the West Indies. Consequently, the merchants and planters of Edenton enjoyed a comfortable lifestyle, with some of the best architecture in the Colony, stylish furniture, fine imported tablewares, wines from Europe, and tea from the Orient. In the 19th century Edenton lost ground to other harbors such as Elizabeth City and Wilmington, and it entered a decline, one that fortunately contributed to the preservation of so much of its early architecture and allows Edenton's quiet streetscapes to still evoke the grace and charm of the 18th century. Examples of period architecture are spectacular, from the 1758 Cupola House overlooking Edenton Bay; the Penelope Barker House, where in 1774 Penelope and 51 of the ladies of Edenton signed a declaration that they would support the American cause in whatever way possible; the 1767 Chowan County Courthouse, considered one of the finest examples of Georgian architecture in the South (set overlooking a green leading down to the bay); and the house of legislator James Iredell, a well-appointed homestead. Tours of the historic district and the sites listed below begin at the Historic Edenton Visitor Center. *Contact Edenton-Chowan Tourism Authority | 116 E. King St., Edenton 27932 | 800/775–0011 | www.edenton.com.*

Historic Edenton Visitor Center. This historic district has a superb grouping of period edifices and attractions. The hours of admission listed here are for all the sites in the district, found below. | 108 N. Broad St. | 252/482–2637 | www.ah.dcr.state.nc.us | Guided tour $6 | Apr.–Oct., Mon.–Sat. 9–5, Sun. 1–5; Nov.–Mar., Tues.–Sat. 10–4, Sun. 1–4. Last tour begins 1 hr before closing.

Chowan County Courthouse. As well as being one of the most refined examples of Georgian architecture in the South, this building is the oldest courthouse in continuous use in North Carolina—the courtroom witnessed many a debate leading up to the Revolution. The simplicity of the courthouse exterior belies the elegance of the chambers within, which are stylishly outfitted with gracefully proportioned columns and beautiful wainscoting. | E. King St. | 252/482–2637 | $7.

Cupola House. The overhanging, or jettied, upper story marks this structure as a rare example of Jacobean architecture in the South. Insides, salons are paneled and decorated with elaborate woodwork. While some elements of the house may be older, the house is dated to 1758. | W. Water and S. Broad Sts. | 252/482–2637.

James Iredell House. James Iredell, like many an Edenton resident, was a trendsetter. His forte was not fashion, but legislature: he was the first state attorney general in North Carolina and was appointed by George Washington to the first U.S. Supreme Court. His house, built in 1773, and outbuildings form an excellent example of a late 18th-century homestead. | 105 E. Church St. | 252/482–2637.

St. Paul's Episcopal Church. Nestled in a tree-lined cemetery, St. Paul's has the oldest charter and is the second oldest standing church in the state. The congregation still uses liturgical silver from 1725. | W. Church and S. Broad Sts. | 252/482–2637 | Free.

Merchants Millpond State Park—Great Dismal Swamp. An enigmatic feature of the state's coastal plain that has caught the imagination of generations of explorers and romantics of all stripes is the Great Dismal Swamp, which straddles the North Carolina–Virginia line. The vast forests of cypress and tupelo trees that rise from its shallows have swallowed explorers, hidden runaway slaves, and inspired entrepreneurs. George Washington invested in the Dismal Swamp Land Company in the 1760s, hoping to turn a profit from the swamp's lumber. The swamp proved to be too much of a challenge, however, and has survived efforts to log it, canal it, drain it, and civilize it. A separate but similar watershed is Merchants Millpond State Park, near Sunbury, outside Gatesville. Here, a coastal pond and a swamp forest mingle to create one of the state's rarest ecological communities. The 760-acre mill pond is stocked with a variety of fish, which makes flyfishing a popular pastime here. For a fee, campers and canoeists are welcome to enjoy the eerie beauty of the park, where towering trees are draped in Spanish moss. | 71 U.S. 158 E, Gatesville | 252/357–1191 | fax 252/357–0149 | www.ils.unc.edu/parkproject/memi.html | Free | Daily 8–sunset.

HISTORIC LODGING

Lords Proprietors' Inn. Housed in three historic buildings, including an 1801 house, this B&B shows extraordinary attention to detail—note the guest beds, many of them four-posters, all crafted by a local cabinetmaker. Complimentary breakfast. | 300 N. Broad St. | 252/482–3641 | fax 252/482–2432 | www.lordspropedenton.com | 16 rooms | $120–$170 | AE, D, MC, V.

GREENSBORO
▼▼

Incorporated in 1808, Greensboro was named for General Nathanael Greene. The area had been settled in the mid-18th century by Quakers and Scots-Irish. The Quakers of New Garden, near modern-day Guilford College, were active in the Underground Railroad from the 1830s. Later in the 19th century, Greensboro became an important textile-producing town with a lively economy. *Contact Greensboro Area Convention and Visitors Bureau | 317 S. Greene St., Greensboro 27401 | 336/274–2282 or 800/344–2282 | www.greensboronc.org.*

Guilford Courthouse National Military Park. General Greene's troops faced British forces at this site in March 1781. While Greene allowed Cornwallis to take command of the battle-field, he had inflicted such losses on the British general and his men that they could hardly claim it as a victory. The battle is commemorated here with a film and exhibits of arms and uniforms, walking trails of key points in the conflict, and 28 monument markers. Occasionally, costumed reenactors bring the battle to life. | 2332 New Garden Rd. | 336/288–1776 | www.nps.gov/guco | Free | Daily 8:30–5.

Mendenhall Plantation. This offers a unique perspective on the "Other South"—a settlement run by early 19th-century Quaker dissenters who lived and practiced anti-slavery and paci-fist views. The plantation has a fine brick house and a variety of outbuildings, including an 1811 school house, spring house, barn, and old medical school house. In the barn is a false-bottomed wagon used to carry slaves north to freedom. The plantation also includes 3 acres of meadow and walking trails. In September, a Heritage Day annually presents living-history Quaker crafts, food, and demonstrations. | 603 W. Main St., Jamestown | 336/545–5315 | www.triadneighbors.com/mendenhall | $2 | Tues.–Fri. 11–2, Sat. 1–4, Sun. 2–4.

Tannenbaum Park. Adjoining Guilford Courthouse National Military Park, this site draws you into the lives of Colonial-era settlers. With advance notice, costumed reenactors will escort you through exhibits at the Colonial Heritage Center. Visit the restored 1778 Hoskins House (tours by appointment), with its blacksmith shop and barn. | 2200 New Garden Rd. | 336/545–5315 | Free | Apr.–Nov., Tues.–Sat. 9–5, Sun. 1–5; Dec.–Mar., Tues.–Sat. 10–4:30, Sun. 1–4:30.

HILLSBOROUGH
▼▼

Hillsborough's sleepy demeanor, with tree-lined streets of 18th- and 19th-century houses, belies its turbulent role in North Carolina history. Rioting Regulators disrupted court sessions and dragged the hated tax collector David Fanning through the streets by his heels. During the Revolution, British troops bivouacked here, bringing a threat of devastation that fortu-nately never materialized. Once independence was won, Hillsborough unsuccessfully sought the honor of being chosen for the new state's capital, but it proved to be the site of debate over ratifying the Constitution in 1788–89. Top historic landmarks include the 1790 Alexan-der Dickson House (which houses the visitor center) and the Orange County Historical Museum. *Contact Orange County Visitor Center/Alexander Dickson House | 150 E. King St., Hillsborough 27278 | 919/732–7741 | fax 919/732–6322 | www.historichillsborough.org.*

Occaneechi Village. When explorer John Lawson first opened this region to European settlers in 1701, the people who greeted him were the Occaneechi tribes, Today, their contact-period Saponi settlement has been excavated and reconstructed on its original loca-tion on the banks of the Eno River. Explore the palisade, dwellings, and a sweat lodge and learn about the remarkable archaeological excavations that enabled the site to be recon-structed in its original form. | S. Cameron St. | 919/304–3723 | www.occaneechi-saponi.org | Free | Daily during daylight hrs.

Orange County Historical Society. Explore the region's Colonial and Revolutionary periods—with special emphasis on the Regulators' uprising—through this museum's regular displays and changing exhibits. | 201 N. Churton St. | 919/732–2201 | www.historichillsborough.org | Free | Tues.–Sun. 11–4.

University of North Carolina at Chapel Hill. A short drive from Hillsborough, this famous insti-tute of learning was the first state university to open its doors to students, in 1795. Its streets may now be dotted with Walkmen and Mohawks, but you can still pace its stately Green and admire the "neat and plain" architecture of its early buildings, especially Old East, built in 1793, and South Building, completed in 1814. The Visitor Center offers a guided walk-ing tour weekdays at 1:30; self-guided tour maps are available. The Wilson Library's North Carolina Collection presents exhibitions on early North Carolina history, from Native American peoples to Colonial settlement to the Gold Rush era. The Walter Raleigh Rooms trace the life and tragic end of the daring explorer who masterminded the first Carolina settlements. | Wilson Library, South Rd. | 919/962–1172 | www.lib.unc.edu/ncc/gallery.html | Free | Weekdays 9–5, Sat. 9–1, Sun. 1–5.

HISTORIC LODGING

Inn at Teardrops. This 1768 saltbox, named for the distinctive shapes in its lead-framed, front-door windows, offers a charming pied-à-terre in the heart of historic Hillsborough. Restaurant. | 6329 Glenwood Ave. | 919/732–1120 | fax 919/571–8385 | 12 rooms | $49–$79 | AE, D, DC, MC, V.

NEW BERN
▼▼

Home to Tryon Palace—the "most beautiful building of Colonial America"—and dotted with more than 150 sites included in the National Register of Historic Places, New Bern is a place where History is taken seriously. The town, the second oldest in North Carolina, was originally settled in 1710 by Swiss and German explorers led by Christopher de Graffenried, who named it after his hometown in Switzerland. It grew to prominence when it was chosen as the permanent site of the colonial government under William Tryon, who built an extraordinarily elegant Georgian edifice to serve as the Governor's Palace. Symbol of the reigning Tidewater aristocracy, "the governor's folly"—as it was called by many settlers in the Backcountry—was funded in part by settlers forced to pay a hefty tax for its building. The cost of the mansion brought the Regulator Movement to a head in an early revolt against "taxation without representation" that presaged the American Revolution.

The royal governor's troubles were not over after the Regulators were squelched. In 1774, when Tryon's successor Josiah Martin convened the Colonial Assembly, he discovered they had switched sides—the entire Assembly was now the Provincial Congress, ready to send delegates to Philadelphia to build a dream of freedom. After the Revolution and the move of the state capital to Raleigh in 1794, Tryon Palace, as it is now called, was destroyed by fire. It was rebuilt in the 1950s from the original plans in the most ambitious restoration of its kind. *Contact Convention and Visitors Bureau | 314 S. Front St., New Bern 28560 | 252/637–9400.*

Attmore-Oliver House. Built in 1790, this house museum shows off fine 18th- and 19th-century furnishings and a lovely antique doll collection. | 511 Broad St. | 252/638–8558 | newbern-history.org | $2.50 | Tues.–Sat. 1–4:30.

First Presbyterian Church. Built between 1819 and 1822 as a handsome example of Federal architecture, the church was used as a hospital during the Civil War. | 418 New St. (near Middle St.) | 252/637–3270 | Free | Mon.–Wed., Fri. 9–2; Sun. services 8:30 and 11.

New Bern Academy Museum. Founded in 1764, the Academy is one of the oldest secondary schools in the country. The museum, set in an 1809 school building, traces the community's history from the early 1700s to the Civil War. Exhibits change periodically. | Corner of Hancock and New Sts. | 252/672–1690 | Free with ticket to Tryon Palace. | Weekdays 10–4.

Tryon Palace. When it was first built in 1770, William Tryon's Governor's Palace was considered the finest example of Georgian architecture in the colonies. In many ways, it still is. Residence of North Carolina's royal governors, then statehouse until the capital moved from New Bern to Raleigh, this magnificent redbrick and white-sash residence is the quintessence of Neoclassical symmetry, grandly bookended by two colonnaded wings and fronted by an allée of trees, forecourt green, and grand iron gates. Tryon had his own English architect, John Hawks, at hand when he arrived to rule over North Carolina in 1764. The enormous expenses incurred to build this sumptuous pile meant supplemental taxes; Before long, the Regular movement was formed to protest these taxes and soon met met with bloody suppression. Tryon added injury to insult by living in the house for only a year before decamping to New York where he had been appointed governor. Dining at the "Pallace" in 1791, George Washington remarked that it was "hastening to Ruins"; seven years later it was largely destroyed by fire. A multimillion dollar restoration in the 1950s, however, has re-created some of the splendor enjoyed by William Tryon. Furnished with furniture and decorative arts appropriate for a representative of the English Crown, the interior is suavely ornamented with grand doorways, impressive mouldings, and elegant antiques. The beautiful formal gardens were probably never planted, since Tryon left before doing so, but they are based on detailed plans he commissioned. A visit to Tryon Palace includes the elegant 1779 home of John Wright Stanley, a wealthy merchant; the Dixon-Stevenson House, built between 1826 and 1833, which was the home of a mayor of New Bern; and the 1816 home of wagon and carriage builder Robert Hay. | 600 block of Pollock St. | 252/514–4900 or 800/767–1560 | www.tryonpalace. org | $15; garden only, $8 | Tues.–Sat. 9–5, Sun. 1–5.

✦ ON THE CALENDAR: Apr. **Historic Homes and Gardens Tour.** Sponsored by New Bern Historical Society every spring. | 252/638–8558 | newbernhistory.org.

Dec. **Tryon Palace Holiday Candlelight Tours.** Period decorations adorn the interior of the fabulous Tryon Palace for the holidays. | 252/514–4900.

RALEIGH

▼▼▼

In 1792, the site for the new state capital was carved out of farmland in a spot accessible to both the Piedmont and the coastal plain. The city's original plan is still visible in the blocks around the State House (the original state house burned in 1831; this structure dates from 1840). *Contact Greater Raleigh Convention and Visitors Bureau | Box 1879, Raleigh 27602 | 919/ 834–5900 or 800/849–8499. Visitor Center | Bank of America Building, 421 Fayetteville St. Mall, Suite 1505 | 919/834–5900 or 800/849–8499 | www.raleighcvb.org.*

Joel Lane House. Dating from 1760, this is the oldest house in Raleigh. Joel Lane entertained state legislators at his house on a number of occasions, which may have led to their purchase of 1,000 acres of his land for the capital. Costumed docents tell the story and show the authentically restored house and period gardens. | 728 W. Hargett St. | 919/833–3431 | $3 | Mar.–mid-Dec., Tues.–Fri. 10–2; 1st and 3rd Sat. 1–4.

Mordecai Historic Park. The centerpiece of this site is the Mordecai House, built in 1785, once a farmstead that with its land was gradually enveloped by the sprawling capital. Other historic buildings have been located on the site, including the cabin in which Andrew Jackson was born in 1808. | 1 Mimosa St. | 919/834–4844 | $4 | Mon. and Wed.–Sat. 10–3, Sun. 1–3.

North Carolina Museum of History. Here old meets new—art and artifacts are introduced through audiovisual programs and interactive exhibits. Learn about Colonial-era history or folkways of the Appalachians, or explore the impact world events have had on North Carolina. | 5 E. Edenton St. | 919/715–0200 | http://ncmuseumofhistory.org | Free | Tues.–Sat. 9–5, Sun. noon–5.

State Capitol. A beautifully preserved example of Greek Revival architecture from 1840, the capitol occupies the location of the original 1794 state house. It once housed all the functions of state government, but today it is part museum, part executive offices. | Capitol Sq., 1 E. Edenton St. | 919/733–4994 | Free | Mon.–Sat. 9–5, Sun. 1–4.

ROANOKE ISLAND (MANTEO)

As site of the legendary "lost colony of Roanoke," this island bears strange and mysterious witness to the very first English settlements in the New World, both in its monuments and along its windswept coastline. The isle's most prominent towns—Manteo and Wanchese—are named for the Roanoke Indian leaders who met the first settlers and traveled to England as exotic trophies (examples of what was then called the "noble savage"). While the first explorers who landed on the island in 1584 declared it a "goodly land" filled with valuable timber, wild grapes, and game, the initial attempts to establish a foothold on the new continent were famously beset by tragedy. The soldiers of a 1585 expedition built a fort, but only occupied it for a winter before they departed, driven away by exposure and the lack of supplies. A 1586 expedition of 15 men—attacked by native tribes in retaliation for English attacks by earlier expeditions—fled the site in a boat and were never seen again.

Then Sir Walter Raleigh, favorite of Queen Elizabeth I, strode upon the stage. Although the great English explorer never set foot in the New World, he was determined to claim its riches for the English crown. He masterminded yet another expedition that included 117 men, women, and boys. Soon after they settled in at Fort Raleigh in August 1587, the first English child was born in the New World: Virginia Dare. Shortly thereafter, the colony's leader, John White, sailed back to England to obtain supplies and make a report to Raleigh, but—due to piracy, bad bouts of weather, and the battles with the Spanish Armada—could not return for three years. When he did, he found his colony abandoned, the settlers vanished without a trace. In fact, the enigmatic letters "CRO" were scratched on a tree, "CROATAN" on another, but no obvious signs of distress were to be discerned and searches in the nearby island of Croatan for settlers were in vain. Nowhere to be found was the sign of a Maltese cross, the agreed-upon symbol to declare that woes had forced an abrupt departure from the colony. Then again, most of the houses had been leveled.

What happened to the Lost Colonists, as they have been called? What was the fate of little Virginia Dare? Were these first settlers lost at sea? Did they die in an attack? Did they live with the Indians, gradually merging their lives with theirs? The mystery may never be solved. Historians have long felt that rising tensions between the colonists—who had grown dependent on food supplies of native Indians, run out of trinkets as gifts, and had introduced smallpox to the tribal population—and the natives erupted; the English were probably killed or taken into enforced slavery. The latest attempt, outlined in Lee Miller's *Roanoke: Solving the Mystery of the Lost Colony* (2001), lays the blame with political treachery in the inner circle of Queen Elizabeth I. Today, Manteo and Roanoke Island offer many keys for you to unlock the past and explore its mysteries: Fort Raleigh; Roanoke Island Festival Park with its replica of the 16th-century ship the *Elizabeth II* and other attractions; the Elizabethan Gardens; and the *Lost Colony* theater production, which has been staged every summer since 1937. *Contact Dare County Tourist Bureau | 704 S. U.S. 64/264, Manteo 27954 | 252/473–2138 or 800/446–6262 | fax 252/473–5106 | www.outerbanks.org/visitor-info.*

Elizabethan Gardens. Part of the Fort Raleigh National Historic Site, these gardens are a lush re-creation of a 16th-century English garden, established as a memorial to the first English colonists who arrived between 1584 and 1587. | 1411 U.S. 64/264, Manteo | 252/473–3234 | $5 | Mar.–Nov., daily 9–5; Dec.–Feb., weekdays 9–4.

Fort Raleigh National Historic Site. To unlock the mystery of the "Lost Colony of Roanoke," all historical Sherlock Holmeses will want to first venture here, where the first English attempts (1585–87) at colonizing the New World were made. These initial settlements, sponsored by Sir Walter Raleigh, led to the ultimate disappearance of 117 men, women, and children. Today, at this restoration of the original 1585 earthworks that mark the beginning of English Colonial history in America, you can view an orientation film before taking a guided tour of the fort. At the visitor center, enjoy the Elizabethan Room, adorned with oak panel-ing and a stone fireplace from a 16th century house of the kind lived in by the original Roanoke colony investors. Artifacts from the site and copies of the watercolors that John White created help fill in details. Overlooking the sound, the fort was surrounded by a moat and encircled by a parapet that was shaped like a square with pointed bastions on two sides, with an octag-onal bastion on the third. Historians believe that the "Cittie of Ralegh"—the settlement of houses—stood near the road leading from the earthwork entrance. A visitor center nature trail leads to an outlook over Roanoke Sound. Presented in the adjacent Waterside Theater is a must-see for all interested in American history: Paul Green's *The Lost Colony,* a fascinating historical pageant which reenacts during summer months the story of the first colonists in a magnificent outdoor theater. The saga of Raleigh's Roanoke Voyages is told through music and drama against a thrilling scenic backdrop that re-creates the first wooden settlement. Offer-ing a stark contrast to the bleak and harsh landscape the colonists must have endured are re-created Elizabethan-style gardens, set on the outskirts of the park site. | 1411 U.S. 64/264, Manteo | 252/473–5772 | www.nps.gov/fora | Free | Daily 9–5; hrs may be extended June–Aug.

Roanoke Island Festival Park. The centerpiece of this park is the *Elizabeth II,* floating proudly along the waterfront in Manteo. Costumed interpreters conduct tours of the 69-ft-long ship, a re-creation of a 16th-century vessel (except when it is on educational voyages in the off-season—call ahead). The park also includes a re-created Settlement Site, where interpreters describe the colonists' early life in the ringing tones of Elizabethan speech, and the Roanoke Adventure Museum, a hands-on center where visitors can explore the past. | 1 Festival Park | 252/475–1506; 252/475–1500 information | www.roanokeisland.com | $8 | Apr.–Oct., daily 9–6; Mar. and Nov.–Dec., daily 10–5.

WASHINGTON
▼▼

This port town, which played a strategic role during the War of Independence, calls itself "the original Washington" because it was the first town in the nation named for Gen. George Washington. Its historic district along the Pamlico River, which is listed in the National Register of Historic Places, includes some 30 noteworthy structures dating from the late 1700s. *Contact Washington–Beaufort County Tourism Development Authority | Box 665, Washington 27889 | 800/999–3857 | www.washnctourism.com.*

Historic Washington. The Arts Council suggests that you begin your walking tour of this nation-ally noted district at the old Atlantic Coast Line railroad station. As you wend your way through the riverside area, you'll see nearly 30 buildings constructed when George Washington himself was alive and probably the best-known person in the young United States. | Main, 2nd, and Gladden Sts. | 252/946–9168 or 800/999–3857 | Free | Daily.

WILMINGTON
▼▼

Founded in 1734 as the best deep-water port on the North Carolina coast, Wilmington built its fortune on shipping rice and other products of the Cape Fear region. Thanks to its strate-gic location, the small but busy city played a major role in the American Revolution. It served as Corwallis's headquarters as he prepared the fateful march to Yorktown. The 200-block historic district, the largest in the state, is not far from the tannin-colored Cape Fear River. At the Visitors Bureau you can pick up a self-guided tour map of historic sites. *Contact Cape Fear Coast Convention and Visitors Bureau | 24 N. 3rd St., Wilmington 28401 | 800/222–4757 | www.cape-fear.nc.us.*

Brunswick Town–Fort Anderson State Historic Site. Explore the excavations of a Colonial port town, see the remains of Fort Anderson, a Civil War earthworks fort, and picnic. Founded in 1726, the 18th-century seaport village of Brunswick was named in homage to the German state of Brunswick, one of the fatherlands of George I, the German-born King of England. Always overshadowed by bustling Wilmington, the town was decimated by, in turn, Spanish privateers, a hurricane, and British troops, then abandoned after 1776. Ruins of the town buildings includes those of the courthouse and inn, while towering over all is St. Philips Church. The visitor center has exhibits and artifacts. | 8884 St. Phillips Rd. SE, Winnabow | 910/371–6613 | www.ah.dcr.state.nc.us/sections/hs/brunswic | Free | Apr.–Oct., Mon.–Sat. 9–5, Sun. 1–5; Nov.–Mar., Tues.–Sat. 10–4, Sun. 1–4.

Burgwin-Wright Museum House. In April 1781, the British leader General Cornwallis used this three-story 1770 house as his headquarters. It has been restored to the style of a Colonial gentleman's town house and includes a period garden. | 224 Market St. | 910/762–0570 | $6 | Feb.–late Dec., Tues.–Sat. 10–4; last tour at 3:30.

Cape Fear Museum. The oldest history museum in the state traces the natural, cultural, and social history of the lower Cape Fear region from its beginnings to the present. | 814 Market St. | 910/341–4350 | $4 | Tues.–Sat. 9–5, Sun. 2–5.

Moore's Creek National Battlefield. American patriots defeated the Loyalists here in 1776. You can view an audiovisual program and exhibits in the small museum, go off on your own self-guided history tours, or stroll along the nature trails. | 200 Moore's Creek Rd., Currie | 910/283–5591 | Free | Daily 9–5.

✦ ON THE CALENDAR: Dec. **Old Wilmington by Candlelight Tour.** The holly, the ivy, and all the other signs of the season await on tours of holiday-bedecked homes and churches, with horse-drawn carriage rides through the historic downtown area, which is lit by luminaria. | 910/762–0492.

HISTORIC LODGING
Taylor House. When you step from the cobblestone streets and into this Classic Revival house you'll find that many architectural elements are as they always were: a large open staircase, stained-glass windows, parquet floors, along with fireplaces and the original claw-foot tubs in the guest rooms. Complimentary breakfast. | 14 N. 7th St. | 800/382–9982 | www.bbonline.com | 5 rooms | $110–$225 | AE, MC, V.

WINDSOR
▼▼

Originally called Gray's Landing, Windsor had its origin as a river port, exporting turpentine, pitch, and agricultural products from the surrounding countryside. *Contact Windsor Chamber of Commerce | 102 S. York St., Windsor 27983 | 252/794–4277 | www.albemarle-nc.com/windsor.*

Historic Windsor. Tour a variety of 18th- and early 19th-century buildings as part of a walking tour through the heart of Windsor. | 252/946–9168 or 800/999–3857 | www.albemarle-nc.com/windsor/history | Free | Daily.

Hope Plantation. Built in 1803 by Gov. David Stone, the clapboard mansion has Federal and Georgian architecture, the governor's library, and period furnishings. You can also visit an earlier house, the 1763 King-Bazemore House, a gambrel-roofed, brick and clapboard structure. | 132 Hope House Rd. | 252/794–3140 | $6.50 | Mon.–Sat. 10–5, Sun. 2–5.

WINSTON-SALEM

In 1753, a band of Moravians carved out 100,000 acres of wilderness to build Utopia—a planned community where God's laws and man's ways would be one. A German Protestant group with roots in the 1400s in the Czech lands, the Moravians dedicated the work of their hands to God, and the result was the well-run town of Salem, occupied in 1772. The first settlement of Bethabara and other villages did well, but Salem thrived as a center of trade and craftmanship. Today, Old Salem is one of the most picturesque and alluring of all historic North Carolina restorations.

In the eyes of outsiders, or "Strangers," as they were called, the hard-working Moravians enjoyed a high standard of living. Girls were educated in their own school and women had a say in community affairs. Music and the arts had a prominent role in daily life. Artisans created beautiful furniture, pottery, and metalwares that were prized across the backcountry. The town's doctor was highly skilled and kept up with scientific breakthroughs in Europe. The price, as outsiders saw it, was conformity: Moravians had to accept the will of the church, from a simple style of dress to the work they did to the man or woman they could marry. The Moravians taught the slaves in their community to read and write, and encouraged them to convert to the Moravian faith. While originally black and white worshiped side by side, in 1821 a separate church was built for the black community. The town of Winston was founded in 1851 as the county seat, and the two communities merged as Winston-Salem in 1913. The visitor center offers materials to help you explore the region, which you can peruse while enjoying a sampling of traditional Moravian sugar cookies! *Contact Greater Winston-Salem Convention and Visitors Bureau | 601 N. Cherry St., Winston-Salem | 336/ 728–4200 or 800/331–7018 | fax 336/728–4220 | www.wscvb.com.*

Historic Bethabara Park. The settlement where the Moravians first put down roots in North Carolina in 1753, this park now contains re-created colonial gardens, foundations of the original houses and workshops, a re-created French and Indian War palisade, and the 1788 Gemeinhaus, or community church, all combining to create a rich impression of a frontier settlement. Nature trails also immerse you in the forests and wildlife that met the Moravians on their arrival here 250 years ago. | 2147 Bethabara Rd. | 336/924–8191 | www.bethabarapark. org | $1; park grounds free | Apr.–Nov., weekdays 9:30–4:30, weekends 1:30–4:30; grounds open year-round.

Old Salem. A living history museum with many faces, Old Salem offers a panoply of 19 restored buildings, many in the simple style Colonial-period Germans favored (needless to say, offering a dramatic contrast to the florid display at New Bern's Tryon Palace). Costumed interpreters demonstrate varied aspects of life here in the 18th and early 19th centuries. Men and boys lived and worked in the Single Brothers House, where you can explore a tinsmith's shop, joiners' and turners' rooms, and communal Saal worship space. Family homes, such as the snug, clapboard 1771 Miksch House and the stylish Federal 1814 Vogler House, open a window onto domestic life. George Washington slept and dined at the 1784 Salem Tavern—built carefully on the outskirts of the community to keep "Strangers" from the brethren (note also the lack of windows on the streetfront first floor in order to keep community members from getting any ideas from the outside world). A shoemaker's, gunsmith's, blacksmith's, and many other shops reveal the many trades the Moravians flourished at. Finally, St. Philip's Moravian Church, built in 1861, is the oldest African-American church building in North Carolina, and its predecessor, the 1821 Negro Moravian Church, has been reconstructed. | 600 S. Main St. | 336/721–7300 or 888/653–7253 | www.oldsalem.org | Old Salem alone, $15; all-in one ticket with Museum of Early Southern Decorative Arts and the Toy Museum, $20 (multiday passes also available) | Mon.–Sat. 9:30–4:30, Sun. 1:30–4:30.

At the **Children's Museum at Old Salem** the message is: Do touch! Do climb on the furniture! In fact, make furniture, cook over a pretend open hearth, and dress as the Moravians did 200 years ago. This hands-on experience lets kids of all ages explore the past—their way. | 924 S. Main St. | 336/721–7300 or 888/653–7253 | $4; with Old Salem ticket, $2 | Tues.–Sat. 9–5, Sun.–Mon. 1–5.

With a courtly bow, enter the world of Southern decorative arts at the **Museum of Early Southern Decorative Arts (MESDA).** Be prepared to be whisked from Virginia in 1660 to Charleston, South Carolina in 1820. The museum, part of Old Salem, has gathered furniture, paintings, ceramics, silver, and textiles in 24 accurately appointed period rooms representing the varied regions of the South. More treasures are showcased in six galleries. | 924 S. Main St. | 336/721–7360 | $10; combination ticket with Old Salem $20 | Mon.–Sat. 9:30–3:30, Sun. 1:30–3:30.

Opened in November 2002, the **Toy Museum at Old Salem** is a stellar collection that brings together 1,700 years of toys and playthings, including a rare regional collection of Moravian dolls and other objects. | 924 S. Main St. | 336/721–7300 or 888/653–7253 | fax 336/721–7335 | Part of all-in-one Old Salem ticket | Mon.–Sat. 9–5, Sun. 1–5.

✦ ON THE CALENDAR: Mar.–Apr. **Moravian Easter Sunrise Service.** Thousands of people make their way to the restored town of Old Salem for the hour-long predawn service that, as tradition dictates, begins in front of the Home Moravian Church and proceeds to God's Acre graveyard as the sun rises. The ritual, which takes place rain or shine, uses hymns, brass instruments, and the spoken word. | 529 S. Church St. | 336/722–6171.

Dec. **Old Salem Christmas.** Hear the sounds and savor the smells of Christmas, as the Moravians would have celebrated 200 years ago. | 600 S. Main St. | 336/721–7300 or 888/653–7253.

HISTORIC DINING AND LODGING

Salem Tavern Restaurant. When you dine here, you're carrying on a tradition of hospitality that reaches back, in these very walls, to 1816. This frame house was built as an extension of the original Salem Tavern, which you can visit as part of the restoration's tour. Costumed servers offer a variety of fare, including some dishes inspired by old Moravian recipes. In summer, you can dine out on the porch. | 736 S. Main St. | 336/748–8585 | $12–$20 | AE, MC, V.

Zevely House. Once set in a remote part of town, this early 19th-century farmhouse is now in the heart of Winston-Salem. Enjoy dining in authentically furnished rooms by an open fire. | 901 W. 4th St. | 336/725–6666 | $20–$30 | AE, MC, V | Closed Mon.

Augustus T. Zevely Inn. In the 1840s, Dr. Zevely took in guests who could not find a bed in the tavern across the street. Now this bed-and-breakfast in the heart of Old Salem carries on the tradition. The guest rooms have been restored and furnished with reproductions of Moravian furniture. Complimentary breakfast. No kids under 16. | 803 S. Main St. | 336/748–9299 | fax 336/721–2211 | 11 rooms, 1 suite | $80–$135; $205 suite | AE, MC, V.

Brookstown Inn. When this building was constructed as a cotton mill in 1837, it ushered the industrial era to Salem. Now, it offers comfortable respite for busy travelers, including wine and cheese served every evening. Early American furnishings keep the interiors true to the mill's origins in the 1830s. Complimentary breakfast. | 200 Brookstown Ave. | 336/725–1120 or 800/845–4262 | fax 336/773–0147 | 40 rooms, 31 suites | $125; $135–$150 suites | AE, DC, MC, V.

By Joyce Eisenberg

Pennsylvania

The Great Declaration

Many fine ingredients were mixed into the hearty stew that was Colonial Pennsylvania. The Germans poured in industriousness and agricultural know-how; the Quakers added equal measures of equality, simplicity, community, and peace; and the Anglicans contributed the spices of style and sophistication. While the stew simmered, Philadelphia became the metropolis of the British colonies and a center of intellectual and commercial life. Who knows? Perhaps it was the radical thinking of the Quakers—who treated Indians as equals and made the earliest protests against slavery—and the intellectual inquiry that Benjamin Franklin encouraged among members of his American Philosophical Society that allowed grumblings over Britain's policies to ferment into the first cries for independence. The questions are there to be mulled over as you walk through the birthplace of the country, "America's most historic square mile," Philadelphia's Independence National Historical Park. Here, in Independence Hall, the Founding Fathers signed the Declaration of Independence one July (even though it was sweltering hot that week, the draftees of the Declaration kept the windows of the hall closed as they didn't want anyone to overhear) and later adopted the Constitution. Here, in Congress Hall, scene of George Washington's second presidential inauguration, debates rang the rafters between 1790 and 1800 when the city functioned as the national capital. Nearby at old City Hall, the first U.S. Supreme Court met. Clearly if seeing such sights as the Liberty Bell Pavilion and the Betsy Ross House doesn't bring out the gee-whiz patriotism in your nine-year-old, nothing will.

Though its homes were handsome and its public buildings finely proportioned, what was most striking about the colony of Pennsylvania was its tolerance for religious diversity; it was home to an alphabet soup of worshipers—from Moravians to Mennonites to Methodists. The atmosphere afforded by William Penn's liberal government and the luxury of time for intellectual pursuits that came with prosperity allowed Philadelphia to earn the title of the "Athens of America" for its rich cultural life. While Penn was the colony's landlord, Benjamin

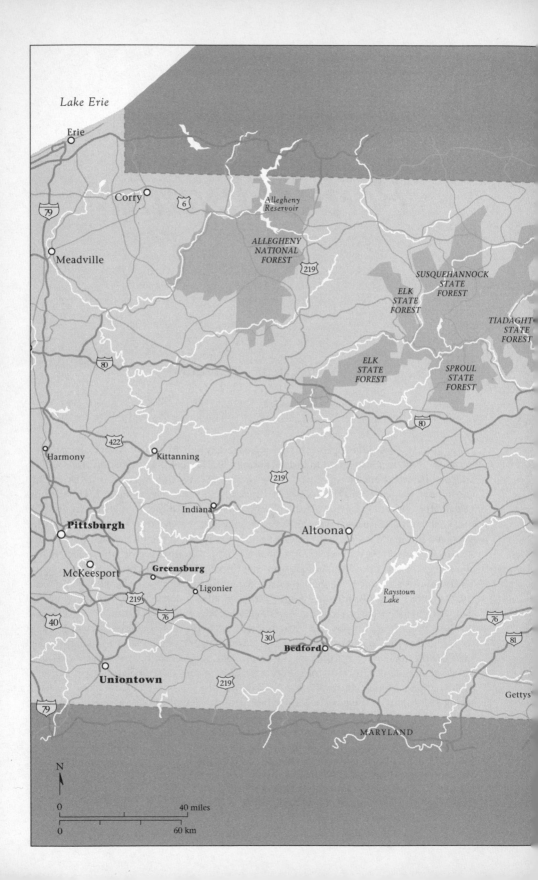

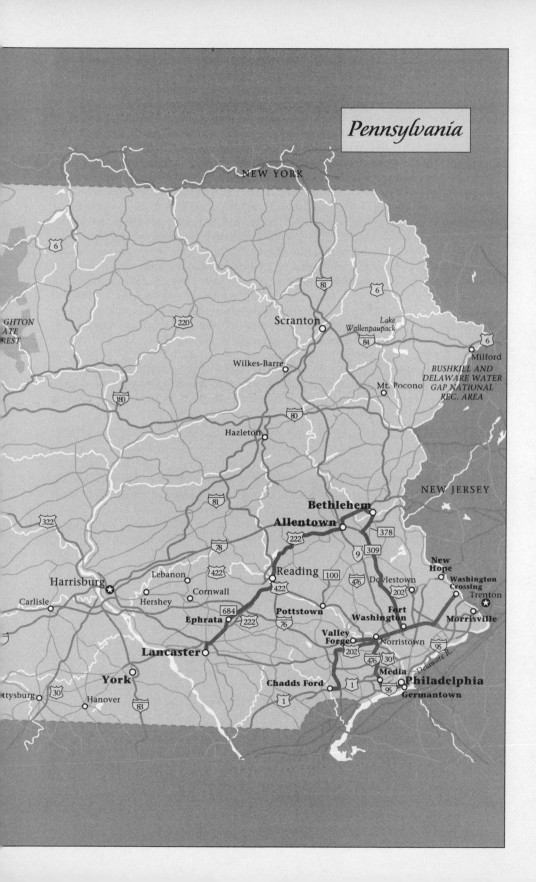

Pennsylvania

NEW YORK

6

81

6

Scranton

Lake
Wallenpaupack

84

Milford

6

Wilkes-Barre

220

180

BUSHKILL AND
DELAWARE WATER
GAP NATIONAL
REC. AREA

80

Mt. Pocono

Hazleton

NEW JERSEY

322

81

Bethlehem

78

Allentown

222

378

9 309

New
Hope

Harrisburg

Lebanon

422

Reading

100

476

Doylestown

Washington
Crossing

Trenton

Carlisle

Cornwall

422

202

Morrisville

Hershey

Pottstown

Fort
Washington

684

76

Ephrata

222

Valley
Forge

Norristown

95

Lancaster

202

476

30

Delaware R.

York

Media

Philadelphia

Chadds Ford

1

95

Germantown

30

Hanover

83

ttysburg

1

Franklin was its most revered tenant. The Renaissance man—statesmen, publisher, philosopher, and scientist—was credited with birthing the first hospital, library, insurance company, and nonsectarian university in the Colonies.

✦ "JOIN, OR DIE"

When the war came to Pennsylvania, the colony was ready. Its iron forges turned to making cannon, its craftsmen reworked the German hunting rifle into the fine Pennsylvania long rifle, its shipbuilders aided in the creation of the Continental Navy, and its troops took part in many key battles of the Revolution. Philadelphia, the nation's capital during the war, provided a place for the greatest minds of the Colonies to meet. After the war, the colony's premier publisher, Franklin, printed the first political cartoon to appear in an American newspaper, a divided serpent with the words "Join, or Die," urging the colonies to unite. At a Jefferson Republican rally in 1802, Pennsylvania was toasted as "the keystone in the federal union" for its key role in the economic, social and political development of the United States.

Though the spotlight remained on Philadelphia through the 1790s, when it was the capital of the new nation, some light was diffused to Pittsburgh in the southwestern corner of the state, which became a gateway to the west as settlers passed through, many in Conestoga wagons that had been developed in Lancaster County. Some in-betweeners consider Philadelphia, primarily, and Pittsburgh, secondarily, world aparts—liberal, cosmopolitan, and out of place in a rural state. The attitude of some corner-dwellers might be best summed up by Democratic political strategist James Carville, who coined the phrase: "Pennsylvania is Philadelphia and Pittsburgh, with Alabama in between." Though this dichotomy may be frustrating for political candidates, it's a delight for travelers, who can sample treasures from French and Indian War–era forts to Amish farms, from medieval cloisters to Quaker meetinghouses, and from historic city taverns to country manors without venturing beyond the borders of the Keystone State.

✦ CHURCH AND STATE

As you sit in a pew in Philadelphia's serene Gloria Dei church, your attention is captured by the ships that hang from the ceiling —models of the vessels that brought the Swedes to the region in 1643. *1643?* In grade-school history, didn't they teach that Pennsylvania was founded in 1682, when William Penn established his colony on land given to him by King Charles II? Just as Columbus didn't "discover" America, the Englishman who wanted a safe haven in the New World for his Quakers wasn't the first to discover Pennsylvania. Some 39 years earlier, the Swedes had made Pennsylvania the capital of New Sweden; they were preceded by Dutch pioneers and the Lenni-Lenape Indians, who had inhabited the land for thousands of years. By 1751, a Dutch official estimated that there were 190,000 souls in Pennsylvania, not including the "pagan inhabitants." The next four decades were an empire-building relay race, with some contenders more reluctant than others to turn over the baton. In 1655, the Dutch took over New Sweden and handed it over to the English who handed it over to Penn.

In the southeastern corner of the colony, Penn established the city of Philadelphia. The Society of Friends (Quakers)—and the Anglicans, Catholics, and Jews who arrived after them—settled in to test the resilience of Penn's "Holy Experiment." Over the next 50 years, the Colonists lived under the governance of Penn's Charter of Privileges, which established liberal provisions for religious freedom and a brilliant model for government. In the southwestern corner of the state, where the Ohio River lay between French possessions in Canada and Louisiana, a different kind of experiment was being conducted: a young George Washington was testing the volatility of the fragile truce between the French and the English. A failed diplomatic mission—and the gunshot that followed—at Jumonville Glen in 1754 sparked the seven-year-long French and Indian War, in which the British finally prevailed.

Sit awhile in a pew at Philadelphia's splendid Christ Church and gaze at the wineglass pulpit from which Bishop White preached for 57 years. If you attended church every Sunday in the 1770s and 1780s along with fellow parishioners George and Martha Washington, Robert Morris, Benjamin Franklin and Betsy Ross, you would bear witness to the coming of inde-

Pennsylvania Timeline

1674 The Treaty of Westminster ends hostilities between the Dutch and the English and turns Dutch colonies, including Pennsylvania, over to the English.

1681 William Penn petitions King Charles II to grant him land in the New World for a Quaker colony as repayment for a debt owed to his late father. Ownership of the huge parcel of land, known as Pennsilvania or Penn's Woods, makes William the largest landholder in the British Empire after the king.

1682 Penn established the city of Philadelphia— Greek for "City of Brotherly Love."

1701 Penn granted the Charter of Privileges, which established forward-looking provisions for religious freedom and a structure for government that became a model for the U.S. Constitution.

1751 To commemorate the 50th anniversary of the Charter of Privileges, and to "Proclaim Liberty thro' all the Land," the Liberty Bell is commissioned from a foundry in England.

1754 Colonial troops commanded by 22-year-old Colonel George Washington are defeated at Fort Necessity, near Uniontown, in the opening battle of the French and Indian Wars.

1774 The First Continental Congress meets in Carpenter's' Hall in Philadelphia to address a declaration of rights and grievances to King George III.

1775 The Second Continental Congress meets in Philadelphia and appoints George Washington as commander-in-chief of the Continental Army.

1776 The Continental Congress, convened in the Assembly Room at the State House, adopts the Declaration of Independence. The Liberty Bell rings to signal the first public reading of the Declaration of Independence. Washington crosses the Delaware River from Bucks County to Trenton to defeat the Hessians on Christmas night.

1777 The British defeat Washington's army at the Battle of Brandywine. Under General Howe, the British take over Philadelphia with no opposition. Washington tries to drive the British out of Germantown but is driven off at the Battle of Germantown. The Continental Army begins its winter encampment at Valley Forge. The Continental Congress flees to York and adopts the Articles of Confederation of the new United States of America.

1778 The British withdraw from Philadelphia. Washington's troops march out of Valley Forge to intercept the British at Monmouth.

1787 The Constitutional Convention, representing 12 states, meets in the Pennsylvania State House in Philadelphia and signs the U.S. Constitution, sending it to the states to ratify. Pennsylvania is the second state to ratify it.

1790 Philadelphia is named capital of the United States.

1800 The nation's capital is moved from Philadelphia to Washington, D.C.

pendence. In September 1774, you might have heard whispers that the First Continental Congress was secreted inside Carpenters' Hall to counter the Intolerable Acts that had closed down Boston's port. Seven months later, it would be hard to find a seat in church when the entire body of delegates to the Second Continental Congress was in attendance. You might notice the worry behind Martha Washington's proud smile; after all, the Congress had just named her husband commander-in-chief of the Continental Army. After the Declaration of Independence's public reading and Washington's brazen Christmas night crossing of the Delaware to victory in Trenton, your spirits would be raised, only to be dashed the following year when the general was defeated at Brandywine and—who would have ever imagined?— the occupation of Philadelphia by the British army! During those tense months, the precious church bells were hidden in Allentown and the members of the Continental Congress found refuge and inspiration in York, where they adopted the Articles of Confederation. While Washington's army wintered at Valley Forge, you wait for the future to unfold.

Once the war is over, the good life has resumed in the largest city in the Colonies. Bishop White hosts delightful parties at his home over on Walnut Street. And there are many reasons to celebrate: on Independence Day 1788, when the church bells—now safely back in their tower—toll all day to celebrate the ratification of the U.S. Constitution, when Philadelphia is christened the capital of the new United States in 1790, and the happy day in 1793, when President Washington begins his second term with inaugural ceremonies at Congress Hall.

A REGIONAL GAZETEER
▼▼▼

✦ PHILADELPHIA AND ITS SUPPORTING CAST
In the southeastern corner of the state, the Delaware River, the longest free-flowing river east of the Mississippi, forms a natural border between Pennsylvania and New Jersey. The long arms of the river cradle **Philadelphia,** the birthplace of the nation and the home of the country's first government. Several chapters of the nation's early history are preserved in Independence National Historical Park in the heart of the city, where Independence Hall and the Liberty Bell take honors as the most popular attractions. Within city limits—in **Germantown** and **Fairmount Park**—are more than a dozen restored Colonial-era mansions to which the wealthy retreated from the city's heat and epidemics. Among these rich deposits of history are all the trappings you'd expect from the nation's fifth-largest city: world-class museums, stunning performing arts centers, and restaurants that regularly make the national top-10 lists.

From Philadelphia, the region known as the Delaware Valley runs in an arc about 40 mi north and west. In Colonial times, the countryside beyond Philadelphia was dotted with iron forges, fields that became battlefields of the American Revolution, stately homes where the moneyed set lived the country life, and roadside taverns where movers and shakers shook up the status quo. Between the Civil War and World War II, this landscape was superimposed with rings of first-generation suburbs with gracious stone homes and towering maples, epitomized by the famous Main Line, and then by rings of newly birthed exurbs. As a result, in the greater metropolitan area, you'll find one of the nation's largest shopping complexes within 2 mi of **Valley Forge National Historical Park,** the commuter borough of **Media** sharing space with the Colonial Pennsylvania Plantation, and the General Lafayette Inn, where the French general fought the Battle of Barren Hill. At the edges of the Delaware Valley are some still-bucolic regions, like the **Chadds Ford** area, home of the Brandywine Battlefield State Park; and **Pottstown,** where you'll find the Hopewell Furnace National Historic Site. North of the city along the upper reaches of the Delaware River is Bucks County, whose beauty lured William Penn himself, who built his country home, Pennsbury Manor, at **Morrisville.** *Towns listed: Chadds Ford, Fort Washington, Germantown, Morrisville, Media, New Hope, Philadelphia, Pottstown, Valley Forge.*

✦ LEHIGH VALLEY: O LITTLE TOWNS OF CHRISTMAS SPIRIT
The bucolic valley nestled between the Lehigh and Delaware rivers, 60 mi north of Philadelphia, reminded the German settlers of their homeland in the Palatinate region. It seemed to be the perfect place to establish their Moravian Church—but it was not sacred ground.

Just three years earlier in 1737, William Penn's sons had swindled the Lenni-Lenape Indians out of their land in the notorious Walking Purchase, where they hired the colony's fastest runners, cleared a straight path, and lay claim to 55 mi of the valley. Today, the straight paths are superhighways—I–78 and U.S 22—that cut through the valley like arrows, keeping the main cities of **Allentown,** Bethlehem, and Easton lined up like ducks in a row. Soon after the English took title to the wilderness, William Allen bought 5,000 acres for his Georgian hunting lodge, Trout Hall. While his unpatriotic son used the manor to entertain Hessian POWs, the Liberty Bell was squirreled away for safekeeping beneath the floorboards of Zion Reformed United Church of Christ. Later on, Allen sold off a piece of his land upstream to the Moravian missionaries, who founded their little town of **Bethlehem.** Today, Christmas City USA bears gifts: the Moravian Museum, housed in the huge log *gemeinhaus*; the Old Chapel, the Moravians' first house of worship; and a month-long Christmas celebration. Although the fertile valley provided crops that sustained its people and the Continental Army, it is industry that forged the region's identity—from the Moravians' Colonial Industrial Quarter to the Lehigh Canal, along which coal and timber floated south to Philadelphia markets, to the factories of the nation's second-largest steelmaker, Bethlehem Steel, which stretched 5 mi along the banks of the Lehigh River and lighted the sky with flames from the blast furnaces. Now the brightest light comes from atop South Mountain, where the 81-ft-tall Star of Bethlehem shines year-round. *Towns listed: Allentown, Bethlehem.*

✦ PENNSYLVANIA DUTCH COUNTRY

Down the country roads that thread through cornfields east of Lancaster, Amish children wave from the backseat of a horse-drawn buggy, signs beckon you to shop for hand-stitched quilts in generations-old patterns, and roadside stands tempt with homemade preserves and shoofly pie. The lush farmlands known as Pennsylvania Dutch Country, an hour's drive west and light years away from Philadelphia, are home to more than 41 still-vital Amish, Mennonite, and Brethren sects who came to Lancaster to escape from religious persecution. They live in towns with colorful names like Intercourse, Bird-in-Hand, and Paradise, in farmhouses devoid of electricity and modern conveniences (if they belong to the stricter Old Order Amish sect). By contrast, the communal society that sequestered itself at the Ephrata Cloister, just north in **Ephrata,** is now just an echo; the last sister died in 1813. Thoroughly modern **Lancaster** has a six-square-block heart clogged with Colonial history—in fact, Lancaster was the nation's capital for one day in September 1777, when Congress, fleeing from the British, convened here. South-southeast of Harrisburg, the state capital, is **York,** which was at the crossroads of history when the Second Continental Congress made its home here for six months. Among the heritage sites is the Colonial Courthouse where the Articles of Confederation were adopted and the nation's first Thanksgiving Day was declared. *Towns listed: Ephrata, Lancaster, York.*

✦ THE WILD WEST: ON THE TRAIL TO PITTSBURGH

The Allegheny Mountains provide an inspired backdrop for the southwest crescent of the state, with Harmony and Bedford at its points and Pittsburgh at its center. From atop **Pittsburgh**'s Duquesne Incline, you get a bird's-eye view of the city of seven hills, of the Allegheny and Monongahela rivers, which flow together to form the Ohio, and of the triangle of land at their juncture. The fort at this golden triangle—originally French-held Fort Duquesne—was the prize during the French and Indian War, when the French and British fought to control the strategic Ohio River Valley. The Fort Pitt Museum and Point State Park are the only Colonial remnants in this city that became a center of the steel industry.

The Laurel Highlands rise to Pittsburgh's south and east; today's recreation—the ski resorts, whitewater rafting outfitters, and hiking trails along scenic gorges—were yesterday's challenges, which settlers had to face on their journey to Pennsylvania's western frontier. In the towns nestled here are poignant reminders of that challenge: the Bushy Run Battlefield near **Greensburg,** where British Col. Henry Bouquet, en route to resupply Fort Pitt, fought off wave after wave of Chief Pontiac's Indian army; **Uniontown**'s Fort Necessity battlefield, where Col. George Washington surrendered for the first and only time in his military career; and, farther east, **Bedford,** where during the 1794 Whiskey Rebellion George Washington led troops into battle. *Towns listed: Bedford, Greensburg, Pittsburgh, Uniontown.*

A Pilgrimage that Pays Tribute to Penn

A DRIVING TOUR FROM LANCASTER TO PHILADELPHIA

▼▼

Distance: Approx. 144 mi (one-way)   **Time:** 3 days (2 nights)
Breaks: Overnight stops in Ephrata and Bethlehem

When William Penn established a haven for Quakers in Pennsylvania in 1682, his "Holy Experiment" left the proverbial door open to other immigrants. The next wave were Anglicans and Presbyterians, who had a running conflict with the "stiff Quakers" and their distaste for music and dancing. But many German religious freethinkers—Amish, Mennonite, and Moravian sects, and the brothers and sisters at Ephrata—had been experimenting with religious communal life for dozens of years. This tour begins near Lancaster, where the Amish community clings to a centuries-old way of life. It goes to Ephrata's extinct cloistered community (celibacy has its consequences) and then to the Moravian-found town of Bethlehem, where church members live as part of the community while following their 500-year-old motto—"In essentials, unity; in nonessentials, liberty; and in all things, love." The tour ends in Philadelphia, where you'll explore the legacy of the Quaker founders and see six 18th-century churches in as many city blocks. On the car rides, you can ponder interesting philosophical questions, such as whether groups benefit by shutting themselves off from society or if Amish children are privileged or deprived (how would your kids feel without their MTV and instant messages?).

Begin your tour about 10 mi east of Lancaster in Intercourse, a town at the intersection, or intercourse, of two roads (Routes 340 and 772), which is how it got its name in Colonial times. Although many attractions in **Lancaster** try to capture the "Amish experience," People's Place is the most tasteful and perceptive introduction to the Amish, Mennonite, and Hutterite communities. A documentary film and interactive family museum give insight into courtship rituals, barn-raising, and how the Amish have survived in today's world. From Intercourse, head west on Route 340 about 4½ mi to Bird-in-Hand. This road, built in 1733 by King George II, was known as King's Highway in Colonial days. Take a 2-mi spin down country roads in a family-style Amish carriage with Abe's Buggy Rides (2596 Old Philadelphia Pike, 717/392–1794). Abe will tell you about the customs of the Pennsylvania Dutch as he leads you past farms and a one-room schoolhouse.

For lunch, head back west on Route 340 about 2 mi to Plain & Fancy Farm, where it's hard not to stuff yourself on hearty Pennsylvania Dutch cuisine. You can walk off your apple dumplings at Lancaster's Landis Valley Museum, about 35 minutes away. Take Route 340 west about 3 mi to U.S. 30 west, follow about 4 mi to Route 272 north. Turn left on Kissel Hill Road. More than two dozen costumed demonstrators are at work spinning, weaving, pottery-making, and tinsmithing at this outdoor museum of Pennsylvania German rural life and folk culture before 1900. Afterward, drive 30 minutes northeast to **Ephrata**; eat dinner in town and spend the night at the Smithton Inn, a 1763 stagecoach inn built by Ephrata Cloister members.

Next morning, take the tour at nearby Ephrata Cloister. After you've just slept beneath a hand-sewn Pennsylvania Dutch quilt and breakfasted on blueberry-apple pancakes, the ascetic life of the Cloister members—wooden pillows, meals of wheat and tuberous vegetables—will seem even more severe. From Ephrata, drive to **Bethlehem,** nicknamed "Christmas City USA," less than two hours away. Take U.S. 322 east to U.S. 222 north about 50 mi to Route 309 north to U.S. 22 east. Follow about 8 mi to Route 378 south to the 8th Avenue ramp to downtown. Have lunch en route or in downtown Bethlehem before you head to the Moravian Museum. It's in the 1741 Gemeinhaus (community house), the largest existing log structure in the country. You'll see their early instruments and learn about the "love-feast" and the religious ideals of this Protestant sect. You can take a self-guided tour of the still-standing mill, tannery, and waterworks of the Colonial Industrial Quarter. Before dinner, peruse the Moravian Book Shop at 428 Main Street, considered the oldest continuously running bookstore in the world, dating from 1745. They have a great selection of Moravian Stars, the 26-point 3-D Christmas star that Moravian schoolchildren made as a exercise in geometry. For dinner, walk across the street to the 1758 The Sun Inn, which John Adams called "the best Inn I ever saw," and stay overnight at one of Bethlehem's hotels.

From Bethlehem, drive to explore the historic district of **Philadelphia.** Take Route 378 for 6 mi to Route 309 south, then follow for 6 mi to Route 663. Follow I–476 south for 28 mi to I–76 east to Philadelphia. Pick up I–676 east toward Central Philadelphia; merge onto the Vine Street Expressway. Follow signs for the Ben Franklin Bridge/6th Street. Begin at the Arch Street Meeting House, a still-active 1804 Quaker house of worship. A museum here honors William Penn and explains the Quaker's role in Colonial politics. Rather than simplicity you'll find sumptuousness at the next stop, Christ Church, where you can sit in the pew where George and Martha Washington worshiped when they attended the nation's founding Episcopal church. For lunch, try Martha Washington's turkey potpie recipe at City Tavern. Within a mile of the restaurant, you can visit any of five Colonial churches: Mother Bethel African Methodist Episcopal Church; the 1768 Old Pine St. Presbyterian Church; St. Peter's Church, an 1761 Episcopal church; the 1733 Old St. Joseph's Church, the first place in the English-speaking world where Catholic mass could be legally celebrated; and Old St. Mary's Church. After three days of reverence, it's time for an unholy break. You'll find it on irreverent South Street, with its pink-haired teens and New Age bookstores.

Battle Cries and Whispers

A DRIVING TOUR FROM WASHINGTON CROSSING TO VALLEY FORGE

▼▼▼

Distance: Approx. 175 mi (one-way)   **Time:** 4 days (3 nights)
Breaks: Overnight stops in Chadds Ford, Lafayette Hill, and Philadelphia

The call to arms signaled by the Declaration of Independence turned the once peaceful countryside surrounding Philadelphia into a battleground. In fact, there were more Revolutionary War battles in the Philadelphia region than in all of the New England states combined. Within 30 mi of the city, the battles of Brandywine and Germantown were fought, Fort Mifflin was under siege, and the Continental Army camped at Valley Forge. This tour takes you to the battlefields, fort, houses, and inns where the war was planned and waged during the period from Christmas 1776 to spring 1778. As you drive from Chadds Ford to Valley Forge, imagine Washington's troops marching on foot—often literally, since their boots were worn beyond repair: Washington wrote: ". . . you might have tracked the army from White Marsh to Valley Forge by the blood of their feet." Savor the victory at Washington Crossing, because it is the only one you'll come across on this tour, although you'll hear many tales of how the young Continental Army showed its pluck and lived to fight another day.

Begin your tour at **Washington Crossing Historic Park,** where on Christmas night 1776 General Washington and 2,400 of his men crossed the icy Delaware River in Durham boats to take the Hessians by surprise at Trenton, New Jersey. Memorials and attractions are divided between the Lower and the Upper Park, which are about 5 mi apart. For lunch, take Route 32/River Road north to New Hope's 1727 Logan Inn. Afterward, on your stroll through town, follow Bridge Street onto the bridge that spans the Delaware River for a broad view of the 1,000-ft-wide river that Washington forded.

Head to **Chadds Ford** for dinner and overnight. The most direct way is to take U.S. 202 south for about 60 mi. Although you've spent just one night, nine months had passed before the war returned to Pennsylvania. After defeating the British at Princeton, New Jersey, Washington wintered in Morristown. The conflict then moved north to New York and New England. In the morning visit the now-peaceful 50-acre Brandywine Battlefield Park, where Washington waited hoping to intercept the British on their march toward Philadelphia. You'll see the house where Washington established his headquarters on the eve of the battle in which British troops found undefended fords of the Brandywine River and attacked the Americans from two sides, forcing Washington to retreat.

Have lunch at the General Warren Inne, where Loyalists plotted against the Revolutionaries and later planned and launched the Paoli Massacre. From Chadds Ford, take U.S. 1 north to U.S. 202 north. Drive about 10 mi to the Route 29 south Malvern exit. Follow Route 29 south to the dead end and turn left onto U.S. 30 east. Turn right onto Old Lincoln Highway and right again onto Old Lancaster Road. After lunch, you can take a walk through the Paoli Battlefield, just 1½ mi away (from the inn, turn right onto Warren Avenue, right onto Monument Avenue, and left onto W. First Avenue), the final resting place for 53 American soldiers who were stabbed with bayonets during a surprise raid, and visit Historic Waynesborough, home of Revolutionary war hero General "Mad Anthony" Wayne, who led the Pennsylvania line in the battles of Brandywine and Germantown. For dinner and overnight, follow Route 252 to U.S. 202 north to I–76 east. Take 1–476 north to the Germantown Pike east exit to the 1732 General Lafayette Inn, where during the Battle of Barren Hill, General Lafayette's men and 50 Indians held off a much larger English force.

Next day, take Germantown Pike northwest to U.S. 202 north. Turn left onto Township Line Road and right onto Valley Forge Road (Route 363) to Peter Wentz Farmstead in Worcester, near **Fort Washington,** for a tour of the home where Washington planned the October 4, 1777 Battle of Germantown, and of the surrounding farm, where guides in period costumes demonstrate how farming was done in the 1700s. From Worcester, follow Route 73 east about 9 mi; turn right onto Bethlehem Pike and then left onto Germantown Avenue. Have lunch at one of the restaurants along **Germantown Avenue** in Chestnut Hill, a posh suburb of Philadelphia (you can image yourself as Loyalist while you have tea at Best of British restaurant.) Then, follow Germantown Avenue southeast to see a few of the country manor houses that played a role in the Battle of Germantown. You first come to Cliveden, which was pounded by cannonballs while British soldiers were holed up inside. The Deshler-Morris House was nicknamed the "Germantown White House" when Washington spent a winter here while the yellow fever epidemic raged in Philadelphia. British General James Agnew died in the parlor of the Wister family home, Grumblethorpe, after being struck by musket balls on the lawn.

From Germantown, go southeast on Germantown Avenue, right onto West Berkley Street and take the U.S. 1 south/Roosevelt Expressway ramp toward Central **Philadelphia** for dinner and overnight. If it's in season, don't miss the Lights of Liberty walking sound-and-light show, which dramatizes the events that led up to the American Revolution on stops at five sites in Independence National Historical Park. Before you leave the city, pick up the makings for a picnic lunch, then head for Fort Mifflin by following I–95 south to Exit 15/Enterprise Avenue toward Island Avenue. Turn left onto Island Avenue, which becomes Hog Island Road. In a 40-day battle that culminated in mid-November 1777, 300 Continental soldiers held off British forces long enough for Washington's troops to retreat to Valley Forge. You, too, can retreat to **Valley Forge** by following I–95 south to I–476 north to I–76 west toward Valley Forge. Call ahead for directions to Valley Forge National Historical Park; new exits are under construction and aren't yet numbered. While the British occupied Philadelphia, Washington and his men camped here during the winter of 1777–78; they fought not the British but cold, hunger, and dysentery. In spring, they were revived with food and training by Prussian drillmaster Baron von Steuben and eventually were able to triumph over the British. While you're heading home to relax after your battlefield tour, consider this: Washington and his troops went on to fight for three more years.

ALLENTOWN

▼▼▼

William Allen's 5,000-acre wilderness hunting lodge was a great place for the Chief Justice of Colonial Pennsylvania's Supreme Court and mayor of Philadelphia to entertain his friends—his own Camp David. In 1763, when Allen launched a business venture to create a market town for the area surrounding his lodge, he was a partner in an iron furnace and a general merchant whose cargo included slaves. He called his village Northampton Towne, but the German farmers and tradesman who had settled here before him dubbed it "Allen's town." In 1777 the Liberty Bell was brought to a church here for safekeeping: a good choice—the Germans were patriots, and nobody would want to come looking for the bell in such a remote outpost. Today people do come to Allentown, which, like its neighbors in the Lehigh Valley, has transformed itself from an iron town to a tourist destination with numerous historic sites and art museums. *Contact Lehigh County Historical Society | Old Courthouse, Hamilton at 5th St., Allentown 18105 | 610/435–1074 | www.voicenet.com/~lchs. Lehigh Valley Convention & Visitors Bureau | Box 20785, Lehigh Valley 18002 | 800/747–0561 | www. lehighvalleypa.org.*

George Taylor House. When 20-year-old George Taylor arrived in the Colonies, this Irish-born son of a clergyman worked as an indentured servant at an iron forge. After the ironmaster died, Taylor married his widow, took over the business, and made a fortune. His interest in politics then led to him the Pennsylvania Assembly and later to the Continental Congress, where he was one of the signers of the Declaration of Independence. This 1768 Georgian home, with its intricate moldings and paneling, is one of several Lehigh Valley properties he owned. The high-style period furnishings on view didn't belong to Taylor, but certainly underline his quintessentially American rags-to-riches story. | Lehigh and Poplar Sts., Catasauqua | 610/435–4664 | www.voicenet.com/~lchs | $2 | June–Oct., weekends 1–4.

Liberty Bell Shrine. "The Redcoats are coming!" The Redcoats *were* coming—straight to Philadelphia after their victory at the Battle of Brandywine. City leaders hatched a plan to save the city's bells from being melted for cannon—a classic bait-and-switch maneuver: tell everyone the bells had been sunken in the Delaware River, and then hide them elsewhere. A train of 700 wagons, accompanied by 200 cavalrymen, transported the Liberty Bell, the State House bells, and the chimes from Christ Church and St. Peter's Church to Allentown, where on the night of September 24, 1777, they were hidden beneath the floor boards of the Zion Reformed United Church of Christ. The shrine, in the exact spot where the Liberty Bell was hidden for that year, includes a bell replica, a 46-ft mural depicting the historic trek to Allentown, and changing exhibits on the American Revolution and the Colonial era. | 622 Hamilton St. | 610/435–4232 | www.geocities.com/athens/ithaca/1760 | Free | Feb.–Apr. and Nov.–Dec., Thurs.–Sat. noon–4; May–Oct., Mon.–Sat. noon–4.

Trout Hall. Son of the patriarch of Allentown, James Allen was given to throwing parties that were the talk of the town. Tongues wagged not because his honored guests were his largely patriotic neighbors but, in fact, Hessian prisoners of war captured during the Battle of Trenton. William Allen's son built his summer house here in 1770 on a piece of his father's huge estate. When the war broke out and his Loyalist sympathies were deemed politically incorrect, he left Philadelphia and made Georgian-style Trout Hall his full-time address. Today it remains Allentown's oldest surviving residence. | 414 Walnut St. | 610/435–4664 | www.voicenet. com/~lchs | $2 | Apr.–May and Sept.–Nov., weekends 1–4; June–Aug., Tues.–Sun. 1–4.

HISTORIC DINING

King George Inn. This 1756 crossroads tavern, a National Historic Site, also served as a town hall, courthouse, and early church. Behind the inn was a drill staging field for citizen-soldiers of the American Revolution. Veal and seafood dishes are the specialities on the Continental menu; you can dine in one of the small hearth-warmed dining rooms or on the porch in season. | 3141 Hamilton Blvd. | 610/435–1723 | $16–$29 | AE, D, DC, MC, V | No lunch Sun.

BEDFORD
▼▼▼

Noted for its working historic village and as a gateway to 14 nearby covered bridges, Bedford will certainly tempt the heritage traveler. Indeed, for a small town in the middle of the state—no towns of importance are nearby—it has an impressive Colonial past. It began as a sparsely settled trading post on the frontier of western Pennsylvania, an area that was ravaged by Indian raids. In 1758, during the French and Indian War, the British built themselves a fort here; their stockade was strategically located to keep supply lines open for an assault on French-held Fort Dusquesne to the west. In the 1794 Whiskey Rebellion, George Washington led troops into battle in Bedford—the first U.S. President ever to do so—to quell a rebellious group of grain farmers who were opposed to his tax on whiskey. Today Bedford's downtown is dotted with antiques shops and even comes with its own walking tour. *Contact Bedford County Visitors Bureau | 141 S. Juliana St., Bedford 15522 | 800/765–3331 | www.bedfordcounty.net.*

Fort Bedford Museum. You can imagine how Fort Bedford's commander treasured the St. George's Cross flag the fourth duke of Bedford had given to him. It was so special that it was kept in the officer's quarters, not fluttering from a flagpole. What did hang over this fort, built in 1758 by the British during the French and Indian War, was an intense fear of Indian raids. Fort Bedford sat at the eastern edge of the military path that General Forbes pieced together from Indian trails to march his army west across the Allegheny Mountains toward French-held Fort Duquesne. The fort stood until the 1770s; a museum on the site today houses a large-scale model of the original fort with its five bastions, Native American artifacts, early period wagons, Flintlock rifles, thousands of household objects from the 1700s and 1800s, and the Fort Bedford flag. | Fort Bedford Dr. | 800/259–4284 | www.bedfordcounty.net | $4 | June–Aug., daily 10–5; May and Sept.–Oct., Wed.–Mon. 10–5.

Historic Downtown Bedford Walking Tour. You'll find this entertaining 90-minute walking tour filled with quirky tales—including one about how Fort Bedford was captured (and why the captors gave it back to the British). The tour includes a stop at Espy House, where President Washington made his headquarters during the Whiskey Rebellion. | 141 S. Juliana St. | 800/765–3331 | www.bedfordcounty.net | Free | June–Oct., Fri. at 3:30.

Old Bedford Village. Just across the Claycomb Covered Bridge, Old Bedford Village is an impressive historic restoration, where you'll find most days the blacksmith hammering fireplace pokers, the cooper drilling a hole in the barrel, and the tourists feasting upon hot apple cider and kettle corn. A tavern, schoolhouse, and village church top the list of 40 buildings set in this mid-1790s pioneer village; about half of the structures are original and were collected from the surrounding area. Costumed interpreters staff the buildings, while craftspeople reenact the daily activities of pioneer life, like broommaking, candlemaking, and weaving. | 220 Sawblade Rd. | 814/623–1156 or 800/238–4347 | www.oldbedfordvillage.org | $8 | Memorial Day–Labor Day, Thurs.–Tues. 9–5; Sept.–Oct., Thurs.–Sun. 10–4.

HISTORIC DINING AND LODGING
Oralee's Golden Eagle. Soon after Dr. John Anderson opened an inn on the ground floor of his mansion, he had distinguished guests: General Washington and his troops, who were in town to quell the Whiskey Rebellion. The 1794 Federal-style tavern serves a seasonal menu. The guest rooms and suites have been updated; several have fireplaces, porches, and Internet connections. Complimentary breakfast. | 131 E. Pitt St. | 814/624–0800 | www.bedford. net/oralee | 16 rooms | $70–$109 | MC, V.

BETHLEHEM

▼▼

"Christmas City USA," Bethlehem was founded on December 24, 1741, by members of a Protestant congregation from Moravia, Czechoslovakia. Sent over by their protector, Count Nikolaus Ludwig von Zinzendorf, they settled on the banks of the Lehigh River. Their purpose was twofold: to preach the gospel to the Native Americans and to be the nerve center of the Moravians' North American empire, providing economic support for the headquarters in Europe. The Moravians' communal efforts produced extraordinary 18th-century industry and handicrafts; their communal buildings represent the largest collection of Germanic style architecture in the United States. Some are on the campus of Moravian College, which was founded in 1742 by 16-year-old Moravian Countess Benigna von Zinzendorf. Today the city is prized for its Moravian legacy, its Bach Festival, and its residential and industrial architecture. With its justly touted nickname, Bethlehem hosts a month-long holiday celebration, which includes Moravian traditions of the lighted 26-point Advent star and Germanic Christmas plays, called *putzes. Contact Historic Bethlehem Partnership | 459 Old York Rd., Bethlehem 18018 | 610/882–0450 | fax 610/882–0460 | www.historicbethlehem.org. Lehigh Valley Convention & Visitors Bureau | Box 20785, Lehigh Valley 18002 | 800/747–0561 | www.lehighvalleypa.org.*

Burnside Plantation. When Moravian missionary James Burnside built a saltbox farmhouse in 1748 for himself and his wife, Mary, he did more than change his address: he moved out of the fold into Bethlehem's first single home. This was a singular act, as the Moravians considered property to be communally owned, with people living together according to gender and marital status. Today Burnside's farmhouse, summer kitchen (with its beehive oven), barns, and orchards give you a feel for rural life between 1748 and 1848. Guided tours of the buildings' interiors are available on summer Saturdays; other times you can take a self-guided tour of the grounds, using a brochure that is in a protected box along the fence nearest the corn crib. | 1461 Schoenersville Rd. | 610/691–0603 | www.historicbethlehem.org | Self-guided tour, free; guided tour, $6 | Daily 8:30–5 for self-guided tours; July–Aug., Sat. noon–4 for guided tours; Christmas season, weekends noon–4.

Central Moravian Church. When Bethlehem's flourishing Moravian community needed a new church in the early 19th century, it succeeded in building Pennsylvania's largest place of worship, consecrated in 1806. | 73 W. Church St. | 610/866–5661 | Free | Weekdays 8:30–4:30.

Colonial Industrial Quarter. The Moravians who immigrated to the New World to bring the Gospel to Native Americans were industrious as well as pious. Guided by a cooperative, communal plan called the "General Economy," in which individuals did not own their own land or businesses, they created thriving industries; in fact, when there were only 395 people living in the town there were 40 different businesses in full swing. The buildings that made up the industrial quarter still stand today. They include the Tannery; the Springhouse; the Waterworks, the first municipal pumping station in the country; and Luckenbach Mill. The latter is home to HistoryWorks!, a children's interactive gallery, open weekends noon–4. Brochures for a free self-guided tour of the area are available at the gristmill weekdays 8:30–5. | 459 Old York Rd. | 610/691–0603 | www.historicbethlehem.org | Self-guided tour, free; guided tour, $6 | Daily 8:30–5 for self-guided tours; July–Aug., Sat. noon–4 for guided tours; Christmas season, weekends noon–4.

Goundie House. A prominent Moravian brewer and community leader, John Sebastian Goundie lived in comfort in his 1810 Federal-style home, Bethlehem's first brick residence. A sampler stitched by his youngest daughter and a child-size spinning wheel share the space with furniture made by Bethlehem's skilled craftsmen, including a pianoforte and bow-back Windsor chairs. | 501 Main St. | 610/691–0603 | www.historicbethlehem.org | Self-guided tour, free | Tues.–Sun. noon–5; Christmas season noon–5.

Moravian Museum of Bethlehem (Gemeinhaus). As you stand in the huge worship room, called the Saal, imagine that it's Christmas Eve 1741 and Count Nikolaus von Zinzendorf, Lutheran minister and benefactor of the Moravians, has come here to give Bethlehem its name. You'd be surrounded by the entire church community in the Gemeinhaus, the community house that the Moravians used as living quarters, home base for missionary work, place of worship, and school. A National Historic Landmark, the building is also the oldest surviving Gemeinhaus in the world, the oldest still-standing building in Bethlehem, and the largest existing log structure in the country. The Moravian Museum of Bethlehem now makes its home here; on a guided tour you'll see the Saal, woodwind and keyboard instruments, hand-drawn fire engines from the 18th century, and exhibits portraying the ideals, art and culture of the early Moravians. | 66 W. Church St. | 610/867–0173 | www.moravianmuseum.org | $6 | Feb.–Dec., Tues.–Sun. noon–4.

Old Historic Bethlehem Walking Tour. This one-hour tour departs from the Moravian Museum and covers a lot of ground—geographically and historically—as it illuminates the history of Bethlehem's Moravian community. Stops include the Brethren's House, which was the bachelors' quarters for the original Moravian community (and later used as a hospital for American soldiers wounded during the Revolution). The tour does not take you inside the buildings. | 66 W. Church St. | 610/867–0173 | www.historicbethlehem.org | $7 | Apr.–Nov., Sat. 2:30; Dec., daily 2:30 and 5.

✦ ON THE CALENDAR: Dec. **Christmas Celebration.** For four weeks, Bethlehem takes a leading role in Christmas pageantry. Events include horse-drawn carriage rides, candlelight concerts, and showings of the Christmas Putz, a musical using miniature lights and antique German figurines. The narrated Bethlehem by Night tour makes the rounds of the holiday lights, including the Star of Bethlehem that hangs on South Mountain. | 610/691–6055 or 800/360–8687.

HISTORIC DINING

Sun Inn. "The best Inn I ever saw," is how John Adams' reviewed this 1758 inn, which was also a way station for such statesmen as George Washington and the Marquis de Lafayette. Pheasant, venison, and "favorites" like Ben Franklin's Almond Trout and John Adams's Peach Duck are served among period furnishings or in the landscaped courtyard in season. Guided one-hour tavern tours are offered Mon.–Sat. 11:30–8 for $2. | 564 Main St. | 610/866–1758 | www.suninnbethlehem.org | $16–$30 | AE, DC, MC, V | Closed Sun. and Mon.

CHADDS FORD
▼▼

Unforgettably immortalized in Andrew Wyeth's paintings, Chadds Ford is the poster child of the bucolic Brandywine Valley. Back in the 18th century, Chadds Ford was less bucolic than bloody: the Battle of Brandywine, one of the largest engagements of the American Revolution, was fought along the east bank of the creek in 1777. While the Wyeth connection draws the crowds, there is, then, much here for the Early American buff. The town was named for John Chads, the man who helped the pioneers head westward by establishing a ferry service across the then-treacherous Brandywine Creek. *Contact Brandywine Conference & Visitors Bureau | 1 Beaver Valley Rd., Chadds Ford 19317 | 610/565–3677 | www.brandywinecvb.org. Chadds Ford Historical Society | 1736 Creek Rd., Chadds Ford 19317 | 610/388–7376 | www. chaddsfordhistory.org.*

Barns-Brinton House. "For ye accommodation of Man and Horse," announced blacksmith William Barns, when he built this country tavern in 1714, ideally located on "Ye Great Road to Nottingham," the major highway between Philadelphia and Maryland. Beyond the original entrance, which is lined with an 18th-century kitchen garden, costumed guides demonstrate crafts and lead you on a tour of the restored and furnished tavern, with its cage bar, fine woodwork, and original hardware. | 630 Baltimore Pike | 610/388-7376 | www.voicenet. com/~cfhs | $5 | May–Sept., weekends noon–5.

Brandywine Battlefield Park. Nightfall on September 11, 1777, found General Washington's defeated men retreating to Chester, and General Howe's victorious soldiers encamped on the Brandywine Battlefield. The day had started out with promise—as the British marched toward Philadelphia from the Chesapeake, Washington planned to engage them at Chadds Ford, an advantageous position. He was confident that his troops were guarding all of the fords along the Brandywine River. With superior reconnaissance information, Howe found an unguarded ford north of the American troops, crossed the river, and in the cover of the heavy morning fog appeared on Washington's right flank. Although they lost the Battle of Brandywine and left Philadelphia vulnerable for the British occupation, one of the king's officers reported that "the Americans had never fought so well before." The 50-acre park is peaceful today, almost as it was that day when the British rested here and drank tea before their assault. On the site are the Quaker farmhouses where Washington established his headquarters on the eve of the battle, and where the young Marquis de Lafayette, a French volunteer, was quartered before his first military action in America (note the famed sycamore tree, which has been standing since before the Revolution). The visitor center's museum has Ferguson rifles, an original cannon, Lafayette memorabilia, and more. You can pick up tickets here for the hour-long tour of the houses. | U.S. 1, at Ring Rd. | 610/459-3342 | www.ushistory. org/brandywine | Park, free; museum, houses $5 | Tues.–Sat. 9–5, Sun. noon–5.

Brandywine River Museum. Set in a a converted Civil War–era gristmill, this museum showcases the art of Chadds Ford native Andrew Wyeth, a major American realist painter, and his family: his father, N. C. Wyeth, illustrator of many children's classics, and his son Jamie. While Andrew rarely approached historical subject matter, his father and relatives, along with such masters as Howard Pyle and Maxfield Parrish, gloried in illustrating tales and episodes from American history, notably paintings of Pilgrims and pirates of the Colonial era. | U.S. 1 and Rte. 100 | 610/388-2700 | www.brandywinemuseum.org | $5 | Museum daily 9:30–4:30; studio Apr.–Oct., Wed.–Sun. 10–3:15.

Brinton 1704 House. Quaker William Brinton, an early settler in Chester County, was not upholding the testimony of simplicity when he built this home in the medieval English style— its 27 original leaded-glass windows were an extravagance in an era when window glass was taxed by the pane, and its abundance of closets was a seldom-seen luxury. Other touches of the good life are the built-in bread-baking oven and the herb garden, still fragrant with plants prized during the Colonial era. Caretakers answer your questions about what life was like during that time. The Brinton House is 2 mi west of the Brandywine Battlefield. | 1435 Oakland Rd. Dilworthtown | 610/399-4588 | www.brintonfamily.org | $3 | May–Oct., weekdays 10–2, weekends 11–6.

John Chads House. From the attic window, Elizabeth Chad had a bird's-eye view of troop movements during the Battle of Brandywine. Her home was perched on the bank of the creek; her husband, a ferryman and farmer, shuttled travelers across the then hard-to-ford waters. Authentically furnished and restored with its original oak floors, paneling, and woodwork, this 1725 home is a fine example of early Pennsylvania architecture. | Route 100 and Creek Rd. | 610/388-7376 | www.voicenet.com/~cfhs | $5 | May–Sept., weekends noon–5.

◆ ON THE CALENDAR: Sept. **Chadds Ford Days.** This Colonial fair, sponsored by the Chadds Ford Historical Society, has period crafts, country rides and games, old-time music, and Brandywine Valley art. | 1736 Creek Rd. | 610/388-7376 | chaddsfordhistory.org.

Sept. **Revolutionary Times.** Soldiers, craftspeople, and reenactors commemorate the anniversary of the Battle of Brandywine with battle reenactments, military encampments, 18th century crafts, and entertainment. | Brandywine Battlefield Park, U.S. 1 at Ring Rd. | 610/459–3342 | www.ushistory.org/brandywine.

HISTORIC DINING AND LODGING

Chadds Ford Inn. A lively rest stop on the Wilmington–Philadelphia–Lancaster commerce route, this 1736 inn entertained Washington's officers before the Battle of Brandywine and housed Martha on her way from Mount Vernon to see George at Valley Forge. Today it's a rest stop for Brandywine Valley visitors, who dine on regional American cuisine in a Colonial-period dining room, complete with candlelight, stone hearths, and Wyeth prints. | Rte. 100 and U.S. 1 | 610/388–7361 | www.chaddsfordinn.com | $17–$24 | AE, DC, MC, V.

Pennsbury Inn. Built in 1714 on land purchased from William Penn's commissioners, the inn is a large but cozy retreat with uneven floorboards, slanted doorways, winding staircases, and huge open fireplaces. Guest rooms have feather beds. Visitors claim to have seen the ghost of Joseph Lancaster, the first innkeeper, around the coachmen's quarters. Complimentary breakfast. No kids under 12. | 883 Baltimore Pike | 610/388–1435 | fax 610/388–1436 | www.pennsburyinn.com | 7 rooms | $140–$225 | AE, DC, MC, V.

EPHRATA

▼▼▼

When Conrad Beissel came to Ephrata to live the life of a hermit, his followers literally followed him and set up their monastic society here in 1732. The group owned most of the land around its Cloister; its "secular concerns"— a gristmill, a paper mill, a flax-seed-oil mill, a printing press, a tannery, etc.—opened up the surrounding area for settlement. Though the Cloister community declined (the members were celibate), the village of Ephrata developed into a classic, Main Street American town with few reminders of its austere beginning. Ephrata, the hub of northeastern Lancaster County, is one of the few places where you can see the rich traditions of the Amish mesh with the modern world. *Contact Pennsylvania Dutch Convention & Visitors Bureau | 501 Greenfield Rd., Lancaster 17601 | 717/299–8901 or 800/723–8824 | fax 717-299-0470 | www.padutchcountry.com.*

Ephrata Cloister. One of the most famous of Early American religious havens, this distinctive group of medieval German-style buildings is all that remains of the communal religious society founded in 1728 by German immigrant Conrad Beissel, a mystic and Seventh-Day Baptist. This spiritual sanctuary was designed to teach humility: as you bend your head to pass through low doorways, observe the sleeping cells with bare benches and wooden pillows, and venture to the dining room, where meals were often a dish of wheat and tuberous vegetables, you'll see how well the Cloister members were taught to maintain the straight and narrow path. The monastic society lived an ascetic life of self-denial, meditation, and simplicity; celibacy was encouraged. The society was best known for its a cappella singing, its *fraktur* (decorated manuscripts now among the most prized and expensive of all Early American antiques), and its publishing skills. It took three years and 15 printers to produce the 1,200 page *Martyr's Mirror,* the largest book printed in Colonial America. After the Battle of Brandywine, 500 sick and wounded soldiers were brought here to be cared for (sadly, a typhus epidemic swept through the Cloister and killed many brothers and sisters). The last sister died in 1813. Guides lead one-hour tours of three restored buildings, after which you can browse through the stable, print shop, and craft shop. | 632 W. Main St. | 717/733–6600 | www.phmc.state.pa.us | $7 | Mar.–Dec., Mon.–Sat. 9–5, Sun. noon–5; Jan.–Feb., Tues.–Sat. 9–5, Sun. noon–5.

HISTORIC LODGING

Historic Smithton Inn. Ephrata Cloister members built and operated this stagecoach inn in 1763, now a cozy bed-and-breakfast with hand-tooled furniture, canopy beds, fireplaces, and Pennsylvania Dutch quilts. The inn is surrounded by a dahlia garden and lily pond with koi. Breakfast is served by candlelight. Feather beds are available on request. Complimentary breakfast. | 900 W. Main St. | 717/733–6094 or 877/755–4590 | www.historicsmithtoninn.com | 7 rooms | $75–$155 | MC, V.

FORT WASHINGTON
▼▼

Gloriously adorned with several period mansions now open to visitors, the Philadelphia suburb of Fort Washington takes its name from the fortifications built here by the Continental Army in the fall of 1777. After their defeat at the Battle of Germantown on October 4, General Washington's army of 12,000 soldiers retreated to the northwest, where they camped for a month before heading to Valley Forge for the winter. Their encampment, along a ridge of hills known today as Militia Hill, is part of Fort Washington State Park. *Contact Valley Forge Convention & Visitors Bureau | 600 W. Germantown Pike, Plymouth Meeting 19462 | 610/834–1550 | www.valleyforge.org.*

Graeme Park. Exceptional surviving Georgian woodwork, original floorboards, Delft-tile fireplace surrounds, and twin closets with graceful fanlights reveal here how miraculously unchanged Graeme Park is since it was built in 1721 for Sir William Keith. Except for some restoration done by the Keith's son-in-law, Dr. Thomas Graeme, in the mid-1700s, the Jacobean-style mansion bears eloquent testimony to the many years Keith lived here as provincial governor of Pennsylvania—that is, until debt from his lavish spending drove him home to England, where he died in debtor's prison. | 859 County Line Rd., Horsham | 215/343–0965 | www.phmc.state.pa.us | $4 | Wed.–Sat. 10–4, Sun. 12–4.

The Highlands. When Quaker lawyer Anthony Morris rose to prominence as the Speaker of the Pennsylvania Senate, he built a suitably distinguished summer house in the late Georgian style on 200 acres of land. By 1808 he had to sell his country manor, with its 14-ft-wide entrance hall and elegant mahogany staircase because of "a total ignorance of the Expenses of building." Subsequent owners are credited with designing the 2-acre formal Colonial Revival garden hidden behind massive stone walls. | 7001 Sheaff La. | 215/641–2687 | ruralhistoryconfederation.org | $4 | Grounds, daily 9–dusk; house weekdays, tours at 1:30 and 3; June–Aug., Sun. by appointment.

Hope Lodge. In the 1920s and '30s, the moneyed set bought up Colonial antiques to decorate their homes in a style known as Colonial Revival. But few had an authentic Colonial home to decorate, as did William and Alice Degn, who lived in this 1748 early Georgian home of Quaker entrepreneur Samuel Morris. Today you'll leave Hope Lodge well schooled in the distinctions between Colonial and Colonial Revival, for the house presents both styles; for example, in Samuel Morris's formal Prussian-blue Colonial parlor the furniture is at the perimeter of the room; the Degns' version uses Colonial antiques in a more modern, comfortable arrangement. The estate is encircled by extensive herb and flower gardens; on their way to Valley Forge after the 1777 Battle of Germantown, Revolutionary troops camped on the fields just beyond. | 553 Bethlehem Pike | 215/646–1595 | www.ushistory.org/hope | $3.50 | June–Oct., Tues.–Sat. 9–5; Oct.–May, Wed.–Sat. 9–5, Sun. noon–5.

Peter Wentz Farmstead. The farmer is tending his Morgan horse, the ox is ploughing the field, and the young Colonial girl is making honey: you've time-traveled to the 1770s, when this farmstead was active not only with husbandry but also military strategy. Washington planned the Oct. 4, 1777, Battle of Germantown in the 1758 Georgian-style farmhouse and later celebrated General Gates's victory at Saratoga. The salute was allegedly fired so close to the house that several of the windows shattered. Volunteers in period costumes demonstrate how farming was done in the 1700s and lead tours of the home, whose odd touches include black polkadots on the wall below the chair rail and a cast-iron stove in the bedroom that is stoked through a hole in the back of the parlor fireplace. | 2100 Schultz Rd., Worcester | 610/584–5104 | www.montcopa.org/culture/history.htm | Free | Tues.–Sat. 10–4, Sun. 1–4.

✦ ON THE CALENDAR: Nov. **1777 Encampment Reenactment.** Hope Lodge hosts two days of military skirmishes and drills, Colonial crafts, and special tours to celebrate the Revolutionary troops' encampment here during the war. | 553 Bethlehem Pike | 215/646–1595 | www. ushistory.org/hope.

HISTORIC DINING AND LODGING

Joseph Ambler Inn. Tucked away on 12 acres, the inn offers accommodations with period furnishings in a stone bank barn, a charming tenant cottage, an 1850s home, and the original fieldstone house, built in 1734 by Joseph Ambler, a skilled wheelwright. The elegant Colonial restaurant, furnished with handcrafted cherry tables and Windsor chairs, serves New American cuisine. Complimentary breakfast. | 1005 Horsham Rd., North Wales | 215/ 362–7500 | www.josephamblerinn.com | 38 rooms | $110–$150 | AE, D, DC, MC, V | No lunch.

GERMANTOWN
▼▼

Set on the outskirts of the "City of Brotherly Love," Germantown spreads out beyond the cobblestoned great road known as Germantown Avenue. It has long been famed as an integrated, progressive community with a tradition of freethinking—the first written protest against slavery came from its residents. Anyone's tour of Philadelphia should include an afternoon here to view some of Germantown's six exceptionally well-preserved 18th-century homes— all lavishly blessed with unique architectural *and* historical pedigrees.

In 1683, when 13 German Quaker and Mennonite families settled here, Germantown was a peaceful place far out in the country, linked to the city 6 mi away by a dirt road. The first settlers soon welcomed English, French, and other Europeans seeking religious freedom. Before long, their modest homes and farms were interspersed with the grand homes of wealthy Philadelphians who hoped to escape the city's summer heat. In the fall of 1777, when the American Revolution came to Germantown, a number of these grand homes were commandeered as military headquarters, bombarded by musket fire, and used as hospitals. During the Battle of Germantown, George Washington led his troops in an audacious four-pronged attack on General Howe's forces that were ensconced here, part of his strategy to retake British-occupied Philadelphia. His plan was spoiled by unexpected British opposition and the heavy early morning fog that cloaked the area. Stalled in front of Cliveden by heavy fire from the British, Washington's troops were unable to meet up with other segments of the army. The Americans retreated—the beginning of their march to Valley Forge. Although they lost 1,000 men (twice as many as the British), their near victory improved the soldiers' morale and swayed the French to join the American side in the war. In 1793–94, when the yellow fever epidemic spread through Philadelphia, President Washington returned to Germantown along with other government officials for fresh air and rest, making the Deshler-Morris House his White House. *Contact Germantown Historical Society | 5501 Germantown Ave., Philadelphia 19144 | 215/844–0514 | www.libertynet.org/ghs. Greater Philadelphia Tourism Marketing Corporation | 30 S. 17th St., Suite 1710, Philadelphia 19103 | 888/GO–PHILA | www.gophila.com.*

Cliveden. Germantown's most noted mansion, Cliveden was the creation of Benjamin Chew, a Quaker-born Chief Justice of the Colonies. He evidently strayed far from his faith, owning slaves, favoring military action, and acquiring the trappings of wealth, which he enjoyed in this, one of the Colonies' finest country homes. A shining example of Middle Georgian style, Cliveden, built in 1763, has many grace notes, including unusual Waterford oil lamps, a mahogany sofa by acclaimed furnituremaker Thomas Affleck, and looking glasses that once reflected powered beauties at the "Meschianza," the fabled ball that Loyalist Philadelphians gave in honor of General Sir William Howe. Beauty gave way to blood, however, when Chew was under house arrest in New Jersey for his Loyalist leanings, and his Germantown abode was under siege. A regiment of British soldiers had barricaded themselves inside Cliveden's thick stone walls as Washington and his Continental Army advanced down Germantown Road on the fog-shrouded morning of October 4, 1777. Cannonballs and musket balls pounded the house for hours, but the British couldn't be dislodged. They left piles of bodies on Cliveden's doorstep and still-visible musket burns on the floor of the elaborate entrance hall, with its Doric columns—built, connoisseurs would tell you, to resemble Chew's court chambers in the Pennsylvania State House (now Independence Hall). | 6401 Germantown Ave. | 215/848–1777 | www.cliveden.org | $8 | Apr.–Dec., Thurs.–Sun. noon–4 and by appointment.

Deshler-Morris House. The "Germantown White House," a finely stuccoed stone house with a gable roof, was erected in 1772 by merchant David Deshler. Five years later, warring forces came to be the new occupants: after the Battle of Germantown, British General Sir William Howe would occupy the house, while in 1793 President George Washington would rent it as an escape from the yellow fever epidemic raging through Philadelphia. The Cabinet met four times at this White House to discuss the nation's position in the war between England and France. You can still see the "green Venetian blinds, a looking glass, four girandoles [branched candle holders], and stuff'd bottom chairs" that were here when the house was occupied by Washington, according to the inventory compiled by then-owner Isaac Franks. The dining room has 72 pieces of "Nankeen China," while the tea room holds a 1765 table that belonged to Declaration of Independence signer James Smith. When the president moved out at the end of the rental period, Franks charged him $2.50 "for Cleaning my house and putting it in the same condition the President rec'd it in." | 5442 Germantown Ave. | 215/596–1748 | www.nps.gov/edal/dmhouse.htm | $3 | Apr.–mid-Dec., Wed., Fri.–Sun. 1–4.

Germantown Historical Society. Although the society's museum and library houses more than 50,000 objects, documents, and photographs, only a fraction is on display, including 17th-century German trunks, Colonial highboys, tall-case clocks, and Peale paintings. If you make an appointment, you can see more, especially the renowned costume and textile collections. The society has an exhibit on Germantown's history. You can pick up brochures describing the historic Colonial houses nearby. | 5501 Germantown Ave. | 215/844–0514 | www.libertynet.org/ghs | Museum, $4; library, $7.50 | Tues. and Thurs. 9–5, Sun. 1–5.

Grumblethorpe. In 1744, Philadelphia merchant and wine importer John Wister built this summer home, then called "Wister's big house"—his brother lived at the smaller Wyck—and not named Grumblethorpe until the next century. Here the Wister family's parlor hints of good times and bad—through its Courting Door young men entered to win the favor of the Wister daughters, while through its front door British General James Agnew staggered after being struck by musket balls during the Battle of Germantown. He died in the arms of a servant girl, and his blood stains remain on the parlor floor. (Agnew lived here for just one week; the Wisters had moved to another home farther from the noisy British troops.) The stones for the house were quarried on the property, and the joists were hewn from oaks in Wister Woods, also owned by the family. The dining room has a chair made by Solomon Fussel, who made the chairs in Independence Hall. From the beginning, the Wisters tended a vegetable garden, orchard, and ornamental bulbs; today the gardens remain a glorious highlight. | 5267 Germantown Ave. | 215/843–4820 | www.ushistory.org/germantown | $3 | Apr.–mid-Dec., Tues., Thurs., and Sun. 1–4.

Stenton. At age 40, James Logan—who first came to Pennsylvania as William Penn's secretary and went on to hold almost every important public office in the Colonies—confided to a friend that he wanted to purchase a plantation to retire to, "for I am heartily out of love with the World." He designed this manor himself—still impressive in its Quaker simplicity—named it after his father's birthplace in Scotland, and proceeded to entertain everyone from Native American tribal delegates to Colonial bigwigs. Logan assembled one of the finest libraries in the Colonies; although the books have been moved to the Library Company, you'll still see his only extant bookcase. Stenton had distinguished guests even after Logan's death: in August 1777 General Washington stayed here on his way to the Battle of Brandywine; two months later British General Howe used it as his headquarters during the Battle of Germantown. Immaculately preserved, Stenton brings the past alive. What did the servant hiding in the dining room's "whispering closet" hear when she eavesdropped on James Logan's guests? An Indian negotiator's strategy? How business was going at the Durham Furnace? Listen closely and these walls may speak. | 4601 18th St. | 215/329–7312 | www.stenton.org | $5 | Apr.–Dec., Tues.–Sat. 1–4.

Upsala. What a threshold to be carried over! John Johnson III built the existing Federal house—with its magnificent fanlight-topped front door and portico with fluted Doric columns—as a wedding present for his bride, Sallie Wheeler, in 1798. Just beyond, the entrance hall is graced with plaster cornices in the design of steer skulls, a prescient symbol of fertility: nine Johnson children were born at Upsala. Fireplaces have splendid wooden mantels, delicately carved and faced with Pennsylvania marble, while the library has been restored to its original deep coral-color walls accented with grained wood. The main reception rooms showcase the family's collection of Sheraton, Hepplewhite, Philadelphia, and English furniture. | 6430 Germantown Ave. | 215/842–1798 | www.upsala-phl.com | $4 | Apr.–mid-Dec., Sat. noon–4.

Wyck. In this Colonial home the "good life" is defined not by the rare large collection of Tucker porcelain or by the fine Jacob Super dining table, but by the child's chair that's drawn up to that table and the toys, dolls, and games strewn about the parlor—signs that this was a happy home where children were cherished. Between the 1690s and 1973 nine generations of the Quaker Wistar-Haines family lived at Wyck; today descendants still stop by to visit. Over time the small stone house was expanded; in 1824 William Strickland, famed architect of the Second Bank of the United States, made the alterations you see today. Though the Duncan Phyfe sofa isn't rare, the letter explaining why it would be delivered late, is: "there have been great pains to select the handsomest wood, the nicest hair, and Phyfe says he must not be hurried as he wishes to finish it in a manner to do himself credit." There are precious receipts, letters, and diary entries about many of the original family furnishings, ceramics, and children's needlework. The garden of old roses, which dates to the 1820s, draws gardeners from around the country. The most prevalent rose is the Germantown Damask, which blooms pink and fades to white. Wyck, which is possibly the oldest house in Germantown, was used as a British field hospital after the Battle of Germantown. | 6026 Germantown Ave. | 215/848–1690 | www.wyck.org | $5 | Apr.–mid-Dec., Tues. and Thurs., noon–4:30, Sat. 1–4.

HISTORIC DINING AND LODGING

General Lafayette Inn and Brewery. This 1732 inn was the site of the Battle of Barren Hill, where General Lafayette, his men, and 50 Indians held off and finally escaped capture by a much larger English force. Today the menu occasionally features wild game. You'll find a fireplace in almost every room, and portraits of Lenni Lenape Indians and early battle scenes on the walls. Complimentary breakfast. | 646 Germantown Pike, Lafayette Hill | 610/941–0600 | www.generallafayetteinn.com | 5 rooms | $99–$159 | AE, D, DC, MC, V.

When you pack your MCI Calling Card, it's like packing your loved ones along too.

Your MCI Calling Card is the easy way to stay in touch when you travel. Use it to call to and from over 125 countries. Plus, every time you call, you can earn frequent flier miles. So wherever your travels take you, call home with your MCI Calling Card. It's even easy to get one. Just visit **www.mci.com/worldphone** or **www.mci.com/partners**.

EASY TO CALL WORLDWIDE

1. Just enter 1-800-888-8000 from the United States.

2. Enter or give the operator your MCI Calling Card number.

3. Enter or give the number you're calling.

EARN FREQUENT FLIER MILES

MCI.

Find America *with a Compass*

Written by local authors and illustrated throughout
with spectacular color images, Compass American
Guides reveal the character and culture of more than
40 of America's most fascinating destinations. Perfect
for residents who want to explore their own backyards
and for visitors who want an insider's perspective
on the history, heritage, and all there is to see and do.

Fodor's COMPASS AMERICAN GUIDES

At bookstores everywhere.

GREENSBURG

▼▼▼

Founded in 1787, Greensburg was named in memory of Revolutionary War hero Gen. Nathanael Greene, who had died in 1786, a year before the town's founding. Thirty miles from Pittsburgh in the heart of the Pennsylvania coal fields, Greensburg is a growing city with many shopping centers, hotels, and restaurants. Through town runs East Pittsburgh Street, which was originally part of a wagon trail that stretched from Philadelphia west over the Appalachian Mountains to Fort Pitt, now Pittsburgh. *Contact Laurel Highlands Visitors Bureau | 120 E. Main St., Ligonier 15658 | 724/238–5661 or 800/333–5661 | www.laurelhighlands. org. Westmoreland County Historical Society | 951 Old Salem Rd., Greensburg 15601 | 724/836– 1800 | www.starofthewest.org.*

Bushy Run Battlefield. The Indians did not wait for darkness to fall. At one o'clock in the afternoon, British Colonel Henry Bouquet and his 400 men found themselves on this hilltop, surrounded by an equal number of Indians. They fought wave after wave of attack, hopelessly outmaneuvered until the Colonel hatched a plan to feign retreat and attack the Indians' flanks and rear. The British prevailed on the battlefield preserved here, a key conflict during Pontiac's Rebellion and a turning point. To remove the British from their tribal lands, Chief Pontiac of the Ottawas and warriors from various tribes had captured nine British forts by late July 1763. The battle on August 5–6, when Pontiac attacked Bouquet en route to resupply Fort Pitt, marked an end to the Indian offensive, opening up the west to further settlement. "The March to Bushy Run" exhibit at the visitor center tells the story of the battle. The 183-acre area has 3 mi of hiking trails and picnic areas; you can take a guided or self-guided tour of the battlefield. | Rte. 993 Jeannette (11 mi northwest of Greensburg) | 724/ 527–5584 | www.bushyrunbattlefield.com | $3 | Park: Wed.–Sun. 9–5; visitor center: Apr.–Oct., Wed.–Sat. 9–5, Sun. noon–5.

Historic Hanna's Town. There's no justice, Robert Hanna must have thought, when the town he founded just 10 years earlier was attacked and burned to the ground by Indians and their English Canadian allies after the Revolution. Ironically, this town on Pennsylvania's western frontier was the site of the first English court west of the Allegheny Mountains. Costumed guides demonstrate Colonial crafts and give tours of the reconstructed village, including the courthouse-tavern, a jail, late 18th-century log houses, a Revolutionary-era fort, and a wagon shed with an authentic Conestoga wagon. An ongoing archaeological dig has unearthed several museums' worth of artifacts to date. | 951 Old Salem Rd. (between U.S. 119 and Rte. 819) | 724/836–1800 | www.starofthewest.org | $3 | June–Aug., Tues.–Sat. 10–4, Sun. 1–4; May, Sept., Oct., Sat. 10–4, Sun. 1–4.

✦ ON THE CALENDAR: June **Colonial Court Days.** Mock trials bring to life court cases that were tried at Old Hanna's Town between 1773 and 1782. There's also a reenactment of Revolutionary War–era military life, a Native American and fur trader encampment; and 18th-century occupations and handicrafts. | 951 Old Salem Rd. | 724/836–1800.

Aug. **Reenactment of the Battle of Bushy Run.** For two days, reenactors portray Colonel Henry Bouquet and his troops' defeat of the Native American forces that ambushed them in 1763 on their way to liberate Fort Pitt. Also featured are period 18th-century camps, a military trades demonstration, and Colonial crafts. | Bushy Run Battlefield, Rte. 993, Jeannette | 724/ 527–5584.

LANCASTER

▼▼▼

Lancaster, which the English named after Lancashire, is in the heart of Pennsylvania Dutch Country. This appealingly residential city of row houses dates from 1710, when eight Mennonite families accepted William Penn's invitation to escape persecution in Switzerland and settle here. The radical religious group named after its leader, Dutch Catholic priest Menno Simons, advocated nonviolence, separation of church and state, and adult baptism. They were soon joined by the Amish, Mennonites who followed Jacob Amman and his stricter interpretation of church tenets. During the French and Indian War and the American Revolution, Lancaster's craftsmen turned out fine guns, building the city's reputation as the arsenal of the Colonies. On September 27, 1777, Lancaster, the largest inland city in the Colonies, became the national capital for a day, as Congress fled the British in Philadelphia and convened here. Today Lancaster hosts busloads of tourists who come for the farmers' markets, family-style restaurants, and a peek at the Amish riding in their horse-drawn buggies. *Contact Pennsylvania Dutch Convention & Visitors Bureau | 501 Greenfield Rd., Lancaster 17601 | 717/299–8901 or 800/723–8824 | fax 717/299–0470 | www.padutchcountry.com.*

Amish Farm and House. In the front room of the stone house, wooden benches are precisely lined up, a reminder that the Old Order Amish hold church services in their homes. As you are guided through the 10-room farmhouse from 1805, you'll find out about Amish clothing, family life, and traditions. A map guides you to the barn, with its hay mows and threshing floor, and overhead scaffolding for air-curing tobacco. You'll also see a windmill, waterwheels, a lime kiln, a blacksmith shop, and animals on the 25-acre working farm, which dates from 1715. | 2395 Lincoln Hwy. E | 717/394–6185 | www.amishfarmandhouse.com | $6.75 | Daily 8:30–6.

Central Market. Andrew Hamilton plotted the land for the market in the center of town in 1730, and in 1743 King George II proclaimed it officially open. This, the oldest operating market in the country, began with open-air stalls; the current Romanesque building was constructed in 1889. It's a good place to shop for Lebanon bologna, shoofly pie, and fruit and vegetables from area farms. | Penn Sq. | 717/291–4723 | Tues. and Fri. 6–4, Sat. 6–2.

Hans Herr House. Andrew Wyeth made the 1719 sandstone Hans Herr house the subject of one of his paintings; perhaps, like many visitors today, he was enchanted by the medieval-style German architecture of this home, which belonged to one of his ancestors. It has the distinction of being the oldest home in Lancaster County and the oldest still-standing Mennonite meetinghouse in the Western Hemisphere. It is part of a museum complex that includes three farmhouses, a working blacksmith shop, an outdoor bake-oven, and a smokehouse. | 1849 Hans Herr Dr. | 717/464–4438 | www.hansherr.org | $4 | Apr.–Nov., Mon.–Sat. 9–4.

Heritage Center of Lancaster County. Why were George Washington's feet switched (the left and right are turned the wrong way) in the sculpture by Johannes Demuth? Why do Amish dolls have no faces? Why is a violin case shaped like a coffin? At the Old City Hall you're invited to discover the answers to these questions in engaging exhibits on the colonial history of the region and the culture of the Pennsylvania German settlers. The skills of Lancaster County artisans and craftspeople are evident in the clocks, furniture, homemade toys, *fraktur*, and Pennsylvania long rifles on display. | King and Queen Sts. on Penn Sq. | 717/299–6440 | www.lancasterheritage.com | Free | Mid-Apr.–Dec., Tue.–Sat. 10–5.

Historic Lancaster Walking Tour. A 90-minute stroll through the six-square-block heart of the Old City is conducted by a Colonial-costumed guide who imparts anecdotes about architecture, history, and the patriots who visited and lived here. Tours depart from the visitor center downtown. | 100 S. Queen St., at Vine St., near Penn Sq. | 717/392–1776 | $7 | Apr.–Oct., Tues. and Fri.–Sat. at 10 and 1, Sun.–Mon. and Wed.–Thurs. at 1; Nov.–Mar., by reservation only.

Historic Rock Ford Plantation. At his refined Georgian-style brick mansion on the banks of the Conestoga River, General Edward Hand spent his postwar years dabbling in experimental farming and cultivating fruit trees (a plum is named for him) until his death in 1802. He had earned the right to retire. Hand served George Washington as adjutant general; before the war, the Irish-born doctor entered politics as a Federalist and served in the Continental Congress. You'll walk on the original 18th-century floors and see original shutters, cupboards, paneling, and window panes. Rooms are filled with 18th century antiques and folk art; afterward, you can stroll through an herb garden, orchards, and landscaped grounds. The last tour is at 3. | 881 Rock Ford Rd. | 717/392–7223 | www.rockfordplantation.org | $5 | Apr.–Oct., Tues.–Fri. 10–4, Sun. noon–4.

Landis Valley Museum. "Demonstrating quilting and presenting the history of quilts is my greatest joy," wrote 75-year-old Arlene Hess, who learned to quilt under her grandma's guidance. She's been a volunteer at this open-air living-history complex for 15 years. But Eugene Smith, third-generation tinsmith, has her beat—he's been at the museum for 27 years. Their commitment speaks to the authenticity and quality of this once-small museum that mushroomed into a huge recreation of the rural lifestyle and folk culture of the Pennsylvania Germans. The museum includes exhibit buildings, a crossroads village with a tavern and country store, and a settler's farmstead with historical breeds of animals and heirloom plants. Over two dozen costumed demonstrators are at work spinning, weaving, pottery-making, tinsmithing. | 2451 Kissel Hill Rd. | 717/569–0401 | www.landisvalleymuseum.org | $9 | Mon.–Sat. 9–5, Sun. noon–5.

People's Place. At this tasteful interpretive center you'll find answers to most of your questions about the Amish, Mennonites, and Hutterites. A 30-minute multiscreen documentary titled *Who Are the Amish?* has close-ups of Amish life and perceptive narration. *20Q* (short for 20 Questions), an interactive family museum, highlights the differences between Amish and Mennonite societies. Children can try on bonnets and play in the "feeling box." Don't miss the collection of wood carvings by Aaron Zook. | 3513 Old Philadelphia Pike, Intercourse | 717/768–7171 or 800/390–8436 | www.thepeoplesplace.com | $5 for documentary or museum; $8 for both | June–Aug., Mon.–Sat. 9:30–7; Sept.–May, Mon.–Sat. 9:30–5.

HISTORIC DINING AND LODGING

Olde Greenfield Inn. A carefully restored 1790 Pennsylvania stone farmhouse is furnished with Early American antiques. You can dine in its wine cellar, by a wood-burning fireplace, or on a balcony overlooking the lounge, where you can hear live piano music on weekends. Don't miss out on the all-lump crab cakes. | 595 Greenfield Rd. | 717/393–0668 | $16–$25 | AE, D, DC, MC, V | No dinner Sun.; no lunch Mon.

Revere Tavern. Dripping with history, this 1740s tavern, formerly called "Sign of the Spread Eagle," was considered one of the state's best inns in its day. Its four dining rooms are warmed by seven working fireplaces; the King George Room features comb-back chairs and its original shutters and plate rail. A century later, it was purchased by President James Buchanan as a parsonage for his brother; Stephen Foster wrote "Oh Susannah!" and "My Olde Kentucky Home" while a guest here. The menu runs to tired-and-true favorites. | 3063 Lincoln Hwy. | 717/687–8601 | $11–$43 | AE, D, DC, MC, V | No lunch Sun. or Mon.

1725 Historic Witmers Tavern Inn. This pre-Revolutionary hostelry is the oldest and most complete Pennsylvania inn still lodging travelers in its original building. When Lancaster was on America's frontier, European immigrants rested here while their Conestoga wagon trains were being outfitted for their journeys to wilderness homesteads. Later, the Witmers hosted members of the Continental Congress and Revolutionary War officers. Restored to authentic pioneer style, the guest rooms have original working wood-burning fireplaces, antiques, and quilts. Complimentary breakfast. | 2014 Old Philadelphia Pike | 717/299–5305 | www.witmerstavern.com | 7 rooms, 2 with bath | $70–$110 | No credit cards.

MEDIA

▼▼

Named for its central location in Delaware County, Media is a primarily a commuter borough for workers in Philadelphia. The borough was settled by Quakers, but wasn't incorporated until 1848, when it became the county seat. *Contact Delaware County Historical Society / 85 N. Malin Rd., Broomall 19008 / 610/359–1148 / www.delcohistory.org/dchs.*

Colonial Pennsylvania Plantation. The smell of fresh-baked bread wafts from the oven, children paddle the butter, and older girls card the wool. It might as well be 1710 here, for the residents in period clothing do a great job of staying in character as they go about their chores. They are re-creating the lives of the Pratt family, three generations of which lived in this 18th-century Quaker plantation that has been farmed for 250 years. You'll see the men mending fences, tending the crops, and feeding the animals. Historical accuracy is important here; in 1973 the plantation buildings were restored using nothing but 18th-century tools. Also check out the state's only operating 18th-century gristmill, Newlin Mill Park, nearby at 219 S. Cheney Road. | Off Rte. 3, in Ridley Creek State Park | 610/566–1725 | www.delcohistory. org/colonialplantation | $4 | Mid-Apr.–mid-Nov., weekends 10–4.

✦ ON THE CALENDAR: May **Plantation Faire.** Colonial Pennsylvania Plantation hosts a hands-on Colonial fair with period entertainment, a "sheep to shawl" spinning demonstration, and the chance to try such skills as candlemaking and metal punching. | Off Rte. 3, Ridley Creek State Park | 610/566–1725.

MORRISVILLE

▼▼

Location, location, location: Morrisville made a name for itself because of its prime location on the "banks of the Delaware at the falls near Trenton." In 1682, William Penn used an outcropping of large gray boulders by the river as the starting point for his first purchase of land from the Indians. A century later, Patrick Colvin started a ferry service across the river; the settlement at the falls became a thriving mill town and was called Colvin's Ferry. Robert Morris, best remembered for his financial contributions to the American Revolution, owned some 2,500 acres in the area. While a senator, he proposed that the town be named the capital of the new nation. Though he didn't prevail, the town was named Morrisville in his honor. *Contact Bucks County Conference & Visitors Bureau / 3207 Street Rd., Bensalem 19020 / 888/359–9110 / www.experiencebuckscounty.com.*

Historic Fallsington. William Penn undoubtedly felt at home here when he attended Quaker meeting in this village established by English Quakers in 1680. The village grew to include four meetinghouses, a general store, and a tavern, the latter to serve the many travelers and farmers who passed through en route to the wharves of the Delaware River. Three of the meetinghouses, plus the homes of the tanner, carpenter, tailor, and saddler still stand, their handsome exteriors virtually untouched, surrounding Meeting House Square. Several restored buildings—including a Federal-period house that boasts one of the most beautiful doorways in Bucks County—the Stagecoach Tavern, and an early settler's log house, are shown on one-hour tours. | 4 Yardley Ave., off Tyburn Rd. W, Fallsington (6 mi northwest of Morrisville) | 215/295–6567 | www.bucksnet.com/hisfalls | $4 | Mid-May–Oct., Mon.–Sat. 10–3:30, Sun. 1–3:30.

Pennsbury Manor. Although William Penn, governor of the colony, preached the Quaker testimony of simplicity, he lived in luxury, importing the finest provisions and keeping a vast retinue of servants in his Georgian-style manor house along the banks of the Delaware River.

"The Country Life is to be preferr'd, for there we see the Works of God; but in Cities little else but the Works of Men," he wrote. The 43-acre country estate, built in the 1680s, with its formal gardens, orchards, ice house, smokehouse, and bake-and-brew house, helps paint a picture of the life of an English gentleman 300 years ago. Penn, his second wife, Hannah, and his daughter Letitia lived in his home—the only one Penn ever built for himself—for less than two years before he had to return to England, where he spent nine months in a debtors' prison. The reconstructed home is furnished with some items Penn owned and other furnishings of the time. Costumed guides conduct 90-minute tours; call for the times. | 400 Pennsbury Memorial Rd. (Tyburn Rd. E off U.S. 13) | 215/946–0400 | www.pennsburymanor. org | $5 | Tues.–Sat. 9–5, Sun. noon–5.

✦ ON THE CALENDAR: Sept. **Manor Fair.** Pennsbury Manor hosts a recreation of a 17th-century fair complete with hucksters, jugglers, and a Colonial court. You can try your hand at quill-pen writing, country dancing, and corn-husk doll making. | 215/946–0400.

Oct. **Historic Fallsington Day.** This one-day outdoor fair at the restored colonial-era village features American Revolution reenactors, Colonial and Native American dancers, puppet shows, hayrides, and demonstrations of papermaking, spinning, and open-hearth cooking. | 215/ 295–6567.

NEW HOPE
▼▼

This former dominion of the Lenni Lenape Indians has had many names in its past. As Coryell's Ferry it played an important role in the American Revolution: when Washington's failing army was driven west from New Jersey to Pennsylvania in the fall of 1776, he set up head-quarters around the ferry to rest his starving troops. After the Revolutionary War, Benjamin Parry began operating two mills here; after burning down in 1790, they were rebuilt and called the "New Hope Mills," offering new possibilities for the town. An arts community of painters and other craftspeople has since sprung up and flourished here for decades. Just across the bridge is Lambertville, New Jersey, studded with antiques dealers. *Contact Bucks County Conference & Visitors Bureau | 3207 Street Rd., Bensalem 19020 | 888/359–9110 | www. experiencebuckscounty.com. New Hope Historical Society | 45 S. Main St., New Hope 18938 | 215/ 862–5652 | www.newhopehistoricalsociety.org.*

Parry Mansion Museum. An impressive fieldstone Georgian-style house built in 1784, this mansion was built by the wealthy lumber-mill owner Benjamin Parry and occupied by five generations of his family. As such, the furnishings of the eight rooms piquantly reflect 125 years of decorative changes wrought by time, from Colonial to American Empire and Victorian. Guests can be easily imagined relaxing in style upon the curved-arm Duncan Phyfe–style sofa, watching a fire in the open Franklin stove (inset with a 13-star design symbolizing the original states). | 45 S. Main St. | 215/862–5652 | www.parrymansion.org | $5 | May–Dec., Fri.–Sun. 1–5.

Washington Crossing Historic Park. It was here, 7 mi south of New Hope, at what is now a lovely Delaware River Park, that on Christmas night in 1776 General Washington and 2,400 of his men crossed the icy Delaware in a blinding snowstorm to attack the British at Trenton. Their victory, which came after months of retreats and defeat, gave new life to the War for Independence. A granite statue of Washington marks the point from which the soldiers embarked that snowy night. Memorials and attractions are divided between the Lower and the Upper Park, which are about 5 mi apart.

In the Lower Park, the Memorial Building and Visitor Center displays a reproduction of Emanuel Leutze's famous painting of the crossing (the original hangs in the Metropolitan

Museum of Art in New York). You can also see the village of Taylorsville, which includes the McKonkey Ferry Inn, where Washington and his staff might have had Christmas dinner before crossing the river. There are also replicas of Durham boats, the shallow-draft boats built to carry iron that Washington used to transport men and artillery across the 1,000-ft-wide river. In the Upper Park, 2 mi south of New Hope, is Bowman's Hill Tower, named after a surgeon who sailed with Captain Kidd. Washington's sentries used the hill as a lookout point to watch for enemy movement before the crossing. The Thompson-Neely House is furnished just as it was when the Colonial leaders planned the attack on Trenton in its kitchen. Hour-long guided tours of historic buildings in the Lower Park leave from the visitor center, preceded by a 15-minute award-winning video titled *Of Dire Necessity.* You can then drive to the Upper Park to see the historic sites there. | 1112 River Rd., at Rte. 532 Washington Crossing | 215/ 493–4076 | www.phmc.state.pa.us | $5 | Tues.–Sat. 9–5, Sun. 12–5.

✦ ON THE CALENDAR: Dec. **Washington Crossing the Delaware.** Colonial reenactors assemble at 1 PM on Christmas Day along the banks of the Delaware River to be addressed by "General George Washington" before boarding the Durham boats to cross the Delaware. | Washington Crossing Historic Park Visitor Center, 1112 River Rd. | 215/493–4076.

HISTORIC DINING AND LODGING

Black Bass Inn. Set 6 mi north of New Hope and built as a haven for river travelers in the 1740s, when hostile Indians roamed the forests, this time-stained, rambling, forest-bordered hotel sits on the bank of the Delaware. Don't look for any GEORGE WASHINGTON SLEPT HERE plaques: the hotel and its clientele were Loyalists and, appropriately, the suave inn today contains a collection of British royal memorabilia. The excellent restaurant is famed for its Charleston Meeting Street Crab. Complimentary breakfast. No kids under 18. | 3774 River Rd., Lumberville (6 mi north of New Hope) | 215/297–5770 | www.blackbasshotel.com | 9 rooms, 2 with bath | $80–$175 | AE, D, DC, MC, V.

Logan Inn. John Wells's Ferry Tavern, the oldest building in New Hope, is at the core of the Logan Inn, in keeping with the Colonial habit of wrapping additions around existing buildings. George Washington is said to have stayed here at least five times. Rooms have Colonial-period furnishings; some have river views. Smack in the noisy center of town, the inn serves three menus: lunch, dinner, and an all-day tavern menu. Complimentary breakfast. | 10 W. Ferry St. | 215/862–2300 | www.loganinn.com | 16 rooms | $155–$200 | AE, D, DC, MC, V.

PHILADELPHIA
▼▼

The City of Brotherly Love is also the birthplace of the United States: it was here on July 4, 1776, that the Declaration of Independence was adopted. But its story begins nearly 100 years earlier, when William Penn began his "Holy Experiment" here in 1682 and named his settlement—Greek for "brotherly love"—after an ancient Syrian city, site of one of the earliest and most venerated Christian churches. Penn's Quakers settled on a tract of land he described as his "greene countrie towne." The next wave of immigrants were Anglicans and Presbyterians, who had a running conflict with the "stiff Quakers" and their distaste for music and dancing. The new residents forged traditions that remain strong in Philadelphia today: closely knit neighborhoods, comfortable houses, handsome furniture, and good education. From these early years came the attitude Mark Twain summed up as: "In Boston, they ask: 'What does he know?' In New York, 'How much does he make?' In Philadelphia, 'Who were his parents?' "

By the mid-1700s, Philadelphia was the largest city and the financial, social, and intellectual heart of the Colonies. The Philadelphia Stock Exchange opened for business in

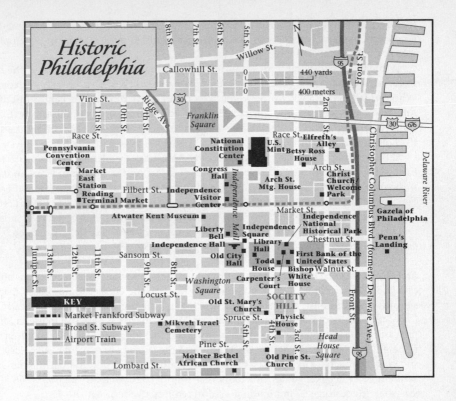

Historic
Philadelphia

1754—transactions took place in the City Tavern. The Assembly Dancing Society held its first social event where experts taught fashionable English and French dances, and Ben Franklin organized the Junto to discuss philosophical and scientific issues of the day. So, when the delegates from the Colonies wanted to meet in a centrally located, thriving city, they chose Philadelphia. They convened the First Continental Congress in 1774 at Carpenters' Hall. The rest, as they say, is history. It is here that the Declaration of Independence was written and adopted, the Constitution was framed, the capital of the United States was established, the Liberty Bell was rung, the nation's flag was sewn by Betsy Ross (though scholars debate this), and George Washington served most of his presidency.

The attractions listed below are scattered throughout Philadelphia, but are usually found within one of four main districts. The Historic District is "America's most historic square mile" and is immediately surrounding Independence National Historical Park. Old City, a melting pot for immigrants, is the area between Front and 5th streets and Chestnut and Vine streets; today it's known for its chic art galleries, restaurants, and its reworked houses and residential lofts. Society Hill is Philadelphia as it has been for 200 years, with its old chimney pots, hidden courtyards, ornate door knockers, and handsome homes; it stretches from the Delaware River to 6th Street, south of Independence National Historical Park. Center City, the city's commercial center, with City Hall as its heart, stretches from 8th Street to the Schuylkill River, and from South to Vine streets.

Any visit to Philadelphia should begin at the Independence Visitor Center; it is both the gateway to Independence National Historical Park and the city's official visitor center, where you can plan your trip to city sights and those in the outlying suburbs. If you have just one day, spend it in the national park; an early start at the Independence Visitor Center lets you pick up timed tickets for Independence Hall and sign up for tours of the Bishop White and Todd Houses; if you can, stay until dark to see the Lights of Liberty walking sound and light show. If Federal and Georgian architecture and period furnishings delight you, you should spend a half or full day visiting the museum homes of Fairmount Park. Or, you could travel 6 mi northwest of Center City to Germantown's museum homes, many of which played a role in the Battle of Germantown.

While many American think they know something about the birthplace of the nation, grade-school facts and figures do little to prepare travelers for the actual Philly experience. Who can fail to be moved by the words "Proclaim Liberty thro' all the Land," inscribed on America's best-loved relic, the Liberty Bell? Or by sitting where James Madison sat in Congress Hall? A walk through Philadelphia is a tour that exercises not only the feet but the spirit— the Spirit of 1776, to be exact.

SEPTA's distinctive purple minibuses, the **PHLASH,** are convenient for visitors. The 33 stops in the loop run from the Philadelphia Museum of Art on the Benjamin Franklin Parkway through Center City to Penn's Landing, and include many of the city's Colonial-era sites. You can get an all-day unlimited-ride pass for $4, or pay $2 for a one-way ticket (215/580–7800). *Contact Greater Philadelphia Tourism Marketing Corporation | 30 S. 17th St., Suite 1710, Philadelphia 19103 | 888/GO-PHILA | www.gophila.com. Independence Hall Association | Carpenters' Hall, 320 Chestnut St., Philadelphia 19106 | 215/925–7877 | www.ushistory.org.*

Arch Street Meeting House. No pulpit, no stained glass, no religious icons: just row after row of wooden pews all facing the center, in keeping with the Quaker testimonies of equality, simplicity, community, and peace. Constructed in 1804 for the Philadelphia Yearly Meeting of the Society of Friends, this is the oldest Friends meetinghouse still in use in Philadelphia and the largest in the world. A "modesty board," a long piece of wood about four inches in height, runs the length of the girls' staircase to the balcony to prevent Quaker lasses from showing too much leg to the Quaker lads climbing on the other side. A small museum honors William Penn. Quaker guides give tours year-round. | 320 Arch St. | 215/627–2667 | www.archstreetfriends.org | $1 minimum donation requested | Mon.–Sat. 10–4.

Atwater Kent Museum. What do you give the man who has everything? Thomas Jefferson brought back an elegant pocketwatch from Paris for President Washington. And what do you give the man who wants nothing? In 1682 at Shakamaxon, the Lenni Lenape thanked William Penn for peacemaking with a wampum belt. Both examples of thoughtful gift-giving are on exhibit in Philadelphia's history museum, which houses thousands of objects, from textiles to toys, that show what everyday life was like for generations of Philadelphians. The Colonial era is showcased in the first-floor Legacy for Philadelphia exhibit, which displays the dining-room chairs and executive desk from the Philadelphia presidential mansion, and portraits of Washington and Franklin by Charles Willson Peale. The museum occupies an elegant 1826 Greek Revival building designed by John Haviland. | 15 S. 7th St. | 215/922–3031 | www.philadelphiahistory.org | $5 | Wed.–Mon. 10–5.

AudioWalk & Tour. Put on your headphones, slip this CD into your Walkman, and let a friendly, virtual tour guide accompany you through the cobblestoned streets of Old Philadelphia at your own pace. It's easier to listen and *then* walk; up to four people can plug in, and there are benches at most of the 20 stops. The 65 tracks, each about two minutes long, offer entertaining anecdotes about history, architecture, and William Penn's vision. | Independence Visitor Center, 6th and Market Sts.; Lights of Liberty, 6th and Chestnut Sts. | 215/965–7676 | www.ushistory.org | $14.95 to purchase, from $10 to $20 for one to four people to rent | Visitor Center, daily 8:30–5; Lights of Liberty, Tues.–Sat. 10–6, Sun. 11–5; later until after the last show, in season.

Bartram's Garden. "There is that of God in every person," reads a Quaker testimony. Quaker farmer John Bartram (1699–1777) evidently found "that of God" in nature, when he was stopped in his tracks by a daisy while plowing his fields; he was so moved by the flower's beauty that he spent the rest of his life studying and collecting plants. With his son William he identified and introduced into cultivation more than 200 of our native plants. By 1765

Bartram's international reputation had earned him the notice of King George III, who made him Royal Botanist. The 45-acre site in now industrialized Southwest Philadelphia includes Bartram's furnished 1728 Swedish farmhouse. In this American birthplace of gardening, you'll see a fragrant flower garden, the country's oldest gingko tree, and the delicate blossoming Franklinia alatamaha tree—the Bartrams' most famous discovery—which they saved from extinction and named for their friend. | 54th St. and Lindbergh Blvd., Southwest Philadelphia | 215/729–5281 | www.bartramsgarden.org | $5 for house tour; garden free | Garden, daily 10–5; house, Mar.–Dec., Tues.–Sun. noon–4.

Betsy Ross House. It's easy to find this little brick house with the gabled roof: just look for the 13-star flag displayed from its second-floor window. Whether Betsy Ross—also known as Elizabeth Griscom Ross Ashbourn Claypoole (1752–1836)—actually lived here and whether she really made the first Stars and Stripes is debatable, but it's an urban legend that Philadelphians aren't anxious to disprove. When the young Betsy Griscom, a skilled seamstress, eloped with Anglican upholsterer John Ross, she was "read out of meeting" (kicked out of the Quaker church). They set up an upholstery business; Betsy's clients included Ben Franklin and members of the Revolutionary Pennsylvania government. The eight tiny rooms in this 1760 home hold her family Bible, chest of drawers, reading glasses, and other pieces that reflect the life of this hardworking woman who married and outlived two more husbands and then returned to her Quaker roots. She's buried along with her third husband, John Claypoole, in the brick-paved courtyard alongside the house. | 239 Arch St. | 215/686–1252 | www.betsyrosshouse.org | $2 donation requested | June–Sept., daily 10–5; Oct.–May, Tues.–Sun. 10–5.

Christ Church. As you sit in the pew where George and Martha Washington worshiped, you can imagine them glancing over their shoulders to see who just arrived late—John and Abigail Adams? Robert Morris? And whether Ben Franklin had missed yet another Sunday service. Fifteen signers of the Declaration of Independence prayed here in the most sumptuous church in the Colonies and the birthplace of the Episcopal Church in the United States. Dr. John Kearsley modeled his Georgian design on the work of famed English architect Sir Christopher Wren; the symmetrical, classical facade with arched windows and a bas-relief of King George II (removed in the pro-Republican 1790s) was furnished with a chandelier from England and a wine-glass pulpit. The bells and the soaring 196-ft steeple, the tallest in the Colonies, were financed by lotteries run by Benjamin Franklin. The mahogany font in which William Penn was baptized in 1644 was sent over from London in 1797. The church was completed in 1754 after 27 years of construction. | 2nd St., north of Market St. | 215/922–1695 | www.christchurchphila.org | Free | Daily 9–5.

Christ Church Burial Ground. Weathered gravestones fill the resting place of five signers of the Declaration of Independence and other Colonial patriots. The best-known is Benjamin Franklin; he lies alongside his wife, Deborah, and their son, Francis, who died at age four. According to local legend, throwing a penny onto Franklin's grave will bring you good luck. Although you can no longer walk through the cemetery, you can toss your penny from outside the iron gate. | 5th and Arch Sts. | 215/922–1695.

Elfreth's Alley. In the 18th century, butchers, bakers, and candlestick makers—and other artisans and tradesmen—rented Philadelphia's modest, narrow row homes, 33 of which survive and thrive on Elfreth's Alley, the oldest continuously occupied residential street in America. The alley, dating from 1702, was named for prosperous blacksmith Jeremiah Elfreth, who owned homes on both sides of the alley; his tenants often lived upstairs above their workshops or small shops. The earliest, Colonial-style pent-eave houses are one room wide and two stories high; the taller homes, built after the Revolution, show the influence of the Federal style. Today, 31 of the homes are owned by folks willing to sacrifice privacy (hundreds of people peek into their windows) for historical pedigree. Nos. 124 and 126, the former homes of a Windsor chair maker and a mantuamaker (an expert needleworker), respectively, are open to the public. | Front and 2nd Sts., between Arch and Race Sts. | 215/574–0560 | www.

elfrethsalley.org | Alley free; museum $2, $5 max. per family | Jan., Sat. 10–4, Sun. noon–4; Feb.–Dec., Tues.–Sat. 10–4, Sun. noon–4.

Fairmount Park Houses. In the late 18th and early 19th centuries, several of Philadelphia's prominent families built grand country manors in William Penn's suburban "Liberty Lands" north and west of Philadelphia. The elevated, forested banks of the Schuylkill River were described by one 18th-century observer as being "finely situated for prospect, health and pleasure"—and it was just a leisurely horseback ride from the city's commercial center. They hired the same expert builders and plasterers who had built Philadelphia's finest homes to craft their summer retreats in what is now Fairmount Park. Seven of these historic homes have been preserved and opened to the public. The Park House Guides of the Philadelphia Museum of Art offer tours of these homes, which are all within a 10-minute drive of each other. The Philadelphia Trolley Works offers tours to the park houses year-round, leaving from the west entrance of the Philadelphia Museum of Art. | 26th St. and Ben Franklin Pkwy. | 215/925–8687 | $10 | Apr.–Dec., Tues.–Sun.

Cedar Grove. Widow Elizabeth Coates Paschall's canopy bed still stands just where it was in the mid-18th century, when she built Cedar Grove in Frankford, 4 mi north of the city, as a summer sanctuary for herself and her children. Two generations later, the Morris family doubled the size of the modest 2½-story stone farmhouse, adding a gambrel roof with a large half-moon window in the gable. When a new railroad encroached on the property, the Morris family paid for the home to be moved—stone by stone—with its original furnishings to Fairmount Park. The remarkable collection of Jacobean, William and Mary, Queen Anne, Chippendale, and Federal furniture reflects the accumulations of five generations of the Paschall-Morris family. Highlights include a Wistar-Morris American black walnut high chest and dressing table. | Lansdowne Dr. off N. Concourse Dr., Fairmount Park West | 215/763–8100 Ext. 4013 | www.philamuseum.org/collections/parkhouse | $2.50 | Tues.–Sun. 10–5.

Laurel Hill. From his portrait perched above the mantle, William Rawle seems to be appraising the elegant octagonal room that a later owner added to his once modest villa. Or perhaps he's sighing with relief that his home was returned after the Americans confiscated it because of his family's Loyalist leanings. The 1767 Middle Georgian two-story, three-bay villa was built by Rebecca Rawle and Samuel Shoemaker on a laurel-covered hill overlooking the Schuylkill River. Later owners (among them Dr. Philip Syng Physick) added wings to the north and south. | Edgeley Dr. and Fairmount Ave., Fairmount Park | 215/235–1776 | www.philamuseum.org/collections/parkhouse | $2.50 | July–mid–Dec., Tues.–Sat. 10–4, Sun. noon–4.

Lemon Hill. When the new Philadelphia Museum of Art opened in the 1920s, the museum's director, distinguished architectural historian Fiske Kimball, chose Lemon Hill for his home. Like visitors today, he was charmed by its distinctive features: three oval parlors with curved doors and fireplaces in the grand Neoclassical style, and, just beyond the double stairs and fanlight-topped door, the entrance hall's checkerboard floor of Valley Forge marble. Kimball renovated the 1800 Federal-style home and lived here for 30 years. | Kelly Dr. and Sedgley Ave., Fairmount Park | 215/232–4337 | www.philamuseum.org/collections/parkhouse | $2.50 | Apr.–mid-Dec., Wed.–Sun. 10–4.

Mount Pleasant. "Symmetrical" and "elegant": ironic, isn't it, that these are the adjectives used to describe the home of John Macpherson, the one-armed, rough-and-tumble Scottish privateer? The sea captain made his fortune in the French and Indian War, and he invested it in real estate. His stunning country home was designed by master builder Thomas Nevell between 1762 and 1765; it is considered a superb example of Philadelphia's Middle Georgian style. John Adams agreed—he once described Mt. Pleasant as the most elegant seat in Pennsylvania. In 1779 Macpherson sold his house to General Benedict Arnold as a wedding gift for Peggy Shippen, but the newlyweds didn't live here before Arnold was charged with treason. The most spectacular of the Chippendale furnishings, culled from the Philadelphia Museum of Art's collection, is the mahogany library bookcase on the second floor. | Fountain Green off Kelly Dr., East Fairmount Park | 215/763–8100 Ext. 4014 | www.philamuseum. org/collections/parkhouse | $2.50 | Tues.–Sun. 10–5.

Strawberry Mansion. Attorney William Lewis, best known for his passage of a law "for the gradual abandonment of slavery in Pennsylvania," built a retreat in 1789, a five-bay Federal home called Summerville. He wouldn't recognize it today. After Lewis's death, U.S. Representative Joseph Hemphill sandwiched the original home between oversized three-story wings in the Greek Revival style. He threw lavish parties in the formal reception room furnished with late Neoclassical gilded furniture in the Restoration style. The room's focal point is a charming *causeuse,* or chatting couch. From the Empire-style bedroom, ornate enough for one of Napoléon's palaces, to the heavenly attic filled with antique dolls and toys, this a fine backdrop for a superb collection of Federal, Regency, and Empire furnishings. In later years the home was rechristened Strawberry Mansion when a Mrs. Grimes lived here and sold strawberries and cream to visitors who arrived by steamboat. | 33rd and Dauphin Sts., Fairmount Park East | 215/228-8364 | www.philamuseum.org/collections/parkhouse | $2.50 | Tues.–Sun. 10–4.

Sweetbriar. When the yellow fever epidemic ravaged Philadelphia in 1797, Samuel and Jean Breck escaped to the west bank of the Schuylkill, where they built a villa in the Neoclassical style. Educated in France, Breck was a friend of the Marquis de Lafayette and a Pennsylvania State senator. He wined and dined his cosmopolitan guests in one of the showplaces of the nation's capital, an elegant drawing room with a French mantel clock and candelabra and a chandelier bought from the Aga Khan's palace. From his floor-to-ceiling Italianate windows he could see the river stretching beyond a sweeping 400-ft lawn. The Brecks refuge—theirs was the first year-round residence in what was then Fairmount Park—did not shelter them from pain; their only daughter died here from typhus in 1828. | Lansdowne Ave., Fairmount Park West | 215/222–1333 | www.philamuseum.org/collections/parkhouse | $2.50 | July–mid-Dec., Wed.–Sun. 10–4.

Woodford. During the British occupation of Philadelphia, owner David Franks invited his Tory friends to congregate at Woodford—but that's not the only way he raised the roof. In 1772 he added a second story to the 20-year-old house to accommodate his large family, giving it its current Middle Georgian appearance. The dining room and drawing room, which contains one of the most finely carved overmantles and chimneybreasts in the city, display the Naomi Wood Collection of decorative arts from the Colonial and Federal periods, including a camelback sofa and tea table and a mahogany shelf clock from the shop of Abner Jones. | 33rd and Dauphin Sts., Fairmount Park East | 215/229–6115 | www.philamuseum. org/collections/parkhouse | $2.50 | Tues.–Sun. 10–4.

Fort Mifflin. From your vantage point atop the torpedo magazine, with the Delaware River spread before you, this looks like a peaceful place. But in the fall of 1777 Fort Mifflin experienced six days of the heaviest bombardment of the American Revolution. The British had laid siege to the fort for seven weeks in the hope of resupplying their troops. Finally, the Pennsylvania artillerists had to destroy and abandon the fort, but their defense held off the British long enough for Washington's troops to retreat to Valley Forge. The fort was rebuilt in 1798 and used until 1962. After a walk around the thick brick walls, you can explore the interior 2 acres, with its officers' and soldiers' barracks, artillery shed, museum, and musket-firing demonstrations. This National Historic Landmark rivals Fort McHenry in importance, but it's mostly unknown to Philadelphians today. | Island and Hog Island Rds., on the Delaware River near Philadelphia International Airport | 215/685–4167 | www.fortmifflin. org | $6 | Daily 10–4.

Franklin Institute Science Museum/Benjamin Franklin National Memorial. A 20-ft-tall marble Benjamin Franklin sits atop a giant pedestal in the rotunda of the city's science museum, a rightful place for the man who was known as much for his scientific inventions as for his role as a Founding Father. Architect John T. Windrim modeled this domed-ceiling marble memorial hall after the Pantheon in Rome, and it's grand, but it's easy to imagine that Franklin would be much happier let loose to run and get his hands on everything. The great news is that you can do exactly that throughout the museum, but on no account should anyone miss the Franklin Gallery's exhibition entitled "Franklin . . . He's Electric!," which explores his scientific genius in spheres from meteorology and music to optics and aquatics. His lightning rod, bifocals, and glass harmonica are on display in a walk-through re-creation of his study and workshop; there's also a model of his Franklin stove and the odometer he used to measure postal routes in Philadelphia. You can experiment with his swim fins, his long-reach device, and static electricity. | 222 N. 20th St. | 215/448–1200 | www.fi.edu | Memorial free, museum $12 | Daily 9:30–5.

Gloria Dei. The Swedes settled the Delaware Valley—"New Sweden"—in the mid-1600s before William Penn, but few traces remain other than their Gloria Dei (Old Swedes') Church in Southwark. The existing building (1698) replaced their original 1642 log house, making Gloria Dei the oldest church in continual use in America. The massive marble baptismal font is still in use; carved cherubim with an open Bible hang on the organ loft; models of the two ships that brought these settlers to the New World hang from the ceiling. The simple exterior shelters other treasures, too, like the 1608 Bible once owned by Sweden's Queen Christina and a delicate silver crown that brides may wear on their wedding day. Since the pastor was a friend of Ben Franklin's, the church was outfitted with a lightning rod. The church sits in the middle of its graveyard; among the patriots buried here is John Hanson, president of the Continental Congress under the Articles of Confederation. | 916 Swanson St., near Christian St. and Columbus Blvd. | 215/389–1513 | www.nps.gov/glde | Free | Daily 9–5.

Historical Society of Pennsylvania. Did Margaret Shippen Arnold feel ashamed after the treason of her husband Benedict? Was it difficult for Quaker Sarah Logan Fisher to exercise passive resistance to the Revolution, as her faith dictated? The answers to these questions can be found in the collection of diaries and letters of Colonial women, which are housed along with 500,000 books, 300,000 graphic works, and 15 million manuscript items in this superlative special collections library. The extensive Penn family papers (1629–1834) include letters that Hannah Callowhill Penn and her husband, William, wrote to each other throughout their courtship and her years of running the colony during her husband's extended illnesses. There's also a printer's proof of the Declaration of Independence and the first draft of the Constitution. | 1300 Locust St. | 215/732–6200 | www.hsp.org | $6. | Tues., Thurs., Fri. 9:30–4, Wed. 1–8, Sat. 10–4.

Independence National Historical Park. On June 28, 1948, President Harry S. Truman signed Public Law 795, creating Independence National Historical Park on 45 acres of Center City real estate. The park has many titles—including "America's most historic square mile" and "the birthplace of the nation"—and they're not hyperbole. Along these cobbled streets, independence was declared, the Liberty Bell was rung, and the U.S. Constitution was created. Close to 40 buildings from Philadelphia's Colonial, Revolutionary, and Federal periods have been preserved; about 20 are open and staffed by National Park Service rangers. Begin your visit at the Independence Visitor Center (*see below*), where you can pick up tickets to Independence Hall (in season), sign up for a tour of the historic houses, and get a map or the AudioWalk & Tour CD.

Bishop White House. Five children, 12 grandchildren, and status as the city's top spiritual leader didn't stop Bishop William White from being a great party-giver. For 50 years, the well-born White lived in this elegant 1786 home with his brood; a founder of the Episcopal Church after the break with England, White was rector of Christ Church and St. Peter's and chaplain to the Continental Congress. The sophisticated clergyman entertained the city's elite, including Washington and Franklin, who was probably delighted with the novelty of the bishop's flush toilet, or "necessary," one of the first in the city. In the parlor are an abundance of Canton china and a sofa that belonged to financier Robert Morris, the bishop's brother-in-law. White's canopy bed is draped with mosquito netting, a reminder that when the yellow fever epidemic hit Philadelphia, White stayed in the city to minister to those who were infected, while many other rich folks fled. | 309 Walnut St. | 215/597–8974 | www.nps.gov/inde/bishop-white.html | Free, sign up at the Independence Visitor Center for a tour of the Bishop White and Todd houses | Tours at 9:30, 10:30, 11:15, and 2.

Carpenters' Hall. Philadelphia is a union town, and the carpenters lay claim to being the city's oldest extant labor organization. In 1770 their headquarters was this handsome, patterned red-and-black brick building that their guild, the Carpenters' Company, founded to support its members, who were both builders and architects in this era. The delegates to the First Continental Congress, indignant over the Intolerable Acts that closed down Boston's port and Massachusetts's Colonial government, met here in September 1774 to sanction a policy of no trade with Great Britain and to address a declaration of rights and grievances to King George III. When the Second Continental Congress convened, it moved to the State House (now Independence Hall). During the Revolution, the hall served as a hospital and an arsenal for American forces. Today's re-created Colonial setting includes original Windsor chairs and candle sconces and displays of 18th-century carpentry tools. The Carpenters' Company still owns and operates the building. | 320 Chestnut St. | 215/597–8974 | www.nps.gov/inde/carpenters-hall.html | Free | Jan.–Feb., Wed.–Sun. 10–4; Mar.–Dec., Tues.–Sun. 10–4.

Congress Hall. During Philadelphia's 10-year tenure as the nation's capital, from 1790 to 1800, Congress adopted the just-built Philadelphia County Court House for its chambers. Within these walls the Bill of Rights was added to the Constitution; Alexander Hamilton's proposals for a mint and a national bank were enacted; and Vermont, Kentucky, and Tennessee became the first new states to join the original 13. On the main floor was the House of Representatives, where President John Adams was inaugurated in 1797. In the upstairs Senate chamber, George Washington was inaugurated for his second term in 1793. | 6th and Chestnut Sts. | 215/597–8974 | www.nps.gov/inde/congress-hall.html | Free | Daily 9–5.

Declaration House. During the summer of 1776, Thomas Jefferson, the 33-year-old delegate from Virginia, rented himself two rooms on Jacob Graff's second floor, settled into his swivel chair, arranged his lap desk, and went to work. The results—a copy of the original draft of the Declaration of Independence—can be seen in this faithfully re-created house-museum, along with that chair and desk. Had that version prevailed, slavery would have been abolished in 1776. But the passage was stricken by a committee that included Benjamin Franklin and John Adams, who feared the slavery matter would ruin the tenuous union. The first floor has exhibits and a short film, *The Extraordinary Creation*. | 701 Market St. | www.nps.gov/inde/declaration-house.html | 215/597–8974 | Free | Daily 10–1.

Franklin Court. One of 17 children, Benjamin Franklin did a good job of getting himself some attention in his pursuits as a statesman, diplomat, scientist, inventor (of bifocals, the lightning rod, and more), printer, and author: in 1763, at the age of 57, Franklin (1706–90) built his first permanent home in Philadelphia, in a courtyard off Market Street. On the site, architect Robert Venturi erected a steel skeleton of Franklin's former home, with cutaways that reveal wall foundations and outdoor privy wells. There's a full restoration of a working print shop and the B. Free Franklin post office; if you mail your postcards home from here, they'll be hand-stamped with Franklin's signature. An underground child-friendly museum pays tribute to his accomplishments. Dial-a-quote to hear his thoughts or pick up a telephone and listen to what his contemporaries really thought of him. A house at 318 Market Street displays ceramics, glassware, and other archaeological artifacts found at the Franklin Court site. | 314–322 Market St. | 215/597–8974 | www.nps.gov/inde/Franklin_Court | Free | Daily 9–5.

Independence Hall. As you stand in the plain and spacious chamber of the Pennsylvania Assembly Room, with George Washington's "Rising Sun" chair, the silver inkstand used to sign to Declaration of Independence and the U.S. Constitution, and the brass candlesticks that lit the way, you're transported back to those hallowed days that made this hall the birthplace of the United States. This stately redbrick building with its clock tower and steeple is one of our nation's greatest icons. America's most historic building was constructed in

1732–56 as the Pennsylvania State House. What happened here between 1775 and 1787 changed the course of American history—and the name of the building to Independence Hall. The delegates to the Second Continental Congress met in the Assembly Room in May 1776, united in anger over the blood that had been shed when British troops fired on citizens in Concord, Massachusetts. In this same room George Washington was appointed commander-in-chief of the Continental Army and Thomas Jefferson's eloquent Declaration of Independence was signed. From May to September 1787, George Washington presided as 12 delegates (Rhode Island didn't send one) framed the Constitution of the United States. Afterward, Benjamin Franklin said about the sun carving on Washington's chair, "I have the happiness to know that it is a rising and not a setting sun." Here the first foreign minister to visit the United States was welcomed; the news of Cornwallis's defeat was announced, signaling the end of the Revolutionary War; and, later, John Adams and Abraham Lincoln lay in state. On the other side of the hall is the chamber occupied by the Pennsylvania Supreme Court, with its jury box, prisoner's dock, and lawyer's table; there's an impressive coat of arms above the judge's bench.

Tours embark from the East Wing, which is attached to Independence Hall by a short colonnade. In the West Wing is the "Great Essentials" exhibit, the park's collection of our nation's founding documents: annotated drafts of the Constitution (with a typo marked by George Washington), and the Articles of Confederation, and an original printed Declaration of Independence, displayed with the inkstand used to sign the documents. From March through October, on Thanksgiving weekend, and the week between Christmas and New Year's Day you'll need a timed ticket in order to take the tour. They can be ordered in advance by calling 800/967–2283 or online at http://reservations.nps.gov. On the day of your visit you can get up to six tickets at the Independence Visitor Center. | Chestnut St. between 5th and 6th Sts. | 215/597–8974 | www.nps.gov/inde/indep-hall.html | Free | Daily 9–5.

Independence Visitor Center. The city's official visitor center is also the gateway to Independence National Historical Park. Park rangers are on hand to answer questions and distribute maps. But before you set off on a walking tour, acquaint yourself with Colonial American history by watching the 30-minute film *Independence* or the shorter *Liberty's Voice*. At the Park Services desk, you can pick up a timed ticket to tour Independence Hall and sign up for a 45-minute tour of the Bishop White and Todd houses. There's also a fully staffed concierge and trip-planning desk, as well as a coffee shop, a bookstore, and exhibit space. | 6th and Market Sts. | 800/537–7676 | www.independencevisitorcenter.com | July–Aug., daily 8:30–6; Sept.–June, daily 8:30–5.

Liberty Bell Pavilion. On July 8, 1776, the Liberty Bell rang out from the tower of Independence Hall, summoning citizens to hear the first public reading of the Declaration of Independence; just 16 years earlier, it had beckoned British subjects to celebrate the coronation of King George III. Originally cast in England in 1751 for the State House, it predates the concept of the separation of church and state; the bell is inscribed with a biblical passage from Leviticus: "Proclaim liberty throughout all the land, unto all the inhabitants thereof." When the 2,000-pound copper and tin bell cracked during testing, Philadelphia craftsmen cast a new bell using metal from the English version. To keep it from falling into British hands during the Revolution—they would have melted it down for ammunition—the bell was spirited away by horse and wagon to Allentown, 60 mi to the north. It didn't get its name until the 1830s, when a group of abolitionists—using it to symbolize their fight against slavery—renamed the State House bell the Liberty Bell. The bell is the subject of much legend; one story says it cracked when tolled at the funeral of Chief Justice John Marshall in 1835. Actually, a thin crack began to affect the bell's tone; despite a repair, it cracked again and hasn't been rung since 1846. The bell was moved to a glass-enclosed pavilion on Independence Mall for the 1976 Bicentennial; in spring of 2003 it was moved again so that it is silhouetted against Independence Hall, rather than 20th-century skyscrapers. The facility includes a shaded outdoor area for waiting in line, the bell chamber, and an interpretive exhibit hall which explains how the bell was made, how it became a symbol of freedom, and shows its reproduction on bottles, ties, lamps, and other everyday objects. | 6th and Market Sts. | 215/597–8974 | www.nps.gov/inde/liberty-bell.html. | Free. | Daily 9–5.

Library Hall. American treasures—a final draft of the Declaration of Independence hand-written by Thomas Jefferson with editorial comments by Richard Henry Lee, a copy of the U.S. Constitution with comments by Ben Franklin, and journals from the Lewis and Clark expedition of 1803–06—are taken from their vaults and displayed each summer in the lobby of Library Hall. The exterior of the building is a reconstruction of the Georgian facade of Ben Franklin's Library Company of Philadelphia, the first public library in the Colonies. Today the hall houses the collection of the American Philosophical Society, one of the country's leading institutions for the study of science. | 105 S. 5th St. | 215/440–3400 | www.amphilsoc.org/about/libhall.htm | Free | Exhibits, mid-June–early Oct., weekdays, 9-5; library year-round, weekdays 9–5.

Lights of Liberty. When you hear the hoofbeats, you will think of horses—and expect them to trample you— thanks to the amazing 3-D surround-sound headphones you wear during this nighttime, multimedia extravaganza billed as the "world's first walkable sound-and-light show." This is a class act: while 50-ft-tall handpainted images are projected onto historic buildings, you'll hear a musical score by the Philadelphia Orchestra, narration by Walter Cronkite and Charlton Heston, and special effects by Skywalker Sound. The one-hour show, which dramatizes the events that led up to the American Revolution, stops at five sites in Independence National Historical Park over a half-mile distance. Whoopi Goldberg narrates a lighter version (she calls King George a brat) for kids. There are four shows per hour; reservations are required. | PECO Energy Liberty Center, 6th and Chestnut Sts. Historic district | 215/542–3789 or 877/462–1776 | www.lightsofliberty.org | $17.76; $49 family package for family of 4 | Evenings beginning at dusk; Memorial Day–Labor Day, Tues.-Sat.; May and Labor Day–October, Thurs.–Sat.

New Hall Military Museum. The Continental soldiers and sailors are well-sung heroes, but did you know that the Marines helped in the fight for independence? Chartered in 1775, the Leathernecks (named for the leather collars they wore during the American Revolution) supported General Washington during his 1776 Christmas crossing of the Delaware. This museum documents the role of the military in early American history, with dioramas, uniforms, and weapons. | Chestnut St. east of 4th St. | 215/597–8974 | www.nps.gov/inde/new-hall.html | Free | Daily 2–4.

Old City Hall. When Philadelphia became the nation's capital in 1790, the just-completed city hall was lent to the federal government to house the U.S. Supreme Court. The high court shared it with the mayor's court, but it wasn't a conflict; the justices met only twice a year; the rest of the time they had to travel the country's backroads to attend circuit courts. The distinctive Federal-style building is on the left flank of Independence Hall; exhibits trace the history of the Supreme Court. | 5th and Chestnut Sts. | www.nps.gov/inde/old-city-hall.html | 215/597–8974 | Free | Daily 2–5.

Second Bank of the United States. While the Continental Army camped at Valley Forge, Charles Willson Peale painted some 40 officers, including Washington. His portraits, along with others by William Rush and Gilbert Stuart, are part of the 185-portrait collection of colonial and Federal leaders, military officers, explorers, and scientists on display in the bank. Washington's death mask, the only known portraits of explorers Meriwether Lewis and William Clark, and Peale's portrait of Jefferson (the only one that shows him with red hair) are highlights. The Doric-columned Second Bank, built between 1819 and 1824 by architect William Strickland, helped establish the popularity of Greek Revival architecture in the United States. The interior banking hall's dramatic, barrel-vault ceiling is Roman. | 420 Chestnut St. | 215/597–8974 | www.nps.gov/inde/second-bank.html | Closed for renovations until October 2003.

Todd House. When yellow fever killed young Quaker lawyer John Todd in 1793, it left his wife Dolley a widow. Within the year, she was married to James Madison, 17 years her senior. She met the future president in her modest second-floor parlor, which you'll see on the tour of this 1775 middle-class home. You'll also be treated to insights into the character of this two-term first lady, a talented hostess who presided over a house containing two children, her younger brother and sister, and two of her husband's law clerks. When one of the clerks died from fever, Dolley sued his parents for back rent. Biblical flash cards belonging to Dolley's sister; pictures of Faith, Hope, and Charity; and a reproduction of Todd's law office are among the items of interest. | 4th and Walnut Sts. | 215/597–8974 | www.nps. gov/inde/todd-house.html | Free, sign up at the Independence Visitor Center for a tour of the Todd and Bishop White houses | Tours at 9:30, 10:30, 11:15, and 2.

Town Crier Summer Theatre. Costumed actors roam the historic district in tricorne hats and petticoats and perform interactive playlets like "Troubling Taxes," while an 18th-century quartet, the Libertytones, sings "Songs of Unrest." Audience members are "recruited" into the Continental Army and inspected down to their teeth, and introduced to Colonial "Instances of Ill Manners." Historic Philadelphia Inc.'s theatre troupe appears at more than a dozen historic sites, from Christ Church to the Betsy Ross House. | Around the historic district | 215/629–5801 | www.historicphiladelphia.org | Free | May–Labor Day, daily 10–6.

Library Company of Philadelphia. Books were too expensive for the middle class to own, so Ben Franklin and his book club, the Junto, pooled their resources to start a subscription library in 1731. Each of the 50 subscribers invested 40 shillings and agreed to pay 10 shillings a year thereafter to buy books; they asked James Logan, "a gentleman of universal learning and the best judge of books in these parts," to choose the volumes and purchase them from England. Although any "civil gentleman" could come in and read the books, only subscribers could take them home. From 1774 to 1800 the Library Company functioned as the de facto Library of Congress. The 400,000-volume collection includes 200,000 rare books. Changing exhibits showcase the library's holdings. | 1314 Locust St. | 215/546–3181 | www.librarycompany. org | Free | Weekdays 9–4:45.

Mikveh Israel Cemetery. When Nathan Levy's ship, the *Myrtilla,* brought the Liberty Bell to America, there were only about 12 Jews living in Philadelphia. But the Colonial merchant knew that the Jewish population would grow—and need a burial ground—so he bought land from the Penn family. It was used as the cemetery for Mikveh Israel, the second oldest Jewish congregation in the United States, which Levy helped found for the city's Spanish-Portuguese Jews. Among the 371 known graves are those of Nathan Levy; Haym Salomon, a financier of the American Revolution who died a pauper; Rebecca Gratz, the inspiration for the character Rebecca in Sir Walter Scott's novel *Ivanhoe*; and 21 Jewish veterans of the Revolutionary War. To visit, contact Mikveh Israel, now at 44 N. 4th St. | Spruce St. between 8th and 9th Sts. | 215/922–5446 | www.mikvehisrael.org | Free | Changing hrs; call for schedule.

Mother Bethel African Methodist Episcopal Church. As Richard Allen preached, anything is possible. In his later years, when Benjamin Chew was Chief Justice of the Supreme Court, Richard Allen was the first bishop of the African Methodist Episcopal church. But if you turn the clock back 56 more years, you'd see Allen being born a slave in the Chew home, helping his family cook and clean for the wealthy attorney. In the interim, Allen had a religious awakening, became a free man and a lay minister, and then led fellow blacks from St. George's Methodist Church as a protest against its segregated worship. In 1791 he bought the land on which the church stands; it's the nation's oldest parcel of land continuously owned by African-Americans. | 6th St. between Pine and Lombard Sts. | 215/925–0616 | www. motherbethel.org | Donation requested. | Museum, Tues.–Sat. 10–3.

National Constitution Center. You can take the presidential oath of office, sit on a Supreme Court bench, and vote in an historic election in the nation's first museum, opening July 4, 2003, dedicated to this founding document; in fact, you can read a 24-ft-high copy that's etched onto glass and wrapped around the exhibits. Designed by Ralph Appelbaum Associates, the firm responsible for the U.S. Holocaust Memorial Museum in Washington, D.C., and Pei Cobb Freed & Partners, known for the expansion of the Louvre, the museum occupies an entire city block on the north end of Independence Mall. The story of the Constitution is brought to life through more than 100 interactive and multimedia exhibits, artifacts, film, music, television, sculpture, and the Internet. With a 360-degree screen and a live actor, *The Founding Story* covers the themes and historical context of the document. A video *Family Tree* tells the stories of 100 ethnically diverse Americans; the Family Theater serves up an irreverent take on the Bill of Rights geared to middle-school students. The visit ends in Signers' Hall among 42 life-size bronze statues of the men who signed, or refused to sign, the Constitution on September 17, 1787. You can decide to add your signature or dissent, by way of custom-made parchment books. | 525 Arch St. | 215/923–0004 | www.constitutioncenter.org | $5 | Daily 9:30–5.

Old Pine St. Presbyterian Church. It's so peaceful inside: the beautifully restored church is painted in soft shades of periwinkle and yellow; the walls are stenciled with thistle and wave motifs, a reminder of Old Pine's true name—Third, Scots, and Mariners Presbyterian Church. It's hard to imagine that during their occupation of Philadelphia, the British used the church as a hospital and then a stable, stripped the sanctuary of its pews (anything that could be sold or burned), and left behind only the bodies of 100 Hessian mercenaries who still lie under the east walk of the churchyard. Today this 1768 church is the only Presbyterian structure in Philadelphia dating back to Colonial times. Its Greek Revival face-lift dates from the mid-19th century. | 412 Pine St. | 215/925–8051 | www.libertynet.org/oldpine | Free | Mon., Wed.–Fri. 8–5, Tues. 10–5, Sat., call ahead.

Old St. Joseph's Church. The open-minded William Penn accepted Catholics in his "Holy Experiment," but he wanted them to worship in secret and not make waves. That's why Philadelphia's 11 Catholic families hid their 1733 church—the first place in the English-speaking world where Catholic mass could be legally celebrated– in an alley. But make waves they did. On one occasion Quakers had to patrol St. Joseph's to prevent a Protestant mob from disrupting the service. The present church, built in 1839, is the third on this site. | 321 Willings Alley | www.oldstjoseph.org | Free | Weekdays 11–4, Sat. 10–7, Sun. 7:30–4.

Old St. Mary's Church. Catholic or not, the city's bright lights came to pray at St. Mary's, including the ecumenical George Washington and the Puritan John Adams. Special pews were reserved for the French, Spanish, and Portuguese ambassadors. The city's second-oldest Catholic church, circa 1763, became its first cathedral when the archdiocese was formed in 1808. A Gothic-style facade was added in 1880. The stained-glass windows, a ceiling mural of St. Mary, and brass chandeliers that hung in the Founders Room of Independence Hall until 1967 are highlights. | 252 S. 4th St. | 215/923–7930 | www.ushistory.org/tour/tour_stmary.htm | Free | Mon.–Sat. 9–5.

Pennsylvania Hospital. As you gaze down from the upper gallery into the surgical amphitheater, imagine that you're a medical student in 1804 watching Dr. Phillip Syng Physick remove a kidney stone, without electricity, sterile technique, or anesthesia—just opium, liquor, or a knock on the head—his swift technique illuminated by the skylight above (unless clouds roll in). Today Pennsylvania Hospital is a full-service modern medical center. In 1751 it was the nation's first hospital, founded by Benjamin Franklin and Dr. Thomas Bond. The hospital has a portrait gallery, early medical instruments, a medicinal herb garden, a rare-book library with holdings dating from 1762, and Benjamin West's painting *Christ Healing the Sick*, which raised $25,000 for the hospital when it was put on exhibition. All of this is housed in one of Philadelphia's most magnificently elegant Federal-style buildings, topped off with a huge octagonal drum, balustraded roof, and stately wings. Pick up a copy of "Pennsylvania Hospital: A Walking Tour" at the Welcome Desk just off the 8th Street entrance. | 800 Spruce St. | 215/829–3971 | www.pahosp.com | Free | Weekdays 8:30–4:30.

Physick House. Touches of Napoléon's France are everywhere: the golden bee motif woven into upholstery; the magenta-hue Aubusson rug (the emperor's favorite color); and stools in the style of Pompeii, the Roman city rediscovered at the time of the house's construction. Built in 1786, this is one of two remaining freestanding houses from this era in Society Hill. It is also one of the most beautiful homes in America, with some of the finest Federal and Empire furniture in Philadelphia, including the one-of-a-kind oval bookcase made for John Penn. Upstairs in the parlor, note the inkstand that still retains Benjamin Franklin's fingerprints. The house's most famous owner was Philip Syng Physick, known as the "Father of American Surgery." Don't miss the lovely 19th-century garden. | 321 S. 4th St. | 215/925–7866 | www.philalandmarks.org | $3 | Sept.–May, Thurs.–Sat. 11–3; June–Aug., Thurs.–Sat. noon–4, Sun. 1–4. Last tour 1 hr before closing.

Powel House. Here, in the second-floor ballroom, you can almost taste the floating islands and whipped syllabubs that Mrs. Powel—the city's hostess-with-the-mostest—served to distinguished guests (including Adams, Franklin, and Lafayette) on Nanking china that was a gift from George and Martha Washington. She lived in this lavish 1765 brick Georgian house with her husband, Samuel, who was the last mayor of Philadelphia under the crown and the first under the new republic. A signed Gilbert Stuart portrait graces the parlor. | 244 S. 3rd St. | 215/627–0364 | www.powelhouse.com | $3 | Thurs.–Sat. noon–5, Sun. 1–5.

St. Peter's Church. When the wealthier members of Christ Church moved from the commercial neighborhood near Second and Market Street to gracious new homes in Society Hill, they built a new church to match. They employed a top architect, Robert Smith, respected for his Carpenters' Hall, to design the Palladian-style building; they had him raise the high-backed cedar pews off the floor to eliminate drafts. William White did double duty, serving as bishop at both Christ Church and St. Peter's. The church, which opened in 1761, has been in continuous use since. In the churchyard lies painter Charles Willson Peale and other notables. | 313 Pine St. | 215/925–5968 | www.stpetersphila.org | Free | Weekdays 8–4, Sat. 8–3, Sun. 1–3; knock on rectory door if church is locked.

Thaddeus Kosciuszko National Memorial. At age 30, Polish military engineer Thaddeus Kosciuszko came to the United States to lend his expertise to the Revolutionary cause; commissioned as a colonel, he went to work planning the forts along the Delaware River. By war's end he was an American hero, promoted to brigadier general. But when he returned to Poland to fight the occupying Russians, he was imprisoned and exiled from his homeland. The wounded soldier returned to Philadelphia to convalesce, spending his time with prominent visitors like Vice President Thomas Jefferson and sketching pictures of local ladies, who were charmed by the handsome general. The memorial has a portrait gallery and a brief film (in English and Polish) about the general's activities during the Revolution. | 301 Pine St. | 215/597–9618 | www.nps.gov/thko | Free | June–Oct., daily 9–5; Nov.–May, Wed.–Sun. 9–5.

Welcome Park. There's no grass in this park named for the ship that brought William Penn to Philadelphia. Instead, you'll find a 60-ft-long marble map showing the city plan for Penn's "greene countrie towne," a model of the Penn statue that tops City Hall, and a wall engraved with his quotations, his philosophy, and a timeline of his life. Penn lived at a home on this site from 1699 to 1701; while here he issued his Charter of Privileges, a document that guaranteed religious and civil liberties and became a model for the U.S. Constitution. | 2nd St. just north of Walnut St.

✦ ON THE CALENDAR: Apr.–June **Philadelphia Open House.** You can peek inside some of the city's Colonial-era homes during this event, when some 150 Philadelphians open up their doors and gardens for tours, which sometimes include lunch, candlelight dinner, or high tea. | 215/928–1188 | ww.friendsofindependence.org.

June **Elfreth's Alley Fete Days.** About 20 of the 30 homes on Elfreth's Alley, the nation's oldest continuously occupied street, are open for tours hosted by guides in Colonial garb at this festival, which includes food, entertainment, and demonstrations of colonial crafts. | Front and 2nd Sts. between Arch and Race Sts. | 215/574–0560 | www.elfrethsalley.org.

Late June–July 4 **Sunoco Welcome America Festival.** Philadelphia's premier event celebrates America's birthday in America's birthplace with 80 free happenings, including big-name outdoor concerts, fireworks, a summer Mummers Parade, and the awarding of the Philadelphia Liberty Medal. | 215/683–2201 | www.americasbirthday.com.

Nov. **Fort Mifflin Reenactment.** With battle reenactments, musket drills, and period crafts, this fortress along the Delaware River brings you back to the fall of 1777, when Fort Mifflin experienced six days of the heaviest bombardment of the American Revolution. | Island and Hog Island Rds., near Philadelphia International Airport | 215/685–4167 | www.fortmifflin.org.

HISTORIC DINING AND LODGING

City Tavern. You can time travel to the 18th century at this authentic re-creation of the original 1773 City Tavern. The food—lobster pie in a pewter casserole, Martha Washington's turkey potpie, and West Indies pepperpot soup—is prepared from enhanced period recipes and served on Colonial-patterned china. Kids' menu. You can eat outside on the patio. Live music Sat. | 138 S. 2nd St. Society Hill | 215/413–1443 | www.citytavern.com | $17–$40 | AE, D, DC, MC, V.

Shippen Way Inn. Two 1750 houses have been restored into a charming period inn with rooms individually decorated with antique four-poster beds, timbered walls, or working fireplaces. Wine and cheese are served each afternoon by the living-room fireplace or in the Colonial herb and rose garden. Complimentary breakfast. | 416–418 Bainbridge St. | 800/245–4873 | http://come.to/shippenwayinn | 9 rooms | $90–$110 | AE, MC, V.

Thomas Bond House. Built in 1769 by a prominent local physician, this four-story Georgian house has undergone a meticulous restoration of everything from its molding and wall sconces to the millwork and flooring. There are pencil-post and cannonball pine beds, Chippendale period furnishings—and 20th-century hot-tub baths. This B&B is within Independence National Historic Park. Complimentary breakfast. No children under 11. | 129 S. 2nd St. | 800/845–2663 | http://www.winston-salem-inn.com/philadelphia | 10 rooms, 2 suites | $95–$175 | AE, D, MC, V.

PITTSBURGH

▼▼▼

What made Pittsburgh great? The confluence of three mighty rivers—the Monongahela, the Allegheny, and the Ohio. In the 1750s Pittsburgh was a strategic frontier outpost from which the fledgling nation could expand west, a prize sought after by both the French and British. At the end of the French and Indian War in 1763, Pittsburgh was officially English. Later, when Pennsylvania and Virginia claimed it, Congress gave it to Pennsylvania. In the early 1800s Pittsburgh earned its title "Gateway to the West" as settlers and goods passed through. Later in the century it became the world's leading producer of steel. The city was home to steel magnate Andrew Carnegie, whose moniker is attached to some of the city's best attractions, including the Carnegie Museum of Art and the Carnegie Science Center. *Contact Greater Pittsburgh Convention and Visitors Bureau | Regional Enterprise Tower, 425 6th Ave., Pittsburgh 15219 | 412/281–7711 or 800/366–0093 | www.visitpittsburgh.com.*

Fort Pitt Museum. Sitting in the fur trader's cabin, you can imagine the comfortless life at this prized frontier outpost at the fork of the Ohio River: the French wanted it to connect their colonies in Louisiana with New France (Canada); the British hoped to expand their colonial power westward, and the Native Americans longed to preserve their lands. Exhibits and dioramas cover the French expeditions, the building of Fort Pitt, and the struggles that exploded in the French and Indian War. You'll see the uncomfortable surroundings of a soldier's barracks and a model of the fort. The museum, housed in the Monongahela Bastion of the old Fort Pitt, is in Point State Park at the tip of Pittsburgh's Golden Triangle. | 101 Commonwealth Pl. | 412/281–9284 | www.fortpittmuseum.com | $2.50 | Wed.–Sat. 10–5, Sun. 12–5.

Point State Park. The triangle of land formed by the Allegheny and Monongahela rivers as they join to form the westward-flowing Ohio was called "the Prize" during the French and Indian War. The strategic point, today the dramatic 36-acre Point State Park, was the site of four different forts built within 10 years by the armies of France and Britain. In 1754, when French forces captured an outpost here erected by Virginians, George Washington was sent to recapture the fort. He suffered his first defeat at Fort Necessity, 50 mi to the southeast. The French then constructed Fort Duquesne and ruled the roost for four years, until they got word that General John Forbes was preparing an assault. Badly outnumbered, the French burned the fort. The British arrived on November 25, 1758, and began construction on Fort Pitt, the most extensive fortification by the British in the American colonies. In the park is Colonel Henry Bouquet's Blockhouse, all that remains of Fort Pitt. Built in 1764, it is the oldest authenticated structure west of the Allegheny Mountains. Three of the fort's five original bastions have been restored. One houses the Fort Pitt Museum; the Music Bastion has been excavated to reveal parts of the original fort's foundation, and the southern-facing Flag Bastion offers a fine view of the Monongahela River. On some summer Sundays the British Royal American Regiment stages a reenactment with cannon firings and fife and drum playing. | 101 Commonwealth Pl. | 412/471–0235 | www.dcnr.state.pa.us | Free | Daily 7 AM–11 PM.

POTTSTOWN
▼▼

This wooded region 35 mi northwest of Philadelphia had what it needed—iron ore, water, and charcoal—to develop a thriving pig-iron industry. John Potts, the area's most successful ironmaster, founded the borough in 1761, laying out the town around his forge. A 1989 study revealed that Pottstown, for its size, contains some of the oldest, most architecturally significant housing in the northeastern United States. More than 1,000 historic homes and buildings occupy its districts. *Contact Reading and Berks County Visitors Bureau | 352 Penn St., Reading 19602 | 610/375–4085 or 800-443-6610 | www.readingberkspa.com.*

Daniel Boone Homestead. The frontiersman who's famous for exploring and settling Kentucky learned the skills of pioneer life—hunting, trapping, exploring unmapped places—while growing up on his family's homestead near Pottstown. He was born here in 1734 and stayed until age 16, when his family began a year-long trek to North Carolina. The site includes the Boone house, blacksmith shop (his father's trade), barn, Bertolet log house, sawmill, and a visitor center. Tours focus on the economic and social lives of the English and Germans who settled in eastern Berks County between 1730 and 1820. | 400 Daniel Boone Rd., Birdsboro (8 mi west of Pottstown) | 610/582–4900 | www.berksweb.com/boone.html | House $4; grounds free | Tue.–Sat. 9–5, Sun. noon–5.

Hopewell Furnace National Historic Site. As you watch the turning waterwheel, puffing bellows, and smoking stack, consider how the fortunes of Mark Bird, Hopewell's ironmaster, went up in smoke. A Berks County militia commander, Bird bought uniforms, tents, and provisions for 300 of Washington's starving men, and in 1778 he sent 1,000 barrels of flour down the Schuylkill River to the general at Valley Forge. But after the war Congress refused to reimburse Bird for his services; that, plus post-war inflation, led to his financial ruin. A fine example of an early American "iron plantation," this charcoal-fueled furnace produced pig iron and finished castings from 1771 until 1883. During the Revolution, Hopewell employees cast cannon, shot, and shells for the patriot forces. The site now has 14 restored structures, including a cold-blast furnace and the ironmaster's mansion. Park brochures, wayside exhibits, and audio stations help you tour the site at your own pace. In summer there's a living-history program that demonstrates molding and casting. | 2 Mark Bird La., Elverson (12 mi southwest of Pottstown) | 610/582–8773 | www.nps.gov/hofu | $5 | Daily 9–5.

Pottsgrove Manor. John Potts, a wealthy ironmaster whose family owned nine furnaces, built this elegant Georgian manor house for his wife and 13 children on 1,000 acres in 1752. Potts, who founded Pottstown and served in Pennsylvania's General Assembly, entertained George and Martha Washington here on several occasions; for five days in September 1777 the general made the manor his headquarters. Its restored interior has antique furnishings, including Philadelphia Chippendale; outside is a Colonial Revival garden. | 100 W. King St. | 610/326–4014 | www.montcopa.org | Free | Tues.–Sat. 10–4, Sun. 1–4.

UNIONTOWN
▼▼

Uniontown, just north of the West Virginia border, was founded on July 4, 1776, a happy coincidence, as news of the nation's independence was still days away. Soon afterward both Pennsylvania and Virginia claimed it; the dispute was settled in 1780 with the drawing of the Mason-Dixon line. The valley around Uniontown was the scene of General George Washington's first military actions in 1754, beginning the French and Indian War. The hard-to-reach, sparsely populated town thrived when statesman Albert Gallatin used his influence to have the new National Road (1811–18) run right through Uniontown. In later years Uniontown was the center of a prosperous coal industry; at one time the town was said to have more millionaires per capita than any other town in the United States. *Contact Laurel Highlands Visitors Bureau | 120 E. Main St., Ligonier 15658 | 724/238–5661 or 800/333–5661 | www. laurelhighlands.org. Ligonier Valley Chamber of Commerce | Town Hall Ligonier 15658 | 724/238–4200 | www.ligonier.com.*

Braddock's Grave. A single marker commemorates the final resting place of British Major General Edward Braddock, commander-in-chief of all British forces in North America. Braddock led an unsuccessful expedition to try and capture French-held Fort Duquesne at the fork of the Ohio River; he was killed on July 13, 1755, along with 900 of his 1,400 men. The general was originally buried in the road his men had built; his men were reported to have then marched over the grave to wipe out any traces of it. | U.S. Rte. 40, Farmington (1½ mi west of Fort Necessity) | 724/329–5512 | www.nps.gov/fone/braddock.htm | Free | Daily 9–5.

Fort Necessity National Battlefield. After encountering the French at Jumonville Glen in the wilderness of the Allegheny Mountains, 22-year-old Colonel George Washington prepared for an attack; he marched to the "Great Meadows" and built a small palisaded fort, which he aptly called Fort Necessity in a journal entry. On July 3, 1754, a French and Indian force captured the fort and forced Washington to surrender, the only time he ever did so in his military career. This, the opening battle of the French and Indian War, began a seven year struggle between Great Britain and France for control of the continent. The site includes the reconstructed circular wooden fortification and a visitor center with a slide show and exhibits on Fort Necessity and the French and Indian War. There are 5 mi of hiking trails, including portions of Braddock Road. | 1 Washington Pkwy. Farmington (11 mi east of Uniontown) | 724/329–5512 | www.nps.gov/fone | $3 | Daily 9–5.

Jumonville Glen. "I heard the bullets whistle, and, believe me there is something charming in the sound," wrote 22-year-old George Washington, describing his first experience under fire. After the 15-minute skirmish—no one knows who fired the first shot—in a wooded glen below a 30-ft wall of rocks, Jumonville, leader of the French detachment hidden here, was killed along with 10 of his men. Washington's diplomatic mission to ask the French to leave the area had turned deadly. Kiosks on the site explain the battle, the first in the Fort Necessity Campaign and the spark that ignited the French and Indian War. | Summit Rd. (7 mi northwest of Fort Necessity) | 724/329–5512 | www.nps.gov/fone/jumglen.htm | Free | Mid–Apr.–Oct. 9–5.

VALLEY FORGE
▼▼▼

A major site of the Revolutionary War is near the suburban village of Valley Forge, which was named for an iron forge built here in the 1740s. The monuments, markers, huts, and headquarters in Valley Forge National Historical Park illuminate a decisive period in U.S. history. The park, with its quiet beauty that seems to whisper of the past, preserves the area where George Washington's Continental Army endured the bitter winter of 1777–78. *Contact Valley Forge Convention and Visitors Bureau | 600 W. Germantown Pike, Plymouth Meeting 19462 | 610/834–1550 | www.valleyforge.org.*

Historic Waynesborough. The fireplace in Anthony and Polly's bedchamber has a curious stain in the shape of a Patriot's portrait, which tour guides suggest is a ghostly reminder of the night of the Paoli Massacre, when British soldiers searched the mansion to find "Mad Anthony" but came back empty-handed. Although George Washington called Wayne "the sanest Brigadier in the Revolutionary Army," his nickname (coined by a drunken soldier who was angry at being put in the guardhouse and given 29 lashes) stuck with him through his illustrious career. The Georgian country manor on 1,000 acres, 5 mi south of Valley Forge, was the birthplace and retirement home of the general, a war hero who led the Pennsylvania Line in the Battles of Brandywine and Germantown. The Elouis portrait of *General Wayne and the Treaty of Greene Ville* (1796) hangs above the mantle in the blue-painted parlor; it is framed by Wayne's officer's sash, dueling pistols, and swords. The house displays his uniforms and medals and Polly's treasures—Chippendale ladder-back side chairs, a 1740 tall-case clock built by Peter Stretch of Philadelphia, and silver, china, and glass. Later in life Wayne came out of retirement to negotiate with the Northwest Indians and open the West to settlement. | 2049 Waynesborough Rd., Paoli | 610/647–1779 | www.madanthonywayne.org | $5 | Mid-Mar.–mid-Dec., Wed. and Thurs. 10–4, Sat. 10–1, Sun. 1–4.

Mill Grove. Haitian-born and adopted by French parents, John James Audubon came to his father's estate in Audubon, 2 mi north of Valley Forge, to escape military service. "I'm not a fighting person," he wrote. He spent his days in the woods, hunting, fishing and sketching birds; he invented a simple wire device for holding his freshly killed birds in realistic poses so that he could draw them in the now famous Audubon style. Although he lived here only two years, it's where the artist, author, and naturalist first encountered American birds and wildlife. Built in 1762, the house is now a museum displaying Audubon's major works, including reproductions, original prints, his paintings of birds and wildlife, and a double-elephant folio of his *Birds of America*. The attic has been restored to a studio and taxidermy room. The surrounding Audubon Wildlife Sanctuary, popular with bird-watchers, has 175 acres with 5 mi of hiking trails. | Pawlings Rd. and Audubon Rd., Audubon | 610/666–5593 | Free | Museum Tues.–Sat. 10–4, Sun. 1–4; grounds Tues.–Sun. dawn–dusk.

Valley Forge National Historical Park. The winter of 1777 was harsh. The Marquis de Lafayette wrote, "The unfortunate soldiers were in want of everything; they had neither coats nor hats, nor shirts, nor shoes. Their feet and their legs froze until they were black, and it was often necessary to amputate them." After losing the battles of Brandywine, White Horse, and Germantown, General George Washington retreated to Valley Forge, while the British occupied Philadelphia. Every 12 men shared a damp 16-by-14-ft log hut, partially below ground; meals were "fire cakes," fried batter of flour and water; and dysentery and typhus spread quickly in the tight quarters. Many men deserted, and although no battle was fought, 2,000 soldiers died. Spring brought hope: the competent General Nathanael Greene was appointed quartermaster general, the shad that surged up the Schuylkill River to spawn were caught, 70 bakers arrived at camp to make each soldier a pound of bread a day, and Prussian drillmaster Baron von Steuben arrived. He worked without pay, leading the troops in dawn-to-dusk training, teaching them about bayonet use and sentry duty. Spirits also lifted in May, when the French recognized the independence of the United States. In June 1778 Washington led his troops away from Valley Forge to intercept British General Henry Clinton at the Battle of Monmouth.

The 3,600-acre park is administered by the National Park Service. Stop first at the visitor center to see the 18-minute orientation film called *Valley Forge: A Winter Encampment,* view exhibits, and board a bus or buy a tape for a self-guided tour. Stops include the National Memorial Arch, built in a style similar to the Arch of Titus in Rome; a bronze equestrian statue of General Anthony Wayne; Artillery Park, where the soldiers stored their cannons; and the Isaac Potts House, which served as Washington's headquarters. The park contains 6 mi of jogging and bicycling paths and hiking trails, and you can picnic at any of three designated areas. A leisurely visit to the park takes no more than half a day. | North Gulph Rd. and Rte. 23 | 610/783–1077 | www.nps.gov/vafo | Free | Visitor center daily 9–5; park grounds daily dawn–dusk.

In the five small rooms of the Isaac Potts house, renamed **Washington's Headquarters,** George Washington and his staff of more than 20 coordinated the efforts of the Continental Army while at Valley Forge. Park volunteers dress in period costumes and discuss life at Valley Forge for Washington, his staff, and his troops. | Apr.–Nov. $3; Dec.–Mar. free | Daily 9–5.

Built in 1904 as a tribute to George Washington, **Washington Memorial Chapel** is still in use today. It's famous for its 26-ton carillon, one of the world's largest, with 58 bronze bells that are played from a keyboard and cover nearly five octaves. Carillon concerts are held Wednesday evenings in July and August. The church also has a Patriots Tower and Veterans Wall of Honor. | 610/783–0120 | www.libertynet.org/chapel | Free | Daily 9–5.

The replicated mud-chinked huts of **Muhlenberg's Bridge** anchored the encampment's outer line of defense. In summer, costumed rangers demonstrate musket loading and how the soldiers lived. | Free | Daily dawn to dusk.

The **Auto Tape Tour** is a do-it-yourself tour in your own car; you're guided by a 60-minute CD or tape that describes the events that took place at Valley Forge. Pull-off areas are available so you can walk through some of the sites. The tape is sold at the visitor center. | 610/783–5788 | $8 tape; $11 CD | Daily 9–5.

A 45-minute **Bus Tour** with a taped narration leaves from the visitor center. Passengers can step off at various locations and pick up another bus as it passes by. Buses run every 30 minutes. | 610/783–5788 | $6 | June–Aug., daily 9:30–4; Sept.–Oct., weekends 9:30–4.

✦ ON THE CALENDAR: June and Dec. **March into Valley Forge.** Each year on December 19, Pennsylvanians commemorate the 1777 march of George Washington and his 12,000 troops into Valley Forge by reenacting the event. If you return to the park in June, on the weekend nearest the 19th, you can celebrate the troops' survival and see them march out. The festivities include the firing of muskets, campfires, and living-history demonstrations. | Valley Forge National Historic Park | 610/783–1077 | www.nps.gov/vafo.

HISTORIC DINING AND LODGING

General Warren Inne. During the Revolution, Loyalists frequently met at his 1745 inn to plot against the revolutionaries and draw maps of the valley, which were given to generals Howe and Cornwallis. The infamous Paoli Massacre, when the British attacked General "Mad Anthony" Wayne with bayonets after midnight on September 20, 1777, was launched from here. You can dine by candlelight indoors or outdoors overlooking the vegetable garden; the menu includes beef Wellington, crab cakes, and snapper soup. The restaurant is closed

Sunday and serves no lunch on Saturday. Complimentary breakfast. No children under 12. | Old Lancaster Hwy. Malvern | 610/296–3637 | www.generalwarren.com | 8 rooms | $120–$170 | AE, DC, MC, V.

YORK

▼▼▼

One of Pennsylvania's first frontier towns west of the Susquehanna, York was named for Yorkshire, England. It was a supply depot during the Revolution. The Second Continental Congress sought refuge here from September 1777 to June 1778, after fleeing British troops marching on Philadelphia. While in York, Congress debated and adopted the Articles of Confederation, which bound the 13 Colonies into the United States of America, providing a legal national government and making York the first U.S. capital. They also declared the first national Thanksgiving to celebrate a victory in Saratoga, New York. Later on, Confederate troops held the town for $100,000 ransom on their way to Gettysburg. Many of its historic buildings and sites remain untouched. *Contact York County Convention and Visitors Bureau | 1 Market Way E, York 17401 | 717/848–4000 or 888/858–9675 | www.yorkpa.org. York County Heritage Trust | 250 E. Market St., York 17401 | 717/848–1587 | www.yorkheritage.org.*

Gates and Plough Complex. When Thomas Paine, John Hancock, and Sam Adams came upon the Golden Plough Tavern on the wooded banks of the Codorus Creek, it must have looked like a scene out of a Brothers Grimm fairy tale with its medieval German architecture. They, with other members of the Second Continental Congress, had retreated to York in 1777 while the British occupied Philadelphia. In 1964, when architectural historian Joe Kindig came upon the tavern, it was buried under wooden siding, except for its chimney. He restored the 1741 tavern, one of several buildings managed by the York County Heritage Trust. The General Horatio Gates House is furnished as it was in 1778, when Gates, president of the Board of War, lived here; it is said to be the site of Lafayette's famous toast to George Washington's health, signalling to conspirators that the French would not support a plot—known as the Conway Cabal—to replace Washington with Gates. You won't find any beer on tap today in the Golden Plough Tavern, but you will see a mix of architectural styles: the first floor is a log structure and the medieval German-style second floor is made with bricks and timber. The Colonial Courthouse is a replica of the building where the Second Continental Congress met in 1777–78. You can listen to a narrative that shows the delegates debating the Articles of the Confederation and see the original Proclamation of the United States of America. The 75-minute tour leaves from the York Downtown Visitor Center. | 149 W. Market St. | 717/848–1587 | www.yorkheritage.org | $6 | Jan.–Feb., Sat. 10–4; Mar.–Dec., Tues.–Sat. 10–4, Sun. 1–4.

By Tracey Minkin

Rhode Island

❧〜❧

The "Lively Experiment"

*I*t all began here. This declared, with a wave of the hand toward a tiny spring along Providence's riverfront, a gesture toward a cluster of white steeples dotting the hillside that rises from that spring, and sometimes, a grand acknowledgment, a flourish away from the steeples, off to the west and upward a hundred feet, to a bronzed statue, Rhode Island's *Independent Man,* who stands high atop the capital city's marble-domed State House. This is what Rhode Islanders, fiercely proud of the stirring beginnings of their tiny, free-thinking (and oft-maligned) state, will tell a visitor. It all began here. Religious dissent. Freedom of worship. Freedom of expression. Prickly resistance to authoritarian control. Independence.

This is not a chronological claim to fame (after all, colonies founded in Virginia and Massachusetts predated the first English settlements along the oceanic wedge later named Narragansett Bay). This, rather, is an ideological claim to fame, beginning with a disgraced minister who sneaked out of snowy Massachusetts and took his Puritan-threatening ideas south. This is about the founding of a new colony based on tolerance, which drew freethinkers from not only nearby settlements but also from across the ocean, and formed the foment, like a pungent sourdough culture, for a local zeitgeist based on independent thought and actions. It made for disagreement, dissent, and sometimes chaos. It allowed for scandal, scurrilous business practices, piracy, and slave-trading. It nourished unparalleled entrepreneurism. And in the more than three centuries since that outcast minister Roger Williams met a small band of welcoming Narragansett Indians who greeted him with "What cheer, Netop?" it has fed a tiny state its wellspring of pride and yielded a modern landscape still alive with the meetinghouses, synagogues, earthworks, trading posts, taverns, wharves, and other still-extant wonders—the literal legacy of Rhode Island's very own "Lively Experiment."

And all of this (with some more hand gesturing, no doubt), within an hour's drive, in any direction! For Rhode Island delivers its historical riches within a tight embrace indeed, making it a place for lingering, strolling, and pausing to reflect. For nothing, no matter what the next destination, can possibly be that far away. And yet so many historic vestiges punc-

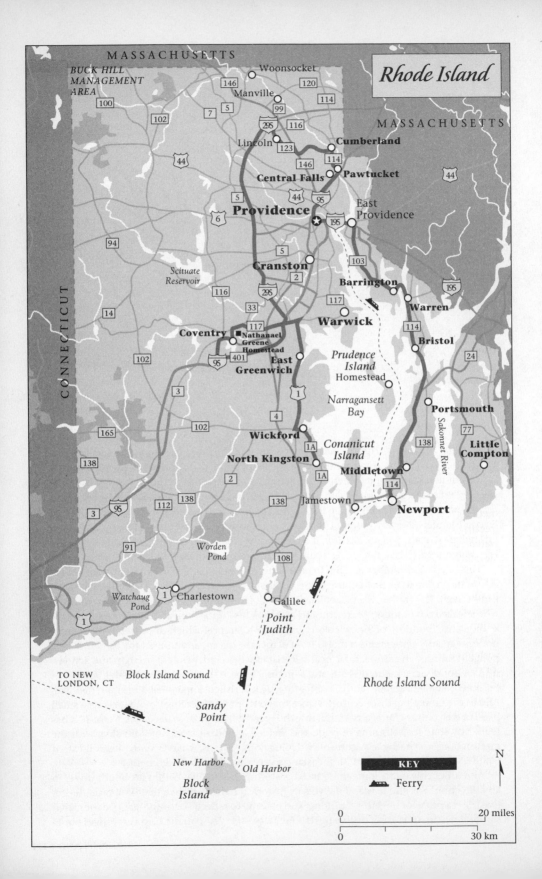

tuate the fields, hills, shorelines, and townscapes of this tiny state, that a happy traveller can spend days in colonial pursuit, Revolutionary discovery, and Federalist delight.

✦ THE TRUE INDEPENDENTS

Although the besieged clergyman Roger Williams may be Rhode Island's best-known arriviste, he was by no means its first. By the time Europeans began their forays in the region a mere 500 years ago, Native Americans made up several distinct (and often warring) tribes, the two most prominent being the Narragansetts, who settled the western side of Narragansett Bay, and their rivals, the Wampanoags, who held the eastern shores. These and other neighboring tribes would play a role in conflicts leading up to (and contributing to) the Revolutionary War, as well as fight in the war itself.

Highly partisan scholars (and highly opinionated Rhode Islanders) bicker over who got here first after these tribes: medieval Irishmen, Norsemen (Newport's Stone Tower continues to spark controversy about whether Vikings built it), Portuguese navigators. But everyone agrees that in 1524 an Italian navigator named Giovanni Verrazano, seeking an all-water route through North America to China, headed north up the Eastern coast and discovered what he called "an island in the form of a triangle, distant from the mainland ten leagues, about the bigness of the Island of Rhodes." Verrazano's small notation begat large tidings. The Rhodes comparison prompted Roger Williams (who mistakenly thought, 90 years later, that Verrazano had been commenting on the Narragansett Bay island called Aquidneck by local tribes) to change Aquidneck's name to "Rhode Island." This led to the official, albeit cumbersome, colonial monicker of "Rhode Island and Providence Plantations." Aquidneck got its name back eventually, but the mouthful continues to be the state's official name.

A smattering of explorers and traders came through in the wake of Verrazano, most notably a Dutchman named Adriaen Block who bumped into the same island off the coast in 1614, and named it after himself. (Block Island, now known mostly for summer splendors and Victorian hotelfronts, did receive a small, incredibly hearty band of colonists who forded ashore in 1661 with their livestock and set up a settlement against brutal weather and later, marauding privateers.) But it was the freethinking minister who really got things rolling. An ardent advocate of the complete separation of church and state as well as the perhaps even more blasphemous notion that Native Americans should be paid for their land by settling Europeans, Williams raised the ire of Massachusetts Bay Colony Puritans. With imprisonment looming, he fled through the snow southward, sleeping in hollowed treetrunks, nearly freezing to death. Sheltered and guided by the Wampanoags, Williams chose a small freshwater spring (now surrounded by the tiny Roger Williams National Memorial) to begin anew. He called the place Providence, with divine implications.

✦ "DIVINE" PROVIDENCE

In short order, word got out. Anne Hutchinson, a revolutionary freethinker with an equally visionary husband, left prickly Massachusetts with her own followers, drawn by the reputation of Williams and what he called a "Lively Experiment" in tolerance. Her band first settled at Portsmouth in 1638, then Newport in 1639. The outpost in Newport, on a deepwater port with good shelter, would thrive and completely outshadow Providence, becoming a center for shipping and trading (and British sympathy). Jews escaping the ever-extending reach of the Inquisition came and prospered and built the nation's first synagogue. Unprecedented wealth (built on legitimate commerce but also on privateering, smuggling, and rampant slave-trading), and a pro-British, colonial yearning to replicate the spoils of the homeland, spawned haute architecture, silversmithing, and the colonies' finest Early American furniture-making.

But the war would not be kind to Newport, now grown—and today magnificently restored—into an opulent town crammed with mansions and shops. Merchants throughout the entire colony (which got its royal charter in 1663) resented British taxation and control, and the freewheeling spirit bridled early. Before the much-heralded Boston Tea Party, Rhode Islanders scuttled and torched a British customs sloop in Newport Harbor (1769), then a British revenue schooner in Warwick (1772), and then held its own Tea Party in Providence (1775).

Rhode Island Timeline

1633 William Blackstone settles near Pawtucket.

1636 Roger Williams moves to Providence.

1638 Aquidneck purchased from Narragansett Indians; Portsmouth is settled.

1663 Charter granted by King Charles II.

1675–76 King Philip's Indian war.

1764 Rhode Island College established (renamed Brown University in 1804).

1769 In first overt act of violence against British authority, British tax ship *Liberty* destroyed in Newport.

1772 British tax ship *Gaspee* burned in Narragansett Bay.

1774 Importation of slaves prohibited.

1776 General Assembly renounces allegiance to Great Britain in May.

1776 General Assembly approves Declaration of Independence in July.

1776 British Army takes Newport in December.

1778 Battle of Rhode Island.

1790 Federal Constitution adopted.

1790 Samuel Slater starts cotton mill in Pawtucket.

And although early Rhode Islanders excelled, it seems, at guerilla-style resistance, they also sought higher, philosophical ground: in May 1776, little more than a year after the skirmishes at Lexington and Concord, Rhode Island became the first colony to renounce allegiance to King George III.

A REGIONAL GAZETEER

✦ THE BLACKSTONE RIVER VALLEY: TINDERBOX OF THAT OTHER REVOLUTION

When a river drops steeply and consistently over 46 mi, great things are bound to happen—and they did. In Pawtucket, "place by the waterfall" to the local Native Americans, the Blackstone River drops most precipitously and culminates in a natural falls. Here in 1793, Moses Brown of Providence installed Samuel Slater, an Englishman with a genius for manufacturing. The result was Slater Mill: the country's first water-powered cotton mill, the first gunshot in America's Industrial Revolution, and today, a tremendous, multibuilding museum that grounds families in the new country's greatest economic shift. But before the Pawtucket Revolution, the Blackstone Valley had already spawned innovation. William Blackstone, an eccentric Anglican minister who was legendary for riding a white bull throughout the region, settled along the banks of the river that would eventually bear his name, and became the first permanent white settler in Rhode Island, beating Roger Williams by a year–see the wilderness park dedicated to him in Cumberland. With country roads and stone walls, orchards and farmstands, and always the presence of the colony's most powerful and influential waterway, the Blackstone Valley is the country's latest National Heritage Corridor. And thanks to **Pawtucket**'s *Spirit of the Blackstone Valley*, a 12-seat riverboat, you can even see the landscape from the most important vista—along the very waters that gave the region its life.
Towns listed: Central Falls, Pawtucket.

✦ WHITE CLAPBOARD AND BLACK SHUTTERS: ELEGANT EAST BAY

With deep roots in local Native American culture, the eastern shores of Narragansett Bay sheltered the Wampanoags and later European farmers, merchants, shipbuilders, and, unfortunately, slave traders. The resulting layers, from Wampanoag ceremonial rocks atop Mount Hope in **Bristol** to pristine colonial farms like Coggeshall and narrow maritime buildings along the **Warren** waterfront, all dotted with Federal white churches and ornate houses, give this jeweled bracelet of towns a deep and very rich story to tell. Bristol especially, with its patriotic red-white-and-blue median stripe down its main thoroughfares, overflows with 17th-, 18th-, and early 19th-century architecture. And like the better-known historic districts of Providence and Newport, Bristol houses its modern citizens in its oldest homes. Guests overnight in the very rooms that Revolutionary generals did. There is nothing remotely museumlike about this town; the lively, postcard-perfect Hope Street, with side streets angling gently toward the waterfront, bustles with local families as much as it does with wide-eyed visitors. *Towns listed: Bristol, Warren.*

✦ PROVIDENCE: AN OUTCAST MINISTER'S LIVELY EXPERIMENT

The secret to the **Providence** Renaissance, as any local can tell you, was a bold move made by one elderly woman named Antoinette Downing in the 1960s to rescue a perishing street of run-down Colonial homes. That was Benefit Street, a mile of nonstop, almost exclusively Colonial architecture that now shines from one end to the other. Lit by period street lamps that locals drape with holiday greenery in December, with its small alleys and cobblestone byways leading down to the riverfront or up to the crest of College Hill, Benefit Street breathes the daily life of its residents—families, artists, students at Brown University and the Rhode Island School of Design—and in that fresh daily mix one never loses the trace of more than 350 years of history. It is everywhere you look in Providence. Small Early Colonial houses such as the Stephen Hopkins homestead recall the first settlers who followed Roger Williams on his quest for a colony that would allow freedom of thought. Churches of every variety, including Williams's own First Baptist Meeting House, punctuate the landscape with their steeples and send a clear symbolic message about Williams's unprecedented stance. Other details—a brick market house at river's edge, tavern buildings from along the waterfront, a stone forge near an old ferry crossing—are reminders of everyday colonial life. And as the city swelled with freethinkers (and free agents), Providence filled with the most sumptuous architecture that money could buy, culminating in the John Brown House, renowned even at the time for its grace and beauty (and now a charming museum). Uncovering the layers of Providence is a delight for the visitor who walks from one end of Benefit to the other. For residents, it is a luxury that weaves into daily life. Either way, as Roger Williams rightly forecast, the result is simply divine. *Towns listed: Providence.*

✦ RADICAL BEGINNINGS: WARWICK AND THE WEST BAY

Was there someone more radical than Roger Williams? It seems there was. Samuel Gorton, kicked out of three colonies, couldn't even behave enough to coexist with the largely tolerant Williams. So Gorton fled south and eventually, through the largesse of the Earl of Warwick, was able to stay put on lands south of Providence, and named his town in honor of his philosophical patron. Thus began a handful of late 17th-century settlements that survive in charming villages such as Pawtuxet along Narragansett Bay's western shores. In fact, one of the colony's finest moments of pre-war revolt, the burning of the British revenue schooner the *Gaspee* in 1772, is commemorated every year in Pawtuxet Village with a mock colonial battle and parade, drums and fifes in evidence. Sometimes the most historically relevant dwellings crop up out of nowhere, it seems, in the West Bay. In **Coventry,** the man who would become Rhode Island's greatest general of the Revolution—Nathanael Greene—built a beautiful homestead that he immediately left at the outbreak of war. With tiny, faded signs pointing the way, his home stands today as a delightful surprise in the midst of a decidedly 20th-century neighborhood. *Towns listed: Cranston, Coventry, Warwick.*

Perhaps it was a blessing in disguise that **Newport** was occupied by the British during the War—the abandoned colonial center that had thrived so headily up to 1776 remained frozen, mostly, in time, and was then remarkably, painstakingly, thrillingly restored to several neighborhoods that hum with activity. Is Newport the country's greatest nonmuseum colonial city? Perhaps. Consider the wealth of 17th- and 18th-century homes in Easton's Point and the Hill, the mix of houses of worship that includes architectural masterpieces Touro Synagogue and Trinity Church, the workaday pleasure in the White Horse Tavern— the country's oldest continuously-operating tavern, hosting travelers since the early 1700s—and the John Stevens Shop, a stonecutting shop that has survived, intact, since 1705 and still produces some of the most lyrical gravestones in the country. And the reason Newport reveals itself so vibrantly is because of the deep preservationist ethic that runs throughout the city—the city teems with knowledgable men and women who lead tours, run museums, and share their arcana with all who slow down to listen. Is there more beyond Newport? Up the coast of Aquidneck Island, **Middletown** and **Portsmouth** reveal beautiful agrarian landscapes dotted with Colonial homesteads such as Prescott Farm, and myriad battle sites from the largest Revolutionary battle fought on New England soil. As you can see at the incredibly picturesque Commons in **Little Compton,** the Sakonnet lands add grace and even more richness to Rhode Island's overflowing historic and aesthetic bounty. *Towns listed: Little Compton, Middletown, Newport, Portsmouth.*

✦ SOUTH COUNTY: PLANTATIONS AND A DUTCHMAN'S CONCEIT
Setting the record straight, there is no real South County. But for Rhode Islanders this stretch of rolling land, encompassing the southern half of the state's mainland to the west of Narragansett Bay, is best known by this name. For European settlers, this fertile land would embrace plantations as wealthy and productive as those of the southern colonies. And for Roger Williams, it would be where he would build his first trading outpost and where his friend Richard Smith would build Smith's Castle, now a museum of colonial life. Here, in **North Kingston,** it would also spawn the new nation's most famous portrait artist—the Gilbert Stuart birthplace, a pristinely restored home and snuff mill that remains one of the state's finest attractions. Today the towns of **East Greenwich** and especially **Wickford** are filled with homes and churches from this period, and make for days of lively strolling. *Towns listed: East Greenwich, North Kingstown, Wickford.*

Jewels in the Crown: Newport, Bristol, and Providence
A DRIVING AND WALKING TOUR FROM NEWPORT TO PROVIDENCE

▼▼

Distance: 41 mi (one-way)   **Time:** 2–3 days (1–2 nights)
Breaks: Can you do this tour in a day? Yes, but you'd be crazy to do so. Each of the main stops—Newport, Bristol, and Providence–is worth a day on its own. Consider sleeping in each of them, or in Bristol's neighbor, Warren.

Freethinking, often freewheeling Rhode Island prospered early on in its Colonial life, and this tour links the three centers where abundance, and its spoils, were most evident. A tour of major sites in Newport reveals why this vital harbor outpost quickly grew to be one of the five largest settlements in the Colonies. No wonder the British chose to invade during the war and the subsequent occupation froze the city in time. Journeying north out of Newport you'll see the battlegrounds that reflect the Continental Army's (unsuccessful) bid to kick the British out. On the mainland, the well-preserved, charming towns of Bristol and neighboring Warren still showcase wealth from the triangle trade. Then farther northwest to Providence for a tour of rich 17th-, 18th-, and early 19th-century neighborhoods that are full of shops, families, and students today. Summer in Newport is a driver's nightmare—so if it is peak season, get to the starting point, the visitor center, early and grab a cheap parking space there. Know also that Route 114, the central road linking all these sites, can be very slow in the summer.

Eighteenth-century **Newport** was as glorious a center as any along the entire eastern seaboard, and this introductory loop will give you a taste of this remarkable city's rich Colonial life—from spiritual freedom to extraordinary architecture. Begin by tucking away your automobile at the Gateway Information Center on America's Cup Avenue and load up on pamphlets and brochures; several bus, trolley, and walking tours leave from here. From the Center, follow the easy-to-spot signs to Washington Square Historic District, just a few blocks away, and take a half hour or so to get your bearings at the small, excellent Museum of Newport History at the Brick Market. Emerge from here at the base of Eisenhower Park (known as The Mall); note here the Rhode Island standard of true separation of church and state—unlike other colonies, no house of worship would sit on a green with houses of commerce and governance. The Mall is bookended by a marketplace at one end, and at the other, the Newport Colony House—this 1739 Georgian structure was one of Rhode Island's five original state houses. Behind you, don't miss the Buliod-Perry House, where Oliver Hazard Perry returned to live after the War of 1812, and take note that what looks like a stone facade on this 1750 building is in fact cleverly carved wood. Just beyond the Colony House, at the base of Broadway, sits the Governor Peleg Sanford House—one of the oldest surviving homes in Newport.

Touro Street, which flanks the park, leads up the hill to Touro Synagogue, one of Newport's proudest buildings. Built in 1763, it is the oldest synagogue in the United States. Its prominent position on a hill in early Newport is a powerful symbol of the colony's open-mindedness. George Washington worshiped here, and you shouldn't miss the excellent short tours. Just next door, pay a visit to the 7th Day Baptist Meeting House, now the home of the Newport Historical Society. Across the street, the very ornate, Greek Revival Levi Gale House was built on Washington Square in 1835, and moved up the hill nearly a century later to make way for the courthouse. Carry on up Touro to a fascinating place, the Colonial Jewish Cemetery, for graves of some of Newport's most prominent Jewish families.

Here's Bellevue Avenue, known for its late 19th- and early 20th-century mansions, but also the location of one of Newport's most important early buildings. Head down just a few blocks to the Redwood Library and Athenaeum, the oldest continuously used library in the country. It was designed by Peter Harrison in 1748 (he also designed Touro Synagogue) in high Classical style. Across Bellevue, Touro Park holds Newport's mysterious Stone Mill. Was it built by meandering Norsemen, as speculation has held for decades? Or is it the base of Benedict Arnold's mill? You decide, and don't miss the John Tillinghast House just across the way—this splendid Georgian, built in 1758, was the base for Nathanael Greene during the Revolution.

Backtrack along Bellevue and down Touro until you reach the back of the courthouse, and bear right along a brick street to Broadway. One block north you can tour the Wanton-Lyman-Hazard House, one of Newport's oldest homes and one that has belonged to some of the city's most prominent families. Just back down the hill, Farewell Street bears right; follow it to the corner of Marlborough. Ready for a rest? The White Horse Tavern awaits. Not only is this the oldest continuously operating tavern in the country (detecting a pattern here in Newport?), it houses a wonderful restaurant open for lunch, dinner, and Sunday brunch. Directly across from the tavern, the massive Great Friends Meeting House (see if you can spot the seams in the exterior that outline the original building in the center), recalls the early arrival of Quakers in Newport (built in 1699, this is the city's oldest surviving house of worship). For straying souls, the nearby Newport Jail House, a 1772 Georgian with Federal additions, held local ruffians and now operates as a bed and breakfast.

If you've been walking, now's the time to backtrack a few blocks, pick up your car, and rejoin the tour at the corner of Marlborough and Farewell; if you're already on wheels, follow Marlborough to the right to Broadway. Head north, and enjoy the range of architecture in this neighborhood that tourists usually miss. Ignore the strip malls coming up, and prepare to emerge, suddenly, after about 4 mi into **Middletown** and Aquidneck Island of old—replete with fields, stonewalls, and glimpses of Narragansett Bay's West Passage. Keep an eye out on the right for Prescott Farm, an 18th-century complex including the home, outbuildings, a wind-powered gristmill, and lovely grounds featuring a freshwater stream. Imagine the surprise of British general Prescott, who was living off the fat of the land here while his troops occupied Newport to the south, when he was kidnapped from this building by brazen rebels. As Routes 114 and 24 split, stay to the left on 114 and follow signs to Patriot's Park, a tidy park that marks the site of part of the Battle of Rhode Island (the largest Revolutionary battle fought in New England), and commemorates the first black regiment in the country. A mile farther, find the parking area on the left, at the crest of Lehigh Hill, for a breathtaking view of open lands (well marked with interpretive signs) where more action took place.

Don't miss a jog left a mile later (follow the sign toward the Bristol Ferry) that runs directly onto the narrow Mount Hope Bridge. Stay on Route 114 for another rural mile, with beautiful views of the Sakonnet River on your left. Soon you'll notice the Colonial houses rising up on either side, and the red-white-and-blue stripe down the middle of the road means you've entered **Bristol,** one of Rhode Island's most historic towns. If you want a detour, take a dogleg away from the water to the Haffenreffer Museum, perched up on Mount Hope (from Route 114, up State Street to Route 136; right and then immediately left up Tower Street 1½ mi to parking lot). Here is where the Wampanoag chief King Philip sat (his rocky throne is still in evidence), and where he was finally murdered in the war named for him. The museum's collection of Native American artifacts is definitely worth a visit as well. Return to the Colonial district by descending any of the downhill streets, and just off the corner of Hope (Route 114) and Court streets, the Bristol Historical and Preservation Society is installed in Bristol's 18th-century jailhouse. Check out slave-trading records for a grim reminder of a major source of wealth that built the beautiful houses that line Bristol's streets. And for what slave trading (and, admittedly, honest trade) can buy, return to Hope Street and tour Linden Place, a stunning Federal mansion designed by Bristol's Russell Warren for George deWolf.

Before the riches of trade built the stunning mansions of Bristol, farmers settled and prospered in the 17th century. One of Rhode Island's loveliest, most educational working Colonial farms, Coggeshall Farm (from Hope Street, follow signs to farm along Poppasquash Road) is well worth the picturesque detour along the waterfront (don't miss the rustic, low-to-the-ground signage on the right). Now, for another best-kept historic secret, leave Bristol behind and journey north 3½ mi to **Warren,** as old as Bristol, not as rich as Bristol, but every bit as interesting (some locals prefer Warren's smaller scale and workaday demeanor). Meander the side streets but don't miss two sites: Maxwell House, the circa 1755 brick home that houses a working museum of the 18th century (from Route 114, left on Washington Street, right on Water Street to corner of Church Street), and Nathaniel Porter Inn (on Water Street), a very Colonial-minded inn that occupies sea captain Samuel Martin's 1790 home. Ask the innkeepers to see their photo album of the house's extensive restoration, and consider a meal in the public rooms, if not an overnight stay.

From Warren, rejoin Route 114 and stay with it as it crosses the Barrington River and enters Barrington, a townscape decidedly "quaint." You can see, as 114 skirts peaceful One Hundred Acre Cove, why the Wampanoags made this route their own long before Europeans arrived. Four miles after the Congregational Church, bear left and follow signs for I–195 east. This utilitarian stretch of interstate will deliver you quickly into the lap of **Providence** (from

I–195 take South Main Street exit), and its true abundance of period homes occupied by families, businesses, and museums. As the off-ramp merges onto South Main, enjoy the lively blending of period architecture and picture, to the left, the now-gone line of wharfs, oyster houses, and other maritime buildings that originally lined the bank of the Providence River. Every block of South Main holds treasures, such as the Captain Joseph Tillinghast House (just at the bottom of the off-ramp on the left at 403 South Main Street), the only restored pre-Revolutionary house in this section; farther down on the left, Providence's original 1775 Market House, and across Main Street the First Baptist Meeting House, the church of the congregation founded by Roger Williams. Just past the Meeting House, enjoy to your right one of Providence's most picturesque blocks, the steep rising of Thomas Street to the east—hereabouts are the Providence Art Club at 10–11 Thomas and, another block north, the Roger Williams Memorial and some of the city's most prominent Colonial and Federal architecture.

From the memorial, climb up Church Street to Benefit Street, a solid mile of unparalleled historic architecture. A quarter-mile south along Benefit, drop into the elegant First Baptist Meeting House you saw from Main Street, completed after a design by Joseph Brown in 1775. Continue south on Benefit Street and consider a stop at the wonderful Museum of Art, Rhode Island School of Design on Benefit Street—many of this small museum's collections are worth a visit, but today pay homage to the great collection of 18th-century American furniture. Two blocks south (is this street not remarkable?), the Stephen Hopkins House at the corner of Hopkins and Benefit streets was home to one of Rhode Island's most prominent Revolutionary-era citizens, whose Quaker background is reflected in the simplicity of his dwelling. Beautifully restored and refurnished, the house opens for tours several days a week. By contrast, another of the colony's most prominent citizens did it up big—the John Brown House (3 blocks south on Benefit to the corner of Power Street) is testimony to the life and achievements of John Brown, considered Providence's most powerful citizen from the mid-1700s to the end of the century. Designed by older brother Joseph Brown in 1785, this extraordinary mansion hosted George Washington in 1790, and John Adams later called it the "most magnificent and elegant mansion" in America. Now the home of the Rhode Island Historical Society and a fascinating museum, this is a not-to-be-missed glimpse into Early American decorative arts in the highest style. Next door, the Joseph Nightingale House was clearly built in homage to the neighboring grandeur (note the pedimented projecting central pavilion, a one-story portico and Palladian window, the balustraded roof), but was built of wood instead of brick.

More Brown influence? For the university that bears the family name, climb one block south on Power Street, then turn left on Brown Street to a dead-end at George, and a side entrance to the Green of Brown University. Founded in Warren in 1764 as Rhode Island College, this seventh-oldest college in America moved to this perch above the city in 1770. If on foot, meander the Green and descend to University Hall (if in a car, take George Street left to Prospect Street, turn right to main gates on the right), the first building of the new college, designed by Robert Smith of Philadelphia in 1770. Carry on along Prospect, heading north to Cushing Street. Take Cushing one block west to Prospect Park for a commanding view of the city, old and new, and a look at an odd statue of Roger Williams. From here on Congdon Street, jog south and descend steep, curvy South Court Street back to Benefit and the Old State House, the very place where the General Assembly of Rhode Island renounced its allegiance to Great Britain on May 4, 1776 (don't forget—a full two months prior to the big-time Declaration of Independence). Peek inside to see the original 18th-century chamber in the southeast corner of the second floor. Is there more? You've barely scratched the surface of all Providence has to offer along its waterfronts and up its hillsides. But that's another day—or, for those lucky enough to live, work, and go to school on these streets, it's a matter of every day.

The Roads Less Taken: Roger Williams, William Blackstone, and Colonial Byways

A DRIVING TOUR BEGINNING AND ENDING IN PROVIDENCE

▼▼▼

Distance: 93 mi (round-trip)   **Time:** 1–2 days (1 night)
Breaks: Any tour in Rhode Island can be completed in a day, but that doesn't mean it should be—consider an overnight in Wickford at one of several period B&Bs.

This tour begins with the Colony's earliest European settlers—Roger Williams and William Blackstone—ventures north, then west and southward, in a bucolic loop linking pastoral Colonial homesteads, farms, and mills, plus lingering in one of the state's most beautiful (and lesser-known) villages, Wickford. A few short stretches (especially the drive linking Roger Williams National Memorial with a monument to William Blackstone) admittedly fall below any traveler's aesthetic expectations, but bear with them—some of Rhode Island's most important historic sites are buried in subsequent layers of modern honky-tonk. Mostly, though, the driving is the backroad variety, particularly along the Great Road and later along Route 1A, the old Boston Neck Road. Except for 1A in the peak of summer beach driving, these are off-the-beaten pathways, and you'll find open roads, lush foliage, meandering stone walls, and even decent signage (not always the case in Rhode Island).

Begin at the wellspring of the Rhode Island colony, in **Providence,** at the literal spring where Roger Williams finally settled, in 1636, after his exile at the hands of the Puritans. The country's smallest national park, Roger Williams Memorial Park, commemorates his homestead with a tiny pocketful of green amid the largely urban landscape. Find the spring, which was declared a public spring in 1721, and spend a half hour in the tiny visitor's center reading some of this visionary minister's writings. From here, head a half-mile north along North Main Street and follow signs to I-95 N, which will run you quickly up to Pawtucket (Exit 28), and follow the excellent signage to the Blackstone River Valley Visitor Center, for an outstanding short film on 18th-century water-powered mills. This will also give you a grounding for what lies across the street—Slater Mill Historic Site, a pristine complex of three impeccably restored period buildings including the original mill that began America's industrial revolution in 1793, all perched along the Blackstone River falls.

When the eccentric Anglican minister William Blackstone rode his white bull home from a book-buying expedition to Providence, his path traced a quiet route through wilderness. No longer—keep your eyes on these pages and ignore the low-slung urban clutter as you retrace Blackstone's steps to the site of his beloved house, apple trees, and rose garden (north from Slater Mill on Roosevelt Street, left on Exchange Street, 3 blocks to Route 114 N). Here, nearly 3 mi up Route 114 in Cumberland, well marked but out-shadowed by a local mill, sits tiny William Blackstone Memorial Park. The somber granite marker doesn't do justice to the spirit of this pioneer, the first European to settle in Boston, and then the first to settle in what became Rhode Island (and it is inaccurate to boot—the memorial reads that Blackstone is buried here, but he's not). Now: into the woods. Backtrack a half-mile to Route 123 W, cross the Blackstone River, and 1½ mi onward bear right onto the Great Road, a historic corridor based on Native American trails and one the later linked farms and early mills in this northern countryside once called "World's End" with Providence. From the town of Lincoln, enjoy pure Rhode Island country driving amid centuries-old stone walls through verdant hills, as Great Road terminates a little more than 3 mi north. Make a right here on Route 116 and take the first U-turn to connect onto Route 146 N for a scant half-mile to I-295 S. For a major highway, this is a pleasure, and enjoy skimming 20 mi among trees and fields to I-95 S.

As you exit the interstate on Hopkins Hill Road (Exit 6A) you'll find yourself again in latter-day, developed Rhode Island, sitting palimpsest-like on one of the oldest colonial regions— **Coventry.** Here, just west of one of the handful of first local settlements, at Warwick,

Nathanael Greene chose to build a beautiful house for his new bride in 1774. Tucked away in an innocuous 20th-century neighborhood, the Nathanael Greene Homestead (from Exit 6A, bear right onto Hopkins Hill Road; then 3 mi to Route 3; right and ½ mi to Route 33, which winds 1.3 mi to Laurel Avenue; turn right and follow the somewhat time-worn signs from here to 50 Taft Street) is a breath of bracing colonial air, and the grounds are worth a stroll. While Greene went on to outfox English commanders in the South, another local boy went on to perhaps even greater notoriety. Pull a dollar bill out of your wallet and check the visage while you retrace to Route 33. Now, turn right and in less than a mile, take Route 117 E to I–95 S. No, you're not going to the Rhode Island hideout of the first president, you're headed to the birthplace of the man who made that face so memorable. Following Route 1A barely a mile to Snuff Mill Road, turn left, and follow the signs to **North Kingston** and the home of the man who gave us the George Washington we best recognize today, the Gilbert Stuart Birthplace, a gorgeous rural house and mill set alongside the quietly rushing waters of the Mattatuxet River. After you've toured the home, don't miss the period herb garden, which has a children's section as well. In fact, children often lead tours here, which is a charming conceit but nonetheless a bit jarring when your colonially dressed guide smiles and reveals a mouth full of distinctly 21st-century orthodonture.

Think this is as beautiful as small-scale colonial Rhode Island gets? Wait. Return to Route 1A and follow it northward for just under 4 mi into the bustling village center of **Wickford.** Start walking where Brown Street meets Main Street, a corner lively with late-19th-century urban architecture. Turn right onto Main and you'll find yourself in a living, breathing architectural gem—house after house, well marked with historical plaques and all inhabited by Wickford residents. Every house is worth a stop, a read, a peek down the alleyway, a pondering of a lintel or a doorway. Some highlights: on the left as you head east, the 1st Baptist Church in Wickford offers the simplicity of rural Federalist architecture. Turn left on Church Lane and follow the narrow road around to the 1707 Old Narragansett Church, a delightful, understated white frame church that's one of the oldest Episcopal churches in America. Take the Greenway from here back to Main, and stroll two more blocks east to Pleasant Street. Turn left for a glimpse of the higher style of the mid-1700s, the John Updike House (no, not the writer—the grandson of Lodowick Updike). Take Main all the way to the pier for a view of Narragansett Bay, and retrace your steps west on Main, with detours on Bay, Washington, and Gold streets. You've been driving all day, so can you believe that Roger Williams used to row down Narragansett Bay to Wickford to debate fellow theologians (he may have been open to all faiths settling in his colony, but he still thought he was the rightest of them all)? He did, and stayed with his friend Richard Smith at the grandiosely dubbed Smith's Castle, just outside Wickford (from town center, W. Main Street west ½ mi to Route 1 north ¾ mi). It remains a splendid period house with frequent tours and special events year-round.

For another view of a town that prospered early in Rhode Island history, head north on Route 1 about 6 mi to **East Greenwich,** and view of one of the five county seats when the Colonial legislature chose to rotate its meeting sites. The Kent County Courthouse, just renovated, at 127 Main Street, is a handsome Federal clapboard structure that replaced, in 1804, its brick colony-house-style predecessor. After the courthouse, turn left on Division Street and climb the hill one block to Pierce, and turn left again for a visit to the General James Mitchell Varnum House Museum, an elegant mansion worth a tour on Sundays for the stories of this general who played a role in creating the first black regiment in the Continental Army. For the site of the Kentish Guards that Varnum also commanded, cross the street to the Kentish Guards Armory, which may have been built at the tail end of the Federalist period but is a charming, clapboard Greek Revival temple. All armories should be this graceful. And so like the Pequot Trail, which later became the Boston Post Road that linked New York to Boston, this road, like all it once seemed in Colonial Rhode Island, leads to Providence. You can poke up Route 1 or dodge west on Division back to I–95 for a straight, connurbistic drive back to the cradle of all that grew from the minister and his spring.

BRISTOL

▼▼

A worthy rival to the twin colonial centers of Newport and Providence, this elegant town, still lined with white clapboard homes and elm trees, has been desirable real estate since the 17th century. Massasoit, chief of the Wampanoag tribe, ruled from the Mount Hope Lands that included Bristol, but sold much of his territory to early colonists who saw the mercantile and maritime value in this fine harbor. In fact, three colonies—Rhode Island, Massachusetts Bay, and Plymouth—each tried to lay hands on Bristol, with temporary successes. But in 1747 Rhode Island regained the thriving town and never let it go again.

But Bristol has seen its share of tragedy. Massasoit's son Metacomet lent his nickname King Philip to a brutal series of conflicts among local Native tribes and settlers called King Philip's War, which broke out on June 20, 1675, in the Mount Hope area. After a year of bloodshed, Metacomet, who had led uprisings as far afield as Maine and New York, was ambushed, murdered, and dismembered in his stronghold on Mount Hope. A century later, Bristol would see more warfare in 1775, when the British (already holding and plundering Newport to the south) sailed into Bristol harbor and tried to take the town by siege. The local citizenry fought back, but by 1778 England would take its revenge: some 500 British soldiers marched on the town from neighboring Warren, stormed Hope Street, and burned buildings in their wake. Still, the legacy of 18th-century and early 19th-century structures distinguishes this postcard-perfect township (about 50 18th-century homes remain), and the red-white-and-blue stripe down the middle of Bristol's main street reminds every visitor of the town's greatest claim to fame: America's longest-running Fourth of July parade. *Contact East Bay Tourism Council | 654 Metacom Ave., Suite 2, Warren 02885 | 401/245–0750 | www. eastbayritourism.com.*

Bristol Historical and Preservation Society Museum & Library. Originally built as a county jail in 1828, using ballast stones from Bristol sailing ships, this museum displays 300 years of memorabilia from Bristol's seafaring past. The DeWolf room houses early records, charts, and accounts of slave ships. Architectural and walking tours can be arranged by appointment, and the Society's excellent guide to historic homes is worth the investment. | 48 Court St. | 401/253–7223 | Donation suggested | Wed. and Fri. 1–5, Sun. 1–4.

Coggeshall Farm Museum. Just outside town center in Colt State Park, the bucolically charming Coggeshall Farm Museum works daily in the colonial way (although the Coggeshalls themselves didn't take over the circa-1750 property until the 1830s). Offering families a hand at sampling 18th-century farm life from sugaring to shearing, Coggeshall boasts a kid-pleasing assortment of period farm animals (including oxen) plus weaving and blacksmithing buildings, as well as a gardener-pleasing historical herb and vegetable plot. Call for summer weekend program. | Colt State Park | 401/253–9062 | $1 | Oct.–Feb., daily 10–5; Mar.–Sept., daily 10–6.

First Baptist Church. With a stylistic nod to Providence's First Baptist Meeting House and Newport's Trinity Church, this early Federal conflation of Gothic and Classical elements, built in 1814, is the oldest original church in Bristol still standing. | 250 High St. | 401/253–6131.

James DeWolf House. After a visit to Linden Place, the public declaration of the DeWolf penchant for moneymaking, stop by this private home of Bristol's most successful–and notorious—slave-trader. James DeWolf was born into poverty in 1764, made his fortune by the age of 25, and labored to circumvent every anti-slavery law passed in Rhode Island during his lifetime. His labors, sadly, were not in vain—he alone was responsible for shipping nearly 4,000 slaves to Charlestown, South Carolina, in a mere four years. By 1812 DeWolf laundered his ill-got gains by funding early textile mills in Coventry, then married the governor's daughter Nancy Bradford, and eventually represented Rhode Island in the U.S. Senate. And yet his home is indeed a beauty—an elegant Federal home built in 1793, with a pair of Victorian-era bays added later. | 56 High St. (private).

Linden Place. The architectural centerpiece of a rich and varied downtown, this Federal mansion was designed by Rhode Island architect Russell Warren and built in 1810 for George DeWolf of the famous Bristol maritime (and slave-trading) family. The home set a new standard for wealth and display: from lacy parapets to giant Corinthian columns, Linden Place represented the apogee of trade and all that it bought. Now open to the public, the home is surrounded by rose gardens adorned with pieces of 19th-century sculpture. | 500 Hope St. | 401/253–0390 | $5 | May–mid-Oct., Thurs.–Sat. 10–4, Sun. noon–4.

✦ ON THE CALENDAR: July **Bristol 4th of July Parade.** The nation's oldest celebration of U.S. independence, Bristol's has been celebrated continuously since 1785. The center line down Hope Street is painted red, white, and blue for a celebration that begins June 14 (Flag Day) and continues through July 4 (homes along the parade route are said to fetch higher prices and in fact advertise their Fourth of July location). Locals will tell you that to get a curbside spot you may want to spend the night, or park outside of town and walk or bicycle in. | Hope St. | 401/245–0750.

HISTORIC LODGING
Joseph Reynolds House Inn. A night at this 1693, red-clapboard inn includes a lesson in colonial history: George Washington and Thomas Jefferson planned the Revolutionary War Battle of Rhode Island here with the Marquis de Lafayette. The Marquis's room is period-accurate, with a 17th-century marbleized fireplace. If that room is taken, take comfort in the four-poster beds elsewhere. Complimentary breakfast. | 956 Hope St. | 800/754–0230 | fax 401/254–2610 | 5 rooms | $95–$175 | AE, D, MC, V.

CENTRAL FALLS
▼▼

A tiny, overshadowed mill town just west of Pawtucket on the Blackstone, Central Falls used to be called Chocolate Mill for a 1790 chocolate factory there. Today it's best known for hosting two sightseeing boats that ply the Blackstone. *Contact Blackstone Valley Tourism Council | 175 Main St., Pawtucket 02860 | 800/454–2882 | www.tourblackstone.com.*

Blackstone Valley Explorer Riverboat. A wonderful way to get to the heart of the valley, these regular flat-bottomed boat tours run by the Blackstone Valley Tourism Council leave from a Central Falls landing (which is, in fact, just over the Cumberland town line) and vary thematically throughout the year. Best bet: on Rivers Day, which falls in June, tours are free. | Madeira Ave., just off Broad St. | 401/724–2200.

Jenks Park and Pierce Park. In Jenks Park, the Cogswell clock tower is your landmark for Dexter's Ledge, which played a role in grim happenings at next-door Pierce Park. During King Philip's War, in 1676, Captain Michael Pierce led 63 colonists and Native American allies in a surprise attack on the local Narragansetts, but the ambushers were themselves ambushed by the Narragansetts, who'd spotted their approach from Dexter's Ledge. The ambush itself is commemorated in Pierce Park. Not one colonist survived. | Broad St. and High St. | 401/727–7480.

HISTORIC LODGING
Samuel Slater Canal Boat B&B. Truth be told, the boat is only two years old and was made in England—but it re-creates, charmingly, the boats that plied the waters of the Blackstone

Canal as early as 1828, and it accommodates four people for overnight stays. (It can also be booked for 12 passengers for day trips). It is named for the father of America's industrial revolution. Complimentary breakfast. | Broad St. and Madeira Ave. | 401/724–2200 | www.tourblackstone.com | Accommodates 4 | $109–$179 | No credit cards.

COVENTRY

▼▼

Now a collection of rural mill villages, Coventry began much earlier as an offshoot of Warwick to the east—it separated and established its own town in 1741 and, most famously, played hometown to Rhode Island's best-known general, Nathanael Greene, for one brief year. *Contact Coventry Historical Society | Box 401, Coventry 02816 | 401/385–9126 | Appointment required.*

General Nathanael Greene Homestead. War was coming, but Nathanael Greene had a family forge to oversee in Coventry and a new bride to support. He managed, in 1774, to build this simple, handsome farmhouse for their new life together on his 2,000-acre lot. But after the news from Lexington and Concord broke to the north, Greene left home for the Continental Army, and the farmhouse ended up serving, during the first year of the war, as a hospital for officers recovering from smallpox vaccination (with his wife, Catherine Greene, supervising). Greene never fully returned to Coventry after the war, eventually settling on a confiscated plantation in Georgia in 1785 and dying there two years later. Meanwhile, other members of the Greene family remained in control of the Coventry house until 1899. Now open as a museum, it contains Greene furnishings, memorabilia, and hardware that's said to have been forged at the family's ironworks. | 50 Taft St., off Rte. 117 | 401/821–8630 | $3 | Mar.–Nov., Wed. and Sat. 10–5, Sun. noon–5.

CRANSTON

▼▼

You'd never know it at first glimpse, but sprawling and industrial Cranston, just southwest of Providence, is one of the earliest settlements in the region (1638). William Arnold, a colleague of Roger Williams as well as father of Benedict Arnold, founded the town but fought long with Williams over jurisdiction. By 1754 the settlements along the Pawtuxet River here were finally incorporated as a town named after Colonial governor Samuel Cranston, of Newport. *Contact Cranston Historical Society | 1353 Cranston St., Cranston 02190 | 401/944–9226.*

Governor Sprague Mansion. One of Rhode Island's most important homes, this 28-room mansion built in 1790 and enlarged in 1864 reflects the rise (and later fall) of a powerful local family (although most of the wealth, earned from milling, and tragedy, including a murder and financial collapse, occurred later in the 19th century). Nonetheless the house is worth touring, particularly for an impressive collection of Asian art objects and a famous collection of carriages. | 1351 Cranston St. | 401/944–9226 | $5 | July–Labor Day, Tues., Sun. 2–5.

EAST GREENWICH

▼▼

Nestled into the northwestern shore of Narragansett Bay, the confusingly named East Greenwich prospered early on in Rhode Island life as a center for both maritime and agricultural pursuits. Europeans had put down roots here in the early 17th century, but the entire settlement was wiped out during King Philip's War. In a quick show of support the next year, the General Assembly granted some 5,000 acres around Greenwich Cove to a group of families to rebuild. They did, divvying up the waterfront land into 50 lots and leaving a large tract west of the town for farming. A wise idea, for by the early 18th century produce from the west was flowing down Division Street to thriving wharves on Greenwich Cove. From trade grew fishing and shipbuilding, and the town drew enough luster to be named one of the five county seats visited by Rhode Island's rotating General Assembly. Further, East Greenwich was home to some of Rhode Island's most illustrious military men, including James Varnum (a Continental army general) and William Greene (governor during the Revolution, who used his East Greenwich home as the capitol). The Kentish Guards, one of the oldest military units in the country, were formed here, and their white clapboard building still stands in town. *Contact Chamber of Commerce | 5853 Post Rd., Suite 106, East Greenwich 02818-0514 | 401/885–0020 | www.eastgreenwichri.com.*

General James Mitchell Varnum House. Not only was James Varnum an honor student in the first class to graduate from what became Brown University, he became a successful lawyer and, in 1773, built this beautiful mansion high above the town. Soon, however, he was drawn into the Revolution. He founded the Kentish Guards and helped create the black regiment that served so honorably in the Battle of Rhode Island, and rose to the rank of brigadier general in the Continental Army. Lafayette and Washington were both welcomed here. Much of the home's original paneling and hardware survives. | 57 Pierce St. | 401/884–1776 | www.varnumcontinentals.org | $4 | June–Labor Day, Thurs.–Sat. 10–2; Sept., Sat. 10–2.

Old Kent County Courthouse. Not only was this site the center of Kent County public life in the 18th century, it housed the circulating Rhode Island General Assembly, and therefore served as a capitol of sorts. The original county seat was built on this site in 1750, but this very handsome Federal, 1804 Court House took over with style that some say echoes, in proportion and form, the earlier colony/state houses in Newport (1739) and Providence (1736). The Declaration of Independence was read to the public on this site in 1776, and now the town of East Greenwich claims the structure as its city hall. | 125 Main St. | 401/886–8606 | Free | Daily 8:30–4:30.

Varnum Memorial Armory and Military Museum. The exterior—faux-medieval circa 1914—may confuse the eye, but the contents within will delight the mind, particularly the military mind. Among a wide assortment of weaponry from the late 16th century through World War II, don't miss a 17th-century crossbow and a Revolutionary War artillery helmet, one of only three in existence. | 6 Main St. | 401/884–4110 | www.varnumcontinentals.org | $4 | By appointment only.

LITTLE COMPTON

▼▼▼

Local Native Americans called this rocky coastline dotted with salt marshes and swamplands Sakonnet, or "haunt of the wild black goose." The natural beauty of this area still embraces the small village that barely appears to have changed in the centuries since Plymouth settlers divided a 20-acre plot into farmland in 1674. *Contact Little Compton Historical Society | 548 West Main Rd., Little Compton 02837 | 401/635–4035 | www.littlecompton.org.*

Little Compton Commons. One of the loveliest sites in Rhode Island, and interesting because it shows the difference in the Puritan view of the common (Little Compton belonged to the Plymouth Colony until 1747). Here the house of worship shares quarters with the town meeting hall. This common's burial ground, laid out in 1675, hosts a handful of colorful monuments. One marks the grave of Elizabeth Pabodie, who, as the daughter of John and Priscilla

Mullins Alden was the first white woman born in New England. Another commemorates Benjamin Church, the wily diplomat and fierce fighter against Native tribes during King Philip's War. Elizabeth's marker bears the humorous epitaph: "should have been the wife of Simeon Palmer." | Meeting House La.

Wilbor House. Kept in the same family from its building in the 1680s to the 1920s, this home has been updated and displays the changing of architectural tastes in rural New England. You can still see, in the house's original section, the two-story, two-room structure with low unplastered ceilings supported by exposed corner posts and anchored by a huge summer beam. The simplicity of later 18th- and 19th-century additions attests to the family's Quaker aesthetic. Don't miss the Barn Museum on the property, with antique farm tools and household equipment. | 548 W. Main Rd. | 401/635–4035 | Call for price (variable every year) | Late June–Labor Day, Thurs.–Sun.; Sept.–Oct., weekends (call for hrs; variable every year).

MIDDLETOWN
▼▼

When this village of far-flung homes was incorporated in 1743 it chose a name that reflected its geographical location and also distinguished it from urban Newport to the south. Though part of the original Newport plantation, it had remained agricultural. This rolling, rich farmland that still hosts some of Rhode Island's largest nurseries still failed to escape the coming of war—on December 7, 1776, the British and Hessian occupation force of eleven ships landed here and spent a night pillaging local homes. Then they set off for Newport. *Contact Middletown Historical Society | Paradise Schoolhouse, Paradise and Prospect Aves., 02842 | 401/849–1870 | www.middletownhistory.org.*

Green End Fort. A British installation, built in 1777 as the easternmost outpost of the defense of Aquidneck Island. | North side of Vernon Ave. extension.

Prescott Farm. Historically minded locals bristle at the fact that this beautiful Colonial farm, so painstakingly preserved and open as an example of agrarian life on Aquidneck, is named for the annoying British General who made this his bachelor's retreat while he ran the occupation of Newport. But perhaps what happened to General Prescott here may soothe local tempers, for it is a great story of patriot derring-do. On July 9, 1777, Lieutenant Colonel William Barton, a Continental officer based across the bay in Tiverton, learned that Prescott planned a rendezvous with a young woman at the Middletown farm then called Overing House. Slipping away from Warwick Neck under the cover of darkness with a party of about 40 men, Barton eluded three British frigates and landed about 2 mi from Overing House. Using blackberry brambles and trees for cover, they evaded British notice and crashed through the house from all sides, grabbed the general and pulled him naked from his bed. The Continental Army gained bragging rights with this bold kidnapping and was able to trade Prescott back for an American major general named Charles Lee. Now, in calmer days, the house is open seasonally for touring, and the grounds make a lovely respite among the still-open fields of Middletown. | 2009 West Main Rd. | 401/847–6230 | www.newportrestoration.com/prescott | $3 | May–Oct., weekdays 10–4.

Whitehall Museum House. One of the great intellectual lights to burn in the Newport firmament lived here in Middletown. In September 1728, George Berkeley, dean of Derry, left England for Bermuda to train churchmen and missionaries for the British colonies. But his ship ran off course and landed, after six months, at Newport. Waiting for financial support to carry on to Bermuda, Berkeley grew attached to Newport and decided to settle down for a three-year stay. This house, purchased in 1729 from Joseph Whipple, was very small—Berkeley greatly expanded it to what you see now. After Berkeley returned to England the home was used as a tavern. | 311 Berkeley Ave. | 401/846–3116 | July–Labor Day, Tues.–Sun. daily 10–5.

NEWPORT

▼▼

It is the 1960s. Doris Duke, the extravagantly rich heiress and preservation doyenne, is hoofing around Newport with a coterie of experts from Williamsburg. Duke, who's visited the new historic theme park to the south, has brought the Williamsburg brain trust up to her beloved city to see what can be done about the scores of dilapidated clapboard homes, most more than two centuries old, that are falling down around her. She wants to save Colonial Newport, but she's not sure how to do it. "Wall it off," she's told. "Buy up all the property, knock down what isn't from the original period, restore, and open a northern Williamsburg. Make Colonial Newport into the country's next great historic theme park." Duke looks around at the run-down streets. She has enough money, and more, to do this. Newport could become New England's greatest outdoor museum of colonial history. She could make it happen. "No," she says.

No? In a manner of speaking. For Doris Duke, a Newporter herself, the city needed its daily life, its citizenry, its lively mix of old and new—it didn't need to become an outdoor museum. And so, in a move even more radical, Duke commits to buying what ends up being more than 80 early American buildings, restoring them to pristine historic condition, and renting them out to Newporters at barely market rates. Duke's vision brings us the incredible Colonial Newport we enjoy today—modern neighborhoods made up of gorgeous 17th- and 18th-century architecture, dotted with museums, houses of worship, shops, restaurants, B&Bs, and many, many homes—a truly living legacy. Often overshadowed by the waterfront's yachting hubbub and the internationally known Gilded Age mansions, this Colonial Newport core, thanks to Duke and many other ardent preservationists, is the city's finest asset. It is the true reason to make a pilgrimage to this rocky island outpost, and to stay and marvel for days on end.

And what a history has been preserved. Like Providence, Newport sprang from religious dissidence and grew in a spirit of tolerance. William Coddington and John Clarke left the Massachusetts Bay Colony with a handful of Antinomian supporters and headed south in 1638 to seek counsel from Roger Williams, who'd established Providence a few years earlier. Williams brokered a purchase of land on Aquidneck Island (again, a remarkable event, that English settlers paid for Native lands rather than merely seizing them), and Coddington, Clarke et al., settled first at the northern end, in what is now Portsmouth. But Anne Hutchinson, another dissident who brought followers to Portsmouth, began to rule the roost. Looking for more self-governance, the original settlers headed farther south in 1639, to a rocky natural harbor at the base of the island, and started over. They called it Newport. And they got down to business. Thames Street came first, with 4-acre lots squared off in what is now the northern end of Washington Square. A year later Newport made peace with Portsmouth and formed an early federation to be overseen by one governor.

Meanwhile, maritime life and commerce quickly sprang up around this deepwater harbor at the mouth of Narragansett Bay. As early as 1646, Newporters were building ships for other coastal colonies and Aquidneck plantations began furnishing exports for the southern colonies, the West Indies, and Europe. Despite not being a whaling center, the town cornered the market on spermaceti candles. It also cornered the market on the era's grimmest commerce—trading in slaves. (Rhode Island, the acknowledged bastion of tolerance and freethinking, was the continent's most active slave-trading colony—up to 60 Rhode Island ships engaged in the movement of slaves in the 18th century.) This particular harvest of shame is evident in Newport to this day: from 1707 to 1732 the Colony charged an import tax of three pounds on each slave, and used the money to pave the city's streets and build its bridges.

By the mid-18th century Newport was one of the New World's wealthiest seaports, and culture followed in affluence's wake. Local carpenters and architects sought out, and applied, grand Classical influences in European design. Craftsmen made furniture, clocks, silver, and

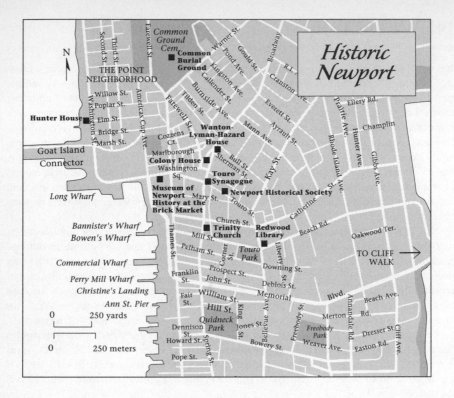

Historic
Newport

pewter for local homes as well as those throughout the colonies. Even the headstones bore the imprimatur of a city on the rise—today the graves of Colonial Newport are among the most ornate in the country. This flourishing community may have drawn its distinctive ardor from the astonishing diversity of its citizenry, and that in turn is directly attributable to the colony's religious tolerance. Quakers, Jews, and Baptists, shunned in England, in Inquisition-bled Spain, and in the rigid New World colonies, flocked to Newport in the 17th century. They brought trading savvy and intellectual aspirations—how remarkable that Newport's Redwood Library (the oldest continuously operating library in the country) was founded by an Anglican churchman, a Jewish merchant, and a Quaker. And although Newport would become the resort of choice in the late 19th century, it was a Colonial vacation hotspot as well. Upper-class families from the Carolinas, Georgia, and Maryland, as well as plantation owners from the West Indies, sought out the hospitable oceanic climate in the summertime coupled with a sophisticated society, and rented homes in the town's center.

This would all change, abruptly, in 1776. Newport, unlike many other Rhode Island settlements, had survived the burning and looting of King Philip's War, and had in fact prospered during the French and Indian War (more than 50 privateer vessels worked for England). But by the mid-18th century England had taken note of the extraordinary wealth of Newport's merchants and sought a bigger take. The Crown began cracking down on antismuggling and tax laws, but the result, as elsewhere in the colonies, was the first surge of anti-English sentiment. In July 1764 the Rhode Island General Assembly sanctioned firing upon the customs schooner *St. John,* and barely a year later a riled-up mob of Newporters set the tender of the frigate *Maidstone* on fire. More directed statements would follow: on a July night in 1769 Newporters cut the anchor line of the *Liberty,* and as the British sloop drifted toward the city's Long Wharf, she was set afire. But Newport maintained a staunch Loyalist community as well. As Newport trembled under the weight of divided loyalties, ships carrying 6,000 English and Hessian soldiers made for the shores of Aquidneck Island. On a cold day in December the ships landed at Middletown just to the north and marched south to take away one of the Colonies' finest treasures.

And take it they did. Patriots fled to join freer forces in Providence, merchants fled to salvage what the British hadn't already destroyed. The occupation of Newport would not only decimate the local economy, but would send shock waves of deprivation throughout the settlements along Narragansett Bay. Three long years later, in October 1779, when the British moved their force to New York, the beleaguered Newporters who had endured were forced to tear down empty houses for firewood to survive the winter. The French occupied, much more gently, by necessity, beginning in July of 1780, when 5,000 troops landed by General Rochambeau to aid the Continental Army were bottled up in Newport by an offshore British fleet. In fact, the forever inventive and party-loving French did much to bolster local spirits during their ten-month occupation.

Newport was free at last, but the damage done was seemingly irreversible. Momentum had shifted to Providence, which remained essentially untouched by the British during the war. Further, the War of 1812 and the ascendancy of the railroads dealt death blows to the maritime economy in Newport. Although some textile mills sprang up along southern Thames Street in the mid-19th century, these also burned down. Newport then lay dormant until the Victorians rediscovered it and created an entirely new economy based on leisure. But Colonial Newport—the pockets close to the harbor—reaped little from the Gilded Age, and it was only in the second half of the 20th century that the rescue began. Strolling the many Colonial streets around Washington Square, it is hard to believe that Newport ever faced near-extinction, or entombment as a museum. So smile at the ghost of Doris Duke gliding along beside you on these narrow streets, and thank her and the many preservationists who fought to bring this remarkable, unparalleled city back to life. *Contact Newport Historical Society | 82 Touro St., Newport 02840 | 401/846–0813 | www.newporthistorical.com. Newport Restoration Foundation | 51 Touro St., Newport 02840 | 401/849–1300 | www.newportrestoration. com. Preservation Society of Newport County | 424 Bellevue Ave., Newport 02840 | 401/847–1000 | www.newportmansions.org.*

Bowen's Wharf. This wharf is part of the original Newport harbor, although it may be hard to picture the clipper ships amid the decidedly modern commerce here today. Do note the Clarke Cooke House restaurant, a beautiful mid-18th-century sea captain's house that was moved here from Thames Street in 1971. | Thames St., at the base of Pelham St.

Colony House. One of Newport's most notable buildings, and anchoring the city's earliest common area (note the distinct absence of churches, in Rhode Island–style) with the market-place at the other end, this 1739 replacement of an earlier wooden structure has hosted a long list of dramatic events. From that elaborate second-floor balcony, clearly designed for great things, the death of King George II was announced in 1760, the English repeal of the Stamp Act was declared in 1766, and the Declaration of Independence was read in September 1776. Step inside, and imagine the British taking over these rooms for barracks during their occupation, then the French using them as a hospital. Picture George Washington meeting with Rochambeau here in 1781 to plan the Battle of Yorktown, then Washington's triumphant return nine years later for a gala reception. Listen for the remarkable strains of the first Catholic mass said in Rhode Island, performed here on the death of France's Admiral de Ternay. Even the architectural details are noteworthy. Only six pre-Revolution buildings in Newport were made of brick, which was imported from Britain—Richard Munday, the ships' carpenter and innkeeper who designed and built the Colony House, clearly wanted to make a statement with his materials. While the rusticated belt course, quoins, and window surrounds recall a typical 17th-century English manor house, the central bay balcony with its ornately carved broken pediments, as well as the broken line of the roof and the cupola, make a public declaration. | Eastern end of Washington Sq. | 401/846–0813 | Weekdays 9:30–4:30, Sat. 9:30–noon.

Common Burial Ground. The Common Burial Ground was hardly common. In fact, this early Colonial cemetery was segregated racially: the southern section, where you can see the crowded stones practically leaning against one another, was for freemen, while the more spacious northern section held slaves. Eight hundred of the 3,000 monuments here date from before 1800; the earliest are from the 1660s. Browsing here is endlessly fascinating. Look especially for the John Ward Stone (1698), carved by William Mumford, the Boston sculptor who brought stonecarving to Newport, and note the central crest that symbolized the door to the other world. Seek out Governor Samuel Ward and his wife (1776), as well as Pompey Brenton (in the slave section) for the work of stonecutter John Stevens II. | Farewell St.

Easton's Point. Newport's second Colonial neighborhood, this quiet cove with land now bordered by Thames and Farewell streets to the east and Washington Street to the west, was bought up by the Eastons, a Quaker family, and subdivided into lots and sold in 1725. The first settlers were maritime tradesmen and craftsmen, including ships' carpenters, sail makers, and rope makers. This easy water access also suited furniture makers and silversmiths, and Easton's Point soon became a thriving artisans' neighborhood. Sea captains followed, and larger homes on Washington Street cropped up, surrounded along the water by docks, warehouses, and shops. The British occupation was very hard on this neighborhood, which withstood regular artillery barrages from Goat Island just across the water. Of the 500 homes destroyed in Newport during the War, many were in this area, and the British were not above tearing down unoccupied houses for firewood. What survived, though, has been remarkably restored. Look elsewhere in these listings for homes with addresses on Thames (29–44), Bridge (16–77), Washington (31–64), as well as Second, Third, Chestnut, Walnut, Poplar, Farewell and Coddington streets. (Note that in Quaker fashion, emulating the plan of William Penn in Philadelphia, the east–west streets are named after trees and the north–south streets bear numbers. The only exception to this plan in Easton's Point is the waterfront homage to George Washington, which needs no further explanation.

Fort Adams. Newporters had the right idea when they built a fort on this site in May 1776, but all to little avail. The British invaded seven months later, took over the place, and destroyed it before leaving in 1779. Twenty years on the fort was rededicated and named after President John Adams, but then fell into disrepair. After the War of 1812 exposed vulnerability of the country's coastline, work began anew on a network of fortifications in 1824. Today the site is better known for hosting jazz and folk festivals, but a renewed effort to present its history is underway. | Ford Adams State Park, Harrison Ave. | 401/841–0707 | www.fortadams.org | $5 | Mid-May–Oct., daily 10–5.

Frigate Rose. A lovely, and historically accurate, reconstruction of the British 24-gun frigate, this ship arrived in Newport in December 1774 to prowl for smugglers. Irritated colonists refused to sell food to the crew, and fired more than once on the frigate from shore. When the now equally irritated commander of the *Rose* fired back by closing Newport Harbor to all shipping, Stephen Hopkins stepped in—in a big way. The feisty governor and delegate to the Continental Congress introduced a bill that established, in 1775, the American Navy. When the *Rose* withdrew from Newport Harbor on May 4, 1776, Rhode Island officially renounced its allegiance to King George III (two months before any other colony). | Bannister's Wharf | www.tallshiprose.org | Hrs vary.

Governor Benedict Arnold Cemetery. Old man Arnold and his family lie here, eternally trying to forget what that great-grandson did. | Pelham St.

The Hill. This Colonial neighborhood is bordered by the harbor to the south, Bellevue Avenue to the north, and Touro Street and Memorial Boulevard to the west and east, respectively. Most of this area once belonged to Benedict Arnold, the great-grandfather of the Revolution's most famous traitor (Arnold bought the land soon after arriving from England in 1653). Thames, the settlement's original commercial street, was once so crowded with merchants' homes on the north side that they were built two rows deep. For sites on the Hill, look for addresses on Cotton's Court, Thames, Spring, Pelham, Corne, Church, Division, Clarke, Touro, and Mill streets and Bellevue Avenue; also Bannister's and Bowen's wharves.

Hunter House. A brilliant remaining example of the high life enjoyed in Newport before the war, this handsome home was built by Jonathan Nichols (colonial deputy-governor from 1748 to 1754) and was originally part of a large complex of house, garden, wharf, and shops typical of wealthy merchants and sea captains. Look to the doorway with its segmented pediment embracing a pineapple—the exotic fruit, often stuck onto a pike by the door of a home to indicate a sea captain's return (coupled with an invitation to visit him), came to symbolize hospitality and welcome. Inside, this home (now managed by the Preservation Society of Newport County) is elaborately paneled and decorated with magnificent Townsend and Goddard pieces, Newport silver, and china and paintings of the period. | 54 Washington St. | 401/847–1000 | www.newportmansions.org | $10 | May 18–Oct. 14, daily 10–5.

King Park. A statue of Comte de Rochambeau stands at the very spot where the French general arrived with his 5,000 troops, pledged to help the besieged Continental Army. | Wellington Ave.

Long Wharf. Now the setting for shopping and noshing, this wharf central to Colonial Newport is worth a pause, and a squint into the past. Picture the hum of activity here, beginning as early as 1685—West Indian ships pulling up, under full sail, with their loads of molasses, spices, sugar, and slaves; British ships hauling manufactured goods and bricks. Other British ships leaving port loaded with tar, lumber, wool, pork, beef, cheese, butter, and horses headed for Barbados and the West Indies. Other ships carrying Newport's finest furniture, clocks, and silver raising sail for Charleston, and points south. Local whaling ships from New Bedford and Boston bringing whale oil to port. And on the wharf, a thriving butchery, where residents would designate the sections of a live cow they'd like to purchase—when the poor animal was completely marked up in chalk, it would be slaughtered on the spot and sold. Newport didn't hum with commerce—it roared. In 1761 this city of 888 residences could boast of 438 warehouses; in 1763 (the last year of the French and Indian War), more than 500 ships left Newport Harbor—a number boosted no doubt by the unfettered privateering supported by the British during the war. | At Thames St., extending from the western side of the Brick Market.

Lucas-Johnston House. What hasn't this house seen since its early 18th-century construction? Slave trading: Augustus Lucas, a French Huguenot merchant who traded in both African and Indian slaves, bought the home in 1713. Botany: Robert Gardner, who rented the house afterward, conducted well-known pear-grafting experiments in the garden. Infamy: Grandson Augustus Lucas Johnston, who served as attorney general of the colony at the young age of 28 and owned so much land that Johnston, Rhode Island, was named for him, accepted the British offer of stamp master in the wake of the Stamp Act of 1765. When locals began rioting over the act, Johnston hid in the basement of his house until his friends could hold off the mob by promising that he would resign his post. He did, and sneaked away to the Carolinas, where he died in 1778. What else? The French stayed here during their occupation, and even Oliver Hazard Perry lived here in 1813–14. | 40 Division St. (private).

Museum of Newport History at the Brick Market. This charming and informative museum should be the embarkation point for any visit to Colonial Newport; the building itself is central to the town's history. Firstly, when Peter Harrison designed this marketplace in 1760, he placed this building at the head of Long Wharf, the settlement's central commercial avenue. Secondly, just two decades after the creation of the Colony House at the other end of the square, Harrison harnessed the newest winds of design that were all the rage in London — Palladian architecture. Note the Classical design motifs—giant Ionic pilasters and pedimented and segmented window frames—and picture the marketplace with the ground floor open, which was Harrison's original plan (the arches were walled up in 1842, when the building became Newport's town hall). Note also that the Brick Market has no proper facade—it was created to be approached, equally, from every angle. Inside, take time to explore the museum, which houses a number of valuable remnants of the period—perhaps most importantly a printing press. The colony's first, it was brought by Benjamin Franklin's brother, James, when he moved to Newport from Boston in 1726. (Six years later he would produce the first newspaper here.) Also look here for guided walking tours of Historic Newport, which leave regularly during the summer (call 401/846–0813 for a schedule). | 127 Thames St., western end of Washington Sq. | 401/841–8770 | $5 | Mon. 10–5, Wed.–Sat. 10–5, Sun. 1–5.

Newport Historical Society/Sabbatarian Meeting House. Many of the society's best items are on display down the hill at the Museum of Newport History at the Brick Market, but this site now also contains the Sabbatarian Meeting House, the oldest of the sect of the Seventh Day Baptists in the nation. Stephen Mumford founded the congregation in Newport in 1671, and the meetinghouse you see was erected in 1729. Ezra Stiles preached here during the war, when his own meetinghouse became a hospital for the French. While the exterior is simple, the interior's delicate panels and moldings recall those of Trinity Church and therefore point to Richard Munday as the likely architect. Don't miss the Claggett clock, which has been keeping time for the congregation for more than 200 years. | 82 Touro St. | 401/846–0813 | www.newporthistorical.com | Tues.–Fri. 9:30–4:30, Sat. 9:30–noon.

Quaker Meeting House/Great Friends Meeting House. Fleeing persecution in the Connecticut and Massachusetts colonies, Quaker families sailed toward Rhode Island via Narragansett Bay—they hit Aquidneck Island first, and many naturally stayed at this first landfall in the colonies' haven of tolerance. (Although Roger Williams didn't much care for the sect, he was bound by his own statements on tolerance.) The Quakers who came to Newport were from wealthy families, and several scions of these families went on to become governors, including William Coddington, Nicholas Easton, and John Coggeshall. The original meetinghouse built in 1700 is bracketed by extensions and barely visible in the seams between the clapboards. | Marlborough and Farewell Sts. | 401/846–0813 | $4 | Summer, Thurs.–Sat. (call for hrs).

Redwood Library and Athenaeum. There may be no greater testimony to Newport's cultural and intellectual vigor than this temple (literally) designed by Peter Harrison in 1748. The library has its roots in the 1730 Philosophical Club founded by Dean Berkeley, Henry Collins, Abraham Redwood, and other like-minded colonists who sought to promote "Knowledge and Virtue by Free Conversation." Harrison's design features rusticated stone—wooden blocks sanded and cut to look like the stone blocks used in Classical architecture. The oldest continuously used library in the country, the building also houses a remarkable collection of paintings and a map of Newport made in 1758 by the indefatigable Ezra Stiles. | 50 Bellevue Ave. | 401/847–0292 | www.redwood1747.org | Mon., Wed., Fri., and Sat. 9:30–5:30; Tues. and Thurs. 9:30–9; Sun. 1–5.

Samuel Whitehorne House Museum. Federal mansions are rare in Newport, because the bottom fell out of the local economy during British occupation, but Samuel Whitehorne, Jr., made such a fortune through rum distilling, banking, shipping, and possibly slave trading, he survived the collapse. Built in 1811, the house features an elegant hipped roof, a Neoclassical circular entry portico, and a formal garden. But Whitehorne never saw his greatest home completed—with two ships lost at sea he went bankrupt and sold the house at auction. Doris Duke's Newport Restoration Foundation purchased the home in 1969 (it had been converted to apartments and shops and was rapidly deteriorating) and Duke decided to finance a purchase of important Newport-created furniture to fill it as a museum. | 416 Thames St. | 401/847–2448 | $8 | Mon., Thurs., and Fri., 11–4; weekends 10–4.

Stevens Family Homes and Shop. The Stevens family were among Newport's proudest stonecutters, and much of their refined artistry can be seen in the Common Burial Ground and

Coddington Cemetery. The family's first home, the John Stevens House at 30 Thames, was built in 1709; the Phillip Stevens House is at 34 Thames. At 29 Thames, the John Stevens shop was opened by the family when they arrived in Newport in 1705. Currently owned and operated by stonecutter John E. Benson, it is one of the oldest continuously operated businesses in the United States. | 29, 30, and 34 Thames St.

Touro Synagogue. One of Newport's proudest and most graceful colonial buildings, this is the longest-standing Jewish house of worship in North America. A mere 20 years after the founding of the colony at Newport, Jews began arriving from Lisbon and Amsterdam with the promise of religious tolerance. Many of the new settlers were merchants, and they founded the candlemaking industry in Newport and embarked on varied marine trades. And while Newport embraced its Jewish merchants, the overall colony denied them citizenship. In 1684 the General Assembly thinly offered "as good protection here as any stranger residing among us," but no true rights, which would have included voting (suffrage wouldn't arrive until after the Revolution).

For a century, therefore, Newport Jews worshipped in private homes. By 1759, however, a now-thriving community led by Isaac de Touro began work on this synagogue. The design was the last important commission by Peter Harrison, who had no English tradition on which to draw and therefore relied on inspiration from descriptions of synagogues in Amsterdam and Lisbon, the works of Inigo Jones, and frankly, his own genius. The result—a simple, elegant building, set at an angle so as to properly face the east (i.e., Jerusalem) and set upon a hill, making for a profound statement of the place Jews enjoyed in Newport society. The architectural design so impressed Thomas Jefferson (who visited Newport as George Washington's secretary of state in 1790), that he incorporated it into his later plans for Monticello, the Capitol in Richmond, and the University of Virginia. But more profound than the architectural statement is perhaps the effect this synagogue had on a new president, who worshipped here during his 1790 visit to Newport. Pressed to define his emerging country's attitude toward Jews (and other religious minorities), George Washington wrote in his 1790 letter to "the Hebrew Congregation in Newport" that this new nation would "give to bigotry no sanction, to persecution no assistance." The stirring words sit outside this remarkable synagogue, and the entire letter, in facsimile, can be read within. | 85 Touro St. | 401/847–4794 | www.tourosynagogue.org | Free | July–Labor Day, Sun.-Fri. 10–5; May, June, and Labor Day–Oct., weekdays 1–3, Sun. 11–3; Nov.–Apr., Sun. 11–3. Tours conducted every half hr; no tours Sat. or Jewish holidays.

Trinity Church. Interesting that the Church of England should find a welcome home in the Colonies, but so it did. Protestants sickened by the Salem witchcraft trials of 1692 sought new affiliations and found comfort in the Anglican Church—so did French Huguenot families driven from their homeland by the revocation of the Edict of Nantes in 1685. Meanwhile, back in England the Society for the Propagation of the Gospel in Foreign Parts (talk about a revealing moniker) backed growing Anglican movements abroad, and in fact provided architects' plans for its newest outpost, Newport's Trinity Church. In 1725 local builder Richard Munday leaned on designs of Christopher Wren and the literal example of Christ Church (Old North) in Boston, and raised this soaring clock tower, one of the few such steeples left from the period. George Washington worshiped here, and George Berkeley, dean of Derry, one of England's most celebrated churchmen and an ardent contributor to Newport's cultural life, preached here often during his three-year stay (1729–31). Berkeley's daughter, who died in infancy, is buried in Trinity's churchyard, as is Admiral de Ternay. | Queen Anne Sq., Spring and Church Sts. | 401/846–0660 | www.trinitynewport.org | Call for hrs.

Wanton-Lyman-Hazard House. Restored, owned, and managed by the Newport Historical Society, this 1675 dwelling houses a small museum that showcases early colonial life, including the famous period furniture made in Newport. Stay for a tour, for this oldest surviving house in Newport has seen its share of action—among many highlights, it was the birthplace of Rhode Island governor and patriot Samuel Ward, it was the home of an infamous Tory, Martin Howard, and it was the site of the Stamp Act riot of 1765. Even the French loved it—during the friendly occupation of Newport, the Wanton family often threw parties that included French officers. | 17 Broadway | 401/846–0813 | www.newporthistorical.com | $4 | June–Sept., Thurs.–Sat. 10–4.

✦ SIGHTSEEING TOURS/TOUR COMPANIES

Ghost Tours. Not all the ghosts in town are pre-Victorian, but plenty are, and this entertaining, lantern-led evening stroll will fill your ears with 90 minutes of historic legends. | 401/841–8600 | www.ghostsofnewport.com. **Newport 101.** An interactive walking tour that promises "101 Unique Points of Interest!" in just over, yes, 101 minutes. Not only will you be treated to cemeteries, churchyards, and accounts of heroes and scoundrels, but you'll also emerge knowing how to hang a pirate, make a wax seal, and sign with a quill pen. Not necessarily in that order. | 401/841–8600 | www.newportwalks.com. **Newport on Foot Guided Tours.** Anita Rafael may be the most knowledgable tour guide around, so don't miss her leisurely, jam-packed strolls through Historic Newport. | 401/846–5391.

✦ ON THE CALENDAR: April **Neighborhoods of Newport House Tour.** A peek inside historic neighborhood homes, sponsored by a local private school. | 401/849–5970.

May **Fort Adams Opening Day.** A family celebration sponsored by the Fort Adams Foundation, along with the Museum of Yachting and the Sail Newport Family Sailing Festival. | 401/841–0707.

June **Secret Garden Tour.** A not-to-be-missed, self-guided walking tour of more than 15 hidden gardens in Newport's Colonial neighborhoods. | 401/847–0514.

HISTORIC DINING AND LODGING

Clarke Cooke House. This home was built for a sea captain, and began its life on nearby Thames Street. Moved to Bannister's Wharf, it now houses a popular restaurant mini-complex that includes formal dining upstairs and fireplace-warmed casual dining below, plus a rocking club in the basement. The refined, pricey Mediterranean menu incorporates local seafood; game dishes often appear as specials. Dress elegantly here. | Bannister's Wharf | 401/849–2900 | $18–$27 | AE, D, MC, V.

White Horse Tavern. As historic and genuine as it gets. Built in 1673, nearly a century before the Colony House, this large and comfortable tavern hosted meetings of the Colony's General Assembly and Criminal Court, and the City Council (members are said to have dined here and charged their meals to the public treasury). Owner William Mayes, who obtained his tavern license in 1687, was the father of a notorious pirate who returned to Newport and, to the consternation of British officials, succeeded his father as tavern-keeper. The tavern moved through several families, billeted Hessian troops during the war, became a boarding house in the early 1900s and was rescued, restored, and reopened as a restaurant in 1957. Today the menu embraces sophisticated European and American fare (and features a *Wine Spectator*–award winning wine list), but the interior is purely Colonial, from the giant beams to the small stairway, tiny front halls, and cavernous fireplaces. Call ahead to see if local historian Anita Rafael is running one of her lunchtime fireside chats—they're worth a trip to Newport alone. Be sure to reserve when dining here. | 26 Marlborough St. | 401/849–3600 | $14–$19 | AE, D, DC, MC, V | No lunch Sun.–Wed.

Admiral Farragut Inn. The meticulous restoration of this Colonial-style bed-and-breakfast showcases its hardwood floors and exposed ceiling beams. The breakfast room with its pewter chandelier and high-backed Pilgrim booths is a sheer delight. Complimentary breakfast. | 31 Clarke St. | 401/848–8015 | fax 401/848–8017 | www.innsofnewport.com | 9 rooms (8 with shower only) | $85–$150 | AE, D, MC, V.

Francis Malbone House. This section of Thames Street was a favorite location for well-off merchants to build homes during the mid-1700s, with a large house on the east side of the street and their gardens on the west side, near their wharfs. This is the only survivor of that era—now a luxury B&B, the house was built in 1760 by Peter Harrison for shipping merchant Francis Malbone. Enjoy the splendors restored, with period furnishing, working fireplaces, and a private courtyard. And ask about the house's underground tunnels to the waterside that are thought to have been used for smuggling goods past the Crown's customs agents. Complimentary breakfast. | 392 Thames St. | 401/846–0392 | fax 401/848–5956 | www. malbone.com | 16 rooms (2 with shower only) | $205–$395 | AE, MC, V.

Melville House. Tucked away in the Hill district and just a short walk from Touro Synagogue and Trinity Church, this 1750 home offers refreshing simplicity in its adherence to Colonial restraint. Rochambeau quartered some of his troops here—imagine their spirits treading the floors, and look across quiet Clarke Street to the house where the French general met with George Washington. Complimentary breakfast. | 39 Clarke St. | 401/847–0640 | fax 401/847–0956 | www.melvillehouse.com | 7 rooms (2 with shared bath) | $125–$165 | AE, D, MC, V.

NORTH KINGSTOWN

▼▼

Roger Williams, not content to sit at home in Providence, ventured south into the Narragansett lands and eventually established a trading post here. Not long after, Williams's friend Richard Smith followed suit and built his own trading post and house, and both men enjoyed friendly relations with the Narragansetts. Planters soon followed, and by 1674 a large parcel stretching from the southern boundary of East Greenwich to the Atlantic coast and west to the Connecticut border, was tidily wrapped up and incorporated as Kings Towne. Later, in 1723, the plantation-rich territory was split into North Kingstown and South Kingstown. The plantations needed a seaport, and the harbor of Wickford grew quickly into a vital and lively village. Today its wealth of remaining Colonial homes makes it one of Rhode Island's most-loved but lesser-known treasures (see separate listing, below). *Contact South County Tourism Council / Stedman Government Center, 4808 Tower Hill Rd., Wakefield 02879 | 800/548–4662 | www.southcountyri.com.*

Casey Farm. This 300-acre working farm overlooking Narragansett Bay was a prosperous plantation in the mid-18th century. Five generations of the Casey family improved and farmed the land—now a community-supported farm organically raises vegetables, herbs, and flowers. Tour the farmyard and cemetery and enjoy the hiking trails. | 2325 Boston Neck Rd. | 401/295–1030 | $4 | June 1–Oct. 15, Sat. 11–5.

Gilbert Stuart Birthplace and Museum. Although this quiet corner of North Kingstown can only claim the first seven years of early America's foremost portrait artist, it has created a fitting tribute. This 18th-century, gambrel-roofed house was not only a workingman's home, but a place of industry as well—the Stuart family ran a snuff mill on the Mettatuxet Stream, the first in all the colonies. Now, a restored gristmill (with two original granite stones once used to mill corn for Rhode Island's famous johnnycakes) is available for touring, along with the pristinely restored home where America's most celebrated portraitist of the Federal era, Gilbert Stuart, was born in 1755. Stuart lived here until his family moved to Newport when he was seven. He traveled to London to study painting with such masters as Benjamin West and Sir Joshua Reynolds. On his return, Stuart lived in Philadelphia, New York, and Washington D.C., all the while immortalizing more than 1,000 sitters. While he painted everyone from Jefferson to Monroe, his most famed portraits were of George Washington; Stuart's many renditions hang in great museums and one adorns the dollar bill. Stuart finished his days in Boston, where he died in 1828 at the age of 72. While here, inquire into renting rowboats for a serene session on Pettasquamscutt Pond. | 815 Gilbert Stuart Rd. | 401/294–3001 | www.gilbertstuartmusem.com | $5 | Apr.–Oct., Thurs.–Mon. 11–4.

Smith's Castle. It may not appear to be much of a castle, but when Richard Smith built his garrison, or castle, here in 1640, the name stuck (although the original buildings were burned to the ground during King Philip's War). The core of the house you see, built by Smith's son in 1678, even contains some of the charred timbers from its forebear. When Daniel Updike, a lawyer, attorney general of the colony, and part-time Newporter who helped found the Redwood Library inherited the house in 1736, he upgraded Smith's Castle to reflect his standing in the colony. The result: a massive central chimney, a full two stories, and two more rooms. Updike also cased the beams, paneled the walls, and put in a handsome simple staircase. The house maintains a museum and hosts a number of special events, plus regular tours. On the grounds, don't miss an 18th-century garden, plus a burial ground with the graves of 40 settlers killed in King Philip's War. | 55 Richard Smith Dr. | 401/294–3521 | www.smithscastle.org | $5 | Docents lead tours at 12:15, 1:30, 2:15, and 3, Fri.–Sun. in May, Sept., Oct.; Thurs.–Mon. from June–Aug.

PAWTUCKET
▼▼

Pawtucket is best known, and rightly so, for having set the stage for Samuel Slater, the Englishman who brought (with the backing of Moses Brown of Providence) his homeland's newest technology—the water-powered milling of cotton thread. Slater Mill, established in 1793, remains to this day a vibrant museum of the first shot of the American industrial revolution. And it was a shot heard, if not throughout the world, at least all over Pawtucket—local John Thorpe invented the hand and water loom for weaving in 1812, and a power loom four years later. And as industrialization continued to seize the vision of a rapidly growing America, Pawtucket would lead, with bigger and faster mills. The result today is a mixed architectural landscape, but several important sites remain amid the brick and smokestacks. *Contact Blackstone Valley Tourism Council | 175 Main St., Pawtucket 02860 | 800/454–2882 | www.tourblackstone.com.*

Daggett House. After John Daggett's house burned to the ground during King Philip's War, he built this gambrel-roofed one with its central chimney in 1685, and this one lasted: eight generations of Daggetts lived on the farm, the grounds of which now comprise Slater Memorial Park. As for the house, the Daughters of the American Revolution, Pawtucket Chapter, leased the house in 1902 and began restoring it. Thanks to the DAR, Daggett house houses an impressive collection of Revolutionary and 18th- and 19th-century memorabilia and antiques, including the dress worn by Catherine Littlefield Greene on the night she danced with General Lafayette. | Slater Memorial Park | 401/722–2631 | $2 | Tours most Sat. and Sun., June–Sept., 2–5.

Slater Mill Historic Site. This is one of Rhode Island's most popular sites, and with good reason. Pristine and fully renovated, perched on the steep falls of the Blackstone River, this multibuilding museum conducts excellent educational programs, leads regular tours, and hosts a variety of historic and cultural events. The central building, Slater Mill, is indeed the original site of Samuel Slater's successful industrial experiment. Up to this point, textile production was slow and tedious—it might take 10 yarn-spinners just to supply one weaver. In England the Arkwright spinning frame was already speeding up this process and, contrary to popular belief, some colonists were already aware of the machine but unable to replicate it effectively—and consistently. Slater, who came to Rhode Island in 1789 supported by Moses Brown and William Almy, was not a master mechanic who memorized the Arkwright's design (as is popularly believed), but an executive who knew how to get the bugs out. Four years later,

Slater's Arkwright-style machines were humming, and production would never be the same again. Nor would America. Today the Slater Mill building exhibits early cotton machines and illustrates each step in turning bale cotton into finished cloth. Also on the property, the Wilkinson Mill, built in 1810, housed Oziel Wilkinson and his sons, who were the first to make steel from iron, and made many of the original machines in Slater's Mill. Today the Wilkinson Mill includes an archaeological excavation revealing an early water system that drove the machines. Finally, the Sylvanus Brown House, a 1758 home that later housed transient millworkers, displays furnishings from a typical 1828 household. | 67 Roosevelt Ave. | 401/725–8638 | www.slatermill.org | $8 | May–Sept., Tues.–Sun. 10–5.

◆ SIGHTSEEING TOURS/TOUR COMPANIES
Spirit of the Blackstone Valley. Regular tours on this 12-passenger rivercraft offer insightful historical presentations. | 401/724–2200. **Autumn in the Blackstone River Valley.** A narrated Conway bus tour that begins in Pawtucket at the Blackstone Valley Visitors Center takes in Slater Mill Historic Site, the Museum of Work and Culture in Woonsocket, and then crosses the border into Massachusetts for more touring along the riverway | 800/888–4661 | $48 (includes all admissions and lunch) | On certain autumn days—call for schedule.

PORTSMOUTH
▼▼▼

When dissidents John Clarke and William Coddington got Roger Williams's advice on settling on Aquidneck Island, they purchased land from the local native tribe and founded Pocasset here at the hilly, northern end of the island. That was in 1638. Within the year, more freethinkers fled Massachusetts and headed for Clarke and Coddington's new settlement, including the revolutionary Anne Hutchinson and her followers. By May of 1639 Clarke and Coddington decided to start over again, taking all their town records with them, and founded Newport. Hutchinson stayed, and her settlement eventually joined with Newport in a loose association. While Newport quickly thrived as a maritime port, Portsmouth remained a quiet agricultural community. It was the war that would give the town its place in history—first, the bold capture of British general Richard Prescott from the country getaway he used during the British occupation of Newport, and second, the Battle of Rhode Island, the largest Revolutionary battle fought on New England soil and the first in the new nation to employ the services of a largely black regiment.

With a white population of only 54,000 at the time of the war and the need to keep five regiments in the field because of the British occupation of Newport, Rhode Island was unable to meet its obligation to the Continental Army. So in February 1778 the General Assembly offered freedom to every able-bodied African-American or Native American slave who would enlist for the length of the war. The First Rhode Island Regiment, comprised not only of to-be-freed slaves but also free black men of the colony, joined General John Sullivan in Providence after only three months' training. And yet, in a pitched battle against a British and Hessian assault during the ill-fated military attempt to drive the English from Newport, this regiment inflicted heavy injuries and took on few. The overall Battle did not fare as well. General Sullivan committed 10,000 American troops to Aquidneck, depending on the support of the French fleet offshore, which began attacking the British fleet relentlessly in the middle of a thundering storm. But in the clearing weather the French found themselves badly damaged and withdrew, surprisingly, to Boston for repairs. This left the Americans badly exposed and potentially surrounded. Sullivan quickly mustered emergency support for evacuation, and engaged the British, in pursuit, around these hills of Portsmouth. The delay worked, and the troops made it safely onto the mainland and out of British hands. But was it a lost cause? Not entirely. The British suffered tremendous damage, and soon gave up on trying to hold the intricate network of shoreline and islands. To protect their mobility, the British withdrew after their three-year occupation, in 1779. *Contact Portsmouth Historical Society | 870 East Main Rd., 02871 | 401/683–9178.*

Butts Hill Fort. Take a look around, and you'll see why this was a natural choice for a military outpost—that's the Sakonnet River to the east, Narragansett Bay to the west, and Middletown to the south. Actually, the British had the idea first, and built an earthworks and walls of a fort in 1777; American forces occupied it in 1778, and it played a major role in the Battle of Rhode Island. | Sprague St., behind the American Legion Post.

Founder's Rock. Clarke and Coddington landed here in 1638. The Portsmouth Compact, outlining a democratic government, is inscribed on a stone marker. | Off Boyd's La.

Friends' Meeting House. Quakers dominated Portsmouth society for its first century and a half; until the early 1800s this meetinghouse was the community's sole church (the original building was raised in 1656; the present, larger building was built in 1702). Surviving Hessian occupation during the war, the building later housed a Friends boarding school in 1784. | Rte. 138 and Hedley Ave.

Hessian Hole. Where many patriots no doubt felt the German mercenaries deserved to lie, the "Hessian Hole" is about 700 yards down the lane from the Portsmouth priory. This depression holds the graves of 30 Hessian soldiers who died during the Battle of Rhode Island on August 29, 1778. The brook that runs past here is said to have been red with blood for days after the fighting. | Off Cory La.

Patriot's Park. A peaceful stretch of green, this is marked with a memorial to Rhode Island First Regiment, the nation's first African- and Native American regiment. | At the junction of Rtes. 24 and 114.

Southernmost School. The first one-room schoolhouse built in Portsmouth, this is one of the oldest remaining schoolhouses in Rhode Island. Dating from the early 18th century, the house originally had a stone end with a bake oven, for the preparation of the master's food. Now part of the Portsmouth Historical Society, the school operates as a museum and displays antique desks and a variety of textbooks. | Rte. 138 and Union St. | 401/683–9178 | Call for hrs.

PROVIDENCE
▼▼

How fitting that the revitalization of today's Providence has had so much to do with rediscovering the city's waterfront—both the head of Narragansett Bay and the shores of the rivers that feed it—because it was this network of waterways that drew the earliest settlers here in the first place. When Roger Williams arrived in 1636, he realized the great bounty these waterways provided. Here, 27 mi from the Atlantic, was a natural harbor, with two rivers—the Moshassuck and the Woonasquatucket—meeting in a great salt cove (just adjacent to today's Providence Place Mall) that was fed by the Providence River, a tidal estuary. Water, water, everywhere. What sustained the first planters and farmers quickly drew merchants, traders, captains, and eventually, manufacturers.

Williams, like other English settlers, could have played his Manifest Destiny card and seized the land from the local Narragansett Indians. But the minister believed in ownership as defined by possession, not from the grant of an absent monarch. So he offered to pay—an amazing notion in the mid-17th century. Contrary to popular belief, though, Williams never had to spend a dime on the settlement he called Providence Plantations, because the Narragansetts gave it to him outright. Barely 10 years later, 200 settlers had built houses along what was then called Towne Street (today, North and South Main Street) and along the river shores. But the focus would remain at the water's edge, and by 1680 Pardon Tillinghast built the first wharf at the base of what is still called Transit Street; by the turn of the century, the waterfront was crowded with wharves and bristling with masts of ships trading raw materials, manufactured goods, and slaves, throughout the Colonies and the West Indies (the settlement's market building still sits at the center of Providence's life today).

The War for Independence changed everything. Already a center of patriot activity producing outspoken British critics such as Stephen Hopkins and Silas Downer, Providence committed what is often considered the first overt acts of aggression of the Revolution when locals not only burned the British schooner *Gaspee*, but then resisted extreme British pressure (including large rewards) to give up the perpetrators. So when the British occupied Newport in 1776, it made perfect sense that Providence would surge to the fore, well-fortified and essentially untouched during the entire war. The momentum would carry the city into the post-war economic boom (the final hurrah of the sea trade segued perfectly into the local explosion in water-powered manufacturing) while Newport languished without rivers and a decimated local economy strangled by a three-year occupation. And although the two cities shared capital status into the dawn of the 20th century, the writing was clear—Providence would lead Rhode Island into the Victorian era, and never look back. *Contact Providence Preservation Society | 21 Meeting St., Providence 02906 | 401/831–8586 | www.ppsri.org. Providence Warwick Convention and Visitors Bureau | 1 W. Exchange St., Providence 02903 | 800/233–1636 | fax 401/351–2090 | www.providencecvb.com.*

Brick School House. Home of one of the first free schools in the country, this 1768 building now houses the venerable Providence Preservation Society. | 24 Meeting St.

Brown University. What began in 1764 as Rhode Island College moved from Warren in 1770 to this hillside perch, but wasn't named for the illustrious local family until 1804, when a whopping gift of land and funds from Nicholas Brown, Jr., cinched the renaming. The campus, tucked tightly among its 17th-, 18th-, and 19th-century neighbors, is full of architectural treasure (and some terrifying architectural blunders as well) and a delight to stroll any time of year. Don't miss University Hall, the heart of the university, which was built in 1770 from designs by Robert Smith of Philadelphia (who also designed Old Nassau Hall at Princeton University). Originally created to house students and provide classrooms, the building became a barracks and hospital for American and French soldiers during the War. Also, the John Carter Brown Library at the southeast corner of the College Green, is a gift to the university from the John Nicholas Brown estate in 1904 and contains a tremendous collection of rare books and early Americana. | Waterman, George, Prospect, and Thayer Sts.

John Brown House. John Quincy Adams called it "the most magnificent and elegant mansion" in America. He may have been right. This extraordinary mansion, which still commands a huge corner lot along Benefit Street, is the supreme statement of richesse acquired in Providence during the mid-18th century, not to mention the way Providence managed to thrive after the War while Newport, and other wealthy (or wealthier) towns were ravaged and never recovered. And what a homeowner: John Brown was Providence's most powerful citizen mid-century. Along with his brothers Nicholas, Joseph and Moses, John Brown seemed to corner every market: sea trading, privateering, manufacturing (iron and spermacetti candles), and distilling rum. He applied the same fervor to the foundling cause of freedom—known as an ardent patriot, Brown led the conspiracy in Providence to burn the *Gaspee* near Warwick. In the years following the War, Brown reached into the Far East with shipping. This gorgeous home was designed by Brown's brother Joseph (who died during its erection) in 1785, who brought every detail of refinement and wealth to the interior and the exterior, including elaborately carved woodwork. Brown entertained here in high style (Washington, on his triumphant return to Rhode Island after the War, was entertained here by Brown in August of 1790); lucky for later arrivistes to Providence, the house remains in pristine condition and is both a headquarters for the Rhode Island Historical Society and open as a museum highlighting early American decorative arts and painting, making this a must-visit. | 52 Power St. | 401/331–8575 | www.rihs.org | $7 | Mar.–Dec., Tues.–Sat. 10–5, Sun. noon–4; Jan. and Feb., Fri. and Sat. 10–5, Sun. noon–4.

Commercial Blocks. Much has changed on this stretch of what was originally called Towne Street: houses cheek-by-jowl lined both sides of the road, and just behind them to the west, sailing ships pulled in near wharves and warehouses lining the Providence River, and did business right out of these houses. Unfortunately, this entire seafaring landscape was destroyed by a massive fire in 1801, which wiped out the entire area. What you see now was rebuilt in the quarter-century following, with, it must be noted, considerable charm. | 293–245 South Main St.

First Baptist Church in America. This National Historic Landmark may be Providence's most historic, for it houses the very congregation that Roger Williams founded in 1639. Two earlier structures, built in 1700 and 1775, are long gone, but this elegant Joseph Brown creation remains as a proud testimony to the freethinking minister who founded the Providence settlement and the Rhode Island Colony. Built in 1775 and based in part on London architect James Gibbs' designs for St. Martin's-in-the-Fields Church, this simple New England meeting house with its pedimented projecting foretower seats up to 1,400 people. And since Brown University first began matriculating in the late 18th century, those students have walked down the hill to First Baptist for their graduation exercises (and still do every year). | 75 North Main St. | 401/454–3418 | www.fbcia.com.

Market House. This 1775 building, designed by Joseph Brown and set directly on the waterfront, was the beating heart of the both civic and political life in the first century of the settlement. Where a modern bridge spans the Providence River, a drawbridge rose regularly to allow ships passage to more wharves farther north, and lowered to let farmers and merchants bring wagons loaded with goods from Weybosset Neck on the western shore (the arches on the Market House you see were originally open to public traffic). In the years surrounding the war, the Market House also hosted resistance meetings and French soldiers, and served as the seat of Providence's city government until 1880. The building now houses part of the Rhode Island School of Design. | Market Square, South Main St.

Museum of Art, Rhode Island School of Design. Renown as one of the country's finest small art museums, RISD—as it is called by locals—also may boast of the one of the most extensive collections of Early American furniture as well. A legacy of many of the grandees of Rhode Island, the collection is particularly famous for its holdings of furniture created by the Townsend and Goddard families of Newport cabinetmakers, including two of the legendary block-front, carved-shell desks-and-bookcases (one of which sold for $12 million at a New York auction in 1969). Period rooms fill Pendleton House—the "wing" of the Museum devoted to the exhibition of decorative arts—with important examples of 18th-century Boston, New York, Philadelphia, and Newport furniture, along with elegant examples of English pottery, Chinese export porcelain, and a comprehensive survey of Rhode Island silver. | 224 Benefit St. | 401/454–6500 | www.risd.edu | $6; free Sun. 10–1 and last Sat. of the month | Tues.–Sun. 10–5.

Nightingale–Brown House. Glowing in yellow clapboard and white rusticated trim and one more challenger to the grandeur of the Brown House, this is another remarkable Federal-era mansion, probably designed and built by Caleb Ormsbee in 1791 for Nightingale who, unfortunately, died soon after its completion. Nicholas Brown, Jr., bought it soon thereafter and added it to the family's remarkable string of real estate along Benefit Street. Made of wood instead of the more expensive brick—presumably the largest such structure to remain from 18th-century America—it is nonetheless an elegant statement with its heavy quoining, portico and Palladian window. It is well-known in Providence that the sale of one piece of Goddard furniture—a nine-shell mahogany secretary desk that had been made for Joseph

Brown—financed the entire renovation of the Nightingale-Brown House, which is now open as a museum. Many of the first floor salons (the only ones on public view) have been refurbished in 1890s style, unfortunately, but there are also several rooms which are interesting relics of the early 20th-century vogue for "Colonial Revival." | 357 Benefit St. | 401/272–0357 | www.brown.edu/Research/JNBC/house | $3 | Fri. 1–4 only.

Old State House. Still charming but hardly the way it looked in 1762 (try to picture a simple brick building *sans* foretower, Italianate entryway, and extensions on the Benefit Street side). Then picture the setting: overlooking the wharves on the river below, the Boston Post Road running by. Then imagine those truly revolutionary Rhode Islanders renouncing their allegiance to Great Britain—two months prior to the Declaration of Independence (on May 4, 1776, to be precise). This vastly important building housed the shared seat of colonial government. It now houses various historic commissions, but you can ask to see the extant 18th-century chamber on the second floor. | North Main St. (backs onto 150 Benefit St.) | Free. | Weekdays 9–4:30.

Providence Art Club. Part of what is surely Providence's most picturesque block, these two homes were both built by Seril Dodge. The earlier of the two, at 10 Thomas Street, offers the whimsical view of a two-and-a-half-story wooden house that was built as such in 1789 but was later lifted up another story to allow a store front at street level (note the beautiful central pedimented doorway in mid-air). Next door, connected with a brick archway, is 11 Thomas, which Dodge built in 1791 to engage in silversmithing with his brother, Nehemiah (the house is made of wood but has a brick veneer). Since 1880, the well-known and beloved Providence Art Club has made its home here, and the galleries in both buildings are frequently open to the public with shows featuring works by current members and friends. | 10–11 Thomas St. | 401/331–1114 | Weekdays 11–4, weekends 2–4.

Providence Preservation Society Heritage Tours. In addition to running a nationally recognized house and garden tour in June, the Providence Preservation Society also offers regular tours of the city's historic neighborhoods with excellent tour guides. | 21 Meeting St. | 401/831–8586 | www.ppsri.org.

Roger Williams National Memorial. His home may have been burned during King Philip's War, but water springs eternal. Here, the spring (declared to be for the public's use since 1721) anchors a pristine and peaceful (and the nation's smallest) national park. The old-fashioned home at the corner of the park is faux-colonial, but houses friendly rangers and good information on Williams, early colonial days, and tours and travel in Rhode Island. | 282 North Main St. | 401/521–7266 | www.nps.gov/rowi.

Shakespeare's Head. A hotbed of activism, journalistically speaking. It all began with John Carter, a printer who'd trained under Benjamin Franklin, and built himself a home and printing office here in 1722. Inside these walls, Carter published *The Providence Gazette and Country Journal,* the town's first newspaper, which had been founded by William Goddard and his mother, Sarah, in 1762. When William left for Philadelphia, Sarah ran the paper with Carter and the two published a long string of dissenting articles in the months before the war. Having been appointed local postmaster by none other than Franklin, Carter also ran the post office from here (along with print and book shops) "at the sign of Shakespeare's Head." While the house is not literally open (it is home to the Junior League of Rhode Island), the lovely gardens behind the building are and are worth a pause. | 21 Meeting St. (private).

Stephen Hopkins House. Perhaps the colony's most outspoken—and hard-working—patriot, Hopkins was nonetheless a modest man whose Quaker views pervaded his choice of home and domestic style. In other words, a little house for the larger-than-life man who served as colonial governor 10 times, chief justice of the Rhode Island Superior Court, representative at the colonial congresses, delegate to the Continental Congress, and signer of the Declaration of Independence. Originally built in 1708, near the corner of South Main and Hopkins streets, the two-room house—stunningly clad in burgundy-red clapboard—with an end chimney was bought by Hopkins and enlarged (the home was moved to its present site in 1927) in 1742. Today, furnished with period antiques, the home serves as a quiet indicator of Colonial daily life. Outside is a Colonial-style parterre garden designed by Alden Hopkins, initial landscape architect at Williamsburg. | 15 Hopkins St. | 401/421–0694 | www.nscda. org/museums/rhodeisland.htm | $3 | Apr.–Dec. 1, Wed. and Sat. 1–4.

Tillinghast Burial Ground. Families with houses on Towne Street (now North and South Main) would have located personal burial grounds in their backyards, as it were. When Providence boosters wanted to lay another street along the hillside here, families were forced to see their burial grounds bisected, or worse. But Benefit Street arrived—and with it, increasing development that relocated many of Providence's oldest graves and headstones to the North Burial Ground. The Tillinghast plot is a reminder of what must have been a regular feature of Providence's earliest landscape. | Benefit St., just adjacent to the Barker Playhouse.

Weybosset Neck. Standing along the shore of the Providence River with College Hill behind you, imagine the landscape to the west, where downtown Providence now stands: in the 18th century, a quiet meadowland with a smattering of businesses, wharves, and shipyards. Westminster Street, named for the City of Westminster in London, was laid out as early as 1763, and the inhabitants there resented the thriving East Siders on the other side of the river (some even proposed seceding from Providence and becoming a city within a city). But the two sides would eventually unite: the first permanent bridge across the Providence River was built in 1816, limiting the northern section of the river (and the salt cove approximately where today's Waterplace Park circles around near the Providence Place Mall) to tall ships. With the decline of shipping after the War of 1812 (and the subsequent boom in manufacturing on the rivers), Weybosset blossomed with modest gable houses along the shoreline and mansions on Westminster and Weybosset streets. Most of these buildings were replaced over time, but a good stock of late 19th-century commercial buildings still give downtown Providence some character. Do not miss an opportunity to shop in the nation's oldest shopping mall, the Arcade (between Weybosset and Westminster), a wonderful example of an early 19th-century American commercial arcade. Architects Russell Warren and James Bucklin designed this charming structure with its three layers of shops opening onto interior balconies, protected by rose-colored skylights set into a gable roof, and each took a facade: the Weybosset facade with its paneled parapet is generally considered to be the work of Warren, while the Westminster facade with pedimented portico atop monolithic Ionic columns is attributed to Bucklin. | Weybosset and Westminster Sts.

HISTORIC LODGING

Annie Brownell House. A grand stairway with carved banister adorns this lovely 1899 Colonial Revival home, 1 mi from city hall and about 4 blocks from Brown University. Rooms are individually appointed with period furniture and reproductions; one has a majestic four-poster bed. Complimentary breakfast. No kids under 12. | 400 Angell St. | 401/454–2934 | fax 401/454–2934 | members.home.net/satunder | 3 rooms (with showers only) | $95–$105 | AE, MC, V.

C. C. Ledbetter Bed & Breakfast. A downtown location, a most cheerful C. C. herself, and the charm of this 1770 mansard-roof home make this a special place to stay. The garden has two hammocks and blooms with roses, lilies, and peonies. Its proximity to Brown and RISD makes it a favorite for visiting parents. Complimentary breakfast. | 326 Benefit St. | phone/fax 401/351–4699 | 4 rooms (2 with shared bath) | $95–$110 | MC, V.

WARREN

▼▼

Often overshadowed by glitzier Bristol, Warren boasts as rich a history and as extensive a catalog of period architecture, and is the true local's favorite because of its underdog status. The Wampanoags knew a good thing when they saw it, and so they settled on the banks of the Warren River, next to a freshwater spring. By 1621 pilgrims Edward Winslow and Stephen Hopkins had found the Wampanoag village called Sowams, and they brought a red-laced coat and a copper chain for the chief, Massasoit. Two years later the English would save the chief's life, and these good relations paved the way for Roger Williams's smooth arrival 13 years later. But in the turmoil of King Philip's War local settlements were burned to the ground, and Warren would not redevelop until peace returned to the area. The town's deep harbor was a draw, and the community rebuilt and thrived in maritime trade and whaling until the British stormed through Warren on May 25, 1778. That, combined with the occupation of Newport, nearly starved the settlement. Warren (named for British admiral Sir Peter Warren in 1746) would rise again. Today the waterfront is dotted with post-Revolutionary buildings erected in the rubble of that conflict, when Warren reclaimed its title as a rich and prosperous whaling and maritime center. *Contact Massasoit Historical Association / Box 203, Warren 02885 / 401/245–0392. Warren Town Hall / 514 Main St., Warren 02885 / 401/245–7340 / www. townofwarren.org.*

Burr's Tavern. Long gone, but not forgotten. Look for the plaque in front of Old Stone Bank commemorating the night George Washington stayed at the tavern on this site—March 13, 1781. Other luminaries passing through Burr's doors include Thomas Jefferson, the Marquis de Chastellux, and the Marquis de Lafayette, who, it is said, ate his first johhnycakes here. | Washington and Main Sts.

James Maxwell House. This is Warren's oldest waterfront home. Elder Samuel Maxwell built it in 1743, and son James was born here in 1752. James, who served in the Revolutionary War, was captured and imprisoned on the HMS *Jersey,* an infamous prison ship anchored in New York Harbor. But this Maxwell survived, returned to Warren, and in two marriages sired 13 children. The nine who survived were all girls, and Maxwell made wedding gifts of houses to each of them (five of the homes are still standing). Today this building also houses a museum worth a visit, and is home to the Massasoit Historical Association. | 59 Church St. | www.massasoithistoricalassociation.org | Free | Sat. 10–2.

Masonic Temple. A fine example of early (and philosophically correct) recycling, this 1796 temple was built with timbers salvaged from British frigates sunk in Newport Harbor. The second-oldest Masonic Temple in Rhode Island (the oldest is in Newport), this building also served as town hall, and in 1803 it was recorded as the home of the Warren Academy. The exterior details, with hand-carved quoins and Ionic capitals topping the doorway's fluted pilasters, are truly exceptional. | Baker St. (private).

Polly Saunders House. She built this house all by herself in 1802. Enough said. | 390 Main St. (private).

Warren Baptist Church. This Gothic 1844 church designed by Russell Warren may be a little young for inclusion, but the site on which it stands is considered to have more historical associations than any other in Warren. Consider: the First Baptist Church in Warren, built in 1762, would be the first home of Rhode Island College, founded by the Philadelphia Baptist Association (which chose Rhode Island because of the colony's already-well-known reputation for religious freedom). The college opened in 1765, graduated seven students four years later, but moved in 1770 and changed its name to Brown University to honor the largesse of the Brown family. In a lovely turn, that first class's valedictorian, Charles Thompson, would return to Warren and become second pastor of the Baptist Church. On the day the British invaded, looted, and burned Warren (May 25, 1778), soldiers burned the Baptist Church and parsonage (they also captured Thompson). The church is just open for Sunday services. | 407 Main St. | 401/245–3669.

HISTORIC DINING AND LODGING
Nathaniel Porter Inn. A charming small inn, this has benefited from painstaking renovation of a 1750 sea captain's home. Pencil-post beds with lacy canopies set the stage on wide-plank floors, and even the little electric candlesticks in the windows seem period somehow. The public rooms downstairs house a cozy tavern and restaurant. Restaurant. | 125 Water St. | 401/ 245–6622 | fax 401/247–2277 | www.nathanielporterinn.com | 3 rooms | $80 | AE, D, MC, V.

WARWICK
▼▼

Roger Williams may have been able to claim exile from two colonies, but his contemporary Samuel Gorton had him beat. A nonconformist of epic proportions—a religious freethinker and a disbeliever in civic authority—Gorton first got himself banished from the Plymouth Bay and Portsmouth colonies. On arrival in Providence in 1640 he challenged the government there, claiming that without a royal charter it had no basis for existence. Williams, who would not obtain a charter from England until 1664, tolerated Gorton's gadflying, and allowed him to remain in Providence provided he behave himself. Gorton refused and stirred up trouble that erupted into a riot on November 15, 1641. When the Gortonites fled Providence that day, they sought sanctuary in Shawomet, which he purchased from local Native Americans, and he and his followers began putting up houses on a neck of land north of the present lighthouse. The Massachusetts Bay Colony thought the land belonged to it, and Massachusetts officials actually imprisoned Gorton for a while, but he was released and sailed to England for vindication. There Robert Rich, Earl of Warwick and head of the parliamentary commission on foreign plantations, heard Gorton's case and upheld his right of colonization. In thanks, Gorton named his vindicated new home after the earl. Today's Warwick doesn't show much of its early, radical roots—a steady stream of modernization has smothered most of the legacy. Perhaps the most important landmark is a natural one—Gaspee Point, where colonists grounded and burned a hated British revenue schooner, and committed one of the first truly aggressive acts of Colonial resistance. *Contact Warwick Historical Society | 25 Roger Williams Circle, Warwick 02888 | 401/467–7647. Warwick Tourism Office | 3275 Post Rd., Warwick 02886 | 800/492–7942 | www.warwickri.com.*

Gaspee Point. Forget the Boston Tea Party—at least temporarily. In 1772, this point set the stage for one of the very first acts of overt hostility in colonial-British relations. The *Gaspee* had sailed into Narragansett Bay in early 1772 to enforce the Crown's repressive trade laws, and it infuriated the freewheeling, entrepreneurial traders of Providence and elsewhere. So what were irate colonists to do on the morning of June 9, 1772, when the ship ran aground off the sandy spit of land near Warwick called Namquit Point? A gang led by merchant John Brown met up at the Sabin Tavern on Towne Street in Providence, where they plotted an ambush. Sometime after midnight, Captain Abraham Whipple led a party of 50 men, including Captain John Hopkins (nephew of former colonial governor Stephen Hopkins), rowing eight longboats, quietly out to the point. The colonists jumped the sleeping crew, put them ashore, then returned and set fire to the ship. More remarkable than this audacious act was the patriotic stonewalling that followed: even in the face of several rewards from King George III for information on the conspirators, the Providence gang kept its confidence, and the *Gaspee*'s untimely conflagration was never avenged. | Access east of Warwick Ave.

John Waterman Arnold House. John Waterman Arnold inherited this land from his ancestor William Arnold, an early settler of Pawtuxet who was granted the land in 1638. The house he built here around 1800 remains a fine example of an 18th-century rural residence; the simple 2½-story home sits on a stone foundation and features a gambrel roof and a central chimney plan. Inside, original details such as wide plank floors and unadorned mantels underscore the simplicity of life outside Providence. | 25 Roger Williams Circle | 401/467-7647 | Donation suggested | Sun 1–4.

WICKFORD

▼▼

Tucked away from the spotlight of Providence and Newport, this harbor is one of the richest historic villages in Rhode Island, and its compact network of narrow streets and alleyways lined with small-scale Colonial and Federal homes are a pure delight to walk. Wickford's history ties in with the Williams and Smith trading posts nearby: Smith named a whole section of his plantation at Cocumscussoc "Wickford," in somewhat indirect homage to Elizabeth Winthrop, wife of the governor of Connecticut (she was born in Wickford, England). In 1707 one of Smith's heirs laid out a small matrix of streets and sold the first town lots in what would become Wickford Village (although the speculator, named Lodowick Updike, first called the development "Updike's Newtown"). The venture drew settlers to this small, well-protected harbor, and soon plantations were shipping goods to Wickford to move up and down Narragansett Bay.

Like the ports on the opposite side of the Bay that suffered during the British occupation of Newport, Wickford's economy sagged, but it did not endure the harsh looting and burning that plagued Bristol and Warren. And even after the Revolution, with Newport now out of the commercial running and the plantations declining, Wickford thrived because locals turned their shipping, shipbuilding, and fishing activities outward. This flush of commerce and success can be seen in the concentration of homes dating from this period, 1780–1830. And the now-charming crowding of the original village streets shows that real estate was at a premium, even then. *Contact South County Room, North Kingstown Free Library | 100 Boone St., North Kingstown 02852 | 401/294-3306 | www.clan.lib.ri.us/nki/index.htm.*

First Baptist Church. Originally erected in 1816, this Greek Revival wooden church (with alterations made about 20 years later) shows how the Classical style adapted itself to more provincial settings. | Main St., north side.

Immanuel Case House. Is there ever a poor tavern keeper? Not Immanuel Case, obviously, from the look of this rather grand home he built, in 1786. Note the beautiful pedimented doorway and the two interior chimneys—status symbols both. | 41 Main St. (private).

Old Narragansett Church/Old St. Paul's. Although this simple, understated New England Puritan-style meetinghouse looks right at home tucked away from the hurly-burly of Main Street, it didn't start out here. This Episcopal Church (the second established in Rhode Island and one of the oldest Episcopal churches in America) was built in 1707 about 7 mi south, near the then-flourishing Tower Hill settlement. But with the post-Revolution decline of Tower Hill, the church emptied (but not before Gilbert Stuart was baptized here in 1756, and the building housed American troops during the war). The rise of Wickford's population prompted its relocation to this site. | 60 Church La.

By Lea Lane Stern

South Carolina and Georgia

❧━━━✦━━━❧

The Pre-Steel Magnolias

As part of "The Carolinas"—the tough and tender southernmost parcel of the newly settled continent—South Carolina and Georgia were the pre-Steel Magnolias of the 13 Colonies. Gullahs and cotton and rice, churches and hedonism, island plantations and major mountain battlefields, Charleston and Savannah, Beaufort and Augusta—the Colonial, Revolutionary, and Federal eras remain today, not only in hundreds of significant buildings, museums, and war ruins, but in these sister states' stubborn retention of an earlier lifestyle. Venture to those crown jewels, Charleston and Savannah, and you'll still find hundreds of historic houses offering their crystal-laden, parquet-floored, time-burnished versions of Southern Comfort, today a bit flamboyant yet decidedly traditional. The region's drive to achieve was perhaps never better portrayed than by that later antebellum heroine, Scarlett O'Hara. As it turns out, the earlier histories of Colonial Georgia and South Carolina are studded with many other figures who were as determined to win.

Drives to and from early sites pass through areas of varied beauty. From Lowcountry shoreline with wide sand beaches, large bays, and forests of palmettos and moss-draped live oaks, South Carolina extends inland into undulating farmlands, then reaches toward the Blue Ridge Mountains, whose foothills are studded with lakes, forests, and wilderness hideaways. Revolutionary War sites and battlefields and historic towns dot the landscape. Just south and west, Georgia would grow into the largest state east of the Mississippi, with sharp geographical contrasts: from the foothills of the southern Appalachian Mountains in the north, with elevations approaching 5,000 ft, to near-sea level in the south; from bleached, sandy beaches along the Atlantic Ocean, to the flat peanut-rich croplands in the west. Tobacco, peaches, soybeans, and pulpwood pine farms rake in far more money now than the cotton and rice of 250 years ago. Small towns that managed to survive wars and natural disasters were overlooked through recent decades, so many still reflect the 18th and early 19th centuries, when the region thrived. These two states are studded with significant Colonial and Federal architecture.

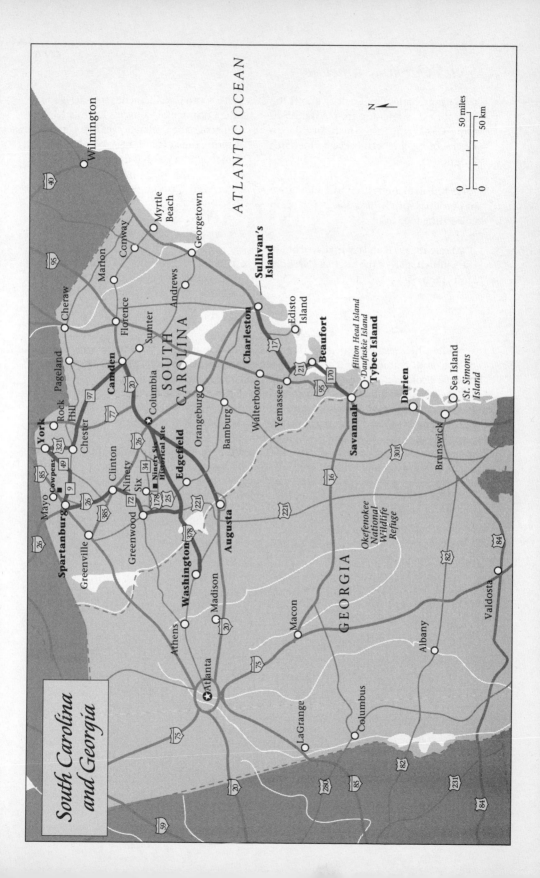

South Carolina and Georgia

South Carolina Timeline

1665 King Charles II of England grants the "Carolinas," stretching from Virginia to Cape Canaveral in Spanish Florida, to several of his financial backers, the Lords Proprietors.

1670s British planters from Barbados arrive in Carolinas with African slaves and begin cultivating the land.

1731 Present-day Georgia is separated out of the southern part of the original Carolinas land grant.

1776 South Carolina sends four delegates to the Continental Congress in Philadelphia. They sign the Declaration of Independence. During the Revolutionary War, 127 battles are fought in South Carolina up until 1783.

1780 British troops occupy Charles Town.

1783 The city of Charles Town is incorporated, and officially becomes Charleston.

1788 South Carolina ratifies the U.S. Constitution and becomes the eighth state in the Union.

Culture here seems to reflect the past as well. Most South Carolinians and Georgians remain church- and community-oriented. Many restaurants and clubs require special liquor permits to serve alcohol after midnight on Saturday, and many shops close on Sundays. The Gullahs still create handicrafts as they did before the Revolution, and their culture continues to make incursions into the modern psyche, most unforgettably in George Gershwin's *Porgy and Bess* opera, inspired in part by Cabbage Row, a neighborhood central to Charleston's African-American history. Integration came late, but manners remain. Small-towners, especially, seem to move and talk a bit more deliberately. It's the old-fashioned aspect of American life, as much a part of history as any battlefield.

✦ THE REAL CIVIL WAR

South Carolina and Georgia's early histories are as connected as their drawls, but as distinct as their cash crops. Each state was influenced early and lastingly by Native American, European, and African cultures, and both flourished during the Colonial, Revolutionary and Federal periods. South Carolina was a rice and rising star; Georgia, a George-come-lately—not because of the Revolution, but a revolutionary invention, the cotton gin.

The Spanish entered St. Helena Sound near what is now Beaufort, South Carolina, in 1520. Six years later, don Lucas Vázquez de Ayllón of Toledo established San Miguel at Winyah Bay, the first European settlement in the state, predating the English at Jamestown, Virginia, by 81 years. After a year and a bitter winter, however, the Spanish abandoned San Miguel. French Huguenots fleeing religious persecution came next, then the English arrived during the 1670s, after King Charles II granted Carolina—encompassing Virginia down to Cape Canaveral in Spanish Florida—to eight of his lord proprietors. Planters from the English colony of Barbados arrived in 1670 at Albemarle Point on the Ashley River. During the next decade, settlers would cross the river to found Charles Town, today's Charleston, soon to become England's wealthiest American city—attracting both planters and pirates.

By 1700, plantations dotted the Lowcountry and Sea Islands; in 1713, a separate governor was appointed for North Carolina, and the Colony was split. By the 1730s, development spread north, thanks to Welsh, Swiss, Irish, Scottish, and German immigrants from northern colonies. By the 1740s, 22,000 slaves toiled in the Colony, most taken from what are today Senegal and Sierra Leone. They outnumbered the whites three to one. Most worked Lowcountry plantations, clearing swamps and building dikes and canals along rivers to plant

Georgia Timeline

1715 South Carolinian Thomas Nairne suggests to the English crown that it colonize the region that is now Georgia. For his reward, unhappy Indians burn him at the stake.

1733 James Oglethorpe and a small contingent of followers debark at the site of Savannah; by March of the following year, they have built 91 log houses overlooking the Savannah River.

1742 English forces under Oglethorpe defeat the Spanish in the battle of Bloody Marsh, ending Spanish influence in the region.

1776 Representing Georgia, Button Gwinnett, George Walton, and Lyman Hall travel to Philadelphia to sign the Declaration of Independence.

1777 Georgia's first constitution is adopted.

1778 During the Revolutionary War, Savannah falls to British naval forces; it is recaptured four years later by the Americans.

1788 Georgia becomes the fourth state to ratify the new federal Constitution.

rice, which they had cultivated in Africa. The Colony's rice crop produced extraordinary wealth for a few hundred plantation owners, Charleston merchants, and seaport shippers.

From one month after the Revolutionary War battle at Bunker Hill in 1775 until the British surrender at Yorktown, Virginia, in 1781, South Carolina became a battleground: there were more battles fought here than in any other state, and more Patriot casualties. The Revolution in this part of the country was the real civil war: father against son, neighbor against neighbor. Most Lowcountry planters took up the rebel cause; the small farmers of the Upcountry, unaffected by British import and export taxes, remained Loyalists. During a major battle—the Tory attack on the Patriot fort at Ninety Six—not a British officer was on the field. Upcountry colonists finally joined forces with Lowcountry rebels against Cornwallis's forces at the Battle of Kings Mountain, in what many historians consider one of the main turning points of the Revolution.

South Carolinia's four young delegates disputed Jefferson's first draft of the Declaration of Independence, and the paragraph condemning slavery was eventually omitted. The state ratified the Constitution on May 23, 1788. Most Upcountry Carolinians were opposed to it; citified Charleston, dependent on commerce, delivered the state to the Federalists.

✦ THAT GEORGE-COME-LATELY

Georgia's history both parallels and veers from its Carolina neighbor. A quarter of a century after Spanish explorer Hernando de Soto entered what is now Georgia in 1540, following landfall in Florida, another Spaniard, Pedro Menéndez de Avilés, was ordered to the New World to drive out a French colony in Florida. Menéndez successfully routed the French, and built a fort on St. Catherines Island, south of present-day Savannah.

In 1629 Charles I of England carved a large land grant out of much of the region, but it was nearly a century later before an English fort was built on the Altamaha River. Soon after, in 1732, King George II issued a land grant to a corporation called the Trustees for Establishing the Colony of Georgia in America. General James Oglethorpe volunteered to lead a party of 120 outcasts and gentlemen across the ocean on a ship called the Anne. Ogelthorpe was a fair, pragmatic leader, whose approach was common sense: he supposedly kept his men in check by suggesting they share a pint of rum when they felt testy. On February 12, 1733, Oglethorpe, by then governor of the new Colony, led his followers to establish the first permanent settlement in Georgia, at the mouth of the Savannah River. They were aided greatly by cooperative Native Americans, led by the charismatic chief, Tomochichi. Nine years later, England and Spain went to war in part over the boundary between Georgia and Florida. When Oglethorpe defeated a Spanish invasion force at Bloody Marsh on St. Simons Island in 1742, Spanish claims to Georgia were extinguished, and the Colony was never again seriously challenged.

When the Revolutionary War began, Georgia's population was about 50,000, one-third of them slaves working on rice and indigo plantations along the seaboard. Georgia was left alone during the first war years, but six months after the Articles of Confederation were approved in July 1778, British troops captured Savannah, and by the end of the next year they had taken control of every major town. The fighting in Georgia, as in the nearby Carolinas, involved guerrilla bands as well as regular troops. The battles may have been small in scale, and fewer than in South Carolina, but they were bitterly contested. In 1779 American troops defeated a British force at Kettle Creek near the town of Washington in northeast Georgia; a short time later they were themselves bested at Brier Creek. The city of Augusta changed hands several times until Andrew Pickens and Light-Horse Harry Lee drove the British out in 1781. The British left Georgia forever when they lost Savannah to American forces in 1782. On January 2, 1788, five years after the Revolutionary War ended, Georgia joined the new United States. The last of the 13 Colonies to be founded, Georgia was the fourth state—and the first Southern state—to ratify the Constitution. Then, in 1793, Eli Whitney, while visiting the plantation of the late General Nathanael Greene near Savannah, designed the cotton gin. Cotton soon became the number-one cash crop in Georgia, and in much of the Southeast. By the mid-1820s, Georgia's export figures for the crop led the world.

In the end, the traveler in search of Colonial America will find much to enjoy and explore in Georgia and South Carolina—after all, pride in the past is a way of life here. And luckily, when it comes to those two jewels, Georgia's Savannah and South Carolina's Charleston, residents have long resisted the modern passion for tearing down the old, and have preserved or restored a multitude of sites and buildings that will take the visitor back in time.

A REGIONAL GAZETEER
▼▼

✦ LOWCOUNTRY COAST AND COLONIAL ISLES

The Atlantic coast of both South Carolina and Georgia is a mix of famed, historic cities and languid islands, southern pines and spiky palmettos. Tabby forts protected the coast against Spanish invasion, British troops in Revolutionary War skirmishes, and the occasional plundering pirate. The great and graceful cities of Charleston and Savannah prospered from rice and cotton. South Carolina Lowcountry is rice country, and the taste for the small grain is, ahem, ingrained in South Carolinians—over 300 historical recipes feature it: red rice, Hoppin' John, rice soups, rice casseroles, rice sausages, rice pâtés, rice pilaus (usually pronounced "puhr-LO" and consisting of rice cooked in a broth until the liquid is absorbed and the rice dry), and rice breads and cakes. Local doctor, Henry Woodward, is said to have obtained the first rice seeds around 1685 when a ship sailing from Madagascar was stranded in Charleston's port—thanks to the knowledge of West Africans slaves, whose native rice lands resembled the Lowcountry, rice soon became a major crop. Gullah culture adds a dash of heat to these regions, especially around Beaufort, and the past meets the present here, enwrapped in the fragrance of magnolias. *Towns listed: Beaufort, Charleston, Sullivan's Island.*

✦ UPCOUNTRY SOUTH CAROLINA

This rolling, rural Carolina countryside in the foothills of the Blue Ridge Mountains reflects an earlier time, and still offers the cool, fresh air that has lured Lowcountry settlers here since the 18th century. Small towns, some filled with grand homes, maintain a country feel. Interspersed are some of the most important Revolutionary War battle sites in the country. *Towns listed: Camden, Edgefield, Spartanburg.*

✦ GEORGIA HISTORIC HEARTLAND

Spreading from middle to southern Georgia, this sprawling semi-rural region offers classic Old South charm—Colonial mansions entwined with wisteria, stately small-town squares, antiques shops, gardens of dogwoods and azaleas, steepled churches, shady verandahs, a great university, legendary golf. Sherman burned his way through much of this area during the Civil War, but much remains, retaining an aura of past centuries. *Towns listed: Augusta, Washington.*

✦ GEORGIA COLONIAL COAST AND GOLDEN ISLES

From Savannah, that great Southern city of squares and Colonial buildings, to the balmy islands that follow the Atlantic coast to the southeast, this beachy, watery setting is also one of the great repositories of American history. Tabby forts built to protect against Spaniards still stand. James Ogelthorpe, plantations, slavery, lighthouses, are only a part of their past. *Towns listed: Darien, Savannah, Tybee Island.*

Upcountry Battlefields of the Southern Campaign

A DRIVING TOUR FROM WASHINGTON TO AUGUSTA

▼▼▼

Distance: 457 mi (approx.)   **Time:** 3–4 days (2–3 nights)
Breaks: Stay in Washington, Cheraw, or Camden, and 1 or 2 nights in Augusta

This circle of Revolutionary War sites starts and ends in Georgia, and ranges from Washington to Augusta (or vice versa). In between you'll visit major battlefields of a regional campaign, which played a major role in the America's victory over the British. The terrain is the green and rolling foothills of the Blue Ridge, and the towns in the area, which focus today on small businesses and agriculture, are often worth a stop for some historic feature, or just a good meal.

Start in **Washington,** with its exceptional courthouse square. Go 1½ mi north and ½ mi west to War Hill, site of the Battle of Kettle Creek. The region was almost completely under British control during the Revolution, but here on February 14, 1779, Col. John Dooly, Col. Elijah Clark, and Col. Andrew Pickens led a company that overcame a far larger group of Tories, turning back the British troops once and for all, in probably the most overwhelming Patriot win for any Georgia or South Carolina battle.

Heading from Washington toward the town of Ninety Six in South Carolina, stay straight on U.S. 378 and go onto U.S. 221-S. This becomes U.S. 178 BYP/U.S. 221, BYP/U.S. 25 BYP. Take the SC-34 ramp, and turn left onto SC-34. **Ninety Six Historical Site** is 9 mi east of Greenwood and 2 mi south of Ninety Six, on S.C. 248. The area was an important backcountry trading village, held by the British. The longest Patriot siege of the war was here, led by American General Nathanael Greene, and this was also the site of the first Southern land battle in the south. You can picnic and camp among earthwork embankments, the remains of two villages, a Colonial plantation and a prehistoric site. Plan to spend a few hours to see all elements.

To get to Cowpens National Battlefield, near **Spartanburg,** the next major Revolutionary War site, go east on S.C. 34/N Main Street in Ninety Six, toward S.C. 248/Cambridge St. Turn left onto S.C. 246/Cambridge St. N. Continue, and turn right onto U.S. 221N/Laurens Hwy/S.C. 72 E and merge onto I-26W. Then merge onto I–85 N via Exit 188, toward Charlotte. Take U.S. 221 Exit 78 toward Chesnee and follow signs to park. The battlefield commemorates the decisive victory at the "Cow Pens" on January 17, 1781, when Daniel Morgan led his tough Continental cavalry and militia to defeat Banastre Tarleton's British regulars. It was the second successive defeat for the Brits under General Charles Cornwallis, and nine months later he surrendered to George Washington at Yorktown, Virginia.

From the town of Mayo, near the battlefield, where you could take a pleasant break, you'll be heading to the site of the Continentals' previous decisive victory at **Kings Mountain.** Go southwest on U.S. 221 toward Gossett Road, and merge onto I–85. Take the N.C. 161 S Exit 8. Take a slight right to York Road and continue toward N.C. 161. Turn left onto S.C. 55. At U.S. 321 turn right. The site is signposted from here. The battle at Kings Mountain on October 7, 1780 was a pivotal one between American Patriots over American Loyalists. The win halted the British advance into nearby North Carolina and forced General Cornwallis to retreat into South Carolina; this gave General Nathanael Greene the chance to reorganize the American troops for later wins. Adjacent to the Military Park is Kings Mountain State Park— picnic, camp, swim, and play miniature golf here. Programs are offered at a reconstructed late 18th-century farm.

Next, you'll head to the Cheraw/Camden area of important battlefields. To get to Cheraw, take S.C. 55, then turn left onto S.C. 557, which becomes S.C. 49 in about 10 mi. Merge onto I– 485 E toward I–77/Columbia. Merge onto U.S. 74 via Exit 518 toward Monroe. Then turn right onto U.S. 52. Stop for a break in Cheraw, to check out where the British troops under Cornwallis set up a strategic line of defense. Nathanael Greene set up camp here to wait out the winter of 1780.

To drive to **Camden,** go southwest on U.S. 52/Market St/U.S.1. Turn onto U,S, 52/U.S. 1 and follow signs to Camden. This town was the main interior British outpost, and 2,500 British troops were stationed here during the Revolution. Cornwallis headquartered here for a year and 14 battles were fought in the area before the Brits evacuated and burned the town. Just south of Camden, on Route 521 is the Historic Camden Revolutionary War Site. Redoubts, powder magazines, reconstructions, and fortifications are on these 90 acres, crisscrossed with walking trails. The most important battles occurred north of town, where the sites can be visited, but are undeveloped. Cornwallis left for Virginia in 1781, but a force of 800 remained in Camden. The British troops could claim technical victories against the Southern commander of American forces, Nathanael Greene, but eventually they were forced to abandon Camden. Greene later marched from here to Ninety Six, and an important Patriot victory.

Heading back to **Augusta,** take 120-W, then GA 28/Washington Rd, Exit 19, toward Augusta. On December 28, 1778, Augusta became the state capital, but its tenure was brief, and the town fell to the British in June 1780 and remained in British occupancy for a spell. Between Augusta and Savannah, British forces converged under the command of Augustine Provost at the Battle of Brier Creek. Camping at the confluence of Brier Creek and the Savannah River, the Patriots were outnumbered and overpowered, but the men defended the camp. Four-hundred Americans, but only five British, died—this terrible defeat would be later remembered as a rallying point for victories to come.

Ringing the Southern Belles

A DRIVING TOUR FROM CHARLESTON THROUGH BEAUFORT TO SAVANNAH

▼▼

Distance: 115 mi (approx.)   **Time:** 4–5 days (3–4 nights)
Breaks: You could spend 2 nights in Charleston, 1 night in Beaufort, 2 nights in Savannah

You can start and end this drive in either Charleston or Savannah, both good transportation hubs, On this trip, you'll head south from Charleston through Beaufort to Savannah, a terrain of Southern pine woods and discount outlets, with the fingers of the Atlantic jutting into the landscape for a bit of drama. But these three historic hubs are the grace notes of this gentle Lowcountry. Each reflects, superbly, our earliest Americana.

Start in **Charleston.** Park your car and hire a horsedrawn carriage, or walk around to get a feel for the 17th- and 18th-century atmosphere. Best to look in the guidebook and create your own itinerary, based on interests. Your two or three days in this gracious city could start at The Battery and include visits to such famed 18th-century sites as the Aiken-Rhett House, the College of Charleston, and the Dock Street Theatre. You could also visit one of the hundreds of houses of worship, including St. Michael's church, with its landmark steeple, and Kahal Kadosh Beth Elohim. the birthplace of American Reform Judaism.

To head toward Beaufort, follow U.S. 17 south for approximately 52 mi, then turn left onto U.S. 21 into Beaufort. Continue 14 mi on U.S. 21, then go into BR/Boundary St. Continue about 2 mi into **Beaufort.** Visit Fort Lyttleton, built before the Revolution. Historic points of interest in this leafy town include the Beaufort Museum, the John Mark Verdier House on Bay Street, and the Tabernacle Baptist Church, built in 1724 and later used as a hospital. Isn't strolling past scores of Federal-style homes a perfect way to spend an afternoon?

To drive to **Savannah,** our third Southern Belle, take U.S. 21-BR, which becomes U.S. 21/ Boundary St. After a mile, turn left onto SC 170-S/Robert Smalls Parkway. Continue for about 26 mi, then turn right onto SC 170. Turn left onto U.S. 17-S. Continue for about 8 mi, then go onto U.S. 17 Alt.S. Take the Ogelthorpe Ave. exit toward GA-25-CO-/Savannah. In about half a mile, go onto GA-25-Conn W/W Oglethorpe Ave. As with Charleston, Savannah is crammed with exceptional Colonial and Federal buildings and historic sites. These include the Isiah Davenport House, Telfair Mansion and Art Museum, and Christ Church. Spend time savoring the Savannah scene out of the car.

South Carolina

BEAUFORT

▼▼

A shy coastal princess, sitting pretty between dowager queens Charleston and Savannah, Beaufort (pronounce it "*b'yew*-furt", darlin') is dressed with lavish 18th- and 19th-century homes and churches lining narrow roads, evoking regal days past as a reigning cotton star. But her patient charm has worked: in 2001 the National Trust for Historic Preservation named Beaufort one of 12 "Distinctive Destinations" in the country. This region goes way, way back— discovered by the Spanish in 1520; the site of the continent's first fort, in 1525; and the first attempted settlement, in 1562. Ruins of other forts date from the mid-16th century and the oldest house dates to 1717; horse-drawn carriages add to the Early American atmosphere, and the Gullah culture (*see* "Gullah of the Sea Islands" box) on nearby islands is showcased. Although many private houses in Old Point, the historic district, are not usually open to visitors, check out the annual Fall House Tour in mid-October and the Spring Tour of Homes and Gardens in April or May. Hollywood has long appreciated Beaufort: *Forrest Gump, The Prince of Tides,* and *The Big Chill* are among the films shot here. *Contact Greater Beaufort Chamber of Commerce | Box 910, 106 Carteret St., Beaufort, SC 29901 | 843/524-3163*

Beaufort Arsenal/Museum. Two galleries here show off everything from stone tools and swords to old bathtubs. Prehistoric relics, native pottery, and Revolutionary and Civil War exhibits are displayed in this brick and tabby arsenal, built in 1798. | 713 Craven St. | 843/525-7077 | www.beaufortcity.sc.com | $2 | Mon.–Tues., Thurs.–Sat. 10–5.

John Mark Verdier House Museum. Note the entrance hallway arch and other architectural details in this exceptionally stylish Federal mansion, built in 1805 by a rich planter and merchant. The Marquis de Lafayette visited here in 1825, and during the Civil War it was headquarters for Union forces. In a more connected mode, this historic home had the first telephone exchange in Beaufort. | 801 Bay St. | 843/524-6335 | www.historic beaufort.org | $4 | Mon.–Sat. 11–4.

Penn Center. Quaker missionaries from the North founded this center for freed slaves in 1862; it is now one of the most important African-American historical sites and preserves the language, culture, and history of the Sea Island Gullah community. The campus 6 mi east of town has 19 buildings, which you can visit on a self-guided tour. | 16 Penn Circle W, St. Helena Island | 843/838–2432 | Free; museum $4 | Grounds, open daily; museum, Mon.–Sat. 11–4.

Sheldon Church Ruins. Massive brick pillars and an imposing outer shell tell the (nearly) Phoenix-like history of Prince William Parish Church, built in 1745–55. During the Revolution, Patriots kept gunpowder here, and sparks would soon fly. Led by a flamboyant local Tory, the British burned the church in 1779. It was rebuilt but burned again by Sherman in 1865. Once a year (on the second Sunday after Easter), services are held at these haunting ruins—missing gables, roof, pediment, and interior—a powerful symbol of war. | Old Sheldon Church Rd. | Free.

✦ SIGHTSEEING TOURS

You can take mule-drawn carriage rides of the historic district with **Carriage Tours of Beaufort.** | 1002 Bay St. | 843/521–1651 | $15 | Mon.–Sat. 10–4, Sun. noon–4. The **Greater Beaufort Chamber of Commerce** offers self-guided walking or driving tours of Beaufort. | 106 Carteret St. | 843/524–3163 | Free | Daily 9–5:30. **Gullah 'n' Geechie Mahn Tours** offer tours of Beaufort and nearby islands, such as St. Helena, that focus on the traditions of African-American culture. | 847 Sea Island Pkwy. | 843/838–7516 | $17 | Tours 9:45 and 1:45.

✦ ON THE CALENDAR: Oct.–Nov. **Beaufort Fall Festival of Homes and Gardens.** Private homes and gardens open up to the public; you can also tour Colonial and Federal sites, and attend lectures and special events. | 208 Scott St. | 843/524–6334.

Nov. **Heritage Days Festival.** This three-day festival at the Penn Center celebrates Gullah culture with storytelling, crafts, tours, and food. | 16 Penn Circle W, St. Helena | 843/838–8563.

HISTORIC LODGING

Cuthbert House Inn. Original Federal fireplaces, crown and rope molding, 18th- and 19th-century antiques, mahogany furniture, and pine floors distinguish this pillared 1790 home overlooking the bay. Complimentary breakfast. | 1203 Bay St. | 800/327–9275 | fax 843/521–1314 | www.cuthberthouseinn.com | 7 rooms | $115–$195 | AE, D, MC, V.

CAMDEN

▼▼▼

Camden is South Carolina's oldest inland town, dating from 1732. British general Lord Cornwallis established a garrison here during the Revolutionary War and burned most of Camden before evacuating it. But during the Civil War, General Sherman spared it, and many of the town's antebellum homes still stand. Horse training and breeding are now major industries, and some of the roads in the fanciest and oldest neighborhoods remain unpaved, as they were some 200 years ago. Many famed battlegrounds are within a short drive—including, sadly, some will note, the worst defeat of the American forces during the war, the tragic Battle of Camden, where more than 1,000 American troops died in a single encounter. Today, the town has a nice array of antiques stores along Broad Street. *Contact Kershaw County Chamber of Commerce | Box 605, 724 S. Broad St., Camden, SC 29020 | 803/432–2525.*

Buford Massacre. Granite monuments mark where more than 100 American soldiers are buried. These retreating Virginia Continentals, defending Charleston, fell on this battleground, May 29, 1780—victims of Lt. Col. Banastre Tarleton's superior tactical skills. Tarleton (*see* Spartanburg–Cowpens, *below*) was the infamous figure, known as "Bloody Tarleton," because of his three missing fingers, cut off by Patriot Col. William Washington. The British officer looted area farmers and drove many to fight for the Revolutionaries. "Tarleton's Quarter" became a rallying cry for Patriot vengeance in later battles. His infamy as a "butcher" was such that while it was customary for American generals to share dinner with their defeated British peers at Terms of Surrender, no American would ever share his table with "Bloody." | North of Camden, east of Lancaster at S.C. 9 and S.C. 22 | Free.

DeKalb Monument. At the 1822 Bethesda Presbyterian Church, close your eyes and see if you can guess the names of the 24 states in existence at the time of the Buford Massacre (1780), which are featured on this monument in honor of Revolutionary hero Baron Johann de Kalb, buried here. Who designed this state-by-state tribute? The ubiquitous Robert Mills. | 502 DeKalb St. | 803/432–2525.

Camden Archives and Museum. Camden's circa 1825 town clock and a rare early American medical chest are among folksy exhibits of local and regional history here. You can search for your ancestry in the extensive materials on genealogical research. | 1314 Broad St. | 803/425–2525 | Free | Weekdays 8–5, 1st Sun. of month 1–5.

Hanging Rock. No one was hanged here; the huge boulder near the Revolutionary battle-field is among several impressive rock formations. The Prince of Wales American Regiment—aligned with British troops and a large Loyalist force—were all commanded by Maj. John Carden. Outnumbered two to one and short on ammo, a scrappy band of Patriots led by General Tom Sumter trounced them, on August 6, 1780. | North of Camden, and 2 mi south of Heath Springs, across Hanging Rock Creek.

Historic Boykin. Strange name, but the working Boykin Grist Mill, Swift Creek Baptist Church (circa 1827), and Boykin Company Store are among the structures set 10 mi north of Camden at this small, scenic farm community. Also here you will find Broom Place, where you can see brooms being made on 100-year-old equipment and set—wistfully perhaps—in a restored 1760 slave cabin. | Rte. 261, Boykin | 803/425–0933 | Free | Broom Place: week-days 10–5, Sat. 10:30–2.

Historic Camden Revolutionary War Park. More than 1,000 American soldiers were killed, and another 1,000 taken prisoner, at the Battle of Camden, one of the saddest landmarks of the Southern Campaign. With its quick access to conquered Charleston, British General Cornwallis established a post here as the main British supply center. One result: 14—count 'em—Revolutionary War battles were fought in this area, including the Camden disaster, waged on August 16, 1780. American forces were that day routed simply because 50 men of the Virginia and North Carolina militia panicked and broke rank once they were counter-attacked by British bayonets; The Delaware and Maryland regiments held under the noble German general Baron Johann de Kalb (to die of wounds suffered in the battle), but the damage was done and most American forces, under the ungallant leadership of General Horatio Gates, took to the hills. A marker on Flat Rock Road indicates the site of the battle, while a stone monument marks the spot de Kalb fell. The village, restored with emphasis on the British occupation, comprises some 100 acres and includes the furnished 1785 John Craven House, two restored log cabins with exhibitions, some reconstructions of fortifi-cations, and the grandly reconstructed and refurbished Joseph Kershaw Mansion, headquarters for Lord Cornwallis himself. Beyond its two-story exterior—grandly adorned with pillars and balconies—lie some refurnished rooms with period artifacts. Inside the log cabins are some lovely miniature dioramas; here even the soldiers' buttons are perfectly detailed. There is a model of the original town of 80 buildings, adapted from General Nathanael Greene's maps. Trails cover much of the 60 wooded acres, and helpful guides will show you every-thing when you arrive and treat you to something the British never got in Camden at the time—true Southern hospitality. | 222 S. Broad St. | 803/432–9841 | www.historic-camden. net | $5 | Tues.–Sat. 10–5, Sun. 1–5.

Mills Court House and Kershaw County Visitors Center. The Kershaw County Chamber of Commerce is in this 1826 building designed by Robert Mills. You can pick up maps and rent cassette tapes for self-guided walking tours. Inquire here about Old South Carriage Co. tours of the historic district that are conducted in horse-drawn carriages. | 603 Broad St. | 803/432–2525 or 800/968–4037 | www.camden-sc.org | Free | Daily 9–5.

✦ ON THE CALENDAR: Nov. **Revolutionary War Field Days.** Battle skirmishes, living-history demonstrations, military courts and competitions, a period fashion show, frontier weddings, and traditional craftsmen are fascinating re-creations of the era during our War for Independence. | 803/432–9841.

HISTORIC LODGING

Camden B&B. Working fireplaces and Belgian stained-glass windows decorate this original Federal-style home, surrounded by acres of pine forest. Complimentary breakfast. No smoking. | 127 Union St. | 803/432–2366 | fax 803/432–9767 | www.camdenscbandb.com | 1–3 bedroom suite; 2 cottages | $85–$109 | AE, D, MC, V.

CHARLESTON
▼▼

Charleston is comely and cosmopolitan, remarkably unchanged from its early 18th-century heyday, when it gloried in being named after rakish British King Charles II. It started life as "Charles Town" during the rule of Lord Proprietors (1670–1720), became "Charlestown" through the Revolution, and was incorporated as "Charleston" in 1783. Huguenots, Irish, and Barbadians were among the many settlers influencing the new community, laid out presciently, in "regular streets, for be the buildings never so mean and thin at first, yet as the town increase in riches and people, the void places will be filled up and the buildings will grow more beautiful."

Snuggled at the confluence of the Ashley and Coopers rivers on the Atlantic coast, Charleston became a leading port by the early 1700s and was a center of protest against the British Stamp Tax. Here was the only harbor where the East India Company's tea shipment landed, and the Patriots would promptly then sell the tea for money to fight the British. The first decisive battle of the Revolution was in Charleston Harbor, at the Battle of Fort Sullivan in 1776. Four years later the British besieged the city until General Benjamin Lincoln surrendered, and Charleston remained under British rule till December, 1782, 15 months after the victory at Yorktown.

Charleston had been the richest city in the richest Colony, the aristocrat's place to be and be seen—temperate in climate, but not in lifestyle. It was the fourth largest city in 1775 (12,000 residents), after Philadelphia, New York, and Boston. While much of its magnificence was due to the cash commodities of rice, indigo, and shipping, misery—or, rather, Charleston's huge market for slave trading—also played its part in bringing continued wealth to plantation owners and nouveau riche merchants, lolling on the breezy piazzas of their true Colonial McMansions with time to spare. One Puritan's take in 1773: "Cards, dice, the bottle and horses engross prodigious portions of time and attention: the gentlemen (planters and merchants) are mostly men of the turf and gamesters." By 1820 there were more slaves than whites, and the high life continued. But all parties end. Antebellum years became stagnant. Reconstruction after the Civil War was difficult—and the lucky result was that precious early Americana was left untouched. An early protest to the widening of Charleston streets resulted in model preservation laws: today you can enjoy approximately 73 pre-Revolutionary homes, 136 late 18th century buildings, and more than 600 structures built before 1840, including more than 180 houses of worship (vice-tolerant locals ironically refer to Charleston as "The Holy City"). Museums are filled with Colonial and Federal arts and artifacts, forts are sites for fun and festivals, and each blooming spring the city celebrates its heritage with candlelight tours. Fires, earthquakes, fearsome pirates, hurricanes, political scoundrels, smallpox and yellow fever epidemics, economic downturns, and major wars have barely weathered Charleston's original grace. *Contact Charleston Area Convention and Visitors Bureau | Box 975, 81 Mary St., Charleston, SC 29402 | 843/853–8000 | fax 843/853–0444 | www.charlestoncvb.com.*

Aiken-Rhett House. From privies to cattle sheds, the kitchen, slave quarters, and work yard (one of the most complete examples of African-American life in the United States) exist much as they were when last occupied. The palatial main house—built in 1817, and one of Charleston's most lavish—was basically remodeled in 1833, but the original wallpaper, paint, and some furnishings still remain in some rooms to conjure up the earlier era. Governor Aiken—a lover of all things foreign and beautiful—brought many of the chandeliers, sculptures, and paintings in Europe. | 48 Elizabeth St. | 843/723–1159 | www.historiccharleston. org | $7 | Mon.–Sat. 10–5, Sun. 2–5.

Battery and White Point Gardens. Stede Bonnet was one of the pirates who was hanged at these former gallows, now a harborfront park at the southernmost point of the peninsula. From here you can see Fort Sumter. The artillery that remains protected the area from maritime invasions. The old seawall was decimated by the hurricanes of 1752 and 1804, when the city rebuilt using stone, which looked better too. The first time the Townshend Revenue Act of 1767 authorized tax on coastal shipping right here, citizen Henry Laurens twisted the nose of the Chief Customs Agent. Assault on Battery? | Battery St. | 843/853–8000 | Free | Daily.

Boone Hall Plantation. A "slave street" is here, made up of nine brick cabins (circa 1743)— it's the last of its kind in the United States. Set just across the Cooper River from the city, the original smokehouse and cotton gin house remain also, while the present 1935 mansion has a main floor open for tours. A famed ½-mi avenue of moss-draped oaks leads up to this former cotton plantation 13 mi east of Charleston on 738 acres. The property, with gardens of antique roses, was established in 1681 by Major John Boone, one of South Carolina's original settlers. He remains, too—buried by an oak he planted in 1743. | 1235 Long Point Rd., Mount Pleasant | 843/884–4371 | $12.50 | Apr.–Labor Day, Mon.–Sat. 8:30–6:30, Sun. 1–5; Labor Day–Mar., Mon.–Sat. 9–5, Sun. 1–4.

Charles Towne Landing Historic Site. Set a few miles northwest of downtown Charlestown over the Ashley River Bridge along Route 171 (accessed from U.S. 61) and commemorating the site of the original 1670 Charleston settlement—the British's only fortified city in America—this park has a reconstructed village and fortifications, English park gardens with tram tours and bicycle trails, a replica 17th-century trading ketch—*The Adventure*—and an animal forest replete with native species of alligators, bison, pumas, and bears. The park recently began a multimillion dollar renovation with an archaeological dig and visitors center. | 1500 Old Town Rd. (Rte. 171) | 843/852–4200 | www.southcarolinaparks.com | $5 | Daily 8:30–6.

Charleston Visitor Center. *Forever Charleston,* an entertaining 20-minute film, runs at this center at this former train depot. You'll find a useful materials about the city, and tickets for shuttle services to downtown. Parking is 65¢ per hour (with the first hour free if you purchase a shuttle pass). | 375 Meeting St. | 843/853–8000 | www.charlestoncvb.com | Film $2.50 | Mar.– Oct., daily 8:30–5:30; Nov.–Feb., daily 8:30–5; film screening daily 9–5 on the ½ hr.

City Hall Art Gallery. John Trumbull's famous 1791 painting of George Washington is among the many portraits of leaders that hang in the historic Council Chamber here. Built circa 1801, City Hall is part of the Four Corners of Law, dubbed so by "Ripley's Believe it or Not" newspaper column. At the intersection of Meeting and Broad streets are represented the laws of: nation (Federal Court, in the present post office building); state (Courthouse); city (City Hall), and church (St. Michael's). The Charleston County courthouse was designed in 1792 by architect James Hoban, who went on to base his design of "The President's House" in Washington,

D.C. (a.k.a. the White House) on this imposing structure. This area was originally designed as the grand square of Charleston. | 80 Broad St. | 843/724–3799 | Free | Weekdays 9–5.

College of Charleston. The founders of the college include three signers of the Declaration of Independence, and three fathers of the United States Constitution. Set on land dedicated to educational purposes in 1724, this was the first municipal college in America, and it's the 13th-oldest college in the country, founded in 1770. The 1828 Randolph House, the graceful main building designed by Philadelphia architect William Strickland, was paid for voluntarily by Charleston residents. The entrance to the campus green, called "The Cistern," was once the janitor's house. Nineteenth-century records show "the presence of the janitor's cow . . . interfered with the gymnastic exercises and was . . . a nuisance." | 66 George St. | 843/953–5507 | www.cofc.edu | Free | Daily dawn–dusk; tours Sept.–Dec. and Feb.–May, weekdays 10 and 2.

Dock Street Theatre. Built on the site of one of the nation's first playhouses—opened in 1736, and burned down in 1740—the building combines the reconstructed early Georgian playhouse and the preserved Old Planter's Hotel (circa 1809), in use until the mid-19th century. The theater offers fascinating backstage views. Charleston built several theatres in the vicinity and was considered the drama center of the Colonies. The first play here was *The Recruiting Officer,* offering a popular "breeches part," where an 18th-century actress could show off her body in a tight British uniform. | 135 Church St. | 843/965–4032 | Weekdays 9–5; call for show times.

Drayton Hall. Many consider this immense, circa-1742 plantation mansion, set 13 mi north of Charleston, as one of the nation's finest examples of Georgian Palladian architecture. Built as a homage to the Whig aristocracy of England, aglow with redbrick and white sash, magnificently facaded with a Palladian double-story balcony and staircase, it remains the oldest plantation house open to the public—neither restored nor furnished—and the only one on the Ashley to survive the Civil War. Built by John Drayton, of His Majesty's Council, it remains little changed, with original plaster moldings and paint and opulent hand-carved woodwork. In a sublimely symmetrical fashion, all the rooms of the house feed off the Grand Hall. As there are no furnishings to be seen here (oddly enough: you would think that Charleston's antiques overflow might have enriched the salons here), the emphasis in the wonderful guided tours is on the people who once inhabited and built this fabled house. "Connections: Africans, Americans, and Europeans," for instance, details the roles that African-Americans—before and after slavery—played here, as among their number were the craftsmen who created many of the house's most gorgeous details. Two scenic trails—the marsh walk and the river walk—allow you to explore some beauteous stretches of the Lowcountry (you're permitted to partake of a picnic under ancient live oak trees). Take U. S. 61, the Ashley River Road, to get to Drayton. | 3380 Ashley River Rd. | 843/766–0188 | www.draytonhall.org | $8; $10 Mar.–Apr. and Sept.–Oct. | Mar.–Oct., daily 10–4; Nov.–Feb., daily 10–3.

Heyward–Washington House. The George himself slept here in 1791. Thomas Heyward, rice king, patriot leader (he was caught by the British, then exiled to Florida, then exchanged), and signer of the Declaration of Independence, lived in this house, built in 1772, and it's now a National Historic Landmark. The salons here are a treasure trove of mid-18th century Charleston furniture, notably the Withdrawing Room's fabled Holmes Bookcase, a huge Chippendale version of today's home-entertainment center and considered among the top 10 pieces of furniture in America. Other priceless Charleston furnishings dot the other rooms, including dressing tables, inlaid bedsteads, and grand armchairs. Of particular note is the original kitchen building—the only such structure open to public view in Charleston; The formal garden is landscaped with period plants. The three-story brick house is near Cabbage Row, a neighborhood central to Charleston's African-American history, and the setting for the book *Porgy,* which inspired Gershwin's opera. | 87 Church St. | 843/722–0354 | www.charlestonmuseum.com | $8 | Mon.–Sat. 10–5, Sun. 1–5.

Colonial Charleston: For Leisure, Best of Show

If you were rich and white in Charleston's colonial heydey, you had plenty of opportunity for high life, according to *A Short History of Charleston* by Robert Rosen. "The people of Charleston live rapidly, not willingly letting go untasted any of the pleasures of life. Few of them, therefore, reach a great age." So noted first-hand observer Dr. Johann Schoepf, adding ". . . their manner of life, dress, equipages, furniture, everything, denotes a higher degree of taste and love of show, and less frugality than in the northern provinces."

In the mid-18th century, cockfighting was a half-time event between horse races, and pampered, high-style Charleston ladies dressed up to attend. Among the private men's clubs for gambling and imbibing were: the Amiable, the Meddlers Laughing Club, the Fryday-Night Club (for "elderly and substantial" men), the Beef-Steak Club, the Fort Jolly Volunteers, and the Brooms (who advertised "a special Sweep").

The "punch house," or tavern, was the main gathering place, and there were more than 100 of these watering holes in Colonial Charleston. Entertainment was one of the main draws, featuring the weird and wacky. One traveling show in 1738 advertised "Ourangnogang (or Man of the Woods), Tho this is . . . a female of that species."

Concerts were popular, and society balls, open to anyone for a high subscription price, were major social events, for music and dancing. Theaters were abundant, and in 1733–34, 188 performances, including eleven Shakespearean dramas made the year "the most brilliant dramatic season in Colonial America."

Joseph Manigault House. Considered by many to be the finest example of Federal-style architecture in the South, this 1803 home was built for a rich rice-planting family of Huguenot heritage. Having toured Europe as a gentleman architect, Gabriel Manigault returned to design this house for his brother Joseph as the city's first essay in Neoclassicism. The house glows in red brick and is adorned with a two-story piazza (the better to catch the breezes: "One does not boast in Charleston of having the most beautiful house, but the coolest," said the Duc de la Rochefoucauld, who visited in 1796). Inside, marvels await: a fantastic "flying" staircase in the central hall, a gigantic Venetian window, elegant plasterwork and mantels, notable Charleston-made furniture, tri-color Wedgewood accents, and a bevy of French, English and American antiques. Don't miss the garden, enhanced by a Gate Temple. | 350 Meeting St. | 843/723–2926 | www.charlestonmuseum.com | $8 | Mon.–Sat. 10–5, Sun. 1–5.

Magnolia Plantation and Gardens. Owner Thomas Drayton came from Barbados in 1671 and created this tropical garden, the country's oldest. The 300-year-old plantation has 50 acres of blooming azaleas and camellias (one of the largest collections in the country), theme gardens—including a Biblical one, and a Reconstruction plantation house. | 355 Ashley River Rd. | 843/571–1266 | www.magnoliaplantation.com | $10 | Apr.–Oct., daily 8–5:30; Nov.–Mar., daily 9–5.

Middleton Place Gardens, House, and Stableyards. These landscaped grounds are America's oldest, started in 1741; the camellias are the oldest in the New World, planted in 1783; and the Middleton Oak was planted about a thousand years ago. The lovely stretch of aged lawn ends in the Butterfly Lakes. Henry Middleton, President of the First Continental Congress, and his son, Arthur, a signer of the Declaration of Independence, were the proud owners, and Arthur is buried near the ruins of of the main house, which, alas, was torched like so many others during the Civil War. The restored wing of the original mansion showcases silver, furniture, paintings, and historic documents. Re-created stable yards of a self-sustaining, working plantation are the home to roaming peacocks and other not-as pretty creatures. You can dip candles, grind corn, and milk cows, and if all this makes you peckish, The Middleton Place restaurant serves Lowcountry specialties for lunch and dinner. The setting is so expansively beautiful that films clamor to shoot: most recently, Mel Gibson's *The Patriot*. The estate lies northwest of Charlestown, over the Ashley River Bridge, and accessed via U.S. 61. | 4300 Ashley River Rd. | 843/556–6020 | www.middletonplace.org | $15, house tours $8 | Daily 9–5; house tours Tues.–Sun. 10–4:30, Mon. 1:30–4:30.

Nathaniel Russell House. One of Charleston's grandest Federal houses, this abode is famed for its projecting oval bay rooms and spectacular "flying" staircase (it circles upward with no visible support). Russell, born in Bristol, Rhode Island, came to Charleston at age 27 and became one of of the city's leading merchants and Federalist fathers in post-Revolutionary times. Salons here are graced with elaborate plasterwork, Pembroke sideboards, Chippendale chairs, and glorious portraits by England's George Romney. Completed in 1808 by Russell and wife Sarah, the house is surrounded by extensive formal gardens. | 843/723–1623 | www. historiccharleston.org | $7 | Mon.–Sat. 10–5, Sun. 2–5.

Old City Market. A series of low sheds that once housed produce and fish markets, this area is often called the Slave Market, though Charlestonians dispute that slaves were ever sold here. Restaurants, shops, and gimcracks and geegaws for children now occupy the area, along with vegetable and fruit vendors and local Gullah "basket ladies" who weave and sell distinctive sweetgrass, pine-straw, and palmetto-leaf baskets—a craft passed down through generations from their West African ancestors. Note their lilting dialect. | Market St. (from Meeting to E. Bay Sts.) | 843/724–3796 | Free | Daily 8:30–5, open evenings Thurs.–Sat. 8:30–11.

Old Dorchester State Historic Site. This outstanding archaeological complex spans much of South Carolina history. Congregationalists from Massachusetts arrived at this bluff overlooking the Ashley River in 1696, and the town prospered for 100 years as a trade center. Today, the 1752 brick bell tower of St. George's Parish Church looms over the graveyard; the rest is fascinating ruins. The Patriots used Fort Dorchester, built during the French and Indian War and repaired in 1775, to store public records and ammunition; it is now the best-preserved example of a tabby-walled fort in the country. The British posted here until 1781, when they escaped as General Greene's army arrived. You can watch the ongoing excavations, and nearby picnic tables provide a nice lunch spot. | 300 State Park Rd. (northwest of Charleston on SC 642 and 4 mi south of Summerville) | 843/873–1740 | Free | Thurs.–Mon. 9–6.

Old Exchange and Provost Dungeon. Pirates and presidents are part of this enlightening attraction, built by the British as The Exchange and Customs House in 1771. Kids love the display of the Half-Moon Battery of Charles Town's seawall, built to protect the town from pirate plunder. During the Revolutionary War, men and women of all classes were imprisoned—and some died—in the "damp, dark cellar under the Exchange." The state ratified the Constitution here in 1788; it is only one of three buildings still remaining where that portentious signing happened. In the ballroom here in 1791, George Washington moved to the beat of the time at a magnificent "dancing assembly." On that trip, Washington noted the beauties of Charleston in his journal: ". . . went to a concert where there were 400 ladies, the number and appearance . . . exceeded anything I have ever seen . . ." | 122 E. Bay St. | 843/727–2165 | $4 | Thurs.–Mon. 9–6.

Old Powder Magazine. When Charles Town was still a walled city ringed with forts, this munitions storage building was an integral part of the defenses against marauders. The oldest public building in the Carolinas, completed in 1712, it was replaced in 1748 by a newer magazine, and used during the Revolution. For awhile it languished as a storage shed and livery stable, but The Colonial Dames restored it. Now a National Historic Landmark, it offers an audiovisual tour of costumes, armor, and other artifacts from 18th-century Charleston. | 79 Cumberland St. | 843/723–1623 | Free | Mon.–Sat. 10–5, Sun. 2–5.

St. Michael's Church. Washington worshipped at this oldest church building in Charleston on his southern tour in 1791, and members include two presidents of the Continental Congress (Henry Laurens and Henry Middleton), and a signer of the Declaration of Independence (Thomas Heyward, Jr.). The 186-ft steeple, Charleston's most famous, punctuates the cityscape. The church was modeled after London's St. Martin-in-the-Fields, took nine years to build, and dates to 1761; the clock tower to 1764. Inside, the original pulpit remains in front of old-fashioned pews. The cherished steeple bells traveled farther than most Charlestonians: removed to England as a Revolutionary War prize; returned to the new nation; sent back to England for recasting after being burned in the Civil War; and then back home again. | Meeting and Broad Sts. | 843/723–0603 | Free | Weekdays 9–4:45, services Sun. 8, 9, 10:30, and 6.

✦ SIGHTSEEING TOURS/TOUR COMPANIES

Charleston Tea Party Walking Tour. This informative tour takes participants into private gardens and ends with tea in the guide's garden. Tours start at 198 King Street. | 198 King St. | 843/577–5896; 843/722–1779 for 2 PM tour | $15 | Mon.–Sat. tours at 9:30 and 2. **Gray Line Bus Tours.** This company offers tours of the historic district, as well as seasonal trips to gardens and plantations. Tours either pick you up from your hotel, or meet you at the Visitors Center. | 374 Meeting St. | 843/722–4444 | $17–$22 | Daily 9:30–4; tours leave every 30 min. **Gullah Tours.** This bus tour, which leaves from Gallery Chuma, focuses on African-American influences on Charleston architecture, history, and culture, and includes Gullah stories. | 43 John St. | 843/763–7551 | www.gullahtours.com | $15 | Weekdays 11 and 1, Sat., 11, 1, and 3. **Old South Carriage Co.** You can do it the old-fashioned way on a one-hour narrated tour of Charleston's historic district by horse-drawn carriage. | 14 Anson St. | 843/577–0042 | www.oldsouthcarriagetours.com | $17 | Daily 9–dusk.

✦ ON THE CALENDAR: May–June **Spoleto Festival USA.** This huge, internationally acclaimed 14-day festival features theater, dance, musical performances, and art in downtown venues, many of them dating back to the Colonial era. | 14 George St. | 843/722–2764 | www.spoletousa.org.

Sept.–Oct. **Fall Candlelight Tour of Homes and Gardens.** Along candlelit sidewalks and into private homes and gardens, this self-guided walking tour is especially evocative in the mild South Carolina autumn. Pick up a map at the Preservation Society Book Shop. No high-heeled shoes allowed—for preservation purposes. | 147 King St. | 843/722–4630.

HISTORIC DINING AND LODGING

McCrady's. Exposed brick walls and antique mirrors complement this lovely Colonial building, today housing a local favorite. | 2 Unity Alley | 843/577–0025 | $17–$29 | AE, MC, V.

Barksdale House. George Barksdale, a wealthy Charleston planter and former member of the South Carolina House of Representatives, built this house in 1778 to serve as city residence when the family wasn't at Youghall Plantation. In 1817, George's nephew sold the town house, which passed through numerous hands until 1985, when the property was meticulously restored into one of Charleston's most elegant accommodations. Complimentary breakfast. No kids under 10. | 27 George St. | 843/577–4800 | fax 843/853–0482 | 14 rooms | $90–$95 | MC, V.

John Rutledge House. The Revolutionary-era main house was built by the eponymous Revolutionary, Judge, Governor, and one of the framers of the Constitution. Two carriage houses (each with four rooms) frame this luxurious 1763 inn. High ceilings make the guest rooms feel airy, while wood floors, antique furnishings, fireplaces, and four-poster beds make them appealing. Complimentary breakfast. | 116 Broad St. | 800/476–9741 | fax 843/720–2615 | www.charminginns.com | 19 rooms | $135–$325 | AE, D, DC, MC, V.

EDGEFIELD

▼▼

Set in the middle of more than a million peach trees, known as The Ridge, Edgefield is, well, peachy. Indeed, all of Edgefield is listed in the National Register of Historic Places—40 19th-century structures are laid out around the courthouse square alone. This little town also spawned a legion of South Carolina leaders: 10 governors and five lieutenant governors. Edgefield's thick clay deposits have been an inexpensive source of material for pottery. Potters developed followings shortly after 1800, supplying pioneers with jars, pitchers, pans, and bowls. The tradition lives on at Old Edgefield Pottery, a business created by the Edgefield County Historical Society. *Contact Edgefield County Chamber of Commerce | 416 Calhoun St., Box 23, Johnston, SC 29832 | 803/275–0010.*

National Wild Turkey Federation. Benjamin Franklin lobbied that the wild turkey be our national bird, rather than the bald eagle. That fizzled faster than lightening on his kite, but just the same, the Wild Turkey Federation, headquartered here, offers a series of exhibits and artifacts on wild turkeys, including efforts to protect them. Dioramas, turkey calls, and hunting-related artifacts include a 4,000 year-old-wingbone used by Native Americans to attract the gobblers. | 770 Augusta Rd. | 803/637–3106 | www.nwtf.org | Free | Weekdays 9–5.

Ninety Six National Historic Site. One of the best-preserved battle sites of the Revolution includes a restored frontier settlement, an intact 200-year old Star Fort, plus remains of other fortifications. The South's first land battle of the Revolution started here in November, 1775, when Patriots were besieged by Loyalists. The British made the site a major outpost. In the spring of 1781, the entire force of Continentals almost retrieved the post until 2,000 British troops, under Lord Rawdon, burst on the scene to relieve the Loyalists. The National Park Service maintains a museum and self-guiding trails. | North on U.S. 25, just south of the town of Ninety Six | 864/543–4068 | www.nps.gov/nisi | Free | Open daily.

Old Edgefield Pottery. A resident potter demonstrates the making of alkaline-glazed traditional pottery, an art form dating to the 1800s, used by African-Americans, who adapted ancient techniques. Old and new pottery is for sale, and you can see examples of the famed work of Dave the Potter, who also wrote poems. | 230 Simkins St. | 803/637–2060 | Tues.–Sat. 10–6.

HISTORIC LODGING

Cedar Grove Plantation. You can stay at one of the oldest plantations in the area (circa 1790) and savor carved moldings, fireplaces, gardens, and porches. The restored slave quarters are the more disturbing remnants of South Carolina's history. Complimentary breakfast. | 1365 Hwy. 25N | 803/637–3056 | 2 rooms | $75–$95 | AE, D, DC, MC, V.

SPARTANBURG (COWPENS)

▼▼

The famed Battle of Cowpens was fought and won near this city, which dates from 1785 (and is now part of the state's largest peach-producing area and an international business center). The Revolutionary battlefield of Cowpens remains the hallowed ground where the War of Independence's momentum changed—for good. *Contact Spartanburg Convention and Visitors Bureau | 298 Magnolia St., Spartanburg, SC 29306 | 864/594–5050 or 800/374–8326 | fax 864/594–5055 | www.spartanburgsc.org.*

Cowpens National Battlefield. Here, on January 17, 1781, Virginian Daniel Morgan led a rustic militia and Continental troops against the better-trained British, led by the notorious Lieutenant Colonel "Bloody" Tarleton. The Patriots won decisively—in less than an hour—and in no small way turned the tide of the entire War of Independence. The British had, in effect, forsaken the North (many regarding New England as a lost cause) and had refocused their attentions on the South, to them a region dense with Loyalists—Highland Scots, Anglicans in the ports, Indian traders, and the like. Indeed, as they trooped through the Carolinas and Georgia, Cornwallis's army amassed a number of important victories, notably the capture of Charleston. What they didn't count on was the extreme Patriot feeling rife in the Back-country, where the populace was often rent by Patriot-Loyalist conflicts, even among single families. Worn down by the guerrilla tactics of the Patriot rebels in backwoods encounters, the British troops decided to track down the main Continental Army, which had been cutting British supply lines and "spiriting up the people" as they went. Cornwallis unleashed Tarleton—a handsome, small, pit-bull of an officer who had become feared as a "butcher" because his troops would often continue to slaughter American troops even after they had surrendered (giving rise to the call "Tarleton's quarter," meaning "no quarter," a rallying cry which came back to haunt the Brits when they were routed by the Americans).

The morning of January 17 broke clear and cold. General Daniel Morgan had sounded a quick retreat once his scouts relayed the fact that Tarleton was growing close, but with his back against a flooded Broad River 6 mi away, Morgan decided to make for a 500-yard-long foraging field, known as the Cowpens, to settle in for battle. Having heard rumors of Over-mountain men on the way, Tarleton knew he had little time to spare and mercilessly had his troops march from 2 AM that morning to arrive and face Morgan's Continental Army—and their guerrilla-ish tactics. First, Morgan had sharpshooters (hidden behind trees) pick off 18 officers, then Andrew Pickens's militias sounded two volleys, retreating then to the line made up of John Eager Howard's Continentals. Tarleton set free his troops, led by his dreaded Dragoons, but they were then scattered by William Washington's Patriot Cavalry, which had arrived out of nowhere. They, in turn, were brought into check by Tartelon's 71st Highlanders, awail with their bagpipes.

But here is where a "mistake" created victory. Howard's troops misunderstood a command as a call to retreat, did so, then realized their miscall. By that time, the British had pursued them—only to be virtually surrounded by their foes. The Americans turned about face and sounded off a devastating volley, followed by a Cavalry charge. When the smoke had cleared, the British had suffered 110 dead, more than 200 wounded, and 500 captured (the Americans lost 12 men), Tarleton escaped with his tail between his legs (incidentally, he wound up back in England, acclaimed a hero, and lived to a ripe old 78), and the news spread like wildfire through the Colonies that David had, indeed, slain Goliath: the propaganda effect of this battle virtually turned the tide of the war, damping Loyalist recruitment and strengthening the Patriot resolve until the final British defeat at Yorktown, nine months later.

After visitors discover the museum area of the Visitor Center, they can view an 8-minute fiber-optic map program and a 22-minute laser disc presentation on the battle, then walk the 1-mi interpretive battlefield trail, or drive the 4-mi auto tour road. There is a small calendar of special events through the year, including a "Mighty Moo" festival head in mid-June, July 4th festivities (which mark the anniversary of Daniel Morgan's death), and occasional reenactments, including the Encampment of the 1st Maryland Continental Line. | 4001 Chesnee Hwy. | 864/461–2828 | www.nps.gov/cowp | Free; fee for slide show | Daily 9–5.

Walnut Grove Plantation. Family antiques furnish this plantation, built in 1765 on a land grant from King George III; the smokehouse, barn, well house, and 1777 kitchen remain intact. Patriots such as the Moores and their neighbors aided General Daniel Morgan and helped enlarge the ranks of his army just before the crucial Battle of Cowpens. Daughter Kate served as a scout for the battle. Children will enjoy the plantation's living history day camp, offered in mid-July—activities including playing Colonial games, candle dipping, and quill-pen writing. | 1200 Otts Shoals Rd. | 864/576–6546 | www.spartanarts. org/history/Walnut_Grove/WG_text.htm | $4.50 | Apr.–Oct., Mon.–Sat. 11–5, Sun. 2–5; Nov.–Mar., Sat. 11–5, Sun. 2–5.

HISTORIC LODGING

Juxa Plantation. A goldfish pond, waterfall, rose and azalea gardens, wooded paths, and a grape arbor dot the grounds of the 225-acre former plantation, complete with horse stable and pasture. Antiques fill the antebellum home, which was built in 1828 and still has its old kitchen and smokehouse. Picnic lunches and dinner are available. Complimentary breakfast. | 117 Wilson Rd., Union | 864/427–8688 | 3 rooms | $85 | AE, MC, V.

SULLIVAN'S ISLAND

The island was named for (Mr.) Florence Sullivan, the first person to land here, in 1670. The island was besieged by hurricanes more than military foes, but that didn't stop Charlestonians from building summer cottages and year-round homes here starting in the 19th century. Fort Moultrie, an important Revolutionary War site and part of the Fort Sumter National Monument Park, stands with its lighthouse at the southwest end of the island. Edgar Allan Poe was stationed at Fort Moultrie in 1827–28. *Contact Charleston Area Convention and Visitors Bureau | Box 975, 81 Mary St., Charleston, SC 29402 | 843/853–8000 or 800/868–8118 | fax 843/853–0444 | www.charlestoncvb.com.*

Fort Moultrie National Historic Site. Little Fort Sullivan, as it was originally known, was built of spongy native palmetto logs, and was, before it was completed, attacked by British warships in 1776. William Moultrie and his Patriots held off the assault, called The Battle of Sullivan's Island. The British ships ran aground, and troops were in a tizzy; a witness reported a British officer had "the hindpart of his breeches shot away, which laid his posteriors bare." When the British shot part of the state flag on the fort, a plucky Patriot quickly replaced it. The British lost more than 100 men and a ship; the Patriots, only 12 men, in the first decisive victory of the Revolution. In honor of the battle, the Palmetto tree was later added to the flag; South Carolina became known as The Palmetto State and the fort was renamed after Moultrie. When that great American general was later captured and offered the chance to head a British regiment, he retorted, "Good God! Is it possible that such an idea could arise in the breast of a man of honor?" Moultrie later led American troops into Charleston. The current fort was built in 1809 and is restored as an example of seacoast defense. | 1214 Middle St. | 843/883–3123 | www.nps.gov/forno | $5 | Daily 9–5.

YORK

Historic York, near the North Carolina border, grew up around the intersection of two stagecoach routes in the late 18th century. The town prospered with the cotton industry and the coming of the railroad in the late 1800s. Wealthy planters built stately town houses and public buildings, which remain as the heart of York's extensive historic district. Close by is a major Revolutionary battlefield, where Patriots routed the Tories. *Contact Greater York Chamber of Commerce | 23 E. Liberty St., York, SC 29745 | 803/684–2590 | www.yorkcountychamber.com.*

Historic District. Settled by Scotch-Irish, Scots, English, and Germans in the mid-1700s, the town of York was established as the county seat in 1785. It was named after York, Pennsylvania, where the settlers originated. Its historic district is one of the largest in the country, with more than 70 structures, dating from the 18th to the early 20th centuries. The Greater York Chamber of Commerce has maps for self-guided tours. | 803/684–2590 | Free | Daily.

Kings Mountain National Military and State Park. A major turning point in the Revolutionary War occurred on this craggy summit, October 7, 1780, when ragtag Patriot forces from the southern Appalachians surrounded and trounced the overconfident British Provincial Troops and Loyalist militia, commanded by British major Patrick Ferguson. The Patriot Visitor center exhibits dioramas, has an orientation film describing the action, and offers a paved self-guided trail through the battlefield. The 6,000-acre state park, next to the national military site, offers camping, swimming, fishing, boating, and nature and hiking trails. | 2625 Park Rd., Blacksburg | 864/936–7921 or 803/222–3209 | www.southcarolinaparks.com | Free | Memorial Day–Labor Day, daily 9–6; Labor Day–Memorial Day, daily 9–5.

Georgia

AUGUSTA

▼▼

Gin—as in "cotton"—made Augusta, but even before it had found its way onto the map. Named (prettily) for the then Princess of Wales, Augusta was state capital from 1785–95. James Oglethorpe founded Augusta in 1736, only three years after landing at the site of Savannah, where he organized the Colony. Located on the headwaters of the Savannah River, Augusta built its reputation on its cotton crop. Near here, on General Nathanael Greene's plantation, Eli Whitney took things one step further in 1793 by inventing the cotton gin. This enabled farmers ever after to plant cotton fields without worrying about extracting the peppery black seeds from the bolls. With mechanical production by the 19th century you could walk for miles along the stacked up bales that lined the river. *Contact Augusta Metropolitan Convention and Visitors Bureau | 14-50 Green St., Suite 110, Augusta, GA 30901 | 706/823–6600 or 800/726–0243 | fax 706/823–6609 | www.augustaga.org.*

Augusta Museum of History. From prehistoric Indians to Master's green jackets and James Brown's costumes, Augusta is presented from past to present. Paintings, Native American artifacts, and Colonial and Revolutionary memorabilia fill the museum's permanent collection. | 560 Reynolds St. | 706/722–8454 | fax 706/724–5192 | www.rightguide.com/civilwar/poi/arcm.htm | $4 | Tues.–Sat. 10–5, Sun. 1–5.

Brier Creek Battlefield. On the night of Feb, 14, 1779, the British evacuated Augusta. Some 15,000 Patriot militia, led by Gen. John Ashe, trailed them and settled in to repair a bridge that the Redcoats had destroyed on the Savannah River by swampy Brier Creek. On March 3, the British surprised the militia, who fled or drowned. More than 200 Patriots were killed, and about the same number were injured. The British victory was complete, with only 17 casualties. A large marker describes the losing battle, and a map shows the movement of the forces. The woodsy landcape remains much the same as during the Revolution, except for the new bridge and the highway beyond. Camping is popular in the area. | South of Augusta along the Savannah River | Free | Weekdays 8–5.

Ezekiel Harris House. Smokers alert: this unusual late-18th-century gambrel-roof frame house originally belonged to prosperous Ezekiel, a tobacco entrepreneur. Traveling tobacco merchants perhaps used the exterior staircase to enter their guest rooms without disturbing the rest of the house (and maybe to grab an extra puff of their smokin' goods). The fine furnishings date to the late 18th and early 19th centuries. | 1822 Broad St. | 706/724–0436 | $2 | Sat. 10–1.

Meadow Garden. George Walton, the youngest signer of the Declaration of Independence and twice Georgia governor, moved into this house in 1792 and named it for its 121 sprawling acres. The earliest part of the house dates to around 1777; the most recent addition, to the early 1800s. It is documented as the oldest residence in Augusta and the first historic preservation site in Georgia. | 1320 Independence Dr. | 706/724–4174 | www.downtownaugusta.com/meadowgarden | $3 | Weekdays 10–4.

HISTORIC LODGING

1810 West Inn. With its screened veranda and period furnishings, this early 19th-century inn is a real Southern romantic. Pull up a fan, take a seat, and savor a cool julep. Complimentary breakfast. No kids under 12. | 254 N. Seymour Dr., Thomson | 800/515–1810 | fax 706/595–3155 | www.gomm.com | 10 rooms | $95–$245 | AE, D, MC, V.

DARIEN

▼▼

Georgia's oldest fort, and a Gullah community named Hog Hammock, are reasons to visit this area, a strategic location from Colonial times through the Revolution. The Altamaha River delta was a natural barrier between Spanish Florida and the English Colonies, and it kept the French from expanding from the Mississipi River to the Atlantic coast. Darien dates to 1736, when Oglethorpe, protecting the Altamaha River frontier from Spaniards to the south, settled a group of Scots Highlanders in the area. The Scots went on to found the town and become wealthy plantation owners. *Contact McIntosh County Chamber of Commerce | 105 Fort King Georgia Dr., Box 1497, Darien, GA 31305 | 912/437–4192 | fax 912/437–5251 | www. mcintoshcounty.com.*

Fort King George State Historic Site. Georgia was essentially meant as a buffer state between English settlements and the southern encroachments of the Spanish in Florida and the western advance of the French from Louisiana. As its southernmost outpost of defense of the British Empire, Fort King George—the Colony's oldest fort was named for England's George I—has a saga behind it that makes for grueling reading. First settled by invalid pensioners from British armies, patrolled by Scottish scouts ("continually Sotting if they can gett any Rum or money"), and built by "swampers" who died from malarial mosquitoes and brackish water, the cypress blockhouse, earthen fort, and barracks finally rose in 1721. Colonel John "Tuscarora Jack" Barnwell decided the fort should rise on a stretch of the Inland Passage, not on St. Simons Island (which would have been a more effective barrier against raiders). After years, Barnwell retreated to his Beaufort plantation a few months before his death, worn out by bad meat, insects, and unfriendly locals. Fresh fruit and veggies were hard to preserve, and salt meat rotted in the heat, so many of his men died of "the flux" and scurvy; the British cemetery here is one of the oldest in the country. But the fort finally took hold—from 1721 to 1727— and with it, the British Colony of Georgia. Battle reenactments and demonstrations of 18th-century life bring the site to life—in late March are two Scottish Heritage Days (with a re-creation of the Battle of Bloody Marsh) and mid-April sees a Pirate Invasion ("ransom notes will be handed out among the children"). An on-site museum interprets history from prehistoric times. Later sawmill ruins are from a time when timber floated down nearby Georgia rivers named Oconee, Ocmulgee, and Ohoopee. | Fort King George Dr. | 912/437–4770 | www. darientel.net/~ftkgeo | $3 | Tues.–Sat. 9–5, Sun. 2–5:30.

✦ ON THE CALENDAR: Nov. **Drums Along the Altamaha.** Not an old Western, but battle reenactments and living-history demonstrations (without having to sit through coming attractions). Britain's southernmost outpost is definitely live—and lively—as it comes under Revolutionary War fire at Fort King George, during the annual fall weekend. | 912/437–4770 | $10.

SAVANNAH

▼▼

Savannah. Soft-syllabled, the name is altogether fitting a beauteous, classic city of a certain age. Savannah, a place of history and substance, a quintessential Steel Magnolia. Here in Georgia's oldest city is the nation's largest historic district, its rhythmic pattern of streets interspersed with 21 cobblestone squares, chockablock with 18th- and early 19th-century mansions, churches, and monuments, giant parterre gardens with iron scrollwork, and languid parks. In March, when azaleas and dogwoods bloom profusely in mild, perfumed air, no American city is lovelier.

The site was founded in 1733 on the Yamacraw Bluff by a river bend, 15 mi from the ocean. It was a cold November day when James Oglethorpe arrived from England on the small ship *Anne,* with 120 mostly poor, mostly idealistic settlers. Savannah's sandy streets were filled immediately by the ambitious and the displaced: English, Jews, Central Europeans, Greeks, Highland Scots. Until 1749, there were few African-Americans, as slavery had been prohibited until then. Numerous Native American tribes looked on, many befriending the newcomers. Antagonism toward England was early and strong, but by the early days of the Revolutionary War, Savannah was a thriving port city, a fact not overlooked by the British, who occupied it in December 1778. Despite a valiant American effort to regain the strategic port in 1779, Savannah remained in British hands until its liberation by General Anthony Wayne's troops in 1782, when it became Georgia's first state capital, a role it held until 1785.

Warehouses stuffed with cotton once lined River Street along the Savannah River, a prime shipping area to Europe. Farther along the river, City Market was the hub of commerce and socializing. But the years brought problems: a yellow fever epidemic in 1818, when half the city was under quarantine; devastating fires, storms, and other calamities; the area fell into gentle decline for decades. Today, Savannah's vigorous and well-organized historic zoning effort has maintained the integrity of the central areas, with 1,400 restored or reconstructed buildings dating from the 18th century. Here you can sense as well as learn about our country's earliest days: the clip-clop of horse carriages passing ancient live oaks bearded with Spanish moss; the splash of fountains in the necklace of tidy squares; bronze statues of Colonial heros; cool mint juleps on the veranda of a porticoed mansion: Savannah remains a walker's city, an aesthetic, unforgettable sampling of our earliest history. *Contact Savannah Area Convention and Visitors Bureau | 101 E. Bay St., Savannah, GA 31401 |912/644–6401 or 877/728–2662 | www.savannahvisit.com.*

Chippewa Square. Daniel Chester French's imposing bronze statue of General James Edward Oglethorpe, founder of Savannah—and Georgia, anchors the square. Also note the Savannah Theatre on Bull Street, opened in 1818, which claims to be the oldest continuously operated theater site in North America. | Bull St. between Hull and Perry Sts.

Christ Church. John Wesley, founder of Methodism, preached here and is believed to have established the Colony's first Sunday school at this home church to Georgia's first congregation. The current building is the third on this site and dates to 1838, but the bell (the only one in the state crafted by the famed Revere and Son, founded by Paul in Massachusetts) dates to 1816. | 28 Bull St. | 912/232–4131 | Free | Tours: Wed., Fri. 10–3.

Colonial Park Cemetery. The second burial ground for Savannah's founders (1750–1853), this is the final resting place for many of the state's historic luminaries, including Button Gwinnett, whose signature remains the rarest of all the signers of the Declaration of Independence; and Joseph Habersham, an early governor. A Tabby composite sidewalk of lime and shells winds under old shade trees. | Oglethorpe Ave. and Abercorn St. | 912/651–6610 | Free | Daily dawn–dusk.

Congregation Mickve Israel. Ashkenazic and Sephardic Jews sailed from London to Savannah without the blessing of the Colony's trustees and were welcomed by Oglethorpe despite orders from London to bar them. Among the temple's members was Samuel Nunes, a Portuguese physician who saved the Colonists from ravaging disease. Founded in 1733, this Reform congregation (the country's third oldest) is now housed in a splendid 19th-century Gothic synagogue on Monterey Square. Its collection includes documents and letters from Washington, Madison, and Jefferson. Washington called upon "the wonder-working Deity" to water the congregation with "the dews of heaven. " | 20 E. Gordon St. | 912/233–1547 | www.mickveisrael.org | Free | Weekdays 10–noon and 2–4.

Fort Jackson. On Salter's Island, just 3½ mi downstream from Savannah, sits the oldest standing fort in Georgia, garrisoned in 1812. The site is just above Five Fathom Hole, where sailing ships lightened their load to enter the shallow Savannah River. The masonry fort, surrounded by a 9-ft-deep tidal moat, holds 13 exhibit areas in arched rooms, with cannon above. In the river under a red buoy, the scuttled ironclad CSS *Georgia* awaits raising, and a group of history enthusiasts is working feverishly to accomplish that goal. | 1 Ft. Jackson Rd. | 912/232–3945 | www.chsgeorgia.org | $3.50 | Daily 9–5.

Historic Savannah Waterfront Area. Stones carried in ships as ballast line the streets leading to River Street, where the waterfront has traded in its rough-and-tumble for fine shops and dining establishments. Lots of festivals and sights and sounds keep the area busy and filled with visitors. | John P. Rousakis Riverfront Plaza | Free | Daily.

Isaiah Davenport House. The threatened demolition of this great Federal mansion jump-started Savannah's historic preservation movement in 1954, when seven stalwart woman bought the house for $22,000, saving it from becoming a parking lot. Master builder Isaiah Davenport constructed his home from 1815 to 1820. The wrought-iron-trimmed, semicircular staircase leading to the front door, polished hardwood floors, fine woodwork and plasterwork, and a soaring, elliptical interior staircase are among its significant features. Furnishings from the 1820s are Hepplewhite, Chippendale, and Sheraton. | 324 E. State St. | 912/236–8097 | $6 | Mon.–Sat. 10–4:30, Sun. 1–4:30.

Johnson Square. The oldest of Ogelthorpe's original squares was laid out in 1733, and named for South Carolina governor Robert Johnson. A monument marks the grave of Nathanael Greene, a Revolutionary War hero. The square was once a popular gathering place: Savannahians came here to welcome President Monroe in 1819, to greet the Marquis de Lafayette in 1825, and to cheer for Georgia's secession in 1861. | Bull St. between Bryan and Congress Sts.

Midway Museum and Church. Early 18th- to 19th-century furniture, artifacts, and documents are crammed in this evocative reproduction of an 18th-century raised cottage. The museum has an excellent bookshop; get the key for the adjacent Puritan church, built in 1792. Two of its congregants, Button Gwinnett and Lyman Hall, were signers of the Declaration of Independence. Don't miss the old cemetery, where Revolutionary War generals Daniel Stewart and James Screven are buried. Supreme Court Justice Oliver Wendell Holmes's grandfather is also among the interred. | U.S. 17 in Midway | 912/884–5837 | $3 | Tues.–Sat. 10–4, Sun. 2–4.

New Ebenezer. Who are Georgia's Salzburgers? In 1736 Lutheran religious refugees from Salzburg, Austria, arrived in Savannah, and Oglethorpe sent them upriver to found a new colony to grow food for Savannah. Devising a town plan similar to that of Savannah, the Salzburgers developed a thriving silkworm industry, but the settlement did not survive long past the Revolution. The historic cemetery is still used by their descendants. Today, surviving buildings include 1769 Jerusalem Church, on its original site, and assorted buildings moved to the site for preservation. A retreat center accommodates up to 170 guests ($13–$40), mostly for groups. There's a museum and small gift shop with books about the Salzburgers. The Georgia Salzburger Society operates the enterprise and serves as caretaker of the site. | 2887 Ebenezer Rd., Rincon (23 mi northwest of Savannah) | 912/754–9242 | www.newebenezer.org | Free | Museum Wed., weekends 3–5.

Owens-Thomas House and Museum. Displays of simple items used and constructed by slaves are juxtaposed within this Regency architectural marvel designed by English architect William Jay in 1819 soon after his arrival in Savannah. Curved walls, half-moon arches, and

Greek-inspired ornamental details highlight the design. Here, after spending the night, Lafayette bade a two-hour au revoir from a wrought-iron balcony to the crowd below. | 124 Abercorn St. | 912/233–9743 | $8 | Mon. noon–5.

Savannah History Museum. The site of this museum is a mass grave for soldiers, interred where they fell at the Revolutionary War's Siege of Savannah. In 1779, Colonial forces led by Polish count Casimir Pulaski were beaten back by the Redcoats, and Pulaski was killed while leading a cavalry charge; a diorama details the battle. Indian poker chips, a 1760 Flintlock pistol, and costumes from the Highlander Regiment are included in exhibits highlighting the entire coastal region, especially the founding of Savannah in 1733. | 303 Martin Luther King, Jr. Blvd. | 912/238–1779 | www.chsgeorgia.org | $2 | Weekdays 8:30–5, weekends 9–5.

Main Theater. Films on the history of Savannah are shown every half hour. | 303 Martin Luther King, Jr. Blvd. | 912/238–1779 | www.chsgeorgia.org | Film $1.50; admission and film $2.90 | Weekdays 8:30–5, weekends 9–5.

Ships of the Sea Museum. Savannah merchant William Scarborough was a major investor of the *The Savannah,* the first steamship to cross the Atlantic. He hired the brilliant designer William Jay to build his exuberant Greek Revival mansion during the 1819 cotton boom. The house has a Doric portico topped by one of Jay's characteristic half-moon windows, and four massive Doric columns form a peristyle in the atrium entrance hall. Today the building houses a nautical museum, exhibiting scale models of famous ships. Included are models of *The Anne,* which bore James Oglethorpe and his settlers to the new Colony; *The Savannah;* and many examples of the famous China clippers. The scrimshaw collection includes an ostrich egg with a ship etching, and a fearsome-looking pirate figurehead. | 41 Martin Luther King, Jr. Blvd. | 912/232–1511 | www.shipsofthesea.org | $5 | Tues.–Sun. 10–4:15.

Telfair Mansion and Art Museum. William Jay, Savannah's principal architect in the early 19th century, designed the Telfair Mansion, now the oldest public art museum in the Southeast. Commissioned by Alexander Telfair, son of the governor, it features marbled rooms exhibiting some historic artifacts, including Telfair family furnishings, such as a Duncan Phyfe sideboard and Savannah-made silver. In addition, American, French, and Dutch Impressionist paintings; German tonalist paintings; plaster casts of the Elgin Marbles, the Venus de Milo, and the Laocoön are on view. | 121 Barnard St. | 912/232–1177 | www.telfair.org | $6 | Tues.–Sat. 10–5, Sun. 1–5, Mon. noon–5.

Wormsloe State Historic Site. Hunger, plague, civil strife—Nobel Jones survived these difficulties to establish himself and his family as colonists. Jones, a native of Surrey, England, was a physician and carpenter who came to Savannah with Oglethorpe in 1733. A road lined with moss-draped live oaks leads to the ruins of his fine mansion. A nature trail leads to the visitor center, where you can watch a film and examine artifacts. Special programs often feature costumed docents. | 7601 Skidaway Rd. | 912/353–3023 | www.gastateparks.org | $2.50 | Tues.–Sat. 9–5, Sun. 2–5:30.

✦ SIGHTSEEING TOURS/TOUR COMPANIES

Gray Line bus tours. Historic Savannah is the focus of the company's bus tours. | 215 W. Boundary St. | 912/234–8687 or 800/426–2318 | www.grayline.com | $16–$21 | Daily 9–4:20. **Old Savannah Tours.** City tours and weddings are their specialties. Tours run every 15 to 20 minutes. | 250 Martin Luther King, Jr. Blvd. | 912/234–8128 | www.oldsavtour.com | $15–$21 | Daily 9–4:30.

HISTORIC DINING AND LODGING

Elizabeth on 37th. Founding chef Elizabeth Terry has won numerous awards, including the James Beard designation as Best Chef in the Southeast. This elegant restaurant, housed in a Beaux Arts mansion, focuses on regional and local specialties—some that date to the

18th century—including Bluffton oysters in season, shrimp on grits, and Savannah cream cake. | 105 E. 37th St. | 912/236–5547 | $21–$31 | AE, D, DC, MC, V | No lunch.

Olde Pink House. SouthernUpstairs you're in the refined atmosphere you'd expect in the brick Georgian mansion built in 1771 for James Habersham, one of America's wealthiest citizens. The downstairs tavern is more hot-pink than old, with live entertainment. She-crab soup, a light version, is a Lowcountry specialty. | 23 Abercorn St. | 912/232–4286 | $15–$25 | AE, MC, V | No lunch.

Jesse Mount. One of the six guest rooms at this 19th-century brick rowhouse is a carriage house suite, complete with a full kitchen and a garden view. Most rooms have original oil paintings, and all have polished hardwood floors and antiques. Complimentary breakfast. | 209 W. Jones St. | 912/236–1774 | 6 rooms | $195–$240 | AE, D, DC, MC, V.

Marshall House. Savannah's history, from its founding to the Civil War is the focus at this restored hotel, with original pine floors, woodwork, and bricks. It caters to business travelers but with the intimacy of a bed-and-breakfast inn. Restaurant. | 123 E. Broughton St. | 800/589–6304 | fax 912/234–3334 | www.marshallhouse.com | 68 rooms | $159–$209 | AE, D, MC, V.

TYBEE ISLAND
▼▼▼

Tybee is an Indian word meaning "salt." The Yamacraws came here to hunt and fish, and pirates came later for a sneakier kind of hunting and fishing. Legend has it they buried the treasures they swiped right here on the island. Flags fluttered here for the Spanish, English, French, and Confederates, who occupied in sequence and often at odds. This popular resort lies right on the Atlantic, some 18 mi east of downtown Savannah. On the island are the third-oldest lighthouse in America, and interesting remains of early coastal defenses that once protected the mainland with batteries of artillery. And here, in a pasture, John Wesley, founder of the Methodist Church, declared his faith in America. *Contact Tybee Island Beach Visitor Information | Box 491, Tybee Island, GA 31328 | 800/868–2322.*

Fort Pulaski National Monument. "I came here, where freedom is being defended, to serve it, and to live or die for it . . ." So declaimed Count Casimir Pulaski, a soldier-patriot mortally wounded in his efforts to save the city of Savannah from the British during its famous siege. Drafted to the American cause by no less than Benjamin Franklin, Pulaski was the son of a Polish noble. Among the engineers working on the fortification honoring him was the young lieutenant and West Point graduate Robert E. Lee. Severely shelled by Federal troops during the Civil War, the fort is a well-preserved testament to 19th-century engineering. Now restored, it's operated by the National Park Service, and contains moats, drawbridges, massive ramparts, and towering walls. An excellent gift shop sells memorabilia and numerous informative books. A nature trail (part of the area's Rails to Trails system) and picnic areas make this a must-visit. The fort is on Cockspur Island. You'll see the entrance on your left just before U.S. 80 reaches Tybee Island. | U.S. 80 | 912/786–5787 | www.nps.gov/fopu | $12 | June–Aug., daily 8:30–6:45; Sept.–May, daily 8:30–5:15.

Tybee Museum and Lighthouse. Imagine timber-hulled, tall-masted ships passing this beacon, whose lower part dates to 1773. Another 94 ft was added in 1866, and today, at 154 ft, the lighthouse is Georgia's oldest and tallest; its observation deck sits 135 ft above the sea, with a panoramic view. Leading to the Tybee Light are 178 steps. | 30 Meddin Dr. | 912/786–5801 | www.tybeelighthouse.org | $4 | Apr.–Labor Day, Wed.–Mon. 9–6; Labor Day–Mar., Wed.–Mon. 9–4.

WASHINGTON

▼▼

First in the United States to be named in honor of our first president, this quaint town was chartered in 1780. George Washington visited nearby Augusta and environs in 1791, and his tour of the region no doubt inspired locals to bestow the honor. The town is landmarked by its noted Courthouse Square, where structures proclaim their construction dates—1815, 1896, 1910—a Flemish-style courthouse presides over all, and the Heard Building saw, on May 4, 1865, the Confederacy officially and finally dissolved, and its treasury, including gold, disposed of (but no one knows exactly where, which is why treasure hunters still explore the woods here). *Contact Washington-Wilkes Chamber of Commerce | 104 E. Liberty St., Washington, GA 30673 | 706/678–2013 | www.washingtonga.org.*

Callaway Plantation. This supersize plantation may be unequaled for understanding 19th-century plantation life. The land goes back to a 3,000-acre 1783 land grant for Jacob Callaway. In 1784 he built a cabin, which burned; exhibited is a similar 1785 log cabin from the Heard plantation, also located in Wilkes County. Callaway's house, dating to 1790, in the Federal plain style, is also on-site. The main house, a redbrick Greek Revival structure, was built by Aristedes Callaway beginning in 1865 and finished in 1869. Period pieces, largely from Washington families, are on display together with simple items that reveal the character of daily life, such as kitchen implements. | 2160 Lexington Rd. | 706/678–7060 | www. washingtonga.org | $4 | Tues.–Sat. 10–5, Sun. 2–5.

Elijah Clark State Park. This popular camping and recreational site is named for the Revolutionary War general, whose reproduced house is a museum. Besides 165 camping sites, facilities include cabins and miniature golf. Is a hole-in-one here called "Elijah's cup"? | 2959 McCormick Hwy. | 706/359–3458 | www.gastateparks.org | $2 vehicle | Mon.–Tues. 8–5, Wed.–Sun. 8–10.

Kettle Creek Battleground. In one of the last battles of the Revolution, a Patriotic force of 300 defeated a group over twice its size, preventing a link-up of Georgia and South Carolina Tories. Col. Andrew Pickens' band of Americans held off "bandits and murderers" led by Colonel Boyd, "a bold, notorious, and dishonest Tory," who died in the surprise attack. A dirt road leads up a hill, to a state historic marker and 20-ft granite obelisk monument commemorating the site where the Revolutionary War ended in Georgia, on February 14, 1779. Today the forested battlefield appears much as it did almost 225 years ago. The Daughters of the American Revolution and the city of Washington jointly manage it. | War Hill Rd. | Free | Daily.

Washington Historical Museum. This restored home was built on land once owned by the town's original surveyor, Micajah Williamson. The back part of the house was built in 1835 by Albert Semmes, and in 1847 Samuel and Elizabeth Barnett bought it and added the front three stories. Most furnishings come from the family of Francis Willis, who was Samuel's half brother. The museum showcases area Native American culture, Revolutionary and Civil War artifacts, and other items related to local history. | 308 E. Robert Toombs Ave. | 706/678–2105 | $2 | Tues.–Sat. 10–5, Sun. 2–5.

By David and Steele Sartwell

Vermont

❧

Valleys of War, Mountains of Resistance

*H*ave a care. When you gaze upon the white-clapboard facades and elegant church steeples of olden Vermont, be aware that such beauty and peace was hard won by the early settlers of the Colonial era, some of whom engaged in battles so bloody they they seem to fit into today's action thrillers. Across Vermont's sylvan hills and by its tranquil lakes, such figures as Benedict Arnold (when he was fighting for the good guys), Remember Baker—fathers still tell their sons the tale of his hacked-off thumb, lost in a struggle against English constables—and Ethan Allen's fabled Green Mountain Boys waged their daring acts of rebellion. Today, of course, they remain heroes to many fifth-grade schoolchildren. But after all their strife and struggle it comes as a surprise to learn that Vermont was not even one of "the Original Thirteen." So, you ask, why is a chapter devoted to it in this guide to those founding states? Well, one way to answer that is with another question, one that is, granted, more college level than grade school:

During the Colonial period, and for approximately 16 years after the Declaration of Independence was adopted, the area that is now Vermont was:

a. controlled by France
b. a part of the colony of New York
c. a part of the colony of New Hampshire
d. a part of the colony of Massachusetts
e. an independent republic
f. all of the above

The answer is: (f) all of the above. This small area of New England was indeed the grinding edge of the early struggle for control of the continent by the French and the British. To add to the brouhaha, the differing Indian tribes now had invading Europeans to fight as well. In turn the first Vermont settlers were abandoned by New Hampshire, which first granted them their land, bullied by New York, which wanted to take their farms away, then rebuffed by the colonies when Vermont wanted to join as an independent state. In self-defense the territory became, from 1777 to 1791, no less than an independent country. One has to wonder if this is taking independence a bit too far. But let's begin at the beginning.

✦ A DISPUTED LAND

From 1675 to 1762 the French and their Abenaki tribe allies headed south from the Champlain islands to be pitted against the British and their Iroquois tribe allies in the never-ending skirmish historians now called the French and Indian Wars. The last of the French were driven out in 1759 when the British defeated them up in Québec. During these formative years, Colonial boundaries were often unclear, and much of the land remained uncharted. In 1760 there were roughly 300 non-Indians in Vermont. By 1790, just 30 years later, there were just over 85,000. Then came the famous land-grab. It turns out that governors of each colony were in charge of the selling of land plots, allowing them to keep a portion of the sale price of each parcel. Needless to say, it was to their monetary advantage to claim as much territory as they could. To the east, the fledgling colony of New Hampshire started the land stake. It had been part of Massachusetts, but King George made it separate, appointing Benning Wentworth the first Governor of the new colony in 1741. Although he had no firm legal authority, and without much complaint from New York, he started selling land in the area around Vermont's Bennington; over the next fifteen years he disposed of these New Hampshire Grants, making himself rich in the process.

Then, seeing gold in these hills—the rich bottomland along Lake Champlain, Otter Creek, and the Battenkill River had proved immensely fertile farmland—the governor of neighboring New York set up business selling land in the *same* area. In 1763, Governor Colden got King George to certify that New York—and not New Hampshire—owned the land. Coldon then got greedy, insisting that all of the New Hampshire Grant landowners had to pay him *again* for the right to the lands they had bought in good faith from New Hampshire. Needless to say, many settlers dug in their heels and refused to pay. Samuel Robinson, from Bennington, went to England and got the King to agree that although New York could govern the land, the New Hampshire Grants were legal, and that New York's Governor had no right to ask them to pay again. Governor Coldon, however, ignored the king and sent in surveyors and sheriffs to throw the early settlers off their land. Many insist this started the distrust between Vermonters and New Yorkers that still lingers to this day!

✦ ETHAN ALLEN AND THE GREEN MOUNTAIN BOYS

In 1770, Ethan Allen—a "flatlander" newly arrived from Connecticut—represented the Grants homesteaders in court in Albany, New York. In direct contradiction of the King's orders, the court ruled that the landowners had to pay and that New York's claims were legitimate. In response, the Bennington area settlers joined together at the Catamount Tavern and decided to resist. The celebrated Green Mountain Boys were born. Over the next five years the Yorkers and the Green Mountain Boys had some rough and tumble confrontations. Happily, there were no armed battles and by 1775 delegates from every town were deciding how to deal the situation. They were mad at the Yorkers for trying to take their land by force, they were upset at the governor of New Hampshire for not defending them, and they were furious at the King for not controlling his governors. As fate would have it, their uprising was preempted a week later by that other set of angry colonists who came to fire "the shot heard round the world" at Lexington and Concord.

Rallying to the larger cause, Ethan Allen, Seth Warner, and the men who had been fighting the Yorkers knew that Fort Ticonderoga and the fort at Crown Point were lightly defended and had cannon the colonists would desperately need in their battle in Boston. The Green Mountain Boys met in Castleton on May 8, 1775, to start out on their raid; the British were surprised and overwhelmed by the colonists. During that fall and the following winter the Colonial army, with the help of the Green Mountain Boys led by Seth Warner, captured Montréal and, under Benedict Arnold, lay siege to Québec City. In the meantime, Mount (Fort) Independence was hastily built on the narrow piece of land across the lake from Fort

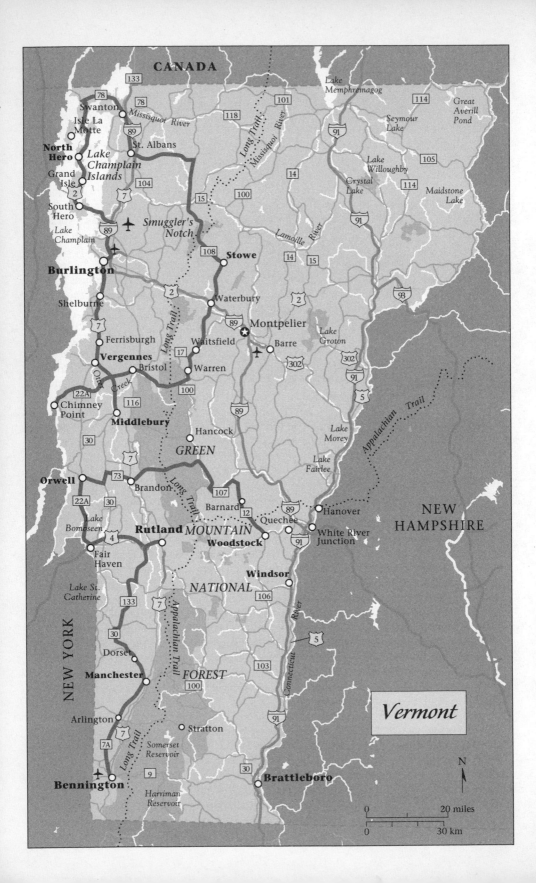

Vermont Timeline

1609 On July 4 Samuel D. Champlain enters Lake Champlain.

1666 French establish Fort Anne and shrine at Isle la Motte.

1689 During King William's War the English construct a small fort at Chimney Point.

1700 Chief Greylock of the Abenaki, from his stronghold on the Missisquoi, wages a war to drive the colonists from Vermont.

1749 First land grant by New Hampshire Governor Benning Wentworth establishes the town of Bennington.

1763 The Treaty of Paris forces France to relinquish claims to Vermont.

1764 On petition from New York, King George sets the Connecticut River as the boundary between New York and New Hampshire.

1770 Ethan Allen chosen to represent the people in their fight against New York claims.

1774 An assembly in Westminster votes to support the Continental Congress.

1775 The Yorkers Westminster "Massacre." Green Mountain Boys capture Fort Ticon-deroga on May 10. Seth Warner takes Crown Point.

1776 Fort Independence is built on Lake Champlain opposite Fort Ticonderoga. The Battle of Valcour in October delays the English advance up Lake Champlain.

1777 Vermont becomes a Republic, declaring its independence from both New Hampshire and New York on January 17. The Vermont Constitution is adopted. Fort Ticonderoga and Fort Independence are evacuated on the night of July 5. Battle of Hubbardton, July 7, successfully delays the British advance. Battle of Bennington, August 16, defeats the British, who fall farther back into New York.

1778 First general elections held. Thomas Chittenden is elected Governor. Ethan Allen returns from captivity.

1791 Vermont admitted to the Union as the 14th State.

1812 The War of 1812 comes to Lake Champlain. An invasion force into Canada is unsuccessful. Boats return to Shelburne Bay, where they are refitted in preparation for the coming summer campaign.

Ticonderoga. It was here that the Colonial army was digging in to defend the northern frontier. Benedict Arnold and the American forces slowed the British attack at the Battle of Valcour Island near South Hero, but in the summer of 1777 the British decided to try to separate the colonies with a three-pronged attack that was to eventually meet near Albany. General St. Ledger was to drive up the Mohawk Valley from Lake Ontario, General Howe was assigned to attack up the Hudson River, and General Burgoyne, with an assist from hired German troops, was to control the shores of Lake Champlain. Burgoyne was victorious for the most part, but as his troops chased retreating Colonials east and south, they were famously halted for a time at Hubbardton by the rearguard action by Seth Warner and the Green Mountain Boys, allowing Colonial troops to regroup. The momentum swung to the other side and the Brits were ultimately defeated at Saratoga, New York.

✦ THE "REPUBLIC" OF VERMONT

During the War of Independence, Vermonters petitioned to be accepted into the Union as a separate colony. They were rebuffed by the opposition led by New York. So in January 1777, in the middle of the Revolutionary War, they set themselves up as an independent republic. Obviously, from the very beginning these Vermonters had decidedly independent ways of looking at the role of the individual in relationship to government. In June they declared their new name as Vermont, and at a convention on July 2 they adopted a constitution that was considered radical at the time—the first in America to prohibit slavery, to allow men to vote without being landholders, and to establish a system of public schools. But it was not until the war had ended and border problems had been straightened out with New York that Vermont, in 1791, was finally admitted to the Union as the fourteenth state.

Vermonters of today still reflect many of the values of their forefathers. They have a fierce allegiance to their land, and have passed some of the most aggressive land protection laws in the country. They jealously guard their right to think independently, yet friendliness and civility join a strong sense of community. As one Vermonter put it, every one who lives here has the right to "make a damn fool of himself." Life as it was lived in old-time Vermont—Arcadian or hardscrabble, depending on how you look at it—gave a certain cast to the land and to the character of the inhabitants. Today, the state offers up many a site to fascinate Revolutionary and Colonial era buffs. They now join the thousands of other visitors who find this tiny state—long after its "baptism of thunder, lightning, and rain"—one of the most peaceful in all the land.

A REGIONAL GAZETEER
▼▼

✦ SOUTHERN VERMONT: BIRTH OF THE REBELLION
Southern Vermont was the site of the state's first permanent settlement, near Brattleboro, and it was also the region first extensively affected by tourism. Well over a century ago, Manchester and environs were already an outpost of fashionable society, but southern Vermont still has plenty of rough edges, thanks in part to the huge swath of land given over to the Green Mountain National Forest. Fanciful stories—part-true–part myth—of Ethan and Ira Allen, Seth Warner, Remember Baker, and the Green Mountain Boys abound. This whole area shouts history at you: from the Catamount Tavern site in **Bennington** to the top of the 306-ft Bennington Monument, where you can look out over the countryside and almost hear the thunder of the cannons and the rattle of musket fire as the green-coated Green Mountain Boys and the rest of the Colonial Army attacked the Redcoats during the Battle of Bennington. At **Mount Independence,** "living interpreters" from the past speak about the struggles there and the hardships they had to endure during the winter of 1776–77. You can look across the narrows at Fort Ticonderoga—once connected to Vermont by a log bridge—or take a historic boat tour on the lake where so many battles were fought. Near **Rutland,** you can walk the Hubbardton Battlefield where carefully placed signs tell you of the engagement that was so dearly fought there. In **Windsor,** the the first Vermont Constitution is on view at the Old Constitution House. *Towns listed: Bennington, Brattleboro, Manchester, Orwell, Rutland, Windsor.*

✦ NORTHERN VERMONT: LAND OF RESISTANCE
The twin cities of Barre and Montpelier—one the world's granite capital, the other the capital of Vermont—mark the fringes of northern Vermont. Here vistas broaden—Mt. Mansfield, Vermont's highest peak, is visible across much of the state's northern tier of counties—and many small towns and villages look as if they spend more effort preparing for the onslaught of winter than the onslaught of tourists. Northern Vermont is where Lake Champlain is deepest—and laden with Revolutionary-era shipwrecks—and allures many who wish to stroll along **Burlington**'s cosmopolitan waterfront and enjoy what has been called the world's most beautiful sunset. Battery Park (where cannons were mounted to stave off the British in the War of 1812) and the Ethan Allen Homestead are two main sights here. To the north are the islands

of Lake Champlain: **North and South Hero** and **Isle La Motte**—here visitors will find St. Anne's Shrine and the Hyde Log Cabin, one of the oldest log cabins in the United States. To the southeast near **Stowe,** along the spine of the Green Mountains, you can drive up through Smugglers' Notch, where legend has it smugglers used this gap to push animals and goods north in illegal trade with British-controlled Canada. Not far away is Ben & Jerry's Ice Cream Factory, which usually has some patriotic-themed ice-cream available in July. To the west along Lake Champlain from **Chimney Point** north to **Burlington** there is a pleasant mix of historical sites, museums, and art galleries, including the Lake Champlain Maritime Museum—its exhibits of the naval battles fought on the lake are a must-see—and the expansive Shelburne Museum, with its incredible collection of 37 historic structures and Early American artifacts, a true history buff's paradise. *Towns listed: Burlington, Middlebury, North Hero, Stowe, Vergennes.*

Southern Vermont: Birth of the Rebellion

A DRIVING TOUR FROM BENNINGTON TO MANCHESTER

▼▼▼

Distance: Approx. 110 mi (one-way)   **Time:** 3 days (2 nights)
Breaks: Manchester and Woodstock offer the best bets for an overnight stay

This multiday tour moves through southern Vermont, where more than two centuries ago settlers struggled for their lives against the French, the Yorkers, the British, the native tribes, and, ultimately, nature itself. **Bennington** is an excellent place from which to start your journey through the southwestern Vermont countryside, which consists mainly of small picturesque villages and large dairy farms. Delightfully, much of this land looks just as it did 200 years ago. Arrive there by taking Route 9 west from Brattleboro, U.S. 7 north from Williamstown, Massachusetts, or Route 7 east from Troy, New York. Start the journey by looking for the 306-ft Bennington Monument, which dominates the landscape. The Bennington Museum and Grandma Moses Gallery is home to many Revolutionary War artifacts including one of the oldest stars-and-stripes flags in existence. The cemetery is the resting-place of Robert Frost, and the famously beautiful 1806 Congregational Church, impeccably restored in 1937, is a must-see. It was from Bennington on May 5, 1775, that Ethan Allen led the raid that captured Fort Ticonderoga. There is a marker on Monument Avenue at the site of the Catamount Tavern—the patriots' meeting place.

To get to the Bennington Battlefield, take Fairview Road from the monument and make a right turn on Silk Road; follow Silk Road through a covered bridge. Turn left on 67A, left again on 67, and follow it to the battlefield (the route is about 8 mi). From the battlefield, retrace your steps on Route 67 east until you reach Route 7A. Go north on 7A about 9 mi to Arlington. (U.S. 7 is faster to Manchester, but 7A is much more scenic.) Arlington, once the capitol of the "Republic of Vermont," has one of Vermont's oldest frame buildings (1764), former home of Thomas Chittenden, Vermont's first governor (and also has a Norman Rockwell Art Gallery), or you can visit an inn which used to be Ira Allen's house just north on U.S. 7 in the town of Sunderland.

About 7 mi north is **Manchester**—with its famed Equinox Hotel and other hostelries (a good place for overnighting)—while historic Dorset is only 5 mi northwest on Route 30. Here, at Cephas Kent's tavern Vermonters pledged to support the Continental Congress in its fight against the British. At Pawlet take Route 133 north to Middletown Springs, then continue north to West Rutland. You have a choice here: a short right takes you into **Rutland,** the largest city in this part of the state. If you want to stay in the country, take 4A west for a scenic 6-mi ride to Castleton: here, on May 8,1775, Ethan Allen and more than 250 soldiers started their march toward Fort Ticonderoga. Look for a marker near the Congregational Church. Backtrack on 4A about a mile and turn north onto the East

Hubbardton Road. There is a marker here indicating that Fort Warren stood on this site, guarding the old military road where on July 7, 1777, General St. Clair and 2,500 soldiers streamed by on their retreat from Fort Ticonderoga. Go 5 mi north on this highway that turns into Monument Hill Road until you get to the Hubbardton Battlefield. At Hubbardton you will find one of the most pristine battlefield sites in America, a magnificent panorama of uncluttered countryside where it is easy to follow the battlefield descriptions. This is the only Revolutionary War battle fought entirely on Vermont soil. The automated display re-creates the action.

From here, continue north on Monument Road. It is a narrow passageway that turns to dirt, but have faith and follow it to Route 30. Turn right, go 3 mi and then cut left onto Route 144. At Route 22A go north to the traffic light at the junction of Route 73, then go left toward the New York Ferry. After a few hundred yards, turn left and follow the signs to **Mount Independence.** This historic landmark is one of the best Colonial-era fortifications in Vermont—the automated characters inside the reception center are a must-see. Be sure to take the two-hour narrated Carillon Cruise from here to Fort Ticonderoga directly across the lake. Upon leaving Mount Independence, retrace your route out Route 73 east and drive through **Orwell.** By following Route 73 some 13 mi to Brandon, and then over the Brandon Gap, you will see some of the state's most scenic roads. This is winding-two-lane-road, go-slow country, but the ride is spectacular. This section will let you see why east–west travel was so difficult in Colonial times.

Take Route 100 south 19 mi along the Green Mountain National Forest to U.S. 4. At this point head east 6 mi to West Bridgewater, then go south on Route 100 about 5 mi to Route 100A at Plymouth Union (with its famous 19th-century historic district), forging on ahead so you can spend the evening about 10 mi east in **Woodstock** where you will find the Billings Farm Museum, the gracious Woodstock Inn, and several outstanding restaurants. **Windsor,** the birthplace of Vermont, is found 20 mi south by following Route 12 and then U.S. 5. Here is found Elijah West's Tavern, now the Old Constitution House, the site of the signing of the Vermont Constitution in 1777. The 460-ft Cornish-Windsor Covered Bridge is the longest in Vermont. Head south on U.S. 5. From Springfield go west on Route 11. You will pass through the beautiful Vermont towns of Chester and Londonderry on this pastoral 40-mi ride back to Manchester.

Northern Vermont:
Islands of War, Peaks of Glory

A DRIVING TOUR FROM BURLINGTON TO THE ISLANDS AND THE GREEN MOUNTAINS AND BACK TO BURLINGTON

▼▼▼

Distance: Approx. 250 mi (round-trip)   **Time:** 3 days (2 nights)
Breaks: Smuggler's Notch Ski Area, Stowe and Middlebury are excellent spots for overnight stays

Northern Vermont is where a sense of history lives easily beside modern industry; where different cultures maintain their individuality while not overwhelming others; and where respect for the environment permeates every expansionist movement. Come and enjoy a scenic three-day ride that offers everything from small B&Bs to gracious hotels, tiny cafés to bustling restaurants, I–89 to the narrow, twisting passway through Smuggler's Notch, the city of Burlington to the small hamlet of Lincoln, and landmarks hallowed by Ethan Allen and Benedict Arnold. Begin in **Burlington,** the largest city in Vermont. Take Route 127 onto North Street and start with a walk through Battery Park to take in some of the best views of Lake Champlain and the Adirondack Mountains. Just below this bluff you'll find the Lake Champlain Basin Science Center—kids love its many hands-on exhibits. Then head north on Route 127 to the area outside of Burlington called the the Intervale to find the Ethan Allen Homestead. Follow twisting Route 127 along the beautiful shores of Malletts Bay until you come to U.S. 2, then go north about 3 mi to I–89 and head toward the islands of North Hero and Isle La Motte. You will soon cross the Lamoille River and onto the islands of South and North Hero. The village of South Hero is roughly 2 mi east of the bridge (at South Street and U.S. 2 is a grocery that is a great spot to buy an ice cream cone or a homemade apple pie). Turn left on South Street and, after a mile, look for West Shore Drive on your right— this will bring you along the shore of Lake Champlain. In the distance you will be able to see Valcour Island, site of a Revolutionary War naval battle. Gordon Landing is where you can catch the car ferry to Plattsburgh, New York. Go left on Route 314 about 3 mi, back to U.S. 2 north. The Hyde Log Cabin, built in 1783 and believed to be the oldest existing log cabin in the United States, can be found on the right about 2 mi north.

Continuing north on U.S. 2, cross the bridge on to **North Hero.** The road winds along through the island north for about 8 mi and then crosses back onto the mainland at South Alburg. Turn left onto Route 129 and follow it out to Isle La Motte, the smallest of the islands. Take Shrine Road to the St. Anne Shrine—the first Catholic Mass in Vermont was celebrated here in 1666. These islands were the battleground for centuries for those that wanted to control the waterways. The Main Road and then Route 128 will take you back off the island. Take Summit Road to Route U.S. 2. About 5 mi north, go right onto Route 78. Swanton is 10 mi south on Route 78. From there take U.S. Route 7 south to St. Albans and then Route 36 east. It is roughly 7 mi to Fairfield through rural Vermont countryside. A 15-mi ride south on Route 108 will bring you to Jeffersonville, the gateway to the mountains. Follow Route 108 up into Smugglers' Notch—the pass through which smugglers brought their goods north to the British during the years leading up to the War of 1812. Just before the summit is the Smuggler's Notch ski area. The Notch pass is not open from November through April, but it does offer spectacular views of northern Vermont the rest of the year. Descend down Route 108 into the village of **Stowe.** Here there are countless eateries and shops that can consume you for a day (speaking of consumption, 7 mi south of the village on Route 100 in Waterbury is the famous Ben & Jerry's Ice Cream Factory). Head southwest along U.S. Route 100, turning west on Route 17 to head up over the Appalachian Gap, a narrow pass between Stark and Molly Stark mountains. Lower in elevation than the Lincoln Gap a few miles south, this is one of the few that are open during the winter. You'll pass by both the Sugarbush and Mad River Glen ski areas. Drop out of the mountains some 16 mi down to Bristol, and then follow Route 17 to the region surrounding **Vergennes.** From Bristol it is 24 mi to Addison and the Chimney Point Historical Site, which chronicles some 12,000 years of settlements. Then backtrack north on Route 17 about 2 mi to the General John Strong D.A.R. Mansion, near **Middlebury** and built in 1796. It is filled with period furnishings and has a Colonial herb garden. Turn left onto Lake Street about 1 mi north and follow along the lake and go left 8 mi to the Button Bay Road. Drive by the Button Bay State Park and follow the signs to Basin Harbor and the Lake Champlain Maritime Museum—top sight here is the replica of the Benedict Arnold's 54-ft-long gunboat *Philadelphia*.

Drive east on Basin Harbor Road along the Otter Creek where Benedict Arnold beached and then burned his boats as his sailors retreated before the British in October of 1776. At the end of Basin Harbor Road go left onto Sand Road and left again onto Route 22A. This 7-mi ride will bring you through Vergennes to Route U.S. 7 north. In the 22 mi along this road from Vergennes to **Burlington,** there are a number of interesting stops to make, the headliners being 9 mi north of Ferrisburg—the world-famous Shelburne Museum—45 acres, 37 buildings, with a vast horde of Americana. The traffic can be tough the 10 mi on to Burlington, but remember the great three days you have just spent riding through some of the most beautiful country in the world.

BENNINGTON

▼▼▼

We owe no allegiance; we bow to no throne, Our ruler is law, and the law is our own. –from the *Song of Vermonters* (1779)

Bennington became the flash point in a land ownership battle between the governors of the colonies of New Hampshire and New York from the 1760s through the 1780s. England's King George ruled that although New York did own the land eastward to the Connecticut River, New York's Governor Colden was to honor the grants that had been already given by the governor of New Hampshire. It came to a boiling point when Colden, in direct opposition to rulings from the king, ordered that Vermonters who already had pre-existing New Hampshire Grants pay him for the title as well. The winds of rebellion began to stir— thanks to Ethan Allen, Seth Warner, Remember Baker, and the Green Mountain Boys.

In a series of nonfatal confrontations, the Green Mountain Boys drove out of the area any "Yorkers" that tried to take over lands already purchased from New Hampshire. The long-vanished Catamount Tavern (look for the catamount—a species of mountain lion—set on a pedestal about half-way up Monument Avenue) in Bennington became the unofficial head-quarters of the "Bennington Mob." Bennington was also the religious and social focal point of the area. The Old First Church, dedicated in 1806, stands on the ground where the orig-inal Protestant meeting house was built in 1763. The adjacent cemetery contains the graves of many of Vermont's early heroes, and the site of Ethan Allen's home is next door. It was here in 1791 that delegates met to ratify the Constitution of the United States in order to become the first state to be admitted to the Union. For history buffs, Bennington is best known for a battle that was never fought here: The Battle of Bennington should probably be known as the Battle "for" Bennington, as the actual fighting occurred along the Wallomsac River some 5 mi west of Bennington on land now belonging to New York. Within the lively little city are three National Register Historic Districts within the town, one in each of its historic village centers: Old Bennington, Downtown Bennington, and North Bennington. *Contact Bennington Area Chamber of Commerce | 100 Veterans Memorial Dr., Bennington 05201 | 802/ 447–3311 | www.bennington.com. Green Mountains Regional Marketing Association | 5046 Main St., Manchester Center 05255 | 800/362–4144 | www.sovermont.com.*

Bennington Battle Monument. The verdant hills of Vermont, New York, and Massachusetts can all be studied from the observation deck atop this 306-ft-tall memorial (reached by eleva-tor), completed in 1891, to honor the famous Battle of Bennington, here immortalized in a diorama depicting the moment Seth Warner and his Green Mountain Boys arrived to fight the British. A huge iron kettle captured from the Brits is hung inside. Outside are statues honoring Seth Warner and General Stark. As for the battle itself, in August of 1779, Benning-ton was a waypoint for settlers fleeing south from the advancing British army and a staging point for Colonial troops. British General Burgoyne, desperately needing supplies, sent troops toward Bennington to capture the stores gathered there. General John Stark brought 800 men from New Hampshire to reinforce the Colonial troops and the Green Mountain Boys. In the first of three battles—fought along the Wallomsac River some 5 mi west of Benning-ton—that ultimately led to the British surrender at Saratoga, the estimated 1,600–1,800 regi-ment of patriots drove the attacking force back. Stark famously urged his militia to attack the British-paid Hessian troops across the New York border by proclaiming, "There are the Redcoats; they will be ours or tonight Molly Stark sleeps a widow!" | 15 Monument Circle, Old Bennington | 802/447–0550 | $1.50 | Mid-Apr.–Oct., daily 9–5.

Bennington Museum. A terrific museum featuring memorabilia from the Battle of Benning-ton, this collection has a fascinating array of exhibits, including one of the oldest Revolu-tionary War flags in existence. Also on view are showcases filled with Early American glass and Bennington Pottery. Folk-art lovers take note: the largest public collection of paintings by Grandma Moses, who lived in the area, is also on show. | W. Main St., Bennington | 802/447–1571 | www.benningtonmuseum.com | $6 | Daily 9–5.

Old Burying Ground. Here lies the graves of many early American patriots. As many as 75 regimental soldiers are buried here as well as a number of British and Hessian troops killed in the Battle of Bennington. Here also is the grave of famed poet Robert Frost (note the inscription on his stone, "I had a lover's quarrel with the world"). | Monument Ave., Bennington | 802/467–8696 | Free | Daily.

Old First Church. Built on the site of the first Protestant meetinghouse in Vermont (1763), the present church was dedicated in 1806. It has remained virtually unchanged since then and is a wonderful example of Early Colonial architecture. | Monument Ave., Bennington | 802/447–1223 | Memorial Day–June, weekends only 10–12 and 1–4; July–Columbus Day, daily 10–noon and 1–4, Sun. 1–4.

✦ ON THE CALENDAR: Aug. **Battle of Bennington Celebration.** August 16 is a state holiday celebrating the Battle of Bennington. Reenactments and other events occur each year on the weekend closest to the 16th. | 802/447–3311.

HISTORIC LODGING

Henry House. The house of Lt. William Henry, Revolutionary War hero and participant in the Battle of Bennington, was built in 1769 and is listed on the National Register of Historic Places. The Henry House crowns 25 acres of tranquil pinelands and meadows. The original charm of this landmark home is retained, replete with working fireplaces and a beautiful open front porch overlooking the Henry Covered Bridge and Walloomsac River. Complimentary breakfast. | 124 Elm St. | 802/447–3839 | www.henryhouseinn.com | 5 rooms. | $105–$180 | MC, V.

BRATTLEBORO

▼▼

In the early 1700s what is now Vermont was truly wild and uncharted country. Because water was the way to move most goods into the wilderness, the Connecticut River became the thoroughfare for the northward expansion of the English settlers. Unfortunately, it was also the route that the French-aligned Abnaki used to raid south into Massachusetts. As it turns out, the rich and fertile soil along the river valley was ideal for farming so settlers moved north along the waterway, building small forts to protect themselves from the local tribes. There was Fort Dummer, Fort Bridgeman, Fort Sartwell, and, farther north across the river from Springfield, a large structure was built with the imaginative name of Fort Number Four. It was from Fort Bridgeman in Vernon that Jemima Sartwell Howe and her children were taken north to Montréal—her tombstone and other historic markers there still tell the story, here told in a box *below*.

In October of 1774, long before the Revolutionary War began, area residents voiced their support of the Continental Congress. It was in March 1775, in the village of Westminster (just north of Brattleboro), when the long-brewing fight over the New York land claims came to a climax with the "Westminster Massacre." About 100 local settlers took over the courthouse on March 13, and while unarmed, refused to come out of the building when the sheriff with a posse of "Yorkers" showed up. Two casualties resulted, and those who didn't escape were locked up, only to be freed the next day by a group of 400 angry settlers. In April, town delegates decided to fight the "Yorkers"—but events just a week later in Concord and Lexington overshadowed their land concerns.

Route 9 will take you the 40 mi west from Brattleboro to Bennington. It is along this approximate route that, in 1777, General Stark led his troops from Fort Number Four to help the Colo-

The Fair Captive

The story of Jemima Sartwell Howe—ancestor of this chapter's author—exemplifies the incredible struggle early settlers faced in their efforts to tame the northern wilderness of New England. This battleground fought over by the French, British, and Indians tested the mettle of even the hardiest of pioneers. Among the hardiest, as it turns out, was the fair Jemima.

On June 27, 1755, 12 Abenaki Indians ambushed Caleb Howe, Hezekiah Grout, and Benjamin Garfield as they were returning from hoeing corn on their plot of land near Fort Sartwell on the Connecticut River. While Grout got away, Garfield drowned in the river, and Howe, shot in the thigh, pierced several times by spears, and scalped, died soon after other settlers found him. The Indians took as captives his wife Jemima Howe, their seven children ranging in age from six months to 11 years, among others. After eight days of walking over the Green Mountains, the raiding party reached Otter Creek on Lake Champlain. Recovering their hidden canoes, the Abenaki paddled up the Richelieu River to the French and Indian stronghold of St. Francis village. Jemima's baby died of small-pox in the Abenaki stronghold near Swainton and her two daughters were sent to a convent in Montréal. During her captivity, Jemima was befriended by Colonel Schuyler, captured in Oswego. Through his efforts, the French released Jemima, her four sons, and 84 other redeemed captives. In October, three years after her forced march north, Jemima Sartwell Howe and the others sailed up Lake Champlain toward home.

A year later, after the British defeated the French, Jemima returned to Québec for her daughters, only to find that her youngest, Mary, had been taken to France by the former Governor de Vaudreuil. However, her eldest, Submit, was still there. Her ordeal over, Jemima Sartwell Howe returned to her home. She subsequently married Amos Tute and died on March 7, 1805, at the age of 82. A historical marker and her gravestone with its long epitaph describing her life can be seen in Vernon, Vermont.

---

nials defeat the British at the Battle of Bennington. Look for markers along the way. The current Brattleboro is the economic hub of southeastern Vermont. The region's picturesque towns—Newfane, Putney, and Dover—siphon off much of the tourist trade. *Contact Brattleboro Area Chamber of Commerce | 180 Main St., Brattleboro 05301 | 802/254–4565 | www.brattleboro.com.*

Brattleboro Historical Society. The society has a history room filled with more than 7,000 photographs from the mid-1800s on and a plethora of material dating back to before the Revolutionary War. | 3rd Floor, 230 Main St. | 802/258–4957 | www.brattleborohistoricalsociety. org | Free | Thurs. 1–4 and Sat. 9–noon.

Connecticut River Cruises. A relaxing, narrated trip aboard the *Belle of Brattleboro* provides a combination of spectacular scenery, American history, and bountiful wildlife. The *"Belle"* is a flat-bottom 49-passenger wooden vessel, similar in design to boats that plied the river a century earlier but hand-built by Vermont craftsmen in 1985. Bring a picnic to enjoy while you view scenic beauty rarely seen from highways. | 28 Springtree Rd. | 802/254–1263 | www. belleofbrattleboro.com | $10 | Memorial Day–Columbus Day, Wed.–Sun.

Rockingham Meetinghouse. The building, part of the now vanished village of Rockingham, is the country's oldest community meetinghouse still in use. Many of its features, like the sash windows and box pews, are original to the 1787 structure. The building is 4 mi north of Bellows Falls, just off Route 103. | Meeting House Rd., Bellows Falls (28 mi north of Brattleboro) | 802/463–4280.

Scott Covered Bridge. Closed to traffic and maintained as a state historic site, the Scott Bridge, located 1 mi north of Townsend and 17 mi north of Brattleboro on Route 30, was built in 1870 and extends 276 ft. There's good swimming below, so why not leap off the bridge for a splash? | Rte. 30, north of Townsend | Free.

✦ ON THE CALENDAR: Aug. **Rockingham Old Home Days.** Held on the weekend of August's first Sunday, this festival celebrates the history of the town and its surrounding villages. The festivities include bands, one of the northeast's largest fireworks displays, and a pilgrimage to the Rockingham Meetinghouse. | Bellows Falls | 802/466–4280.

HISTORIC DINING AND LODGING

Old Newfane Inn. The quiet, country-formal dining room in this 1787 inn has a heavy timbered ceiling, brick fireplaces, and pewter plates, all bestowing a fine Colonial-era feel. Chef Eric Wendl blends his European style with American preferences—breast of capon cordon rouge is a winner. | 4 Court St., Newfane (8 mi north of Brattleboro) | 802/365–4427 | $32 | No credit cards | Closed Mon.

Four Columns Inn. Located on the classic green of Newfane, this 1830 Greek Revival mansion is one of the most romantic and charming of all Vermont inns. Twelve of the 16 guest rooms are beautifully appointed with gas fireplaces. Gardens enhance the natural beauty of the inn's stream and two ponds. Complimentary breakfast. | 21 West St., Newfane (8 mi north of Brattleboro) | 800/787–6633 | www.fourcolumnsinn.com | 20 rooms | $125–$340 | AE, D, MC, V.

BURLINGTON
▼▼

"Waubanakees–Winooski!" was the cry that sent fear coursing through the veins of early Vermont settlers. These words meant that the Indians were attacking along the Winooski River, one of the main thoroughfares of war at the time. They would canoe up this river, portage over the height of the land, then descend into the Connecticut River for raids south. As the events of the Revolutionary War and the War of 1812 unfolded, Burlington became an important battleground for the defense of the republic. During the 1700s, this northwestern part of Vermont was in constant turmoil. The French were the first to settle along the lake, but in 1759 the British drove them out. Although Burlington was chartered in 1763, very few settlers occupied this region at that time because of the constant war conflicts in the area. At the conclusion of the War for Independence, however, they poured into the region. At the first falls, about 2 mi up the Winooski River, Remember Baker built the first gristmill. Ethan Allen spent his years after the Revolution (he died in 1789) on his farm in the Intervale just north of the city. Ira Allen, the more educated of the Allens, established the University of Vermont in 1791 (the first four students graduated in 1804). Today, Burlington is a charming college town, a wonderfully livable address with a brick pedestrian mall, miles of bike paths along the water, and acres of city-owned parks. *Contact Lake Champlain Valley Regional Marketing Organization | 60 Main St., Suite 100, Burlington 05401 | 877/686–5253 | www.vermont.org.*

Battery Park. This site on the bluff overlooking the lake was once an important staging area for the American army in the War of 1812. There is a small plaque here that commemorates the battle. The spot offers spectacular views of the lake and the Adirondack Mountains in the distance, making this a perfect place to watch the sunset. | Battery St., Burlington.

Ethan Allen Homestead and Museum. No name is more associated with Vermont history than that of Ethan Allen. Flamboyant leader, land speculator, prisoner of war and, some say, a collaborator with the British on the matter of Vermont Independence, this site was his last homestead. Located on the shores of the Winooski River, the restored 1787 farmhouse, gardens (often abloom with plants that would have been cultivated during his lifetime), descriptive exhibits, and a multimedia show all reveal the man, the myths, and a true measure of his place in Vermont history. This famed leader of the Green Mountain Boys represented the New Hampshire Grant settlers in their legal fights with the courts in New York. Leading the Green Mountain Boys into battle at the beginning of the Revolution, he captured Fort Ticonderoga and fought in several subsequent engagements. Captured in September 1775 during an ill-fated attack on Montréal, he was a prisoner of the British for more than two years. He was eventually paroled on Long Island and later exchanged for a British officer in 1778. After the war he retired to his landholdings in northern Vermont with his second wife, Fanny, and died in 1789. On the grounds, enjoy hiking trails, guided tours, and picnic areas. | 1 Ethan Allen Homestead (1 mi north of Burlington on Rte. 127) | 802/865–4556 | www.ethanallenhomestead.org | $5 | May–mid-Oct., Mon.–Sat. 10–5, Sun. 1–5; mid-Oct.–mid-May, weekends 12–4.

Ethan Allen Monument. Located in the Greenmount Cemetery, close to the Ethan Allen Homestead and Museum, this 1857 monument marks the burial site of General Ethan Allen. Resting on an 8-ft-high granite base with marble tablets, the 35-ft tall Doric column is topped by an 8-ft-tall Carrara marble statue of a youthful Allen in a strident pose demanding the surrender of Fort Ticonderoga. | Greenmount Cemetery, Colchester Ave.

Lake Champlain Basin Science Center. This science center concentrates on the ecology, history, and culture of the Lake Champlain Basin with many "hands-on" activities. | 1 College St. | 802/864–1848 | www.lakechamplaincenter.org | $3 | Mid-June–Labor Day, daily 11–5; Labor Day–mid-June, weekends 12:30–4:30.

Shelburne Museum. In Old World Europe, dukes and duchesses were fond of shifting entire villages when they built their stately houses. Here, Lila Webb's Vanderbilt money went them one better by enabling her to build her own "village." She and her Vanderbilt husband moved together 37 venerable and historic structures, then stuffed them with extraordinary collections, ranging from antique duck decoys to great 18th-century American paintings. All in all, there are some 80,000 pieces of American decorative arts in the collection, including weathervanes, quilts, decoys, toys, dolls, paintings, sculptures, and much more. But the reason a visit here is a must is to see the historic buildings, including the 1773 Prentiss House, the 1783 Stagecoach Inn, the 1832 Dorset House, the 1782 Dutton House, a 1790 Hat and Fragrance Textile Gallery, and the 1800 Stencil House. In addition, there are any number of other wonders, including a complete side-wheeler *Ticonderoga* from the 19th century. In more modern gallery structures you will find a trove of American antiquities and paintings, such as Edward Hicks *William Penn and the Indians*. Across town is Mrs. Webb's Shelburne Farms, a model agricultural estate farm created in 1886 by Frederic Law Olmsted, designer of New York City's Central Park—here you can try your hand at milking a Brown Swiss cow, watch maple syrup being made, or take a sleigh ride during the winter months. All in all, the Shelburne estates remain an incomparable time-machine to the American past. | 6000 Shelburne Rd., Shelburne (15 mi south of Burlington) | 802/985–3346 | www.shelburnemuseum.org | $10, Apr.–May; $17.50, May–Oct. | Mid-Apr.–mid-May, daily 1–4; mid-May–late Oct., daily 10–5.

HISTORIC LODGING
Burlington Redstone Bed-and-Breakfast. Listed on the National Historic Register, this warm and hospitable building offers spectacular lake and mountain views. The guest rooms are filled with art and antiques, with lovely gardens just outside. Another plus: this is only a short walk to downtown. Complimentary breakfast. No children under 13. | 497 S. Willard St. | 802/862–0508 | www.burlingtonredstone.com | 3 rooms | $99–$159 | No credit cards.

MANCHESTER

▼▼▼

The Revolutionary War swirled all around Manchester from 1775 to 1777, and it was here that Ira Allen famously proposed financing Vermont's participation in the American Revolution by confiscating Tory estates. It was through Manchester that 200 Green Mountain Boys marched on their way to capture Fort Ticonderoga—the first in a series of battles with the British for control of the northern border. Then in the retreat from Fort Independence in 1777, Major General Arthur St. Clair led his 2,500 troops through Manchester on the way toward Bennington. The rearguard action at Hubbardton by Seth Warner's troops stopped the British pursuit. After the battle, Warner and his troops encamped just behind where the Equinox Hotel now sits. A month later they rejoined the Colonial troops and stopped the southern advance of General Burgoyne. Across the street from the Equinox there is a Veterans Memorial with a Green Mountain Boy on top. Today Manchester, filled with stately homes (including Hildene, a beautiful 24-room mansion that was the summer home of Robert Todd Lincoln, the son of Abraham Lincoln) of the late 19th century, seems to be one huge mall for the wealthy. *Contact Manchester and the Mountains Chamber of Commerce | 5046 Main St., Manchester Center 05255 | 802/362–2100 | www.manchestervermont.net.*

Ira Allen House. The house where Ira Allen—Ethan's brother and noted Surveyor-General of Vermont during the turbulent Revolutionary years—once lived is now a B&B. It is one of the oldest Inns in Vermont, although it has been fairly extensively restored with a modern clapboard trim. Inside, the tavern and the guest rooms are over 200 years old, with some time-burnished touches, including large hand-hewn beams, the handmade bricks of the fireplace, and some hand-blown panes of glass. The "new" part of the inn was added around 1846. | Rte. 7A, Sunderland (16 mi north of Arlington on Rte. 7A | 888/733–8666 | www. iraallenhouse.com | By appointment only.

Southern Vermont Arts Center. The original Georgian Revival home that housed the Arts Center has been supplemented by the addition, in July of 2000, of the stunning Elizabeth de C. Wilson Museum wing. This 12,500-square-ft structure houses several hundred pieces of art and photography in 10 different galleries. | West Rd. | 802/362–1405 | http://svac.org | $6 | Late May–Oct., Tues.–Sat. daily 10–5, Sun. noon–5; Dec.–Mar., Mon.–Sat. 10–5.

✦ ON THE CALENDAR: June **Ethan Allen Days.** This encampment in nearby Sunderland reenacts famous skirmishes with period uniforms and arms. Performers replicate the daily life of the Revolutionary War soldier. | 802/375–2800.

HISTORIC DINING AND LODGING

Ye Olde Tavern. The wide floorboards and the low exposed beams give this old tavern a Colonial feel. The food—venison port sausage served with blackberry sauce, Vermont raised–buffalo meat loaf, and warm cranberry apple crisp—is yummy. | 5183 Main St. | 802/362–0611 | $27 | AE, DC, MC, V.

1811 House. Built in the 1770s, this house has operated as an inn since 1811 except for a period when it was the private residence of Mary Lincoln Isham, the granddaughter of President Lincoln. Listed in the National Registry of Historic Places, it proffers fireplaces, oriental rugs, fine paintings, authentic antiques, and canopied beds in an elegant but relaxed atmosphere. Complimentary breakfast. No children under 16. | Rte. 7A | 802/362–1811 | www.1811house.com. | 14 rooms | $140–$280 | AE, D, MC, V.

The Equinox. The Equinox has been one of Vermont's most luxurious hotels for more than 200 years. The hotel consists of the main building, the 1769 Marsh Tavern, and the intimate Charles Orvis Inn. Activities could include learning to fly a falcon or drive a Land Rover, while the dining rooms offer superlative meals. A new spa, set to open, includes an enormous pool. Restaurant. | 3567 Main St. | 802/362–4700 | www.equinoxresort.com | 150 rooms, 23 suites. | $199–$669 | AE, D, MC, V.

MIDDLEBURY
▼▼

One of the flash points of the French and Indian Wars, this region has some notable sites for the Colonial buff. Beginning in 1731, the French started what grew to be a large community at Chimney Point on the shore, and instigating almost constant warfare for the next 85 years. The French and their Indian allies would raid south to the Connecticut River. However, during the Seven Years War in the late 1750s, the British pushed the French north into Canada, replacing them with Colonists from the south. During the Revolutionary War this region became a demilitarized zone where the British sent patrols south from Canada and the Colonists raided north from Bennington. Interestingly, settlers with claims here often returned only long enough to tend their crops on this incredibly fertile plain, but it was just too dangerous to stay, as the 30 mi between the steep Green Mountains to the east and the lake to the west was a thoroughfare for hostile forces.

Gamaliel Painter erected the first house in Middlebury in 1773 (it now houses the Information center for the town, the Addison County Chamber). He fought in the Revolutionary War, was with Ethan Allen when they captured Fort Ticonderoga, and was also a principal founder of Middlebury College (est. 1800) and left it $10,000 on his death in 1819. Today, Middlebury is a delightful college town that remains the economic center of the region. *Contact Addison County Chamber of Commerce | 2 Court St., Middlebury 05753 | 802/388–7951 | www. midvermont.com.*

Congregational Church. This elegant church, built in 1809, is capped with a 136-ft spire and is considered by many the most graceful in Vermont. | Main St. at U.S. 7 | 802/388–7634 | Free | Daily; summer services, Sun. 10.

Henry Sheldon Museum of Vermont History. Built in 1829, this marble merchant's house gives a visitor a look at the household items, tools, clothes, and written material of early Vermont. | 1 Park St. | 802/388–2117 | www.henrysheldonmuseum.org | $4 | Nov.–May, weekdays 10–5; late May–Oct., Mon.–Sat. 10–5.

John Strong D.A.R. Mansion. Built in the mid-1790s by General John Strong and his wife Agnes McClure Strong, this redbrick mansion—constructed of bricks fired on the property—was meant to replace the family cabin destroyed by the Indian and Tory forces under the aegis of General John Burgoyne. Five generations of the Strong family occupied this home until around the Civil War. The salons on view here lovingly display period furnishings and exhibits and the story of a Colonial family in the northern wilderness comes alive—outside, literally, thanks to the flowers and herbs still blooming in their perennial gardens. | 6656 Rte. 17, west of Rte. 22A, West Addison | 802/759–2309 | www.vmga.org/addison/jstrong.html | $3 | Memorial Day–Labor day, weekends 10–5.

HISTORIC LODGING
Inn on the Green. This lovingly renovated 1803 Federal-style inn has been a recipient of the Vermont Preservation Trust Award. Both cozy and elegant, it's located conveniently on the

green in the center of town. Complimentary breakfast. | 71 S. Pleasant St. | 802/388–7512 | www.innonthegreen.com | 9 rooms. | $160–$260 | AE, D, MC, V.

1796 House. Travelers will be drawn to the welcoming lights of this historic building—built by Moses Stow of the Ethan Allen Green Mountain Boys—sitting high on a hill nestled between the Adirondack and Green mountains. The views are spectacular as are some of the specials served at Roland's Place Restaurant. Restaurant, complimentary breakfast. | 3629 Ethan Allen Highway, New Haven | 802/453–6309 | www.virtualcities.com/vt/rolands.htm | 3 rooms | $19–$28 | AE, MC, V.

NORTH HERO

▼▼

For thousands of years the tiny islands of Isle la Motte, North Hero, and South Hero had been awash in the waters of war. Whoever possessed these small pieces of land controlled the access to the waterway that divided the region. It was on Isle la Motte in 1666 that the French established Fort St. Anne, their first settlement in Vermont. It was not until the end of the French and Indian Wars in 1759 that the British finally drove the French back into Québec. Then, 16 years later, Benedict Arnold anchored his fleet off Windmill Point prior to the Battle of Valcour against the British Navy. Gen. Guy Carleton's largest ship, the 400-ton *Thunder,* once bombarded a small rock formation called Carleton's Folly in White's Bay in South Hero, thinking it was one of Benedict Arnold's ships. Legend has it that the Heroes were named for the Allen brothers, Ethan and Ira. They, along with other relatives and friends, owned the New Hampshire Grants that included these islands. The islands are now treasured by tourists as a quiet spot with rural beauty. Bicyclists find these flat venues relatively traffic free and the view of the lake and both the Adirondack and Green mountains are to be greatly enjoyed. Huge apple orchards and, more recently, vineyards take advantage of the warm lake breezes. *Contact Vermont's Islands and Farms Regional Marketing Organization | 3501 U.S. 2, North Hero 05474 | 800/262–5226 | www.islandsandfarms.com.*

Franklin County Historical Society. The three-story brick schoolhouse that holds the collections was built in 1861. An 18-ft-by-14-ft made-to-scale diorama equipped with lights and sound presents history of northwest corner of Vermont and St. Albans. Old farm tools, a maple-sugaring exhibit, period costumes, and railroad memorabilia make it an interesting stop. | 7 Church St., St. Albans | 802/527–7933 | Free | May–Oct., weekdays 1–4.

Hyde Log Cabin. Capt. Jedediah Hyde was a member of the Colonial Army and fought at the Battle of Bunker Hill, arriving at these islands as a surveyor, along with his son. They purchased several pieces of land from Ethan and Ira Allen, the deeds still kept at the office of the South Hero Town Clerk. Built by the son Jedediah Hyde, Jr., in 1783, this tiny home built of cedar logs is believed to be one of the oldest in the United States. Members of the Hyde family lived it in for the next 150 years. | U.S. 2, Grand Isle | 802/828–3051 | $1. | July 4–Labor Day, Thurs.–Mon. 11–5.

St. Anne's Shrine. The Shrine is on the site of Fort St. Anne where, in 1666, the French established the first settlement in Vermont by Europeans. The first Mass in Vermont was celebrated here. Large crowds gather here on Sundays to celebrate Mass. The simple structure creates a feeling of closeness with nature. There is a majestic granite statue of Champlain where it is claimed he landed in 1609. | 92 St. Anne's Rd., Isle La Motte | 802/928–3362 | Free | Mid-May–mid-Oct., daily 9–7.

HISTORIC LODGING
Ransom Bay Inn. Originally a stagecoach stop and inn built by Amos Ransom in 1795, this beautiful stone marble inn has antique furnishings and original period details throughout.

Three fireplaces, an old-fashioned cook-stove, and old jelly cupboards filled with jam make this a place for a quiet getaway. Complimentary breakfast. | 4 Center Bay Rd., Alburg | 802/796–3399 | www.bedandbreakfast.com | 4 rooms | $60–$85 | AE, D, MC, V.

ORWELL

▼▼▼

Control of Fort Ticonderoga, set on a strategic spot on the New York side of Lake Champlain, changed hands many times—first belonging to the French (the original name of Fort Ticonderoga was actually Carillon), then British, then American, then British again, and finally, American. At the outset of the Revolutionary War, Ethan Allen and the Green Mountain Boys captured this fort. At the same time, Seth Warner pushed north and captured the fort at Crown Point, whose cannons were hauled overland to Boston where they were used to attack the British. Then, in 1776 the British, under Gen. Guy Carlton, sailed south in October defeating the small American Navy led by Benedict Arnold. It was during that summer that the American troops started to build a fortification they called Mount Independence on the Vermont side, directly across from Fort Ticonderoga, near Orwell. *Contact Crossroads of Vermont Regional Marketing Organization | 256 N. Main St., Rutland 05701 | 800/756–8880 | www.vermontcrossroads.com.*

Carillon Cruises. This informative tour lets visitors see this historically important part of Lake Champlain from the water. Visit Hands Cove, Thunder Meadow, Mount Independence, Mount Defiance, and Fort Ticonderoga. You can get off at the major sites and then catch a later boat. Live narration is offered aboard this 60-ft., 49-passenger replica of a Thousand Islands wooden motor launch. You can catch the boat for this 1-½ hour cruise at Mount Independence or at their main marina just to the north. | Larrabees Point, Shoreham | 802/897–5331 | www.paxp.com/carillon | $8.50 | July–Aug., Sat.–Tues. Cruises leave at 11, 1, and 3.

Mount Independence. It was said that the combined sight of Mount Independence and Fort Ticonderoga—lying directly across the narrows from each other on Lake Champlain—was such a show of American might that British Gen. Guy Carleton abandoned his attempted invasion of the area from Canada in October 1776. Fortified in the summer of 1776 to prevent such an invasion on orders from Gen. Philip Schuyler, this outpost soon comprised a major shore battery, a horseshoe-shaped battery, and a picket fort. Although the ranks swelled to some 12,000 troops, only 2,500 remained over the winter—sadly, many died of sickness or simply froze to death in the harsh conditions. However, the Americans were forced to withdraw from both forts in early July when attacked by General Burgoyne's troops. Those at Fort Independence fled southeast past Orwell. It was just south of here at Hubbardton where Seth Warner and others fought a pitched battle with the advancing British and German troops. British and German forces camped out at the Mount until November 1777 when, after Burgoyne's surrender at Saratoga, they burned and destroyed the fort. Today, in fact, there are only archaeological remains left of the complex, including the batteries, blockhouses, hospital, and barracks. The visitor center, which is fashioned to look like an upside-down bateau, features "speaking" military figures from the past who tell the story of the life at the fort. Exhibitions reveal artifacts recovered during recent digs. Several miles of trails lead the visitor around the Mount and there are many special events, lectures, and encampments throughout the summer that offer insights into this remarkable time in Vermont history. | Rte. 73A | 802/948–2000 | www.historicvermont.org | $3 | Late May–mid-Oct., daily 9:30–5:30.

HISTORIC LODGING
Brookside Farms Country Inn. This restored 1789 farmhouse and 1843 Greek Revival Mansion sits on 300 acres with views of the Adirondacks and the lake. There is a large antiques shop

to browse through. Complimentary breakfast. | Rte. 22A | 802/948–2727 | www.brooksideinn. com | 7 rooms | $95–$175 | No credit cards.

RUTLAND

▼▼

The Green Mountain Boys marched through Rutland on their way to capture Fort Ticonderoga. But after the fall of Mount (Fort) Independence across Lake Champlain on July 5, 1777 to the British, the American commander General St. Clair and his 2,500 troops retreated through nearby Hubbardton. The German troops tried to cut off their escape, but in a rearguard action designed to give St. Clair and his troops a time, Col. Seth Warner was given the task of slowing the British and German forces. In a terrific running battle at Hubbardton, their advancing forces were stopped. St. Clair was then able to rest his weary troops at Fort Rutland (located at the present day North and South Main streets) before moving to Bennington to prepare for the battles that would ultimately spell doom for the British. Later, Rutland grew rapidly and, until recently, was the second largest city in Vermont. Known as the "Marble Capital," it was from here that the area marble quarries shipped their stone southward. Now there are many shops, museums, and galleries that make this the business center for the region—truly a "crossroads" town. The four-lane U.S. 4 from Whitehall, New York, crosses through the city and into ski areas along the mountain road of Route 100 (this adds to the traffic coming north from Manchester on U.S. 7, causing back-ups on busy weekends). Routes 30 and 133 are good alternates when heading north from Manchester. *Contact Rutland Chamber of Commerce | 256 N. Main St., Rutland 05701 | 802/773–2747 | www.rutlandvermont.com.*

Hubbardton Battlefield and Museum. Left behind to protect the rear of the retreating Colonial troops of General St. Clair, Col. Seth Warner and a detachment of Green Mountain Boys; a detail of Massachusetts militia under Colonel Francis; and Colonel Hale with a regiment from New Hampshire fought the advancing British and German troops to a standstill. Although the enemy captured the ground, the action so exhausted the pursuers that they advanced no farther, allowing General St. Clair to rest his troops for the coming Battle of Bennington. This is one of the few Revolutionary War battle sites that has remained virtually unchanged since the time of the conflict. Equipped with a map of the battle obtained from the visitors center and following the markers that are posted there, visitors at this remote site can stand where the fighters stood and thrillingly re-create the battle in their minds. | E. Hubbardton Rd., East Hubbardton | 802/759–2412 | www.historicvermont.com | $2 | Late May–mid-Oct., Wed.–Sun. 9:30–5.

New England Maple Museum. Eight miles north of Rutland on U.S. Route 7, this museum offers a trip through 200 years of maple-sugaring history. It all started with the Native American discovery that maple sap cooked over a fire produces a sweet syrup. This, along with molasses, became one of the main sources of sweeteners in Colonial times. There is an exhibit of antique sugaring equipment, a tasting area, a video, and a scrumptious gift shop. | U.S. 7, Pittsford | 802/483–9414 | www.maplemuseum.com | $2.50 | Late May–Oct., daily 8:30–5:30; Nov.–Dec. 31, daily 10–4; mid-Mar.–late May, daily 10–4.

✦ ON THE CALENDAR: July **Hubbardton Encampment**. Activities include tactical maneuvers, enactment of military camp life in the 1700s, and displays of historic equipment and clothing. | 802/273–2282.

HISTORIC LODGING

Baker's Bed and Breakfast. This 1826 redbrick Colonial is located on 3 acres of landscaped grounds just outside the city. The large bedrooms are furnished with period antiques—the common room have a burnished and warm feel. Complimentary breakfast. | 80 Campbell Rd. | 802/775–4835 | www.members.aol.com/bakersbnb | 3 rooms | $150 | AE.

STOWE

Stowe was changed forever in the 1930s when the Civilian Conservation Corps cut the first ski trails to the top of Mt. Mansfield. Since then skiers have flocked here to careen down the state's highest mountain. More than 50 restaurants and 100 shops now serve the influx of tourists that come here year-round. Nature and history intertwine here in the famous mountain pass, Smugglers' Notch. *Contact Stowe/Smugglers' Notch Regional Marketing Organization | 51 Main St., Stowe 05672 | 877/247–8693 | www.stowesmugglers.org.*

Smugglers' Notch. In the years just after the Revolutionary War, Vermont prospered. Settlers flooded north with the prospects of good farmland and no military threat from the Québecois. In fact, the British soon became lucrative trading partners, as it was quite easy to float goods down Lake Champlain to the St. Lawrence River. However, when President Jefferson imposed an embargo on trading with Britain just before the War of 1812, it resulted in quite a hardship for northern Vermont. Smuggling became a way of life for some and revenue agents tried to dry up the flow of goods going north by patrolling the river systems. Of course, that did not stop the more adventurous. Legend has it that one of the favorite overland routes north went through the narrow gap between Mt. Mansfield and Spruce Peak that is now known as Smuggler's Notch. According to one story, a sheriff from Jeffersonville caught a smuggler with his stash in a cave along the notch. He blew up the hiding place—with the poor fellow inside. Two years later the same sheriff was found dead up on the side of the mountain, some saying it was the work of the ghost of the smuggler. Today, the Smugglers Notch narrow passageway—only open during the summer—still claws its way up to 2,162 ft above sea level before it drops away into the Lamoille Valley below. Crossed by the Long Trail, the 1,000 ft cliffs on either side make this a slow but interesting car ride. | Rte. 108 north of Stowe.

HISTORIC LODGING
Black Locust. Lady, the resident Golden Retriever, will greet you at this restored 1832 farmhouse, which is surrounded with black locust trees and spectacular views of Sugarbush, Mt. Mansfield, and other Green Mountains. The three-course candlelight breakfast features many Vermont products. Complimentary breakfast. No kids under 12. | 5088 Waterbury/Stowe Rd. Waterbury Center (7 mi south on Rte. 11) | 802/244–7490 | www.blacklocustinn.com | 6 rooms | $115–$235 | AE, D, MC, V | Closed Nov. and Apr.

VERGENNES

Like so many other early Vermont villages, Vergennes sprung up around a waterfall. Although founded by Donald McIntosh in 1764, it was named by Ethan Allen for the French minister of foreign affairs, Charles Gravier, Comte de Vergennes, who had come to the aid of the fledgling country during the Revolutionary War. Located on Otter Creek 6 mi upstream from Lake Champlain, the mills here proved invaluable in building the naval ships necessary to combat the British in the War of 1812. A pleasant community with a rich history, Vergennes has a tiny downtown that is charming and friendly and is a great jumping-off point for several area attractions. *Contact Vergennes Chamber of Commerce | Box 335, Vergennes 05491 | 802/ 877–0080 | www.virtualvermont.com/chamber/vergennes.*

Bixby Memorial Library. This Greek Revival library has a large collection of Indian artifacts, paintings by Vermont artists, maps, documents, manuscripts, cup plates, Vermont stamps and covers, and items of local interest. | 256 Main St. | www.state.vt.us/vhs/hs | Free | Mon. and Fri. 12:30–8, Tues. and Thurs. 12:30–5, Wed. 10–5.

Chimney Point State Historic Site. Lake Champlain narrows dramatically at this point where Native Americans once regularly camped. Artifacts discovered here reveal that this was an important trading site. Worked copper, shell, stone, and other materials not normally found in this area had been brought from distant locations. The French were the first Europeans to see this area in 1609, but only around 1731 did the first settlers arrive. A small stockade called Fort de Pieux was soon replaced with a permanent fort, St. Fréderic, across the narrows on the New York side. This site fell to the British who built His Majesty's Fort at Crown Point, the largest British fort in the New World. It was subsequently captured by the Colonials during the Revolutionary War and is now maintained by New York as the Crown Point Historic Site, where Crown Point now stands. When the French were driven out at the close of the Seven Years War, they burned their houses. All that was left were the chimneys—thus, Chimney Point. A 1780s tavern now houses the Chimney Point State Historic Site. It has excellent displays on Native American culture and the early French settlement. Just across the bridge in New York is the Crown Point State Historic site. | 7305 Rte. 125, West Addison (12 mi southwest of Vergennes) | 802/759–2412 | www.historicvermont.org | $3 | Late May–mid-Oct., Wed.–Sun. 9:30–5:30.

Lake Champlain Maritime Museum. For those interested in the histories of the Revolutionary War and the War of 1812, this is a must stop. You can climb aboard the *Philadelphia II*, Benedict Arnold's gunboat, completely rigged, armed, and ready to take to sea. There is a working blacksmith shop, a boatbuilding shop, an extensive exhibit about the history of naval battles and boats on the lake, and you can see the lab where current artifact recovery and exploration is taking place. | 4472 Basin Harbor Rd. | 802/475–2022 | www.lcmm.org | $8 | May–mid-Oct, daily 10–5.

WINDSOR
▼▼▼

Site of Elijah West's Tavern, where Vermont's Constitution was famously adopted in 1777, Windsor was also widely known as a leader in the machine-tool industry. In the early 1800s, inventors such as Lemuel Hedge, Asahel Hubbard, and Niconar Kendall were designing pumps, scales, and rifles with interchangeable parts. Yankee ingenuity brought prosperity to the region. At the same time, William Jarvis, of nearby Wethersfield, brought in Marino sheep from Spain. Although Vermont is known for its dairy farming, by the middle 1800s it was sheep that were driving the agricultural engine. Today, Windsor is a lively place that serves as the regional hub for the many small towns in the area. It has a pocket-size downtown with many beautiful homes built in the mid-19th century. The township's covered bridge—the longest in the state—spans the Connecticut River. To the north are the tourist towns of Woodstock and Quechee, while to the east are the ski areas of Ascutney, Okemo, and Killington. *Contact Upper Valley Chamber of Commerce | 61 Old River Rd., White River Junction 05001 | 802/295–6200 | www.uppervalley.com.*

American Precision Museum. This museum celebrates the ingenuity and creativity of the designers of machine tools. It is one of 12 sites on the Machine Tool Trail, which encompasses the area from Springfield to Windsor. | 196 Main St. | 802/674–5781 | www.americanprecision.org | $5 | Memorial Day–Oct., daily 10–5.

Billings Farm and Museum. Step back a century or so and visit this working dairy farm that is a "museum" of rural life at the time. Old varieties of vegetables bloom in the heritage garden, oxen are used to plow the fields, and Jersey cows are still milked twice a day. | Rte. 12 and River Rd., Woodstock | 802/457–4663 | $8 | May–Oct., daily 10–5.

Old Constitution House. It was on July 8, 1777, in the midst of a violent rain storm, that the first constitution of the "Free and Independent State of Vermont" was adopted. Meeting in the Windsor Tavern owned by Elijah West—now called the Old Constitution House—the delegates hammered out a Constitution that was quite radical for the time. It was the first in America to prohibit slavery, the first to allow every man to vote regardless of income or property holdings, and the first to establish a system of public schools. This document is even more impressive in its construction considering that at the time it was being written, Seth Warner and the Green Mountain boys were fighting a rearguard action to protect the Colonial army fleeing southward from Fort Independence. Period rooms, reflecting its use as an 18th-century tavern, include the original table upon which the document was signed. A large interpretive area re-creates the events surrounding its writing and signing. | N. Main St. | 802/672–3773 | www.historicvermont.org | $3 | Late May–mid-Oct., Wed.–Sun. 11–5.

✦ ON THE CALENDAR: July **Windsor Heritage Days.** Celebrating the signing of Vermont's Constitution, there are historic reenactments, a parade, and folk music. | 802/674–5910.

HISTORIC LODGING

Inn at Windsor. The 1786 Green Mansion that sits above Windsor's Main Street has been lovingly restored. A collection of original late 18th- and early 19th-century buildings set around a central, open courtyard have bedrooms with fireplaces, underground stone chambers, elegant "Indian-shuttered" parlors, and even some messages from the past (so they tell us). Complimentary breakfast. | 106 Apothecary La. | 802/674–5670 | 2 rooms, 1 suite | $125–$165 | AE, MC, V.

By CiCi Williamson

Virginia

❧❧

"Give Me Liberty, or Give Me Death!"

t's 1607 and it's May, a glorious time in the region we know as the Tidewater. Close your eyes and picture yourself gliding up peaceful Chesapeake Bay, watching the blossoms of jasmine and dogwood float by and bluefish arc free of the water. Imagine that you've been crossing the Atlantic for five months now and you're anxious to get off the ship. But Indians—the unknown tribes said to inhabit this presumed "India"—are on the shore, so you patiently look for a secure spot. Sixty miles up the bay, a wide river flows in from the west and you follow the river 30 mi upstream. On your starboard side is a lush island connected to the mainland by a narrow, easily defensible isthmus, and just the place to set foot. You anchor, clamber ashore on wobbly sea-legs, and name the island Jamestown for your king. By August, the stifling-hot, humid, gnat-filled summer typical of the area proves you made a mistake; "James Swamp" is more like it.

Fast forward 174 years, 20 mi, and a gazillion mosquitoes. Your new enterprise: to defeat the world's most disciplined army with a ragtag regiment of farmers and a few Frenchmen. Incredibly, history strikes again. Yorktown—situated on the very same Virginia peninsula that anchored Jamestown, historically dubbed "the first permanent English settlement in the New World"—now plays host to the battle in which America decisively wins its independence.

Centered chronologically and spatially in this incredible triangle of coincidences, Williamsburg—the largest and most visited attraction in Virginia today—was the state's Colonial capital from 1699 to 1780, before the seat of government was moved to Richmond for greater protection during the Revolutionary War. With Jamestown, Yorktown, and Williamsburg taking center stage, it is little wonder that Virginia played a starring role in the early history of America. If these three great attractions helped set the scene, bring down the curtain (on the British), and underscore Virginia's status as a haven for patriots, there are scores of other historic destinations that deserve the tourist's applause. In fact, through its hundreds of national historic sites, including presidential homes, plantations, excavations, and restorations, the story of

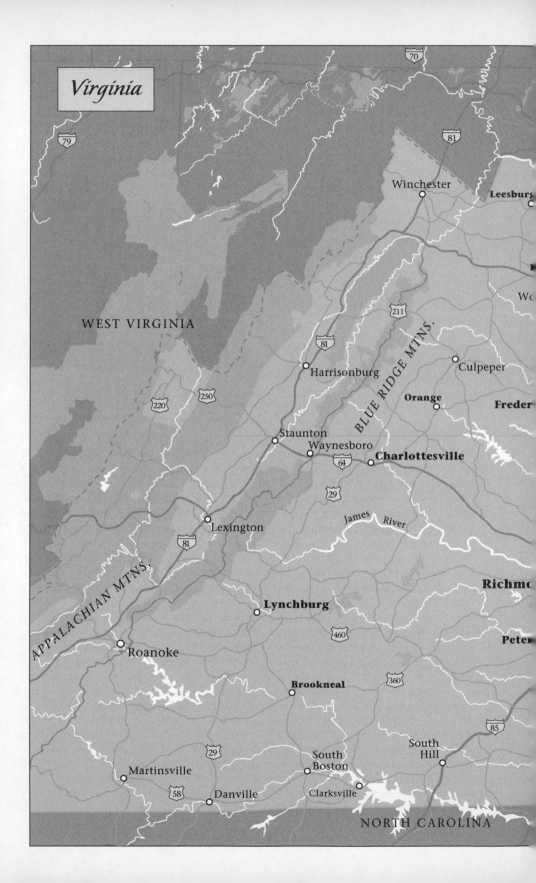

early Virginia unfolds across the state like a red carpet before a dignitary—Jamestown to York-town, Mount Vernon to Monticello, and Colonial Williamsburg to Richmond.

Many things were born in Virginia. Of the state's many nicknames (the name itself is a reference to the "Virgin Queen," England's Elizabeth I), several have a decidedly matriarchal bent. Virginia is proudly called "Mother of Presidents"—it produced four of America's first five presidents and seven of its first 12; "Mother of Statesmen"—Thomas Jefferson framed the Declaration of Independence and James Madison fathered the new country's Constitution and wrote the Bill of Rights; and "Mother of States." The latter moniker is due to the fact that, from the mid-16th century to the late 18th century almost all the English-dominated continent we know today as the U.S.—from Florida to Canada and from the Atlantic to beyond the Mississippi River—was called Virginia. As the first to be settled, Virginia was vast almost beyond measure (in the ensuing centuries, the domain shrunk as portions of land were deeded away or reassigned by the crown to needy proprietors).

The first English "tourists" arrived in 1607, many attracted by the writings of Captain John Smith—America's first "time-share" salesman—who lauded the new land's attributes in pamphlets and broadsides to lure adventurous settlers to the Colony on behalf of the Virginia Company of London. Thanks to the captain's excessively complimentary words (they would also later seduce Pocahontas), Virginia became, in their minds, as much an "ideal" as a place. In short order, land-hungry Englishmen viewed the name "Virginia" as a synonym for paradise.

That was before they arrived. This "virgin" territory, whose lush forests were indeed filled with sufficient game and whose waters held a plenitude of fish, defiantly stood her ground when approached by these arrivals from the sea. She launched a plague of malarial mosquitoes at them, resisted their efforts to cultivate crops, withheld fresh water, and allowed her native people to pelt them with defensive arrows. Once tamed, however, Virginia gave birth to many commonwealths and like any loving parent, offered up parts of her domain to her offspring, retaining only the smallish triangle of land that places it 36th in size among the states today. But although small of stature, Virginia remains today as it was then—a giant in substance. Land under the jurisdiction of the Plymouth Virginia Company eventually yielded states stretching from New York to Maine; its sister, the London Virginia Company, yielded the states from North Carolina to New Jersey. After Virginia became a state, she brought forth Illinois, Indiana, Kentucky, Michigan, Minnesota, Ohio, West Virginia, and Wisconsin from her western lands (such lands were never actually colonies but joined the Union as states in the following years: Illinois (1818), Indiana (1816), Kentucky (1792), Michigan (1837), Minnesota (1858), Ohio (1803), West Virginia (1863), and Wisconsin (1848)—somewhat like grandchildren or descendants that have been dispersed far and wide).

Perseverando—Latin for "By Persevering"—reads the reverse of Virginia's great seal, designed in 1779. Only through strong-headed perseverance were her adopted sons John Smith and John Rolfe, the pair instrumental in settling Jamestown, able to develop a viable economy. By 1624 only 1,218 of the original 8,500 colonists had survived, the rest having been taken by the ravages of starvation, disease, and Native American attacks. Then, in an amazing success story, by 1700 the now thriving Colony numbered 58,000, most of them hardy souls.

An overflow of free-spirited energy made Virginia the "California" of its time. During the long and evolving period—over 200 years—when she was the most populous Colony, then state, she set in motion numerous innovative trends in agriculture, entertainment, architecture, and government. As the wealthiest and most architecturally advanced of the Colonies, her capital boasted the most impressive group of Colonial-Georgian public buildings, and this is still true today. The vast plantations of the James River (Shirley, Berkeley, Evelynton, Sherwood Forest, Westover, Carter's Grove), the Potomac (Mount Vernon and Gunston Hall) and the Piedmont (Monticello and Montpelier) were legendary for their hospitality and for the trendy Continental foods prepared in their kitchens. Recipes considered *nouveau* today—gazpacho, polenta, pasta, crème bruleé, chicken marengo, veal with Madeira sauce—were being served in Virginia dining rooms in the 1700s. The Virginia Reel was one of the oldest dances enjoyed in the New World by the colonists. A look beyond the Chippendale chairs, the silver tea-caddies, and the love of all things reflecting the Georgian English style reveals that "Old Dominion" was a hotbed of reactionary thoughts. Although most loyal to the British crown among the Colonies—another nickname for Virginians was "Cavaliers," the term describing supporters of King Charles I in the English civil war—some of her citizens were becoming vociferous in the growing outcry for revolution. As history later recorded, Patrick Henry was far from the only native fanning the flames of the War for Independence.

✦ STAYING ALIVE

Although Patrick Henry pronounced the phrase "Give me liberty, or give me death" in 1775, relating to the imminent American Revolution, the words could very well have been uttered almost 200 years earlier at Jamestown, the first permanent English settlement. Holding onto this river island on the edge of a 3,000-mi-wide continent cost most of the arrivals their lives. Of the 800 arrivals, more than 600 died from hunger, sickness, and the tomahawk, without winning the liberty they sought in the New World. Yet still they came, boatloads of men— and later, women—in search of land, fortune, or religious freedom. Captain John Smith's writings lured many from their English hearths, but his words were often false. Indeed, some say Smith (or Smyth, as he is listed on the 1607 passenger list) even concocted the story that 12-year old princess Pocahontas saved his life.

Wounded in an explosion, the captain left for England in October 1609, never to return. But while on American shores Smith had saved the fledgling Colony from starvation by enforcing the rule that "he that will not worke, shall not eate." He was sorely missed—the following winter so many settlers died from lack of food that the period became known as "the starveing tyme." Settlers ate anything they could to stay alive. One poor wretch thought his wife looked good enough to eat, and so he did, "for which hee was executed, as hee well deserved; now whether shee was better roasted, boyled or carbonado'd I know not." (Billings, *The Old Dominion*).

Also associated with Pocahontas and this time in Virginia history, John Rolfe arrived at Jamestown after John Smith had left. Rolfe, too, saved the Colony by introducing tobacco seeds from Trinidad, a much more desirable variety than what the Indians grew, which became a profitable item of export. He married Pocahontas, a daughter of Powhatan, chief of the Indian confederation around Jamestown. Their marriage brought a period of peace between the Indians and the colonists. In 1616 Rolfe took his new wife and infant son Thomas to England, but Pocahontas died at Gravesend seven months later. A sad John Rolfe returned to continue efforts to improve the quality and quantity of Virginia tobacco. In 1617 tobacco exports to England totaled 20,000 pounds but 12 years later some 1,500,000 pounds were exported. Rolfe wouldn't live to see it, however, dying sometime in 1622, when 400 colonists—nearly a third of the Colony—were killed in an Indian uprising. But he had given the Colony its economic base, and his son Thomas would survive to become the progenitor of a long line of Virginians, among them Thomas Jefferson. The main problem for colonists until late in the 17th century was staying alive. Indian attacks, dearth of food and supplies, and diseases from the malarial swamps shortened life expectancy in the Colony. The majority of Virginians were small farmers, not plantation owners with indentured servants or slaves to do the back-breaking work. The Colony also suffered from a lack of sufficient financial backing from the Virginia Company of London, a speculative stock company granted the Colony's charter.

✦ GOVERNMENT FOR THE PEOPLE

In 1624 King James I revoked the Virginia Company's charter and made the territory England's first royal Colony. The company had established a parliament for the Colony in 1619, marking the beginning of popular representation in the New World. The House of Burgesses met in Jamestown with 22 burgesses representing 11 plantations. Now the Colony would have a royal governor, councilors, and burgesses who eventually stabilized the Colony by skillful management. All was not smooth, however. The overthrow of the royal government in England, Cromwellian rule, and subsequent restoration of the monarchy had its effects on Virginia. According to tradition, Charles II was touched by the Colony's loyalty during his exile and conferred the nickname "The Old Dominion," which gave Virginia equal rank with his other dominions—England, Scotland, and Ireland. The return of the monarchy brought few benefits to Virginia, however. The Navigation Acts of 1660 restricted commerce to England and resulted in a fall in the price of tobacco, the Colony's great staple. Native American raiding became a problem and, in response, royal governor William Berkeley built forts—and taxed Virginians dearly to pay for them. So much so that in 1676 a group of discontented colonists were led by Nathaniel Bacon, a young planter, to rebel against the government. "Bacon's Rebellion" collapsed when Bacon died of a fever, only to have the crown tighten its hold by sending a succession of firm-handed governors. The capital was moved from Jamestown to Williamsburg in 1699, partly to escape the unhealthy island. Williamsburg already had the College of William and Mary, founded in 1693, the second institution of higher learning in British North America. By 1700, the Virginia population totaled 58,000 of the 250,000 Anglos living in the Colonies.

◆ GOING WEST
In the 17th century Virginia settlement extended only to the head of the Tidewater. The new century saw settlement reach into the Piedmont and west of the Blue Ridge as soil depletion and continued immigration stimulated the need for new land. In the 18th century Virginia grew in wealth and population and many fine estates and mansions were erected. Towns such as Alexandria, Fredericksburg, Richmond, and Petersburg sprang up along major rivers. Although the Blue Ridge Mountains hindered immigration from the east, southward travel from Pennsylvania was easy, and German and Scotch-Irish settlers poured down the Great Wagon Road into the Shenandoah and Roanoke valleys. The Indians were not happy about this development and teamed up with the French, who also claimed the territory, to repulse and terrorize frontier residents. It was at this time, in 1754, that the young George Washington was first sent with a small militia to try capturing Fort Duquesne at the fork of the Ohio River. He did not succeed, and there would be three more years before the French and Indian War would end with the Treaty of Paris. With France ceding to Great Britain all claim to territories east of the Mississippi, it would seem that Virginians could happily begin occupying her western lands. However, hoping to prevent hostilities between Indians and settlers, the British government forbade settlement west of the mountains, unwittingly raising a divisive issue that contributed to the Revolutionary War.

◆ DEATH AND TAXES
Another issue that set Virginians on the road to independence was the 1764 Stamp Act, a levy on printed matter—newspapers, legal documents, and even playing cards—to pay for Britain's engagement in the French and Indian Wars. Virginians in the House of Burgesses maintained that only the elected representatives of the colonists could levy taxes. Patrick Henry sponsored resolutions against the Act that put Virginia in the vanguard of Colonial resistance. Although the Stamp Act was repealed two years later, Parliament imposed other duties against which Virginia also led protests. At Williamsburg's Raleigh Tavern in May 1774, the Burgesses convened as *private* citizens and called upon the other Colonies to send representatives to Philadelphia for the First Continental Congress. Peyton Randolph was elected its president, and others representing Virginia included Patrick Henry, Richard Henry Lee, George Washington, and Benjamin Harrison. The Congress adopted a non-importation policy developed by the Virginia Convention, but this did not cause Parliament to give in. It was on March 23, 1775, at Virginia's second Revolutionary Convention held at St. John's Church in Richmond that Patrick Henry made his plea, "Give me liberty, or give me death!"

Open conflict broke out in Norfolk that September, and on New Year's Day 1776, the British burned the city. At Virginia's last Revolutionary Convention, the members called for independence, and the representatives went to Congress, where Richard Henry Lee moved that "the Colonies

Virginia Timeline

1584 Sir Walter Raleigh founds Roanoke Colony (in what is now North Carolina) and names the new territory Virginia after Queen Elizabeth I, the "Virgin Queen." The Colony soon perishes.

1607 On May 14 Jamestown is established by 104 men; by the end of the year, only 32 are alive.

1614 Rolfe marries Pocahontas, a daughter of Powhatan, chief of the Indian confederation around Jamestown, bringing a period of peace between the Indians and the colonists.

1619 The House of Burgesses, first representative legislative body in the New World, meets in Jamestown with 22 burgesses representing 11 plantations.

1624 King James I revokes the Virginia Company of London's charter and makes Virginia a royal Colony.

1676 A group of discontented colonists led by Nathaniel Bacon, a young planter, rebels against the government (Bacon's Rebellion).

1760 Population of the Colonies reaches 1.5 million; Virginia has 340,000 people.

1775 The Second Virginia Convention meets on March 23, 1775, at St. John's Church in Richmond; Patrick Henry makes his plea, "Give me liberty, or give me death!"

1776 Congress adopts the Declaration of Independence, drafted by Virginia's native son, Thomas Jefferson. The Virginia Declaration of Rights and Virginia's first constitution, drafted by George Mason, also receive Congressional approval.

1781 British General Charles Cornwallis surrenders to American and French forces at Yorktown, Virginia, ending the Revolutionary War.

1788 Virginia becomes the 10th state of the Union by ratifying the Constitution on June 25. James Madison and other Virginians lead in creating the Constitution of the United States to replace the Articles.

1789 Washington, Virginia-born, is elected first U.S. president. He appoints Jefferson the first secretary of state, and Edmund Randolph first attorney general.

1801 Thomas Jefferson is elected third president on the 36th House ballot.

1809 James Madison is elected fourth president; serves two terms with dynamic Dolley by his side. She is the first president's wife to be called "First Lady."

1817 James Monroe is elected fifth president and serves two terms.

---

were, of right ought to be, free and independent states." Congress passed Lee's motion and two days later Thomas Jefferson presented his famous Declaration of Independence.

The state was, for the most part, spared from Revolutionary War battles because the British were battling to her north and south. However, Virginia regiments fought and died in four states and suffered through the winter at Valley Forge. The British didn't attack Virginia until late in 1780, when they twice swept through the Tidewater and struck as far inland as Charlottesville, burning the new capital city of Richmond. In the spring of 1781, Continental troops commanded by the Marquis de Lafayette forced Cornwallis toward the Chesapeake Bay and the British took defensive positions in Yorktown. When a French fleet prevented the British navy from entering the Bay to help Cornwallis, Washington forced him to surrender on October 19, and the Peace of Paris was finally signed in 1783.

◆ VIRGINIA LEADS THE NEW NATION

The agricultural economy of Virginia recovered fast after the war but the nation was in disarray. Virginians led the movement to strengthen the national government, when a plan by James Madison became the Constitution. Madison subsequently drafted the Bill of Rights and included provisions suggested by the Virginia Convention of 1788. George Washington was unanimously elected the country's first president and Thomas Jefferson served as his secretary of state. When Jefferson narrowly defeated John Adams for president, he began a 24-year period in which all the presidents were from Virginia. Washington and Jefferson, along with James Madison and James Monroe, came to be called "the Virginia Dynasty." John Marshall, chief justice of the Supreme Court under Jefferson, served 34 years—longer than any in history, and strengthened the power of the central government. As the first 200 years of Virginia history shows, the Old Dominion was the most populous, the largest, and the wealthiest from 1607 to until the War of 1812.

A REGIONAL GAZETEER

▼▼▼

◆ THE COASTAL PLAIN—NURSERY OF THE NATION

Like a winning poker hand, Virginia has four aces up her regional sleeve. Distinctly different but ever appealing, you can bet that each of the state's four regions has allure for the Early American history buff (note that many of its farthest-flung corners are not covered in this guide since they were so unsettled during the Colonial era). First settled, needless to say, was the flat, sandy land that fronts the Atlantic Ocean and Chesapeake Bay; today, these areas have the most prodigious assemblage of Colonial and Revolutionary-era sites to visit. This cradle area for first settlements and first presidents extends inland about 100 mi from the Chesapeake Bay. The Coastal Plain envelops the Tidewater plus the Eastern Shore that fronts on both the Bay and the Atlantic Ocean. Along the mainland are three peninsulas or "necks" cut out by the long, wide mouths of the region's four tidal rivers—the Potomac, the Rappahannock, the York, and the James. The peninsulas jut into the Chesapeake Bay and are named the Northern Neck, the Middle Peninsula, and simply the Peninsula. Most of the early settlers lived between the Atlantic Ocean and the "fall line," an imaginary demarcation running north to south at points where the tidal rivers are no longer navigable owing to the presence of rapids or waterfalls.

The enormous harbor of Hampton Roads, where the James, Elizabeth, and Nansemond rivers flow together into the Chesapeake Bay, played a crucial role in the discovery and settlement of the nation. Encompassing the cities of **Portsmouth** and Virginia Beach, this area is a huge shipping port. Remarkably, the first permanent English settlement at **Jamestown** and the decisive battle for the nation's independence at **Yorktown** are located on the same peninsula about 20 mi apart. **Colonial Williamsburg**—Virginia's top tourist attraction—is between the two. Northwest in **Charles City County** are the magnificent **James River plantations** (Shirley, Berkeley, Evelynton, Sherwood Forest, Westover, and Carter's Grove), birthplace of two presidents—William Henry Harrison and John Tyler—and home to the original Virginia families—Byrds, Carters, Harrisons, Hills, and Randolphs (all of whom would have easily ranked at the top if *Fortune* magazine had been doing its 500 Wealthiest Americans list back when).

The Northern Neck peninsula between the Potomac and Rappahannock rivers gave birth to three presidents and the famous Lee family. Today it's characterized by small villages and plantation homes such as the Lee family's Stratford Hall and George Washington's Birthplace National Monument, both set near **Montross.** Part of northern Virginia up to the Great Falls of the Potomac is also in the Coastal Plain. George made his adult home at **Mount Vernon,** about 8 mi south of Alexandria; his good friend George Mason lived nearby along the Potomac at **Gunston Hall** in Mason's Neck. Both rich and cultured men ventured to nearby

Alexandria to enjoy its feast of grand houses and cultural delights, still there to ravish the visitor. *Towns listed: Alexandria, Charles City, Fredericksburg, Jamestown, Montross, Mount Vernon, Portsmouth, Surry, Williamsburg, Yorktown.*

✦ THE PIEDMONT PLATEAU—"FOOT OF THE MOUNTAINS"
The Piedmont bears the brilliant stamp of its famous resident Thomas Jefferson, who likened the lush countryside to Eden. His architectural achievements can be seen throughout the region, particularly in **Charlottesville** at his home Monticello and at the University of Virginia. Many other famous Virginians, such as Patrick Henry and Presidents James Madison and James Monroe, lived in this region bounded by the Blue Ridge Mountains to the west and the Tidewater region to the east. The region is home to Red Hill, orator Patrick Henry's final residence and grave, in **Brookneal,** near Lynchburg. The state's capital, **Richmond,** also offers visual evidence that Jefferson was here. He designed the capitol building, and the government was moved here from Williamsburg in 1780, largely through his efforts. Straddling the Tidewater and Piedmont regions of Virginia, Richmond is built on seven hills and was home to Chief Justice John Marshall. The final resting place for two presidents is in the city's Hollywood Cemetery. Patrick Henry delivered his famous speech at St. John's Episcopal Church.

Piedmont is Italian for "foot of the mountains," and it is a region of gently rolling terrain that extends the full length of the state, bordered by Maryland on the north and by North Carolina on the south. This region was originally settled by the Colony's leading families, who acquired the best acreage and immense estates such as Montpelier, near **Orange**; Oatlands, near **Leesburg**; and **Sully,** in Fairfax County. *Towns listed: Brookneal, Charlottesville, Fairfax County, Leesburg, Lynchburg, Orange, Petersburg, Richmond.*

The Tricorne Tour

A DRIVING TOUR FROM JAMESTOWN TO RICHMOND
▼▼

Distance: Approx. 75 mi (one-way; 100 mi if starting in Washington, D.C.)   **Time:** 5–6 days (4–5 nights)
Breaks: Overnight stops in Williamsburg and James City County or Richmond

It began life as an ordinary wide-brimmed hat. When long-barreled rifles were presented, the hat got in the way. An inventive soldier folded one side of the brim toward the crown to avoid the rifle barrel. To make the hat look uniform, three sides were folded. Gadzooks! The "tricorne" or three-cornered hat was born. Fashionable during the 18th century, it eventually yielded to a more protective soldierly headgear. However, at interpretive Colonial American sites, the tricorne is the hat of choice, both among interpreters and patrons of the gift shops.

Virginia also has another sort of "tricorne"—a triangle that includes the top Colonial-era sights in the state: Jamestown, Williamsburg, and Yorktown, enclosed by a region that includes the great James River plantation houses and the state capital, Richmond. Any really good story (and the Historic Triangle is one of the best) should be enjoyed in its proper sequence—from the beginning, through the middle, to the end. This story is no exception and therefore this tour begins on the marsh lowlands along the James, moves inland to a new and vigorous Colonial town, moves on to the fields south of Yorktown and Virginia's greatest plantation houses, and then concludes at the state capital.

Begin your Tricorne Tour by driving southeast 9 mi from Williamsburg on the Colonial Parkway, the scenic 23-mi roadway that connects Jamestown, Williamsburg, and Yorktown. The parkway, mostly fronting the James River, winds through marshy areas, pine trees, and scrub that replaced the original hardwood forests chopped down or shipped back to England by early colonists. Today there are not one but two Jamestowns on the peninsula. Continue straight on the Colonial Parkway to its terminus at **Jamestown, The Original Site,** an ongoing archaeological study of the first permanent English settlement in the New World. Driving onto the island, you'll almost immediately enter the parking lot of the Jamestown Visitor Center to the right, while an island loop drive is to the left. A walking tour south of the center takes you to the site of the original town and fort area. Along with statues of Pocahontas and Capt. John Smith, you can explore a reconstructed First Landing Site, New Towne, and remains of the original 1607 James Fort. Returning to your car, drive the Jamestown Island Loop Drive, which begins at the far end of the parking lot and is marked with significant sites of the early settlers. Reversing your course, exit the Original Site and turn left after the ticket booth to reach the other **Jamestown Settlement.** Most visitors start by viewing *Jamestown: The Beginning,* a 15-minute docudrama film. Outdoors, costumed interpreters demonstrate daily tasks in the Indian village and palisaded James Fort. Walk downhill to the James River pier and board replicas of the *Godspeed, Discovery,* and *Susan Constant,* the pitifully small vessels that delivered the first settlers to Jamestown. Enter James Fort, which surrounds thatched-roof buildings where the settlers lived, prayed, and cooked. Historical interpreters farm, do metalwork and carpentry, fire muskets, and play games with visitors such as quoits and ninepins. Some of the gentlemen settlers preferred gaming to farming, and later found bowling balls to be less than nutritious.

The midpoint of the Colonial era—and your tour—is represented by **Colonial Williamsburg,** Virginia's re-created capital and a living-history museum on a colossal scale. Covering 173 acres, reconstructed and build over a span of forty years, it is a recreation of the city that was the capital of Virginia from 1699 to 1780. Here, where no vehicles are allowed, you're transported back to the 18th century. Tour the Historic Area, which includes exhibition buildings such as the Capitol, the center of Virginia's political power from 1699 to 1781, the reconstructed Governor's Palace, the Courthouse, the DeWitt Wallace Decorative Arts Gallery, and the Abby Aldrich Rockefeller Folk Art Center. Along the way you can pop into the craftsmen's shops to see costumed interpreters making products by Colonial methods, and visit retail shops where you can buy their wares, other Colonial gifts, and maybe a tricorne hat.

At last you're at the beginning—of a new nation. Drive north and east on the Colonial Parkway 12 mi along the York River to **Yorktown** and its Yorktown Victory Center. After parking at the Victory Center, follow the open-air walkway that depicts events leading to the Declaration of Independence as you connect between the ticket/orientation building with its movie *A Time of Revolution* and exhibition galleries. Outdoors, interpreters describe and depict a soldier's daily life in the Continental Army Encampment, firing muskets and a cannon to the delight of young visitors. The Farm of 1781 illustrates how many Americans lived in the decade following the Revolution. The real Yorktown Battlefield is at the easternmost end of the Colonial Parkway. Drive to the visitor center to buy tickets, look at the battlefield from an observation deck, watch a 16-minute film about the siege, and pick up leaflets and tapes for a nine-mile automobile tour. Natural sand dunes and open fields let you see how vulnerable the British were with their backs to the water and, courtesy of the French navy, no ships waiting to rescue them.

Allow two days to see the fabulous 18th-century mansions of Virginia's planters. From Yorktown, follow Route 238 to U.S. 60 and drive west to **Carter's Grove Plantation,** 8 mi distant from Colonial Williamsburg. As you enter the property from the visitor center you'll pass the slave quarters on your left, which reveals much about the lives of African-Virginians who supported the vast acreage. After touring the elegant mansion and gardens, tour Wolstenholme Towne, settled by a group of English "adventurers" who arrived in 1619. Returning to your car, take the country road back to Williamsburg. Heading toward Richmond, take Route 5, a Virginia Byway and one of the loveliest roads in the state. In some places the trees join over the road, creating a cool, shady umbrella, and in others, planted fields make a patchwork quilt for a giant's picnic. On the way to and from **Charles City** along this road are four glorious James River plantations, including the beautifully decorated Georgian Revival manor house at Evelynton Plantation that sits on the original foundation of a mansion burned by Union forces. The next site Berkeley Plantation is where Virginians claim the real first Thanksgiving was celebrated in 1619 and was home to generations of Harrisons. The closest to Richmond, Shirley Plantation is Virginia's oldest and also the oldest continuously owned family business in the United States.

A great way to pace your house tours and experience the early history of the area is to book an overnight in one of the plantation B&Bs in Charles City. After your tour of the great patrician plantation estates of Virginia, continue northwest on Route 5 about 20 mi to check out the state capital, **Richmond.** Give your greetings to the famous life-size statue of George Washington sculpted by the famed Jean-Antoine Houdon, just one of many statues of Virginia presidents found at the Virginia State Capitol, designed by Thomas Jefferson in 1785, located in the center of downtown. Also downtown in a restored 1812 house is the Valentine Museum, which deals with city history. From here you can walk south on 10th Street and then right on Marshall to reach the John Marshall House, home to Jefferson's Supreme Court chief justice. Hop in your car and drive east of downtown to the Church Hill Historic District for a visit to St. John's Episcopal Church, where Patrick Henry delivered his memorable "Give me liberty, or give me death!" speech in 1775. On the west side of town, about 10 minutes from the Virginia Historical Society Museum is the fabulous Georgian-era estate of Wilton, ending your tour with a true Virginia flourish.

George Washington Really Did Sleep Here!

A DRIVING TOUR FROM RICHMOND TO ALEXANDRIA

▼▼

Distance: 133 mi one-way (83 mi if starting in Washington, DC)   **Time:** 3–4 days (2–3 nights)
Breaks: Stay overnight in Fredericksburg and Alexandria

No one is buried in the U.S. Capitol building, but if the nation's first president hadn't had his way, there would have been a tomb designed in the magnificent building as his final resting place. Instead, George Washington chose to sleep eternally at his beloved Mount Vernon estate some 20 mi south of Washington, D.C. This illustrates the essence of the gentle farmer, mapmaker, and reluctant president, father of no children but "father of us all."

Many sites claim that "Washington slept here." Whether many can prove such claims is uncertain—but what is certain is that he did spend major parts of his life at three riverfront homes where he was born, grew up, and lived out his final days. By visiting Pope's Creek Plantation, Ferry Farm, and Mount Vernon, one can trace the life of our remarkable founding father. Today it's necessary to have a car to pursue Washington's life journey—unless you prefer to ride astride a horse as he did. This tour begins at Washington's birthplace, which is on a peninsula called the Northern Neck. Amazingly, there is no public transportation at all to this 90-mi-long, million-acre peninsula bathed on three sides by the Potomac and Rappahannock rivers and the mighty Chesapeake Bay.

Begin this tour from **Richmond,** the capital of Virginia. Perhaps more fittingly, you can alternatively start from **Washington, D.C.,** the nation's capital in the District of Columbia. Here you can, appropriately, visit the Washington Monument, tallest structure in the city, to look out over the beautiful capital city laid out by Pierre L'Enfant, a French engineer who had fought in the Revolutionary War. GW himself chose the diamond-shaped site comprising the thriving tobacco ports of Alexandria and Georgetown plus low-lying swamp and farmland at the confluence of the Anacostia and Potomac rivers. Not coincidentally, it happened to be near his home at Mount Vernon.

Vestiges of our first president can also be seen in Richmond. The Jefferson-designed Virginia State Capitol houses the noted life-size statue by Houdon of the 6′2½″-tall Virginian. Unlike TJ, however, Washington never served as governor of his state. To head to Washington's birthplace, one route from either Washington, D.C. or Richmond is to follow I–95 to Fredericksburg, about 50 mi equidistant from the two capitals. Leave the interstate at Exit 130 East (Route 3) and follow it east 32 mi to the town of Oak Grove, where on Pope's Creek you'll find the George Washington Birthplace National Monument. If you'd like to travel a slower, more picturesque route from Fredericksburg, take Route 218, a Virginia Byway. The two-lane road passes under large weeping willows and hardwood forests with occasional glimpses of the Potomac and nature sanctuaries. If you take this route, you'll pass the birthplace marker of President James Monroe 1.8 mi south of Colonial Beach on Route 205.

A shorter but possibly slower route from Richmond leaves I–95 at Exit 104 (U.S. 301). Travel north 27 mi to Route 3; then turn right and follow it about 15 mi to Washington's birthplace. Along this route, you'll pass the birthplace marker of the third president born on the Northern Neck, President James Madison, ½ mi north of Port Royal on U.S. 301. A second route from D.C. meanders through Maryland. Take I–295 south to the Beltway (I–95) and go east three exits. Take Exit 7 South (Route 5 or Branch Avenue), and join U.S. 301 in Waldorf. This route may be just as fast as I–95, depending on traffic. If you take this route, you will cross the toll bridge over the Potomac River at Dahlgren and immediately encounter Virginia's excellent Potomac Gateway Visitors Center on the right side of the highway. Here you can pick up free maps and brochures for the entire state of Virginia. Drive about 9 mi, turn left on Route 3, and drive about 15 mi to the vicinity of **Montross.**

Although the name of this site operated by the National Park Service may sound like a highway marker, the George Washington Birthplace National Monument is a re-created 18th-century working plantation on 550 beautiful waterfront acres of the original Washington family property. The visitor center and excellent museum containing 16,000 artifacts recovered from the property is set among a glorious upland forest of tall, shady trees. The land fronts the Potomac River—here 5 mi wide, about 80 mi downriver from Mount Vernon. The house where George was born on February 22, 1732, burned in 1779, but you will enjoy touring the reconstructed, furnished Georgian-style Memorial House set upon the original home's foundations. Here also is the Family Burial Ground, containing 32 Washington family graves. While still on the Northern Neck, visit George's former neighbors, the famous Lee family, who lived at magnificent Stratford Hall, about 4 mi east on Route 3. It is the birthplace of Richard Henry Lee and Francis Lightfoot Lee, signers of the Declaration of Independence, and Robert E. Lee, born in 1807.

From ages 6 to 19 George lived on a farm in **Fredericksburg,** on another river, the Rappahannock. To reach Ferry Farm, drive east on Route 3 about 30 mi—about a day's journey in those days. The property will be on your left just before you cross the Rappahannock into historic Fredericksburg. George's second home was so named because a ferry landing was there for crossing the river. The house where Washington slept at Ferry Farm is long gone, but there are exhibits and ongoing excavations at this mainly archaeological site. George Washington started his own surveying business when he was 17 years old and left to live at Mount Vernon, home of his half-brother Lawrence. But he returned to Fredericksburg often to visit his married sister Betty, who lived at beautiful Kenmore plantation—awash in elegant plaster moldings that outdo the ones at Mount Vernon, his mother at the Mary Washington House, and his friend William Fitzhugh at Chatham Manor. He also visited the Rising Sun Tavern, a "watering hole" for patriots such as the Lee brothers, Patrick Henry, and Thomas Jefferson, and patronized the Hugh Mercer Apothecary Shop.

Now you are just an hour's drive from the finale of this tour through the Lifestyles of the Rich and Patrician. But in advance of George's beloved mansion are four sites that are an intrinsic part of this region for you to see: two remarkable 18th-century homes, a church, and a gristmill. Drive north on I–95 from Fredericksburg about 25 mi. Use Exit 161 off I–95 and take U.S. 1 north 1.4 mi. Turn right on Route 242 and drive 3½ mi to the entrance of **Gunston Hall,** the plantation home of Washington's compatriot George Mason, author of the Virginia Declaration of Rights. About 12 mi south of Mount Vernon and also fronting the Potomac, Mason's home on 5,500 acres was built circa 1755. In the formal gardens you'll see the famed boxwood gardens planted by Mason himself. The Georgian-style mansion built of native brick, black walnut, and yellow pine has some of the finest hand-carved ornamented interiors in the country. It is the handiwork of one of the 18th century's foremost architects, William Buckland.

After returning to U.S. 1—a Colonial route known as the King's Highway—drive 1.9 mi north to Lorton, outside Alexandria, to see Pohick Episcopal Church. Named for the nearby creek of the same name, Pohick is a Dogue Indian word for "hickory," a plentiful tree in Virginia. The vestrymen of the parish included George Mason, George William Lord Fairfax, and George Washington, who largely selected the site and plans for the Georgian-style building constructed of locally made bricks. You can actually see the workers' hand prints in some of the bricks. Continue north up U.S. 1 about 3.6 mi and turn left at Route 235 to visit **Woodlawn,** the home built for Washington's step-granddaughter Nellie Parke Custis, who married his favorite nephew, Lawrence Lewis. The riverfront mansion and its formal gardens are on land that was originally part of the Mount Vernon estate. From here you can still see traces of the bowling green that fronted Washington's home. Stay on Route 235 and about ¼ mi after crossing U.S. 1 you'll see George Washington's Gristmill on your left side. After many years of research, George Washington's Gristmill opened in 2002 on the site of his original mill and distillery. Then continue on Route 235 almost 3 mi to Mount Vernon.

Probably the best-known country house in the nation—and certainly one of its most magnificent and stirring homes—**Mount Vernon** has been restored to appear as it did when George Washington lived here in the late 1700s. The 40 acres of grounds contain restored outbuildings, pleasure gardens, two museums, a full-scale farm (George was a full-blown gentleman farmer), palatial Georgian interiors, and the tombs of Washington and his wife Martha. For some, however, the real treasure of the estate is the view from around back: beneath a 90-ft-long portico (Washington's own idea), the home's dramatic riverside porch looks out on a Cinerama vista of the Potomac. After leaving Mount Vernon, turn right out of the parking lot and drive 8 mi up the George Washington Parkway to **Alexandria,** where he spent a lot of time. Tour Old Town Alexandria—with more than 2,000 historic structures, including 18th-century churches, taverns, and redbrick houses. Tour Carlyle House, the home of his friend John Carlyle and the finest home in the city. Pick up maps and brochures in Ramsay House—the current visitor center—where he posted letters. See the pew at Christ Church where the "Father of Our Country" worshiped. Top it all off with a meal featuring "George Washington's Favorite Duck" at Gadsby's Tavern, where the great general once attended birthday celebrations in his honor.

GARDEN WEEK
▼▼▼

Travelers to Virginia will want to note the state's famous Historic Garden Week, now entering its eighth decade as the nation's oldest and largest statewide house and garden tour event. On view during "America's Largest Open House"—typically the last week of April—are more than 250 of Virginia's most beautiful gardens, homes, and historic landmarks. Three dozen Historic Garden Week tours present some of the country's finest properties at the peak of Virginia's springtime color. Sponsored by the **Garden Club of Virginia,** local events are scheduled for gardens located from the Atlantic Ocean to the Allegheny Mountains. You can see gardens of all types—walled, cottage, cutting, annual, perennial, herb, water, and even secret—as well as beautifully renovated historic properties, exceptional artwork, and some of the country's best collections of glass, china, and American, European, and Asian antiques. In many houses you'll see how many interesting family histories are intertwined with Virginia's own early history. Included are Belle Air, Brandon and Westover, historic James River plantations—not normally open to the public—and Tuckahoe Plantation, a boyhood home of Thomas Jefferson. Proceeds from tours benefit the restoration of important historic grounds and gardens throughout the state. | 12 E. Franklin St., Richmond | 804/644–7776 | www.vagardenweek.org.

ALEXANDRIA

▼▼

George Washington's "home" town (Mount Vernon is only 8 mi away), Alexandria once lured Colonial visitors with the same temptations it offers today's travelers—elegant streets of Georgian redbrick houses, candlelit parlors at Lord Fairfax House, tempting victuals at Gadsby's Tavern, and a general civilizing air that Revolutionary generals once cottoned to and D.C. lawyers still do. On the western bank of the Potomac River, just across from Washington, D.C., Alexandria was founded in 1749 by Scottish merchants eager to capitalize on the booming tobacco trade and named in honor of John Alexander, who bought the land of the present-day city from an English sea captain in 1699. The town emerged as one of the most important ports in Colonial America, and its history is linked to significant events and individuals of the Revolutionary period.

For architecture and history buffs, the city offers a host of house museums, some of which are star attractions of the famous historic district Old Town Alexandria. A few streets here are still paved with cobblestones (according to research, the rounded stones served as ballast aboard early sailing ships), while restored 18th- and 19th-century churches, taverns, and houses line the streets; Among the scores of Georgian Colonial and early Federal buildings are a few long, narrow structures called "Flounder Houses" that resemble halves of gabled houses—an unusual architectural style born of the owners' attempts to evade taxation by reporting construction unfinished.

Washington often came to Alexandria. He made maps of the township in 1740s, represented it in the House of Burgesses, and made so many visits from Mount Vernon that in the 1760s he finally decided to build a house on Cameron Street as a pied-à-terre so as to be able to attend the main parties and gatherings he frequented here—a replica has been constructed on the site. History buffs will delight in the main sites, in fact, that were once visited by George Washington, including taverns, gorgeous Christ Church, the educational Alexandria Academy, and the Stabler-Leadbeater Apothecary. There is a month-long celebration honoring Washington's birthday, complete with a reading of his Farewell Address and a Birthnight Banquet and Ball. Outside the city are such important sights as Mount Veron and Gunston Hall. *Contact Alexandria Convention and Visitors Association | 221 King St., Alexandria 22314 | 703/838–4200 or 800/388–9119 | www.funside.com.*

Arlington House. Looking like a grand Greek temple, the centerpiece of Arlington National Cemetery, and envisioned by George Washington's adopted grandson as a virtual "shrine" to the first president, Arlington House (also known as the Custis-Lee Mansion) is now part of the city of Arlington, a few miles from Alexandria. It was the manor house of a 1,100-acre estate where two famous names in Virginia history—Washington and Lee—became intertwined. George Washington Parke Custis—raised by Martha and George Washington, his grandmother and step-grandfather—built Arlington House between 1802 and 1817 on his estate overlooking the Potomac. His daughter, Mary Anna Randolph Custis, inherited the property and married Lieutenant Robert E. Lee. The Custis-Lee family lived at Arlington House until the federal government "stole" the estate during the Civil War. If most of the period furnishings are Antebellum in style, many of the gigantic rooms are adorned with the Washingtoniana—vast portraits, painted battle scenes, Washington's personal papers and clothes, and the command tent the president had used at Yorktown—that Custis acquired through his life. Washington, who loved the virtues of ancient Greece and Rome, would have loved the facade designed by George Hadfield, a young English architect who for a while supervised construction of the Capitol. Next to a flag that flies at half staff whenever there is a funeral in the cemetery is the flat-top grave of Pierre L'Enfant, designer of the Federal City. L'Enfant died in 1825, a penniless, bitter man who felt he hadn't been recognized for his planning genius. | Between Lee and Sherman Drs. | 703/557–0613 | Free | Daily 9:30–4:30.

Carlyle House. Considered the grandest of Alexandria's older homes, this beautiful stone Georgian house in the Palladian style was built in 1753 by Scottish merchant John Carlyle, and modeled after the manor houses of his homeland. Carlyle House interprets the lifestyle of an 18th-century Virginia family, its servants, and slaves. Inside are regal salons, the Large Parlor taking pride of place, with its robin's-egg-blue painted trim, Georgian doorways, and rows of framed pictures. Take one of the tours that run every half-hour and admire the Chippendale furniture and beautiful decorative objects, such as the exquisite Chinese porcelain. Outside is a stunning garden planted in the Colonial style, accented with hedgerows, strawberry, and snapdragon. General Edward Braddock and five Colonial governors met at the house to plot strategy during the French and Indian War. John Carlyle married the very rich Sarah Fairfax of Belvoir Plantation (now Fort Belvoir), the home of William Fairfax, one of the founders of Alexandria, which is one reason the house is as magnificent as it is. | 121 N. Fairfax St. | 703/549–2997 | www.carlylehouse.org | $4 | Tues.–Sat. 10–4:30, Sun. noon–4:30.

Christ Church. The very quintessence of Colonial Good Taste, this imposing architectural statement was composed in redbrick and stone, modeled after the country churches of England, and is enlivened by an elegant Palladian window. It's no surprise to learn that both George Washington and Robert E. Lee belonged to this church, which was completed in 1773 and remains in nearly original condition. Washington was a vestry member and his pew is marked with a plaque. The general attended services here when he made his last visit to Alexandria on November 17, 1799. Note the cut-glass chandelier brought from England at Washington's expense. | 118 N. Washington St. | 703/549–1450 | www.funside.com/attractions | $1 (suggested) | Mon.–Sat. 9–4, Sun. 2–4:30.

Gadsby's Tavern Museum. If *People* magazine were covering the grand parties of the Colonial era, they definitely would have hung out at this Georgian-style tavern, built circa 1770, and Federal-style City Hotel constructed in 1792. The elegant tavern—named for barkeep John Gadsby, who operated the place between 1796 and 1808—was once the gathering place of the age's *crème de la crème*. Power lunches were undoubtedly served in the taproom (back when dinner was a much less important meal). In the evening, dancing assemblies, theatrical and musical performances, and meetings of local organizations filled the establishment—some of those who attended were John Adams, Thomas Jefferson, and the Marquis de Lafayette. George Washington was feted with birthday celebrations in the ballroom in 1798 and 1799, and, happily, patrons today can still take dancing lessons here (George danced with Martha here on his last birthday) or attend the annual Birthnight Ball. All in all, the taproom, dining room, assembly room, ballroom, and communal bedrooms have been convincingly restored to how they probably appeared in the 1770s. Tours of the tavern leave 15 minutes before and after the hour. | 134 N. Royal St. | 703/838–4242 | www.gadsbys.com | $4 | Oct.–Mar., Tues.–Sat. 11–4, Sun. 1–4, last tour at 3:15; Apr.–Sept., Tues.–Sat. 10–5, Sun. 1–5, last tour at 4:15.

George Washington Masonic National Memorial. George Washington became a Mason in 1753 and served as Master of the Alexandria-Washington Lodge No. 22 in 1788–89, while president. Of special historic interest inside this 333-ft-tall landmark dedicated in 1932 is a replica of the Lodge room, which was located in "Old Town Alexandria." It contains the original furniture used by Washington as well as his old leather library chair, which he personally donated to the lodge and was used by the presiding Masters for 118 years. Memorabilia include Washington's bedchamber clock, stopped at 10:20 PM December 14, 1799, the exact minute he died, his Masonic apron, and a silver trowel that he used at the cornerstone ceremony for the United States Capitol in 1793, and also the only portrait of the general said to depict him as he actually looked. Washington is said to have admonished the artist to "Paint me as I am," so the artist included the pock marks resulting from an attack of small pox contracted when he was nineteen years old; there is a small brown mole under his right ear, and a scar along his left cheek. The monument's ninth-floor observation deck gives a spectacular view of Alexandria, with Washington, D.C., in the distance. | 101 Callahan Dr. | 703/683–2007 | www.gwmemorial.org | Free | Daily 9–5.

Lee-Fendall House. George Washington's journal recorded that he "dined at Mr. Fendall's" on November 10, 1785, and again on August 13 and October 25, 1786. Built in 1785 by local civic leader Philip R. Fendall (cousin of "Light Horse Harry" Lee), this clapboard house was the address of several illustrious members of the Lee family; a total of 37 members of the household lived here from 1785 to 1903. The house is furnished with a splendid collection of Lee family heirlooms as well as period pieces produced by local and regional cabinetmakers and silversmiths. | 614 Oronoco St. | 703/548–1789 | www.leefendallhouse.org | $4 | Tues.– Sat. 10–4, Sun. 1–4.

Lloyd House. This late Georgian-style house was built in 1797 by John Wise, who also built Gadsby's Tavern. In the early 1800s, Charles Lee, Attorney General in the Washington and Adams administrations, lived here. It was owned by John Lloyd, whose wife, Anne Harriotte Lee, was a cousin of Robert E. Lee. Restored in 1976, Lloyd House is a branch of the Alexandria Library; the first floor is a museum with 18th- and 19th-century books from the Alexandria Library Company, a subscription library formed in 1794. Furnishings, artifacts, and paintings belonging to former residents of the house and city are also displayed. | 220 N. Washington St. | 703/838–4577 | www.cybvis.com/alex/lloyd.htm | Free | Mon.–Sat. 9–5.

Old Presbyterian Meeting House. Scottish merchants established the meeting house in 1774, a gathering place for patriots during the American Revolution. George Washington's funeral service was held here on December 29, 1799; the Tomb of the Unknown Soldier of the American Revolution lies in a corner of the churchyard, where many prominent Alexandrians also are interred. To visit the sanctuary, obtain a key from the church office on Royal Street. Sanctuary is on S. Fairfax St. | 321 S. Fairfax St. | 703/549–6670 | Free | Sanctuary open weekdays 9–5.

Pohick Episcopal Church. Located outside Alexandria, Pohick was the "New Church" that George Washington often favored for Sunday worship. In its day, it was a shining example of brickmason elegance, and even today it seems eminently more a "Temple of Enlightenment" than a religious meetinghouse, due to its lack of a steeple, its superbly cadenced windows, and severe Georgian presence. Erected in 1774—Washington and George Mason both were long-standing vestrymen at this parish church and oversaw some of its major architectural decisions—it was graced inside with woodwork carved by William Bernard Sears (between his work at Gunston Hall and Mount Vernon)—the two-story pulpit, altarpiece ("done after the Ionic manner"), and other woodcarved details were inspired by the English tastemaker Batty Langham, whose pattern books had much influence on Colonial design. Pohick has pew boxes; the walls around the pews were built fairly high to help keep the worshipers warm, and during the winter worshipers would bring heated bricks into church to put their feet on. Unfortunately, Union troops tore out much of the interior during the Civil War to create a makeshift stable. The stone baptismal font was discovered on a nearby farm and was probably brought from England. Washington's family pew was actually off to the side, "No. 28," near the communion table. On Sunday, the general—who also served as Pohick's "Overseer of the Poor"—would ride to the church, where it was "not the custom for Gentlemen to go into Church until Service is beginning, when they enter in a Body, in the same manner as they come out." Take the Fort Belvoir exit off I–95 to the Telegraph Road exit of the Fairfax County Parkway. | 9301 Richmond Hwy., Lorton | 703/550–9449 | www.pohick.org | Free | Daily 9–4:30.

Ramsay House. Believed to be the oldest house in Alexandria, the Ramsey House was built in 1724 in Dumfries (about 30 mi south of Alexandria) and barged up the river to the new town in 1749. It was home to the city's founder and first postmaster, a Scotsman named William Ramsay. It is thought that both William Ramsay and John Carlyle, whose mansion is five doors from the Ramsay House, situated their homes facing the Potomac River so they could watch their trading vessels sail in and out of the harbor. His wife Anne McCarty Ramsay was praised by Thomas Jefferson for having raised over $75,000 in funds to support the American Revolution. When William Ramsay died in 1785, his close personal friend George Washington walked in his funeral. The gambrel roof design is rarely found today in the Alexandria region, but was typical between 1675 and 1725 in parts of Maryland, Delaware, New England, and the Virginia Tidewater region. Today the house is the headquarters of the Alexandria Convention and Visitors Association, where travel counselors dispense information, brochures, and maps for self-guided walking tours. You can also obtain a free 24-hour parking permit here. | 221 King St. | 800/388–9119 | www.alexandriacity.com/visitorscenter.htm | Free | Daily 9–5.

Stabler-Leadbeater Apothecary Museum. Apothecary memorabilia from the 18th and 19th centuries is displayed, including old account books, medical wares, and one of the finest collections of apothecary jars in the country (some 800 in all). The museum is housed in what is believed to be Alexandria's oldest mercantile establishment, and was once patronized by George Washington, James Monroe, and the Lee family. Early medicines were ground only from natural products—roots, seeds, barks, and minerals. These medicines were then administered in the form of brewed teas, syrups, suspensions, and emulsions, fine powders for pills, or ointments. Over the years the store sold botanicals and drugs, farm and garden equipment, paint and perfume, tobacco and turpentine, tea and thermometers, deodorizers, dyestuffs, and chocolates. Martha Washington's last prescription was presumably filled here. | 105–107 S. Fairfax St. | 703/836–3713 | www.apothecary.org | $2.50 | Mon.–Sat. 10–4, Sun. 1–5.

✦ SIGHTSEEING TOURS/TOUR COMPANIES

Ghost and Graveyard Tours Sponsored by Doorways to Old Virginia. Guides dressed in 18th-century attire lead you on a walk through Old Town, describing the histories of the many 18th- and 19th-century homes that line the cobblestone streets. The tour begins at the Ramsay House Visitor Center. Inquire here also about Alexandria's popular boat tours. | 221 King St. | 703/548–0100 | www.funside.com | $6 | Apr.–Nov., tours Fri. and Sat. at 7:30 and 9, Sun. at 7:30 only.

✦ ON THE CALENDAR: Feb. **George Washington Birthday Celebrations.** Festivities include a George Washington Birthday Parade through Old Town Alexandria, a 10K race and 2K fun run, and the Birthnight Banquet and Ball, a black-tie dinner followed by Colonial dancing at Gadsby's Tavern. A Revolutionary War encampment and reenactment are held at Fort Ward Park | 703/838–4200 or 800/388–9119.

Apr., Sept., Dec. **House Tours.** Privately owned Old Town homes and gardens open their doors to the public. Tickets are available at Ramsay House Visitor Center. | 703/838–4200.

Dec. **Scottish Christmas Walk.** More than 100 Scottish clans in traditional tartans play bagpipes and march through the streets of Old Town Alexandria to celebrate the city's Scottish heritage. Other activities include holiday crafts workshops, children's events, and musical performances. | 703/549–0111.

HISTORIC DINING AND LODGING

Gadsby's Tavern. Want to try "George Washington's Favorite Duck"—half a duck roasted over a peach apricot dressing and served with Madiera sauce? Just head to this famed, circa 1792 tavern, set in the heart of Old Town, for a taste of the decor, cuisine, and entertainment of Colonial days. A strolling balladeer makes the rounds on Tuesday and Wednesday nights. The tavern was a favorite of George Washington and other greats of his time (*see* the entry on Gadsby's Tavern *above*), who came for such delights as Gentlemen's Pye made with veal, Sally Lunn bread, and a rich English trifle. | 138 N. Royal St. | 703/548–1288 | $17–$24 | D, DC, MC, V.

Seaport Inn. This stone building dates from the 1770s, and the first two floors served its owner John Fitzgerald— General Washington's military aide during the Revolutionary War—as warehouse and salesroom. The top floor housed a sail loft, where men busied themselves with needle and cord, sewing and lacing the great pieces of canvas into sails that powered Alexandria's ships. Today the mark of the adze can be seen on the huge beams and the oyster-shell mortar is still readily visible in the George Washington Tavern Room. Old Town's first restaurant offers fireside dining and views of the Potomac River. Shrimp and scallops in wine sauce round out the menu of seafood standards, chicken, and steak. | 6 King St. | $18–$28 | AE, D, DC, MC, V.

Morrison House. The architecture, parquet floors, crystal chandeliers, sconces, and furnishings of the stunning Morrison House, in Old Town, are so faithful to the style of the Federal period (1790–1820) that it's often mistaken for a renovation of a historic building rather than one built in 1985. Guest rooms blend the Federal Period reproductions of four-poster beds and armoires with modern conveniences. An attentive staff makes sure your stay is equally warm. | 116 S. Alfred St. | 800/367–0800 | fax 703/684–6283 | www.morrissonhouse.com | 45 rooms | $150–$295 | AE, DC, MC, V.

BROOKNEAL
▼▼

Near the confluence of the Falling and Staunton rivers in the south-central part of the state, Brookneal is most noted for Red Hill, a frame house where that Colonial-era hero Patrick Henry lived until his death in 1799. The town itself was named after the Brooke and Neal families. The settlement started as a tobacco inspection depot in the 1790s and got its town charter in 1802. The present-day economy is based on a mix of service and manufacturing firms. *Contact Town of Brookneal | 215 Main St., Box 450, Brookneal 24528 | 804/376–3124 | www.brookneal.com.*

Patrick Henry National Memorial (Red Hill). Red Hill was the final home of "the Voice of the Revolution," the famed patriot and firebrand Patrick Henry (1736–99), whose "Give me liberty, or give me death" speech inspired a generation. Throughout his career, Henry proved the word was often mightier than the sword—with glowing Ciceronian eloquence, Henry crafted many of the sound bites that helped inflame the public and launch the Revolution (perhaps not surprisingly, he was trained as a lawyer). "He appeared to speak to me as Homer wrote," Thomas Jefferson noted. Even early in his career, arguing for fair pricing practices in tobacco, he struck the major chords of the revolutionary storm that was to follow by arguing "a king, by disallowing acts of a salutary nature, from being the father of his people, degenerates into a tyrant, and forfeits all right to his subjects' obedience." Elected to the First Continental Congress, he went on to pronounce "I am not a Virginian, but an American." Then on May 29, 1765 (his 29th birthday), he heralded a number of resolutions defining the rights of the Virginia Colony against the loathed Stamp Act. Arguing in the Virginia House of Burgesses, he carried the day and his published speeches and "If this be treason, make the most of it!" stance helped arouse the public. He was among the first to call for a Constitution (but helped delay its passage until a Bill of Rights could accompany it), sent out American troops to colonize Ohio, and foresaw the end of slavery in one sensational speech.

More an executive than a soldier, he retired to his life as a lawyer and landowner after serving as Virginia's first governor after independence. Red Hill's grounds overlook the Staunton River valley and are still landmarked by a 60-ft-tall Osage orange tree. There are seven historic buildings on the site, including the main house, an original law office, and a coachman's cabin and stable. The residence is on the small side. Inside, pride of place goes to one of the greatest history paintings in America, Peter Rothermel's 19th-century take on

Patrick Henry Arguing Before the House of Burgesses. Not far from the boxwood garden is Henry's grave, whose stone eloquently announces "His fame his best epitaph." The estate runs special events throughout the year, capped by a July 4th hosted by Revolutionary War–era reenactors and patriotic fireworks. | 1250 Red Hill Rd. | 804/376–2044 | www.redhill.org | $3 | Apr.–Oct., daily 9–5; Nov.–Mar., daily 9–4.

CHARLES CITY AND THE JAMES RIVER PLANTATIONS

▼▼▼

The Tidewater Plantations of the Old Dominion are among the most fabled sights of Colonial America—Charles City Country is the geographic region that includes these idyllic realms, including such estates as Berkeley, Evelynton, and Shirley (note that these three can be visited on one combination ticket for $28). Back when, Williamsburg—18 mi to the west—may have attracted all by its glittering (candle)lights, but as soon as "Publick Times" halted, their stocks purchased at the blacksmith, and gossip traded at the taverns, the lords and ladies of Colonial Virginia retreated to their very private realms, their plantation homes built in homage to the great houses of England. Here, along four rivers—the James, the York, the Rappahannock, and the Potomac—Virginia's country gentlemen emulated the squirearchy of the mother country in mansions groaning with silver plate, Chippendale sideboards, and carved marble fireplaces. For a trip back into the Lifestyles of the Rich and Revolutionary—1726 version—the James River plantations can't be beat.

Life here in the Colonial era was something out of Henry Fielding's *Tom Jones.* English expatriates—and that's exactly what they were—created a plantation society much like the England of Squire Western and his neighbors. It was a society that valued land above any other wealth. It had an Old Testament faith in the moral superiority of tilling the soil and reaping the harvest. The great plantation of the James River was the world in embryo, sufficient unto itself. Unlike the Puritan town-dwellers who settled most of New England, Virginia's colonists turned naturally to the cultivation of tobacco, wheat, and corn. By the end of the 17th century much of the coastal plain of the Mid-Atlantic—called "the Low Country" in South Carolina and "Tidewater" in Virginia—had been divided into plantations. And thanks to the fact that many rivers and creeks emptied into the sea, these estates could be reached by sailing ships from the British Isles, which brought British manufactured goods and the finest furnishings—Chinese porcelains, Sheraton desks, Oriental carpets, and Palladian wood paneling—of the good life to American soil. Much of this beauty can still be seen in the "great rooms" of the plantation houses.

Colonial Virginia was divided into four political units in 1619, and Charles City County is one of the oldest "incorporated" settlements in America. Its early glory days are best glimpsed along Route 5, a scenic road that follows the nine James River plantations, the oldest dating from 1723. Benjamin Harrison, presidents William Henry Harrison and John Tyler, and the family of Robert E. Lee rank among the county's famous residents. Ironically, there is no city in Charles City County; despite its proximity to Richmond and Williamsburg, Charles City is largely rural, with extensive timberlands and cultivated farmland. *Contact Charles City County Tourism Board | 501 Shirley Plantation Rd., Charles City 23030 | 804/829–5121.*

Berkeley. Virginians say that the first Thanksgiving was celebrated at Berkeley on December 14, 1619, not in Massachusetts in 1621, when early settlers from England came ashore here and broke bread. A hundred years later, in 1726, this grand, brick riverfront Georgian was constructed; it is believed to be the oldest three-story brick house in Virginia that can prove its date—note the initials of the owners, Benjamin Harrison IV and his wife, Anne, that appear in a datestone over the side door—and the first designed with a pediment roof. Harrison IV married Anne Carter, daughter of Robert "King" Carter of Lancaster County, Virginia, one of the Colony's great land barons and owner of Carter's Grove. With white sash windows and glowing red brick (fired in kilns on the plantation grounds), the house itself is stately and Georgian in appearance, framed by elegant white gates and gardens. The Harrisons were to give the nation not only Benjamin Harrison, a signer of the Declaration of Independence (and three-time governor of Virginia), but also his third son, William Henry Harrison, born at Berkeley, the famous Indian fighter known as "Tippecanoe," who later became the ninth president of the United States, in 1841, and also his grandson, Benjamin Harrison, the 23rd president. Note that this is still a family home—only the first floor can be visited.

Inside, the "great rooms" are still adorned with impressive Adamesque woodwork and double arches, constructed by Benjamin Harrison VI in 1790 at the direction of that tastemaker Thomas Jefferson. Great may be pushing it—most of these salons are on the small side, and today are stuffed with a fine array of period furnishings, including old English silver, Heppelwhite chairs, Waterford glass, Chinese porcelain, while a Aubusson rug and Louis XV settee add a French touch to the main hall. To the dining room, replete with a grand view of the James, came the famous and powerful, including George Washington and the succeeding nine presidents of the United States. Later, no doubt, they all walked off their pheasant and port with a stroll through the 10 acres of terraced boxwood gardens, the floral Ladies Garden, and the lawn that extends a quarter-mile from the front door to the river. You will want to do the same after enjoying a meal at the estate's Coach House Tavern restaurant (seating indoors and out). Berkeley Plantation is 18 mi west of Williamsburg and 35 mi east of Richmond on Route 5, the John Tyler Memorial Highway. The Plantation is 3 mi east of the Charles City County Courthouse. | 12602 Harrison Landing Rd. | 804/829–6018 | www.jamesriverplantations.org | $8.50 | Daily 9–5.

Evelynton Plantation. This is Colonial Revival—not Colonial. Originally part of the Wover estate, the 2,500-acre working plantation had been the dowry of William Byrd II's eldest daughter, Evelyn. However, her father refused to allow her to wed her favorite suitor, and she never married. The plantation was purchased in 1846 by the Ruffin family, who had actually settled on the south shore of the James as long ago as the 1650s. Edmund Ruffin was a Secessionist who fired the shot at Fort Sumter that officially began the Civil War, and the family's real glory days came in the 19th century. After many of the estate buildings were destroyed in the Civil War, Evelynton slowly came back to life. In 1937 architect W. Duncan Lee, who had done the restoration of Carters Grove in Williamsburg, designed a "new" Georgian Revival manor house, currently listed on the National Register of Historic Places and filled with authentic period England and American antiques. This is not an overly inspired piece of architecture—perfectly correct, it glows in "Georgian" brick, white trim, and does it best to underwhelm the viewer. However, the landscaped lawns are a favorite place for weddings, and the floral arrangements through the house, using garden blooms, are famous. | 6701 John Tyler Memorial Hwy. | 804/829–5075 | www.jamesriverplantations.org | $9 | Daily 9–5.

Shirley. The oldest plantation in Virginia and also the oldest continuously owned family business in the United States, Shirley was founded six years after the settlers arrived at Jamestown in 1607 and once covered 18,000 acres. It has been occupied by a single family, the Carters, for 10 generations; in fact, the current owners famously still live on the upper floors of the beautiful 1723 Georgian manor (that are not open to the public). The home stands at the end of a drive lined by towering Lombardy poplars, and a stunning 350-year old willow-oak tree shades the magnificent lawn that faces the James River. A number of superb brick outbuildings, also built in 1723, form a unique Queen Anne forecourt. Robert E. Lee's mother, Anne Hill Carter, was born here, and his parents were married in the parlor of the present mansion built by Edward Hill III, a member of the house of Burgesses in the Virginia Colony, for his daughter Elizabeth, who married John Carter, eldest son of King Carter. Robert received part of his schooling in the converted laundry house. This architectural treasure was finished in 1738 and is largely in its original state. The mansion contains a famous carved walnut staircase that rises for three stories without visible means of support and is the only one of its kind in America. Every room is elaborately paneled in local wood from floor to ceiling, each in a different classic design. Some woodwork features the pineapple (the Colonial symbol of hospitality), and a pineapple serves as a 3-ft finial on the peak of the roof. And for good reason—Shirley was a well-known center of hospitality, as the Hills and Carters entertained the Byrds and Harrisons, not to mention Washington, Jefferson, and other prominent Virginians, let alone a horse on occasion. Topping the Sheraton dining room table is Nestor's punch bowl, a heavy silver piece engraved with both the Carter coat of arms and a portrait of Nestor, the famous Carter thoroughbred. Whenever Nestor won his race, the bowl was filled with champagne and served to the stallion in his stable. | 501 Shirley Plantation Rd. | 804/829–5121 | www.jamesriverplantations.org | $9 | Daily 9–5.

Westover. During the Revolutionary War, the Marquis de Castelleux called Westover "the most beautiful house in America"—and you might agree if this house was ever open to the public. It is, but one week a year, during Garden Week in late April. However, the lovely grounds are open to the public daily. This estate was built about 1730 by Col. William Byrd II, an American aristocrat who served in both the upper and lower houses of the Colonial legislature at Williamsburg; he also wrote one of the first travel books about the region. As you approach Westover from the north, you pass through wrought-iron gates constructed by Colonel Byrd, flanked by massive columns supporting beautifully detailed eagles, symbol of the family name. To the south the plantation fronts on the broad James River. The grounds feature rose and other flowering gardens as well as Byrd's grave site. The house remains a renowned example of Georgian architecture. | 7000 Westover Rd. | 804/829–2882 | www.jamesriverplantations.org | $2 | Garden Week.

✦ ON THE CALENDAR: July **Independence Day Celebrations at James River Plantations.** Benjamin Harrison, a signer of the Declaration of Independence, is honored at a wreath-laying ceremony at Berkeley Plantation. An ice-cream social and 19th-century games are held at Sherwood Forest Plantation. | 804/829–5377.

Nov. **First Thanksgiving Festival.** Food, music, and special events commemorate the first official celebration of Thanksgiving in the New World, which occurred at Berkeley Plantation in 1619. There are living-history performances, dances, demonstrations by local Native American tribes, Southern-style food, and arts and crafts. | 804/829–6018.

HISTORIC DINING AND LODGING

Coach House Tavern. This tavern on the Berkley Plantation defines rustic elegance with fresh flowers and double linens. French doors open to a view over the gardens. Oyster stew, crabcakes, homemade breads, and desserts are choice selections on the menu. | 12604 Harrison Landing Rd. | 804/829–6003 | $25–$40 | AE, DC, MC, V | No dinner Sun.–Thurs.

North Bend Plantation. A National Registry property, this bed-and-breakfast on a working plantation is one of the finest examples of Federal-period Greek Revival architecture in Charles City. Original antiques, rare books, and old dolls furnish the building that has a rich history. While much of that dates to the Civil War era, there is a period air that extends further back. Rooms have canopy beds, antique armoires, fireplaces, and chaise longues, plus private baths. | 12200 Weyanoke Rd. (Rte. 5) | 804/829–5176 | fax 804/829–6828 | www.jamesriverplantations.org/NorthBend.html | 4 rooms | $120–$135 | MC, V | Closed Jan.

CHARLOTTESVILLE
▼▼▼

Before there was Charlottesville, there was Thomas Jefferson. He was born nearby in 1743, well before the founding of the city in 1762. At this point, Albemarle County leaders established a new county seat on the Three Notch'd Road, an early Monacan Indian trail used by explorers and traders. Named Charlottesville in honor of Princess Charlotte, who had become the Queen of England that year as wife of George III, the town was laid out on a hilltop overlooking the Rivanna River, a branch of the James. By 1800 the city was a popular business and social community for the 12,585 Albemarle County residents (the county was created in 1744 and named for William Keppel, Second Earl of Albemarle and governor of Virginia at the time). The courthouse, one tavern, and a dozen dwellings of 1797 had become a bustling small town boasting tailors, milliners, a jeweler, a cabinetmaker, a gunsmith, a carriage shop, and a printer.

Owing to the prominence of our third president, Charlottesville, 71 mi northwest of Richmond, is today the heart of what Virginians call Mr. Jefferson's Country. While his influence is inescapable throughout the commonwealth, in Albemarle and Orange counties Jefferson's presence is especially visible. Here are buildings and sites associated with "Tom" and the locales of many crucial events in early American history. Roughly in the center of the state, the rapidly growing city has been an important crossroads since Colonial times; Main Street follows one of the first trails from Tidewater to the West. Charlottesville's leading attraction, of course, is Monticello, Jefferson's glorious mountaintop home. Nearby are the estates of Jefferson's presidential friends James Monroe (Ash Lawn-Highland) and James Madison (Montpelier). The University of Virginia, founded in 1819 and designed by Jefferson, is renowned for its beauty, and remains one of Virginia's top cultural meccas. The Albemarle County Historical Society (434/296–1492) offers Charlottesville walking tours by appointment for groups of 6 or more (between April and October). *Contact Charlottesville/Albemarle Convention and Visitors Bureau | 600 College Dr., Charlottesville 22902 | 434/ 977–1783 or 877/386–1102 | www.charlottesvilletourism.org.*

Albemarle County Court House. Albemarle County's first frame courthouse, constructed between 1763 and 1781, was replaced in 1803 by what now serves as the north wing of the present building. The front of the building was built just before the Civil War. Thomas Jefferson visited the courthouse many times, as did his neighbors and presidential successors James Madison and James Monroe. The only large public building in the village during the early 1800s, the courthouse was used for a range of activities, from meetings of the University of Virginia's Board of Visitors to religious services. | 501 E. Jefferson St. | 804/972–4083 | Free | Weekdays 8:30–4:30.

Ash Lawn-Highland. Two miles from Monticello, modest Ash Lawn-Highland is—like its grand neighbor—marked by the personality of the president who lived in it and who held more major national offices than any other man of his era. This idyllic and fairly small farmhouse retreat was James Monroe's residence from 1799 to 1826, chosen, in part, so that he could be close to his friend Thomas Jefferson. It was built after the vogue for "cabin-castles" then fashionable. It is no longer the simple farmhouse built in 1799 for Monroe, who lived in the L-shape single story at the rear; a later owner added the more prominent two-story section, though the furniture is mostly original. However, the small rooms are crowded with gifts from notable persons and with souvenirs from his time as envoy to France. Such coziness befits the fifth U.S. president, the first to come from the middle class.

Raised by his family of "small planters," Monroe studied at the College of William and Mary in Williamsburg, Virginia, from 1774, subsequently crossed the Delaware with General Washington in December 1776, was wounded at the Battle of Trenton, and survived the next winter at Valley Forge. After the war he returned to Virginia, and there met Governor Thomas Jefferson, who became a mentor. Monroe held many posts in the fledgling republic, including senator; minister to France, Britain, and Spain; governor of Virginia; President James Madison's Secretary of State and Secretary of War during the War of 1812; and president (elected in 1816 and 1820). He helped arrange the Louisiana Purchase in 1803 and acquired Florida from the Spanish in 1819. But he is most famous for his proclamation of the Monroe Doctrine in 1823, which held that the lands of the Western Hemisphere should be free from any European supervision or intervention.

Which makes the interior of the house a bit of a surprise, since it is positively aglitter with sumptuous French and Continental antiques of the 19th century. Well, if Jefferson adored the chic of France, so would Monroe. The drawing room is a virtual museum on the Napoleonic style, graced as it is with Neoclassical chairs, an Empire-style mantel clock, a bust of the emperor (a gift from Napoléon himself), Zuber hand-painted wallpapers, and portraits given by Queen Hortense of Holland. The dining room is also charming. In the study is a Louis XVI desk that mirrors the "Monroe Doctrine Desk" now in the James Monroe Museum in Fredericksburg. The 550-acre property is still a working plantation—vegetable plots sit next to more stylish boxwood gardens, while peacocks roam the grounds with spectacular vistas over the countryside. The outdoor Ash Lawn-Highland Summer Festival, one of the country's top-ranked summer opera companies, draws music lovers June through August. | 1000 James Monroe Pkwy. | 804/293–9539 | www.monticello.avenue. org/ashlawn | $8 | Mar.–Oct. daily 9–6; Nov.–Feb. daily 10–5.

Historic Michie Tavern. Don't be surprised if your waitress here addresses you as "Stranger"—the term was used in the 18th century to refer to travelers, and, as such, has often been in the air hereabouts since Michie Tavern was opened by Scotsman William Michie way back in 1784. Back when, you would come here to dine on chicken potpie in The Ordinary—today the place still serves up Colonial fare "cafeteria-style" to hoards of visitors. But taverns in the 18th century were much more than eating houses—Michie's second-floor Assembly Room once served as a ballroom, school room, place for worship, and extra sleeping accommodations. Today your costumed hostess leads tours through antiques-filled rooms that turn the clock back to Michie's era. Afternoons, April through October, you may be invited to dance the Virginia Reel in the Assembly Room or try your hand with a quill pen. After visiting the original Inn, the tour ends up in the tavern's "dependencies" and the Virginia Wine Museum, now housed in the tavern's old wine cellar. The old gristmill has been converted into a gift shop. Tours are every 10 minutes. | 683 Thomas Jefferson Pkwy. | 804/977–1234 | www.michietavern.com | $8 | Daily 9–5.

Jefferson Vineyards. The winery, which offers free tours and tastings, occupies the same land that Thomas Jefferson gave in 1773 to Italian winemaker Filippo Mazzei to establish a European-style vineyard. Mazzei is said to have found Virginia's soil and climate better than Italy's, and the modern-day operation has consistently produced award-winning wines. | 1399 Thomas Jefferson Pkwy. | 434/977–3042 or 800/272–3042 | www.jeffersonvineyards.com | Free | Daily 11–5.

Monticello. As one of America's greatest presidents and thinkers, Thomas Jefferson helped forge its road to liberty, most famously through his authorship of the Declaration of Independence. But Jefferson was at the forefront of another "revolution"—this one in art and architecture. For as designer of Monticello, his house set on the flank of Carter's Mountain, he all but declared war on the hyper-elegant Georgian style then used by his fellow colonists in building such sumptuous showpieces as the James River plantations in Charles City County. With the construction of his "Little Mountain" (*monticello* in Italian), he returned to the ideals of ancient building. Why shouldn't the architecture of Greece, the world's first democracy, and the Roman Empire, the first super-power, be the most appropriate models for the fledging nation?

Declaring his independence from the foldcrol of the Georgian style (whose very name was a homage to England's King George)—carved and painted plasterwork, florid Corinthian pillars and pilasters, super-ornamental doorways—he cast aside the main mentor of the style, Sir Christopher Wren, architect of London's St. Paul's Cathedral, and daringly pledged allegiance to Palladio, the 16th-century Italian designer who found fame by building little "temple" countryside homes for the Venetian rich. His pattern books reenvisioned ancient structures and influenced all who saw them. Having fallen under the spell of France and Italy, Jefferson decided to create his home using their architectural styles, but imbuing them with a novel Colonial quirkiness. In these respects and in its overall conception, Monticello was a revolutionary structure and typical of no single architectural style—a Neoclassical repudiation of the prevalent English Georgian style and of the "colonial" mentality behind it.

Constructed over a 40-year period, Monticello was fussed and fretted over by its owner (who sometimes went AWOL from his pressing government tasks elsewhere) between 1769 and 1809—he was in his twenties when he inherited the estate, in his sixties when he completed his work there. "Architecture is my delight . . . and pulling up and pulling down one of my favorite amusements." Indeed, Jefferson must have been thinking of his house when he wrote this, for he tore down his original two-story porticoed manse and almost completely rebuilt it. With a Greek temple front—note the sober Doric order of the columns—round Palladian windows, and a "Chinese Chippendale" latticed fretwork to serve as balustrades and window embrasures (the latter, reportedly, because one gentleman had leaned out on his chair through the floor-to-ceiling window and toppled to the lawn), his inspiration was obviously many-sided. Also many-sided was the octagonal form—probably inspired by the gigantic roof of the Pantheon—used to top the west facade and give the house its signature look. This crowning touch can even be viewed on the U.S. nickel coin.

Visitors, however, enter from the east portico—note the compass in the portico ceiling, which shows the directions of the wind (it is connected by cable to the weathervane atop the house). In this hall, which combines stately marble busts with elk and moose antlers brought back from the Lewis and Clark expeditions, you'll find Jefferson's famous cannonball clock, a Rube Goldbergian device that tells hours and days of the week (marked off on the side walls) with weighted balls. The ladder here collapses into poles, the windows slide like a streetcar's. Jefferson's "devices" can be seen in many other rooms. In the library is a "polygraph," a two-pen contraption that allowed him to make a copy of his correspondence as he wrote it, and his tall desk, which allowed him to do office work while standing up (this man could never sit still). In his bedroom is his famous swivel-chair—the arms both hold candles—while elsewhere there is a swivel chaise longue, a multi-sided music stand (three people could accompany Jefferson on his violin), and a magical Wedgewood mantelpiece in the dining room (one side has a tiny dumbwaiter to bring up bottles from the cellar, the other another dumbwaiter to lower the empties). The bedrooms really can't be called bedrooms per se, since Jefferson did his best to save space by having most of them contain alcove-beds built into the wall. His own bed is ingeniously positioned in a wall between his bedroom and study—he could roll out of bed to either look up a copy of Milton or go through his morning ablutions (he always washed his feet first thing with cold water). Having been minister to France for five years, Jefferson wined and dined in the finest houses, and much of the Neoclassical elegance seen at Monticello—the swag-curtains on the windows, the Louis XVI chairs, the pedestaled portrait busts—is influenced by Parisian styles.

Contrary to plantation tradition, his outbuildings are in the rear, not on the side. His gardens have now been restored according to Jefferson's specifications and include many rare varieties of fruits and vegetables. The Thomas Jefferson Center for Historic Plants, located on the grounds, includes gardens, exhibits, and a sales area. April through October, interpreters give tours of Mulberry Row, the plantation "street" where Jefferson's slaves lived and labored, and they can fill you in on the details on TJ's "liaison" with Sally Hemings. In every direction from Monticello, Jefferson left his mark. Not only could he espy the construction work going on at the University of Virginia—his biggest architectural statement— through his telescope, but many of the neighboring "templed hills" bore his mark, as he helped design mansions for his friends, such as John Cocke's Bremo, George Divers' Farmington, John Coles III's Estouteville, and Robert Carter's Redlands. In the end, Jefferson became the *arbiter elegantorum* for the Good Life for many of Virginia's gentry. Fittingly—"All my wishes . . . end at Monticello," he once wrote—he and members of his family are buried in a graveyard on the site. | Rte. 53 | 434/984–9822; 434/984–9800 for recorded info | www. monticello.org | $11 | Mar.–Oct., daily 8–5; Nov.–Feb., daily 9–4:30.

The **Monticello Visitors Center** provides extensive background information on both Thomas Jefferson and the construction of Monticello. Exhibits include a wide assortment of personal memorabilia—from drafting instruments to financial ledgers—as well as artifacts recovered during recent archaeological excavations. A free film that delves into Jefferson's political career is shown every half hour. Tours leave every 15 minutes. | Rte. 20 S | 434/977–1783 | www.monticello.org | Free | Mar.–Oct., daily 9–5:30; Nov.–Feb., daily 9–5.

University of Virginia. Thomas Jefferson founded this great university in 1819, drafted its first curriculum, helped select its first faculty, designed the original buildings, and served as the first rector of its Board of Visitors. He triumphed in all these tasks, especially his artistic vision—a poll of experts at the time of the U.S. bicentennial designated this complex "the proudest achievement of American architecture of the past 200 years." Jefferson first set to work on building plans that would mirror his philosophical vision. He believed the college experience should take place within an "academical village" where shared learning infused daily life, and he developed plans for 10 Pavilions built around a rectangular, terraced green space called The Lawn. These stately faculty homes, each in a different classical style, had living quarters upstairs and classrooms downstairs attached to two rows of student rooms and connected by an inward-facing colonnade. To counteract the law of perspective, Jefferson increased the number of student rooms in the Pavilions and made the wooden railings above the colonnades higher as they progress away from the Rotunda. As a result, the Pavilions appear to be the same size rather than receding into the distance. The most expensive Pavilion to build has Corinthian capitals made from Carrara marble. Jefferson's Italian masons found the local stone unsuitable for this ornate work, so they were carved in Italy. To save the Virginia taxpayer customs duty, Jefferson declared them "educational materials."

Each Pavilion was identified with a subject to be studied and inhabited by the professor who taught that subject. At the head of the shared lawn would stand the library, its dome inspired by Rome's Pantheon. The plans grew to include two more colonnades of student rooms facing outwards and attached to a set of "hotels" where private businessmen served food for the students. Behind are public gardens delineated by serpentine brick walls. Jefferson designed the Pavilion Gardens as both a place of study and a subject of study—residents were to design, plant, and maintain their own gardens. Jefferson corresponded with scholars in America and Europe, seeking the best faculty to teach in the areas of philosophy, arts, foreign languages, science, law, and medicine. Construction and transatlantic travel delayed the date of opening, but in March 1825 the University of Virginia opened to serve its first 123 students. For more than its first year of operation, Thomas Jefferson was a living legacy among university students and faculty. Each Sunday he hosted students for dinner at Monticello. Among those was Edgar Allan Poe, a university student in 1826–27. Poe was among the students, too, who journeyed up the mountain to pay their respects at the funeral of their university's founder, who died on July 4, 1826. It is little wonder that today's students and faculty speak of "Mr. Jefferson" as if he were a living presence. | 804/924–1019 or 804/924–7969 | fax 804/924–3587 | www.virginia.edu | Free | Daily; closed during winter break in Dec.–Jan. and during spring exams (1st 3 wks of May); tours daily at 10, 11, 2, 3, and 4.

Anchoring the north end of The Lawn, the domed **Rotunda** is a half-scale replica of the Pantheon in Rome and the last building Thomas Jefferson designed. While a typical focal point of many universities is a chapel, and one might think Jefferson would have made this highly prominent structure fulfill the same function, the great man designed the Rotunda as the university's library, with rooms for drawing, music, and examinations. The Rotunda's pine doors are "grained" in 19th-century fashion to simulate costlier mahogany or walnut. The ground and main floors contain oval-shaped classrooms, resulting in hourglass shaped hallways. The two double-curved staircases are unique in North America—they have been restored with handcarved black walnut railings (that get "polished" as hands slide along them). Displayed on the main floor is a life-size marble statue of Jefferson (which students saved from a 19th-century fire in the Rotunda by carrying it out on a mattress). The portrait of Jefferson standing in his Monticello study, which hangs over the mantel in the East Oval Room, is one of the few full-length portraits for which he posed. The third-floor dome room originally housed the university library, and two years before he died Jefferson made a list of 6,860 volumes to be acquired for it. The room is now used for lectures, banquets, and chamber music concerts. | Main St. | 804/924–7969 | Free | Daily 9–4:45; tours at 10, 11, 2, 3, and 4.

Maps and other brochures about the university can be picked up at the **Visitors Center,** located about ½ mi from campus. | 2304 Ivy Rd. (at U.S. 250) | 804/924–7166 | www.virginia. edu | Free | Daily.

✦ ON THE CALENDAR: Apr. **Commemoration of Thomas Jefferson's Birth.** A wreath-laying ceremony at Thomas Jefferson's grave at Monticello includes a speech and music by a fife-and-drum corps. | Monticello, Rte. 53 | 804/984–9822.

HISTORIC DINING AND LODGING

Ivy Inn. Regional food is served in four dining rooms warmed by fireplaces in this Federal-style toll house built in 1815. The tent-covered garden patio is open April to October. Locally raised bison and loin of veal from the nearby Summerfield Farms are house specialties. | 2244 Old Ivy Rd. | 434/977–1222 | $17–$27 | AE, MC, V | Closed Sun. No lunch.

Clifton—the Country Inn. This historic 18th-century manor house has a large columned veranda and beautiful views of Monticello (4 mi away). Rooms are luxuriously designed with down comforters, antique beds, and fireplaces. The 40-acre grounds include a croquet court and gazebo. Tea is served at 4. Restaurant, complimentary breakfast. | 1296 Clifton Inn Dr. | 434/971–1800 | fax 434/971–7098 | www.cliftoninn.com | 14 rooms | $150–$265 | MC, V.

1817 Historic Bed and Breakfast. A block from the University of Virginia campus, this Federal-period bed-and-breakfast was constructed by one of Charlottesville's master artisans: James Dinsmore, who also worked on Monticello. Antiques and period reproductions, complemented by lemon and burgundy walls, grace the rooms. Complimentary breakfast. | 1211 W Main St. | 800/730–7443 | www.1817Inn.com | 5 rooms | $89–$259 | AE, D, MC, V.

Inn at Court Square. This Federal-style home, built in 1785, gets top honors as the oldest house in Charlottesville. Opened as an inn in 2000, the building touts modern amenities and improvements, such as whirlpools in all baths, but still casts a period charm with polished antiques and fireplaces in every room. The bed-and-breakfast is surrounded by charming shops and restaurants; the county courthouse is across the street. Complimentary breakfast. | 410 E Jefferson St. | 434/295–2800 | 4 rooms, 1 suite | $149–$259 | AE, D, DC, MC, V.

FAIRFAX COUNTY

▼▼

In 1694, King Charles II of England gave the land that would become Fairfax County to seven English noblemen. In 1741 the land became a county named after Thomas, sixth Lord Fairfax. During the 18th century the dominant industry in the area was tobacco farming, but increasingly depleted lands helped steer the county toward a more industrial base. Today Fairfax County is a suburb of Washington, D.C., and has one of the highest per-capita incomes in the country. In Fairfax, the county seat, the County Courthouse, built in 1800, displays the wills of George and Martha Washington. Elsewhere in the county waiting to be explored are a Colonial-era farm, a historic mill, spectacular waterfalls, and a 1794 mansion. *Contact Fairfax County Convention and Visitors Bureau | 8300 Boone Blvd., Suite 450, Tysons Corner 22182 | 703/790–3329 | www.cvb.co.fairfax.va.us. Fairfax Visitors Center | 10209 Main St., Fairfax 22030 | 703/385–8414 | www.visitfairfax.org.*

Claude Moore Colonial Farm. A family in costume re-creates the activities of a tenant farm in the 1770s—planting, cultivating, and harvesting corn, wheat, and tobacco crops, and tending livestock (old breeds of cows, chickens, and hogs). Special events include seasonal harvest celebrations with flax processing and cheese-making, and 18th-century market fairs. | 6310 Georgetown Pike | 703/442–7557 | www.cvb.co.fairfax.va.us | $2 | Apr.–mid-Dec., Wed.–Sun. 10–4:30.

Fairfax County Court House. This national landmark has been in continuous use ever since it was built in 1800, except for a period during the Civil War when Union troops occupied the town and used the building as a stable. The original wills of George and Martha Washington are kept in the Archives Department on the lower level, along with a Truro Church pew paid for by Washington, some original documents signed by George Mason, and a 1742 original land grant by Lord Fairfax. Genealogists may search for family records with the help of archivist Sandy Rathbun. | 4000 Chain Bridge Rd. | 703/246–4168 | www.fairfax.va.us/courts | Free | Weekdays 8:30–4:30.

Falls Church. The original Episcopal church building, erected in 1733, stood on a road leading to the falls of the Potomac River—hence its name. Still standing in Falls Church, it served as a recruiting station during the Revolution and as a hospital during the Civil War. The current building dates from 1769. | 115 E. Fairfax St. | 703/532–7600 | Free | Weekdays 9–4, weekends 9–1.

Sully Historic Site. This Federal-period home was the home of northern Virginia's first representative to Congress, Richard Bland Lee. He built this country home for his wife Elizabeth Collins Lee in 1794 on land inherited by his father, Henry Lee II (originally a 3,111 acre tract between Cub and Flatlick runs). From Philadelphia, Lee ordered the necessary supplies and forwarded building instructions to his agent in Virginia. Nails, plaster of Paris, linseed oil, window weights and ropes, even two marble hearths were among the cargoes shipped by sloop to the port of Alexandria and transported by wagon the remaining 20 mi to Sully. Because of Lee's responsibilities in the new Federal City of Washington, D.C., he sold Sully in 1811 to a cousin, Francis Lightfoot Lee. Now restored to its original appearance, the home is furnished with Federal-period antiques including the Lees' original mirrors, Chinese export blue-and-white porcelain, a pair of heartback Hepplewhite dining-room chairs, and a sampler stitched by a Lee family child. Sully has formal and kitchen gardens;, plus several outbuildings, including a reproduction slave quarters. | 3601 Sully Rd., at U.S. 28, Chantilly | 703/437–1794 | www.co.fairfax.va.us/parks/sully/ | $5 | Wed.–Mon. 11–4.

HISTORIC LODGING

Bailiwick Inn. Across from the old courthouse, this Federal-style inn was built in 1800. Rooms, named for early American heroes, are luxurious and plush with period furnishings and fireplaces. There is a fine, excellent restaurant, complete with rose-strewn garden. Restaurant, complimentary breakfast. | 4023 Chain Bridge Rd. at Rte. 123 | 800/366–7666 | fax 703/934–2112 | http://bailiwickinn.com/inn/ | 14 rooms | $225–$330 | AE, MC, V.

FREDERICKSBURG

▼▼▼

Established as a frontier port to serve nearby tobacco farmers and iron miners, Fredericksburg took its name from England's crown prince at the time, and the streets still bear names of his family members: George, Caroline, Sophia, Princess Anne, Hanover, William, and Amelia. The city prospered in the decades after independence, benefiting from its location midway along the 100-mi route between Washington and Richmond, and remains a strategic halfway point between Richmond and Washington, D.C., on Interstate 95, near the falls of the Rappahannock River.

Fredericksburg is a popular destination for history buffs. The town's 40-block National Historic District contains more than 350 original 18th- and 19th-century structures, and the city's relationship with the Washington family is deep. George grew up just across the river on Ferry Farm and Washington family buildings open to the public include the house he bought for his mother, Mary; the Rising Sun Tavern; and Kenmore, the magnificent 1752 plantation home of George Washington's sister. In addition, the town is a favorite with antiques collectors, who enjoy cruising the dealers' shops along Caroline Street on land once favored by Indian tribes as fishing and hunting ground. The short drive across the Rappahannock to George Washington's Ferry Farm, Chatham Manor, and Belmont is well worth it to see where our first president grew up, tour the beautiful residences, and enjoy their splendid views of all of Fredericksburg. *Contact Fredericksburg Office of Economic Development and Tourism | 706 Caroline St., Fredericksburg 22401 | 800/678–4748 | www.fredericksburgva.com.*

Chatham Manor. A fine example of Georgian architecture, Chatham Manor was built between 1768 and 1771 by William Fitzhugh, on a site overlooking the Rappahannock River and the northeast side of Fredericksburg. Fitzhugh, a noted plantation owner, frequently hosted such luminaries of his day as George Washington and Thomas Jefferson. During the Civil War, Union forces commandeered the house and converted it into a headquarters and hospital. President Abraham Lincoln conferred with his generals here; Clara Barton (founder of the American Red Cross) and poet Walt Whitman tended the wounded. The home itself is now a museum housing exhibits spanning several centuries. | 120 Chatham La., Chatham Heights | 540/371–0802 | www.nps.gov/frsp | Free | Daily 9–5.

Ferry Farm. George Washington spent his early years from 1738 to 1752 at this now-hallowed farm, just across the Rappahannock River from downtown Fredericksburg. Living here from ages 6 to 19, Washington received his formal education and taught himself surveying. But for the outcries of historians and citizens, a Wal-Mart store would have been built on this site of our first president's boyhood home (happily, the land was saved by the Historic Kenmore Foundation, and the discount store found a location farther out on the same road). Here Washington allegedly chopped down the cherry tree, a legend as untrue as the story that he threw a silver dollar across the Potomac. In truth the tall, blue-eyed athlete threw a rock across the Rappahannock River (the Potomac, indeed, is a mile wide as it flows past Mount Vernon). Besides, there were no silver dollars in those days! The mainly archaeological site, now with exhibits and ongoing excavations, became a major artillery base and river-crossing site for Union forces during the Battle of Fredericksburg. Archaeological exploration has found evidence of early Native American habitation as well as building foundations and family artifacts. | Ferry Farm Rd., East of Rte. 3 | 540/373–3381 | $2 | Mon.–Sat. 10–5, Sun. 12–5.

George Washington Masonic Museum. Our first president was "raised," or became a Master Mason, in Lodge No. 4 AF and AM in 1752. The lodge museum now contains memorabilia and relics relating to his membership, including an original Gilbert Stuart portrait of him. | 803 Princess Anne St. | 540/373–5885 | www.fredericksburgva.com | $2 | Mon.–Sat. 9–4, Sun. 1–4.

Hugh Mercer Apothecary Shop. Offering a close-up view of 18th- and 19th-century medicine, including instruments and procedures, Hugh Mercer Apothecary Shop was established in 1771 by Dr. Mercer, a Scotsman who served as a brigadier general of the Continental Army (he was killed at the Battle of Princeton). Dr. Mercer might have been more careful than other Colonial physicians, but his methods will make you cringe. A costumed guide describes amputations and other operations performed before the advent of anesthetics, and exhibits include the devices used in Colonial dentistry. | 1020 Caroline St. | 540/373–3362 | www.fredericksburgva.com | $4 | Mar.–Nov., daily 9–5; Dec.–Feb., daily 10–4.

James Monroe Museum and Memorial Library. This tiny one-story building—on the site where Monroe, who became the fifth president of the United States, practiced law from 1787 to 1789—contains many of Monroe's possessions, collected and preserved by his family until the present day. They include a mahogany dispatch box used during the negotiation of the Louisiana Purchase and the desk on which Monroe signed the doctrine named for him. | 908 Charles St. | 540/654–1043 | www.jamesmonroemuseum.mwc.edu | $4 | Mar.–Nov., daily 9–5; Dec.–Feb., daily 10–4.

Kenmore. This late 18th-century home belonged to Colonel Fielding Lewis, a patriot, plantation owner, and his wife, Betty Washington, Lewis, sister to George Washington. The mansion was built in 1775 on a 1,300-acre plantation originally surveyed by her brother. During the Revolutionary War, Lewis sacrificed his fortune to operate a gun factory and otherwise supply General Washington's forces. As a result, his debts forced his widow to sell the home following his death. The plaster moldings in Kenmore's ceilings are outstanding, even more ornate than those at Mount Vernon. It is believed that a French artisan called simply "the Stucco Man" worked frequently in both homes; his name is unknown, possibly because he was an indentured servant. The furnishings, which include a large standing clock that belonged to Mary Washington, are original 18th-century Virginia pieces. In the beautiful dining room is a portrait of Betty, who strongly resembles her famous brother. Until 2004 the usual house tour has been shortened to an "architectural tour," because the mansion is undergoing a methodical historic renovation. Some of the beautiful furnishings are on display in the subterranean Crowningshield Museum on the grounds, which includes family portraits and changing exhibits on Fredericksburg life. On Washington Avenue on the estate grounds stands the Mary Washington Grave and Monument, dedicated by President Grover Cleveland in 1894, and placed near "Meditation Rock," a spot on her daughter's property where Mrs. Washington liked to read. Just a minute's stroll away is the Mary Washington House. | 1201 Washington Ave. | 540/373–3381 | www.kenmore.org | $6 | Mar.–Nov., Mon.–Sat. 10–5, Sun. noon–5; Jan.–Feb., Sat. noon–4, weekdays by reservation only.

Mary Ball Washington House. Due to his mother's advanced age and care, George purchased this modest white-painted house for her in 1772. She spent the last 17 years of her life here, tending the charming Old English garden containing her sundial and where her boxwood still flourishes. Inside, displays include Mrs. Washington's "best dressing glass"—a silver-over-tin mirror—and her teapot, as well as period furniture. Tours begin on the back porch with a history of the house. Mrs. Washington's only daughter, Betty, lived just a few blocks away at Kenmore. | 1200 Charles St. | 540/373–1569 | www.apva.org | $4 | Mar.–Nov., daily 9–5; Dec.–Feb., daily 10–4.

Rising Sun Tavern. In 1760 George Washington's brother Charles built as his home what became the Rising Sun Tavern, a watering hole for such patriots as the Lee brothers, Patrick Henry, the five-term governor of Virginia who said "Give me liberty, or give me death," and future presidents Washington and Jefferson. A "wench" in period costume leads a tour without stepping out of character. From her perspective you watch the activity—day and night, upstairs and down—at this busy institution. Of antiquarian note is the tavern's fine collection of eighteenth- and nineteenth-century English and American pewter. In the taproom enjoy a cup of spiced tea. | 1304 Caroline St. | 540/371–1494 | www.fredericksburgva.com | $4 | Mar.–Nov., daily 9–5; Dec.–Feb., daily 10–4.

St. James House. Built in the 1760s, this is a rare example of a typical pre-Revolutionary Fredericksburg house. Called a "gentleman's cottage," it was the residence of James Mercer, Fredericksburg's first judge. The interior is furnished with period antiques. | 1300 Charles St. | 540/373–1569 | $4 | 3rd wk of Apr. (Garden Week) and 1st wk of Oct., daily 9–5.

Visitor Center. Beyond the usual booklets, pamphlets, and maps, this visitor center has passes that enable you to park for a whole day in what are usually two-hour zones, as well as money-saving passes to city attractions ($19.75 for entry to seven sights; $13.75 for four sights). It also offers lodging reservation services. The building itself was constructed in 1824 as a residence and confectionery. Before touring Fredericksburg, you should see the center's free 14-minute film on the area's history. | 706 Caroline St. | 800/678–4748 | www.fredericksburgva.com | Free | Memorial Day–Labor Day, daily 9–7; Labor Day–Memorial Day, daily 9–5.

✦ ON THE CALENDAR: May **Market Square Fair.** An arts-and-crafts fair at 1200 Caroline St. It features demonstrations of 18th- and 19th-century work by artisans in period garb. | 540/373–1776 or 800/678–4748.

HISTORIC DINING AND LODGING

Smythe's Cottage and Tavern. Taking a step into this cozy dining room—once a blacksmith's house—is like taking a step back in time. The decor is Colonial; the lunch and dinner menus, classic Virginia. Lots of windows make this cozy dining room bright and airy by day; candlelight sets the tone by night. | 303 Fauquier St. | 540/373–1645 | $10–$18 | MC, V.

Richard Johnston. This elegant B&B was constructed in the late 1700s and served as the home of Richard Johnston, mayor of Fredericksburg from March 1809 to March 1810. Guest rooms—each with a private bath—are decorated with period antiques, reproduction furniture, quilts, fine linen, and canopy beds. The aroma of freshly baked breads and muffins entices you to breakfast in the large Federal-style dining room set with fine china, silver, and linens. The inn is just across from the visitor center and two blocks from the train station. Complimentary breakfast. No kids under 12. | 711 Caroline St. | 540/899–7606 | www.inns.com | 6 rooms, 2 suites | $115–$135 | AE, MC, V.

GUNSTON HALL
▼▼▼

"That all Men are by Nature equally free and independent, and have certain inherent Rights . . . namely, the Enjoyment of Life and Liberty . . . and obtaining Happiness and Safety." These words flowed from the pen of another important George—George Mason, who wrote the above for the Virginia Declaration of Rights, and, in turn, probably inspired the words used in the Declaration of Independence and the Bill of Rights. A colonel of the Fairfax militia, Mason's Declaration of Rights called for freedom of the press, tolerance of religion, and other fundamental democratic principles. He was a framer of the Constitution but refused to sign the final document because it didn't stop the importation of slaves or adequately restrain the powers of the federal government—and his objections spurred the movement for the inclusion of the Bill of Rights into the Constitution. As it turns out, Mason wrote many responses to crises of the age—such as the Stamp Act and the Townshend Acts—so much so that he could have become a leading statesmen. He opted, instead, to remain a gentleman farmer, and when you see his vast estate you may understand why.

His Potomac plantation set in Mason Neck (12 mi south of Mount Vernon) is replete with grand gardens and a sumptuous brick house, Georgian in style and finished in 1755. Inside, carved woodwork done by William Buckland—one of the foremost architects of the age—in styles from Chinese to Gothic and Palladian has been meticulously restored throughout, with paints made from the original formulas and carefully carved replacements for the intricate mahogany medallions in the moldings. Wing-back armchairs, Turkish carpets, and Chippendale tables are some finishing touches. Just off the parking lot, you'll enter the modern Ann Mason Reception Center, which houses interpretive exhibits, an orientation video, and a high-quality gift shop. Leaving the center for the mansion house, you'll walk down a magnolia allée, a long walkway lined on both sides with the *grandiflora* evergreen trees so typical of Virginia and the South. The formal gardens are famous for their boxwoods—some, now 12 ft high and dating from the 1760s, are thought to be among the oldest in the country and were planted during George Mason's time. Also on the grounds is an active farmyard with livestock and crops resembling those of Mason's time. With vistas of the Potomac visible past the expansive deer park, this is truly one of the great houses of the Tidewater. | 10709 Gunston Rd., Mason Neck | 800/811–6966 | www.gunstonhall.org | $7 | Daily 9:30–5; first tour at 10, last tour at 4:30.

JAMESTOWN
▼▼

Known today as the "Original Site," Jamestown Island, separated from the mainland by a narrow isthmus, was the area of the first permanent English settlement in North America. Colonists sent by the Virginia Company of London arrived on May 14, 1607, on three sailing vessels: the *Susan Constant,* the *Godspeed,* and the *Discovery*; they called the new enterprise "James Towne" after their king. The Colony served as the capital of Virginia until 1699. Now uninhabited, the island is beginning to reveal the buildings and lives of its early colonists through the Jamestown Rediscovery Project, central to Virginia's 400th anniversary commemoration in 2007. So far, remains of the 1607 Fort (long believed lost to the James River) have been found, as have more than 350,000 artifacts that reveal the early life of the settlement—including what people ate and how they prepared food. The ruin of a church tower from the 1640s, brick foundation walls, and other structural relics help give us an idea of what the settlement looked like, together with some artists' renderings. Two miles from the park on the mainland is Jamestown Settlement, a separate museum complex. *Contact National Park Service, Colonial National Historical Park | Box 210, Yorktown 23690 | 757/898–2410 or 757/229–1733 | www.nps.gov/colo.*

Jamestown, the Original Site. This is the site of an ongoing archaeological study of the first permanent English settlement in the New World, dating to 1607. Nothing of Jamestown remains above ground except the Old Church Tower. Since 1934, the National Park Service has conducted archaeological explorations and has now made the outline of the town clear. Cooperative efforts by the park service and the Association for the Preservation of Virginia Antiquities (which owns 22 acres of the island, including the Old Church Tower) have exposed foundations, streets, property ditches, fences, and the James Fort site. Markers, recorded messages, and paintings around the park supplement the tour. The island is part of the Colonial National Historical Park. | Jamestown Island | 757/229–1733 | www.nps.gov/colo | $5 (includes admission to all sites on the island) | Daily 9–5.

At the reconstructed **Glasshouse** on Jamestown Island, artisans demonstrate glassblowing, an unsuccessful business venture of the early colonists. The original ruins of Jamestown's 1608 glass furnace are all that remain of their efforts. | Jamestown Island | 757/229–1733 | Free with entrance to the Original Site | Daily 9–5.

In addition to maps and information about special programs and ranger-led tours, the **Jamestown Visitor Center** on Jamestown Island contains one of the most extensive collections of 17th-century artifacts in the United States. A 15-minute film provides a perspective of the island's history. Audio tapes for self-guided tours can be rented here, and books and other educational materials are sold in the gift shop. | Jamestown Island | 757/229–1733 | Free with entrance to the Original Site | Daily 9–5 (gates close at 4:30).

While no particular spot on Jamestown Island has been identified as the first landing site in 1607, a 103-ft obelisk at **First Landing Site** commemorates its founding. | 757/229–1733 | Free with entrance to the Original Site | Daily 9–5.

Jamestown Island Loop Drive winds through Jamestown Island's woods and marshes for 5 mi and is posted with historically informative signs and interpretive paintings that show what a building might have looked like where only ruins or foundations now stand. | Jamestown Island | 757/229–1733 | Free with entrance to the Original Site | Daily 9–5.

The **Memorial Church,** which dates to 1907, contains the foundations of two earlier, 17th-century churches—a wooden structure built in 1617 that was the first assembly place and a 1640s brick church. | Jamestown Island | 757/229–1733 | Free with entrance to the Original Site | Daily 9–5.

New Towne contains the ruins of an early country house belonging to Henry Hartwell, a founder of the College of William and Mary. Other ruins include Ambler House and a part of the old James City, which dates to the 1620s. Foundations of several statehouses also are visible. A 1-mi self-guided walking tour takes you along the old streets, where markers indicate the sites of former structures. | Jamestown Island | 757/229–1733 | Free with entrance to the Original Site | Daily 9–5.

Old Church Tower is the only structure that remains standing on Jamestown Island, marking the site of the first permanent English settlement in North America (1607). Dating from the 1640s, the tower was part of Jamestown's first brick church, which was used until about 1750 and then fell into ruin. The tower is now part of Memorial Church. | Jamestown Island | 757/229–1733 | Free with entrance to the Original Site | Daily 9–5.

Dale House. This building holds the laboratories and offices of the Jamestown Rediscovery Project, an ongoing archaeological investigation headed by the Association for the Preservation of Virginia Antiquities. A gallery allows you to observe the workings of an archaeological lab and see some of the items unearthed in recent digs. Archaeologists have found pieces of armor like those worn by soldiers in Europe in the late 16th and early 17th centuries, plus animal bones that indicate the early colonists survived on fish and turtles. Coins, tobacco pipes, ceramic fragments, and more are on display. | Jamestown Island | 757/229–1733 | Free with entrance to the Original Site | Daily 9–5.

Jamestown Settlement. Not to be confused with Jamestown Island, Jamestown Settlement is an adjacent living-history museum complex. Built in 1957 to celebrate the 350th anniversary of Jamestown's founding, the museum has several indoor exhibits as well as outdoor areas that provide a glimpse of life during the early 1600s. A 20-minute film and three permanent galleries—the English Gallery, the Powhatan Indian Gallery, and the Jamestown Gallery—focus on the conditions that led to the English colonization of America, the culture of its indigenous Indian tribes, and the development of Jamestown from an outpost into an economically secure entity. At the pier are full-scale reproductions of the ships in which the settlers arrived: *Godspeed, Discovery,* and *Susan Constant.* You can climb aboard the *Susan Constant,* which is manned with sailor interpreters. | Rte. 31 at Colonial Pkwy. | 757/253–4838 | www.historyisfun.org | $10.25 | Daily 9–5.

James Fort is a recreation of the three-cornered fort that was home to the first Jamestown settlers. Within the fort at Jamestown Settlement, colonists (interpreters in costume) cook, make armor, and describe their hard life under thatched roofs and between walls of wattle and daub (stick framework covered with mud plaster). | Rte. 31 at Colonial Pkwy. | 757/253–4838 | www.historyisfun.org | Free with entrance to Jamestown Settlement | Daily 9–5.

At the **Powhatan Indian Village,** the Powhatan Indian tribe once lived between Jamestown and Richmond in Quanset huts. Today, those huts have been reconstructed as the Powhatan Indian Village, part of the Jamestown Settlement. As you walk through this living history village, you'll see people tanning furs, cooking, preserving food, and making tools. | Rte. 31 | 888/593–4682 | www.visitwilliamsburg.com | Free with admission to Jamestown Settlement | Daily 9–5.

Down at the dock on the James River, you'll find the **Replica of the Three Ships,** full-size replicas of the boats that brought the first settlers to the Colonies: the *Susan Constant,* the *Discovery,* and the *Godspeed.* You're welcome aboard the *Susan Constant* (unless it is out at sea, which is rare), where interpreters are on board to share stories about the 104 men and boys who landed here in 1607. Sometimes the other two ships are open to the public, too. | Rte. 31 | 888/593–4682 | www.visitwilliamsburg.com | Free with admission to Jamestown Settlement | Daily 9–5.

◆ **ON THE CALENDAR: May Founders' Weekend.** An encampment, tactical demonstrations, lectures, and a concert of patriotic music commemorate the founding of the Original Site of Jamestown in 1607. | 757/898–3400.

Nov. Foods and Feasts of Colonial Virginia. Learning how Jamestown's colonists and Virginia's Powhatan Indians gathered, preserved, and prepared food on land and at sea is the intent of this event. | Jamestown Settlement | 757/253–4838 or 888/593–4682.

LEESBURG
▼▼

Founded in 1758, Leesburg is one of the oldest towns in northern Virginia, and happily has numerous well-preserved Colonial- and Revolutionary-era buildings. County seat of Loudoun County, the town has a rich history spanning three centuries. Originally a settlement called George Town in honor of the reigning monarch of Great Britain, it was a staging area for the British during the French and Indian War. In fact, Leesburg was renamed to honor the influential Lee family of Virginia. During the War of 1812, Leesburg served as the temporary capital of the United States when the valuable papers of the Federal Archives (including the Declaration of Independence and Constitution) were brought to town for safekeeping. President James Monroe resided just south of town at Oak Hill, where he wrote the Monroe Doctrine in 1823. The town is in the heart of Virginia's "hunt country," at the foothills of the Blue Ridge Mountains. Nearby, two historic and ravishing mansions, Oatlands and Morven Park, are open for tours. *Contact Loudoun Tourism Council | 108D South St. SE, Leesburg 20175 | 800/752–6118 | www.visitloudoun.org.*

Morven Park. At this 1,200-acre estate you'll find the Westmoreland Davis Equestrian Institute, a private riding school, and two museums—the Morven Park Carriage Museum and the Museum of Hounds and Hunting. The 1781 Greek Revival building bears a striking resemblance to the White House (it's been used as a stand-in for films) and has been the home of two governors, Westmoreland Davis and Thomas Swann Jr. (a Maryland governor). The mansion is fully furnished with pieces Mrs. Davis inherited and collected on travels throughout Europe and Asia. The tour takes you through 16 rooms decorated in differing styles. You can also stroll the estate's gardens, which include a boxwood garden and reflecting pool. On the grounds is the Winmill Carriage Museum, with more than 100 historic horse-drawn vehicles, while the Museum of Hounds and Hunting is set in the house's north wing. | Old Waterford Rd. (Rte. 7) | 703/777–2414 | www.morvenpark.com | $6 | Apr.–Nov. and Christmas season, Fri.–Mon. noon–4.

Oatlands. Formerly a 3,400-acre plantation, Oatlands was built in 1803 by a great-grandson of Robert "King" Carter, one of the wealthiest planters in Virginia before the Revolution. In 1903, William Corcoran Eustis bought the property and restored the Greek Revival mansion to its original beauty (some historians believe that Greek Revival can only be dated to the 1820—but Virginia must have simply been ahead of the times!). Pieces from Eustis's collection of French and American art and antiques furnish the rooms, and a 4-acre formal English garden highlights the grounds. Beyond the gardens, a self-guided walking tour allows visitors to explore the plantation, aided by interpretive signs that explain the history and significance of Oatlands dependencies. Most notable of these buildings is the country's second oldest propagation greenhouse. Built in 1810 with bricks fired on the plantation, George Carter's greenhouse housed a variety of exotic fruits and plants. In 2002, the greenhouse was undergoing restoration. | 20850 Oatlands Plantation La. | 703/777–3174 | www.oatlands.org | $8 | Apr.–Dec., Mon.–Sat. 10–4:30, Sun. 1–4:30.

◆ ON THE CALENDAR: Aug. **August Court Days.** More than 200 costumed characters interpret Leesburg's Colonial history with street dramas and demonstrations. A children's fair, music, and crafts are part of the festivities. | Downtown | 703/777–2617.

HISTORIC DINING AND LODGING

Green Tree. Originally an 18th-century wayside inn, this restaurant retains much of its original tone—with some changes for the better. The tap room is no longer open only to men, and women don't have to dine alone upstairs. There's a walk-in fireplace large enough to roast a pig on a spit, and the dining room has long wooden tables, tall wicker chairs, wide-plank flooring, and tin ceilings. The dishes are prepared according to authentic 18th-century recipes—including cabbage pie, green herb soup, and rabbit fricassee, and seasonal drinks are made from original recipes researched in the National Archives. | 15 S. King St. | 703/777–7246 | $24–$40 | AE, D, MC, V.

Colonial. This redbrick inn is in the heart of the downtown historic district. Early American furniture, hardwood floors, and fireplaces give each room a special warmth. In keeping with the name, the restaurant serves early American food in an old-fashioned atmosphere—cherry and apple pies are always in season. Restaurant. Complimentary breakfast. | 19 S. King St. | 703/777–5000 | fax 703/777–7000 | 10 rooms | $78–$120 | AE, D, MC, V.

LYNCHBURG
▼▼

Established in 1786, this city of more than 65,000 takes its name from John Lynch, the owner of the original town site. Tobacco was the economic stimulus of this largely Quaker community. Before the days of canal and railroad, bateaus (flat-bottomed boats) used to carry tobacco down the James River to Richmond, where it was sold—every June, the Bateau Festival celebrates this part of the city's history. Walking tours cover some of Lynchburg's 19th- and early 20th-century residential districts; five of the seven hill neighborhoods are National Register Historic Districts. In the heart of the city is Blackwater Creek Natural Area, which has walking trails. Thomas Jefferson's retreat, Poplar Forest, is minutes south of town. *Contact Lynchburg Visitor Information Center | 216 12th St., Lynchburg 24504 | 804/847–1811 or 800/732–5821 | www.lynchburgchamber.org.*

Point of Honor. This mansion, built on Daniel's Hill (the site of a duel) in 1815, was home to Dr. George Cabell Sr., a prominent Lynchburg physician and friend to Patrick Henry. Once part of a 900-acre estate, the house has matching polygonal bay windows and a commanding view of the James River. The restored interior is furnished with pieces from the 19th-century Federal period. | 112 Cabell St. | 804/847–1459 | www.pointofhonor.org | $5 | Daily 10–4.

Thomas Jefferson's Poplar Forest. Conceived of and built by Thomas Jefferson as his "occasional retreat" for solitude and contemplation, Poplar Forest is considered one of his most creative and original architectural designs, an octagonal house that is both simple and compact. Just as he did with Monticello, his other home 90 mi north in Charlottesville, Jefferson built Poplar Forest after his retirement from the presidency. He began work on the house in 1809, and in 1823, at the age of 80, was still supervising interior work. The 4,800-acre plantation, which came to Jefferson as part of his wife Martha Skelton's inheritance, provided him with substantial cash income from tobacco and wheat. Here, Jefferson utilized many of the architectural ideas he had collected throughout his years of study and his travels abroad. The 16th-century Italian architect, Andrea Palladio, greatly influenced Jefferson's plan for Poplar Forest. He utilized Palladio's rules of design and the idea of blending landscape with architecture. Jefferson also incorporated many French design ideas and conveniences he had observed in Paris, such as floor-to-ceiling windows, alcove beds, a skylight, and an indoor privy. From his earliest use of architectural handbooks, Jefferson became fascinated with octagons. Although he included them in many designs, the house at Poplar Forest is the only octagonal structure Jefferson designed that was actually constructed. Every July 4—not only Independence Day but the anniversary of Jefferson's death in 1826—a free celebration is held here. | 2100 Poplar Forest Dr., Forest | 804/525–1806 | www.poplarforest.org | $7 | Apr.–Nov., daily 10–4.

✦ ON THE CALENDAR: June **James River Batteau Festival.** Crews pole authentic replicas of 18th-century merchant boats down the James River from Lynchburg to Richmond, camping at various points along the route, in this eight-day event. Music, food, and exhibits add to the fun. | James Riverfront | 804/528–3950.

MONTROSS
▼▼▼

This small village on the Northern Neck in eastern Virginia (the region between the Potomac and Rappahannock Rivers) is known principally for the George Washington Birthplace National Monument and the Lee family's ancestral estate, Stratford Hall. Montross is located in historic Westmoreland County, best known for its host of Revolutionary leaders. In 1766 Richard Henry Lee of Stratford Hall wrote the Leedstown Resolutions. Considered the forerunner of the Declaration of Independence, the resolutions were the first organized resistance to British tyranny and were signed by 115 patriots protesting the Stamp Act including six Lees, five Washingtons and Spence Monroe, father of President James Monroe. Ten years later, Lee and his brother, Francis Lightfoot Lee, signed the Declaration of Independence. At that same time another Westmoreland native, George Washington, took command of the Continental Army. George Washington's Birthplace is now a 550-acre national park located on Pope's Creek between Montross and Oak Grove. Westmorelander James Monroe served as the fifth U.S. President from 1817–25. His birthplace can be seen on Route 205 between Oak Grove and Colonial Beach. *Contact Northern Neck Tourism Council | 479 Main St., Warsaw 22472 | 800/393–6180 | www.northernneck.org.*

George Washington Birthplace National Monument. Maintained by the National Park Service, the 550-acre George Washington Birthplace National Monument has been restored to resemble the farm where our first president was born. Set amid upland forest with stands of historic trees and pristine beaches along the 5-mi-wide Potomac River, the site includes the Colonial Living Farm, Memorial House, kitchen, garden, family cemetery, and a combination visitor center and museum. The "monument" part of the site is a 55-ft, ⅒ replica of the Washington Monument in Washington, D.C. The house in which Mary Ball Washington gave birth to our first president in 1732 burned on Christmas Day in 1779, but archaeologists uncovered the ruins of the home yielding 16,000 artifacts, many of which had been intensely heated by the fire. A typical 18th-century Tidewater plantation house called the Memorial House has been reconstructed at the site. The house, resembling George Mason's Gunston Hall, is a good example of Georgian architecture used in such notable homes as Fielding Lewis' Kenmore, Gunston Hall, and the basic design of Mount Vernon prior to George Washington's -Federal-style alterations. The dining room's centerpiece is the Jacobean-style gateleg table made in 1720. The other notable piece of furniture is the Jacobean-style court cupboard made in 1700. The dishes found on both the table and the cupboard are Lambeth Delft manufactured in the middle of the 18th century. Delft ceramics were popular with the American Colonists from the late 1600s until about 1750. The wine bottle on the table was found in an excavation near the original home. It bears the "AW" stamp of Augustine Washington, George's father.

The livestock and gardens at the Colonial Living Farm are tended by methods employed in Colonial days. Historical varieties of crops are planted in an effort to re-create the milieu of George Washington's boyhood. The Family Burial Ground contains the graves of 32 members of the Washington family, including Washington's father, grandfather, and great-grandfather. The Visitor Center screens a 14-minute orientation film and provides a chrono-logical history of the site, beginning with the purchase of the land in 1718 by Augustine Washington. On display are some of the roughly 16,000 artifacts recovered during a 1930s archaeological survey of the property. The park includes natural areas inhabited by bald eagles and whistling swans. Picnic facilities are available year-round. In February, the site hosts a President's Day, complete with Colonial-era music and dancing, plus demonstrations of weav-ing, blacksmithing, and ox-driving; hot cider and gingerbread are served. | 1732 Popes Creek Rd., Oak Grove | 804/224–1732 | www.nps.gov/gewa | $2 | Daily 9–5.

Stratford Hall Plantation. Thomas Lee (1690–1750), grandfather of Robert E. Lee, was a member of the governing Council of the Colony, and acting Governor of Virginia from 1749 to 1750. In 1717, he purchased the land for Stratford Hall Plantation and, during 1730–38, built the brick Georgian "Great House." A successful tobacco planter and land speculator, he owned more than 16,000 acres in Virginia and Maryland. The home overlooking the Potomac River is the birthplace of Richard Henry Lee and Francis Lightfoot Lee, two sign-ers of the Declaration of Independence (the only brothers to do such), and of Confederate General Robert E. Lee. The H-shaped building, constructed with brick and timber produced on the site, is considered one of the finest examples of Colonial-era architecture in the coun-try. Four generations of the Lee family lived here, from the 1730s until 1822; period furnish-ings include some original possessions, such as Robert E. Lee's crib. Outbuildings include an 18th-century kitchen, a coach house, stables, and a school house. In the early 1930s, the Garden Club of Virginia restored the formal East Garden in a typical 18th-century English style; the West Garden is an period flower garden containing old-fashioned daffodils, heritage roses, sweet-faced johnny jumpups, and many other heirloom perennials, annuals, and bulbs. Lunch is served in a log cabin April through October. Stratford Hall is 3 mi northeast of Montross. The estate hosts a grand July 4th celebration every year. | Rte. 214, Stratford | 804/493–8038 | www.stratfordhall.org | $7 | Daily 9–5.

HISTORIC DINING AND LODGING
Inn at Montross. This rustic inn was destroyed by fire in the mid-1700s and rebuilt with the original timbers in 1790. Five guest rooms on the second floor over the pub are furnished with Colonial reproductions and tasteful watercolors. The adjacent John Minors Pub was has original red heart-pine floorboards, which were salvaged, and give the main dining area an old-world rustic charm. For dinner, try the Northern Neck asparagus soup, hickory-smoked Magret, and other specialties. Restaurant. | 21 Polk St. | 804/493–0573 | fax 804/493–9118 | www.theinnatmontross.com | 5 rooms | $95–$115 | AE, MC, V.

MOUNT VERNON
▼▼▼

Contact Alexandria Convention and Visitors Association. | 221 King St. Alexandria 22314 | 703/838–4200 or 800/388–9119 | www.funside.com.

"No estate in United America is more pleasantly situated than this. It lyes in a high, dry and healthy Country . . . on one of the finest Rivers in the world." –George Washington to Arthur Young, British agriculturist, December 12, 1793

Washington may have conjured up these thoughts while sitting beneath the 90-ft portico on the back of his mansion—almost as famous during his lifetime as it is today—gazing down the sloping lawn to his formal gardens and his own "Potomack" glittering beyond. The view, framed by blossoms of wild plum and dogwood in springtime, still inspires visitors and lets them understand that of all his roles—Revolutionary hero, first president, forger of the Constitution—the one Washington preferred was . . . squire of Mount Vernon. He retired here after wining the war, eager to return to private life, only to be drafted as the nation's first president. It is a bit startling to realize that even though Washington chose to lead the fight against the mother country, his Mount Vernon was meant to be a veritable homage to English style: carved marble chimneypieces, raised plaster ceilings, fine china, glittering crystal lamps, bottle-green Windsor chairs, white dimity curtains tassled with green, and an Adamesque large dining room all helped create an ambience almost as fitting to a lord as a gentlemen farmer. The great squires of Tidewater Virginia were as intent on "keeping up with the Joneses" as the flashy moguls of the 1980s, and Washington, some believe, spent almost as much time consulting the pattern books of Batty Langley (the Martha Stewart of his day) as he did governmental reports.

Today the estate that countless visitors see has been restored to its appearance in 1799, the last year of Washington's life. By 9 AM, when the visitors' gate opens, the owner would have been long gone. The industrious farmer awoke at sunrise, read until 7 AM, ate his favorite breakfast of three hoe cakes swimming in butter and honey along with three cups of tea without cream, and rode out to his farms to oversee their operation. Even though Washington—"Straight as an Indian, measuring six feet 2 inches in stockings . . . A pleasing and benevolent tho a commanding countenance, with dark brown hair which he wears in a cue"— won't be there, Mount Vernon's employees will still make you welcome. Back when, the Washingtons' reputation for hospitality was known far and wide, and in 1798 alone no fewer than 656 came for dinner and at least 677 stayed overnight. Washington once described his home as a "well-resorted tavern." Today, of course, more than a million visitors troop through the house every year (small groups are ushered from room to room, each of which is staffed by a guide).

Mount Vernon and the surrounding lands had been in the Washington family for nearly 90 years by the time George inherited it all in 1761. The estate, covering 2,000 acres, was first known as Little Hunting Creek Plantation and originally granted to Washington's great grandfather John Washington in 1674. It passed to Washington's older half-brother, Lawrence, who renamed the property "Mount Vernon" after his commanding officer, Admiral Edward Vernon of the British navy. George inherited the property upon the death of his brother's widow in 1761, when he was 29 and before taking over the command of the Continental Army. Over the course of 45 years he added to the estate until it totaled some 8,000 acres (3,000 of which were under cultivation) and oversaw the transformation of the main house from an ordinary farm dwelling into what was, for the time, a grand mansion. The inheritance of his widowed bride, Martha, is largely what made that transformation possible.

Washington's major additions to the Georgian mansion (the central portion of which dates from 1740) were done in 1759 and 1778; among his architectural achievements is the dramatic portico. The exterior of the house—80% original—is made of yellow pine painted and coated with layers of sand to resemble white-stone blocks. Some historians point to the fact that there were no nearby quarries, so stone would have been prohibitively expensive. The first-floor rooms are quite ornate, especially the formal large dining room, with its molded ceiling decorated with agricultural motifs by the same nameless French "Stucco Man" who embellished his sister's Kenmore mansion ceilings in Fredericksburg. The bright colors of the verdigris-green walls may surprise those who associate the period with pastels.

Each object seems to have a story—throughout the house are smaller symbols of the owner's eminence, such as Washington's hunting horn, a miniature of Martha painted by Charles Wilson Peale at Mount Vernon in 1776, a key to the main portal of the Bastille—presented to Washington by the Marquis de Lafayette—and Washington's presidential chair. The study has his desk, chair, books, letters, surveyor's tripod, clocks, and wearing apparel. Legend has it that the grand mantelpiece in the large dining room was sent from England on a ship that fell into the hands of pirates, but when they noticed the addressee's name, they sent it on its way with thanks. In the music room is the harpsichord he gave to Martha's grand-daughter, Nelly Custis—Washington never played it, but it is known he loved to dance. During the cold winter months more than a dozen fireplaces warmed the house.

Visitors grow silent as they stop before a chamber door where it is explained that Washington died in that room. His bed is 6 ft wide and 6½ ft long. Elsewhere in the room are his dressing table, washstand, and mirror. Washington died on December 14, 1799 (after making the rounds of his plantation in the snow). His final illness was described by his doctors as quinsy; the most recent medical opinion is that he died of a virulent infection, known as "acute epiglottitis," which even today can be fatal without aggressive treatment with antibiotics. For some time, historians pointed to the practice of bleeding, and wondered if Washington was "bled to death." According to medical books of the period, bleeding was the standard treatment for quinsy at that time; while it may have weakened him, however, death was caused by lack of oxygen resulting from the swelling in the throat due to the infection. Tobias Lear, his secretary and assistant for decades, noted "He resigned his breath with the greatest composure, having the full possession of his reason to the last moment." Note the plaster bust—wrinkles and pockmarks included—as sculpted by the great French artist Houdon and today housed in a glass case in the the the George Washington Museum, an adjacent structure built in 1928 to house the growing collection of objects and artifacts related to the lives of General and his wife—the family's china, articles of clothing and jewelry, and pistols and silver spurs worn by Washington during the Revolutionary War, to name just a few items.

Making a wonderful link between interior and exterior—between art and nature—is "the Piazza," the verandah which rises two stories along the east facade of the house. A design of Washington himself and set with Windsor chairs, it was meant to catch the slightest breeze off the Potomac—a sort of 18th-century version of air-conditioning. "Half rustic and half sophisticated," to quote Robert F. Dalzell and Lee Baldwin Dalzell's *George Washington's Mount Vernon: At Home in Revolutionary America* (Oxford University Press, 1998), "making of its something simultaneously simple and grand," it was an appropriate grace note for this most elegant but understated of houses. Outside you can stroll around the estate's 500 acres and three gardens, visiting the workshops, the kitchen, the carriage house, the greenhouse, the slave quarters, and—down the hill toward the boat landing—the tomb of George and Martha Washington, where the man who could have been "king" peacefully sleeps today. Looking like a village in miniature, the estate's dozen outbuildings have been restored; a highlight is the kitchen, complete with iron skillets, washhouse tubs, and stage-prop hams. Here cooks would whip up house specialities, including Martha's "great cake" ("Take 40 eggs . . . work four pounds of butter"). There are three gardens, glowing in season with boxwood-edged flower beds. Among the souvenirs sold at the plantation are stripling boxwoods that began life as clippings from bushes planted in 1798, the year before Washington died.

Emphasizing Washington's role as a farmer, a hands-on, pioneer farmer exhibit has Washington's treading barn as its centerpiece. Before taking command of the Continental Army, Washington spent years farming his "plantation." Initially the plantation (a farm growing primarily one crop) concentrated on tobacco, the most valuable crop for colonists. However it severely depleted the soil—so Washington tested over 60 different crops and many different planting techniques. Modern-day farmers who support methods called "sustainable agriculture" mirror Washington's concern for the long-term productivity of his land. He advocated the production of wheat and other grains and resolved to make America a "granary to the world." Be sure to see his most dramatic invention, America's first 16-sided treading barn for processing wheat and other grains as part of the exhibit "George Washington: Pioneer Farmer." His working gristmill is 3 mi from the mansion. The Potomac River was also "farmed" by Washington. Every spring the catch, mostly shad and herring, was salted and stored in large barrels in the salt house for use on the plantation and for sale. Elsewhere, such "living exhibits" (for instance, the estate beehives) underscore the fact that life here at Mount Vernon remains much the same as it was in the general's day.

But the future has come knocking, and major plans are afoot: beginning in 2004, Mount Vernon will be constructing a new state-of-the art Orientation Center, Education Center and Museum on the grounds, scheduled for completion in 2007. Included in the 50,000-square-ft facility will be 17 galleries and two theaters—rumor had it that Steven Spielberg was going to film a special film presentation for the center, but it seems the Mount Vernon Ladies Association (the very august owners of the estate) decided not to give The George the full Hollywood treatment. Just outside the front gate you will find the museum shop, a food court, and the Mount Vernon Inn, a fine dining restaurant. Ask the museum staff about the Mount Vernon Trail, a nature hike that winds along the river for some 18 mi over Washington's beloved hills and dales. | George Washington Memorial Pkwy. Mount Vernon | 703/780–2000 | www.mountvernon.org | $9 | Mar. and Sept.–Oct., daily 9–5; Apr.–Aug., daily 8–5; Nov.–Feb., daily 9–4.

After many years of research, **George Washington's Gristmill** opened in 2002 on the site of his original mill and distillery. During the guided tours, led by interpreters, you'll meet an 18th-century miller and watch the water-powered wheel grind grain into flour just as it did 200 years ago. The mill is 3 mi from Mount Vernon on Route 235. Tickets can be purchased either at the Gristmill itself or at Mount Vernon's main gate. | Southern end of George Washington Pkwy., Mount Vernon | 703/780–2000 | www.mountvernon.org | $4 | Mar., Sept., and Oct., daily 9–5; Apr.–Aug., daily 8–5; Nov.–Feb., daily 9–4.

Woodlawn Plantation. George Washington gave 2,000 acres, originally part of the Mount Vernon estate (8 mi south of Alexandria), to his wife's granddaughter, Nelly Parke Custis, who married his favorite nephew, Lawrence Lewis. Washington secured the services of Dr. William Thornton, first architect of the U.S. Capitol, to design the house and its formal gardens for the young couple. Finished in 1805, this grand house overlooking the Potomac River interprets the lives of the Lewis family as well as the numerous African-Americans, both free and enslaved, who lived and worked on this Virginia plantation. Like Mount Vernon, the Woodlawn house is made entirely of native materials, including the clay for its bricks and the yellow pine used throughout the interior. In the tradition of Southern riverfront mansions, Woodlawn has a central hallway that provides a cool refuge in summer. At one corner of the passage is a bust of George Washington set on a pedestal so that the crown of the head is at 6 ft, 2 inches—Washington's actual height. The music room has a ceiling that's 2 ft higher than any other in the house, built that way to improve the acoustics for the harp and harpsichord recitals that the Lewises and their children enjoyed. Tours are given of the 19th-century period rooms. | 9000 Richmond Hwy., Mount Vernon | 703/780–4000 | www.nthp. org/national_trust_sites/woodlawn.html | $6 | Mar.–Dec., daily 10–5.

✦ ON THE CALENDAR: Sept. **Crafts Fair at Mount Vernon.** More than 75 artisans demonstrate their craft and hock handmade wares at this juried, 18th-century-style crafts festival at Mount Vernon. Colonial music, entertainment, and food also draw crowds. | 703/780–2000.

Nov.–Dec. **Mount Vernon by Candlelight.** Learn about George Washington's Christmas traditions and take a candlelight tour of his Mount Vernon estate that includes the rarely seen third floor. On the grounds there's a bonfire and caroling with free cookies and hot cider served. | 703/780–2000.

HISTORIC DINING

Mount Vernon Inn. The hearty American Colonial-style food of this restaurant just outside George Washington's estate is served by waiters in character and period dress. One room has a wall of windows—so when it's cold, sit by one of the three crackling fireplaces. | 703/780–0011 | $12–$24 | AE, D, MC, V | No dinner Sun.

ORANGE

▼▼

Formed in 1734 and named in honor of William IV, Prince of Orange, the town of Orange became Orange County's judicial seat in 1749, when Culpeper County was created from it. The town was incorporated in 1872, and many history buffs venture here to visit nearby Montpelier, the lifelong home of James Madison and his wife, Dolley. The town of Orange is historically significant—the courthouse and St. Thomas' Episcopal Church, Robert E. Lee's place of worship during the winter of 1863–64, are listed on the National Register of Historic Places. The present courthouse was constructed in 1858. Although fire destroyed much of the town in 1908, many buildings from the 1800s still remain. *Contact Orange County Visitors Bureau | Box 133, 122 E. Main St., Orange 22960 | 540/672–1653 | www.visitocva.com.*

Barboursville Vineyards. The historic ruins of one of the largest and finest residences in the region are located on Barboursville's 830 acres of lovely rolling hills. Preserved as a ruin after its destruction by fire on Christmas Day 1884, the elegant mansion for which the vineyard was named was the only building in Orange County known to have been designed by Thomas Jefferson. The mansion was constructed between 1814 and 1822 for Jefferson's friend James Barbour, governor of Virginia (1812–14), U.S. senator, secretary of war, and ambassador to Great Britain. The remains—four massive columns, brick walls, and the foundation—are pictured on the label of Barboursville wine bottles and are the stage for the yearly Shakespeare in the Ruins theater. The vineyards are owned by the wine-growing Zonin family of Italy, and the award-winning wines produced by vintner Luca Paschina are in Italian and French styles. They are located 20 mi northeast of Charlottesville at the intersection of Routes 33 and 20 —from Route 29, turn east on Route 33 east and drive 6 mi; turn right on Route 20 south for 200 yards, take the first left on Route 678 and proceed ½ mi; turn right on Route 777 (Vineyard Road), then right at the first driveway and follow the signs. | Rte. 777, Box 136 Barboursville | 540/832–3824 | www.vawine.com | Free; Tasting fees $3 | Tastings Mon.–Sat. 10–5, Sun. 11–5; tours weekends noon–4.

James Madison Museum. James Madison's Campeachy chair, an 18th-century piece made for him by his friend Thomas Jefferson, is featured in this museum, which celebrates the fourth U.S. president. Other artifacts include furnishings from his nearby home, Montpelier; presidential correspondence; and china and glassware recovered from the White House before the British torched it during the War of 1812. Another permanent exhibit details the history of Orange. The museum also houses Orange County historical exhibits, a Hall of Agriculture composed of early farm equipment and machinery, and a restored 1730s house. | 129 Caroline St. | 540/672–1776 | www.jamesmadisonmuseum.org | $4 | Mar.–Nov., weekdays 9–4, Sat. 10–4, Sun. 1–4; Dec.–Feb., weekdays 9–4.

Montpelier. The history of the mansion that today is known as Montpelier began when Ambrose Madison purchased 4,675 acres of land on the Virginia frontier in 1723 to start a tobacco plantation in an area that would later be known as Orange County. Ambrose, his wife Frances, and their children moved to their new plantation (which they called Mount Pleasant) in 1732. Frances ran the plantation until her eldest son, James Madison, was old enough to take over. James was an excellent farmer and businessman, and the plantation turned a good profit. In 1749 James married Nelly Conway, who in 1751 gave birth to James Madison, Jr., the future president. Around 1755 the Madisons began construction on Montpelier, which was completed about five years later and was the second largest brick dwelling in Orange County. When James, Jr., returned from Philadelphia with his new bride Dolley, he found the house to be too small to share with his parents, so a 30-ft, four-room addition was created; two wings on either side of the house were added in 1809. After her husband's death in 1836, Dolley ran the plantation until 1844 when she sold it because she was no longer able to do so. Today, the estate includes 2,700 acres, more than 130 buildings, extensive gardens and forests, and a steeplechase course. The visitor center has an exhibit and video detailing the life and times of James and Dolley Madison. From here, you're given headphones for an audio tour, which provides descriptions of historical and natural features. The main-house exhibit does not attempt to re-create Madison's home but uses the mostly empty rooms as evocative spaces to weave a story of plantation life. The landscape walking tour includes a stop at the family cemetery where Madison and his wife are buried. | 11407 Constitution Hwy. | 540/672–2728 | www.montpelier.org | $7.50 | Apr.–Nov., daily 10–4; Dec.–Mar., daily 11–3.

St. Thomas's Episcopal Church. This 1833 church is believed to be the lone surviving example of Jeffersonian church architecture. It was modeled after Charlottesville's demolished Christ Church, which Thomas Jefferson—famed creator of Monticello and the University of Virginia—designed. During the Civil War, the building served as a hospital following four different battles; Robert E. Lee worshiped here during the winter of 1863–64. | 119 Caroline St. | 540/672–3761 | Donations suggested | Daily, 9–1.

HISTORIC DINING AND LODGING

Holladay House. This restored 1830s, Federal-style home is now a bed-and-breakfast furnished with Victorian and Colonial antiques, rocking chairs in all rooms, and fireplaces in two of the guest rooms. The inn includes a parlor and veranda and is surrounded by flower and herb gardens. Complimentary breakfast. | 155 W. Main St. | 800/358–4422 | fax 540/672–3028 | www.vawinetoursbandb.com | 8 rooms | $95–$205 | AE, D, MC, V.

Inn at Meander Plantation. Today a beloved landmark, this beautiful 1776 historic country inn was the first plantation patented in Madison County. Its owner, Colonel Joshua Fry, was the partner of Peter Jefferson (father of Thomas Jefferson), who surveyed and drew the first official map of the State of Virginia. Originally named Elim, the manor was enlarged in 1766 by Joshua's son, Henry Fry. His lifelong friend, Thomas Jefferson, visited here often, as did General Lafayette. The property has been a working plantation throughout its history, and it is operated as a horse farm in addition to an inn. The gracious dining room serves up meals Thursday to Saturday, while a French basket takeaway is available other days. | HCR 5 Box 460, James Madison Hwy. 15 Locust Dale | 540/672–4912 | fax 540/672–0405 | www.meander.net | 7 rooms | $120–$195 | AE, D, MC, V.

PETERSBURG

▼▼

Twenty miles south of Richmond, Petersburg flanks the Appomattox River. It began in 1645 as Fort Henry, a frontier fort and trading center. The city was important during the Revolutionary War. The Virginia militia put up a heroic fight at Petersburg in late April 1781. Outnumbered by the British army of 2,500 to the militia strength of barely more than 1,000 men, the Virginians denied the King's soldiers the opportunity of capturing the city without fighting for it. The battle actually bought a full day's time for Lafayette to entrench his army on the heights of Richmond, and ultimately prevented a second "sacking" of Richmond—as was seen in the previous January, when British Brigadier Benedict Arnold assaulted and burned much of that city. By the early 19th century, Petersburg outshone Richmond both economically and culturally. *Contact Petersburg Visitor Center | Box 2107, 425 Cockade Alley, Petersburg 23804 | 800/368–3595 | www.petersburg-va.org.*

✦ ON THE CALENDAR: Apr. **Battle of Petersburg Reenactment.** Each year since 1992, the City of Petersburg has hosted a Revolutionary War encampment and commemorative reenactment of the battle fought here on April 25, 1781. Normally hosted on the third weekend of April, this event draws many authentically re-created American, British, German, French, Native American, and Spanish units that document their lineage to actual service in the American Revolution. The Battle of Petersburg reenactment is held at the historic Battersea Plantation (a grand house closed for some years due to renovations) on the west end of Washington Street, about 2 mi from Exit 52 off I–95. There are 35 acres for encampment and tactical demonstrations on the actual site that Lord Charles Cornwallis's troops occupied in May 1781. There's free admission and ample free parking. | Battersea La. and Upper Appomattox St. | 804/733–2400 or 800/368–3595 | www.petersburg-va.org.

PORTSMOUTH
▼▼

The area now known as Portsmouth was first explored by Capt. John Smith, one of the famous "first citizens" of Jamestown, in 1608. This water-locked point of flat land near the mouth of Hampton Roads harbor, surrounded by the James and Elizabeth rivers, was recognized as suitable shipbuilding location by John Wood, a shipbuilder who petitioned King James for a land grant in 1620. The site was established as the Town of Portsmouth in 1752. Gosport Shipyard, "The Most Considerable in America," was established in 1767 by Andrew Sprowle. However, a dozen years later, the British fleet torched the shipyard and 137 vessels and captured Fort Nelson. In 1781 Benedict Arnold—the infamous traitor—with 2,500 British troops occupied and fortified Portsmouth in 1781, and later the Army of Lord Cornwallis evacuated Portsmouth for Yorktown, where he surrendered. Today Portsmouth is home to the Norfolk Naval Shipyard, now the world's largest ship repair yard. The Olde Towne Historic District, a restored 18th-century neighborhood, is said to have the largest collection of historically important homes of any place between Alexandria and Charleston, South Carolina. *Contact Portsmouth Convention and Visitors Bureau | 505 Crawford St., Suite 2, Portsmouth 23704 | 800/ 767–8782 | www.ci.portsmouth.va.us.*

Olde Towne Historic District. The handsome 18th- and 19th-century buildings here are in diverse architectural styles—Colonial, Federal, Greek Revival, Georgian, and Victorian. Imported English street lanterns stand before structures of historic or architectural significance. Bordered by Crawford, Effingham, and South streets and Crawford Parkway. | 757/ 393–5327 or 800/767–8782.

Trinity Church. Portsmouth's first Episcopal church dates to 1762. During the Civil War, it was a Union field hospital for wounded black soldiers. | 500 Court St. | 757/393–0431 | Free | Weekdays by appointment.

♦ SIGHTSEEING TOURS
Olde Towne Historic District Trolley Tours. You can view the district's many historically notable homes aboard vintage mass transit—trolleys operated by Tidewater Regional Transit. They depart from the Visitor Center, where you can also inquire about the Olde Towne Lantern Tours. | Crawford St. | 757/393–5327 or 800/767–8782 | $3.50 | May–Sept., daily 10:45, noon, 1:15, 2:30.

HISTORIC DINING AND LODGING
Smithfield Inn. George Washington slept here—truly. Set 25 mi northwest of Portsmouth in Smithfield, a town with its own notable Revolutionary history, this house, built in 1752 by Henry Woodley, served as an inn when the main stage-coach route passed through from Norfolk to Richmond. In 1756, it was sold to William Rand. In in 1759, he applied for a license to operate an inn and tavern. Thus began some 240 years of innkeeping for travelers coming by ship and later by stagecoach and steamboat, then motor cars. Adjacent to the formal dining room, the English-style William Rand Tavern is a perfect meeting spot for drinks or dessert. Restaurant. Complimentary breakfast. | 112 Main St. | 757/357–1752 | fax 757/ 365–4425 | www.smithfieldinn.com | 5 suites, 4 rooms | $70–$125 | AE, D, DC, MC, V.

RICHMOND

▼▼

Purchased by Capt. John Smith in 1609 from Chief Powhatan, father of Pocahontas, the land was advantageous for its location at the fall line—the farthest point inland accessible to water transport—of the James River. Only with the construction of Fort Charles in 1644 did the settlement begin attracting residents and soon grew into a popular trading post for furs, hides and tobacco. Built on seven hills straddling the Tidewater and Piedmont regions of Virginia, the town was founded in 1737 by Colonel William Byrd II. He inherited the lands on both sides of the James River from his father and became known as the "Father of Richmond." He named it after the English borough Richmond-upon-Thames. The state capital was temporarily moved here from Williamsburg at the request of the General Assembly, which wanted a central location that was less exposed to British incursions. In May of 1782, eight months after the British surrendered at Yorktown, Richmond was incorporated as a city and officially became Virginia's new capital, largely through the efforts of Thomas Jefferson. Despite the plethora of Revolutionary history in and around Richmond, the city is most known as the capital of the Confederacy. *Contact Metropolitan Richmond Convention and Visitors Bureau | 550 E. Marshall St., Richmond 23219 | 804/782–2777 or 800/370–9004 | www.richmond.org.*

Canal Walk. George Washington proposed the James River–Kanawha Canal as a way of bringing ships around the falls of the James River. Dating from 1785, it was the country's first canal system. The 1¼-mi Canal Walk meanders through downtown Richmond along the Haxall Canal, the James River, and the Kanawha Canal, and can be enjoyed on foot or in boats. Along the way, look for history exhibits, such as the Flood Wall Gallery and bronze medallions placed on Brown's Island and Canal Walk by the Richmond Historical Riverfront Foundation. | 12th and Byrd Sts. | 804/358–5511 | Free | Daily 9–5.

Richmond Canal Cruises (139 Virginia St. | 804/649–2800) operates a 35-minute ride on the canal in a 38-seat open boat. Tours, which cost $5, depart from the Turning Basin near 14th and Virginia streets. If you're in a car, try to find the site before parking. Lack of prominent signage makes it challenging to find, and parking lots are a few blocks away.

Edgar Allan Poe Museum. Reputedly the oldest residential dwelling in Richmond, this modest house is now surrounded by the Shockoe Valley commercial district. Dendrochronoly (tree ring dating) suggests that the house was built in 1754. The house features a hall and parlor plan with unevenly spaced openings and dormered gable roofs. The small stone house is now a part of the Edgar Allen Poe Museum complex, which contains a collection of items relating to the life and work of this famous American poet and storywriter who grew up in Richmond. The Raven Room has James Carling illustrations inspired by the writer's most famous poem. | 1914 E. Main St. | 804/648–5523 | $6 | www.poemuseum.org | Tues.–Sat. 10–5, Sun.–Mon. 11–5.

John Marshall House. John Marshall built his home in Richmond in 1790, 11 years prior to becoming the third Chief Justice of the U.S. Supreme Court—and also serving as secretary of state and ambassador to France. He lived here from 1791 until his death in 1835. The home is one of the last remaining structures of the neighborhood that existed in what is now downtown Richmond. Fully restored, this house in Court End combines the Federal style with Neoclassical motifs: it has wood paneling and wainscoting, and narrow arched passageways. Inside the house is the largest collection of Marshall family furnishings and memorabilia in America. The garden features plants popular in the 18th and early 19th centuries. | 818 E. Marshall St. | 804/648–7998 | $3 | Apr.–Sept., Tues.–Sat. 10–5; Oct.–Dec., Tues.–Sat. 10–4:30.

St. John's Episcopal Church. Virginia's second revolutionary convention met here in 1775, and it was in this church that Patrick Henry made his celebrated "Give me liberty or give me death!" speech. Richmond's oldest place of worship, its original frame building was erected in 1741. Edgar Allan Poe's mother and many famous early Virginians are buried in its cemetery. You can hear a reenactment of Henry's speech every summer on Sundays at 2 PM. | 2401 E. Broad St. | 804/648–5015 | $3 | Mon.–Sat. 10–4, Sun. 1–4.

State Capitol. Thomas Jefferson designed this State Capitol in 1785, modeling it on a Roman temple: the Maison Carrée, in Nîmes, France. The central portion was completed in 1792; the wings were added in 1906. The Virginia General Assembly, the oldest legislative body in the Western Hemisphere, still meets here. A wealth of sculpture is contained within: busts of Virginia's eight presidents and a famous life-size statue of George Washington by Jean-Antoine Houdon, the only work for which Washington posed. Guided tours operate continuously throughout the day and delve into the building's history and architectural highlights. | 804/698–1788 | www.legis.state.va.us/vaonline | Free | Apr.–Nov., daily 9–5; Dec.–Mar., Mon.–Sat. 9–5, Sun. 1–5.

Tuckahoe Plantation. Built in 1712 by Thomas Randolph, this boyhood home of Thomas Jefferson stands as the most complete 18th-century plantation layout, including kitchen, overseer's office, stables, smokehouse, three servants' quarters, and the schoolhouse where Thomas Jefferson studied. He lived here as a child when his father took over the Plantations' management from his cousin. Its wonderful Palladian elements were prototypes for American design. Built on a bluff overlooking the James River valley, the plantation and its collection of historic buildings are in a setting that remains remarkably untouched by the passage of time. The mansions "H" shape plan is unique among frame buildings. | 12601 River Rd. | 804/784–5736 | By appointment.

Valentine Museum. The museum documents the life and history of Richmond with changing exhibits that cover everything from architecture to relationships between the races. The museum's collection includes costumes, decorative arts, textiles, and paintings, in addition to more than 500,000 photographs of the city. The core of the holdings is from Edward Valentine, a former owner of the Wickham House mansion. The museum admission includes a tour of the restored 1812 Wickham House, a Neoclassical mansion designed by architect Alexander Parris, the creater of Boston's Faneuil Hall. | 1015 E. Clay St. | 804/649–0711 | www. valentinemuseum.com | $5 | Mon.–Sat. 10–5, Sun. noon–5.

Wilton. William Randolph III built this elegant Georgian house in 1753 on the only James River plantation in Richmond. Once 14 mi downriver and the centerpiece of a 2,000–acre tobacco plantation, the home was moved brick-by-brick to its present site when industry encroached upon its former location. The redbrick house, with its low-pitched hip roof of Buckingham slate and four great chimneys, has identical facades on both its land and its river sides. The most extraordinary feature of Wilton is the floor to ceiling heart-of-pine paneling in every room—including the closets, and the pastel-painted panels and sunlit alcoves are part of its beauty. Its effect is especially breathtaking in the parlor, which has the most elaborate Georgian design, a culmination of that great period of English woodwork begun by Sir Christopher Wren a century before. | 215 S. Wilton Rd. | 804/282–5936 | $5 | Mar.–Jan., Tues.–Sat. 10–4:30. Last tour at 3:45.

✦ SIGHTSEEING TOURS

Paddle wheeler Annabel Lee. The narrated tours include a day-long plantation cruise 25 mi down the James River, where you can disembark and tour Berkeley and Evelynton plantations and the Westover gardens. There are also lunch, brunch, and dinner cruises, with live music, dancing, and a southern buffet. | Intermediate Terminal, 3011 Dock St. | 804/644–5700 or 800/752–7093 | fax 804/644–5760 | www.annabellee.com | $20–$46 | Mar.–Dec., daily Tues.–Sun.; plantation cruise Apr.–Oct., Tues.

HISTORIC LODGING

Linden Row Inn. This downtown inn, built in 1833, is a four-story building with balconies. The main building is conjoined Greek Revival town houses—the carriage-house garden quarters are decorated in Old English style while the main house is furnished in antiques and period reproductions. Edgar Allan Poe played in the garden, which local legends say was the "enchanted garden" Poe mentions in his poem, "To Helen." Complimentary breakfast. | 100 E. Franklin St. | 804/783–7000 | fax 804/648–7504 | www.lindenrowinn.com | 70 rooms | $99–$179 | AE, D, DC, MC, V.

SURRY

▼▼▼

On the south bank of the James River in southeastern Virginia, Surry is home to one of the country's oldest working farms, which is the centerpiece of Chippokes Plantation State Park. The park has a farm museum, tours of an antebellum mansion, swimming, hiking, and fishing. Surry, founded in 1652, was named after the English county of Surrey. The area was one of Virginia's eight original shires, designated in 1634. *Contact Surry County Visitors Center | Courthouse Green, Box 444, Surry 23883 | 757/294–0066.*

Chippokes Farm and Forestry Museum. A working farm since the 1600s, the 1,683-acre Chippokes Plantation State Park on the south shore of the James River is home to the Chippokes Farm and Forestry Museum, an antebellum plantation house, and interpretive hiking trails. Life on an early 19th-century farm in rural Virginia is portrayed via exhibits, on display in a series of farm buildings. Chippokes, one of the oldest continually farmed plantations in the country, is endowed with thousands of artifacts—many have been generously donated so that the story of Virginia's agriculture and forestry communities may be told. | 695 Chippokes Park Rd. | 757/294–3439 | www.dcr.state.va.us/parks/chipffmu.htm | Mansion $3, museum $2; parking $2 weekends, $1 weekdays | Apr.–May and Sept.–Oct., Sat. 10–4, Sun. 1–4; June–Aug., Wed.–Sun. 10–6.

Smith's Fort Plantation. Directly across the James River from Jamestown on Gray's Creek is this site where in 1609 Captain John Smith—who was worried that an Indian attack or Spanish invasion might threaten the safety of the settlement—had his men build a second fort to serve as a strategic retreat position. Later, Powhatan gifted some of the land to his son-in-law John Rolfe when he married the chief's daughter, Pocahontas. Smith's Fort Plantation was built on this property between 1751 and 1765. The 1½-story redbrick house is laid in Flemish bond–brickwork patterns was the abode of one Jacob Faulcon and family. A gabled roof accented with dormer windows shields the interior—which is significant because much of the original woodwork still exists. The restored house has a fine collection of English and American furnishings. The Blue Room holds a special charm, with its chimney piece, fluted pilasters, cornice, arched cupboards with butterfly shelves, and paneling. The site of the retreat fort, the house, a gift shop, and a small herb garden are open to visitors. Take the Jamestown Ferry to Surry. The site is 2 mi from the ferry landing on the right side of John Rolfe Highway (Rte. 31). | 217 Smith Fort La. (Rte. 31, Box 240) | 757/294–3872 | www.apva. org/apva/smithfort.html | $6 | Apr.–Oct., Tues.–Sat. 10–4, Sun. noon–4; Mar. and Nov., weekends noon–4.

HISTORIC DINING

Surrey House Restaurant. AmericanThe food here is about as "down-home Virginia" as it "gits." Dig in to hams (smoked down the street), crab cakes, peanut soup, apple fritters, and peanut raisin pies. | 11865 Rolfe Hwy. | 757/294–3389 | $9–$17 | AE, MC, V.

WILLIAMSBURG

▼▼▼

Today the Disneyland of Colonial America, the restored township of Colonial Williamsburg, the former Virginia capital, gives you the chance to walk into another century and see how earlier Americans lived. Studded with glorious examples of 18th-century architecture, restored through Rockefeller millions, Williamsburg is a must-see—the rich detail of the recreation and the sheer size of the city could hold your attention for days. Of course, you may be amused to see "Patrick Henry" cocking his tricorn over his eye and straightening out his blue velvet coat only to bump into a lady in sunglasses and Spandex—but welcome to the wonder of traveling through Colonial Virginia in 2003. Here you'll be able to watch the wheelwright at work in the Carriage House; keep an eye and an ear out for the current "inhabitants," who will be only too glad to chat with you about the town. Their speech as well as their dress may belong to the 18th century, and you may find yourself conversing about "Mr. Franklin's experiment."

On the peninsula between the York and James rivers in eastern Virginia, Williamsburg was first established as Middle Plantation in 1633. After the capitol building in Jamestown burned in 1698, the capital of the Colony was moved here, and Middle Plantation was renamed Williamsburg in honor of King William III. Jamestown had been a rather shiftless, scraggly little town in a bug-infested malarial swamp, so when its House of Burgesses burned down for the third time, everyone decided to move the capital to Williamsburg, which wound up serving as Virginia's cultural and political center until 1780, when the capital was moved yet again to Richmond to escape the invading British. Its political role diminished, Williamsburg faded in significance and fell into general decay in the 19th century.

Revival came at the hands of the local rector, W. A. R. Goodwin, who convinced John D. Rockefeller, Jr., to bequeath part of the family fortune to fund a restoration project. Work began in 1926, and by the 1930s restored buildings were being opened to the public. In 40 years, Rockefeller spent more than $80 million on the project. Roughly 600 post-Colonial structures were demolished, more than 80 period buildings were restored, and 40 replicas were reconstructed over excavated foundations. The historic district is approximately a mile long and ½ mi wide and is surrounded by a greenbelt to preserve the illusion of a Colonial city. Bordering the historic district is the leafy campus of the College of William and Mary. Outside the restored area is a modern city with plenty of dining and lodging options and attractions such as outlet shops and a large water park. *Contact Williamsburg Area Convention and Visitors Bureau | 201 Penniman Rd., Box 3585, Williamsburg 23187 | 757/253–0192 or 800/368–6511 | www.visitwilliamsburg.com | Daily 8:30–5. Colonial Williamburg Foundation | Box 1776, Williamsburg 23187 | 757/220–7645 or 800/447–8679 | www.colonialwilliamsburg. org | Weekdays 9–5.*

College of William and Mary. The second-oldest college in the United States after Harvard University, William and Mary was chartered in 1693 by the reigning king and queen of England, William III and Mary II. It severed formal ties with Britain in 1776 and became state-supported in 1906. Today it has an enrollment of about 7,500 students and is regarded as a "public Ivy" for its high academic standards. Among its distinguished alumni are Thomas Jefferson, James Monroe, John Marshall, and John Tyler. | Richmond Rd. and Jamestown Rd. at Duke of Gloucester St. | 757/221–4000 | www.wm.edu.

The college's original structure, the **Wren Building,** dates from 1695; its design is attributed to the celebrated London architect Sir Christopher Wren. The redbrick outer walls are original, but fire gutted the interior several times, and the present quarters are largely 20th-century reconstructions. It is the oldest academic building in use in America; there are faculty offices on the third floor and classrooms throughout. Undergraduates lead tours of the building, including the chapel where Peyton Randolph, prominent Colonist and revolutionary

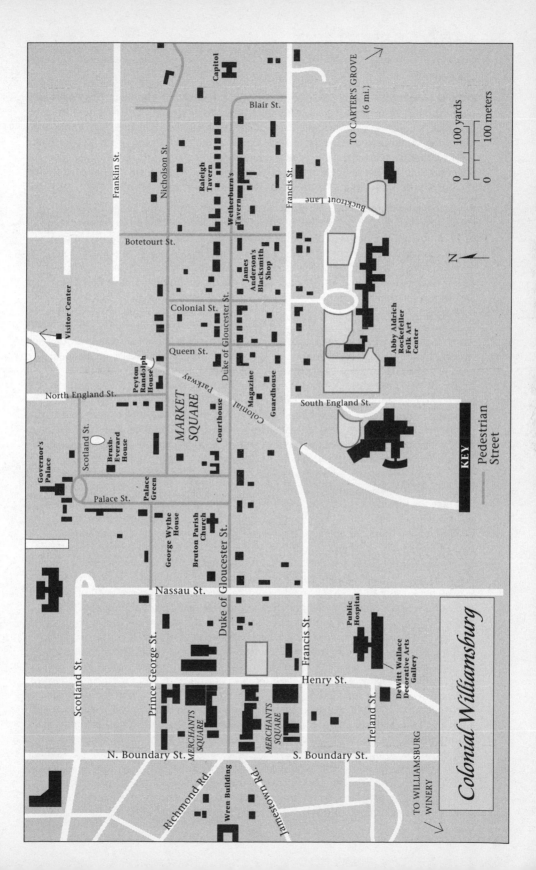

Colonial Williamsburg

KEY

Pedestrian
Street

N

0   100 yards
0   100 meters

TO CARTER'S GROVE
(6 mi.)

Capitol

Blair St.

Raleigh
Tavern

Wetherburn's
Tavern

Francis St.

Bucktrout Lane

Nicholson St.

Franklin St.

Botetourt St.

James
Anderson's
Blacksmith
Shop

Abby Aldrich
Rockefeller
Folk Art
Center

Colonial St.

Duke of Gloucester St.

Queen St.

Visitor Center

Peyton
Randolph
House

Magazine

Guardhouse

South England St.

North England St.

MARKET
SQUARE

Colonial Parkway

Courthouse

Scotland St.

Brush-
Everard
House

Governor's
Palace

Palace
Green

Palace St.

George Wythe
House

Bruton Parish
Church

Nassau St.

Duke of Gloucester St.

Francis St.

Public
Hospital

DeWitt Wallace
Decorative Arts
Gallery

Scotland St.

Prince George St.

Henry St.

Ireland St.

MERCHANTS
SQUARE

MERCHANTS
SQUARE

N. Boundary St.

S. Boundary St.

Richmond Rd.

Jamestown Rd.

Wren Building

TO WILLIAMSBURG
WINERY

who served as president of the First Continental Congress, is buried. | Duke of Gloucester St. | 757/221–4000 or 757/221–1540 | Free | Tours Mon.–Sat. 9–5, Sun. noon–5 during the academic year.

Colonial Parkway. This scenic 23-mi roadway connects three historic sites—Jamestown, the site of the first permanent English settlement in North America; Williamsburg, the former Colonial capital; and Yorktown, the scene of the last major battle of the American Revolution, where America won its independence. Created in the 1930s by the Depression-era Public Works Administration, the parkway has a number of turnouts with unobstructed views of the James and York rivers; many of these are good spots for a quiet picnic. | Colonial National Historical Park, Yorktown | 757/898–3400 | www.nps.gov/colo/index.htm | Free | Daily.

Colonial Williamsburg. Williamsburg was the capital of Virginia from 1699 until 1780, when it was succeeded by Richmond. Restoration of the town to its 18th-century appearance began in 1926 through the efforts of William A. R. Goodwin, rector of Bruton Parish Church, and John D. Rockefeller, Jr., who financed the massive undertaking. The work of archaeologists and historians of the Colonial Williamsburg Foundation continue, and the 173-acre restored area is operated as a living-history museum. There are 88 original 18th-century buildings and another 40 that have been reconstructed on their original sites. In all, 225 period rooms have been furnished from the foundation's collection of more than 100,000 pieces of furniture, pottery, china, glass, silver, textiles, and tools. Period authenticity also governs the grounds, which include 90 acres of gardens. Costumed interpreters lead house tours and demonstrate historic trades; you can step inside nearly two dozen workshops to watch a shoemaker, gunsmith, blacksmith, musical-instrument maker, silversmith, or wig maker.

Despite its huge scale, Colonial Williamsburg can seem almost cozy. One million visitors come here annually, and all year long hundreds of costumed interpreters, wearing bonnets or three-corner hats, rove and ride through the streets (you can even rent outfits for your children). Dozens of skilled craftspersons, also in costume, demonstrate and explain their trades inside their workshops. They include the shoemaker, the cooper, the gunsmith, the blacksmith, the musical-instrument maker, the silversmith, and the wig maker. Their wares are for sale nearby. Four taverns serve food and drink that approximate the fare of more than 220 years ago.

Once the substitute capital for Jamestown in times of pestilence and fire, Williamsburg was initially a small hamlet; in 1695 the Colony's first educational institution, the College of William and Mary, set up shop. The village was relatively undeveloped and thus ready for a planned town to be built. Francis Nicholson, Royal Governor of the Colony of Virginia by appointment of His Majesty William III, was qualified to plan such a town. He had already designed one—Annapolis—when he was governor of the Maryland Colony. Here, the land was higher but not hilly. Several small creeks drained it well. At the west end of his sketch pad he drew in the College, its few buildings in place, attractive, and proclaiming "Culture!" The roadway for the small settlement of Middle Plantation ran up to the doors of the College on a fine east-west axis, so Nicholson only had to draw a straight line, a scaled mile, to the east side of his pad for his town to begin to take form. As a balance to the College, the east end would be the Capitol. Exactly midway between the two would be the Market Place. Here the town would govern itself (ergo a courthouse), carry on its commerce (ergo wide green spaces for vendors), and marshall its defenses (ergo the powder magazine and the guardhouse). And just to make sure everyone remembered who was what, Nicholson went about a quarter of a mile north of the town center and sketched in the Governor's Palace. During the 80 years of its vibrant existence as the state capital, Williamsburg grew from an outpost to a bustling town of nearly 2,000 people—a complex community of pastoral and urban elements where the living was good.

For many, that is. The foundation has made an effort not just to represent the lives of a privileged few, but also to reveal other perspectives of the country's history. African-Americans now play a prominent role in reenactments and vignettes. During "The Gentlemen's

Men," slaves discuss the prestige of their masters in the Colonial town. The emotional "Healing Hands" is the story of a slave named Flora who gains the trust of her owners as she practices folk medicine. "No More Slavery Chains" depicts slaves Peter and Sarah, who must decide whether to join the British army and be free or remain with their masters, enslaved. A nighttime performance ($10) at Carter's Grove of "Broken Spirit," which is not suitable for young children, dramatizes the plight of an African family just brought to America. During the winter months, you can also attend a disturbing mock trial of a witch accused of heresy. Several reenactments focus on specific days that brought Virginia closer to revolution. In "Raise the Alarm," British soldiers encircle a group discussing the rumors and possibility of a slave insurrection. "The Gathering Storm" puts visitors up close to the drama of April 28, 1775, when town leaders met to defuse a potential bloody battle days before the Second Continental Congress convened in Philadelphia.

Because of the size of Colonial Williamsburg and the large numbers of visitors (especially in the warmer months), the best plan may be to begin a tour early in the day; it's a good idea to spend the night before in the area. The foundation claims that visitors must allow three or four days to do Colonial Williamsburg justice, but that will depend on your own interest in the period—and that interest often increases on arrival. Everyone should allow at least one full day to tour the city. Museums, exhibits, and stores close at 5 PM, but the town is open 24 hours, and walks and events take place in the evenings, usually ending by 10 PM. Some sites close in winter on a rotating basis.

You must tour the restored area on foot because all vehicular traffic is prohibited to preserve the Colonial atmosphere. Shuttle buses run continuously to and from the visitor center. Vans for people with disabilities are permitted by prior arrangement, and some structures have wheelchair ramps. Other services for visitors with disabilities are also available. Colonial Williamsburg offers several types of admission tickets. The Patriot's Pass, valid for one year, includes admission to all of the exhibition buildings, trade sites, homes, shops, the DeWitt Wallace Gallery, the Abby Aldrich Rockefeller Folk Art Center, an orientation walk, seasonal history walks, Carter's Grove, and Bassett Hall; there's also a discount on evening programs. The two-day Colonist's Pass includes an orientation walk and admission to all of the exhibition buildings, trade sites, homes and shops, plus the DeWitt Wallace Gallery and Abby Aldrick Rockefeller Folk Art Center. The basic one-day admission ticket includes an orientation walk, trade sites, homes, shops, and most exhibition buildings (it excludes the Governor's Palace and Wheelwright); it also includes the DeWitt Wallace Gallery and Abby Aldrich Rockefeller Folk Art Center. You can also buy a single ticket to some specific attractions. Arrangements for visitors with disabilities can be made in advance (757/220–7644).

Note that if you wish to dine at one of Colonial Williamsburg's noted taverns—including Raleigh Tavern (where Jefferson and his friends set up Virginia's Committee of Correspondence), it is really imperative that you have a reservation. Don't plan to merely stop in for lunch, dinner, or even a cup of coffee—remember, 18th-century innkeepers were rarely confronted by more than a half a dozen guests at a time, and *they* put a strain on the facilities. Of course, if your desire for a hamburger or hot dog outweighs your striving for authenticity, head to the west end of Duke of Gloucester Street to **Merchants Square,** where you'll find more than 40 shops and restaurants, some serving fast food. | Rte. 5 and Jamestown Rd. (Rte. 31) | 757/220–7644, 757/220–7645, or 800/447–8679 | www.colonialwilliamsburg.org | Patriot's Pass $34, valid for 1 yr; Colonist's Pass $30, valid for 2 days; basic admission $26; single admission to Governor's Palace or Carter's Grove $17; museums $10; annual museums pass $17; Tickets also sold at the Lumber House in historic area and at the Williamsburg Attraction Center in Berkeley Commons Outlet Center | Daily 9–5.

The **Visitor Center** is the logical first stop at Colonial Williamsburg. Here you can park free; buy tickets; see a 35-minute introductory movie, *Williamsburg—the Story of a Patriot*; and pick up the very useful *Visitors Companion* guide, with a list of regular events and special programs and a map of the Historic Area. | 102 Information Center Dr., off U.S. 60 | 757/220–7645 or 800/447–8679.

The spine of Colonial Williamsburg's restored area is the broad, 1-mi-long **Duke of Gloucester Street.** On Saturday at noon, from March to October, the Junior Fife and Drum Corps marches the length of the street and performs a stirring drill. Along this artery alone, or just off it, are two dozen attractions. Walking west on Duke of Gloucester Street from the Capitol, you'll find a dozen 18th-century shops—including the Pasteur and Galt Apothecary Shop, the Raleigh Tavern and Bake shop, the Silversmith, the Millner, the Grocers Shop, the Printer-Bookbinder and Post Office, Prentis Store, the famed Chowning's Tavern, the Courthouse, the Geddy House and Foundry, and the Bruton Parish Church.

The **Capitol** is the building that made this town so important. It was here that the pre-Revolutionary House of Burgesses (dominated by the ascendant gentry) challenged the royally appointed council (an almost medieval body made up of the bigger landowners). In 1765, the House eventually arrived at the resolutions, known as Henry's Resolves (after Patrick Henry), that amounted to rebellion. An informative tour explains the development, stage by stage, of American democracy from its English parliamentary roots. In the courtroom a guide recites the harsh Georgian sentences that were meted out: for instance, theft of more than 12 shillings was a capital crime. Occasional reenactments, such as witch trials, dramatize the evolution of American jurisprudence. What stands on the site today is a reproduction of the 1705 structure that burned down in 1747. Dark-wood wainscoting, pewter chandeliers, and towering ceilings contribute to a handsome impression. That an official building would have so ornate an interior was characteristic of aristocratic 18th-century Virginia. This was in telling contrast to the plain town meeting halls of Puritan New England, where other citizens were governing themselves at the same time. | East end of Duke of Gloucester St.

Raleigh Tavern was the scene of pre-Revolutionary revels and rallies that were often joined by Washington, Jefferson, Patrick Henry, and other major figures. The spare but elegant blue-and-white Apollo Room is said to have been the first meeting place of Phi Beta Kappa, the scholastic honorary society founded in 1776. The French general Marquis de Lafayette was feted here in 1824. In 1859 the original structure burned, and today's building is a reconstruction based on archaeological evidence and period descriptions and sketches of the building. | Duke of Gloucester St., just west of the Capitol.

Wetherburn's Tavern, which offered refreshment, entertainment, and lodging beginning in 1743, is possibly the most accurately furnished building in Colonial Williamsburg, with contents that conform to a room-by-room inventory taken in 1760. Excavations at this site have yielded more than 200,000 artifacts. The outbuildings include the original dairy and a reconstructed kitchen. Vegetables are still grown in the small garden. | Duke of Gloucester St. across from Raleigh Tavern.

James Anderson's Blacksmith Shop, smiths forge the nails, tools, and other iron hardware used in construction throughout the town. The shop itself was reconstructed by costumed carpenters using 18th-century tools and techniques—a project that was featured on public television. | Between Botetourt and Colonial Sts. on the south side of Duke of Gloucester St.

The original **Magazine** (1715), an octagonal brick warehouse, was used for storing arms and ammunition—at one time, 60,000 pounds of gunpowder and 3,000 muskets. It was used for this purpose by the British, then by the Continental army, and again by the Confederates during the Civil War. Today, 18th-century firearms are on display within the arsenal. | West of Queen St. on the south side of Duke of Gloucester St.

Market Square, an open green between Queen and Palace streets along Duke of Gloucester Street, was the outdoor site for the vending of cattle, seafood, dairy products, fruit, and vegetables. It was also the venue for slave auctions. Both the market and auctions are sometimes re-enacted.

The **Guardhouse** once served in the defense of the Magazine's lethal inventory; now it contains a replica fire engine (1750) that is seen on the town streets in the warmer months. Special interpretive programs about the military are scheduled here. | Duke of Gloucester St. near Queen St.

The original **Courthouse** of 1770 was used by municipal and county courts until 1932. Civil and minor criminal matters and cases involving slaves were adjudicated here; other trials were conducted at the Capitol. Stocks, once used to punish misdemeanors, are located outside the building; modern-day visitors take perverse pleasure in photographing each other clapped in the stocks. The exterior of the courthouse has been restored to its original appearance. Visitors often participate in scheduled reenactments of court sessions. | North side of Duke of Gloucester St. west of Queen St.

The handsome **Palace Green** runs north from Duke of Gloucester Street up the center of Palace Street, with the Governor's Palace at the far end and a notable historic house on each side of it.

The **George Wythe House** was the residence of Thomas Jefferson's law professor; Wythe was also a signer of the Declaration of Independence. General Washington used the house as a headquarters just before his victory at Yorktown. The large brick structure, built in the mid-18th century, is conspicuously symmetrical: Each side has a chimney, and each floor has two rooms on either side of a center hallway. The garden in back is similarly divided. The outbuildings, including a smokehouse, kitchen, laundry, privies, and a chicken coop, are reconstructions. | West side of Palace Green.

Residence of seven royal governors and the first two governors of the Commonwealth of Virginia—Patrick Henry and Thomas Jefferson, the **Governor's Palace** is perhaps the most elegant building of 18th-century America. Today's completely refurbished reconstruction on the original foundations is surrounded by formal gardens, outbuildings, a graveyard, a canal, and a host of indications that this was, indeed, a most impressive place to live. His Majesty's Governor Alexander Spotswood built the original palace in 1720, and seven British viceroys, the last of them Lord Dunmore in 1775, lived in this appropriately showy mansion.— note Britain's royal lion and unicorn prancing above the main doorway in the royal seal, recalling the nearly 170 years Virginians lived under British rule. Eight hundred guns and swords arrayed on the walls and ceilings of several rooms herald the power of the Crown. Some of the gorgeous furnishings—Gainsborough chairs, mahogany tea caddies, and ancestral portraits—are original, and the rest are matched to an extraordinary inventory of 16,000 items. Lavishly appointed as it is, the palace is furnished to the time just before the Revolution. The original residence burned down in 1781. A costumed guide greets visitors at the door and a tour through the building, offering commentary and answering questions. Notable among the furnishings are several pieces made in Williamsburg and actually owned by Lord Dunmore, the last royal governor. Social events are described on the walk through the great formal ballroom, where you might even hear the sounds of an 18th-century harp, clavichord, or piano, or see colonists dancing to the hit tunes of the times. The supper room— adazzle with 18th-century floral wallpaper, Georgian furniture, and glittering chandlier— leads to the formal garden and the planted terraces beyond. | Northern end of Palace Green.

The **Brush-Everard House** was built in 1717 by John Brush, a gunsmith, and later owned by Thomas Everard, who was twice mayor of Williamsburg. The yellow wood-frame house contains remarkable ornate carving work but is open only for special-focus tours. Temporary exhibits on slaves' lives are held here during the summer. | Scotland St. and Palace Green.

On the outskirts of the Historic Area, you can follow the pleasant fragrance of wood burning to **Robertson's Windmill,** where rural trades such as basket making, pit sawing, and coopering (barrel making) are demonstrated. When the weather is willing, the windmill powers the fires inside that tradespeople use for their craft. The coopers smolder metal strands that wrap around the barrels, keeping them taut. | N. England St.

The **Peyton Randolph House** was the home of a prominent Colonist and revolutionary who served as attorney general under the British, then as Speaker of the House of Burgesses, and later as president of the first and second Continental Congresses. The oak-paneled bedroom and Randolph family silver are remarkable. | Nicholson at N. England Sts.

East of the Peyton-Randolph House, on Nicholson Street, is the **Military Encampment,** where you can get a feeling for military life in the 18th century. During warm weather, "Join the Continental Army," an interactive theater performance, lets you experience military life on the eve of the Revolution. Under the guidance of costumed militiamen, drill and make camp in a 45-minute participatory program. If you want to join the ranks for a little while, you can volunteer at the site.

Built in 1715, the lovely brick Episcopal **Bruton Parish Church** has served continuously as a house of worship. One of its 20th-century pastors, W. A. R. Goodwin, provided the impetus for Williamsburg's restoration. The church tower, topped by a beige wooden steeple, was added in 1769; during the Revolution its bell served as the local liberty bell. The white pews, tall and boxed in, are characteristic of the starkly graceful Colonial ecclesiastical architecture of the region. When sitting in a pew, listening to the history of the church, keep in mind that you could be sitting where Thomas Jefferson, Ben Franklin, or George Washington once sat for long hours listening to sermons. George was godfather to 14 slaves baptized here—the stone baptismal font is believed to have come from an older Jamestown church. Many local eminences, including one royal governor, are interred in the graveyard. The fully operational church is open to the public; contributions are accepted. | Duke of Gloucester St. west of Palace St.

The **Wren Building** is part of the College of William and Mary, founded in 1693. The campus extends to the west; the Wren Building (1695) was based on the work of the celebrated London architect Sir Christopher Wren. Its redbrick outer walls are original, but fire gutted the interiors several times, and the present quarters are largely reconstructions of the 20th century. The faculty common room, with a table covered with green felt and an antique globe, suggests Oxford and Cambridge universities, the models for this New World institution. Jefferson studied and later taught law here to James Monroe and others. College undergraduates lead tours of the building, including the chapel where Colonial leader Peyton Randolph is buried. | West end of Duke of Gloucester St.

The **Public Hospital,** a reconstruction of a 1773 insane asylum, provides an informative, if sometimes shocking, look at the treatment of the mentally ill in the 18th and 19th centuries. It also serves as cover for a modern edifice that houses very different exhibitions; visitors pass through the hospital lobby into the DeWitt Wallace Decorative Arts Gallery (*see below*). | Francis St.

The famous **DeWitt Wallace Decorative Arts Gallery** adds another cultural dimension that goes well beyond Colonial history. Grouped by medium are English and American furniture, textiles, prints, metals, and ceramics of the 17th to the early 19th century. If you're yawning at the thought of fancy tableware, stop: you'll be surprised at the exhibits' creative presentations. Prizes among the 8,000 pieces in the collection are a full-length portrait of George Washington by Charles Willson Peale and a royally commissioned case clock surmounted by the detailed figure of a Native American. You can enter the museum through the Public Hospital. | Francis St.

The **Abby Aldrich Rockefeller Folk Art Center** showcases American "decorative usefulware"— toys, furniture, weather vanes, coffeepots, and quilts—within typical 19th-century domestic interiors. There are also folk paintings, rustic sculptures, and needlepoint pictures. Since the 1920s, the 2,000-piece collection has grown from the original 400 pieces acquired by the wife of Colonial Williamsburg's first and principal benefactor. | S. England St.

The reconstructed **Carter's Grove plantation,** created after extensive archaeological investigation, examines 400 years of history, starting in 1619 with Wolstenholme Towne. Exhibits in the Winthrop Rockefeller Archaeology Museum provide further insight. The 18th century is represented by slave dwellings on their original foundations, where costumed interpreters explain the crucial role African-Americans played on plantations. A play that focuses on a newly arrived African slave, "Broken Spirit," takes place here during the evening. Finally, you may tour the mansion, built in 1755 by Carter Burwell, whose grandfather "King" Carter made the family fortune as one of Virginia's wealthiest landowners and greatest explorers. The mansion was extensively remodeled in 1919 to express its owner's fascination with the past, and additions were made in the 1930s. The interior is notable for the original wood paneling and elaborate carvings. A one-way scenic country road, also used for biking, leads from Carter's Grove through woods, meadows, marshes, and streams back to Williamsburg. | U.S. 60, 8 mi east of Colonial Williamsburg | 757/229–1000. | $18 (included in Williamsburg $30 general admission ticket or the annual pass). Play $10. | Mid-Mar.–Dec., daily 9–5.

The **Williamsburg Winery** carries on a Virginia tradition of winemaking that began with early settlers. The winery offers guided tours, a well-stocked wine shop, a unique 17th-century tasting room, and a museum of winemaking artifacts. A casual luncheon is served in the Gabriel Archer Tavern. Be sure to try the selection of cabernets and merlots, as they surprise even the most finicky of tastes. | 5800 Wessex Hundred, off Lake Powell Rd. and Rte. 199 | 757/229–0999. | $5. | Feb. 15–Jan. 15, Mon.–Sat. 10–6, Sun. noon–6.

✦ ON THE CALENDAR: Feb. **Washington's Birthday Celebration.** Reenactments, lectures, and a military tribute are part of the festivities in the historic district on President's Day weekend; the event includes a traditional review of the troops by General George Washington. | 800/246–2099.

Mar. **English Country Dance Ball.** Held on the first Saturday in March at the Newport House B&B, this ball attracts more than 200 dancers who come out in full period costume. The $25 ticket includes dinner. The inn also hosts free English country dancing every Tuesday night from 8 to 10. | 757/229–1775.

Mar. **Learning Weekend.** During this event conducted by the Williamsburg Institute, you can explore the complex decisions faced by Virginians on the eve of Revolution, and experience "living history" through encounters with 18th-century character interpreters. | 800/603–0948.

Mar.–Oct. **Military Drill.** You can observe interpreters costumed as 18th-century soldiers every afternoon as they undergo military training in the historic district. | 757/253–0192.

Apr.–Oct. **Fife and Drum Corps.** Listen to Colonial Williamsburg's Fife and Drum Corps perform daily throughout the historic district; typically, the corps parades down Duke of Gloucester Street, the main thoroughfare. | 757/253–0192.

May **Prelude to Independence.** Watch a debate by Virginia's Colonial leaders at the Second Continental Congress as they prepared to vote for independence from Great Britain, performed in the historic district. | 757/253–0192.

Sept. **Publick Times.** At the Capitol, you can see a reenactment of "publick times" during the Colonial era, when planters and merchants gathered in Williamsburg for the spring and fall sessions of the General Court and House of Burgesses on | Labor Day weekend | 757/253–0192.

Dec. **Traditional Christmas Activities.** Holiday programs, tours, workshops, and concerts take place in the historic district during the Christmas season. A highlight is the Grand Illumination, when all the windows in the historic district are lit with candles; the evening event also features fireworks and 18th-century-style entertainment. | 757/253–0192.

HISTORIC DINING AND LODGING

Colonial Williamsburg Taverns. Four reconstructed taverns within Colonial Williamsburg serve Colonial-style foods for lunch, dinner, and Sunday brunch. The dishes are a bit overpriced, but a meal at any tavern is a great way to get into the spirit of the era. No reservations are taken for lunch, but it's recommended that you make dinner reservations up to two or three weeks in advance. Hours also change according to season, so check by calling the reservations number (800/447–8679).

In the Historic Area, there are four authentic 18th-century taverns with costumed waiters and oversize napkins and cutlery. The fare is all hearty early American but differs in each tavern. All offer outdoor dining. **Chownings,** a reconstructed ale-house, serves casual meals including Welsh rarebit, oyster fritters, and sandwiches, and heartier fare such as Brunswick stew, duckling, and prime rib. **Christiana Campbell's** was George Washington's favorite tavern; its specialty is seafood and it looks out upon the Capitol just across the street. **King's Arms** is the most upscale of the Colonial taverns catered to the gentry in its day. This spot comes complete with costumed servers waiting tables and Colonial balladeers. The genteel atmosphere and the fare here might still please Thomas Jefferson, who sometimes came here to chow down on Virginia ham, game pie, and Sally Lunn bread. The tavern is now famous for peanut soup, chicken breast with crab stuffing, cavalier's rack of lamb, and a venison, rabbit, and duck game pie. Williamsburg pecan pie is its dessert specialty. **Shields Tavern** serves 18th-century low-country cuisine in eight dining rooms and the garden, while strolling balladers entertain diners. | 800/447–8679 | Reservations essential | $15–$30 | AE, D, MC, V.

Colonial Houses. A stay here is particularly transporting at night, when the town's historic area is quiet, and you have Williamsburg pretty much to yourself. Five of the 25 homes and two lodging taverns are 18th-century structures; the others have been rebuilt on their original foundations. Lodgings are furnished with antiques, period reproductions, and are serviced by costumed staff. A very hospitable touch is the complimentary bottle of wine and fruit basket delivered to each room. The Colonial Houses share the facilities of the adjacent Williamsburg Inn, and the Williamsburg Lodge. Cable TV. | 302 E. Francis St. | 800/447–8679 | fax 757/565–8444 | 76 rooms | $100–$515 | AE, D, DC, MC, V.

Governor Spottswood Motel. This one-story redbrick motel has been extended gradually, section by section, over the past 50 years. The decor reflects the influence of Colonial Williamsburg, but in classic motel design each room faces its parking space. There's lawn space and a sunken garden setting for the swimming pool. Seven cottages sleep four to seven people, and 14 rooms have kitchens. It's a good value for the location. Pool. | 1508 Richmond Rd. | 757/ 229–6444 | fax 757/253–2410 | 78 rooms | $32–$64 | AE, D, DC, MC, V.

Williamsburg Inn. This award-winning grand hotel—built in 1937—is owned and operated by Colonial Williamsburg. Rooms are beautifully and individually furnished with reproductions and antiques in the English Regency style, and genteel service and tradition reign. Complimentary morning coffee and afternoon tea, free daily newspaper, turndown service, and bathrobes contribute to the pampering. The Providence Wings, adjacent to the inn, have a less formal atmosphere; rooms have contemporary decor with Asian accents and overlook the tennis courts, a private pond, and a wooded area. Restaurant. | 136 E. Francis St. | 757/ 229–1000 | fax 757/220–7096 | www.colonialwilliamsburg.com | 124 rooms, 11 suites | $259– $363; $410–$750 suites | AE, D, DC, MC, V.

Williamsburg Sampler. Charming and hospitable, this redbrick inn near the historic district is modeled after an 18th-century plantation-style home. It features 18th- and 19th-century antiques, pewter pieces, four-poster beds, pleasant views of the city, and a warm atmosphere. The suites are particularly inviting as each has a separate sitting room, French doors, and a porch overlooking gardens. Complimentary breakfast. | 922 Jamestown Rd. | 757/253–0398 | fax 757/253–2669 | www.williamsburgsampler.com | 2 rooms, 2 suites | $110; $160 suites | MC, V.

YORKTOWN
▼▼

Famously, the combined American and French forces surrounded British troops under Lord Cornwallis in 1781 at Yorktown, forcing an end to the American War of Independence. In Yorktown today, as at Jamestown, two major attractions complement each other. Yorktown Battlefield, the historical site, is operated by the National Park Service; and Yorktown Victory Center, an informative entertainment, is operated by the state's Jamestown-Yorktown Foundation. The town of Yorktown remains a living community, albeit a small one that time seems to have forgotten. Route 238 leads into Yorktown, whose Main Street is an array of preserved 18th-century buildings on a bluff overlooking the York River. Its quiet character actually calls attention to itself amid the area's theme park-like attractions.

First settled in 1691, Yorktown had become a thriving tobacco port and a prosperous community of several hundred houses by the time of the Revolution. Nine buildings from that time still stand, not all of them open to visitors. Moore House, where the terms of surrender were negotiated, and the elegant Nelson House, the residence of a Virginia governor and a signer of the Declaration of Independence, are open for tours in summer and are part of the Yorktown Victory Center's entrance fee. The Swan Tavern, a reconstruction of a structure of 1722, houses an antiques shop. On Church Street, Grace Church, built in 1697 and damaged in the War of 1812 and the Civil War, was rebuilt and remains an active Episcopal congregation; its walls are made of native marl (a mixture of clay, sand, and limestone containing fragments of seashells). On Main Street, the Somerwell House, built before 1707, and the Sessions House (before 1699)—the oldest houses in town—are privately owned and closed to the public. The latter was used as local headquarters by the Union forces during General George McClellan's Peninsula Campaign of the Civil War. *Contact Colonial National Historical Park / Box 210, Yorktown 23690 / 757/898–3400 / www.nps.gov/colo.*

Colonial National Historic Park. This parkland commemorates the English Colonial Period of American History and includes Jamestown, the first permanent English settlement in America, and Yorktown, battlefield site of the last major battle of the American Revolution. | Visitors Center, Colonial Pkwy. at Rte. 238, Yorktown | 757/898–3400 | www.nps.gov/colo | Jamestown $5, Yorktown $4, combination $7 | Daily 9–5.

Yorktown Battlefield. Witness to the final military denouement of the Revolutionary War, this battlefield preserves the land where the British surrendered to American and French forces in 1781. This culmination had begun with the movements of the British troops. After suffering a string of defeats in South Carolina and North Carolina, the British Major-General Charles Cornwallis headed his army north and marched to Virginia, turning to the coast in late June of 1781 and settling in at the tiny port town of Yorktown as a winter base from which he could maintain sea communication with British naval forces in New York. What he didn't expect was that the French forces, led by Admiral De Grasse on the way from the West Indies decided not to sail to New York but make for Chesapeake Bay, and effectively blockaded Cornwallis's troops. On the way was Washington and Rochambeau, marching south with 9,000 soldiers to begin what became known as the Siege of Yorktown. With their arrival, Cornwallis drew his 8,000 soldiers closer to town, abandoning his outer defenses and setting up big guns in trenches, which over days of hand-to-hand fighting, gave way to American forces. General Cornwallis made one final attempt on October 16 to retake the redoubts. When it failed, he made plans to evacuate his troops across the York River to the Gloucester Point defenses with, he hoped, the protection of the few British ships that lay bottled up in the river. When an Indian Summer Chesapeake storm blew up that afternoon, he sued for peace. On the morning of October 17, 1781, Cornwallis sent his proposal for a truce to the allied commanders and "terms" were worked out at a meeting at a plantation down the road from the main battle point, "Mr. Moore's house." The following day, the thousands of British and Hessian troops marched 2 mi through meadows to finally lay down their arms and have their General O'Hara present his sword, final symbol of a turned tide. Wild cheering broke forth from the Americans and French as the English and Germans were called to rank and began to march from the field. His Majesty's pipers accompanied them away to the old British marching tune, "The World Turned Upside Down." The war had not ended, in fact, but fully a third of the British forces in the Colonies had been lost, and what battles remained were not much more than skirmishes between Patriots and Redcoats. King George's cabinet resigned, and the new one opened peace negotiations that were to take nearly two more years before becoming final.

The Hero of Yorktown

"He was a hot-tempered redhead with little formal education. He stood nearly 6 feet 4 inches tall, could crush walnuts with his bare hands, and loved to dance. A natural athlete, he was called the Greatest Horseman in Virginia by Thomas Jefferson. He explored the frontier, won the heart of the most eligible widow on the continent, and helped create a new nation by the force of his character. Why, then, do so many Americans think of George Washington as the grumpy old man on the dollar bill?" So asks the Web site of New York City's Fraunces Tavern Museum. Perhaps the answer lies in the fact that the gentleman had a mangled, bloody, broken, uneven, and, by all accounts, shockingly painful collection of teeth that made him miserable, irritable, and unpleasant. Perhaps not, but the hero of Yorktown remains a conundrum in many other respects. Born in 1732, George was to become a father himself some 50 years later—the father of his country. His older stepbrother was George's idol and when Lawrence married into the rich Fairfax family, this connection led to George's first office—official surveyor of Culpeper County. If he didn't cut down the famous cherry tree, he certainly did cut down a lot of *other* trees in that job. Although George's first forays on the military field were filled with blunders, he had better luck in love, sort of—it was said that he was in love with his neighbor's wife, but he married a rich widow, Martha Custis, instead. In the end, his trump card was his strength of character, a strength seen today in the many portrait statues of him that stand everywhere, from Washington, D.C. to (believe it or not) London's Trafalgar Square.

The museum in the visitor center has on exhibit part of Gen. George Washington's original field tent. Dioramas, illuminated maps, and a short movie about the battle make the sobering point that Washington's victory was hardly inevitable. A look around from the roof's observation deck can help you visualize the events of the campaign. Guided by an audio tour ($2) rented from the gift shop, you can explore the battlefield by car, stopping at the site of Washington's headquarters, a couple of crucial redoubts (breastworks dug into the ground), and the field where surrender took place. | Rte. 238 off Colonial Pkwy. | 757/898–3400 | $5. | Visitor center daily 9–5 (extended hrs from spring to fall).

On the western edge of Yorktown Battlefield, the **Yorktown Victory Center** has wonderful exhibits and demonstrations that bring to life the era of the American Revolution. The exhibits here lift you from the gentle and somewhat genteel aura of Williamsburg to the fever pitch of patriotism that compelled men to offer "their Lives, their Fortunes, and their sacred Honor" to the cause of liberty. Textual and graphic displays along the Road to Revolution walkway cover the principal events and personalities. The trail enters the main museum, where the story of Yorktown's critical role in the achievement of American independence is told, and where life-size tableaux show 10 "witnesses," including an African-American patriot, a loyalist, a Native American leader, two Continental Army soldiers, and the wife of a Virginia plantation owner. The exhibit galleries contain more than 500 period artifacts, including many recovered during underwater excavations of "Yorktown's Sunken Fleet" (British ships lost during the siege of 1781). Outdoors, in a Continental Army encampment, interpreters costumed as soldiers and female auxiliaries reenact and discuss daily camp life. In another outdoor area, interpreters re-create 18th-century farm life. | Rte. 238 off Colonial Pkwy. | 757/253–4838 | $8; combination ticket for Yorktown Victory Center and Jamestown Settlement, $12 | Daily 9–5.

Resources

To enrich your travels back in time to the events of Colonial, Revolutionary, and Federal America and to enhance your heritage-tourism vacation, this chapter offers an array of historical organizations, Internet sites (with hundreds of fascinating Web links), and a state-by-state list of tourism offices and tour-group companies. In addition there are tempting panoplies of books to give you the latest and greatest research on America's founding fathers, daughters, and times. Any of the selections found in the "Further Reading: Classic Histories and Biographies" section below would be a grand overture to the field. They range from groundbreaking works like Alan Taylor's *American Colonies* and magisterial overviews such as Bernard Bailyn's *To Begin the World Anew* to brilliant biographies like Richard Norton Smith's *Patriarch* and sumptuous art books such as Wendell Garrett's *American Colonial*. For the newest volumes of historical research, consult scholarly journals such as *Early American Literature*. And if you want to go from being a mere observer to becoming a real participant, check out the feature on the Reenactors movement in "Liberty's Road," at the beginning of this book. There's nothing like the thrill of "being there" when Washington crosses the Delaware—as you can still discover *every* Christmas Day at Washington Crossing, New Jersey.

The Thirteen Colonies

HISTORICAL ORGANIZATIONS AND INTERNET RESOURCES

American Revolution.Org | www.americanrevolution.org/home.html.
Archiving Early America | www.earlyamerica.com.

American Antiquarian Society | 165 Salisbury St., Worcester, MA 01609 | 508/471–2160 | www.common-place.org/contact.shtml.
National Society of the Daughters of the American Revolution | 1776 D Street, NW, Washington, DC 20006 | 202/628–1776 | www.dar.org.
National Society of the Sons of the American Revolution | 1000 S. 4th St., Louisville, KY 40203 | 502/589–1776 | www.sar.org.
On-Line Institute for Advanced Loyalist Studies | www.royalprovincial.com/index.htm.
Reenactor.net | www.reenactor.net/colonial/rev_units_amer.html | www.reenactor.net/colonial/rev_units_brit.html.
Society of Early Americanists | www.humanities.uci.edu/~mclark/seapage.htm.
American Revolution | revolution.h-net.msu.edu.
Continental Line | www.continentalline.org.
UShistory.org | www.ushistory.org.

FURTHER READING: CLASSIC HISTORIES AND BIOGRAPHIES

Alden, John R. *A History of the American Revolution,* Knopf, 1969.
Anderson, Fred. *Crucible of War: The Seven Years' War and the Fate of Empire in British North America, 1754–1766,* Knopf, 2001.
Bailyn, Bernard. *To Begin the World Anew: The Genius and Ambiguities of the American Founders,* Knopf, 2003.
___. *The Ideological Origins of the American Revolution,* Belknap Press, 1992.
Berkin, Carol. *A Brilliant Solution: Inventing the American Constitution,* Harcourt, 2002.
Blackburn, Roderick and Geoffrey Gross. *Dutch Colonial Homes in America,* Rizzoli, 2002.
Bobrick, Benson. *Angel in the Whirlwind: Triumph of the American Revolution,* Penguin, 1997.
Boorstin, Daniel J. *The Americans: The Colonial Experience,* Random House, 1958.
Bowne, Russell. *Gods of War, Gods of Peace: How the Meeting of Natives and Colonial Religions Shaped Early America,* Harcourt, 2002.

Brands, H. W. *The First American: The Life and Times of Benjamin Franklin,* Anchor, 2002.

Brodie, Fawn. *Thomas Jefferson: An Intimate History,* W. W. Norton, 1974.

Brookhiser, Richard. *Rediscovering George Washington,* Free Press, 1996.

Burstein, Andrew. *The Inner Jefferson,* University Press of Virginia, 1997.

Commager, Henry Steele (Editor). *The Spirit of Seventy-six,* Bobbs-Merrill, 1958.

Dalzell, Robert F. and Lee Baldwin Dalzell. *George Washington's Mount Vernon: At Home in Revolutionary America,* Oxford University Press, 1998.

Elkins, Stanley. *The Age of Federalism: The Early Republic, 1788–1820,* Overlook, 1993.

Ellis, Joseph L. *American Sphinx: The Character of Thomas Jefferson,* Vintage, 1998.

Ellis, Joseph L. *Founding Brothers: The Revolutionary Generation,* Vintage, 2000.

Garrett, Wendell. *Colonial America: Puritan Simplicity to Georgian Grace,* Monacelli, 1995.

Hibbert, Christopher. *Redcoats and Rebels,* W. W. Norton, 2002.

Howard, Hugh. *Thomas Jefferson, Architect,* Rizzoli, 2003.

Jennings, Francis. *The Creation of America: Through Revolution to Empire,* Cambridge University Press, 2000.

Landsman, Ned. *From Colonials to Provincials: American Thought and Culture 1680–1760,* Twayne, 1997.

McCullough, David. *John Adams,* Simon and Schuster, 2001.

Morgan, Edmund. *Benjamin Franklin,* Yale University Press, 2002.

Purcell, J. Edward, and David F. Burg. *The World Almanac of the American Revolution,* World Almanac, 1992.

Randall, William. *Thomas Jefferson: A Life,* Harper Collins, 1993.

___. *George Washington: A Life,* Henry Holt, 1997.

___. *Alexander Hamilton: A Life,* Harper Collins, 2003.

Smith, Richard Norton. *Patriarch: George Washington and the New American Nation,* Bantam, 1987.

Taylor, Alan. *American Colonies,* Viking, 2001.

Tree, Christina. *How New England Happened,* Little, Brown, 1976.

Wills, Garry. *Cincinnatus: George Washington and the Enlightenment—Images of Power in Early America,* Doubleday, 1984.

Wood, Gordon S. *The American Revolution: A History,* Modern Library, 2001.

Connecticut

HISTORICAL AND TOURISM ORGANIZATIONS

Antiquarian & Landmarks Society | 66 Forest St., Hartford, CT 06105 | 860/247–8996 | www.hartnet.org/als.

Connecticut Historical Commission | 59 S. Prospect St., Hartford, CT 06106 | 860/566–3005 | www.chc.state.ct.us.

Connecticut Historical Society | 1 Elizabeth St., Hartford, CT 06105 | 860/236–5621. | www.chs.org.

Connecticut Office of Tourism | 550 Hudson St., Hartford, CT 06106 | 860/270–8080 | www.ctbound.org.

HISTORY TOURS AND PACKAGES

Antiquarian & Landmarks Society | 66 Forest St., Hartford, CT 06105 | 860/247–8996 | www.hartnet.org/als/alshtours.html

Heritage Trails Sightseeing Tours | Box 138 Farmington, CT 06034 | 860/677–8867 | www.charteroaktree.com.

Travels with a Connecticut Yankee/Friendship Tours | 533 Cottage Grove Rd., Bloomfield, CT 06002 | 860/243–1630.

FURTHER READING

Buel, Joy Day, and Buel, Richard, Jr. *The Way of Duty: A Woman and Her Family in Revolutionary Connecticut,* W.W. Norton, 1984.

Buel, Richard, Jr., and McNulty, J. Bard, eds. *Connecticut Observed: Three Centuries of Visitors' Impressions, 1676–1940,* Acorn Club and the Connecticut Humanities Council, 1999.

Bushman, Richard. *Puritan to Yankee: Character and Social Order in Connecticut, 1690–1765,* Harvard University Press, 1967.

Cave, Alfred A. *The Pequot War,* University of Massachusetts Press, 1996.

Collier, Christopher. *Roger Sherman's Connecticut: Yankee Politics and the American Revolution,* Wesleyan University Press, 1971.

Daniels, Bruce C. *The Connecticut Town: Growth and Development, 1635–1790,* Wesleyan University Press, 1979.

Fraser, Bruce. *A Land of Steady Habits: A Brief History of Connecticut,* Connecticut Historical Commission, 1988.

Grant, Marion Hepburn. *The Infernal Machine of Saybrook's David Bushnell, Patriot Inventor of the American Revolution,* Bicentennial Committee of Old Saybrook, 1976.

Hosley, William, and Ward, Gerald, eds. *The Great River: Art and Society of the Connecticut Valley, 1635–1820,* Wadsworth Atheneum, 1985.

Jones, Mary Jeanne. *Congregational Commonwealth: Connecticut, 1636–1662,* Wesleyan University Press, 1968.

Taylor, Robert. *Colonial Connecticut: A History,* KTO Press, 1979.

Tomlinson, R.G. *Witchcraft Trials of Connecticut,* Bond Press, 1978.

Van Dusen, Albert E. *Connecticut,* Random House, 1961.

Zeichner, Oscar. *Connecticut's Years of Controversy, 1750–1776,* Archon Books, 1970.

Delaware

HISTORICAL AND TOURISM ORGANIZATIONS

Delaware Tourism Office | 99 Kings Hwy., Dover, DE 19901 | 302/739–4271 | fax 302/739–5749 | www.visitdelaware.com.

Greater Wilmington Convention & Visitors Bureau | 100 W. 10th St., Suite 20, Wilmington, DE 19801 | 800/489–6664 | www.visitwilmingtonde.com.

Historical Society of Delaware | 505 Market St., Wilmington, DE 19801 | 302/655–7161 | fax 302/655–7844 | www.hsd.org.

Kent County Convention & Visitors Bureau | 435 N. Dupont Hwy., Dover, DE 19901 | 800/233–KENT or 302/734–1736 | fax 302/734–0167 | www.visitdover.com.

Southern Delaware Tourism | Box 240, Georgetown, DE 19947 | 800/357–1818 | www.visitsoutherndelaware.com.

HISTORY TOURS AND PACKAGES

Alternative Tours | Box 8492, Cherry Hill, NJ 08002 | 856/854–6396

Centipede Tours | 1315 Walnut St., Philadelphia, PA 19107 | 215/735–3123 | www.centipedeinc.com.

Colonial Pathway Tours | Box 30789, Chadds Ford, PA 19317 | 610/388–2654 | www.colonialpathways.com.

Cornucopia Tours | 1408 N. Union St., Wilmington, DE 19806 | 302/427–9037 | fax 302/427–0888 | www.cornucopiatours.com.

Shadows of the Past Walking Tours | 420 S. State St, Dover, DE 19901 | 302/677–0719

FURTHER READING

Cooper, Wendy A., T. A. Gleason, and K. A. John. *An American Vision: Henry Francis Du Pont's Winterthur Museum*, Lund Humphries, 2002.

Dale, Frank. *Delaware Diary: Episodes in the Life of a River*, Rutgers University Press, 1996.

Dickinson, John (eds. R. H. Lee and F. McDonald). *Empire and Nation: Letters from a Farmer in Pennsylvania*, Liberty Fund, Inc.,1998.

Hancock, Harold B. *Delaware: Two Hundred Years Ago: 1780–1800*, Middle Atlantic Press, 1987.

Hancock, Harold. *The Delaware Loyalists*, Irvington Publishing, 1940.

Hoffecker, Carol E. *Delaware: The First State*, Middle Atlantic Press, 1988.

Levy, Barry. *Quakers and the American Family: British Settlement in the Delaware Valley*, Oxford University Press, 1992.

Scott, Jane. *A Gentleman As Well As a Whig: Caesar Rodney and the American Revolution*, University of Delaware Press, 2000.

Wamsley, James, with photos by Steven Mays. *The Brandywine Valley: An Introduction to its Cultural Treasures*, H. A. Abrams, Inc., 1992.

Wilkinson, Norman. *E. I. du Pont, Botaniste: The Beginning of a Tradition*, University of Virginia Press, 1972.

Weslager, C. W. *The Swedes and Dutch at New Castle*, Middle Atlantic Press, 1987.

Weslager, C. W. *A Man and His Ship: Peter Minuit and the Kalmar Nyckel.*, Middle Atlantic Press, 1990.

Zeidner, Lisa, with photos by Anthony Edgeworth. *Brandywine: A Legacy of Tradition in Du Pont–Wyeth Country*, Lickle Publishing, 1996.

Maine

HISTORICAL AND TOURISM ORGANIZATIONS

Brigade of the American Revolution | Box 14, Westwood, NJ 07675 | www.brigade.org.

Coalition of Historical Trekkers | Maine Representative: J. LeDoux: 135 Shepard St., Rochester, NY 14620 | www.coht.org.

Maine Historical Society | 489 Congress St., Portland, ME 04101 | 207/774–1822 | www.mainehistory.org.

Maine Office of Tourism | 59 State House Station Augusta, ME 04333 | 888/624–6345 | www.visitmaine.com.

HISTORY TOURS AND PACKAGES

Country Walkers | Box 180, Waterbury, VT 05676 | 800/464–9255 | fax 802/244–1387 | www.countrywalkers.com.

Downeast Windjammer Cruises–Historic Vessel Tours | Box 28, Cherryfield, ME 04622 | Summer, 207/288–4585; winter, 207/546–2927 | www.downeastwindjammer.com.

Elderhostel Adventures in Lifelong Learning | 11 Ave. de Lafayette, Boston, MA 02111 | 877/426-8056 | fax 617/426–0701 | www.elderhostel.org.

Yankee Vacations | Box 520, Dublin, NH 03444 | 877/481–5986 | www.yankeemagazine.com/vacations.

FURTHER READING

Caldwell, Bill. *Islands of Maine: Where America Really Began*, Down East Books, 2001.

Calvert, Mary. *Dawn Over the Kennebec*, Down East Books, 1984.

Coffin, Robert Tristram. *Kennebec: Cradle of Americans*, Down East Books, 2002.

Conkling, Philip. *Islands in Time: A Natural and Human History of the Islands of the Gulf of Maine*, Down East Books, 1999.

Coolidge, Olivia. *Colonial Entrepreneur: Dr. Silvester Gardiner and the Settlement of Maine's Kennebec Valley*, Tilbury House Publishers, 1999.

Fisher, Carelton Edward. *Maine Soldiers, Sailors and Patriots of the Revolutionary War*, Picton Press, 1982.

Jewett, Sarah Orne. *The Country of Pointed Firs and Other Stories*, Modern Library, 2001.

___. *The Country Doctor,* New American Library Trade, 1994.

Leamon, James. *Revolution Downeast: The War for American Independence in Maine,* University of Massachusetts Press, 1995.

Paine, Lincoln. *Down East: A Maritime History of Maine,* Down East Books, 2002.

Shain, Charles. *The Maine Reader/The Down East Experience, 1614 to Present,* Houghton Mifflin, 1991.

Taylor, Alan. *Liberty Men and Great Proprietors: The Revolutionary Settlement on the Maine Frontier, 1760–1820,* University of North Carolina Press, 1990.

Thoreau, Henry David. *The Maine Woods,* Penguin, 1988.

Maryland

HISTORICAL AND TOURISM ORGANIZATIONS

Maryland Historical Society | 201 W. Monument St., Baltimore, MD 21201 | 410/685–3750 | fax 410/385–2105 | www.mdhs.org
Maryland Office of Tourism Development | 217 E. Redwood St., Baltimore, MD 21202 | 410/767–3400 | www.mdwelcome.org.

HISTORY TOURS AND PACKAGES

Brendan Worldwide Vacations | 21625 Prairie St., Chatsworth, CA 91311 | 800/421–8446 | fax 818/772–6492 | www.brendantours.com.
Elderhostel Adventures in Lifelong Learning | 11 Ave. de Lafayette, Boston, MA 02111 | 877/426–8056 | fax 617/426–0701 | www.elderhostel.org.
Historic Fells Point Walking Tours | 808 S. Ann St., Baltimore, MD 21231 | 410/675–6750 | www.preservationsociety.com/fellspointwalkingtours.html.
Washington D.C. Sightseeing | 9009 Paddock La., Potomac, MD 20854 | 301/294–9514 | fax 301/309–0753 | dcsightseeing.com.

FURTHER READING

Arnett, Earl, Robert J. Brugger, and Edward C. Papenfuse. *Maryland: A New Guide to the Old Line State,* Johns Hopkins University Press, 1999.

Brugger, Robert J. *Maryland: A Middle Temperament, 1634–1980,* Johns Hopkins University Press, 1988.

Dorsey, John, and James D. Dilts. *A Guide to Baltimore Architecture,* Tidewater Press, 1997.

George, Christopher T. *Terror on the Chesapeake: The War of 1812 on the Bay,* White Mane, 2000.

Lord, Walter. *The Dawn's Early Light,* W.W. Norton, 1972.

Scharf, J. Thomas. *Chronicles of Baltimore (1874),* Tradition Press, 1976.

Scharf, J. Thomas. *History of Maryland from the Earliest Period to the Present Day (1879),* Tradition Press, 1976.

Shivers, Frank R., Jr. *Walking in Baltimore: An Intimate Guide to the Old City,* Johns Hopkins University Press, 1995.

Weeks, Christopher. *A.I.A. Guide to the Architecture of Washington, D.C,* Johns Hopkins University Press, 1994.

Massachusetts

HISTORICAL AND TOURISM ORGANIZATIONS

Massachusetts Historical Commission | 220 Morrissey Blvd., Boston, MA 02125-3314 | 617/727–8470 | www.state.ma.us/sec/mhc
Massachusetts Historical Society | 1154 Boylston St., Boston, MA 02215 | 617/536–1608 | www.masshist.org
Massachusetts Office of Travel and Tourism | 10 Park Plaza, Suite 4510 Boston, MA 02116 | 617/973–8500 or 800/227–6277 | www.mass-vacation.com
Society for the Preservation of New England Antiquities | 141 Cambridge St., Boston, MA 02114 | 617/227–3956 | www.spnea.org
Trustees of Reservations | Long Hill, 572 Essex St., Beverly, MA 01915-1530 | 978/921–1944 | www.thetrustees.org

HISTORY TOURS AND PACKAGES

Boston by Foot | 77 N. Washington St., Boston, MA 02114 | 617/367–3766 or 617/367–2345 | fax 617/720–7873 | www.bostonbyfoot.com.
Boston History Collaborative | 650 Beacon St., Boston, MA 02215 | 617/350–0358 | fax 617/350–0357 | www.bostonhistorycollaborative.org.
Brush Hill Tours | 16 Charles St. South, Boston, MA 02116-5430 | 781/986–6100 or 800/343–1328 | fax 781/986–0167 | www.brushhilltours.com.
Elderhostel Adventures in Lifelong Learning | 11 Ave. de Lafayette, Boston, MA 02111-1746 | 877/426–8056 | fax 617/426–0701 | www.elderhostel.org.

FURTHER READING

Adams, Abigail and Adams, John (Butterfield, L.H., editor). *The Book of Abigail and John: Selected Letters of the Adams Family, 1762–1784,* Northeastern University Press, 2002.

Bahne, Charles. *The Complete Guide to Boston's Freedom Trail.* Cambridge, MA: Newtowne Publishing, 1993.

Boyer, Paul, and Nissenbaum, Stephen. *Salem Possessed.* Cambridge, MA: Harvard University Press, 1974.

Bradford, William. *History of Plymouth Plantation 1620–1647.* Edited by Worthington C. Ford. Boston: Massachusetts Historical Society (Houghton Mifflin), 1912.

Brown, Richard D. and Tager, Jack. *Massachusetts: A Concise History.* Amherst, MA: University of Massachusetts Press, 2000.

Fischer, David Hackett. *Paul Revere's Ride*. New York: Oxford University Press, 1995.

Forbes, Esther. *Johnny Tremain*. New York: Yearling Books, 1987.

Frazier, Patrick. *The Mohicans of Stockbridge*. Lincoln, NE: University of Nebraska Press, 1992.

Gross, Robert A. *The Minutemen and Their World*. New York: Hill & Wang, 2001.

Hawthorne, Nathaniel. *The House of the Seven Gables*. New York: Bantam, 1987.

Hutchinson, Thomas. *The History of the Colony and Province of Massachusetts-Bay*. Cambridge, MA: Harvard University Press, 1936.

Labaree, Benjamin W. *The Boston Tea Party*. Boston: Northeastern University Press, 1979.

Laska, Vera. *Remember the Ladies: Outstanding Women of the American Revolution*. Boston: Massachusetts Bicentennial Commission, 1976.

Lasky, Kathryn. *A Journey to the New World: The Diary of Remember Patience Whipple, Mayflower, 1620 (Dear America series)*. New York : Scholastic, 1996.

Kaufman, Polly Welts; Smith, Bonnie Hurd; Smoyer, Mary Howland; and Wilson, Susan. *Boston Women's Heritage Trail: Four Centuries of Boston Women*. Gloucester, MA: The Curious Traveller Press, 1999.

McNulty, Elizabeth. *Boston Then and Now*. San Diego: Thunder Bay Press, 1999.

Melvoin, Richard I. *New England Outpost: War and Society in Colonial Deerfield*. New York: W. W. Norton, 1989.

Miller, Arthur. *The Crucible*. New York: Penguin, 1976.

Norton, Mary Beth. *In the Devil's Snare: The Salem Witchcraft Crisis of 1692*, Knopf, 2002.

National Park Service. *Boston and the American Revolution*. Washington, DC: U.S. Department of the Interior, 1998.

O'Connor, Thomas H. *The Hub: Boston Past and Present*. Boston: Northeastern University Press, 2001.

Ott, John Harlow. *Hancock Shaker Village: A Guidebook and History*. Pittsfield, MA: Shaker Community, Inc., 1976.

Rosenthal, Bernard. *Salem Story*. Cambridge, East Anglia, U.K.: Cambridge University Press, 1993.

Schofield, William G. *Freedom by the Bay: The Boston Freedom Trail*. Wellesley, MA: Branden Publishing Co., 1988.

Taylor, Robert J. *Western Massachusetts in the Revolution*. Providence: Brown University Press, 1954.

Williams, John. *The Redeemed Captive Returning to Zion*. Originally published Boston, 1707. Bedford, MA: Applewood Books, 1987.

Zobel, Hiller. *The Boston Massacre*. New York: W. W. Norton, 1996.

New Hampshire

HISTORICAL AND TOURISM ORGANIZATIONS

New Hampshire Division of Historical Resources | Box 2043, Concord, NH 03302 | 603/271–3558 | www.state.nh.us/nhdhr.

New Hampshire Division of Travel and Tourism | 172 Pembroke Rd., (Box 1856), Concord, NH 03302 | 603/271–2665 | fax 603/271–6870 | www.visitnh.gov

New Hampshire Historical Society | The Tuck Library, 30 Park St., Concord, NH 03301 | 603/228–6688 | fax 603/224–0463 | www.nhhistory.org.

HISTORY TOURS AND PACKAGES

Elderhostel Adventures in Lifelong Learning | 11 Ave. de Lafayette, Boston, MA 02111 | 877/426–8056 | fax 617/426–0701 | www.elderhostel.org.

New England Journeys | 419 Ledgeview Dr., Rochester, NH 03839 | 603/332–9595 | fax 530/452–2013 | nejourneys@metrocast.net.

Yankee Vacations | Box 520, Dublin, NH 03444 | 877/481–5986 | www.yankeemagazine.com/vacations.

FURTHER READING

Bailyn, Bernard. *The New England Merchants of the Seventeenth Century*, Harvard University Press, 1955.

Conforti, Joseph A. *Imagining New England: Explorations of Regional Identity from the Pilgrims to the Mid-Twentieth Century*, University of Chapel Hill, 2001.

Daniell, Jere. *Colonial New Hampshire*, Kraus Thomson Press, 1981.

Goen, C. C. *Revivalism and Separatism in New England, 1740–1800: Strict Congregationalists and Separate Baptists in the Great Awakening*, Yale University Press, 1963.

Heffernan, Nancy and Stecker, A. *New Hampshire: Crosscurrents in Its Development*, University Press of New England, 1996.

Howells, John Mead. *The Architectural Heritage of the Piscataqua*, Architectural Book, reprinted 1965.

Howells, John Mead. *The Architectural Heritage of the Merrimack*, Architectural Book, reprinted 1978.

Remini, Robert. *Daniel Webster: The Man and His Time*, W.W. Norton, 1997.

Tolles, Bryan. *New Hampshire Architecture*, University Press of New England, 1979.

Turner, Lynn. *The Ninth State: New Hampshire's Formative Years*, University of North Carolina Press, 1983.

Van Deventer, David E. *The Emergence of Provincial New Hampshire, 1623–1741*, Johns Hopkins University Press, 1976.

Wilderson, Paul W. *Governor John Wentworth and The American Revolution*, University Press of New England, 1994.

Wood, Joseph S. *The New England Village,* Johns Hopkins University Press, 1997.

Workers of the Federal Writers' Project of the WPA. *New Hampshire: A Guide to the Granite State,* Houghton Mifflin, 1938.

New Jersey

HISTORICAL AND TOURISM ORGANIZATIONS

New Jersey Commerce and Economic Growth Commission, Office of Travel and Tourism | Box 820, 20 W. State St. Trenton 08625 | 800/847–4865 | www.visitnj.org.

New Jersey Department of Environmental Protection, Division of Parks and Forestry | Box 404, 501 E. State St., Trenton 08625 | 800/843–6420 | www.state.nj.us/dep/forestry/parks

New Jersey Historical Commission | 225 W. State St., Trenton 08625 | 609/292–6062 | www.newjerseyhistory.org.

New Jersey Historical Society | 52 Park Pl., Newark 07102 | 973/596–8500.

Trenton Convention and Visitors Bureau | Lafayette and Barrack Sts., Trenton 08608 | 609/777–1771 recording; 609/777–1770 voice | www.trentonnj.com

FURTHER READING

Di Ionno, Mark. *A Guide to New Jersey's Revolutionary War Trail: For Families and History Buffs,* Rutgers University Press, 2000.

Dwyer, William. *The Day is Ours!: November 1776–January 1777: An Inside View of the Battles of Trenton and Princeton,* Viking, 1983.

Fast, Howard. *The Crossing,* IBooks, 1996.

Groff, Sibyl McC. *New Jersey's Historic Houses: A Guide to Homes Open to the Public,* A.S. Barnes, 1971.

Ketchum, Richard. *The Winter Soldiers: the Battles for Trenton and Princeton,* Henry Holt, 1999.

McCormick, Richard, ed. *New Jersey from Colony to State 1609–1789,* New Jersey Historical Society, 1981.

Miers, Earl Schenck. *Crossroads of Freedom; the American Revolution and the Rise of a New Nation,* Rutgers University Press, 1971.

Ryan, Dennis. *New Jersey in the American Revolution, 1763–1783: A Chronology,* New Jersey Historical Commission, 1975.

Stockton, Frank. *Stories of New Jersey,* Rutgers University Press, 1987.

Raphael, Ray. *A People's History of the American Revolution: How Common People Shaped the Fight for Independence,* New Press, 2001.

Tunis, Edwin. *The Tavern at the Ferry: Washington's 1776 Crossing,* Crowell, 1973.

New York

HISTORICAL AND TOURISM ORGANIZATIONS

Historic Hudson Valley | 150 White Plains Rd., Tarrytown, NY 10591 | 914/631–8200 | fax 914/631–0089 | www.hudsonvalley.org.

Long Island Convention and Visitors Bureau and Sports Commission | 330 Motor Pkwy., Suite 203, Hauppage, NY 11788 | 877/386–6654 | www.licvb.com.

Mohawk Valley Heritage Corridor Commission | 66 Montgomery St., Canajoharie, NY 13317 | 518/673–1045 | fax 518/673–1078 | www.mohawkvalleyheritage.com.

New York State Division of Tourism | Empire State Plaza, Main Concourse, Room 110, Albany, NY 12220 | 518/474–4116 | www.iloveny.com.

New York State Historical Association | Lake Road (Rte. 80) (Box 800), Cooperstown, NY 13326 | 888/547–1450 | www.nysha.org.

New York State Office of Parks, Recreation, and Historic Preservation | Empire State Plaza, Agency Building #1, 20th Floor, Albany, NY 12238 | 518/474–0456 | fax 518/292–5893 | www.nysparks.com.

HISTORY TOURS AND PACKAGES

Upstate Tours | Box 325, Geyser Rd., Saratoga Springs, NY 12886 | 518/584–5252 | fax 518/584–1092 | www.upstatetours.com.

Tauck World Discovery | 276 Post Rd. W, Westport, CT 06880 | 800/788–7885 | www.tauck.com.

World Wide Country Tours | 5939 Country La., Greendale, WI 53129 | 800/344–6918 | fax 414/423–3944 | www.countrytours.com.

FURTHER READING

Bonomi, Patricia U. *A Factious People: Politics and Society in Colonial New York,* Columbia University Press, 1971.

Carmer, Carl. *The Hudson,* Farrar & Rinehart, 1939.

Countryman, Edward. *A People in Revolution: The American Revolution and Political Society in New York, 1760–1790,* Johns Hopkins University Press, 1981.

Irving, Washington. *Knickerbocker's History of New York,* F. Ungar Pub. Co. 1959.

Johnson, Donald, ed. *Charting the Sea of Darkness: The Four Voyages of Henry Hudson,* International Marine, 1993.

Kammen, Michael G. *Colonial New York: A History,* New York: KTO Press, 1987.

Ketchum, Richard M. *Saratoga: Turning Point of America's Revolutionary War,* H. Holt, 1997

Kierner, Cynthia A., *Traders and Gentlefolk : the Livingstons of New York, 1675–1790,* Cornell University Press, 1992.

Kim, Sung Bok. *Landlord and Tenant in Colonial New York: Manorial Society, 1664–1775,* University of North Carolina Press, 1978.
Jackson, Kenneth T., ed. *The Encyclopedia of New York City,* Yale University Press, 1995.
Merwick, Donna. *Possessing Albany, 1630–1710: The Dutch and English Experiences,* Cambridge University Press, 1990.
Mintz, Max M. *Seeds of Empire: the American Revolutionary Conquest of the Iroquois,* New York University Press, 1999.
Rink, Oliver A. *Holland on the Hudson: An Economic and Social History of Dutch New York,* Cornell University Press, 1986.
Rogow, Arnold. *A Fatal Friendship: Alexander Hamilton and Aaron Burr,* Hill and Wang, 1998.
Steele, Ian K. *Betrayals: Fort William Henry and the "Massacre,"* Oxford University Press, 1990.
Taylor, Alan. *William Cooper's Town: Power and Persuasion on the Frontier of the Early American Republic,* Knopf, 1995.
Zandt, Roland van. *Chronicles of the Hudson: Three Centuries of Travel and Adventure,* Black Dome Press, 1992.

North Carolina

HISTORICAL AND TOURISM ORGANIZATIONS

North Carolina Division of Tourism | 301 N. Wilmington St., Raleigh, NC 27601 | 800/VISITNC | fax 919/733–8582 | www.visitnc.com.
North Carolina ECHO (Exploring Cultural Heritage Online) | www.ncecho.org/ncecho.asp.
North Carolina State Archives | 109 E. Jones St. Raleigh NC 27699 | 919/733–3952 | fax 919/733–1354 | www.ah.dcr.state.nc.us/sections/archives/arch/default.htm

HISTORY TOURS AND PACKAGES

Allways Tours | 3978 Old Greensboro Rd. Winston-Salem, NC 27101 | 800/942–3301.
Elderhostel Adventures in Lifelong Learning | 11 Ave. de Lafayette, Boston, MA 02111 | 877/426–8056 | fax 617/426–0701 | www.elderhostel.org.
Historic Albemarle Tour, Inc. | Box 1604, Washington, NC 27889 | 800/734–1117 | fax 252/926–9312 | www.albemarle-nc.com/hat.
Overmountain Victory National Historic Trail | Kings Mountain National Military Park, 2625 Park Rd., Blacksburg, SC 29702 | 864/936–7921 | fax 864/936–9897 | www.nps.gov/ovvi

FURTHER READING

Barnett, Colin. *The Impact of Historic Preservation of New Bern, North Carolina, from Tryon Palace to the Coor-Cook House,* Bandit Books/John F. Blair, 1995.
Bishir, Catherine. *A Guide to the Historic Architecture of Eastern North Carolina,* University of North Carolina Press, 1996.
Bishir, Catherine, M. Southern, and J. Martin. *A Guide to the Historic Architecture of Western North*

Carolina, University of North Carolina Press, 1999.
Bivins, John, and Forsyth, Alexander. *The Regional Arts of the Early South,* Museum of Early Southern Decorative Arts, 1991.
Cecelski, David. *The Waterman's Song: Slavery and Freedom in Maritime North Carolina,* University of North Carolina Press, 2001.
Fischer, Kirsten. *Suspect Relations: Sex, Race, and Resistance in Colonial North Carolina,* Cornell University Press, 2002.
Fries, Adelaide. *The Road to Salem,* John F. Blair, 1993.
Green, Paul. *The Lost Colony: A Symphonic Drama of American History,* University of North Carolina Press, 2001.
Hudson, Marjorie. *Searching for Virginia Dare: A Fool's Errand,* Coastal Carolina Press, 2002.
Hume, Ivor Noel. *The Virginia Adventure: Roanoke to Jamestown, an Archaeological and Historical Odyssey,* University Press of Virginia, 1997.
Kars, Marjoleine. *Breaking Loose Together: The Regulator Rebellion in Pre-Revolutionary North Carolina,* University of North Carolina Press, 2002.
Kupperman, Karen Ordahl. *Indians and English: Facing Off in Early America,* Cornell University Press, 2000.
Kupperman, Karen Ordahl. *Roanoke: The Abandoned Colony,* Bowman and Littlefield, 1991.
Miller, Lee. *Roanoke: Solving the Mystery of the Lost Colony,* Arcade, 2001.
Nelson, Paul David. *William Tryon and the Course of Empire: A Life in British Imperial Service,* University of North Carolina Press, 1990.
Niven, Penelope, with Cornelia B. Wright. *The Old Salem Official Guidebook,* Old Salem, Inc., 2000.
Wood, Peter H. *Natives and Newcomers: The Way We Lived in North Carolina before 1770,* University of North Carolina Press, 2001.

Pennsylvania

HISTORICAL AND TOURISM ORGANIZATIONS

Greater Philadelphia Tourism Marketing Corporation. | 30 S.17th St., Suite 1710, Philadelphia PA 19103 | 888/GO–PHILA | www.gophila.com.
Independence Hall Association | Carpenters' Hall, 320 Chestnut St., Philadelphia, PA 19106 | 215/925–7877 | www.ushistory.org.
National Park Service | Northeast Region, U.S. Custom House, 200 Chestnut St., Philadelphia, PA 19106 | 215/597–7013 | www.nps.gov
Pennsylvania Dutch Convention & Visitors Bureau | 501 Greenfield Rd., Lancaster, PA, 17601 | 717/299–8901 | fax 717/299–0470 | www.padutchcountry.com

Pennsylvania Historical and Museum Commission | 300 North St., Harrisburg, PA 17120 | 717/787–3362 | www.phmc.state.pa.us

HISTORY TOURS AND PACKAGES

Collette Vacations | 162 Middle St., Pawtucket, RI 02860 | 800/340–5158 | www.collettevacations.com

Mid Atlantic Tour & Receptive Services | 174 Garber La., Winchester, VA 22604 | 540/665–1939 | www.takeafuntrip.com

Philadelphia Hospitality, Inc. | 123 S. Broad St, Suite 1330, Philadelphia, PA 19109 | 215/790–9901 | fax 215/790–9906 | www.philahospitality.org.

Philadelphia On Foot–Personal Tours by Eg Mauger | 215/627–8680 or 800/340–9869 | www.ushistory.org/more/mauger

Poor Richard's Walking Tours–Led by Scholars | Box 8193, Philadelphia, PA 19101 | 215/206–1682 | www.phillywalks.com

FURTHER READING

Avery, Ron. *A Concise History of Philadelphia,* Philadelphia 1999.

Durham, Michael S. *The Smithsonian Guide to Historic America: The Mid-Atlantic States: New York, New Jersey, Pennsylvania,* Stewart, Tabori & Chang, New York, 1989.

Geiter, Mary. *William Penn, Profiles in Power Series,* Longman, 2000.

Gregory, Kristiana. *The Winter of Red Snow: The Revolutionary War Diary of Abigail Jane Stewart, Valley Forge, Pennsylvania, 1777,* Scholastic Trade, 1996.

Miller, Randall and W. Pencak, eds. *Pennsylvania: History of the Commonwealth,* Pennsylvania State University Press, 2002.

Marion, John Francis. *Walking Tours of Historic Philadelphia,* ISHI Publications, 1984.

Merrell, James. *Into the American Woods: Negotiators on the Pennsylvania Frontier,* W.W. Norton, 2000.

Moss, Roger. *Historic Houses of Philadelphia: A Tour of the Region's Museum Homes,* University of Pennsylvania Press, 1998.

Nash, Gary. *Forging Freedom: The Formation of Philadelphia's Black Community, 1720-1840* Harvard University Press, 1991.

Nolt, Steven. *Foreigners in Their Own Land: Pennsylvania Germans in the Early Republic,* Pennsylvania State Univesity Press, 2002.

Powell, J. H. *Bring Out Your Dead: The Great Plague of Yellow Fever in Philadelphia in 1793,* University of Pennsylvania Press, 1993.

Wallace, Paul. *Indians in Pennsylvania,* Pennsylvania Historical and Museum Commission, 2000.

Weigley, Russell. *Philadelphia: A 300-Year History,* W.W. Norton, 1992.

Rhode Island

HISTORICAL AND TOURISM ORGANIZATIONS

Rhode Island Historical Society | 110 Benevolent St., Providence, RI 02906 | 401/331–8575 | www.rihs.org.

Rhode Island Tourism Division | 1 W. Exchange St., Providence, RI 02906 | 800/556–2484 | www.visitrhodeisland.com.

HISTORY TOURS AND PACKAGES

Conway Tours Gray Line | 10 Nate Whipple Hwy., Cumberland, RI 02864 | 401/658–3400 or 800/888–4661 | fax 401/658-3411 | www.conwaytours.com.

Trek Tours, Ltd. | 128 Main St., Westerly, RI 02891 | 800/370–0357 | fax 402/596–2757 | www.trektours.com.

FURTHER READING

Conley, Patrick. *An Album of Rhode Island History 1636-1986,* Rhode Island Publication Society, 1986.

Conley, Patrick. *Liberty and Justice: A History of Law and Lawyers in Rhode Island, 1636-1998,* Rhode Island Publications Society, 1998.

Beals, Carleton. *Colonial Rhode Island,* Thomas Nelson and Sons, 1970.

Coughtry, Jay. *The Notorious Triangle: Rhode Island and the African Slave Trade,* Temple University Press, 1981.

Demos, John. *The Unredeemed Captive: A Family Story from Early America,* Vintage, 1995.

Greene, Janet. *Epitaphs to Remember: Remarkable Inscriptions from New England Gravestones,* Alan C. Hood & Company, 1993.

James, Sydney. *Colonial Rhode Island: A History,* Scribner, 1975.

Karlsen, Carol F. *The Devil in the Shape of a Woman: Witchcraft in Colonial New England,* W. W. Norton, 1998.

Lederer, Richard, Jr. *Colonial American English,* Verbatim, 1985.

Lepore, Jill. *The Name of War: King Philip's War and the Origins of American Identity,* Vintage, 1998.

McLoughlin, William G. *Rhode Island: A History,* W.W. Norton, 1986.

Settle, Mary Lee. *I, Roger Williams,* W.W. Norton, 2001.

Walker, Anthony. *So Few The Brave: Rhode Island Continentals, 1775–1783,* Seafield Press, 1981.

Whitehead, Russell F. *Colonial Architecture in New England,* Arno Press, 1977.

Thorson, Robert. *Stone by Stone: The Magnificent History in New England's Stone Walls,* Walker & Company, 2002.

South Carolina and Georgia

HISTORICAL AND TOURISM ORGANIZATIONS

Byron Convention & Visitors Bureau/Historic Heartland | 101 E. Heritage Blvd., Byron, GA 31501 | 912/283–3744 | fax 912/283–0121 | www.okefenokeetourism.com.

Georgia Tourism | 285 Peachtree Center Ave., Suite 1100, Atlanta, GA 30303 | 800/847-4842 | fax 803/734–0138 | www.georgia.org/tourism.

Historic High Country Travel Association | 527 Broad St., Rome, GA 30161 | www.georgiahighcountry.org/.

South Carolina Department of Parks, Recreation & Tourism | Box 71, Columbia, SC 29202 | 803/734–1700 | fax 803/734–0138 | www.discoversouthcarolina.com.

HISTORY TOURS AND PACKAGES

Caravan Tours | 401 N. Michigan Ave., Chicago, IL 60611 | 800/227–2826 | fax 312/321–9845 | www.caravantours.com.

Coastal Tours | 46 Lanier Rd., Jekyll Island, GA | 800/260–0470 | fax 912/635–2699 | www.coastaltours.com.

Historic Savannah Foundation Special Tours | 117 W. Perry St., Savannah, GA | 912/234–4088 | fax 912/234–4065 | www.savatours.com.

Patriots to Pizzazz and Custom Tours | Camden, SC | 800/968–4037 | www.camden-sc.org.

Savannah Seen Historic Tours | 426 Abercorn St., Savannah, GA 31401 | 912/234–8204 | fax 912/447–1077.

FURTHER READING

Cashin, J. Edward. *The King's Ranger: Thomas Brown and the American Revolution on the Southern Frontier,* Fordham University Press, 1999.

Colanis, Peter. *The Shadow of a Dream: Economic Life and Death in the South Carolina Low Country, 1670–1920.* Oxford Univeristy Press, 1993.

Edgar, Walter. *Partisans and Redcoats: The Southern Conflict That Turned the Tide of the American Revolution,* William Morrow, 2001.

Fenn, Elizabeth A. *Pox Americana: The Great Small Pox Epidemic of 1775–82,* Hill & Wang, 2001.

Fraser, Walter. *Charleston! Charleston! The History of a Southern City,* University of South Carolina Press, 1989.

Hall, Leslie. *Land and Allegiance in Revolutionary Georgia,* University of Georgia Press, 2001.

Sully, Susan. *Charleston Style: Past and Present,* Rizzoli, 1999.

Sully, Susan. *Savannah Style: Mystery and Manners,* Rizzoli, 2001.

Vermont

HISTORICAL AND TOURISM ORGANIZATIONS

Vermont Department of Tourism and Marketing | 6 Baldwin St., 4th Floor, Drawer 33, Montpelier, VT 05633 | 802/828–3237 | fax 802/828–3233 | www.1-800-Vermont.com.

Vermont Chamber of Commerce | Box 37, Montpelier, VT 05602 | 802/223–3443 | fax 802/828–4257 | www.vtchamber.com.

Vermont Historical Society | 60 Washington St., Barre, VT 05641 | 802/479–8500 | www.state.vt.us/vhs.

Vermont Division for Historic Preservation | National Life Building, Drawer 20, Montpelier, VT 05620 | 802/828–3211 | fax 802/828–3206 | www.historicvermont.com.

HISTORY TOURS AND PACKAGES

Adventure Vacation Packages | Box 3, North Ferrisburg, VT 05473 | 800/747–5905 | www.adventureguidesvt.com.

Carillon Cruises | Teachout's Lakehouse Store and Wharf, Larabee's Point, Shoreham, VT 05770 | 802/897–5331 | www.paxp.com/carillon.

Country Walkers | Box 180, Waterbury, VT 05676 | 800/464–9255 | fax 802/244–1387 | www.countrywalkers.com.

Trains Around Vermont | Box 498, Depot St., Bellows Falls, VT 05101 | 800/707–3530 | www.rails-vt.com.

Lake Champlain Transportation Company | King St. Dock, Burlington, VT 05401 | 802/864–9804 | www.ferries.com.

FURTHER READING

Calhoon, R.M. *The Loyalists in Revolutionary America, 1760–1781,* Harcourt Brace Jovanovich, 1973.

Calloway, Colin G. *The American Revolution in Indian Country,* Cambridge University Press, 1995.

Cheney, Cora. *Vermont: The State with the Storybook Past,* New England Press, 1996.

Demos, John. *The Unredeemed Captive: A Family Story from Early America,* Knopf, 1994.

Howe, Dennis E. *This Ragged, Starved Lousy, Pocky Army,* The Printed Word, 1996.

Hoyt, Edwin P. *The Damndest Yankees: Ethan Allen and his Clan,* Stephen Greene Press, 1976.

Jellison, Charles A. *Ethan Allen: Frontier Rebel,* Syracuse University Press, 1985.

Ketchum, Richard. *Saratoga: Turning Point of the American Revolution,* Henry Holt, 1997.

Morrissey, Charles T. *Vermont: A Bicentennial History,* W.W. Norton, 1981.

Randall, Willard Stearne. *Benedict Arnold: Patriot and Traitor,* Dorset Press, 1990.

Robinson, Rowland E. *Vermont: A Study of Independence.* Charles E. Tuttle, 1976.

Shultz, Eric B., and Tougias, Michael J. *King Philip's War: The History and Legacy of America's Forgotten Conflict,* Countryman Press, 1999.

Shalhope, Robert E. *Bennington and the Green Mountain Boys: The Emergence of Liberal Democracy in Vermont, 1760–1850.* John Hopkins University Press, 1996.

Washington, Carol E., and Washington, Ida H. *The Green Mountain Boys,* Cherry Tree Books, 2000.

Wickman, Donald H. "Built with Spirit, Deserted in Darkness: the American Occupation of Mount Independence, 1776–1777," Master's thesis, University of Vermont, 1993.

Williams, John. *The Battle of Hubbardton: The American Rebels Stem the Tide,* Sharp Offset Printing, 1988.

Virginia

HISTORICAL AND TOURISM ORGANIZATIONS

Association for the Preservation of Virginia Antiquities (APVA) | 204 W. Franklin St., Richmond, VA 23220 | 804/648–1889 | www.apva.org.

Virginia Historical Society, The Center for Virginia History | 428 North Blvd., Richmond, VA 23220 | 804/358–4901 | fax 804/355–2399 | www.vahistorical.org.

Virginia Tourism Corporation | 901 E. Byrd St., Richmond, VA 23219 | 804/786–2051 | fax 804/786–1919 | www.vatc.org.

HISTORY TOURS AND PACKAGES

Mid-Atlantic Receptive Services (MARS) | Box 3099, Winchester, VA 22604 | 800/769–5912 | fax 540/678–9460 | www.takeafuntrip.com.

Old Dominion Tours & Virginia Destinations, Inc. | 723 Twinridge La., Richmond, VA 23235 | 800/868–7782 | fax 804/320–5885 | tourva@richmonder.com.

Rsvp Tours & Guides–Pepper Bird | 121 Meredith St., Hampton, VA 23669 | 804/722–7485.

Traveling America | 199 Spotnap Rd., Suite 3, Charlottesville, VA 22911 | 804/984–1000 | fax 434/984–1010 | www.travelingamerica.com.

Triangle Tours of Virginia | 105 Powhatan Overlook, Williamsburg, VA 23188 | 757/259–0697 | fax 757/259–0697 | triangletours.port5.com.

FURTHER READING

Ambrose, Stephen E. *Undaunted Courage: Meriwether Lewis, Thomas Jefferson, and the Opening of the American West,* Simon & Schuster; 1996.

Ayers, Edward L. *The Edge of the South: Life in Nineteenth-Century Virginia,* University Press of Virginia, 1991.

Bailyn, Bernard, ed. *The Debate on the Constitution: Part One: September 1787 to February 1788; Part Two: January to August 1788,* Library of America, 1993.

Beiswanger, William L. *Thomas Jefferson's Monticello,* University of North Carolina Press, 2002.

Campbell, Norine Dickson. *Patrick Henry: Patriot and Statesman,* Devin-Adair, 1975.

Dowdey, Clifford. *The Virginia Dynasties: The Emergence Of "King" Carter and the Golden Age,* Little, Brown & Co., 1969.

Edwards, Betsy Wells. *Virginia Country: Inside the Private Historic Homes of the Old Dominion,* Simon & Schuster, 1998.

Ellis, Joseph J. *American Sphinx: The Character of Thomas Jefferson,* Vintage Books, 1998.

Ellis, Joseph J. *Founding Brothers: The Revolutionary Generation,* Knopf, 2000.

Fischer, David Hackett. *Bound Away: Virginia and the Westward Movement,* University Press of Virginia, 2000.

Garrett, Wendell. *George Washington's Mount Vernon,* Monacelli Press, 1999.

Gerson, Noel B. *Velvet Glove, a Life of Dolly Madison,* Thomas Nelson Inc., 1975.

Griswold, Mac. *Washington's Gardens at Mount Vernon,* Houghton Mifflin, 1999.

Hardwick, Kevin R. *Virginia Reconsidered: New Histories of the Old Dominion,* University of Virginia Press, 2003.

Jones, Robert F. *George Washington: Ordinary Man, Extraordinary Leader,* Fordham University Press, 2002.

Lewis, Charlene M. Boyer. *Ladies and Gentlemen on Display: Planter Society at the Virginia Springs,* University Press of Virginia, 2001.

Neider, Charles, ed., and Washington Irving. *George Washington: A Biography,* DaCapo Press, 1994.

Styron, Arthur. *The Last of the Cocked Hats: James Monroe and the Virginia Dynasty,* University of Oklahoma Press, 1945.

Whichard, Rogers Dey. *The History of Lower Tidewater Virginia,* Lewis Historical Pubishing. Co., 1959.

Index

Notes

Notes

Fodor's Key to the Guides

America's guidebook leader publishes guides for every kind of traveler. Check out our many series and find your perfect match.

Fodor's Gold Guides
America's favorite travel-guide series offers the most detailed insider reviews of hotels, restaurants, and attractions in all price ranges, plus great background information, smart tips, and useful maps.

Fodor's Road Guide USA
Big guides for a big country—the most comprehensive guides to America's roads, packed with places to stay, eat, and play across the U.S.A. Just right for road warriors, family vacationers, and cross-country trekkers.

COMPASS AMERICAN GUIDES
Stunning guides from top local writers and photographers, with gorgeous photos, literary excerpts, and colorful anecdotes. A must-have for culture mavens, history buffs, and new residents.

Fodor's CITYPACKS
Concise city coverage with a foldout map. The right choice for urban travelers who want everything under one cover.

Fodor's EXPLORING GUIDES
Hundreds of color photos bring your destination to life. Lively stories lend insight into the culture, history, and people.

Fodor's POCKET GUIDES
For travelers who need only the essentials. The best of Fodor's in pocket-size packages for just $9.95.

Fodor's To Go
Credit-card–size, magnetized color microguides that fit in the palm of your hand—perfect for "stealth" travelers or as gifts.

Fodor's FLASHMAPS
Every resident's map guide. 60 easy-to-follow maps of public transit, parks, museums, zip codes, and more.

Fodor's CITYGUIDES
Sourcebooks for living in the city: Thousands of in-the-know listings for restaurants, shops, sports, nightlife, and other city resources.

Fodor's AROUND THE CITY WITH KIDS
68 great ideas for family days, recommended by resident parents. Perfect for exploring in your own backyard or on the road.

Fodor's ESCAPES
Fill your trip with once-in-a-lifetime experiences, from ballooning in Chianti to overnighting in the Moroccan desert. These full-color dream books point the way.

Fodor's FYI
Get tips from the pros on planning the perfect trip. Learn how to pack, fly hassle-free, plan a honeymoon or cruise, stay healthy on the road, and travel with your baby.

Fodor's Languages for Travelers
Practice the local language before hitting the road. Available in phrase books, cassette sets, and CD sets.

Karen Brown's Guides
Engaging guides to the most charming inns and B&Bs in the U.S.A. and Europe, with easy-to-follow inn-to-inn itineraries.

Baedeker's Guides
Comprehensive guides, trusted since 1829, packed with A–Z reviews and star ratings.

At bookstores everywhere.   www.fodors.com/books